LIT

LITERATURE
AND
INTERPRETIVE TECHNIQUES

WILFRED L. GUERIN,
Louisiana State University in Shreveport

MICHAEL L. HALL,
Centenary College of Louisiana

EARLE LABOR,
Centenary College of Louisiana

LEE MORGAN,
Centenary College of Louisiana

BARRY NASS,
C.W. Post Center, Long Island University

JOHN R. WILLINGHAM,
University of Kansas

1817

HARPER & ROW, PUBLISHERS, New York
Cambridge, Philadelphia, San Francisco,
London, Mexico City, São Paulo, Singapore, Sydney

For
Wilda
Joy
Betty
Lucy
Helen and Mannie
Yvonne

Sponsoring Editor: Phillip Leininger
Project Editor: Brigitte Pelner
Text and Cover Design: Suzanne Bennett & Associates/Graphic Design
Production: Jeanie Berke/Delia Tedoff
Compositor: ComCom Division of Haddon Craftsmen, Inc.
Printer and Binder: R. R. Donnelley & Sons Company

LIT: Literature and Interpretive Techniques
Copyright © 1986 by Harper & Row, Publishers, Inc.

Library of Congress Cataloging in Publication Data

Main entry under title:

LIT-literature and interpretive techniques.
    Includes index.
        1. Literature—Collections.   I. Guerin, Wilfred L.
II. Title: LIT.   III. Title: Literature and interpretive
techniques.
PN6014.L556   1986   808'.0427   85-21857
ISBN 0-06-042553-9

86 87 88 9 8 7 6 5 4 3 2 1

Acknowledgments

Sherwood Anderson: "Death in the Woods," copyright © 1926 by *The American Mercury*, Inc. Renewed 1953 by Eleanor Copenhaver Anderson. Reprinted by permission of Harold Ober Associates, Inc.

Aristophanes: "Lysistrata," translated by Donald Sutherland. (Chandler Publishing Co.) Copyright © 1959 by Donald Sutherland. Copyright © 1961 by Harper & Row, Publishers, Inc. Reprinted by permission of Harper & Row, Publishers, Inc.

W. H. Auden: "Musée des Beaux Arts," "In Memory of W. B. Yeats," "The Unknown Citizen." Copyright © 1940 and renewed 1968 by W.H. Auden. Reprinted from *Collected Poems by W. H. Auden*, edited by Edward Mendelson. Reprinted by permission of Random House, Inc., and Faber and Faber Ltd.

John Berryman: "Life, Friends, Is Boring," from *The Dream Songs* by John Berryman. Copyright © 1959, 1962, 1963, 1964, 1969 by John Berryman. Reprinted by permission of Farrar, Straus & Giroux, Inc.

Elizabeth Bishop: "The Fish," from *The Complete Poems*, by Elizabeth Bishop. Copyright © 1940, 1969 by Elizabeth Bishop. Copyright renewed © 1976 by Elizabeth Bishop. Reprinted with the permission of Farrar, Straus & Giroux, Inc.

Michael Blumenthal: "The Woman Inside," originally published in *The Missouri Review* and "Jungians and Freudians at the Joseph Campbell Lecture," originally published in *The Bennington Review*, from *Days We Would Rather Know* by Michael Blumenthal. Copyright © 1980, 1981, 1982, 1983, 1984 by Michael Blumenthal. Reprinted by permission of Viking Penguin Inc.

Jorge Luis Borges: "The Circular Ruins," from *Ficciones* by Jorge Luis Borges, translated from the Spanish, copyright © 1956 by Emece Editores, S.A., Buenos Aires. Copyright © 1962 by Grove Press, Inc. Reprinted by permission of Grove Press, Inc.

Elizabeth Bowen: "The Demon Lover," copyright © 1946 and renewed 1974 by Elizabeth Bowen. Reprinted from *The Collected Stories of Elizabeth Bowen*, by permission of Alfred A. Knopf, Inc.

Gwendolyn Brooks: "The Rites for Cousin Vit." Copyright © 1949 by Gwendolyn Brooks Blakely, "We Real Cool: The Pool Players, Seven at the Golden Shovel," Copyright © 1959 by Gwendolyn Brooks. Both from *The World of Gwendolyn Brooks*, by Gwendolyn Brooks. Reprinted by permission of Harper & Row, Publishers, Inc.

John Cheever: "The Swimmer," copyright © 1964 by John Cheever. Reprinted from *The Stories of John Cheever*, by permission of Alfred A. Knopf, Inc.

Anton Chekov: "A Work of Art," translated by Joel A. Huberman. Reprinted by permission of Joel A. Huberman.

John William Corrington: "Pastoral," from *Where We Are* by John William Corrington. Reprinted by permission of Charioteer Press.

Hart Crane: "At Melville's Tomb," "Voyages I," from *The Complete Poems and Selected Letters of Hart Crane*, edited by Brown Weber. Copyright © 1933, 1958, 1966 by Liveright Publishing Corp. Reprinted by permission of Liveright Publishing Corp.

Robert Creeley: "Kore," "Just Friends," in *For Love: Poems 1950–1960*. Copyright © 1962 by Robert Creeley. Reprinted by permission of Charles Scribner's Sons.

E. E. Cummings: "anyone lived in a pretty how town," copyright © 1940 by E.E. Cummings, renewed 1968 by Marion Morehouse Cummings. Reprinted from his volume *Complete Poems 1913–1962* by permission of Harcourt Brace Jovanovich, Inc. "Buffalo Bill's," "the Cambridge ladies who live in furnished souls," from *Tulips & Chimneys* by E. E. Cummings. Reprinted by permission of Liveright Publishing Corp., copyright © 1923, 1925, and renewed 1951, 1953 by E. E. Cummings. Copyright © 1973, 1976 by the Trustees for the E. E. Cummings Trust. Copyright © 1973, 1976

Contents

CONTENTS

POETRY

READING POETRY

CONTENTS

CONTENTS

CONTENTS

DRAMA   581

READING DRAMA

WRITING ABOUT LITERATURE   1119

Thematic Table of Contents

NOTE: Neither the range of themes nor the selections listed under each theme is intended to exhaust the interpretive possibilities of a thematic approach to the selections in this anthology.

THE INDIVIDUAL VERSUS SOCIETY

LOVE

VARIETIES OF RELIGIOUS EXPERIENCE

DEATH AND DYING

YOUTH AND AGE

IMAGES OF WOMEN

JOURNEYS AND QUESTS

HUMOR AND THE HUMAN COMEDY

Critical Table of Contents

NOTE: As with the Thematic Table of Contents, the following table of critical approaches is intended merely to suggest a few works that lend themselves to these techniques. In fact, virtually all of the works in this anthology lend themselves to multiple approaches.

Preface

Our title, *LIT: Literature and Interpretive Techniques,* indicates the dual emphasis of this book. We want to introduce students to literature as well as to a variety of critical techniques for interpreting literature. Our assumption is that an introduction to literature is also an introduction to reading. Every work of literature, even the simplest, supposes interaction between author and reader, a shared experience of written language. We recognize that no two experiences are exactly alike and that all are valid to some extent, although some may be more imaginative or sophisticated than others. For that reason we have included an "Introduction to Reading Literature" which demonstrates some of the more popular techniques of interpretation and presents a variety of critical approaches. More elaborate demonstrations introduce genres: fiction, poetry, and drama.

In the expectation that these introductions will serve as examples of critical reading, we have avoided overburdening them with the usual apparatus of literary instruction. Instead, discussion and demonstration of the more technical details and language of literary criticism have been reserved for the Glossary and the afterword "Writing About Literature." In the Glossary, students will find brief definitions of the technical vocabulary of literary criticism that are customarily italicized in the introductions and questions; in the afterword, we have discussed the kinds of questions students often have when confronting writing assignments. We have also included examples of interpretive papers and the new MLA style of documentation.

Another distinctive feature of this text is chronological order. Although we have grouped works by genre—fiction, poetry, and drama—we have arranged the authors chronologically by date of birth within each genre. There are several advantages to this approach. First, individual works and authors retain a certain amount of autonomy and independence. In addition, we feel that readers will learn to find their way around such a large collection much more quickly and easily with this arrangement. But our principal reason for choosing a chronological order was to avoid arbitrary thematic groupings that tend to impose an editor's own preconceptions and prejudices on works and on readers. The experience of reading literature is certainly cumulative and comparative; each work we read becomes instruction and commentary for further reading.

Learning about literature, like all other learning, relies on comparison and contrast between the known or familiar and the unknown or unfamiliar. For that reason we have included thematic and critical tables of contents as well as a number of writing assignments that encourage comparison and contrast. But as teachers (and students) of literature, we recognize that no two readers will always agree on precisely the same thematic groupings. Few works of literature fit in only one thematic or critical category. The poem that illustrates metaphor or figurative language may just as well be a fine demonstration of irony or social comment or psychological insight. We are convinced that an introductory text is more useful to both teachers and students when it allows them to make their own selections and move about freely from one work to another.

Finally, *LIT* offers richness and variety. Among the 34 stories, more than 200 poems, and 11 plays, readers will find literature to suit every taste: familiar classics as well as more recent and contemporary works. For some poets we have included a greater number of poems to suggest the range of both poetic achievement and interpretive possibilities. Our guiding principle throughout has been to choose works that are "teachable." We have chosen literature that students enjoy reading and works that lend themselves to a variety of critical approaches and interpretations. Nearly every selection is followed by questions intended to reveal some of the work's richness without limiting interpretation. Writing topics follow some selections as guides for student composition, but the distinction between questions for class discussion and topics for student writing may often be slight. In either case our aim has been to provoke discussion and individual exploration by suggesting some points of departure. We hope that the teachers and students who use this anthology will discover many more questions and answers of their own. We will be delighted if our readers in this way join us in the making of this book.

To those friends and colleagues who have encouraged us at various points in the editing of this book, we editors wish to express our kindest thanks. We are especially indebted to Gerry Dollar, Jeff Hendricks, Katherine Hill-Miller, David Jackson, Laurence Perrine, James Pickering, Anne Rogers, Gayle Johnson Rogers, and Karl-Heinz Westarp. We are also indebted to Phillip Leininger, Senior Editor of the College Division at Harper & Row, for his sound advice and continuing patience. We are grateful for the expert professional assistance we have received from Ella Edwards and Anna White of the Magale Library at Centenary College. Two of the editors wish to express special appreciation to the Centenary College Alumni Association for the generous summer grant which enabled them to commence work on this project. Finally, scarcely enough can be said in praise of Joy Hall, Betty Labor, and Florence Martin for their assistance in the preparation of this manuscript.

We would also like to express our appreciation to the following colleagues throughout the country who read and commented on earlier versions of this text. We have benefited greatly from their criticism, encouragement, and suggestions: Lawrence Berkove, T. Y. Booth, Harry B. Caldwell, Glenn Carey, William E. Carigan, James Culp, Huston Diehl, Clyde Dornbusch, Herbert Fackler, Suzanne Ferguson, Billy Ferris, Jack Folsom, Susan Fox, Donna Gerstenberger, Kevin Harty, Forrest Hazard, Ronald Herzman, Edward Huberman, Elizabeth Huberman, John J. Joyce, Donald D. Kummings, Howard Lachtman, Walton Litz, Ralph Loomis, John Matthews, Randy Nelson, Mary B. Pulleyn, Kenneth Rothwell, William Shaw, Donald Stone, Eric Sundquist, Cynthia Thomiszer, Vincent L. Toller, Linda Wagner, Winston Weathers, Seth Weiner, Robert E. Yarber.

Introduction to Reading Literature

I

Some anonymous versifier, in a playful mood one day, sat down and wrote:

> There's a notable family named Stein,
> There's Gert and there's Ep and there's Ein.
>> Gert's prose is all bunk
>> Ep's sculpture just junk
> And nobody understands Ein.

A well-known poet, Ezra Pound, even more incisive, once wrote:

> *In a Station of the Metro*
>
> The apparition of these faces in the crowd;
> Petals on a wet, black bough.

Here we have two complete poems, accessible, and easy enough, although the limerick seems more immediate because of its conventional shape and obvious tradition, its rhymes and rhythm, and because it makes a statement. Pound's two lines, however, also have a tradition and a structure, and, in fewer words, possibly more meaning. In both cases, we can make an immediate response to the pieces. They are not forbidding; they are inviting, or almost so.

The writer of the limerick invites us in to share his light laughter. He is in a playful mood, and he wants company. We join him. We may not have met Gert or Ep before, but perhaps by the end of the limerick we suspect we have met Ein: There was, after all a Stein named Ein, except that he was really Einstein, and we know we didn't understand him when we met him. Gert and Ep must be just as challenging, although obviously their fields were different. The author has invited us in, and whether or not we comprehend it all, we are smiling with him.

Pound does not quite invite us in. But he allows us to listen in. His speaker seems to be musing, for himself and to himself, as much as for our benefit. We know where he is, and we are with him, there in a station in a subway, very likely in Paris: The title has implied that. The speaker does not look directly at us, perhaps, but maybe forward or slightly downward, at faces in a crowd. They resemble something; they are like white petals of flowers, fruit blossoms possibly, stuck to a wet, black bough. We have overheard the muser or walking beside him have been addressed by him as he continued to look downward at these faces. We are not invited in; we simply are in the metro.

These are our first impressions of these poems, our initial responses, although having gone this far in our musing with the speaker in Pound's lines, we have already deepened our response. Still, we have not gone as far as we might. Good literature always invites us further in, and good literature always invites us through multiple doors. We may enter by means of one, or several, and often we may enter

1

by one only to return and enter by means of another later on. When we do, however, we may not see quite the same interior that we saw earlier.

Let's look at that limerick through another door. As we said already, there's a structure and there's a tradition here. But we did not really get into either yet. The limerick has a long history and a prescribed structure, with only slight variations—five lines (or four with two half-lines playing against each other), generally anapestic (triple) rhythm, the first, second, and fifth lines longer than the third and fourth, with rhymes according. We like the limerick partly for its traditional humor, to be sure, but partly for its predictability coupled with unpredictability. There's a definite structure, with which we are familiar and therefore comfortable. There's also a twist and a surprise waiting for us at the end. The juncture of the known and the unknown gives us something of the form of the poem. Or put differently, we are starting to see something of what critics in this century have called the *formalistic approach* to a poem—an awareness of the close relationship between the very specific details and shapes and the meanings of a piece of literature, a form so closely bound with the full experience of the piece that we can say that it is organic or integral to the work.

Pound's lines at first do not seem nearly so conventional, for there is no stanzaic pattern or rhyming pattern giving us traditional signposts along the way —at least not for the average reader in the Western tradition. And the poem is so brief that it is over before we have blinked twice. Is it a poem? Can it have a tradition and a structure? Indeed it can, for the poem is modeled on a form about as old as the limerick—the Japanese haiku. To be sure, the lines from Pound do not exemplify in every detail the definition of the haiku, but the length is near the prescribed seventeen syllables, and even more important is the interplay of a fairly prosaic statement or phrase (the first line) with the sudden, vivid image of the second line, an image that we do not expect to see but which, like the last line of a limerick, is crucial for what we finally do see. It is, again, an organic form, a living interplay of lines that shapes our feelings and our response to the scene.

Let's now open another door or two, and enter these pieces anew. Who, after all, are Gert and Ep in the limerick? (Remember, we recognized Ein earlier.) Maybe the names are further tricks, and then again maybe they are not. A brief comment will clue us in. For some of us already suspect that Gert *is* a Stein, the only true one in the group. She's Gertrude Stein, patroness of literary figures, shaper of ideas in the Paris of the 1920s, namer of the Lost Generation, "a rose is a rose is a rose," and all that, and possibly the writer of prose bunk. Ep is not a Stein, but Jacob Epstein is a well-known sculptor: As with Gert, some may like his work and some may not, but clearly the author of the limerick is inviting us to lump the author, the sculptor, and the scientist in a group that we can enjoy poking fun at.

We would not care to break a butterfly upon a wheel—but let's get serious about humor for a moment. Why do we smile at this poem or its disparagement of famous figures? What is the nature of the bond that the author sets up between himself and us? If we engage in a bit of soul-searching, the answer we get may not be flattering. Most of us are not gifted, most of us will not leave a mark on the

2

worlds of science or art or literature and ideas. But these three figures, makers of junk and developers of ideas beyond our ken, have made a mark, whether or not we like it. They have presented a world beyond us, a world that we fear we may not be able to enter. So we enter the world of the author of the limerick and laugh at those whose worlds we may not enter. That's not a flattering idea. It means that we have a sense of inadequacy and want to cover it with scorn and laughter. It means that we are looking for a scapegoat on whom or on which we can place our sense of guilt so that we are free again. Not a pleasant thought, after all, as we see that the psychological roots of our laughter go deep, deep into the unconscious where *archetypes* lurk.

And what about another door that leads us into the Pound lines? That first line is fairly prosaic, as we said. But the word "apparition" has connotations. The word does not suggest only something that appears: Rather, the suggestion is of something that appears, and disappears, like ghosts perhaps. Also there's a crowd, but it's a lonely crowd, for apparitions come and go, with little or no bond among them. There's a ghostly, ephemeral, lonely feeling here, deep within the earth. Suddenly the counterthrust of the second line comes to us. It's a scene from nature, above the surface of the earth, coupled, however, with that below the earth. The scene is at once lovely and foreboding. The petals are in themselves lovely, white, or pink perhaps, the residue of a fruit blossom. It has rained, the bough is wet, the petals are knocked from the blossom and are sticking to the wet, black bough. Although the seed they helped engender may live on, these petals are dying, dying on the blackness of the bough. Like the faces in the metro, they are stark against a dark background—apparitions. There's a somberness amid the beauty, a hint of death and loneliness, a theme of nature's being born to die, with man amongst it all. The metro takes on the proportions of the ancient myths of Charon and the river Styx, of Pluto and Hades. There's a hint that archetypally we are dealing with the myths of nature, renewing itself to be sure, but the myths also of the unredeemed loneliness of the human being, whether it be the loneliness of the ancient Hades or that of alienated modern humanity.

So what have we here in this meditation on two short poems? We have several means of literary interpretation. We have techniques for entering a piece of literature to make it our own, so that within it we may experience it in different ways. We have a felt response, a *precritical response*. We have a sense of structure or form. We have traditions and *genres*. We have some hints of psychology and some of the abiding archetypes that lie below the surface of these responses. We have enduring concerns that speak directly to our experiences as human beings.

II

Stories too, no less than poems, are universal in their appeal. There's something inherently human about listening to and reading stories, probably because stories, whatever their subject, usually tell us something about ourselves. That's no doubt a large part of the appeal in Somerset Maugham's little tale, "Appointment in Samarra," told by the character Death in the play *Sheppy*.

There was a merchant in Bagdad who sent his servant to market to buy provisions, and in a little while the servant came back, white and trembling, and said, "Master, just now when I was in the marketplace I was jostled by a woman in the crowd and when I turned I saw it was Death that jostled me. She looked at me and made a threatening gesture; now, lend me your horse, and I will ride away from this city and avoid my fate. I will go to Samarra and there Death will not find me." The merchant lent him his horse, and the servant mounted it, and he dug his spurs in its flanks and as fast as the horse could gallop he went. Then the merchant went down to the marketplace and he saw Death standing in the crowd and he came to Death and said, "Why did you make a threatening gesture to my servant when you saw him this morning?" "That was not a threatening gesture," Death said. "It was only a start of surprise. I was astonished to see him in Bagdad, for I had an appointment with him tonight in Samarra."

Many readers find in this brief story an uncanny fascination, a familiarity, almost a feeling of *déjà vu*. But why should that be so? To answer this question, let's use some of the same interpretive techniques we employed with our limerick and with Pound's "In a Station of the Metro."

What is our initial or precritical response to "Appointment in Samarra"? Many of us are probably struck by the "surprise ending," although some might refine that a bit and suggest that what we appreciate is the story's wonderful *irony*. Still, there's more to it than that. Even a story as short as this has many layers of meaning. Let's see if we can find our way to some of its deeper levels.

As we have seen, a good starting place for any interpretation is with form and structure. A story only one paragraph long may not seem to offer much form to analyze; but when we look more closely, we find that Maugham's brief paragraph has all of the necessary elements of good fiction: setting, plot, character, mood, and theme.

One of the first things we notice is the setting: Bagdad, the mysterious land of flying carpets, magic lamps, and *The Thousand and One Nights*. And Maugham reinforces our initial impression through mood and style. The story is told in a straightforward manner. The style is economical, almost terse; the language is plain, but the tone is slightly formal and sounds somewhat foreign, perhaps like a translation from the original Arabic. The opening action appears perfectly commonplace: A merchant has sent his servant to market to buy provisions. Then an extraordinary thing happens. The servant reports that he has been "jostled" in the marketplace by a woman—something we know happens all the time—but on closer inspection the servant discovers that this woman is, in fact, Death and that she is looking at him with a "threatening gesture."

In Bagdad, in that magical time of the *Arabian Nights*, perhaps it was normal to encounter Death in a marketplace. At any rate, that's the impression Maugham gives us through his matter-of-fact style and direct manner. The story is told as though the narrator or storyteller has absolute faith in the accuracy of what he is reporting, and that tone draws us directly into the story.

As we have already observed, one of the most delightful things about this story is Maugham's use of *irony*. But for that irony to work on us, we must not be given time to contemplate what is coming next or to analyze the action as it unfolds. Irony results, in large measure, from things not being what they seem. Sometimes readers are aware of the discrepancy between what appears to be true and what is actually so; sometimes they discover the discrepancy at the same time as does one of the characters or the narrator. In either case there is that delicious sense of uncovering the difference between appearance and reality. But let's examine the ways in which Maugham builds the irony in his plot. There are at least two major ironic turns before we come to the final one. The first occurs almost immediately when the servant is "jostled by a woman," but that woman turns out to be Death. The next turn comes when the merchant discovers that Death was not making a "threatening gesture" at all but was only surprised to see the servant in Bagdad. The final irony, of course, is that the servant who has fled to Samarra to escape his fate has only helped to bring it about and will now be able to keep his appointment with Death.

This *formal* analysis has uncovered quite a lot, but let's try another technique. We said earlier that the story has a theme. We might have said that it has a moral. Maugham's little story, like the limerick and the haiku, has a long tradition behind it. Some of us, no doubt, have recognized its similarity to the moral tale or parable. "Appointment in Samarra" teaches us a rather familiar lesson: that none of us can escape our fate and that Death has an appointment with each of us. Similar stories appear in every culture, often with Death *personified* and given a role to play. Other examples include Chaucer's "Pardoner's Tale" and Poe's "Masque of the Red Death." But even Sophocles's play *Oedipus the King* touches the same theme, for both Oedipus and his father Laius attempt to escape their fates. In fact, in a very condensed version, Maugham's tale offers us one of the most pervasive themes in all literature and one to which we will frequently return in this anthology.

But why should such a theme be so pervasive? Perhaps another approach will lead us toward an answer. In *Hero with a Thousand Faces,* Joseph Campbell records the following dream taken from an actual case history:

> I was on a bridge where I met a blind fiddler. Everyone was tossing coins into his hat. I came close and perceived that the musician was not blind. He had a squint, and was looking at me with a crooked glance from the side. Suddenly, there was a little old woman sitting at the side of a road. It was dark and I was afraid. "Where does this road lead?" I thought. A young peasant came along the road and took me by the hand. "Do you want to come home," he said, "and drink coffee?" "Let me go! You are holding too tight!" I cried, and awoke.

The dream lacks the artistry and unity of Maugham's story, but there are some interesting parallels. Death appears in several "avatars" or incarnations—as the blind fiddler, the man with a squint, the little old woman, and the peasant—all of which seem frightening to the dreamer. This is clearly an anxiety dream, and the dreamer is afraid not only of death's touch, but of "a crooked glance," which sounds very much like Maugham's woman who "looks" at the servant and makes a "threatening gesture." Maugham seems to have tapped a deep psychological fear. And if, as we said, the story appears to have an uncanny familiarity, perhaps we recognize in it some version of our own dreams.

But let's consider still another possible reason for the story's fascination—the fact that in Maugham's tale Death is a woman. This may at first seem unusual to us, although in the dream we just read death appears both as a man and as a woman. In fact, it isn't all that uncommon for death to be represented even as a beautiful woman, which she is in Washington Irving's "Adventure of the German Student" and John Keats's "La Belle Dame sans Merci." In *The Archetypes and the Collective Unconscious,* C. G. Jung points out that death may often appear, especially to men, in the form of a woman, a version of the "terrible mother" or the dark side of the anima, the female spirit that is buried deep in the male psyche. When Maugham gives Death a woman's form, he is reaching back into mythology and giving further life to one of our most haunting archetypes.

And so, as with the two poems we glanced at earlier, we have found several doors opening into Maugham's brief tale. We have noticed the importance of form, of style and irony, and have recognized a familiar moral; we have also found a suggestion of a common psychological fear of death and hints of a familiar archetype. All of this we have uncovered within a very short story, no more than a paragraph in length.

III

We have said a great deal about opening critical doors of various dimensions leading more or less directly into the interior of literary works. Although there are many possible interpretive techniques—countless doors, front, back, and within a work of literature—there are some convenient groupings or categories to which we would like to pay particular attention. We have already mentioned most of them, but perhaps we should review the principal ones now in a more systematic way before attempting to go further.

Traditional Techniques

Traditionally, the study of literature has always included a certain amount of historical and biographical background. Some works of literature make more sense when we look at them in their historical context and when we know something about the lives of their authors. It helps us, for example, to know something about the "three Steins" in our limerick or to discover that Ezra Pound was thinking of the Japanese haiku when he wrote "In a Station of the Metro." Later on we may want to know something about nineteenth-century imperialism when we read Joseph Conrad's *Heart of Darkness* or some of the details of Sylvia Plath's tragic life when we read her poem "Daddy."

Traditional techniques of literary criticism also include textual study. Before we can say with confidence what a literary work is about or what an author means, we must have faith that our text is accurate. For the most part this is a matter for textual scholars who study manuscript evidence and early editions to establish the most accurate possible text. But from time to time textual problems can lead to interesting critical problems. Shakespeare's *Hamlet* offers a famous example: "O that this too too solid flesh would melt." Hamlet speaks this line in his first soliloquy, Act I, scene ii. The word "solid" appears in the first folio edition (1623) of Shakespeare's complete works. Yet the second quarto edition (1604–1605), probably printed from Shakespeare's own manuscript, has "sallied," a legitimate sixteenth-century form of "sully" (to dirty, or make foul). These words pose two rather different interpretations of the line. "Solid" suggests that Hamlet regrets the corporeality of flesh, whereas "sullied" reveals his revulsion upon contemplating life's impurity. Most textual problems occur in manuscripts and early printed works, but modern literature also must have accurate texts before we can interpret it with confidence, as we can see by glancing at the controversy surrounding the final lines of Keats's "Ode on a Grecian Urn."

Not all of the techniques we have lumped together under the general heading of traditional criticism are historical, biographical, or textual. Many traditional critics have sought in literature moral and philosophical meanings. In fact, moral and philosophical interpretations are as old as classical Greek and Roman critics. Plato emphasized morality and utilitarianism; and his greatest student, Aristotle, furthered these concepts in his definitions of tragedy and its cathartic effect. Horace suggested a work should be delightful and instructive *(dulce et utile)*. Among English critics, Samuel Johnson stressed the moral purpose of eighteenth-century, neoclassical writers, and Matthew Arnold urged "sweetness and light" as critical criteria for his fellow Victorians. The basic position of all such critics is that the larger function of literature is to teach morality and probe philosophical issues. Although there are many useful ways of discussing morality and literature, moral-philosophical interpretations tend to direct us to the work's message. In Maugham's "Appointment in Samarra," for example, we would dwell at some length on the theme of death's inevitability, not so much because the work can be reduced to that moral, but because the moral emerges with such clarity through Maugham's little parable.

Finally, we should mention again the work of Aristotle under the heading of traditional techniques. For in his *Poetics,* he dealt with more than the moral dimension alluded to previously, and his theories have come to be absorbed into the thinking of many subsequent generations of readers and interpreters of literature. We may even say that Aristotle laid the foundation for multiple critical approaches to literature, and in that respect he is our most eminent "traditional" critic. He contributed insights into the nature of drama and of the epic, the concept that mimesis (imitation) is the very basis of art. Aristotle also introduced several key critical terms in dramatic analysis: catharsis (purging), the tragic hero, and hubris (overweening pride). He called attention to the moral dimensions of literature and to the psychology of characters. His concepts of the unity of plot are also a beginning point of the formalist approach to literature, a subject to which we now turn.

7

Formalistic Techniques

Although formalism has played some part in literary criticism at least since Aristotle's *Poetics,* the American New Critics of the 1930s—especially John Crowe Ransom, Allen Tate, Robert Penn Warren, and Cleanth Brooks—have been its most influential modern proponents. Formalistic criticism, as the name suggests, concentrates attention on the *form* of a literary work. In fact, this technique often assumes that the work itself is autonomous and that we can read and understand it without concerning ourselves about historical background or the author's life and without seeking moral or philosophical "messages." The formalistic interpretation seeks to discover what the work is, its shape and effect, and how these are achieved. And it usually insists that all relevant answers to such questions should come from the work itself.

Formalists begin with a careful, close reading of the text. The reader pays close attention to the language, to the meanings of individual words, as well as to such things as *imagery, connotation,* and *tone.* After individual words, formalists concern themselves with structures and patterns: the interrelationships of words, the overall form of the work. Thus formalism is sensitive to any repetition of words, images, or structural patterns in the theme, plot, or setting.

Formalism may seem most suited to the study of poetry, where, as we have seen, great emphasis is placed on individual words and images; however, it can also be helpful to readers of fiction and drama, where we may find ourselves affected not only by specific words and images but by elaborate structural patterns in the overall form of the work. Maugham's "Appointment in Samarra" is too brief to make this absolutely clear, but when we read longer works we will discover some of these patterns. We might, for example, trace Conrad's repetition of his title *Heart of Darkness,* noting the many variations on the meaning of that phrase as the story progresses and observing the important role these words play in structuring our journey through Conrad's text. Finally, we come to recognize that the "heart of darkness" is at the same time a geographical reference to the "darkness" of the "heart" of the African jungle, a psychological reference to the "darkness" within the tormented Mr. Kurtz (and every human being), and a formal or structural reference to the "darkness" of the mystery at the heart of Conrad's story. Nor is it formally insignificant that all of these references are bound together by the journey into darkness on the great river that runs through the book.

Psychological Techniques

Like traditional and formalistic techniques, psychological interpretations of literature have a distinguished history. Aristotle included psychological analysis both in his *Poetics* and in his *Art of Rhetoric.* In fact, any study of the characters in a literary work or the relationship between an author's life and his writing will include a certain amount of psychological analysis. It is well to remember that psychology means the study of the soul *(psyche)* or being, although recently we have tended to think of it as an analysis of the mind. The most systematic psychological techniques of literary criticism, however, derive from Sigmund Freud's theory of psychoanalysis.

Freud drew many of his insights into the workings of the mind from his consideration of literature and the literary process. In "Creative Writers and Day-Dreaming," he suggested that a writer's unconscious wishes and ambitions, which cannot be fulfilled in actual life, are imaginatively transformed into the work of art. Literature is in effect an artistic daydream: The writer creates a fantasy generated by repressed desires that take on symbolic guises and appear as plot, imagery, characterization, and other aspects of the text. This "symbolic" material, like the imagery and events of a dream, can be analyzed to reveal the fantasy at the heart of the literary work. Psychoanalysis can also illuminate the emotional reasons we turn, as writers and as readers, to literature, and it can help us discover the ways a poem, story, or play affect us psychologically.

Using a spatial metaphor, Freud divided the human psyche into several layers. The surface layer, the *conscious* mind, is in command of most of our waking mental activity. But below the layer of consciousness are the *preconscious,* which contains psychic material that can easily become conscious and just as easily become hidden (or *latent*) again, and the *unconscious,* which contains psychic material repressed by some opposing force (or *resistance*) and which cannot become conscious nor be explained without the psychoanalytic process to remove the resistance. During sleep, however, this resistance lowers naturally and unconscious desires and fears manifest themselves symbolically as dreams. This same unconscious material may also be the stuff of the literary text.

In illuminating these mental processes, Freud distinguished three psychic areas of the mind: the *id,* the *ego,* and the *superego.* The id is the source of all instinctual drives for physical and sexual satisfaction, regardless of consequences to the individual or society. Freud believed that the id's psychic energy, the *libido,* derived from sexual instincts or *Eros.* Consequently, he suggested, nearly all actions and neuroses may be explained in terms of their sexual origin. The ego controls the baser impulses of the id, by either postponing or suppressing them. Thus the ego, representing reason and common sense, substitutes the *reality principle* (the influence of the external world) for the *pleasure principle* (the id's unrestrained desire for gratification). The superego, the repository of social customs and prohibitions inherited from parents and authority figures, exercises influence over both the id and the ego. Although this voice of morality and higher ideals makes its demands unconsciously, we often experience its dictates as the *conscience.*

Psychoanalytic criticism, as we have stated, concerns itself with interpreting the forms these unconscious processes take in the imagery and plot of a work of literature. Much of this imagery may be interpreted in terms of sexuality. Concave images (such as cups, ships, vessels, or caves) are often taken to be female or yonic symbols. Images longer than they are wide (such as towers, rifles, snakes, knives, or swords) are taken as male or phallic symbols. Activities such as dancing, riding, or flying also become symbols of sexual pleasure. For example, in *The Life and Works of Edgar Allan Poe: A Psycho-Analytic Interpretation,* Marie Bonaparte interprets the flying figure of Psyche in "Ulalume" in terms of sexual imagery: "Psyche's drooping trailing wings in this poem symbolise in concrete form Poe's physical impotence. We know that flying, to all races, unconsciously symbolises the sex act, and that antiquity often represented the penis erect and winged."

Mythological and Archetypal Techniques

There's a close connection between psychological techniques of interpretation and mythological-archetypal techniques. Although risking the danger of oversimplification, we might say that what psychoanalysis attempts to disclose about the individual personality, the study of myths reveals about the mind and character of a people or culture. And just as dreams reflect the unconscious desires and anxieties of the individual, so myths are the symbolic projections of a people's hopes, values, fears, and aspirations.

According to the common misconceptions and misuse of the term, *myths* are merely primitive fictions, illusions, or opinions based upon false reasoning. Actually, mythology encompasses more than stories about Greek and Roman deities or clever fables invented for the amusement of children. It may be true that myths do not meet our current standards of factual reality, but then neither does any great literature. Instead, they both reflect a more profound reality. Myths are, by nature, collective and communal; they bind a tribe or a nation together in that particular people's common psychological and spiritual activities. Moreover, myth is ubiquitous in time as well as place. It is a dynamic factor everywhere in human society; it transcends time, uniting the past (traditional modes of belief) with the present (current values) and reaching toward the future (spiritual and cultural aspirations).

Mythological interpretations of literature tend to delve beneath the surfaces of individual works to seek common mythic patterns. One such pattern, for example, may be distinguished in stories about death in which Death is *personified* as one of the characters, as in "Appointment in Samarra." These stories appear in many versions. Indeed, there are several others in this anthology, but they all seem to derive from the fact that we human beings are aware of our own mortality and often fear and even seek some escape from our inevitable demise. Virtually every culture seems to have at least one version of this old story about a man or woman attempting to outwit Death.

Another somewhat more contemporary example of a mythic pattern is our own myth of the American Dream, which has its origins in the idea that America is a new Eden, an earthly paradise or promised land, and has continued in more recent American mythology to be the land of opportunity where everyone has an equal chance to enjoy both material prosperity and spiritual fulfillment: "the right to life, liberty, and the pursuit of happiness." Quite a lot of American literature deals in one way or another with this particular myth. Often, in fact, American authors ask us to contemplate some failure to achieve the dream, as in John Cheever's "The Swimmer," James Thurber's "The Secret Life of Walter Mitty," or Arthur Miller's *Death of a Salesman*.

10

One of the major influences on mythological criticism is the work of C. G. Jung, the great psychologist-philosopher and one-time student of Freud who broke with the master because of what he regarded as a too narrow approach to psycho-analysis. Jung believed libido (psychic energy) to be more than sexual; also, he considered Freudian theories too negative because of Freud's emphasis on the neurotic rather than on the healthy aspects of the psyche.

Jung's primary contribution to myth criticism is his theory of racial memory and archetypes. In developing this concept, Jung expanded Freud's theories of the personal unconscious, asserting that beneath this is a primeval, collective uncon-scious shared in the psychic inheritance of all members of the human family. Just as certain instincts are inherited by the lower animals, so more complex psychic predispositions (that is, a "racial memory") are inherited by human beings. And one of the ways in which the psychic inheritance is transmitted is through myths. In other words, myths are the means by which archetypes, essentially unconscious forms, become manifest and articulate to the conscious mind. Jung indicated fur-ther that archetypes reveal themselves in the dreams of individuals, so that we might say that dreams are "personalized myths" and myths are "depersonalized dreams." Jung detected an intimate relationship among dreams, myths, and art in that all three serve as media through which archetypes become accessible to consciousness.

Another of Jung's major contributions is his theory of *individuation* as related to those archetypes designated as the *shadow,* the *persona,* and the *anima.* Individua-tion is a psychological "growing up," the process of discovering those aspects of one's self that make one an individual different from other members of our species. It is basically a process of self-recognition, which requires extraordinary courage and honesty but is absolutely essential if we are to become well-balanced individu-als. Jung theorizes that neuroses are the results of the person's failure to confront and accept some archetypal component of his or her consciousness.

The *shadow, persona,* and *anima* (or *animus* in the female psyche) are struc-tural components of the psyche that humans have inherited; they are part of the collective unconscious we all share. The shadow is the darker side of our uncon-scious self, the inferior and less pleasing aspect of the personality, which we wish to suppress. The most common variant of this archetype, when projected, is the Devil and, in literature, evil characters such as Conrad's Kurtz. The anima is a more complex archetype. It is the "soul-image," the spirit of human life force or vital energy. Jung gives the anima a feminine designation in the male psyche, pointing out that the "anima-image is usually projected upon women," whereas its counter-part, the animus, is projected on men. The anima thus represents the image of the opposite sex that each of us carries within us. Moreover, the projections of the anima may be both good and evil. Positive projections would include such ideal literary females as Poe's Helen, but on occasion a darker side may emerge, and the anima projection may be a personification of the "terrible mother" or a temptress as in Maugham's "Appointment in Samarra" and Irving's "Adventure of the German Student." Finally, the obverse of the anima is the persona, our social personality, the actor's mask we show to the world.

11

Sociological Techniques

The interaction between literature and society can flow in either direction. Nearly every literary work bears some relationship to the society out of which it has grown and toward which it is directed for either instruction or entertainment or both. For this reason sociologists and social critics often use works of literature as evidence or data in their studies of societies, of social customs and manners. Although some literary critics may object to this particular use of literature, it has proven valuable to sociologists and historians. Classical history and anthropology, for example, have benefited considerably from the study of literary works by classical Greek authors such as Homer, Sophocles, and Aristophanes because these works give insights into the values and manners of early Greek civilization. But literature itself may have an impact on society and may even be written to force or at least facilitate social awareness and change. That was certainly a part of Charles Dickens's purpose in novels like *Nicholas Nickleby* and *Oliver Twist,* which exposed the abuses of Victorian England, especially toward children and the poor. And there is a large measure of social protest against the evils of European imperialism and colonialism in Joseph Conrad's *Heart of Darkness.*

Sociological techniques have been particularly popular among those who demand a more active role for literature and criticism. Marxist critics, for example, place considerable stress on the uses of literature as an instrument of proletarian revolt as well as a projection of the currents of social history. They prefer to see literature as one part of a total program of social and political reform. Thus Marxists have accused formalists of restricting their attention to the art work itself, its internal and aesthetic form, without paying sufficient attention to the social milieu in which it found its being or the social circumstances to which it ought to speak. Feminist critics have directed attention to the literary treatment of women and to images of women in literature. They have brought to literary and social criticism a distinctly female perspective, altering and correcting male-dominated histories of literature and culture. Books like Elaine Showalter's *A Literature of Their Own* have focused critical interest on women writers and their visions of the world and the roles of women in society. The study of regional literature or the literature of racial or ethnic minorities may also be classified with sociological criticism, especially when the emphasis is on social relationships between groups or between the individual and society. Virtually all literature about human beings has this social dimension; sociological techniques bring that dimension to the fore.

Reader-Response Criticism

Recently, literary theory and interpretation has been concerned with the role of the reader and the reader's response to the literary experience or to reading a literary work. These reader-response critics have emphasized the way readers "respond" to the written language of a literary text. Some have even reminded us that every reader has a unique and individual experience. In spite of this uniqueness of response, authors usually write to be read, and one of the things authors do through literary artistry is manipulate and attempt to control the reader's response by manipulating the language, imagery, organization, and structure of a work of literature. Critics who stress the role of the reader or the reading process or the ways an author attempts to influence the reader's response may be grouped together in this category.

For example, a reader-response critic might point to the significance of the many compound sentences and the repetition of the conjunction "and" in Maugham's "Appointment in Samarra." The conjunction tends to link the many simple statements into a chain and to propel the reader forward so that we do not have time to pause and think about what is happening until the final ironic remark of Death. Perhaps the tone and the choice of words represent additional strategies designed to influence the reader's response to the story. The opening words, "There was a merchant in Bagdad . . . ," recall a familiar formula of storytelling and alert us to the pattern of the unfolding tale. To some extent the author counts on our recognizing such formulas and responding to them, for instance, by suspending our disbelief when we read that the servant has encountered Death in the marketplace, a fact we might otherwise question in ordinary conversation but are willing to accept as part of a story or fiction.

In some ways reader-response criticism resembles older forms of literary criticism. Rhetorical criticism, for example, has (at least since Aristotle's *Art of Rhetoric*) stressed the importance of the audience and has explored ways in which an author can manipulate an audience or readers by manipulating language. Among modern critics Wayne Booth, author of *The Rhetoric of Fiction,* has insisted on the importance of literary rhetoric. Furthermore, reader-response criticism in practice often resembles formalist criticism, especially when employing the techniques of close reading. Certainly, reader-response critics, like other literary critics, must rely to some extent on close study of the text, but, as Stanley Fish has emphasized in *Is There a Text in This Class?,* affective criticism (or criticism that emphasizes the reader's response to the literary work) should be focused on the reader and the role that the reader plays in the interpretive act. In books such as *The Dynamics of Literary Response* and *5 Readers Reading* Norman Holland, a licensed psychoanalyst as well as a practicing literary critic, has pointed to links between reader-response criticism and psychoanalysis. He has even stressed the importance of a reader's personal response to the literary work. The fact that a reader of Pound's "In a Station of the Metro" has lived in Paris and experienced the Paris subway will be a part of that reader's experience of the poem. Finally, many recent theorists—some of whom would not be comfortably grouped with these we have labeled reader-response critics—have placed great importance on the reading and interpretation of literature as a creative act, finding validity in interpretations that may lead to sometimes brilliant though unusual and even idiosyncratic readings of familiar works. The impulse behind much reader-response criticism is to challenge authority, especially the authority of the literary text, and to open the text to a variety of readings and interpretations, emphasizing the reader's experience of literature.

Clearly, in such a brief survey we have not been able to give adequate treatment to any of these critical approaches. We hope we have provided a useful introductory survey of the interpretive techniques. But most important of all, we hope we have been able to indicate the many available critical doors that lead into literature. No one door is the right one or the only one. As we said earlier, good literature always invites us to go further in and to enter through multiple doors.

"TWENTY QUESTIONS": A CHECKLIST

One way to apply these various interpretive techniques to individual works of literature is to begin by asking some general questions. The following list is certainly not exhaustive or definitive, but it should help get the process of interpretation started. We have grouped the following questions according to specific critical approaches in order to reveal the ways in which different techniques call for different responses or presume different critical attitudes toward the same work of literature.

Reader-response

1. How do you feel about this work? For example, what feelings did it evoke when you read it—pity, fear, suspense, surprise, joy, humor?
2. Does your attitude toward or understanding of the work change as you read it? What brings about or conditions that change? How many different ways can the work be read?
3. By manipulating such literary devices as tone and point of view, authors try to establish a relationship between their work and their readers. What relationship to the reader does this work (or author) assume? What elements of the work help establish this relationship?

Formal

4. Make an inventory of the key words, symbols, and images in the work by listing those that seem most significant to you. What "meanings" seem to be attached to these words, symbols, and images?
5. How do these words, symbols, and images help to provide unity or define the overall pattern or structure of the work?
6. Under what genre should the work be classified? What generic conventions are readily apparent? If it is fiction or drama, what does each of the five structural elements—plot, character, setting, theme, and mood—contribute to the work? If it is poetry, how do meter, rhythm, rhyme, and figurative language contribute to your experience of the poem? (See the glossary for definitions of these key critical terms.)

14

Traditional

7. How does the work reflect the biographical or historical background of the author or the time during which it was written?
8. What are the principal themes of the work?
9. What moral statement, if any, does the work make? What philosophical view of life or the world does the work present?

Psychological

10. What are the principal characteristics or defining traits of the protagonist or main character(s) in the work?
11. What psychological relationships exist between and among the characters? Try to determine which characters are stronger and which are weaker. What is the source of their strength or weakness?
12. Are there unconscious conflicts within or between characters? How are these conflicts portrayed in the work? Is the Freudian concept of the id-ego-superego applicable?
13. Is sexuality or sexual imagery employed in the work? Does the work contain Freudian or psychoanalytic symbolism: for example, the Oedipus complex, the pleasure principle, wish fulfillment?
14. How do the principal characters view the world around them and the other characters in the work? Is that view accurate or trustworthy, or do you sense some distortion? If you do, what do you think causes that distortion?

Mythological-Archetypal

15. Does the work contain mythic elements in plot, theme, or character? If not specific ancient myths or modern ones like the American Dream, are there recognizable mythic patterns such as rebirth/fertility, quest/journey, struggle/return of the hero?
16. Are there archetypal characters, images, or symbols, such as the great mother, the wise old man, the sea, the seasons? How do these archetypal elements contribute to the work?
17. Do you find a pattern of growth or "individuation" such as C. G. Jung describes? Are certain characters identifiable as shadow, persona, or anima types?

Sociological

18. What is the relationship between the work and the society it presents or grew out of? Does it address particular social issues either directly or indirectly—for example, race, sex, class, religion, politics?

19. What is the sex of the main character(s)? Does that affect your reading of the work? Does sexual identity affect the relationships among characters in the work?

*   *   *

20. Finally, does the story, poem, or play lend itself to one of the various interpretive techniques more than to others?

Reading Fiction

The short story is one of the oldest forms of literature. The fairy tales our mothers and fathers told us at the bedside are in a direct line of descent from the ancient myths, legends, and folktales that our ancestors recounted to amuse and instruct one another even before they had a written language. And these two elements, amusement and instruction, have remained an important part of storytelling and reading for us as well. As we observed in the "Introduction to Reading Literature," good literature always invites us to look beneath the surface, to seek deeper levels of meaning and enjoyment. Let's take, for example, the following story by Edgar Allan Poe.

The Masque of the Red Death

The "Red Death" had long devastated the country. No pestilence had ever been so fatal or so hideous. Blood was its Avatar and its seal—the redness and the horror of blood. There were sharp pains, and sudden dizziness, and then profuse bleeding at the pores, with dissolution. The scarlet stains upon the body, and especially upon the face of the victim, were the pest ban which shut him out from the aid and from the sympathy of his fellow-men; and the whole seizure, progress, and termination of the disease, were the incidents of half-an-hour.

But the Prince Prospero was happy and dauntless and sagacious. When his dominions were half-depopulated, he summoned to his presence a thousand hale and light-hearted friends from among the knights and dames of his court, and with these retired to the deep seclusion of one of his castellated abbeys. This was an extensive and magnificent structure, the creation of the prince's own eccentric yet august taste. A strong and lofty wall girdled it in. This wall had gates of iron. The courtiers, having entered, brought furnaces and massy hammers and welded the bolts. They resolved to leave means neither of ingress or egress to the sudden impulses of despair from without or of frenzy from within. The abbey was amply provisioned. With such precautions the courtiers might bid defiance to contagion. The external world could take care of itself. In the meantime it was folly to grieve or to think. The prince had provided all the appliances of pleasure. There were buffoons, there were improvisatori, there were ballet dancers, there were musicians, there was beauty, there was wine. All these and security were within. Without was the "Red Death."

It was toward the close of the fifth or sixth month of his seclusion, and while the pestilence raged most furiously abroad, that the Prince Prospero entertained his thousand friends at a masked ball of the most unusual magnificence.

It was a voluptuous scene, that masquerade. But first let me tell of the rooms in which it was held. There were seven—an imperial suite. In many palaces, however, such suites form a long and straight vista, while the folding doors slide back nearly to the walls on either hand, so that the view of the whole extent is scarcely impeded. Here the case was very different, as might have been expected from the duke's love of the *bizarre.* The apartments were so irregularly disposed that the vision embraced but little more than one at a time. There was a sharp turn at every twenty or thirty yards, and at each turn a novel effect. To the right and left, in the middle of each wall, a tall and narrow Gothic window looked out upon a closed corridor which pursued the windings of the suite. These windows were of stained glass whose color varied in accordance with the prevailing hue of the decorations of the chamber into which it opened. That at the eastern extremity was hung, for example, in blue, and vividly blue were its windows. The second chamber was purple in its ornaments and tapestries, and here the panes were purple. The third was green throughout, and so were the casements. The fourth was furnished and lighted with orange, the fifth with white, the sixth with violet. The seventh apartment was closely shrouded in black velvet tapestries that hung all over the ceiling and down the walls, falling in heavy folds upon a carpet of the same material and hue. But in this chamber only the colour of the windows failed to correspond with the decorations. The panes here were scarlet—a deep blood-color. Now in no one of the seven apartments was there any lamp or candelabrum amid the profusion of golden ornaments that lay scattered to and fro or depended from the roof. There was no light of any kind emanating from lamp or candle within the suite of chambers; but in the corridors that followed the suite there stood opposite to each window a heavy tripod bearing a brazier of fire that projected its rays through the tinted glass and so glaringly illuminated the room. And thus were produced a multitude of gaudy and fantastic appearances. But in the western or black chamber the effect of the firelight that streamed upon the dark hangings, through the blood-tinted panes, was ghastly in the extreme, and produced so wild a look upon the countenances of those who entered that there were few of the company bold enough to set foot within its precincts at all.

It was in this apartment also that there stood against the western wall a gigantic clock of ebony. Its pendulum swung to and fro with a dull, heavy, monotonous clang; and when the minute-hand made the circuit of the face, and the hour was to be stricken, there came from the brazen lungs of the clock a sound which was clear and loud, and deep, and exceedingly musical, but of so peculiar a note and emphasis that, at each lapse of an hour, the musicians of the orchestra were constrained to pause momentarily in their performance to hearken to the sound; and thus the waltzers perforce ceased their evolutions, and there was a brief disconcert of the whole gay company, and while the chimes of the clock yet rang it was observed that the giddiest grew pale, and the more aged and sedate passed their hands over their brows as if in confused reverie or meditation; but when the echoes had fully ceased a light laughter at once pervaded the assembly; the musicians looked at each other and smiled as if at their own nervousness and folly, and made whispering vows each to the other that the next chiming of the clock should produce in them no similar emotion, and then, after the lapse of sixty minutes (which embrace three thousand and six hundred seconds of the time that flies), there came yet another chiming of the clock, and then were the same disconcert and tremulousness and meditation as before.

But in spite of these things it was a gay and magnificent revel. The tastes of the duke were peculiar. He had a fine eye for colors and effects. He disregarded the *decora* of mere fashion. His plans were bold and fiery, and his conceptions glowed with barbaric lustre. There are some who would have thought him mad. His followers felt that he was not. It was necessary to hear, and see, and touch him to be sure that he was not.

He had directed, in great part, the moveable embellishments of the seven chambers, upon occasion of this great *fête;* and it was his own guiding taste which had given character to the masqueraders. Be sure they were grotesque. There were much glare and glitter and piquancy and phantasm—much of what has been since seen in "Hernani." There were arabesque figures with unsuited limbs and appointments. There were delirious fancies such as the madman fashions. There were much of the beautiful, much of the wanton, much of the *bizarre,* something of the terrible, and not a little of that which might have excited disgust. To and fro in the seven chambers there stalked, in fact, a multitude of dreams. And these—the dreams—writhed in and about, taking hue from the rooms, and causing the wild music of the orchestra to seem as the echo of their steps. And, anon, there strikes the ebony clock which stands in the hall of the velvet; and then, for a moment, all is still, and all is silent save the voice of the clock. The dreams are stiff-frozen as they stand. But the echoes of the chime die away—they have endured but an instant—and a light, half-subdued laughter floats after them as they depart. And now again the music swells, and the dreams live, and writhe to and fro more merrily than ever, taking hue from the many tinted windows through which stream the rays from the tripods. But to the chamber which lies most westwardly of the seven, there are now none of the maskers who venture; for the night is waning away; and there flows a ruddier light through the blood-coloured panes; and the blackness of the sable-drapery appals; and to him whose foot falls upon the sable carpet, there comes from the near clock of ebony a muffled peal more solemnly emphatic than any which reaches their ears who indulge in the more remote gaieties of the other apartments.

But these other apartments were densely crowded, and in them beat feverishly the heart of life. And the revel went whirlingly on, until at length there commenced the sounding of midnight upon the clock. And then the music ceased, as I have told; and the evolutions of the waltzers were quieted; and there was an uneasy cessation of all things as before. But now there were twelve strokes to be sounded by the bell of the clock; and thus it happened, perhaps, that more of thought crept, with more of time, into the meditations of the thoughtful among those who revelled. And thus, too, it happened, perhaps, that before the last echoes of the last chime had utterly sunk into silence, there were many individuals in the crowd who had found leisure to become aware of the presence of a masked figure which had arrested the attention of no single individual before. And the rumor of this new presence having spread itself whisperingly around, there arose at length from the whole company a buzz, or murmur, expressive of disapprobation and surprise —then, finally, of terror, of horror, and of disgust.

In an assembly of phantasms such as I have painted, it may well be supposed that no ordinary appearance could have excited such sensation. In truth the masquerade license of the night was nearly unlimited; but the figure in question had out-Heroded Herod, and gone beyond the bounds of even the prince's indefinite decorum. There are chords in the hearts of the most reckless which cannot be touched without emotion. Even with the utterly lost, to whom life and death are equally jests, there are matters of which no jest can be made. The whole company indeed seemed now deeply to feel that in the costume and bearing of the stranger neither wit nor propriety existed. The figure was tall and gaunt, and shrouded from head to foot in the habiliments of the grave. The mask which concealed the visage was made so nearly to resemble the countenance of a stiffened corpse that the closest scrutiny must have had difficulty in detecting the cheat. And yet all this might have been endured, if not approved, by the mad revellers around. But the mummer had gone so far as to assume the type of the Red Death. His vesture was dabbled in blood—and his broad brow, with all the features of the face, was be-sprinkled with the scarlet horror.

When the eyes of Prince Prospero fell upon this spectral image (which with a slow and solemn movement, as if more fully to sustain its *rôle,* stalked to and fro among the waltzers) he was seen to be convulsed in the first moment with a strong shudder either of terror or distaste; but in the next his brow reddened with rage.

"Who dares?" he demanded hoarsely of the courtiers who stood near him—"who dares insult us with this blasphemous mockery? Seize him and unmask him, that we may know whom we have to hang at sunrise from the battlements!"

It was in the eastern or blue chamber in which stood the Prince Prospero as he uttered these words. They rang throughout the seven rooms loudly and clearly—for the prince was a bold and robust man, and the music had become hushed at the waving of his hand.

It was in the blue room where stood the prince, with a group of pale courtiers by his side. At first, as he spoke, there was a slight rushing movement of this group in the direction of the intruder, who, at the moment was also near at hand, and now, with deliberate and stately step, made closer approach to the speaker. But, from a certain nameless awe with which the mad assumptions of the mummer had inspired the whole party, there were found none who put forth hand to seize him; so that unimpeded he passed within a yard of the prince's person; and while the vast assembly, as if with one impulse, shrank from the centers of the rooms to the walls, he made his way uninterruptedly, but with the same solemn and measured step which had distinguished him from the first, through the blue chamber to the purple—through the purple to the green—through the green to the orange—through this again to the white—and even thence to the violet, ere a decided movement had been made to arrest him. It was then, however, that the Prince Prospero, maddening with rage and the shame of his own momentary cowardice, rushed hurriedly through the six chambers, while none followed him on account of a deadly terror that had seized upon all. He bore aloft a drawn dagger, and had approached in rapid impetuosity, to within three or four feet of the retreating figure, when the latter, having attained the extremity of the velvet apartment, turned suddenly and confronted his pursuer. There was a sharp cry—and the dagger dropped gleaming upon the sable carpet upon which, instantly afterwards, fell prostrate in death the Prince Prospero. Then, summoning the wild courage of despair, a throng of the revellers at once threw themselves into the black apartment, and, seizing the mummer, whose tall figure stood erect and motionless within the shadows of the ebony clock, gasped in unutterable horror at finding the grave cerements and corpse-like mask which they handled with so violent a rudeness, untenanted by any tangible form.

And now was acknowledged the presence of the Red Death. He had come like a thief in the night; and one by one dropped the revellers in the blood-bedewed halls of their revel, and died each in the despairing posture of his fall; and the life of the ebony clock went out with that of the last of the gay; and the flames of the tripods expired; and darkness and decay and the Red Death held illimitable dominion over all.

Most of us have read stories by Poe before. Many are probably familiar with this one. And some of us no doubt are thinking of those old "B" movies based loosely on Poe's tales, usually with Vincent Price or Christopher Lee as narrator and principal character. One reason Poe is so popular is that he amuses us. He tells us stories that divert our attention from everyday life. And he does it with a certain unmistakable flair. In this particular story we are probably attracted by Poe's *tone* and the *mood* it creates. From the first paragraph we know we are in another world—a world of the bizarre and the horrible. But then we expect that even from the story's title: "The Masque of the Red Death."

We may also be attracted by the swift pace of the story and its surprise ending. True to the horror story tradition, Poe introduces an element of the supernatural or inexplicable. When we have finished reading the tale, we probably find ourselves wondering just who the mysterious masquerader is. If it isn't some gruesome practical joker, is it really the "Red Death" *personified?* And what kills Prince Prospero? Is it the plague, or does he die of fright? And if he dies of fright, what does he see that is so frightening?

Of course, one reason we read Poe's stories—or any other horror stories— is to be shocked if not actually frightened, to feel the hairs on our necks standing on end, a chill crawling up our spines. Also, a sufficient reason for reading any kind of story is simply to find out what happens next, to divert ourselves for a few moments from our everyday thoughts and concerns, to get a thrill or some similar reaction.

But sometimes we may find ourselves asking questions about the stories we have read, wondering not only about the ending but also about details in the plot, the setting, or the theme. Many of us may even go so far as to read a story over again, no longer simply to find out what happens or how it ends, nor for the sheer pleasure that the rereading brings, but to discover more about the story and our responses to it.

The first reading, which is often all we are really interested in (and sometimes all the story will sustain), usually results in amusement or pleasure. Our response is not necessarily a critical one. We may not even wish to judge the author's skill or technique, but only seek to be entertained or diverted. This is a perfectly normal reaction to any work of literature. We have called this initial response the *precritical response,* and it is a necessary part of our enjoyment of all forms of art.

However, when we begin asking questions, of ourselves or of the work, we are moving from the precritical response into the realm of criticism, which is what we are most concerned with. When we begin finding answers to our questions, we have become critics or interpreters; we have found the work of art not merely entertaining but instructive as well.

Let's consider, for example, some of the questions we have already asked ourselves about Poe's "Masque of the Red Death," questions having to do with the story's ending. Who or what is the mysterious masquerader dressed as the Red Death? And why does Prince Prospero fall "prostrate in death" at the mere sight of him?

When we reread the story, we find that Poe has included much richness in a very short tale. There are many possible interpretations. Let's begin with the "Red Death" itself. On the most obvious level the Red Death is a plague, something like the Black Death or bubonic plague that ravaged Europe in the Middle Ages. Its symptoms suggest a horrible disease: "There were sharp pains, and sudden dizziness, and then profuse bleeding at the pores." The bleeding is the reason for the name Red Death. We also know that the disease acts very quickly; the whole progress of the illness takes only half an hour.

But Poe seems to intend his story about the Red Death to suggest something more than the historical plagues that ravaged Europe. When Prince Prospero and his group of "lighthearted" friends retire to the seclusion of one of his abbeys, they appear to be attempting to escape from death itself in any form. Perhaps we notice that the bleeding associated with the Red Death is a particularly vivid way of suggesting the loss of our life substance, through the loss of blood, one of the essentials for sustaining life. At least one critic, Joseph Roppolo, has suggested in *Tulane Studies in English* that the Red Death, the death whose "seal" and "avatar" · is the body's own blood, is the disease of living itself, of mortality, since everyone who lives must one day die.

When the figure of the Red Death appears at the great masquerade dressed in the "habiliments of the grave," it reminds Prince Prospero and his guests of death, which they now must realize they cannot escape simply by locking themselves away in an abbey, any more than the servant in Maugham's "Appointment in Samarra" can escape death by fleeing the city. When the mysterious masquerader apparently vanishes after being confronted by Prospero, we suspect, of course, that this is not one of the guests but some spirit or demon or even *Death* itself.

But what kills the prince when he looks at the figure? Does the Red Death enter his body? Or does he die of fright when suddenly confronted by the masquerader? And why should the prince die of fright? Is he frightened by what he sees? Some readers believe Prospero looks at the face of Death; others think he sees his own likeness afflicted with the Red Death, as though he were looking in a mirror. All of these are possible interpretations, but Poe does not tell us what the prince sees. He leaves that up to us as readers to decide, and our interpretations may depend on what else we see in the story.

So far we have simply skimmed along the surface of Poe's tale, dipping slightly beneath the surface, perhaps, to suggest what Poe may have meant by the Red Death and some of the events at the end of the story. If we were to continue this sort of interpretation, we might construct a fully developed moral or *allegorical* reading of the tale. We might see in it a parable about our fear of death and our fruitless attempts to escape the inevitable—what the Middle Ages or Renaissance would have called a *memento mori,* a reminder of death or of our own mortality, like the skull of the jester Yorick that Hamlet finds in the scene with the gravedigger. Prospero and his friends try to shut themselves away from death and spend their time dancing and feasting, but death finds them anyway. We remember Poe's final words in the story: "and darkness and decay and the Red Death held illimitable dominion over all." Are there other details in the story to support such an interpretation?

We have demonstrated one way of discovering some of the reasons we find Poe's story interesting, but there are many other ways of discussing short stories and longer fiction, some of which may complement this moral or allegorical interpretation and some of which may suggest other interpretations of Poe's tale. For example, rather than seeking immediately the moral or meaning of the story, we might have begun by examining its structure, its form or shape, the details of language and *imagery.* We might look, for example, in a more traditional manner at the familiar elements of *plot, character, setting,* and *mood* as well as at the *theme* or meaning.

Poe believed that stories should be well made, carefully constructed. In his review of Nathaniel Hawthorne's *Twice-Told Tales,* published in 1842 in the same issue of *Graham's Lady and Gentleman's Magazine* as "The Masque of the Red Death," Poe writes:

> A skilful literary artist has constructed a tale. If wise, he has not fashioned his thoughts to accommodate his incidents; but having conceived, with deliberate care, a certain unique or single *effect* to be wrought out, he then invents such incidents—he then combines such events as may best aid him in establishing this preconceived effect. If his very initial sentence tend not to the outbringing of this effect, then he has failed in his first step. In the whole composition there should be no word written, of which the tendency, direct or indirect, is not to the one preestablished design.

In other words, Poe insists on both unity and economy in storytelling: Everything included in the story, every word and image, should contribute to the single "preestablished design"; and nothing that does not contribute to the design should be included in the story.

When we examine "The Masque of the Red Death," using Poe's own criteria of judgment, we find few words wasted. In fact, Poe relies on a simple plot and very little character development. Stated briefly the plot is quite economical: While plague ravages his land, Prince Prospero withdraws with a thousand friends to the safety of one of his abbeys. Within the security of the abbey, they indulge in endless merrymaking, ignoring the terrible plague outside. Eventually, during a magnificent ball, the Red Death enters the secluded stronghold and kills everyone.

As for character development, the only character we learn very much about is Prospero himself. And even he remains mysterious. For instance, do we know where his country is? Is he married? Does he have children? How old is he? What we do know, however, contributes to the mystery. Poe tells us, perhaps with considerable irony, that Prospero is "happy and dauntless and sagacious." He is certainly vain and afflicted with pride enough to think he can escape death. We also learn that his taste is "peculiar," "eccentric yet august," and that he loves the *"bizarre."*

We might ask ourselves why Poe doesn't provide more details of plot and character. But what further details do we require? Instead of wasting time and words on an overelaborate plot or on character development, Poe concentrates primarily on mood and setting to achieve his single effect. From the first paragraph, to which we will return in a moment, the mood of the story is somber and ominous. The image of the Red Death is pervasive, and the setting, the "castellated abbey," is fantastic and bizarre. In fact, the mood seems to be created largely by the setting, especially by Poe's somewhat exaggerated descriptions of the abbey, the rooms decorated for the masked ball, and the masqueraders themselves. The center of the story is the great masquerade that Prospero plans during the fifth or sixth month of seclusion, "while the pestilence raged most furiously abroad." We can picture Prospero and his guests hiding away in their abbey, a kind of sanctuary, while the Red Death destroys the world around them.

Poe describes the masked ball in great detail. He tells us that the arrangement of the seven chambers is unusual, that they appear gaudy and fantastic, that the clanging of the clock and chiming of the hours has a disconcerting effect on the revelers, that the decorations and the costumes of the masqueraders are not only beautiful but grotesque, wanton, and even disgusting, that they "were delirious fancies such as the madman fashions." The masqueraders themselves are like figures from a dream. And in their midst is the ebony clock, ticking away the moments and finally sounding the fateful hour of midnight.

After he has sketched the essential details of plot and character and set the bizarre scene for the masked ball, Poe moves quickly to the *climax* (high point) and *dénouement* (conclusion) of his tale. The Red Death appears or, as Poe puts it, the revelers "become aware of the presence of a masked figure which had arrested the attention of no single individual before." Prince Prospero challenges him, chases him, and falls dead when he confronts him.

All of the details of description and language contribute to Poe's "preestablished design." He has carefully chosen words to convey a mood of horror and apprehension. In the first paragraph, for example, we notice the repetition of words like "red," "blood," "bleeding," and "scarlet." These words not only refer directly to the title of the story and reinforce the emphasis on *red* death or *bloody* death, but they also prepare us for the use of color imagery throughout the story, especially in the visual effects that Prospero strives for in the seven chambers.

Red is certainly the dominant color in the tale; the color of blood, which is the "seal" and "avatar" of the Red Death, is vividly recalled, for example, by the red stained-glass windowpanes in the seventh chamber of Prospero's fantastic suite. And, appropriately, that is the black chamber, the last in the series of seven, and the one that all of the revelers avoid as the ball progresses into the evening. It is the chamber also in which the ebony clock marks the passing of the hours with a disconcerting chime.

Both red and black signify death in Poe's story. Red reminds us of the blood of the Red Death, and black is traditionally the color of death and funerals. The fact that both colors appear in the seventh chamber suggests that the room itself is to be associated with death, an association further reinforced by the presence of the ominous ebony clock. A careful formalist reading, however, would not stop with these, Poe's most conventional color images, but would attempt to explain the color scheme of the other rooms that constitute the setting for the very important masked ball.

Some readers have remarked that the colors of the rooms progress from blue to black and that the rooms are laid out from east to west, suggesting the movement of the sun from dawn to night, or *symbolically* the passage of time from the beginning of life to its end, from birth to death. The other colors may then represent stages in the day or in the life of an individual. Thus the purple of the second room must stand for the first stages of growth after birth; the green of the third room would symbolize further growth and maturity; the orange of the fourth chamber suggests the sun at midday, or perhaps the color of autumn, the season of full maturity and harvest; the fifth room is white suggesting hoary old age; the sixth room is violet, the color of twilight and late evening. The seventh room, as we observed earlier, is black—an almost universal symbol for night and death; the red windows recall, for the reader as well as the revelers, the blood of the Red Death.

If we take Poe's tale to be an allegory of life and death, these meanings seem to fit. Further, the fact that there are seven chambers in Prospero's suite has led a number of interpreters to point to a parallel with Shakespeare's "seven ages of man" in the comedy *As You Like It,* which are very likely derived from the seven decades or seventy years allotted to each individual in the Bible, where three score and ten years is given as the length of a human life. Shakespeare's seven ages are: the infant, the schoolboy, the lover, the soldier, the judge, the piping schoolboy again (second childhood), and the dotard. But do these seven ages of man parallel Poe's seven chambers or the color symbolism we discussed in the previous paragraph? Neither seems a perfect fit, though perhaps both give us some indication of the symbolism Poe is developing in the story.

Another organizing motif that we may want to examine also has to do with the passing of time: the significance of the "gigantic clock of ebony." In fact, the clock extends the meaning of Poe's color imagery. It is an ebony clock, a dark black clock, and it stands in the seventh chamber, the chamber of death. The clock reminds the reader and the revelers of the inevitable and inexorable passage of time—the minutes ticking away, the hours marked by a disconcerting chime. It is important to notice that with each tolling of the hour everything comes to a halt; the revelry ceases as musicians and masqueraders alike note the hour. When the clock strikes midnight, the mysterious masked figure appears in the likeness of the Red Death. Time has run out for Prospero and his lighthearted band of friends.

These formalistic elements, we should notice, complement rather than contradict the allegorical interpretation we mentioned earlier. Poe's story is not simply a horror story; it is a parable of life and death. We might further observe that these allegorical and symbolical elements in the story—the colors (especially red and black); the clock marking the passage of time; the chiming of the hour of midnight (the witching hour) marking the appearance of the Red Death; and even the figure of Death dressed in the "habiliments of the grave"—are all familiar to readers of horror stories the world over. We might even remark that they are conventions of the horror story *genre.* But, as some interpreters would point out, many of these conventional elements of the horror story are also *archetypes*—emblems or symbols so universal and ancient that their meanings are recognized by most readers with little or no critical effort.

There are many archetypal elements present in Poe's tale, but in a much larger sense the story itself is archetypal. Interpreters who use the methods of archetypal criticism tend to look beneath the surface of particular stories to uncover more universal patterns. And one of the most familiar of these universal stories (or myths) has to do with the attempt to flee or in some way defeat death. Maugham's

"Appointment in Samarra" and Chaucer's "Pardoner's Tale" are two well-known stories based on this type. But the archetype itself is familiar to us in myth and ritual as well as in literature. It is the story that stands behind the ancient practice of carnival, a farewell to flesh before a period of fasting, a festive time during which normal rules and restraints are suspended and we are allowed to lose ourselves in a fantasy world of parties and merrymaking, which is actually a celebration of the forces of life and an attempt to forget or deny the power of death over all living things. The most famous carnival in the United States is *Mardi Gras* in New Orleans, where revelry and feasting on Fat Tuesday precede Ash Wednesday and the fasting of Lent. Not uncommonly *Mardi Gras* revelers mock death by dressing up as skeletons or in the "habiliments of the grave" and indulge in a parody of the dance of death.

All of this seems to lurk somewhere in the background of Poe's "Masque of the Red Death," for, as we observed, a "masque" or masquerade is very often quite similar to a carnival, a festive celebration, a party celebrating life and mocking death. When Prospero and his lighthearted companions withdraw from the real world into their own fantasy world of dancing and masquerades, they are fleeing and attempting to forget the ravages of the Red Death. It is a familiar reaction and recalls the ancient saying: "Eat, drink, and be merry, for tomorrow you die."

Archetypes like these exist not only in myth and literature, in folklore and fairy tales, but may also be familiar to us from the symbolism of our dreams. According to the psychologist C. G. Jung, archetypes have their origin in what he calls the *collective unconscious,* a kind of racial or group memory of unconscious wishes and fears shared by all human cultures and the source of much of the symbolism we encounter in our private dreams and public myths. The frightening figure of the Red Death, dressed in grave-clothes, may have stepped directly out of one of Poe's nightmares, but even more importantly, we can recognize that figure as universal, one any of us may encounter in other stories or even in our own dreams.

The suggestion that Poe's "Masque of the Red Death," like most horror stories, is a nightmare brought to life by literary artifice is further borne out by some of Poe's descriptions. He compares the masqueraders to "a multitude of dreams" that stalk "to and fro in the seven chambers," writhing "in and about, taking hue from the rooms, and causing the wild music of the orchestra to seem as the echo of their steps." When the ebony clock strikes the hour, "the dreams are stiff-frozen as they stand. But the echoes of the chime die away—they have endured but an instant—and a light, half-subdued laughter floats after them as they depart. And now again the music swells, and the dreams live, and writhe to and fro more merrily than ever, taking hue from the many tinted windows through which stream the rays from the tripods."

The relationship between literature and dreaming is an important one. In his essay "Creative Writers and Day-Dreaming," Sigmund Freud points out that although most of us daydream and indulge in fantasies of various kinds, only the literary artist seems able to turn these fantasies into works of art. Creative writers may also bring into their stories their own preoccupations and obsessions. Many psychological critics have suggested that authors sometimes draw on their own psychological conflicts to build their world of art. This seems especially likely for an artist as troubled as Edgar Allan Poe, who often found the inspiration for his stories and poems in dreams and waking visions, the "fancies" and "psychal impressions," as he called them, that "arise in the soul . . . at those mere points of time where the confines of the waking world blend with those of the world of dreams."

In *The Life and Works of Edgar Allan Poe: A Psycho-Analytic Interpretation,* Marie Bonaparte describes some of the obsessions and preoccupations that find their way into Poe's stories and poems. While still a child, not quite three years old, Poe watched his mother, a beautiful actress, waste away and die of tuberculosis. This may or may not be sufficient explanation for his apparent obsession with the death of beautiful women in his literary works, but, unfortunately for Poe, it was the beginning of a pattern that repeated itself throughout his life. He watched a number of beautiful women, mother figures and lovers, including his foster mother and protectress Frances Allan, die in a similar fashion. Add to this the fact that Poe very early developed an intense animosity toward his guardian, John Allan, and we have the principal ingredients for the Oedipus complex that Bonaparte sees in the background of most of Poe's works.

The Oedipus complex is a psychological state that Freud named after the mythological character Oedipus, who unwittingly kills his father and marries his mother. Given dramatic expression in Sophocles's play *Oedipus the King,* the Oedipus complex is a central part of Freud's theory of psychoanalysis. According to Freud, everyone must come to terms (usually in early childhood) with this hidden conflict involving an erotic attraction to the parent of the opposite sex and feelings of jealousy and hatred toward the parent of the same sex. Such feelings are part of growing up, and Oedipus's mother, Jocasta, recognizes their universality in the play when she tells Oedipus: "Many men before this have dreamt that they/Have shared their mother's bed. The man to whom/These things are nothing lives the easiest life."

Sometimes this Oedipal phase is accompanied by what Freud describes as a desire to return to the security of the mother's womb. According to Bonaparte, "The Masque of the Red Death" is one of several stories in which Poe, perhaps quite unconsciously, expresses this Oedipal theme. Prospero, by withdrawing to the seclusion of the labyrinthine abbey, is attempting to return to the womb. The Red Death represents the figure of the avenging father whom Prospero has tried to lock outside. In a symbolic way both the Red Death and the ebony clock, with its human characteristics ("hands," "face," and "brazen lungs"), are *personifications* of Father Time. For time is the real enemy, and Prospero in fleeing the Red Death—mortality—is attempting to turn back the hands of the clock. The *irony,* of course, is that in running away from death, Prospero and his companions do not return to a nurturing womb but withdraw into the abbey that becomes their tomb. However, as Freud points out in his essay on "The 'Uncanny,'" there's a definite relationship between the desire to return to the womb and the fear of premature burial or entombment.

Bonaparte's psychological or psychoanalytic interpretation fits some of the details of the story, but it becomes much more convincing when we take into consideration the known facts of Poe's biography. Certainly, that's why her study begins with an elaborate psychological analysis of Poe's life. In some ways, then, the psychological or psychoanalytic interpretation is a variant of the biographical interpretation and depends on careful study of an author's career and biography. But not all psychological interpretation must include an analysis of the author himself. Some psychoanalytic readings focus on the characters in the story (or poem or play). For instance, Prospero, named after the artist/magician in Shakespeare's *Tempest,* may be an alter ego for Poe, the writer of the story. But he is also a character in his own right, and one who (as Poe suggests) suffers from some form of madness. What can we learn from psychoanalyzing Prospero? For instance, why does he withdraw into the abbey? And what is he attempting to achieve with his fantastic masked ball? These are the kinds of questions we might ask in applying the psychological technique to an examination of the central character in the story.

Finally, applying the sociological perspective, we might approach the story as a parable of the struggle between the privileged and the downtrodden members of society. We note, for example, that Prospero is a prince or duke who attempts to escape his responsibilities as a ruler and to save himself and his privileged friends from the fate of those less fortunate, less wealthy. While his dominions are "half-depopulated," he and the chosen "knights and dames of his court . . . retired to the deep seclusion of one of his castellated abbeys." Notice the tone of Poe's description of this retirement:

> The courtiers, having entered, brought furnaces and massy hammers and welded the bolts. They resolved to leave means neither of ingress or egress to the sudden impulses of despair from without or of frenzy from within. The abbey was amply provisioned. With such precautions the courtiers might bid defiance to contagion. The external world could take care of itself.

This act of irresponsible selfishness, however, cannot save these privileged few. Even they must suffer and die at the hands of the Red Death, as Poe makes clear at the conclusion of the story. According to such an interpretation, "The Masque of the Red Death" carries a social and political message, a reminder that wealth cannot protect the privileged classes from a final reckoning.

Although here the Red Death may seem to be a form of retribution, this sociological interpretation is not unrelated to the moral or allegorical reading with which we began. And it is worth remarking again that many of these different interpretive techniques tend to overlap and support one another. That may not be the case with every story, nor can every work of literature be approached with equal success from all of these various critical viewpoints. Nearly all works will yield insights through formalistic interpretation, but only a certain few may seem suited to the moral-philosophical approach, whereas others may best be considered using the techniques of archetypal, psychological, or sociological criticism.

As we have seen, Poe's "Masque of the Red Death" can be discussed from a number of different critical perspectives. Admittedly, some of these may seem to be taking us away from the story itself, but that is perfectly all right—so long as we are reading "out of" rather than "into" the story. One of the higher pleasures of literature derives from the discussion that it can provoke, and we want to provoke discussion and encourage readers themselves to participate in discussing literary works. Some interpreters and some kinds of interpretation seek in literature the means to understand the world around us and our reactions to that world, including the world of our dreams and fantasies. Others limit interpretation only to those things that can help us understand the work of literature itself, the world of the story, poem, or play.

But it is difficult to know sometimes where one world leaves off and the other begins. As far as anyone knows, Poe's "Masque of the Red Death" describes no incident that ever happened, nor any place that ever existed. Yet it is a very recognizable world (Poe used the term "verisimilitude" to describe this quality), and it may even remind us of things familiar to us either in waking reality or in our nightmares, if not in other stories. If we find Poe's story chilling, maybe it is for a variety of reasons, some of them having nothing to do with stories or literature but with our own conscious and unconscious knowledge of the world we live in and dream about. And who is to say which interpretations help us understand our responses or the story itself more clearly?

Some students will ask, "But how do I know all of that is really *in* the story? How do I know what Poe really intended?" And these are very reasonable and even necessary questions. Of course, no one—not even Poe himself—can know everything the story means. The story has a life of its own, and Poe was drawing on his unconscious fears and desires as well as on his conscious intentions. Bonaparte points out, for example, that "The Masque of the Red Death" was published in May of 1842 and that in January of that same year Poe's young wife Virginia, who later died of tuberculosis, had her first hemorrhage, coughing up blood while singing for Poe and some friends. Perhaps that awful episode influenced Poe's conception of the Red Death, whether or not he was consciously aware of it. The story recalls Poe's dreams and nightmares as well as our own, and none of us can say for sure what our dreams are all about. It is better not to restrict ourselves by saying that we are trying to understand the story completely, but instead, to point out that we are first attempting to understand something about our own responses and to identify the things in the story that provoke a response. As we proceed, we may find our interpretation growing.

Another problem we often confront as readers is knowing where to look for help in understanding a work of literature. Of course, we can always go to the library and look at books of criticism and articles in literary journals. But the best place to begin is with our own responses and our own experiences in life and literature—the things we already know. For example, we might ask ourselves why the colors in Poe's story seem to have meaning. Where did we learn that black is a color associated with death? Why should red, the color of blood, which is the source of life, also suggest death? How many of us have had dreams about a figure

29

like the Red Death, the dead coming to life, the "grim reaper"? Do these dreams have anything in common with Poe's story?

These are only the first tentative critical steps. The next step is to begin to ask ourselves why something works. Why is Poe so successful? What makes "The Masque of the Red Death" succeed? We have made some small progress in answering that question. We have mentioned Poe's use of mood; noticed his economical style, his description of the seven chambers, his use of the image of the ebony clock; identified universal or archetypal symbols like the colors black and red and the figure of death dressed in grave-clothes; found both moral and socio-logical meanings in the story. And after all of this we have left much unsaid. There are, no doubt, many things that contribute to Poe's effectiveness that we have not mentioned. But that is as it should be. Our discussion here was never intended to be exhaustive, only suggestive of ways we can learn from reading and interpreting stories by using multiple interpretive techniques.

GEOFFREY CHAUCER (c. 1340–1400) Soldier, diplomat, civil servant, father of English poetry. Written mostly in verse, his *Canterbury Tales* is a fascinating grab bag of narrative forms: for example, the chivalric romance, the fairy tale, the beast fable, the fabliau. The following excerpt from the "Pardoner's Tale" is an exemplum: a short, action-packed narrative used by a preacher to vivify the moral lesson of his sermon. Omitted here is the sermon itself, which is the frame for the exemplum and in which the hypocritical pardoner berates those guilty of gluttony, avarice, luxury, and gambling—then concludes by trying to sell worthless "saints' relics" to his fellow pilgrims.

FROM "THE PARDONER'S TALE"

Translated by Michael L. Hall

Here begins the Pardoner's Tale: In Flanders there once was a gang of young men who spent their time in folly—gambling, rioting, and hanging around brothels and taverns, where they danced to harps, lutes, and guitars and played dice all day and night. They also ate and drank to excess, and through these vices made sacrifices to the devil in his temple, the tavern, where their excesses knew no limits. Their oaths were so great and damnable that just hearing them was a frightening thing. They tore the Lord's body in their swearing—apparently they thought the Jews had not torn him enough—and each of them laughed at the sins of the others. Some-times a group of young girls would come tumbling and dancing, selling fruit and cakes, singing and playing their harps. For the most part they were bawds, who are the devil's own officers to kindle and blow on the flames of lechery, which often accompanies gluttony.

Now these three rioters of whom I'm telling, long before the breakfast bell, were sitting in the tavern ready to drink. And as they sat there they heard a death bell clang before a body that was being carried to its grave. Then one called to his boy and said, "Go quickly and ask what body that is that's passing by, and see to it you get the name right." "Sir," the boy answered, "there's no need for that. It was told to me two hours before you came here. He was, by the Lord, an old friend of yours, and suddenly he was slain last night, completely drunk and sitting upright on his bench. There came a sneaking thief that men call Death, who slays all the people in this country, and with his spear he struck his heart in two, then went his way without saying another word. He has slain a thousand in this plague and, Master, before you come into his presence, it seems to me you should beware such an adversary. Be ready to meet him at any time; that's what my mother taught me. I'll say no more."

"By Saint Mary," said the barkeeper, "this boy speaks the truth, for this year Death has slain in a village over a mile away both men and women, children, laborers, and pages. I'll wager his home is there. It would be wise to be forewarned before he did you some dishonor."

"Yea, God's arms," said this rioter, "is it such peril to meet with him? I'll seek him out on the byways and highways, I swear by God's worthy Bones! Listen here, fellows, we three are all in this together. Let each of us hold up his hand to the others, and each become the others' brother, and we'll slay this false traitor Death. He that slays so many shall be slain himself before nightfall."

And so these three pledged to one another to live and die each for the others, as though they were born brothers. And up they started, in their drunken rage, and went forth toward that village which the barkeeper had mentioned before. And many a grisly oath they swore then, and Christ's holy body tore limb from limb—Death shall be dead if they ever get hold of him.

When they had gone not quite half a mile, just as they were about to walk over a stile, they met a poor old man who greeted them meekly and said, "Now, Lords, God be with you."

The proudest of these three rioters answered, "Curse you, old man. Why are you all wrapped up except your face? Why do you live so long, to such a great age?"

The old man began to look him in the face and said, "Because I can't find anyone, even if I walked to India, neither in any city or village, that will change his youth for my age; and so I must keep my age as long as it's God's will. Not even Death, alas, will have my life. Thus I walk like a restless prisoner, and on the ground, which is my mother's gate, I knock with my staff all day long and say, 'Dear Mother, let me in! Look how I vanish, flesh, blood, and skin. Alas, when shall my bones be at rest? Mother, I'd gladly exchange with you the chest that's been in my chamber all this time for a burial cloth to wrap me in.' But yet she won't do me that kindness, and therefore my face is all pale and withered.

"But, sires, it's no courtesy in you to speak so villainously to an old man unless he harms you either in word or deed. You may read yourselves in the Holy Scripture: 'Before an old man, with white hairs upon his head, you should rise.' Therefore, I give you warning not to do any harm to an old man now, no more than you'd want me to do to you in your old age, if you should live so long. Now, God be with you wherever you walk or ride. I must go where I have to go."

"Not so fast, old man; by God, you're not going anywhere," said another of the gamblers. "You're not getting away so easily, by Saint John! You spoke just now of this traitor Death, who slays all our friends in this country. Here's my word on it—you're obviously one of his spies—tell me where he is, or you'll pay for it, by God and the Holy Sacrament! For, certainly, you're in league with him to kill us young folk, you false thief!"

"Now, sirs," he answered, "if you're so anxious to find Death, turn up this crooked path; for in that grove I left him, by my faith, under a tree, and there he'll stay. Not for all your threats will he hide himself. Do you see that oak? Right there you'll find him. Now may the Lord, who died for all mankind, save and amend you!"

Thus the old man spoke, and every one of these rioters ran until he came to that tree, and there they found, it seemed to them, nearly eight bushels of fine gold florins. No longer then did they seek after Death, but each of them was so glad at that sight, those fair, bright florins, that they sat themselves down by this precious horde. The worst of them spoke the first word.

"Brothers," he said, "take heed what I say. My wits are keen, though I joke and play. Fortune has given this treasure to us to live our lives in mirth and jollity, and as lightly as it comes, so we will spend it. Hey, by God's worthiness, who would have thought that today we'd have such good luck? But shouldn't this gold be carried from this place home to my house, or else to yours—for well you know it's all ours—then we'd be as happy as possible. But certainly, we can't do it in broad daylight. Men would say that we were strangers and thieves and hang us on account of our treasure. This treasure must be carried away by night as wisely and slyly as possible. Therefore, I suggest we draw lots and see how they fall, and he who wins the draw shall run into town happily and quickly and bring back some bread and wine, but without attracting any attention. The other two will carefully guard the treasure. And if he doesn't tarry, when it's night we'll carry this treasure where we all agree it will be best." Then he took the straws in his fist and told them to draw and see where the lot would fall, and it fell on the youngest one of them. So right away he went off to the town.

As soon as he was gone, one said to the other: "You're well aware that you're my sworn brother. I'll tell you something that will profit you. You can see very clearly that one companion is gone. And the gold is right here—and plenty of it —that is to be divided among the three of us. But if I can devise a way to divide it among the two of us, won't I have done you a friendly turn?"

The other answered, "I can't see how that could be. He knows, certainly, that the gold is with the two of us. What'll we do? What'll we tell him?"

"Can you keep it secret?" said the first villain. "Then I'll tell you in few words what we'll do to bring it about."

"I promise," said the other, "on my honor, I'll not betray you."

"Now," said the first, "you know very well that there are two of us, and two are stronger than one. Watch him when he sits down, then get up and go for him in jest, and I'll stab him in the side while you pretend to struggle with him. Then take your dagger and do the same, and all this gold can be divided, my dear friend, between me and you. Then we can fulfill all our desires and play dice as much as we like." And so these two traitors agreed to slay the third, as you've heard me say.

The youngest, who went to town, kept turning over in his heart the beauty of those bright, new florins. "Oh, Lord," he said, "if only I could have all this treasure to myself, there's no man on God's earth would live so merry as I." And at last the devil, our enemy, put this thought in his mind, that he should buy poison with which he might slay his two fellows. Since the fiend found him living such a sinful life, he had leave to bring him to sorrow. For this fellow's intention was to kill both of his companions and never repent. And off he went, without delay, into the town, up to an apothecary, and asked him to sell him some poison to kill some rats, and also, he said, there was a polecat in his yard that was killing his chickens, and he'd like to get even with these vermin that were ruining him by night.

And the apothecary answered, "You shall have something, God save my soul. There is no creature in all this world that may eat or drink of this preparation —even as little as a kernel of wheat—and not yield up his life immediately. Yes, he shall die, and die in less time than you would walk the distance of a mile, this poison is so strong and violent."

This wicked man took the poison in a box. Then he ran into the next street and borrowed three large bottles from another man, and into two of these he poured his poison. He kept the third clean for his own drink. For all that night he planned to labor in carrying the gold out of that place. And when this rioter —a curse upon him—had filled his three great bottles with wine, he returned to his fellows again.

What need is there to continue longer with this sermon? For just as they had planned his death earlier, so they killed him as soon as he returned. And when that was done, one of them said, "Now let us sit and drink and make merry, and afterward we'll bury his body." And with that word he chanced to take one of the bottles with the poison in it and drank and gave his fellow drink also, from which they both soon died. Thus these two murderers met their end, as did the false poisoner also.

DISCUSSION TOPICS

1. Like many other short stories, Chaucer's "Pardoner's Tale" builds up to a "surprise" ending. What are some of the things that prepare you for the conclusion and make it work?
2. "The Pardoner's Tale" qualifies as an example of allegory, a story in which abstractions such as "Death" appear as characters or personifications. Does Death actually appear in this story?
3. What is irony? In what ways is this story ironic? (Compare the discussion of "Appointment in Samarra" in the Introduction.)

4. One of Chaucer's strengths is his ability to draw enduring portraits of human nature. What universal characteristics do you see in his portraits of the three young men? In what ways do you suppose readers might be expected to identify with these rioters?
5. What are some of the symbolic implications of the gold, of the crooked path to the tree, and of the tree itself?
6. Many readers have been fascinated by the old man in this story. What do you think is his function? In what ways does he appear to be a mythic or archetypal character? What is the meaning of his plea, "Dear Mother, let me in . . ."?
7. Edgar Allan Poe said that a story should not be didactic. How well does Chaucer's tale hold up under this criticism? In what way is your response affected by the fact that Chaucer's Pardoner teaches, or preaches, a moral lesson by telling a story?
8. "The Pardoner's Tale" appears in a sermon preached against familiar sins, especially gluttony and avarice. Do you think the story is particularly Christian? Does the tale present religious values or social values? What is the difference?

WASHINGTON IRVING (1783–1859) Literary ambassador of good will; first American writer to win international literary recognition; regarded by many critics as "the father of the modern short story." *The Sketch Book* (1820), containing such universally appealing tales as "Rip Van Winkle" and "The Legend of Sleepy Hollow," demonstrated that short fiction could be a worthy field for the true literary artist. Irving's narratives, written explicitly for entertainment through what he called "the half-concealed vein of humor that is often playing through the whole," combine a neoclassical wit and polish with romantic subject matter. Often based on folktales from the Old World, his short fiction also possesses elements of myth and archetype.

ADVENTURE OF THE GERMAN STUDENT

On a stormy night, in the tempestuous times of the French revolution,[1] a young German was returning to his lodgings, at a late hour, across the old part of Paris. The lightning gleamed, and the loud claps of thunder rattled through the lofty narrow streets—but I should first tell you something about this young German.

Gottfried Wolfgang was a young man of good family. He had studied for some time at Gottingen, but being of a visionary and enthusiastic character, he had wandered into those wild and speculative doctrines which have so often bewildered German students. His secluded life, his intense application and the singular nature of his studies, had an effect on both mind and body. His health was impaired; his imagination diseased. He had been indulging in fanciful speculations on spiritual essences, until, like Swedenborg,[2] he had an ideal world of his own around him. He took up a notion, I do not know from what cause, that there was an evil influence hanging over him; an evil genius of spirit seeking to ensnare him and ensure his perdition. Such an idea working on his melancholy temperament, produced the most gloomy effects. He became haggard and desponding. His friends discovered the mental malady preying upon him, and determined that the best cure was a change of scene; he was sent, therefore, to finish his studies amidst the splendors and gayeties of Paris.

Wolfgang arrived at Paris at the breaking out of the revolution. The popular delirium at first caught his enthusiastic mind, and he was captivated by the political and philosophical theories of the day: but the scenes of blood which followed shocked his sensitive nature, disgusted him with society and the world, and made him more than ever a recluse. He shut himself up in a solitary apartment in the Pays Latin, the quarter of students. There, in a gloomy street not far from the monastic walls of the Sorbonne,[3] he pursued his favorite speculations. Sometimes he spent hours together in the great libraries of Paris, those catacombs of departed authors, rummaging among their hoards of dusty and obsolete works in quest of food for his unhealthy appetite. He was, in a manner, a literary ghoul, feeding in the charnel-house of decayed literature.

Wolfgang, though solitary and recluse, was of an ardent temperament, but for a time it operated merely upon his imagination. He was too shy and ignorant of the world to make any advances to the fair, but he was a passionate admirer of female beauty, and in his lonely chamber would often lose himself in reveries on forms and faces which he had seen, and his fancy would deck out images of loveliness far surpassing the reality.

While his mind was in this excited and sublimated state, a dream produced an extraordinary effect upon him. It was of a female face of transcendent beauty. So strong was the impression made, that he dreamt of it again and again. It haunted his thoughts by day, his slumbers by night; in fine, he became passionately enamoured of this shadow of a dream. This lasted so long that it became one of those fixed ideas which haunt the minds of melancholy men, and are at times mistaken for madness.

Such was Gottfried Wolfgang, and such his situation at the time I mentioned. He was returning home late one stormy night, through some of the old and gloomy streets of the Marais, the ancient part of Paris. The loud claps of thunder rattled among the high houses of the narrow streets. He came to the Place de Grève, the square where public executions are performed. The lightning quivered about the pinnacles of the ancient Hôtel de Ville,[4] and shed flickering gleams over the open space in front. As Wolfgang was crossing the square, he shrank back with horror at finding himself close by the guillotine. It was the height of the reign of terror, when this dreadful instrument of death stood ever ready, and its scaffold was continually running with the blood of the virtuous and the brave. It had that very day been actively employed in the work of carnage, and there it stood in grim array, amidst a silent and sleeping city, waiting for fresh victims.

Wolfgang's heart sickened within him, and he was turning shuddering from the horrible engine, when he beheld a shadowy form, cowering as it were at the foot of the steps which led up to the scaffold. A succession of vivid flashes of lightning revealed it more distinctly. It was a female figure, dressed in black. She was seated on one of the lower steps of the scaffold, leaning forward, her face hid in her lap; and her long dishevelled tresses hanging to the ground, streaming with the rain which fell in torrents. Wolfgang paused. There was something awful in this solitary monument of woe. The female had the appearance of being above the common order. He knew the times to be full of vicissitude, and that many a fair head, which had once been pillowed on down, now wandered houseless. Perhaps this was some poor mourner whom the dreadful axe had rendered desolate, and who sat here heartbroken on the strand of existence, from which all that was dear to her had been launched into eternity.

He approached, and addressed her in the accents of sympathy. She raised her head and gazed wildly at him. What was his astonishment at beholding, by the bright glare of the lightning, the very face which had haunted him in his dreams. It was pale and disconsolate, but ravishingly beautiful.

Trembling with violent and conflicting emotions, Wolfgang again accosted her. He spoke something of her being exposed at such an hour of the night, and to the fury of such a storm, and offered to conduct her to her friends. She pointed to the guillotine with a gesture of dreadful signification.

"I have no friend on earth!" said she.

"But you have a home," said Wolfgang.

"Yes—in the grave!"

The heart of the student melted at the words.

"If a stranger dare make an offer," said he, "without danger of being misunderstood, I would offer my humble dwelling as a shelter; myself as a devoted friend. I am friendless myself in Paris, and a stranger in the land; but if my life could be of service, it is at your disposal, and should be sacrificed before harm or indignity should come to you."

There was an honest earnestness in the young man's manner that had its effect. His foreign accent, too, was in his favor; it showed him not to be a hackneyed inhabitant of Paris. Indeed, there is an eloquence in true enthusiasm that is not to be doubted. The homeless stranger confided herself implicitly to the protection of the student.

He supported her faltering steps across the Pont Neuf,[5] and by the place where the statue of Henry the Fourth had been overthrown by the populace. The storm had abated, and the thunder rumbled at a distance. All Paris was quiet; that great volcano of human passion slumbered for awhile, to gather fresh strength for the next day's eruption. The student conducted his charge through the ancient streets of the Pays Latin, and by the dusky walls of the Sorbonne, to the great dingy hotel which he inhabited. The old portress who admitted them stared with surprise at the unusual sight of the melancholy Wolfgang with a female companion.

On entering his apartment, the student, for the first time, blushed at the scantiness and indifference of his dwelling. He had but one chamber— an old-fashioned saloon—heavily carved, and fantastically furnished with the remains of former magnificence, for it was of those hotels in the quarter of the Luxembourg palace which had once belonged to nobility. It was lumbered with books and papers, and all the usual apparatus of a student, and his bed stood in a recess at one end.

When lights were brought, and Wolfgang had a better opportunity of contemplating the stranger, he was more than ever intoxicated by her beauty. Her face was pale, but of a dazzling fairness, set off by a profusion of raven hair that hung clustering about it. Her eyes were large and brilliant, with a singular expression approaching almost to wildness. As far as her black dress permitted her shape to be seen, it was of perfect symmetry. Her whole appearance was highly striking, though she was dressed in the simplest style. The only thing approaching to an ornament which she wore, was a broad black band round her neck, clasped by diamonds.

The perplexity now commenced with the student how to dispose of the helpless being thus thrown upon his protection. He thought of abandoning his chamber to her, and seeking shelter for himself elsewhere. Still he was so fascinated by her charms, there seemed to be such a spell upon his thoughts and senses, that he could not tear himself from her presence. Her manner, too, was singular and unaccountable. She spoke no more of the guillotine. Her grief had abated. The attentions of the student had first won her confidence, and then, apparently, her heart. She was evidently an enthusiast like himself, and enthusiasts soon understand each other.

In the infatuation of the moment, Wolfgang avowed his passion for her. He told her the story of his mysterious dream, and how she had possessed his heart before he had even seen her. She was strangely affected by his recital, and acknowledged to have felt an impulse towards him equally unaccountable. It was the time for wild theory and wild actions. Old prejudices and superstitions were done away; everything was under the sway of the "Goddess of Reason."[6] Among other rubbish of the old times, the forms and ceremonies of marriage began to be considered superfluous bonds for honorable minds. Social compacts were the vogue. Wolfgang was too much of a theorist not to be tainted by the liberal doctrines of the day.

"Why should we separate?" said he: "our hearts are united; in the eye of reason and honor we are as one. What need is there of sordid forms to bind high souls together?"

The stranger listened with emotion: she had evidently received illumination at the same school.

"You have no home nor family," continued he; "let me be everything to you, or rather let us be everything to one another. If form is necessary, form shall be observed—there is my hand. I pledge myself to you forever."

"For ever?" said the stranger, solemnly.

"For ever!" repeated Wolfgang.

The stranger clasped the hand extended to her: "Then I am yours," murmured she, and sank upon his bosom.

The next morning the student left his bride sleeping, and sallied forth at an early hour to seek more spacious apartments, suitable to the change in his situation.

When he returned, he found the stranger lying with her head hanging over the bed, and one arm thrown over it. He spoke to her, but received no reply. He advanced to awaken her from her uneasy posture. On taking her hand, it was cold —there was no pulsation—her face was pallid and ghastly.—In a word—she was a corpse.

Horrified and frantic, he alarmed the house. A scene of confusion ensued. The police was summoned. As the officer of police entered the room, he started back on beholding the corpse.

"Great heaven!" cried he, "how did this woman come here?"

"Do you know anything about her?" said Wolfgang, eagerly.

"Do I?" exclaimed the police officer: "she was guillotined yesterday."

He stepped forward; undid the black collar round the neck of the corpse, and the head rolled on the floor!

The student burst into a frenzy. "The fiend! the fiend has gained possession of me!" shrieked he: "I am lost for ever."

They tried to soothe him, but in vain. He was possessed with the frightful belief that an evil spirit had reanimated the dead body to ensnare him. He went distracted, and died in a madhouse.

Here the old gentleman with the haunted head finished his narrative.

"And is this really a fact?" said the inquisitive gentleman.

"A fact not to be doubted," replied the other. "I had it from the best authority. The student told it to me himself. I saw him in a madhouse at Paris."

[1] 1789–1799.
[2] Emanuel Swedenborg (1688–1772), Swedish philosophical and religious writer.
[3] The University of Paris.
[4] Headquarters of city government ("city hall").
[5] Literally, "New Bridge"; actually, the oldest bridge over the Seine River in Paris.
[6] The patron "deity" of the anticlerical revolutionary radicals. A papier-mâché effigy of this goddess was frequently substituted for the crucifix over the altar in churches, and orgies of various kinds were celebrated in her "worship."

DISCUSSION TOPICS

1. "Adventure of the German Student," from *Tales of a Traveller* (1824), is a version of the Gothic tale of terror that achieved widespread popularity in the late eighteenth and early nineteenth centuries. Clearly, the author does not intend his reader to take this tale too seriously. What evidence can you find in the story indicating that Irving intended a parody of the Gothic fad? How is your reading of the story changed by the last three paragraphs?

2. Do you think Irving intended to suggest any kind of moral lesson through the example of his protagonist? Why—or why not?

3. Why is historical setting—both time and place—especially important in this story?

4. If you were a psychiatrist (or a psychologist), how would you diagnose Gott-fried's problem?
5. Why does the student believe he has been possessed by the fiend? Why would the fiend come to him in the guise of a beautiful woman? What is the Jungian (or archetypal) name for this kind of woman?
6. What present-day evidence (in literature, TV, and the movies) can you cite of the continuing popularity of the Gothic thriller?

NATHANIEL HAWTHORNE (1804–1864) Strong Puritan influence on his works. His writing is characterized by archetypal richness. One of our greatest authors, he added moral depth and psychological substance to the American short story.

MY KINSMAN, MAJOR MOLINEUX

After the kings of Great Britain had assumed the right of appointing the colonial governors, the measures of the latter seldom met with the ready and general approbation which had been paid to those of their predecessors, under the original charters. The people looked with most jealous scrutiny to the exercise of power which did not emanate from themselves, and they usually rewarded their rulers with slender gratitude for the compliances by which, in softening their instructions from beyond the sea, they had incurred the reprehension of those who gave them. The annuals of Massachusetts Bay will inform us, that of six governors in the space of about forty years from the surrender of the old charter, under James II, two were imprisoned by a popular insurrection; a third, as Hutchinson[1] inclines to believe, was driven from the province by the whizzing of a musket-ball; a fourth, in the opinion of the same historian, was hastened to his grave by continual bickerings with the House of Representatives; and the remaining two, as well as their successors, till the Revolution, were favored with few and brief intervals of peaceful sway. The inferior members of the court party, in times of high political excitement, led scarcely a more desirable life. These remarks may serve as a preface to the following adventures, which chanced upon a summer night, not far from a hundred years ago.[2] The reader, in order to avoid a long and dry detail of colonial affairs, is requested to dispense with an account of the train of circumstances that had caused much temporary inflammation of the popular mind.

It was near nine o'clock of a moonlight evening, when a boat crossed the ferry with a single passenger, who had obtained his conveyance at that unusual hour by the promise of an extra fare. While he stood on the landing-place, searching in either pocket for the means of fulfilling his agreement, the ferryman lifted a lantern, by the aid of which, and the newly risen moon, he took a very accurate survey of the stranger's figure. He was a youth of barely eighteen years, evidently country-bred, and now, as it should seem, upon his first visit to town. He was clad in a coarse gray coat, well worn, but in excellent repair; his under garments[3] were durably constructed of leather, and fitted tight to a pair of serviceable and well-shaped limbs; his stockings of blue yarn were the incontrovertible work of a mother or a sister; and on his head was a three-cornered hat, which in its better days had perhaps sheltered the graver brow of the lad's father. Under his left arm was a heavy cudgel formed of an oak sapling, and retaining a part of the hardened root; and his equipment was completed by a wallet, not so abundantly stocked as to incommode the vigorous shoulders on which it hung. Brown, curly hair, well-shaped features, and bright, cheerful eyes were nature's gifts, and worth all that art could have done for his adornment.

The youth, one of whose names was Robin, finally drew from his pocket the half of a little providence bill of five shillings, which, in the depreciation in that sort of currency, did but satisfy the ferryman's demand, with the surplus of a sexangular piece of parchment, valued at three pence. He then walked forward into the town, with as light a step as if his day's journey had not already exceeded thirty miles, and with as eager an eye as if he were entering London city, instead of the little metropolis of a New England colony. Before Robin had proceeded far, however, it occurred to him that he knew not whither to direct his steps; so he paused, and looked up and down the narrow street, scrutinizing the small and mean wooden buildings that were scattered on either side.

"This low hovel cannot be my kinsman's dwelling," thought he, "nor yonder old house, where the moonlight enters at the broken casement; and truly I see none hereabouts that might be worthy of him. It would have been wise to inquire my way of the ferryman, and doubtless he would have gone with me, and earned a shilling from the Major for his pains. But the next man I meet will do as well."

He resumed his walk, and was glad to perceive that the street now became wider, and the houses more respectable in their appearance. He soon discerned a figure moving on moderately in advance, and hastened his steps to overtake it. As Robin drew nigh, he saw that the passenger was a man in years, with a full periwig of gray hair, a wideskirted coat of dark cloth, and silk stockings rolled above his knees. He carried a long and polished cane, which he struck down perpendicularly before him at every step; and at regular intervals he uttered two successive hems, of a peculiarly solemn and sepulchral intonation. Having made these observations, Robin laid hold of the skirt of the old man's coat, just when the light from the open door and windows of a barber's shop fell upon both their figures.

"Good evening to you, honored sir," said he, making a low bow, and still retaining his hold of the skirt. "I pray you tell me whereabouts is the dwelling of my kinsman, Major Molineux."

The youth's question was uttered very loudly; and one of the barbers, whose razor was descending on a well-soaped chin, and another who was dressing a Ramillies wig,[4] left their occupations, and came to the door. The citizen, in the mean time, turned a long favored countenance upon Robin, and answered him in a tone of excessive anger and annoyance. His two sepulchral hems, however, broke into the very centre of his rebuke, with most singular effect, like a thought of the cold grave obtruding among wrathful passions.

"Let go my garment, fellow! I tell you, I know not the man you speak of. What! I have authority, I have—hem, hem—authority; and if this be the respect you show for your betters, your feet shall be brought acquainted with the stocks by daylight, tomorrow morning!"

Robin released the old man's skirt, and hastened away, pursued by an ill-mannered roar of laughter from the barber's shop. He was at first considerably surprised by the result of his question, but, being a shrewd youth, soon thought himself able to account for the mystery.

"This is some country representative," was his conclusion, "who has never seen the inside of my kinsman's door, and lacks the breeding to answer a stranger civilly. The man is old, or verily—I might be tempted to turn back and smite him on the nose. Ah, Robin, Robin! even the barber's boys laugh at you for choosing such a guide! You will be wiser in time, friend Robin."

He now became entangled in a succession of crooked and narrow streets, which crossed each other, and meandered at no great distance from the water-side. The smell of tar was obvious to his nostrils, the masts of vessels pierced the moonlight above the tops of the buildings, and the numerous signs, which Robin paused to read, informed him that he was near the centre of business. But the streets were empty, the shops were closed, and lights were visible only in the second stories of a few dwelling-houses. At length, on the corner of a narrow lane, through which he was passing, he beheld the broad countenance of a British hero swinging before the door of an inn,[5] whence proceeded the voices of many guests. The casement of one of the lower windows was thrown back, and a very thin curtain permitted Robin to distinguish a party at supper, round a well-furnished table. The fragrance of the good cheer steamed forth into the outer air, and the youth could not fail to recollect that the last remnant of his travelling stock of provision had yielded to his morning appetite, and that noon had found and left him dinnerless.

"Oh, that a parchment three-penny might give me a right to sit down at yonder table!" said Robin with a sigh. "But the Major will make me welcome to the best of his victuals; so I will even step boldly in, and inquire my way to his dwelling."

He entered the tavern, and was guided by the murmur of voices and the fumes of tobacco to the public-room. It was a long and low apartment, with oaken walls, grown dark in the continual smoke, and a floor which was thickly sanded, but of no immaculate purity. A number of persons—the larger part of whom appeared to be mariners, or in some way connected with the sea—occupied the wooden benches, or leather-bottomed chairs, conversing on various matters, and occasionally lending their attention to some topic of general interest. Three or four little groups were draining as many bowls of punch, which the West India trade had long since made a familiar drink in the colony. Others, who had the appearance of men who lived by regular and laborious handicraft, preferred the insulated bliss of an unshared potation, and became more taciturn under its influence. Nearly all, in short, evinced a predilection for the Good Creature[6] in some of its various shapes, for this is a vice to which, as Fast Day sermons of a hundred years ago will testify, we have a long hereditary claim. The only guests to whom Robin's sympathies inclined him were two or three sheepish countrymen, who were using the inn somewhat after the fashion of a Turkish caravansary;[7] they had gotten themselves into the darkest corner of the room, and heedless of the Nicotian[8] atmosphere, were supping on the bread of their own ovens, and the bacon cured in their own chimney-smoke. But though Robin felt a sort of brotherhood with these strangers, his eyes were attracted from them to a person who stood near the door, holding whispered conversation with a group of ill-dressed associates. His features were separately striking almost to grotesqueness, and the whole face left a deep impression on the memory. The forehead bulged out into a double prominence, with a vale between; the nose came boldly forth in an irregular curve, and its bridge was of more than a finger's breadth; the eyebrows were deep and shaggy, and the eyes glowed beneath them like fire in a cave.

While Robin deliberated of whom to inquire respecting his kinsman's dwelling, he was accosted by the innkeeper, a little man in a stained white apron, who had come to pay his professional welcome to the stranger. Being in the second generation from a French Protestant, he seemed to have inherited the courtesy of his parent nation; but no variety of circumstances was ever known to change his voice from the one shrill note in which he now addressed Robin.

"From the country, I presume, sir?" said he, with a profound bow. "Beg leave to congratulate you on your arrival, and trust you intend a long stay with us. Fine town here, sir, beautiful buildings, and much that may interest a stranger. May I hope for the honor of your commands in respect to supper?"

"The man sees a family likeness! the rogue has guessed that I am related to the Major!" thought Robin, who had hitherto experienced little superfluous civility.

All eyes were now turned on the country lad, standing at the door, in his worn three-cornered hat, gray coat, leather breeches, and blue yarn stockings, leaning on an oaken cudgel, and bearing a wallet on his back.

Robin replied to the courteous innkeeper, with such an assumption of confidence as befitted the Major's relative. "My honest friend," he said, "I shall make it a point to patronize your house on some occasion, when"—here he could not help lowering his voice—"when I may have more than a parchment threepence in my pocket. My present business," continued he, speaking with lofty confidence, "is merely to inquire my way to the dwelling of my kinsman, Major Molineux."

There was a sudden and general movement in the room, which Robin interpreted as expressing the eagerness of each individual to become his guide. But the innkeeper turned his eyes to a written paper on the wall, which he read, or seemed to read, with occasional recurrences to the young man's figure.

"What have we here?" said he, breaking his speech into little dry fragments. " 'Left the house of the subscriber, bounden servant;[9] Hezekiah Mudge,—had on, when he went away, gray coat, leather breeches, master's third-best hat. One pound currency reward to whosoever shall lodge him in any jail of the province.' Better trudge, boy; better trudge!"

Robin had begun to draw his hand towards the lighter end of the oak cudgel, but a strange hostility in every countenance induced him to relinquish his purpose of breaking the courteous innkeeper's head. As he turned to leave the room, he encountered a sneering glance from the bold-featured personage whom he had before noticed; and no sooner was he beyond the door, than he heard a general laugh, in which the innkeeper's voice might be distinguished, like the dropping of small stones into a kettle.

"Now, is it not strange," thought Robin, with his usual shrewdness,—"is it not strange that the confession of an empty pocket should outweigh the name of my kinsman, Major Molineux? Oh, if I had one of those grinning rascals in the woods, where I and my oak sapling grew up together, I would teach him that my arm is heavy though my purse be light!"

On turning the corner of the narrow lane, Robin found himself in a spacious street, with an unbroken line of lofty houses on each side, and a steepled building at the upper end, whence the ringing of a bell announced the hour of nine. The light of the moon, and the lamps from the numerous shop-windows, discovered people promenading on the pavement, and amongst them Robin hoped to recognize his hitherto inscrutable relative. The result of his former inquiries made him unwilling to hazard another, in a scene of such publicity, and he determined to walk slowly and silently up the street, thrusting his face close to that of every elderly gentleman, in search of the Major's lineaments. In his progress, Robin encountered many gay and gallant figures. Embroidered garments of showy colors, enormous periwigs, gold-laced hats, and silver-hilted swords glided past him and dazzled his optics. Travelled youths, imitators of the European fine gentlemen of the period, trod jauntily along, half dancing to the fashionable tunes which they hummed, and making poor Robin ashamed of his quiet and natural gait. At length, after many pauses to examine the gorgeous display of goods in the shop-windows, and after suffering some rebukes for the impertinence of his scrutiny into people's faces, the Major's kinsman found himself near the steepled building, still unsuccessful in his search. As yet, however, he had seen only one side of the thronged street; so Robin crossed, and continued the same sort of inquisition down the opposite pavement, with stronger hopes than the philosopher seeking an honest man, but with no better fortune. He had arrived about midway towards the lower end, from which his course began, when he overheard the approach of some one who struck down a cane on the flag-stones at every step, uttering, at regular intervals, two sepulchral hems.

"Mercy on us!" quoth Robin, recognizing the sound.

Turning a corner, which chanced to be close at his right hand, he hastened to pursue his researches in some other part of the town. His patience now was wearing low, and he seemed to feel more fatigue from his rambles since he crossed the ferry, than from his journey of several days on the other side. Hunger also pleaded loudly within him, and Robin began to balance the propriety of demanding, violently, and with lifted cudgel, the necessary guidance from the first solitary passenger whom he should meet. While a resolution to this effect was gaining strength, he entered a street of mean appearance, on either side of which a row of ill-built houses was straggling towards the harbor. The moonlight fell upon no passenger along the whole extent, but in the third domicile which Robin passed there was a half-opened door, and his keen glance detected a woman's garment within.

"My luck may be better here," said he to himself.

Accordingly, he approached the door, and beheld it shut closer as he did so; yet an open space remained, sufficing for the fair occupant to observe the stranger, without a corresponding display on her part. All that Robin could discern was a strip of scarlet petticoat, and the occasional sparkle of an eye, as if the moonbeams were trembling on some bright thing.

"Pretty mistress," for I may call her so with a good conscience, thought the shrewd youth, since I know nothing to the contrary,—"my sweet pretty mistress, will you be kind enough to tell me whereabouts I must seek the dwelling of my kinsman, Major Molineux?"

Robin's voice was plaintive and winning, and the female, seeing nothing to be shunned in the handsome country youth, thrust open the door, and came forth into the moonlight. She was a dainty little figure, with a white neck, round arms, and a slender waist, at the extremity of which her scarlet petticoat jutted out over a hoop, as if she were standing in a balloon. Moreover, her face was oval and pretty, her hair dark beneath the little cap, and her bright eyes possessed a sly freedom, which triumphed over those of Robin.

"Major Molineux dwells here," said this fair woman.

Now, her voice was the sweetest Robin had heard that night, the airy counterpart of a stream of melted silver; yet he could not help doubting whether that sweet voice spoke Gospel truth. He looked up and down the mean street, and then surveyed the house before which they stood. It was a small, dark edifice of two stories, the second of which projected over the lower floor, and the front apartment had the aspect of a shop for petty commodities.

"Now, truly, I am in luck," replied Robin, cunningly, "and so indeed is my kinsman, the Major, in having so pretty a housekeeper. But I prithee trouble him to step to the door; I will deliver him a message from his friends in the country, and then go back to my lodgings at the inn."

"Nay, the Major has been abed this hour or more," said the lady of the scarlet petticoat; "and it would be to little purpose to disturb him to-night, seeing his evening draught was of the strongest. But he is a kind-hearted man, and it would be as much as my life's worth to let a kinsman of his turn away from the door. You are the good old gentleman's very picture, and I could swear that was his rainy-weather hat. Also he has garments very much resembling those leather small-clothes. But come in, I pray, for I bid you hearty welcome in his name."

So saying, the fair and hospitable dame took our hero by the hand; and the touch was light, and the force was gentleness, and though Robin read in her eyes what he did not hear in her words, yet the slender-waisted woman in the scarlet petticoat proved stronger than the athletic country youth. She had drawn his half-willing footsteps nearly to the threshold, when the opening of a door in the neighborhood startled the Major's housekeeper, and, leaving the Major's kinsman, she vanished speedily into her own domicile. A heavy yawn preceded the appearance of a man, who, like the Moonshine of Pyramus and Thisbe,[10] carried a lantern, needlessly aiding his sister luminary in the heavens. As he walked sleepily up the street, he turned his broad, dull face on Robin, and displayed a long staff, spiked at the end.

"Home, vagabond, home!" said the watchman, in accents that seemed to fall asleep as soon as they were uttered. "Home, or we'll set you in the stocks by peep of day!"

"This is the second hint of the kind," thought Robin. "I wish they would end my difficulties, by setting me there to-night."

Nevertheless, the youth felt an instinctive antipathy towards the guardian of midnight order, which at first prevented him from asking his usual question. But just when the man was about to vanish behind the corner, Robin resolved not to lose the opportunity, and shouted lustily after him,—

"I say, friend! will you guide me to the house of my kinsman, Major Molineux?"

The watchman made no reply, but turned the corner and was gone; yet Robin seemed to hear the sound of drowsy laughter stealing along the solitary street. At that moment, also, a pleasant titter saluted him from the open window above his head; he looked up, and caught the sparkle of a saucy eye; a round arm beckoned to him, and next he heard light footsteps descending the staircase within. But Robin, being of the household of a New England clergyman, was a good youth, as well as a shrewd one; so he resisted temptation, and fled away.

He now roamed desperately, and at random, through the town, almost ready to believe that a spell was on him, like that by which a wizard of his country had once kept three pursuers wandering, a whole winter night, within twenty paces of the cottage which they sought. The streets lay before him, strange and desolate, and the lights were extinguished in almost every house. Twice, however, little parties of men, among whom Robin distinguished individuals in outlandish attire, came hurrying along; but, though on both occasions they paused to address him, such intercourse did not at all enlighten his perplexity. They did but utter a few words in some language of which Robin knew nothing, and perceiving his inability to answer, bestowed a curse upon him in plain English and hastened away. Finally, the lad determined to knock at the door of every mansion that might appear worthy to be occupied by his kinsman, trusting that perseverance would overcome the fatality that had hitherto thwarted him. Firm in this resolve, he was passing beneath the walls of a church, which formed the corner of two streets, when, as he turned into the shade of its steeple, he encountered a bulky stranger, muffled in a cloak. The man was proceeding with the speed of earnest business, but Robin planted himself full before him, holding the oak cudgel with both hands across his body as a bar to further passage.

"Halt, honest man, and answer me a question," said he, very resolutely.

"Tell me, this instant, whereabouts is the dwelling of my kinsman, Major Molineux!"

"Keep your tongue between your teeth, fool, and let me pass!" said a deep, gruff voice, which Robin partly remembered. "Let me pass, I say, or I'll strike you to the earth!"

"No, no, neighbor!" cried Robin, flourishing his cudgel, and then thrusting its larger end close to the man's muffled face. "No, no, I'm not the fool you take me for, nor do you pass till I have an answer to my question. Whereabouts is the dwelling of my kinsman, Major Molineux?"

The stranger, instead of attempting to force his passage, stepped back into the moonlight, unmuffled his face, and stared full into that of Robin.

"Watch here an hour, and Major Molineux will pass by," said he.

Robin gazed with dismay and astonishment on the unprecedented physiognomy of the speaker. The forehead with its double prominence, the broad hooked nose, the shaggy eyebrows, and fiery eyes were those which he had noticed at the inn, but the man's complexion had undergone a singular, or, more properly a twofold change. One side of the face blazed an intense red, while the other was black as midnight, the division line being in the broad bridge of the nose; and a mouth which seemed to extend from ear to ear was black or red, in contrast to the color of the cheek. The effect was as if two individual devils, a fiend of fire and a fiend of darkness, had united themselves to form this infernal visage. The stranger grinned in Robin's face, muffled his parti-colored features, and was out of sight in a moment.

"Strange things we travellers see!" ejaculated Robin.

He seated himself, however, upon the steps of the church-door, resolving to wait the appointed time for his kinsman. A few moments were consumed in philosophical speculations upon the species of man who had just left him; but having settled this point shrewdly, rationally, and satisfactorily, he was compelled to look elsewhere for his amusement. And first he threw his eyes along the street. It was of more respectable appearance than most of those into which he had wandered; and the moon, creating, like the imaginative power, a beautiful strangeness in familiar objects, gave something of romance to a scene that might not have possessed it in the light of day. The irregular and often quaint architecture of the houses, some of whose roofs were broken into numerous little peaks, while others ascended, steep and narrow, into a single point, and others again were square; the pure snow-white of some of their complexions, the aged darkness of others, and the thousand sparklings, reflected from bright substances in the walls of many; these matters engaged Robin's attention for a while, and then began to grow wearisome. Next he endeavored to define the forms of distant objects, starting away, with almost ghostly indistinctness, just as his eye appeared to grasp them; and finally he took a minute survey of an edifice which stood on the opposite side of the street, directly in front of the church-door, where he was stationed. It was a large, square mansion, distinguished from its neighbors by a balcony, which rested on tall pillars, and by an elaborate Gothic window, communicating therewith.

46

"Perhaps this is the very house I have been seeking," thought Robin.

Then he strove to speed away the time, by listening to a murmur which swept continually along the street, yet was scarcely audible, except to an unaccustomed ear like his; it was a low, dull, dreamy sound, compounded of many noises, each of which was at too great a distance to be separately heard. Robin marvelled at this snore of a sleeping town, and marvelled more whenever its continuity was broken by now and then a distant shout, apparently loud where it originated. But altogether it was a sleep-inspiring sound, and, to shake off its drowsy influence, Robin arose, and climbed a window-frame, that he might view the interior of the church. There the moonbeams came trembling in, and fell down upon the deserted pews, and extended along the quiet aisles. A fainter yet more awful radiance was hovering around the pulpit, and one solitary ray had dared to rest upon the open page of the great Bible. Had nature, in that deep hour, become a worshipper in the house which man had builded? Or was that heavenly light the visible sanctity of the place—visible because no earthly and impure feet were within the walls? The scene made Robin's heart shiver with a sensation of loneliness stronger than he had ever felt in the remotest depths of his native woods; so he turned away and sat down again before the door. There were graves around the church, and now an uneasy thought obtruded into Robin's breast. What if the object of his search, which had been so often and so strangely thwarted, were all the time mouldering in his shroud? What if his kinsman should glide through yonder gate, and nod and smile to him in dimly passing by?

"Oh that any breathing thing were here with me!" said Robin.

Recalling his thoughts from this uncomfortable track, he sent them over forest, hill, and stream, and attempted to imagine how that evening of ambiguity and weariness had been spent by his father's household. He pictured them assembled at the door, beneath the tree, the great old tree, which had been spared for its huge twisted trunk and venerable shade, when a thousand leafy brethren fell. There, at the going down of the summer sun, it was his father's custom to perform domestic worship, that the neighbors might come and join with him like brothers of the family, and that the wayfaring man might pause to drink at that fountain, and keep his heart pure by freshening the memory of home. Robin distinguished the seat of every individual of the little audience; he saw the good man in the midst, holding the Scriptures in the golden light that fell from the western clouds; he beheld him close the book and all rise up to pray. He heard the old thanksgiving for daily mercies, the old supplications for their continuance, to which he had so often listened in weariness, but which were now among his dear remembrances. He perceived the slight inequality of his father's voice when he came to speak of the absent one; he noted how his mother turned her face to the broad and knotted trunk; how his elder brother scorned, because the beard was rough upon his upper lip, to permit his features to be moved; how the younger sister drew down a low hanging branch before her eyes; and how the little one of all, whose sports had hitherto broken the decorum of the scene, understood the prayer for her playmate, and burst into clamorous grief. Then he saw them go in at the door; and when Robin would have entered also, the latch tinkled into its place, and he was excluded from his home.

"Am I here, or there?" cried Robin, starting; for all at once, when his thoughts had become visible and audible in a dream, the long, wide, solitary street shone out before him.

He aroused himself, and endeavored to fix his attention steadily upon the large edifice which he had surveyed before. But still his mind kept vibrating between fancy and reality; by turns, the pillars of the balcony lengthened into the tall, bare stems of pines, dwindled down to human figures, settled again into their true shape and size, and then commenced a new success of changes. For a single moment, when he deemed himself awake, he could have sworn that a visage—one which he seemed to remember, yet could not absolutely name as his kins-man's—was looking towards him from the Gothic window. A deeper sleep wrestled with and nearly overcame him, but fled at the sound of footsteps along the opposite pavement. Robin rubbed his eyes, discerned a man passing at the foot of the balcony, and addressed him in a loud, peevish, and lamentable cry.

"Hallo, friend! must I wait here all night for my kinsman, Major Molineux?"

The sleeping echoes awoke, and answered the voice; and the passenger, barely able to discern a figure sitting in the oblique shade of the steeple, traversed the street to obtain a nearer view. He was himself a gentleman in his prime, of open, intelligent, cheerful, and altogether prepossessing countenance. Perceiving a country youth, apparently homeless and without friends, he accosted him in a tone of real kindness, which had become strange to Robin's ears.

"Well, my good lad, who are you sitting here?" inquired he. "Can I be of service to you in any way?"

"I am afraid not, sir," replied Robin, despondingly; "yet I shall take it kindly, if you'll answer me a single question. I've been searching, half the night, for one Major Molineux; now, sir, is there really such a person in these parts, or am I dreaming?"

"Major Molineux! The name is not altogether strange to me," said the gentleman, smiling. "Have you any objection to telling me the nature of your business with him?"

Then Robin briefly related that his father was a clergyman, settled on a small salary, at a long distance back in the country, and he and Major Molineux were brothers' children. The Major, having inherited riches, and acquired civil and military rank, had visited his cousin, in great pomp, a year or two before; had manifested much interest in Robin and an elder brother, and, being childless himself, had thrown out hints respecting the future establishment of one of them in life. The elder brother was destined to succeed to the farm which his father cultivated in the interval of sacred duties; it was therefore determined that Robin should profit by his kinsman's generous intentions, especially as he seemed to be rather the favorite, and was thought to possess other necessary endow-ments.

"For I have the name of being a shrewd youth," observed Robin, in this part of his story.

"I doubt not you deserve it," replied his new friend, good-naturedly; "but pray proceed."

"Well, sir, being nearly eighteen years old, and well grown, as you see," continued Robin, drawing himself up to his full height, "I thought it high time to begin the world. So my mother and sister put me in handsome trim, and my father gave me half the remnant of his last year's salary, and five days ago I started for this place, to pay the Major a visit. But, would you believe it, sir! I crossed the ferry a little after dark, and have yet found nobody that would show me the way to his dwelling; only, an hour or two since, I was told to wait here, and Major Molineux would pass by."

"Can you describe the man who told you this?" inquired the gentleman.

"Oh, he was a very ill-favored fellow, sir," replied Robin, "with two great bumps on his forehead, a hook nose, fiery eyes; and, what struck me as the strangest, his face was of two different colors. Do you happen to know such a man, sir?"

"Not intimately," answered the stranger, "but I chanced to meet him a little time previous to your stopping me. I believe you may trust his word, and that the Major will very shortly pass through this street. In the mean time, as I have a singular curiosity to witness your meeting, I will sit down here upon the steps and bear you company."

He seated himself accordingly, and soon engaged his companion in animated discourse. It was but a brief continuance, however, for a noise of shouting, which had long been remotely audible, drew so much nearer that Robin inquired its cause.

"What may be the meaning of this uproar?" asked he. "Truly, if your town be always as noisy, I shall find little sleep while I am an inhabitant."

"Why, indeed, friend Robin, there do appear to be three or four riotous fellows abroad to-night," replied the gentleman. "You must not expect all the stillness of your native woods here in our streets. But the watch will shortly be at the heels of these lads and"—

"Ay, and set them in the stocks by peep of day," interrupted Robin, recollecting his own encounter with the drowsy lantern-bearer. "But, dear sir, if I may trust my ears, an army of watchmen would never make head against such a multitude of rioters. There were at least a thousand voices went up to make that one shout."

"May not a man have several voices, Robin, as well as two complexions?" said his friend.

"Perhaps a man may; but Heaven forbid that a woman should!" responded the shrewd youth, thinking of the seductive tones of the Major's housekeeper.

The sounds of a trumpet in some neighboring street now became so evident and continual, that Robin's curiosity was strongly excited. In addition to the shouts, he heard frequent bursts from many instruments of discord, and a wild and confused laughter filled up the intervals. Robin rose from the steps, and looked wistfully towards a point whither people seemed to be hastening.

"Surely some prodigious merry-making is going on," exclaimed he. "I have laughed very little since I left home, sir, and should be sorry to lose an opportunity. Shall we step round the corner by that darkish house, and take our share of the fun?"

"Sit down again, sit down, good Robin," replied the gentleman, laying his hand on the skirt of the gray coat. "You forget that we must wait here for your kinsman; and there is reason to believe that he will pass by, in the course of a very few moments."

The near approach of the uproar had now disturbed the neighborhood; windows flew open on all sides; and many heads, in the attire of the pillow, and confused by sleep suddenly broken, were protruded to the gaze of whoever had leisure to observe them. Eager voices hailed each other from house to house, all demanding the explanation, which not a soul could give. Half-dressed men hurried towards the unknown commotion, stumbling as they went over the stone steps that thrust themselves into the narrow foot-walk. The shouts, the laughter, and the tuneless bray, the antipodes of music, came onwards with increasing din, till scattered individuals, and then denser bodies, began to appear round a corner at the distance of a hundred yards.

"Will you recognize your kinsman, if he passes in this crowd?" inquired the gentleman.

"Indeed, I can't warrant it, sir; but I'll take my stand here, and keep a bright lookout," answered Robin, descending to the outer edge of the pavement.

A mighty stream of people now emptied into the street, and came rolling slowly towards the church. A single horseman wheeled the corner in the midst of them, and close behind him came a band of fearful wind-instruments, sending forth a fresher discord now that no intervening buildings kept it from the ear. Then a redder light disturbed the moonbeams, and a dense multitude of torches shone along the street, concealing, by their glare, whatever object they illuminated. The single horseman, clad in a military dress, and bearing a drawn sword, rode onward as the leader, and, by his fierce and variegated countenance, appeared like war personified; the red of one cheek was an emblem of fire and sword; the blackness of the other betokened the mourning that attends them. In his train were wild figures in the Indian dress, and many fantastic shapes without a model, giving the whole march a visionary air, as if a dream had broken forth from some feverish brain, and were sweeping visibly through the midnight streets. A mass of people, inactive, except as applauding spectators, hemmed the procession in; and several women ran along the sidewalk, piercing the confusion of heavier sounds with their shrill voices of mirth or terror.

"The double-faced fellow has his eye upon me," muttered Robin, with an indefinite but an uncomfortable idea that he was himself to bear a part in the pageantry.

The leader turned himself in the saddle, and fixed his glance full upon the country youth, as the steed went slowly by. When Robin had freed his eyes from those fiery ones, the musicians were passing before him, and the torches were close at hand; but the unsteady brightness of the latter formed a veil which he could not penetrate. The rattling of wheels over the stones sometimes found its way to his ear, and confused traces of a human form appeared at intervals, and then melted into the vivid light. A moment more, and the leader thundered a command to halt: the trumpets vomited a horrid breath, and then held their peace; the shouts and laughter of the people died away, and there remained only a universal hum, allied to silence. Right before Robin's eyes was an uncovered cart. There the torches blazed the brightest, there the moon shone out like day, and there, in tar-and-feathery dignity, sat his kinsman, Major Molineux!

He was an elderly man, of large and majestic person, and strong, square features, betokening a steady soul; but steady as it was, his enemies had found means to shake it. His face was pale as death, and far more ghastly; the broad forehead was contracted in his agony, so that his eyebrows formed one grizzled line; his eyes were red and wild, and the foam hung white upon his quivering lip. His whole frame was agitated by a quick and continual tremor, which his pride strove to quell, even in those circumstances of overwhelming humiliation. But perhaps the bitterest pang of all was when his eyes met those of Robin; for he evidently knew him on the instant, as the youth stood witnessing the foul disgrace of a head grown gray in honor. They stared at each other in silence, and Robin's knees shook, and his hair bristled, with a mixture of pity and terror. Soon, however, a bewildering excitement began to seize upon his mind; the preceding adventures of the night, the unexpected appearance of the crowd, the torches, the confused din and the hush that followed, the spectre of his kinsman reviled by that great multitude,—all this, and, more than all, a perception of tremendous ridicule in the whole scene, affected him with a sort of mental inebriety. At that moment a voice of sluggish merriment saluted Robin's ears; he turned instinctively, and just behind the corner of the church stood the lantern-bearer, rubbing his eyes, and drowsily enjoying the lad's amazement. Then he heard a peal of laughter like the ringing of silvery bells; a woman twitched his arm, a saucy eye met his, and he saw the lady of the scarlet petticoat. A sharp, dry cachinnation appealed to his memory, and, standing on tiptoe in the crowd, with his white apron over his head, he beheld the courteous little innkeeper. And lastly, there sailed over the heads of the multitude a great, broad laugh, broken in the midst of two sepulchral hems; thus, "Haw, haw, haw,—hem, hem,—haw, haw, haw, haw!"

The sound proceeded from the balcony of the opposite edifice, and thither Robin turned his eyes. In front of the Gothic window stood the old citizen wrapped in a wide gown, his gray periwig exchanged for a nightcap, which was thrust back from his forehead, and his silk stockings hanging about his legs. He supported himself on his polished cane in a fit of convulsive merriment, which manifested itself on his solemn old features like a funny inscription on a tombstone. Then Robin seemed to hear the voices of the barbers, of the guests of the inn, and of all who had made sport of him that night. The contagion was spreading among the multitude, when all at once, it seized upon Robin, and he sent forth a shout of laughter that echoed through the street,—every man shook his sides, every man emptied his lungs, but Robin's shout was the loudest there. The cloud-spirits peeped from their silvery islands, as the congregated mirth went roaring up the sky! The Man in the Moon heard the far bellow. "Oho," quoth he, "the old earth is frolicsome to-night!"

When there was a momentary calm in that tempestuous sea of sound, the leader gave the sign, the procession resumed its march. On they went, like fiends that throng in mockery around some dead potentate, mighty no more, but majestic still in his agony. On they went, in counterfeited pomp, in senseless uproar, in frenzied merriment, trampling all on an old man's heart. On swept the tumult, and left a silent street behind.

"Well, Robin, are you dreaming?" inquired the gentleman, laying his hand on the youth's shoulder.

Robin started, and withdrew his arm from the stone post to which he had instinctively clung, as the living stream rolled by him. His cheek was somewhat pale, and his eye not quite as lively as in the earlier part of the evening.

"Will you be kind enough to show me the way to the ferry?" said he, after a moment's pause.

"You have, then, adopted a new subject of inquiry?" observed his companion, with a smile.

"Why, yes, sir," replied Robin, rather dryly. "Thanks to you, and to my other friends, I have at last met my kinsman, and he will scarce desire to see my face again. I begin to grow weary of a town life, sir. Will you show me the way to the ferry?"

"No, my good friend Robin,—not tonight, at least," said the gentleman. "Some few days hence, if you wish it, I will speed you on your journey. Or, if you prefer to remain with us, perhaps, as you are a shrewd youth, you may rise in the world without the help of your kinsman, Major Molineux."

---

¹ Thomas Hutchinson (1711–1780), last royal governor of Massachusetts Bay Colony and author of a two-volume history of the colony.

² 1728 or 1729.

³ Knee breeches.

⁴ Fashionable wig named after a small Belgian city. It had a long plait behind tied with a bow at top and bottom.

⁵ Inns were often named after a notable person whose picture would be displayed on a sign projecting from above the entrance.

⁶ Humorous epithet for intoxicating liquor. It originally meant that part of God's creation that contributes to man's comfort. See I Timothy 4:4, "For every creature of God is good, and nothing to be refused, if it be received with thanksgiving . . . ." (KJV)

⁷ A public place where travelers prepare and eat their own food.

⁸ An allusion to Jacques Nicot, introducer of tobacco into France in 1560; hence a smoky atmosphere.

⁹ A servant bound to a master for a set time, after which he is free. The common expression is "indentured servant."

¹⁰ An allusion to Shakespeare's *A Midsummer Night's Dream,* Act V, Scene 1, wherein a comic character with a lantern represents the moon in a hilariously inept portrayal of the tragic love story of Pyramus and Thisbe.

DISCUSSION TOPICS

1. Cite evidence that Hawthorne (in contrast with Irving in "Adventure of the German Student") intends his reader to sympathize with his protagonist.
2. This story has been referred to as "The American Revolution in Miniature." Why is this label significant? Note especially the historical details in the opening paragraph.
3. At least one psychological critic has suggested that Robin does not really want to find his kinsman. Discuss this notion with particular reference to his series of encounters with various authority figures in the narration.
4. What is the significance (archetypal as well as psychological) of the woman with the scarlet petticoat—and of the kindly stranger?
5. Robin's experience mirrors the universal ordeal that youth must endure in passing from innocence into adulthood. This initiation is often labeled the rite or rites of passage. What episodes in the story make up this ritual for Robin?
6. Compare Robin's experiences with your own. What are some of the typical experiences of modern young persons passing from youth to adulthood? What stages mark that passage? Has this ritual changed significantly since Hawthorne's time?
7. Why does Robin finally laugh?

Herman Melville (1819–1891) Mariner, schoolteacher, friend and admirer of Hawthorne, customs officer, poet. He is regarded by many critics as America's greatest prose fictionist. He was a pioneer in complex narrative point of view in his magnum opus, *Moby-Dick*, as well as in *Bartleby*.

BARTLEBY THE SCRIVENER

A STORY OF WALL STREET

I am a rather elderly man. The nature of my avocations for the last thirty years has brought me into more than ordinary contact with what would seem an interesting and somewhat singular set of men, of whom as yet nothing that I know of has ever been written:—I mean the law-copyists or scriveners. I have known very many of them, professionally and privately, and if I pleased, could relate divers histories, at which good-natured gentlemen might smile, and sentimental souls might weep. But I waive the biographies of all other scriveners for a few passages in the life of Bartleby, who was a scrivener the strangest I ever saw or heard of. While of other law-copyists I might write the complete life, of Bartleby nothing of that sort can be done. I believe that no materials exist for a full and satisfactory biography of this man. It is an irreparable loss to literature. Bartleby was one of those beings of whom nothing is ascertainable, except from the original sources, and in his case those are very small. What my own astonished eyes saw of Bartleby, *that* is all I know of him, except, indeed, one vague report which will appear in the sequel.

Ere introducing the scrivener, as he first appeared to me, it is fit I make some mention of myself, my *employés,* my business, my chambers, and general surroundings; because some such description is indispensable to an adequate understanding of the chief character about to be presented.

Imprimis: I am a man who, from his youth upward, has been filled with a profound conviction that the easiest way of life is the best. Hence, though I belong to a profession proverbially energetic and nervous, even to turbulence, at times, yet nothing of that sort have I ever suffered to invade my peace. I am one of those unambitious lawyers who never addresses a jury, or in any way draws down public applause; but in the cool tranquillity of a snug retreat, do a snug business among rich men's bonds and mortgages and title-deeds. All who know me, consider me an eminently *safe* man. The late John Jacob Astor,[1] a personage little given to poetic enthusiasm, had no hesitation in pronouncing my first grand point to be prudence; my next, method. I do not speak it in vanity, but simply record the fact, that I was not unemployed in my profession by the late John Jacob Astor; a name which, I admit, I love to repeat, for it hath a rounded and orbicular sound to it, and rings like unto bullion. I will freely add, that I was not insensible to the late John Jacob Astor's good opinion.

Some time prior to the period at which this little history begins, my avocations had been largely increased. The good old office, now extinct in the State of New York, of a Master in Chancery,[2] had been conferred upon me. It was not a very arduous office, but very pleasantly remunerative. I seldom lose my temper; much more seldom indulge in dangerous indignation at wrongs and outrages; but I must be permitted to be rash here and declare, that I consider the sudden and violent abrogation of the office of Master in Chancery, by the new Constitution,[3] as a———premature act; inasmuch as I had counted upon a life-lease of the profits, whereas I only received those of a few short years. But this is by the way.

My chambers were upstairs at No.———Wall Street. At one end they looked upon the white wall of the interior of a spacious sky-light shaft, penetrating the building from top to bottom. This view might have been considered rather tame than otherwise, deficient in what landscape painters call "life." But if so, the view from the other end of my chambers offered, at least, a contrast, if nothing more. In that direction my windows commanded an unobstructed view of a lofty brick wall, black by age and everlasting shade; which wall required no spy-glass to bring out its lurking beauties, but for the benefit of all near-sighted spectators, was pushed up to within ten feet of my window panes. Owing to the great height of the surrounding buildings, and my chambers being on the second floor, the interval between this wall and mine not a little resembled a huge square cistern.

At the period just preceding the advent of Bartleby, I had two persons as copyists in my employment, and a promising lad as an office-boy. First, Turkey; second, Nippers; third, Ginger Nut. These may seem names, the like of which are not usually found in the Directory.[4] In truth they were nicknames, mutually conferred upon each other by my three clerks, and were deemed expressive of their respective persons or characters. Turkey was a short, pursy Englishman of about my own age, that is, somewhere not far from sixty. In the morning, one might say, his face was of a fine florid hue, but after twelve o'clock, meridian—his dinner hour—it blazed like a grate full of Christmas coals; and continued blazing—but, as it were, with a gradual wane—till 6 o'clock P.M. or thereabouts, after which I saw no more of the proprietor of the face, which, gaining its meridian with the sun, seemed to set with it, to rise, culminate, and decline the following day, with the like regularity and undiminished glory. There are many singular coincidences I have known in the course of my life, not the least among which was the fact, that exactly when Turkey displayed his fullest beams from his red and radiant countenance, just then, too, at that critical moment, began the daily period when I considered his business capacities as seriously disturbed for the remainder of the twenty-four hours. Not that he was absolutely idle, or averse to business then; far from it. The difficulty was, he was apt to be altogether too energetic. There was a strange, inflamed, flurried, flighty recklessness of activity about him. He would be incautious in dipping his pen into his inkstand. All his blots upon my documents, were dropped there after twelve o'clock, meridian. Indeed, not only would he be reckless and sadly given to making blots in the afternoon, but some days he went further, and was rather noisy. At such times, too, his face flamed with augmented blazonry, as if cannel coal had been heaped on anthracite.[5] He made an unpleasant racket with his chair; spilled his sandbox;[6] in mending his pens, impatiently split them all to pieces, and threw them on the floor in a sudden passion; stood up and leaned over his table, boxing his papers about in a most indecorous manner, very sad to behold in an elderly man like him. Nevertheless, as he was in many ways a most valuable person to me, and all the time before twelve o'clock, meridian, was the quickest, steadiest creature, too, accomplishing a great deal of work in a style not easy to be matched—for these reasons, I was willing to overlook his eccentricities, though indeed, occasionally, I remonstrated with him. I did this very gently, however, because, though the civilest, nay, the blandest and most reverential of men in the morning, yet in the afternoon he was disposed, upon provocation, to be slightly rash with his tongue, in fact, insolent. Now, valuing his morning services as I did, and resolving not to lose them—yet, at the same time, made uncomfortable by his inflamed ways after twelve o'clock; and being a man of peace, unwilling by my admonitions to call forth unseemly retorts from him—I took upon me, one Saturday noon (he was always worse on Saturdays), to hint to him, very kindly, that perhaps now that he was growing old, it might be well to abridge his labours; in short, he need not come to my chambers after twelve o'clock, but, dinner over, had best go home to his lodgings and rest himself till tea-time. But no; he insisted upon his afternoon devotions. His countenance became intolerably fervid, as he oratorically assured me—gesticulating, with a long ruler, at the other side of the room—that if his services in the morning were useful, how indispensable, then, in the afternoon?

"With submission, sir," said Turkey on this occasion, "I consider myself your right-hand man. In the morning I but marshal and deploy my columns; but in the afternoon I put myself at their head, and gallantly charge the foe, thus!"—and he made a violent thrust with the ruler.

"But the blots, Turkey," intimated I.

"True,—but, with submission, sir, behold these hairs! I am getting old. Surely, sir, a blot or two of a warm afternoon is not to be severely urged against grey hairs. Old age—even if it blot the page—is honourable. With submission, sir, we *both* are getting old."

This appeal to my fellow-feeling was hardly to be resisted. At all events, I saw that go he would not. So I made up my mind to let him stay, resolving, nevertheless, to see to it, that during the afternoon he had to do with my less important papers.

Nippers, the second on my list, was a whiskered, sallow, and, upon the whole, rather piratical-looking young man of about five and twenty. I always deemed him the victim of two evil powers—ambition and indigestion. The ambition was evinced by a certain impatience of the duties of a mere copyist—an unwarrantable usurpation of strictly professional affairs, such as the original drawing up of legal documents. The indigestion seemed betokened in an occasional nervous testiness and grinning irritability, causing the teeth to audibly grind together over mistakes committed in copying; unnecessary maledictions, hissed, rather than spoken, in the heat of business; and especially by a continual discontent with the height of the table where he worked. Though of a very ingenious mechanical turn, Nippers could never get this table to suit him. He put chips under it, blocks of various sorts, bits of pasteboard, and at last went so far as to attempt an exquisite adjustment by final pieces of folded blotting-paper. But no invention would answer. If, for the sake of easing his back, he brought the table lid at a sharp angle well up toward his chin, and wrote there like a man using the steep roof of a Dutch house for his desk—then he declared that it stopped the circulation in his arms. If now he lowered the table to his waistbands, and stooped over it in writing, then there was a sore aching in his back. In short, the truth of the matter was, Nippers knew not what he wanted. Or, if he wanted anything, it was to be rid of a scrivener's table altogether. Among the manifestations of his diseased ambition was a fondness he had for receiving visits from certain ambiguous-looking fellows in seedy coats, whom he called his clients. Indeed I was aware that not only was he, at times, considerable of a ward-politician, but he occasionally did a little business at the Justices' courts, and was not unknown on the steps of the Tombs.[7] I have good reason to believe, however, that one individual who called upon him at my chambers, and who, with a grand air, he insisted was his client, was no other than a dun, and the alleged title-deed, a bill. But with all his failings, and the annoyances he caused me, Nippers, like his compatriot Turkey, was a very useful man to me; wrote a neat, swift hand; and, when he chose, was not deficient in a gentlemanly sort of deportment. Added to this, he always dressed in a gentlemanly sort of way; and so, incidentally, reflected credit upon my chambers. Whereas with respect to Turkey, I had much ado to keep him from being a reproach to me. His clothes were apt to look oily and smell of eating-houses. He wore his pantaloons very loose and baggy in summer. His coats were execrable; his hat not to be handled. But while the hat was a thing of indifference to me, inasmuch as his natural civility and deference, as a dependent Englishman, always led him to doff it the moment he entered the room, yet his coat was another matter. Concerning his coats, I reasoned with him; but with no effect. The truth was, I suppose, that a man with so small an income, could not afford to sport such a lustrous face and a lustrous coat at one and the same time. As Nippers once observed, Turkey's money went chiefly for red ink. One winter day I presented Turkey with a highly-respectable looking coat of my own, a padded grey coat, of a most comfortable warmth, and which buttoned straight up from the knee to the neck. I thought Turkey would appreciate the favour, and abate his rashness and obstreperousness of afternoons. But no. I verily believe that buttoning himself up in so downy and blanket-like a coat had a pernicious effect upon him; upon the same principle that too much oats are bad for horses. In fact, precisely as a rash, restive horse is said to feel his oats, so Turkey felt his coat. It made him insolent. He was a man whom prosperity harmed.

Though concerning the self-indulgent habits of Turkey I had my own private surmises, yet touching Nippers I was well persuaded that whatever might be his faults in other respects, he was, at least, a temperate young man. But, indeed, nature herself seemed to have been his vintner, and at his birth charged him so thoroughly with an irritable, brandy-like disposition, that all subsequent potations were needless. When I consider how, amid the stillness of my chambers, Nippers would sometimes impatiently rise from his seat, and stooping over his table, spread his arms wide apart, seize the whole desk, and move it, and jerk it, with a grim, grinding motion on the floor, as if the table were a perverse voluntary agent, intent on thwarting and vexing him; I plainly perceive that for Nippers, brandy and water were altogether superfluous.

It was fortunate for me that, owing to its peculiar cause—indigestion—the irritability and consequent nervousness of Nippers, were mainly observable in the morning, while in the afternoon he was comparatively mild. So that Turkey's paroxysms only coming on about twelve o'clock, I never had to do with their eccentricities at one time. Their fits relieved each other like guards. When Nippers's was on, Turkey's was off; and *vice versa.* This was a good natural arrangement under the circumstances.

Ginger Nut, the third on my list, was a lad some twelve years old. His father was a carman,[8] ambitious of seeing his son on the bench instead of a cart, before he died. So he sent him to my office as student at law, errand boy, and cleaner and sweeper, at the rate of one dollar a week. He had a little desk to himself, but he did not use it much. Upon inspection, the drawer exhibited a great array of the shells of various sorts of nuts. Indeed, to this quick-witted youth the whole noble science of the law was contained in a nut-shell. Not the least among the employments of Ginger Nut, as well as one which he discharged with the most alacrity, was his duty as cake and apple purveyor for Turkey and Nippers. Copying law papers being proverbially a dry, husky sort of business, my two scriveners were fain to moisten their mouths very often with Spitzenbergs[9] to be had at the numerous stalls nigh the Custom House and Post Office. Also, they sent Ginger

Nut very frequently for that peculiar cake—small, flat, round, and very spicy—after which he had been named by them. Of a cold morning, when business was but dull, Turkey would gobble up scores of these cakes, as if they were mere wafers —indeed they sell them at the rate of six or eight for a penny—the scrape of his pen blending with the crunching of the crisp particles in his mouth. Of all the fiery afternoon blunders and flurried rashness of Turkey, was his once moistening a gingercake between his lips, and clapping it on a mortgage for a seal. I came within an ace of dismissing him then. But he mollified me by making an oriental bow and saying—"With submission, sir, it was generous of me to find[10] you in stationery on my own account."

Now my original business—that of a conveyancer and title hunter, and drawer-up of recondite documents of all sorts—was considerably increased by receiving the master's office. There was now great work for scriveners. Not only must I push the clerks already with me, but I must have additional help. In answer to my advertisement, a motionless young man one morning stood upon my office threshold, the door being open, for it was summer. I can see that figure now— pallidly neat, pitiably respectable, incurably forlorn! It was Bartleby.

After a few words touching his qualifications, I engaged him, glad to have among my corps of copyists a man of so singularly sedate an aspect, which I thought might operate beneficially upon the flighty temper of Turkey, and the fiery one of Nippers.

I should have stated before that ground glass folding-doors divided my premises into two parts, one of which was occupied by my scriveners, the other by myself. According to my humour I threw open these doors, or closed them. I resolved to assign Bartleby a corner by the folding-doors, but on my side of them, so as to have this quiet man within easy call, in case any trifling thing was to be done. I placed his desk close up to a small side-window in that part of the room, a window which originally had afforded a lateral view of certain grimy back-yards and bricks, but which, owing to subsequent erections, commanded at present no view at all, though it gave some light. Within three feet of the panes was a wall, and the light came down from far above, between two lofty buildings, as from a very small opening in a dome. Still further to a satisfactory arrangement, I procured a high green folding screen, which might entirely isolate Bartleby from my sight, though not remove him from my voice. And thus, in a manner, privacy and society were conjoined.

At first Bartleby did an extraordinary quantity of writing. As if long famishing for something to copy, he seemed to gorge himself on my documents. There was no pause for digestion. He ran a day and night line, copying by sun-light and by candle-light. I should have been quite delighted with his application, had he been cheerfully industrious. But he wrote on silently, palely, mechanically.

It is, of course, an indispensable part of a scrivener's business to verify the accuracy of his copy, word by word. Where there are two or more scriveners in an office, they assist each other in this examination, one reading from the copy, the other holding the original. It is a very dull, wearisome, and lethargic affair. I can readily imagine that to some sanguine temperaments it would be altogether intolerable. For example, I cannot credit that the mettlesome poet Byron would have contentedly sat down with Bartleby to examine a law document of, say five hundred pages, closely written in a crimpy hand.

Now and then, in the haste of business, it had been my habit to assist in comparing some brief document myself, calling Turkey or Nippers for this purpose. One object I had in placing Bartleby so handy to me behind the screen, was to avail myself of his services on such trivial occasions. It was on the third day, I think, of his being with me, and before any necessity had arisen for having his own writing examined, that, being much hurried to complete a small affair I had in hand, I abruptly called to Bartleby. In my haste and natural expectancy of instant compliance, I sat with my head bent over the original on my desk, and my right hand sideways, and somewhat nervously extended with the copy, so that immediately upon emerging from his retreat, Bartleby might snatch it and proceed to business without the least delay.

In this very attitude did I sit when I called to him, rapidly stating what it was I wanted him to do—namely, to examine a small paper with me. Imagine my surprise, nay, my consternation, when without moving from his privacy, Bartleby in a singularly mild, firm voice, replied, "I would prefer not to."

I sat awhile in perfect silence, rallying my stunned faculties. Immediately it occurred to me that my ears had deceived me, or Bartleby had entirely misunderstood my meaning. I repeated my requst in the clearest tone I could assume. But in quite as clear a one came the previous reply, "I would prefer not to."

"Prefer not to," echoed I, rising in high excitement, and crossing the room with a stride. "What do you mean? Are you moon-struck?[11] I want you to help me compare this sheet here—take it," and I thrust it toward him.

"I would prefer not to," said he.

I looked at him steadfastly. His face was leanly composed; his grey eye dimly calm. Not a wrinkle of agitation rippled him. Had there been the least uneasiness, anger, impatience or impertinence in his manner; in other words, had there been anything ordinarily human about him; doubtless I should have violently dismissed him from the premises. But as it was, I should have as soon thought of turning my pale plaster-of-paris bust of Cicero[12] out of doors. I stood gazing at him awhile, as he went on with his own writing, and then reseated myself at my desk. This is very strange, thought I. What had one best do? But my business hurried me. I concluded to forget the matter for the present, reserving it for my future leisure. So calling Nippers from the other room, the paper was speedily examined.

A few days after this, Bartleby concluded four lengthy documents, being quadruplicates of a week's testimony taken before me in my High Court of Chancery. It became necessary to examine them. It was an important suit, and great accuracy was imperative. Having all things arranged, I called Turkey, Nippers and Ginger Nut from the next room, meaning to place the four copies in the hands of my four clerks, while I should read from the original. Accordingly Turkey, Nippers and Ginger Nut had taken their seats in a row, each with his document in hand, when I called to Bartleby to join this interesting group.

"Bartleby! quick, I am waiting."

I heard a slow scrape of his chair legs on the uncarpeted floor, and soon he appeared standing at the entrance of his hermitage.

"What is wanted?" said he mildly.

"The copies, the copies," said I hurriedly. "We are going to examine them. There"—and I held toward him the fourth quadruplicate.

"I would prefer not to," he said, and gently disappeared behind the screen.

For a few moments I was turned into a pillar of salt,[13] standing at the head of my seated column of clerks. Recovering myself, I advanced toward the screen, and demanded the reason for such extraordinary conduct.

"*Why* do you refuse?"

"I would prefer not to."

With any other man I should have flown outright into a dreadful passion, scorned all further words, and thrust him ignominiously from my presence. But there was something about Bartleby that not only strangely disarmed me, but in a wonderful manner touched and disconcerted me. I began to reason with him.

"These are your own copies we are about to examine. It is labour saving to you, because one examination will answer for your four papers. It is common usage. Every copyist is bound to help examine his copy. Is it not so? Will you not speak? Answer!"

"I prefer not to," he replied in a flute-like tone. It seemed to me that while I had been addressing him, he carefully revolved every statement that I made; fully comprehended the meaning; could not gainsay the irresistible conclusion; but, at the same time, some paramount consideration prevailed with him to reply as he did.

"You are decided, then, not to comply with my request—a request made according to common usage and common sense?"

He briefly gave me to understand that on that point my judgment was sound. Yes: his decision was irreversible.

It is not seldom the case that when a man is browbeaten in some unprecedented and violently unreasonable way, he begins to stagger in his own plainest faith. He begins, as it were, vaguely to surmise that, wonderful as it may be, all the justice and all the reason are on the other side. Accordingly, if any disinterested persons are present, he turns to them for some reinforcement for his own faltering mind.

"Turkey," said I, "what do you think of this? Am I not right?"

"With submission, sir," said Turkey, with his blandest tone, "I think that you are."

"Nippers," said I, "what do *you* think of it?"

"I think I should kick him out of the office."

(The reader of nice perceptions will here perceive that, it being morning, Turkey's answer is couched in polite and tranquil terms but Nippers's reply in ill-tempered ones. Or, to repeat a previous sentence, Nippers's ugly mood was on duty, and Turkey's off.)

"Ginger Nut," said I, willing to enlist the smallest suffrage[14] in my behalf, "what do *you* think of it?"

"I think, sir, he's a little *luny*,"[15] replied Ginger Nut, with a grin.

"You hear what they say," said I, turning towards the screen, "come forth and do your duty."

But he vouchsafed no reply. I pondered a moment in sore perplexity. But once more business hurried me. I determined again to postpone the consideration of this dilemma to my future leisure. With a little trouble we made out to examine the papers without Bartleby, though at every page or two, Turkey deferentially dropped his opinion that this proceeding was quite out of the common; while Nippers, twitching in his chair with a dyspeptic nervousness, ground out between his set teeth occasional hissing maledictions against the stubborn oaf behind the screen. And for his (Nippers's) part, this was the first and the last time he would do another man's business without pay.

Meanwhile Bartleby sat in his hermitage, oblivious to everything but his own peculiar business there.

Some days passed, the scrivener being employed upon another lengthy work. His late remarkable conduct led me to regard his ways narrowly. I observed that he never went to dinner; indeed that he never went any where. As yet I had never of my personal knowledge known him to be outside of my office. He was a perpetual sentry in the corner. At about eleven o'clock though, in the morning, I noticed that Ginger Nut would advance towards the opening in Bartleby's screen, as if silently beckoned thither by a gesture invisible to me where I sat. The boy would then leave the office jingling a few pence, and reappear with a handful of ginger-nuts which he delivered in the hermitage, receiving two of the cakes for his trouble.

He lives, then, on ginger-nuts, thought I; never eats a dinner, properly speaking; he must be a vegetarian then; but no; he never eats even vegetables, he eats nothing but ginger-nuts. My mind then ran on in reveries concerning the probable effects upon the human constitution of living entirely on ginger-nuts. Ginger-nuts are so called because they contain ginger as one of their peculiar constituents, and the final flavouring one. Now what was ginger? A hot, spicy thing. Was Bartleby hot and spicy? Not at all. Ginger, then, had no effect upon Bartleby. Probably he preferred it should have none.

Nothing so aggravates an earnest person as a passive resistance. If the individual so resisted be of a not inhumane temper, and the resisting one perfectly harmless in his passivity; then, in the better moods of the former, he will endeavour charitably to construe to his imagination what proves impossible to be solved by his judgment. Even so, for the most part, I regarded Bartleby and his ways. Poor fellow! thought I, he means no mischief; it is plain he intends no insolence; his aspect sufficiently evinces that his eccentricities are involuntary. He is useful to me. I can get along with him. If I turn him away, the chances are he will fall in with some less indulgent employer, and then he will be rudely treated, and perhaps driven forth miserably to starve. Yes. Here I can cheaply purchase a delicious self-approval. To befriend Bartleby; to humour him in his strange wilfulness, will cost me little or nothing, while I lay up in my soul what will eventually prove a sweet morsel for my conscience. But this mood was not invariable with me. The passiveness of Bartleby sometimes irritated me. I felt strangely goaded on to encounter him in new opposition, to elicit some angry spark from him answerable to my own. But indeed I might as well have essayed to strike fire with my knuckles against a bit of Windsor soap.[16] But one afternoon the evil impulse in me mastered me, and the following little scene ensued:

"Bartleby," said I, "when those papers are all copied, I will compare them with you."

"I would prefer not to."

"How? Surely you do not mean to persist in that mulish vagary?"

No answer.

I threw open the folding-doors near by, and turning upon Turkey and Nippers, exclaimed in an excited manner:

"He says, a second time, he won't examine his papers. What do you think of it, Turkey?"

It was afternoon, be it remembered. Turkey sat glowing like a brass boiler, his bald head steaming, his hands reeling among his blotted papers.

"Think of it?" roared Turkey; "I think I'll just step behind his screen, and black his eyes for him!"

So saying, Turkey rose to his feet and threw his arms into a pugilistic position. He was hurrying away to make good his promise, when I detained him, alarmed at the effect of incautiously rousing Turkey's combativeness after dinner.

"Sit down, Turkey," said I, "and hear what Nippers has to say. What do you think of it, Nippers? Would I not be justified in immediately dismissing Bartleby?"

"Excuse me, that is for you to decide, sir. I think his conduct quite unusual, and indeed unjust, as regards Turkey and myself. But it may only be a passing whim."

"Ah," exclaimed I, "you have strangely changed your mind then—you speak very gently of him now."

"All beer," cried Turkey; "gentleness is effects of beer—Nippers and I dined together today. You see how gentle *I* am, sir. Shall I go and black his eyes?"

"You refer to Bartleby, I suppose. No, not today, Turkey," I replied; "pray, put up your fists."

I closed the doors, and again advanced towards Bartleby. I felt additional incentives tempting me to my fate. I burned to be rebelled against again. I remembered that Bartleby never left the office.

"Bartleby," said I, "Ginger Nut is away; just step round to the Post Office, won't you? (it was but a three minutes' walk), and see if there is anything for me."

"I would prefer not to."

"You *will* not?"

"I *prefer* not."

I staggered to my desk, and sat there in a deep study. My blind inveteracy returned. Was there any other thing in which I could procure myself to be ignominiously repulsed by this lean, penniless wight?—my hired clerk? What added thing is there, perfectly reasonable, that he will be sure to refuse to do?

"Bartleby!"

No answer.

"Bartleby," in a louder tone.

No answer.

"Bartleby," I roared.

Like a very ghost, agreeably to the laws of magical invocation, at the third summons, he appeared at the entrance of his hermitage.

"Go to the next room, and tell Nippers to come to me."

"I prefer not to," he respectfully and slowly said, and mildly disappeared.

"Very good, Bartleby," said I, in a quiet sort of serenely severe self-possessed tone, intimating the unalterable purpose of some terrible retribution very close at hand. At the moment I half intended something of the kind. But upon the whole, as it was drawing towards my dinnerhour, I thought it best to put on my hat and walk home for the day, suffering much from perplexity and distress of mind.

Shall I acknowledge it? The conclusion of this whole business was, that it soon became a fixed fact of my chambers, that a pale young scrivener, by the name of Bartleby, had a desk there; that he copied for me at the usual rate of four cents a folio (one hundred words); but he was permanently exempt from examining the work done by him, that duty being transferred to Turkey and Nippers, out of compliment doubtless to their superior acuteness; moreover, said Bartleby was never on any account to be despatched on the most trivial errand of any sort; and that even if entreated to take upon him such a matter, it was generally understood that he would prefer not to—in other words, that he would refuse point-blank.

As days passed on, I became considerably reconciled to Bartleby. His steadiness, his freedom from all dissipation, his incessant industry (except when he chose to throw himself into a standing revery behind his screen), his great stillness, his unalterableness of demeanour under all circumstances, made him a valuable acquisition. One prime thing was this,—*he was always there;*—first in the morning, continually through the day, and the last at night. I had a singular confidence in his honesty. I felt my most precious papers perfectly safe in his hands. Sometimes to be sure I could not, for the very soul of me, avoid falling into sudden spasmodic passions with him. For it was exceeding difficult to bear in mind all the time those strange peculiarities, privileges, and unheard of exemptions, forming the tacit stipulations on Bartleby's part under which he remained in my office. Now and then, in the eagerness of dispatching pressing business, I would inadvertently summon Bartleby, in a short, rapid tone, to put his finger, say, on the incipient tie of a bit of red tape with which I was about compressing some papers. Of course, from behind the screen the usual answer, "I prefer not to," was sure to come; and then, how could a human creature with the common infirmities of our nature, refrain from bitterly exclaiming upon such perverseness—such unreasonableness? However, every added repulse of this sort which I received only tended to lessen the probability of my repeating the inadvertence.

Here it must be said, that according to the custom of most legal gentlemen occupying chambers in densely-populated law buildings, there were several keys to my door. One was kept by a woman residing in the attic, which person weekly scrubbed and daily swept and dusted my apartments. Another was kept by Turkey for convenience sake. The third I sometimes carried in my own pocket. The fourth I knew not who had.

Now, one Sunday morning I happened to go to Trinity Church,[17] to hear a celebrated preacher, and finding myself rather early on the ground, I thought I would walk round to my chambers for awhile. Luckily I had my key with me; but upon applying it to the lock, I found it resisted by something inserted from the inside. Quite surprised, I called out; when to my consternation a key was turned from within; and thrusting his lean visage at me, and holding the door ajar, the apparition of Bartleby appeared, in his shirt sleeves, and otherwise in a strangely tattered dishabille, saying quietly that he was sorry, but he was deeply engaged just then, and—preferred not admitting me at present. In a brief word or two, he moreover added, that perhaps I had better walk round the block two or three times, and by that time he would probably have concluded his affairs.

Now, the utterly unsurmised appearance of Bartleby, tenanting my lawchambers of a Sunday morning, with his cadaverously gentlemanly *nonchalance,* yet withal firm and self-possessed, had such a strange effect upon me, that incontinently I slunk away from my own door, and did as desired. But not without sundry twinges of impotent rebellion against the mild effrontery of this unaccountable scrivener. Indeed, it was his wonderful mildness chiefly, which not only disarmed me, but unmanned me, as it were. For I consider that one, for the time, is in a way unmanned when he tranquilly permits his hired clerk to dictate to him, and order him away from his own premises. Furthermore, I was full of uneasiness as to what Bartleby could possibly be doing in my office in his shirt sleeves, and in an otherwise dismantled condition of a Sunday morning. Was anything amiss going on? Nay, that was out of the question. It was not to be thought of for a moment that Bartleby was an immoral person. But what could he be doing there—copying? Nay again, whatever might be his eccentricities, Bartleby was an eminently decorous person. He would be the last man to sit down to his desk in any state approaching to nudity. Besides, it was Sunday; and there was something about Bartleby that forbade the supposition that he would by any secular occupation violate the proprieties of the day.

Nevertheless, my mind was not pacified; and full of a restless curiosity, at last I returned to the door. Without hindrance I inserted my key, opened it, and entered. Bartleby was not to be seen. I looked round anxiously, peeped behind his screen; but it was very plain that he was gone. Upon more closely examining the place, I surmised that for an indefinite period Bartleby must have ate, dressed, and slept in my office, and that too without plate, mirror, or bed. The cushioned seat of a rickety old sofa in one corner bore the faint impress of a lean, reclining form. Rolled away under his desk, I found a blanket; under the empty grate, a blacking box[18] and brush; on a chair, a tin basin, with soap and a ragged towel; in a newspaper a few crumbs of ginger-nuts and a morsel of cheese. Yes, thought I, it is evident enough that Bartleby has been making his home here, keeping bachelor's hall all by himself. Immediately then the thought came sweeping across me. What miserable friendlessness and loneliness are here revealed! His poverty is great; but his solitude, how horrible! Think of it. Of a Sunday, Wall Street is deserted as Petra;[19] and every night of every day it is an emptiness. This building too, which of week-days hums with industry and life, at nightfall echoes with sheer vacancy, and all through Sunday is forlorn. And here Bartleby makes his home; sole spectator of a solitude which he has seen all populous—a sort of innocent and transformed Marius brooding among the ruins of Carthage![20]

For the first time in my life a feeling of overpowering stinging melancholy seized me. Before, I had never experienced aught but a not-unpleasing sadness. The bond of a common humanity now drew me irresistibly to gloom. A fraternal melancholy! For both I and Bartleby were sons of Adam. I remembered the bright silks and sparkling faces I had seen that day, in gala trim, swan-like sailing down the Mississippi of Broadway; and I contrasted them with the pallid copyist, and thought to myself, Ah, happiness courts the light, so we deem the world is gay; but misery hides aloof, so we deem that misery there is none. These sad fancyings —chimeras, doubtless, of a sick and silly brain—led on to other and more special thoughts, concerning the eccentricities of Bartleby. Presentiments of strange discoveries hovered round me. The scrivener's pale form appeared to me laid out, among uncaring strangers, in its shivering winding sheet.

Suddenly I was attracted by Bartleby's closed desk, the key in open sight left in the lock.

I mean no mischief, seek the gratification of no heartless curiosity, thought I; besides, the desk is mine, and its contents, too, so I will make bold to look within. Everything was methodically arranged, the papers smoothly placed. The pigeon holes were deep, and removing the files of documents, I groped into their recesses. Presently I felt something there, and dragged it out. It was an old bandana handkerchief, heavy and knotted. I opened it, and saw it was a saving's bank.

I now recalled all the quiet mysteries which I had noted in the man. I remembered that he never spoke but to answer; that though at intervals he had considerable time to himself, yet I had never seen him reading—no, not even a newspaper; that for long periods he would stand looking out, at his pale window behind the screen, upon the dead brick wall; I was quite sure he never visited any refectory or eating-house; while his pale face clearly indicated that he never drank beer like Turkey, or tea and coffee even, like other men; that he never went anywhere in particular that I could learn; never went out for a walk, unless indeed that was the case at present; that he had declined telling who he was, or whence he came, or whether he had any relatives in the world; that though so thin and pale, he never complained of ill health. And more than all, I remembered a certain unconscious air of pallid—how shall I call it?—of pallid haughtiness, say, or rather an austere reserve about him, which had positively awed me into my tame compliance with his eccentricities, when I had feared to ask him to do the slightest incidental thing for me, even though I might know, from his long-continued motionlessness, that behind his screen he must be standing in one of those dead-wall reveries of his.

Revolving all these things, and coupling them with the recently discovered fact that he made my office his constant abiding place and home, and not forgetful of his morbid moodiness; revolving all these things, a prudential feeling began to steal over me. My first emotions had been those of pure melancholy and sincerest pity; but just in proportion as the forlornness of Bartleby grew and grew to my imagination, did that same melancholy merge into fear, that pity into repulsion. So true it is, and so terrible, too, that up to a certain point the thought or sight of misery enlists our best affections; but, in certain special cases, beyond that point it does not. They err who would assert that invariably this is owing to the inherent selfishness of the human heart. It rather proceeds from a certain hopelessness of remedying excessive and organic ill. To a sensitive being, pity is not seldom pain. And when at last it is perceived that such pity cannot lead to effectual succour, common sense bids the soul be rid of it. What I saw that morning persuaded me that the scrivener was the victim of innate and incurable disorder. I might give alms to his body; but his body did not pain him; it was his soul that suffered, and his soul I could not reach.

I did not accomplish the purpose of going to Trinity Church that morning. Somehow, the things I had seen disqualified me for the time from church-going. I walked homeward, thinking what I would do with Bartleby. Finally, I resolved upon this:—I would put certain calm questions to him the next morning, touching his history, &c., and if he declined to answer them openly and unreservedly (and I supposed he would prefer not), then to give him a twenty dollar bill over and above what I might owe him, and tell him his services were no longer required; but that if in any other way I could assist him, I would be happy to do so, especially if he desired to return to his native place, wherever that might be, I would willingly help to defray the expenses. Moreover, if, after reaching home, he found himself at any time in want of aid, a letter from him would be sure of a reply.

The next morning came.

"Bartleby," said I, gently calling to him behind his screen.

No reply.

"Bartleby," said I, in a still gentler tone, "come here; I am not going to ask you to do anything you would prefer not to do—I simply wish to speak to you."

Upon this he noiselessly slid into view.

"Will you tell me, Bartleby, where you were born?"

"I would prefer not to."

"Will you tell me *anything* about yourself?"

"I would prefer not to."

"But what reasonable objection can you have to speak to me? I feel friendly towards you."

He did not look at me while I spoke, but kept his glance fixed upon my bust of Cicero, which, as I then sat, was directly behind me, some six inches above my head.

"What is your answer, Bartleby?" said I, after waiting a considerable time for a reply, during which his countenance remained immovable, only there was the faintest conceivable tremor of the white attenuated mouth.

"At present I prefer to give no answer," he said, and retired into his hermitage.

It was rather weak in me I confess, but his manner on this occasion nettled me. Not only did there seem to lurk in it a certain calm disdain, but his perverseness seemed ungrateful, considering the undeniable good usage and indulgence he had received from me.

Again I sat ruminating what I should do. Mortified as I was at his behaviour, and resolved as I had been to dismiss him when I entered my office, nevertheless I strangely felt something superstitious knocking at my heart, and forbidding me to carry out my purpose, and denouncing me for a villain if I dared to breathe one bitter word against this forlornest of mankind. At last, familiarly drawing my chair behind his screen, I sat down and said: "Bartleby, never mind then about revealing your history; but let me entreat you, as a friend, to comply as far as may be with the usages of this office. Say now you will help to examine papers tomorrow or next day: in short, say now that in a day or two you will begin to be a little reasonable:—say so, Bartleby."

"At present I would prefer not to be a little reasonable," was his mildly cadaverous reply.

Just then the folding-doors opened, and Nippers approached. He seemed suffering from an unusually bad night's rest, induced by severer indigestion than common. He overheard those final words of Bartleby.

"*Prefer not*, eh?" gritted Nippers—"I'd *prefer* him, if I were you, sir," addressing me—"I'd *prefer* him; I'd give him preferences, the stubborn mule! What is it, sir, pray, that he *prefers* not to do now?"

Bartleby moved not a limb.

"Mr. Nippers," I said, "I'd prefer that you would withdraw for the present."

Somehow, of late I had got into the way of involuntarily using this word "prefer" upon all sorts of not exactly suitable occasions. And I trembled to think that my contact with the scrivener had already and seriously affected me in a mental way. And what further and deeper aberration might it not yet produce? This apprehension had not been without efficacy in determining me to summary means.

As Nippers, looking very sour and sulky, was departing, Turkey blandly and deferentially approached.

"With submission, sir," said he, "yesterday I was thinking about Bartleby here, and I think that if he would but prefer to take a quart of good ale every day, it would do much towards mending him, and enabling him to assist in examining his papers."

"So you have got the word, too," said I, slightly excited.

"With submission, what word, sir?" asked Turkey, respectfully crowding himself into the contracted space behind the screen, and by so doing, making me jostle the scrivener. "What word, sir?"

"I would prefer to be left alone here," said Bartleby, as if offended at being mobbed in his privacy.

"*That's* the word, Turkey," said I—"*that's* it."

"Oh, *prefer?* oh, yes—queer word. I never use it myself. But, sir, as I was saying, if he would but prefer—"

"Turkey," interrupted I, "you will please withdraw."

"Oh, certainly, sir, if you prefer that I should."

As he opened the folding-door to retire, Nippers at his desk caught a glimpse of me, and asked whether I would prefer to have a certain paper copied on blue paper or white. He did not in the least roguishly accent the word prefer. It was plain that it involuntarily rolled from his tongue. I thought to myself, surely I must get rid of a demented man, who already has in some degree turned the tongues, if not the heads, of myself and clerks. But I thought it prudent not to break the dismission at once.

The next day I noticed that Bartleby did nothing but stand at his window in his dead-wall revery. Upon asking him why he did not write, he said that he had decided upon doing no more writing.

"Why, how now? what next?" exclaimed I, "do no more writing?"

"No more."

"And what is the reason?"

"Do you not see the reason for yourself?" he indifferently replied.

I looked steadfastly at him, and perceived that his eyes looked dull and glazed. Instantly it occurred to me, that his unexampled diligence in copying by his dim window for the first few weeks of his stay with me might have temporarily impaired his vision.

I was touched. I said something in condolence with him. I hinted that, of course, he did wisely in abstaining from writing for a while, and urged him to embrace that opportunity of taking wholesome exercise in the open air. This, however, he did not do. A few days after this, my other clerks being absent, and being in a great hurry to despatch certain letters by the mail, I thought that, having nothing else earthly to do, Bartleby would surely be less inflexible than usual, and carry these letters to the Post Office. But he blankly declined. So, much to my inconvenience, I went myself.

Still added days went by. Whether Bartleby's eyes improved or not, I could not say. To all appearance, I thought they did. But when I asked him if they did, he vouchsafed no answer. At all events, he would do no copying. At last, in reply to my urgings, he informed me that he had permanently given up copying.

"What!" exclaimed I; "suppose your eyes should get entirely well—better than ever before—would you not copy then?"

"I have given up copying," he answered and slid aside.

He remained, as ever, a fixture in my chamber. Nay—if that were possible —he became still more of a fixture than before. What was to be done? He would do nothing in the office: why should he stay there? In plain fact, he had now become a millstone[21] to me, not only useless as a necklace, but afflictive to bear. Yet I was sorry for him. I speak less than truth when I say that, on his own account, he occasioned me uneasiness. If he would but have named a single relative or friend, I would instantly have written, and urged their taking the poor fellow away to some convenient retreat. But he seemed alone, absolutely alone in the universe. A bit of wreckage in the mid-Atlantic. At length, necessities connected with my business tryannized over all other considerations. Decently as I could, I told Bartleby that in six days' time he must unconditionally leave the office. I warned him to take measures, in the interval, for procuring some other abode. I offered to assist him in this endeavour, if he himself would but take the first step towards a removal. "And when you finally quit me, Bartleby," added I, "I shall see that you go away not entirely unprovided. Six days from this hour, remember."

At the expiration of that period, I peeped behind the screen, and lo! Bartleby was there.

I buttoned up my coat, balanced myself; advanced slowly towards him, touched his shoulder, and said, "The time has come; you must quit this place; I am sorry for you; here is money; but you must go."

"I would prefer not," he replied, with his back still towards me.

"You *must.*"

He remained silent.

Now I had an unbounded confidence in this man's common honesty. He had frequently restored to me sixpences and shillings carelessly dropped upon the floor, for I am apt to be very reckless in such shirt-button affairs. The proceeding then which followed will not be deemed extraordinary.

"Bartleby," said I, "I owe you twelve dollars on account; here are thirty-two; the odd twenty are yours.—Will you take it?" and I handed the bills towards him.

But he made no motion.

"I will leave them here then," putting them under a weight on the table. Then taking my hat and cane and going to the door, I tranquilly turned and added —"After you have removed your things from these offices, Bartleby, you will of course lock the door—since every one is now gone for the day but you—and if you please, slip your key underneath the mat, so that I may have it in the morning. I shall not see you again; so good-bye to you. If hereafter in your new place of abode I can be of any service to you, do not fail to advise me by letter. Good-bye, Bartleby, and fare you well."

But he answered not a word; like the last column of some ruined temple, he remained standing mute and solitary in the middle of the otherwise deserted room.

As I walked home in a pensive mood, my vanity got the better of my pity. I could not but highly plume myself on my masterly management in getting rid of Bartleby. Masterly I call it, and such it must appear to any dispassionate thinker. The beauty of my procedure seemed to consist in its perfect quietness. There was no vulgar bullying, no bravado of any sort, no choleric hectoring, no striding to and fro across the apartment, jerking out vehement commands for Bartleby to bundle himself off with his beggarly traps.[22] Nothing of the kind. Without loudly bidding Bartleby depart—as an inferior genius might have done—I *assumed* the ground that depart he must; and upon that assumption built all I had to say. The more I thought over my procedure, the more I was charmed with it. Nevertheless, next morning, upon awakening, I had my doubts,—I had somehow slept off the fumes of vanity. One of the coolest and wisest hours a man has, is just after he awakes in the morning. My procedure seemed as sagacious as ever,—but only in theory. How it would prove in practice—there was the rub. It was truly a beautiful thought to have assumed Bartleby's departure; but, after all, that assumption was simply my own, and none of Bartleby's. The great point was, not whether I had assumed that he would quit me, but whether he would prefer so to do. He was more a man of preferences than assumptions.

After breakfast, I walked down town, arguing the probabilities *pro* and *con.* One moment I thought it would prove a miserable failure, and Bartleby would be found all alive at my office as usual; the next moment it seemed certain that I should see his chair empty. And so I kept veering about. At the corner of Broadway and Canal Street, I saw quite an excited group of people standing in earnest conversation.

"I'll take odds he doesn't," said a voice as I passed.

"Doesn't go?—done!" said I, "put up your money."

I was instinctively putting my hand in my pocket to produce my own, when I remembered that this was an election day. The words I had overheard bore no reference to Bartleby, but to the success or nonsuccess of some candidate for the mayoralty. In my intent frame of mind, I had, as it were, imagined that all Broadway shared in my excitement, and were debating the same question with me. I passed on, very thankful that the uproar of the street screened my momentary absentmindedness.

As I had intended, I was earlier than usual at my office door. I stood listening for a moment. All was still. He must be gone. I tried the knob. The door was locked. Yes, my procedure had worked to a charm; he indeed must be vanished. Yet a certain melancholy mixed with this: I was almost sorry for my brilliant success. I was fumbling under the door mat for the key, which Bartleby was to have left there for me, when accidentally my knee knocked against a panel, producing a summoning sound, and in response a voice came to me from within—"Not yet; I am occupied."

It was Bartleby.

I was thunderstruck. For an instant I stood like the man who, pipe in mouth, was killed one cloudless afternoon long ago in Virginia, by summer lightning; at his own warm open window he was killed, and remained leaning out there upon the dreamy afternoon, till some one touched him, and he fell.

"Not gone!" I murmured at last. But again obeying that wondrous ascendancy which the inscrutable scrivener had over me—and from which ascendancy, for all my chafing, I could not completely escape—I slowly went down stairs and out into the street, and while walking round the block, considered what I should next do in this unheard-of perplexity. Turn the man out by an actual thrusting I could not; to drive him away by calling him hard names would not do; calling in the police was an unpleasant idea; and yet, permit him to enjoy his cadaverous triumph over me,—this too I could not think of. What was to be done? or, if nothing could be done, was there anything further that I could *assume* in the matter? Yes, as before I had prospectively assumed that Bartleby would depart, so now I might retrospectively assume that departed he was. In the legitimate carrying out of this assumption, I might enter my office in a great hurry, and pretending not to see Bartleby at all, walk straight against him as if he were air. Such a proceeding would in a singular degree have the appearance of a home-thrust.[23] It was hardly possible that Bartleby could withstand such an application of the doctrine of assumptions. But, upon second thought, the success of the plan seemed rather dubious. I resolved to argue the matter over with him again.

"Bartleby," said I, entering the office, with a quietly severe expression. "I am seriously displeased. I am pained, Bartleby. I had thought better of you. I had imagined you of such a gentlemanly organization, that in any delicate dilemma a slight hint would suffice—in short, an assumption; but it appears I am deceived. Why," I added, unaffectedly starting, "you have not even touched that money yet," pointing to it, just where I had left it the evening previous.

He answered nothing.

"Will you, or will you not, quit me?" I now demanded in a sudden passion, advancing close to him.

"I would prefer *not* to quit you," he replied, gently emphasizing the *not*.

"What earthly right have you to stay here? Do you pay any rent? Do you pay my taxes? Or is this property yours?"

He answered nothing.

"Are you ready to go on and write now? Are your eyes recovered? Could you copy a small paper for me this morning? or help examine a few lines? or step round to the Post Office? In a word, will you do any thing at all, to give a colouring to your refusal to depart the premises?"

He silently retired into his hermitage.

I was now in such a state of nervous resentment that I thought it but prudent to check myself, at present, from further demonstrations. Bartleby and I were alone. I remembered the tragedy of the unfortunate Adams and the still more unfortunate Colt[24] in the solitary office of the latter; and how poor Colt, being dreadfully incensed by Adams, and imprudently permitting himself to get wildly excited, was at unawares hurried into his fatal act—an act which certainly no man could possibly deplore more than the actor himself. Often it had occurred to me in my ponderings upon the subject, that had that altercation taken place in the public street, or at a private residence, it would not have terminated as it did. It was the circumstance of being alone in a solitary office, upstairs, of a building entirely unhallowed by humanizing domestic associations—an uncarpeted office, doubtless, of a dusty, haggard sort of appearance;—this it must have been, which greatly helped to enhance the irritable desperation of the hapless Colt.

But when this old Adam[25] of resentment rose in me and tempted me concerning Bartleby, I grappled him and threw him. How? Why, simply by recalling the divine injunction: "A new commandment give I unto you, that ye love one another."[26] Yes, this it was that saved me. Aside from higher considerations, charity often operates as a vastly wise and prudent principle—a great safeguard to its possessor. Men have committed murder for jealousy's sake, and anger's sake, and hatred's sake, and selfishness' sake, and spiritual pride's sake; but no man that ever I heard of, ever committed a diabolical murder for sweet charity's sake. Mere self-interest, then, if no better motive can be enlisted, should, especially with high-tempered men, prompt all beings to charity and philanthropy. At any rate, upon the occasion in question, I strove to drown my exasperated feelings toward the scrivener by benevolently construing his conduct. Poor fellow, poor fellow! thought I, he doesn't mean anything; and besides, he has seen hard times, and ought to be indulged.

I endeavoured also immediately to occupy myself, and at the same time to comfort my despondency. I tried to fancy that in the course of the morning, at such time as might prove agreeable to him, Bartleby, of his own free accord, would emerge from his hermitage, and take up some decided line of march in the direction of the door. But no. Half-past twelve o'clock came; Turkey began to glow in the face, overturn his inkstand, and become generally obstreperous; Nippers abated down into quietude and courtesy; Ginger Nut munched his noon apple; and Bartleby remained standing at his window in one of his profoundest dead-wall reveries. Will it be credited? Ought I to acknowledge it? That afternoon I left the office without saying one further word to him.

Some days now passed, during which at leisure intervals I looked a little into "Edwards on the Will," and "Priestly on Necessity."[27] Under the circumstances, those books induced a salutary feeling. Gradually I slid into the persuasion that these troubles of mine, touching the scrivener, had been all predestinated from eternity, and Bartleby was billeted upon me for some mysterious purpose of an all-wise Providence, which it was not for a mere mortal like me to fathom. Yes, Bartleby, stay there behind your screen, thought I; I shall persecute you no more; you are harmless and noiseless as any of these old chairs; in short, I never feel so private as when I know you are here. At last I see it, I feel it; I penetrate to the predestinated purpose of my life. I am content. Others may have loftier parts to enact; but my mission in this world, Bartleby, is to furnish you with office room for such period as you may see fit to remain.

I believe that this wise and blessed frame of mind would have continued with me had it not been for the unsolicited and uncharitable remarks obtruded upon me by my professional friends who visited the rooms. But thus it often is, that the constant friction of illiberal minds wears out at last the best resolves of the more generous. Though to be sure, when I reflected upon it, it was not strange that people entering my office should be struck by the peculiar aspect of the unaccountable Bartleby, and so be tempted to throw out some sinister observations concerning him. Sometimes an attorney having business with me, and calling at my office, and finding no one but the scrivener there, would undertake to obtain some sort of precise information from him touching my whereabouts; but without heeding his idle talk, Bartleby would remain standing immovable in the middle of the room. So, after contemplating him in that position for a time, the attorney would depart, no wiser than he came.

Also, when a Reference[28] was going on, and the room full of lawyers and witnesses and business was driving fast, some deeply occupied legal gentleman present, seeing Bartleby wholly unemployed, would request him to run round to his (the legal gentleman's) office and fetch some papers for him. Thereupon, Bartleby would tranquilly decline, and yet remain idle as before. Then the lawyer would give a great stare, and turn to me. And what could I say? At last I was made aware that all through the circle of my professional acquaintance, a whisper of wonder was running round, having reference to the strange creature I kept at my office. This worried me very much. And as the idea came upon me of his possibly turning out a long-lived man, keep occupying my chambers, and denying my authority; and perplexing my visitors; and scandalizing my professional reputation; and casting a general gloom over the premises; keeping soul and body together to the last upon his savings (for doubtless he spent but half a dime a day), and in the end perhaps outlive me, and claim possession of my office by right of his perpetual occupancy: as all these dark anticipations crowded upon me more and more, and my friends continually intruded their relentless remarks upon the apparition in my room, a great change was wrought in me. I resolved to gather all my faculties together, and for ever rid me of this intolerable incubus.

Ere revolving any complicated project, however, adapted to this end, I first simply suggested to Bartleby the propriety of his permanent departure. In a calm and serious tone, I commended the idea to his careful and mature consideration. But having taken three days to meditate upon it, he apprised me that his original determination remained the same; in short, that he still preferred to abide with me.

What shall I do? I now said to myself, buttoning up my coat to the last button. What shall I do? what ought I to do? what does conscience say I *should* do with this man, or rather ghost? Rid myself of him, I must; go, he shall. But how? You will not thrust him, the poor, pale, passive mortal,—you will not thrust such a helpless creature out of your door? you will not dishonour yourself by such cruelty? No, I will not, I cannot do that. Rather would I let him live and die here, and then mason up his remains in the wall. What then will you do? For all your coaxing, he will not budge. Bribes he leaves under your own paperweight on your table; in short, it is quite plain that he prefers to cling to you.

Then something severe, something unusual must be done. What! surely you will not have him collared by a constable, and commit his innocent pallor to the common jail? And upon what ground could you procure such a thing to be done? —a vagrant, is he? What! he a vagrant, a wanderer, who refuses to budge? It is because he will *not* be a vagrant, then, that you seek to count him *as* a vagrant. That is too absurd. No visible means of support: there I have him. Wrong again: for indubitably he *does* support himself, and that is the only unanswerable proof that any man can show of his possessing the means so to do. No more then. Since he will not quit me, I must quit him. I will change my offices; I will move elsewhere; and give him fair notice, that if I find him on my new premises I will then proceed against him as a common trespasser.

Acting accordingly, next day I thus addressed him: "I find these chambers too far from the City Hall; the air is unwholesome. In a word, I propose to remove my offices next week, and shall no longer require your services. I tell you this now, in order that you may seek another place."

He made no reply, and nothing more was said.

On the appointed day I engaged carts and men, proceeded to my chambers, and having but little furniture, everything was removed in a few hours. Throughout all, the scrivener remained standing behind the screen, which I directed to be removed the last thing. It was withdrawn; and being folded up like a huge folio, left him the motionless occupant of a naked room. I stood in the entry watching him a moment, while something from within me upbraided me.

I re-entered, with my hand in my pocket—and—and my heart in my mouth.

"Good-bye, Bartleby; I am going—good-bye, and God some way bless you; and take that," slipping something in his hand. But it dropped upon the floor and then—strange to say—I tore myself from him whom I had so longed to be rid of.

Established in my new quarters, for a day or two I kept the door locked, and started at every footfall in the passages. When I returned to my rooms after any little absence, I would pause at the threshold for an instant, and attentively listen, ere applying my key. But these fears were needless. Bartleby never came nigh me.

I thought all was going well, when a perturbed looking stranger visited me, inquiring whether I was the person who had recently occupied rooms at No.———— Wall Street.

Full of forebodings, I replied that I was.

"Then sir," said the stranger, who proved a lawyer, "you are responsible for the man you left there. He refuses to do any copying, he refuses to do anything; and he says he prefers not to, and he refuses to quit the premises."

"I am very sorry, sir," said I, with assumed tranquillity, but an inward tremor, "but, really, the man you allude to is nothing to me—he is no relation or apprentice of mine, that you should hold me responsible for him."

"In mercy's name, who is he?"

"I certainly cannot inform you. I know nothing about him. Formerly I employed him as a copyist; but he has done nothing for me now for some time past."

"I shall settle him then,—good morning, sir."

Several days passed, and I heard nothing more; and though I often felt a charitable prompting to call at the place and see poor Bartleby, yet a certain squeamishness of I know not what withheld me.

All is over with him, by this time, thought I at last, when through another week no further intelligence reached me. But coming to my room the day after, I found several persons waiting at my door in a high state of nervous excitement.

"That's the man—here he comes," cried the foremost one, whom I recognized as the lawyer who had previously called upon me alone.

"You must take him away, sir, at once," cried a portly person among them, advancing upon me, and whom I knew to be the landlord of No.————Wall Street. "These gentlemen, my tenants, cannot stand it any longer; Mr. B————," pointing to the lawyer, "has turned him out of his room, and he now persists in haunting the building generally, sitting upon the banisters of the stairs by day, and sleeping in the entry by night. Everybody here is concerned; clients are leaving the offices; some fears are entertained of a mob; something you must do, and that without delay."

Aghast at this torrent, I fell back before it, and would fain have locked myself in my new quarters. In vain I persisted that Bartleby was nothing to me—no more than to any one else there. In vain:—I was the last person known to have anything to do with him, and they held me to the terrible account. Fearful then of being exposed in the papers (as one person present obscurely threatened) I considered the matter, and at length said, that if the lawyer would give me a confidential interview with the scrivener, in his (the lawyer's) own room, I would that afternoon strive my best to rid them of the nuisance they complained of.

Going up stairs to my old haunt, there was Bartleby silently sitting upon the banister at the landing.

"What are you doing here, Bartleby?" said I.

"Sitting upon the banister," he mildly replied.

I motioned him into the lawyer's room, who then left us.

"Bartleby," said I, "are you aware that you are the cause of great tribulation to me, by persisting in occupying the entry after being dismissed from the office?"

No answer.

"Now one of two things must take place. Either you must do something, or something must be done to you. Now what sort of business would you like to engage in? Would you like to re-engage in copying for some one?"

"No; I would prefer not to make any change."

"Would you like a clerkship in a dry-goods store?"

"There is too much confinement about that. No, I would not like a clerkship; but I am not particular."

"Too much confinement," I cried, "why you keep yourself confined all the time!"

"I would prefer not to take a clerkship," he rejoined, as if to settle that little item at once.

"How would a bartender's business suit you? There is no trying of the eyesight in that."

"I would not like it at all; though, as I said before, I am not particular."

His unwonted wordiness inspirited me. I returned to the charge.

"Well then, would you like to travel through the country collecting bills for the merchants? That would improve your health."

"No, I would prefer to be doing something else."

"How then would going as a companion to Europe to entertain some young gentleman with your conversation,—how would that suit you?"

"Not at all. It does not strike me that there is anything definite about that. I like to be stationary. But I am not particular."

"Stationary you shall be then," I cried, now losing all patience, and for the first time in all my exasperating connection with him fairly flying into a passion. "If you do not go away from these premises before night, I shall feel bound— indeed I *am* bound—to—to—to quit the premises myself!" I rather absurdly concluded, knowing not with what possible threat to try to frighten his immobility into compliance. Despairing of all further efforts, I was precipitately leaving him, when a final thought occurred to me—one which had not been wholly unindulged before.

"Bartleby," said I, in the kindest tone I could assume under such exciting circumstances, "will you go home with me now—not to my office, but my dwelling

—and remain there till we can conclude upon some convenient arrangement for you at our leisure? Come, let us start now, right away."

"No: at present I would prefer not to make any change at all."

I answered nothing; but effectually dodging every one by the suddenness and rapidity of my flight, rushed from the building, ran up Wall Street toward Broadway, and then jumping into the first omnibus was soon removed from pursuit. As soon as tranquillity returned I distinctly perceived that I had now done all that I possibly could, both in respect to the demands of the landlord and his tenants, and with regard to my own desire and sense of duty, to benefit Bartleby, and shield him from rude persecution. I now strove to be entirely care-free and quiescent; and my conscience justified me in the attempt; though indeed it was not so successful as I could have wished. So fearful was I of being again hunted out by the incensed landlord and his exasperated tenants, that, surrendering my business to Nippers, for a few days I drove about the upper part of the town and through the suburbs, in my rockaway; crossed over to Jersey City and Hoboken, and paid fugitive visits to Manhattanville and Astoria. In fact I almost lived in my rockaway for the time.

When again I entered my office, lo, a note from the landlord lay upon the desk. I opened it with trembling hands. It informed me that the writer had sent to the police, and had Bartleby removed to the Tombs as a vagrant. Moreover, since I knew more about him than any one else, he wished me to appear at that place, and make a suitable statement of the facts. These tidings had a conflicting effect upon me. At first I was indignant; but at last almost approved. The landlord's energetic, summary disposition had led him to adopt a procedure which I do not think I would have decided upon myself; and yet as a last resort, under such peculiar circumstances, it seemed the only plan.

As I afterwards learned, the poor scrivener, when told that he must be conducted to the Tombs, offered not the slightest obstacle, but in his own pale, unmoving way silently acquiesced.

Some of the compassionate and curious bystanders joined the party; and headed by one of the constables, arm-in-arm with Bartleby, the silent procession filed its way through all the noise, and heat, and joy of the roaring thoroughfares at noon.

The same day I received the note I went to the Tombs, or, to speak more properly, the Halls of Justice. Seeking the right officer, I stated the purpose of my call, and was informed that the individual I described was indeed within. I then assured the functionary that Bartleby was a perfectly honest man, and greatly to be compassionated, however unaccountably eccentric. I narrated all I knew, and closed by suggesting the idea of letting him remain in as indulgent confinement as possible till something less harsh might be done—though indeed I hardly knew what. At all events, if nothing else could be decided upon, the almshouse must receive him. I then begged to have an interview.

Being under no disgraceful charge, and quite serene and harmless in all his ways, they had permitted him freely to wander about the prison, and especially in the inclosed grass-platted yards thereof. And so I found him there, standing all alone in the quietest of the yards, his face toward a high wall—while all around, from the narrow slits of the jail windows, I thought I saw peering out upon him the eyes of murderers and thieves.

"Bartleby!"

"I know you," he said, without looking round,—"and I want nothing to say to you."

"It was not I that brought you here, Bartleby," said I, keenly pained at his implied suspicion. "And to you, this should not be so vile a place. Nothing reproachful attaches to you by being here. And see, it is not so sad a place as one might think. Look, there is the sky and here is the grass."

"I know where I am," he replied, but would say nothing more, and so I left him.

As I entered the corridor again a broad, meat-like man in an apron accosted me, and jerking his thumb over his shoulder said—"Is that your friend?"

"Yes."

"Does he want to starve? If he does, let him live on the prison fare, that's all."

"Who are you?" asked I, not knowing what to make of such an unofficially speaking person in such a place.

"I am the grub-man. Such gentlemen as have friends here, hire me to provide them with something good to eat."

"Is this so?" said I, turning to the turnkey.

He said it was.

"Well then," said I, slipping some silver into the grub-man's hands (for so they called him), "I want you to give particular attention to my friend there; let him have the best dinner you can get. And you must be as polite to him as possible."

"Introduce me, will you?" said the grub-man, looking at me with an expression which seemed to say he was all impatience for an opportunity to give a specimen of his breeding.

Thinking it would prove of benefit to the scrivener, I acquiesced; and asking the grub-man his name, went up with him to Bartleby.

"Bartleby, this is Mr. Cutlets; you will find him very useful to you."

"Your sarvant, sir, your sarvant," said the grub-man, making a low salutation behind his apron. "Hope you find it pleasant here, sir;—spacious grounds—cool apartments, sir—hope you'll stay with us some time—try to make it agreeable. May Mrs. Cutlets and I have the pleasure of your company to dinner, sir, in Mrs. Cutlets' private room?"

"I prefer not to dine today," said Bartleby, turning away. "It would disagree with me; I am unused to dinners." So saying, he slowly moved to the other side of the inclosure and took up a position fronting the dead-wall.

"How's this?" said the grub-man, addressing me with a stare of astonishment. "He's odd, ain't he?"

"I think he is a little deranged," said I, sadly.

"Deranged? deranged is it? Well now, upon my word, I thought that friend of yourn was a gentleman forger; they are always pale and genteel-like, them forgers. I can't help pity 'em—can't help it, sir. Did you know Monroe Edwards?''[29] he added touchingly, and paused. Then, laying his hand pityingly on my shoulder, sighed, "he died of the consumption at Sing-Sing.[30] So you weren't acquainted with Monroe?"

"No, I was never socially acquainted with any forgers. But I cannot stop longer. Look to my friend yonder. You will not lose by it. I will see you again."

Some few days after this, I again obtained admission to the Tombs, and went through the corridors in quest of Bartleby; but without finding him.

"I saw him coming from his cell not long ago," said a turnkey, "maybe he's gone to loiter in the yards."

So I went in that direction.

"Are you looking for the silent man?" said another turnkey passing me. "Yonder he lies—sleeping in the yard there. 'Tis not twenty minutes since I saw him lie down."

The yard was entirely quiet. It was not accessible to the common prisoners. The surrounding walls, of amazing thickness, kept off all sounds behind them. The Egyptian character of the masonry weighed upon me with its gloom. But a soft imprisoned turf grew under foot. The heart of the eternal pyramids, it seemed, wherein by some strange magic, through the clefts grass-seed, dropped by birds, had sprung.

Strangely huddled at the base of the wall—his knees drawn up, and lying on his side, his head touching the cold stones—I saw the wasted Bartleby. But nothing stirred. I paused; then went close up to him; stooped over, and saw that his dim eyes were open; otherwise he seemed profoundly sleeping. Something prompted me to touch him. I felt his hand, when a tingling shiver ran up my arm and down my spine to my feet.

The round face of the grub-man peered upon me now. "His dinner is ready. Won't he dine today, either? Or does he live without dining?"

"Lives without dining," said I, and closed the eyes.

"Eh!—He's asleep, ain't he?"

"With kings and counsellors,"[31] murmured I.

There would seem little need for proceeding further in this history. Imagination will readily supply the meagre recital of poor Bartleby's interment. But ere parting with the reader, let me say, that if this little narrative has sufficiently interested him, to awaken curiosity as to who Bartleby was, and what manner of life he led prior to the present narrator's making his acquaintance, I can only reply, that in such curiosity I fully share—but am wholly unable to gratify it. Yet here I hardly know whether I should divulge one little item of rumour, which came to my ear a few months after the scrivener's decease. Upon what basis it rested, I could never ascertain; and hence, how true it is I cannot now tell. But inasmuch as this vague report has not been without a certain strange suggestive interest to me, however sad, it may prove the same with some others; and so I will briefly mention it. The report was this: that Bartleby had been a subordinate clerk in the

Dead Letter Office³² at Washington, from which he had been suddenly removed by a change in the administration. When I think over this rumour I cannot adequately express the emotions which seize me. Dead letters! does it not sound like dead men? Conceive a man by nature and misfortune prone to a pallid hopelessness: can any business seem more fitted to heighten it than that of continually handling these dead letters, and assorting them for the flames? For by the cartload they are annually burned. Sometimes from out the folded paper the pale clerk takes a ring:—the finger it was meant for, perhaps, moulders in the grave; a bank-note sent in swiftest charity:—he whom it would relieve, nor eats nor hungers any more; pardon for those who died despairing; hope for those who died unhoping; good tidings for those who died stifled by unrelieved calamities. On errands of life, these letters speed to death.

Ah, Bartleby! Ah, humanity!

---

¹ New York capitalist and fur merchant (1763–1848). The richest American of his era, his name was a synonym for great wealth.

² An officer of the court that deals with conscience and natural justice in settling controversies. The office was abolished in 1846.

³ In 1847.

⁴ Post Office Directory.

⁵ Cannel coal is oily and burns brightly; anthracite is slow burning and gives off almost no flame.

⁶ Box containing sand to be sprinkled on a sheet of paper to dry ink.

⁷ A prison in New York City.

⁸ Driver of a cart.

⁹ Red and yellow American apples.

¹⁰ To provide or furnish.

¹¹ Crazy.

¹² Marcus Tullius Cicero (106–43 BC), Roman statesman, orator, and author.

¹³ Dumbstruck. An allusion to Genesis 19:26. The Lord turned Lot's wife into a pillar of salt for disobeying Him by looking back at the destruction of Sodom.

¹⁴ Favorable vote.

¹⁵ Loony. Melville's spelling suggests the etymology "lunatic."

¹⁶ Scented soap, usually brown.

¹⁷ Episcopal Church in the Wall Street district.

¹⁸ Box of black shoe polish.

¹⁹ Ancient city, once a Middle Eastern trade center. Now in ruins, it is located in modern-day Jordan.

²⁰ Gaius (or Caius) Marius (157–86 BC), Roman general and consul expelled in 88 BC by Sulla. He is represented as brooding among the ruins of Carthage, comparing its condition to his own broken and forlorn state.

²¹ Traditional image of a burden hung on someone. See Matthew 18:6, "But whoso shall offend one of these little ones which believe in me, it were better for him that a millstone were hanged about his neck, and that he were drowned in the depth of the sea." (KJV)

²² Luggage, personal effects.

²³ A term in sword-fighting or fencing meaning a thrust that finds its mark; by extension, any action that accomplishes its purpose.

²⁴ John C. Colt, brother of the famous firearms manufacturer. He killed Samuel Adams, a printer, in 1841, by hitting him an unpremeditated blow on the head during a fight. The episode resulted in a famous New York murder case in which Colt was sentenced to death. He committed suicide before the sentence could be executed.

²⁵ The sinful element in human nature.

26 John 13:34. (KJV)
27 Jonathan Edwards (1703–1758), New England Calvinist theologian and clergyman, argued in *The Freedom of the Will* that the human will is not free. Joseph Priestly (1733–1804), English Dissenting minister who discovered oxygen, was also a grammarian and a philosopher. In *The Doctrine of Philosophical Necessity*, he argued against free will on theological, metaphysical, and moral grounds.
28 A conference.
29 (1808–1847). A Wall Street broker who forged credit documents in schemes to swindle clients.
30 New York State Prison at Ossining.
31 See Job 3:13–14, "then had I been at rest, With kings and counsellors of the earth. . . ." (KJV)
32 Repository for mail that is undeliverable and unreturnable by the post office.

DISCUSSION TOPICS

1. How do you respond to Melville's story? Do you feel sympathetic or exasperated with Bartleby? Why? How do you feel about the narrator—do your feelings toward him change during the course of the story?
2. Many readers of *Bartleby* have felt that the story is about the narrator as much as it is about Bartleby himself. What do you think? What is the narrative point of view? What would the story be like told from Bartleby's point of view?
3. What is the nature of the narrator's initiation and its consequences? Trace the decisive steps (or stages) of his initiation.
4. How do Turkey, Ginger Nut, and Nippers function in the story?
5. Psychologically speaking, what is Bartleby's problem? How can you account for his condition? (Note especially the position he has assumed when he dies.)
6. Critic Henry A. Murray has observed that "In Melville's narrative we have a miniature social system with its traditions and customs, laws and regulations, rewards and penalties, operating within the frame of the Protestant ethic and the utilitarian philosophy, in terms of which, as usual, rationality and sanity are defined." With this observation in mind, who is truly sane in the story? In what ways might the story be interpreted as an indictment of the American system of exploitative capitalism versus humanistic concern for the common worker? (Note the narrator's repeated comment that Bartleby and his other employees are "useful" to him.) Why is it particularly significant that the story's setting is Wall Street?

GUY DE MAUPASSANT (1850–1893) Friend and disciple of the great French novelist Gustave Flaubert. His tales are distinguished by compression and unity of effect. He is perhaps best known for his brilliant and sometimes relentless irony.

MOONLIGHT

Translated by Theodore Toulon Beck

Father Marignan's military name[1] suited him well. He was a tall, lean priest, bigoted, highly emotional, yet righteous. All his beliefs were fixed, without ever varying. He believed sincerely that he knew his God, was able to penetrate His plans, His will, His intentions.

When he walked with great strides along the path of his little country rectory, sometimes a question arose in his mind: "Why has God made that?" And he persistently searched for the answer, in his mind putting himself in God's place, and he almost always found the answer. He was not one who would have murmured in a burst of pious humility: "Lord, your designs are inscrutable!" He would say to himself: "I am God's servant, I ought to know His motives for acting, and to guess them if I do not know them."

Everything in nature appeared to him to have been created with an admirable and absolute logic. The "whys" and "becauses" always came out even. Dawns were made to make our awaking joyful, days to ripen the harvests, rains to water them, evenings to prepare for sleep, and dark nights for sleeping.

The four seasons corresponded perfectly to all the needs of agriculture, and never could the priest have suspected that nature has no intentions and that, on the contrary, everything that lives is forced to yield to the harsh demands of the times, climates, and matter.

But he hated woman; he hated her unconsciously, and despised her instinctively. Often he repeated the words of Christ: "Woman, what is there in common between us?"[2] and he would add: "One would say that God Himself was dissatisfied with that work of His." Woman was really for him the child twelve times impure of which the poet speaks. She was the tempter who had led astray the first man, who was still continuing her work of damnation, the weak creature, dangerous, and mysteriously disturbing man. And even more than her sinful body, he hated her loving heart.

He had often sensed her affection directed toward himself, and, although he knew himself to be invulnerable, he would become angry at this need of loving which is always vibrating in them.

God, in his opinion, had created woman only to tempt man and to test him. Man must not approach her except with defensive precautions and the fear of potential snares. She was, indeed, very much like a snare with her outstretched arms and her lips open to man.

He had no tolerance except for the nuns, whose vows made them inoffensive; but he treated them sternly just the same, because he perceived that deep down in their meek and fettered hearts was burning brightly that eternal affection which constantly went out even to him, although he was a priest.

He sensed it in their looks more moist with piety than those of the monks, in their raptures in which their sex was intermingled, in their transports of love towards Christ, which shocked him because it was woman's love, carnal love; he felt this accursed affection in their very submissiveness, in the softness of their voice when speaking to him, in their lowered eyes, and in their resigned tears when he reproved them harshly.

And he would shake his cassock on leaving the doors of the convent, and would walk away lengthening his strides as if he were fleeing from some peril.

He had a niece who lived with her mother in a little house nearby. He had set his heart on making a Sister of Charity of her.

She was a pretty, scatterbrained, and scoffing youngster. When the priest would lecture her, she would laugh; and when he became angry with her, she would hug him impetuously, holding him close to her heart, while he tried unconsciously to extricate himself from this embrace which, nevertheless, caused him to enjoy a sweet pleasure, arousing deep down inside him that paternal feeling which is dormant in every man.

Often while walking beside her through the country lanes, he would speak to her about God, his God. She would hardly listen to him and would look at the sky, the grass, the flowers, with the joy of being alive gleaming in her eyes. Sometimes she would dart ahead to catch some flying creature, exclaiming as she brought it back: "Look, uncle, how pretty it is; how I would like to hug and kiss it." And this desire to hug bugs and kiss lilac buds worried, irritated, and revolted the priest, who could find even in that the ineradicable affection that is always sprouting in women's hearts.

Then one day the sexton's wife, who kept house for Father Marignan, informed him, cautiously, that his niece had a lover.

He experienced a frightful emotion from it, and remained almost choking with his face full of soap, for he was in the process of shaving.

When he found himself once more in a condition to think and speak, he exclaimed: "That's not true, you are lying, Melanie!"

But the good woman placed her hand over her heart: "May Our Lord judge me if I am lying, Father. I tell you that she goes to him every evening as soon as your sister goes to bed. They meet each other along the river. You only have to go there and see for yourself between ten o'clock and midnight."

He stopped scraping his chin, and began to pace back and forth violently, as he always did when he was in deep meditation. When he started to shave again, he cut himself three times from his nose to his ear.

All day long he remained silent, swollen with anger and indignation. To his priestly frenzy, confronted with unconquerable love, was added the exasperation of a spiritual father, a guardian, a keeper of souls, who has been cheated, tricked, outwitted by a little girl; that egotistical rage of parents to whom their daughter announces that she has selected a husband without them and in spite of them.

After dinner he tried to read a bit, but could not manage to do so; and he became more and more enraged. When ten o'clock rang, he took his cane, a formidable oaken stick, which he was accustomed to carry when he had to go out at night to visit sick parishioners. And smiling, he looked at the enormous club which he was twirling, in his solid, countryman's fist, cutting threatening circles. Then, suddenly, he raised it and, gnashing his teeth, brought it down on a chair whose back, split in two, fell on the floor.

He opened the door to go out; but he stopped on the threshold, surprised by a splendor of moonlight such as is almost never seen.

And as he was endowed with an emotional nature, such as the Fathers of the Church, those poetic dreamers, must have had, he felt suddenly diverted and moved by the grandiose, serene beauty of the pale night.

In his little garden, completely bathed in soft light, his fruit trees, lined up in a row, cast in shadowy outline on the path their frail wooden branches, scarcely in leaf; while the giant honeysuckle, climbing along the wall of his house, exhaled delightful, sugared breaths and caused to float in the warm, clear evening a kind of perfumed soul.

He began to breathe deeply, drinking in the air as drunkards drink wine, and he walked along with slow steps, delighted, marveling, almost forgetting his niece.

As soon as he was in open country, he stopped to contemplate the whole plain flooded by this caressing light, drowned in that tender, languishing charm of serene nights. The frogs at each moment threw into space their short, metallic notes, and distant nightingales mingled their fitful music which sets one dreaming without thinking—their light, vibrant music made for kisses—with the seduction of the moonlight.

The priest walked on again, his courage failing, though he knew not why. He felt as if he were weakened, suddenly exhausted; he wanted very much to sit down, to remain there, to think and to admire God in all His works.

Farther down, following the undulations of the stream, a great line of poplar trees meandered in and out. A fine mist, a white haze through which the moonbeams passed, silvered it and made it gleam, hovered around and above the banks, enveloping all the tortuous course of the water with a sort of light, transparent cotton wadding.

The priest stopped once more, penetrated to the very bottom of his soul by an increasing, irresistible affection.

And a doubt, a vague uneasiness, spread over him; he sensed being born in him one of those questions that he sometimes asked himself.

Why had God made that? Since night is destined for sleep, unconsciousness, rest, forgetfulness of everything, why make it more delightful than day, sweeter than dawns and evenings, and why had this slow, seductive astral body,—more poetic than the sun and which appears destined, so discreet it is, to illuminate things too delicate and mysterious for daylight,—come to make the darkness so transparent?

Why didn't the most expert of feathered songsters go to rest like the others, and why did it start singing in the heady darkness?

Why this half-veil thrown over the world? Why these heart flutters, this emotion of the soul, this languor of the flesh?

Why this display of enticements that men would not see, since they were lying in bed? For whom was this sublime spectacle destined, this abundance of poetry cast from heaven to earth?

And the priest just could not understand it at all.

But look over there, along the edge of the meadow, under the arch of trees drenched in a shining mist, two figures appeared walking side by side.

The man was the taller and had his arm around his sweetheart's neck, and, from time to time, kissed her on the forehead. They brought life all at once to this placid landscape which enveloped them as if it were a divine frame made for them alone. They both seemed a single being, the being for whom this calm and silent night was destined; and they were heading towards the priest as a living answer, the answer that his Master flung down to his questioning.

He remained standing stock-still, his heart beating, overwhelmed, and he believed he was seeing something biblical, something like the loves of Ruth and Boaz,[3] the accomplishment of the Lord's will in one of those great settings spoken of in the holy scriptures. Through his head began to run the verses of the Song of Songs,[4] the appeals of passion, all the warm poetry of that poem burning with love.

And he said to himself: "Perhaps God made such nights to idealize the loves of men."

He shrank back before this couple who were still advancing arm in arm. It was his niece; but now he wondered if he had not been on the point of disobeying God. For does not God allow love since He surrounds it with such visible splendor?

And he fled, bewildered, almost ashamed, as if he had intruded into a temple where he had no right to enter.

[1] The battle of Marignano (1515), where the French king Francis I defeated Massimiliano Sforza, heir of the deposed Lodovico, duke of Milan, thus consolidating French control over Lombardy.

[2] John 2:4, "Woman, what have I to do with thee?" (KJV) The context is the wedding at Cana. Jesus is speaking to His mother, who has just informed Him that the hosts have run out of wine.

[3] A famous pair of lovers in the Old Testament. When Ruth's first husband died, she elected to stay with her mother-in-law, Naomi. She subsequently met Boaz, a rich landowner in whose fields she was gleaning. He fell in love with her and married her.

[4] Another name for the Song of Solomon, an Old Testament book composed of sensuous love lyrics. Scholars think there is not much basis for attributing them to Solomon.

DISCUSSION TOPICS

1. Why does Father Marignan hate "woman"? What are the psychological implications of this hatred?
2. What is the psychological significance of Father Marignan's "formidable oaken stick"?
3. Why does Father Marignan feel "bewildered, almost ashamed" at the end of the story?
4. What do the garden and the moonlight symbolize?

Kate Chopin (1851–1904) Short story writer, novelist, interpreter of Creole and Cajun life. Born into a wealthy and aristocratic family in St. Louis, Kate Chopin married a Creole cotton broker at 19 and moved south, first to New Orleans and later to another part of Louisiana. She is famous for her stories and sketches of the Acadians and Creoles of south Louisiana, many of which were collected in *Bayou Folk* (1894) and *A Night in Acadie* (1897). When her novel *The Awakening* (1899), which deals with extramarital love, was severely criticized for its morbidity and eroticism, her interest in writing seemed to fade. Many Chopin stories, like "The Dream of an Hour," are characterized by economy and irony.

THE DREAM OF AN HOUR

Knowing that Mrs. Mallard was afflicted with a heart trouble, great care was taken to break to her as gently as possible the news of her husband's death.

It was her sister Josephine who told her, in broken sentences; veiled hints that revealed in half concealing. Her husband's friend Richards was there, too, near her. It was he who had been in the newspaper office when intelligence of the railroad disaster was received, with Brently Mallard's name leading the list of "killed." He had only taken the time to assure himself of its truth by a second telegram, and had hastened to forestall any less careful, less tender friend in bearing the sad message.

She did not hear the story as many women have heard the same, with a paralyzed inability to accept its significance. She wept at once, with sudden, wild abandonment, in her sister's arms. When the storm of grief had spent itself she went away to her room alone. She would have no one follow her.

There stood, facing the open window, a comfortable, roomy armchair. Into this she sank, pressed down by a physical exhaustion that haunted her body and seemed to reach into her soul.

She could see in the open square before her house the tops of trees that were all aquiver with the new spring life. The delicious breath of rain was in the air. In the street below a peddler was crying his wares. The notes of a distant song which some one was singing reached her faintly, and countless sparrows were twittering in the eaves.

There were patches of blue sky showing here and there through the clouds that had met and piled one above the other in the west facing her window.

She sat with her head thrown back upon the cushion of the chair, quite motionless, except when a sob came up into her throat and shook her, as a child who has cried itself to sleep continues to sob in its dreams.

She was young, with a fair, calm face, whose lines bespoke repression and even a certain strength. But now there was a dull stare in her eyes, whose gaze was fixed away off yonder on one of those patches of blue sky. It was not a glance of reflection, but rather indicated a suspension of intelligent thought.

There was something coming to her and she was waiting for it, fearfully. What was it? She did not know; it was too subtle and elusive to name. But she felt it, creeping out of the sky, reaching toward her through the sounds, the scents, the color that filled the air.

Now her bosom rose and fell tumultuously. She was beginning to recognize this thing that was approaching to possess her, and she was striving to beat it back with her will—as powerless as her two white slender hands would have been.

When she abandoned herself a little whispered word escaped her slightly parted lips. She said it over and over under her breath: "free, free, free!" The vacant stare and the look of terror that had followed it went from her eyes. They stayed keen and bright. Her pulses beat fast, and the coursing blood warmed and relaxed every inch of her body.

She did not stop to ask if it were or were not a monstrous joy that held her. A clear and exalted perception enabled her to dismiss the suggestion as trivial.

She knew that she would weep again when she saw the kind, tender hands folded in death; the face that had never looked save with love upon her, fixed and gray and dead. But she saw beyond that bitter moment a long procession of years to come that would belong to her absolutely. And she opened and spread her arms out to them in welcome.

There would be no one to live for her during those coming years; she would live for herself. There would be no powerful will bending hers in that blind persistence with which men and women believe they have a right to impose a private will upon a fellow-creature. A kind intention or a cruel intention made the act seem no less a crime as she looked upon it in that brief moment of illumination.

And yet she had loved him—sometimes. Often she had not. What did it matter! What could love, the unsolved mystery, count for in face of this possession of self-assertion which she suddenly recognized as the strongest impulse of her being!

"Free! Body and soul free!" she kept whispering.

Josephine was kneeling before the closed door with her lips to the keyhole, imploring for admission. "Louise, open the door! I beg; open the door—you will make yourself ill. What are you doing, Louise? For heaven's sake open the door."

"Go away. I am not making myself ill." No; she was drinking in a very elixir of life through that open window.

Her fancy was running riot along those days ahead of her. Spring days, and summer days, and all sorts of days that would be her own. She breathed a quick prayer that life might be long. It was only yesterday she had thought with a shudder that life might be long.

She arose at length and opened the door to her sister's importunities. There was a feverish triumph in her eyes, and she carried herself unwittingly like a goddess of Victory. She clasped her sister's waist, and together they descended the stairs. Richards stood waiting for them at the bottom.

Some one was opening the front door with a latchkey. It was Brently Mallard who entered, a little travel-stained, composedly carrying his grip-sack and umbrella. He had been far from the scene of accident, and did not even know there had been one. He stood amazed at Josephine's piercing cry; at Richards' quick motion to screen him from the view of his wife.

But Richards was too late.

When the doctors came they said she had died of heart disease—of joy that kills.

DISCUSSION TOPICS

1. Why do you think Mrs. Mallard died suddenly of heart disease? Was the cause simply the sudden loss of her newfound freedom, or was there perhaps a more complicated reason?
2. Why was Mrs. Mallard relieved by the news of her husband's death? Was she herself surprised by this reaction? Does her relief indicate that she does not love her husband?
3. Chopin's stories are famous for their irony. Where are the ironic turns in the plot of this story? Discuss the rich ironic implications of the story's final phrase —"of joy that kills."
4. What are the sociological implications of this story? What social conventions are challenged or criticized?

JOSEPH CONRAD (1857–1924) Born Teodor Jozef Konrad Korzeniowski of Polish parents in Russian Ukraine. A multilinguist and ship's captain, he became a British citizen in 1884 and wrote all of his fiction in English because of the myriad nuances of meaning offered by this language. His famous preface to *The Nigger of the Narcissus* (1898) ranks with Henry James's essay "The Art of Fiction" as one of the great documents of modern critical theory. Much of his work is based on his experiences in the tropics. One of his recurrent themes is human isolation and the need for fellowship.

HEART OF DARKNESS

1

The Nellie, a cruising yawl, swung to her anchor without a flutter of the sails, and was at rest. The flood had made, the wind was nearly calm, and being bound down the river, the only thing for it was to come to and wait for the turn of the tide.

The sea-reach[1] of the Thames stretched before us like the beginning of an interminable waterway. In the offing[2] the sea and the sky were welded together without a joint, and in the luminous space the tanned sails of the barges drifting up with the tide seemed to stand still in red clusters of canvas sharply peaked, with gleams of varnished sprits. A haze rested on the low shores that ran out to sea in vanishing flatness. The air was dark above Gravesend;[3] and farther back still seemed condensed into a mournful gloom, brooding motionless over the biggest, and the greatest, town on earth.

The Director of Companies was our captain and our host. We four affectionately watched his back as he stood in the bows looking to seaward. On the whole river there was nothing that looked half so nautical. He resembled a pilot, which to a seaman is trustworthiness personified. It was difficult to realize his work was not out there in the luminous estuary, but behind him, within the brooding gloom.

Between us there was, as I have already said somewhere, the bond of the sea. Besides holding our hearts together through long periods of separation, it had the effect of making us tolerant of each other's yarns—and even convictions. The Lawyer—the best of old fellows—had, because of his many years and many virtues, the only cushion on deck, and was lying on the only rug. The Accountant had brought out already a box of dominoes, and was toying architecturally with the bones. Marlow sat cross-legged right aft, leaning against the mizzen-mast. He had sunken cheeks, a yellow complexion, a straight back, an ascetic aspect, and, with his arms dropped, the palms of hands outwards, resembled an idol. The director, satisfied the anchor had good hold, made his way aft and sat down amongst us. We exchanged a few words lazily. Afterwards there was silence on board the yacht. For some reason or other we did not begin that game of dominoes. We felt meditative, and fit for nothing but placid staring. The day was ending in a serenity of still and exquisite brilliance. The water shone pacifically; the sky, without a speck, was a benign immensity of unstained light; the very mist on the Essex marshes[4] was like a gauzy and radiant fabric, hung from the wooded rises inland, and draping the low shores in diaphanous folds. Only the gloom to the west, brooding over the upper reaches, became more somber every minute, as if angered by the approach of the sun.

And at last, in its curved and imperceptible fall, the sun sank low, and from glowing white changed to a dull red without rays and without heat, as if about to go out suddenly, stricken to death by the touch of that gloom brooding over a crowd of men.

Forthwith a change came over the waters, and the serenity became less brilliant but more profound. The old river in its broad reach rested unruffled at the decline of day, after ages of good service done to the race that peopled its banks, spread out in the tranquil dignity of a waterway leading to the uttermost ends of the earth. We looked at the venerable stream not in the vivid flush of a short day that comes and departs forever, but in the august light of abiding memories. And indeed nothing is easier for a man who has, as the phrase goes, "followed the sea" with reverence and affection, than to evoke the great spirit of the past upon the lower reaches of the Thames. The tidal current runs to and fro in its unceasing service, crowded with memories of men and ships it had borne to the rest of home or to the battles of the sea. It had known and served all the men of whom the nation is proud, from Sir Francis Drake[5] to Sir John Franklin,[6] knights all, titled and untitled—the knights-errant of the sea. It had borne all the ships whose names are like jewels flashing in the night of time, from the *Golden*

Hind returning with her round flanks full of treasure, to be visited by the Queen's Highness and thus pass out of the gigantic tale to the *Erebus* and *Terror,* bound on other conquests—and that never returned. It had known the ships and the men. They had sailed from Deptford; from Greenwich, from Erith[7]—the adventurers and the settlers; kings' ships and the ships of men on 'Change,[8] captains, admirals, the dark "interlopers"[9] of the Eastern trade, and the commissioned "generals"[10] of East India fleets. Hunters for gold or pursuers of fame, they all had gone out on that stream, bearing the sword, and often the torch, messengers of the might within the land, bearers of a spark from the sacred fire. What greatness had not floated on the ebb of that river into the mystery of an unknown earth! . . . The dreams of men, the seed of commonwealths, the germs of empires.

The sun set; the dusk fell on the stream, and lights began to appear along the shore. The Chapman lighthouse, a three-legged thing erect on a mudflat, shone strongly. Lights of ships moved in the fairway—a great stir of lights going up and going down. And farther west on the upper reaches the place of the monstrous town[11] was still marked ominously on the sky, a brooding gloom in sunshine, a lurid glare under the stars.

"And this also," said Marlow suddenly, "has been one of the dark places on the earth."

He was the only man of us who still "followed the sea." The worst that could be said of him was that he did not represent his class. He was a seaman, but he was a wanderer, too, while most seamen lead, if one may so express it, a sedentary life. Their minds are of the stay-at-home order, and their home is always with them—the ship; and so is their country—the sea. One ship is very much like another, and the sea is always the same. In the immutability of their surroundings the foreign shores, the foreign faces, the changing immensity of life, glide past, veiled not by a sense of mystery but by a slightly disdainful ignorance; for there is nothing mysterious to a seaman unless it be the sea itself, which is the mistress of his existence and as inscrutable as Destiny. For the rest, after his hours of work, a casual stroll or a casual spree on shore suffices to unfold for him the secret of a whole continent, and generally he finds the secret not worth knowing. The yarns of seamen have a direct simplicity, the whole meaning of which lies within the shell of a cracked nut. But Marlow was not typical (if his propensity to spin yarns be excepted), and to him the meaning of an episode was not inside like a kernel but outside, enveloping the tale which brought it out only as a glow brings out a haze, in the likeness of one of these misty halos that sometimes are made visible by the spectral illumination of moonshine.

His remark did not seem at all surprising. It was just like Marlow. It was accepted in silence. No one took the trouble to grunt even; and presently he said, very slow—

"I was thinking of very old times, when the Romans first came here, nineteen hundred years ago—the other day. . . . Light came out of this river since—you say Knights? Yes; but it is like a running blaze on a plain, like a flash of lightning in the clouds. We live in the flicker—may it last as long as the old earth keeps rolling! But darkness was here yesterday. Imagine the feelings of a commander of a fine

—what d'ye call 'em—trireme[12] in the Mediterranean, ordered suddenly to the north; run overland across the Gauls[13] in a hurry; put in charge of one of these craft the legionaries—a wonderful lot of handy men they must have been, too—used to build, apparently by the hundred, in a month or two, if we may believe what we read. Imagine him here—the very end of the world, a sea the color of lead, a sky the color of smoke, a kind of ship about as rigid as a concertina—and going up this river with stores, or orders, or what you like. Sandbanks, marshes, forests, savages,—precious little to eat fit for a civilized man, nothing but Thames water to drink. No Falernian wine[14] here, no going ashore. Here and there a military camp lost in a wilderness, like a needle in a bundle of hay—cold, fog, tempests, disease, exile, and death,—death skulking the air, in the water, in the bush. They must have been dying like flies here. Oh, yes—he did it. Did it very well, too, no doubt, and without thinking much about it either, except afterwards to brag of what he had gone through in his time, perhaps. They were men enough to face the darkness. And perhaps he was cheered by keeping his eye on a chance of promotion to the fleet at Ravenna[15] by and by, if he had good friends in Rome and survived the awful climate. Or think of a decent young citizen in a toga—perhaps too much dice, you know—coming out here in the train of some prefect,[16] or tax-gatherer, or trader even, to mend his fortunes. Land in a swamp, march through the woods, and in some inland post feel the savagery, the utter savagery, had closed round him,—all that mysterious life of the wilderness that stirs in the forest, in the jungles, in the hearts of wild men. There's no initiation either into such mysteries. He had to live in the midst of the incomprehensible, which is also detestable. And it has a fascination, too, that goes to work upon him. The fascination of the abomination—you know, imagine the growing regrets, the longing to escape, the powerless disgust, the surrender, the hate."

He paused.

"Mind," he began again, lifting one arm from the elbow, the palm of the hand outwards, so that, with his legs folded before him, he had the pose of a Buddha preaching in European clothes and without a lotus-flower—"Mind, none of us would feel exactly like this. What saves us is efficiency—the devotion to efficiency. But these chaps were not much account, really. They were no colonists; their administration was merely a squeeze, and nothing more, I suspect. They were conquerors, and for that you want only brute force—nothing to boast of, when you have it, since your strength is just an accident arising from the weakness of others. They grabbed what they could get for the sake of what was to be got. It was just robbery with violence, aggravated murder on a great scale, and men going at it blind—as is very proper for those who tackle a darkness. The conquest of the earth, which mostly means the taking it away from those who have a different complexion or slightly flatter noses than ourselves, is not a pretty thing when you look into it too much. What redeems it is the idea only. An idea at the back of it; not a sentimental pretense but an idea; and an unselfish belief in the idea—something you can set up, and bow down before, and offer a sacrifice to. . . ."

He broke off. Flames glided in the river, small green flames, red flames, white flames, pursuing, overtaking, joining, crossing each other—then separating slowly or hastily. The traffic of the great city went on in the deepening night upon the sleepless river. We looked on, waiting patiently—there was nothing else to do till the end of the flood; but it was only after a long silence, when he said, in a hesitating voice, "I suppose you fellows remember I did once turn fresh-water sailor for a bit," that we knew we were fated, before the ebb began to run, to hear one of Marlow's inconclusive experiences.

"I don't want to bother you much with what happened to me personally," he began, showing in this remark the weakness of many tellers of tales who seem so often unaware of what their audience would best like to hear; "yet to understand the effect of it on me you ought to know how I got out there, what I saw, how I went up that river to the place where I first met the poor chap. It was the farthest point of navigation and the culminating point of my experience. It seemed somehow to throw a kind of light on everything about me—and into my thoughts. It was somber enough, too—and pitiful—not extraordinary in any way—not very clear either. No, not very clear. And yet it seemed to throw a kind of light.

"I had then, as you remember, just returned to London after a lot of Indian Ocean, Pacific, China Seas—a regular dose of the East—six years or so, and I was loafing about, hindering you fellows in your work and invading your homes, just as though I had got a heavenly mission to civilize you. It was very fine for a time, but after a bit I did get tired of resting. Then I began to look for a ship—I should think the hardest work on earth. But the ships wouldn't even look at me. And I got tired of that game, too.

"Now when I was a little chap I had a passion for maps. I would look for hours at South America, or Africa, or Australia, and lose myself in all the glories of exploration. At that time there were many blank spaces on the earth, and when I saw one that looked particularly inviting on a map (but they all look that) I would put my finger on it and say, When I grow up I will go there. The North Pole was one of these places, I remember. Well, I haven't been there yet, and shall not try now. The glamour's off. Other places were scattered about the Equator, and in every sort of latitude all over the two hemispheres. I have been in some of them, and . . . well, we won't talk about that. But there was one[17] yet—the biggest, the most blank, so to speak—that I had a hankering after.

"True, by this time it was not a blank space any more. It had got filled since my childhood with rivers and lakes and names. It had ceased to be a blank space of delightful mystery—a white patch for a boy to dream gloriously over. It had become a place of darkness. But there was in it one river especially, a mighty big river, that you could see on the map, resembling an immense snake uncoiled, with its head in the sea, its body at rest curving afar over a vast country, and its tail lost in the depths of the land. And as I looked at the map of it in a shop-window, it fascinated me as a snake would a bird—a silly little bird. Then I remembered there was a big concern, a Company for trade on that river. Dash it all! I thought to myself, they can't trade without using some kind of craft on that lot of fresh water —steamboats! Why shouldn't I try to get charge of one? I went on along Fleet Street, but could not shake off the idea. The snake had charmed me.

"You understand it was a Continental concern, that Trading society; but I have a lot of relations living on the Continent, because it's cheap and not so nasty as it looks, they say.

"I am sorry to own I began to worry them. This was already a fresh departure for me. I was not used to getting things that way, you know. I always went my own road and on my own legs where I had a mind to go. I wouldn't have believed it of myself; but, then—you see—I felt somehow I must get there by hook or by crook. So I worried them. The men said 'My dear fellow,' and did nothing. Then —would you believe it?—I tried the women. I, Charlie Marlow, set the women to work—to get a job. Heavens! Well, you see, the notion drove me. I had an aunt, a dear enthusiastic soul. She wrote: 'It will be delightful. I am ready to do anything, anything for you. It is a glorious idea. I know the wife of a very high personage in the Administration, and also a man who has lots of influence with,' etc., etc. She was determined to make no end of fuss to get me appointed skipper of a river steamboat, if such was my fancy.

"I got my appointment—of course; and I got it very quick. It appears the Company had received news that one of their captains had been killed in a scuffle with the natives. This was my chance, and it made me the more anxious to go. It was only months and months afterwards, when I made the attempt to recover what was left of the body, that I heard the original quarrel arose from a misunderstanding about some hens. Yes, two black hens. Fresleven—that was the fellow's name, a Dane—thought himself wronged somehow in the bargain, so he went ashore and started to hammer the chief of the village with a stick. Oh, it didn't surprise me in the least to hear this, and at the same time to be told that Fresleven was the gentlest, quietest creature that ever walked on two legs. No doubt he was; but he had been a couple of years already out there engaged in the noble cause, you know, and he probably felt the need at last of asserting his self-respect in some way. Therefore he whacked the old nigger mercilessly, while a big crowd of his people watched him, thunderstruck, till some man—I was told the chief's son—in desperation at hearing the old chap yell, made a tentative jab with a spear at the white man —and of course it went quite easy between the shoulder-blades. Then the whole population cleared into the forest, expecting all kinds of calamities to happen, while, on the other hand, the steamer Fresleven commanded left also in a bad panic, in charge of the engineer, I believe. Afterwards nobody seemed to trouble much about Fresleven's remains, till I got out and stepped into his shoes. I couldn't let it rest, though; but when an opportunity offered at last to meet my predecessor, the grass growing through his ribs was tall enough to hide his bones. They were all there. The supernatural being had not been touched after he fell. And the village was deserted, the huts gaped black, rotting, all askew within the fallen enclosures. A calamity had come to it, sure enough. The people had vanished. Mad terror had scattered them, men, women, and children, through the bush, and they had never returned. What became of the hens I don't know either. I should think the cause of progress got them, anyhow. However, through this glorious affair I got my appointment, before I had fairly begun to hope for it.

"I flew around like mad to get ready, and before forty-eight hours I was crossing the Channel to show myself to my employers, and sign the contract. In a very few hours I arrived in a city that always makes me think of a whited sepulcher.[18] Prejudice no doubt. I had no difficulty in finding the Company's offices. It was the biggest thing in the town, and everybody I met was full of it. They were going to run an over-sea empire, and make no end of coin by trade.

"A narrow and deserted street in deep shadow, high houses, innumerable windows with venetian blinds, a dead silence, grass sprouting between the stones, imposing carriage archways right and left, immense double doors standing ponderously ajar. I slipped through one of these cracks, went up a swept and ungarnished staircase, as arid as a desert, and opened the first door I came to. Two women, one fat and the other slim, sat on strawbottomed chairs, knitting black wool. The slim one got up and walked straight at me—still knitting with down-cast eyes—and only just as I began to think of getting out of her way, as you would for a somnambulist, stood still, and looked up. Her dress was as plain as an umbrella-cover, and she turned round without a word and preceded me into a waiting-room. I gave my name, and looked about. Deal table in the middle, plain chairs all around the walls, on one end a large shining map, marked with all the colors of a rainbow.[19] There was a vast amount of red—good to see at any time, because one knows that some real work is done in there, a deuce of a lot of blue, a little green, smears of orange, and, on the East Coast, a purple patch, to show where the jolly pioneers of progress drink the jolly lager-beer. However, I wasn't going into any of these. I was going into the yellow. Dead in the center. And the river was there—fascinating—deadly —like a snake. Ough! A door opened, a white-haired secretarial head, but wearing a compassionate expression, appeared, and a skinny forefinger beckoned me into the sanctuary. Its light was dim, and a heavy writing-desk squatted in the middle. From behind that structure came out an impression of pale plumpness in a frockcoat. The great man himself. He was five feet six, I should judge, and had his grip on the handle-end of ever so many millions. He shook hands, I fancy, murmured vaguely, was satisfied with my French. *Bon voyage.*[20]

"In about forty-five seconds I found myself again in the waiting-room with the compassionate secretary, who, full of desolation and sympathy, made me sign some document. I believe I undertook amongst other things not to disclose any trade secrets. Well, I am not going to.

"I began to feel slightly uneasy. You know I am not used to such ceremonies, and there was something ominous in the atmosphere. It was just as though I had been let into some conspiracy—I don't know—something not quite right; and I was glad to get out. In the outer room the two women knitted black wool feverishly. People were arriving, and the younger one was walking back and forth introducing them. The old one sat on her chair. Her flat cloth slippers were propped up on a foot-warmer, and a cat reposed on her lap. She wore a starched white affair on her head, had a wart on one cheek, and silver-rimmed spectacles hung on the tip of her nose. She glanced at me above the glasses. The swift and indifferent placidity of that look troubled me. Two youths with foolish and cheery countenances were being piloted over, and she threw at them the same quick glance of unconcerned wisdom. She seemed to know all about them and about me, too. An eerie feeling came over me. She seemed uncanny and fateful. Often far away there I thought of these two, guarding the door of Darkness, knitting black wool as for a warm pall, one introducing, introducing continuously to the unknown, the other scrutinizing the cheery and foolish faces with unconcerned old eyes. *Ave!* Old knitter of black wool. *Morituri te salutant.* [21] Not many of those she looked at ever saw her again—not half, by a long way.

"There was yet a visit to the doctor. 'A simple formality,' assured me the secretary, with an air of taking an immense part in all my sorrows. Accordingly a young chap wearing his hair over the left eyebrow, some clerk I suppose,—there must have been clerks in the business, though the house was as still as a house in a city of the dead—came from somewhere upstairs, and led me forth. He was shabby and careless, with inkstains on the sleeves of his jacket, and his cravat was large and billowy, under a chin shaped like the toe of an old boot. It was a little too early for the doctor, so I proposed a drink, and thereupon he developed a vein of joviality. As we sat over our vermouths he glorified the Company's business, and by and by I expressed casually my surprise at him not going out there. He became very cool and collected all at once. 'I am not such a fool as I look, quoth Plato to his disciples,' he said sententiously, emptied his glass with great resolution, and we rose.

"The old doctor felt my pulse, evidently thinking of something else the while. 'Good, good for there,' he mumbled, and then with a certain eagerness asked me whether I would let him measure my head. Rather surprised, I said Yes, when he produced a thing like calipers and got the dimensions back and front and every way, taking notes carefully. He was an unshaven little man in a thread-bare coat like a gaberdine, with his feet in slippers, and I thought him a harmless fool. 'I always ask leave, in the interests of science, to measure the crania of those going out there,' he said. 'And when they come back, too?' I asked. 'Oh, I never see them,' he remarked; 'and, moreover, the changes take place inside, you know.' He smiled, as if at some quiet joke. 'So you are going out there. Famous. Interesting, too.'' He gave me a searching glance, and made another note. 'Ever any madness in your family?' he asked, in a matter-of-fact tone. I felt very annoyed. 'Is that question in the interests of science, too?' 'It would be,' he said, without taking notice of my irritation, 'interesting for science to watch the mental changes of individuals, on the spot, but . . .' 'Are you an alienist?'[22] I interrupted. 'Every doctor should be—a little,' answered that original, imperturbably. 'I have a little theory which you Messieurs who go out there must help me to prove. This is my share in the advantages my country shall reap from the possession of such a magnificent dependency. The mere wealth I leave to others. Pardon my questions, but you are the first Englishman coming under my observation . . .' I hastened to assure him I was not in the least typical. 'If I were,' said I, 'I wouldn't be talking like this with you.' 'What you say is rather profound, and probably erroneous,' he said, with a laugh. 'Avoid irritation more than exposure to the sun. Adieu. How do you English say, eh? Good-by. Ah! Good-by. Adieu. In the tropics one must before everything keep calm.' . . . He lifted a warning forefinger. . . . *'Du calme, du calme. Adieu.'*[23]

"One thing more remained to do—say good-by to my excellent aunt. I found her triumphant. I had a cup of tea—the last decent cup of tea for many days—and in a room that most soothingly looked just as you would expect a lady's drawing-room to look, we had a long quiet chat by the fireside. In the course of these confidences it became quite plain to me I had been represented to the wife of the high dignitary, and goodness knows to how many more people besides, as an exceptional and gifted creature—a piece of good fortune for the Company—a man you don't get hold of every day. Good heavens! and I was going to take charge of a twopenny-half-penny river-steamboat with a penny whistle attached! It appeared, however, I was also one of the Workers, with a capital—you know. Something like an emissary of light, something like a lower sort of apostle. There had been a lot of such rot let loose in print and talk just about that time, and the excellent woman, living right in the rush of all that humbug, got carried off her feet. She talked about 'weaning those ignorant millions from their horrid ways,' till, upon my word, she made me quite uncomfortable. I ventured to hint that the Company was run for profit.

" 'You forget, dear Charlie, that the laborer is worthy of his hire,'[24] she said, brightly. It's queer how out of touch with truth women are. They live in a world of their own, and there has never been anything like it, and never can be. It is too beautiful altogether, and if they were to set it up it would go to pieces before the first sunset. Some confounded fact we men have been living contentedly with ever since the day of creation would start up and knock the whole thing over.

"After this I got embraced, told to wear flannel, be sure to write often, and so on—and I left. In the street—I don't know why—a queer feeling came to me that I was an impostor. Odd thing that I, who used to clear out for any part of the world at twenty-four hours' notice, with less thought than most men give to the crossing of a street, had a moment—I won't say of hesitation, but of startled pause, before this common-place affair. The best way I can explain it to you is by saying that, for a second or two, I felt as though, instead of going to the center of a continent, I were about to set off for the center of the earth.

"I left in a French steamer, and she called in every blamed port they have out there,[25] for, as far as I could see, the sole purpose of landing soldiers and custom-house officers. I watched the coast. Watching a coast as it slips by the ship is like thinking about an enigma. There it is before you—smiling, frowning, inviting, grand, mean, insipid, or savage, and always mute with an air of whisper-ing, Come and find out. This one was almost featureless, as if still in the making, with an aspect of monotonous grimness. The edge of a colossal jungle, so dark-green as to be almost black, fringed with white surf, ran straight, like a ruled line, far, far away along a blue sea whose glitter was blurred by a creeping mist. The sun was fierce, the land seemed to glisten and drip with steam. Here and there grayish-whitish specks showed up clustered inside the white surf, with a flag flying above them perhaps. Settlements some centuries old, and still no bigger than pinheads on the untouched expanse of their background. We pounded along, stopped, landed soldiers; went on, landed custom-house clerks to levy toll in what looked like a God-forsaken wilderness, with a tin shed and a flag-pole lost in it;

95

landed more soldiers—to take care of the custom-house clerks, presumably. Some, I heard, got drowned in the surf; but whether they did or not, nobody seemed particularly to care. They were just flung out there, and on we went. Every day the coast looked the same, as though we had not moved; but we passed various places—trading places—with names like Gran' Bassam, Little Popo; names that seemed to belong to some sordid farce acted in front of a sinister back-cloth. The idleness of a passenger, my isolation amongst all these men with whom I had no point of contact, the oily and languid sea, the uniform somberness of the coast, seemed to keep me away from the truth of things, within the toil of a mournful and senseless delusion. The voice of the surf heard now and then was a positive pleasure, like the speech of a brother. It was something natural, that had its reason, that had a meaning. Now and then a boat from the shore gave one a momentary contact with reality. It was paddled by black fellows. You could see from afar the white of their eyeballs glistening. They shouted, sang; their bodies streamed with perspiration; they had faces like grotesque masks—these chaps; but they had bone, muscle, a wild vitality, an intense energy of movement, that was as natural and true as the surf along their coast. They wanted no excuse for being there. They were a great comfort to look at. For a time I would feel I belonged still to a world of straightforward facts; but the feeling would not last long. Something would turn up to scare it away. Once, I remember, we came upon a man-of-war anchored off the coast. There wasn't even a shed there, and she was shelling the bush. It appears the French had one of their wars going on thereabouts. Her ensign[26] dropped limp like a rag; the muzzles of the long six-inch guns stuck out all over the low hull; the greasy, slimy swell swung her up lazily and let her down, swaying her thin masts. In the empty immensity of earth, sky, and water, there she was, incomprehensible, firing into a continent. Pop, would go one of the six-inch guns; a small flame would dart and vanish, a little white smoke would disappear, a tiny projectile would give a feeble screech—and nothing happened. Nothing could happen. There was a touch of insanity in the proceeding, a sense of lugubrious drollery in the sight; and it was not dissipated by somebody on board assuring me earnestly there was a camp of natives—he called them enemies!—hidden out of sight somewhere.

"We gave her her letters (I heard the men in that lovely ship were dying of fever at the rate of three a day) and went on. We called at some more places with farcical names, where the merry dance of death and trade goes on in a still and earthy atmosphere as of an overheated catacomb; all along the formless coast bordered by dangerous surf, as if Nature herself had tried to ward off intruders; in and out of rivers, streams of death in life, whose banks were rotting into mud, whose waters, thickened into slime, invaded the contorted mangroves, that seemed to writhe at us in the extremity of an impotent despair. Nowhere did we stop long enough to get a particularized impression, but the general sense of vague and oppressive wonder grew upon me. It was like a weary pilgrimage amongst hints for nightmares.

"It was upward of thirty days before I saw the mouth of the big river.[27] We anchored off the seat of the government.[28] But my work would not begin till some

96

two hundred miles farther on. So as soon as I could I made a start for a place thirty miles higher up.

"I had my passage on a little sea-going steamer. Her captain was a Swede, and knowing me for a seaman, invited me on the bridge. He was a young man, lean, fair, and morose, with lanky hair and a shuffling gait. As we left the miserable little wharf, he tossed his head contemptuously at the shore. 'Been living there?' he asked. I said, 'Yes.' 'Fine lot these government chaps—are they not?' he went on, speaking English with great precision and considerable bitterness. 'It is funny what some people will do for a few francs a month. I wonder what becomes of that kind when it goes up-country?' I said to him I expected to see that soon. 'So-o-o!'' he exclaimed. He shuffled athwart, keeping one eye ahead vigilantly. 'Don't be too sure,' he continued. 'The other day I took up a man who hanged himself on the road. He was a Swede, too.' 'Hanged himself! Why, in God's name?' I cried. He kept on looking out watchfully. 'Who knows? The sun was too much for him, or the country perhaps.'

"At last we opened a reach.[29] A rocky cliff appeared, mounds of turned-up earth by the shore, houses on a hill, others with iron roofs, amongst a waste of excavations, or hanging to the declivity.[30] A continuous noise of the rapids above hovered over this scene of inhabited devastation. A lot of people, mostly black and naked, moved about like ants. A jetty projected into the river. A blinding sunlight drowned all this at times in a sudden recrudescence of glare. 'There's your Company's station,' said the Swede, pointing to three wooden barrack-like structures on the rocky slope. 'I will send your things up. Four boxes did you say? So. Farewell.'

"I came upon a boiler wallowing in the grass, then found a path leading up the hill. It turned aside for the bowlders, and also for an under-sized railway-truck lying there on its back with its wheels in the air. One was off. The thing looked as dead as the carcass of some animal. I came upon more pieces of decaying machinery, a stack of rusty rails. To the left a clump of trees made a shady spot, where dark things seemed to stir feebly. I blinked, the path was steep. A horn tooted to the right, and I saw the black people run. A heavy and dull detonation shook the ground, a puff of smoke came out of the cliff, and that was all. No change appeared on the face of the rock. They were building a railway. The cliff was not in the way or anything; but this objectless blasting was all the work going on.

"A slight clinking behind me made me turn my head. Six black men advanced in a file, toiling up the path. They walked erect and slow, balancing small baskets full of earth on their heads, and the clink kept time with their footsteps. Black rags were wound round their loins, and the short ends behind waggled to and fro like tails. I could see every rib, the joints of their limbs were like knots in a rope; each had an iron collar on his neck, and all were connected together with a chain whose bights[31] swung between them, rhythmically clinking. Another report from the cliff made me think suddenly of that ship of war I had seen firing into a continent. It was the same kind of ominous voice; but these men could by no stretch of imagination be called enemies. They were called criminals, and the outraged law, like the bursting shells, had come to them, an insoluble mystery from the sea. All their meager breasts panted together, the violently dilated nostrils quivered, the eyes stared stonily up-hill. They passed me within six inches, without a glance, with that complete, deathlike indifference of unhappy savages. Behind this raw matter one of the reclaimed, the product of the new forces at work, strolled despondently, carrying a rifle by its middle. He had a uniform jacket with one button off, and seeing a white man on the path, hoisted his weapon to his shoulder with alacrity. This was simple prudence, white men being so much alike at a distance that he could not tell who I might be. He was speedily reassured, and with a large, white rascally grin, and a glance at his charge, seemed to take me into partnership in his exalted trust. After all, I also was a part of the great cause of these high and just proceedings.

"Instead of going up, I turned and descended to the left. My idea was to let that chain-gang get out of sight before I climbed the hill. You know I am not particularly tender; I've had to strike and to fend off. I've had to resist and to attack sometimes—that's only one way of resisting—without counting the exact cost, according to the demands of such sort of life as I had blundered into. I've seen the devil of violence, and the devil of greed, and the devil of hot desire; but, by all the stars! these were strong, lusty, red-eyed devils, that swayed and drove men —men, I tell you. But as I stood on this hillside, I foresaw that in the blinding sunshine of that land I would become acquainted with a flabby, pretending, weak-eyed devil of a rapacious and pitiless folly. How insidious he could be, too, I was only to find out several months later and a thousand miles farther. For a moment I stood appalled, as though by a warning. Finally I descended the hill, obliquely, towards the trees I had seen.

"I avoided a vast artificial hole somebody had been digging on the slope, the purpose of which I found it impossible to divine. It wasn't a quarry or a sandpit, anyhow. It was just a hole. It might have been connected with the philanthropic desire of giving the criminals something to do. I don't know. Then I nearly fell into a very narrow ravine, almost no more than a scar in the hillside. I discovered that a lot of imported drainage-pipes for the settlement had been tumbled in there. There wasn't one that was not broken. It was a wanton smash-up. At last I got under the trees. My purpose was to stroll into the shade for a moment; but no sooner within than it seemed to me I had stepped into the gloomy circle of some Inferno. The rapids were near, and an uninterrupted, uniform, headlong, rushing noise filled the mournful stillness of the grove, where not a breath stirred, not a leaf moved, with a mysterious sound—as though the tearing pace of the launched earth had suddenly become audible.

"Black shapes crouched, lay, sat between the trees leaning against the trunks, clinging to the earth, half coming out, half effaced within the dim light, in all the attitudes of pain, abandonment, and despair. Another mine[32] on the cliff went off, followed by a slight shudder of the soil under my feet. The work was going on. The work! And this was the place where some of the helpers had withdrawn to die.

"They were dying slowly—it was very clear. They were not enemies, they were not criminals, they were nothing earthly now,—nothing but black shadows of disease and starvation, lying confusedly in the greenish gloom. Brought from all the recesses of the coast in all the legality of time contracts, lost in uncongenial surroundings, fed on unfamiliar food, they sickened, became inefficient, and were then allowed to crawl away and rest. These moribund shapes were free as air—and nearly as thin. I began to distinguish the gleam of the eyes under the trees. Then, glancing down, I saw a face near my hand. The black bones reclined at full length with one shoulder against the tree, and slowly the eyelids rose and the sunken eyes looked up at me, enormous and vacant, a kind of blind, white flicker in the depths of the orbs, which died out slowly. The man seemed young—almost a boy—but you know with them it's hard to tell. I found nothing else to do but to offer him one of my good Swede's ship's biscuits I had in my pocket. The fingers closed slowly on it and held—there was no other movement and no other glance. He had tied a bit of white worsted round his neck—Why? Where did he get it? Was it a badge—an ornament—a charm—a propitiatory act? Was there any idea at all connected with it? It looked startling round his black neck, this bit of white thread from beyond the seas.

"Near the same tree two more bundles of acute angles sat with their legs drawn up. One, with his chin propped on his knees, stared at nothing, in an intolerable and appalling manner: his brother phantom rested its forehead, as if overcome with a great weariness; and all about others were scattered in every pose of controlled collapse, as in some picture of a massacre or a pestilence. While I stood horror-struck, one of these creatures rose to his hands and knees, and went off on all-fours towards the river to drink. He lapped out of his hand, then sat up in the sunlight, crossing his shins in front of him, and after a time let his woolly head fall on his breastbone.

"I didn't want any more loitering in the shade, and I made haste towards the station. When near the buildings I met a white man, in such an unexpected elegance of get-up that in the first moment I took him for a sort of vision. I saw a high starched collar, white cuffs, a light alpaca jacket, snowy trousers, a clean necktie, and varnished boots. No hat. Hair parted, brushed, oiled, under a green-lined parasol held in a big white hand. He was amazing, and had a penholder behind his ear.

"I shook hands with this miracle, and I learned he was the Company's chief accountant, and that all the book-keeping was done at this station. He had come out for a moment, he said, 'to get a breath of fresh air.' The expression sounded wonderfully odd, with its suggestion of sedentary desk-life. I wouldn't have mentioned the fellow to you at all, only it was from his lips that I first heard the name of the man who is so indissolubly connected with the memories of that time. Moreover, I respected the fellow. Yes; I respected his collars, his vast cuffs, his brushed hair. His appearance was certainly that of a hairdresser's dummy; but in the great demoralization of the land he kept up his appearance. That's backbone. His starched collars and got-up shirt-fronts were achievements of character. He had been out nearly three years; and, later, I could not help asking him how he managed to sport such linen. He had just the faintest blush, and said modestly, 'I've been teaching one of the native women about the station. It was difficult. She had a distaste for the work.' Thus this man had verily accomplished something. And he was devoted to his books, which were in apple-pie order.

"Everything else in the station was in a muddle,—heads, things, buildings. Strings of dusty niggers with splay feet arrived and departed; a stream of manufactured goods, rubbishy cottons, beads, and brass-wire set into the depths of darkness, and in return came a precious trickle of ivory.

"I had to wait in the station for ten days—an eternity. I lived in a hut in the yard, but to be out of the chaos I would sometimes get into the accountant's office. It was built of horizontal planks, and so badly put together that, as he bent over his high desk, he was barred from neck to heels with narrow strips of sunlight. There was no need to open the big shutter to see. It was hot there, too; big flies buzzed fiendishly, and did not sting, but stabbed. I sat generally on the floor, while, of faultless appearance (and even slightly scented), perching on a high stool, he wrote, he wrote. Sometimes he stood up for exercise. When a trucklebed with a sick man (some invalid agent from up-country) was put in there, he exhibited a gentle annoyance. 'The groans of this sick person,' he said, 'distract my attention. And without that it is extremely difficult to guard against clerical errors in this climate.'

"One day he remarked, without lifting his head, 'In the interior you will no doubt meet Mr. Kurtz.' On my asking who Mr. Kurtz was, he said he was a first-class agent; and seeing my disappointment at this information, he added slowly, laying down his pen, 'He is a very remarkable person.' Further questions elicited from him that Mr. Kurtz was at present in charge of a trading post, a very important one, in the true ivory-country, at 'the very bottom of there. Sends in as much ivory[33] as all the others put together. . . .' He began to write again. The sick man was too ill to groan. The flies buzzed in a great peace.

"Suddenly there was a growing murmur of voices and a great tramping of feet. A caravan had come in. A violent babble of uncouth sounds burst out on the other side of the planks. All the carriers were speaking together, and in the midst of the uproar the lamentable voice of the chief agent was heard 'giving it up' tearfully for the twentieth time that day. . . . He rose slowly. 'What a frightful row,' he said. He crossed the room gently to look at the sick man, and returning, said to me, 'He does not hear.' 'What! Dead?' I asked, startled. 'No, not yet,' he answered, with great composure. Then, alluding with a toss of the head to the tumult in the stationyard, 'When one has got to make correct entries, one comes to hate those savages—hate them to the death.' He remained thoughtful for a moment. 'When you see Mr. Kurtz,' he went on, 'tell him for me that everything here'—he glanced at the desk—'is very satisfactory. I don't like to write to him —with those messengers of ours you never know who may get hold of your letter —at that Central Station.' He stared at me for a moment with his mild, bulging eyes. 'Oh, he will go far, very far,' he began again. 'He will be a somebody in the Administration before long. They, above—the Council in Europe, you know— mean him to be.'

"He returned to his work. The noise outside had ceased, and presently in going out I stopped at the door. In the steady buzz of flies the homeward-bound agent was lying flushed and insensible; the other, bent over his books, was making correct entries of perfectly correct transactions; and fifty feet below the doorstep I could see the still treetops of the grove of death.

"Next day I left that station at last, with a caravan of sixty men, for a two-hundred-mile tramp.

"No use telling you much about that. Paths, paths, everywhere; a stamped-in network of paths spreading over the empty land, through long grass, through burnt grass, through thickets, down and up chilly ravines, up and down stony hills ablaze with heat; and a solitude, a solitude, nobody, not a hut. The population had cleared out a long time ago. Well, if a lot of mysterious niggers armed with all kinds of fearful weapons suddenly took to traveling on the road between Deal and Gravesend,[34] catching the yokels right and left to carry heavy loads for them, I fancy every farm and cottage thereabouts would get empty very soon. Only here the dwellings were gone, too. Still I passed through several abandoned villages. There's something pathetically childish in the ruins of grass walls. Day after day, with the stamp and shuffle of sixty pair of bare feet behind me, each pair under a sixty-lb. load. Camp, cook, sleep, strike camp, march. Now and then a carrier dead in harness, at rest in the long grass near the path, with an empty water-gourd and his long staff lying by his side. A great silence around and above. Perhaps on some quiet night the tremor of far-off drums, sinking, swelling, a tremor vast, faint; a sound weird, appealing, suggestive, and wild—and perhaps with as profound a meaning as the sound of bells in a Christian country. Once a white man in an unbuttoned uniform, camping on the path with an armed escort of lank Zanzibars,[35] very hospitable and festive—not to say drunk. Was looking after the upkeep of the road, he declared. Can't say I saw any road or any upkeep, unless the body of a middle-aged Negro, with a bullet-hole in the forehead, upon which I absolutely stumbled three miles farther on, may be considered as a permanent improvement. I had a white companion, too, not a bad chap, but rather too fleshy and with the exasperating habit of fainting on the hot hillsides, miles away from the least bit of shade and water. Annoying, you know, to hold your own coat like a parasol over a man's head while he is coming to. I couldn't help asking him once what he meant by coming there at all. 'To make money, of course. What do you think?' he said, scornfully. Then he got fever, and had to be carried in a hammock slung under a pole. As he weighed sixteen stone[36] I had no end of rows with the carriers. They jibbed, ran away, sneaked off with their loads in the night—quite a mutiny. So, one evening, I made a speech in English with gestures, not one of which was lost to the sixty pairs of eyes before me, and the next morning I started the hammock off in front all right. An hour afterwards I came upon the whole concern wrecked in a bush—man, hammock, groans, blankets, horrors. The heavy pole had skinned his poor nose. He was very anxious for me to kill somebody, but there wasn't the shadow of a carrier near. I remember the old doctor—'It would be interesting for science to watch the mental changes of individuals, on the spot.' I felt I was becoming scientifically interesting. However, all that is to no purpose. On the fifteenth day I came in sight of the big river again, and hobbled into the Central Station. It was on a back water surrounded by scrub and forest, with a pretty border of smelly mud on one side, and on the three others enclosed by a crazy fence of rushes. A neglected gap was all the gate it had, and the first glance at the place was enough to let you see the flabby devil was running that show. White men with long staves in their hands appeared languidly from amongst the buildings, strolling up to take a look at me, and then retired out of sight somewhere. One of them, a stout, excitable chap with black mustaches, informed me with great volubility and many digressions, as soon as I told him who I was, that my steamer was at the bottom of the river. I was thunder-struck. What, how, why? Oh, it was 'all right.' The 'manager himself' was there. All quite correct. 'Everybody had behaved splendidly! splendidly!'—'you must,' he said in agitation, 'go and see the general manager at once. He is waiting!'

"I did not see the real significance of that wreck at once. I fancy I see it now, but I am not sure—not at all. Certainly the affair was too stupid—when I think of it—to be altogether natural. Still. . . . But at the moment it presented itself simply as a confounded nuisance. The steamer was sunk. They had started two days before in a sudden hurry up the river with the manager on board, in charge of some volunteer skipper, and before they had been out three hours they tore the bottom out of her on stones, and she sank near the south bank. I asked myself what I was to do there, now my boat was lost. As a matter of fact, I had plenty to do in fishing my command out of the river. I had to set about it the very next day. That, and the repairs when I brought the pieces to the station, took some months.

"My first interview with the manager was curious. He did not ask me to sit down after my twenty-mile walk that morning. He was commonplace in complexion, in feature, in manners, and in voice. He was of middle size and of ordinary build. His eyes, of the usual blue, were perhaps remarkably cold, and he certainly could make his glance fall on one as trenchant and heavy as an ax. But even at these times the rest of his person seemed to disclaim the intention. Otherwise there was only an indefinable, faint expression of his lips, something stealthy—a smile—not a smile—I remember it, but I can't explain. It was unconscious, this smile was, though just after he had said something it got intensified for an instant. It came at the end of his speeches like a seal applied on the words to make the meaning of the commonest phrase appear absolutely inscrutable. He was a common trader, from his youth up employed in these parts—nothing more. He was obeyed, yet he inspired neither love nor fear, nor even respect. He inspired uneasiness. That was it! Uneasiness. Not a definite mistrust—just uneasiness—nothing more. You have no idea how effective such a . . . a . . . faculty can be. He had no genius for organizing, for initiative, or for order even. That was evident in such things as the deplorable state of the station. He had no learning, and no intelligence. His position had come to him—why? Perhaps because he was never ill. . . . He had served three terms of three years out there. . . . Because triumphant health in the general rout of constitutions is a kind of power in itself. When he went home on leave he rioted on a large scale—pompously. Jack ashore[37]—with a difference— in externals only. This one could gather from his casual talk. He originated nothing, he could keep the routine going—that's all. But he was great. He was great by this little thing that it was impossible to tell what could control such a man. He never gave that secret away. Perhaps there was nothing within him. Such a suspicion made one pause—for out there there were no external checks. Once when various tropical diseases had laid low almost every 'agent' in the station, he was heard to say, 'Men who come out here should have no entrails.' He sealed the utterance with that smile of his, as though it had been a door opening into a darkness he had in his keeping. You fancied you had seen things—but the seal was on. When annoyed at meal-times by the constant quarrels of the white men about precedence, he ordered an immense round table to be made, for which a special house had to be built. This was the station's mess-room. Where he sat was the first place—the rest were nowhere. One felt this to be his unalterable conviction. He was neither civil nor uncivil. He was quiet. He allowed his 'boy'—an over-fed young Negro from the coast—to treat the white men, under his very eyes, with provoking insolence.

"He began to speak as soon as he saw me. I had been very long on the road. He could not wait. Had to start without me. The upriver stations had to be relieved. There had been so many delays already that he did not know who was dead and who was alive, and how they got on—and so on, and so on. He paid no attention to my explanations, and, playing with a stick of sealing-wax, repeated several times that the situation was 'very grave, very grave.' There were rumors that a very important station was in jeopardy, and its chief, Mr. Kurtz, was ill. Hoped it was not true. Mr. Kurtz was . . . I felt weary and irritable. Hang Kurtz, I thought. I interrupted him by saying I had heard of Mr. Kurtz on the coast. 'Ah! So they talk of him down there,' he murmured to himself. Then he began again, assuring me Mr. Kurtz was the best agent he had, an exceptional man, of the greatest importance to the Company; therefore I could understand his anxiety. He was, he said, 'very, very uneasy.' Certainly he fidgeted on his chair a good deal, exclaimed, 'Ah, Mr. Kurtz!' broke the stick of sealing-wax and seemed dumfounded by the accident. Next thing he wanted to know 'how long it would take to . . . I interrupted him again. Being hungry, you know, and kept on my feet too, I was getting savage. 'How can I tell?' I said. 'I haven't even seen the wreck yet —some months, no doubt.' All this talk seemed to me so futile. 'Some months,' he said. 'Well, let us say three months before we can make a start. Yes. That ought to do the affair.' I flung out of his hut (he lived all alone in a clay hut with a sort of veranda) muttering to myself my opinion of him. He was a chattering idiot. Afterwards I took it back when it was borne in upon me startlingly with what extreme nicety he had estimated the time requisite for the 'affair.'

"I went to work the next day, turning, so to speak, my back on that station. In that way only it seemed to me I could keep my hold on the redeeming facts of life. Still, one must look about sometimes; and then I saw this station, these men strolling aimlessly about in the sunshine of the yard. I asked myself sometimes what it all meant. They wandered here and there with their absurd long staves in their hands, like a lot of faithless pilgrims bewitched inside a rotten fence. The word 'ivory' rang in the air, was whispered, was sighed. You would think they were praying to it. A taint of imbecile rapacity blew through it all, like a whiff from some corpse. By Jove! I've never seen anything so unreal in my life. And outside, the silent wilderness surrounding this cleared speck on the earth struck me as something great and invincible, like evil or truth, waiting patiently for the passing away of this fantastic invasion.

"Oh, these months! Well, never mind. Various things happened. One evening a grass shed full of calico, cotton prints, beads, and I don't know what else, burst into a blaze so suddenly that you would have thought the earth had opened to let an avenging fire consume all that trash. I was smoking my pipe quietly by my dismantled steamer, and saw them all cutting capers in the light, with their arms lifted high, when the stout man with mustaches came tearing down to the river, a tin pail in his hand, assured me that everybody was 'behaving splendidly, splendidly,' dipped about a quart of water and tore back again. I noticed there was a hole in the bottom of his pail.

"I strolled up. There was no hurry. You see the thing had gone off like a box of matches. It had been hopeless from the very first. The flame had leaped high, driven everybody back, lighted up everything—and collapsed. The shed was already a heap of embers glowing fiercely. A nigger was being beaten near by. They said he had caused the fire in some way; be that as it may, he was screeching most horribly. I saw him, later, for several days, sitting in a bit of shade looking very sick and trying to recover himself: afterwards he arose and went out—and the wilderness without a sound took him into its bosom again. As I approached the glow from the dark I found myself at the back of two men, talking. I heard the name of Kurtz pronounced, then the words, 'take advantage of this unfortunate accident.' One of the men was the manager. I wished him a good evening. 'Did you ever see anything like it—eh? it is incredible,' he said, and walked off. The other man remained. He was a first-class agent, young, gentlemanly, a bit reserved, with a forked little beard and a hooked nose. He was stand-offish with the other agents, and they on their side said he was the manager's spy upon them. As to me, I had hardly even spoken to him before. We got into talk, and by and by we strolled away from the hissing ruins. Then he asked me to his room, which was in the main building of the station. He struck a match, and I perceived that this young aristocrat had not only a silver-mounted dressing-case but also a whole candle all to himself. Just at that time the manager was the only man supposed to have any right to candles. Native mats covered the clay walls; a collection of spears, assegais,³⁸ shields, knives was hung up in trophies. The business intrusted to this fellow was the making of bricks—so I had been informed; but there wasn't a fragment of a brick anywhere in the station, and he had been there more than a year—waiting. It seems he could not make bricks without something, I don't know what—straw, maybe. Anyway, it could not be found there, and as it was not likely to be sent from Europe, it did not appear clear to me what he was waiting for. An act of special creation perhaps. However, they were all waiting—all the sixteen or twenty pilgrims of them—for something; and upon my word it did not seem an uncongenial occupation from the way they took it, though the only thing that ever came to them was disease—as far as I could see. They beguiled the time by backbiting and intriguing against each other in a foolish kind of way. There was an air of plotting about that station, but nothing came of it, of course. It was as unreal as everything else—as the philanthropic pretense of the whole concern, as their talk, as their government, as their show of work. The only real feeling was a desire to get appointed to a trading-post where ivory was to be had, so that they could earn percentages. They intrigued and slandered and hated each other only on that account,—but as to effectually lifting a little finger—oh, no. By heavens! there is something after all in the world allowing one man to steal a horse while another must not look at a halter. Steal a horse straight out. Very well. He has done it. Perhaps he can ride. But there is a way of looking at a halter that would provoke the most charitable of saints into a kick.

"I had no idea why he wanted to be sociable, but as we chatted in there it suddenly occurred to me the fellow was trying to get at something—in fact, pumping me. He alluded constantly to Europe, to the people I was supposed to know there—putting leading questions as to my acquaintances in the sepulchral city, and so on. His little eyes glittered like mica discs—with curiosity—though he tried to keep up a bit of superciliousness. At first I was astonished, but very soon I became awfully curious to see what he would find out from me. I couldn't possibly imagine what I had in me to make it worth his while. It was very pretty to see how he baffled himself, for in truth my body was full only of chills, and my head had nothing in it but that wretched steamboat business. It was evident he took me for a perfectly shameless prevaricator. At last he got angry, and, to conceal a movement of furious annoyance, he yawned. I rose. Then I noticed a small sketch in oils, on a panel, representing a woman, draped and blindfolded, carrying a lighted torch. The background was somber—almost black. The movement of the woman was stately, and the effect of the torchlight on the face was sinister.

"It arrested me, and he stood by civilly, holding an empty half-pint champagne bottle (medical comforts) with the candle stuck in it. To my question he said Mr. Kurtz had painted this—in this very station more than a year ago—while waiting for means to go to his trading-post. "Tell me, pray,' said I, 'who is this Mr. Kurtz?'

" 'The chief of the Inner Station,' he answered in a short tone, looking away. 'Much obliged,' I said, laughing. 'And you are the brick-maker of the Central Station. Every one knows that.' He was silent for a while. 'He is a prodigy,' he said at last. 'He is an emissary of pity, and science, and progress, and devil knows what else. We want,' he began to declaim suddenly, 'for the guidance of the cause intrusted to us by Europe, so to speak, higher intelligence, wide sympathies, a singleness of purpose.' 'Who says that?' I asked. 'Lots of them,' he replied. 'Some even write that; and so *he* comes here, a special being, as you ought to know.' 'Why ought I to know?' I interrupted, really surprised. He paid no attention. 'Yes. To-day he is chief of the best station, next year he will be assistant-manager, two years more and . . . but I daresay you know what he will be in two years' time. You are of the new gang—the gang of virtue. The same people who sent him specially also recommended you. Oh, don't say no. I've my own eyes to trust.' Light dawned upon me. My dear aunt's influential acquaintances were producing an unexpected effect upon that young man. I nearly burst into a laugh. 'Do you read the Company's confidential correspondence?' I asked. He hadn't a word to say. It was great fun. 'When Mr. Kurtz,' I continued, severely, 'is General Manager, you won't have the opportunity.'

"He blew the candle out suddenly, and we went outside. The moon had risen. Black figures strolled about listlessly, pouring water on the glow, whence proceeded a sound of hissing; steam ascended in the moonlight, the beaten nigger groaned somewhere. 'What a row the brute makes!' said the indefatigable man with the mustaches, appearing near us. 'Serves him right. Transgression—punishment—bang! Pitiless, pitiless. That's the only way. This will prevent all conflagrations for the future. I was just telling the manager. . . .' He noticed my companion, and became crest-fallen all at once. 'Not in bed yet,' he said, with a kind of servile heartiness; 'it's so natural. Ha! Danger—agitation.' He vanished. I went on to the river-side, and the other followed me. I heard a scathing murmur at my ear, 'Heap of mugs[39]—go to.' The pilgrims could be seen in knots gesticulating, discussing. Several had still their staves in their hands. I verily believe they took these sticks to bed with them. Beyond the fence the forest stood up spectrally in the moonlight, and through the dim stir, through the faint sounds of that lamentable courtyard, the silence of the land went home to one's very heart—its mystery, its greatness, the amazing reality of its concealed life. The hurt nigger moaned feebly somewhere near by, and then fetched a deep sigh that made me mend my pace away from there. I felt a hand introducing itself under my arm. 'My dear sir,' said the fellow, 'I don't want to be misunderstood, and especially by you, who will see Mr. Kurtz long before I can have that pleasure. I wouldn't like him to get a false idea of my disposition. . . .'

"I let him run on, this papier-mâché Mephistopheles,[40] and it seemed to me that if I tried I could poke my forefinger through him, and would find nothing inside but a little loose dirt, maybe. He, don't you see, had been planning to be assistant-manager by and by under the present man, and I could see that the coming of that Kurtz had upset them both not a little. He talked precipitately, and I did not try to stop him. I had my shoulders against the wreck of my steamer, hauled up on the slope like a carcass of some big river animal. The smell of mud, of primeval mud, by Jove! was in my nostrils, the high stillness of primeval forest was before my eyes; there were shiny patches on the black creek. The moon had spread over everything a thin layer of silver—over the rank grass, over the mud, upon the wall of matted vegetation standing higher than the wall of a temple, over the great river I could see through a somber gap glittering, glittering, as it flowed broadly by without a murmur. All this was great, expectant, mute, while the man jabbered about himself. I wondered whether the stillness on the face of the immensity looking at us two were meant as an appeal or as a menace. What were we who had stayed in here? Could we handle that dumb thing, or would it handle us? I felt how big, how confoundedly big, was that thing that couldn't talk, and perhaps was deaf as well. What was in there? I could see a little ivory coming out from there, and I had heard Mr. Kurtz was in there. I had heard enough about it, too —God knows! Yet somehow it didn't bring any image with it—no more than if I had been told an angel or a fiend was in there. I believed it in the same way one of you might believe there are inhabitants in the planet Mars. I knew once a Scotch sailmaker who was certain, dead sure, there were people in Mars. If you asked him for some idea how they looked and behaved, he would get shy and mutter something about 'walking on all-fours.' If you as much as smiled, he would—though a man of sixty-four—offer to fight you. I would not have gone so far as to fight for Kurtz, but I went for him near enough to a lie. You know I hate, detest, and can't bear a lie, not because I am straighter than the rest of us, but simply because it appalls me. There is a taint of death, a flavor of mortality in lies—which is exactly what I hate and detest in the world—what I want to forget. It makes me miserable and sick, like biting something rotten would do. Temperament, I suppose. Well, I went near enough to it by letting the young fool there believe anything he liked to imagine as to my influence in Europe. I became in an instant as much of a pretense as the rest of the bewitched pilgrims. This simply because I had a notion it somehow would be of help to that Kurtz whom at the time I did not see—you understand. He was just a word for me. I did not see the man in the name any more than you do. Do you see him? Do you see the story? Do you see anything? It seems to me I am trying to tell you a dream—making a vain attempt, because no relation of a dream can convey the dream-sensation, that commingling of absurdity, surprise, and bewilderment in a tremor of struggling revolt, that notion of being captured by the incredible which is of the very essence of dreams. . . ."

He was silent for a while.

". . . No, it is impossible; it is impossible to convey the life-sensation of any given epoch of one's existence—that which makes its truth, its meaning—its subtle and penetrating essence. It is impossible. We live, as we dream—alone. . . ."

He paused again as if reflecting, then added—

"Of course in this you fellows see more than I could then. You see me, whom you know. . . ."

It had become so pitch dark that we listeners could hardly see one another. For a long time already he, sitting apart, had been no more to us than a voice. There was not a word from anybody. The others might have been asleep, but I was awake. I listened, I listened on the watch for the sentence, for the word, that would give me the clew to the faint uneasiness inspired by this narrative that seemed to shape itself without human lips in the heavy night-air of the river.

". . . Yes—I let him run on," Marlow began again, "and think what he pleased about the powers that were behind me. I did! And there was nothing behind me! There was nothing but that wretched, old, mangled steamboat I was leaning against, while he talked fluently about 'the necessity for every man to get on.' 'And when one comes out here, you conceive, it is not to gaze at the moon.' Mr. Kurtz was a 'universal genius,' but even a genius would find it easier to work with 'adequate tools—intelligent men.' He did not make bricks—why, there was a physical impossibility in the way—as I was well aware; and if he did secretarial work for the manager, it was because 'no sensible man rejects wantonly the confidence of his superiors.' Did I see it? I saw it. What more did I want? What I really wanted was rivets, by heaven! Rivets. To get on with the work—to stop the hole. Rivets I wanted. There were cases of them down at the coast—cases—

piled up—burst—split! You kicked a loose rivet at every second step in that station yard on the hillside. Rivets had rolled into the grove of death. You could fill your pockets with rivets for the trouble of stooping down—and there wasn't one rivet to be found where it was wanted. We had plates that would do, but nothing to fasten them with. And every week the messenger, a lone negro, letter-bag on shoulder and staff in hand, left our station for the coast. And several times a week a coast caravan came in with trade goods—ghastly glazed calico that made you shudder only to look at it; glass beads, valued about a penny a quart, confounded spotted cotton handkerchiefs. And no rivets. Three carriers could have brought all that was wanted to set that steamboat afloat.

"He was becoming confidential now, but I fancy my unresponsive attitude must have exasperated him at last, for he judged it necessary to inform me he feared neither God nor devil, let alone any mere man. I said I could see that very well, but what I wanted was a certain quantity of rivets—and rivets were what really Mr. Kurtz wanted, if he had only known it. Now letters went to the coast every week. . . . 'My dear sir,' he cried, 'I write from dictation.' I demanded rivets. There was a way—for an intelligent man. He changed his manner; became very cold, and suddenly began to talk about a hippopotamus; wondered whether sleeping on board the steamer (I stuck to my salvage night and day) I wasn't disturbed. There was an old hippo that had the bad habit of getting out on the bank and roaming at night over the station grounds. The pilgrims used to turn out in a body and empty every rifle they could lay hands on at him. Some even had sat up o' nights for him. All this energy was wasted, though. 'That animal has a charmed life,' he said; 'but you can say this only of brutes in this country. No man—you apprehend me?—no man here bears a charmed life.' He stood there for a moment in the moonlight with his delicate hooked nose set a little askew, and his mica eyes glittering without a wink, then, with a curt good night, he strode off. I could see he was disturbed and considerably puzzled, which made me feel more hopeful than I had been for days. It was a great comfort to turn from that chap to my influential friend, the battered, twisted, ruined, tin-pot steamboat. I clambered on board. She rang under my feet like an empty Huntley & Palmer biscuit-tin kicked along a gutter; she was nothing so solid in make, and rather less pretty in shape, but I had expended enough hard work on her to make me love her. No influential friend would have served me better. She had given me a chance to come out a bit—to find out what I could do. No. I don't like work. I had rather laze about and think of all the fine things that can be done. I don't like work—no man does—but I like what is in the work,—the chance to find yourself. Your own reality—for yourself, not for others—what no other man can ever know. They can only see the mere show, and never can tell what it really means.

"I was not surprised to see somebody sitting aft, on the deck, with his legs dangling over the mud. You see I rather chummed with the few mechanics there were in that station, whom the other pilgrims naturally despised—on account of their imperfect manners, I suppose. This was the foreman—a boiler-maker by trade —a good worker. He was a lank, bony, yellow-faced man, with big intense eyes. His aspect was worried, and his head was as bold as the palm of my hand; but his

108

hair in falling seemed to have stuck to his chin, and had prospered in the new locality, for his beard hung down to his waist. He was a widower with six young children (he had left them in charge of a sister of his to come out there), and the passion of his life was pigeon-flying. He was an enthusiast and a connoisseur. He would rave about pigeons. After work hours he used sometimes to come over from his hut for a talk about his children and his pigeons; at work, when he had to crawl in the mud under the bottom of the steamboat, he would tie up that beard of his in a kind of white serviette he brought for the purpose. It had loops to go over his ears. In the evening he could be seen squatted on the bank rinsing that wrapper in the creek with great care, then spreading it solemnly on a bush to dry.

"I slapped him on the back and shouted, 'We shall have rivets!' He scrambled to his feet exclaiming. 'No! Rivets!' as though he couldn't believe his ears. Then in a low voice, 'You . . . eh?' I don't know why we behaved like lunatics. I put my finger to the side of my nose and nodded mysteriously. 'Good for you!' he cried, snapped his fingers above his head, lifting one foot. I tried a jig. We capered on the iron deck. A frightful clatter came out of that hulk, and the virgin forest on the other bank of the creek sent it back in a thundering roll upon the sleeping station. It must have made some of the pilgrims sit up in their hovels. A dark figure obscured the lighted doorway of the manager's hut, vanished, then, a second or so after, the doorway itself vanished, too. We stopped, and the silence driven away by the stamping of our feet flowed back again from the recesses of the land. The great wall of vegetation, an exuberant and entangled mass of trunks, branches, leaves, boughs, festoons, motionless in the moonlight, was like a rioting invasion of soundless life, a rolling wave of plants, piled up, crested, ready to topple over the creek, to sweep every little man of us out of his little existence. And it moved not. A deadened burst of mighty splashes and snorts reached us from afar, as through an ichthyosaurus had been taking a bath of glitter in the great river. 'After all,' said the boiler-maker in a reasonable tone, 'why shouldn't we get the rivets?' Why not, indeed? I did not know of any reason why we shouldn't. 'They'll come in three weeks,' I said, confidently.

"But they didn't. Instead of rivets there came an invasion, an infliction, a visitation. It came in sections during the next three weeks, each section headed by a donkey carrying a white man in new clothes and tan shoes, bowing from that elevation right and left to the impressed pilgrims. A quarrelsome band of footsore sulky niggers trod on the heels of the donkeys; a lot of tents, campstools, tin boxes, white cases, brown bales would be shot down in the courtyard, and the air of mystery would deepen a little over the muddle of the station. Five such installments came, with their absurd air of disorderly flight with the loot of innumerable outfit shops and provision stores, that, one would think, they were lugging, after a raid, into the wilderness for equitable division. It was an inextricable mess of things decent in themselves but that human folly made look like the spoils of thieving.

"This devoted band called itself the Eldorado Exploring Expedition, and I believe they were sworn to secrecy. Their talk, however, was the talk of sordid buccaneers: it was reckless without hardihood, greedy without audacity, and cruel without courage; there was not an atom of foresight or of serious intention in the whole batch of them, and they did not seem aware these things are wanted for the work of the world. To tear treasure out of the bowels of the land was their desire, with no more moral purpose at the back of it than there is in burglars breaking into a safe. Who paid the expenses of the noble enterprise I don't know; but the uncle of our manager was leader of that lot.

"In exterior he resembled a butcher in a poor neighborhood, and his eyes had a look of sleepy cunning. He carried his fat paunch with ostentation on his short legs, and during the time his gang infested the station spoke to no one but his nephew. You could see these two roaming about all day long with their heads close together in an everlasting confab.

"I had given up worrying myself about the rivets. One's capacity for that kind of folly is more limited than you would suppose. I said Hang!—and let things slide. I had plenty of time for meditation, and now and then I would give some thought to Kurtz. I wasn't very interested in him. No. Still, I was curious to see whether this man, who had come out equipped with moral ideas of some sort, would climb to the top after all and how he would set about his work when there."

2

"One evening as I was lying flat on the deck of my steamboat, I heard voices approaching—and there were the nephew and the uncle strolling along the bank. I laid my head on my arm again, and had nearly lost myself in a doze, when somebody said in my ear, as it were: 'I am as harmless as a little child, but I don't like to be dictated to. Am I the manager—or am I not? I was ordered to send him there. It's incredible.' . . . I became aware that the two were standing on the shore alongside the forepart of the steamboat, just below my head. I did not move; it did not occur to me to move: I was sleepy. "It *is* unpleasant,' grunted the uncle. 'He has asked the Administration to be sent there,' said the other, 'with the idea of showing what he could do; and I was instructed accordingly. Look at the influence that man must have. Is it not frightful?' They both agreed it was frightful, then made several bizarre remarks: 'Make rain and fine weather—one man—the Council—by the nose'—bits of absurd sentences that got the better of my drowsiness, so that I had pretty near the whole of my wits about me when the uncle said, 'The climate may do away with this difficulty for you. Is he alone there?' 'Yes,' answered the manager; 'he sent his assistant down the river with a note to me in these terms: "Clear this poor devil out of the country, and don't bother sending more of that sort. I had rather be alone than have the kind of men you can dispose of with me." It was more than a year ago. Can you imagine such impudence!' 'Anything since then?' asked the other, hoarsely. 'Ivory,' jerked the nephew; 'lots of it—prime sort—lots—most annoying, from him.' 'And with that?' questioned the heavy rumble. 'Invoice,' was the reply fired out, so to speak. Then silence. They had been talking about Kurtz.

"I was broad awake by this time, but, lying perfectly at ease, remained still, having no inducement to change my position. 'How did that ivory come all this way?' growled the elder man, who seemed very vexed. The other explained that it had come with a fleet of canoes in charge of an English half-caste clerk Kurtz had with him; that Kurtz had apparently intended to return himself, the station being by that time bare of goods and stores, but after coming three hundred miles, had suddenly decided to go back, which he started to do alone in a small dugout with four paddlers, leaving the half-caste to continue down the river with the ivory. The two fellows there seemed astounded at anybody attempting such a thing. They were at a loss for an adequate motive. As to me, I seemed to see Kurtz for the first time. It was a distinct glimpse: the dugout, four paddling savages, and the lone white man turning his back suddenly on the headquarters, on relief, on thoughts of home—perhaps; setting his face towards the depths of the wilderness, towards his empty and desolate station. I did not know the motive. Perhaps he was just simply a fine fellow who stuck to his work for its own sake. His name, you understand, had not been pronounced once. He was 'that man.' The half-caste, who, as far as I could see, had conducted a difficult trip with great prudence and pluck, was invariably alluded to as 'that scoundrel.' The 'scoundrel' had reported that the 'man' had been very ill—had recovered imperfectly. . . . The two below me moved away then a few paces, and strolled back and forth at some little distance. I heard: 'Military post—doctor—two hundred miles—quite alone now—unavoidable delays—nine months—no news—strange rumors.' They approached again, just as the manager was saying, 'No one, as far as I know, unless a species of wandering trader—a pestilential fellow, snapping ivory from the natives.' Who was it they were talking about now? I gathered in snatches that this was some man supposed to be in Kurtz's district, and of whom the manager did not approve. 'We will not be free from unfair competition till one of these fellows is hanged for an example,' he said. 'Certainly,' grunted the other; 'get him hanged! Why not? Anything—anything can be done in this country. That's what I say; nobody here, you understand, here, can endanger your position. And why? You stand the climate —you outlast them all. The danger is in Europe; but there before I left I took care to—' They moved off and whispered, then their voices rose again. 'The extraordi-nary series of delays is not my fault. I did my best.' The fat man sighed. 'Very sad,' 'And the pestiferous absurdity of his talk,' continued the other; 'he bothered me enough when he was here. "Each station should be like a beacon on the road towards better things, a center for trade, of course, but also for humanizing, improving, instructing." Conceive you—that ass! And he wants to be manager! No, it's—' Here he got choked by excessive indignation, and I lifted my head the least bit. I was surprised to see how near they were—right under me. I could have spat upon their hats. They were looking on the ground, absorbed in thought. The manager was switching his leg with a slender twig: his sagacious relative lifted his head. 'You have been well since you came out this time?' he asked. The other gave a start. 'Who? I? Oh! Like a charm—like a charm. But the rest—oh, my goodness! All sick. They die so quick, too, that I haven't the time to send them out of the country—it's incredible!' 'H'm. Just so,' grunted the uncle. 'Ah! my boy, trust to this—I say, trust to this.' I saw him extend his short flipper of an arm for a gesture that took in the forest, the creek, the mud, the river,—seemed to beckon with a dishonoring flourish before the sunlit face of the land a treacherous appeal to the lurking death, to the hidden evil, to the profound darkness of its heart. It was so startling that I leaped to my feet and looked back at the edge of the forest, as though I had expected an answer of some sort to that black display of confidence. You know the foolish notions that come to one sometimes. The high stillness confronted these two figures with its ominous patience, waiting for the passing away of a fantastic invasion.

"They swore aloud together—out of sheer fright, I believe—then pretending not to know anything of my existence, turned back to the station. The sun was low; and leaning forward side by side, they seemed to be tugging painfully uphill their two ridiculous shadows of unequal length, that trailed behind them slowly over the tall grass without bending a single blade.

"In a few days the Eldorado Expedition went into the patient wilderness, that closed upon it as the sea closes over a diver. Long afterwards the news came that all the donkeys were dead. I know nothing as to the fate of the less valuable animals. They, no doubt, like the rest of us, found what they deserved. I did not inquire. I was then rather excited at the prospect of meeting Kurtz very soon. When I say very soon I mean it comparatively. It was just two months from the day we left the creek when we came to the bank below Kurtz's station.

"Going up that river was like traveling back to the earliest beginnings of the world, when vegetation rioted on the earth and the big trees were kings. An empty stream, a great silence, an impenetrable forest. The air was warm, thick, heavy, sluggish. There was no joy in the brilliance of sunshine. The long stretches of the waterway ran on, deserted, into the gloom of overshadowed distances. On silvery sandbanks hippos and alligators sunned themselves side by side. The broadening waters flowed through a mob of wooded islands; you lost your way on that river as you would in a desert, and butted all day long against shoals, trying to find the channel, till you thought yourself bewitched and cut off forever from everything you had known once—somewhere—far away—in another existence perhaps. There were moments when one's past came back to one, as it will sometimes when you have not a moment to spare to yourself; but it came in the shape of an unrestful and noisy dream, remembered with wonder amongst the overwhelming realities of this strange world of plants, and water, and silence. And this stillness of life did not in the least resemble a peace. It was the stillness of an implacable force brooding over an inscrutable intention. It looked at you with a vengeful aspect. I got used to it afterwards; I did not see it any more; I had no time. I had to keep guessing at the channel; I had to discern, mostly by inspiration, the signs of hidden banks; I watched for sunken stones; I was learning to clap my teeth smartly before my heart flew out, when I shaved by a fluke some infernal sly old snag that would have ripped the life out of the tin-pot steamboat and drowned all the pilgrims; I had to keep a look-out for the signs of dead wood we could cut up in the night for next day's steaming. When you have to attend to things of that sort, to the mere incidents of the surface, the reality—the reality, I tell you—fades. The inner truth is hidden—luckily, luckily. But I felt it all the same; I felt often its mysterious stillness watching me at my monkey tricks, just as it watches you fellows performing on your respective tight-ropes for—what is it? half-a-crown a tumble—"

"'Try to be civil, Marlow,' growled a voice, and I knew there was at least one listener awake besides myself.

"I beg your pardon. I forgot the heartache which makes up the rest of the price. And indeed what does the price matter, if the trick be well done? You do your tricks very well. And I didn't do badly either, since I managed not to sink that steamboat on my first trip. It's a wonder to me yet. Imagine a blindfolded man set to drive a van over a bad road. I sweated and shivered over that business considerably, I can tell you. After all, for a seaman, to scrape the bottom of the thing that's supposed to float all the time under his care is the unpardonable sin. No one may know of it, but you never forget the thump—eh? A blow on the very heart. You remember it, you dream of it, you wake up at night and think of it— years after—and go hot and cold all over. I don't pretend to say that steamboat floated all the time. More than once she had to wade for a bit, with twenty cannibals splashing around and pushing. We had enlisted some of these chaps on the way for a crew. Fine fellows—cannibals—in their place. They were men one could work with, and I am grateful to them. And, after all, they did not eat each other before my face: they had brought along a provision of hippo-meat which went rotten, and made the mystery of the wilderness stink in my nostrils. Phoo! I can sniff it now. I had the manager on board and three or four pilgrims with their staves —all complete. Sometimes we came upon a station close by the bank, clinging to the skirts of the unknown, and the white men rushing out of a tumble-down hovel, with great gestures of joy and surprise and welcome, seemed very strange—had the appearance of being held there captive by a spell. The word ivory would ring in the air for a while—and on we went again into the silence, along empty reaches, round the still bends, between the high walls of our winding way, reverberating in hollow claps the ponderous beat of the stern-wheel. Trees, trees, millions of trees, massive, immense, running up high; and at their foot, hugging the bank against the stream, crept the little begrimed steamboat, like a sluggish beetle crawling on the floor of a lofty portico. It made you feel very small, very lost, and yet it was not altogether depressing, that feeling. After all, if you were small, the grimy beetle crawled on—which was just what you wanted it to do. Where the pilgrims imagined it crawled to I don't know. To some place where they expected to get something, I bet! For me it crawled towards Kurtz—exclusively; but when the steam-pipes started leaking we crawled very slow. The reaches opened before us and closed behind, as if the forest had stepped leisurely across the water to bar the way for our return. We penetrated deeper and deeper into the heart of darkness. It was very quiet there. At night sometimes the roll of drums behind the curtain of trees would run up the river and remain sustained faintly, as if hovering in the air high over our heads, till the first break of day. Whether it meant war, peace, or prayer we could not tell. The dawns were heralded by the descent of a chill stillness; the wood-cutters slept, their fires burned low; the snapping of a twig would make you start. We were wanderers on a prehistoric earth, on an earth that wore the aspect of an unknown planet. We could have fancied ourselves the first of men taking possession of an accursed inheritance, to be subdued at the cost of profound anguish and of excessive toil. But suddenly, as we struggled round a bend, there would be a glimpse of rush walls, of peaked grass-roofs, a burst of yells, a whirl of black limbs, a mass of hands clapping, of feet stamping, of bodies swaying, of eyes rolling, under the droop of heavy and motionless foliage. The streamer toiled along slowly on the edge of a black and incomprehensible frenzy. The prehistoric man was cursing us, praying to us, welcoming us—who could tell? We were cut off from the comprehension of our surroundings; we glided past like phantoms, wondering and secretly appalled, as sane men would be before an enthusiastic outbreak in a madhouse. We could not understand because we were too far and could not remember, because we were traveling in the night of first ages, of those ages that are gone, leaving hardly a sign—and no memories.

"The earth seemed unearthly. We are accustomed to look upon the shackled form of a conquered monster, but there—there you could look at a thing monstrous and free. It was unearthly, and the men were—No, they were not inhuman. Well, you know, that was the worst of it—this suspicion of their not being inhuman. It would come slowly to one. They howled and leaped, and spun, and made horrid faces; but what thrilled you was just the thought of their humanity—like yours—the thought of your remote kinship with this wild and passionate uproar. Ugly. Yes, it was ugly enough; but if you were man enough you would admit to yourself that there was in you just the faintest trace of a response to the terrible frankness of that noise, a dim suspicion of there being a meaning in it which you —you so remote from the night of first ages—could comprehend. And why not? The mind of man is capable of anything—because everything is in it, all the past as well as all the future. What was there after all? Joy, fear, sorrow, devotion, valor, rage—who can tell?—but truth—truth stripped of its cloak of time. Let the fool gape and shudder—the man knows, and can look on without a wink. But he must at least be as much of a man as these on the shore. He must meet that truth with his own true stuff—with his own inborn strength. Principles won't do. Acquisitions, clothes, pretty rags—rags that would fly off at the first good shake. No; you want a deliberate belief. An appeal to me in this fiendish row—is there? Very well; I hear; I admit, but I have a voice, too, and for good or evil mine is the speech that cannot be silenced. Of course, a fool, what with sheer fright and fine sentiments, is always safe. Who's that grunting? You wonder I didn't go ashore for a howl and a dance? Well, no—I didn't. Fine sentiments, you say? Fine sentiments, be hanged! I had no time. I had to mess about with whitelead and strips of woolen blanket helping to put bandages on those leaky steam-pipes—I tell you. I had to watch the steering, and circumvent those snags, and get the tinpot along by hook or by crook. There was surface-truth enough in these things to save a wiser man. And between whiles I had to look after the savage who was fireman. He was an improved specimen; he could fire up a vertical boiler.[41] He was there below me, and, upon my word, to look at him was as edifying as seeing a dog in a parody of breeches and a feather hat, walking on his hind-legs. A few months of training had done for that really fine chap. He squinted at the steam-gauge and at the water-gauge with an evident effort of intrepidity—and he had filed teeth, too, the poor devil, and the wool of his pate shaved into queer patterns, and three ornamental scars on each of his cheeks. He ought to have been clapping his hands and

114

stamping his feet on the bank, instead of which he was hard at work, a thrall to strange witchcraft, full of improving knowledge. He was useful because he had been instructed; and what he knew was this—that should the water in that transparent thing disappear, the evil spirit inside the boiler would get angry through the greatness of his thirst, and take a terrible vengeance. So he sweated and fired up and watched the glass fearfully (with an impromptu charm, made of rags, tied to his arm, and a piece of polished bone, as big as a watch, stuck flatways through his lower lip), while the wooden banks slipped past us slowly, the short noise was left behind, the interminable miles of silence—and we crept on, toward Kurtz. But the snags were thick, the water was treacherous and shallow, the boiler seemed indeed to have a sulky devil in it, and thus neither that fireman nor I had any time to peer into our creepy thoughts.

"Some fifty miles below the Inner Station we came upon a hut of reeds, an inclined and melancholy pole, with the unrecognizable tatters of what had been a flag of some sort flying from it, and a neatly stacked woodpile. This was unexpected. We came to the bank, and on the stack of firewood found a flat piece of board with some faded pencil-writing on it. When deciphered it said: 'Wood for you. Hurry up. Approach cautiously.' There was a signature, but it was illegible —not Kurtz—a much longer word. 'Hurry up.' Where? Up the river? 'Approach cautiously.' We had not done so. But the warning could not have been meant for the place where it could be only found after approach. Something was wrong above. But what—and how much? That was the question. We commented adversely upon the imbecility of that telegraphic style. The bush around said nothing, and would not let us look very far, either. A torn curtain of red twill hung in the doorway of the hut, and flapped sadly in our faces. The dwelling was dismantled; but we could see a white man had lived there not very long ago. There remained a rude table—a plank on two posts; a heap of rubbish reposed in a dark corner, and by the door I picked up a book. It had lost its covers, and the pages had been thumbed into a state of extremely dirty softness; but the back had been lovingly stitched afresh with white cotton thread, which looked clean yet. It was an extraordinary find. Its title was, *An Inquiry into some Points of Seamanship,* by a man Towser, Towson—some such name—Master in his Majesty's Navy. The matter looked dreary reading enough, with illustrative diagrams and repulsive tables of figures, and the copy was sixty years old. I handled this amazing antiquity with the greatest possible tenderness, lest it should dissolve in my hands. Within, Towson or Towser was inquiring earnestly into the breaking strain of ships' chains and tackle, and other such matters. Not a very enthralling book; but at the first glance you could see there a singleness of intention, an honest concern for the right way of going to work, which made these humble pages, thought out so many years ago, luminous with another than a professional light. The simple old sailor, with his talk of chains and purchases,[42] made me forget the jungle and the pilgrims in a delicious sensation of having come upon something unmistakably real. Such a book being there was wonderful enough; but still more astounding were the notes penciled in the margin, and plainly referring to the text. I couldn't believe my eyes! They were in cipher! Yes, it looked like cipher. Fancy a man lugging with him a book of that description into this nowhere and studying it—and making notes—in cipher at that! It was an extravagant mystery.

"I had been dimly aware for some time of a worrying noise, and when I lifted my eyes I saw the wood pile was gone, and the manager, aided by all the pilgrims, was shouting at me from the river-side. I slipped the book into my pocket. I assure you to leave off reading was like tearing myself away from the shelter of an old and solid freindship.

"I started the lame engine ahead. 'It must be this miserable trader—this intruder,' exclaimed the manager, looking back malevolently at the place we had left. 'He must be English,' I said. 'It will not save him from getting into trouble if he is not careful,' muttered the manager darkly. I observed with assumed innocence that no man was safe from trouble in this world.

"The current was more rapid now, the steamer seemed at her last gasp, the stern-wheel flopped languidly, and I caught myself listening on tiptoe for the next beat of the boat,[43] for in sober truth I expected the wretched thing to give up every moment. It was like watching the last flickers of a life. But still we crawled. Sometimes I would pick out a tree a little way ahead to measure our progress towards Kurtz by, but I lost it invariably before we got abreast. To keep the eyes so long on one thing was too much for human patience. The manager displayed a beautiful resignation. I fretted and fumed and took to arguing with myself whether or no I would talk openly with Kurtz; but before I could come to any conclusion it occurred to me that my speech or my silence, indeed any action of mine, would be a mere futility. What did it matter what any one knew or ignored? What did it matter who was manager? One gets sometimes such a flash of insight. The essentials of this affair lay deep under the surface, beyond my reach, and beyond my power of meddling.

"Towards the evening of the second day we judged ourselves about eight miles from Kurtz's station. I wanted to push on; but the manager looked grave, and told me the navigation up there was so dangerous that it would be advisable, the sun being very low already, to wait where we were till next morning. Moreover, he pointed out that if the warning to approach cautiously were to be followed, we must approach in daylight—not at dusk, or in the dark. This was sensible enough. Eight miles meant nearly three hours' steaming for us, and I could also see suspicious ripples at the upper end of the reach. Nevertheless, I was annoyed beyond expression at the delay, and most unreasonably, too, since one night more could not matter much after so many months. As we had plenty of wood, and caution was the word, I brought up in the middle of the stream. The reach was narrow, straight, with high sides like a railway cutting. The dusk came gliding into it long before the sun had set. The current ran smooth and swift, but a dumb immobility sat on the banks. The living trees, lashed together by the creepers and every living bush of the undergrowth, might have been changed into stone, even to the slenderest twig, to the lightest leaf. It was not sleep—it seemed unnatural, like a state of trance. Not the faintest sound of any kind could be heard. You looked on amazed, and began to suspect yourself of being deaf—then the night came suddenly, and struck you blind as well. About three in the morning some large fish leaped, and the loud splash made me jump as though a gun had been fired. When the sun rose there was a white fog, very warm and clammy, and more blinding than the night. It did not shift or drive; it was just there, standing all round you like something solid. At eight or nine, perhaps, it lifted as a shutter lifts. We had a glimpse of the towering multitude of trees, of the immense matted jungle, with the blazing little ball of the sun hanging over it—all perfectly still—and then the white shutter came down again, smoothly, as if sliding in greased grooves. I ordered the chain, which we had begun to heave in, to be paid out again. Before it stopped running with a muffled rattle, a cry, a very loud cry, as of infinite desolation, soared slowly in the opaque air. It ceased. A complaining clamor, modulated in savage discords, filled our ears. The sheer unexpectedness of it made my hair stir under my cap. I don't know how it struck the others: to me it seemed as though the mist itself had screamed, so suddenly, and apparently from all sides at once, did this tumultuous and mournful uproar arise. It culminated in a hurried outbreak of almost intolerably excessive shrieking, which stopped short, leaving us stiffened in a variety of silly attitudes, and obstinately listening to the nearly as appalling and excessive silence. 'Good God! What is the meaning—' stammered at my elbow one of the pilgrims,—a little fat man, with sandy hair and red whiskers, who wore side-spring boots, and pink pajamas tucked into his socks. Two others remained open-mouthed a whole minute, then dashed into the little cabin, to rush out incontinently and stand darting scared glances, with Winchesters[44] at 'ready' in their hands. What we could see was just the steamer we were on, her outlines blurred as though she had been on the point of dissolving, and a misty strip of water, perhaps two feet broad, around her—and that was all. The rest of the world was nowhere, as far as our eyes and ears were concerned. Just nowhere. Gone, disappeared; swept off without leaving a whisper or a shadow behind.

"I went forward, and ordered the chain to be hauled in short, so as to be ready to trip the anchor and move the steamboat at once if necessary. 'Will they attack?' whispered an awed voice. 'We will be all butchered in this fog,' murmured another. The faces twitched with the strain, the hands trembled slightly, the eyes forgot to wink. It was very curious to see the contrasts of expressions of the white men and of the black fellows of our crew, who were as much strangers to that part of the river as we, though their homes were only eight hundred miles away. The whites, of course, greatly discomposed, had besides a curious look of being painfully shocked by such an outrageous row. The others had an alert, naturally interested expression; but their faces were essentially quiet, even those of the one or two who grinned as they hauled at the chain. Several exchanged short, grunting phrases, which seemed to settle the matter to their satisfaction. Their headman, a young, broad-chested black, severely draped in dark-blue fringed clothes, with fierce nostrils and his hair all done up artfully in oily ringlets, stood near me. 'Aha!' I said, just for good fellowship's sake. 'Catch 'im,' he snapped, with a bloodshot widening of his eyes and a flash of sharp teeth—'catch 'im. Give 'im to us.' 'To you, eh?' I asked; 'what would you do with them?' 'Eat 'im!' he said, curtly, and, leaning his elbow on the rail, looked out into the fog in a dignified and profoundly pensive attitude. I would no doubt have been properly horrified, had it not occurred to me that he and his chaps must be very hungry: that they must have been growing increasingly hungry for at least this month past. They had been engaged for six months (I don't think a single one of them had any clear idea of time, as we at the end of countless ages have. They still belonged to the beginnings of time —had no inherited experience to teach them as it were), and of course, as long as there was a piece of paper written over in accordance with some farcical law or other made down the river, it didn't enter anybody's head to trouble how they would live. Certainly they had brought with them some rotten hippo-meat, which couldn't have lasted very long, anyway, even if the pilgrims hadn't, in the midst of a shocking hullabaloo, thrown a considerable quantity of it overboard. It looked like a high-handed proceeding; but it was really a case of legitimate self-defense. You can't breathe dead hippo waking, sleeping, and eating, and at the same time keep your precarious grip on existence. Besides that, they had given them every week three pieces of brass wire, each about nine inches long; and the theory was they were to buy their provisions with that currency in river-side villages. You can see how *that* worked. There were either no villages, or the people were hostile, or the director, who like the rest of us fed out of tins, with an occasional old he-goat thrown in, didn't want to stop the steamer for some more or less recondite reason. So, unless they swallowed the wire itself, or made loops of it to snare the fishes with, I don't see what good their extravagant salary could be to them. I must say it was paid with a regularity worthy of a large and honorable trading company. For the rest, the only thing to eat—though it didn't look eatable in the least—I saw in their possession was a few lumps of some stuff like half-cooked dough, of a dirty lavender color, they kept wrapped in leaves, and now and then swallowed a piece of, but so small that it seemed done more for the looks of the thing than for any serious purpose of sustenance. Why in the name of all the gnawing devils of hunger they didn't go for us—they were thirty to five—and have a good tuck-in[45] for once, amazes me now when I think of it. They were big powerful men, with not much capacity to weigh the consequences, with courage, with strength, even yet, though their skins were no longer glossy and their muscles no longer hard. And I saw that something restraining, one of those human secrets that baffle probability, had come into play there. I looked at them with a swift quickening of interest—not because it occurred to me I might be eaten by them before very long, though I own to you that just then I perceived—in a new light, as it were—how unwholesome the pilgrims looked and I hoped, yes, I positively hoped, that my aspect was not so —what shall I say?—so—unappetizing: a touch of fantastic vanity which fitted well with the dream-sensation that pervaded all my days at that time. Perhaps I had a little fever, too. One can't live with one's finger everlastingly on one's pulse. I had often 'a little fever,' or a little touch of other things—the playful paw-strokes of the wilderness, the preliminary trifling before the more serious onslaught which came in due course. Yes; I looked at them as you would on any human being, with a curiosity of their impulses, motives, capacities, weaknesses, when brought to the test of an inexorable physical necessity. Restraint! What possible restraint? Was it superstition, disgust, patience, fear—or some kind of primitive honor? No fear can stand up to hunger, no patience can wear it out, disgust simply does not exist where hunger is; and as to superstition, beliefs, and what you may call principles, they are less than chaff in a breeze. Don't you know the devilry of lingering starvation, its exasperating torment, its black thoughts, its somber and brooding ferocity? Well, I do. It takes a man all his inborn strength to fight hunger properly. It's really easier to face bereavement, dishonor, and the perdition of one's soul—than this kind of prolonged hunger. Sad, but true. And these chaps, too, had no earthly reason for any kind of scruple. Restraint! I would just as soon have expected restraint from a hyena prowling amongst the corpses of a battlefield. But there was the fact facing me—the fact dazzling, to be seen, like the foam on the depth of the sea, like a ripple on an unfathomable enigma, a mystery greater—when I thought of it—than the curious, inexplicable note of desperate grief in this savage clamor that had swept by us on the river-bank, behind the blind whiteness of the fog.

"Two pilgrims were quarreling in hurried whispers as to which bank. 'Left.' 'No, no; how can you? Right, right, of course.' 'It is very serious,' said the manager's voice behind me; 'I would be desolated if anything should happen to Mr. Kurtz before we came up.' I looked at him, and had not the slightest doubt he was sincere. He was just the kind of man who would wish to preserve appearances. That was his restraint. But when he muttered something about going on at once, I did not even take the trouble to answer him. I knew, and he knew, that it was impossible. Were we to let go our hold of the bottom, we would be absolutely in the air—in space. We wouldn't be able to tell where we were going to—whether up or down stream, or across—till we fetched against one bank or the other,—and then we wouldn't know at first which it was. Of course I made no move. I had no mind for a smash-up. You couldn't imagine a more deadly place for a shipwreck. Whether drowned at once or not, we were sure to perish speedily in one way or another. 'I authorize you to take all the risks,' he said, after a short silence. 'I refuse to take any,' I said, shortly; which was just the answer he expected, though its tone might have surprised him. 'Well, I must defer to your judgment. You are captain,' he said, with marked civility. I turned my shoulder to him in sign of my appreciation, and looked into the fog. How long would it last? It was the most hopeless look-out. The approach to this Kurtz grubbing for ivory in the wretched bush was beset by as many dangers as though he had been an enchanted princess sleeping in a fabulous castle. 'Will they attack, do you think?' asked the manager, in a confidential tone.

"I did not think they would attack, for several obvious reasons. The thick fog was one. If they left the bank in their canoes they would get lost in it, as we would be if we attempted to move. Still, I had also judged the jungle of both banks quite impenetrable—and yet eyes were in it, eyes that had seen us. The river-side bushes were certainly very thick; but the undergrowth behind was evidently penetrable. However, during the short lift I had seen no canoes anywhere in the reach—certainly not abreast of the steamer. But what made the idea of attack inconceivable to me was the nature of the noise—of the cries we had heard. They had not the fierce character boding immediate hostile intention. Unexpected, wild, and violent as they had been, they had given me an irresistible impression of sorrow. The glimpse of the steamboat had for some reason filled those savages with unrestrained grief. The danger, if any, I expounded, was from our proximity to a great human passion let loose. Even extreme grief may ultimately vent itself in violence —but more generally takes the form of apathy. . . .

"You should have seen the pilgrims stare! They had no heart to grin, or even to revile me: but I believe they thought me gone mad—with fright, maybe. I delivered a regular lecture. My dear boys, it was no good bothering. Keep a look-out? Well, you may guess I watched the fog for the signs of lifting as a cat watches a mouse; but for anything else our eyes were of no more use to us than if we had been buried miles deep in a heap of cotton-wool. It felt like it, too— choking, warm, stifling. Besides, all I said, though it sounded extravagant, was absolutely true to fact. What we afterwards alluded to as an attack was really an attempt at repulse. The action was very far from being aggressive—it was not even defensive, in the usual sense: it was undertaken under the stress of desperation, and in its essence was purely protective.

"It developed itself, I should say, two hours after the fog lifted, and its commencement was at a spot, roughly speaking, about a mile and a half below Kurtz's station. We had just floundered and flopped round a bend, when I saw an islet, a mere grassy hummock of bright green, in the middle of the stream. It was the only thing of the kind; but as we opened the reach more, I perceived it was the head of a long sandbank, or rather of a chain of shallow patches stretching down the middle of the river. They were discolored, just awash, and the whole lot was seen just under the water, exactly as a man's backbone is seen running down the middle of his back under the skin. Now, as far as I did see, I could go to the right or to the left of this. I didn't know either channel, of course. The banks looked pretty well alike, the depth appeared the same; but as I had been informed the station was on the west side, I naturally headed for the western passage.

"No sooner had we fairly entered it than I became aware it was much narrower than I had supposed. To the left of us there was the long uninterrupted shoal, and to the right a high, steep bank heavily overgrown with bushes. Above the bush the trees stood in serried ranks. The twigs overhung the current thickly, and from distance to distance a large limb of some tree projected rigidly over the stream. It was then well on in the afternoon, the face of the forest was gloomy, and a broad strip of shadow had already fallen on the water. In this shadow we steamed up—very slowly, as you may imagine. I sheered her well inshore—the water being deepest near the bank, as the sounding-pole informed me.

"One of my hungry and forbearing friends was sounding[46] in the bows just below me. This steamboat was exactly like a decked scow. On the deck, there were two little teakwood houses, with doors and windows. The boiler was in the fore-end, and the machinery right astern. Over the whole there was a light roof, supported on stanchions. The funnel projected through that roof, and in front of the funnel a small cabin built of light planks served for a pilot-house. It contained a couch, two camp-stools, a loaded Martini-Henry[47] leaning in one corner, a tiny table, and the steering-wheel. It had a wide door in front and a broad shutter at each side. All these were always thrown open, of course. I spent my days perched up there on the extreme fore-end of that roof, before the door. At night I slept, or tried to, on the couch. An athletic black belonging to some coast tribe, and educated by my poor predecessor, was the helmsman. He sported a pair of brass earrings, wore a blue cloth wrapper from the waist to the ankles, and thought all the world of himself. He was the most unstable kind of fool I had ever seen. He steered with no end of a swagger while you were by; but if he lost sight of you, he became instantly the prey of an abject funk, and would let that cripple of a steamboat get the upper hand of him in a minute.

"I was looking down at the sounding-pole, and feeling much annoyed to see at each try a little more of it stick out of that river, when I saw my poleman give up the business suddenly, and stretch himself flat on the deck, without even taking the trouble to haul his pole in. He kept hold on it though, and it trailed in the water. At the same time the fireman, whom I could also see below me, sat down abruptly before his furnace and ducked his head. I was amazed. Then I had to look at the river mighty quick, because there was a snag in the fairway. Sticks, little sticks, were flying about—thick: they were whizzing before my nose, dropping below me, striking behind me against my pilot-house. All this time the river, the shore, the woods, were very quiet—perfectly quiet. I could only hear the heavy splashing thump of the stern-wheel and the patter of these things. We cleared the snag clumsily. Arrows, by Jove! We were being shot at! I stepped in quickly to close the shutter on the land-side. That fool-helmsman, his hands on the spokes, was lifting his knees high, stamping his feet, champing his mouth, like a reined-in horse. Confound him! And we were staggering within ten feet of the bank. I had to lean right out to swing the heavy shutter, and I saw a face amongst the leaves on the level with my own, looking at me very fierce and steady; and then suddenly, as though a veil had been removed from my eyes, I made out, deep in the tangled gloom, naked breasts, arms, legs, glaring eyes,—the bush was swarming with human limbs in movement, glistening, of bronze color. The twigs shook, swayed, and rustled, the arrows flew out of them, and then the shutter came to. 'Steer her straight,' I said to the helmsman. He held his head rigid, face forward; but his eyes rolled, he kept on lifting and setting down his feet gently, his mouth foamed a little. 'Keep quiet!' I said in a fury. I might just as well have ordered a tree not to sway in the wind. I darted out. Below me there was a great scuffle of feet on the iron deck; confused exclamations; a voice screamed, 'Can you turn back?' I caught sight of a V-shaped ripple on the water ahead. What? Another snag! A fusillade burst out under my feet. The pilgrims had opened with their Winchesters, and were simply squirting lead into that bush. A deuce of a lot of smoke came up and drove slowly forward. I swore at it. Now I couldn't see the ripple or the snag either. I stood in the doorway, peering, and the arrows came in swarms. They might have been poisoned, but they looked as though they wouldn't kill a cat. The bush began to howl. Our wood-cutters raised a warlike whoop; the report of a rifle just at my back deafened me. I glanced over my shoulder, and the pilot-house was yet full of noise and smoke when I made a dash at the wheel. The fool-nigger had dropped everything, to throw the shutter open and let off[48] that Martini-Henry. He stood before the wide opening, glaring, and I yelled at him to come back, while I straightened the sudden twist out of that steamboat. There was no room to turn even if I had wanted to, the snag was somewhere very near ahead in that confounded smoke, there was no time to lose, so I just crowded her into the bank—right into the bank, where I knew the water was deep.

"We tore slowly along the overhanging bushes in a whirl of broken twigs and flying leaves. The fusillade below stopped short, as I had foreseen it would when the squirts got empty. I threw my head back to a glinting whizz that traversed the pilot-house, in at one shutter-hole and out at the other. Looking past that mad helmsman, who was shaking the empty rifle and yelling at the shore, I saw vague forms of men running bent double, leaping, gliding, distinct, incomplete, evanescent. Something big appeared in the air before the shutter, the rifle went overboard, and the man stepped back swiftly, looked at me over his shoulder in an extraordinary, profound, familiar manner, and fell upon my feet. The side of his head hit the wheel twice, and the end of what appeared a long cane clattered round and knocked over a little camp-stool. It looked as though after wrenching that thing from somebody ashore he had lost his balance in the effort. The thin smoke had blown away, we were clear of the snag, and looking ahead I could see that in another hundred yards or so I would be free to sheer off, away from the bank; but my feet felt so very warm and wet that I had to look down. The man had rolled on his back and stared straight up at me; both his hands clutched that cane. It was the shaft of a spear that, either thrown or lunged through the opening, had caught him in the side just below the ribs; the blade had gone in out of sight, after making a frightful gash; my shoes were full; a pool of blood lay very still, gleaming dark-red under the wheel; his eyes shone with an amazing luster. The fusillade burst out again. He looked at me anxiously, gripping the spear like something precious, with an air of being afraid I would try to take it away from him. I had to make an effort to free my eyes from his gaze and attend to steering. With one hand I felt above my head for the line of the steam whistle, and jerked out screech after screech hurriedly. The tumult of angry and warlike yells was checked instantly, and then from the depths of the woods went out such a tremulous and prolonged wail of mournful fear and utter despair as may be imagined to follow the flight of the last hope from the earth. There was a great commotion in the bush; the shower of arrows stopped, a few dropping shots rang out sharply—then silence, in which the languid beat of the stern-wheel came plainly to my ears. I put the helm hard a-starboard at the moment when the pilgrim in pink pajamas, very hot and agitated, appeared in the doorway. 'The manager sends me—' he began in an official tone, and stopped short. 'Good God!' he said, glaring at the wounded man.

"We two whites stood over him, and his lustrous and inquiring glance enveloped us both. I declare it looked as though he would presently put to us some question in an understandable language; but he died without uttering a sound, without moving a limb, without twitching a muscle. Only in the very last moment, as though in response to some sign we could not see, to some whisper we could not hear, he frowned heavily, and that frown gave to his black death-mask an inconceivably somber, brooding, and menacing expression. The luster of inquiring glance faded swiftly into vacant glassiness. 'Can you steer?' I asked the agent eagerly. He looked very dubious; but I made a grab at his arm, and he understood at once I meant him to steer whether or no. To tell you the truth, I was morbidly anxious to change my shoes and socks. 'He is dead,' murmured the fellow, immensely impressed. 'No doubt about it,' said I, tugging like mad at the shoe-laces. 'And by the way, I suppose Mr. Kurtz is dead as well by this time.'

"For the moment that was the dominant thought. There was a sense of extreme disappointment, as though I had found out I had been striving after something altogether without a substance. I couldn't have been more disgusted if I had traveled all this way for the sole purpose of talking with Mr. Kurtz. Talking with . . . I flung one shoe overboard, and became aware that that was exactly what I had been looking forward to—a talk with Kurtz. I made the strange discovery that I had never imagined him as doing, you know, but as discoursing. I didn't say to myself, 'Now I will never see him,' or 'Now I will never shake him by the hand,' but, 'Now I will never hear him.' The man presented himself as a voice. Not of course that I did not connect him with some sort of action. Hadn't I been told in all the tones of jealousy and admiration that he had collected, bartered, swindled, or stolen more ivory than all the other agents together? That was not the point. The point was in his being a gifted creature, and that of all his gifts the one that stood out preëminently, that carried with it a sense of real presence, was his ability to talk, his words—the gift of expression, the bewildering, the illuminating, the most exalted and the most contemptible, the pulsating stream of light, or the deceitful flow from the heart of an impenetrable darkness.

"The other shoe went flying unto the devil-god of that river. I thought, by Jove! it's all over. We are too late; he has vanished—the gift has vanished, by means of some spear, arrow, or club. I will never hear that chap speak after all,—and my sorrow had a startling extravagance of emotion, even such as I had noticed in the howling sorrow of these savages in the bush. I couldn't have felt more lonely desolation somehow, had I been robbed of a belief or had missed my destiny in life. . . . Why do you sigh in this beastly way, somebody? Absurd? Well, absurd. Good Lord! musn't a man ever—Here, give me some tobacco." . . .

There was a pause of profound stillness, then a match flared, and Marlow's lean face appeared, worn, hollow, with downward folds and drooped eyelids, with an aspect of concentrated attention; and as he took vigorous draws at his pipe, it seemed to retreat and advance out of the night in the regular flicker of the tiny flame. The match went out.

"Absurd!" he cried. "This is the worst of trying to tell. . . . Here you all are, each moored with two good addresses, like a hulk with two anchors, a butcher round one corner, a policeman round another, excellent appetites, and temperature normal—you hear—normal from year's end to year's end. And you say, Absurd! Absurd be—exploded! Absurd! My dear boys, what can you expect from a man who out of sheer nervousness had just flung overboard a pair of new shoes! Now I think of it, it is amazing I did not shed tears. I am, upon the whole, proud of my fortitude. I was cut to the quick at the idea of having lost the inestimable privilege of listening to the gifted Kurtz. Of course I was wrong. The privilege was waiting for me. Oh, yes, I heard more than enough. And I was right, too. A voice. He was very little more than a voice. And I heard—him—it—this voice—

other voices— all of them were so little more than voices—and the memory of that time itself lingers around me, impalpable, like a dying vibration of one immense jabber, silly, atrocious, sordid, savage, or simply mean, without any kind of sense. Voices, voices—even the girl herself—now—"

He was silent for a long time.

"I laid the ghost of his gifts at last with a lie," he began, suddenly. "Girl! What? Did I mention a girl? Oh, she is out of it—completely. They—the women I mean—are out of it—should be out of it. We must help them to stay in that beautiful world of their own, lest ours gets worse. Oh, she had to be out of it. You should have heard the disinterred body of Mr. Kurtz saying, 'My Intended.' You would have perceived directly then how completely she was out of it. And the lofty frontal bone of Mr. Kurtz! They say the hair goes on growing sometimes, but this —ah—specimen, was impressively bald. The wilderness had patted him on the head, and, behold, it was like a ball—an ivory ball; it had caressed him, and—lo! —he had withered; it had taken him, loved him, embraced him, got into his veins, consumed his flesh, and sealed his soul to its own by the inconceivable ceremonies of some devilish initiation. He was its spoiled and pampered favorite. Ivory? I should think so. Heaps of it, stacks of it. The old mud shanty was bursting with it. You would think there was not a single tusk left either above or below the ground in the whole country. 'Mostly fossil,' the manager had remarked, disparagingly. It was no more fossil than I am; but they call it fossil when it is dug up. It appears these niggers do bury the tusks sometimes—but evidently they couldn't bury this parcel deep enough to save the gifted Mr. Kurtz from his fate. We filled the steamboat with it, and had to pile a lot on the deck. Thus he could see and enjoy as long as he could see, because the appreciation of this favor had remained with him to the last. You should have heard him say, 'My ivory.' Oh, yes, I heard him. 'My Intended, my ivory, my station, my river, my—' everything belonged to him. It made me hold my breath in expectation of hearing the wilderness burst into a prodigious peal of laughter that would shake the fixed stars in their places. Everything belonged to him—but that was a trifle. The thing was to know what he belonged to, how many powers of darkness claimed him for their own. That was the reflection that made you creepy all over. It was impossible—it was not good for one either—trying to imagine. He had taken a high seat amongst the devils of the land—I mean literally. You can't understand. How could you?—with solid pavement under your feet, surrounded by kind neighbors ready to cheer you or to fall on you, stepping delicately between the butcher and the policeman, in the holy terror of scandal and gallows and lunatic asylums—how can you imagine what particular region of the first ages a man's untrammeled feet may take him into by the way of solitude—utter solitude without a policeman—by the way of silence —utter silence, where no warning voice of a kind neighbor can be heard whispering of public opinion? These little things make all the great difference. When they are gone you must fall back upon your own innate strength, upon your own capacity for faithfulness. Of course you may be too much of a fool to go wrong —too dull even to know you are being assaulted by the powers of darkness. I take it, no fool ever made a bargain for his soul with the devil: the fool is too much of a fool, or the devil too much of a devil—I don't know which. Or you may be such a thunderingly exalted creature as to be altogether deaf and blind to anything but heavenly sights and sounds. Then the earth for you is only a standing place —and whether to be like this is your loss or your gain I won't pretend to say. But most of us are neither one nor the other. The earth for us is a place to live in, where we must put up with sights, with sounds, with smells, too, by Jove!—breathe dead hippo, so to speak, and not be contaminated. And there, don't you see? your strength comes in, the faith in your ability for the digging of unostentatious holes to bury the stuff in—your power of devotion, not to yourself, but to an obscure, back-breaking business. And that's difficult enough. Mind, I am not trying to excuse or even explain—I am trying to account to myself for—for—Mr. Kurtz— for the shade of Mr. Kurtz. This initiated wraith from the back of Nowhere honored me with its amazing confidence before it vanished altogether. This was because it could speak English to me. The original Kurtz had been educated partly in England, and—as he was good enough to say himself—his sympathies were in the right place. His mother was half-English, his father was half-French. All Europe contributed to the making of Kurtz; and by and by I learned that, most appropriately, the International Society for the Suppression of Savage Customs had intrusted him with the making of a report, for its future guidance. And he had written it, too. I've seen it. I've read it. It was eloquent, vibrating with eloquence, but too high-strung, I think. Seventeen pages of close writing he had found time for! But this must have been before his—let us say—nerves, went wrong, and caused him to preside at certain midnight dances ending with unspeakable rites, which—as far as I reluctantly gathered from what I heard at various times—were offered up to him—do you understand?—to Mr. Kurtz himself. But it was a beautiful piece of writing. The opening paragraph, however, in the light of later information, strikes me now as ominous. He began with the argument that we whites, from the point of development we had arrived at, 'must necessarily appear to them [savages] in the nature of supernatural beings—we approach them with the might as of a deity,' and so on, and so on. 'By the simple exercise of our will we can exert a power for good practically unbounded,' etc. etc. From that point he soared and took me with him. The peroration was magnificent, though difficult to remember, you know. It gave me the notion of an exotic Immensity ruled by an august Benevolence. It made me tingle with enthusiasm. This was the unbounded power of eloquence— of words—of burning noble words. There were no practical hints to interrupt the magic current of phrases, unless a kind of note at the foot of the last page, scrawled evidently much later, in an unsteady hand, may be regarded as the exposition of a method. It was very simple, and at the end of that moving appeal to every altruistic sentiment it blazed at you, luminous and terrifying, like a flash of lightning in a serene sky: 'Exterminate all the brutes!' The curious part was that he had apparently forgotten all about the valuable postscriptum, because, later on, when he in a sense came to himself, he repeatedly entreated me to take good care of 'my pamphlet' (he called it), as it was sure to have in the future a good influence upon his career. I had full information about all these things, and, besides, as it turned out, I was to have the care of his memory. I've done enough for it to give me the indisputable right to lay it, if I choose, for an everlasting rest in the dustbin of progress, amongst all the sweepings and, figuratively speaking, all the dead cats of civilization. But then, you see, I can't choose. He won't be forgotten. Whatever he was, he was not common. He had the power to charm or frighten rudimentary souls into an aggravated witch-dance in his honor; he could also fill the small souls of the pilgrims with bitter misgivings: he had one devoted friend at least, and he had conquered one soul in the world that was neither rudimentary nor tainted with self-seeking. No; I can't forget him, though I am not prepared to affirm the fellow was exactly worth the life we lost in getting to him. I missed my late helmsman awfully,—I missed him even while his body was still lying in the pilot-house. Perhaps you will think it passing strange this regret for a savage who was no more account than a grain of sand in a black Sahara. Well, don't you see, he had done something, he had steered; for months I had him at my back—a help—an instrument. It was a kind of partnership. He steered for me—I had to look after him, I worried about his deficiencies, and thus a subtle bond had been created, of which I only became aware when it was suddenly broken. And the intimate profundity of that look he gave me when he received his hurt remains to this day in my memory—like a claim of distant kinship affirmed in a supreme moment.

"Poor fool! If he had only left that shutter alone. He had no restraint, no restraint—just like Kurtz—a tree swayed by the wind. As soon as I had put on a dry pair of slippers, I dragged him out, after first jerking the spear out of his side, which operation I confess I performed with my eyes shut tight. His heels leaped together over the little door-step; his shoulders were pressed to my breast; I hugged him from behind desperately. Oh! he was heavy, heavy; heavier than any man on earth, I should imagine. Then without more ado I tipped him overboard. The current snatched him as though he had been a wisp of grass, and I saw the body roll over twice before I lost sight of it forever. All the pilgrims and the manager were then congregated on the awning-deck about the pilot-house, chattering at each other like a flock of excited magpies, and there was a scandalized murmur at my heartless promptitude. What they wanted to keep that body hanging about for I can't guess. Embalm it, maybe. But I had also heard another, and a very ominous, murmur on the deck below. My friends the wood-cutters were likewise scandalized, and with a better show of reason—though I admit that the reason itself was quite inadmissible. Oh, quite! I had made up my mind that if my late helmsman was to be eaten, the fishes alone should have him. He had been a very second-rate helmsman while alive, but now he was dead he might have become a first-class temptation, and possibly cause some startling trouble. Besides, I was anxious to take the wheel, the man in pink pajamas showing himself a hopeless duffer at the business.

"This I did directly the simple funeral was over. We were going half-speed, keeping right in the middle of the stream, and I listened to the talk about me. They had given up Kurtz, they had given up the station; Kurtz was dead, and the station had been burnt—and so on—and so on. The red-haired pilgrim was beside himself with the thought that at least this poor Kurtz had been properly avenged. 'Say!' We must have made a glorious slaughter of them in the bush. Eh? What do you think? Say?' He positively danced, the bloodthirsty little gingery beggar.[49] And he had nearly fainted when he saw the wounded man! I could not help saying, 'You made a glorious lot of smoke, anyhow.' I had seen, from the way the tops of the bushes rustled and flew, that almost all the shots had gone too high. You can't hit anything unless you take aim and fire from the shoulder; but these chaps fired from the hip with their eyes shut. The retreat, I maintained—and I was right—was caused by the screeching of the steam-whistle. Upon this they forgot Kurtz, and began to howl at me with indignant protests.

"The manager stood by the wheel murmuring confidentially about the necessity of getting well away down the river before dark at all events, when I saw in the distance a clearing on the river-side and the outlines of some sort of building. 'What's this?' I asked. He clapped his hands in wonder. 'The station!' he cried. I edged in at once, still going half-speed.

"Through my glasses I saw the slope of a hill interspersed with rare trees and perfectly free from undergrowth. A long decaying building on the summit was half buried in the high grass; the large hole in the peaked roof gaped black from afar; the jungle and the woods made a background. There was no enclosure or fence of any kind; but there had been one apparently, for near the house half-a-dozen slim posts remained in a row, roughly trimmed, and with their upper ends ornamented with round carved balls. The rails, or whatever there had been between, had disappeared. Of course the forest surrounded all that. The river-bank was clear, and on the water-side I saw a white man under a hat like a cartwheel beckoning persistently with his whole arm. Examining the edge of the forest above and below, I was almost certain I could see movements—human forms gliding here and there. I steamed past prudently, then stopped the engines and let her drift down. The man on the shore began to shout, urging us to land. 'We have been attacked,' screamed the manager. 'I know—I know. It's all right,' yelled back the other, as cheerful as you please. 'Come along. It's all right. I am glad.'

"His aspect reminded me of something I had seen—something funny I had seen somewhere. As I maneuvered to get alongside, I was asking myself, 'What does this fellow look like? Suddenly I got it. He looked like a harlequin. His clothes had been made of some stuff that was brown holland probably, but it was covered with patches all over, with bright patches, blue, red and yellow,—patches on the back, patches on the front, patches on elbows, on knees; colored binding around his jacket, scarlet edging at the bottom of his trousers; and the sunshine made him look extremely gay and wonderfully neat withal, because you could see how beautifully all this patching had been done. A beardless, boyish face, very fair, no features to speak of, nose peeling, little blue eyes, smiles and frowns chasing each other over that open countenance like sunshine and shadow on a windswept plain. 'Look out, captain!' he cried; 'there's a snag lodged in here last night.' 'What! Another snag?' I confess I swore shamefully. I had nearly holed my cripple, to finish off that charming trip. The harlequin on the bank turned his little pug-nose up to me. 'You English?' he asked, all smiles. 'Are you?' I shouted from the wheel. The smiles vanished, and he shook his head as if sorry for my disappointment. Then he brightened up. 'Never mind!' he cried, encouragingly. 'Are we in time?' I asked. 'He is up there,' he replied, with a toss of the head up the hill, and becoming gloomy all of a sudden. His face was like the autumn sky, overcast one moment and bright the next.

"When the manager, escorted by the pilgrims, all of them armed to the teeth, had gone to the house this chap came on board. 'I say, I don't like this. These natives are in the bush,' I said. He assured me earnestly it was all right. 'They are simple people,' he added; 'well, I am glad you came. It took me all my time to keep them off.' 'But you said it was all right,' I cried. 'Oh, they meant no harm,' he said; and as I stared he corrected himself, 'Not exactly.' Then vivaciously, 'My faith, your pilot-house wants a clean-up!' In the next breath he advised me to keep enough steam on the boiler to blow the whistle in case of any trouble. 'One good screech will do more for you than all your rifles. They are simple people,' he repeated. He rattled away at such a rate he quite overwhelmed me. He seemed to be trying to make up for lots of silence, and actually hinted, laughing, that such was the case. 'Don't you talk with Mr. Kurtz?' I said. 'You don't talk with that man —you listen to him,' he exclaimed with severe exaltation. 'But now—' He waved his arm, and in the twinkling of an eye was in the uttermost depths of despondency. In a moment he came up again with a jump, possessed himself of both my hands, shook them continuously, while he gabbed: 'Brother sailor . . . honor . . . pleasure . . . delight . . . introduce myself . . . Russian . . . son of an arch-priest . . . Government of Tambov. . . . What? Tobacco! English tobacco; the excellent English tobacco! Now, that's brotherly. Smoke? Where's a sailor that does not smoke?'

"The pipe soothed him, and gradually I made out he had run away from school, had gone to sea in a Russian ship; ran away again; served some time in English ships; was now reconciled with the arch-priest. He made a point of that. 'But when one is young one must see things, gather experience, ideas; enlarge the mind.' 'Here!' I interrupted. 'You can never tell! Here I met Mr. Kurtz,' he said, youthfully solemn and reproachful. I held my tongue after that. It appears he had persuaded a Dutch trading house on the coast to fit him out with stores and goods, and had started for the interior with a light heart, and no more idea of what would happen to him than a baby. He had been wandering about that river for nearly two years alone, cut off from everybody and everything. 'I am not so young as I look. I am twenty-five,' he said. 'At first old Van Shuyten would tell me to go to the devil,' he narrated with keen enjoyment; 'but I stuck to him, and talked and talked, till at last he got afraid I would talk the hind-leg off his favorite dog, so he gave me some cheap things and a few guns, and told me he hoped he would never see my face again. Good old Dutchman, Van Shuyten. I've sent him one small lot of ivory a year ago, so that he can't call me a little thief when I get back. I hope he got it. And for the rest I don't care. I had some wood stacked for you. That was my old house. Did you see?'

"I gave him Towson's book. He made as though he would kiss me, but restrained himself. 'The only book I had left, and I thought I had lost it,' he said, looking at it ecstatically. 'So many accidents happen to a man going about alone, you know. Canoes get upset sometimes—and sometimes you've got to clear out so quick when the people get angry.' He thumbed the pages. 'You made notes in Russian?' I asked. He nodded. 'I thought they were written in cipher,' I said. He laughed, then became serious. 'I had lots of trouble to keep these people off,' he said. 'Did they want to kill you?' I asked. 'Oh, no!' he cried, and checked himself. 'Why did they attack us?' I pursued. He hesitated, then said shamefacedly, 'They don't want him to go.' 'Don't they?' I said curiously. He nodded a nod full of mystery and wisdom. 'I tell you,' he cried, 'this man has enlarged my mind.' He opened his arms wide, staring at me with his little blue eyes that were perfectly round."

3

"I looked at him, lost in astonishment. There he was before me, in motley, as though he had absconded from a troupe of mimes, enthusiastic, fabulous. His very existence was improbable, inexplicable, and altogether bewildering. He was an insoluble problem. It was inconceivable how he had existed, how he had succeeded in getting so far, how he had managed to remain—why he did not instantly disappear. 'I went a little farther,' he said, 'then still a little farther—till I had gone so far that I don't know how I'll ever get back. Never mind. Plenty time. I can manage. You take Kurtz away quick—quick—I tell you.' The glamour of youth enveloped his parti-colored rags, his destitution, his loneliness, the essential desolation of his futile wanderings. For months—for years—his life hadn't been worth a day's purchase; and there he was gallantly, thoughtlessly alive, to all appearance indestructible solely by the virtue of his few years and of his unreflecting audacity. I was seduced into something like admiration—like envy. Glamour urged him on, glamour kept him unscathed. He surely wanted nothing from the wilderness but space to breathe in and to push on through. His need was to exist, and to move onwards at the greatest possible risk, and with a maximum of privation. If the absolutely pure, uncalculating, unpractical spirit of adventure had ever ruled a human being, it ruled this be-patched youth. I almost envied him the possession of this modest and clear flame. It seemed to have consumed all thought of self so completely, that even while he was talking to you, you forgot that it was he—the man before your eyes—who had gone through these things. I did not envy him his devotion to Kurtz, though. He had not meditated over it. It came to him and he accepted it with a sort of eager fatalism. I must say that to me it appeared about the most dangerous thing in every way he had come upon so far.

"They had come together unavoidably, like two ships becalmed near each other, and lay rubbing sides at last. I suppose Kurtz wanted an audience, because on a certain occasion, when encamped in the forest, they had talked all night, or more probably Kurtz had talked. 'We talked of everything,' he said, quite transported at the recollection. 'I forgot there was such a thing as sleep. The night did not seem to last an hour. Everything! Everything! . . . Of love, too.' 'Ah, he talked to you of love!' I said, much amused. 'It isn't what you think' he cried, almost passionately. 'It was in general. He made me see things—things.'

"He threw his arms up. We were on deck at the time, and the headman of my woodcutters, lounging near by, turned upon him his heavy and glittering eyes. I looked around, and I don't know why, but I assure you that never, never before, did this land, this river, this jungle, the very arch of this blazing sky, appear to me so hopeless and so dark, so impenetrable to human thought, so pitiless to human weakness. 'And ever since, you have been with him, of course?' I said.

"On the contrary. It appears their intercourse had been very much broken by various causes. He had, as he informed me proudly, managed to nurse Kurtz through two illnesses (he alluded to it as you would to some risky feat), but as a rule Kurtz wandered alone far in the depths of the forest. 'Very often coming to this station, I had to wait days and days before he would turn up,' he said. 'Ah, it was worth waiting for!—sometimes.' 'What was he doing? exploring or what?' I asked. 'Oh, yes, of course'; he had discovered lots of villages, a lake, too—he did not know exactly in what direction; it was dangerous to inquire too much—but mostly his expeditions had been for ivory. 'But he had no goods to trade with by that time,' I objected. 'There's a good lot of cartridges left even yet,' he answered, looking away. 'To speak plainly, he raided the country,' I said. He nodded. 'Not alone, surely!' He muttered something about the villages round that lake. 'Kurtz got the tribe to follow him, did he?' I suggested. He fidgeted a little. 'They adored him,' he said. The tone of these words was so extraordinary that I looked at him searchingly. It was curious to see his mingled eagerness and reluctance to speak of Kurtz. The man filled his life, occupied his thoughts, swayed his emotions. 'What can you expect?' he burst out; 'he came to them with thunder and lightning, you know—and they had never seen anything like it—and very terrible. He could be very terrible. You can't judge Mr. Kurtz as you would an ordinary man. No, no, no! Now—just to give you an idea—I don't mind telling you he wanted to shoot me, too, one day—but I don't judge him.' 'Shoot you!' I cried. 'What for?' 'Well, I had a small lot of ivory the chief of that village near my house gave me. You see I used to shoot game for them. Well, he wanted it, and wouldn't hear reason. He declared he would shoot me unless I gave him the ivory and then cleared out of the country, because he could do so, and had a fancy for it, and there was nothing on earth to prevent him killing whom he jolly well pleased. And it was true, too. I gave him the ivory. What did I care! But I didn't clear out. No, no, I couldn't leave him. I had to be careful, of course, till we got friendly again for a time. He had his second illness then. Afterwards I had to keep out of the way; but I didn't mind. He was living for the most part in those villages on the lake. When he came down to the river, sometimes he would take to me, and sometimes it was better for me to be careful. This man suffered too much. He hated all this, and somehow he couldn't get away. When I had a chance I begged him to try and leave while there was time; I offered to go back with him. And he would say yes, and then he would remain; go off on another ivory hunt; disappear for weeks; forget himself amongst these people—forget himself—you know.' 'Why! he's mad,' I said. He protested indignantly. Mr. Kurtz couldn't be mad. If I had heard him talk, only two days ago, I wouldn't dare hint at such a thing. . . . I had taken up my binoculars while we talked, and was looking at the shore, sweeping the limit of the forest at each side and at the back of the house. The consciousness of there

being people in that bush, so silent, so quiet—as silent and quiet as the ruined
house on the hill—made me uneasy. There was no sign on the face of nature of
this amazing tale that was not so much told as suggested to me in desolate exclamations, completed by shrugs, in interrupted phrases, in hints ending in deep sighs.
The woods were unmoved, like a mask—heavy, like the closed door of a prison
—they looked with their air of hidden knowledge, of patient expectation, of
unapproachable silence. The Russian was explaining to me that it was only lately
that Mr. Kurtz had come down to the river, bringing along with him all the fighting
men of that lake tribe. He had been absent for several months—getting himself
adored, I suppose—and had come down unexpectedly, with the intention to all
appearance of making a raid either across the river or down stream. Evidently the
appetite for more ivory had got the better of the—what shall I say?—less material
aspirations. However, he had got much worse suddenly. 'I heard he was lying
helpless, and so I came up—took my chance,' said the Russian. 'Oh, he is bad, very
bad.' I directed my glass to the house. There were no signs of life, but there was
the ruined roof, the long mud wall peeping above the grass, with three little square
window-holes, no two of the same size; all this brought within reach of my hand,
as it were. And then I made a brusque movement, and one of the remaining posts
of that vanished fence leaped up in the field of my glass. You remember I told you
I had been struck at the distance by certain attempts at ornamentation, rather
remarkable in the ruinous aspect of the place. Now I had suddenly a nearer view,
and its first result was to make me throw my head back as if before a blow. Then
I went carefully from post to post with my glass, and I saw my mistake. These round
knobs were not ornamental but symbolic; they were expressive and puzzling,
striking and disturbing—food for thought and also for vultures if there had been
any looking down from the sky; but at all events for such ants as were industrious
enough to ascend the pole. They would have been even more impressive, those
heads on the stakes, if their faces had not been turned to the house. Only one, the
first I had made out, was facing my way. I was not so shocked as you may think.
The start back I had given was really nothing but a movement of surprise. I had
expected to see a knob of wood there, you know. I returned deliberately to the
first I had seen—and there it was, black, dried, sunken, with closed eyelids,—a
head that seemed to sleep at the top of that pole, and with the shrunken dry lips
showing a narrow white line of the teeth, was smiling, too, smiling continuously
at some endless and jocose dream of that eternal slumber.

"I am not disclosing any trade secrets. In fact, the manager said afterwards
that Mr. Kurtz's methods had ruined the district. I have no opinion on that point,
but I want you clearly to understand that there was nothing exactly profitable in
these heads being there. They only showed that Mr. Kurtz lacked restraint in the
gratification of his various lusts, that there was something wanting in him—some
small matter which, when the pressing need arose, could not be found under his
magnificent eloquence. Whether he knew of this deficiency himself I can't say. I
think the knowledge came to him at last—only at the very last. But the wilderness
had found him out early, and had taken on him a terrible vengeance for the
fantastic invasion. I think it had whispered to him things about himself which he

did not know, things of which he had no conception till he took counsel with this great solitude—and the whisper had proved irresistibly fascinating. It echoed loudly within him because he was hollow at the core. . . . I put down the glass, and the head that had appeared near enough to be spoken to seemed at once to have leaped away from me into inaccessible distance.

"The admirer of Mr. Kurtz was a bit crestfallen. In a hurried indistinct voice he began to assure me he had not dared to take these—say, symbols—down. He was not afraid of the natives; they would not stir till Mr. Kurtz gave the word. His ascendancy was extraordinary. The camps of these people surrounded the place, and the chiefs came every day to see him. They would crawl. . . . 'I don't want to know anything of the ceremonies used when approaching Mr. Kurtz,' I shouted. Curious, this feeling that came over me that such details would be more intolerable than those heads drying on the stakes under Mr. Kurtz's windows. After all, that was only a savage sight, while I seemed at one bound to have been transported into some lightless region of subtle horrors, where pure, uncomplicated savagery was a positive relief, being something that had a right to exist—obviously—in the sunshine. The young man looked at me with surprise. I suppose it did not occur to him that Mr. Kurtz was no idol of mine. He forgot I hadn't heard any of these splendid monologues on, what was it? on love, justice, conduct of life—or what not. If it had come to crawling before Mr. Kurtz, he crawled as much as the veriest savage of them all. I had no idea of the conditions, he said: these heads were the heads of rebels. I shocked him excessively by laughing. Rebels! What would be the next definition I was to hear? There had been enemies, criminals, workers— and these were rebels. Those rebellious heads looked very subdued to me on their sticks. 'You don't know how such a life tries a man like Kurtz,' cried Kurtz's last disciple. 'Well, and you?' I said. 'I! I! I am a simple man. I have no great thoughts. I want nothing from anybody. How can you compare me to . . . ?' His feelings were too much for speech, and suddenly he broke down. 'I don't understand,' he groaned, 'I've been doing my best to keep him alive and that's enough. I had no hand in all this. I have no abilities. There hasn't been a drop of medicine or a mouthful of invalid food for months here. He was shamefully abandoned. A man like this, with such ideas. Shamefully! Shamefully! I—I—haven't slept for the last ten nights. . . .'

"His voice lost itself in the calm of the evening. The long shadows of the forest had slipped downhill while we talked, had gone far beyond the ruined hovel, beyond the symbolic row of stakes. All this was in the gloom, while we down there were yet in the sunshine, and the stretch of the river abreast of the clearing glittered in a still and dazzling splendor, with a murky and overshadowed bend above and below. Not a living soul was seen on the shore. The bushes did not rustle.

"Suddenly round the corner of the house a group of men appeared, as though they had come up from the ground. They waded waist-deep in the grass, in a compact body, bearing an improvised stretcher in their midst. Instantly, in the emptiness of the landscape, a cry arose whose shrillness pierced the still air like a sharp arrow flying straight to the very heart of the land; and, as if by enchantment, streams of human beings—of naked human beings—with spears in their hands, with bows, with shields, with wild glances and savage movements, were poured into the clearing by the dark-faced and pensive forest. The bushes shook, the grass swayed for a time, and then everything stood still in attentive immobility.

" 'Now, if he does not say the right thing to them we are all done for,' said the Russian at my elbow. The knot of men with the stretcher had stopped, too, halfway to the steamer, as if petrified. I saw the man on the stretcher sit up, lank and with an uplifted arm, above the shoulders of the bearers. 'Let us hope that the man who can talk so well of love in general will find some particular reason to spare us this time,' I said. I resented bitterly the absurd danger of our situation, as if to be at the mercy of that atrocious phantom had been a dishonoring necessity. I could not hear a sound, but through my glasses I saw the thin arm extended command-ingly, the lower jaw moving, the eyes of that apparition shining darkly far in its bony head that nodded with grotesque jerks. Kurtz—Kurtz—that means short in German—don't it? Well, the name was as true as everything else in his life—and death. He looked at least seven feet long. His covering had fallen off, and his body emerged from it pitiful and appalling as from a winding-sheet. I could see the cage of his ribs all astir, the bones of his arm waving. It was as though an animated image of death carved out of old ivory had been shaking its hand with menaces at a motionless crowd of men made of dark and glittering bronze. I saw him open his mouth wide—it gave him a weirdly voracious aspect, as though he had wanted to swallow all the air, all the earth, all the men before him. A deep voice reached me faintly. He must have been shouting. He fell back suddenly. The stretcher shook as the bearers staggered forward again, and almost at the same time I noticed that the crowd of savages was vanishing without any perceptible movement of retreat, as if the forest that had ejected these beings so suddenly had drawn them in again as the breath is drawn in a long aspiration.

"Some of the pilgrims behind the stretcher carried his arms—two shotguns, a heavy rifle, and a light revolver-carbine[50]—the thunderbolts of that pitiful Jupi-ter.[51] The manager bent over him murmuring as he walked beside his head. They laid him down in one of the little cabins—just a room for a bedplace and a camp-stool or two, you know. We had brought his belated correspondence, and a lot of torn envelopes and open letters littered his bed. His hand roamed feebly amongst these papers. I was struck by the fire of his eyes and the composed languor of his expression. It was not so much the exhaustion of disease. He did not seem in pain. This shadow looked satiated and calm, as though for the moment it had had its fill of all the emotions.

"He rustled one of the letters, and looking straight in my face said, 'I am glad.' Somebody had been writing to him about me. These special recommenda-tions were turning up again. The volume of tone he emitted without effort, almost without the trouble of moving his lips, amazed me. A voice! a voice! It was grave, profound, vibrating, while the man did not seem capable of a whisper. However, he had enough strength in him—factitious no doubt—to very nearly make an end of us, as you shall hear directly.

"The manager appeared silently in the doorway; I stepped out at once and he drew the curtain after me. The Russian, eyed curiously by the pilgrims, was staring at the shore. I followed the direction of his glance.

"Dark human shapes could be made out in the distance, flitting indistinctly against the gloomy border of the forest, and near the river two bronze figures, leaning on tall spears, stood in the sunlight under fantastic headdresses of spotted skins, warlike and still in statuesque repose. And from right to left along the lighted shore moved a wild and gorgeous apparition of a woman.

"She walked with measured steps, draped in striped and fringed cloths, treading the earth proudly, with a slight jingle and flash of barbarous ornaments. She carried her head high; her hair was done in the shape of a helmet; she had brass leggings to the knee, brass wire gauntlets to the elbow, a crimson spot on her tawny cheek, innumerable necklaces of glass beads on her neck; bizarre things, charms, gifts of witch-men, that hung about her, glittered and trembled at every step. She must have had the value of several elephant tusks upon her. She was savage and superb, wild-eyed and magnificent; there was something ominous and stately in her deliberate progress. And in the hush that had fallen suddenly upon the whole sorrowful land, the immense wilderness, the colossal body of the fecund and mysterious life seemed to look at her, pensive, as though it had been looking at the image of its own tenebrous and passionate soul.

"She came abreast of the steamer, stood still, and faced us. Her long shadow fell to the water's edge. Her face had a tragic and fierce aspect of wild sorrow and of dumb pain mingled with the fear of some struggling, half-shaped resolve. She stood looking at us without a stir, and like the wilderness itself, with an air of brooding over an inscrutable purpose. A whole minute passed, and then she made a step forward. There was a low jingle, a glint of yellow metal, a sway of fringed draperies, and she stopped as if her heart had failed her. The young fellow by my side growled. The pilgrims murmured at my back. She looked at us all as if her life had depended upon the unswerving steadiness of her glance. Suddenly she opened her bared arms and threw them up rigid above her head, as though in an uncontrollable desire to touch the sky, and at the same time the swift shadows darted out on the earth, swept around on the river, gathering the steamer into a shadowy embrace. A formidable silence hung over the scene.

"She turned away slowly, walked on, following the bank, and passed into the bushes to the left. Once only her eyes gleamed back at us in the dusk of the thickets before she disappeared.

"'If she had offered to come aboard I really think I would have tried to shoot her,' said the man of patches, nervously. 'I have been risking my life every day for the last fortnight to keep her out of the house. She got in one day and kicked up a row about those miserable rags I picked up in the storeroom to mend my clothes with. I wasn't decent. At least it must have been that, for she talked like a fury to Kurtz for an hour, pointing at me now and then. I don't understand the dialect of this tribe. Luckily for me, I fancy Kurtz felt too ill that day to care, or there would have been mischief. I don't understand. . . . No—it's too much for me. Ah, well, it's all over now.'

"At this moment I heard Kurtz's deep voice behind the curtain: 'Save me!

—save the ivory, you mean. Don't tell me. Save *me!* Why, I've had to save you. You are interrupting my plans now. Sick! Sick! Not so sick as you would like to believe. Never mind. I'll carry my ideas out yet—I will return. I'll show you what can be done. You with your little peddling notions—you are interfering with me. I will return. I. . . .'

"The manager came out. He did me the honor to take me under the arm and lead me aside. 'He is very low, very low,' he said. He considered it necessary to sigh, but neglected to be consistently sorrowful. 'We have done all we could for him—haven't we? But there is no disguising the fact, Mr. Kurtz has done more harm than good to the Company. He did not see the time was not ripe for vigorous action. Cautiously, cautiously—that's my principle. We must be cautious yet. The district is closed to us for a time. Deplorable! Upon the whole, the trade will suffer. I don't deny there is a remarkable quantity of ivory—mostly fossil. We must save it, at all events—but look how precarious the position is—and why? Because the method is unsound.' 'Do you,' said I, looking at the shore, 'call it "unsound method?"' 'Without doubt,' he exclaimed hotly. 'Don't you?' . . . 'No method at all,' I murmured after a while. 'Exactly,' he exulted. 'I anticipated this. Shows a complete want of judgment. It is my duty to point it out in the proper quarter.' 'Oh,' said I, 'that fellow—what's his name?—the brickmaker, will make a readable report for you.' He appeared confounded for a moment. It seemed to me I had never breathed an atmosphere so vile, and I turned mentally to Kurtz for relief —positively for relief. 'Nevertheless I think Mr. Kurtz is a remarkable man,' I said with emphasis. He started, dropped on me a cold heavy glance, said very quietly, 'he *was,*' and turned his back on me. My hour of favor was over; I found myself lumped along with Kurtz as a partisan of methods for which the time was not ripe: I was unsound! Ah! but it was something to have at least a choice of nightmares.

"I had turned to the wilderness really, not to Mr. Kurtz, who, I was ready to admit, was as good as buried. And for a moment it seemed to me as if I also were buried in a vast grave full of unspeakable secrets. I felt an intolerable weight oppressing my breast, the smell of the damp earth, the unseen presence of victorious corruption, the darkness of an impenetrable night. . . . The Russian tapped me on the shoulder. I heard him mumbling and stammering something about 'brother seaman—couldn't conceal—knowledge of matters that would affect Mr. Kurtz's reputation.' I waited. For him evidently Mr. Kurtz was not in his grave; I suspect that for him Mr. Kurtz was one of the immortals. 'Well!' said I at last, 'speak out. As it happens, I am Mr. Kurtz's friend—in a way.'

"He stated with a good deal of formality that had we not been 'of the same profession,' he would have kept the matter to himself without regard to consequences. 'He suspected there was an active ill will towards him on the part of these white men that—' 'You are right,' I said, remembering a certain conversation I had overheard. 'The manager thinks you ought to be hanged.' He showed a concern at this intelligence which amused me at first. 'I had better get out of the way quietly,' he said, earnestly. 'I can do no more for Kurtz now, and they would soon find some excuse. What's to stop them? There's a military post three hundred miles from here.' 'Well, upon my word,' said I, 'perhaps you had better go if you have any friends amongst the savages near by.' 'Plenty,' he said. 'They are simple people—and I want nothing, you know.' He stood biting his lip, then: 'I don't want any harm to happen to these whites here, but of course I was thinking of Mr. Kurtz's reputation—but you are a brother seaman and—' 'All right,' said I, after a time. 'Mr. Kurtz's reputation is safe with me.' I did not know how truly I spoke.

"He informed me, lowering his voice, that it was Kurtz who had ordered the attack to be made on the steamer. 'He hated sometimes the idea of being taken away—and then again. . . . But I don't understand these matters. I am a simple man. He thought it would scare you away—that you would give it up, thinking him dead. I could not stop him. Oh, I had an awful time of it this last month.' 'Very well,' I said. 'He is all right now.' 'Ye-e-es,' he muttered, not very convinced apparently. 'Thanks,' said I; 'I shall keep my eyes open.' 'But quiet—eh?' he urged, anxiously. 'It would be awful for his reputation if anybody here—' I promised a complete discretion with great gravity. 'I have a canoe and three black fellows waiting not very far. I am off. Could you give me a few Martini-Henry cartridges?' I could, and did, with proper secrecy. He helped himself, with a wink at me, to a handful of my tobacco. 'Between sailors—you know—good English tobacco.' At the door of the pilot-house he turned round—'I say, haven't you a pair of shoes you could spare?' He raised one leg. 'Look.' The soles were tied with knotted strings sandal-wise under his bare feet. I rooted out an old pair, at which he looked with admiration before tucking them under his left arm. One of his pockets (bright red) was bulging with cartridges, from the other (dark blue) peeped 'Towson's Inquiry,' etc., etc. He seemed to think himself excellently well equipped for a renewed encounter with the wilderness. 'Ah! I'll never, never meet such a man again. You ought to have heard him recite poetry—his own, too, it was, he told me. Poetry!' He rolled his eyes at the recollection of these delights. 'Oh, he enlarged my mind!' 'Good-by,' said I. He shook hands and vanished in the night. Sometimes I ask myself whether I had ever really seen him—whether it was possible to meet such a phenomenon! . . .

"When I woke up shortly after midnight his warning came to my mind with its hint of danger that seemed, in the starred darkness, real enough to make me get up for the purpose of having a look round. On the hill a big fire burned, illuminating fitfully a crooked corner of the station-house. One of the agents with a picket of a few of our blacks, armed for the purpose, was keeping guard over the ivory; but deep within the forest, red gleams that wavered, that seemed to sink and rise from the ground amongst confused columnar shapes of intense blackness, showed the exact position of the camp where Mr. Kurtz's adorers were keeping their uneasy vigil. The monotonous beating of a big drum filled the air with muffled shocks and a lingering vibration. A steady droning sound of many men chanting each to himself some weird incantation came out from the black, flat wall of the woods as the humming of bees comes out of a hive, and had a strange narcotic effect upon my half-awake senses. I believe I dozed off leaning over the rail, till an abrupt burst of yells, an overwhelming outbreak of a pent-up and mysterious frenzy, woke me up in a bewildered wonder. It was cut short all at once, and the low droning went on with an effect of audible and soothing silence. I glanced casually into the little cabin. A light was burning within, but Mr. Kurtz was not there.

"I think I would have raised an outcry if I had believed my eyes. But I didn't believe them at first—the thing seemed so impossible. The fact is I was completely unnerved by a sheer blank fright, pure abstract terror, unconnected with any distinct shape of physical danger. What made this emotion so overpowering was —how shall I define it?—the moral shock I received, as if something altogether monstrous, intolerable to thought and odious to the soul, had been thrust upon me unexpectedly. This lasted of course the merest fraction of a second, and then the usual sense of commonplace, deadly danger, the possibility of a sudden on-slaught and massacre, or something of the kind, which I saw impending, was positively welcome and composing. It pacified me, in fact, so much, that I did not raise an alarm.

"There was an agent buttoned up inside an ulster[52] and sleeping on a chair on deck within three feet of me. The yells had not awakened him; he snored very slightly; I left him to his slumbers and leaped ashore. I did not betray Mr. Kurtz —it was ordered I should never betray him—it was written I should be loyal to the nightmare of my choice. I was anxious to deal with this shadow by myself alone, —and to this day I don't know why I was so jealous of sharing with any one the peculiar blackness of that experience.

"As soon as I got on the bank I saw a trail—a broad trail through the grass. I remember the exultation with which I said to myself, 'He can't walk—he is crawling on all-fours—I've got him.' The grass was wet with dew. I strode rapidly with clenched fists. I fancy I had some vague notion of falling upon him and giving him a drubbing. I don't know. I had some imbecile thoughts. The knitting old woman with the cat obtruded herself upon my memory as a most improper person to be sitting at the other end of such an affair. I saw a row of pilgrims squirting lead in the air out of Winchesters held to the hip. I thought I would never get back to the steamer, and imagined myself living alone and unarmed in the woods to an advanced age. Such silly things—you know. And I remember I confounded the beat of the drum with the beating of my heart, and was pleased at its calm regularity.

"I kept to the track though—then stopped to listen. The night was very clear; a dark blue space, sparkling with dew and starlight, in which black things stood very still. I thought I could see a kind of motion ahead of me. I was strangely cocksure of everything that night. I actually left the track and ran in a wide semicircle (I verily believe chuckling to myself) so as to get in front of that stir, of that motion I had seen—if indeed I had seen anything. I was circumventing Kurtz as though it had been a boyish game.

"I came upon him, and, if he had not heard me coming, I would have fallen over him, too, but he got up in time. He rose, unsteady, long, pale, indistinct, like a vapor exhaled by the earth, and swayed slightly misty and silent before me; while at my back the fires loomed between the trees, and the murmur of many voices issued from the forest. I had cut him off cleverly; but when actually confronting him I seemed to come to my senses, I saw the danger in its right proportion. It was by no means over yet. Suppose he began to shout? Though he could hardly stand, there was still plenty of vigor in his voice. 'Go away—hide yourself,' he said, in that profound tone. It was very awful. I glanced back. We were within thirty yards from the nearest fire. A black figure stood up, strode on long black legs, waving long black arms, across the glow. It had horns—antelope horns, I think—on its head. Some sorcerer, some witch-man, no doubt: it looked fiend-like enough. 'Do you know what you are doing?' I whispered. 'Perfectly,' he answered, raising his voice for that single word: it sounded to me far off and yet loud, like a hail through a speaking-trumpet. If he makes a row we are lost, I thought to myself. This clearly was not a case for fisticuffs, even apart from the very natural aversion I had to beat that Shadow—this wandering and tormented thing. 'You will be lost,' I said—'utterly lost.' One gets sometimes such a flash of inspiration, you know. I did say the right thing, though indeed he could not have been more irretrievably lost than he was at this very moment, when the foundations of our intimacy were being laid—to endure—to endure—even to the end—even beyond.

" 'I had immense plans,' he muttered irresolutely. 'Yes,' said I; 'but if you try to shout I'll smash your head with—' There was not a stick or a stone near. 'I will throttle you for good,' I corrected myself. 'I was on the threshold of great things,' he pleaded, in a voice of longing, with a wistfulness of tone that made my blood run cold. 'And now for this stupid scoundrel—' 'Your success in Europe is assured in any case,' I affirmed, steadily. I did not want to have the throttling of him, you understand—and indeed it would have been very little use for any practical purpose. I tried to break the spell—the heavy, mute spell of the wilderness—that seemed to draw him to its pitiless breast by the awakening of forgotten and brutal instincts, by the memory of gratified and monstrous passions. This alone, I was convinced, had driven him out to the edge of the forest, to the bush, towards the gleam of fires, the throb of drums, the drone of weird incantations; this alone had beguiled his unlawful soul beyond the bounds of permitted aspirations. And, don't you see, the terror of the position was not in being knocked on the head—though I had a very lively sense of that danger, too—but in this, that I had to deal with a being to whom I could not appeal in the name of anything high or low. I had, even like the niggers, to invoke him—himself—his own exalted and incredible degradation. There was nothing either above or below him, and I knew it. He had kicked himself loose of the earth. Confound the man! he had kicked the very earth to pieces. He was alone, and I before him did not know whether I stood on the ground or floated in the air. I've been telling you what we said—repeating the phrases we pronounced—but what's the good? They were common everyday words—the familiar, vague sounds exchanged on every waking day of life. But what of that? They had behind them, to my mind, the terrific suggestiveness of words heard in dreams, of phrases spoken in nightmares. Soul! If anybody had ever struggled with a soul, I am the man. And I wasn't arguing with a lunatic either. Believe me or not, his intelligence was perfectly clear—concentrated, it is true, upon himself with horrible intensity, yet clear; and therein was my only chance—barring, of course, the killing him there and then, which wasn't so good, on account of unavoidable noise. But his soul was mad. Being alone in the wilderness, it had looked within itself, and, by heavens! I tell you, it had gone mad. I had—for my sins, I suppose—to go through the ordeal of looking into it myself. No eloquence could have been so withering to one's belief in mankind as his final burst of sincerity. He struggled with himself, too. I saw it,—I heard it. I saw the inconceivable mystery of a soul that knew no restraint, no faith, and no fear, yet struggling blindly with itself. I kept my head pretty well; but when I had him at last stretched on the couch, I wiped my forehead, while my legs shook under me as though I had carried half a ton on my back down that hill. And yet I had only supported him, his bony arm clasped round my neck—and he was not much heavier than a child.

"When next day we left at noon, the crowd, of whose presence behind the curtain of trees I had been acutely conscious all the time, flowed out of the woods again, filled the clearing, covered the slope with a mass of naked, breathing, quivering, bronze bodies. I steamed up a bit, then swung downstream, and two thousand eyes followed the evolutions of the splashing, thumping, fierce river-demon beating the water with its terrible tail and breathing black smoke into the air. In front of the first rank, along the river, three men, plastered with bright red earth from head to foot, strutted to and fro restlessly. When we came abreast again, they faced the river, stamped their feet, nodded their horned heads, swayed their scarlet bodies; they shook towards the fierce river-demon a bunch of black feathers, a mangy skin with a pendent tail—something that looked like a dried gourd; they shouted periodically together strings of amazing words that resembled no sounds of human language; and the deep murmurs of the crowd, interrupted suddenly, were like the responses of some satanic litany.

"We had carried Kurtz into the pilot-house: there was more air there. Lying on the couch, he stared through the open shutter. There was an eddy in the mass of human bodies, and the woman with helmeted head and tawny cheeks rushed out to the very brink of the stream. She put out her hands, shouted something, and all that wild mob took up the shout in a roaring chorus of articulated, rapid, breathless utterance.

" 'Do you understand this?' I asked.

"He kept on looking out past me with fiery, longing eyes, with a mingled expression of wistfulness and hate. He made no answer, but I saw a smile, a smile of indefinable meaning, appear on his colorless lips that a moment after twitched convulsively. 'Do I not?' he said slowly, gasping, as if the words had been torn out of him by a supernatural power.

"I pulled the string of the whistle, and I did this because I saw the pilgrims on deck getting out their rifles with an air of anticipating a jolly lark. At the sudden screech there was a movement of abject terror through that wedged mass of bodies. 'Don't! don't you frighten them away,' cried some one on deck disconsolately. I pulled the string time after time. They broke and ran, they leaped, they crouched, they swerved, they dodged the flying terror of the sound. The three red chaps had fallen flat, face down on the shore, as though they had been shot dead. Only the barbarous and superb woman did not so much as flinch, and stretched tragically her bare arms after us over the somber and glittering river.

"And then that imbecile crowd down on the deck started their little fun, and I could see nothing more for smoke.

"The brown current ran swiftly out of the heart of darkness, bearing us down towards the sea with twice the speed of our upward progress; and Kurtz's life was running swiftly, too, ebbing, ebbing out of his heart into the sea of inexorable time. The manager was very placid, he had no vital anxieties now, he took us both in with a comprehensive and satisfied glance: the 'affair' had come off as well as could be wished. I saw the time approaching when I would be left alone of the party of 'unsound method.' The pilgrims looked upon me with disfavor. I was, so to speak, numbered with the dead. It is strange how I accepted this unforeseen partnership, this choice of nightmares forced upon me in the tenebrous land invaded by these mean and greedy phantoms.

"Kurtz discoursed. A voice! a voice! It rang deep to the very last. It survived his strength to hide in the magnificent folds of eloquence the barren darkness of his heart. Oh, he struggled! he struggled! The wastes of his weary brain were haunted by shadowy images now—images of wealth and fame revolving obsequiously round his unextinguishable gift of noble and lofty expression. My Intended, my station, my career, my ideas—these were the subjects for the occasional utterances of elevated sentiments. The shade of the original Kurtz frequented the bedside of the hollow sham, whose fate it was to be buried presently in the mold of primeval earth. But both the diabolic love and the unearthly hate of the mysteries it had penetrated fought for the possession of that soul satiated with primitive emotions, avid of lying fame, of sham distinction, of all the appearances of success and power.

"Sometimes he was contemptibly childish. He desired to have kings meet him at railway stations on his return from some ghastly Nowhere, where he intended to accomplish great things. 'You show them you have in you something that is really profitable, and then there will be no limits to the recognition of your ability,' he would say. 'Of course you must take care of the motives—right motives —always.' The long reaches that were like one and the same reach, monotonous bends that were exactly alike, slipped past the steamer, with their multitude of secular[53] trees looking patiently after this grimy fragment of another world, the forerunner of change, of conquest, of trade, of massacres, of blessings. I looked ahead—piloting. 'Close the shutter,' said Kurtz suddenly one day; 'I can't bear to look at this.' I did so. There was a silence. 'Oh, but I will wring your heart yet!' he cried at the invisible wilderness.

"We broke down—as I had expected—and had to lie up for repairs at the head of an island. This delay was the first thing that shook Kurtz's confidence. One morning he gave me a packet of papers and a photograph—the lot tied together with a shoestring. 'Keep this for me,' he said. 'This noxious fool' (meaning the manager) 'is capable of prying into my boxes when I am not looking.' In the afternoon I saw him. He was lying on his back with closed eyes, and I withdrew quietly, but I heard him mutter, 'Live rightly, die, die. . . .' I listened. There was nothing more. Was he rehearsing some speech in his sleep, or was it a fragment of a phrase from some newspaper article? He had been writing for the papers and meant to do so again, 'for the furthering of my ideas. It's a duty.'

"His was an impenetrable darkness. I looked at him as you peer down at a man who is lying at the bottom of a precipice where the sun never shines. But I had not much time to give him, because I was helping the engine-driver to take to pieces the leaky cylinders, to straighten a bent connecting-rod, and in other such matters. I lived in an infernal mess of rust, filings, nuts, bolts, spanners,⁵⁴ hammers, ratchet-drills—things I abominate, because I don't get on with them. I tended the little forge we fortunately had aboard; I toiled wearily in a wretched scrapheap—unless I had the shakes too bad to stand.

"One evening coming in with a candle I was startled to hear him say a little tremulously, 'I am lying here in the dark waiting for death.' The light was within a foot of his eyes. I forced myself to murmur, 'Oh, nonsense!' and stood over him as if transfixed.

"Anything approaching the change that came over his features I have never seen before, and hope never to see again. Oh, I wasn't touched. I was fascinated. It was as though a veil had been rent. I saw on that ivory face the expression of somber pride, of ruthless power, of craven terror—of an intense and hopeless despair. Did he live his life again in every detail of desire, temptation, and surrender during that supreme moment of complete knowledge? He cried in a whisper at some image, at some vision—he cried out twice, a cry that was no more than a breath—

" 'The horror! The horror!'

"I blew the candle out and left the cabin. The pilgrims were dining in the mess-room, and I took my place opposite the manager, who lifted his eyes to give me a questioning glance, which I successfully ignored. He leaned back, serene, with that peculiar smile of his sealing the unexpressed depths of his meanness. A continuous shower of small flies streamed upon the lamp, upon the cloth, upon our hands and faces. Suddenly the manager's boy put his insolent black head in the doorway, and said in a tone of scathing contempt—

" 'Mistah Kurtz—he dead.'

"All the pilgrims rushed out to see. I remained, and went on with my dinner. I believe I was considered brutally callous. However, I did not eat much. There was a lamp in there—light, don't you know—and outside it was so beastly, beastly dark. I went no more near the remarkable man who had pronounced a judgment upon the adventures of his soul on this earth. The voice was gone. What else had been there? But I am of course aware that next day the pilgrims buried something in a muddy hole.

"And then they very nearly buried me.

"However, as you see I did not go to join Kurtz there and then. I did not. I remained to dream the nightmare out to the end, and to show my loyalty to Kurtz once more. Destiny. My destiny! Droll thing life is—that mysterious arrangement of merciless logic for a futile purpose. The most you can hope from it is some knowledge of yourself—that comes too late—a crop of unextinguishable regrets.

I have wrestled with death. It is the most unexciting contest you can imagine. It takes place in an impalpable grayness, with nothing underfoot, with nothing around, without spectators, without clamor, without glory, without the great desire of victory, without the great fear of defeat, in a sickly atmosphere of tepid skepticism, without much belief in your own right, and still less in that of your adversary. If such is the form of ultimate wisdom, then life is a greater riddle than some of us think it to be. I was within a hair's breadth of the last opportunity for pronouncement, and I found with humiliation that probably I would have nothing to say. This is the reason why I affirm that Kurtz was a remarkable man. He had something to say. He said it. Since I had peeped over the edge myself, I understand better the meaning of his stare, that could not see the flame of the candle, but was wide enough to embrace the whole universe, piercing enough to penetrate all the hearts that beat in the darkness. He had summed up—he had judged. 'The horror!' He was a remarkable man. After all, this was the expression of some sort of belief; it had candor, it had conviction, it had a vibrating note of revolt in its whisper, it had the appalling face of a glimpsed truth—the strange commingling of desire and hate. And it is not my own extremity I remember best—a vision of grayness without form filled with physical pain, and a careless contempt for the evanescence of all things—even of this pain itself. No! It is his extremity that I seem to have lived through. True, he had made that last stride, he had stepped over the edge, while I had been permitted to draw back my hesitating foot. And perhaps in this is the whole difference; perhaps all the wisdom, and all truth, and all sincerity, are just compressed into the inappreciable moment of time in which we step over the threshold of the invisible. Perhaps! I like to think my summing-up would not have been a word of careless contempt. Better his cry—much better. It was an affirmation, a moral victory paid for by innumerable defeats, by abominable terrors, by abominable satisfactions. But it was a victory! That is why I have remained loyal to Kurtz to the last, and even beyond, when a long time after I heard once more, not his own voice, but the echo of his magnificent eloquence thrown to me from a soul as translucently pure as a cliff of crystal.

"No, they did not bury me, though there is a period of time which I remember mistily, with a shuddering wonder, like a passage through some inconceivable world that had no hope in it and no desire. I found myself back in the sepulchral city resenting the sight of people hurrying through the streets to filch a little money from each other, to devour their infamous cookery, to gulp their unwholesome beer, to dream their insignificant and silly dreams. They trespassed upon my thoughts. They were intruders whose knowledge of life was to me an irritating pretense, because I felt so sure they could not possibly know the things I knew. Their bearing, which was simply the bearing of commonplace individuals going about their business in the assurance of perfect safety, was offensive to me like the outrageous flauntings of folly in the face of a danger it is unable to comprehend. I had no particular desire to enlighten them, but I had some difficulty in restraining myself from laughing in their faces, so full of stupid importance. I daresay I was not very well at that time. I tottered about the streets—there were various affairs to settle—grinning bitterly at perfectly respectable persons. I admit my behavior was inexcusable, but then my temperature was seldom normal in these days. My dear aunt's endeavors to 'nurse up my strength' seemed altogether beside the mark. It was not my strength that wanted nursing, it was my imagination that wanted soothing. I kept the bundle of papers given me by Kurtz, not knowing exactly what to do with it. His mother had died lately, watched over, as I was told, by his Intended. A clean-shaved man, with an official manner and wearing gold-rimmed spectacles, called on me one day and made inquiries, at first circuitous, afterwards suavely pressing, about what he was pleased to denominate certain 'documents.' I was not surprised, because I had two rows with the manager on the subject out there. I had refused to give up the smallest scrap out of that package, and I took the same attitude with the spectacled man. He became darkly menacing at last, and with much heat argued that the Company had the right to every bit of information about its 'territories.' And said he, 'Mr. Kurtz's knowledge of unexplored regions must have been necessarily extensive and peculiar—owing to his great abilities and to the deplorable circumstances in which he had been placed: therefore—' I assured him Mr. Kurtz's knowledge, however extensive, did not bear upon the problems of commerce or administration. He invoked then the name of science. 'It would be an incalculable loss, if,' etc., etc. I offered him the report on the 'Suppression of Savage Customs,' with the postscriptum torn off. He took it up eagerly, but ended by sniffing at it with an air of contempt. "This is not what we had a right to expect,' he remarked. 'Expect nothing else,' I said. 'There are only private letters.' He withdrew upon some threat of legal proceedings, and I saw him no more; but another fellow, calling himself Kurtz's cousin, appeared two days later, and was anxious to hear all the details about his dear relative's last moments. Incidentally he gave me to understand that Kurtz had been essentially a great musician. 'There was the making of an immense success,' said the man, who was an organist, I believe, with lank gray hair flowing over a greasy coat-collar. I had no reason to doubt his statement; and to this day I am unable to say what was Kurtz's profession, whether he ever had any—which was the greatest of his talents. I had taken him for a painter who wrote for the papers, or else for a journalist who could paint—but even the cousin (who took snuff during the interview) could not tell me what he had been—exactly. He was a universal genius —on that point I agreed with the old chap, who thereupon blew his nose noisily into a large cotton handkerchief and withdrew in senile agitation, bearing off some family letters and memoranda without importance. Ultimately a journalist anxious to know something of the fate of his 'dear colleague' turned up. This visitor informed me Kurtz's proper sphere ought to have been politics 'on the popular side.' He had furry straight eyebrows, bristly hair cropped short, an eye-glass on a broad ribbon, and, becoming expansive, confessed his opinion that Kurtz really couldn't write a bit—'but heavens! how that man could talk. He electrified large meetings. He had faith—don't you see?—he had the faith. He could get himself to believe anything—anything. He would have been a splendid leader of an extreme party.' 'What party?' I asked. 'Any party,' answered the other. 'He was an—an—extremist.' Did I not think so? I assented. Did I know, he asked, with a sudden flash of curiosity, 'what it was that had induced him to go out there?' 'Yes,' said I, and forthwith handed him the famous Report for publication, if he thought fit. He glanced through it hurriedly, mumbling all the time, judged 'it would do,' and took himself off with this plunder.

"Thus I was left at last with a slim packet of letters and the girl's portrait. She struck me as beautiful—I mean she had a beautiful expression. I know that the sunlight can be made to lie, too, yet one felt that no manipulation of light and pose could have conveyed the delicate shade of truthfulness upon those features. She seemed ready to listen without mental reservation, without suspicion, without a thought for herself. I concluded I would go and give her back her portrait and those letters myself. Curiosity? Yes; and also some other feeling perhaps. All that had been Kurtz's had passed out of my hands: his soul, his body, his station, his plans, his ivory, his career. There remained only his memory and his Intended—and I wanted to give that up, too, to the past, in a way—to surrender personally all that remained of him with me to that oblivion which is the last word of our common fate. I don't defend myself. I had no clear perception of what it was I really wanted. Perhaps it was an impulse of unconscious loyalty, or the fulfillment of one of those ironic necessities that lurk in the facts of human existence. I don't know. I can't tell. But I went.

"I thought his memory was like the other memories of the dead that accumulate in every man's life—a vague impress on the brain of shadows that had fallen on it in their swift and final passage; but before the high and ponderous door, between the tall houses of a street as still and decorous as a well-kept alley in a cemetery, I had a vision of him on the stretcher, opening his mouth voraciously, as if to devour all the earth with all its mankind. He lived then before me; he lived as much as he had ever lived—a shadow insatiable of splendid appearances, of frightful realities; a shadow darker than the shadow of the night, and draped nobly in the folds of a gorgeous eloquence. The vision seemed to enter the house with me—the stretcher, the phantom-bearers, the wild crowd of obedient worshippers, the gloom of the forest, the glitter of the reach between the murky bends, the beat of the drum, regular and muffled like the beating of a heart—the heart of a conquering darkness. It was a moment of triumph for the wilderness, an invading and vengeful rush which, it seemed to me, I would have to keep back alone for the salvation of another soul. And the memory of what I had heard him say afar there, with the horned shapes stirring at my back, in the glow of fires, within the patient woods, those broken phrases came back to me, were heard again in their ominous and terrifying simplicity. I remembered his abject pleading, his abject threats, the colossal scale of his vile desires, the meanness, the torment, the tempestuous anguish of his soul. And later on I seemed to see his collected languid manner, when he said one day, 'This lot of ivory now is really mine. The Company did not pay for it. I collected it myself at a very great personal risk. I am afraid they will try to claim it as theirs though. H'm. It is a difficult case. What do you think I ought to do—resist? Eh? I want no more than justice.' . . . He wanted no more than justice—no more than justice. I rang the bell before a mahogany door on the first floor, and while I waited he seemed to stare at me out of the glassy panel—stare with that wide and immense stare embracing, condemning, loathing all the universe. I seemed to hear the whispered cry, 'The horror! The horror!'

"The dusk was falling. I had to wait in a lofty drawing room with three long windows from floor to ceiling that were like three luminous and bedraped columns. The bent gilt legs and backs of the furniture shone in indistinct curves. The tall marble fireplace had a cold and monumental whiteness. A grand piano stood massively in a corner; with dark gleams on the flat surfaces like a somber and polished sarcophagus. A high door opened—closed. I rose.

"She came forward, all in black, with a pale head, floating towards me in the dusk. She was in mourning. It was more than a year since his death, more than a year since the news came; she seemed as though she would remember and mourn forever. She took both my hands in hers and murmured, 'I had heard you were coming.' I noticed she was not very young—I mean not girlish. She had a mature capacity for fidelity, for belief, for suffering. The room seemed to have grown darker, as if all the sad light of the cloudy evening had taken refuge on her forehead. This fair hair, this pale visage, this pure brow, seemed surrounded by an ashy halo from which the dark eyes looked out at me. Their glance was guileless, profound, confident, and trustful. She carried her sorrowful head as though she were proud of that sorrow, as though she would say, I—I alone know how to mourn him as he deserves. But while we were still shaking hands, such a look of awful desolation came upon her face that I perceived she was one of those creatures that are not the playthings of Time. For her he had died only yesterday. And, by Jove! the impression was so powerful that for me, too, he seemed to have died only yesterday—nay, this very minute. I saw her and him in the same instant of time —his death and her sorrow—I saw her sorrow in the very moment of his death. Do you understand? I saw them together—I heard them together. She had said, with a deep catch of the breath, 'I have survived' while my strained ears seemed to hear distinctly, mingled with her tone of despairing regret, the summing up whisper of his eternal condemnation. I asked myself what I was doing there, with a sensation of panic in my heart as though I had blundered into a place of cruel and absurd mysteries not fit for a human being to behold. She motioned me to a chair. We sat down. I laid the packet gently on the little table, and she put her hand over it. . . . 'You knew him well,' she murmured, after a moment of mourning silence.

" 'Intimacy grows quickly out there,' I said. 'I knew him as well as it is possible for one man to know another.'

" 'And you admired him,' she said. 'It was impossible to know him and not to admire him. Was it?'

" 'He was a remarkable man,' I said, unsteadily. Then before the appealing fixity of her gaze, that seemed to watch for more words on my lips, I went on, 'It was impossible not to—'

" 'Love him,' she finished eagerly, silencing me into an appalled dumbness. 'How true! how true! But when you think that no one knew him so well as I! I had all his noble confidence. I knew him best.'

" 'You knew him best,' I repeated. And perhaps she did. But with every word spoken the room was growing darker, and only her forehead, smooth and white, remained illumined by the unextinguishable light of belief and love.

"'You were his friend,' she went on. 'His friend,' she repeated, a little louder. 'You must have been, if he had given you this, and sent you to me. I feel I can speak to you—and oh! I must speak. I want you—you have heard his last words—to know I have been worthy of him. . . . It is not pride. . . . Yes! I am proud to know I understood him better than any one on earth—he told me so himself. And since his mother died I have had no one—no one—to—to—'

"I listened. The darkness deepened. I was not even sure he had given me the right bundle. I rather suspect he wanted me to take care of another batch of his papers which, after his death, I saw the manager examining under the lamp. And the girl talked, easing her pain in the certitude of my sympathy; she talked as thirsty men drink. I had heard that her engagement with Kurtz had been disapproved by her people. He wasn't rich enough or something. And indeed I don't know whether he had not been a pauper all his life. He had given me some reason to infer that it was his impatience of comparative poverty that drove him out there.

"'. . . Who was not his friend who had heard him speak once?' she was saying. 'He drew men towards him by what was best in them.' She looked at me with intensity. 'It is the gift of the great,' she went on, and the sound of her low voice seemed to have the accompaniment of all the other sounds, full of mystery, desolation, and sorrow, I had ever heard—the ripple of the river, the soughing of the trees swayed by the wind, the murmurs of the crowds, the faint ring of incomprehensible words cried from afar, the whisper of a voice speaking from beyond the threshold of an eternal darkness. 'But you have heard him! You know!' she cried.

"'Yes, I know,' I said with something like despair in my heart, but bowing my head before the faith that was in her, before that great and saving illusion that shone with an unearthly glow in the darkness, in the triumphant darkness from which I could not have defended her—from which I could not even defend myself.

"'What a loss to me—to us!'—she corrected herself with beautiful generosity; then added in a murmur, 'To the world.' By the last gleams of twilight I could see the glitter of her eyes, full of tears—of tears that would not fall.

"'I have been very happy—very fortunate—very proud,' she went on. 'Too fortunate. Too happy for a little while. And now I am unhappy for—for life.'

"She stood up; her fair hair seemed to catch all the remaining light in a glimmer of gold. I rose, too.

"'And of all this,' she went on, mournfully, 'of all his promise, and of all his greatness, of his generous mind, of his noble heart, nothing remains—nothing but a memory. You and I—'

"'We shall always remember him,' I said, hastily.

"'No!' she cried. 'It is impossible that all this should be lost—that such a life should be sacrificed to leave nothing—but sorrow. You know what vast plans he had. I knew of them, too—I could not perhaps understand—but others knew of them. Something must remain. His words, at least, have not died.'

146

" 'His words will remain,' I said.

" 'And his example,' she whispered to herself. 'Men looked up to him—his goodness shone in every act. His example—'

" 'True,' I said; 'his example, too. Yes, his example, I forgot that.'

" 'But I do not. I cannot—I cannot believe—not yet. I cannot believe that I shall never see him again, that nobody will see him again, never, never, never.'

"She put out her arms as if after a retreating figure, stretching them back and with clasped pale hands across the fading and narrow sheen of the window. Never see him! I saw him clearly enough then. I shall see this eloquent phantom as long as I live, and I shall see her, too, a tragic and familiar Shade, resembling in this gesture another one, tragic also, and bedecked with powerless charms, stretching bare brown arms over the glitter of the infernal stream, the stream of darkness. She said suddenly very low, 'He died as he lived.'

" 'His end,' said I, with dull anger stirring in me, 'was in every way worthy of his life.'

" 'And I was not with him,' she murmured. My anger subsided before a feeling of infinite pity.

" 'Everything that could be done—' I mumbled.

" 'Ah, but I believed in him more than any one on earth—more than his own mother, more than—himself. He needed me! Me! I would have treasured every sigh, every word, every sign, every glance.'

"I felt like a chill grip on my chest. 'Don't,' I said, in a muffled voice.

" 'Forgive me. I—I—have mourned so long in silence—in silence. . . . You were with him—to the last? I think of his loneliness. Nobody near to understand him as I would have understood. Perhaps no one to hear. . . .'

" 'To the very end,' I said, shakily. 'I heard his very last words. . . .' I stopped in a fright.

" 'Repeat them,' she murmured in a heartbroken tone. 'I want—I want—something—something—to—live with.'

"I was on the point of crying at her, 'Don't you hear them?' The dusk was repeating them in a persistent whisper all around us, in a whisper that seemed to swell menacingly like the first whisper of a rising wind. 'The horror! The horror!'

" 'His last word—to live with,' she insisted. 'Don't you understand I loved him—I loved him—I loved him!'

"I pulled myself together and spoke slowly.

" 'The last word he pronounced was—your name.'

"I heard a light sigh and then my heart stood still, stopped dead short by an exulting and terrible cry, by the cry of inconceivable triumph and of unspeakable pain. 'I knew it—I was sure!' . . . She knew. She was sure. I heard her weeping; she had hidden her face in her hands. It seemed to me that the house would collapse before I could escape, that the heavens would fall upon my head. But nothing happened. The heavens do not fall for such a trifle. Would they have fallen, I wonder, if I had rendered Kurtz that justice which was his due? Hadn't he said he wanted only justice? But I couldn't. I could not tell her. It would have been too dark—too dark altogether. . . ."

Marlow ceased, and sat apart, indistinct and silent, in the pose of a meditating Buddha. Nobody moved for a time. "We have lost the first of the ebb," said the Director, suddenly. I raised my head. The offing was barred by a black bank of clouds, and the tranquil waterway leading to the uttermost ends of the earth flowed somber under an overcast sky—seemed to lead into the heart of an immense darkness.

[1] Tidal part of the river as it broadens toward the sea.
[2] Part of the sea visible from the river's mouth.
[3] A seaport on the Thames, 26 miles east of London.
[4] On the north bank of the Thames.
[5] Drake (1540–1596) sailed around the world; defeated the Spanish Armada. The *Golden Hind* was his ship.
[6] Franklin (1786–1847), Arctic explorer; led expedition, including the ships *Erebus* and *Terror,* that was lost searching for the Northwest Passage.
[7] Deptford, Greenwich, and Erith are seaports on the Thames.
[8] The financial district of London.
[9] Unauthorized competitors of the Crown-chartered East India Company.
[10] The East India Company had the right to put troops in India and to appoint "generals."
[11] London.
[12] A Roman galley propelled by three tiers of oars.
[13] The inhabitants of France in Roman times.
[14] A wine much celebrated among the Romans.
[15] Roman naval base on the Adriatic, a choice tour of duty.
[16] An important government official.
[17] The Congo Free State, at that time the Belgian Congo; in the Congo River Basin. Present-day Zaire.
[18] Brussels. See also Matthew 23:27 (KJV).
[19] Map's colors represent nations controlling each area: red-British; green-Italians; orange-Portuguese; purple-Germans; yellow-Belgians.
[20] *Bon voyage.* "Have a good trip." (French)
[21] *Ave! Morituri te salutant.* "Hail! they who are about to die salute you." (Latin) The supposed greeting of the Roman gladiator.
[22] A physician who treats mental disorders.
[23] *Du calme, du calme. Adieu.* "Keep calm, keep calm. Good-bye." (French)
[24] Luke 10:7.
[25] France's colonial empire extended down the West African coast to the mouth of the Congo River. Dakar and Casablanca are two of the major ports.
[26] Flag.
[27] The Congo.
[28] Boma, in the mouth of the Congo.
[29] Sailed into a clear and unobstructed part of the river.
[30] Matadi, a town.
[31] Loops.
[32] Explosive charge.
[33] One of the main resources of the Congo Free State.
[34] English coastal cities.
[35] Mercenaries from the island of Zanzibar.
[36] British unit of weight equal to 14 pounds. The man weighed 224 pounds.
[37] A sailor on shore leave.
[38] Slender javelins.
[39] Bunglers.

[40] Cardboard devil.
[41] Primitive but easily operated boiler.
[42] Rigging used to apply leverage.
[43] Some editions print "float" and gloss it variously as the blade of a paddle wheel or a water regulator on a water supply valve.
[44] A Winchester is a famous repeating rifle, named for its American maker.
[45] A good meal.
[46] Gauging the water's depth by means of a weighted line.
[47] A make of military rifle.
[48] Fired.
[49] Slang expression for "red-haired rascal."
[50] Short-barreled rifle with revolving cylinder.
[51] Principal Roman god; thunderbolts were his weapons.
[52] A long, loose overcoat made of heavy material.
[53] Age-old.
[54] Wrenches.

DISCUSSION TOPICS

1. "Before the Congo I was just a mere animal," Conrad confessed about his own journey into the heart of Africa in 1890—an initiatory ordeal that, according to biographer G. Jean-Aubry, "killed Conrad the sailor and strengthened Conrad the novelist." About his personal reaction to the colonial exploitation of the dark continent, Conrad wrote: "A great melancholy descended on me [in reflecting on] the distasteful knowledge of the vilest scramble for loot that ever disfigured the history of human conscience and geographical exploration. What an end to the idealized realities of a boy's daydreams!" In what ways are Conrad's sentiments expressed through his fictive persona Charlie Marlow?

2. How does Marlow's prologue function as a thematic epitome of the whole story? What major images and symbols are introduced in this first part of the story?

3. Discuss the element of comedy that counterpoints the basically tragic nature of Marlow's tale, giving it and its narrator a sense of balance.

4. In his *Journey of a Novel,* John Steinbeck has said: "The craft of writing is the clumsy attempt to find symbols for the wordlessness. In utter loneliness a writer tries to explain the inexplicable." Similarly Conrad advised his reader: "My task which I am trying to achieve is, by the power of the written word, to make you hear, to make you feel—it is, before all, to make you *see.* That—and no more, and it is everything. If I succeed, you shall find there according to your deserts: encouragement, consolation, fear, charm—all you demand and, perhaps, also that glimpse of truth for which you have forgotten to ask" (Preface to *The Nigger of the "Narcissus"*). And the narrator of the frame in *Heart of Darkness* comments on Marlow's characteristically oblique narrative strategy: "to him the meaning of an episode was not inside like a kernel but outside, enveloping the tale which brought it out only as a glow brings out a haze, in the likeness of one of these misty halos that sometimes are made visible by the spectral illumination of moonshine." With these observations in mind, discuss the rea-

sons for Marlow's developing a complex symbolism in order to cope with the nature of his narrative. Why wouldn't a straightforward, factual, realistic account of Marlow's journey work?

5. Francis Ford Coppola's film *Apocalypse Now* transports Conrad's *Heart of Darkness* from the Belgian Congo of the nineteenth century to twentieth-century Vietnam. What is there in Conrad's story that enables the modern filmmaker to translate it into a twentieth-century context? How does Conrad's story relate to African and other Third World nations today?

6. Marlow remarks that "The mind of man is capable of anything—because everything is in it, all the past as well as all the future." Clearly, Marlow's journey (and that of the reader) is more than a physical one. It requires no profound knowledge of Freudian theory to realize that the "Heart of Darkness" is psychological (and moral) as well as geographic. However, Freudian theory lends itself especially well to this story. What characters, for example, might be seen as representing the Freudian id, ego, and superego?

7. Conrad's story is rich with mythological and archetypal implications. Discuss, for example, the archetypal significance of the ship, the river, the quest, blackness, the woman (Kurtz's Intended as well as his jungle woman), the death-and-rebirth motif, and the Jungian theory of individuation (psychological and spiritual maturing by coming to terms with the persona, shadow, and anima).

WRITING TOPIC

Compare this initiation story with others such as "My Kinsman, Major Molineux" and "Bartleby the Scrivener."

ANTON CHEKHOV (1860–1904) Russian physician and humanist. He was a groundbreaker in modern realistic drama and short fiction: a consummate craftsman. His works are concerned with drabness, boredom, and waste of human life—especially among the materialistic middle class—as well as with social inequities and universal human frailties. He was a subtle ironist and humorist.

A WORK OF ART

Translated by Joel A. Huberman

Carrying under his arm an object wrapped in Number 223 of the *Stock Exchange News,* Sasha Smirnov, his mother's only son, twitched his face and walked into the office of Dr. Koshelkov.

"Ah, my dear lad!" the doctor greeted him. "How are you? And what is your good news?"

150

Sasha blinked, put his hand to his heart, and said in an excited voice:

"My mother sends you her greetings, Ivan Nikolaevich, and she asks me to thank you . . . I am my mother's only son, and you saved my life . . . cured me of a dangerous disease, and . . . neither of us knows how to thank you."

"Don't mention it, young man!" interrupted the doctor, melting with pleasure. "I did no more than any other in my place would have done."

"I am my mother's only son . . . We are poor and cannot pay for your services, and . . . we are very embarrassed, doctor. However, my mother and I, my mother's only son, beg you to accept as an expression of gratitude . . . this gift . . . which is of great value . . . an antique bronze . . . a truly rare work of art."

"It is not necessary," replied the doctor, looking askance. "Why must you do this?"

"No, please don't refuse it," Sasha stammered, unwrapping his bundle. "You will offend both Mother and me if you don't take it. It's a very fine piece . . . an antique bronze . . . It was bequeathed to us by my father, and we have treasured it in his memory . . . My father bought antique bronzes and sold them to collectors . . . Now Mother and I carry on the business . . ."

Sasha finished unwrapping the object and ceremoniously placed it on the table. It was a low candelabrum of weathered bronze, a work of genuine artistic merit. On its pedestal stood two female figures in the costume of Eve and in poses which I have neither the nerve nor the temperament to describe. The figures smiled flirtatiously, and, apart from the necessity of supporting the candelabrum, seemed ready to jump down from the pedestal and engage in such debauchery in the room that the mere thought of it, dear reader, would be indecent.

After glancing at the gift, the doctor slowly scratched behind his ear, snorted, and blew his nose.

"Yes, it is really beautiful," he murmured. "But . . . How shall I put it? It's not . . . not suitable for public display . . . This is more than décolleté; it's the devil knows what . . ."

"What is it, then?"

"The serpent-tempter himself could not have fashioned anything more lewd. Such an obscenity on my table would deface the whole room."

"What a strange way to regard art, doctor," replied Sasha, affronted. "This is most certainly a work of art. Just look! It has so much beauty and taste that it exalts the soul and brings a lump to one's throat. The sight of such beauty makes one forget all earthly things. See how much movement and expression there is! It is breath-taking!"

"I see that perfectly well, my dear fellow," interrupted the doctor, "but, as you know, I am a family man, my children run in and out of this room, and ladies come to visit me."

"Of course, if you look at it from the point of view of the multitude," said Sasha, "then this piece of pure art appears in another light. But, doctor, rise above the multitude, especially since your refusal would deeply distress both my Mother and me. I am my mother's only son . . . You saved my life . . . We give you, in return, our most precious possession, and . . . only regret that we do not have its mate."

"Thank you, dear boy, I am most grateful. My greetings to your mother, but do try to realize that my children run around in here and ladies come to visit me! Oh, well, leave it here anyway. It's no use arguing with you."

"There is nothing to argue about," exclaimed Sasha delightedly. "Place the candelabrum there, beside the vase. What a pity the mate is missing! What a pity! Well, good-by, doctor."

After Sasha's departure, the doctor stared at the candelabrum for a long time, scratched behind his ear, and pondered.

"A fine piece—of that there can be no doubt," he thought. "It's impossible to keep it here, yet it would be a pity to throw it away. Hmm! What a problem! To whom can I give it? To what charity can I donate it?"

After prolonged consideration, he remembered his good friend, the lawyer Ukhov, to whom he was indebted for some legal services.

"Excellent," decided the doctor. "It would be awkward for him as a friend to accept money from me, so a present of this candelabrum would be just the thing. I'll take this fiendish object to him! Fortunately, he is a gay bachelor."

Without delay, the doctor put on his hat and coat, took the candelabrum, and went to Ukhov's.

"Good morning, my friend," he said, finding the lawyer at home. "I've come . . . I've come to thank you, my dear fellow, for your efforts on my behalf. Since you won't take money, please accept this trifling gift. This little object . . . is truly magnificent."

On seeing it, the lawyer was enraptured.

"What a work!" he burst out laughing. "What fiendish artistry! Wonderful! Ravishing! Where did you find such an attractive piece?"

Having shown his delight, the lawyer timidly glanced at the door and said:

"But no, brother, you must take it away. I cannot possibly accept it."

"Why not?" asked the doctor, looking worried.

"Because . . . sometimes my mother calls on me here; at other times clients come . . . and, besides, it would shame me before the servants."

"No, no, no . . . don't dare to refuse!" exclaimed the doctor with a frantic gesture. "That would be churlish of you! This is a masterpiece. What movement! What expression! Say no more about it! You will deeply offend me if you don't take it."

"If only it were painted over, or fig leaves were attached . . ."

But the doctor rushed from Ukhov's apartment and returned home, satisfied with his success in disposing of the gift.

After his departure, the lawyer examined the candelabrum, touched it all over with his fingers, and, like the doctor, considered for a long time what to do with it.

"It is a beautiful thing," he reasoned, "and it would be a pity to throw it away, but I can't possibly keep it here. I had best give it to someone as a present.

That's it, I'll take it this very afternoon to the comedian Shashkin. That rogue adores such pieces, and, as luck would have it, he's giving a benefit performance today."

No sooner said than done. That afternoon the carefully wrapped candelabrum was delivered to the comedian Shashkin. And all through the afternoon men stormed his dressing room to admire it. Their joyous laughter (which sounded like the neighing of horses) filled the place. Whenever an actress approached the door, demanding to be let in, the comedian's husky voice promptly replied:

"No, no, my sweet! I'm not dressed."

After the show, the comedian shrugged his shoulders, folded his arms, and said:

"Well, well, what shall I do with this disgusting object? After all, I live in a private apartment. Actresses come to visit me. This is no photograph; one can't hide it in a desk drawer."

"Why not sell it?" recommended the wigmaker who was helping the comedian change his clothes. "There's an old woman hereabouts who buys old bronzes. Ask for Smirnova . . . Everyone knows her."

The comedian listened. . . .

Two days later, Dr. Koshelkov was sitting alone in his office, and, with his finger to his head, was thinking about bile acids, when the door suddenly flew open and in burst Sasha Smirnov. He was smiling, and looked delighted with himself. In his hand he carried a parcel wrapped in a newspaper.

"Doctor," he began, catching his breath, "imagine my joy! Luckily, we have found the mate to your candelabrum. Mother is so pleased . . . I am my mother's only son . . . you saved my life . . ."

And Sasha, trembling with gratitude, placed the candelabrum before the doctor. The doctor's jaw dropped. He tried to speak, but could say nothing. Words failed him.

DISCUSSION TOPICS

1. How would you describe the character of the narrator—and his tone of voice —in the story?
2. Apply the saying "Beauty is in the eye of the beholder" to this story. Discuss particularly Sasha's reaction to Dr. Koshelkov's remark that the candelabrum is "an obscenity." Where do you think the line should be drawn between art and pornography? How would you classify the work of art in Chekhov's story —on the basis of the narrator's description of it?
3. Chekhov was a brilliant social satirist. Why do you think he has chosen males only—specifically, a physician, a lawyer, and a comedian—as recipients of the candelabrum? Discuss the reaction of each recipient to this "gift."
4. What do you think Dr. Koshelkov does with the gift when he receives it the second time?

Stephen Crane (1871–1900) Son of a Methodist minister, college baseball star, journalist. The "Wonderful Boy" of American literary naturalism, he published the now classic *Red Badge of Courage* when he was 24. He died of tuberculosis before he was 30. A forerunner of Hemingway in the stylized treatment of violence and war, he is noted for the poetic qualities of his fiction.

THE OPEN BOAT

A tale intended to be after the fact: being the experience of four men from the sunk steamer "Commodore"

I

None of them knew the color of the sky. Their eyes glanced level, and were fastened upon the waves that swept toward them. These waves were of the hue of slate, save for the tops, which were of foaming white, and all of the men knew the colors of the sea. The horizon narrowed and widened, and dipped and rose, and at all times its edge was jagged with waves that seemed thrust up in points like rocks.

Many a man ought to have a bathtub larger than the boat which here rode upon the sea. These waves were most wrongfully and barbarously abrupt and tall, and each froth-top was a problem in small-boat navigation.

The cook squatted in the bottom, and looked with both eyes at the six inches of gunwale which separated him from the ocean. His sleeves were rolled over his fat forearms, and the two flaps of his unbuttoned vest dangled as he bent to bail out the boat. Often he said, "Gawd! that was a narrow clip." As he remarked it he invariably gazed eastward over the broken sea.

The oiler, steering with one of the two oars in the boat, sometimes raised himself suddenly to keep clear of water that swirled in over the stern. It was a thin little oar, and it seemed often ready to snap.

The correspondent, pulling at the other oar, watched the waves and wondered why he was there.

The injured captain, lying in the bow, was at this time buried in that profound dejection and indifference which comes, temporarily at least, to even the bravest and most enduring when, willy-nilly, the firm fails, the army loses, the ship goes down. The mind of the master of a vessel is rooted deep in the timbers of her, though he command for a day or a decade; and this captain had on him the stern impression of a scene in the grays of dawn of seven turned faces, and later a stump of a topmast with a white ball on it, that slashed to and fro at the waves, went low and lower, and down. Thereafter there was something strange in his voice. Although steady, it was deep with mourning, and of a quality beyond oration or tears.

"Keep 'er a little more south, Billie," said he.

"A little more south, sir," said the oiler in the stern.

A seat in this boat was not unlike a seat upon a bucking broncho, and by the same token a broncho is not much smaller. The craft pranced and reared and plunged like an animal. As each wave came, and she rose for it, she seemed like a horse making at a fence outrageously high. The manner of her scramble over these walls of water was a mystic thing, and, moreover, at the top of them were ordinarily these problems in white water, the foam racing down from the summit of each wave requiring a new leap, and a leap from the air. Then, after scornfully bumping a crest, she would slide and race and splash down a long incline, and arrive bobbing and nodding in front of the next menace.

A singular disadvantage of the sea lies in the fact that after successfully surmounting one wave you discover that there is another behind it just as important and just as nervously anxious to do something effective in the way of swamping boats. In a ten-foot dinghy one can get an idea of the resources of the sea in the line of waves that is not probable to the average experience, which is never at sea in a dinghy. As each slaty wall of water approached, it shut all else from the view of the men in the boat, and it was not difficult to imagine that this particular wave was the final outburst of the ocean, the last effort of the grim water. There was a terrible grace in the move of the waves, and they came in silence, save for the snarling of the crests.

In the wan light the faces of the men must have been gray. Their eyes must have glinted in strange ways as they gazed steadily astern. Viewed from a balcony, the whole thing would, doubtless, have been weirdly picturesque. But the men in the boat had no time to see it, and if they had had leisure, there were other things to occupy their minds. The sun swung steadily up the sky, and they knew it was broad day because the color of the sea changed from slate to emerald-green streaked with amber lights, and the foam was like tumbling snow. The process of the breaking day was unknown to them. They were aware only of this effect upon the color of the waves that rolled toward them.

In disjointed sentences the cook and the correspondent argued as to the difference between a life-saving station and a house of refuge. The cook had said: "There's a house of refuge just north of the Mosquito Inlet Light, and as soon as they see us they'll come off in their boat and pick us up."

"As soon as who see us?" said the correspondent.

"The crew," said the cook.

"Houses of refuge don't have crews," said the correspondent. "As I understand them, they are only places where clothes and grub are stored for the benefit of shipwrecked people. They don't carry crews."

"Oh, yes, they do," said the cook.

"No, they don't," said the correspondent.

"Well, we're not there yet, anyhow," said the oiler, in the stern.

"Well," said the cook, "perhaps it's not a house of refuge that I'm thinking of as being near Mosquito Inlet Light; perhaps it's a life-saving station."

"We're not there yet," said the oiler in the stern.

As the boat bounced from the top of each wave the wind tore through the hair of the hatless men, and as the craft plopped her stern down again the spray slashed past them. The crest of each of these waves was a hill, from the top of which the men surveyed for a moment a broad tumultuous expanse, shining and wind-riven. It was probably splendid, it was probably glorious, this play of the free sea, wild with lights of emerald and white and amber.

"Bully good thing it's an on-shore wind," said the cook. "If not, where would we be? Wouldn't have a show."

"That's right," said the correspondent.

The busy oiler nodded his assent.

Then the captain, in the bow, chuckled in a way that expressed humor, contempt, tragedy, all in one. "Do you think we've got much of a show now, boys?" said he.

Whereupon the three were silent, save for a trifle of hemming and hawing. To express any particular optimism at this time they felt to be childish and stupid, but they all doubtless possessed this sense of the situation in their minds. A young man thinks doggedly at such times. On the other hand, the ethics of their condition was decidedly against any open suggestion of hopelessness. So they were silent.

"Oh, well," said the captain, soothing his children, "we'll get ashore all right."

But there was that in his tone which made them think; so the oiler quoth, "Yes! if this wind holds."

The cook was bailing. "Yes! if we don't catch hell in the surf."

Canton-flannel[1] gulls flew near and far. Sometimes they sat down on the sea, near patches of brown seaweed that rolled over the waves with a movement like carpets on a line in a gale. The birds sat comfortably in groups, and they were envied by some in the dinghy, for the wrath of the sea was no more to them than it was to a covey of prairie chickens a thousand miles inland. Often they came very close and stared at the men with black bead-like eyes. At these times they were uncanny and sinister in their unblinking scrutiny, and the men hooted angrily at them, telling them to be gone. One came, and evidently decided to alight on the top of the captain's head. The bird flew parallel to the boat and did not circle, but made short sidelong jumps in the air in chicken fashion. His black eyes were wistfully fixed upon the captain's head. "Ugly brute," said the oiler to the bird. "You look as if you were made with a jackknife." The cook and the correspondent swore darkly at the creature. The captain naturally wished to knock it away with the end of the heavy painter, but he did not dare do it, because anything resembling an emphatic gesture would have capsized this freighted boat; and so, with his open hand, the captain gently and carefully waved the gull away. After it had been discouraged from the pursuit the captain breathed easier on account of his hair, and others breathed easier because the bird struck their minds at this time as being somehow gruesome and ominous.

In the meantime the oiler and the correspondent rowed; and also they rowed.

They sat together in the same seat, and each rowed an oar. Then the oiler took both oars; then the correspondent took both oars, then the oiler; then the correspondent. They rowed and they rowed. The very ticklish part of the business was when the time came for the reclining one in the stern to take his turn at the oars. By the very last star of truth, it is easier to steal eggs from under a hen than it was to change seats in the dinghy. First the man in the stern slid his hand along the thwart and moved with care, as if he were of Sèvres.[2] Then the man in the rowing-seat slid his hand along the other thwart. It was all done with the most extraordinary care. As the two sidled past each other, the whole party kept watchful eyes on the coming wave, and the captain cried: "Look out, now! Steady, there!"

The brown mats of seaweed that appeared from time to time were like islands, bits of earth. They were travelling, apparently, neither one way nor the other. They were, to all intents, stationary. They informed the men in the boat that it was making progress slowly toward the land.

The captain, rearing cautiously in the bow after the dinghy soared on a great swell, said that he had seen the lighthouse at Mosquito Inlet. Presently the cook remarked that he had seen it. The correspondent was at the oars then, and for some reason he too wished to look at the lighthouse; but his back was toward the far shore, and the waves were important, and for some time he could not seize an opportunity to turn his head. But at last there came a wave more gentle than the others, and when at the crest of it he swiftly scoured the western horizon.

"See it?" said the captain.

"No," said the correspondent, slowly; "I didn't see anything."

"Look again," said the captain. He pointed. "It's exactly in that direction."

At the top of another wave the correspondent did as he was bid, and this time his eyes chanced on a small, still thing on the edge of the swaying horizon. It was precisely like the point of a pin. It took an anxious eye to find a lighthouse so tiny.

"Think we'll make it, Captain?"

"If this wind holds and the boat don't swamp, we can't do much else," said the captain.

The little boat, lifted by each towering sea and splashed viciously by the crests, made progress that in the absence of seaweed was not apparent to those in her. She seemed just a wee thing wallowing, miraculously top up, at the mercy of five oceans. Occasionally a great spread of water, like white flames, swarmed into her.

"Bail her, cook," said the captain, serenely.

"All right, Captain," said the cheerful cook.

III

It would be difficult to describe the subtle brotherhood of men that was here established on the seas. No one said that it was so. No one mentioned it. But it dwelt in the boat, and each man felt it warm him. They were a captain, an oiler, a cook, and a correspondent, and they were friends—friends in a more curiously iron-bound degree than may be common. The hurt captain, lying against the water-jar in the bow, spoke always in a low voice and calmly; but he could never command a more ready and swiftly obedient crew than the motley three of the dinghy. It was more than a mere recognition of what was best for the common safety. There was surely in it a quality that was personal and heart-felt. And after this devotion to the commander of the boat, there was this comradeship, that the correspondent, for instance, who had been taught to be cynical of men, knew even at the time was the best experience of his life. But no one said that it was so. No one mentioned it.

"I wish we had a sail," remarked the captain. "We might try my overcoat on the end of an oar, and give you two boys a chance to rest." So the cook and the correspondent held the mast and spread wide the overcoat; the oiler steered; and the little boat made good way with her new rig. Sometimes the oiler had to scull sharply to keep a sea from breaking into the boat, but otherwise sailing was a success.

Meanwhile the lighthouse had been growing slowly larger. It had now almost assumed color, and appeared like a little gray shadow on the sky. The man at the oars could not be prevented from turning his head rather often to try for a glimpse of this little gray shadow.

At last, from the top of each wave, the men in the tossing boat could see land. Even as the lighthouse was an upright shadow on the sky, this land seemed but a long black shadow on the sea. It certainly was thinner than paper. "We must be about opposite New Smyrna,"[3] said the cook, who had coasted this shore often in schooners. "Captain, by the way, I believe they abandoned that life-saving station there about a year ago."

"Did they?" said the captain.

The wind slowly died away. The cook and the correspondent were not now obliged to slave in order to hold high the oar. But the waves continued their old impetuous swooping at the dinghy, and the little craft, no longer under way, struggled woundily over them. The oiler or the correspondent took the oars again.

Shipwrecks are *apropos* of nothing. If men could only train for them and have them occur when the men had reached pink condition, there would be less drowning at sea. Of the four in the dinghy none had slept any time worth mentioning for two days and two nights previous to embarking in the dinghy, and in the excitement of clambering about the deck of a foundering ship they had also forgotten to eat heartily.

For these reasons, and for others, neither the oiler nor the correspondent was fond of rowing at this time. The correspondent wondered ingenuously how in the name of all that was sane could there be people who thought it amusing to row a boat. It was not an amusement; it was a diabolical punishment, and even a genius of mental aberrations could never conclude that it was anything but a horror to the muscles and a crime against the back. He mentioned to the boat in general how the amusement of rowing struck him, and the weary-faced oiler smiled in full sympathy. Previously to the foundering by the way, the oiler had worked a double watch in the engine-room of the ship.

"Take her easy now, boys," said the captain. "Don't spend yourselves. If we have to run a surf you'll need all your strength, because we'll sure have to swim for it. Take your time."

Slowly the land arose from the sea. From a black line it became a line of black and a line of white—trees and sand. Finally the captain said that he could make out a house on the shore. "That's the house of refuge, sure," said the cook. "They'll see us before long, and come out after us."

The distant lighthouse reared high. "The keeper ought to be able to make us out now, if he's looking through a glass," said the captain. "He'll notify the life-saving people."

"None of those other boats could have got ashore to give word of this wreck," said the oiler, in a low voice, "else the life-boat would be out hunting us."

Slowly and beautifully the land loomed out of the sea. The wind came again. It had veered from the northeast to the southeast. Finally a new sound struck the ears of the men in the boat. It was the low thunder of the surf on the shore. "We'll never be able to make the lighthouse now," said the captain. "Swing her a little more north, Billie."

"A little more north, sir," said the oiler.

Whereupon the little boat turned her nose once more down the wind, and all but the oarsman watched the shore grow. Under the influence of this expansion doubt and direful apprehension were leaving the minds of the men. The management of the boat was still most absorbing, but it could not prevent a quiet cheerfulness. In an hour, perhaps, they would be ashore.

Their backbones had become thoroughly used to balancing in the boat, and they now rode this wild colt of a dinghy like circus men. The correspondent thought that he had been drenched to the skin, but happening to feel in the top pocket of his coat, he found therein eight cigars. Four of them were soaked with sea-water; four were perfectly scatheless. After a search, somebody produced three dry matches; and thereupon the four waifs rode impudently in their little boat and, with an assurance of an impending rescue shining in their eyes, puffed at the big cigars, and judged well and ill of all men. Everybody took a drink of water.

IV

"Cook," remarked the captain, "there don't seem to be any signs of life about your house of refuge."

"No," replied the cook. "Funny they don't see us!"

A broad stretch of lowly coast lay before the eyes of the men. It was of low dunes topped with dark vegetation. The roar of the surf was plain, and sometimes they could see the white lip of a wave as it spun up the beach. A tiny house was blocked out black upon the sky. Southward, the slim lighthouse lifted its little gray length.

Tide, wind, and waves were swinging the dinghy northward. "Funny they don't see us," said the men.

159

The surf's roar was here dulled, but its tone was nevertheless thunderous and mighty. As the boat swam over the great rollers the men sat listening to this roar. "We'll swamp sure," said everybody.

It is fair to say here that there was not a life-saving station within twenty miles in either direction; but the men did not know this fact, and in consequence they made dark and opprobrious remarks concerning the eyesight of the nation's life-savers. Four scowling men sat in the dinghy and surpassed records in the invention of epithets.

"Funny they don't see us."

The light-heartedness of a former time had completely faded. To their sharpened minds it was easy to conjure pictures of all kinds of incompetency and blindness and, indeed, cowardice. There was the shore of the populous land, and it was bitter and bitter to them that from it came no sign.

"Well," said the captain, ultimately, "I suppose we'll have to make a try for ourselves. If we stay out here too long, we'll none of us have strength left to swim after the boat swamps."

And so the oiler, who was at the oars, turned the boat straight for the shore. There was a sudden tightening of muscles. There was some thinking.

"If we don't all get ashore," said the captain—"if we don't all get ashore, I suppose you fellows know where to send news of my finish?"

They then briefly exchanged some addresses and admonitions. As for the reflections of the men, there was a great deal of rage in them. Perchance they might be formulated thus: "If I am going to be drowned—if I am going to be drowned —if I am going to be drowned, why, in the name of the seven mad gods who rule the sea, was I allowed to come thus far and contemplate sand and trees? Was I brought here merely to have my nose dragged away as I was about to nibble the sacred cheese of life? It is preposterous. If this old ninny-woman, Fate, cannot do better than this, she should be deprived of the management of men's fortunes. She is an old hen who knows not her intention. If she has decided to drown me, why did she not do it in the beginning and save me all this trouble? The whole affair is absurd. . . . But no; she cannot mean to drown me. She dare not drown me. She cannot drown me. Not after all this work." Afterward the man might have had an impulse to shake his fist at the clouds. "Just you drown me, now, and then hear what I call you!"

The billows that came at this time were more formidable. They seemed always just about to break and roll over the little boat in a turmoil of foam. There was a preparatory and long growl in the speech of them. No mind unused to the sea would have concluded that the dinghy could ascend these sheer heights in time. The shore was still afar. The oiler was a wily surfman. "Boys," he said swiftly, "she won't live three minutes more, and we're too far out to swim. Shall I take her to sea again, Captain?"

"Yes; go ahead!" said the captain.

This oiler, by a series of quick miracles and fast and steady oarsmanship, turned the boat in the middle of the surf and took her safely to sea again.

There was a considerable silence as the boat bumped over the furrowed sea to deeper water. Then somebody in gloom spoke: "Well, anyhow, they must have seen us from the shore by now."

The gulls went in slanting flight up the wind toward the gray, desolate east. A squall, marked by dingy clouds and clouds brick-red, like smoke from a burning building, appeared from the southeast.

"What do you think of those life-saving people? Ain't they peaches?"

"Funny they haven't seen us."

"Maybe they think we're out here for sport! Maybe they think we're fishin'. Maybe they think we're damned fools."

It was a long afternoon. A changed tide tried to force them southward, but wind and wave said northward. Far ahead, where coast-line, sea, and sky formed their mighty angle, there were little dots which seemed to indicate a city on the shore.

"St. Augustine?"

The captain shook his head. "Too near Mosquito Inlet."

And the oiler rowed and then the correspondent rowed; then the oiler rowed. It was a weary business. The human back can become the seat of more aches and pains than are registered in books for the composite anatomy of a regiment. It is a limited area, but it can become the theater of innumerable muscular conflicts, tangles, wrenches, knots, and other comforts.

"Did you ever like to row, Billie?" asked the correspondent.

"No," said the oiler; "hang it!"

When one exchanged the rowing-seat for a place in the bottom of the boat, he suffered a bodily depression that caused him to be careless of everything save an obligation to wiggle one finger. There was cold sea-water swashing to and fro in the boat, and he lay in it. His head, pillowed on a thwart, was within an inch of the swirl of a wave-crest, and sometimes a particularly obstreperous sea came inboard and drenched him once more. But these matters did not annoy him. It is almost certain that if the boat had capsized he would have tumbled comfortably out upon the ocean as if he felt sure that it was a great soft mattress.

"Look! There's a man on the shore!"

"Where?"

"There! See 'im? See 'im?"

"Yes, sure! He's walking along."

"Now he's stopped. Look! He's facing us!"

"He's waving at us!"

"So he is! By thunder!"

"Ah, now we're all right! Now we're all right! There'll be a boat out here for us in half an hour."

"He's going on. He's running. He's going up to that house there."

The remote beach seemed lower than the sea, and it required a searching glance to discern the little black figure. The captain saw a floating stick, and they rowed to it. A bath towel was by some weird chance in the boat, and, tying this on the stick, the captain waved it. The oarsman did not dare turn his head, so he was obliged to ask questions.

"What's he doing now?"

"He's standing still again. He's looking, I think. . . . There he goes again—toward the house. . . . Now he's stopped again."

"Is he waving at us?"

"No, not now; he was, though."

"Look! There comes another man!"

"He's running."

"Look at him go, would you!"

"Why, he's on a bicycle. Now he's met the other man. They're both waving at us. Look!"

"There comes something up the beach."

"What the devil is that thing?"

"Why, it looks like a boat."

"Why, certainly, it's a boat."

"No; it's on wheels."

"Yes, so it is. Well, that must be the life-boat. They drag them along shore on a wagon."

"That's the life-boat, sure."

"No, by God, it's—it's an omnibus."

"I tell you it's a life-boat."

"It is not! It's an omnibus. I can see it plain. See? One of these big hotel omnibuses."

"By thunder, you're right. It's an omnibus, sure as fate. What do you suppose they are doing with an omnibus? Maybe they are going around collecting the life-crew, hey?"

"That's it, likely. Look! There's a fellow waving a little black flag. He's standing on the steps of the omnibus. There come those other two fellows. Now they're all talking together. Look at the fellow with the flag. Maybe he ain't waving it!"

"That ain't a flag, is it? That's his coat. Why, certainly, that's his coat."

"So it is; it's his coat. He's taken it off and is waving it round his head. But would you look at him swing it!"

"Oh, say, there isn't any life-saving station there. That's just a winter-resort hotel omnibus that has brought over some of the boarders to see us drown."

"What's that idiot with the coat mean? What's he signalling, anyhow?"

"It looks as if he were trying to tell us to go north. There must be a life-saving station up there."

"No; he thinks we're fishing. Just giving us a merry hand. See? Ah, there, Willie!"

"Well, I wish I could make something out of those signals. What do you suppose he means?"

"He don't mean anything; he's just playing."

"Well, if he'd just signal us to try the surf again, or to go to sea and wait, or go north, or go south, or go to hell, there would be some reason in it. But look at him! He just stands there and keeps his coat revolving like a wheel. The ass!"

162

"There come more people."

"Now there's quite a mob. Look! Isn't that a boat?"

"Where? Oh, I see where you mean. No, that's no boat."

"That fellow is still waving his coat."

"He must think we like to see him do that. Why don't he quit it? It don't mean anything."

"I don't know. I think he is trying to make us go north. It must be that there's a life-saving station there somewhere."

"Say, he ain't tired yet. Look at 'im wave!"

"Wonder how long he can keep that up. He's been revolving his coat ever since he caught sight of us. He's an idiot. Why aren't they getting men to bring a boat out? A fishing-boat—one of those big yawls—could come out here all right. Why don't he do something?"

"Oh, it's all right now."

"They'll have a boat out here for us in less than no time, now that they've seen us."

A faint yellow tone came into the sky over the low land. The shadows on the sea slowly deepened. The wind bore coldness with it, and the men began to shiver.

"Holy smoke!" said one, allowing his voice to express his impious mood, "if we keep on monkeying out here! If we've got to flounder out here all night!"

"Oh, we'll never have to stay here all night! Don't you worry. They've seen us now, and it won't be long before they'll come chasing out after us."

The shore grew dusky. The man waving a coat blended gradually into this gloom, and it swallowed in the same manner the omnibus and the group of people. The spray, when it dashed uproariously over the side, made the voyagers shrink and swear like men who were being branded.

"I'd like to catch the chump who waved the coat. I feel like socking him one, just for luck."

"Why? What did he do?"

"Oh, nothing, but then he seemed so damned cheerful."

In the meantime the oiler rowed, and then the correspondent rowed, and then the oiler rowed. Gray-faced and bowed forward, they mechanically, turn by turn, plied the leaden oars. The form of the lighthouse had vanished from the southern horizon, but finally a pale star appeared, just lifting from the sea. The streaked saffron in the west passed before the all-merging darkness, and the sea to the east was black. The land had vanished, and was expressed only by the low and drear thunder of the surf.

"If I am going to be drowned—if I am going to be drowned—if I am going to be drowned, why, in the name of the seven mad gods who rule the sea, was I allowed to come thus far and contemplate sand and trees? Was I brought here merely to have my nose dragged away as I was about to nibble the sacred cheese of life?"

The patient captain, drooped over the water-jar, was sometimes obliged to speak to the oarsman.

"Keep her head up! Keep her head up!"

"Keep her head up, sir." The voices were weary and low.

This was surely a quiet evening. All save the oarsman lay heavily and listlessly in the boat's bottom. As for him, his eyes were just capable of noting the tall black waves that swept forward in a most sinister silence, save for an occasional subdued growl of a crest.

The cook's head was on a thwart, and he looked without interest at the water under his nose. He was deep in other scenes. Finally he spoke, "Billie," he murmured, dreamfully, "what kind of pie do you like best?"

V

"Pie!" said the oiler and the correspondent, agitatedly. "Don't talk about those things, blast you!"

"Well," said the cook, "I was just thinking about ham sandwiches, and—"

A night on the sea in an open boat is a long night. As darkness settled finally, the shine of the light, lifting from the sea in the south, changed to full gold. On the northern horizon a new light appeared, a small bluish gleam on the edge of the waters. These two lights were the furniture of the world. Otherwise there was nothing but waves.

Two men huddled in the stern, and distances were so magnificent in the dinghy that the rower was enabled to keep his feet partly warm by thrusting them under his companions. Their legs indeed extended far under the rowing-seat until they touched the feet of the captain forward. Sometimes, despite the efforts of the tired oarsman, a wave came piling into the boat, an icy wave of the night, and the chilling water soaked them anew. They would twist their bodies for a moment and groan, and sleep the dead sleep once more, while the water in the boat gurgled about them as the craft rocked.

The plan of the oiler and the correspondent was for one to row until he lost the ability, and then arouse the other from his seawater couch in the bottom of the boat.

The oiler plied the oars until his head drooped forward and the overpowering sleep blinded him; and he rowed yet afterward. Then he touched a man in the bottom of the boat, and called his name. "Will you spell me for a little while?" he said meekly.

"Sure, Billie," said the correspondent, awaking and dragging himself to a sitting position. They exchanged places carefully, and the oiler, cuddling down in the sea-water at the cook's side, seemed to go to sleep instantly.

The particular violence of the sea had ceased. The waves came without snarling. The obligation of the man at the oars was to keep the boat headed so that the tilt of the rollers would not capsize her, and to preserve her from filling when the crests rushed past. The black waves were silent and hard to be seen in the darkness. Often one was almost upon the boat before the oarsman was aware.

In a low voice the correspondent addressed the captain. He was not sure that the captain was awake, although this iron man seemed to be always awake. "Captain, shall I keep her making for that light north, sir?"

The same steady voice answered him. "Yes. Keep it about two points off the port bow."

The cook had tied a life-belt around himself in order to get even the warmth which this clumsy cork contrivance could donate, and he seemed almost stove-like when a rower, whose teeth invariably chattered wildly as soon as he ceased his labor, dropped down to sleep.

The correspondent, as he rowed, looked down at the two men sleeping underfoot. The cook's arm was around the oiler's shoulders, and, with their fragmentary clothing and haggard faces, they were the babes of the sea—a grotesque rendering of the old babes in the wood.

Later he must have grown stupid at his work, for suddenly there was a growling of water, and a crest came with a roar and a swash into the boat, and it was a wonder that it did not set the cook afloat in his life-belt. The cook continued to sleep, but the oiler sat up, blinking his eyes and shaking with the new cold.

"Oh, I'm awful sorry, Billie," said the correspondent, contritely.

"That's all right, old boy," said the oiler, and lay down again and was asleep.

Presently it seemed that even the captain dozed, and the correspondent thought that he was the one man afloat on all the ocean. The wind had a voice as it came over the waves, and it was sadder than the end.

There was a long, loud swishing astern of the boat, and a gleaming trail of phosphorescence, like blue flame, was furrowed on the black waters. It might have been made by a monstrous knife.

Then there came a stillness, while the correspondent breathed with open mouth and looked at the sea.

Suddenly there was another swish and another long flash of bluish light, and this time it was alongside the boat, and might almost have been reached with an oar. The correspondent saw an enormous fin speed like a shadow through the water, hurling the crystalline spray and leaving the long glowing trail.

The correspondent looked over his shoulder at the captain. His face was hidden, and he seemed to be asleep. He looked at the babes of the sea. They certainly were asleep. So, being bereft of sympathy, he leaned a little way to one side and swore softly into the sea.

But the thing did not then leave the vicinity of the boat. Ahead or astern, on one side or the other, at intervals long or short, fled the long sparkling streak, and there was to be heard the *whirroo* of the dark fin. The speed and power of the thing was greatly to be admired. It cut the water like a gigantic and keen projectile.

The presence of this biding thing did not affect the man with the same horror that it would if he had been a picnicker. He simply looked at the sea dully and swore in an undertone.

Nevertheless, it is true that he did not wish to be alone with the thing. He wished one of his companions to awake by chance and keep him company with it. But the captain hung motionless over the water-jar, and the oiler and the cook in the bottom of the boat were plunged in slumber.

VI

"If I am going to be drowned—if I am going to be drowned—if I am going to be drowned, why, in the name of the seven mad gods who rule the sea, was I allowed to come thus far and contemplate sand and trees?"

During this dismal night, it may be remarked that a man would conclude that it was really the intention of the seven mad gods to drown him, despite the abominable injustice of it. For it was certainly an abominable injustice to drown a man who had worked so hard, so hard. The man felt it would be a crime most unnatural. Other people had drowned at sea since galleys swarmed with painted sails, but still—

When it occurs to a man that nature does not regard him as important, and that she feels she would not maim the universe by disposing of him, he at first wishes to throw bricks at the temple, and he hates deeply the fact that there are no bricks and no temples. Any visible expression of nature would surely be pelleted with his jeers.

Then, if there be no tangible thing to hoot, he feels, perhaps, the desire to confront a personification and indulge in pleas, bowed to one knee, and with hands supplicant, saying, "Yes, but I love myself."

A high cold star on a winter's night is the word he feels that she says to him. Thereafter he knows the pathos of his situation.

The men in the dinghy had not discussed these matters, but each had, no doubt, reflected upon them in silence and according to his mind. There was seldom any expression upon their faces save the general one of complete weariness. Speech was devoted to the business of the boat.

To chime the notes of his emotion, a verse mysteriously entered the correspondent's head. He had even forgotten that he had forgotten this verse, but it suddenly was in his mind.

> *A soldier of the Legion lay dying in Algiers;*
> *There was lack of woman's nursing, there was dearth of woman's tears;*
> *But a comrade stood beside him, and he took that comrade's hand,*
> *And he said, "I never more shall see my own, my native land."*[4]

In his childhood the correspondent had been made acquainted with the fact that a soldier of the Legion lay dying in Algiers, but he had never regarded it as important. Myriads of his schoolfellows had informed him of the soldier's plight, but the dinning had naturally ended by making him perfectly indifferent. He had never considered it his affair that a soldier of the Legion lay dying in Algiers, nor had it appeared to him as a matter for sorrow. It was less to him than the breaking of a pencil's point.

Now, however, it quaintly came to him as a human, living thing. It was no longer merely a picture of a few throes in the breast of a poet, meanwhile drinking tea and warming his feet at the grate; it was an actuality—stern, mournful, and fine.

The correspondent plainly saw the soldier. He lay on the sand with his feet out straight and still. While his pale left hand was upon his chest in an attempt to thwart the going of his life, the blood came between his fingers. In the far Algerian distance, a city of low square forms was set against a sky that was faint with the last sunset hues. The correspondent, plying the oars and dreaming of the slow and slower movements of the lips of the soldier, was moved by a profound and perfectly impersonal comprehension. He was sorry for the soldier of the Legion who lay dying in Algiers.

The thing which had followed the boat and waited had evidently grown bored at the delay. There was no longer to be heard the slash of the cutwater, and there was no longer the flame of the long trail. The light in the north still glimmered, but it was apparently no nearer to the boat. Sometimes the boom of the surf rang in the correspondent's ears, and he turned the craft seaward then and rowed harder. Southward, some one had evidently built a watch-fire on the beach. It was too low and too far to be seen, but it made a shimmering, roseate reflection upon the bluff in back of it, and this could be discerned from the boat. The wind came stronger, and sometimes a wave suddenly raged out like a mountain-cat, and there was to be seen the sheen and sparkle of a broken crest.

The captain, in the bow, moved on his water-jar and sat erect. "Pretty long night," he observed to the correspondent. He looked at the shore. "Those life-saving people take their time."

"Did you see that shark playing around?"

"Yes, I saw him. He was a big fellow, all right."

"Wish I had known you were awake."

Later the correspondent spoke into the bottom of the boat. "Billie!" There was a slow and gradual disentanglement. "Billie, will you spell me?"

"Sure," said the oiler.

As soon as the correspondent touched the cold, comfortable sea-water in the bottom of the boat and had huddled close to the cook's life-belt he was deep in sleep, despite the fact that his teeth played all the popular airs. This sleep was so good to him that it was but a moment before he heard a voice call his name in a tone that demonstrated the last stages of exhaustion. "Will you spell me?"

"Sure, Billie."

The light in the north had mysteriously vanished, but the correspondent took his course from the wide-awake captain.

Later in the night they took the boat farther out to sea, and the captain directed the cook to take one oar at the stern and keep the boat facing the seas. He was to call out if he should hear the thunder of the surf. This plan enabled the oiler and the correspondent to get respite together. "We'll give those boys a chance to get into shape again," said the captain. They curled down and, after a few preliminary chatterings and trembles, slept once more the dead sleep. Neither knew they had bequeathed to the cook the company of another shark, or perhaps the same shark.

As the boat caroused on the waves, spray occasionally bumped over the side and gave them a fresh soaking, but this had no power to break their repose. The ominous slash of the wind and the water affected them as it would have affected mummies.

"Boys," said the cook, with the notes of every reluctance in his voice, "she's drifted in pretty close. I guess one of you had better take her to sea again." The correspondent, aroused, heard the crash of the toppled crests.

As he was rowing, the captain gave him some whiskey-and-water, and this steadied the chills out of him. "If I ever get ashore and anybody shows me even a photograph of an oar—"

At last there was a short conversation.

"Billie! . . . Billie, will you spell me?"

"Sure," said the oiler.

VII

When the correspondent again opened his eyes, the sea and the sky were each of the gray hue of the dawning. Later, carmine and gold was painted upon the waters. The morning appeared finally, in its splendor, with a sky of pure blue, and the sunlight flamed on the tips of the waves.

On the distant dunes were set many little black cottages, and a tall white windmill reared above them. No man, nor dog, nor bicycle appeared on the beach. The cottages might have formed a deserted village.

The voyagers scanned the shore. A conference was held in the boat. "Well," said the captain, "if no help is coming, we might better try a run through the surf right away. If we stay out here much longer we will be too weak to do anything for ourselves at all." The others silently acquiesced in this reasoning. The boat was headed for the beach. The correspondent wondered if none ever ascended the tall wind-tower, and if then they never looked seaward. This tower was a giant, standing with its back to the plight of the ants. It represented in a degree, to the correspondent, the serenity of nature amid the struggles of the individual—nature in the wind, and nature in the vision of men. She did not seem cruel to him then, nor beneficent, nor treacherous, nor wise. But she was indifferent, flatly indifferent. It is, perhaps, plausible that a man in this situation, impressed with the unconcern of the universe, should see the innumerable flaws of his life, and have them taste wickedly in his mind, and wish for another chance. A distinction between right and wrong seems absurdly clear to him, then, in this new ignorance of the grave-edge, and he understands that if he were given another opportunity he would mend his conduct and his words, and be better and brighter during an introduction or at a tea.

"Now, boys," said the captain, "she is going to swamp sure. All we can do is to work her in as far as possible, and then when she swamps, pile out and scramble for the beach. Keep cool now, and don't jump until she swamps sure."

The oiler took the oars. Over his shoulders he scanned the surf. "Captain," he said, "I think I'd better bring her about and keep her head-on to the seas and back her in."

"All right, Billie," said the captain. "Back her in." The oiler swung the boat

168

then, and, seated in the stern, the cook and the correspondent were obliged to look over their shoulders to contemplate the lonely and indifferent shore.

The monstrous inshore rollers heaved the boat high until the men were again enabled to see the white sheets of water scudding up the slanted beach. "We won't get in very close," said the captain. Each time a man could wrest his attention from the rollers, he turned his glance toward the shore, and in the expression of the eyes during this contemplation there was a singular quality. The correspondent, observing the others, knew that they were not afraid, but the full meaning of their glances was shrouded.

As for himself, he was too tired to grapple fundamentally with the fact. He tried to coerce his mind into thinking of it, but the mind was dominated at this time by the muscles, and the muscles said they did not care. It merely occurred to him that if he should drown it would be a shame.

There were no hurried words, no pallor, no plain agitation. The men simply looked at the shore. "Now, remember to get well clear of the boat when you jump," said the captain.

Seaward the crest of a roller suddenly fell with a thunderous crash, and the long white comber came roaring down upon the boat.

"Steady now," said the captain. The men were silent. They turned their eyes from the shore to the comber and waited. The boat slid up the incline, leaped at the furious top, bounced over it, and swung down the long back of the wave. Some water had been shipped, and the cook bailed it out.

But the next crest crashed also. The tumbling, boiling flood of white water caught the boat and whirled it almost perpendicular. Water swarmed in from all sides. The correspondent had his hands on the gunwale at this time, and when the water entered at that place he swiftly withdrew his fingers, as if he objected to wetting them.

The little boat, drunken with this weight of water, reeled and snuggled deeper into the sea.

"Bail her out, cook! Bail her out!" said the captain.

"All right, Captain," said the cook.

"Now, boys, the next one will do for us sure," said the oiler. "Mind to jump clear of the boat."

The third wave moved forward, huge, furious, implacable. It fairly swallowed the dinghy, and almost simultaneously the men tumbled into the sea. A piece of life-belt had lain in the bottom of the boat, and as the correspondent went overboard he held this to his chest with his left hand.

The January water was icy, and he reflected immediately that it was colder than he had expected to find it off the coast of Florida. This appeared to his dazed mind as a fact important enough to be noted at the time. The coldness of the water was sad; it was tragic. This fact was somehow mixed and confused with his opinion of his own situation, so that it seemed almost a proper reason for tears. The water was cold.

When he came to the surface he was conscious of little but the noisy water. Afterward he saw his companions in the sea. The oiler was ahead in the race. He

169

was swimming strongly and rapidly. Off to the correspondent's left, the cook's great white and corked back bulged out of the water; and in the rear the captain was hanging with his one good hand to the keel of the overturned dinghy.

There is a certain immovable quality to a shore, and the correspondent wondered at it amid the confusion of the sea.

It seemed also very attractive; but the correspondent knew that it was a long journey, and he paddled leisurely. The piece of life-preserver lay under him, and sometimes he whirled down the incline of a wave as if he were on a hand-sled.

But finally he arrived at a place in the sea where travel was beset with difficulty. He did not pause swimming to inquire what manner of current had caught him, but there his progress ceased. The shore was set before him like a bit of scenery on a stage, and he looked at it and understood with his eyes each detail of it.

As the cook passed, much farther to the left, the captain was calling to him, "Turn over on your back, cook! Turn over on your back and use the oar."

"All right, sir." The cook turned on his back, and, paddling with an oar, went ahead as if he were a canoe.

Presently the boat also passed to the left of the correspondent, with the captain clinging with one hand to the keel. He would have appeared like a man raising himself to look over a board fence if it were not for the extraordinary gymnastics of the boat. The correspondent marvelled that the captain could still hold to it.

They passed on nearer to shore—the oiler, the cook, the captain—and following them went the water-jar, bouncing gaily over the seas.

The correspondent remained in the grip of this strange new enemy, a current. The shore, with its white slope of sand and its green bluff topped with little silent cottages, was spread like a picture before him. It was very near to him then, but he was impressed as one who, in a gallery, looks at a scene from Brittany or Algiers.

He thought: "I am going to drown? Can it be possible? Can it be possible? Can it be possible?" Perhaps an individual must consider his own death to be the final phenomenon of nature.

But later a wave perhaps whirled him out of this small deadly current, for he found suddenly that he could again make progress toward the shore. Later still he was aware that the captain, clinging with one hand to the keel of the dinghy, had his face turned away from the shore and toward him, and was calling his name. "Come to the boat! Come to the boat!"

In his struggle to reach the captain and the boat, he reflected that when one gets properly wearied drowning must really be a comfortable arrangement—a cessation of hostilities accompanied by a large degree of relief; and he was glad of it, for the main thing in his mind for some moments had been horror of the temporary agony; he did not wish to be hurt.

Presently he saw a man running along the shore. He was undressing with most remarkable speed. Coat, trousers, shirt, everything flew magically off him.

"Come to the boat!" called the captain.

"All right, Captain." As the correspondent paddled, he saw the captain let himself down to bottom and leave the boat. Then the correspondent performed his one little marvel of the voyage. A large wave caught him and flung him with ease and supreme speed completely over the boat and far beyond it. It struck him even then as an event in gymnastics and a true miracle of the sea. An overturned boat in the surf is not a plaything to a swimming man.

The correspondent arrived in water that reached only to his waist, but his condition did not enable him to stand for more than a moment. Each wave knocked him into a heap, and the undertow pulled at him.

Then he saw the man who had been running and undressing, and undressing and running, come bounding into the water. He dragged ashore the cook, and then waded toward the captain; but the captain waved him away and sent him to the correspondent. He was naked—naked as a tree in winter; but a halo was about his head, and he shone like a saint. He gave a strong pull, and a long drag, and a bully heave at the correspondent's hand. The correspondent, schooled in the minor formulae, said, "Thanks, old man." But suddenly the man cried, "What's that?" He pointed a swift finger. The correspondent said, "Go."

In the shallows, face downward, lay the oiler. His forehead touched sand that was periodically, between each wave, clear of the sea.

The correspondent did not know all that transpired afterward. When he achieved safe ground he fell, striking the sand with each particular part of his body. It was as if he had dropped from a roof, but the thud was grateful to him.

It seems that instantly the beach was populated with men with blankets, clothes, and flasks, and women with coffee-pots and all the remedies sacred to their minds. The welcome of the land to the men from the sea was warm and generous; but a still and dripping shape was carried slowly up the beach, and the land's welcome for it could only be the different and sinister hospitality of the grave.

When it came night, the white waves paced to and fro in the moonlight, and the wind brought the sound of the great sea's voice to the men on the shore, and they felt that they could then be interpreters.

---

[1] Cotton fabric. The gulls' feathers resembled this material.
[2] A type of very good French china.
[3] Florida coastal town south of Daytona Beach.
[4] A stanza from "Bingen on the Rhine" by Caroline E. S. Norton (1808–1877).

DISCUSSION TOPICS

1. Critic John T. Frederick has pointed out that there is a *fifth* person in "The Open Boat": the reader. How does Crane manage to get you into the boat?
2. Crane's story is a model of literary naturalism, an aspect of which is the pitting of puny man against the overwhelming and pitiless forces of Nature. What other major thematic element redeems the story from bleak pessimism?

3. Especially praiseworthy in this story is Crane's firm control of point of view: third-person limited (excepting the effective use of "you" in the third paragraph on p. 155 and of the occasional ironic speculations on the "quaint" and "picturesque" view of the boat from the shore). What is the appropriateness of Crane's use of the correspondent as "central intelligence"?

4. Discuss the relationship between life as experienced in the raw and life as encountered in literature, with specific attention to the following passage: "To chime the notes of his emotion, a verse mysteriously entered the correspondent's head. . . . He had never considered it his affair that a soldier of the Legion lay dying in Algiers, nor had it appeared to him as a matter for sorrow. . . . Now, however, it quaintly came to him as a human, living thing. . . . He was sorry for the soldier of the Legion who lay dying in Algiers."

5. Analyze the boat and its occupants as a metaphor for human society. Consider how the four men—a captain, a cook, an oiler, and a correspondent—constitute a composite man, or a microcosm of society.

6. Like several other selections in *LIT,* "The Open Boat" deals with the archetypal theme of initiation: the gaining of wisdom through ordeal. For example, compare the initiatory experience of Crane's "babes of the sea" with the awakening of the poet's creative demon by the "savage old mother" in Whitman's "Out of the Cradle Endlessly Rocking." Comment particularly on the meaning of Crane's concluding statement "they felt that they could then be interpreters."

WRITING TOPIC

In 1897 Joseph Conrad wrote to Crane: "The boat thing is immensely interesting. I don't use the word in its common sense. It is fundamentally interesting to me. Your temperament makes old things new and new things amazing. . . . You are an everlasting surprise to one. You shock—and the next moment you give the perfect artistic satisfaction. Your method is fascinating. You are a complete impressionist. The illusions of life come out of your hand without a flaw. It is not life—which nobody wants—it is art—art for which everyone—the abject and the great —hanker—mostly without knowing it." Explain the manifold significance of Conrad's last remark, pointing out the difference between "life" and "art" in Crane's "The Open Boat" and Conrad's *Heart of Darkness.*

JACK LONDON (1876–1916) Born illegitimate, the son of an itinerant astrologer and a spiritualist; reared in poverty; a newsboy, oyster pirate, hobo, and convict during his youth. London produced over fifty books on a wide range of subjects during his brief, spectacular career; and his world classic, *The Call of the Wild,* has been translated into more than seventy languages. A literary disciple of Poe, Melville, and Conrad, London was also the first major writer to incorporate the theories of Freud and Jung into his fiction.

THE RED ONE

There it was! The abrupt liberation of sound, as he timed it with his watch, Bassett likened to the trump of an archangel. Walls of cities, he meditated, might well fall down before so vast and compelling a summons. For the thousandth time vainly he tried to analyze the tone-quality of that enormous peal that dominated the land far into the strongholds of the surrounding tribes. The mountain gorge which was its source rang to the rising tide of it until it brimmed over and flooded earth and sky and air. With the wantonness of a sick man's fancy, he likened it to the mighty cry of some Titan of the Elder World vexed with misery or wrath. Higher and higher it arose, challenging and demanding in such profounds of volume that it seemed intended for ears beyond the narrow confines of the solar system. There was in it, too, the clamor of protest in that there were no ears to hear and comprehend its utterance.

—Such the sick man's fancy. Still he strove to analyze the sound. Sonorous as thunder was it, mellow as a golden bell, thin and sweet as a thrummed taut cord of silver—no; it was none of these, nor a blend of these. There were no words nor semblances in his vocabulary and experience with which to describe the totality of that sound.

Time passed. Minutes merged into quarters of hours, and quarters of hours into half hours, and still the sound persisted, ever changing from its initial vocal impulse yet never receiving fresh impulse—fading, dimming, dying as enormously as it had sprung into being. It became a confusion of troubled mutterings and babblings and colossal whisperings. Slowly it withdrew, sob by sob, into whatever great bosom had birthed it, until it whimpered deadly whispers of wrath and as equally seductive whispers of delight, striving still to be heard, to convey some cosmic secret, some understanding of infinite import and value. It dwindled to a ghost of sound that had lost its menace and promise, and became a thing that pulsed on in the sick man's consciousness for minutes after it had ceased. When he could hear it no longer, Bassett glanced at his watch. An hour had elapsed ere that archangel's trump had subsided into tonal nothingness.

Was this, then, *his* dark tower?[1]—Bassett pondered, remembering his Browning and gazing at his skeletonlike and fever-wasted hands. And the fancy made him smile—of Childe Roland bearing a slughorn to his lips with an arm as feeble as his was. Was it months, or years, he asked himself, since he first heard that mysterious call on the beach at Ringmanu? To save himself he could not tell. The long sickness had been most long. In conscious count of time he knew of months, many of them; but he had no way of estimating the long intervals of delirium and stupor. And how fared Captain Bateman of the blackbirder *Nari?* he wondered; and had Captain Bateman's drunken mate died of delirium tremens yet?

From which vain speculations, Bassett turned idly to review all that had occurred since that day on the beach of Ringmanu when he first heard the sound and plunged into the jungle after it. Sagawa had protested. He could see him yet, his queer little monkeyish face eloquent with fear, his back burdened with specimen cases, in his hands Bassett's butterfly net and naturalist's shotgun, as he quavered in bêche de mer English: "Me fella too much fright along bush. Bad fella boy too much stop'm along bush."

Bassett smiled sadly at the recollection. The little New Hanover boy had been frightened, but had proved faithful, following him without hesitancy into the bush in the quest after the source of the wonderful sound. No fire-hollowed tree trunk, that, throbbing war through the jungle depths, had been Bassett's conclusion. Erroneous had been his next conclusion, namely, that the source or cause could not be more distant than an hour's walk and that he would easily be back by midafternoon to be picked up by the *Nari's* whaleboat.

"That big fella noise no good, all the same devil-devil," Sagawa had adjudged. And Sagawa had been right. Had he not had his head hacked off within the day? Bassett shuddered. Without doubt Sagawa had been eaten as well by the bad fella boys too much that stopped along the bush. He could see him, as he had last seen him, stripped of the shotgun and all the naturalist's gear of his master, lying on the narrow trail where he had been decapitated barely the moment before. Yes, within a minute the thing had happened. Within a minute, looking back, Bassett had seen him trudging patiently along under his burdens. Then Bassett's own trouble had come upon him. He looked at the cruelly healed stumps of the first and second fingers of his left hand, then rubbed them softly into the indentation in the back of his skull. Quick as had been the flash of the long-handled tomahawk, he had been quick enough to duck away his head and partially to deflect the stroke with his upflung hand. Two fingers and a nasty scalp wound had been the price he paid for his life. With one barrel of his ten-gauge shotgun he had blown the life out of the bushman who had so nearly got him; with the other barrel he had peppered the bushmen bending over Sagawa, and had the pleasure of knowing that the major portion of the charge had gone into the one who leaped away with Sagawa's head. Everything had occurred in a flash. Only himself, the slain bushman, and what remained of Sagawa, were in the narrow, wild-pig run of a path. From the dark jungle on either side came no rustle of movement or sound of life. And he had suffered distinct and dreadful shock. For the first time in his life he had killed a human being, and he knew nausea as he contemplated the mess of his handiwork.

Then had begun the chase. He retreated up the pig-run before his hunters, who were between him and the beach. How many there were, he could not guess. There might have been one, or a hundred, for aught he saw of them. That some of them took to the trees and traveled along through the jungle roof he was certain; but at the most he never glimpsed more than an occasional flitting of shadows. No bowstrings twanged that he could hear; but every little while, whence discharged he knew not, tiny arrows whispered past him or struck tree boles and fluttered to the ground beside him. They were bone-tipped and feather-shafted, and the feathers, torn from the breasts of hummingbirds, iridesced like jewels.

Once—and now, after the long lapse of time, he chuckled gleefully at the recollection—he had detected a shadow above him that came to instant rest as he turned his gaze upward. He could make out nothing, but, deciding to chance it, had fired at it a heavy charge of number-five shot. Squalling like an infuriated cat, the shadow crashed down through tree ferns and orchids and thudded upon the earth at his feet, and, still squalling its rage and pain, had sunk its human teeth into the ankle of his stout tramping boot. He, on the other hand, was not idle, and with his free foot had done what reduced the squalling to silence. So inured to savagery had Bassett since become, that he chuckled again with the glee of the recollection.

What a night had followed! Small wonder that he had accumulated such a virulence and variety of fevers, he thought, as he recalled that sleepless night of torment, when the throb of his wounds was as nothing compared with the myriad stings of the mosquitoes. There had been no escaping them, and he had not dared to light a fire. They had literally pumped his body full of poison, so that, with the coming of day, eyes swollen almost shut, he had stumbled blindly on, not caring much when his head should be hacked off and his carcass started on the way of Sagawa's to the cooking fire. Twenty-four hours had made a wreck of him—of mind as well as body. He had scarcely retained his wits at all, so maddened was he by the tremendous inoculation of poison he had received. Several times he fired his shotgun with effect into the shadows that dogged him. Stinging day insects and gnats added to his torment, while his bloody wounds attracted hosts of loathsome flies that clung sluggishly to his flesh and had to be brushed off and crushed off.

Once, in that day, he heard again the wonderful sound, seemingly more distant, but rising imperiously above the nearer war drums in the bush. Right there was where he had made his mistake. Thinking that he had passed beyond it and that, therefore, it was between him and the beach of Ringmanu, he had worked back toward it when in reality he was penetrating deeper and deeper into the mysterious heart of the unexplored island. That night, crawling in among the twisted roots of a banyan tree, he had slept from exhaustion while the mostquitoes had had their will of him.

Followed days and nights that were vague as nightmares in his memory. One clear vision he remembered was of suddenly finding himself in the midst of a bush village and watching the old men and children fleeing into the jungle. All had fled but one. From close at hand and above him, a whimpering as of some animal in pain and terror had startled him. And looking up he had seen her—a girl, or young woman, rather, suspended by one arm in the cooking sun. Perhaps for days she had so hung. Her swollen, protruding tongue spoke as much. Still alive, she gazed at him with eyes of terror. Past help, he decided, as he noted the swellings of her legs which advertised that the joints had been crushed and the great bones broken. he resolved to shoot her, and there the vision terminated. He could not remember whether he had or not, any more than could he remember how he chanced to be in that village or how he succeeded in getting away from it.

Many pictures, unrelated, came and went in Bassett's mind as he reviewed that period of his terrible wanderings. He remembered invading another village of a dozen houses and driving all before him with his shotgun save for one old man, too feeble to flee, who spat at him and whined and snarled as he dug open a ground oven and from amid the hot stones dragged forth a roasted pig that steamed its essence deliciously through its greenleaf wrappings. It was at this place that a wantonness of savagery had seized upon him. Having feasted, ready to depart with a hind quarter of the pig in his hand, he deliberately fired the grass thatch of a house with his burning glass.

But seared deepest of all in Bassett's brain, was the dank and noisome jungle. It actually stank with evil, and it was always twilight. Rarely did a shaft of sunlight penetrate its matted roof a hundred feet overhead. And beneath that roof was an aerial ooze of vegetation, a monstrous, parasitic dripping of decadent life-forms that rooted in death and lived on death. And through all this he drifted, ever pursued by the flitting shadows of the anthropophagi, themselves ghosts of evil that dared not face him in battle but that knew, soon or late, that they would feed on him. Bassett remembered that at the time, in lucid moments, he had likened himself to a wounded bull pursued by plains' coyotes too cowardly to battle with him for the meat of him, yet certain of the inevitable end of him when they would be full gorged. As the bull's horns and stamping hoofs kept off the coyotes, so his shotgun kept off these Solomon Islanders, these twilight shades of bushmen of the island of Guadalcanal.[2]

Came the day of the grasslands. Abruptly, as if cloven by the sword of God in the hand of God, the jungle terminated. The edge of it, perpendicular and as black as the infamy of it, was a hundred feet up and down. And, beginning at the edge of it, grew the grass—sweet, soft, tender, pasture grass that would have delighted the eyes and beasts of any husbandman and that extended, on and on, for leagues and leagues of velvet verdure, to the backbone of the great island, the towering mountain range flung up by some ancient earth cataclysm, serrated and gullied but not yet erased by the erosive tropic rains. But the grass! He had crawled into it a dozen yards, buried his face in it, smelled it, and broken down in a fit of involuntary weeping.

And, while he wept, the wonderful sound had pealed forth—if by *peal,* he had often thought since, an adequate description could be given of the enunciation of so vast a sound so melting sweet. Sweet it was as no sound ever heard. Vast it was, of so mighty a resonance that it might have proceeded from some brazen-throated monster. And yet it called to him across that leagues-wide savannah, and was like a benediction to his long-suffering, pain-wracked spirit.

He remembered how he lay there in the grass, wet-cheeked but no longer sobbing, listening to the sound and wondering that he had been able to hear it on the beach of Ringmanu. Some freak of air pressures and air currents, he reflected, had made it possible for the sound to carry so far. Such conditions might not happen again in a thousand days or ten thousand days; but the one day it had happened had been the day he landed from the *Nari* for several hours' collecting. Especially had he been in quest of the famed jungle butterfly, a foot across from wing tip to wing tip, as velvet-dusky of lack of color as was the gloom of the roof, of such lofty arboreal habits that it resorted only to the jungle roof and could be brought down only by a dose of shot. It was for this purpose that Sagawa had carried the twenty-gauge shotgun.

Two days and nights he had spent crawling across that belt of grassland. He had suffered much, but pursuit had ceased at the jungle edge. And he would have died of thirst had not a heavy thunderstorm revived him on the second day.

And then had come Balatta. In the first shade, where the savannah yielded to the dense mountain jungle, he had collapsed to die. At first she had squealed with delight at sight of his helplessness, and was for beating his brain out with a stout forest branch. Perhaps it was his very utter helplessness that had appealed to her, and perhaps it was her human curiosity that made her refrain. At any rate, she had refrained, for he opened his eyes again under the impending blow, and saw her studying him intently. What especially struck her about him were his blue eyes and white skin. Coolly she had squatted on her hams, spat on his arm, and with her fingertips scrubbed away the dirt of days and nights of muck and jungle that sullied the pristine whiteness of his skin.

And everything about her had struck him especially, although there was nothing conventional about her at all. He laughed weakly at the recollection, for she had been as innocent of garb as Eve before the fig-leaf adventure. Squat and lean at the same time, asymmetrically limbed, string-muscled as if with lengths of cordage, dirt-caked from infancy save for casual showers, she was as unbeautiful a prototype of woman as he, with a scientist's eye, had ever gazed upon. Her breasts advertised at the one time her maturity and youth; and, if by nothing else, her sex was advertised by the one article of finery with which she was adorned, namely a pig's tail, thrust through a hole in her left earlobe. So lately had the tail been severed, that its raw end still oozed blood that dried upon her shoulder like so much candle droppings. And her face! A twisted and wizened complex of apish features, perforated by upturned, sky-open, Mongolian nostrils, by a mouth that sagged from a huge upper lip and faded precipitately into a retreating chin, and by peering querulous eyes that blinked as blink the eyes of denizens of monkey cages.

Not even the water she brought him in a forest leaf, and the ancient and half-putrid chunk of roast pig, could redeem in the slightest the grotesque hideousness of her. When he had eaten weakly for a space, he closed his eyes in order not to see her, although again and again she poked them open to peer at the blue of them. Then had come the sound. Nearer, much nearer, he knew it to be; and he knew equally well, despite the weary way he had come, that it was still many hours distant. The effect of it on her had been startling. She cringed under it, with averted face, moaning and chattering with fear. But after it had lived its full life of an hour, he closed his eyes and fell asleep with Balatta brushing the flies from him.

When he awoke it was night, and she was gone. But he was aware of renewed strength, and, by then too thoroughly inoculated by the mosquito poison to suffer further inflammation, he closed his eyes and slept an unbroken stretch till sunup. A little later Balatta had returned, bringing with her a half dozen women who, unbeautiful as they were, were patently not so unbeautiful as she. She evidenced by her conduct that she considered him her find, her property, and the pride she took in showing him off would have been ludicrous had his situation not been so desperate.

Later, after what had been to him a terrible journey of miles, when he collapsed in front of the devil-devil house in the shadow of the breadfruit tree, she had shown very lively ideas on the matter of retaining possession of him. Ngurn, whom Bassett was to know afterward as the devil-devil doctor, priest, or medicine man of the village, had wanted his head. Others of the grinning and chattering monkey men, all as stark of clothes and bestial of appearance as Balatta, had wanted his body for the roasting oven. At that time he had not understood their language, if by *language* might be dignified the uncouth sounds they made to represent ideas. But Bassett had thoroughly understood the matter of debate, especially when the men pressed and prodded and felt of the flesh of him as if he were so much commodity in a butcher's stall.

Balatta had been losing the debate rapidly, when the accident happened. One of the men, curiously examining Bassett's shotgun, managed to cock and pull a trigger. The recoil of the butt into the pit of the man's stomach had not been the most sanguinary result, for the charge of shot, at a distance of a yard, had blown the head of one of the debaters into nothingness.

Even Balatta joined the others in flight, and, ere they returned, his senses already reeling from the oncoming fever attack, Bassett had regained possession of the gun. Whereupon, although his teeth chattered with the ague and his swimming eyes could scarcely see, he held onto his fading consciousness until he could intimidate the bushmen with the simple magics of compass, watch, burning glass, and matches. At the last, with due emphasis of solemnity and awfulness, he had killed a young pig with his shotgun and promptly fainted.

Bassett flexed his arm muscles in quest of what possible strength might reside in such weakness, and dragged himself slowly and totteringly to his feet. He was shockingly emaciated; yet, during the various convalescences of the many months of his long sickness, he had never regained quite the same degree of strength as this time. What he feared was another relapse such as he had already frequently experienced. Without drugs, without even quinine, he had managed so far to live through a combination of the most pernicious and most malignant of malarial and blackwater fevers. But could he continue to endure? Such was his everlasting query. For, like the genuine scientist he was, he would not be content to die until he had solved the secret of the sound.

Supported by a staff, he staggered the few steps to the devil-devil house where death and Ngurn reigned in gloom. Almost as infamously dark and evil-stinking as the jungle was the devil-devil house—in Bassett's opinion. Yet therein was usually to be found his favorite crony and gossip, Ngurn, always willing for a yarn or a discussion, the while he sat in the ashes of death and in a slow smoke shrewdly revolved curing human heads suspended from the rafters. For, through the months' interval of consciousness of his long sickness, Bassett had mastered the psychological simplicities and lingual difficulties of the language of the tribe of Ngurn and Balatta, and Gngngn—the latter the addleheaded[3] young chief who was ruled by Ngurn, and who, whispered intrigue had it, was the son of Ngurn.

"Will the Red One speak to-day?" Bassett asked, by this time so accustomed to the old man's gruesome occupation as to take even an interest in the progress of the smoke-curing.

With the eye of an expert Ngurn examined the particular head he was at work upon.

"It will be ten days before I can say 'finish,' " he said. "Never has any man fixed heads like these."

Bassett smiled inwardly at the old fellow's reluctance to talk with him of the Red One. It had always been so. Never, by any chance, had Ngurn or any other member of the weird tribe divulged the slightest hint of any physical characteristic of the Red One. Physical the Red One must be, to emit the wonderful sound, and though it was called the Red One, Bassett could not be sure that red represented the color of it. Red enough were the deeds and powers of it, from what abstract clews he had gleaned. Not alone, had Ngurn informed him, was the Red One more bestial powerful than the neighbor tribal gods, ever athirst for the red blood of living human sacrifices, but the neighbor gods themselves were sacrificed and tormented before him. He was the god of a dozen allied villages similar to this one, which was the central and commanding village of the federation. By virtue of the Red One many alien villages had been devastated and even wiped out, the prisoners sacrificed to the Red One. This was true today, and it extended back into old history carried down by word of mouth through the generations. When he, Ngurn, had been a young man, the tribes beyond the grasslands had made a war raid. In the counterraid, Ngurn and his fighting folk had made many prisoners. Of children alone over five score living had been bled white before the Red One, and many, many more men and women.

The Thunderer, was another of Ngurn's names for the mysterious deity. Also at times was he called The Loud Shouter, The God-Voiced, The Bird-Throated, The One with the Throat Sweet as the Throat of the Honey-Bird, The Sun Singer, and The Star-Born.

Why The Star-Born? In vain Bassett interrogated Ngurn. According to that old devil-devil doctor, the Red One had always been, just where he was at present, forever singing and thundering his will over men. But Ngurn's father, wrapped in decaying grass matting and hanging even then over their heads among the smoky rafters of the devil-devil house, had held otherwise. That departed wise one had believed that the Red One came from out of the starry night, else why—so his argument had run—had the old and forgotten ones passed his name down as the Star-Born? Bassett could not but recognize something cogent in such argument. But Ngurn affirmed the long years of his long life, wherein he had gazed upon many starry nights, yet never had he found a star on grassland or in jungle depth—and he had looked for them. True, he had beheld shooting stars (this in reply to Bassett's contention); but likewise had he beheld the phosphorescence of fungoid growths and rotten meat and fireflies on dark nights, and the flames of wood fires and of blazing candlenuts; yet what were flame and blaze and glow when they had flamed, and blazed and glowed? Answer: memories, memories only, of things which had ceased to be, like memories of matings accomplished, of feasts forgotten, of desires that were the ghosts of desires, flaring, flaming, burning, yet unrealized in achievement of easement and satisfaction. Where was the appetite of yesterday? the roasted flesh of the wild pig the hunter's arrow failed to slay? the maid, unwed and dead, ere the young man knew her?

A memory was not a star, was Ngurn's contention. How could a memory be

179

a star? Further, after all his long life he still observed the starry night sky unaltered. Never had he noted the absence of a single star from its accustomed place. Besides, stars were fire, and the Red One was not fire—which last involuntary betrayal told Bassett nothing.

"Will the Red One speak tomorrow?" he queried.

Ngurn shrugged his shoulders as who should say.

"And the day after?—and the day after that?" Bassett persisted.

"I would like to have the curing of your head," Ngurn changed the subject. "It is different from any other head. No devil-devil has a head like it. Besides, I would cure it well. I would take months and months. The moons would come and the moons would go, and the smoke would be very slow, and I should myself gather the materials for the curing smoke. The skin would not wrinkle. It would be as smooth as your skin now."

He stood up, and from the dim rafters grimed with the smoking of countless heads, where day was no more than a gloom, took down a matting-wrapped parcel and began to open it.

"It is a head like yours," he said, "but it is poorly cured."

Bassett had pricked up his ears at the suggestion that it was a white man's head; for he had long since come to accept that these jungle dwellers, in the midmost center of the great island, had never had intercourse with white men. Certainly he had found them without the almost universal bêche de mer English of the west South Pacific. Nor had they knowledge of tobacco, nor of gunpowder. Their few precious knives, made from lengths of hoop iron, and their few and more precious tomahawks, made from cheap trade hatchets, he had surmised they had captured in war from the bushmen of the jungle beyond the grasslands, and that they, in turn, had similarly gained them from the saltwater men who fringed the coral beaches of the shore and had contact with the occasional white men.

"The folk in the out beyond do not know how to cure heads," old Ngurn explained, as he drew forth from the filthy matting and placed in Bassett's hands an indubitable white man's head.

Ancient it was beyond question; white it was as the blond hair attested. He could have sworn it once belonged to an Englishman, and to an Englishman of long before by token of the heavy gold circlets still threaded in the withered earlobes.

"Now your head . . ." the devil-devil doctor began on his favorite topic.

"I'll tell you what," Bassett interrupted, struck by a new idea. "When I die I'll let you have my head to cure, if, first, you take me to look upon the Red One."

"I will have your head anyway when you are dead," Ngurn rejected the proposition. He added, with the brutal frankness of the savage: "Besides, you have not long to live. You are almost a dead man now. You will grow less strong. In not many months I shall have you here turning and turning in the smoke. It is pleasant, through the long afternoons, to turn the head of one you have known as well as I know you. And I shall talk to you and tell you the many secrets you want to know. Which will not matter, for you will be dead."

"Ngurn," Bassett threatened in sudden anger. "You know the Baby Thunder in the Iron that is mine." (This was in reference to his all-potent and all-awful shotgun.) "I can kill you any time, and then you will not get my head."

"Just the same, will Gngngn, or some one else of my folk get it," Ngurn complacently assured him. "And just the same will it turn and turn here in the devil-devil house in the smoke. The quicker you slay me with your Baby Thunder, the quicker will your head turn in the smoke."

And Bassett knew he was beaten in the discussion.

What was the Red One?—Bassett asked himself a thousand times in the succeeding week, while he seemed to grow stronger. What was the source of the wonderful sound? What was this Sun Singer, this Star-Born One, this mysterious deity, as bestial-conducted as the black and kinky-headed and monkeylike human beasts who worshiped it, and whose silver-sweet, bull-mouthed singing and commanding he had heard at the taboo distance for so long?

Ngurn had he failed to bribe with the inevitable curing of his head when he was dead. Gngngn, imbecile and chief that he was, was too imbecilic, too much under the sway of Ngurn, to be considered. Remained Balatta, who, from the time she found him and poked his blue eyes open to recrudescence of her grotesque, female hideousness, had continued his adorer. Woman she was, and he had long known that the only way to win from her treason to her tribe was through the woman's heart of her.

Bassett was a fastidious man. He had never recovered from the initial horror caused by Balatta's female awfulness. Back in England, even at best, the charm of woman, to him, had never been robust. Yet now, resolutely, as only a man can do who is capable of martyring himself for the cause of science, he proceeded to violate all the fineness and delicacy of his nature by making love to the unthinkably disgusting bushwoman.

He shuddered, but with averted face hid his grimaces and swallowed his gorge as he put his arm around her dirt-crusted shoulders and felt the contact of her rancid-oily and kinky hair with his neck and chin. But he nearly screamed when she succumbed to that caress so at the very first of the courtship and mowed and gibbered and squealed little, queer, piglike gurgly noises of delight. It was too much. And the next he did in the singular courtship was to take her down to the stream and give her a vigorous scrubbing.

From then on he devoted himself to her like a true swain as frequently and for as long at a time as his will could override his repugnance. But marriage, which she ardently suggested, with due observance of tribal custom, he balked at. Fortunately, taboo rule was strong in the tribe. Thus, Ngurn could never touch bone, or flesh, or hide of crocodile. This had been ordained at his birth. Gngngn was denied ever the touch of woman. Such pollution, did it chance to occur, could be purged only by the death of the offending female. It had happened once, since Bassett's arrival, when a girl of nine, running in play, stumbled and fell against the sacred chief. And the girl-child was seen no more. In whispers, Balatta told Bassett that she had been three days and nights in dying before the Red One. As for Balatta, the breadfruit was taboo to her. For which Bassett was thankful. The taboo might have been water.

For himself, he fabricated a special taboo. Only could he marry, he explained, when the Southern Cross rode highest in the sky. Knowing his astronomy, he thus gained a reprieve of nearly nine months; and he was confident that within that time he would either be dead or escaped to the coast with full knowledge of the Red One and of the source of the Red One's wonderful voice. At first he had fancied the Red One to be some colossal statue, like Memnon, rendered vocal under certain temperature conditions of sunlight. But when, after a war raid, a batch of prisoners was brought in and the sacrifice made at night, in the midst of rain, when the sun could play no part, the Red One had been more vocal than usual, Bassett discarded that hypothesis.

In company with Balatta, sometimes with men and parties of women, the freedom of the jungle was his for three quadrants of the compass. But the fourth quadrant, which contained the Red One's abiding place, was taboo. He made more thorough love to Balatta—also saw to it that she scrubbed herself more frequently. Eternal female she was, capable of any treason for the sake of love. And, though the sight of her was provocative of nausea and the contact of her provocative of despair, although he could not escape her awfulness in his dream-haunted nightmares of her, he nevertheless was aware of the cosmic verity of sex that animated her and that made her own life of less value than the happiness of her lover with whom she hoped to mate. Juliet[4] or Balatta? Where was the intrinsic difference? The soft and tender product of ultracivilization, or her bestial prototype of a hundred thousand years before her?—there was no difference.

Bassett was a scientist first, a humanist afterward. In the jungle heart of Guadalcanal he put the affair to the test, as in the laboratory he would have put to the test any chemical reaction. He increased his feigned ardor for the bushwoman, at the same time increasing the imperiousness of his will of desire over her to be led to look upon the Red One face to face. It was the old story, he recognized, that the woman must pay, and it occurred when the two of them, one day, were catching the unclassified and unnamed little black fish, an inch long, half-eel and half-scaled, rotund with salmon-golden roe, that frequented the fresh water and that were esteemed, raw and whole, fresh or putrid, a perfect delicacy. Prone in the muck of the decaying jungle floor, Balatta threw herself, clutching his ankles with her hands, kissing his feet and making slubbery noises that chilled his backbone up and down again. She begged him to kill her rather than exact this ultimate love payment. She told him of the penalty of breaking the taboo of the Red One—a week of torture, living, the details of which she yammered out from her face in the mire until he realized that he was yet a tyro in knowledge of the frightfulness the human was capable of wreaking on the human.

Yet did Bassett insist on having his man's will satisfied, at the woman's risk, that he might solve the mystery of the Red One's singing, though she should die long and horribly and screaming. And Balatta, being mere woman, yielded. She led him into the forbidden quadrant. An abrupt mountain, shouldering in from the north to meet a similar intrusion from the south, tormented the stream in which they had fished into a deep and gloomy gorge. After a mile along the gorge, the way plunged sharply upward until they crossed a saddle of raw limestone which

182

attracted his geologist's eye. Still climbing, although he paused often from sheer physical weakness, they scaled forest-clad heights until they emerged on a naked mesa or tableland. Bassett recognized the stuff of its composition as black volcanic sand, and knew that a pocket magnet could have captured a full load of the sharply angular grains he trod upon.

And then, holding Balatta by the hand and leading her onward, he came to it—a tremendous pit, obviously artificial, in the heart of the plateau. Old history, the South Seas Sailing Directions, scores of remembered data and connotations swift and furious, surged through his brain. It was Mendana[5] who had discovered the islands and named them Solomon's, believing that he had found that monarch's fabled mines. They had laughed at the old navigator's childlike credulity; and yet here stood himself, Bassett, on the rim of an excavation for all the world like the diamond pits of South Africa.

But no diamond this that he gazed down upon. Rather was it a pearl, with the depth of iridescence of a pearl; but of a size all pearls of earth and time welded into one, could not have totaled; and of a color undreamed of any pearl, or of anything else, for that matter, for it was the color of the Red One. And the Red One himself Bassett knew it to be on the instant. A perfect sphere, fully two hundred feet in diameter, the top of it was a hundred feet below the level of the rim. He likened the color quality of it to lacquer. Indeed, he took it to be some sort of lacquer, applied by man, but a lacquer too marvelously clever to have been manufactured by the bush folk. Brighter than bright cherry-red, its richness of color was as if it were red builded upon red. It glowed and iridesced in the sunlight as if gleaming up from underlay under underlay of red.

In vain Balatta strove to dissuade him from descending. She threw herself in the dirt; but, when he continued down the trail that spiraled the pit wall, she followed, cringing and whimpering her terror. That the red sphere had been dug out as a precious thing, was patent. Considering the paucity of members of the federated twelve villages and their primitive tools and methods, Bassett knew that the toil of a myriad generations could scarcely have made that enormous excavation.

He found the pit bottom carpeted with human bones, among which, battered and defaced, lay village gods of wood and stone. Some, covered with obscene totemic figures and designs, were carved from solid tree trunks forty or fifty feet in length. He noted the absence of the shark and turtle gods, so common among the shore villages, and was amazed at the constant recurrence of the helmet motive. What did these jungle savages of the dark heart of Guadalcanal know of helmets? Had Mendana's men-at-arms worn helmets and penetrated here centuries before? And if not, then whence had the bush folk caught the motive?

Advancing over the litter of gods and bones, Balatta whimpering at his heels, Bassett entered the shadow of the Red One and passed on under its gigantic overhang until he touched it with his fingertips. No lacquer that. Nor was the surface smooth as it should have been in the case of lacquer. On the contrary, it was corrugated and pitted, with here and there patches that showed signs of heat and fusing. Also, the substance of it was metal, though unlike any metal or combi-

183

nation of metals he had ever known. As for the color itself, he decided it to be no application. It was the intrinsic color of the metal itself.

He moved his fingertips, which up to that had merely rested, along the surface, and felt the whole gigantic sphere quicken and live and respond. It was incredible! So light a touch on so vast a mass! Yet did it quiver under the fingertip caress in rhythmic vibrations that became whisperings and rustlings and mutterings of sound—but of sound so different; so elusive thin that it was shimmeringly sibilant; so mellow that it was maddening sweet, piping like an elfin horn, which last was just what Bassett decided would be like a peal from some bell of the gods reaching earthward from across space.

He looked to Balatta with swift questioning; but the voice of the Red One he had evoked had flung her face-downward and moaning among the bones. He returned to contemplation of the prodigy. Hollow it was, and of no metal known on earth, was his conclusion. It was right-named by the ones of old time as the Star-Born. Only from the stars could it have come, and no thing of chance was it. It was a creation of artifice and mind. Such perfection of form, such hollowness that it certainly possessed, could not be the result of mere fortuitousness. A child of intelligences, remote and unguessable, working corporally in metals, it indubitably was. He stared at it in amaze, his brain a racing wild fire of hypotheses to account for this far-journeyer who had adventured the night of space, threaded the stars, and now rose before him and above him, exhumed by patient anthropophagi, pitted and lacquered by its fiery bath in two atmospheres.

But was the color a lacquer of heat upon some familiar metal? Or was it an intrinsic quality of the metal itself? He thrust in the blade point of his pocketknife to test the constitution of the stuff. Instantly the entire sphere burst into a mighty whispering, sharp with protest, almost twanging goldenly if a whisper could possibly be considered to twang, rising higher, sinking deeper, the two extremes of the registry of sound threatening to complete the circle and coalesce into the bull-mouthed thundering he had so often heard beyond the taboo distance.

Forgetful of safety, of his own life itself, entranced by the wonder of the unthinkable and unguessable thing, he raised his knife to strike heavily from a long stroke, but was prevented by Balatta. She upreared on her own knees in an agony of terror, clasping his knees and supplicating him to desist. In the intensity of her desire to impress him, she put her forearm between her teeth and sank them to the bone.

He scarcely observed her act, although he yielded automatically to his gentler instincts and withheld the knife hack. To him, human life had dwarfed to microscopic proportions before this colossal portent of higher life from within the distances of the sidereal universe. As had she been a dog, he kicked the ugly little bushwoman to her feet and compelled her to start with him on an encirclement of the base. Part way around, he encountered horrors. Even, among the others, did he recognize the sun-shriveled remnant of the nine-years girl who had accidentally broken Chief Gngngn's personality taboo. And, among what was left of these that had passed, he encountered what was left of one who had not yet passed. Truly had the bush folk named themselves into the name of the Red One, seeing in him their own image which they strove to placate and please with such red offerings.

Farther around, always treading the bones and images of humans and gods that constituted the floor of this ancient charnel house of sacrifice, he came upon the device by which the Red One was made to send his call singing thunderingly across the jungle belts and grasslands to the far beach of Ringmanu. Simple and primitive was it as was the Red One's consummate artifice. A great king post, half a hundred feet in length, seasoned by centuries of superstitious care, carven into dynasties of gods, each superimposed, each helmeted, each seated in the open mouth of a crocodile, was slung by ropes, twisted of climbing vegetable parasites, from the apex of a tripod of three great forest trunks, themselves carved into grinning and grotesque adumbrations of man's modern concepts of art and god. From the striker king post, were suspended ropes of climbers to which men could apply their strength and direction. Like a battering ram, this king post could be driven end-onward against the mighty, red-iridescent sphere.

Here was where Ngurn officiated and functioned religiously for himself and the twelve tribes under him. Bassett laughed aloud, almost with madness, at the thought of this wonderful messenger, winged with intelligence across space, to fall into a bushman stronghold and be worshiped by apelike, man-eating and head-hunting savages. It was as if God's Word had fallen into the muck mire of the abyss underlying the bottom of hell; as if Jehovah's Commandments had been presented on carved stone[6] to the monkeys of the monkey cage at the Zoo; as if the Sermon on the Mount had been preached in a roaring bedlam of lunatics.

The slow weeks passed. The nights, by election, Bassett spent on the ashen floor of the devil-devil house, beneath the ever-swinging, slow-curing heads. His reason for this was that it was taboo to the lesser sex of woman, and, therefore, a refuge for him from Balatta, who grew more persecutingly and perilously loverly as the Southern Cross rode higher in the sky and marked the imminence of her nuptials. His days Bassett spent in a hammock swung under the shade of the great breadfruit tree before the devil-devil house. There were breaks in this program, when, in the comas of his devastating fever attacks, he lay for days and nights in the house of heads. Ever he struggled to combat the fever, to live, to continue to live, to grow strong and stronger against the day when he would be strong enough to dare the grasslands and the belted jungle beyond, and win to the beach, and to some labor-recruiting, blackbirding ketch or schooner, and on to civilization and the men of civilization, to whom he could give news of the message from other worlds that lay, darkly worshiped by beastmen, in the black heart of Guadalcanal's mid-most center.

On other nights, lying late under the breadfruit tree, Bassett spent long hours watching the slow setting of the western stars beyond the black wall of jungle where it had been thrust back by the clearing for the village. Possessed of more than a cursory knowledge of astronomy, he took a sick man's pleasure in speculating as to the dwellers on the unseen worlds of those incredibly remote suns, to haunt whose houses of light, life came forth, a shy visitant, from the rayless crypts of matter. He could no more apprehend limits to time than bounds to space. No subversive radium speculations had shaken his steady scientific faith in the conservation of energy and the indestructibility of matter. Always and forever must there have been stars. And surely, in that cosmic ferment, all must be comparatively alike, comparatively of the same substance, or substances, save for the freaks of the ferment. All must obey, or compose, the same laws that ran without infraction through the entire experience of man. Therefore, he argued and agreed, must worlds and life be appanages to all the suns as they were appanages to the particular sun of his own solar system.

Even as he lay here, under the breadfruit tree, an intelligence that stared across the starry gulfs, so must all the universe be exposed to the ceaseless scrutiny of innumerable eyes, like his, though grantedly different, with behind them, by the same token, intelligences that questioned and sought the meaning and the construction of the whole. So reasoning, he felt his soul go forth in kinship with that august company, that multitude whose gaze was forever upon the arras of infinity.

Who were they, what were they, those far distant and superior ones who had bridged the sky with their gigantic, red-iridescent, heaven-singing message? Surely, and long since, had they, too, trod the path on which man had so recently, by the calendar of the cosmos, set his feet. And to be able to send such a message across the pit of space, surely they had reached those heights to which man, in tears and travail and bloody sweat, in darkness and confusion of many counsels, was so slowly struggling. And what were they on their heights? Had they won Brotherhood? Or had they learned that the law of love imposed the penalty of weakness and decay? Was strife, life? Was the rule of all the universe the pitiless rule of natural selection? And, and most immediately and poignantly, were their far conclusions, their long-won wisdoms, shut even then in the huge, metallic heart of the Red One, waiting for the first earth-man to read? Of one thing he was certain: No drop of red dew shaken from the lion mane of some sun in torment, was the sounding sphere. It was of design, not chance, and it contained the speech and wisdom of the stars.

What engines and elements and mastered forces, what lore and mysteries and destiny controls, might be there! Undoubtedly, since so much could be inclosed in so little a thing as the foundation stone of public building, this enormous sphere should contain vast histories, profounds of research achieved beyond man's wildest guesses, laws and formulæ that, easily mastered, would make man's life on earth, individual and collective, spring up from its present mire to inconceivable heights of purity and power. It was Time's greatest gift to blindfold, insatiable, and sky-aspiring man. And to him, Bassett, had been vouchsafed the lordly fortune to be the first to receive this message from man's interstellar kin!

No white man, much less no outland man of the other bush tribes, had gazed upon the Red One and lived. Such the law expounded by Ngurn to Bassett. There was such a thing as blood brotherhood, Bassett, in return, had often argued in the past. But Ngurn had stated solemnly no. Even the blood brotherhood was outside the favor of the Red One. Only a man born within the tribe could look upon the Red One and live. But now, his guilty secret known only to Balatta, whose fear of immolation before the Red One fast-sealed her lips, the situation was different. What he had to do was to recover from the abominable fevers that weakened him and gain to civilization. Then would he lead an expedition back, and, although the entire population of Guadalcanal be destroyed, extract from the heart of the Red One the message of the world from other worlds.

But Bassett's relapses grew more frequent, his brief convalescences less and less vigorous, his periods of coma longer, until he came to know, beyond the last promptings of the optimism inherent in so tremendous a constitution as his own, that he would never live to cross the grasslands, perforate the perilous coast jungle, and reach the sea. He faded as the Southern Cross rose higher in the sky, till even Balatta knew that he would be dead ere the nuptial date determined by his taboo. Ngurn made pilgrimage personally and gathered the smoke materials for the curing of Bassett's head, and to him made proud announcement and exhibition of the artistic perfectness of his intention when Bassett should be dead. As for himself, Bassett was not shocked. Too long and too deeply had life ebbed down in him to bite him with fear of its impending extinction. He continued to persist, alternating periods of unconsciousness with periods of semiconsciousness, dreamy and unreal, in which he idly wondered whether he had ever truly beheld the Red One or whether it was a nightmare fancy of delirium.

Came the day when all mists and cobwebs dissolved, when he found his brain clear as a bell, and took just appraisement of his body's weakness. Neither hand nor foot could he lift. So little control of his body did he have, that he was scarcely aware of possessing one. Lightly indeed his flesh sat upon his soul, and his soul, in its briefness of clarity, knew by its very clarity, that the black of cessation was near. He knew the end was close; knew that in all truth he had with his eyes beheld the Red One, the messenger between the worlds; knew that he would never live to carry that message to the world—that message, for aught to the contrary, which might already have waited man's hearing in the heart of Guadalcanal for ten thousand years. And Bassett stirred with resolve, calling Ngurn to him, out under the shade of the breadfruit tree, and with the old devil-devil doctor discussing the terms and arrangements of his last life effort, his final adventure in the quick of the flesh.

"I know the law, O Ngurn," he concluded the matter. "Whoso is not of the folk may not look upon the Red One and live. I shall not live anyway. Your young men shall carry me before the face of the Red One, and I shall look upon him, and hear his voice, and thereupon die, under your hand, O Ngurn. Thus will the three things be satisfied: the law, my desire, and your quicker possession of my head for which all your preparations wait."

To which Ngurn consented, adding:

"It is better so. A sick man who cannot get well is foolish to live on for so little a while. Also, it is better for the living that he should go. You have been much in the way of late. Not but what it was good for me to talk to such a wise one. But for moons of days we have held little talk. Instead, you have taken up room in the house of heads, making noises like a dying pig, or talking much and loudly in your own language which I do not understand. This has been a confusion to me, for I like to think on the great things of the light and dark as I turn the heads in the smoke. Your much noise has thus been a disturbance to the long learning and hatching of the final wisdom that will be mine before I die. As for you, upon whom the dark has already brooded, it is well that you die now. And I promise you, in the long days to come when I turn your head in the smoke, no man of the tribe shall come in to disturb us. And I will tell you many secrets, for I am an old man and very wise, and I shall be adding wisdom to wisdom as I turn your head in the smoke."

So a litter was made, and, borne on the shoulders of half a dozen of the men, Bassett departed on the last little adventure that was to cap the total adventure, for him, of living. With a body of which he was scarcely aware, for even the pain had been exhausted out of it, and with a bright clear brain that accommodated him to a quiet ecstasy of sheer lucidness of thought, he lay back on the lurching litter and watched the fading of the passing world, beholding for the last time the breadfruit tree before the devil-devil house, the dim day beneath the matted jungle roof, the gloomy gorge between the shouldering mountains, the saddle of raw limestone, and the mesa of black, volcanic sand.

Down the spiral path of the pit they bore him, encircling the sheening, glowing Red One that seemed ever imminent to iridesce from color and light into sweet singing and thunder. And over bones and logs of immolated men and gods they bore him, past the horrors of other immolated ones that yet lived, to the three-king-post tripod and the huge king-post striker.

Here Bassett, helped by Ngurn and Balatta, weakly sat up, swaying weakly from the hips, and with clear, unfaltering, all-seeing eyes gazed upon the Red One.

"Once, O Ngurn," he said, not taking his eyes from the sheening, vibrating surface whereon and wherein all the shades of cherry-red played unceasingly, ever aquiver to change into sound, to become silken rustlings, silvery whisperings, golden thrummings of cords, velvet pipings of elfland, mellow distances of thunderings.

"I wait," Ngurn prompted after a long pause, the long-handled tomahawk unassumingly ready in his hand.

"Once, O Ngurn," Bassett repeated, "let the Red One speak so that I may see it speak as well as hear it. Then strike, thus, when I raise my hand; for, when I raise my hand, I shall drop my head forward and make place for the stroke at the base of my neck. But, O Ngurn, I, who am about to pass out of the light of day forever, would like to pass with the wonder voice of the Red One singing greatly in my ears."

"And I promise you that never will a head be so well cured as yours," Ngurn assured him, at the same time signaling the tribesmen to man the propelling ropes suspended from the kingpost striker. "Your head shall be my greatest piece of work in the curing of heads."

Bassett smiled quietly to the old one's conceit, as the great carved log, drawn back through two-score feet of space, was released. The next moment he was lost in ecstasy at the abrupt and thunderous liberation of sound. But such thunder! Mellow it was with preciousness of all sounding metals. Archangels spoke in it; it was magnificently beautiful before all other sounds; it was invested with the intelligence of supermen of planets of other suns; it was the voice of God, seducing and commanding to be heard. And—the everlasting miracle of that interstellar metal! Bassett, with his own eyes, saw color and colors transform into sound till the whole visible surface of the vast sphere was acrawl and titillant and vaporous with what he could not tell was color or was sound. In that moment the interstices of matter were his, and the interfusings and intermating transfusings of matter and force.

Time passed. At the last Bassett was brought back from his ecstasy by an impatient movement of Ngurn. He had quite forgotten the old devil-devil one. A quick flash of fancy brought a husky chuckle into Bassett's throat. His shotgun lay beside him in the litter. All he had to do, muzzle to head, was press the trigger and blow his head into nothingness.

But why cheat him? was Bassett's next thought. Headhunting, cannibal beast of a human that was as much ape as human, nevertheless Old Ngurn had, according to his lights, played squarer than square. Ngurn was in himself a forerunner of ethics and contract, of consideration, and gentleness in man. No, Bassett decided; it would be a ghastly pity and an act of dishonor to cheat the old fellow at the last. His head was Ngurn's, and Ngurn's head to cure it would be.

And Bassett, raising his hand in signal, bending forward his head as agreed so as to expose cleanly the articulation to his taut spinal cord, forgot Balatta, who was merely a woman, a woman merely and only and undesired. He knew, without seeing, when the razor-edged hatchet rose in the air behind him. And for that instant, ere the end, there fell upon Bassett the shadow of the Unknown, a sense of impending marvel of the rending of walls before the imaginable. Almost, when he knew the blow had started and just ere the edge of steel bit the flesh and nerves, it seemed that he gazed upon the serene face of the Medusa, Truth—And, simultaneous with the bite of the steel on the onrush of the dark, in a flashing instant of fancy, he saw the vision of his head turning slowly, always turning, in the devil-devil house beside the breadfruit tree.

[1] An allusion to Robert Browning's "Childe Roland to the Dark Tower Came."
[2] In the southeast Solomons; location of a major World War II battle between American and Japanese forces.
[3] Confused; eccentric, mixed up.
[4] Beautiful tragic heroine of Shakespeare's *Romeo and Juliet*.
[5] Alvaro de Mendaña de Niera (1541–1595), Spanish mariner.
[6] The Ten Commandments, given by God on tablets of stone to Moses on Mount Sinai (Exodus 20:3–17; 24:12; 32:15–16, 19; 34:1, 29).

DISCUSSION TOPICS

1. What, according to your own understanding of this story, is the Red One—and where did it come from?
2. What is the significance of the statement that "Bassett was a scientist first, a humanist afterward"—and how does this relate to the central theme of the story?

3. What role does Ngurn play in Bassett's initiation? What is the nature of Bassett's transformation? How does his initiation differ from that of the correspondent in Crane's "The Open Boat"?
4. What is the function of Balatta? What is Bassett's attitude toward her—and toward women in general?
5. What are the indications that this is essentially a religious story?

WRITING TOPICS

1. "The Red One" is obviously rich in those universal symbols Jung called "archetypes." Discuss some of the "key" archetypal images and patterns in the story.
2. London was strongly influenced by his reading of Joseph Conrad's works (in fact, the two writers exchanged appreciative letters), and several critics have noted the similarities, both texturally and thematically, between "The Red One" and *Heart of Darkness.* What especially noteworthy resemblances do you find between these two works? Consider, for example, such matters as setting, mood, and atmosphere; themes and symbolism (especially archetypal motifs); and significant similarities and differences between the central characters.

SHERWOOD ANDERSON (1876–1941) Financial success in manufacturing and advertising. He suddenly terminated business and family connections in his late thirties to give himself to a full-time career as a writer. His first collection of stories, *Winesburg, Ohio* (1919), assured his fame as the creator of poignant, realistic sketches of small-town "grotesques" (individuals warped by obsessions, frustrations, neuroses, loneliness) and anticipated the Freudian vogue of the twenties. Anderson befriended promising young writers like Ernest Hemingway and William Faulkner. His seemingly unstudied, groping method of narration effectively mirrors the psychological problems and insecurity of his characters.

DEATH IN THE WOODS

She was an old woman and lived on a farm near the town in which I lived. All country and small-town people have seen such old women, but no one knows much about them. Such an old woman comes into town driving an old worn-out horse or she comes afoot carrying a basket. She may own a few hens and have eggs to sell. She brings them in a basket and takes them to a grocer. There she trades them in. She gets some salt pork and some beans. Then she gets a pound or two of sugar and some flour.

Afterwards she goes to the butcher's and asks for some dog-meat. She may spend ten or fifteen cents, but when she does she asks for something. Formerly the butchers gave liver to anyone who wanted to carry it away. In our family we were always having it. Once one of my brothers got a whole cow's liver at the slaughterhouse near the fair grounds in our town. We had it until we were sick of it. It never cost a cent. I have hated the thought of it ever since.

The old farm woman got some liver and a soup-bone. She never visited with anyone, and as soon as she got what she wanted she lit out for home. It made quite a load for such an old body. No one gave her a lift. People drive right down a road and never notice an old woman like that.

There was such an old woman who used to come into town past our house one summer and fall when I was a young boy and was sick with what was called inflammatory rheumatism. She went home later carrying a heavy pack on her back. Two or three large gaunt-looking dogs followed at her heels.

The old woman was nothing special. She was one of the nameless ones that hardly anyone knows, but she got into my thoughts. I have just suddenly now, after all these years, remembered her and what happened. It is a story. Her name was Grimes, and she lived with her husband and son in a small unpainted house on the bank of a small creek four miles from town.

The husband and son were a tough lot. Although the son was but twenty-one, he had already served a term in jail. It was whispered about that the woman's husband stole horses and ran them off to some other county. Now and then, when a horse turned up missing, the man had also disappeared. No one ever caught him. Once, when I was loafing at Tom Whitehead's liverybarn, the man came there and sat on the bench in front. Two or three other men were there, but no one spoke to him. He sat for a few minutes and then got up and went away. When he was leaving he turned around and stared at the men. There was a look of defiance in his eyes. "Well, I have tried to be friendly. You don't want to talk to me. It has been so wherever I have gone in this town. If, some day, one of your fine horses turns up missing, well, then what?" He did not say anything actually. "I'd like to bust one of you on the jaw," was about what his eyes said. I remember how the look in his eyes made me shiver.

The old man belonged to a family that had had money once. His name was Jake Grimes. It all comes back clearly now. His father, John Grimes, had owned a sawmill when the country was new, and had made money. Then he got to drinking and running after women. When he died there wasn't much left.

Jake blew in the rest. Pretty soon there wasn't any more lumber to cut and his land was nearly all gone.

He got his wife off a German farmer, for whom he went to work one June day in the wheat harvest. She was a young thing then and scared to death. You see, the farmer was up to something with the girl—she was, I think, a bound girl and his wife had her suspicions. She took it out on the girl when the man wasn't around. Then, when the wife had to go off to town for supplies, the farmer got after her. She told young Jake that nothing really ever happened, but he didn't know whether to believe it or not.

He got her pretty easy himself, the first time he was out with her. He wouldn't have married her if the German farmer hadn't tried to tell him where to get off. He got her to go riding with him in his buggy one night when he was threshing on the place, and then he came for her the next Sunday night.

She managed to get out of the house without her employer's seeing, but when she was getting into the buggy he showed up. It was almost dark, and he just popped up suddenly at the horse's head. He grabbed the horse by the bridle and Jake got out his buggy-whip.

They had it out all right! The German was a tough one. Maybe he didn't care whether his wife knew or not. Jake hit him over the face and shoulders with the buggy-whip, but the horse got to acting up and he had to get out.

Then the two men went for it. The girl didn't see it. The horse started to run away and went nearly a mile down the road before the girl got him stopped. Then she managed to tie him to a tree beside the road. (I wonder how I know all this. It must have stuck in my mind from small-town tales when I was a boy.) Jake found her there after he got through with the German. She was huddled up in the buggy seat, crying, scared to death. She told Jake a lot of stuff, how the German had tried to get her, how he chased her once into the barn, how another time, when they happened to be alone in the house together, he tore her dress open clear down the front. The German, she said, might have got her that time if he hadn't heard his old woman drive in at the gate. She had been off to town for supplies. Well, she would be putting the horse in the barn. The German managed to sneak off to the fields without his wife seeing. He told the girl he would kill her if she told. What could she do? She told a lie about ripping her dress in the barn when she was feeding the stock. I remember now that she was a bound girl and did not know where her father and mother were. Maybe she did not have any father. You know what I mean.

Such bound children were often enough cruelly treated. They were children who had no parents, slaves really. There were very few orphan homes then. They were legally bound into some home. It was a matter of pure luck how it came out.

II

She married Jake and had a son and daughter, but the daughter died.

Then she settled down to feed stock. That was her job. At the German's place she had cooked the food for the German and his wife. The wife was a strong woman with big hips and worked most of the time in the fields with her husband. She fed them and fed the cows in the barn, fed the pigs, the horses and the chickens. Every moment of every day, as a young girl, was spent feeding something.

Then she married Jake Grimes and he had to be fed. She was a slight thing, and when she had been married for three or four years, and after the two children were born, her slender shoulders became stooped.

Jake always had a lot of big dogs around the house, that stood near the unused sawmill near the creek. He was always trading horses when he wasn't stealing something and had a lot of poor boney ones about. Also he kept three or four pigs and a cow. They were all pastured in the few acres left of the Grimes place and Jake did little enough work.

He went into debt for a threshing outfit and ran it for several years, but it did not pay. People did not trust him. They were afraid he would steal the grain at night. He had to go a long way off to get work and it cost too much to get there. In the winter he hunted and cut a little firewood, to be sold in some nearby town. When the son grew up he was just like the father. They got drunk together. If there wasn't anything to eat in the house when they came home the old man gave his old woman a cut over the head. She had a few chickens of her own and had to kill one of them in a hurry. When they were all killed she wouldn't have any eggs to sell when she went to town, and then what would she do?

She had to scheme all her life about getting things fed, getting the pigs fed so they would grow fat and could be butchered in the fall. When they were butchered her husband took most of the meat off to town and sold it. If he did not do it first the boy did. They fought sometimes and when they fought the old woman stood aside trembling.

She had got the habit of silence anyway—that was fixed. Sometimes, when she began to look old—she wasn't forty yet—and when the husband and son were both off, trading horses or drinking or hunting or stealing, she went around the house and the barnyard muttering to herself.

How was she going to get everything fed?—that was her problem. The dog had to be fed. There wasn't enough hay in the barn for the horses and the cow. If she didn't feed the chickens how could they lay eggs? Without eggs to sell how could she get things in town, things she had to have to keep the life of the farm going? Thank heaven, she did not have to feed her husband—in a certain way. That hadn't lasted long after their marriage and after the babies came. Where he went on his long trips she did not know. Sometimes he was gone from home for weeks, and after the boy grew up they went off together.

They left everything at home for her to manage and she had no money. She knew no one. No one ever talked to her in town. When it was winter she had to gather sticks of wood for her fire, had to try to keep the stock fed with very little grain.

The stock in the barn cried to her hungrily, the dogs followed her about. In the winter the hens laid few enough eggs. They huddled in the corners of the barn and she kept watching them. If a hen lays an egg in the barn in the winter and you do not find it, it freezes and breaks.

One day in winter the old woman went off to town with a few eggs and the dogs followed her. She did not get started until nearly three o'clock and the snow was heavy. She hadn't been feeling very well for several days and so she went muttering along, scantily clad, her shoulders stooped. She had an old grain bag in which she carried her eggs, tucked away down in the bottom. There weren't many of them, but in winter the price of eggs is up. She would get a little meat in exchange for the eggs, some salt pork, a little sugar, and some coffee perhaps. It might be the butcher would give her a piece of liver.

When she had got to town and was trading in her eggs the dogs lay by the door outside. She did pretty well, got the things she needed, more than she had hoped. Then she went to the butcher and he gave her some liver and some dog-meat.

It was the first time anyone had spoken to her in a friendly way for a long time. The butcher was alone in his shop when she came in and was annoyed by the thought of such a sick-looking old woman out on such a day. It was bitter cold and the snow, that had let up during the afternoon, was falling again. The butcher said something about her husband and her son, swore at them, and the old woman stared at him, a look of mild surprise in her eyes as he talked. He said that if either the husband or the son were going to get any of the liver or the heavy bones with scraps of meat hanging to them that he had put into the grain bag, he'd see him starve first.

Starve, eh? Well, things had to be fed. Men had to be fed, and the horses that weren't any good but maybe could be traded off, and the poor thin cow that hadn't given any milk for three months.

Horses, cows, pigs, dogs, men.

III

The old woman had to get back before darkness came if she could. The dogs followed at her heels, sniffing at the heavy grain bag she had fastened on her back. When she got to the edge of town she stopped by a fence and tied the bag on her back with a piece of rope she had carried in her dress-pocket for just that purpose. That was an easier way to carry it. Her arms ached. It was hard when she had to crawl over fences and once she fell over and landed in the snow. The dogs went frisking about. She had to struggle to get to her feet again, but she made it. The point of climbing over the fences was that there was a short cut over a hill and through a woods. She might have gone around by the road, but it was a mile farther that way. She was afraid she couldn't make it. And then, besides, the stock had to be fed. There was a little hay left and a little corn. Perhaps her husband and son would bring some home when they came. They had driven off in the only buggy the Grimes family had, a rickety thing, a rickety horse hitched to the buggy, two other rickety horses led by halters. They were going to trade horses, get a little money if they could. They might come home drunk. It would be well to have something in the house when they came back.

The son had an affair with a woman at the county seat, fifteen miles away. She was a rough enough woman, a tough one. Once, in the summer, the son had brought her to the house. Both she and the son had been drinking. Jake Grimes was away and the son and his woman ordered the old woman about like a servant. She didn't mind much; she was used to it. Whatever happened she never said anything. That was her way of getting along. She had managed that way when she was a young girl at the German's and ever since she had married Jake. That time her son brought his woman to the house they stayed all night, sleeping together just as though they were married. It hadn't shocked the old woman, not much. She had got past being shocked early in life.

With the pack on her back she went painfully along across an open field, wading in the deep snow, and got into the woods.

There was a path, but it was hard to follow. Just beyond the top of the hill, where the woods was thickest, there was a small clearing. Had someone once thought of building a house there? The clearing was as large as a building lot in town, large enough for a house and a garden. The path ran along the side of the clearing, and when she got there the old woman sat down to rest at the foot of a tree.

It was a foolish thing to do. When she got herself placed, the pack against the tree's trunk, it was nice, but what about getting up again? She worried about that for a moment and then quietly closed her eyes.

She must have slept for a time. When you are about so cold you can't get any colder. The afternoon grew a little warmer and the snow came thicker than ever. Then after a time the weather cleared. The moon even came out.

There were four Grimes dogs that had followed Mrs. Grimes into town, all tall gaunt fellows. Such men as Jake Grimes and his son always keep just such dogs. They kick and abuse them, but they stay. The Grimes dogs, in order to keep from starving, had to do a lot of foraging for themselves, and they had been at it while the old woman slept with her back to the tree at the side of the clearing. They had been chasing rabbits in the woods and in adjoining fields and in their ranging had picked up three other farm dogs.

After a time all the dogs came back to the clearing. They were excited about something. Such nights, cold and clear and with a moon, do things to dogs. It may be that some old instinct, come down from the time when they were wolves and ranged the woods in packs on winter nights, comes back into them.

The dogs in the clearing, before the old woman, had caught two or three rabbits and their immediate hunger had been satisfied. They began to play, running in circles in the clearing. Round and round they ran, each dog's nose at the tail of the next dog. In the clearing, under the snow-laden trees and under the wintry moon they made a strange picture, running thus silently, in a circle their running had beaten in the soft snow. The dogs made no sound. They ran around and around in the circle.

It may have been that the old woman saw them doing that before she died. She may have awakened once or twice and looked at the strange sight with dim old eyes.

She wouldn't be very cold now, just drowsy. Life hangs on a long time. Perhaps the old woman was out of her head. She may have dreamed of her girlhood, at the German's, and before that, when she was a child and before her mother lit out and left her.

Her dreams couldn't have been very pleasant. Not many pleasant things had happened to her. Now and then one of the Grimes dogs left the running circle and came to stand before her. The dog thrust his face close to her face. His red tongue was hanging out.

The running of the dogs may have been a kind of death ceremony. It may have been that the primitive instinct of the wolf, having been aroused in the dogs by the night and the running, made them somehow afraid.

"Now we are no longer wolves. We are dogs, the servants of men. Keep alive, man! When man dies we become wolves again."

When one of the dogs came to where the old woman sat with her back against the tree and thrust his nose close to her face he seemed satisfied and went back to run with the pack. All the Grimes dogs did it at some time during the evening, before she died. I knew all about it afterward, when I grew to be a man, because once in a woods in Illinois, on another winter night, I saw a pack of dogs act just like that. The dogs were waiting for me to die as they had waited for the old woman that night when I was a child, but when it happened to me I was a young man and had no intention whatever of dying.

The old woman died softly and quietly. When she was dead and when one of the Grimes dogs had come to her and had found her dead all the dogs stopped running.

They gathered about her.

Well, she was dead now. She had fed the Grimes dogs when she was alive, what about now?

There was the pack on her back, the grain bag containing the piece of salt pork, the liver the butcher had given her, the dog-meat, the soup bones. The butcher in town, having been suddenly overcome with a feeling of pity, had loaded her grain bag heavily. It had been a big haul for the old woman.

It was a big haul for the dogs now.

IV

One of the Grimes dogs sprang suddenly out from among the others and began worrying the pack on the old woman's back. Had the dogs really been wolves that one would have been the leader of the pack. What he did, all the others did.

All of them sank their teeth into the grain bag the old woman had fastened with ropes to her back.

They dragged the old woman's body out into the open clearing. The worn-out dress was quickly torn from her shoulders. When she was found, a day or two later, the dress had been torn from her body clear to the hips, but the dogs had not touched her body. They had got the meat out of the grain bag, that was all. Her body was frozen stiff when it was found, and the shoulders were so narrow and the body so slight that in death it looked like the body of some charming young girl.

Such things happened in towns of the Middle West, on farms near town, when I was a boy. A hunter out after rabbits found the old woman's body and did not touch it. Something, the beaten round path in the little snow-covered clearing, the silence of the place, the place where the dogs had worried the body trying to pull the grain bag away or tear it open—something startled the man and he hurried off to town.

I was in Main Street with one of my brothers who was town newsboy and who was taking the afternoon papers to the stores. It was almost night.

The hunter came into a grocery and told his story. Then he went to a hardware shop and into a drugstore. Men began to gather on the sidewalks. Then they started out along the road to the place in the woods.

My brother should have gone on about his business of distributing papers but he didn't. Everyone was going to the woods. The undertaker went and the town marshal. Several men got on a dray and rode out to where the path left the road and went into the woods, but the horses weren't very sharply shod and slid about on the slippery roads. They made no better time than those of us who walked.

The town marshal was a large man whose leg had been injured in the Civil War. He carried a heavy cane and limped rapidly along the road. My brother and I followed at his heels, and as we went other men and boys joined the crowd.

It had grown dark by the time we got to where the old woman had left the road but the moon had come out. The marshal was thinking there might have been a murder. He kept asking the hunter questions. The hunter went along with his gun across his shoulders, a dog following at his heels. It isn't often a rabbit hunter has a chance to be so conspicuous. He was taking full advantage of it, leading the procession with the town marshal. "I didn't see any wounds. She was a beautiful young girl. Her face was buried in the snow. No, I didn't know her." As a matter of fact, the hunter had not looked closely at the body. He had been frightened. She might have been murdered and someone might spring out from behind a tree and murder him. In a woods, in the late afternoon, when the trees are all bare and there is white snow on the ground, when all is silent, something creepy steals over the mind and body. If something strange or uncanny has happened in the neighborhood all you think about is getting away from there as fast as you can.

The crowd of men and boys had got to where the old woman had crossed the field and went, following the marshal and the hunter, up the slight incline and into the woods.

My brother and I were silent. He had his bundle of papers in a bag slung across his shoulder. When he got back to town he would have to go on distributing his papers before he went home to supper. If I went along, as he had no doubt already determined I should, we would both be late. Either mother or our older sister would have to warm our supper.

Well, we would have something to tell. A boy did not get such a chance very often. It was lucky we just happened to go into the grocery when the hunter came in. The hunter was a country fellow. Neither of us had ever seen him before.

Now the crowd of men and boys had got to the clearing. Darkness comes quickly on such winter nights, but the full moon made everything clear. My brother and I stood near the tree, beneath which the old woman had died.

She did not look old, lying there in that light, frozen and still. One of the men turned her over in the snow and I saw everything. My body trembled with some strange mystical feeling and so did my brother's. It might have been the cold.

Neither of us had ever seen a woman's body before. It may have been the snow, clinging to the frozen flesh, that made it look so white and lovely, so like

197

marble. No woman had come with the party from town; but one of the men, he was the town blacksmith, took off his overcoat and spread it over her. Then he gathered her into his arms and started off to town, all the others following silently. At that time no one knew who she was.

V

I had seen everything, had seen the oval in the snow, like a miniature race track, where the dogs had run, had seen how the men were mystified, had seen the white bare young-looking shoulders, had heard the whispered comments of the men.

The men were simply mystified. They took the body to the undertaker's, and when the blacksmith, the hunter, the marshal and several others had got inside they closed the door. If father had been there perhaps he could have got in, but we boys couldn't.

I went with my brother to distribute the rest of his papers and when we got home it was my brother who told the story.

I kept silent and went to bed early. It may have been I was not satisfied with the way he told it.

Later, in the town, I must have heard other fragments of the old woman's story. She was recognized the next day and there was an investigation.

The husband and son were found somewhere and brought to town and there was an attempt to connect them with the woman's death, but it did not work. They had perfect enough alibis.

However, the town was against them. They had to get out. Where they went I never heard.

I remember only the picture there in the forest, the men standing about, the naked girlish-looking figure, face down in the snow, the tracks made by the running dogs and the clear cold winter sky above. White fragments of clouds were drifting across the sky. They went racing across the little open space among the trees.

The scene in the forest had become for me, without my knowing it, the foundation for the real story I am now trying to tell. The fragments, you see, had to be picked up slowly, long afterwards.

Things happened. When I was a young man I worked on the farm of a German. The hired-girl was afraid of her employer. The farmer's wife hated her.

I saw things at that place. Once later, I had a half-uncanny, mystical adventure with dogs in an Illinois forest on a clear, moonlit winter night. When I was a schoolboy, and on a summer day, I went with a boy friend out along a creek some miles from town and came to the house where the old woman had lived. No one had lived in the house since her death. The doors were broken from the hinges; the window lights were all broken. As the boy and I stood in the road outside, two dogs, just roving farm dogs no doubt, came running around the corner of the house. The dogs were tall, gaunt fellows and came down to the fence and glared through at us, standing in the road.

The whole thing, the story of the old woman's death, was to me as I grew older like music heard from far off. The notes had to be picked up slowly one at a time. Something had to be understood.

The woman who died was one destined to feed animal life. Anyway, that is all she ever did. She was feeding animal life before she was born, as a child, as a young woman working on the farm of the German, after she married, when she grew old and when she died. She fed animal life in cows, in chickens, in pigs, in horses, in dogs, in men. Her daughter had died in childhood and with her one son she had no articulate relations. On the night when she died she was hurrying homeward, bearing on her body food for animal life.

She died in the clearing in the woods and even after her death continued feeding animal life.

You see it is likely that, when my brother told the story, that night when we got home and my mother and sister sat listening, I did not think he got the point. He was too young and so was I. A thing so complete has its own beauty.

I shall not try to emphasize the point. I am only explaining why I was dissatisfied then and have been ever since. I speak of that only that you may understand why I have been impelled to try to tell the simple story over again.

DISCUSSION TOPICS

1. Point of view is crucially important in establishing a relationship between the reader and this story. What does Anderson gain by using the first-person narrator instead of the third-person point of view? Why does he occasionally shift to the second person?
2. Like "The Open Boat" and several other stories we have studied, "Death in the Woods" deals with the theme of initiation. What is the narrator's newfound insight? What does he mean when he says, "I saw everything. My body trembled with some strange mystical feeling and so did my brother's"?
3. How would the story change if Mrs. Grimes, rather than the male narrator, were the "central intelligence"?
4. What is the symbolic significance of Mrs. Grimes's name?

WRITING TOPIC

This story is extraordinarily rich in mythological and archetypal meaning. Write an interpretive essay in which you discuss Anderson's effective use of the following symbols:

> The circle (sphere, egg) = the life cycle, life in primordial form, wholeness; also associated with the Earth Mother.

> The Earth Mother (also Good Mother) = birth, warmth, protection, fertility, growth, nourishment; also associated with the number *four*.

The number *four* (quaternity) = the life cycle (as in the four seasons); associated with the Earth Mother and the circle.

The number *seven* (combining the female *four* and male *three*) = the most potent of all numbers, symbolizing perfect order and the completion of a period or cycle.

The moon = the feminine principle, fecundity, the rhythm of life, and the mysteries of creation and death.

JAMES JOYCE (1882–1941) Dubliner who experimented brilliantly with new stream-of-consciousness narrative techniques and with linguistic symbolism in *Ulysses* (1922) and *Finnegans Wake* (1939). Although he produced only a half-dozen books, he is regarded as a major twentieth-century author. Virtually every selection in his one volume of short stories, *Dubliners* (1914), has been honored by multiple anthologizing. One of Joyces's best-known contributions to the modern short story is his theory of "epiphany"—a sudden insight or revelation.

ARABY

North Richmond Street,[1] being blind,[2] was a quiet street except at the hour when the Christian Brothers'[3] School set the boys free. An uninhabited house of two storeys stood at the blind end, detached from its neighbors in a square ground. The other houses of the street, conscious of decent lives within them, gazed at one another with brown imperturbable faces.

The former tenant of our house, a priest, had died in the back drawing-room. Air, musty from having been long enclosed, hung in all the rooms, and the waste room behind the kitchen was littered with old useless papers. Among these I found a few paper-covered books, the pages of which were curled and damp: *The Abbot,*[4] by Walter Scott, *The Devout Communicant*[5] and *The Memoirs of Vidocq.*[6] I liked the last best because its leaves were yellow. The wild garden behind the house contained a central apple-tree and a few straggling bushes under one of which I found the late tenant's rusty bicycle-pump. He had been a very charitable priest; in his will he had left all his money to institutions and the furniture of his house to his sister.

When the short days of winter came dusk fell before we had well eaten our dinners. When we met in the street the houses had grown sombre. The space of sky above us was the colour of ever-changing violet and towards it the lamps of the street lifted their feeble lanterns. The cold air stung us and we played till our bodies glowed. Our shouts echoed in the silent street. The career of our play brought us through the dark muddy lanes behind the houses where we ran the gauntlet of the rough tribes from the cottages, to the back doors of the dark dripping gardens where odours arose from the ashpits, to the dark odorous stables where a coachman smoothed and combed the horse or shook music from the buckled harness. When we returned to the street, light from the kitchen windows had filled the areas. If my uncle was seen turning the corner we hid in the shadow until we had seen him safely housed. Or if Mangan's sister came out on the doorstep to call her brother in to his tea we watched her from our shadow peer up and down the street. We waited to see whether she would remain or go in and, if she remained, we left our shadow and walked up to Mangan's steps resignedly. She was waiting for us, her figure defined by the light from the half-opened door. Her brother always teased her before he obeyed and I stood by the railings looking at her. Her dress swung as she moved her body and the soft rope of her hair tossed from side to side.

Every morning I lay on the floor in the front parlour watching her door. The blind was pulled down to within an inch of the sash so that I could not be seen. When she came out on the doorstep my heart leaped. I ran to the hall, seized my books and followed her. I kept her brown figure always in my eye and, when we came near the point at which our ways diverged, I quickened my pace and passed her. This happened morning after morning. I had never spoken to her, except for a few casual words, and yet her name was like a summons to all my foolish blood.

Her image accompanied me even in places the most hostile to romance. On Saturday evenings when my aunt went marketing I had to go to carry some of the parcels. We walked through the flaring streets, jostled by drunken men and bargaining women, amid the curses of labourers, the shrill litanies of shop-boys who stood on guard by the barrels of pigs' cheeks, the nasal chanting of street-singers, who sang a *come-all-you* about O'Donovan Rossa[7] or a ballad about the troubles in our native land. These noises converged in a single sensation of life for me: I imagined that I bore my chalice safely through a throng of foes. Her name sprang to my lips at moments in strange prayers and praises which I myself did not understand. My eyes were often full of tears (I could not tell why) and at times a flood from my heart seemed to pour itself out into my bosom. I thought little of the future. I did not know whether I would ever speak to her or not or, if I spoke to her, how I could tell her of my confused adoration. But my body was like a harp and her words and gestures were like fingers running upon the wires.

One evening I went into the back drawing-room in which the priest had died. It was a dark rainy evening and there was no sound in the house. Through one of the broken panes I heard the rain impinge upon the earth, the fine incessant needles of water playing in the sodden beds. Some distant lamp or lighted window gleamed below me. I was thankful that I could see so little. All my senses seemed to desire to veil themselves and, feeling that I was about to slip from them, I pressed the palms of my hands together until they trembled, murmuring: *"O love! O love!"* many times.

At last she spoke to me. When she addressed the first words to me I was so confused that I did not know what to answer. She asked me was I going to *Araby*.[8] I forgot whether I answered yes or no. It would be a splendid bazaar, she said she would love to go.

"And why can't you?" I asked.

While she spoke she turned a silver bracelet round and round her wrist. She could not go, she said, because there would be a retreat that week in her convent. Her brother and two other boys were fighting for their caps and I was alone at the railings. She held one of the spikes, bowing her head towards me. The light from the lamp opposite our door caught the white curve of her neck, lit up her hair that rested there and, falling, lit up the hand upon the railing. It fell over one side of her dress and caught the white border of a petticoat, just visible as she stood at ease.

"It's well for you," she said.

"If I go," I said, "I will bring you something."

What innumerable follies laid waste my waking and sleeping thoughts after that evening! I wished to annihilate the tedious intervening days. I chafed against the work of school. At night in my bedroom and by day in the classroom her image came between me and the page I strove to read. The syllables of the word *Araby* were called to me through the silence in which my soul luxuriated and cast an Eastern enchantment over me. I asked for leave to go to the bazaar on Saturday night. My aunt was surprised and hoped it was not some Freemason[9] affair. I answered few questions in class. I watched my master's face pass from amiability to sternness; he hoped I was not beginning to idle. I could not call my wandering thoughts together. I had hardly any patience with the serious work of life which, now that it stood between me and my desire, seemed to me child's play, ugly monotonous child's play.

On Saturday morning I reminded my uncle that I wished to go to the bazaar in the evening. He was fussing at the hallstand, looking for the hat-brush, and answered me curtly:

"Yes, boy, I know."

As he was in the hall I could not go into the front parlour and lie at the window. I left the house in bad humour and walked slowly towards the school. The air was pitilessly raw and already my heart misgave me.

When I came home to dinner my uncle had not yet been home. Still it was early. I sat staring at the clock for some time and, when its ticking began to irritate me, I left the room. I mounted the staircase and gained the upper part of the house. The high cold empty gloomy rooms liberated me and I went from room to room singing. From the front window I saw my companions playing below in the street. Their cries reached me weakened and indistinct and, leaning my forehead against the cool glass, I looked over at the dark house where she lived. I may have stood there for an hour, seeing nothing but the brown-clad figure cast by my imagination, touched discreetly by the lamplight at the curved neck, at the hand upon the railings and at the border below the dress.

When I came downstairs again I found Mrs. Mercer sitting at the fire. She was an old garrulous woman, a pawnbroker's widow, who collected used stamps for some pious purpose. I had to endure the gossip of the tea-table. The meal was prolonged beyond an hour and still my uncle did not come. Mrs. Mercer stood up to go: she was sorry she couldn't wait any longer, but it was after eight o'clock and she did not like to be out late, as the night air was bad for her. When she had gone I began to walk up and down the room, clenching my fists. My aunt said:

"I'm afraid you may put off your bazaar for this night of Our Lord."

At nine o'clock I heard my uncle's latchkey in the halldoor. I heard him talking to himself and heard the hallstand rocking when it had received the weight of his overcoat. I could interpret these signs. When he was midway through his dinner I asked him to give me the money to go to the bazaar. He had forgotten.

"The people are in bed and after their first sleep now," he said.

I did not smile. My aunt said to him energetically:

"Can't you give him the money and let him go? You've kept him late enough as it is."

My uncle said he was very sorry he had forgotten. He said he believed in the old saying: "All work and no play makes Jack a dull boy." He asked me where I was going and, when I had told him a second time he asked me did I know *The Arab's Farewell to His Steed*. [10] When I left the kitchen he was about to recite the opening lines of the piece to my aunt.

I held a florin tightly in my hand as I strode down Buckingham Street towards the station. The sight of the streets thronged with buyers and glaring with gas recalled to me the purpose of my journey. I took my seat in a third-class carriage of a deserted train. After an intolerable delay the train moved out of the station slowly. It crept onward among ruinous houses and over the twinkling river. At Westland Row Station a crowd of people pressed to the carriage doors; but the porters moved them back, saying that it was a special train for the bazaar. I remained alone in the bare carriage. In a few minutes the train drew up beside an improvised wooden platform. I passed out on to the road and saw by the lighted dial of a clock that it was ten minutes to ten. In front of me was a large building which displayed the magical name.

I could not find any sixpenny entrance and, fearing that the bazaar would be closed, I passed in quickly through a turnstile, handing a shilling to a weary-looking man. I found myself in a big hall girdled at half its height by a gallery. Nearly all the stalls were closed and the greater part of the hall was in darkness. I recognised a silence like that which pervades a church after a service. I walked into the centre of the bazaar timidly. A few people were gathered about the stalls which were still open. Before a curtain, over which the words *Café Chantant* [11] were written in coloured lamps, two men were counting money on a salver. I listened to the fall of the coins.

Remembering with difficulty why I had come I went over to one of the stalls and examined porcelain vases and flowered tea-sets. At the door of the stall a young lady was talking and laughing with two young gentlemen. I remarked their English accents and listened vaguely to their conversation.

"O, I never said such a thing!"

"O, but you did!"

"O, but I didn't!"

"Didn't she say that?"

"Yes. I heard her."

"O, there's a . . . fib!"

Observing me the young lady came over and asked me did I wish to buy anything. The tone of her voice was not encouraging; she seemed to have spoken to me out of a sense of duty. I looked humbly at the great jars that stood like eastern guards at either side of the dark entrance to the stall and murmured:

"No, thank you."

The young lady changed the position of one of the vases and went back to the two young men. They began to talk of the same subject. Once or twice the young lady glanced at me over her shoulder.

I lingered before her stall, though I knew my stay was useless, to make my interest in her wares seem the more real. Then I turned away slowly and walked down the middle of the bazaar. I allowed the two pennies to fall against the sixpence in my pocket. I heard a voice call from one end of the gallery that the light was out. The upper part of the hall was now completely dark.

Gazing up into the darkness I saw myself as a creature driven and derided by vanity; and my eyes burned with anguish and anger.

---

[1] In Dublin.
[2] Dead-end street.
[3] Conservative Irish lay order.
[4] Historical novel by Sir Walter Scott (1771–1834). Published in 1820, the story deals with Mary Queen of Scots.
[5] Catholic religious tract.
[6] Purportedly written by François Vidocq (1775–1857), French criminal turned chief of detectives.
[7] *Come, all you Irishmen:* standard beginning for a type of popular song. O'Donovan Rossa was a sobriquet of Jeremiah O'Donovan (1831–1915), Irish revolutionary banished to the United States for terrorist activities. Also known as "Dynamite Rossa."
[8] A bazaar to raise money for a hospital. It was advertised as a "Grand Oriental Fête."
[9] Masonic Order, considered enemies by Catholics.
[10] Sentimental poem by Caroline E. S. Norton (1808–1877).
[11] Café featuring musical entertainment.

DISCUSSION TOPICS

1. Any reader who has experienced "young love" should be able to identify with Joyce's protagonist. How old do you think he is? Why is his age a significant factor in the story?

2. Joyce said that his *Dubliners* was written "to betray the soul of that hemiplegia or paralysis which many consider a city" and that he hoped "people might be willing to pay for the special odour of corruption" that floated over these stories. Discuss the devices (particularly images) used in "Araby" to convey a sense of moral paralysis, decay, and corruption. Also discuss the counterbalancing devices Joyce uses to sublimate or refine the sordidness of Dublin: Note especially Joyce's curious blending of romantic, erotic, and religious images throughout the story. What does this technique suggest about the nature of love as it is defined in this story?

3. Why is Mangan's sister not named?
4. It has been noted that Joyce used irony as a defense against his own sentimentality. In what ways does irony counterpoint the narrator's poignant remembrance in this story?
5. Discuss the significance of the uncle's reference to "The Arab's Farewell to His Steed," a popular sentimental poem dramatizing the Arab's remorse for having sold his most cherished mount.
6. This story may be compared in many ways with Sherwood Anderson's "Death in the Woods": for example, both are told from the first-person point of view, in retrospect, many years after the unforgettable, illuminating experiences; both are initiation stories (each protagonist is recounting a traumatic experience); both deal with female archetypes (Earth Mother and Soul-Mate or "beautiful lady"); both are strongly autobiographical; both deal with the transfiguring powers of the human imagination. In each story what has the narrator gained in the passage of years since the event itself?

WRITING TOPIC

In *Stephen Hero* Joyce defined "epiphany" as "a sudden spiritual manifestation, whether in the vulgarity of speech or of gesture or in a memorable phase of the mind itself," adding that "it was for the man of letters to record these epiphanies with extreme care, seeing that they themselves are the most delicate and evanescent of moments." What is the nature of the epiphany in "Araby"?

WILLIAM CARLOS WILLIAMS (1883–1963) New Jersey physician, realist, essayist, imagist poet. He was known among his patients as "Uncle Billy." His essential compassion is saved from sentimentality by a tough honesty and ironic understatement similar to Ernest Hemingway's.

THE USE OF FORCE

They were new patients to me, all I had was the name, Olson. Please come down as soon as you can, my daughter is very sick.

When I arrived I was met by the mother, a big startled looking woman, very clean and apologetic who merely said, Is this the doctor? and let me in. In the back, she added. You must excuse us, doctor, we have her in the kitchen where it is warm. It is very damp here sometimes.

The child was fully dressed and sitting on her father's lap near the kitchen table. He tried to get up, but I motioned for him not to bother, took off my overcoat and started to look things over. I could see that they were all very nervous, eyeing me up and down distrustfully. As often, in such cases, they weren't telling me more than they had to, it was up to me to tell them; that's why they were spending three dollars on me.

The child was fairly eating me up with her cold, steady eyes, and no expression to her face whatever. She did not move and seemed, inwardly, quiet; an unusually attractive little thing, and as strong as a heifer in appearance. But her face was flushed, she was breathing rapidly, and I realized that she had a high fever. She had magnificent blonde hair, in profusion. One of those picture children often reproduced in advertising leaflets and the photogravure sections of the Sunday papers.

She's had a fever for three days, began the father and we don't know what it comes from. My wife has given her things, you know, like people do, but it don't do no good. And there's been a lot of sickness around. So we tho't you'd better look her over and tell us what is the matter.

As doctors often do I took a trial shot at it as a point of departure. Has she had a sore throat?

Both parents answered me together, No . . . No, she says her throat don't hurt her.

Does your throat hurt you? added the mother to the child. But the little girl's expression didn't change nor did she move her eyes from my face.

Have you looked?

I tried to, said the mother, but I couldn't see.

As it happens we had been having a number of cases of diphtheria in the school to which this child went during that month and we were all, quite apparently, thinking of that, though no one had as yet spoken of the thing.

Well, I said, suppose we take a look at the throat first. I smiled in my best professional manner and asking for the child's first name I said, come on, Mathilda, open your mouth and let's take a look at your throat.

Nothing doing.

Aw, come on, I coaxed, just open your mouth wide and let me take a look. Look, I said opening both hands wide, I haven't anything in my hands. Just open up and let me see.

Such a nice man, put in the mother. Look how kind he is to you. Come on, do what he tells you to. He won't hurt you.

At that I ground my teeth in disgust. If only they wouldn't use the word "hurt" I might be able to get somewhere. But I did not allow myself to be hurried or disturbed but speaking quietly and slowly I approached the child again.

As I moved my chair a little nearer suddenly with one catlike movement both her hands clawed instinctively for my eyes and she almost reached them too. In fact she knocked my glasses flying and they fell, though unbroken, several feet away from me on the kitchen floor.

Both the mother and father almost turned themselves inside out in embarrassment and apology. You bad girl, said the mother, taking her and shaking her by one arm. Look what you've done. The nice man . . .

For heaven's sake, I broke in. Don't call me a nice man to her. I'm here to look at her throat on the chance that she might have diphtheria and possibly die of it. But that's nothing to her. Look here, I said to the child, we're going to look at your throat. You're old enough to understand what I'm saying. Will you open it now by yourself or shall we have to open it for you?

Not a move. Even her expression hadn't changed. Her breaths however were coming faster and faster. Then the battle began. I had to do it. I had to have a throat culture for her own protection. But first I told the parents that it was entirely up to them. I explained the danger but said that I would not insist on a throat examination so long as they would take the responsibility.

If you don't do what the doctor says you'll have to go to the hospital, the mother admonished her severely.

Oh yeah? I had to smile to myself. After all, I had already fallen in love with the savage brat, the parents were contemptible to me. In the ensuing struggle they grew more and more abject, crushed, exhausted while she surely rose to magnificent heights of insane fury of effort bred of her terror of me.

The father tried his best, and he was a big man but the fact that she was his daughter, his shame at her behavior and his dread of hurting her made him release her just at the critical times when I had almost achieved success, till I wanted to kill him. But his dread also that she might have diphtheria made him tell me to go on, go on though he himself was almost fainting, while the mother moved back and forth behind us raising and lowering her hands in an agony of apprehension.

Put her in front of you on your lap, I ordered, and hold both her wrists.

But as soon as he did the child let out a scream. Don't, you're hurting me. Let go of my hands. Let them go I tell you. Then she shrieked terrifyingly, hysterically. Stop it! Stop it! You're killing me!

Do you think she can stand it, doctor! said the mother.

You get out, said the husband to his wife. Do you want her to die of diphtheria?

Come on now, hold her, I said.

Then I grasped the child's head with my left hand and tried to get the wooden tongue depressor between her teeth. She fought, with clenched teeth, desperately! But now I also had grown furious—at a child. I tried to hold myself down but I couldn't. I know how to expose a throat for inspection. And I did my best. When finally I got the wooden spatula behind the last teeth and just the point of it into the mouth cavity, she opened up for an instant but before I could see anything she came down again and gripping the wooden blade between her molars she reduced it to splinters before I could get it out again.

Aren't you ashamed, the mother yelled at her. Aren't you ashamed to act like that in front of the doctor?

Get me a smooth-handled spoon of some sort, I told the mother. We're going through with this. The child's mouth was already bleeding. Her tongue was cut and she was screaming in wild hysterical shrieks. Perhaps I should have desisted and come back in an hour or more. No doubt it would have been better. But I have seen at least two children lying dead in bed of neglect in such cases, and feeling that I must get a diagnosis now or never I went at it again. But the worst of it was that I too had got beyond reason. I could have torn the child apart in my own fury and enjoyed it. It was a pleasure to attack her. My face was burning with it.

The damned little brat must be protected against her own idiocy, one says to one's self at such times. Others must be protected against her. It is a social necessity. And all these things are true. But a blind fury, a feeling of adult shame, bred of a longing for muscular release are the operatives. One goes on to the end.

In a final unreasoning assault I overpowered the child's neck and jaws. I forced the heavy silver spoon back of her teeth and down her throat till she gagged. And there it was—both tonsils covered with membrane. She had fought valiantly to keep me from knowing her secret. She had been hiding that sore throat for three days at least and lying to her parents in order to escape just such an outcome as this.

Now truly she was furious. She had been on the defensive before but now she attacked. Tried to get off her father's lap and fly at me while tears of defeat blinded her eyes.

DISCUSSION TOPICS

1. How is your response to this story enhanced by knowing that the author himself was a physician who had many patients like the family in "The Use of Force"? Do you think he was a really good doctor? Why—or why not?
2. Discuss the significance of point of view, particularly as it works to reveal character (in other characters as well as the protagonist). Consider what the story might have been like if told in retrospect from the antagonist's viewpoint; for example, like the youngster in "Araby," she might have concluded that her own eyes "burned with anguish and anger" after the initiation and epiphany. But, of course, as Williams has handled the story, the central focus is upon the revelation of a "force" within the physician's character (revealed to himself as well as to the reader).
3. The story vibrates with violence. Trace the motifs of violence with which Williams has unified the tone of his story; also trace the various strands of conflict with which the story is interwoven: for example, doctor versus patient, doctor versus parents, doctor versus self.
4. Several critics have interpreted this story from the psychological viewpoint as a symbolic rape. Do you find any consistent evidence that supports such an interpretation? What does the story gain or lose from this interpretation?

WRITING TOPIC

How do you feel about this story? Do you relate to the child or to the doctor— or to both? Have you ever had an experience comparable to the one dramatized by Williams? Answer at least two of these questions in a brief (500-word) essay.

ISAK DINESEN (1885–1962) Short story writer, novelist, poet, dramatist, essayist. Isak Dinesen is the pseudonym of Karen Blixen, a Danish author who was famous for her finely crafted stories—written in English—of wonder and enchantment. After her marriage in 1914, she spent 17 years on a coffee plantation in Kenya (then British East Africa), at first with her husband and later, after her divorce, alone. Her African experiences are recounted in *Out of Africa* (1937). Her best-known collections of stories are *Seven Gothic Tales* (1934), *Winter's Tales* (1942), and *Last Tales* (1957).

THE SAILOR-BOY'S TALE

The barque *Charlotte* was on her way from Marseille to Athens, in grey weather, on a high sea, after three days' heavy gale. A small sailor-boy, named Simon, stood on the wet, swinging deck, held on to a shroud, and looked up towards the drifting clouds, and to the upper top-gallant yard of the main-mast.

A bird, that had sought refuge upon the mast, had got her feet entangled in some loose tackle-yarn of the halliard, and, high up there, struggled to get free. The boy on the deck could see her wings flapping and her head turning from side to side.

Through his own experience of life he had come to the conviction in this world everyone must look after himself, and expect no help from others. But the mute, deadly fight kept him fascinated for more than an hour. He wondered what kind of bird it would be. These last days a number of birds had come to settle in the barque's rigging: swallows, quails, and a pair of peregrine falcons; he believed that this bird was a peregrine falcon. He remembered how, many years ago, in his own country and near his home, he had once seen a peregrine falcon quite close, sitting on a stone and flying straight up from it. Perhaps this was the same bird. He thought: "That bird is like me. Then she was there, and now she is here."

At that a fellow-feeling rose in him, a sense of common tragedy; he stood looking at the bird with his heart in his mouth. There were none of the sailors about to make fun of him; he began to think out how he might go up by the shrouds to help the falcon out. He brushed his hair back and pulled up his sleeves, gave the deck round him a great glance, and climbed up. He had to stop a couple of times in the swaying rigging.

It was indeed, he found when he got to the top of the mast, a peregrine falcon. As his head was on a level with hers, she gave up her struggle, and looked at him with a pair of angry, desperate yellow eyes. He had to take hold of her with one hand while he got his knife out, and cut off the tackle-yarn. He was scared as he looked down, but at the same time he felt that he had been ordered up by nobody, but that this was his own venture, and this gave him a proud, steadying sensation, as if the sea and the sky, the ship, the bird and himself were all one. Just as he had freed the falcon, she hacked him in the thumb, so that the blood ran, and he nearly let her go. He grew angry with her, and gave her a clout on the head, then he put her inside his jacket, and climbed down again.

When he reached the deck the mate and the cook were standing there, looking up; they roared to him to ask what he had had to do in the mast. He was so tired that the tears were in his eyes. He took the falcon out and showed her to them, and she kept still within his hands. They laughed and walked off. Simon set the falcon down, stood back and watched her. After a while he reflected that she might not be able to get up from the slippery deck, so he caught her once more, walked away with her and placed her upon a bolt of canvas. A little after she began to trim her feathers, made two or three sharp jerks forward, and then suddenly flew off. The boy could follow her flight above the troughs of the grey sea. He thought: "There flies my falcon."

When the *Charlotte* came home, Simon signed aboard another ship, and two years later he was a light hand on the schooner *Hebe* lying at Bodø, high up on the coast of Norway, to buy herrings.

To the great herring-markets of Bodø ships came together from all corners of the world; here were Swedish, Finnish and Russian boats, a forest of masts, and on shore a turbulent, irregular display of life, with many languages spoken, and mighty fights. On the shore booths had been set up, and the Lapps, small yellow people, noiseless in their movements, with watchful eyes, whom Simon had never seen before, came down to sell bead-embroidered leather-goods. It was April, the sky and the sea were so clear that it was difficult to hold one's eyes up against them —salt, infinitely wide, and filled with bird-shrieks—as if someone were incessantly whetting invisible knives, on all sides, high up in Heaven.

Simon was amazed at the lightness of these April evenings. He knew no geography, and did not assign it to the latitude, but he took it as a sign of an unwonted good-will in the Universe, a favour. Simon had been small for his age all his life, but this last winter he had grown, and had become strong of limb. That good luck, he felt, must spring from the very same source as the sweetness of the weather, from a new benevolence in the world. He had been in need of such encouragement, for he was timid by nature; now he asked for no more. The rest he felt to be his own affair. He went about slowly, and proudly.

One evening he was ashore with land-leave, and walked up to the booth of a small Russian trader, a Jew who sold gold watches. All the sailors knew that his watches were made from bad metal, and would not go, still they bought them, and paraded them about. Simon looked at these watches for a long time, but did not buy. The old Jew had divers goods in his shop, and amongst others a case of oranges. Simon had tasted oranges on his journeys; he bought one and took it with him. He meant to go up on a hill, from where he could see the sea, and suck it there.

As he walked on, and had got to the outskirts of the place, he saw a little girl in a blue frock, standing at the other side of a fence and looking at him. She was thirteen or fourteen years old, as slim as an eel, but with a round, clear, freckled face, and a pair of long plaits. The two looked at one another.

"Who are you looking out for?" Simon asked, to say something. The girl's face broke into an ecstatic, presumptuous smile. "For the man I am going to marry, of course," she said. Something in her countenance made the boy confident and happy; he grinned a little at her. "That will perhaps be me," he said. "Ha, ha," said the girl, "he is a few years older than you, I can tell you." "Why," said Simon, "you are not grown up yourself." The little girl shook her head solemnly. "Nay," she said, "but when I grow up I will be exceedingly beautiful, and wear brown shoes with heels, and a hat." "Will you have an orange?" asked Simon, who could give her none of the things she had named. She looked at the orange and at him. "They are very good to eat," said he. "Why do you not eat it yourself then?" she asked. "I have eaten so many already," said he, "when I was in Athens. Here I had to pay a mark for it." "What is your name?" asked she. "My name is Simon," said he. "What is yours?" "Nora," said the girl. "What do you want for your orange now, Simon?"

When he heard his name in her mouth Simon grew bold. "Will you give me a kiss for the orange?" he asked. Nora looked at him gravely for a moment. "Yes," she said, "I should not mind giving you a kiss." He grew as warm as if he had been running quickly. When she stretched out her hand for the orange he took hold of it. At that moment somebody in the house called out for her. "That is my father," said she, and tried to give him back the orange, but he would not take it. "Then come again tomorrow," she said quickly, "then I will give you a kiss." At that she slipped off. He stood and looked after her, and a little later went back to his ship.

Simon was not in the habit of making plans for the future, and now he did not know whether he would be going back to her or not.

The following evening he had to stay aboard, as the other sailors were going ashore, and he did not mind that either. He meant to sit on the deck with the ship's dog, Balthasar, and to practise upon a concertina that he had purchased some time ago. The pale evening was all round him, the sky was faintly roseate, the sea was quite calm, like milk-and-water, only in the wake of the boats going inshore it broke into streaks of vivid indigo. Simon sat and played; after a while his own music began to speak to him so strongly that he stopped, got up and looked upwards. Then he saw that the full moon was sitting high on the sky.

The sky was so light that she hardly seemed needed there; it was as if she had turned up by a caprice of her own. She was round, demure and presumptuous. At that he knew that he must go ashore, whatever it was to cost him. But he did not know how to get away, since the others had taken the yawl with them. He stood on the deck for a long time, a small lonely figure of a sailor-boy on a boat, when he caught sight of a yawl coming in from a ship farther out, and hailed her. He found that it was the Russian crew from a boat named *Anna,* going ashore. When he could make himself understood to them, they took him with them; they first asked him for money for his fare, then, laughing, gave it back to him. He thought: "These people will be believing that I am going in to town, wenching." And then he felt, with some pride, that they were right, although at the same time they were infinitely wrong, and knew nothing about anything.

When they came ashore they invited him to come in and drink in their company, and he would not refuse, because they had helped him. One of the Russians was a giant, as big as a bear; he told Simon that his name was Ivan. He got drunk at once, and then fell upon the boy with a bear-like affection, pawed him, smiled and laughed into his face, made him a present of a gold watchchain, and kissed him on both cheeks. At that Simon reflected that he also ought to give Nora a present when they met again, and as soon as he could get away from the Russians he walked up to a booth that he knew of, and bought a small blue silk handkerchief, the same colour as her eyes.

It was Saturday evening, and there were many people amongst the houses; they came in long rows, some of them singing, all keen to have some fun that night. Simon, in the midst of this rich, bawling life under the clear moon, felt his head light with the flight from the ship and the strong drinks. He crammed the handkerchief in his pocket; it was silk, which he had never touched before, a present for his girl.

He could not remember the path up to Nora's house, lost his way, and came back to where he had started. Then he grew deadly afraid that he should be too late, and began to run. In a small passage between two wooden huts he ran straight into a big man, and found that it was Ivan once more. The Russian folded his arms round him and held him. "Good! Good!" he cried in high glee, "I have found you, my little chicken. I have looked for you everywhere, and poor Ivan has wept because he lost his friend." "Let me go, Ivan," cried Simon. "Oho," said Ivan, "I shall go with you and get you what you want. My heart and my money are all yours, all yours; I have been seventeen years old myself, a little lamb of God, and I want to be so again tonight." "Let me go," cried Simon, "I am in a hurry." Ivan held him so that it hurt, and patted him with his other hand. "I feel it, I feel it," he said. "Now trust to me, my little friend. Nothing shall part you and me. I hear the others coming; we will have such a night together as you will remember when you are an old grandpapa."

Suddenly he crushed the boy to him, like a bear that carries off a sheep. The odious sensation of male bodily warmth and the bulk of a man close to him made the lean boy mad. He thought of Nora waiting, like a slender ship in the dim air, and of himself, here, in the hot embrace of a hairy animal. He struck Ivan with all his might. "I shall kill you, Ivan," he cried out, "if you do not let me go." "Oh, you will be thankful to me later on," said Ivan, and began to sing. Simon fumbled in his pocket for his knife, and got it opened. He could not lift his hand, but he drove the knife, furiously, in under the big man's arm. Almost immediately he felt the blood spouting out, and running down in his sleeve. Ivan stopped short in the song, let go his hold of the boy and gave two long deep grunts. The next second he tumbled down on his knees. "Poor Ivan, poor Ivan," he groaned. He fell straight on his face. At that moment Simon heard the other sailors coming along, singing, in the by-street.

He stood still for a minute, wiped his knife, and watched the blood spread into a dark pool underneath the big body. Then he ran. As he stopped for a second to choose his way, he heard the sailors behind him scream out over their dead comrade. He thought: "I must get down to the sea, where I can wash my hand." But at the same time he ran the other way. After a little while he found himself

212

on the path that he had walked on the day before, and it seemed as familiar to him, as if he had walked it many hundred times in his life.

He slackened his pace to look round, and suddenly saw Nora standing on the other side of the fence; she was quite close to him when he caught sight of her in the moonlight. Wavering and out of breath he sank down on his knees. For a moment he could not speak. The little girl looked down at him. "Good evening, Simon," she said in her small coy voice. "I have waited for you a long time," and after a moment she added: "I have eaten your orange."

"Oh, Nora," cried the boy. "I have killed a man." She stared at him, but did not move. "Why did you kill a man?" she asked after a moment. "To get here," said Simon. "Because he tried to stop me. But he was my friend." Slowly he got on to his feet. "He loved me!" the boy cried out, and at that burst into tears. "Yes," said she slowly and thoughtfully. "Yes, because you must be here in time." "Can you hide me?" he asked. "For they are after me." "Nay," said Nora, "I cannot hide you. For my father is the parson here at Bodo, and he would be sure to hand you over to them, if he knew that you had killed a man." "Then," said Simon, "give me something to wipe my hands on." "What is the matter with your hands?" she asked, and took a little step forward. He stretched out his hands to her. "Is that your own blood?" she asked. "No," said he, "it is his." She took the step back again. "Do you hate me now?" he asked. "No. I do not hate you," said she. "But do put your hands at your back."

As he did so she came up close to him, at the other side of the fence, and clasped her arms round his neck. She pressed her young body to his, and kissed him tenderly. He felt her face, cool as the moonlight, upon his own, and when she released him, his head swam, and he did not know if the kiss had lasted a second or an hour. Nora stood up straight, her eyes wide open. "Now," she said slowly and proudly, "I promise you that I will never marry anybody, as long as I live." The boy kept standing with his hands on his back, as if she had tied them there. "And now," she said, "you must run, for they are coming." They looked at one another. "Do not forget Nora," said she. He turned and ran.

He leapt over a fence, and when he was down amongst the houses he walked. He did not know at all where to go. As he came to a house, from where music and noise streamed out, he slowly went through the door. The room was full of people; they were dancing in here. A lamp hung from the ceiling, and shone down on them; the air was thick and brown with the dust rising from the floor. There were some women in the room, but many of the men danced with each other, and gravely or laughingly stamped the floor. A moment after Simon had come in the crowd withdrew to the walls to clear the floor for two sailors, who were showing a dance from their own country.

Simon thought: "Now, very soon, the men from the boat will come round to look for their comrade's murderer, and from my hands they will know that I have done it." These five minutes during which he stood by the wall of the dancing-room, in the midst of the gay, sweating dancers, were of great significance to the boy. He himself felt it, as if during this time he grew up, and became like other people. He did not entreat his destiny, nor complain. Here he was, he had killed a man, and had kissed a girl. He did not demand any more from life, nor did life now demand more from him. He was Simon, a man like the men round him, and going to die, as all men are going to die.

He only became aware of what was going on outside him, when he saw that a woman had come in, and was standing in the midst of the cleared floor, looking round her. She was a short, broad old woman, in the clothes of the Lapps, and she took her stand with such majesty and fierceness as if she owned the whole place. It was obvious that most of the people knew her, and were a little afraid of her, although a few laughed; the din of the dancing-room stopped when she spoke.

"Where is my son?" she asked in a high shrill voice, like a bird's. The next moment her eyes fell on Simon himself, and she steered through the crowd, which opened up before her, stretched out her old skinny, dark hand, and took him by the elbow. "Come home with me now," she said. "You need not dance here tonight. You may be dancing a high enough dance soon."

Simon drew back, for he thought that she was drunk. But as she looked him straight in the face with her yellow eyes, it seemed to him that he had met her before, and that he might do well in listening to her. The old woman pulled him with her across the floor, and he followed her without a word. "Do not birch your boy too badly, Sunniva," one of the men in the room cried to her. "He has done no harm, he only wanted to look at the dance."

At the same moment as they came out through the door, there was an alarm in the street, a flock of people came running down it, and one of them, as he turned into the house, knocked against Simon, looked at him and the old woman, and ran on.

While the two walked along the street, the old woman lifted up her skirt, and put the hem of it into the boy's hand. "Wipe your hand on my skirt," she said. They had not gone far before they came to a small wooden house, and stopped; the door to it was so low that they must bend to get through it. As the Lapp-woman went in before Simon, still holding on to his arm, the boy looked up for a moment. The night had grown misty; there was a wide ring round the moon.

The old woman's room was narrow and dark, with but one small window to it; a lantern stood on the floor and lighted it up dimly. It was all filled with reindeer skins and wolf skins, and with reindeer horn, such as the Lapps use to make their carved buttons and knife-handles, and the air in here was rank and stifling. As soon as they were in, the woman turned to Simon, took hold of his head, and with her crooked fingers parted his hair and combed it down in Lapp fashion. She clapped a Lapp cap on him and stood back to glance at him. "Sit down on my stool, now," she said. "But first take out your knife." She was so commanding in voice and manner that the boy could not but choose to do as she told him; he sat down on the stool, and he could not take his eyes off her face, which was flat and brown, and as if smeared with dirt in its net of fine wrinkles. As he sat there he heard many people come along outside, and stop by the house; then someone knocked at the door, waited a moment and knocked again. The old woman stood and listened, as still as a mouse.

214

"Nay," said the boy and got up. "This is no good, for it is me that they are after. It will be better for you to let me go out to them." "Give me your knife," said she. When he handed it to her, she stuck it straight into her thumb, so that the blood spouted out, and she let it drip all over her skirt. "Come in, then," she cried.

The door opened, and two of the Russian sailors came and stood in the opening; there were more people outside. "Has anybody come in here?" they asked. "We are after a man who has killed our mate, but he has run away from us. Have you seen or heard anybody this way?" The old Lapp-woman turned upon them, and her eyes shone like gold in the lamplight. "Have I seen or heard anyone?" she cried. "I have heard you shriek murder all over the town. You frightened me, and my poor silly boy there, so that I cut my thumb as I was ripping the skin-rug that I sew. The boy is too scared to help me, and the rug is all ruined. I shall make you pay me for that. If you are looking for a murderer, come in and search my house for me, and I shall know you when we meet again." She was so furious that she danced where she stood, and jerked her head like an angry bird of prey.

The Russian came in, looked round the room, and at her and her blood-stained hand and shirt. "Do not put a curse on us now, Sunniva," he said timidly. "We know that you can do many things when you like. Here is a mark to pay you for the blood you have spilled." She stretched out her hand, and he placed a piece of money in it. She spat on it. "Then go, and there shall be no bad blood between us," said Sunniva, and shut the door after them. She stuck her thumb in her mouth, and chuckled a little.

The boy got up from his stool, stood straight up before her and stared into her face. He felt as if he were swaying high up in the air, with but a small hold. "Why have you helped me?" he asked her. "Do you not know?" she answered. "Have you not recognised me yet? But you will remember the peregrine falcon which was caught in the tackle-yarn of your boat, the *Charlotte,* as she sailed in the Mediterranean. That day you climbed up by the shrouds of the top-gallantmast to help her out, in a stiff wind, and with a high sea. That falcon was me. We Lapps often fly in such a manner, to see the world. When I first met you I was on my way to Africa, to see my younger sister and her children. She is a falcon too, when she chooses. By that time she was living at Takaunga, within an old ruined tower, which down there they call a minaret." She swathed a corner of her skirt round her thumb, and bit at it. "We do not forget," she said. "I hacked your thumb, when you took hold of me; it is only fair that I should cut my thumb for you tonight."

She came close to him, and gently rubbed her two brown, claw-like fingers against his forehead. "So you are a boy," she said, "who will kill a man rather than be late to meet your sweetheart? We hold together, the females of this earth. I shall mark your forehead now, so that the girls will know of that, when they look at you, and they will like you for it." She played with the boy's hair, and twisted it round her finger.

"Listen now, my little bird," said she. "My great grandson's brother-in-law is lying with his boat by the landing-place at this moment; he is to take a consignment of skins out to a Danish boat. He will bring you back to your boat, in time, before your mate comes. The *Hebe* is sailing tomorrow morning, is it not so? But when you are aboard, give him back my cap for me." She took up his knife, wiped it in her skirt and handed it to him. "Here is your knife," she said. "You will stick it into no more men; you will not need to, for from now you will sail the seas like a faithful seaman. We have enough trouble with our sons as it is."

The bewildered boy began to stammer his thanks to her. "Wait," said she, "I shall make you a cup of coffee, to bring back your wits, while I wash your jacket." She went and rattled an old copper kettle upon the fireplace. After a while she handed him a hot, strong, black drink in a cup without a handle to it. "You have drunk with Sunniva now," she said; "you have drunk down a little wisdom, so that in the future all your thoughts shall not fall like raindrops into the salt sea."

When he had finished and set down the cup, she led him to the door and opened it for him. He was surprised to see that it was almost clear morning. The house was so high up that the boy could see the sea from it, and a milky mist about it. He gave her his hand to say good-bye.

She stared into his face. "We do not forget," she said. "And you, you knocked me on the head there, high up in the mast. I shall give you that blow back." With that she smacked him on the ear as hard as she could, so that his head swam. "Now we are quits," she said, gave him a great, mischievous, shining glance, and a little push down the doorstep, and nodded to him.

In this way the sailor-boy got back to his ship, which was to sail the next morning, and lived to tell the story.

DISCUSSION TOPICS

1. Birds often appear in myths and fairy tales as agents of spiritual transformation. How does Dinesen use this symbol in her story? What is the significance of Simon's thought, "That bird is like me. Then she was there, and now she is here"?
2. By what means does Dinesen achieve the fairy-tale atmosphere in her story?
3. What is the thematic function of Ivan? Why is he killed? Are you troubled by the fact that his killer goes unpunished? Why—or why not?
4. Why does Sunniva mark Simon's forehead? What does she mean when she says, "We have enough trouble with our sons as it is"?
5. Compare and contrast this tale with Anderson's "Death in the Woods" and Hemingway's "Indian Camp."

KATHERINE ANNE PORTER (1890–1980) Spent childhood on Texas ranch and in convent schools. Although her short stories had won critical esteem, her allegorical novel, *Ship of Fools* (1962), was her first widely popular work. The autobiographical character Miranda appears in several of her stories.

THE GRAVE

The grandfather, dead for more than thirty years, had been twice disturbed in his long repose by the constancy and possessiveness of his widow. She removed his bones first to Louisiana and then to Texas as if she had set out to find her own burial place, knowing well she would never return to the places she had left. In Texas she set up a small cemetery in a corner of her first farm, and as the family connection grew, and oddments of relations came over from Kentucky to settle, it contained at last about twenty graves. After the grandmother's death, part of her land was to be sold for the benefit of certain of her children, and the cemetery happened to lie in the part set aside for sale. It was necessary to take up the bodies and bury them again in the family plot in the big new public cemetery, where the grandmother had been buried. At last her husband was to lie beside her for eternity, as she had planned.

The family cemetery had been a pleasant small neglected garden of tangled rose bushes and ragged cedar trees and cypress, the simple flat stones rising out of uncropped sweet-smelling wild grass. The graves were lying open and empty one burning day when Miranda and her brother Paul, who often went together to hunt rabbits and doves, propped their twenty-two Winchester rifles carefully against the rail fence, climbed over and explored among the graves. She was nine years old and he was twelve.

They peered into the pits all shaped alike with such purposeful accuracy, and looking at each other with pleased adventurous eyes, they said in solemn tones: "These were graves!" trying by words to shape a special, suitable emotion in their minds, but they felt nothing except an agreeable thrill of wonder: they were seeing a new sight, doing something they had not done before. In them both there was also a small disappointment at the entire commonplaceness of the actual spectacle. Even if it had once contained a coffin for years upon years, when the coffin was gone a grave was just a hole in the ground. Miranda leaped into the pit that had held her grandfather's bones. Scratching around aimlessly and pleasurably as any young animal, she scooped up a lump of earth and weighed it in her palm. It had a pleasantly sweet, corrupt smell, being mixed with cedar needles and small leaves, and as the crumbs fell apart, she saw a silver dove no larger than a hazel nut, with spread wings and a neat fan-shaped tail. The breast had a deep round hollow in it. Turning it up to the fierce sunlight, she saw that the inside of the hollow was cut in little whorls. She scrambled out, over the pile of loose earth that had fallen back into one end of the grave, calling to Paul that she had found something, he must guess what. . . . His head appeared smiling over the rim of another grave. He waved a closed hand at her. "I've got something too!" They ran to compare treasures, making a game of it, so many guesses each, all wrong, and a final showdown with opened palms. Paul had found a thin wide gold ring carved with intricate flowers and leaves. Miranda was smitten at sight of the ring and wished to have it. Paul seemed more impressed by the dove. They made a trade, with some little bickering. After he had got the dove in his hand, Paul said. "Don't you know what this

217

is? This is a screw head for a *coffin!* . . . I'll bet nobody else in the world has one like this!''

Miranda glanced at it without covetousness. She had the gold ring on her thumb; it fitted perfectly. "Maybe we ought to go now," she said, "maybe one of the niggers'll see us and tell somebody." They knew the land had been sold, the cemetery was no longer theirs, and they felt like trespassers. They climbed back over the fence, slung their rifles loosely under their arms—they had been shooting at targets with various kinds of firearms since they were seven years old—and set out to look for the rabbits and doves or whatever small game might happen along. On these expeditions Miranda always followed at Paul's heels along the path, obeying instructions about handling her gun when going through fences; learning how to stand it up properly so it would not slip and fire unexpectedly; how to wait her time for a shot and not just bang away in the air without looking, spoiling shots for Paul, who really could hit things if given a chance. Now and then, in her excitement at seeing birds whizz up suddenly before her face, or a rabbit leap across her very toes, she lost her head, and almost without sighting she flung her rifle up and pulled the trigger. She hardly ever hit any sort of mark. She had no proper sense of hunting at all. Her brother would be often completely disgusted with her. "You don't care whether you get your bird or not," he said. "That's no way to hunt." Miranda could not understand his indignation. She had seen him smash his hat and yell with fury when he had missed his aim. "What I like about shooting," said Miranda, with exasperating inconsequence, "is pulling the trigger and hearing the noise."

"Then, by golly," said Paul, "whyn't you go back to the range and shoot at bulls-eyes?"

"I'd just as soon," said Miranda, "only like this, we walk around more."

"Well, you just stay behind and stop spoiling my shots," said Paul, who, when he made a kill, wanted to be certain he had made it. Miranda, who alone brought down a bird once in twenty rounds, always claimed as her own any game they got when they fired at the same moment. It was tiresome and unfair and her brother was sick of it.

"Now, the first dove we see, or the first rabbit, is mine," he told her. "And the next will be yours. Remember that and don't get smarty."

"What about snakes?" asked Miranda idly. "Can I have the first snake?"

Waving her thumb gently and watching her gold ring glitter, Miranda lost interest in shooting. She was wearing her summer roughing outfit: dark blue overalls, a light blue shirt, a hired-man's straw hat, and thick brown sandals. Her brother had the same outfit except his was a sober hickory-nut color. Ordinarily Miranda preferred her overalls to any other dress, though it was making rather a scandal in the countryside, for the year was 1903, and in the back country the law of female decorum had teeth in it. Her father had been criticized for letting his girls dress like boys and go careering around astride barebacked horses. Big sister Maria, the really independent and fearless one, in spite of her rather affected ways, rode at a dead run with only a rope knotted around her horse's nose. It was said the motherless family was running down, with the Grandmother no longer there

218

to hold it together. It was known that she had discriminated against her son Harry in her will, and that he was in straits about money. Some of his old neighbors reflected with vicious satisfaction that now he would probably not be so stiffnecked, nor have any more high-stepping horses either. Miranda knew this, though she could not say how. She had met along the road old women of the kind who smoked corncob pipes, who had treated her grandmother with most sincere respect. They slanted their gummy old eyes side-ways at the granddaughter and said, "Ain't you ashamed of yoself, Missy? It's aginst the Scriptures to dress like that. Whut yo Pappy thinkin about?" Miranda, with her powerful social sense, which was like a fine set of antennae radiating from every pore of her skin, would feel ashamed because she knew well it was rude and ill-bred to shock anybody, even bad-tempered old crones, though she had faith in her father's judgment and was perfectly comfortable in the clothes. Her father had said, "They're just what you need, and they'll save your dresses for school. . . ." This sounded quite simple and natural to her. She had been brought up in rigorous economy. Wastefulness was vulgar. It was also a sin. These were truths; she had heard them repeated many times and never once disputed.

Now the ring, shining with serene purity of fine gold on her rather grubby thumb, turned her feelings against her overalls and sockless feet, toes sticking through the thick brown leather straps. She wanted to go back to the farmhouse, take a good cold bath, dust herself with plenty of Maria's violet talcum powder—provided Maria was not present to object, of course—put on the thinnest, most becoming dress she owned, with a big sash, and sit in a wicker chair under the trees. . . . These things were not all she wanted, of course; she had vague stirrings of desire for luxury and a grand way of living which could not take precise form in her imagination but were founded on family legend of past wealth and leisure. These immediate comforts were what she could have, and she wanted them at once. She lagged rather far behind Paul, and once she thought of just turning back without a word and going home. She stopped, thinking that Paul would never do that to her, and so she would have to tell him. When a rabbit leaped, she let Paul have it without dispute. He killed it with one shot.

When she came up with him, he was already kneeling, examining the wound, the rabbit trailing from his hands. "Right through the head," he said complacently, as if he had aimed for it. He took out his sharp, competent bowie knife and started to skin the body. He did it very cleanly and quickly. Uncle Jimbilly knew how to prepare the skins so that Miranda always had fur coats for her dolls, for though she never cared much for her dolls she liked seeing them in fur coats. The children knelt facing each other over the dead animal. Miranda watched admiringly while her brother stripped the skin away as if he were taking off a glove. The flayed flesh emerged dark scarlet, sleek, firm; Miranda with thumb and finger felt the long fine muscles with the silvery flat strips binding them to the joints. Brother lifted the oddly bloated belly. "Look," he said, in a low amazed voice. "It was going to have young ones."

Very carefully he slit the thin flesh from the center ribs to the flanks, and a scarlet bag appeared. He slit again and pulled the bag open, and there lay a bundle of tiny rabbits, each wrapped in a thin scarlet veil. The brother pulled these off and there they were, dark gray, their sleek wet down lying in minute, even ripples, like a baby's head just washed, their unbelievably small delicate ears folded close, their little blind faces almost featureless.

Miranda said, "Oh, I want to *see*," under her breath. She looked and looked —excited but not frightened, for she was accustomed to the sight of animals killed in hunting—filled with pity and astonishment and a kind of shocked delight in the wonderful little creatures for their own sakes, they were so pretty. She touched one of them ever so carefully, "Ah, there's blood running over them," she said and began to tremble without knowing why. Yet she wanted most deeply to see and to know. Having seen, she felt at once as if she had known all along. The very memory of her former ignorance faded, she had always known just this. No one had ever told her anything outright, she had been rather unobservant of the animal life around her because she was so accustomed to animals. They seemed simply disorderly and unaccountably rude in their habits, but altogether natural and not very interesting. Her brother had spoken as if he had known about everything all along. He may have seen all this before. He had never said a word to her, but she knew now a part at least of what he knew. She understood a little of the secret, formless intuitions in her own mind and body, which had been clearing up, taking form, so gradually and so steadily she had not realized that she was learning what she had to know. Paul said cautiously, as if he were talking about something forbidden: "They were just about ready to be born." His voice dropped on the last word. "I know," said Miranda, "like kittens. I know, like babies." She was quietly and terribly agitated, standing again with her rifle under her arm, looking down at the bloody heap. "I don't want the skin," she said, "I won't have it." Paul buried the young rabbits again in their mother's body, wrapped the skin around her, carried her to a clump of sage bushes, and hid her away. He came out again at once and said to Miranda, with an eager friendliness, a confidential tone quite unusual in him, as if he were taking her into an important secret on equal terms: "Listen now. Now you listen to me, and don't ever forget. Don't you ever tell a living soul that you saw this. Don't tell a soul. Don't tell Dad because I'll get into trouble. He'll say I'm leading you into things you ought not to do. He's always saying that. So now don't you go and forget and blab out sometime the way you're always doing. . . . Now, that's a secret. Don't you tell."

Miranda never told, she did not even wish to tell anybody. She thought about the whole worrisome affair with confused unhappiness for a few days. Then it sank quietly into her mind and was heaped over by accumulated thousands of impressions, for nearly twenty years. One day she was picking her path among the puddles and crushed refuse of a market street in a strange city of a strange country, when without warning, plain and clear in its true colors as if she looked through a frame upon a scene that had not stirred nor changed since the moment it happened, the episode of that far-off day leaped from its burial place before her mind's eye. She was so reasonlessly horrified she halted suddenly staring, the scene before her eyes dimmed by the vision back of them. An Indian vendor had held up before her a tray of dyed sugar sweets, in the shapes of all kinds of small creatures: birds, baby chicks, baby rabbits, lambs, baby pigs. They were in gay colors and smelled of vanilla, maybe. . . . It was a very hot day and the smell in the market, with its piles of raw flesh and wilting flowers, was like the mingled sweetness and corruption she had smelled that other day in the empty cemetery at home: the day she had remembered always until now vaguely as the time she and her brother had found treasure in the opened graves. Instantly upon this thought the dreadful vision faded, and she saw clearly her brother, whose childhood face she had forgotten, standing again in the blazing sunshine, again twelve years old, a pleased sober smile in his eyes, turning the silver dove over and over in his hands.

DISCUSSION TOPICS

1. This is the story of a young girl's initiation or passage into the world of women and, simultaneously, into the mystery of death and birth. Is Miranda's initiation a success or failure? Explain why.
2. Pay particular attention to the ending of the story, and to the image in her mind's eye. Is it affirmative or negative? How does it relate to the opening paragraph?
3. Explain how the following passages work to reveal Miranda's character and how they relate to her subsequent behavior: "she had vague stirrings of desire for luxury and a grand way of living which could not take precise form in her imagination but were founded on family legend of past wealth and leisure . . . though she never cared much for her dolls she liked seeing them in fur coats. . . . [She was] filled with pity and astonishment and a kind of shocked delight in the wonderful little creatures for their own sakes, they were so pretty."
4. Writers often use animals as "objective correlatives" (see the glossary). Discuss Porter's use of this technique. Also discuss the symbolism of the wedding ring and the dove-shaped coffin-screw that Miranda and Paul exchange.
5. Why is Paul so intent upon keeping the killing a secret?

WRITING TOPIC

Compare this story with Anderson's "Death in the Woods," focusing upon the initiation archetype and "mystery of life and death" motif.

JAMES THURBER (1894–1961) Satirist: cartoonist, essayist, fabulist. A long-time contributor to *The New Yorker,* he collaborated with E. B. White on *Is Sex Necessary?* (1929), a parody on sex books, and with Elliot Nugent on the successful Broadway play *The Male Animal* (1940). The war between the sexes is a recurrent theme throughout his essays, cartoons, poems, and stories.

"We're going through!" The Commander's voice was like thin ice breaking. He wore his full-dress uniform, with the heavily braided white cap pulled down rakishly over one cold gray eye. "We can't make it, sir. It's spoiling for a hurricane, if you ask me." "I'm not asking you, Lieutenant Berg," said the Commander. "Throw on the power lights! Rev her up to 8,500! We're going through!" The pounding of the cylinders increased: ta-pocketa-pocketa-pocketa-*pocketa-pocketa.* The Commander stared at the ice forming on the pilot window. He walked over and twisted a row of complicated dials. "Switch on No. 8 auxiliary!" he shouted. "Switch on No. 8 auxiliary!" repeated Lieutenant Berg. "Full strength in No. 3 turret!" shouted the Commander. "Full strength in No. 3 turret!" The crew, bending to their various tasks in the huge, hurtling eight-engined Navy hydroplane, looked at each other and grinned. "The Old Man'll get us through," they said to one another. "The Old Man ain't afraid of Hell!" . . .

"Not so fast! You're driving too fast!" said Mrs. Mitty. "What are you driving so fast for?"

"Hmm?" said Walter Mitty. He looked at his wife, in the seat beside him, with shocked astonishment. She seemed grossly unfamiliar, like a strange woman who had yelled at him in a crowd. "You were up to fifty-five," she said. "You know I don't like to go more than forty. You were up to fifty-five." Walter Mitty drove on toward Waterbury in silence, the roaring of the SN202 through the worst storm in twenty years of Navy flying fading in the remote, intimate airways of his mind. "You're tensed up again," said Mrs. Mitty. "It's one of your days. I wish you'd let Dr. Renshaw look you over."

Walter Mitty stopped the car in front of the building where his wife went to have her hair done. "Remember to get those overshoes while I'm having my hair done," she said. "I don't need overshoes," said Mitty. She put her mirror back into her bag. "We've been all through that," she said, getting out of the car. "You're not a young man any longer." He raced the engine a little. "Why don't you wear your gloves? Have you lost your gloves?" Walter Mitty reached in a pocket and brought out the gloves. He put them on, but after she had turned and gone into the building and he had driven on to a red light, he took them off again. "Pick it up, brother!" snapped a cop as the light changed, and Mitty hastily pulled on his gloves and lurched ahead. He drove around the streets aimlessly for a time, and then he drove past the hospital on his way to the parking lot.

. . . "It's the millionaire banker, Wellington McMillan," said the pretty nurse. "Yes?" said Walter Mitty, removing his gloves slowly. "Who has the case?" "Dr. Renshaw and Dr. Benbow, but there are two specialists here, Dr. Remington from New York and Mr. Pritchard-Mitford from London. He flew over." A door opened down a long, cool corridor and Dr. Renshaw came out. He looked distraught and haggard. "Hello, Mitty," he said. "We're having the devil's own time with McMillan, the millionaire banker and close personal friend of Roosevelt. Obstreosis[1] of the ductal tract. Tertiary. Wish you'd take a look at him." "Glad to," said Mitty.

In the operating room there were whispered introductions: Dr. Remington, Dr. Mitty. Mr. Pritchard-Mitford, Dr. Mitty." "I've read your book on strepto-thricosis,"[2] said Pritchard-Mitford, shaking hands. "A brilliant performance, sir." "Thank you." said Walter Mitty." "Didn't know you were in the States, Mitty," grumbled Remington. "Coals to Newcastle,[3] bringing Mitford and me here for a tertiary." "You are very kind," said Mitty. A huge, complicated machine, connected to the operating table, with many tubes and wires, began at this moment to go pocketa-pocketa-pocketa. "The new anesthetizer is giving way!" shouted an interne. "There is no one in the East who knows how to fix it!" "Quiet, man!" said Mitty, in a low, cool voice. He sprang to the machine, which was now going pocketa-pocketa-queep-pocketa-queep. He began fingering delicately a row of glistening dials. "Give me a fountain pen!" he snapped. Someone handed him a fountain pen. He pulled a faulty piston out of the machine and inserted the pen in its place. "That will hold for ten minutes," he said. "Get on with the operation." A nurse hurried over and whispered to Renshaw, and Mitty saw the man turn pale. "Coreopsis[4] has set in," said Renshaw nervously. "If you would take over, Mitty?" Mitty looked at him and at the craven figure of Benbow, who drank, and at the grave, uncertain faces of the two great specialists. "If you wish," he said. They slipped a white gown on him; he adjusted a mask and drew on thin gloves; nurses handed him shining . . .

"Back it up, Mac! Look out for that Buick!" Walter Mitty jammed on the brakes. "Wrong lane, Mac," said the parking-lot attendant, looking at Mitty closely. "Gee. Yeh," muttered Mitty. He began cautiously to back out of the lane marked "Exit Only." "Leave her sit there," said the attendant. "I'll put her away." Mitty got out of the car. "Hey, better leave the key." "Oh," said Mitty, handing the man the ignition key. The attendant vaulted into the car, backed it up with insolent skill, and put it where it belonged.

They're so damn cocky, thought Walter Mitty, walking along Main Street; they think they know everything. Once he had tried to take his chains off, outside New Milford, and he had got them wound around the axles. A man had had to come out in a wrecking car and unwind them, a young, grinning garageman. Since then Mrs. Mitty always made him drive to a garage to have the chains taken off. The next time, he thought, I'll wear my right arm in a sling; they won't grin at me then. I'll have my right arm in a sling and they'll see I couldn't possibly take the chains off myself. He kicked at the slush on the sidewalk. "Overshoes," he said to himself, and he began looking for a shoe store.

When he came out into the street again, with the overshoes in a box under his arm, Walter Mitty began to wonder what the other thing was his wife had told him to get. She told him twice, before they set out from their house for Waterbury. In a way he hated these weekly trips to town—he was always getting something wrong. Kleenex, he thought, Squibb's, razor blades? No. Toothpaste, toothbrush, bicarbonate, carborundum, initiative and referendum? He gave it up. But she would remember it. "Where's the what's-its-name?" she would ask. "Don't tell me you forgot the what's-it's name." A newsboy went by shouting something about the Waterbury trial.

223

... "Perhaps this will refresh your memory." The District Attorney suddenly thrust a heavy automatic at the quiet figure on the witness stand. "Have you ever seen this before?" Walter Mitty took the gun and examined it expertly. "This is my Webley-Vickers 50.80," he said calmly. An excited buzz ran around the courtroom. The judge rapped for order. "You are a crack shot with any sort of firearms, I believe?" said the District Attorney, insinuatingly. "Objection!" shouted Mitty's attorney. "We have shown that the defendant could not have fired the shot. We have shown that he wore his right arm in a sling on the night of the fourteenth of July." Walter Mitty raised his hand briefly and the bickering attorneys were stilled. "With any known make of gun," he said evenly, "I could have killed Gregory Fitzhurst at three hundred feet with *my left hand.*" Pandemonium broke loose in the courtroom. A woman's scream rose above the bedlam and suddenly a lovely, dark-haired girl was in Walter Mitty's arms. The District Attorney struck at her savagely. Without rising from his chair, Mitty let the man have it on the point of the chin. "You miserable cur!" ...

"Puppy biscuit," said Walter Mitty. He stopped walking and the buildings of Waterbury rose up out of the misty courtroom and surrounded him again. A woman who was passing laughed. "He said 'Puppy biscuit,'" she said to her companion. "That man said 'Puppy biscuit' to himself." Walter Mitty hurried on. He went into an A. & P., not the first one he came to but a smaller one farther up the street. "I want some biscuit for small, young dogs," he said to the clerk. "Any special brand, sir?" The greatest pistol shot in the world thought a moment. "It says 'Puppies Bark for It' on the box," said Walter Mitty.

His wife would be through at the hairdresser's in fifteen minutes, Mitty saw in looking at his watch, unless they had trouble drying it; sometimes they had trouble drying it. She didn't like to get to the hotel first; she would want him to be there waiting for her as usual. He found a big leather chair in the lobby, facing a window, and he put the overshoes and the puppy biscuit on the floor beside it. He picked up an old copy of *Liberty*[5] and sank down into the chair. "Can Germany Conquer the World Through the Air?" Walter Mitty looked at the pictures of bombing planes and of ruined streets.

... "The cannonading has got the wind up in young Raleigh, sir," said the sergeant. Captain Mitty looked up at him through tousled hair. "Get him to bed," he said wearily. "With the others. I'll fly alone." "But you can't, sir," said the sergeant anxiously. "It takes two men to handle that bomber and the Archies[6] are pounding hell out of the air. Von Richtman's circus[7] is between here and Saulier." "Somebody's got to get that ammunition dump," said Mitty. "I'm going over. Spot of brandy?" He poured a drink for the sergeant and one for himself. War thundered and whined around the dugout and battered at the door. There was a rending of wood and splinters flew through the room. "A bit of a near thing," said Captain Mitty carelessly. "The box barrage[8] is closing in," said the sergeant. "We only live once, Sergeant," said Mitty, with his faint, fleeting smile. "Or do we?" He poured another brandy and tossed it off. "I never see a man could hold his brandy like you, sir," said the sergeant. "Begging your pardon, sir." Captain Mitty stood up and strapped on his huge Webley-Vickers automatic. "It's forty kilometers through hell, sir," said the sergeant. Mitty finished one last brandy. "After all," he said softly, "what isn't?" The pounding of the cannon increased; there was the rat-tat-tatting of machine guns, and from somewhere came the menacing pocketa-pocketa-pocketa of the new flame-throwers. Walter Mitty walked to the door of the dugout humming "Auprès de Ma Blonde."[9] He turned and waved to the sergeant. "Cheerio!" he said. . . .

Something struck his shoulder. "I've been looking all over this hotel for you," said Mrs. Mitty. "Why do you have to hide in this old chair? How did you expect me to find you?" "Things close in," said Walter Mitty vaguely. "What?" Mrs. Mitty said. "Did you get the what's-its-name? The puppy biscuit? What's in that box?" "Overshoes," said Mitty. "Couldn't you have put them on in the store?" "I was thinking," said Walter Mitty. "Does it ever occur to you that I am sometimes thinking?" She looked at him. "I'm going to take your temperature when I get you home," she said.

They went out through the revolving doors that made a faintly derisive whistling sound when you pushed them. It was two blocks to the parking lot. At the drugstore on the corner she said, "Wait here for me. I forgot something, I won't be a minute." She was more than a minute. Walter Mitty lighted a cigarette. It began to rain, rain with sleet in it. He stood up against the wall of the drugstore, smoking. . . . He put his shoulders back and his heels together. "To hell with the handkerchief," said Walter Mitty scornfully. He took one last drag on his cigarette and snapped it away. Then, with that faint, fleeting smile playing about his lips, he faced the firing squad; erect and motionless, proud and disdainful, Walter Mitty the Undefeated, inscrutable to the last.

[1] A nonsense word.
[2] Another nonsense word.
[3] "Carrying coals to Newcastle [a coal-mining center]" is an old saying to indicate a superfluous action. An analogy would be "Hauling ice to the North Pole."
[4] A species of herb, not a medical condition.
[5] A popular weekly magazine (1924–1951).
[6] The slang term of the day for antiaircraft batteries.
[7] An allusion to Baron Manfred von Richtofen (1892–1918), German fighter pilot ace of World War I. Fighter squadrons on both the Allied and German sides were known as "flying circuses."
[8] Artillery attack from all four sides.
[9] "Close to My Blonde," World War I popular song.

DISCUSSION TOPICS

1. "The Secret Life of Walter Mitty" has become a classic among American comic tales. What are the keys to Thurber's humor? Why do we laugh when we read the story? Are we really laughing at Mitty—or at ourselves? About 40 years ago the story was made into a movie by Hollywood. In the film version Mitty (played by comedian Danny Kaye) is unmarried; in the end he proves himself

a real hero and wins the beautiful heroine (Virginia Mayo). What does the story lose in this version?

2. What narrative devices does Thurber use to give his story unity and coherence? Pay particular attention to the transitions between the "real" world and Mitty's fantasy world.

3. The war between the sexes, especially the struggle between meek, henpecked husbands and domineering, shrewish wives, has been a familiar comic theme from Greek and Roman drama to television's situation comedies. Identify some of the comic stereotypes in "The Secret Life of Walter Mitty." Do you think the story is "sexist," even though Mitty seems to be the object of satirical attack?

4. In addition to portraying comic stereotypes, Thurber's Walter Mitty also exemplifies, in his daydreams at any rate, some well-known heroic archetypes. What kind of hero does Mitty imagine himself to be? How does the story reveal some of the differences between stereotypes and archetypes?

5. Which of Mitty's qualities is distinctly "American" or associated with the "American Dream"?

6. How would the story be changed if told from Mrs. Mitty's point of view?

WILLIAM FAULKNER (1897–1962) Mississippi fictionist; hunter; creator, sole owner and proprietor of mythic Yoknapatawpha County. Although his characters are Southerners, his subject is humanity. He called himself a "failed poet," but he is unquestionably one of the great literary artists of the twentieth century. Many of his novels and stories depict the fall of the decadent Old Southern aristocracy and rise of the vulgar, opportunistic *nouveaux riches.* He won the Nobel prize in 1950.

A ROSE FOR EMILY

When Miss Emily Grierson died, our whole town went to her funeral: the men through a sort of respectful affection for a fallen monument, the women mostly out of curiosity to see the inside of her house, which no one save an old manservant —a combined gardener and cook—had seen in at least ten years.

It was a big, squarish frame house that had once been white, decorated with cupolas and spires and scrolled balconies in the heavily lightsome style of the Seventies, set on what had once been our most select street. But garages and cotton gins had encroached and obliterated even the august names of that neighborhood; only Miss Emily's house was left, lifting its stubborn and coquettish decay above the cotton wagons and the gasoline pumps—an eyesore among eyesores. And now Miss Emily had gone to join the representatives of those august names where they lay in the cedar-bemused cemetery among the ranked and anonymous graves of Union and Confederate soldiers who fell at the battle of Jefferson.

Alive, Miss Emily had been a tradition, a duty, and a care; a sort of hereditary obligation upon the town, dating from that day in 1894 when Colonel Sartoris, the mayor—he who fathered the edict that no Negro woman should appear on the streets without an apron—remitted her taxes, the dispensation dating from the death of her father on into perpetuity. Not that Miss Emily would have accepted charity. Colonel Sartoris invented an involved tale to the effect that Miss Emily's father had loaned money to the town, which the town, as a matter of business, preferred this way of repaying. Only a man of Colonel Sartoris' generation and thought could have invented it, and only a woman could have believed it.

When the next generation, with its more modern ideas, became mayors and aldermen, this arrangement created some little dissatisfaction. On the first of the year they mailed her a tax notice. February came, and there was no reply. They wrote her a formal letter, asking her to call at the sheriff's office at her convenience. A week later the mayor wrote her himself, offering to call or to send his car for her, and received in reply a note on paper of an archaic shape, in a thin, flowing calligraphy in faded ink, to the effect that she no longer went out at all. The tax notice was also enclosed, without comment.

They called a special meeting of the Board of Aldermen. A deputation waited upon her, knocked at the door through which no visitor had passed since she ceased giving china-painting lessons eight or ten years earlier. They were admitted by the old Negro into a dim hall from which a stairway mounted into still more shadow. It smelled of dust and disuse—a close, dank smell. The Negro led them into the parlor. It was furnished in heavy, leather-covered furniture. When the Negro opened the blinds of one window, they could see that the leather was cracked; and when they sat down, a faint dust rose sluggishly about their thighs, spinning with slow motes in the single sun-ray. On a tarnished gilt easel before the fireplace stood a crayon portrait of Miss Emily's father.

They rose when she entered—a small, fat woman in black, with a thin gold chain descending to her waist and vanishing into her belt, leaning on an ebony cane with a tarnished gold head. Her skeleton was small and spare; perhaps that was why what would have been merely plumpness in another was obesity in her. She looked bloated, like a body long submerged in motionless water, and of that pallid hue. Her eyes, lost in the fatty ridges of her face, looked like two small pieces of coal pressed into a lump of dough as they moved from one face to another while the visitors stated their errand.

She did not ask them to sit. She just stood in the door and listened quietly until the spokesman came to a stumbling halt. Then they could hear the invisible watch ticking at the end of the gold chain.

Her voice was dry and cold. "I have no taxes in Jefferson. Colonel Sartoris explained it to me. Perhaps one of you can gain access to the city records and satisfy yourselves."

"But we have. We are the city authorities, Miss Emily. Didn't you get a notice from the sheriff, signed by him?"

"I received a paper, yes," Miss Emily said. "Perhaps he considers himself the sheriff . . . I have no taxes in Jefferson."

"But there is nothing on the books to show that, you see. We must go by the—"

"See Colonel Sartoris. I have no taxes in Jefferson."

"But, Miss Emily—"

"See Colonel Sartoris." (Colonel Sartoris had been dead almost ten years.) "I have no taxes in Jefferson. Tobe!" The Negro appeared. "Show these gentlemen out."

2

So she vanquished them, horse and foot,[1] just as she had vanquished their fathers thirty years before about the smell. That was two years after her father's death and a short time after her sweetheart—the one we believed would marry her—had deserted her. After her father's death she went out very little; after her sweetheart went away, people hardly saw her at all. A few of the ladies had the temerity to call, but were not received, and the only sign of life about the place was the Negro man—a young man then—going in and out with a market basket.

"Just as if a man—any man—could keep a kitchen properly," the ladies said; so they were not surprised when the smell developed. It was another link between the gross, teeming world and the high and mighty Griersons.

A neighbor, a woman, complained to the mayor, Judge Stevens, eighty years old.

"But what will you have me do about it, madam?" he said.

"Why, send her word to stop it," the woman said. "Isn't there a law?"

"I'm sure that won't be necessary," Judge Stevens said. "It's probably just a snake or a rat that nigger of hers killed in the yard. I'll speak to him about it."

The next day he received two more complaints, one from a man who came in diffident deprecation. "We really must do something about it, Judge. I'd be the last one in the world to bother Miss Emily, but we've got to do something." That night the Board of Aldermen met—three graybeards and one younger man, a member of the rising generation.

"It's simple enough," he said. "Send her word to have her place cleaned up. Give her a certain time to do it in, and if she don't . . ."

"Dammit, sir," Judge Stevens said, "will you accuse a lady to her face of smelling bad?"

So the next night, after midnight, four men crossed Miss Emily's lawn and slunk about the house like burglars, sniffing along the base of the brickwork and at the cellar openings while one of them performed a regular sowing motion with his hand out of a sack slung from his shoulder. They broke open the cellar door and sprinkled lime there, and in all the outbuildings. As they recrossed the lawn, a window that had been dark was lighted and Miss Emily sat in it, the light behind her, and her upright torso motionless as that of an idol. They crept quietly across the lawn and into the shadow of the locusts that lined the street. After a week or two the smell went away.

That was when people had begun to feel really sorry for her. People in our

228

town, remembering how Old Lady Wyatt, her great-aunt, had gone completely crazy at last, believed that the Griersons held themselves a little too high for what they really were. None of the young men was quite good enough for Miss Emily and such. We had long thought of them as a tableau: Miss Emily a slender figure in white in the background, her father a spraddled silhouette in the foreground, his back to her and clutching a horsewhip,[2] the two of them framed by the back-flung front door. So when she got to be thirty and was still single, we were not pleased exactly, but vindicated; even with insanity in the family she wouldn't have turned down all of her chances if they had really materialized.

When her father died, it got about that the house was all that was left to her; and in a way, people were glad. At last they could pity Miss Emily. Being left alone, and a pauper, she had become humanized. Now she too would know the old thrill and the old despair of a penny more or less.

The day after his death all the ladies prepared to call at the house and offer condolence and aid, as is our custom. Miss Emily met them at the door, dressed as usual and with no trace of grief on her face. She told them that her father was not dead. She did that for three days, with the ministers calling on her, and the doctors, trying to persuade her to let them dispose of the body. Just as they were about to resort to law and force, she broke down, and they buried her father quickly.

We did not say she was crazy then. We believed she had to do that. We remembered all the young men her father had driven away, and we knew that with nothing left, she would have to cling to that which had robbed her, as people will.

3

She was sick for a long time. When we saw her again, her hair was cut short, making her look like a girl, with a vague resemblance to those angels in colored church windows—sort of tragic and serene.

The town had just let the contracts for paving the sidewalks, and in the summer after her father's death they began the work. The construction company came with niggers and mules and machinery, and a foreman named Homer Barron, a Yankee—a big, dark, ready man, with a big voice and eyes lighter than his face. The little boys would follow in groups to hear him cuss the niggers, and the niggers singing in time to the rise and fall of picks. Pretty soon he knew everybody in town. Whenever you heard a lot of laughing anywhere about the square, Homer Barron would be in the center of the group. Presently we began to see him and Miss Emily on Sunday afternoons driving in the yellow-wheeled buggy and the matched team of bays from the livery stable.

At first we were glad that Miss Emily would have an interest, because the ladies all said, "Of course a Grierson would not think seriously of a Northerner, a day laborer." But there were still others, older people, who said that even grief could not cause a real lady to forget *noblesse oblige*—without calling it *noblesse oblige*. They just said, "Poor Emily. Her kinsfolk should come to her." She had some kin in Alabama; but years ago her father had fallen out with them over the estate of Old Lady Wyatt, the crazy woman, and there was no communication between the two families. They had not even been represented at the funeral.

And as soon as the old people said, "Poor Emily," the whispering began. "Do you suppose it's really so?" they said to one another. "Of course it is. What else could . . ." This behind their hands; rustling of craned silk and satin behind jalousies closed upon the sun of Sunday afternoon as the thin, swift clop-clop-clop of the matched team passed: "Poor Emily."

She carried her head high enough—even when we believed that she was fallen. It was as if she demanded more than ever the recognition of her dignity as the last Grierson; as if it had wanted that touch of earthiness to reaffirm her imperviousness. Like when she bought the rat poison, the arsenic. That was over a year after they had begun to say "Poor Emily," and while the two female cousins were visiting her.

"I want some poison," she said to the druggist. She was over thirty then, still a slight woman, though thinner than usual, with cold, haughty black eyes in a face the flesh of which was strained across the temples and about the eye-sockets as you imagine a lighthouse-keeper's face ought to look. "I want some poison," she said.

"Yes, Miss Emily. What kind? For rats and such? I'd recom—"

"I want the best you have. I don't care what kind."

The druggist named several. "They'll kill anything up to an elephant. But what you want is—"

"Arsenic," Miss Emily said. "Is that a good one?"

"Is . . . arsenic? Yes, ma'am. But what you want—"

"I want arsenic."

The druggist looked down at her. She looked back at him, erect, her face like a strained flag. "Why, of course," the druggist said. "If that's what you want. But the law requires you to tell what you are going to use it for."

Miss Emily just stared at him, her head tilted back in order to look him eye for eye, until he looked away and went and got the arsenic and wrapped it up. The Negro delivery boy brought her the package; the druggist didn't come back. When she opened the package at home there was written on the box, under the skull and bones: "For rats."

4

So the next day we all said, "She will kill herself"; and we said it would be the best thing. When she had first begun to be seen with Homer Barron, we had said, "She will marry him." Then we said, "She will persuade him yet," because Homer himself had remarked—he liked men, and it was known that he drank with the younger men in the Elks' Club—that he was not a marrying man. Later we said, "Poor Emily" behind the jalousies as they passed on Sunday afternoon in the glittering buggy, Miss Emily with her head high and Homer Barron with his hat cocked and a cigar in his teeth, reins and whip in a yellow glove.

Then some of the ladies began to say it was a disgrace to the town and a bad example to the young people. The men did not want to interfere, but at last the ladies forced the Baptist minister—Miss Emily's people were Episcopal—to call upon her. He would never divulge what happened during that interview, but he refused to go back again. The next Sunday they again drove about the streets, and the following day the minister's wife wrote to Miss Emily's relations in Alabama.

So she had blood-kin under her roof again and we sat back to watch developments. At first nothing happened. Then we were sure that they were to be married. We learned that Miss Emily had been to the jeweler's and ordered a man's toilet set in silver, with the letters H.B. on each piece. Two days later we learned that she had bought a complete outfit of men's clothing, including a nightshirt, and we said, "They are married." We were really glad. We were glad because the two female cousins were even more Grierson than Miss Emily had ever been.

So we were not surprised when Homer Barron—the streets had been finished some time since—was gone. We were a little disappointed that there was not a public blowing-off, but we believed that he had gone on to prepare for Miss Emily's coming, or to give her a chance to get rid of the cousins. (By that time it was a cabal, and we were all Miss Emily's allies to help circumvent the cousins.) Sure enough, after another week they departed. And, as we had expected all along, within three days Homer Barron was back in town. A neighbor saw the Negro man admit him at the kitchen door at dusk one evening.

And that was the last we saw of Homer Barron. And of Miss Emily for some time. The Negro man went in and out with the market basket, but the front door remained closed. Now and then we would see her at a window for a moment, as the men did that night when they sprinkled the lime, but for almost six months she did not appear on the streets. Then we knew that this was to be expected too; as if that quality of her father which had thwarted her woman's life so many times had been too virulent and too furious to die.

When we next saw Miss Emily, she had grown fat and her hair was turning gray. During the next few years it grew grayer and grayer until it attained an even pepper-and-salt iron-gray, when it ceased turning. Up to the day of her death at seventy-four it was still that vigorous iron-gray, like the hair of an active man.

From that time on her front door remained closed, save for a period of six or seven years, when she was about forty, during which she gave lessons in china-painting. She fitted up a studio in one of the downstairs rooms, where the daughters and granddaughters of Colonel Sartoris' contemporaries were sent to her with the same regularity and in the same spirit that they were sent to church on Sundays with a twenty-five-cent piece for the collection plate. Meanwhile her taxes had been remitted.

Then the newer generation became the backbone and the spirit of the town, and the painting pupils grew up and fell away and did not send their children to her with boxes of color and tedious brushes and pictures cut from the ladies' magazines. The front door closed upon the last one and remained closed for good. When the town got free postal delivery, Miss Emily alone refused to let them fasten the metal numbers above her door and attach a mailbox to it. She would not listen to them.

231

Daily, monthly, yearly we watched the Negro grow grayer and more stooped, going in and out with the market basket. Each December we sent her a tax notice, which would be returned by the post office a week later, unclaimed. Now and then we would see her in one of the downstairs windows—she had evidently shut up the top floor of the house—like the carven torso of an idol in a niche, looking or not looking at us, we could never tell which. Thus she passed from generation to generation—dear, inescapable, impervious, tranquil, and perverse.

And so she died. Fell ill in the house filled with dust and shadows, with only a doddering Negro man to wait on her. We did not even know she was sick; we had long since given up trying to get any information from the Negro. He talked to no one, probably not even to her, for his voice had grown harsh and rusty, as if from disuse.

She died in one of the downstairs rooms, in a heavy walnut bed with a curtain, her gray head propped on a pillow yellow and moldy with age and lack of sunlight.

5

The Negro met the first of the ladies at the front door and let them in, with their hushed, sibilant voices and their quick, curious glances, and then he disappeared. He walked right through the house and out the back and was not seen again.

The two female cousins came at once. They held the funeral on the second day, with the town coming to look at Miss Emily beneath a mass of bought flowers, with the crayon face of her father musing profoundly above the bier and the ladies sibilant and macabre; and the very old men—some in their brushed Confederate uniforms—on the porch and the lawn, talking of Miss Emily as if she had been a contemporary of theirs, believing that they had danced with her and courted her perhaps, confusing time with its mathematical progression, as the old do, to whom all the past is not a diminishing road but, instead, a huge meadow which no winter ever quite touches, divided from them now by the narrow bottle-neck of the most recent decade of years.

Already we knew that there was one room in that region above stairs which no one had seen in forty years, and which would have to be forced. They waited until Miss Emily was decently in the ground before they opened it.

The violence of breaking down the door seemed to fill this room with pervading dust. A thin, acrid pall as of the tomb seemed to lie everywhere upon this room decked and furnished as for a bridal: upon the valance curtains of faded rose color, upon the rose-shaded lights, upon the dressing table, upon the delicate array of crystal and the man's toilet things backed with tarnished silver, silver so tarnished that the monogram was obscured. Among them lay a collar and tie, as if they had just been removed, which, lifted, left upon the surface a pale crescent in the dust. Upon a chair hung the suit, carefully folded; beneath it the two mute shoes and the discarded socks.

The man himself lay in the bed.

For a long while we just stood there, looking down at the profound and fleshless grin. The body had apparently once lain in the attitude of an embrace, but now the long sleep that outlasts love, that conquers even the grimace of love, had cuckolded him. What was left of him, rotted beneath what was left of the nightshirt, had become inextricable from the bed in which he lay; and upon him and upon the pillow beside him lay that even coating of the patient and biding dust.

Then we noticed that in the second pillow was the indentation of a head. One of us lifted something from it, and leaning forward, that faint and invisible dust dry and acrid in the nostrils, we saw a long strand of iron-gray hair.

[1] A military metaphor: cavalry and infantry.

[2] The traditional American instrument of punishment for particularly "heinous" infractions of manners. Unwelcome callers on a young girl would be prime candidates for a "horse-whipping" by her father or other of her male relatives.

DISCUSSION TOPICS

1. What are your feelings toward Miss Emily—shock, horror, revulsion, pity, admiration? How does Faulkner manage to elicit these emotions from his readers?
2. Our knowledge of the biographical and historical backgrounds of this story should substantially enrich our understanding and appreciation of Faulkner's creation of this little masterpiece. It may be helpful to know, for example, that "Jefferson" is modeled after the author's own hometown, Oxford, Mississippi. What else do you know about Southern history, particularly late-nineteenth- and early twentieth-century Southern history, that might enhance your response to this story? What are the principal differences between the old Southern aristocrats (represented by such characters as Colonel Sartoris and Judge Stevens) and the "newer generation"? How may the story be read as a moral parable? As a story of the Old South versus the New South (and the Northern economic invasion of the South)?
3. What is the meaning of Faulkner's title, and how does his opening sentence force us to interpret Miss Emily as something more than a psychological case study?
4. What key images and symbols does Faulkner use to reinforce the themes of the story? Note especially his description of the Grierson house in the second paragraph.
5. Compare Miss Emily with the women in Keats's "La Belle Dame Sans Merci" and Irving's "Adventure of the German Student." What archetypal manifestation of the Great Mother do all three characters represent?

WRITING TOPIC

Explain the role of the narrator as teller and participant in "A Rose for Emily." Notice, for example, the shifts in point of view.

ELIZABETH BOWEN (1899–1973) Born in Dublin; reared in England. She is considered by many critics to be among the finest novelists of her generation. During World War II she worked days in the Ministry of Information and nights as an air raid warden in London.

THE DEMON LOVER

Towards the end of her day in London Mrs. Drover went round to her shut-up house to look for several things she wanted to take away. Some belonged to herself, some to her family, who were by now used to their country life. It was late August; it had been a steamy, showery day: at the moment the trees down the pavement glittered in an escape of humid yellow afternoon sun. Against the next batch of clouds, already piling up ink-dark, broken chimneys and parapets stood out. In her once familiar street, as in any unused channel, an unfamiliar queerness had silted up; a cat wove itself in and out of railings, but no human eye watched Mrs. Drover's return. Shifting some parcels under her arm, she slowly forced round her latchkey in an unwilling lock, then gave the door, which had warped, a push with her knee. Dead air came out to meet her as she went in.

The staircase window having been boarded up, no light came down into the hall. But one door, she could just see, stood ajar, so she went quickly through into the room and unshuttered the big window in there. Now the prosaic woman, looking about her, was more perplexed than she knew by everything that she saw, by traces of her long former habit of life—the yellow smoke-stain up the white marble mantelpiece, the ring left by a vase on the top of the escritoire; the bruise in the wallpaper where, on the door being thrown open widely, the china handle had always hit the wall. The piano, having gone away to be stored, had left what looked like claw-marks on its part of the parquet. Though not much dust had seeped in, each object wore a film of another kind; and, the only ventilation being the chimney, the whole drawing-room smelled of the cold hearth. Mrs. Drover put down her parcels on the escritoire and left the room to proceed upstairs; the things she wanted were in a bedroom chest.

She had been anxious to see how the house was—the part-time caretaker she shared with some neighbours was away this week on his holiday, known to be not yet back. At the best of times he did not look in often, and she was never sure that she trusted him. There were some cracks in the structure, left by the last bombing, on which she was anxious to keep an eye. Not that one could do anything—

A shaft of refracted daylight now lay across the hall. She stopped dead and stared at the hall table—on this lay a letter addressed to her.

She thought first—then the caretaker *must* be back. All the same, who, seeing the house shuttered, would have dropped a letter in at the box? It was not a circular, it was not a bill. And the post office redirected, to the address in the country, everything for her that came through the post. The caretaker (even if he *were* back) did not know she was due in London to-day—her call here had been planned to be a surprise—so his negligence in the matter of this letter, leaving it to wait in the dusk and the dust, annoyed her. Annoyed, she picked up the letter, which bore no stamp. But it cannot be important, or they would know. . . . She took the letter rapidly upstairs with her, without a stop to look at the writing till she reached what had been her bedroom, where she let in light. The room looked over the garden and other gardens: the sun had gone in; as the clouds sharpened and lowered, the trees and rank lawns seemed already to smoke with dark. Her reluctance to look again at the letter came from the fact that she felt intruded upon —and by someone contemptuous of her ways. However, in the tenseness preceding the fall of rain she read it: it was a few lines.

DEAR KATHLEEN,
    You will not have forgotten that to-day is our anniversary, and the day we said. The years have gone by at once slowly and fast. In view of the fact that nothing has changed, I shall rely upon you to keep your promise. I was sorry to see you leave London, but was satisfied that you would be back in time. You may expect me, therefore, at the hour arranged.

Until then . . .
K.

Mrs. Drover looked for the date: it was to-day's. She dropped the letter on to the bed-springs, then picked it up to see the writing again—her lips, beneath the remains of lipstick, beginning to go white. She felt so much the change in her own face that she went to the mirror, polished a clear patch in it and looked at once urgently and stealthily in. She was confronted by a woman of forty-four, with eyes starting out under a hatbrim that had been rather carelessly pulled down. She had not put on any more powder since she left the shop where she ate her solitary tea. The pearls her husband had given her on their marriage hung loose round her now rather thinner throat, slipping into the V of the pink wool jumper her sister knitted last autumn as they sat round the fire. Mrs. Drover's most normal expression was one of controlled worry, but of assent. Since the birth of the third of her little boys, attended by a quite serious illness, she had had an intermittent muscular flicker to the left of her mouth, but in spite of this she could always sustain a manner that was at once energetic and calm.

Turning from her own face as precipitately as she had gone to meet it, she went to the chest where the things were, unlocked it, threw up the lid and knelt to search. But as rain began to come crashing down she could not keep from looking over her shoulder at the stripped bed on which the letter lay. Behind the blanket of rain the clock of the church that still stood struck six—with rapidly heightening apprehension she counted each of the slow strokes. "The hour arranged. . . . My God," she said, "*what* hour? How should I . . . ? After twenty-five years. . . ."

The young girl talking to the soldier in the garden had not ever completely seen his face. It was dark; they were saying good-bye under a tree. Now and then —for it felt, from not seeing him at this intense moment, as though she had never

235

seen him at all—she verified his presence for these few moments longer by putting out a hand, which he each time pressed, without very much kindness, and painfully, on to one of the breast buttons of his uniform. That cut of the button on the palm of her hand was, principally, what she was to carry away. This was so near the end of a leave from France that she could only wish him already gone. It was August 1916. Being not kissed, being drawn away from and looked at intimidated Kathleen till she imagined spectral glitters in the place of his eyes. Turning away and looking back up the lawn she saw, through branches of trees, the drawing-room window alight: she caught a breath for the moment when she could go running back there into the safe arms of her mother and sister, and cry: "What shall I do, what shall I do? He has gone."

Hearing her catch her breath, her fiancé said, without feeling: "Cold?"

"You're going away such a long way."

"Not so far as you think."

"I don't understand?"

"You don't have to," he said. "You will. You know what we said."

"But that was—suppose you—I mean, suppose."

"I shall be with you," he said, "sooner or later. You won't forget that. You need do nothing but wait."

Only a little more than a minute later she was free to run up the silent lawn. Looking in through the window at her mother and sister, who did not for the moment perceive her, she already felt that unnatural promise drive down between her and the rest of all human kind. No other way of having given herself could have made her feel so apart, lost and foresworn. She could not have plighted a more sinister troth.

Kathleen behaved well when, some months later, her fiancé was reported missing, presumed killed. Her family not only supported her but were able to praise her courage without stint because they could not regret, as a husband for her, the man they knew almost nothing about. They hoped she would, in a year or two, console herself—and had it been only a question of consolation things might have gone much straighter ahead. But her trouble, behind just a little grief, was a complete dislocation from everything. She did not reject other lovers, for these failed to appear: for years she failed to attract men—and with the approach of her thirties she became natural enough to share her family's anxiousness on this score. She began to put herself out, to wonder; and at thirty-two she was very greatly relieved to find herself being courted by William Drover. She married him, and the two of them settled down in this quiet, arboreal part of Kensington[1]: in this house the years piled up, her children were born and they all lived till they were driven out by the bombs of the next war. Her movements as Mrs. Drover were circumscribed, and she dismissed any idea that they were still watched.

As things were—dead or living the letter-writer sent her only a threat. Unable, for some minutes, to go on kneeling with her back exposed to the empty room, Mrs. Drover rose from the chest to sit on an upright chair whose back was firmly against the wall. The desuetude of her former bedroom, her married London home's whole air of being a cracked cup from which memory, with its reassuring power, had either evaporated or leaked away, made a crisis—and at just this crisis the letter-writer had, knowledgeably, struck. The hollowness of the house this evening cancelled years on years of voices, habits and steps. Through the shut windows she only heard rain fall on the roofs around. To rally herself, she said she was in a mood—and, for two or three seconds shutting her eyes, told herself that she had imagined the letter. But she opened them—there it lay on the bed.

On the supernatural side of the letter's entrance she was not permitting her mind to dwell. Who, in London, knew she meant to call at the house to-day? Evidently, however, this had been known. The caretaker, *had* he come back, had had no cause to expect her: he would have taken the letter in his pocket, to forward it, at his own time, through the post. There was no other sign that the caretaker had been in—but, if not? Letters dropped in at doors of deserted houses do not fly or walk to tables in halls. They do not sit on the dust of empty tables with the air of certainty that they will be found. There is needed some human hand—but nobody but the caretaker had a key. Under circumstances she did not care to consider, a house can be entered without a key. It was possible that she was not alone now. She might be being waited for, downstairs. Waited for—until when? Until "the hour arranged." At least that was not six o'clock: six had struck.

She rose from the chair and went over and locked the door.

The thing was, to get out. To fly? No, not that: she had to catch her train. As a woman whose utter dependability was the keystone of her family life she was not willing to return to the country, to her husband, her little boys and her sister, without the objects she had come up to fetch. Resuming work at the chest she set about making up a number of parcels in a rapid, fumbling-decisive way. These, with her shopping parcels, would be too much to carry; these meant a taxi—at the thought of the taxi her heart went up and her normal breathing resumed. I will ring up the taxi now; the taxi cannot come too soon: I shall hear the taxi out there running its engine, till I walk calmly down to it through the hall. I'll ring up—But no: the telephone is cut off. . . . She tugged at a knot she had tied wrong.

The idea of flight . . . He was never kind to me, not really. I don't remember him kind at all. Mother said he never considered me. He was set on me, that was what it was—not love. No love, not meaning a person well. What did he do, to make me promise like that? I can't remember—But she found that she could.

She remembered with such dreadful acuteness that the twenty-five years since then dissolved like smoke and she instinctively looked for the weal left by the button on the palm of her hand. She remembered not only all that he said and did but the complete suspension of *her* existence during that August week. I was not myself—they all told me so at the time. She remembered—but with one white burning blank as where acid has dropped on a photograph: *under no conditions* could she remember his face.

So, wherever he may be waiting, I shall not know him. You have no time to run from a face you do not expect.

The thing was to get to the taxi before any clock struck what could be the hour. She would slip down the street and round the side of the square to where the square gave on the main road. She would return in the taxi, safe, to her own door, and bring the solid driver into the house with her to pick up the parcels from room to room. The idea of the taxi driver made her decisive, bold: she unlocked her door, went to the top of the staircase and listened down.

She heard nothing—but while she was hearing nothing the *passé* air of the staircase was disturbed by a draught that travelled up to her face. It emanated from the basement: down there a door or window was being opened by someone who chose this moment to leave the house.

The rain had stopped; the pavements steamily shone as Mrs. Drover let herself out by inches from her own front door into the empty street. The unoccupied houses opposite continued to meet her look with their damaged stare. Making towards the thoroughfare and the taxi, she tried not to keep looking behind. Indeed, the silence was so intense—one of those creeks of London silence exaggerated this summer by the damage of war—that no tread could have gained on hers unheard. Where her street debouched on the square where people went on living she grew conscious of and checked her unnatural pace. Across the open end of the square two buses impassively passed each other: women, a perambulator, cyclists, a man wheeling a barrow signalized, once again, the ordinary flow of life. At the square's most populous corner should be—and was—the short taxi rank. This evening, only one taxi—but this, although it presented its blank rump, appeared already to be alertly waiting for her. Indeed, without looking round the driver started his engine as she panted up from behind and put her hand on the door. As she did so, the clock struck seven. The taxi faced the main road: to make the trip back to her house it would have to turn—she had settled back on the seat and the taxi *had* turned before she, surprised by its knowing movement, recollected that she had not "said where." She leaned forward to scratch at the glass panel that divided the driver's head from her own.

The driver braked to what was almost a stop, turned round and slid the glass panel back: the jolt of this flung Mrs. Drover forward till her face was almost into the glass. Through the aperture driver and passenger, not six inches between them, remained for an eternity eye to eye. Mrs. Drover's mouth hung open for some seconds before she could issue her first scream. After that she continued to scream freely and to beat with her gloved hands on the glass all round as the taxi, accelerating without mercy, made off with her into the hinterland of deserted streets.

---

[1] A section in the west of London.

DISCUSSION TOPICS

1. Reread the opening paragraphs of the story. What hints does Bowen provide that this is a tale of horror and the supernatural?
2. What role does the wartime setting play in your response to the story?

3. Some readers have tried to "explain" the story as the result of Mrs. Drover's hysteria. What evidence can you find that Mrs. Drover is under some kind of psychological pressure?
4. What elements of the story foreshadow the demonic nature of Mrs. Drover's lover?
5. The "demon lover" is a well-known mythic or archetypal figure. Read the anonymous poem with that same title in the poetry section of this anthology. What similarities and differences can you find in character, plot, setting, mood, and theme between the story and the poem? Which do you prefer and why?

WRITING TOPICS

1. Compare and contrast the "demon lover" theme in this story and in Irving's "Adventure of the German Student."
2. See if you can construct an interpretation of the story that "explains" or accounts for all of the seemingly supernatural occurrences in the story.

ERNEST HEMINGWAY (1899–1961) Fisherman, journalist, bullfight aficionado, war correspondent, big-game hunter, inimitable prose stylist, and master of dialogue. As spokesman for the "lost generation," he articulated the sense of trauma and the "unreasonable wound" suffered by modern man. In the famous Hemingway "code," he transferred the principles of "grace under pressure" and "purity of line" from the bullfight to the arenas of life and art. He was awarded the Nobel prize in 1953.

INDIAN CAMP

At the lake shore there was another rowboat drawn up. The two Indians stood waiting.

Nick and his father got in the stern of the boat and the Indians shoved it off and one of them got in to row. Uncle George sat in the stern of the camp rowboat. The young Indian shoved the camp boat off and got in to row Uncle George.

The two boats started off in the dark. Nick heard the oarlocks of the other boat quite a way ahead of them in the mist. The Indians rowed with quick choppy strokes. Nick lay back with his father's arm around him. It was cold on the water. The Indian who was rowing them was working very hard, but the other boat moved further ahead in the mist all the time.

"Where are we going, Dad?" Nick asked.

"Over to the Indian camp. There is an Indian lady very sick."

"Oh," said Nick.

Across the bay they found the other boat beached. Uncle George was smoking a cigar in the dark. The young Indian pulled the boat way up on the beach. Uncle George gave both the Indians cigars.

They walked up from the beach through a meadow that was soaking wet with dew, following the young Indian who carried a lantern. Then they went into the woods and followed a trail that led to the logging road that ran back into the hills. It was much lighter on the logging road as the timber was cut away on both sides. The young Indian stopped and blew out his lantern and they all walked on along the road.

They came around a bend and a dog came out barking. Ahead were the lights of the shanties where the Indian bark-peelers lived. More dogs rushed out at them. The two Indians sent them back to the shanties. In the shanty nearest the road there was a light in the window. An old woman stood in the doorway holding a lamp.

Inside on a wooden bunk lay a young Indian woman. She had been trying to have her baby for two days. All the old women in the camp had been helping her. The men had moved off up the road to sit in the dark and smoke out of range of the noise she made. She screamed just as Nick and the two Indians followed his father and Uncle George into the shanty. She lay in the lower bunk, very big under a quilt. Her head was turned to one side. In the upper bunk was her husband. He had cut his foot very badly with an ax three days before. He was smoking a pipe. The room smelled very bad.

Nick's father ordered some water to be put on the stove, and while it was heating he spoke to Nick.

"This lady is going to have a baby, Nick," he said.

"I know," said Nick.

"You don't know," said his father. "Listen to me. What she is going through is called being in labor. The baby wants to be born and she wants it to be born. All her muscles are trying to get the baby born. That is what is happening when she screams."

"I see," Nick said.

Just then the woman cried out.

"Oh, Daddy, can't you give her something to make her stop screaming?" asked Nick.

"No. I haven't any anaesthetic," his father said. "But her screams are not important. I don't hear them because they are not important."

The husband in the upper bunk rolled over against the wall.

The woman in the kitchen motioned to the doctor that the water was hot. Nick's father went into the kitchen and poured about half of the water out of the big kettle into a basin. Into the water left in the kettle he put several things he unwrapped from a handkerchief.

"Those must boil," he said, and began to scrub his hands in the basin of hot water with a cake of soap he had brought from the camp. Nick watched his father's hands scrubbing each other with the soap. While his father washed his hands very carefully and thoroughly, he talked.

240

"You see, Nick, babies are supposed to be born head first but sometimes they're not. When they're not they make a lot of trouble for everybody. Maybe I'll have to operate on this lady. We'll know in a little while."

When he was satisfied with his hands he went in and went to work.

"Pull back that quilt, will you, George?" he said. "I'd rather not touch it."

Later when he started to operate Uncle George and three Indian men held the woman still. She bit Uncle George on the arm and Uncle George said, "Damn squaw bitch!" and the young Indian who had rowed Uncle George over laughed at him. Nick held the basin for his father. It all took a long time.

His father picked the baby up and slapped it to make it breathe and handed it to the old woman.

"See, it's a boy, Nick," he said. "How do you like being an interne?"

Nick said, "All right." He was looking away so as not to see what his father was doing.

"There. That gets it," said his father and put something into the basin.

Nick didn't look at it.

"Now," his father said, "there's some stitches to put in. You can watch this or not, Nick, just as you like. I'm going to sew up the incision I made."

Nick did not watch. His curiosity had been gone for a long time.

His father finished and stood up. Uncle George and the three Indian men stood up. Nick put the basin out in the kitchen.

Uncle George looked at his arm. The young Indian smiled reminiscently.

"I'll put some peroxide on that, George," the doctor said.

He bent over the Indian woman. She was quiet now and her eyes were closed. She looked very pale. She did not know what had become of the baby or anything.

"I'll be back in the morning," the doctor said, standing up. "The nurse should be here from St. Ignace by noon and she'll bring everything we need."

He was feeling exalted and talkative as football players are in the dressing room after a game.

"That's one for the medical journal, George," he said. "Doing a Caesarian with a jack-knife and sewing it up with nine-foot, tapered gut leaders."

Uncle George was standing against the wall, looking at his arm.

"Oh, you're a great man, all right," he said.

"Ought to have a look at the proud father. They're usually the worst sufferers in these little affairs," the doctor said. "I must say he took it all pretty quietly."

He pulled back the blanket from the Indian's head. His hand came away wet. He mounted on the edge of the lower bunk with the lamp in one hand and looked in. The Indian lay with his face toward the wall. His throat had been cut from ear to ear. The blood had flowed down into a pool where his body sagged the bunk. His head rested on his left arm. The open razor lay, edge up, in the blankets.

"Take Nick out of the shanty, George," the doctor said.

There was no need of that. Nick, standing in the door of the kitchen, had a good view of the upper bunk when his father, the lamp in one hand, tipped the Indian's head back.

It was just beginning to be daylight when they walked along the logging road back toward the lake.

"I'm terribly sorry I brought you along, Nickie," said his father, all his post-operative exhilaration gone. "It was an awful mess to put you through."

"Do ladies always have such a hard time having babies?" Nick asked.

"No, that was very, very exceptional."

"Why did he kill himself. Daddy?"

"I don't know, Nick. He couldn't stand things, I guess."

"Do many men kill themselves, Daddy?"

"Not very many, Nick."

"Do many women?"

"Hardly ever."

"Don't they ever?"

"Oh, yes. They do sometimes."

"Daddy?"

"Yes."

"Where did Uncle George go?"

"He'll turn up all right."

"Is dying hard, Daddy?"

"No, I think it's pretty easy, Nick. It all depends."

They were seated in the boat. Nick in the stern, his father rowing. The sun was coming up over the hills. A bass jumped, making a circle in the water. Nick trailed his hand in the water. It felt warm in the sharp chill of the morning.

In the early morning on the lake sitting in the stern of the boat with his father rowing, he felt quite sure that he would never die.

DISCUSSION TOPICS

1. Sheridan Baker has said that "Indian Camp" is "perhaps the most appalling birth–death story ever written." What makes it so "appalling"?

2. Hemingway's own father was a physician and often took young Ernest fishing at a camp in the Michigan woods similar to the one in this story. Do these biographical parallels help in our appreciation of this story? Why—or why not?

3. In *The Paris Review* interview, when George Plimpton questioned him about symbolism in his fiction, Hemingway replied: "I suppose there are symbols since critics keep finding them. . . . Read anything I write for the pleasure of reading it. Whatever else you find will be the measure of what you brought to the reading. . . . You can be sure that there is much more there than will be read at any first reading." Discuss this statement with reference to "Indian Camp."

4. In the same interview, Hemingway said, "If it is any use to know it, I always try to write on the principle of the iceberg. There are seven eighths of it under

water for every part that shows. Anything you know you can eliminate and it only strengthens your iceberg. It is the part that doesn't show. . . . I have tried to eliminate everything unnecessary to conveying experience to the reader so that after he or she has read something it will become a part of his or her experience and seem actually to have happened. This is very hard to do and I've worked at it very hard." How does Hemingway succeed in this respect with "Indian Camp"?

5. What is the function of Uncle George? Where did he go (in answer to Nick's question) at the end of the story? Why did he give the Indians cigars after they had rowed him across the lake? Why did the Indian woman bite him? Why do you think her husband killed himself? What are the larger sociological implications of Hemingway's theme in the light of our understanding of Uncle George's role in the narrative?

WRITING TOPIC

Compare and contrast Hemingway's "Indian Camp" and Porter's "The Grave" as initiation stories. Pay special attention to the birth-and-death symbolism in these two stories.

JORGE LUIS BORGES (1899–   ) Short story writer, poet, essayist. Borges is a blind Argentine writer and intellectual, the leading figure in South America's literary renaissance. A widely read and learned man, past director of Argentina's National Library, Borges is known for his brief essays and short narratives that mingle fantasy and absurdity with serious philosophical insights and the arcane details of literary and cultural history. Borges's works have spawned an international following among authors and critics. Developing archetypal concepts of myth through fantasy, he creates a fictional world without the constants of time and reality, searching for another, interior kind of truth existing within the mind and memory. "The Circular Ruins" is taken from *Ficciones* (1962), his best-known collection of stories. He was awarded the Nobel prize in 1982.

THE CIRCULAR RUINS

And if he left off dreaming about you . . .
—*Through the Looking Glass,* VI.

No one saw him disembark in the unanimous night, no one saw the bamboo canoe sink into the sacred mud, but in a few days there was no one who did not know that the taciturn man came from the South and that his home had been one of those numberless villages upstream in the deeply cleft side of the mountain, where the Zend language has not been contaminated by Greek and where leprosy is infrequent. What is certain is that the gray man kissed the mud, climbed up the bank without pushing aside (probably, without feeling) the blades which were lacerating his flesh, and crawled, nauseated and bloodstained, up to the circular enclosure crowned with a stone tiger or horse, which sometimes was the color of flame and now was that of ashes. This circle was a temple which had been devoured by ancient fires, profaned by the miasmal jungle, and whose god no longer received the homage of men. The stranger stretched himself out beneath the pedestal. He was awakened by the sun high overhead. He was not astonished to find that his wounds had healed; he closed his pallid eyes and slept, not through weakness of flesh but through determination of will. He knew that this temple was the place required for his invincible intent; he knew that the incessant trees had not succeeded in strangling the ruins of another propitious temple downstream which had once belonged to gods now burned and dead; he knew that his immediate obligation was to dream. Toward midnight he was awakened by the inconsolable shriek of a bird. Tracks of bare feet, some figs and a jug warned him that the men of the region had been spying respectfully on his sleep, soliciting his protection or afraid of his magic. He felt a chill of fear, and sought out a sepulchral niche in the dilapidated wall where he concealed himself among unfamiliar leaves.

The purpose which guided him was not impossible, though supernatural. He wanted to dream a man; he wanted to dream him in minute entirety and impose him on reality. This magic project had exhausted the entire expanse of his mind; if some one had asked him his name or to relate some event of his former life, he would not have been able to give an answer. This uninhabited, ruined temple suited him, for it contained a minimum of visible world; the proximity of the workmen also suited him, for they took it upon themselves to provide for his frugal needs. The rice and fruit they brought him were nourishment enough for his body, which was consecrated to the sole task of sleeping and dreaming.

At first, his dreams were chaotic; then in a short while they became dialectic in nature. The stranger dreamed that he was in the center of a circular amphitheater which was more or less the burnt temple; clouds of taciturn students filled the tiers of seats; the faces of the farthest ones hung at a distance of many centuries and as high as the stars, but their features were completely precise. The man lectured his pupils on anatomy, cosmography, and magic: the faces listened anxiously and tried to answer understandingly, as if they guessed the importance of that examination which would redeem one of them from his condition of empty illusion and interpolate him into the real world. Asleep or awake, the man thought over the answers of his phantoms, did not allow himself to be deceived by impostors, and in certain perplexities he sensed a growing intelligence. He was seeking a soul worthy of participating in the universe.

After nine or ten nights he understood with a certain bitterness that he could expect nothing from those pupils who accepted his doctrine passively, but that he could expect something from those who occasionally dared to oppose him. The former group, although worthy of love and affection, could not ascend to the level of individuals; the latter pre-existed to a slightly greater degree. One afternoon (now afternoons were also given over to sleep, now he was only awake for a couple of hours at daybreak) he dismissed the vast illusory student body for good and kept only one pupil. He was a taciturn, sallow boy, at times intractable, and whose sharp features resembled those of his dreamer. The brusque elimination of his fellow students did not disconcert him for long; after a few private lessons, his progress was enough to astound the teacher. Nevertheless, a catastrophe took place. One day, the man emerged from his sleep as if from a viscous desert, looked at the useless afternoon light which he immediately confused with the dawn, and understood that he had not dreamed. All that night and all day long, the intolerable lucidity of insomnia fell upon him. He tried exploring the forest, to lose his strength; among the hemlock he barely succeeded in experiencing several short snatches of sleep, veined with fleeting, rudimentary visions that were useless. He tried to assemble the student body but scarcely had he articulated a few brief words of exhortation when it became deformed and was then erased. In his almost perpetual vigil, tears of anger burned his old eyes.

He understood that modeling the incoherent and vertiginous matter of which dreams are composed was the most difficult task that a man could undertake, even though he should penetrate all the enigmas of a superior and inferior order; much more difficult than weaving a rope out of sand or coining the faceless wind. He swore he would forget the enormous hallucination which had thrown him off at first, and he sought another method of work. Before putting it into execution, he spent a month recovering his strength, which had been squandered by his delirium. He abandoned all premeditation of dreaming and almost immediately succeeded in sleeping a reasonable part of each day. The few times that he had dreams during this period, he paid no attention to them. Before resuming his task, he waited until the moon's disk was perfect. Then, in the afternoon, he purified himself in the waters of the river, worshiped the planetary gods, pronounced the prescribed syllables of a mighty name, and went to sleep. He dreamed almost immediately, with his heart throbbing.

He dreamed that it was warm, secret, about the size of a clenched fist, and of a garnet color within the penumbra of a human body as yet without face or sex; during fourteen lucid nights he dreamt of it with meticulous love. Every night he perceived it more clearly. He did not touch it; he only permitted himself to witness it, to observe it, and occasionally to rectify it with a glance. He perceived it and lived it from all angles and distances. On the fourteenth night he lightly touched the pulmonary artery with his index finger, then the whole heart, outside and inside. He was satisfied with the examination. He deliberately did not dream for a night; he then took up the heart again, invoked the name of a planet, and undertook the vision of another of the principal organs. Within a year he had come to the skeleton and the eyelids. The innumerable hair was perhaps the most difficult task. He dreamed an entire man—a young man, but who did not sit up or talk, who was unable to open his eyes. Night after night, the man dreamt him asleep.

In the Gnostic cosmogonies, demiurges fashion a red Adam who cannot stand; as clumsy, crude and elemental as this Adam of dust was the Adam of dreams forged by the wizard's nights. One afternoon, the man almost destroyed his entire work, but then changed his mind. (It would have been better had he destroyed it.) When he had exhausted all supplications to the deities of the earth, he threw himself at the feet of the effigy which was perhaps a tiger or perhaps a colt and implored its unknown help. That evening, at twilight, he dreamt of the statue. He dreamt it was alive, tremulous: it was not an atrocious bastard of a tiger and a colt, but at the same time these two fiery creatures and also a bull, a rose, and a storm. This multiple god revealed to him that his earthly name was Fire, and that in this circular temple (and in others like it) people had once made sacrifices to him and worshiped him, and that he would magically animate the dreamed phantom, in such a way that all creatures, except Fire itself and the dreamer, would believe it to be a man of flesh and blood. He commanded that once this man had been instructed in all the rites, he should be sent to the other ruined temple whose pyramids were still standing downstream, so that some voice would glorify him in that deserted edifice. In the dream of the man that dreamed, the dreamed one awoke.

The wizard carried out the orders he had been given. He devoted a certain length of time (which finally proved to be two years) to instructing him in the mysteries of the universe and the cult of fire. Secretly, he was pained at the idea of being separated from him. On the pretext of pedagogical necessity, each day he increased the number of hours dedicated to dreaming. He also remade the right shoulder, which was somewhat defective. At times, he was disturbed by the impression that all this had already happened. . . . In general, his days were happy; when he closed his eyes, he thought: *Now I will be with my son.* Or, more rarely: *The son I have engendered is waiting for me and will not exist if I do not go to him.*

Gradually, he began accustoming him to reality. Once he ordered him to place a flag on a faraway peak. The next day the flag was fluttering on the peak. He tried other analogous experiments, each time more audacious. With a certain bitterness, he understood that his son was ready to be born—and perhaps impatient. That night he kissed him for the first time and sent him off to the other temple whose remains were turning white downstream, across many miles of inextricable jungle and marshes. Before doing this (and so that his son should never know that he was a phantom, so that he should think himself a man like any other) he destroyed in him all memory of his years of apprenticeship.

His victory and peace became blurred with boredom. In the twilight times of dusk and dawn, he would prostrate himself before the stone figure, perhaps imagining his unreal son carrying out identical rites in other circular ruins downstream; at night he no longer dreamed, or dreamed as any man does. His perceptions of the sounds and forms of the universe became somewhat pallid: his absent son was being nourished by these diminutions of his soul. The purpose of his life had been fulfilled; the man remained in a kind of ecstasy. After a certain time, which some chroniclers prefer to compute in years and others in decades, two oarsmen awoke him at midnight; he could not see their faces, but they spoke to him of a charmed man in a temple of the North, capable of walking on fire without burning himself. The wizard suddenly remembered the words of the god. He remembered that of all the creatures that people the earth, Fire was the only one who knew his son to be a phantom. This memory, which at first calmed him, ended by tormenting him. He feared lest his son should meditate on this abnormal privilege and by some means find out he was a mere simulacrum. Not to be a man, to be a projection of another man's dreams—what an incomparable humiliation, what madness! Any father is interested in the sons he has procreated (or permitted) out of the mere confusion of happiness; it was natural that the wizard should fear for the future of that son whom he had thought out entrail by entrail, feature by feature, in a thousand and one secret nights.

His misgivings ended abruptly, but not without certain forewarnings. First (after a long drought) a remote cloud, as light as a bird, appeared on a hill; then, toward the South, the sky took on the rose color of leopard's gums; then came clouds of smoke which rusted the metal of the nights; afterwards came the panic-stricken flight of wild animals. For what had happened many centuries before was repeating itself. The ruins of the sanctuary of the god of Fire were destroyed by fire. In a dawn without birds, the wizard saw the concentric fire licking the walls. For a moment, he thought of taking refuge in the water, but then he understood that death was coming to crown his old age and absolve him from his labors. He walked toward the sheets of flame. They did not bite his flesh, they caressed him and flooded him without heat or combustion. With relief, with humiliation, with terror, he understood that he also was an illusion, that someone else was dreaming him.

DISCUSSION TOPICS

1. Like many of Borges's stories, this one is clearly fabulous and symbolic. What signals does the author give you in his manner of telling the tale that it is not to be read merely on a literal level?
2. What are some of the key images and symbols in the story?
3. What archetypal or universal meanings are attached to circles and fire?
4. Why is it appropriate that these ruins are circular?
5. Discuss the relationship between dreaming and reality in the story.
6. What are the implications of the main character's understanding in the final sentence that "he also was an illusion, that someone else was dreaming him"?
7. Many of Borges's stories confront the mysteries of creation and creativity. In what ways is this story about creating works of art?

JOHN STEINBECK (1902–1968) Californian who immortalized himself and "Okies" in his epic novel of the Great Depression: *The Grapes of Wrath* (1939). He dignifies the common man by means of myth and archetype. His naturalism is tempered by humanism; his primitivism is enriched with psychological symbolism. He was awarded the Nobel prize in 1962.

THE SNAKE

It was almost dark when young Dr. Phillips swung his sack to his shoulder and left the tide pool. He climbed up over the rocks and squashed along the street in his rubber boots. The street lights were on by the time he arrived at his little commercial laboratory on the cannery street of Monterey.[1] It was a tight little building, standing partly on piers over the bay water and partly on the land. On both sides the big corrugated-iron sardine canneries crowded in on it.

Dr. Phillips climbed the wooden steps and opened the door. The white rats in their cages scampered up and down the wire, and the captive cats in their pens mewed for milk. Dr. Phillips turned on the glaring light over the dissection table and dumped his clammy sack on the floor. He walked to the glass cages by the window where the rattlesnakes lived, leaned over and looked in.

The snakes were bunched and resting in the corners of the cage, but every head was clear; the dusty eyes seemed to look at nothing, but as the young man leaned over the cage the forked tongues, black on the ends and pink behind, twittered out and waved slowly up and down. Then the snakes recognized the man and pulled in their tongues.

Dr. Phillips threw off his leather coat and built a fire in the tin stove; he set a kettle of water on the stove and dropped a can of beans into the water. Then he stood staring down at the sack on the floor. He was a slight young man with the mild, preoccupied eyes of one who looks through a microscope a great deal. He wore a short blond beard.

The draft ran breathily up the chimney and a glow of warmth came from the stove. The little waves washed quietly about the piles under the building. Arranged on shelves about the room were tier above tier of museum jars containing the mounted marine specimens the laboratory dealt in.

Dr. Phillips opened a side door and went into his bedroom, a booklined cell containing an army cot, a reading light and an uncomfortable wooden chair. He pulled off his rubber boots and put on a pair of sheepskin slippers. When he went back to the other room the water in the kettle was already beginning to hum.

He lifted his sack to the table under the white light and emptied out two dozen common starfish. These he laid out side by side on the table. His preoccupied eyes turned to the busy rats in the wire cages. Taking grain from a paper sack, he poured it into the feeding troughs. Instantly the rats scrambled down from the wire and fell upon the food. A bottle of milk stood on a glass shelf between a small mounted octopus and a jellyfish. Dr. Phillips lifted down the milk and walked to the cat cage, but before he filled the containers he reached in the cage and gently picked out a big rangy alley tabby. He stroked her for a moment and then dropped her in a small black painted box, closed the lid and bolted it and then turned on a petcock which admitted gas into the killing chamber. While the short soft struggle went on in the black box he filled the saucers with milk. One of the cats arched against his hand and he smiled and petted her neck.

The box was quiet now. He turned off the petcock, for the airtight box would be full of gas.

On the stove the pan of water was bubbling furiously about the can of beans. Dr. Phillips lifted out the can with a big pair of forceps, opened it, and emptied the beans into a glass dish. While he ate he watched the starfish on the table. From between the rays little drops of milky fluid were exuding. He bolted his beans and when they were gone he put the dish in the sink and stepped to the equipment cupboard. From this he took a microscope and a pile of little glass dishes. He filled the dishes one by one with sea water from a tap and arranged them in a line beside the starfish. He took out his watch and laid it on the table under the pouring white light. The waves washed with little sighs against the piles under the floor. He took an eyedropper from a drawer and bent over the starfish.

At that moment there were quick soft steps on the wooden stairs and a strong knocking at the door. A slight grimace of annoyance crossed the young man's face as he went to open. A tall, lean woman stood in the doorway. She was dressed in a severe dark suit—her straight black hair, growing low on a flat forehead, was mussed as though the wind had been blowing it. Her black eyes glittered in the strong light.

She spoke in a soft throaty voice, "May I come in? I want to talk to you."

"I'm very busy just now," he said half-heartedly. "I have to do things at times." But he stood away from the door. The tall woman slipped in.

"I'll be quiet until you can talk to me."

He closed the door and brought the uncomfortable chair from the bedroom. "You see," he apologized, "the process is started and I must get to it." So many people wandered in and asked questions. He had little routines of explanations for the commoner processes. He could say them without thinking. "Sit here. In a few minutes I'll be able to listen to you."

The tall woman leaned over the table. With the eyedropper the young man gathered fluid from between the rays of the starfish and squirted it into a bowl of water, and then he drew some milky fluid and squirted it in the same bowl and stirred the water gently with the eyedropper. He began his little patter of explanation.

"When starfish are sexually mature they release sperm and ova when they are exposed at low tide. By choosing mature specimens and taking them out of the water, I give them a condition of low tide. Now I've mixed the sperm and eggs. Now I put some of the mixture in each one of these ten watch glasses. In ten minutes I will kill those in the first glass with menthol, twenty minutes later I will kill the second group and then a new group every twenty minutes. Then I will have arrested the process in stages, and I will mount the series on miscroscope slides for biologic study." He paused. "Would you like to look at this first group under the microscope?"

"No, thank you."

He turned quickly to her. People always wanted to look through the glass. She was not looking at the table at all, but at him. Her black eyes were on him, but they did not seem to see him. He realized why—the irises were as dark as the pupils, there was no color line between the two. Dr. Phillips was piqued at her

249

answer. Although answering questions bored him, a lack of interest in what he was doing irritated him. A desire to arouse her grew in him.

"While I'm waiting the first ten minutes I have something to do. Some people don't like to see it. Maybe you'd better step into that room until I finish."

"No," she said in her soft flat tone. "Do what you wish. I will wait until you can talk to me." Her hands rested side by side on her lap. She was completely at rest. Her eyes were bright but the rest of her was almost in a state of suspended animation. He thought, "Low metabolic rate, almost as low as a frog's, from the looks." The desire to shock her out of her inanition possessed him again.

He brought a little wooden cradle to the table, laid out scalpels and scissors and rigged a big hollow needle to a pressure tube. Then from the killing chamber he brought the limp dead cat and laid it in the cradle and tied its legs to hooks in the sides. He glanced sidewise at the woman. She had not moved. She was still at rest.

The cat grinned up into the light, its pink tongue stuck out between its needle teeth. Dr. Phillips deftly snipped open the skin at the throat; with a scalpel he slit through and found an artery. With flawless technique he put the needle in the vessel and tied it in with gut. "Embalming fluid," he explained. "Later I'll inject yellow mass into the veinous system and red mass into the arterial system—for bloodstream dissection—biology classes."

He looked around at her again. Her dark eyes seemed veiled with dust. She looked without expression at the cat's open throat. Not a drop of blood had escaped. The incision was clean. Dr. Phillips looked at his watch. "Time for the first group." He shook a few crystals of menthol into the first watch-glass.

The woman was making him nervous. The rats climbed about on the wire of their cage again and squeaked softly. The waves under the building beat with little shocks on the piles.

The young man shivered. He put a few lumps of coal in the stove and sat down. "Now," he said. "I haven't anything to do for twenty minutes." He noticed how short her chin was between lower lip and point. She seemed to awaken slowly, to come up out of some deep pool of consciousness. Her head raised and her dark dusty eyes moved about the room and then came back to him.

"I was waiting," she said. Her hands remained side by side on her lap. "You have snakes?"

"Why, yes," he said rather loudly. "I have about two dozen rattlesnakes. I milk out the venom and send it to the anti-venom laboratories."

She continued to look at him but her eyes did not center on him, rather they covered him and seemed to see in a big circle all around him. "Have you a male snake, a male rattlesnake?"

"Well, it just happens I know I have. I came in one morning and found a big snake in—in coition with a smaller one. That's very rare in captivity. You see, I do know I have a male snake."

"Where is he?"

"Why, right in the glass cage by the window there."

Her head swung slowly around but her two quiet hands did not move. She turned back toward him. "May I see?"

He got up and walked to the case by the window. On the sand bottom the knot of rattlesnakes lay entwined, but their heads were clear. The tongues came out and flickered a moment and then waved up and down feeling the air for vibrations. Dr. Phillips nervously turned his head. The woman was standing beside him. He had not heard her get up from the chair. He had heard only the splash of water among the piles and the scampering of the rats on the wire screen.

She said softly, "Which is the male you spoke of?"

He pointed to a thick, dusty grey snake lying by itself in one corner of the cage. "That one. He's nearly five feet long. He comes from Texas. Our Pacific coast snakes are usually smaller. He's been taking all the rats, too. When I want the others to eat I have to take him out."

The woman stared down at the blunt dry head. The forked tongue slipped out and hung quivering for a long moment. "And you're sure he's a male."

"Rattlesnakes are funny," he said glibly. "Nearly every generalization proves wrong. I don't like to say anything definite about rattlesnakes, but—yes—I can assure you he's a male."

Her eyes did not move from the flat head. "Will you sell him to me?"

"Sell him?" he cried. "Sell him to you?"

"You do sell specimens, don't you?"

"Oh—yes. Of course I do. Of course I do."

"How much? Five dollars? Ten?"

"Oh! Not more than five. But—do you know anything about rattlesnakes? You might be bitten."

She looked at him for a moment. "I don't intend to take him. I want to leave him here, but—I want him to be mine. I want to come here and look at him and feed him and to know he's mine." She opened a little purse and took out a five-dollar bill. "Here! Now he is mine."

Dr. Phillips began to be afraid. "You could come to look at him without owning him."

"I want him to be mine."

"Oh, Lord!" he cried. "I've forgotten the time." He ran to the table. "Three minutes over. It won't matter much." He shook menthol crystals into the second watch-glass. And then he was drawn back to the cage where the woman still stared at the snake.

She asked, "What does he eat?"

"I feed them white rats, rats from the cage over there."

"Will you put him in the other cage? I want to feed him."

"But he doesn't need food. He's had a rat already this week. Sometimes they don't eat for three or four months. I had one that didn't eat for over a year."

In her low monotone she asked, "Will you sell me a rat?"

He shrugged his shoulders. "I see. You want to watch how rattlesnakes eat. All right. I'll show you. The rat will cost twenty-five cents. It's better than a

251

bullfight if you look at it one way, and it's simply a snake eating his dinner if you look at it another." His tone had become acid. He hated people who made sport of natural processes. He was not a sportsman but a biologist. He could kill a thousand animals for knowledge, but not an insect for pleasure. He'd been over this in his mind before.

She turned her head slowly toward him and the beginning of a smile formed on her thin lips. "I want to feed my snake," she said. "I'll put him in the other cage." She had opened the top of the cage and dipped her hand in before he knew what she was doing. He leaped forward and pulled her back. The lid banged shut.

"Haven't you any sense?" he asked fiercely. "Maybe he wouldn't kill you, but he'd make you damned sick in spite of what I could do for you."

"You put him in the other cage then," she said quietly.

Dr. Phillips was shaken. He found that he was avoiding the dark eyes that didn't seem to look at anything. He felt that it was profoundly wrong to put a rat into the cage, deeply sinful; and he didn't know why. Often he had put rats in the cage when someone or other had wanted to see it, but this desire tonight sickened him. He tried to explain himself out of it.

"It's a good thing to see," he said. "It shows you how a snake can work. It makes you have a respect for a rattlesnake. Then, too, lots of people have dreams about the terror of snakes making the kill. I think because it is a subjective rat. The person is the rat. Once you see it the whole matter is objective. The rat is only a rat and the terror is removed."

He took a long stick equipped with a leather noose from the wall. Opening the trap he dropped the noose over the big snake's head and tightened the thong. A piercing dry rattle filled the room. The thick body writhed and slashed about the handle of the stick as he lifted the snake out and dropped it in the feeding cage. It stood ready to strike for a time, but the buzzing gradually ceased. The snake crawled into a corner, made a big figure eight with its body and lay still.

"You see," the young man explained, "these snakes are quite tame. I've had them a long time. I suppose I could handle them if I wanted to, but everyone who does handle rattlesnakes gets bitten sooner or later. I just don't want to take the chance." He glanced at the woman. He hated to put in the rat. She had moved over in front of the new cage; her black eyes were on the stony head of the snake again.

She said, "Put in a rat."

Reluctantly he went to the rat cage. For some reason he was sorry for the rat, and such a feeling had never come to him before. His eyes went over the mass of swarming white bodies climbing up the screen toward him. "Which one?" he thought. "Which one shall it be?" Suddenly he turned angrily to the woman. "Wouldn't you rather I put in a cat? Then you'd see a real fight. The cat might even win, but if it did it might kill the snake. I'll sell you a cat if you like."

She didn't look at him. "Put in a rat," she said. "I want him to eat."

He opened the rat cage and thrust his hand in. His fingers found a tail and he lifted a plump, red-eyed rat out of the cage. It struggled up to try to bite his fingers and, failing, hung spread out and motionless from its tail. He walked quickly across the room, opened the feeding cage and dropped the rat in on the sand floor. "Now, watch it," he cried.

The woman did not answer him. Her eyes were on the snake where it lay still. Its tongue, flicking in and out rapidly, tasted the air of the cage.

The rat landed on its feet, turned around and sniffed at its pink naked tail and then unconcernedly trotted across the sand, smelling as it went. The room was silent. Dr. Phillips did not know whether the water sighed among the piles or whether the woman sighed. Out of the corner of his eye he saw her body crouch and stiffen.

The snake moved out smoothly, slowly. The tongue flicked in and out. The motion was so gradual, so smooth that it didn't seem to be motion at all. In the other end of the cage the rat perked up in a sitting position and began to lick down the fine white hair on its chest. The snake moved on, keeping always a deep S curve in its neck.

The silence beat on the young man. He felt the blood drifting up in his body. He said loudly, "See! He keeps the striking curve ready. Rattlesnakes are cautious, almost cowardly animals. The mechanism is so delicate. The snake's dinner is to be got by an operation as deft as a surgeon's job. He takes no chances with his instruments."

The snake had flowed to the middle of the cage by now. The rat looked up, saw the snake and then unconcernedly went back to licking its chest.

"It's the most beautiful thing in the world," the young man said. His veins were throbbing. "It's the most terrible thing in the world."

The snake was close now. Its head lifted a few inches from the sand. The head weaved slowly back and forth, aiming, getting distance, aiming. Dr. Phillips glanced again at the woman. He turned sick. She was weaving too, not much, just a suggestion.

The rat looked up and saw the snake. It dropped to four feet and back up, and then—the stroke. It was impossible to see, simply a flash. The rat jarred as though under an invisible blow. The snake backed hurriedly into the corner from which it had come, and settled down, its tongue working constantly.

"Perfect!" Dr. Phillips cried. "Right between the shoulder blades. The fangs must almost have reached the heart."

The rat stood still, breathing like a little white bellows. Suddenly it leaped in the air and landed on its side. Its legs kicked spasmodically for a second and it was dead.

The woman relaxed, relaxed sleepily.

"Well," the young man demanded, "it was an emotional bath, wasn't it?"

She turned her misty eyes to him. "Will he eat it now?" she asked.

"Of course he'll eat it. He didn't kill it for a thrill. He killed it because he was hungry."

The corners of the woman's mouth turned up a trifle again. She looked back at the snake. "I want to see him eat it."

Now the snake came out of its corner again. There was no striking curve in its neck, but it approached the rat gingerly, ready to jump back in case it attacked.

It nudged the body gently with its blunt nose, and drew away. Satisfied that it was dead, the snake touched the body all over with its chin, from head to tail. It seemed to measure the body and to kiss it. Finally it opened its mouth and unhinged its jaws at the corners.

Dr. Phillips put his will against his head to keep it from turning toward the woman. He thought, "If she's opening her mouth, I'll be sick. I'll be afraid." He succeeded in keeping his eyes away.

The snake fitted its jaws over the rat's head and then with a slow peristaltic pulsing, began to engulf the rat. The jaws gripped and the whole throat crawled up, and the jaws gripped again.

Dr. Phillips turned away and went to his work table. "You've made me miss one of the series," he said bitterly. "The set won't be complete." He put one of the watch glasses under a low-power microscope and looked at it, and then angrily he poured the contents of all the dishes into the sink. The waves had fallen so that only a wet whisper came up through the floor. The young man lifted a trapdoor at his feet and dropped the starfish down into the black water. He paused at the cat, crucified in the cradle and grinning comically into the light. Its body was puffed with embalming fluid. He shut off the pressure, withdrew the needle and tied the vein.

"Would you like some coffee?" he asked.

"No, thank you. I shall be going pretty soon."

He walked to her where she stood in front of the snake cage. The rat was swallowed, all except an inch of pink tail that stuck out of the snake's mouth like a sardonic tongue. The throat heaved again and the tail disappeared. The jaws snapped back into their sockets, and the big snake crawled heavily to the corner, made a big eight and dropped its head on the sand.

"He's asleep now," the woman said. "I'm going now. But I'll come back and feed my snake every little while. I'll pay for the rats. I want him to have plenty. And sometime—I'll take him away with me." Her eyes came out of their dusty dream for a moment. "Remember, he's mine. Don't take his poison. I want him to have it. Goodnight." She walked swiftly to the door and went out. He heard her footsteps on the stairs, but he could not hear her walk away on the pavement.

Dr. Phillips turned a chair around and sat down in front of the snake cage. He tried to comb out his thought as he looked at the torpid snake. "I've read so much about psychological sex symbols," he thought. "It doesn't seem to explain. Maybe I'm too much alone. Maybe I should kill the snake. If I knew—no, I can't pray to anything."

For weeks he expected her to return. "I will go out and leave her alone here when she comes," he decided. "I won't see the damned thing again."

She never came again. For months he looked for her when he walked about in the town. Several times he ran after some tall woman thinking it might be she. But he never saw her again—ever.

---

[1] A city in western California on the Monterey peninsula at the southern end of Monterey Bay (inlet of the Pacific).

DISCUSSION TOPICS

1. One of Steinbeck's close friends was marine biologist Ed Rickets, the model for Dr. Phillips. (The two collaborated on the *Sea of Cortez: A Leisurely Journal of Travel and Research,* 1941.) Steinbeck said that he recorded this rattlesnake incident just as it happened and that he didn't know what it meant. What evidence do you find in reading the story that it is, in truth, a carefully wrought work of art—not merely a journalistic account?
2. What is the symbolic significance of Dr. Phillips's occupation? What does the description of his bedroom reveal about his character? How does the starfish experiment fit into the story?
3. Who is this strange female visitor? What does she seem to represent to Dr. Phillips? Why does he identify her with the snake?
4. Discuss the range of symbolic meanings that attach to snakes in the myths of our culture (and other cultures). Which of these meanings are relevant to Steinbeck's story?

WRITING TOPIC

Explicate the meaning of the following quotation: " 'I've read so much about psychological sex symbols,' he thought. 'It doesn't seem to explain. Maybe I'm too much alone. Maybe I should kill the snake. If I knew—no, I can't pray to anything.' "

ANAïS NIN (1903–1977) Fashion model, artist's model, dancer, psychologist, author, feminist. A French-born American writer, Anaïs Nin is best known for the six-volume *Diary of Anaïs Nin,* which chronicles 60 years of her life, recalling her experiences in bohemian Paris and America and containing vivid portraits of well-known contemporaries such as Lawrence Durrell, Henry Miller, and William Carlos Williams. Her stories are often erotic and reflect the influence of her interest in psychoanalysis, which she studied under Otto Rank and practiced in both Europe and New York.

HEJDA

The unveiling[1] of women is a delicate matter. It will not happen overnight. We are all afraid of what we shall find.

Hejda was, of course, born in the Orient. Before the unveiling she was living in an immense garden, a little city in itself, filled with many servants, many sisters and brothers, many relatives. From the roof of the house one could see all the people passing, vendors, beggars, Arabs going to the mosque.

Hejda was then a little primitive, whose greatest pleasure consisted in insert-
ing her finger inside pregnant hens and breaking the eggs, or filling frogs with
gasoline and setting a lighted match to them. She went about without underclothes
in the house, without shoes, but once outside she was heavily veiled and there was
no telling exactly the contours of her body, which were at an early age those of
a full-blown woman, and there was no telling that her smile had that carnivorous
air of smiles with large teeth.

In school she had a friend whose great sorrow was her dark color. The
darkest skin in the many shaded nuances of the Arabian school. Hejda took her
out into the farthest corner of the school garden one day and said to her: "I can
make you white if you want me to. Do you trust me?"

"Of course I do."

Hejda brought out a piece of pumice stone. She very gently but very persistently began to pumice a piece of the girl's forehead. Only when the pain became
unendurable did she stop. But for a week, every day, she continued enlarging the
circle of scraped, scarred skin, and took secret pleasure in the strange scene of the
girl's constant lamentations of pain and her own obstinate scraping. Until they
were both found out and punished.

At seventeen she left the Orient and the veils, but she retained an air of being
veiled. With the most chic and trim French clothes, which molded her figure, she
still conveyed the impression of restraint and no one could feel sure of having seen
her neck, arms or legs. Even her evening dresses seemed to sheathe her. This
feeling of secrecy, which recalled constantly the women of Arabia as they walked
in their many yards of white cotton, rolled like silk around a spool, was due in great
part to her inarticulateness. Her speech revealed and opened no doors. It was
labyrinthian. She merely threw off enough words to invite one into the passageway
but no sooner had one started to walk towards the unfinished phrase than one met
an impasse, a curve, a barrier. She retreated behind half admissions, half promises,
insinuations.

This covering of the body, which was like the covering of the spirit, had
created an unshatterable timidity. It had the effect of concentrating the light, the
intensity in the eyes. So that one saw Hejda as a mixture of elegance, cosmetics,
aesthetic plumage, with only the eyes sending signals and messages. They pierced
the European clothes with the stabbing brilliancy of those eyes in the Orient which
to reach the man had to pierce through the heavy aura of yards of white cotton.

The passageways that led one to Hejda were as tortuous and intricate as the
passageways in the oriental cities in which the pursued women lost themselves, but
all through the vanishing, turning streets the eyes continued to signal to strangers
like prisoners waving out of windows.

The desire to speak was there, after centuries of confinement and repression,
the desire to be invaded and rescued from the secretiveness. The eyes were full
of invitations, in great contradiction to the closed folds of the clothes, the many
defenses of the silk around the neck, the sleeves around the arms.

Her language was veiled. She had no way to say: look at Hejda who is full
of ideas. So she laid out cards and told fortunes like the women of the harem, or

she ate sweets like a stunted woman who had been kept a child by close binding with yards of white cotton, as the feet of the Chinese women had been kept small by bandaging. All she could say was: I had a dream last night (because at breakfast time in the Orient, around the first cup of dark coffee, everyone told their dreams). Or she opened a book accidentally when in trouble and placed her finger on a phrase and decided on her next course of action by the words of this phrase. Or she cooked a dish as colorful as an oriental market place.

Her desire to be noticed was always manifested, as in the Orient, by a bit of plumage, a startling jewel, a spangle pasted on her forehead between the eyes (the third eye of the Oriental was a jewel, as if the secret life so long preserved from openness had acquired the fire of precious stones).

No one understood the signals: look at Hejda, the woman of the Orient who wants to be a woman of tomorrow. The plumage and the aesthetic adornment diverted them like decoration on a wall. She was always being thrust back into the harem, on a pillow.

She had arrived in Paris, with all her invisible veils. When she laughed she concealed her mouth as much as possible, because in her small round face the teeth were extraordinarily large. She concealed her voraciousness and her appetites. Her voice was made small, again as the Chinese make their feet small, small and infantile. Her poses were reluctant and reserved. The veil was not in her timidities, her fears, in her manner of dressing, which covered her throat and compressed her overflowing breasts. The veil was in her liking for flowers (which was racial), especially small roses and innocent asexual flowers, in complicated rituals of politeness (also traditional), but above all in evasiveness of speech.

She wanted to be a painter. She joined the Academie Julien. She painted painstakingly on small canvases—the colors of the Orient, a puerile Orient of small flowers, serpentines, confetti and candy colors, the colors of small shops with metallic lace-paper roses and butterflies.

In the same class there was a dark, silent, timid young Roumanian. He had decadent, aristocratic hands, he never smiled, he never talked. Those who approached him felt such a shriveling timidity in him, such a retraction, that they remained at a distance.

The two timidities observed each other. The two silences, the two withdrawals. Both were oriental interiors, without windows on the external world, and all the greenery in the inner patio, all their windows open on the inside of the house.

A certain Gallic playfulness presides in the painting class. The atmosphere is physical, warm, gay. But the two of them remain in their inner patio, listening to birds singing and fountains playing. He thinks: how mysterious she is. And she thinks: how mysterious he is.

Finally one day, as she is leaving, he watches her repainting the black line on the edge of her eyes out of a silver peacock. She nimbly lifts up the head of the peacock and it is a little brush that makes black lines around her oriental eyes.

This image confounds him, ensorcells him. The painter is captivated, stirred. Some memory out of Persian legends now adorns his concept of her.

257

They marry and take a very small apartment where the only window gives on a garden.

At first they marry to hide together. In the dark caverns of their whisperings, confidences, timidities, what they now elaborate is a stalactitic world shut out from light and air. He initiates her into his aesthetic values. They make love in the dark and in the daytime make their place more beautiful and more refined.

In Molnar's hands she is being remolded, refashioned, stylized. He cannot remold her body. He is critical of her heaviness. He dislikes her breasts and will not let her ever show them. They overwhelm him. He confesses he would like her better without them. This shrinks her within herself and plants the seed of doubt of her feminine value. With these words he has properly subjugated her, given her a doubt which will keep her away from other men. He bound her femininity, and it is now oppressed, bound, even ashamed of its vulgarity, of its expansiveness. This is the reign of aesthetic value, stylization, refinement, art, artifice. He has established his domination in this. At every turn nature must be subjugated. Very soon, with his coldness, he represses her violence. Very soon he polishes her language, her manners, her impulses. He reduces and limits her hospitality, her friendliness, her desire for expansion.

It is her second veiling. It is the aesthetic veils of art and social graces. He designs her dresses. He molds her as far as he can into the stylized figures in his paintings. His women are transparent and lie in hammocks between heaven and earth. Hejda cannot reach this, but she can become an odalisque. She can acquire more silver peacocks, more poetic objects that will speak for her.

Her small canvases look childlike standing beside his. Slowly she becomes more absorbed in his painting than in her own. The flowers and gardens disappear.

He paints a world of stage settings, static ships, frozen trees, crystal fairs, the skeletons of pleasure and color, from which nature is entirely shut off. He proceeds to make Hejda one of the objects in this painting; her nature is more and more castrated by this abstraction of her, the obtrusive breasts more severely veiled. In his painting there is no motion, no nature, and certainly not the Hejda who liked to run about without underwear, to eat herbs and raw vegetables out of the garden.

Her breasts are the only intrusion in their exquisite life. Without them she could be the twin he wanted, and they could accomplish this strange marriage of his feminine qualities and her masculine ones. For it is already clear that he likes to be protected and she likes to protect, and that she has more power in facing the world of reality, more power to sell pictures, to interest the galleries in his work, more courage too. It is she who assumes the active role in contact with the world. Molnar can never earn a living, Hejda can. Molnar cannot give orders (except to her) and she can. Molnar cannot execute, realize, concretize as well as she can, for in execution and action she is not timid.

Finally it is Molnar who paints and draws and it is Hejda who goes out and sells his work.

Molnar grows more and more delicate, more vulnerable, and Hejda stronger. He is behind the scene, and she is in the foreground now.

He permits her love to flow all around him, sustain him, nourish him. In the dark he reconquers his leadership. And not by any sensual prodigality, but on the contrary, by a severe economy of pleasure. She is often left hungry. She never suspects for a moment that it is anything but economy and thinks a great abundance lies behind this aesthetic reserve. There is no delight or joy in their sensual contact. It is a creeping together into a womb.

Their life together is stilted, windowless, facing inward. But the plants and fountains of the patio are all artificial, ephemeral, immobile. A stage setting for a drama that never takes place. There are colonnades, friezes, backgrounds, plush drops but no drama takes place, no evolution, no sparks. His women's figures are always lying down, suspended in space.

But Hejda, Hejda feels compressed. She does not know why. She has never known anything but oppression. She has never been out of a small universe delimited by man. Yet something is expanding in her. A new Hejda is born out of the struggle with reality, to protect the weakness of Molnar. In the outer world she feels larger. When she returns home she feels she must shrink back into submission to Molnar's proportions. The outgoing rhythm must cease. Molnar's whole being is one total negation; negation and rejection of the world, of social life, of other human beings, of success, of movement, of motion, of curiosity, of adventure, of the unknown.

What is he defending, protecting? No consuming passion for one person, but perhaps a secret consuming. He admits no caresses, no invitations to love-making. It is always "no" to her hunger, "no" to her tenderness, "no" to the flow of life. They were close in fear and concealment, but they are not close in flow and development. Molnar is now frozen, fixed. There is no emotion to propel him. And when she seeks to propel him, substitute her élan for his static stagnation, all he can do is break this propeller.

"Your ambitions are vulgar."

(She does not know how to answer: my ambitions are merely the balance to your inertia.)

A part of her wants to expand. A part of her being wants to stay with Molnar. This conflict tears her asunder. The pulling and tearing bring on illness.

Hejda falls.

Hejda is ill.

She cannot move forward because Molnar is tied, and she cannot break with him.

Because he will not move, his being is stagnant and filled with poison. He injects her every day with this poison.

She has taken his paintings into the real world, to sell, and in so doing she has connected with that world and found it larger, freer.

Now he does not let her handle the painting. He even stops painting. Poverty sets in.

Perhaps Molnar will turn about now and protect her. It is the dream of every maternal love: I have filled him with my strength. I have nourished his painting. My painting has passed into his painting. I am broken and weak. Perhaps now he will be strong.

But not at all. Molnar watches her fall, lets her fall. He lets poverty install itself. He watches inertly the sale of their art possessions, the trips to the pawnbroker. He leaves Hejda without care. His passivity and inertia consume the whole house.

It is as if Hejda had been the glue that held the furniture together. Now it breaks. It is as if she had been the cleaning fluid and now the curtains turn gray. The logs in the fireplace now smoke and do not burn: was she the fire in the hearth too? Because she lies ill objects grow rusty. The food turns sour. Even the artificial flowers wilt. The paints dry on the palette. Was she the water, the soap too? Was she the fountain, the visibility of the windows, the gloss of the floors? The creditors buzz like locusts. Was she the fetish of the house who kept them away? Was she the oxygen in the house? Was she the salt now missing from the bread? Was she the delicate feather duster dispelling the webs of decay? Was she the silver polish?

Tired of waiting for her to get well—alone, he goes out.

Hejda and Molnar are now separated. She is free. Several people help her to unwind the binding wrapped around her personality first by the family life, then by the husband. Someone falls in love with her ample breasts, and removes the taboo that Molnar had placed upon them. Hejda buys herself a sheer blouse which will reveal her possessions.

When a button falls off she does not sew it on again.

Then she also began to talk.

She talked about her childhood. The same story of going about without underwear as a child which she had told before with a giggle of confusion and as if saying: "what a little primitive I was," was now told with the oblique glance of the strip-teaser, with a slight arrogance, the *agent provocateur* towards the men (for now exhibitionism placed the possibility in the present, not in the past).

She discards small canvases and buys very large ones. She paints larger roses, larger daisies, larger trellises, larger candied clouds, larger taffy seas. But just as the canvases grow larger without their content growing more important, Hejda is swelling up without growing. There is more of her. Her voice grows louder, her language, freed of Molnar's decadent refinement, grows coarser. Her dresses grow shorter. Her blouses looser. There is more flesh around her small body but Molnar is not there to corset it. There is more food on her table. She no longer conceals her teeth. She becomes proud of her appetite. Liberty has filled her to overflowing with a confidence that everything that was once secret and bound was of immense value. Every puerile detail of her childhood, every card dealer's intuition, every dream, becomes magnified.

And the stature of Hejda cannot bear the weight of her ambition. It is as if compression had swung her towards inflation. She is inflated physically and spiritually. And whoever dares to recall her to a sense of proportion, to a realization that there are perhaps other painters of value in the world, other women, becomes the traitor who must be banished instantly. On him she pours torrents of abuse like the abuse of the oriental gypsies to whom one has refused charity—curses and maledictions.

260

It is not desire or love she brings to the lovers: I have discovered that I am very gifted for love-making!

It is not creativity she brings to her painting: I will show Molnar that I was a better painter!

Her friendships with women are simply one long underground rivalry: to excel in startling dress or behavior. She enters a strained, intense competition. When everything fails she resorts to lifting her dress and arranging her garters.

Where are the veils and labyrinthian evasions?

She is back in the garden of her childhood, back to the native original Hejda, child of nature and succulence and sweets, of pillows and erotic literature.

The frogs leap away in fear of her again.

---

[1] In Moslem countries, women in strict, conservative religious households wear a veil in public so that no man outside their family may gaze on their face.

DISCUSSION TOPICS

1. Discuss the image of the veil in the story. Why must Hejda be veiled a second time by Molnar? What does "veiling" suggest about the relationship between men and women? What are we to make of Hejda's final unveiling?
2. What evidence do you find in this story of Nin's interest in psychoanalysis?
3. There are several archetypes in the story. Hejda's expansive femininity certainly suggests the attributes of the Earth Mother, as does the emphasis on her breasts. In fact, for Molnar her breasts are an "intrusion." He is seeking a twin, a "marriage of his feminine qualities and her masculine ones." Discuss the relationship of Hejda and Molnar as an archetypal or mythic conjunction of male and female. What does Molnar represent to Hejda?
4. What do you think the frogs signify in Nin's story?

ISAAC BASHEVIS SINGER (1904–   ) Journalist, novelist, short story writer, Nobel prize winner. Born in Radzymin, Poland, Singer emigrated to the United States in 1935. His stories, written in Yiddish, owe much to an oral tradition of storytelling; they draw on ancient folk-tale motifs as well as on closely observed details of contemporary Jewish life, often combining straightforward portrayal of quotidian reality with an equally straightforward treatment of the fantastic and the supernatural.

GETZEL THE MONKEY

Translated by the author and Ellen Kantarov

My dear friends, we all know what a mimic is. Once we had such a man living in our town, and he was given a fitting name. In that day they gave nicknames to everybody but the rich people. Still, Getzel was even richer than the one he tried to imitate, Todrus Broder. Todrus himself lived up to his fancy name. He was tall, broad-shouldered like a giant, with a black beard as straight as a squire's and a pair of dark eyes that burned through you when they looked at you. Now, I know what I'm talking about. I was still a girl then, and a good-looking one, too. When he stared at me with those fiery eyes, the marrow in my bones trembled. If an envious man were to have a look like that, he could, God preserve us, easily give you the evil eye. Todrus had no cause for envy, though. He was as healthy as an ox, and he had a beautiful wife and two graceful daughters, real princesses. He lived like a nobleman. He had a carriage with a coachman, and a hansom as well. He went driving to the villages and played around with the peasant women. When he threw coins to them, they cheered. Sometimes he would go horseback riding through the town, and he sat up in the saddle as straight as a Cossack.

His surname was Broder, but Todrus came from Great Poland, not from Brody. He was a great friend of all the nobles. Count Zamoysky used to come to his table on Friday nights to taste his gefilte fish. On Purim the count sent him a gift, and what do you imagine the gift turned out to be? Two peacocks, a male and a female!

Todrus spoke Polish like a Pole and Russian like a Russian. He knew German, too, and French as well. What didn't he know? He could even play the piano. He went hunting with Zamoysky and he shot a wolf. When the Tsar visited Zamosc and the finest people went to greet him, who do you think spoke to him? Todrus Broder. No sooner were the first three words out of his mouth than the Tsar burst out laughing. They say that later the two of them played a game of chess and Todrus won. I wasn't there, but it probably happened. Later Todrus received a gold medal from Petersburg.

His father-in-law, Falk Posner, was rich, and Falk's daughter Fogel was a real beauty. She had a dowry of twenty thousand rubles, and after her father's death she inherited his entire fortune. But don't think that Todrus married her for her money. It is said that she was traveling with her mother to the spas when suddenly Todrus entered the train. He was still a bachelor then, or perhaps a widower. He took one look at Fogel and then he told her mother that he wanted her daughter to be his wife. Imagine, this happened some fifty years ago. . . . Everyone said that it was love at first sight for Todrus, but later it turned out that love didn't mean a thing to him. I should have as many blessed years as the nights Fogel didn't sleep because of him! They joked, saying that if you were to dress a shovel in a woman's skirts, he would chase after it. In those days, Jewish daughters didn't know about love affairs, so he had to run after Gentile girls and women.

Not far from Zamosc, Todrus had an estate where the greatest nobles came to admire his horses. But he was a terrible spendthrift, and over the years his debts grew. He devoured his father-in-law's fortune, and that is the plain truth.

Now, Getzel the Monkey, whose name was really Getzel Bailes, decided to imitate everything about Todrus Broder. He was a rich man, and stingy to boot. His father had also been known as a miser. It was said that he had built up his fortune by starving himself. The son had a mill that poured out not flour but gold.

Getzel had an old miller who was as devoted as a dog to him. In the fall, when there was a lot of grain to mill, this miller stayed awake nights. He didn't even have a room for himself; he slept with the mice in the hayloft. Getzel grew rich because of him. In those times people were used to serving. If they didn't serve God, they served the boss.

Getzel was a moneylender, too. Half the town's houses were mortgaged to him. He had one precious little daughter, Dishke, and a wife, Risha Leah, who was as sick as she was ugly. Getzel could as soon become Todrus as I the rabbi of Turisk. But a rumor spread through the town that Getzel was trying to become another Todrus. At the beginning it was only the talk of the peddlers and the seamstresses, and who pays attention to such gossip? But then Getzel went to Selig the tailor and he ordered a coat just like Todrus's, with a broad fox collar and a row of tails. Later he had the shoemaker fit him with a pair of boots exactly the same as Todrus's, with low uppers and shiny toes. Zamosc isn't Warsaw. Sooner or later everyone knows what everyone else is doing. So why mimic anyone? Still, when the rumors reached Todrus's ears he merely said, "I don't care. It shows that he has a high opinion of my taste." Todrus never spoke a bad word about anyone. If he was going down Lublin Street and a girl of twelve walked by, he would lift his hat to her just as though she were a lady. Had a fool done this, they would have made fun of him. But a clever person can afford to be foolish sometimes. At weddings Todrus got drunk and cracked such jokes that they thought he, not Berish Venngrover, was the jester. When he danced a kozotsky, the floor trembled.

Well, Getzel Bailes was determined to become a second Todrus. He was small and thick as a barrel, and a stammerer to boot. To hear him try to get a word out was enough to make you faint. The town had something to mock. He bought himself a carriage, but it was a tiny carriage and the horses were two old nags. Getzel rode from the marketplace to the mill and from the mill to the marketplace. He wanted to be gallant, and he tried to take his hat off to the druggist's wife. Before he could raise his hand, she had already disappeared. People were barely able to keep from laughing in his face, and the town rascals immediately gave him his nickname.

Getzel's wife, Risha Leah, was a shrew, but she had sense enough to see what was happening. They began to quarrel. There was no lack in Zamosc of curious people who listened at the cracks in the shutters and looked through the keyhole. Risha Leah said to him, "You can as much become Todrus as I can become a man! You are making a fool of yourself. Todrus is Todrus; you stay Getzel."

But who knows what goes on in another person's head? It seemed to be an obsession. Getzel began to pronounce his words like a person from Great Poland and to use German expressions: *mädchen, schmädchen, grädchen.* [1] He found out what Todrus ate, what he drank, and forgive me for the expression, what drawers he wore. He began to chase women, too. And, my dear friends, just as Todrus had succeeded in everything, so Getzel failed. He would crack a joke and get a box on the ear in return. Once, in the middle of a wedding celebration, he tried to seduce a woman, and her husband poured chicken soup down the front of his gaberdine. Dishke cried and implored him, "Daddy, they are making fun of you!" But it is written somewhere that any fancy can become a madness.

Getzel met Todrus in the street and said, "I want to see your furniture."

"With the greatest pleasure," said Todrus and took him into his living room. What harm would it do Todrus, after all, if Getzel copied him?

So Getzel kept on mimicking. He tried to imitate Todrus's voice. He tried to make friends with the squires and their wives. He had studied everything in detail. Getzel had never smoked, but suddenly he came out with cigars and the cigars were bigger than he was. He also started a subscription to a newspaper in Petersburg. Todrus's daughters went to a Gentile boarding school, and Getzel wanted to send Dishke there, even though she was already too old for that. Risha Leah raised an uproar and she was barely able to prevent him from doing it. If he had been a pauper, Getzel would have been excommunicated. But he was loaded with money. For a long time Todrus didn't pay any attention to all of this, but at last in the marketplace he walked over to Getzel and asked: "Do you want to see how I make water?" He used plain language, and the town had something to laugh about.

2

Now, listen to this. One day Risha Leah died. Of what did she die? Really, I couldn't say. Nowadays people run to the doctor; in those times a person got sick and it was soon finished. Perhaps it was Getzel's carryings on that killed her. Anyway, she died and they buried her. Getzel didn't waste any tears over it. He sat on the stool during the seven days of mourning and cracked jokes like Todrus. His daughter Dishke was already engaged. After the thirty days of bereavement the matchmakers showered him with offers, but he wasn't in a hurry.

Two months hadn't passed when there was bedlam in the town. Todrus Broder had gone bankrupt. He had borrowed money from widows and orphans. Brides had invested their dowries with him, and he owed money to nobles. One of the squires came over and tried to shoot him. Todrus's wife wept and fainted, and the girls hid in the attic. It came out that Todrus owed Getzel a large sum of money. A mortgage, or God knows what. Getzel came to Todrus. He was carrying a cane with a silver tip and an amber handle, just like Todrus's, and he pounded on the floor with it. Todrus tried to laugh off the whole business, but you could tell that he didn't feel very good about it. They wanted to auction off all his possessions, tear him to pieces. The women called him a murderer, a robber, and a swindler. The brides howled: "What did you do with our dowries?" and wailed as if it were Yom Kippur. Todrus had a dog as big as a lion, and Getzel had gotten one the image of it. He brought the dog with him, and both animals tried to devour each other. Finally Getzel whispered something to Todrus; they locked themselves in a room and stayed there for three hours. During that time the creditors almost tore the house down. When Todrus came out, he was as pale as death; Getzel was perspiring. He called out to the men: "Don't make such a racket! I'll pay all the debts. I have taken over the business from Todrus." They didn't believe their own ears. Who puts a healthy head into a sickbed? But Getzel took out his purse, long and deep, just like Todrus's. However, Todrus's was empty, and this one was full of bank notes. Getzel began to pay on the spot. To some he paid off the whole debt and to others an advance, but they all knew that he was solvent. Todrus looked on silently. Fogel, his wife, came to herself and smiled. The girls came out of their hiding places. Even the dogs made peace; they began to sniff each other and wag their tails. Where had Getzel put together so much cash? As a rule, a merchant has all his money in his business. But Getzel kept on paying. He had stopped stammering and he spoke now as if he really were Todrus. Todrus had a bookkeeper whom they called the secretary, and he brought out the ledgers. Meanwhile, Todrus had become his old self again. He told jokes, drank brandy, and offered a drink to Getzel. They toasted *l'chayim*. [2]

To make a long story short, Getzel took over everything. Todrus Broder left for Lublin with his wife and daughters, and it seemed that he had moved out altogether. Even the maids went with him. But then why hadn't he taken his featherbeds with him? By law, no creditor is allowed to take these. For three months there was no word of them. Getzel had already become the boss. He went here, he went there, he rode in Todrus's carriage with Todrus's coachman. After three months Fogel came back with her daughters. It was hard to recognize her. They asked her about her husband and she answered simply, "I have no more husband." "Some misfortune, God forbid?" they asked, and she answered no, that they had been divorced.

There is a saying that the truth will come out like oil on water. And so it happened here. In the three hours that Getzel and Todrus had been locked up in the office, Todrus had transferred everything to Getzel—his house, his estate, all his possessions, and on top of it all, his wife. Yes, Fogel married Getzel. Getzel gave her a marriage contract for ten thousand rubles and wrote up a house—it was actually Todrus's—as estate. For the daughters he put away large dowries.

The turmoil in the town was something awful. If you weren't in Zamosc then, you have no idea how excited a town can become. A book could be written about it. Not one book, ten books! Even the Gentiles don't do such things. But that was Todrus. As long as he could, he acted like a king. He gambled, he lost, and then it was all over; he disappeared. It seems he had been about to go to jail. The squires might have murdered him. And in such a situation, what won't a man do to save his life? Some people thought that Getzel had known everything in advance and that he had plotted it all. He had managed a big loan for Todrus and had lured him into his snare. No one would have thought that Getzel was so clever. But how does the saying go? If God wills, a broom will shoot.

Todrus's girls soon got married. Dishke went to live with her in-laws in Lemberg. Fogel almost never showed her face outside. Todrus's grounds had a garden with a pavilion, and she sat there all summer. In the winter she hid inside the house. Todrus Broder had vanished like a stone in the water. Some held that he was in Krakow; others, that he had gone to Warsaw. Still others said that he had converted and had married a rich squiress. Who can understand such a man? If a Jew is capable of selling his wife in such a way, he is no longer a Jew. Fogel had loved him with a great love, and it was clear that she had consented to everything just to save him. In the years that followed, nobody could say a word against Todrus to her. On Rosh Hashanah and Yom Kippur she stood in her pew in the women's section at the grating and she didn't utter a single word to anybody. She remained proud.

Getzel took over Todrus's language and his manners. He even became taller, or perhaps he put lifts in his boots. He became a bosom friend of the squires. It was rumored that he drank forbidden wine with them. After he had stopped stammering, he had begun to speak Polish like one of them.

Dishke never wrote a word to her father. About Todrus's daughters I heard that they didn't have a good end. One died in childbirth. Another was supposed to have hanged herself. But Getzel became Todrus and I saw it happen with my own eyes, from beginning to end. Yes, mimicking is forbidden. If you imitate a person, his fate is passed on to you. Even with a shadow one is not allowed to play tricks. In Zamosc there was a young man who used to play with his shadow. He would put his hands together so that the shadow on the wall would look like a buck with horns, eating and butting. One night the shadow jumped from the wall and gored the young man as if with real horns. He got such a butt that he had two holes in his forehead afterwards. And so it happened here.

Getzel did not need other people's money. He had enough. But suddenly he began to borrow from widows and orphans. Anywhere he could find credit he did, and he paid high interest. He didn't have to renovate his mill either. The flour was as white as snow. But he built a new mill and put in new millstones. His old and devoted miller had died, and Getzel hired a new miller who had long mustaches, a former bailiff. This one swindled him right and left. Getzel also bought an estate from a nobleman even though he already had an estate with a stable and horses. Before this he had kept to his Jewishness, but now he began to dress like a fop. He stopped coming to the synagogue except on High Holy Days. As if this wasn't enough, Getzel started a brewery and he sowed hops for beer. He didn't need any of this. Above all, it cost him a fortune. He imported machines, God knows from where, and they made such a noise at night that the neighbors couldn't sleep. Every few weeks he made a trip to Warsaw. Who can guess what really happened to him? Ten enemies don't do as much harm to a man as he does to himself. One day the news spread that Getzel was bankrupt. My dear friends, he didn't have to go bankrupt; it was all an imitation of Todrus. He had taken over the other's bad luck. People streamed from every street and broke up his window-panes. Getzel had no imitator. No one wanted his wife; Fogel was older than Getzel by a good many years. He assured everyone that he wouldn't take anything away from them. But they beat him up. A squire came and put his pistol to Getzel's forehead in just the same way as the other had to Todrus.

To make a long story short, Getzel ran away in the middle of the night. When he left, the creditors took over and it turned out that there was more than enough for everybody. Getzel's fortune was worth God knows how much. So why had he run away? And where had he gone? Some said that the whole bankruptcy was nothing but a sham. There was supposed to have been a woman involved, but what does an old man want with a woman? It was all to be like Todrus. Had Todrus buried himself alive, Getzel would have dug his own grave. The whole thing was the work of demons. What are demons if not imitators? And what does a mirror do? This is why they cover a mirror when there is a corpse in the house. It is dangerous to see the reflection of the body.

Every piece of property Getzel had owned was taken away. The creditors didn't leave as much as a scrap of bread for Fogel. She went to live in the poorhouse. When this happened I was no longer in Zamosc. But may my enemies have such an old age as they say Fogel had. She lay down on a straw mattress and she never got up again. It was said that before her death she asked to be inscribed on the tombstone not as the wife of Getzel but as the wife of Todrus. Nobody even bothered to put up a stone. Over the years the grave become overgrown and was finally lost.

What happened to Getzel? And what happened to Todrus? No one knew. Somebody thought they might have met somewhere, but for what purpose? Todrus must have died. Dishke tried to get a part of her father's estate, but nothing was left. A man should stay what he is. The troubles of the world come from mimicking. Today they call it fashion. A charlatan in Paris invents a dress with a train in front and everybody wears it. They are all apes, the whole lot of them.

I could also tell you a story about twins, but I wouldn't dare to talk about it at night. They had no choice. They were two bodies with one soul. Both sisters died within a single day, one in Zamosc and the other in Kovle. Who knows? Perhaps one sister was real and the other was her shadow?

I am afraid of a shadow. A shadow is an enemy. When it has the chance, it takes revenge.

---

[1] *Mädchen* is, of course, the German word for maiden. The other two words are humorous nonsense variations on the sound (though *grädchen* is also a girl's name). The phrase is a typically Jewish way of expressing mild criticism of something, as in the following: "Getzel, what are you doing?" "I'm reading the paper." "Paper, schmaper, get in here and carry out the garbage."
[2] "To life." (Hebrew)

DISCUSSION TOPICS

1. What is your initial reaction to "Getzel the Monkey"? What part does the story's humor play in your response?
2. What is the meaning of the story's title? What do you think motivates Getzel to become a "monkey"?
3. There are many examples in literature of the theme of the double or shadow. One of the best known is Robert Louis Stevenson's *The Strange Case of Dr.*

Jekyll and Mr. Hyde. The double or *doppelgänger* may appear as a twin, a shadow, an alter ego or opposite; very often the double represents a dark projection of the soul and suggests C. G. Jung's idea of the *shadow.* Thus sometimes the double may seem to be a demon, an agent of the devil himself. Are there any suggestions in Singer's story that Todrus might be diabolical? What about Getzel?

4. Why should a shadow or a double be frightening?
5. "Getzel the Monkey" sometimes sounds like a parable. What has Singer done to create that impression?
6. Parables usually have a moral or social message. What would you say is the moral of this story?

RICHARD WRIGHT (1908–1960) Novelist, short story writer. Born into a sharecropper's family in Natchez, Mississippi, deserted by his father at an early age, Richard Wright spent part of his youth in orphan asylums and part living with relatives in Memphis, Tennessee. Although he had little formal education, he was determined to be a writer and worked for a time in Chicago for the Federal Writers Project and later in New York, where he wrote the government-sponsored *Guide to Harlem* (1937). His first novel, *Native Son* (1940), was a critical and popular success. After the appearance of his autobiography, *Black Boy* (1945), Wright moved to Paris, where he lived and wrote until his death.

THE MAN WHO WAS ALMOST A MAN

Dave struck out across the fields, looking homeward through paling light. Whuts the usa talkin wid em niggers in the field? Anyhow, his mother was putting supper on the table. Them niggers can't understand *nothing.* One of these days he was going to get a gun and practice shooting, then they can't talk to him as though he were a little boy. He slowed, looking at the ground. Shucks, Ah ain scareda them even ef they are biggern me! Aw, Ah know whut Ahma do. . . . Ahm going by ol Joe's sto n git that Sears Roebuck catlog n look at them guns. Mabbe Ma will lemme buy one when she gits mah pay from ol man Hawkins. Ahma beg her t gimme some money. Ahm ol ernough to hava gun. Ahm seventeen. Almos a man. He strode, feeling his long, loose-jointed limbs. Shucks, a man oughta hava little gun aftah he done worked hard all day. . . .

He came in sight of Joe's store. A yellow lantern glowed on the front porch. He mounted steps and went through the screen door, hearing it bang behind him. There was a strong smell of coal oil and mackerel fish. He felt very confident until he saw fat Joe walk in through the rear door, then his courage began to ooze.

"Howdy, Dave! Whutcha want?"

"How yuh, Mistah Joe? Aw, Ah don wanna buy nothing. Ah jus wanted t see ef yuhd lemme look at tha ol catlog erwhile."

"Sure! You wanna see it here?"

"Nawsuh. Ah wans t take it home wid me. Ahll bring it back termorrow when Ah come in from the fiels."

"You plannin on buyin something?"

"Yessuh."

"Your ma letting you have your own money now?"

"Shucks. Mistah Joe, Ahm gittin t be a man like anybody else!"

Joe laughed and wiped his greasy white face with a red bandanna.

"Whut you plannin on buyin?"

Dave looked at the floor, scratched his head, scratched his thigh, and smiled. Then he looked up shyly.

"Ahll tell yuh, Mistah Joe, ef yuh promise yuh won't tell."

"I promise."

"Waal, Ahma buy a gun."

"A gun? Whut you want with a gun?"

"Ah wanna keep it."

"You ain't nothing but a boy. You don't need a gun."

"Aw, lemme have the catalog, Mistah Joe. Ahll bring it back."

Joe walked through the rear door. Dave was elated. He looked around at barrels of sugar and flour. He heard Joe coming back. He craned his neck to see if he were bringing the book. Yeah, he's got it! Gawddog, he's got it!

"Here; but be sure you bring it back. It's the only one I got."

"Sho, Mistah Joe."

"Say, if you wanna buy a gun, why don't you buy one from me. I gotta gun to sell."

"Will it shoot?"

"Sure it'll shoot."

"Whut kind is it?"

"Oh, it's kinda old. . . . A Lefthand Wheeler. A pistol. A big one."

"Is it got bullets in it?"

"It's loaded."

"Kin Ah see it?"

"Where's your money?"

"Whut yuh wan fer it?"

"I'll let you have it for two dollars."

"Just *two* dollahs? Shucks, Ah could buy tha when Ah git mah pay."

"I'll have it here when you want it."

"Awright, suh. Ah be in fer it."

He went through the door, hearing it slam again behind him. Ahma git some money from Ma n buy me a gun! Only *two* dollahs! He tucked the thick catalogue under his arm and hurried.

"Where yuh been, boy?" His mother held a steaming dish of blackeyed peas.

"Aw, Ma, Ah jus stopped down the road t talk wid th boys."

"Yuh know bettah than t keep suppah waitin."

He sat down, resting the catalogue on the edge of the table.

"Yuh git up from there and git to the well n wash yosef! Ah ain feedin no hogs in mah house!"

She grabbed his shoulder and pushed him. He stumbled out of the room, then came back to get the catalogue.

"Whut this?"

"Aw, Ma, it's jusa catlog."

"Who yuh git it from?"

"From Joe, down at the sto."

"Waal, thas good. We kin use it around the house."

"Naw, Ma." He grabbed for it. "Gimme mah catlog, Ma."

She held onto it and glared at him.

"Quit hollerin at me! Whuts wrong wid yuh? Yuh crazy?"

"But Ma, please. It ain mine! It's Joe's! He tol me t bring it back t im termorrow."

She gave up the book. He stumbled down the back steps, hugging the thick book under his arm. When he had splashed water on his face and hands, he groped back to the kitchen and fumbled in a corner for the towel. He bumped into a chair; it clattered to the floor. The catalogue sprawled at his feet. When he had dried his eyes he snatched up the book and held it again under his arm. His mother stood watching him.

"Now, ef yuh gonna acka fool over that ol book, Ahll take it n burn it up."

"Naw, Ma, please."

"Waal, set down n be still!"

He sat and drew the oil lamp close. He thumbed page after page, unaware of the food his mother set on the table. His father came in. Then his small brother.

"Whutcha got there, Dave?" his father asked.

"Jusa catlog," he answered, not looking up.

"Ywah, here they is!" His eyes glowed at blue and black revolvers. He glanced up, feeling sudden guilt. His father was watching him. He eased the book under the table and rested it on his knees. After the blessing was asked, he ate. He scooped up peas and swallowed fat meat without chewing. Buttermilk helped to wash it down. He did not want to mention money before his father. He would do much better by cornering his mother when she was alone. He looked at his father uneasily out of the edge of his eye.

"Boy, how come yuh don quit foolin wid tha book n eat yo suppah?"

"Yessuh."

"How yuh n ol man Hawkins gittin erlong?"

"Suh?"

"Can't yuh hear? Why don yuh lissen? Ah ast yuh how wuz yuh n ol man Hawkins gittin erlong?"

"Oh, swell, Pa. Ah plows mo lan than anybody over there."

"Waal, yuh oughta keep yo min on whut yuh doin."

"Yessuh."

He poured his plate full of molasses and sopped at it slowly with a chunk of

270

cornbread. When all but his mother had left the kitchen, he still sat and looked again at the guns in the catalogue. Lawd, ef Ah only had tha pretty one! He could almost feel the slickness of the weapon with his fingers. If he had a gun like that he would polish it and keep it shining so it would never rust. N Ahd keep it loaded, by Gawd!

"Ma?"

"Hunh?"

"Ol man Hawkins give yuh mah money yit?"

"Yeah, but ain no usa yuh thinkin bout thowin nona it erway. Ahm keepin tha money sos yuh kin have cloes t go to school this winter."

He rose and went to her side with the open catalogue in his palms. She was washing dishes, her head bent low over a pan. Shyly he raised the open book. When he spoke his voice was husky, faint.

"Ma, Gawd knows Ah wans one of these."

"One of whut?" she asked, not raising her eyes.

"One of these," he said again, not daring even to point. She glanced up at the page, then at him with wide eyes.

"Nigger Is yuh gone plum crazy?"

"Ah, Ma———"

"Git outta here! Don yuh talk t me bout no gun! Yuh a fool!"

"Ma, Ah kin buy one fer *two* dollahs."

"Not ef Ah knows it yuh ain!"

"But yuh promised me one———"

"Ah don care whut Ah promised! Yuh ain nothing but a boy yit!"

"Ma, ef yuh lemme buy one Ahll **never ast** yuh fer nothing no mo."

"Ah tol yuh t git outta here! Yuh ain gonna toucha penny of tha money fer no gun! Thas how come Ah has Mistah Hawkins t pay yo wages t me, cause Ah knows yuh ain got no sense."

"But Ma, we needa gun. Pa ain got no gun. We needa gun in the house. Yuh kin never tell whut might happen."

"Now don yuh try to maka fool outta me, boy! Ef we did hava gun yuh wouldn't have it!"

He laid the catalogue down and slipped his arm around her waist.

"Aw, Ma, Ah done worked hard alla summer n ain ast yuh fer nothin, is Ah, now?"

"Thas whut yuh spose t do!"

"But Ma, Ah wans a gun. Yuh kin lemme have two dollahs outta mah money. Please, Ma. I kin give it to Pa . . . Please, Ma! Ah loves yuh, Ma."

When she spoke her voice came soft and low.

"Whut yuh wan wida gun, Dave? Yuh don need no gun. Yuhll git in trouble. N ef yo Pa jus *thought* Ah let yuh have money t buy a gun he'd hava fit."

"Ahll hide it, Ma, it ain but two dollahs."

"Lawd, chil, whuts wrong wid yuh?"

"Ain nothing wrong, Ma. Ahm almos a man now. Ah wans a gun."

"Who gonna sell yuh a gun?"

"Ol Joe at the sto."

"N it don cos but two dollahs?"

"Thas all, Ma. Just two dollahs. Please, Ma."

She was stacking the plates away; her hands moved slowly, reflectively. Dave kept an anxious silence. Finally, she turned to him.

"Ahll let yuh git tha gun ef yuh promise me one thing."

"Whuts tha, Ma?"

"Yuh bring it straight back t *me*, yuh hear? Itll be fer Pa."

"Yessum! Lemme go now, Ma."

She stooped, turned slightly to one side, raised the hem of her dress, rolled down the top of her stocking, and came up with a slender wad of bills.

"Here," she said. "Lawd knows yuh don need no gun. But yer Pa does. Yuh bring it right back t *me*, yuh hear? Ahma put it up. Now ef yuh don, Ahma have yuh Pa lick yuh so hard yuh won ferget it."

"Yessum."

He took the money, ran down the steps, and across the yard.

"Dave! Yuuuuuh Daaaaave!"

He heard, but he was not going to stop now. "Naw, Lawd!"

The first movement he made the following morning was to reach under his pillow for the gun. In the gray light of dawn he held it loosely, feeling a sense of power. Could killa man wida gun like this. Kill anybody, black er white. And if he were holding his gun in his hand nobody could run over him; they would have to respect him. It was a big gun, with a long barrel and a heavy handle. He raised and lowered it in his hand, marveling at its weight.

He had not come straight home with it as his mother had asked; instead he had stayed out in the fields, holding the weapon in his hand, aiming it now and then at some imaginary foe. But he had not fired it; he had been afraid that his father might hear. Also he was not sure he knew how to fire it.

To avoid surrendering the pistol he had not come into the house until he knew that all were asleep. When his mother had tiptoed to his bedside late that night and demanded the gun, he had first played 'possum; then he had told her that the gun was hidden outdoors, that he would bring it to her in the morning. Now he lay turning it slowly in his hands. He broke it, took out the cartridges, felt them, and then put them back.

He slid out of bed, got a long strip of old flannel from a trunk, wrapped the gun in it, and tied it to his naked thigh while it was still loaded. He did not go in to breakfast. Even though it was not yet daylight, he started for Jim Hawkins' plantation. Just as the sun was rising he reached the barns where the mules and plows were kept.

"Hey! That you, Dave?"

He turned. Jim Hawkins stood eying him suspiciously.

"Whatre yuh doing here so early?"

"Ah didn't know Ah wuz gittin up so early, Mistah Hawkins. Ah wuz fixin t hitch up ol Jenny n take her t the fiels."

"Good. Since you're here so early, how about plowing that stretch down by the woods?"

"Suits me. Mistah Hawkins."

"O.K. Go to it!"

He hitched Jenny to a plow and started across the fields. Hot dog! This was just what he wanted. If he could get down by the woods, he could shoot his gun and nobody would hear. He walked behind the plow, hearing the traces creaking, feeling the gun tied tight to his thigh.

When he reached the woods, he plowed two whole rows before he decided to take out the gun. Finally, he stopped, looked in all directions, then untied the gun and held it in his hand. He turned to the mule and smiled.

"Know whut this is, Jenny? Naw, yuh wouldn't know! Yuhs jusa ol mule! Anyhow, this is a gun, n it kin shoot, by Gawd!"

He held the gun at arm's length. Whut t hell, Ahma shoot this thing! He looked at Jenny again.

"Lissen here, Jenny! When Ah pull this ol trigger Ah don wan yuh t run n acka fool now."

Jenny stood with head down, her short ears pricked straight. Dave walked off about twenty feet, held the gun far out from him, at arm's length, and turned his head. Hell, he told himself, Ah ain afraid. The gun felt loose in his fingers; he waved it wildly for a moment. Then he shut his eyes and tightened his forefinger. *Blooom!* A report half-deafened him and he thought his right hand was torn from his arm. He heard Jenny whinnying and galloping over the field, and he found himself on his knees, squeezing his fingers hard between his legs. His hand was numb; he jammed it into his mouth, trying to warm it, trying to stop the pain. The gun lay at his feet. He did not quite know what had happened. He stood up and stared at the gun as though it were a live thing. He gritted his teeth and kicked the gun. Yuh almos broke mah arm! He turned to look for Jenny; she was far over the fields, tossing her head and kicking wildly.

"Hol on there, ol mule!"

When he caught up with her she stood trembling, walling her big white eyes at him. The plow was far away; the traces had broken. Then Dave stopped short, looking, not believing. Jenny was bleeding. Her left side was red and wet with blood. He went closer. Lawd have mercy! Wondah did Ah shoot this mule? He grabbed for Jenny's mane. She flinched, snorted, whirled, tossing her head.

"Hol on now! Hol on."

Then he saw the hole in Jenny's side, right between the ribs. It was round, wet, red. A crimson stream streaked down the front leg, flowing fast. Good Gawd! Ah wuznt shootin at tha mule. . . . He felt panic. He knew he had to stop that blood, or Jenny would bleed to death. He had never seen so much blood in all his life. He ran the mule for half a mile, trying to catch her. Finally she stopped, breathing hard, stumpy tail half arched. He caught her mane and led her back to where the plow and gun lay. Then he stopped and grabbed handfuls of damp black earth and tried to plug the bullet hole. Jenny shuddered, whinnied, and broke from him.

"Hol on! Hol on now!"

He tried to plug it again, but blood came anyhow. His fingers were hot and sticky. He rubbed dirt hard into his palms, trying to dry them. Then again he attempted to plug the bullet hole, but Jenny shied away, kicking her heels high. He stood helpless. He had to do something. He ran at Jenny; she dodged him. He watched a red stream of blood flow down Jenny's leg and form a bright pool at her feet.

"Jenny . . . Jenny . . ." he called weakly.

His lips trembled. She's bleeding t death! He looked in the direction of home, wanting to go back, wanting to get help. But he saw the pistol lying in the damp black clay. He had a queer feeling that if he only did something, this would not be; Jenny would not be there bleeding to death.

When he went to her this time, she did not move. She stood with sleepy, dreamy eyes; and when he touched her she gave a low-pitched whinny and knelt to the ground, her front knees slopping in blood.

"Jenny . . . Jenny . . ." he whispered.

For a long time she held her neck erect; then her head sank, slowly. Her ribs swelled with a mighty heave and she went over.

Dave's stomach felt empty, very empty. He picked up the gun and held it gingerly between his thumb and forefinger. He buried it at the foot of a tree. He took a stick and tried to cover the pool of blood with dirt—but what was the use? There was Jenny lying with her mouth open and her eyes walled and glassy. He could not tell Jim Hawkins he had shot his mule. But he had to tell something. Yeah, Ahll tell em Jenny started gittin wil n fell on the joint of the plow. . . . But that would hardly happen to a mule. He walked across the field slowly, head down.

It was sunset. Two of Jim Hawkins' men were over near the edge of the woods digging a hole in which to bury Jenny. Dave was surrounded by a knot of people; all of them were looking down at the dead mule.

"I don't see how in the world it happened," said Jim Hawkins for the tenth time.

The crowd parted and Dave's mother, father, and small brother pushed into the center.

"Where Dave?" his mother called.

"There he is," said Jim Hawkins.

His mother grabbed him.

"Whut happened, Dave? Whut yuh done?"

"Nothing."

"C'mon, boy, talk," his father said.

Dave took a deep breath and told the story he knew nobody believed.

"Waal," he drawled. "Ah brung ol Jenny down here sos Ah could do mah plowin. Ah plowed bout two rows, just like yuh see." He stopped and pointed at the long rows of upturned earth. "Then something musta been wrong wid ol Jenny. She wouldn't ack right a-tall. She started snortin n kickin her heels. Ah tried to hol her, but she pulled erway, rearin n goin on. Then when the point of the plow was stickin up in the air, she swung erroun n twisted hersef back on it. . . . She stuck hersef n started t bleed. N fo Ah could do anything, she wuz dead."

"Did you ever hear of anything like that in all your life?" asked Jim Hawkins.

There were white and black standing in the crowd. They murmured. Dave's mother came close to him and looked hard into his face.

"Tell the truth, Dave," she said.

"Looks like a bullet hole ter me," said one man.

"Dave, whut yuh do wid tha gun?" his mother asked.

The crowd surged in, looking at him. He jammed his hands into his pockets, shook his head slowly from left to right, and backed away. His eyes were wide and painful.

"Did he hava gun?" asked Jim Hawkins.

"By Gawd, Ah tol yuh tha wuz a *gun* wound," said a man, slapping his thigh.

His father caught his shoulders and shook him till his teeth rattled.

"Tell whut happened, yuh rascal! Tell whut . . ."

Dave looked at Jenny's stiff legs and began to cry.

"Whut yuh do wid tha gun?" his mother asked.

"Whut wuz he doin wida gun?" his father asked.

"Come on and tell the truth," said Hawkins. "Ain't nobody going to hurt you . . ."

His mother crowded close to him.

"Did yuh shoot tha mule, Dave?"

Dave cried, seeing blurred white and black faces.

"Ahh ddinnt gggo tt sshoooot hher. . . . Ah sssswear off Gawd Ahh ddint. . . . Ah wuz a-tryin t sssee ef the ol gggun would sshoot————"

"Where yuh git the gun from?" his father asked.

"Ah got it from Joe, at the sto."

"Where yuh git the money?"

"Ma give it t me."

"He kept worryin me, Bob. . . . Ah had t. . . . Ah tol im t bring the gun right back t me. . . . It was fer yuh, the gun."

"But how yuh happen to shoot that mule?" asked Jim Hawkins.

"Ah wuznt shootin at the mule, Mistah Hawkins. The gun jumped when Ah pulled the trigger . . . N fo Ah knowed anything Jenny wuz there a-bleedin."

Somebody in the crowd laughed. Jim Hawkins walked close to Dave and looked into his face.

"Well, looks like you have bought you a mule, Dave."

"Ah swear fo Gawd, Ah didn't go t kill the mule, Mistah Hawkins!"

"But you killed her!"

All the crowd was laughing now. They stood on tiptoe and poked heads over one another's shoulders.

"Well, boy, looks like yuh done bought a dead mule! Hahaha!"

"Ain tha ershame."

"Hohohohoho."

Dave stood head down, twisting his feet in the dirt.

"Well, you needn't worry about it, Bob," said Jim Hawkins to Dave's father. "Just let the boy keep on working and pay me two dollars a month."

"Whut yuh wan fer yo mule, Mistah Hawkins?"

Jim Hawkins screwed up his eyes.

"Fifty dollars."

"Whut yuh do wid tha gun?" Dave's father demanded.

Dave said nothing.

"Yuh wan me t take a tree lim n beat yuh till yuh talk!"

"Nawsuh!"

"Whut yuh do wid it?"

"Ah thowed it erway."

"Where?"

"Ah . . . Ah thowed it in the creek."

"Waal, c mon home. N firs thing in the mawnin git to tha creek n fin tha gun."

"Yessuh."

"Whut yuh pay fer it?"

"Two dollahs."

"Take tha gun n git yo money back n carry it t Mistah Hawkins, yuh hear? N don fergit Ahma lam yo black bottom good fer this! Now march yosef on home, suh!"

Dave turned and walked slowly. He heard people laughing. Dave glared, his eyes welling with tears. Hot anger bubbled in him. Then he swallowed and stumbled on.

That night Dave did not sleep. He was glad that he had gotten out of killing the mule so easily, but he was hurt. Something hot seemed to turn over inside him each time he remembered how they had laughed. He tossed on his bed, feeling his hard pillow. *N Pa says he's gonna beat me. . . .* He remembered other beatings, and his back quivered. *Naw, naw, Ah sho don wan im t beat me tha way no mo. . . . Dam em all!* Nobody ever gave him anything. All he did was work. *They treat me lika mule. . . . N then they beat me. . . .* He gritted his teeth. *N Ma had t tell on me.*

Well, if he had to, he would take old man Hawkins that two dollars. But that meant selling the gun. And he wanted to keep that gun. Fifty dollahs fer a dead mule.

He turned over, thinking of how he had fired the gun. He had an itch to fire it again. *Ef other men kin shoota gun, by Gawd, Ah kin!* He was still listening. *Mebbe they all sleepin now. . . .* The house was still. He heard the soft breathing of his brother. *Yes, now!* He would go down and get that gun and see if he could fire it! He eased out of bed and slipped into overalls.

The moon was bright. He ran almost all the way to the edge of the woods. He stumbled over the ground, looking for the spot where he had buried the gun. *Yeah, here it is.* Like a hungry dog scratching for a bone he pawed it up. He puffed

276

his black cheeks and blew dirt from the trigger and barrel. He broke it and found four cartridges unshot. He looked around; the fields were filled with silence and moonlight. He clutched the gun stiff and hard in his fingers. But as soon as he wanted to pull the trigger, he shut his eyes and turned his head. Naw, Ah can't shoot wid mah eyes closed n mah head turned. With effort he held his eyes open; then he squeezed. *Blooooom!* He was stiff, not breathing. The gun was still in his hands. Dammit, he'd done it! He fired again. *Bloooom!* He smiled. *Bloooom! Bloooom!* *Click, click.* There! It was empty. If anybody could shoot a gun, he could. He put the gun into his hip pocket and started across the fields.

When he reached the top of a ridge he stood straight and proud·in the moonlight, looking at Jim Hawkins' big white house, feeling the gun sagging in his pocket. Lawd, ef Ah had jus one mo bullet Ahd taka shot at tha house. Ahd like t scare ol man Hawkins jusa little. . . . Jussa enough t let im know Dave Sanders is a man.

To his left the road curved, running to the tracks of the Illinois Central. He jerked his head, listening. From far off came a faint *boooof-boooof; boooof-boooof; boooof-boooof . . .* Tha's number eight. He took a swift look at Jim Hawkins' white house; he thought of pa, of ma, of his little brother, and the boys. He thought of the dead mule and heard *boooof-boooof; boooof-boooof; boooof-boooof . . .* He stood rigid. Two dollahs a mont. Les see now. . . . Tha means itll take bout two years. Shucks! Ahll be dam!

He started down the road, toward the tracks. Yeah, here she comes! He stood beside the track and held himself stiffly. Here she comes, erroun the ben. . . . C mon, yuh slow poke! C mon! He had his hand on his gun; something quivered in his stomach. Then the train thundered past, the gray and brown box cars rumbling and clinking. He gripped the gun tightly; then he jerked his hand out of his pocket. Ah betcha Bill wouldn't do it! Ah betcha. . . . The cars slid past, steel grinding upon steel. Ahm riding yuh ternight so hep me Gawd! He was hot all over. He hesitated just a moment; then he grabbed, pulled atop of a car, and lay flat. He felt his pocket; the gun was still there. Ahead the long rails were glinting in the moonlight, stretching away, away to somewhere, somewhere where he could be a man. . . .

DISCUSSION TOPICS

1. Setting, social as well as geographic, is crucially important in this story. How does Wright convey this setting, especially the pressures that influence Dave's actions, and how does setting relate to theme and character in the story?

2. How would the theme of the story be changed if the protagonist were white?

3. Wright's story is another tale of initiation (see the discussion of Hawthorne's "My Kinsman, Major Molineux"). What is the outcome of Dave's initiation? What part does the gun play in his rite of passage? Do you think Wright would be an advocate of gun-control laws? Why—or why not?

JOHN CHEEVER (1912–1982) Short story writer, novelist, television scriptwriter. He was born in Quincy, Massachusetts, and was expelled from Thayer Academy at age 17. Cheever's fame rests on his achievement as a writer of short stories, many appearing in *The New Yorker*.

THE SWIMMER

It was one of those midsummer Sundays when everyone sits around saying, "I *drank* too much last night." You might have heard it whispered by the parishioners leaving church, heard it from the lips of the priest himself, struggling with his cassock in the *vestiarium*,[1] heard it from the golf links and the tennis courts, heard it from the wildlife preserve where the leader of the Audubon[2] group was suffering from a terrible hangover. "I *drank* too much," said Donald Westerhazy. "We all *drank* too much," said Lucinda Merrill. "It must have been the wine," said Helen Westerhazy. "I *drank* too much of that claret."

This was at the edge of the Westerhazys' pool. The pool, fed by an artesian well with a high iron content, was a pale shade of green. It was a fine day. In the west there was a massive stand of cumulus cloud so like a city seen from a distance —from the bow of an approaching ship—that it might have had a name. Lisbon.[3] Hackensack.[4] The sun was hot. Neddy Merrill sat by the green water, one hand in it, one around a glass of gin. He was a slender man—he seemed to have the especial slenderness of youth—and while he was far from young he had slid down his banister that morning and given the bronze backside of Aphrodite on the hall table a smack, as he jogged toward the smell of coffee in his dining room. He might have been compared to a summer's day, particularly the last hours of one, and while he lacked a tennis racket or a sail bag the impression was definitely one of youth, sport, and clement weather. He had been swimming and now he was breathing deeply, stertorously as if he could gulp into his lungs the components of that moment, the heat of the sun, the intenseness of his pleasure. It all seemed to flow into his chest. His own house stood in Bullet Park, eight miles to the south, where his four beautiful daughters would have had their lunch and might be playing tennis. Then it occurred to him that by taking a dogleg to the southwest he could reach his home by water.

His life was not confining and the delight he took in this observation could not be explained by its suggestion of escape. He seemed to see, with a cartographer's eye, that string of swimming pools, that quasi-subterranean stream that curved across the county. He had made a discovery, a contribution to modern geography; he would name the stream Lucinda after his wife. He was not a practical joker nor was he a fool but he was determinedly original and had a vague and modest idea of himself as a legendary figure. The day was beautiful and it seemed to him that a long swim might enlarge and celebrate its beauty.

He took off a sweater that was hung over his shoulders and dove in. He had an inexplicable contempt for men who did not hurl themselves into pools. He swam a choppy crawl, breathing either with every stroke or every fourth stroke and counting somewhere well in the back of his mind the one-two one-two of a flutter kick. It was not a serviceable stroke for long distances but the domestication of swimming had saddled the sport with some customs and in his part of the world a crawl was customary. To be embraced and sustained by the light green water was less a pleasure, it seemed, than the resumption of a natural condition, and he would have liked to swim without trunks, but this was not possible, considering his project. He hoisted himself up on the far curb—he never used the ladder—and started across the lawn. When Lucinda asked where he was going he said he was going to swim home.

The only maps and charts he had to go by were remembered or imaginary but these were clear enough. First there were the Grahams, the Hammers, the Lears, the Howlands, and the Crosscups. He would cross Ditmar Street to the Bunkers and come, after a short portage, to the Levys, the Welchers, and the public pool in Lancaster. Then there were the Hallorans, the Sachses, the Biswangers, Shirley Adams, the Gilmartins, and the Clydes. The day was lovely, and that he lived in a world so generously supplied with water seemed like a clemency, a beneficence. His heart was high and he ran across the grass. Making his way home by an uncommon route gave him the feeling that he was a pilgrim, an explorer, a man with a destiny, and he knew that he would find friends all along the way; friends would line the banks of the Lucinda River.

He went through a hedge that separated the Westerhazys' land from the Grahams', walked under some flowering apple trees, passed the shed that housed their pump and filter, and came out at the Grahams' pool. "Why, Neddy," Mrs. Graham said, "what a marvelous surprise. I've been trying to get you on the phone all morning. Here, let me get you a drink." He saw then, like any explorer, that the hospitable customs and traditions of the natives would have to be handled with diplomacy if he was ever going to reach his destination. He did not want to mystify or seem rude to the Grahams nor did he have the time to linger there. He swam the length of their pool and joined them in the sun and was rescued, a few minutes later, by the arrival of two carloads of friends from Connecticut. During the uproarious reunions he was able to slip away. He went down by the front of the Grahams' house, stepped over a thorny hedge, and crossed a vacant lot to the Hammers'. Mrs. Hammer, looking up from her roses, saw him swim by although she wasn't quite sure who it was. The Lears heard him splashing past the open windows of their living room. The Howlands and the Crosscups were away. After leaving the Howlands' he crossed Ditmar Street and started for the Bunkers', where he could hear, even at that distance, the noise of a party.

The water refracted the sound of voices and laughter and seemed to suspend it in midair. The Bunkers' pool was on a rise and he climbed some stairs to a terrace where twenty-five or thirty men and women were drinking. The only person in the water was Rusty Towers, who floated there on a rubber raft. Oh, how bonny and lush were the banks of the Lucinda River! Prosperous men and women gathered by the sapphire-colored waters while caterer's men in white coats passed them cold gin. Overhead a red de Haviland trainer[5] was circling around and around and around in the sky with something like the glee of a child in a swing.

279

Ned felt a passing affection for the scene, a tenderness for the gathering, as if it was something he might touch. In the distance he heard thunder. As soon as Enid Bunker saw him she began to scream: "Oh, look who's here! What a marvelous surprise! When Lucinda said that you couldn't come I thought I'd *die.*" She made her way to him through the crowd, and when they had finished kissing she led him to the bar, a progress that was slowed by the fact that he stopped to kiss eight or ten other women and shake the hands of as many men. A smiling bartender he had seen at a hundred parties gave him a gin and tonic and he stood by the bar for a moment, anxious not to get stuck in any conversation that would delay his voyage. When he seemed about to be surrounded he dove in and swam close to the side to avoid colliding with Rusty's raft. At the far end of the pool he bypassed the Tomlinsons with a broad smile and jogged up the garden path. The gravel cut his feet but this was the only unpleasantness. The party was confined to the pool, and as he went toward the house he heard the brilliant, watery sound of voices fade, heard the noise of a radio from the Bunkers' kitchen, where someone was listening to a ball game. Sunday afternoon. He made his way through the parked cars and down the grassy border of their driveway to Alewives Lane. He did not want to be seen on the road in his bathing trunks but there was no traffic and he made the short distance to the Levys' driveway, marked with a PRIVATE PROPERTY sign and a green tube for *The New York Times.* All the doors and windows of the big house were open but there were no signs of life; not even a dog barked. He went around the side of the house to the pool and saw that the Levys had only recently left. Glasses and bottles and dishes of nuts were on a table at the deep end, where there was a bathhouse or gazebo, hung with Japanese lanterns. After swimming the pool he got himself a glass and poured a drink. It was his fourth or fifth drink and he had swum nearly half the length of the Lucinda River. He felt tired, clean, and pleased at that moment to be alone; pleased with everything.

It would storm. The stand of cumulus cloud—that city—had risen and darkened, and while he sat there he heard the percussiveness of thunder again. The de Haviland trainer was still circling overhead and it seemed to Ned that he could almost hear the pilot laugh with pleasure in the afternoon; but when there was another peal of thunder he took off for home. A train whistle blew and he wondered what time it had gotten to be. Four? Five? He thought of the provincial station at that hour, where a waiter, his tuxedo concealed by a raincoat, a dwarf with some flowers wrapped in newspaper, and a woman who had been crying would be waiting for the local. It was suddenly growing dark; it was that moment when the pin-headed birds seem to organize their song into some acute and knowledgeable recognition of the storm's approach. Then there was a fine noise of rushing water from the crown of an oak at his back, as if a spigot there had been turned. Then the noise of fountains came from the crowns of all the tall trees. Why did he love storms, what was the meaning of his excitement when the door sprang open and the rain wind fled rudely up the stairs, why had the simple task of shutting the windows of an old house seemed fitting and urgent, why did the first watery notes of a storm wind have for him the unmistakable sound of good news, cheer, glad tidings? Then there was an explosion, a smell of cordite, and rain lashed the

Japanese lanterns that Mrs. Levy had bought in Kyoto[6] the year before last, or was it the year before that?

He stayed in the Levys' gazebo until the storm had passed. The rain had cooled the air and he shivered. The force of the wind had stripped a maple of its red and yellow leaves and scattered them over the grass and the water. Since it was midsummer the tree must be blighted, and yet he felt a peculiar sadness at this sign of autumn. He braced his shoulders, emptied his glass, and started for the Welchers' pool. This meant crossing the Lindleys' riding ring and he was surprised to find it overgrown with grass and all the jumps dismantled. He wondered if the Lindleys had sold their horses or gone away for the summer and put them out to board. He seemed to remember having heard something about the Lindleys and their horses but the memory was unclear. On he went, barefoot through the wet grass, to the Welchers', where he found their pool was dry.

This breach in his chain of water disappointed him absurdly, and he felt like some explorer who seeks a torrential headwater and finds a dead stream. He was disappointed and mystified. It was common enough to go away for the summer but no one ever drained his pool. The Welchers had definitely gone away. The pool furniture was folded, stacked, and covered with a tarpaulin. The bathhouse was locked. All the windows of the house were shut, and when he went around to the driveway in front he saw a FOR SALE sign nailed to a tree. When had he last heard from the Welchers—when, that is, had he and Lucinda last regretted an invitation to dine with them? It seemed only a week or so ago. Was his memory failing or had he so disciplined it in the repression of unpleasant facts that he had damaged his sense of the truth? Then in the distance he heard the sound of a tennis game. This cheered him, cleared away all his apprehensions and let him regard the overcast sky and the cold air with indifference. This was the day that Neddy Merrill swam across the county. That was the day! He started off then for his most difficult portage.

Had you gone for a Sunday afternoon ride that day you might have seen him, close to naked, standing on the shoulders of Route 424, waiting for a chance to cross. You might have wondered if he was the victim of foul play, had his car broken down, or was he merely a fool. Standing barefoot in the deposits of the highway—beer cans, rags, and blowout patches—exposed to all kinds of ridicule, he seemed pitiful. He had known when he started that this was a part of his journey —it had been on his maps—but confronted with the lines of traffic, worming through the summery light, he found himself unprepared. He was laughed at, jeered at, a beer can was thrown at him, and he had no dignity or humor to bring to the situation. He could have gone back, back to the Westerhazys', where Lucinda would still be sitting in the sun. He had signed nothing, vowed nothing, pledged nothing, not even to himself. Why, believing as he did, that all human obduracy was susceptible to common sense, was he unable to turn back? Why was he determined to complete his journey even if it meant putting his life in danger? At what point had this prank, this joke, this piece of horseplay become serious? He could not go back, he could not even recall with any clearness the green water

281

at the Westerhazys', the sense of inhaling the day's components, the friendly and relaxed voices saying that they had *drunk* too much. In the space of an hour, more or less, he had covered a distance that made his return impossible.

An old man, tooling down the highway at fifteen miles an hour, let him get to the middle of the road, where there was a grass divider. Here he was exposed to the ridicule of the northbound traffic, but after ten or fifteen minutes he was able to cross. From here he had only a short walk to the Recreation Center at the edge of the village of Lancaster, where there were some handball courts and a public pool.

The effect of the water on voices, the illusion of brilliance and suspense, was the same here as it had been at the Bunkers' but the sounds here were louder, harsher, and more shrill, and as soon as he entered the crowded enclosure he was confronted with regimentation. "ALL SWIMMERS MUST TAKE A SHOWER BEFORE USING THE POOL. ALL SWIMMERS MUST USE THE FOOTBATH. ALL SWIMMERS MUST WEAR THEIR IDENTIFICATION DISKS." He took a shower, washed his feet in a cloudy and bitter solution, and made his way to the edge of the water. It stank of chlorine and looked to him like a sink. A pair of lifeguards in a pair of towers blew police whistles at what seemed to be regular intervals and abused the swimmers through a public address system. Neddy remembered the sapphire water at the Bunkers' with longing and thought that he might contaminate himself—damage his own prosperousness and charm—by swimming in this murk, but he reminded himself that he was an explorer, a pilgrim, and that this was merely a stagnant bend in the Lucinda River. He dove, scowling with distaste, into the chlorine and had to swim with his head above water to avoid collisions, but even so he was bumped into, splashed, and jostled. When he got to the shallow end both lifeguards were shouting at him: "Hey, you, you without the identification disk, get outa the water." He did, but they had no way of pursuing him and he went through the reek of suntan oil and chlorine out through the hurricane fence and passed the handball courts. By crossing the road he entered the wooded part of the Halloran estate. The woods were not cleared and the footing was treacherous and difficult until he reached the lawn and the clipped beech hedge that encircled their pool.

The Hallorans were friends, an elderly couple of enormous wealth who seemed to bask in the suspicion that they might be Communists. They were zealous reformers but they were not Communists, and yet when they were accused, as they sometimes were, of subversion, it seemed to gratify and excite them. Their beech hedge was yellow and he guessed this had been blighted like the Levys' maple. He called hullo, hullo, to warn the Hallorans of his approach, to palliate his invasion of their privacy. The Hallorans, for reasons that had never been explained to him, did not wear bathing suits. No explanations were in order, really. Their nakedness was a detail in their uncompromising zeal for reform and he stepped politely out of his trunks before he went through the opening in the hedge.

Mrs. Halloran, a stout woman with white hair and a serene face, was reading the *Times*. Mr. Halloran was taking beech leaves out of the water with a scoop. They seemed not surprised or displeased to see him. Their pool was perhaps the oldest in the country, a fieldstone rectangle, fed by a brook. It had no filter or pump and its waters were the opaque gold of the stream.

"I'm swimming across the county," Ned said.

"Why, I didn't know one could," exclaimed Mrs. Halloran.

"Well, I've made it from the Westerhazys'," Ned said. "That must be about four miles."

He left his trunks at the deep end, walked to the shallow end, and swam this stretch. As he was pulling himself out of the water he heard Mrs. Halloran say, "We've been *terribly* sorry to hear about all your misfortunes, Neddy."

"My misfortunes?" Ned asked. "I don't know what you mean."

"Why, we heard that you'd sold the house and that your poor children . . ."

"I don't recall having sold the house," Ned said, "and the girls are at home."

"Yes," Mrs. Halloran sighed. "Yes . . ." Her voice filled the air with an unseasonable melancholy and Ned spoke briskly. "Thank you for the swim."

"Well, have a nice trip," said Mrs. Halloran.

Beyond the hedge he pulled on his trunks and fastened them. They were loose and he wondered if, during the space of an afternoon, he could have lost some weight. He was cold and he was tired and the naked Hallorans and their dark water had depressed him. The swim was too much for his strength but how could he have guessed this, sliding down the banister that morning and sitting in the Westerhazys' sun? His arms were lame. His legs felt rubbery and ached at the joints. The worst of it was the cold in his bones and the feeling that he might never be warm again. Leaves were falling down around him and he smelled wood smoke on the wind. Who would be burning wood at this time of year?

He needed a drink. Whiskey would warm him, pick him up, carry him through the last of his journey, refresh his feeling that it was original and valorous to swim across the county. Channel swimmers took brandy. He needed a stimulant. He crossed the lawn in front of the Hallorans' house and went down a little path to where they had built a house for their only daughter, Helen, and her husband, Eric Sachs. The Sachses' pool was small and he found Helen and her husband there.

"Oh, *Neddy*," Helen said. "Did you lunch at Mother's?"

"Not *really*," Ned said. "I *did* stop to see your parents." This seemed to be explanation enough. "I'm terribly sorry to break in on you like this but I've taken a chill and I wonder if you'd give me a drink."

"Why, I'd *love* to," Helen said, "but there hasn't been anything in this house to drink since Eric's operation. That was three years ago."

Was he losing his memory, had his gift for concealing painful facts let him forget that he had sold his house, that his children were in trouble, and that his friend had been ill? His eyes slipped from Eric's face to his abdomen, where he saw three pale, sutured scars, two of them at least a foot long. Gone was his navel, and what, Neddy thought, would the roving hand, bed-checking one's gifts at 3 A.M., make of a belly with no navel, no link to birth, this breach in the succession?

"I'm sure you can get a drink at the Biswangers'," Helen said. "They're having an enormous do. You can hear it from here. Listen!"

She raised her head and from across the road, the lawns, the gardens, the woods, the fields, he heard again the brilliant noise of voices over water. "Well, I'll get wet," he said, still feeling that he had no freedom of choice about his means of travel. He dove into the Sachses' cold water and, gasping, close to drowning, made his way from one end of the pool to the other. "Lucinda and I want *terribly* to see you," he said over his shoulder, his face set toward the Biswangers'. "We're sorry it's been so long and we'll call you *very* soon."

He crossed some fields to the Biswangers' and the sounds of revelry there. They would be honored to give him a drink, they would be happy to give him a drink. The Biswangers invited him and Lucinda for dinner four times a year, six weeks in advance. They were always rebuffed and yet they continued to send out their invitations, unwilling to comprehend the rigid and undemocratic realities of their society. They were the sort of people who discussed the price of things at cocktails, exchanged market tips during dinner, and after dinner told dirty stories to mixed company. They did not belong to Neddy's set—they were not even on Lucinda's Christmas-card list. He went toward their pool with feelings of indifference, charity, and some unease, since it seemed to be getting dark and these were the longest days of the year. The party when he joined it was noisy and large. Grace Biswanger was the kind of hostess who asked the optometrist, the veterinarian, the real-estate dealer, and the dentist. No one was swimming and the twilight, reflected on the water of the pool, had a wintry gleam. There was a bar and he started for this. When Grace Biswanger saw him she came toward him, not affectionately as he had every right to expect, but bellicosely.

"Why, this party has everything," she said loudly, "including a gate crasher."

She could not deal him a social blow—there was no question about this and he did not flinch. "As a gate crasher," he asked politely, "do I rate a drink?"

"Suit yourself," she said. "You don't seem to pay much attention to invitations."

She turned her back on him and joined some guests, and he went to the bar and ordered a whiskey. The bartender served him but he served him rudely. His was a world in which the caterer's men kept the social score, and to be rebuffed by a part-time barkeep meant that he had suffered some loss of social esteem. Or perhaps the man was new and uninformed. Then he heard Grace at his back say: "They went for broke overnight—nothing but income—and he showed up drunk one Sunday and asked us to loan him five thousand dollars. . . ." She was always talking about money. It was worse than eating your peas off a knife. He dove into the pool, swam its length and went away.

The next pool on his list, the last but two, belonged to his old mistress, Shirley Adams. If he had suffered any injuries at the Biswangers' they would be cured here. Love—sexual roughhouse in fact—was the supreme elixir, the pain killer, the brightly colored pill that would put the spring back into his step, the joy of life in his heart. They had had an affair last week, last month, last year. He couldn't remember. It was he who had broken it off, his was the upper hand, and he stepped through the gate of the wall that surrounded her pool with nothing so considered as self-confidence. It seemed in a way to be his pool, as the lover, particularly the illicit lover, enjoys the possessions of his mistress with an authority unknown to holy matrimony. She was there, her hair the color of brass, but her figure, at the edge of the lighted, cerulean water, excited in him no profound memories. It had been, he thought, a light-hearted affair, although she had wept when he broke it off. She seemed confused to see him and he wondered if she was still wounded. Would she, God forbid, weep again?

"What do you want?" she asked.

"I'm swimming across the county."

"Good Christ. Will you ever grow up?"

"What's the matter?"

"If you've come here for money," she said, "I won't give you another cent."

"You could give me a drink."

"I could but I won't. I'm not alone."

"Well, I'm on my way."

He dove in and swam the pool, but when he tried to haul himself up onto the curb he found that the strength in his arms and shoulders had gone, and he paddled to the ladder and climbed out. Looking over his shoulder he saw, in the lighted bathhouse, a young man. Going out onto the dark lawn he smelled chrysanthemums or marigolds—some stubborn autumnal fragrance—on the night air, strong as gas. Looking overhead he saw that the stars had come out, but why should he seem to see Andromeda, Cepheus, and Cassiopeia? What had become of the constellations of midsummer? He began to cry.

It was probably the first time in his adult life that he had ever cried, certainly the first time in his life that he had ever felt so miserable, cold, tired, and bewildered. He could not understand the rudeness of the caterer's barkeep or the rudeness of a mistress who had come to him on her knees and showered his trousers with tears. He had swum too long, he had been immersed too long, and his nose and his throat were sore from the water. What he needed then was a drink, some company, and some clean, dry clothes, and while he could have cut directly across the road to his home he went on to the Gilmartins' pool. Here, for the first time in his life, he did not dive but went down the steps into the icy water and swam a hobbled sidestroke that he might have learned as a youth. He staggered with fatigue on his way to the Clydes' and paddled the length of their pool, stopping again and again with his hand on the curb to rest. He climbed up the ladder and wondered if he had the strength to get home. He had done what he wanted, he had swum the county, but he was so stupefied with exhaustion that his triumph seemed vague. Stooped, holding on to the gateposts for support, he turned up the driveway of his own house.

The place was dark. Was it so late that they had all gone to bed? Had Lucinda stayed at the Westerhazys' for supper? Had the girls joined her there or gone someplace else? Hadn't they agreed, as they usually did on Sunday, to regret all their invitations and stay at home? He tried the garage doors to see what cars were in but the doors were locked and rust came off the handles onto his hands. Going toward the house, he saw that the force of the thunderstorm had knocked one of the rain gutters loose. It hung down over the front door like an umbrella rib, but

285

it could be fixed in the morning. The house was locked, and he thought that the stupid cook or the stupid maid must have locked the place up until he remembered that it had been some time since they had employed a maid or a cook. He shouted, pounded on the door, tried to force it with his shoulder, and then, looking in at the windows, saw that the place was empty.

[1] The room in the church where the priest dons his vestments before the service and where sacred vessels are kept; the sacristy.
[2] John James Audubon (1785–1851), American artist and naturalist. The Audubon Society is one of the oldest and largest conservation organizations in North America.
[3] The capital of Portugal.
[4] A city in New Jersey.
[5] An airplane designed by Sir Geoffrey de Haviland (1882–1965), British aircraft designer and manufacturer and pioneer in commercial jet and long-distance flight. The de Haviland bomber of World War II was one of his most famous planes.
[6] A city in Honshu province, Japan.

DISCUSSION TOPICS

1. How does your attitude toward Ned Merrill change as you read "The Swimmer"? Do you feel differently toward him at different points in the story? How does Cheever influence your reactions?
2. When do you first suspect that Ned Merrill's version of his own life differs significantly from the versions of those around him?
3. What do you think are the central themes of "The Swimmer"? How does Cheever use the characters and the setting of the story to present these themes?
4. In many ways Ned Merrill is a victim of the American Dream or myth of success. What essential features of that dream are revealed in this story? What darker aspects of the American Dream does the story uncover?

WRITING TOPICS

1. Using the evidence presented in the story, construct your own portrait of Ned Merrill's life. Who is he? What kind of man, father, husband do you think he is?
2. Compare and contrast Cheever's Ned Merrill and Arthur Miller's Willy Loman (in *Death of a Salesman*) as casualties of the American Dream.

FLANNERY O'CONNOR (1925–1964) American short story writer, novelist. A native of Georgia and a devout Catholic, O'Connor is known for her stark and often grotesque stories of the struggle of the human spirit in a violent, secular environment. Her *Complete Stories* (1971) won the National Book Award (posthumously).

286

THE LIFE YOU SAVE MAY BE YOUR OWN

The old woman and her daughter were sitting on their porch when Mr. Shiftlet came up their road for the first time. The old woman slid to the edge of her chair and leaned forward, shading her eyes from the piercing sunset with her hand. The daughter could not see far in front of her and continued to play with her fingers. Although the old woman lived in this desolate spot with only her daughter and she had never seen Mr. Shiftlet before, she could tell, even from a distance, that he was a tramp and no one to be afraid of. His left coat sleeve was folded up to show there was only half an arm in it and his gaunt figure listed slightly to the side as if the breeze were pushing him. He had on a black town suit and a brown felt hat that was turned up in the front and down in the back and he carried a tin tool box by a handle. He came on, at an amble, up her road, his face turned toward the sun which appeared to be balancing itself on the peak of a small mountain.

The old woman didn't change her position until he was almost into her yard; then she rose with one hand fisted on her hip. The daughter, a large girl in a short blue organdy dress, saw him all at once and jumped up and began to stamp and point and make excited speechless sounds.

Mr. Shiftlet stopped just inside the yard and set his box on the ground and tipped his hat at her as if she were not in the least afflicted; then he turned toward the old woman and swung the hat all the way off. He had long black slick hair that hung flat from a part in the middle to beyond the tips of his ears on either side. His face descended in forehead for more than half its length and ended suddenly with his features just balanced over a jutting steeltrap jaw. He seemed to be a young man but he had a look of composed dissatisfaction as if he understood life thoroughly.

"Good evening," the old woman said. She was about the size of a cedar fence post and she had a man's gray hat pulled down low over her head.

The tramp stood looking at her and didn't answer. He turned his back and faced the sunset. He swung both his whole and his short arm up slowly so that they indicated an expanse of sky and his figure formed a crooked cross. The old woman watched him with her arms folded across her chest as if she were the owner of the sun, and the daughter watched, her head thrust forward and her fat helpless hands hanging at the wrists. She had long pink-gold hair and eyes as blue as a peacock's neck.

He held the pose for almost fifty seconds and then he picked up his box and came on to the porch and dropped down on the bottom step. "Lady," he said in a firm nasal voice, "I'd give a fortune to live where I could see me a sun do that every evening."

"Does it every evening," the old woman said and sat back down. The daughter sat down too and watched him with a cautious sly look as if he were a bird that had come up very close. He leaned to one side, rooting in his pants pocket, and in a second he brought out a package of chewing gum and offered her a piece. She took it and unpeeled it and began to chew without taking her eyes

287

off him. He offered the old woman a piece but she only raised her upper lip to indicate she had no teeth.

Mr. Shiftlet's pale sharp glance had already passed over everything in the yard—the pump near the corner of the house and the big fig tree that three or four chickens were preparing to roost in—and had moved to a shed where he saw the square rusted back of an automobile. "You ladies drive?" he asked.

"That car ain't run in fifteen year," the old woman said. "The day my husband died, it quit running."

"Nothing is like it used to be, lady," he said. "The world is almost rotten."

"That's right," the old woman said. "You from around here?"

"Name Tom T. Shiftlet," he murmured, looking at the tires.

"I'm pleased to meet you," the old woman said. "Name Lucynell Crater and daughter Lucynell Crater. What you doing around here, Mr. Shiftlet?"

He judged the car to be about a 1928 or '29 Ford. "Lady," he said, and turned and gave her his full attention, "lemme tell you something. There's one of these doctors in Atlanta that's taken a knife and cut the human heart—the human heart," he repeated, leaning forward, "out of a man's chest and held it in his hand," and he held his hand out, palm up, as if it were slightly weighted with the human heart, "and studied it like it was a day-old chicken, and lady," he said, allowing a long significant pause in which his head slid forward and his clay-colored eyes brightened, "he don't know no more about it than you or me."

"That's right," the old woman said.

"Why, if he was to take that knife and cut into every corner of it, he still wouldn't know no more than you or me. What you want to bet?"

"Nothing," the old woman said wisely. "Where you come from, Mr. Shiftlet?"

He didn't answer. He reached into his pocket and brought out a sack of tobacco and a package of cigarette papers and rolled himself a cigarette, expertly with one hand, and attached it in a hanging position to his upper lip. Then he took a box of wooden matches from his pocket and struck one on his shoe. He held the burning match as if he were studying the mystery of flame while it traveled dangerously toward his skin. The daughter began to make loud noises and to point to his hand and shake her finger at him, but when the flame was just before touching him, he leaned down with his hand cupped over it as if he were going to set fire to his nose and lit the cigarette.

He flipped away the dead match and blew a stream of gray into the evening. A sly look came over his face. "Lady," he said, "nowadays, people'll do anything anyways. I can tell you my name is Tom T. Shiftlet and I come from Tarwater, Tennessee, but you never have seen me before: how you know I ain't lying? How you know my name ain't Aaron Sparks, lady, and I come from Singleberry, Georgia, or how you know it's not George Speeds and I come from Lucy, Alabama, or how you know I ain't Thompson Bright from Toolafalls, Mississippi?"

"I don't know nothing about you," the old woman muttered, irked.

"Lady," he said, "people don't care how they lie. Maybe the best I can tell you is, I'm a man; but listen lady," he said and paused and made his tone more ominous still, "what is a man?"

The old woman began to gum a seed. "What you carry in that tin box, Mr. Shiftlet?" she asked.

"Tools," he said, put back. "I'm a carpenter."

"Well, if you come out here to work, I'll be able to feed you and give you a place to sleep but I can't pay. I'll tell you that before you begin," she said.

There was no answer at once and no particular expression on his face. He leaned back against the two-by-four that helped support the porch roof. "Lady," he said slowly, "there's some men that some things mean more to them than money." The old woman rocked without comment and the daughter watched the trigger that moved up and down in his neck. He told the old woman then that all most people were interested in was money, but he asked what a man was made for. He asked her if a man was made for money, or what. He asked her what she thought she was made for but she didn't answer, she only sat rocking and wondered if a one-armed man could put a new roof on her garden house. He asked a lot of questions that she didn't answer. He told her that he was twenty-eight years old and had lived a varied life. He had been a gospel singer, a foreman on the railroad, an assistant in an undertaking parlor, and he come over the radio for three months with Uncle Roy and his Red Creek Wranglers. He said he had fought and bled in the Arm Service of his country and visited every foreign land and that everywhere he had seen people that didn't care if they did a thing one way or another. He said he hadn't been raised thataway.

A fat yellow moon appeared in the branches of the fig tree as if it were going to roost there with the chickens. He said that a man had to escape to the country to see the world whole and that he wished he lived in a desolate place like this where he could see the sun go down every evening like God made it to do.

"Are you married or are you single?" the old woman asked.

There was a long silence. "Lady," he asked finally, "where would you find you an innocent woman today? I wouldn't have any of this trash I could just pick up."

The daughter was leaning very far down, hanging her head almost between her knees watching him through a triangular door she had made in her overturned hair; and she suddenly fell in a heap on the floor and began to whimper. Mr. Shiftlet straightened her out and helped her get back in the chair.

"Is she your baby girl?" he asked.

"My only," the old woman said "and she's the sweetest girl in the world. I would give her up for nothing on earth. She's smart too. She can sweep the floor, cook, wash, feed the chickens, and hoe. I wouldn't give her up for a casket of jewels."

"No," he said kindly, "don't ever let any man take her away from you."

"Any man come after her," the old woman said, " 'll have to stay around the place."

Mr. Shiftlet's eye in the darkness was focused on a part of the automobile bumper that glittered in the distance. "Lady," he said, jerking his short arm up as if he could point with it to her house and yard and pump, "there ain't a broken thing on this plantation that I couldn't fix for you, one-arm jackleg or not. I'm a man," he said with a sullen dignity, "even if I ain't a whole one. I got," he said, tapping his knuckles on the floor to emphasize the immensity of what he was going to say, "a moral intelligence!" and his face pierced out of the darkness into a shaft of doorlight and he stared at her as if he were astonished himself at this impossible truth.

The old woman was not impressed with the phrase. "I told you you could hang around and work for food," she said, "if you don't mind sleeping in that car yonder."

"Why listen, lady," he said with a grin of delight, "the monks of old slept in their coffins!"

"They wasn't as advanced as we are," the old woman said.

The next morning he began on the roof of the garden house while Lucynell, the daughter, sat on a rock and watched him work. He had not been around a week before the change he had made in the place was apparent. He had patched the front and back steps, built a new hog pen, restored a fence, and taught Lucynell, who was completely deaf and had never said a word in her life, to say the word "bird." The big rosy-faced girl followed him everywhere, saying "Burrttddt ddbirrrttdt," and clapping her hands. The old woman watched from a distance, secretly pleased. She was ravenous for a son-in-law.

Mr. Shiftlet slept on the hard narrow back seat of the car with his feet out the side window. He had his razor and a can of water on a crate that served him as a bedside table and he put up a piece of mirror against the back glass and kept his coat neatly on a hanger that he hung over one of the windows.

In the evenings he sat on the steps and talked while the old woman and Lucynell rocked violently in their chairs on either side of him. The old woman's three mountains were black against the dark blue sky and were visited off and on by various planets and by the moon after it had left the chickens. Mr. Shiftlet pointed out that the reason he had improved this plantation was because he had taken a personal interest in it. He said he was even going to make the automobile run.

He had raised the hood and studied the mechanism and he said he could tell that the car had been built in the days when cars were really built. You take now, he said, one man puts in one bolt and another man puts in another bolt and another man puts in another bolt so that it's a man for a bolt. That's why you have to pay so much for a car: you're paying all those men. Now if you didn't have to pay but one man, you could get you a cheaper car and one that had had a personal interest taken in it, and it would be a better car. The old woman agreed with him that this was so.

Mr. Shiftlet said that the trouble with the world was that nobody cared, or stopped and took any trouble. He said he never would have been able to teach Lucynell to say a word if he hadn't cared and stopped long enough.

"Teach her to say something else," the old woman said.

"What you want her to say next?" Mr. Shiftlet asked.

The old woman's smile was broad and toothless and suggestive. "Teach her to say 'sugarpie,'" she said.

Mr. Shiftlet already knew what was on her mind.

The next day he began to tinker with the automobile and that evening he told her that if she would buy a fan belt, he would be able to make the car run.

The old woman said she would give him the money. "You see that girl yonder?" she asked, pointing to Lucynell who was sitting on the floor a foot away, watching him, her eyes blue even in the dark. "If it was ever a man wanted to take her away, I would say, 'No man on earth is going to take that sweet girl of mine away from me!' but if he was to say, 'Lady, I don't want to take her away, I want her right here,' I would say, 'Mister, I don't blame you none. I wouldn't pass up a chance to live in a permanent place and get the sweetest girl in the world myself. You ain't no fool,' I would say."

"How old is she?" Mr. Shiftlet asked casually.

"Fifteen, sixteen," the old woman said. The girl was nearly thirty but because of her innocence it was impossible to guess.

"It would be a good idea to paint it too," Mr. Shiftlet remarked. "You don't want it to rust out."

"We'll see about that later," the old woman said.

The next day he walked into town and returned with the parts he needed and a can of gasoline. Late in the afternoon, terrible noises issued from the shed and the old woman rushed out of the house, thinking Lucynell was somewhere having a fit. Lucynell was sitting on a chicken crate, stamping her feet and screaming, "Burrddttt! bddurrddtttt!" but her fuss was drowned out by the car. With a volley of blasts it emerged from the shed, moving in a fierce and stately way. Mr. Shiftlet was in the driver's seat, sitting very erect. He had an expression of serious modesty on his face as if he had just raised the dead.

That night, rocking on the porch, the old woman began her business, at once. "You want you an innocent woman, don't you?" she asked sympathetically. "You don't want none of this trash."

"No'm, I don't," Mr. Shiftlet said.

"One that can't talk," she continued, "can't sass you back or use foul language. That's the kind for you to have. Right there," and she pointed to Lucynell sitting cross-legged in her chair, holding both feet in her hands.

"That's right," he admitted. "She wouldn't give me any trouble."

"Saturday," the old woman said, "you and her and me can drive into town and get married."

Mr. Shiftlet eased his position on the steps.

"I can't get married right now," he said. "Everything you want to do takes money and I ain't got any."

"What you need with money?" she asked.

"It takes money," he said. "Some people'll do anything anyhow these days, but the way I think, I wouldn't marry no woman that I couldn't take on a trip like she was somebody. I mean take her to a hotel and treat her. I wouldn't marry the Duchesser Windsor[1]," he said firmly, "unless I could take her to a hotel and giver something good to eat.

"I was raised thataway and there ain't a thing I can do about it. My old mother taught me how to do."

"Lucynell don't even know what a hotel is," the old woman muttered. "Listen here, Mr. Shiftlet," she said, sliding forward in her chair, "You'd be getting a permanent house and a deep well and the most innocent girl in the world. You don't need no money. Lemme tell you something: there ain't anyplace in the world for a poor disabled friendless drifting man."

The ugly words settled in Mr. Shiftlet's head like a group of buzzards in the top of a tree. He didn't answer at once. He rolled himself a cigarette and lit it and then he said in an even voice, "Lady, a man is divided into two parts, body and spirit."

The old woman clamped her gums together.

"A body and a spirit," he repeated. "The body, lady, is like a house: it don't go anywhere; but the spirit, lady, is like a automobile: always on the move, always . . ."

"Listen, Mr. Shiftlet," she said, "my well never goes dry and my house is always warm in the winter and there's no mortgage on a thing about this place. You can go to the courthouse and see for yourself. And yonder under that shed is a fine automobile." She laid the bait carefully. "You can have it painted by Saturday. I'll pay for the paint."

In the darkness, Mr. Shiftlet's smile stretched like a weary snake waking up by a fire. After a second he recalled himself and said, "I'm only saying a man's spirit means more to him than anything else. I would have to take my wife off for the weekend without no regards at all for cost. I got to follow where my spirit says to go."

"I'll give you fifteen dollars for a weekend trip," the old woman said in a crabbed voice. "That's the best I can do."

"That wouldn't hardly pay for more than the gas and the hotel," he said. "It wouldn't feed her."

"Seventeen-fifty," the old woman said. "That's all I got so it isn't any use you trying to milk me. You can take a lunch."

Mr. Shiftlet was deeply hurt by the word "milk." He didn't doubt that she had more money sewed up in her mattress but he had already told her he was not interested in her money. "I'll make that do," he said and rose and walked off without treating with her further.

On Saturday the three of them drove into town in the car that the paint had barely dried on and Mr. Shiftlet and Lucynell were married in the Ordinary's office while the old woman witnessed. As they came out of the courthouse, Mr. Shiftlet began twisting his neck in his collar. He looked morose and bitter as if he had been insulted while someone held him. "That didn't satisfy me none," he said. "That was just something a woman in an office did, nothing but paper work and blood tests. What do they know about my blood? If they was to take my heart and cut it out," he said, "they wouldn't know a thing about me. It didn't satisfy me at all."

"It satisfied the law," the old woman said sharply.

"The law," Mr. Shiftlet said and spit. "It's the law that don't satisfy me."

He had painted the car dark green with a yellow band around it just under the windows. The three of them climbed in the front seat and the old woman said, "Don't Lucynell look pretty? Looks like a baby doll." Lucynell was dressed up in a white dress that her mother had uprooted from a trunk and there was a Panama hat on her head with a bunch of red wooden cherries on the brim. Every now and then her placid expression was changed by a sly isolated little thought like a shoot of green in the desert. "You got a prize!" the old woman said.

Mr. Shiftlet didn't even look at her.

They drove back to the house to let the old woman off and pick up the lunch. When they were ready to leave, she stood staring in the window of the car, with her fingers clenched around the glass. Tears began to seep sideways out of her eyes and run along the dirty creases in her face. "I ain't ever been parted with her for two days before," she said.

Mr. Shiftlet started the motor.

"And I wouldn't let no man have her but you because I seen you would do right. Good-by, Sugarbaby," she said, clutching at the sleeve of the white dress. Lucynell looked straight at her and didn't seem to see her there at all. Mr. Shiftlet eased the car forward so that she had to move her hands.

The early afternoon was clear and open and surrounded by pale blue sky. Although the car would go only thirty miles an hour, Mr. Shiftlet imagined a terrific climb and dip and swerve that went entirely to his head so that he forgot his morning bitterness. He had always wanted an automobile but he had never been able to afford one before. He drove very fast because he wanted to make Mobile by nightfall.

Occasionally he stopped his thoughts long enough to look at Lucynell in the seat beside him. She had eaten the lunch as soon as they were out of the yard and now she was pulling the cherries off the hat one by one and throwing them out the window. He became depressed in spite of the car. He had driven about a hundred miles when he decided that she must be hungry again and at the next small town they came to, he stopped in front of an aluminum-painted eating place called The Hot Spot and took her in and ordered her a plate of ham and grits. The ride had made her sleepy and as soon as she got up on the stool, she rested her head on the counter and shut her eyes. There was no one in The Hot Spot but Mr. Shiftlet and the boy behind the counter, a pale youth with a greasy rag hung over his shoulder. Before he could dish up the food, she was snoring gently.

"Give it to her when she wakes up," Mr. Shiftlet said. "I'll pay for it now."

The boy bent over her and stared at the long pink-gold hair and the half-shut sleeping eyes. Then he looked up and stared at Mr. Shiftlet. "She looks like an angel of Gawd," he murmured.

"Hitchhiker," Mr. Shiftlet explained. "I can't wait. I got to make Tuscaloosa."

The boy bent over again and very carefully touched his finger to a strand of the golden hair and Mr. Shiftlet left.

He was more depressed than ever as he drove on by himself. The late afternoon had grown hot and sultry and the country had flattened out. Deep in the sky a storm was preparing very slowly and without thunder as if it meant to drain every drop of air from the earth before it broke. There were times when Mr. Shiftlet preferred not to be alone. He felt too that a man with a car had a responsibility to others and he kept his eye out for a hitchhiker. Occasionally he saw a sign that warned: "Drive carefully. The life you save may be your own."

The narrow road dropped off on either side into dry fields and here and there a shack or a filling station stood in a clearing. The sun began to set directly in front of the automobile. It was a reddening ball that through his windshield was slightly flat on the bottom and top. He saw a boy in overalls and a gray hat standing on the edge of the road and he slowed the car down and stopped in front of him. The boy didn't have his hand raised to thumb the ride, he was only standing there, but he had a small cardboard suitcase and his hat was set on his head in a way to indicate that he had left somewhere for good. "Son," Mr. Shiftlet said, "I see you want a ride."

The boy didn't say he did or he didn't but he opened the door of the car and got in, and Mr. Shiftlet started driving again. The child held the suitcase on his lap and folded his arms on top of it. He turned his head and looked out the window away from Mr. Shiftlet. Mr. Shiftlet felt oppressed. "Son," he said after a minute, "I got the best old mother in the world so I reckon you only got the second best."

The boy gave him a quick dark glance and then turned his face back out the window.

"It's nothing so sweet," Mr. Shiftlet continued, "as a boy's mother. She taught him his first prayers at her knee, she give him love when no other would, she told him what was right and what wasn't, and she seen that he done the right thing. Son," he said, "I never rued a day in my life like the one I rued when I left that old mother of mine."

The boy shifted in his seat but he didn't look at Mr. Shiftlet. He unfolded his arms and put one hand on the door handle.

"My mother was a angel of Gawd," Mr. Shiftlet said in a very strained voice. "He took her from heaven and giver to me and I left her." His eyes were instantly clouded over with a mist of tears. The car was barely moving.

The boy turned angrily in the seat. "You go to the devil!" he cried. "My old woman is a flea bag and yours is a stinking pole cat!" and with that he flung the door open and jumped out with his suitcase into the ditch.

Mr. Shiftlet was so shocked that for about a hundred feet he drove along slowly with the door still open. A cloud, the exact color of the boy's hat and shaped like a turnip, had descended over the sun, and another, worse looking, crouched behind the car. Mr. Shiftlet felt that the rottenness of the world was about to engulf him. He raised his arm and let it fall again to his breast. "Oh Lord!" he prayed. "Break forth and wash the slime from this earth!"

The turnip continued slowly to descend. After a few minutes there was a guffawing peal of thunder from behind and fantastic raindrops, like tin-can tops, crashed over the rear of Mr. Shiftlet's car. Very quickly he stepped on the gas and with his stump sticking out the window he raced the galloping shower into Mobile.

[1] Wallis Warfield Simpson (1896–   ), American divorcée for whom Edward VIII abdicated the British throne. He took the title Duke of Windsor. When he married Mrs. Simpson, she was thereafter known as the Duchess of Windsor, the leading figure of international high society.

DISCUSSION TOPICS

1. Tone and point of view are critically important in this story as devices to establish a relationship between the reader and the work. What is the tone—does it change perceptibly during the course of the narrative? What is the point of view—how does it change, especially near the end of the story? What effect is achieved by this change?
2. A confidence man ("con artist") is a "tempter" who offers something for nothing, or for very little. Tom T. Shiftlet is clearly a "con man." What meanings are suggested by his name "Shiftlet"? Why is he able to "con" old lady Crater?
3. There is considerable Christian symbolism and religious imagery in this story —and the style of Shiftlet's initial appeal to Mrs. Crater is reminiscent of a tent evangelist's. What other religious implication do you find in the story? What is the significance of the story's title?

WRITING TOPIC

Discuss the symbolic function of the automobile in O'Connor's story.

GABRIEL GARCÍA MÁRQUEZ (1928–   ) A Colombian writer, winner of the Nobel prize for literature, and (along with Jorge Luis Borges) a central figure in the South American literary renaissance. His masterpiece is the novel *One Hundred Years of Solitude* (1967, trans. 1970), which like the short story "A Very Old Man with Enormous Wings" combines straightforward, realistic narrative with elements of magic, supernaturalism, folklore, fairy tales, and moral allegory.

A VERY OLD MAN WITH ENORMOUS WINGS

A TALE FOR CHILDREN

Translated by Gregory Rabassa

On the third day of rain they had killed so many crabs inside the house that Pelayo had to cross his drenched courtyard and throw them into the sea, because the newborn child had a temperature all night and they thought it was due to the stench. The world had been sad since Tuesday. Sea and sky were a single ash-gray thing and the sands of the beach, which on March nights glimmered like powdered light, had become a stew of mud and rotten shellfish. The light was so weak at noon that when Pelayo was coming back to the house after throwing away the crabs, it was hard for him to see what it was that was moving and groaning in the rear of the courtyard. He had to go very close to see that it was an old man, a very old man, lying face down in the mud, who, in spite of his tremendous efforts, couldn't get up, impeded by his enormous wings.

Frightened by that nightmare, Pelayo ran to get Elisenda, his wife, who was putting compresses on the sick child, and he took her to the rear of the courtyard. They both looked at the fallen body with mute stupor. He was dressed like a ragpicker. There were only a few faded hairs left on his bald skull and very few teeth in his mouth, and his pitiful condition of a drenched great-grandfather had taken away any sense of grandeur he might have had. His huge buzzard wings, dirty and half-plucked, were forever entangled in the mud. They looked at him so long and so closely that Pelayo and Elisenda very soon overcame their surprise and in the end found him familiar. Then they dared speak to him, and he answered in an incomprehensible dialect with a strong sailor's voice. That was how they skipped over the inconvenience of the wings and quite intelligently concluded that he was a lonely castaway from some foreign ship wrecked by the storm. And yet, they called in a neighbor woman who knew everything about life and death to see him, and all she needed was one look to show them their mistake.

"He's an angel," she told them. "He must have been coming for the child, but the poor fellow is so old that the rain knocked him down."

On the following day everyone knew that a flesh-and-blood angel was held captive in Pelayo's house. Against the judgment of the wise neighbor woman, for whom angels in those times were the fugitive survivors of a celestial conspiracy, they did not have the heart to club him to death. Pelayo watched over him all afternoon from the kitchen, armed with his bailiff's club, and before going to bed he dragged him out of the mud and locked him up with the hens in the wire chicken coop. In the middle of the night, when the rain stopped, Pelayo and Elisenda were still killing crabs. A short time afterward the child woke up without a fever and with a desire to eat. Then they felt magnanimous and decided to put the angel on a raft with fresh water and provisions for three days and leave him to his fate on the high seas. But when they went out into the courtyard with the first light of dawn, they found the whole neighborhood in front of the chicken coop having fun with the angel, without the slightest reverence, tossing him things to eat through the openings in the wire as if he weren't a supernatural creature but a circus animal.

Father Gonzaga arrived before seven o'clock, alarmed at the strange news. By that time onlookers less frivolous than those at dawn had already arrived and they were making all kinds of conjectures concerning the captive's future. The simplest among them thought that he should be named mayor of the world. Others of sterner mind felt that he should be promoted to the rank of five-star general in order to win all wars. Some visionaries hoped that he could be put to stud in order to implant on earth a race of winged wise men who could take charge of the universe. But Father Gonzaga, before becoming a priest, had been a robust wood-cutter. Standing by the wire, he reviewed his catechism in an instant and asked them to open the door so that he could take a close look at that pitiful man who looked more like a huge decrepit hen among the fascinated chickens. He was lying in a corner drying his open wings in the sunlight among the fruit peels and breakfast leftovers that the early risers had thrown him. Alien to the impertinences of the world, he only lifted his antiquarian eyes and murmured something in his dialect when Father Gonzaga went into the chicken coop and said good morning to him in Latin. The parish priest had his first suspicion of an imposter when he saw that he did not understand the language of God or know how to greet His ministers. Then he noticed that seen close up he was much too human: he had an unbearable smell of the outdoors, the back side of his wings was strewn with parasites and his main feathers had been mistreated by terrestrial winds, and nothing about him measured up to the proud dignity of angels. Then he came out of the chicken coop and in a brief sermon warned the curious against the risks of being ingenuous. He reminded them that the devil had the bad habit of making use of carnival tricks in order to confuse the unwary. He argued that if wings were not the essential element in determining the difference between a hawk and an airplane, they were even less so in the recognition of angels. Nevertheless, he promised to write a letter to his bishop so that the latter would write to his primate so that the latter would write to the Supreme Pontiff in order to get the final verdict from the highest courts.

His prudence fell on sterile hearts. The news of the captive angel spread with such rapidity that after a few hours the courtyard had the bustle of a marketplace and they had to call in troops with fixed bayonets to disperse the mob that was about to knock the house down. Elisenda, her spine all twisted from sweeping up so much marketplace trash, then got the idea of fencing in the yard and charging five cents admission to see the angel.

The curious came from far away. A traveling carnival arrived with a flying acrobat who buzzed over the crowd several times, but no one paid any attention to him because his wings were not those of an angel but, rather, those of a sidereal bat. The most unfortunate invalids on earth came in search of health: a poor woman who since childhood had been counting her heartbeats and had run out of num-bers; a Portuguese man who couldn't sleep because the noise of the stars disturbed him; a sleepwalker who got up tonight to undo the things he had done while awake; and many others with less serious ailments. In the midst of that shipwreck disorder that made the earth tremble, Pelayo and Elisenda were happy with fa-tigue, for in less than a week they had crammed their rooms with money and the line of pilgrims waiting their turn to enter still reached beyond the horizon.

The angel was the only one who took no part in his own act. He spent his time trying to get comfortable in his borrowed nest, befuddled by the hellish heat of the oil lamps and sacramental candles that had been placed along the wire. At first they tried to make him eat some mothballs, which, according to the wisdom of the wise neighbor woman, were the food prescribed for angels. But he turned them down, just as he turned down the papal lunches[1] that the penitents brought him, and they never found out whether it was because he was an angel or because he was an old man that in the end he ate nothing but eggplant mush. His only supernatural virtue seemed to be patience. Especially during the first days, when the hens pecked at him, searching for the stellar parasites that proliferated in his wings, and the cripples pulled out feathers to touch their defective parts with, and even the most merciful threw stones at him, trying to get him to rise so they could see him standing. The only time they succeeded in arousing him was when they burned his side with an iron for branding steers, for he had been motionless for so many hours that they thought he was dead. He awoke with a start, ranting in his hermetic language and with tears in his eyes, and he flapped his wings a couple of times, which brought on a whirlwind of chicken dung and lunar dust and a gale of panic that did not seem to be of this world. Although many thought that his reaction had been one not of rage but of pain, from then on they were careful not to annoy him, because the majority understood that his passivity was not that of a hero taking his ease but that of a cataclysm in repose.

Father Gonzaga held back the crowd's frivolity with formulas of maidservant inspiration while awaiting the arrival of a final judgment on the nature of the captive. But the mail from Rome showed no sense of urgency. They spent their time finding out if the prisoner had a naval, if his dialect had any connection with Aramaic, how many times he could fit on the head of a pin,[2] or whether he wasn't just a Norwegian with wings. Those meager letters might have come and gone until the end of time if a providential event had not put an end to the priest's tribulations.

It so happened that during those days, among so many other carnival attractions, there arrived in town the traveling show of the woman who had been changed into a spider for having disobeyed her parents. The admission to see her was not only less than the admission to see the angel, but people were permitted to ask her all manner of questions about her absurd state and to examine her up and down so that no one would ever doubt the truth of her horror. She was a frightful tarantula the size of a ram and with the head of a sad maiden. What was most heart-rending, however, was not her outlandish shape but the sincere affliction with which she recounted the details of her misfortune. While still practically a child she had sneaked out of her parents' house to go to a dance, and while she was coming back through the woods after having danced all night without permission, a fearful thunderclap rent the sky in two and through the crack came the lightning bolt of brimstone that changed her into a spider. Her only nourishment came from the meatballs that charitable souls chose to toss into her mouth. A spectacle like that, full of so much human truth and with such a fearful lesson, was bound to defeat without even trying that of a haughty angel who scarcely deigned to look at mortals. Besides, the few miracles attributed to the angel showed a certain mental disorder, like the blind man who didn't recover his sight but grew three new teeth, or the paralytic who didn't get to walk but almost won the lottery, and the leper whose sores sprouted sunflowers. Those consolation miracles, which were more like mocking fun, had already ruined the angel's reputation when the woman who had been changed into a spider finally crushed him completely. That was how Father Gonzaga was cured forever of his insomnia and Pelayo's courtyard went back to being as empty as during the time it had rained for three days and crabs walked through the bedrooms.

The owners of the house had no reason to lament. With the money they saved they built a two-story mansion with balconies and gardens and high netting so that crabs wouldn't get in during the winter, and with iron bars on the windows so that angels wouldn't get in. Pelayo also set up a rabbit warren close to town and gave up his job as bailiff for good, and Elisenda bought some satin pumps with high heels and many dresses of iridescent silk, the kind worn on Sunday by the most desirable women in those times. The chicken coop was the only thing that didn't receive any attention. If they washed it down with creolin[3] and burned tears of myrrh inside it every so often, it was not in homage to the angel but to drive away the dungheap stench that still hung everywhere like a ghost and was turning the new house into an old one. At first, when the child learned to walk, they were careful that he not get too close to the chicken coop. But then they began to lose their fears and got used to the smell, and before the child got his second teeth he'd gone inside the chicken coop to play, where the wires were falling apart. The angel was no less standoffish with him than with other mortals, but he tolerated the most ingenious infamies with the patience of a dog who had no illusions. They both came down with chicken pox at the same time. The doctor who took care of the child couldn't resist the temptation to listen to the angel's heart, and he found so much whistling in the heart and so many sounds in his kidneys that it seemed impossible for him to be alive. What surprised him most, however, was the logic of his wings. They seemed so natural on that completely human organism that he couldn't understand why other men didn't have them to.

When the child began school it had been some time since the sun and rain had caused the collapse of the chicken coop. The angel went dragging himself about here and there like a stray dying man. They would drive him out of the bedroom with a broom and a moment later find him in the kitchen. He seemed to be in so many places at the same time that they grew to think that he'd been duplicated, that he was reproducing himself all through the house, and the exasperated and unhinged Elisenda shouted that it was awful living in that hell full of angels. He could scarcely eat and his antiquarian eyes had also become so foggy that he went about bumping into posts. All he had left were the bare cannulae of his last feathers. Pelayo threw a blanket over him and extended him the charity of letting him sleep in the shed, and only then did they notice that he had a temperature at night, and was delirious with the tongue twisters of an old Norwegian. That was one of the few times they became alarmed, for they thought he was going to die and not even the wise neighbor woman had been able to tell them what to do with dead angels.

And yet he not only survived his worst winter, but seemed improved with the first sunny days. He remained motionless for several days in the farthest corner of the courtyard, where no one would see him, and at the beginning of December some large, stiff feathers began to grow on his wings, the feathers of a scarecrow, which looked more like another misfortune of decrepitude. But he must have known the reason for those changes, for he was quite careful that no one should notice them, that no one should hear the sea chanteys that he sometimes sang under the stars. One morning Elisenda was cutting some bunches of onions for lunch when a wind that seemed to come from the high seas blew into the kitchen. Then she went to the window and caught the angel in his first attempts at flight. They were so clumsy that his fingernails opened a furrow in the vegetable patch and he was on the point of knocking the shed down with the ungainly flapping that slipped on the light and couldn't get a grip on the air. But he did manage to gain altitude. Elisenda let out a sigh of relief, for herself and for him, when she saw him pass over the last houses, holding himself up in some way with the risky flapping of a senile vulture. She kept watching him even when she was through cutting the onions and she kept on watching until it was no longer possible for her to see him, because then he was no longer an annoyance in her life but an imaginary dot on the horizon of the sea.

---

[1] High-priced, gourmet meals.

[2] A subject on which the medieval Scholastics are said to have debated was how many angels could dance on the head of a pin.

[3] A disinfectant.

DISCUSSION TOPICS

1. What is your initial reaction to this story? García Márquez has called it "A Tale for Children." Do you think it is?
2. The juxtaposition of supernatural with realistic (even homely) details is sometimes referred to as magic realism. What examples of this technique can you find in the story? What effects does García Márquez achieve through his use of "magic realism"?
3. Do you think the old man is an angel?
4. What attitude toward religion does the story present?
5. Do you think this story is a moral allegory? (Compare Chaucer's "Pardoner's Tale.") If so, what is the moral or message? If not, what do you think García Márquez is doing?

SLAWOMIR MROZEK (1930–   ) Polish playwright and fabulist: "an Aesop for our times." He is a brilliant satirist whose works depict the universal absurdities of bureaucracy, pretension, hypocrisy. "Art" is taken from his collection of fables *The Elephant,* the first of Mrozek's works to appear in English.

ART

Translated by Konrad Syrop

"Art educates. That's why writers must know life. Proust[1] is the best example. He knew nothing about life. He cut himself off; he shut himself up in a cork-lined room. An extreme case. One can't write in cork-lined rooms. One can't hear anything. And what are you writing now?"

"It's a story for a competition. I've already worked out the idea. It's about a remote village which is changing very slowly and with difficulty. Little Johnny is a cowhand in the service of a rich peasant. While in the fields he suddenly hears the hum of engines. It's a steel bird, a plane. Johnny looks up and dreams of becoming a pilot. And then—oh wonder—the plane comes lower and lower and lands on the meadow. A figure clad in a flying suit and goggles jumps out of the cockpit. Johnny runs towards him as fast as his legs will go. The stranger smiles at the panting boy and enquires about the nearest smithy. Some small part needs repairing. Johnny brings help. When the repair is completed, the pilot thanks Johnny, and, noticing his eyes shining with curiosity and enthusiasm, says; 'You'd like to fly yourself, wouldn't you?' The boy, struck dumb by excitement, can only nod his head. The engine starts and soon the plane is flying over the meadow. The pilot leans from the cockpit and waves Johnny goodbye.

"Times passes. Johnny continues to look after the cows. But he can't forget the incident with the pilot. At last one day the postman approaches the cabin where Johnny lives with his widowed mother. From far away he's waving a white envelope and there is a smile on his face. An invitation to a school for airmen: the pilot hasn't forgotten his promise. Johnny is beside himself with joy.

"He goes to the city and joins the school. When he has finished his training he is given a plane. In a few seconds his steel bird is airborne. Johnny's mother comes out of the cabin and, shading her eyes with her hand, looks to the sky. Johnny circles the village and waves to his mother. His dream has come true."

"Yes, indeed. If the writer knows life, his work is often progressive, even though his own consciousness may lag behind. Balzac[2] is a typical example. He had a tendency to eulogize the aristocracy and the monarchy, but his realistic work points in the opposite direction. I think I've read your story in the last issue of——"

"Yes. 'Frank's Adventure.' That was commissioned. It was a question of illustrating a typical problem of psychology concerning the life of youth. A group of boys goes on an excursion. They sing as they march along. They all keep together, except Frank, who leaves the party surreptitiously. He rejects his colleagues and wants to cross the forest by himself. Soon he loses his way and falls into a pit. He tries to climb out, but he can't. In the end he cries for help. His colleagues come to the rescue and, amid jokes and jeers, extricate him from the pit. After this experience Frank never separates himself from his colleagues."

"Yes. Art has a noble task: to educate man. That's why the writer's part in our society is a most responsible one. The writers are the architects of human souls

301

and the critics are the architects of the writers' souls. Can you, by any chance, lend me five hundred zlotys?"

"I'm afraid that three hundred is all I can manage."

"All right, three hundred will do."

[1] Marcel Proust (1871–1922), French novelist.
[2] Honoré de Balzac (1799–1850), French novelist.

DISCUSSION TOPICS

1. What tone does the narrator use in Mrozek's story, and how does this tone influence your response to the tale?
2. Who is talking in the story? What is gained by the use of dialogue rather than conventional narrative?
3. What is the thematic purpose of the allusions to Proust and Balzac?
4. What clichés do you find in "Art"—in plot, situation, character, diction? What is the effect of these clichés?
5. What is the significance of the concluding dialogue about the loan?
6. Clearly, this story was written to satirize the official attitude toward art in a socialist or communist state. Is Mrozek's satire also relevant to our own society? Why—or why not?

BRUCE JAY FRIEDMAN (1930–   ) American novelist, short story writer. He is known for his biting wit, which is most often directed at various aspects of contemporary American life.

BLACK ANGELS

Smothered by debt, his wife and child in flight, Stefano held fast to his old house in the country, a life buoy in a sea of despair. Let him but keep up the house, return to it each day; before long, his wife would come to her senses, fly back to him. Yet he dreaded the approach of spring, which meant large teams of gardeners who would charge him killing prices to keep the place in shape. Cheapest of all had been the Angeluzzi Brothers who had gotten him off the ground with a two-hundred-and-fifty-dollar cleanup, then followed through with ninety dollars a month for maintenance. April through October, a hundred extra for the leaf-raking fall windup. Meticulous in April, the four Angeluzzis soon began to dog it; for his ninety, Stefano got only a few brisk lawn cuts and a swipe or two at his flower beds. This spring, unable to work, his life in shreds, Stefano held off on the grounds as

302

long as he could. The grass grew to his shins until one day Swansdowne, a next-door neighbor who had won marigold contests, called on another subject, but with much lawn-mowing and fertilizing in his voice. Stefano dialed the Angeluzzis; then, on an impulse, he dropped the phone and reached for the local paper, running his finger along Home Services. A gardener named Please Try Us caught his fancy. He called the number, asked the deep voice at the other end to come by soon and give him an estimate. The following night, a return call came through.

"I have seen and checked out the place," said the voice, the tones heavy, resonant, solid.

"What'll you take for cleanup?" asked Stefano. "We'll start there."

Long pause. Lip smack. Then, "Thutty dollars."

"Which address did you go to? I'm at 42 Spring. Big old place on the corner of Spring and Rooter."

"That's correct. For fertilizing, that'll be eight extra, making thutty-eight."

"Awful lot of work here," said Stefano, confused, tingling with both guilt and relief. "All right, when can you get at it?"

"Tomorrow morning. Eight o'clock."

"You're on."

Stefano watched them arrive the next day, Sunday, a quartet of massive Negroes in two trucks and two sleek private cars. In stifling heat, they worked in checkered shirts and heavy pants, two with fedoras impossibly balanced on the backs of their great shaved heads. Stefano, a free-lance writer of technical manuals, went back to his work, stopping now and then to check the Negroes through the window. How could they possibly make out on thirty-eight dollars, he wondered. Divided four ways it came to nothing. Gas alone for their fleet of cars would kill their nine-fifty each. He'd give them forty-five dollars to salve his conscience, but still, what about their groceries, rent? Late in the afternoon, he ran out with beers for each. "Plenty of leaves, eh?" he said to Cotten, largest of them, the leader, expressionless in dainty steel-rimmed glasses.

"Take about two and a half days," said the Negro.

"I'm giving you forty-five dollars," said Stefano. "What the hell."

The job actually took three full days, two for the cleanup, a third for the lawn and fertilizing the beds. The last day was a bad one for Stefano. Through his window, he watched the black giants trim the lawn, then kneel in winter clothes and lovingly collect what seemed to be each blade of grass so there'd be no mess. He wanted to run out and tell them to do less work, certainly not at those prices. Yet he loved the prices, too. He could take it all out of expense money, not even bother his regular free-lance payments. At the end of the day, he walked up to Cotten, took out his wallet and said, "I'm giving you cash. So you won't have to bother with a check." It had occurred to him that perhaps the Negroes only did cleanups, no maintenance. By doing enough of them, thousands, perhaps they could sneak by, somehow make a living. "What about maintenance?" he asked the head gardener.

The man scratched his ear, shook his head, finally said, "Can't do your place for less than eighteen dollars a month."

"You guys do some work," said Stefano, shivering with glee. "Best I've seen. I think you're too low. I'll give you twenty-two."

The Negroes came back twice a week, turned Stefano's home into a showplace, hacking down dead trees, planting new ones, filling in dead spots, keeping the earth black and loamy. Swansdowne, who usually let Stefano test-run new gardeners and then swooped down to sign them up if they were good, looked on with envy, yet called one day and said, "I would never let a colored guy touch my place."

"They're doing a great job on mine," said Stefano.

Maybe that explains it, he thought. All of the Swansdownes who won't have Negro gardeners. That's why their rates are low. Otherwise, they'd starve. He felt good, a liberal. Why shouldn't he get a slight break on money?

At the end of May, Stefano paid them their twenty-two dollars and distributed four American-cheese sandwiches. The three assistants took them back to a truck where one had mayonnaise. "You guys do other kinds of work?" Stefano asked Cotten, who leaned on a hoe. "What about painting? A house?"

The gardener looked up at Stefano's colonial. "We do," he said.

"How much would you take?" The best estimate on the massive ten-roomer had been seven hundred dollars.

"Fifty-eight dollars," said the huge Negro, neutral in his steelrims.

"I'll pay for half the paint," said Stefano.

The following day, when Stefano awakened, the four Negroes, on high, buckling ladders, had half the house done, the paint deep brown, rich and gurgling in the sun. Their gardening clothes were spattered with paint. He'd pick up the cleaning bill, thought Stefano. It was only fair.

"It looks great!" he hollered up to Cotten, swaying massively in the wind.

"She'll shape up time we get the fourth coat on."

By mid-June, the four Negroes had cleaned out Stefano's attic for three dollars, waterproofed his basement for another sixteen; an elaborate network of drainage pipes went in for twelve-fifty. One day he came home to find the floors cleaned, sanded, shellacked, his cabinets scrubbed, linen closets dizzying in their cleanliness. Irritated for the first time—I didn't order this—he melted quickly when he saw the bill. A slip on the bread box read: "You owes us $2.80." Loving the breaks he was getting, Stefano threw them bonuses, plenty of sandwiches, all his old sports jackets, venetian blinds that had come out of the attic and books of fairly recent vintage on Nova Scotia tourism. Never in the thick of marriage had his place been so immaculate; cars slowed down to admire his dramatically painted home, his shrubs bursting with fertility. Enter any room; its cleanliness would tear your head off. With all these ridiculously cheap home services going for him, Stefano felt at times his luck had turned. Still, a cloak of loneliness rode his shoulders, aggravation clogged his throat. If only to hate her, he missed his wife, a young, pretty woman, circling the globe with her lover, an assistant director on daytime TV. He saw pictures of her, tumbling with lust, in staterooms, inns, the backs of small foreign cars. He missed his son, too, a boy of ten, needing braces.

304

God only knows what shockers he was being exposed to. The pair had fled in haste, leaving behind mementos, toys lined up on shelves, dresses spilling out of chests. Aging quickly, his confidence riddled, Stefano failed in his quest for dates with young girls, speechless and uncertain on the phone. What could he do with himself. At these prices, he could keep his home spotless. But would that make everything all right. Would that haul back a disgruntled wife and son. One night, his heart weighing a ton, he returned from an "Over 28" dance to find the burly Negroes winding up their work. Sweating long into the night, they had rigged up an elaborate network of gas lamps, the better to show off a brilliantly laid out thicket of tea roses and dwarf fruit trees. Total cost for the lighting: Five dollars and fifty cents.

"Really lovely," said Stefano, inspecting his grounds, counting out some bills. "Here," he said to the head gardener. "Take another deuce. In my condition, money means nothing." The huge Negro toweled down his forehead, gathered up his equipment. "Hey," said Stefano. "Come on in for a beer. If I don't talk to someone I'll bust."

"Got to get on," said Cotten. "We got work to do."

"Come on, come on," said Stefano. "What can you do at this hour. Give a guy a break."

The Negro shook his head in doubt, then moved massively toward the house, Stefano clapping him on the back in a show of brotherhood.

Inside, Stefano went for flip-top beers. The gardener sat down in the living room, his great bulk caving deeply into the sofa. For a moment, Stefano worried about gardening clothes, Negro ones to boot, in contact with living-room furniture, then figured the hell with it, who'd complain.

"I've got the worst kind of trouble," said Stefano, leaning back on a Danish modern slat bench. "Sometimes I don't think I'm going to make it through the night. My wife's checked out on me. You probably figured that out already."

The Negro crossed his great legs, sipped his beer. The steel-rimmed glasses had a shimmer to them and Stefano could not make out his eyes.

"She took the kid with her," said Stefano. "That may be the worst part. You don't know what it's like to have a kid tearing around your house for ten years and then not to hear anything. Or maybe you do?" Stefano asked hopefully. "You probably have a lot of trouble of your own."

Silent, the Negro sat forward and shoved a cloth inside his flannel shirt to mop his chest.

"Anyway, I'll be goddamned if I know what to do. Wait around? Pretend she's never coming back? I don't know what in the hell to do with myself. Where do I go from here?"

"How long she gone?" asked the guest, working on the back of his neck now.

"What's that got to do with it?" asked Stefano. "About four months, I guess. Just before you guys came. Oh, I see what you mean. If she hasn't come back in four months, she's probably gone for good. I might as well start building a new life. That's a good point."

The Negro put away the cloth and folded his legs again, crossing his heavy, blunted fingers, arranging them on the point of one knee.

"It just happened out of the clear blue sky," said Stefano. "Oh, why kid around. It was never any good." He told the Negro about their courtship, the false pregnancy, how he had been "forced" to get married. Then he really started in on his wife, the constant primping, the thousands of ways she had made him jealous, the in-laws to support. He let it all come out of him, like air from a tire, talking with heat and fury; until he realized he had been talking nonstop for maybe twenty minutes, half an hour. The Negro listened to him, patiently, not bothering with his beer. Finally, when Stefano sank back to catch his breath, the gardener asked a question: "You think you any good?"

"What do you mean," said Stefano. "Of course I do. Oh, I get what you're driving at. If I thought I was worth anything, I wouldn't let all of this kill me. I'd just kind of brace myself, dig out and really build something fine for myself. Funny how you make just the right remark. It's really amazing. You know I've done the analysis bit. Never meant a damned thing to me. I've had nice analysts, tough ones, all kinds. But the way you just let me sound off and then asked that one thing. This is going to sound crazy, but what if we just talked this way, couple of times a week. I just sound off and then you come in with the haymaker, the way you just did. Just for fun, what would you charge me? An hour?"

"Fo' hundred," said the Negro.

"Four hundred. That's really a laugh. You must be out of your head. What are you, crazy? Don't you know I was just kidding around."

The Negro took a sip of the beer and rose to leave. "All right, wait a second," said Stefano. "Hold on a minute. Let's just finish up this hour, all right. Then we'll see about other times. This one doesn't count, does it?"

"It do," said the Negro, sinking into the couch and producing pad and pencil.

"That's not really fair, you know," said Stefano. "To count this one. Anyway, we'll see. Maybe we'll try it for awhile. That's some price. Where was I? Whew, all that money. To get back to what I was saying, this girl has been a bitch ever since the day I laid eyes on her. You made me see it tonight. In many ways, I think she's a lot like my mom. . . ."

DISCUSSION TOPICS

1. If humor is often used as a means of "unmasking," what is Bruce Jay Friedman unmasking in "Black Angels"?
2. One of the discussion topics for "The Secret Life of Walter Mitty" suggests that comedy often exploits stereotypes rather than archetypes. In "Black Angels" what stereotypes does Friedman rely on to set up his surprise ending?
3. What is the significance of the title?

HARLAN ELLISON (1934–   ) American short story writer, novelist, editor, screen-writer. Ellison writes in a highly personal literary language, richly allusive and charged with his own brand of myth and moral allegory. His characters are often Americans or recognizable American types living out on the frontiers of civilization and making a frontal attack on the established orders of the universe.

SHATTERDAY

i: Someday

Not much later but later nonetheless, he thought back on the sequence of what had happened, and knew he had missed nothing. How it had gone, was this:

He had been abstracted, thinking about something else. It didn't matter what. He had gone to the telephone in the restaurant, to call Jamie, to find out where the hell she was already, to find out why she'd kept him sitting in the bloody bar for thirty-five minutes. He had been thinking about something else, nothing deep, just woolgathering, and it wasn't till the number was ringing that he realized he'd dialed his own apartment. He had done it other times, not often, but as many as anyone else, dialed a number by rote and not thought about it, and occasionally it was his own number, everyone does it (he thought later), everyone does it, it's a simple mistake.

He was about to hang up, get back his dime and dial Jamie, when the receiver was lifted at the other end.

He answered.

Himself.

He recognized his own voice at once. But didn't let it penetrate.

He had no little machine to take messages after the bleep, he had had his answering service temporarily disconnected (unsatisfactory service, they weren't catching his calls on the third ring as he'd *insisted*), there was no one guesting at his apartment, nothing. He was not at home, he was here, in the restaurant, calling his apartment, and *he* answered.

"Hello?"

He waited a moment. Then said, "Who's this?"

He answered, "Who're you calling?"

"Hold it," he said. "Who *is* this?"

His own voice, on the other end, getting annoyed, said, "Look, friend, what number do you want?"

"This is BEacon 3-6189, right?"

Warily: "Yeah . . . ?"

"Peter Novins's apartment?"

There was silence for a moment, then: "That's right."

He listened to the sounds from the restaurant's kitchen. "If this is Novins's apartment, who're you?"

On the other end, in his apartment, there was a deep breath. "This is Novins."

He stood in the phone booth, in the restaurant, in the night, the receiver to his ear, and listened to his own voice. He had dialed his own number by mistake, dialed an empty apartment . . . *and he had answered.*

Finally, he said, very tightly, *"This* is Novins."

"Where are you?"

"I'm at The High Tide, waiting for Jamie."

Across the line, with a terrible softness, he heard himself asking, "Is that you?"

A surge of fear pulsed through him and he tried to get out of it with one last possibility. "If this is a gag . . . Freddy . . . is that you, man? Morrie? Art?"

Silence. Then, slowly, "I'm Novins. Honest to God."

His mouth was dry. "I'm out here. You can't be, I *can't* be in the apartment."

"Oh yeah? Well, I am."

"I'll have to call you back." Peter Novins hung up.

He went back to the bar and ordered a double Scotch, no ice, straight up, and threw it back in two swallows, letting it burn. He sat and stared at his hands, turning them over and over, studying them to make sure they were his own, not alien meat grafted onto his wrists when he was not looking.

Then he went back to the phone booth, closed the door and sat down, and dialed his own number. Very carefully.

It rang six times before *he* picked it up.

He knew why the voice on the other end had let it ring six times; he didn't want to pick up the snake and hear his own voice coming at him.

"Hello?" His voice on the other end was barely controlled.

"It's me," he said, closing his eyes.

"Jesus God," he murmured.

They sat there, in their separate places, without speaking. Then Novins said, "I'll call you Jay."

"That's okay," he answered from the other end. It was his middle name. He never used it, but it appeared on his insurance policy, his driver's license and his social security card. Jay said, "Did Jamie get there?"

"No, she's late again."

Jay took a deep breath and said, "We'd better talk about this, man."

"I suppose," Novins answered. "Not that I really want to. You're scaring the shit out of me."

"How do you think *I* feel about it?"

"Probably the same way I feel about it."

They thought about that for a long moment. Then Jay said, "Will we be feeling exactly the same way about things?"

Novins considered it, then said, "If you're really me then I suppose so. We ought to try and test that."

"You're taking this a lot calmer than I am, it seems to me," Jay said.

Novins was startled. "You really think so? I was just about to say I thought you were really terrific the way you're handling all this. I think you're *much* more together about it than I am. I'm really startled, I've got to tell you."

"So how'll we test it?" Jay asked.

Novins considered the problem, then said, "Why don't we compare likes and dislikes. That's a start. That sound okay to you?"

"It's as good a place as any, I suppose. Who goes first?"

"It's my dime," Novins said, and for the first time he smiled. "I like, uh, well-done prime rib, end cut if I can get it, Yorkshire pudding, smoking a pipe, Max Ernst's[1] paintings, Robert Altman[2] films, William Goldman's[3] books, getting mail but not answering it, uh . . ."

He stopped. He had been selecting random items from memory, the ones that came to mind first. But as he had been speaking, he heard what he was saying, and it seemed stupid. "This isn't going to work," Novins said. "What the hell does it matter? Was there anything in that list you didn't like?"

Jay sighed. "No, they're all favorites. You're right. If I like it, you'll like it. This isn't going to answer any questions."

Novins said, "I don't even know what the questions *are!*"

"That's easy enough," Jay said. "There's only one question: which of us is me, and how does *me* get rid of *him?*"

A chill spread out from Novins's shoulder blades and wrapped around his arms like a mantilla. "What's *that* supposed to mean? Get rid of *him?* What the hell's *that?*"

"Face it," Jay said—and Novins heard a tone in the voice he recognized, the tone *he* used when he was about to become a tough negotiator—"we can't *both* be Novins. One of us is going to get screwed."

"Hold it, friend," Novins said, adopting the tone. "That's pretty muddy logic. First of all, who's to say you're not going to vanish back where you came from as soon as I hang up . . ."

"Bullshit," Jay answered.

"Yeah, well, maybe; but even if you're here to stay, and I don't concede *that* craziness for a second, even if you *are* real—"

"Believe it, baby, I'm real," Jay said, with a soft chuckle. Novins was starting to hate him.

"—even if you *are* real," Novins continued, "there's no saying we can't both exist, and both lead happy, separate lives."

"You know something, Novins," Jay said, "you're really full of horse puckey. You can't lead a happy life by yourself, man, how the hell are you going to do it knowing I'm over here living your life, too?"

"What do you mean I can't lead a happy life? What do you know about it?" And he stopped; of course Jay knew about it. *All* about it.

"You'd better start facing reality, Novins. You'll be coming to it late in life, but you'd better learn how to do it. Maybe it'll make the end come easier."

Novins wanted to slam the receiver into its rack. He was at once furiously angry and frightened. He knew what the other Novins was saying was true; he

309

had to know, without argument; it was, after all, himself saying it. "Only one of us is going to make it," he said, tightly. "And it's going to be me, old friend."

"How do you propose to do it, Novins? You're out there, locked out. I'm in here, in my home, safe where I'm supposed to be."

"How about we look at it *this* way," Novins said quickly, "you're trapped in there, locked away from the world in three-and-a-half rooms. I've got every-where else to move in. You're limited. I'm free."

There was silence for a moment.

Then Jay said, "We've reached a bit of an impasse, haven't we? There's something to be said for being loose, and there's something to be said for being safe inside. The amazing thing is that we both have accepted this thing so quickly."

Novins didn't answer. He accepted it because he had no other choice; if he could accept that he was speaking to himself, then anything that followed had to be part of that acceptance. Now that Jay had said it bluntly, that only one of them could continue to exist, all that remained was finding a way to make sure it was he, Novins, who continued past this point.

"I've got to think about this," Novins said. "I've got to try to work some of this out better. You just stay celled in there, friend; I'm going to a hotel for the night. I'll call you tomorrow."

He started to hang up when Jay's voice stopped him "What do I say if Jamie gets there and you're gone and she calls me?"

Novins laughed. "That's *your* problem, motherfucker."

He racked the receiver with nasty satisfaction.

ii: Moanday

He took special precautions. First the bank, to clean out the checking account. He thanked God he'd had his checkbook with him when he'd gone out to meet Jamie the night before. But the savings account passbook was in the apartment. That meant Jay had access to almost ten thousand dollars. The checking account was down to fifteen hundred, even with all outstanding bills paid, and the Banks for Cooperatives note came due in about thirty days and that meant . . . he used the back of a deposit slip to figure the interest . . . he'd be getting ten thousand four hundred and sixty-five dollars and seven cents deposited to his account. His *new* account, which he opened at another branch of the same bank, signing the identification cards with a variation of his signature sufficiently different to prevent Jay's trying to draw on the account. He was at least solvent. For the time being.

But all his work was in the apartment. All the public relations accounts he handled. Every bit of data and all the plans and phone numbers and charts, they were all there in the little apartment office. So he was quite effectively cut off from his career.

Yet in a way, that was a blessing. Jay would have to keep up with the work in his absence, would have to follow through on the important campaigns for Topper and McKenzie, would have to take all the moronic calls from Lippman and his insulting son, would have to answer all the mail, would have to keep popping Titralac all day just to stay ahead of the heartburn. He felt gloriously free and almost satanically happy that he was rid of the aggravation for a while, and that Jay was going to find out being Peter Jay Novins wasn't all fun and Jamies.

Back in his hotel room at the Americana he made a list of things he had to do. To survive. It was a new way of thinking, setting down one by one the everyday routine actions from which he was now cut off. He was all alone now, entirely and totally, for the first time in his life, cut off from everything. He could not depend on friends or associates or the authorities. It would be suicide to go to the police and say, "Listen, I hate to bother you, but I've split and one of me has assumed squatter's rights in my apartment; please go up there and arrest him." No, he was on his own, and he had to exorcise Jay from the world strictly by his own wits and cunning.

Bearing in mind, of course, that Jay had the same degree of wit and cunning.

He crossed half a dozen items off the list. There was no need to call Jamie and find out what had happened to her the night before. Their relationship wasn't that binding in any case. Let Jay make the excuses. No need to cancel the credit cards, he had them with him. Let Jay pay the bills from the savings account. No need to contact any of his friends and warn them. He *couldn't* warn them, and if he did, what would he warn them against? Himself? But he did need clothes, fresh socks and underwear, a light jacket instead of his topcoat, a pair of gloves in case the weather turned. And he had to cancel out the delivery services to the apartment in a way that would prevent Jay from reinstating them: groceries, milk, dry cleaning, newspapers. He had to make it as difficult for him in there as possible. And so he called each tradesman and insulted him so grossly they would *never* serve him again. Unfortunately, the building provided heat and electricity and gas and he *had* to leave the phone connected.

The phone was his tie-line to victory, to routing Jay out of there.

When he had it all attended to, by three o'clock in the afternoon, he returned to the hotel room, took off his shoes, propped the pillows up on the bed, lay down and dialed a 9 for the outside line, then dialed his own number.

As it rang, he stared out the forty-fifth floor window of the hotel room, at the soulless pylons of the RCA and Grants Buildings, the other dark-glass filing cabinets for people. It was a wonder *any*one managed to stay sane, stay whole in such surroundings! Living in cubicles, boxed and trapped and throttled, was it any surprise that people began to fall apart . . . even as *he* seemed to be falling apart? The wonder was that it all managed to hold together as well as it did. But the fractures were beginning to appear, culturally and now—as with Peter Novins, he mused—personally. The phone continued to ring. Clouds blocked out all light and the city was swamped by shadows. At three o'clock in the afternoon, the ominous threat of another night settled over Novins's hotel room.

The receiver was lifted at the other end. But Jay said nothing.

"It's me," Novins said. "How'd you enjoy your first day in my skin?"

"How did you enjoy your first day *out* of it?" he replied.

"Listen, I've got your act covered, friend, and your hours are numbered. The checking account is gone, don't try to find it; you're going to go out to get food and when you do I'll be waiting—"

"Terrific," Jay replied. "But just so you don't waste your time, I had the locks changed today. Your keys don't work. And I bought groceries. Remember the fifty bucks I put away in the jewelry box?"

Novins cursed himself silently. He hadn't thought of that.

"And I've been doing some figuring, Novins. Remember that old Jack London novel, *The Star Rover*?[4] Remember how he used astral projection to get out of his body? I think that's what happened to me. I sent you out when I wasn't aware of it. So I've decided I'm me, and you're just a little piece that's wandered off. And I can get along just peachy-keen without that piece, so why don't you just go—"

"Hold it," Novins interrupted, "that's a sensational theory, but it's stuffed full of wild blueberry muffins, if you'll pardon my being so forward as to disagree with a smartass voice that's probably disembodied and doesn't have enough ecto-plasm to take a healthy shit. Remember the weekend I went over to the lab with Kenny and he took that Kirlian photograph of my aura?[5] Well, my theory is that something happened and the aura produced another me, or something . . ."

He slid down into silence. Neither theory was worth thinking about. He had no idea, *really*, what had happened. They hung there in silence for a long moment, then Jay said, "Mother called this morning."

Novins felt a hand squeeze his chest. "What did she say?"

"She said she knew you lied when you were down in Florida. She said she loved you and she forgave you and all she wants is for you to share your life with her."

Novins closed his eyes. He didn't want to think about it. His mother was in her eighties, very sick, and just recovering from her second serious heart attack in three years. The end was near and, combining a business trip to Miami with a visit to her, he had gone to Florida the month before. He had never had much in common with his mother, had been on his own since his early teens, and though he supported her in her declining years, he refused to allow her to impose on his existence. He seldom wrote letters, save to send the check, and during the two days he had spent in her apartment in Miami Beach he had thought he would go insane. He had wanted to bolt, and finally had lied to her that he was returning to New York a day earlier than his plans required. He had packed up and left her, checking into a hotel, and had spent the final day involved in business and that night had gone out with a secretary he dated occasionally when in Florida.

"How did she find out?" Novins asked.

"She called here and the answering service told her you were still in Florida and hadn't returned. They gave her the number of the hotel and she called there and found out you were registered for that night."

Novins cursed himself. Why had he called the service to tell them where he was? He could have gotten away with one day of his business contacts not being able to reach him. "Swell," he said. "And I suppose you didn't do anything to make her feel better."

312

"On the contrary," Jay said, "I did what you never would have done. I made arrangements for her to come live here with me."

Novins heard himself moan with pain. "You did *what*!? Jesus Christ, you're out of your fucking mind. How the hell am I going to take care of that old woman in New York? I've got work to do, places I have to go, I have a life to lead . . ."

"Not any more you don't, you guilty, selfish sonafabitch. Maybe *you* could live with the bad gut feelings about her, but not me. She'll be arriving in a week."

"You're crazy," Novins screamed. "You're fucking crazy!"

"Yeah," Jay said, softly, and added, "and you just lost your mother. Chew on *that* one, you creep."

And he hung up.

iii: Duesday

They decided between them that the one who *deserved* to be Peter Novins should take over the life. They had to make that decision; clearly, they could not go on as they had been; even two days had showed them half an existence was not possible. Both were fraying at the edges.

So Jay suggested they work their way through the pivot experiences of Novins's life, to see if he was really entitled to continue living.

"*Every*one's entitled to go on living," Novins said, vehemently. "That's why we live. To say no to death."

"You don't believe that for a second, Novins," Jay said. "You're a misanthrope. You hate people."

"That's not true; I just don't like some of the things people *do*."

"Like what, for instance? Like, for instance, you're always bitching about kids who wear ecology patches,[6] who throw Dr. Pepper cans in the bushes; like that, for instance?"

"That's good for starters," Novins said.

"You hypocritical bastard," Jay snarled back at him, "you have the audacity to beef about that and you took on the Cumberland account."

"That's another kind of thing!"

"My ass. You know damned well Cumberland's planning to strip mine the guts out of that county, and they're going to get away with it with that publicity campaign you dreamed up. Oh, you're one hell of a good PR man, Novins, but you've got the ethics of a weasel."

Novins was fuming, but Jay was right. He had felt lousy about taking on Cumberland from the start, but they were big, they were international, and the billing for the account was handily in six figures. He had tackled the campaign with the same ferocity he brought to all his accounts, and the program was solid. "I have to make a living. Besides, if I didn't do it, someone else would. I'm only doing a job. They've got a terrific restoration program, don't forget that. They'll put that land back in shape."

Jay laughed. "That's what Eichmann[7] said: 'We have a terrific restoration program, we'll put them Jews right back in shape, just a little gas to spiff 'em up.' He was just doing a job, too, Novins. Have I mentioned lately that you stink on ice?"

Novins was shouting again. "I suppose you'd have turned it down."

"That's exactly what I did, old buddy." Jay said, "I called them today and told them to take their account and stuff it up their nose. I've got a call in to Nader[8] right now, to see what he can do with all the data in the file."

Novins was speechless. He lay there, under the covers, the Tuesday snow drifting in enormous flakes past the forty-fifth floor windows. Slowly, he let the receiver settle into the cradle. Only three days and his life was drifting apart inexorably; soon it would be impossible to knit it together.

His stomach ached. And all that day he had felt nauseated. Room service had sent up pot after pot of tea, but it hadn't helped. A throbbing headache was lodged just behind his left eye, and cold sweat covered his shoulders and chest.

He didn't know what to do, but he knew he was losing.

iv: Woundsday

On Wednesday Jay called Novins. He never told him how he'd located him, he just called. "How do you feel?" he asked. Novins could barely answer, the fever was close to immobilizing.

"I just called to talk about Jeanine and Patty and that girl in Denver," Jay said, and he launched into a long and stately recitation of Novins's affairs, and how they had ended. It was not as Novins remembered it.

"That isn't true," Novins managed to say, his voice deep and whispering, dry and nearly empty.

"It *is* true, Novins. That's what's so sad about it. That it *is* true and you've never had the guts to admit it, that you go from woman to woman without giving anything, always taking, and when you leave them—or they dump you—you've never learned a god damned thing. You've been married twice, divorced twice, you've been in and out of two dozen affairs and you haven't learned that you're one of those men who is simply no bloody good for a woman. So now you're forty-two years old and you're finally coming to the dim understanding that you're going to spend all the rest of the days and nights of your life alone, because you can't stand the company of another human being for more than a month without turning into a vicious prick."

"Not true," murmured Novins.

"True, Novins, true. Flat true. You set after Patty and got her to leave her old man, and when you'd pried her loose, her and the kid, you set her up in that apartment with three hundred a month rent, and then you took off and left her to work it out herself. It's true, old buddy. So don't try and con me with that 'I lead a happy life' bullshit."

Novins simply lay there with his eyes closed, shivering with the fever.

Then Jay said, "I saw Jamie last night. We talked about her future. It took some fast talking; she was really coming to hate you. But I think it'll work out if I go at it hard, and I *intend* to go at it hard. I don't intend to have any more years like I've had, Novins. From this point on it changes."

The bulk of the buildings outside the window seemed to tremble behind the falling snow. Novins felt terribly cold. He didn't answer.

"We'll name the first one after you. Peter," Jay said, and hung up.

That was Wednesday.

v: Thornsday

There were no phone calls that day. Novins lay there, the television set mindlessly playing and replaying the five minute instruction film on the pay-movie preview channel, the ghost-image of a dark-haired girl in a gray suit showing him how to charge a first-run film to his hotel bill. After many hours he heard himself reciting the instructions along with her. He slept a great deal. He thought about Jeanine and Patty, the girl in Denver whose name he could not recall, and Jamie.

After many more hours, he thought about insects, but he didn't know what that meant. There were no phone calls that day. It was Thursday.

Shortly before midnight, the fever broke, and he cried himself back to sleep.

vi: Freeday

A key turned in the lock and the hotel room door opened. Novins was sitting in a mass-produced imitation of a Saarinen[9] pedestal chair, its seat treated with Scotch-Gard. He had been staring out the window at the geometric irrelevancy of the glass-wall buildings. It was near dusk, and the city was gray as cardboard.

He turned at the sound of the door opening and was not surprised to see himself walk in.

Jay's nose and cheeks were still red from the cold outside. He unzipped his jacket and stuffed his kid gloves into a pocket, removed the jacket and threw it on the unmade bed. "Really cold out there," he said. He went into the bathroom and Novins heard the sound of water running.

Jay returned in a few minutes, rubbing his hands together. "That helps," he said. He sat down on the edge of the bed and looked at Novins.

"You look terrible, Peter," he said.

"I haven't been at all well," Novins answered dryly. "I don't seem to be myself these days."

Jay smiled briefly. "I see you're coming to terms with it. That ought to help."

Novins stood up. The thin light from the room-long window shone through him like white fire through milk glass. "You're looking well," he said.

"I'm getting better, Peter. It'll be a while, but I'm going to be okay."

Novins walked across the room and stood against the wall, hands clasped behind his back. He could barely be seen. "I remember the archetypes from Jung.[10] Are you my shadow, my persona, my anima or my animus?"

"What am I now, or what was I when I got loose?"

"Either way."

"I suppose I was your shadow. Now I'm the self."

"And I'm becoming the shadow."

"No, you're becoming a memory. A bad memory."

"That's pretty ungracious."

"I was sick for a long time, Peter. I don't know what the trigger was that broke us apart, but it happened and I can't be too sorry about it. If it hadn't happened I'd have been you till I died. It would have been a lousy life and a miserable death."

Novins shrugged. "Too late to worry about it now. Things working out with Jamie?"

Jay nodded. "Yeah. And Mom comes in Tuesday afternoon. I'm renting a car to pick her up at Kennedy. I talked to her doctors. They say she doesn't have too long. But for whatever she's got, I'm determined to make up for the last twenty-five years since Dad died."

Novins smiled and nodded. "That's good."

"Listen," Jay said slowly, with difficulty, "I just came over to ask if there was anything you wanted me to do . . . anything *you* would've done if . . . if it had been different."

Novins spread his hands and thought about it for a moment. "No, I don't think so, nothing special. You might try and get some money to Jeanine's mother, for Jeanine's care, maybe. That wouldn't hurt."

"I already took care of it. I figured that would be on your mind."

Novins smiled. "That's good. Thanks."

"Anything else . . . ?"

Novins shook his head. They stayed that way, hardly moving, till night had fallen outside the window. In the darkness, Jay could barely see Novins standing against the wall. Merely a faint glow.

Finally, Jay stood and put on his jacket, zipped up and put on his left glove. "I've got to go."

Novins spoke from the shadows. "Yeah. Well, take care of me, will you?"

Jay didn't answer. He walked to Novins and extended his right hand. The touch of Novin's hand in his was like the whisper of a cold wind; there was no pressure.

Then he left.

Novins walked back to the window and stared out. The last remaining daylight shone through him. Dimly.

vii: Shatterday

When the maid came in to make up the bed, she found the room was empty. It was terribly cold in the room on the forty-fifth floor. When Peter Novins did not

316

return that day, or the next, the management of the Americana marked him as a skip, and turned it over to a collection agency.

In due course the bill was sent to Peter Novins's apartment on Manhattan's upper east side.

It was promptly paid, by Peter Jay Novins, with a brief, but *sincere* note of apology.

[1] German painter (1891–1976).
[2] American movie director (1925–   ).
[3] American author (1931–   ).
[4] Published in 1915 by Macmillan, the story is essentially fantasy, although it is sometimes discussed as science fiction.
[5] Semyon Davidovitch Kirlian, Russian scientist who, together with his wife, discovered around 1940 the process of photographing an object by exposing it to a high-frequency electric field. Objects so photographed appear surrounded by discharges of light.
[6] Young people in the 1960s protesting against the dominance of corporations in America frequently sewed patches on their blue jeans that expressed their antiestablishment views.
[7] Adolf Eichmann (1906–1962), infamous Nazi bureaucrat in charge of transporting millions of Jews to concentration camps during World War II. After the war Israeli agents tracked him to Argentina, where he had been hiding out for years. They kidnapped him and brought him to trial in Israel. He was convicted of crimes against humanity and hanged.
[8] Ralph Nader (1934–   ), American consumer advocate. His various campaigns against manufacturing companies have brought about higher standards in production, products, and the environment.
[9] Eero Saarinen (1910–1961), American architect of Finnish descent. He designed the chair mentioned in the story; he also designed the giant stainless steel arch on the banks of the Mississippi River at St. Louis—the Jefferson National Expansion Memorial.
[10] C. G. Jung (1875–1961), Swiss psychologist.

DISCUSSION TOPICS

1. In his Introduction to this story, Ellison writes:

> There is a curse over the door of my tomb. It says, Beware all ye who enter here—because herein lie the proofs of observation that we are all as one, living in the same skin, each of us condemned to handle the responsibility of our past, our memories, our destiny as elements in the great congeries of life. And if you find these dark dreams troubling, perhaps it is because they are *your* dreams.

Discuss this statement in the light of your reading of "Shatterday."
2. Ellison is obviously punning on the names of the days of the week in the section headings of his story. How do these puns relate to his central theme?
3. What do you think is wrong with Peter Jay Novins? What is his fate?
4. Referring explicitly to Jungian archetypes, Peter asks Jay, "Are you my shadow, my persona, my anima or my animus?" What do you think the right answer is?

WRITING TOPIC

Compare Ellison's story with Singer's "Getzel the Monkey" (or Conrad's *Heart of Darkness*) with particular emphasis on the concept of the *alter ego* or *shadow*.

GARY GILDNER (1938–   ) American poet, short story writer, academic. Gildner is a professor of English at Drake University. Much of his early work was poetry, but he has recently turned his creative attention toward works of fiction.

SLEEPY TIME GAL

In the small town in northern Michigan where my father lived as a young man, he had an Italian friend who worked in a restaurant. I will call his friend Phil. Phil's job in the restaurant was as ordinary as you can imagine—from making coffee in the morning to sweeping up at night. But what was not ordinary about Phil was his piano playing. On Saturday nights my father and Phil and their girl friends would drive ten or fifteen miles to a roadhouse by a lake where they would drink beer from schoopers and dance and Phil would play an old beat-up piano. He could play any song you named, my father said, but the song everyone waited for was the one he wrote, which he would always play at the end before they left to go back to the town. And everyone knew of course that he had written the song for his girl, who was as pretty as she was rich. Her father was the banker in their town and he was a tough old German and he didn't like Phil going around with his daughter.

My father, when he told this story, which was not often, would tell it in an offhand way and emphasize the Depression[1] and not having much, instead of the important parts. I will try to tell it the way he did, if I can.

So they would go to the roadhouse by the lake and finally Phil would play his song and everyone would say, Phil, that's a great song, you could make a lot of money from it. But Phil would only shake his head and smile and look at his girl. I have to break in here and say that my father, a gentle but practical man, was not inclined to emphasize the part about Phil looking at his girl. It was my mother who said the girl would rest her head on Phil's shoulder while he played, and that he got the idea for the song from the pretty way she looked when she got sleepy. My mother was not part of the story, but she had heard it when she and my father were younger and therefore had that information. I would like to intrude further and add something about Phil writing the song, maybe show him whistling the tune and going over the words slowly and carefully to get the best ones, while peeling onions or potatoes in the restaurant; but my father is already driving them home from the roadhouse and saying how patched up his tires were and how his car's engine was a gingerbread of parts from different makes, and some parts were

318

his own invention as well. And my mother is saying that the old German had made his daughter promise not to get involved with any man until after college, and they couldn't be late. Also my mother likes the sad parts and is eager to get to their last night before the girl goes away to college.

So they all went out to the roadhouse and it was sad. The women got tears in their eyes when Phil played her song, my mother said. My father said that Phil spent his week's pay on a new shirt and tie, the first tie he ever owned, and people kidded him. Somebody piped up and said, Phil, you ought to take that song down to Bay City—which was like saying New York City to them, only more realistic —and sell it and take the money and go to college too. Which was not meant to be cruel, but that was the result because Phil had never even got to high school. But you can see people were trying to cheer him up, my mother said.

Well, she'd come home for Thanksgiving and Christmas and Easter and they'd all sneak out to the roadhouse and drink beer from schoopers and dance and everything would be like always. And of course there were the summers. And everyone knew Phil and the girl would get married after she made good her promise to her father, because you could see it in their eyes when he sat at the old beat-up piano and played her song.

That last part about their eyes was not of course in my father's telling, but I couldn't help putting it in there even though I know it is making some of you impatient. Remember that this happened many years ago in the woods by a lake in northern Michigan, before television. I wish I could put more in, especially about the song and how it felt to Phil to sing it and how the girl felt when hearing it and knowing it was hers, but I've already intruded too much in a simple story that isn't even mine.

Well, here's the kicker part. Probably by now many of you have guessed that one vacation near the end she doesn't come home to see Phil, because she meets some guy at college who is good-looking and as rich as she is and, because her father knew about Phil all along and was pressuring her into forgetting about him, she gives in to this new guy and goes to his home town during the vacation and falls in love with him. That's how the people in town figured it, because after she graduates they turn up, already married, and right away he takes over the old German's bank—and buys a new Pontiac at the place where my father is the mechanic and pays cash for it. The paying cash always made my father pause and shake his head and mention again that times were tough, but here comes this guy in a spiffy white shirt (with French cuffs, my mother said) and pays the full price in cash.

And this made my father shake his head too: Phil took the song down to Bay City and sold it for twenty-five dollars, the only money he ever got for it. It was the same song we'd just heard on the radio and which reminded my father of the story I just told you. What happened to Phil? Well, he stayed in Bay City and got a job managing a movie theatre. My father saw him there after the Depression when he was on his way to Detroit to work for Ford. He stopped and Phil gave him a box of popcorn. The song he wrote for the girl has sold many millions of records and if I told you the name of it you could probably sing it, or at least whistle the tune. I wonder what the girl thinks when she hears it. Oh yes, my father met Phil's wife too. She worked in the movie theatre with him, selling tickets and cleaning the carpet after the show with one of those sweepers you push. She was also big and loud and nothing like the other one, my mother said.

---

[1] The period in American history from 1929 to, roughly, the beginning of World War II in 1939 (for the United States, 1941). It started with the crash of the stock market and was marked by low economic activity, especially the failures of banks and small businesses and by massive unemployment.

DISCUSSION TOPICS

1. What is the significance of the title, "Sleepy Time Gal"?
2. Gildner's story, like Anderson's "Death in the Woods," involves the reader not only in the telling but also in the creation of the story from a variety of perspectives. (Notice that the last words are "my mother said.") What does a writer accomplish by giving his readers this glimpse behind the scenes?
3. Both Gildner's and Anderson's stories are told from the first-person point of view. What does point of view have to do with this technique of storytelling?
4. What elements of the folktale can you find in this story? Does it have any mythic or archetypal dimensions?

JOYCE CAROL OATES (1938–   ) American poet, critic, fiction writer, academic. She is a prolific writer whose novels and stories are known for their frequent portrayal of violence, madness, and social disorder.

STALKING

The Invisible Adversary is fleeing across a field.

Gretchen, walking slowly, deliberately, watches with her keen unblinking eyes the figure of the Invisible Adversary some distance ahead. The Adversary has run boldly in front of all that traffic—on long spiky legs brisk as colts' legs—and jumped up onto a curb of new concrete, and now is running across a vacant field. The Adversary glances over his shoulder at Gretchen.

Bastard, Gretchen thinks.

Saturday afternoon. November. A cold gritty day. Gretchen is out stalking. She has hours for her game. Hours. She is dressed for the hunt, her solid legs crammed into old blue jeans, her big, square, strong feet jammed into white leather boots that cost her mother forty dollars not long ago, but are now scuffed and filthy with mud. Hopeless to get them clean again, Gretchen doesn't give a

320

damn. She is wearing a dark green corduroy jacket that is worn out at the elbows and the rear, with a zipper that can be zipped swiftly up or down, attached to a fringed leather strip. On her head nothing, though it is windy today.

She has hours ahead.

Cars and trucks and buses from the city and enormous interstate trucks hauling automobiles pass by the highway; Gretchen waits until the way is nearly clear, then starts out. A single car is approaching. *Slow down, you bastard,* Gretchen thinks; and like magic he does.

Following the footprints of the Invisible Adversary. There is no sidewalk here yet, so she might as well cut right across the field. A gigantic sign announces the site of the new Pace & Fischbach Building, an office building of fifteen floors to be completed the following year. The land around here is all dug up and muddy; she can see the Adversary's footsteps leading right past the gouged-up area . . . and there he is, smirking back at her, pretending panic.

I'll get you. Don't worry, Gretchen thinks carefully.

Because the Adversary is so light-footed and invisible, Gretchen doesn't make any effort to be that way. She plods along as she does at school, passing from classroom to classroom, unhurried and not even sullen, just unhurried. She knows she is very visible. She is thirteen years old and weighs one hundred and thirty-five pounds. She's only five feet three—stocky, muscular, squat in the torso and shoulders, with good strong legs and thighs. She could be good at gym, if she bothered; instead, she just stands around, her face empty, her arms crossed and her shoulders a little slumped. If forced, she takes part in the games of volleyball and basketball, but she runs heavily, without spirit, and sometimes bumps into other girls, hurting them. *Out of my way,* she thinks, at such times her face shows no expression.

And now? . . . The Adversary is peeking out at her from around the corner of a gas station. Something flickers in her brain. *I see you,* she thinks, with quiet excitement. The Adversary ducks back out of sight. Gretchen heads in his direction, plodding through a jumbled, bulldozed field of mud and thistles and debris that is mainly rocks and chunks of glass. The gas station is brand new and not yet opened for business. It is all white tile, white concrete, perfect plate-glass windows with white-washed X's on them, a large driveway and eight gasoline pumps, all proudly erect and ready for business. But the gas station has not opened since Gretchen and her family moved here—about six months ago. Something must have gone wrong. Gretchen fixes her eyes on the corner where the Adversary was last seen. He can't escape.

One wall of the gas station's white tile has been smeared with something like tar. Dreamy, snakelike, thick twistings of black. Black tar. Several windows have been broken. Gretchen stands in the empty driveway, her hands jammed into her pockets. Traffic is moving slowly over here. A barricade has been set up that directs traffic out onto the shoulder of the highway, on a narrow, bumpy, muddy lane that loops out and back again onto the pavement. Cars move slowly, carefully. Their bottoms scrape against the road. The detour signs are great rectangular things, bright yellow with black zigzag lines. SLOW. DETOUR. In the two center lanes of the highway are bulldozers not being used today, and gigantic concrete pipes to be used for storm sewers. Eight pipes. They are really enormous; Gretchen's eyes crinkle with awe, just to see them.

She remembers the Adversary.

There he is—headed for the shopping plaza. *He won't get away in the crowds,* Gretchen promises herself. She follows. Now she is approaching an area that is more completed, though there are still no sidewalks and some of the buildings are brand-new and yet unoccupied, vacant. She jumps over a concrete ditch that is stained with rust-colored water and heads up a slight incline in the service drive of the Federal Savings Bank. The drive-in tellers' windows are all dark today, behind their green-tinted glass. The whole bank is dark, closed. Is this the bank her parents go to now? It takes Gretchen a minute to recognize it.

Now a steady line of traffic, a single lane, turns onto the service drive that leads to the shopping plaza. BUCKINGHAM MALL. 101 STORES. Gretchen notices a few kids her own age, boys or girls, trudging in jeans and jackets ahead of her, through the mud. They might be classmates of hers. Her attention is captured again by the Invisible Adversary, who has run all the way up to the Mall and is hanging around the entrance of the Cunningham Drug Store, teasing her.

You'll be sorry for that, you bastard, Gretchen thinks with a smile.

Automobiles pass her slowly. The parking lot for the Mall is enormous, many acres. A city of cars on a Saturday afternoon. Gretchen sees a car that might be her mother's, but she isn't sure. Cars are parked slanted here, in lanes marked LOT K, LANE 15; LOT K, LANE 16. The signs are spheres, bubbles, perched up on long slender poles. At night they are illuminated.

Ten or twelve older kids are hanging around the drugstore entrance. One of them is sitting on top of a mailbox, rocking it back and forth. Gretchen pushes past them—they are kidding around, trying to block people—and inside the store her eye darts rapidly up and down the aisles, looking for the Invisible Adversary.

Hiding here? Hiding?

She strolls along, cunning and patient. At the cosmetics counter a girl is showing an older woman some liquid make-up. She smears a small oval onto the back of the woman's hand, rubs it gently. "That's Peace Pride," the girl says. She has shimmering blond hair and eyes that are penciled to show a permanent exclamatory interest. She does not notice Gretchen, who lets one hand drift idly over a display of marked-down lipsticks, each for only $1.59.

Gretchen slips the tube of lipstick into her pocket. Neatly. Nimbly. Ignoring the Invisible Adversary, who is shaking a finger at her, she drifts over to the newsstand, looks at the magazine covers without reading them, and edges over to another display. Packages in a cardboard barrel, out in the aisle. Big bargains. Gretchen doesn't even glance in the barrel to see what is being offered . . . she just slips one of the packages in her pocket. No trouble.

She leaves by the other door, the side exit. A small smile tugs at her mouth.

The Adversary is trotting ahead of her. The Mall is divided into geometric areas, each colored differently; the Adversary leaves the blue pavement and is now on the green. Gretchen follows. She notices the Adversary going into a Franklin Joseph store.

Gretchen enters the store, sniffs in the perfumy, overheated smell, sees nothing that interests her on the counters or at the dress racks, and so walks right to the back of the store, to the Ladies Room. No one inside. She takes the tube of lipstick out of her pocket, opens it, examines the lipstick. It has a tart, sweet smell. A very light pink: *Spring Blossom.* Gretchen goes to the mirror and smears the lipstick onto it, at first lightly, then coarsely; part of the lipsteak breaks and falls into a hair-littered sink. Gretchen goes into one of the toilet stalls and tosses the tube into the toilet bowl. She takes handfuls of toilet paper and crumbles them into a ball and throws them into the toilet. Remembering the package from the drugstore, she takes it out of her pocket—just toothpaste. She throws it, cardboard package and all, into the toilet bowl, then, her mind glimmering with an idea, she goes to the apparatus that holds the towel—a single cloth towel on a roll—and tugs at it until it comes loose, then pulls it out hand over hand, patiently, until the entire towel is out. She scoops it up and carries it to the toilet. She pushes it in and flushes the toilet.

The stuff doesn't go down, so she tries again. This time it goes part-way down before it gets stuck.

Gretchen leaves the rest room and strolls unhurried through the store. The Adversary is waiting for her outside—peeking through the window—wagging a finger at her. *Don't you wag no finger at me,* she thinks, with a small tight smile. Outside, she follows him at a distance. Loud music is blaring around her head. It is rock music, piped out onto the colored squares and rectangles of the Mall, blown everywhere by the November wind, but Gretchen hardly hears it.

Some boys are fooling around in front of the record store. One of them bumps into Gretchen and they all laugh as she is pushed against a trash can. "Watch it, babe!" the boy sings out. Her leg hurts. Gretchen doesn't look at them but, with a cold, swift anger, her face averted, she knocks the trash can over onto the sidewalk. Junk falls out. The can rolls. Some women shoppers scurry to get out of the way and the boys laugh.

Gretchen walks away without looking back.

She wanders through Sampson Furniture, which has two entrances. In one door and out the other, as always, it is a ritual with her. Again she notices the sofa that is like the sofa in their family room at home—covered with black and white fur, real goatskin. All over the store there are sofas, chairs, tables, beds. A jumble of furnishings. People stroll around them, in and out of little displays, displays meant to be living rooms, dining rooms, bedrooms, family rooms. . . . It makes Gretchen's eyes squint to see so many displays: like seeing the inside of a hundred houses. She slows down, almost comes to a stop. Gazing at a living-room display on a raised platform. Only after a moment does she remember why she is here—whom she is following—and she turns to see the Adversary beckoning to her.

She follows him outside again. He goes into Dodi's Boutique and, with her head lowered so that her eyes seem to move to the bottom of her eyebrows, pressing up against her forehead, Gretchen follows him. *You'll regret this,* she thinks. Dodi's Boutique is decorated in silver and black. Metallic strips hang down from a dark ceiling, quivering. Salesgirls dressed in pants suits stand around with nothing to do except giggle with one another and nod their heads in time to the music amplified throughout the store. It is music from a local radio station. Gretchen wanders over to the dress rack, for the hell of it. Size 14. "The time is now 2:35," a radio announcer says cheerfully. "The weather is 32 degrees with a chance of showers and possible sleet tonight. You're listening to WCKK, Radio Wonderful . . ." Gretchen selects several dresses and a salesgirl shows her to a dressing room.

"Need any help?" the girl asks. She has long swinging hair and a high-shouldered, indifferent, bright manner.

"No," Gretchen mutters.

Alone, Gretchen takes off her jacket. She is wearing a navy blue sweater. She zips one of the dresses open and it falls off the flimsy plastic hanger before she can catch it. She steps on it, smearing mud onto the white wool. *The hell with it.* She lets it lie there and holds up another dress, gazing at herself in the mirror.

She has untidy, curly hair that looks like a wig set loosely on her head. Light brown curls spill out everywhere, bouncy, a little frizzy, a cascade, a tumbling of curls. Her eyes are deep set, her eyebrows heavy and dark. She wears no make-up, her lips are perfectly colorless, pale, a little chapped, and they are usually held tight, pursed tightly shut. She has a firm, rounded chin. Her facial structure is strong, pensive, its features stern and symmetrical as a statue's, blank, neutral, withdrawn. Her face is attractive. But there is a blunt, neutral, sexless stillness to it, as if she were detached from it and somewhere else, uninterested.

She holds the dress up to her body, smooths it down over her breasts, staring.

After a moment she hangs the dress up again, and runs down the zipper so roughly that it breaks. The other dress she doesn't bother with. She leaves the dressing room, putting on her jacket.

At the front of the store the salesgirl glances at her . . . "—Didn't fit?—"

"No," says Gretchen.

She wanders around for a while, in and out of Carmichael's, the Mall's big famous store, where she catches sight of her mother on an escalator going up. Her mother doesn't notice her. She pauses by a display of "winter homes." Her family owns a home like this, in the Upper Peninsula, except theirs is larger. This one comes complete for only $5330: PACKAGE ERECTED ON YOUR LOT—YEAR-ROUND HOME FIBER GLASS INSULATION—BEAUTIFUL ROUGH-SAWN VERTICAL B.C. CEDAR SIDING WITH DEEP SIMULATED SHADOW LINES FOR A RUGGED EXTERIOR.

Only 3:15. For the hell of it, Gretchen goes into the Big Boy restaurant and orders a ground-round hamburger with French fries. Also a Coke. She sits at the crowded counter and eats slowly, her jaws grinding slowly, as she glances at her reflection in the mirror directly in front of her—her mop of hair moving almost imperceptibly with the grinding of her jaws—and occasionally she sees the Adversary waiting outside, coyly. *You'll get yours,* she thinks.

She leaves the Big Boy and wanders out into the parking lot, eating from a bag of potato chips. She wipes her greasy hands on her thighs. The afternoon has turned dark and cold. Shivering a little, she scans the maze of cars for the Adversary —yes, there he is—and starts after him. He runs ahead of her. He runs through the parking lot, waits teasingly at the edge of a field, and as she approaches he runs across the field, trotting along with a noisy crowd of four or five loose dogs that don't seem to notice him.

Gretchen follows him through that field, trudging in the mud, and through another muddy field, her eyes fixed on him. Now he is at the highway—hesitating there—now he is about to run across in front of traffic—now, now—now he darts out—

Now! He is struck by a car! His body knocked backward, spinning backward. Ah, now, *now how does it feel?* Gretchen asks.

He picks himself up. Gets to his feet. Is he bleeding? Yes, bleeding! He stumbles across the highway to the other side, where there is a sidewalk. Gretchen follows him as soon as the traffic lets up. He is staggering now, like a drunken man. *How does it feel? Do you like it now?*

The Adversary staggers along the sidewalk. He turns onto a side street, beneath an archway, *Piney Woods.* He is leading Gretchen into the Piney Woods subdivision. Here the homes are quite large, on artificial hills that show them to good advantage. Most of the homes are white colonials with attached garages. There are no sidewalks here, so the Adversary has to walk in the street, limping like an old man, and Gretchen follows him in the street, with her eyes fixed on him.

Are you happy now? Does it hurt? Does it?

She giggles at the way he walks. He looks like a drunken man. He glances back at her, white-faced, and turns up a flagstone walk . . . goes right up to a big white colonial house. . . .

Gretchen follows him inside. She inspects the simulated brick of the foyer: yes, there are blood spots. He is dripping blood. Entranced, she follows the splashes of blood into the hall, to the stairs . . . forgets her own boots, which are muddy . . . but she doesn't feel like going back to wipe her feet. The hell with it.

Nobody seems to be home. Her mother is probably still shopping, her father is out of town for the weekend. The house empty. Gretchen goes into the kitchen, opens the refrigerator, takes out a Coke, and wanders to the rear of the house, to the family room. It is two steps down from the rest of the house. She takes off her jacket and tosses it somewhere. Turns on the television set. Sits on the goatskin sofa and stares at the screen: a return of a Shotgun Steve show, which she has already seen.

If the Adversary comes crawling behind her, groaning in pain, weeping, she won't even bother to glance at him.

DISCUSSION TOPICS

1. How do you account for Gretchen's behavior? What seem to be the causes of her "antisocial" attitudes? Is she a typical adolescent?
2. From what point of view is the story told? What is its tone? Do you sympathize with Gretchen? Why or why not?
3. Who is the "Invisible Adversary"? What kind of relationship does Gretchen have with him? Why does she want to see him hurt or killed?
4. What psychological dimensions do you find in the story? Are there also archetypal elements? For example, why is Gretchen's adversary *masculine?* How do you think the story would be changed if Gretchen were male?
5. Discuss the story's setting: the suburban landscape, the shopping mall. What does the setting contribute to the story?

WRITING TOPIC

Taking the role of a friend (or teacher or counselor), defend or deplore Gretchen's behavior. Use evidence presented in the story to support your arguments.

Reading Poetry

Poetry is one means of seeing the world, and of seeing it well. Its subjects encompass the range of human experience and all that is open to the imagination. It articulates feelings, perceptions, and ideas we had thought inexpressible, or of which we were unaware. It makes the strange familiar, and the familiar new. Through poetry we can discover more about our language, ourselves, and our world. Consider, for example, the creative possibilities in reading the following poem by William Blake:

The Sick Rose

O Rose, thou art sick.
The invisible worm,
That flies in the night
In the howling storm:

Has found out thy bed
Of crimson joy:
And his dark secret love
Does thy life destroy.

What is our initial reaction—our "felt response"—to the poem? Perhaps it would be helpful to read it once again—preferably aloud this time—to get the full import of Blake's weirdly artful choice of words.

At this stage we are engaged in what is called the "precritical approach" to literature. We are "feeling" the poem rather than interpreting it. And our feelings about Blake's rose are probably a bit uncomfortable: partly because we cannot fully comprehend what is happening, on a literal level, in the poem; partly because the poet has selected words with discomforting associations and put them together in ways that do not quite fit our ordinary sense of things. Why, we may ask ourselves, is a flower addressed as being "sick"? We may think of flowers as being "cankered" or "blighted," but "sick" is a word usually applied to warm-blooded creatures, particularly humans. Why is the word "Rose" capitalized, and why is a flower addressed as "thou"? Why is the worm "invisible," and how does its "dark secret love" (a somber, troubling phrase not generally ascribed to worms) destroy the flower? How does a rose experience joy, or lose it for that matter? Careful attention to the words and images of "The Sick Rose" begins to suggest that much more is at stake here than merely the death of a flower. Having raised these questions, we may now wonder how to resolve them. How, that is, do we get at the heart of this poem, which no longer appears as simple or straightforward as we first thought?

One way into the meanings of "The Sick Rose" is offered by the formalist approach. As we have seen earlier, formalism concerns itself with the discovery and explanation of form in a literary work. Its goal is to determine how the different elements of a text combine to produce its unity and effects. To this end formalism intensively examines the relationships within a poem among its words, ideas, sounds, figures of speech, images, rhythms, rhymes (if present), punctuation, division into stanzas, even its shape on the page. In the interpretation of a text the formalist approach subordinates historical, biographical, and psychoanalytic data: the primary source for all critical observations is the text itself.

Evidently, the rose has been blighted by a worm during a storm. But the word "Rose," we also note, is capitalized. The opening line, then, sets this rose apart from ordinary flowers by combining two figures of speech, *apostrophe* (a form of address to an absent or dead person, abstract quality, animal, or thing) and *personification* (the act of giving human characteristics to an object, animal, or abstract quality). The rose can therefore be expected to share a number of human traits, and we will remain alert to these correspondences as we continue reading. Clearly, there is something special about this particular plant and its sickness—something to do with us perhaps—although we do not yet understand why. Moreover, as a part of the apostrophe and as the first word in the poem, the exclamation "O" immediately colors our response to the plight of the flower. How might the effect be different, for example, if the opening verse were: "Rose, thou art sick"?

Attention to questions of this kind helps define more exactly other important aspects of "The Sick Rose," such as the nature of its speaker or *persona,* the character through whom the poem makes itself heard. Here the exclamation "O" emphasizes the concern—perhaps even the anxiety or despair—of the speaker. (In some editions of the poem, the line ends with an exclamation point, heightening still further the level of emotion.) If we are reading aloud or hearing the poem in our mind's ear, it also becomes apparent that the long "o" in "O" and "Rose" gives vocal unity to the apostrophe, and that the long vowels in the first three words —"O Rose, thou"—lend a plaintive quality to the opening line. With these observations we have begun to establish the *tone* of the poem—the attitude the speaker projects—as one of sadness or distress over the fate of the rose. And in becoming more conscious of the speaker's feelings, we have extended our own range of experience to include the emotional world of "The Sick Rose."

The desire to know why the rose is sick arouses our curiosity—as does any dramatic incident or the opening line of a story—and propels us further into the poem. The destructive force in this garden world is a worm, and like the rose it has unusual properties. Although worms burrow in the ground and might therefore be considered "invisible," this worm is invisible while it "flies in the night / In the howling storm." These traits make the worm both unnatural and ominous. It can't be seen and, like any hidden danger, becomes especially menacing. It moves about in darkness, at night—characteristics that a familiarity with Dracula films might prompt us to associate with evil and some form of vampirism, as opposed to the more positive connotations we attach to words like "day" and "light." Finally, the worm flies "in the howling storm," a source of fury and destruction.

Having examined the first stanza more closely, we now realize that the malady afflicting the rose is not merely botanical. The *apostrophe* and *personification* in the opening line and the attributes of the worm indicate that a literal interpretation of these details fails in a number of ways to do these images justice. In fact, we may well begin to suspect that here we are in a shadowy and enigmatic universe of symbols. A *symbol* may be defined as an image, object, or action that evokes emotions and meanings beyond its denotative value. We sense that a symbol stands for something else, but the multitude of ideas and meanings it suggests cannot be precisely fixed or defined. This situation arises in part because the associations a symbol calls forth are unconscious, and in part because history and experience often allow us to draw out from symbols or detect in them an ever-increasing number of significations. Such is the case with the multiple meanings generated by the rose and worm of "The Sick Rose"; and, when we are prepared to look at Blake's verses in a less literal manner, it may be surprising to find that this brief poem is so rich in symbolic content.

A symbolic reading of the second stanza discloses still more about the nature of the rose and the worm that "Has found out thy bed / Of crimson joy." As a horticultural term the word "bed" denotes both the plot of land in a garden cultivated for plants, and the plants themselves. In a wider sense, though, the word "bed"—including the bed in which humans sleep—carries the connotation of a place where one expects to enjoy rest, security, and peace. The worm, however, "has found out" this sanctuary, the verb suggesting a deliberate search for something hidden from others. Consequently, its invasion and the harm it brings the rose can symbolize the threats that unforeseen, "invisible" dangers pose to happiness and well-being. The stricken rose in turn becomes a symbol for our vulnerabil-

328

ity; or, to borrow John Milton's image of the Fall in *Paradise Lost,* this blighted flower represents humanity's "faded bliss, / Faded so soon."

A bed is also a place for lovemaking. In some way, therefore, "The Sick Rose" may touch on the physical and emotional consequences of love. This insight into another possible dimension of the poem is confirmed by the last two lines of the second stanza: "And his dark secret love / Does thy life destroy." Were we reading solely about flowers and worms, this "dark secret love" might be taken as a figure of speech depicting the worm's desire for food. But we have learned to seek out symbolic meanings to these words. Indeed, we may now begin to suspect—and would be well justified in doing so—that the poem describes the violation of the rose. Corroborating this suspicion is the possessive pronoun "his" in line seven, which identifies the worm as male. Rose is a woman's name; and it is conventional to think of most flowers, especially the rose, as symbols of the female. Tracing this idea further, we can see that the "crimson joy" of the rose signifies both the deep vermilion color of its petals and also its blood when, to use the older metaphor singularly appropriate here, the female is deflowered. In terms of sexual imagery, the adjectives "dark" and "secret" help unify the imagery of the first and second stanzas by recalling the fact that the worm flies in the night (a time of darkness, often linked with love) and that it is "invisible" (a kind of "secret" or hidden love). These adjectives also suggest an initiation into sexual maturity, since this experience involves, among other things, an awareness of secrets once shrouded in darkness. Moreover, the howling storm through which the worm flies is an apt image for the violence so often at the heart of passion.

This brief poem therefore moves from a provocative but mysterious declaration—"O Rose, thou art sick"—through a series of symbols that gradually reveal this sickness to be a love ruinous to life and joy. In charting the direction the poem takes, we have observed that many of its words carry negative meanings: *sick, worm* (which feeds off things living and dead, including human corpses), *night, howling, storm, dark, secret,* and *destroy.* Other formal qualities, such as the short choppy lines of the poem with their constantly shifting accents, enhance the impression of anxiety and agitation evoked by the words themselves. The rhythms of the poem therefore underscore its content, for the orderly patterns of existence that a more regular meter might project have been disrupted by the ravaging worm. We may also feel that this blight is even now a threat to joy and life because the poem is narrated in the present tense: "O Rose thou *art* sick / The invisible worm, / That *flies* in the night / . . . *Does* thy life *destroy.*" The sickness and suffering symbolized by the rose are still occurring in our world; and the sorrow and destruction symbolized by the worm still retain the capacity to destroy the qualities of innocence, beauty, youth, happiness—indeed, whatever characteristics seem appropriate—that we may wish to attach to the rose.

Blake was most unusual as a poet because he published very nearly all his poems in illuminated books in which he unified text and design to an unprecedented degree. A formalist critic might therefore claim that any interpretation of "The Sick Rose" should take into account the relationship between the words of the poem and the illustration that accompanies them. In Blake's own engraving of

"The Sick Rose" the text is framed by the drooping stem of the plant. The rose lies on the ground, so that the position of the stem and flower shows how much the rose has changed from its healthy state and how great the burden of its sickness is. Commenting on the engraving, Geoffrey Keynes, a leading Blake scholar, writes that the worm "is entering the heart of the rose and simultaneously the spirit of joy is extruded." In the upper left-hand corner of the engraving a caterpillar feeds on the already weakened plant, furthering its misery. Two grief-stricken figures rest on the stems, which bristle with jagged thorns. Clearly, these visual details contribute to the atmosphere and meaning of the poem.

The formalist technique reveals that the imagery of "The Sick Rose" is in great measure sexual and that powerful forces are at the heart of the rose's dilemma. These insights are further supported by a psychological interpretation of the poem. On the assumption that actions are motivated by sexuality, Freudian analysis—the basis for the psychoanalytic technique in literary criticism—interprets much of the imagery of dreams and literature in terms of sexual significance. In "The Sick Rose" the flower, with its concave shape, is a female symbol. The worm, with its long, tapering body, is a symbol for the male or phallus, and for death and decay. The fact that the worm "flies" is important psychoanalytically, too, as a symbol of the sex act. The night in which the worm flies may be seen as symbolic of the hidden and sexual desires of the unconscious; and the "howling storm" may also suggest the powerful, chaotic energy of the id and the libido.

Using Freud's descriptions of the interrelationships among the id (or pleasure principle), the ego (or reality principle), and the superego (or morality principle), we may also interpret the plight of the rose as the manifestation of a guilty conscience. A sense of guilt, Freud theorized in *The Ego and the Id* and *Civilization and Its Discontents,* arises when the stern and moralistic superego punishes the ego for its failure to suppress the drives of the id. The ego experiences this tension between itself and the superego in the form of guilt or conscience. "The Sick Rose" might therefore be said to show how the fulfillment of sexual desire deemed illicit by society is being condemned by the superego, and how this condemnation is evidenced, either psychologically or physically, in the sickness of the rose.

There may also be a glimpse in "The Sick Rose" of a provocative theory of Freud's which, it should be noted, remains unaccepted by many psychoanalysts. Over a period of time Freud proposed the existence of two classes of instincts: the *sexual* or *life instincts* (also called *Eros*) and the *death instinct.* The aim of Eros (the love instinct) is to preserve life; that of the death instinct is to seek relief from tension by returning to an inanimate or inorganic state. All existence, Freud argued, consists of a fusion between these two antithetical instincts. Thus the desire for quiescence and death is present even in the life-affirming act of making love, with the result that complete sexual satisfaction is often likened to "dying." The sickness of the rose may therefore be seen as an expression of the death instinct, which Freud found to be so closely linked with sexual passion. The rose and the worm have long been familiar as sexual symbols, and in Blake's illumination to the poem it is clear that the flower is dying as a result of its union with the worm. The striking rhyme between "joy" and "destroy," words closely coupled with "bed" and "dark secret love," further reinforces a perception of this psychological bond between sensual pleasure and death and between Eros and destruction in "The Sick Rose."

Often the same images (water, circles, or the number "three") and motifs (a creation, journey, or initiation) are recounted by individuals or appear in completely different cultures and time periods that have no connection with each other. In such cases we are in the presence of archetypal imagery. According to the psychologist C. G. Jung, *archetypes* are the content of the *collective unconscious,* the unconscious part of the psyche that is innate, universal, and inherited by all human beings. Jung's studies convinced him that the content of the collective unconscious is impersonal and identical in all humankind, whereas in psychological theories such as those of Freud, the content of the unconscious is considered to be exclusively the product of an individual's personal history. Jung was careful to point out that in the collective unconscious the archetypes do not exist as precisely rendered images. Rather, they are formless elements with the propensity or tendency to take perceptible form under certain circumstances. In dreams, myths, and works of art, the archetypes are activated and represented in a multitude of particular images and motifs. Although these images and patterns may differ with respect to specific details in a given myth or poem, they nonetheless can be grouped into categories such as The Hero, The Great Mother, and Death and Rebirth. It is with reference to classifications like these that we can isolate and analyze the archetypes in a work of literature such as "The Sick Rose."

The archetypal and mythological approaches are critical techniques for discovering how archetypal images and patterns found in myths and other enduring works of literature evoke universal and powerful reactions throughout the centuries. The tools of these approaches are the study of comparative religion, anthropology, and cultural history, all of which help to reveal the psychological importance of myth and ritual. Myths and fairy tales, with their panoply of gods, heroes, and monsters, are often dismissed as products of a darker age and as childish stories. But they are in fact projections of humanity's most profound fears, needs, and desires. The myths and their symbols are a way of giving meaning and structure to life and of explaining the world. They are records of a primordial and timeless desire to account for our own existence—how the universe evolved, why we are born and must die, what becomes of us after death. As Jung observes in *Man and His Symbols,* myths allow us to recover the instinctive responses of our deeper, unconscious selves, responses to nature and the universe that have been lost in the shadow of civilization.

As might be expected from an artist of Blake's mythopoeic genius, "The Sick Rose" is rich in archetypal content. The rose itself is one of the most highly charged universal symbols. In *A Dictionary of Symbols,* J. E. Cirlot remarks that "The single rose is, in essence, a symbol of completion, of consummate achievement and perfection." Associated with the rose therefore are ideals of human and divine love, paradise, beauty, and blessedness. In tradition and literature, as Jung observes in *Symbols of Transformation,* the rose is also a symbol of the beloved, of the perfection for which the lover strives.

Whereas the rose represents all that is pure and spiritual, the worm is an archetype for uncontrolled, potentially disruptive energies and desires. It symbolizes the unconscious, the passions, the instincts, sensuality, and knowledge. In these respects the worm has the same archetypal significance as the serpent, snake, or dragon, to all of which it is psychologically and even semantically related. In Old English, for example, the word "worm" signifies either a serpent, snake, or dragon. The last of these is of course a monstrous, serpent-like creature with wings that is capable of flight, as is the flying worm of Blake's poem. Given these similarities, the archetypal battle between the hero and dragon casts considerable light on the malevolent worm in "The Sick Rose." Jung comments in *Symbols of Transformation* that

> the hero represents the positive, favourable action of the unconscious, while the dragon is its negative and unfavourable action—not birth, but a devouring; not a beneficial and constructive deed, but greedy retention and destruction.

The dragon is an image for destructive energy that devours its victim (perhaps a damsel in distress), just as the worm (or caterpillar in Blake's illumination) devours the hapless rose. The worm therefore is a symbol of death and decay, and of the hidden ("invisible") forces that destroy rather than perpetuate life.

Correspondingly, the "night" in which the worm flies is an archetype for death, whereas the *"dark* secret love" represents evil, the unknown, chaos, and nothingness. Crimson, or red, as Cirlot points out, is the archetypal color for blood, life, passion, emotion, and disorder. In its "crimson joy," therefore, the once-untainted rose has fallen prey to violent and destructive forces that are sexual, mysterious, and potentially evil in nature. These have taken their toll on the rose, whose body and perhaps soul are now stricken and waste away.

The garden, where we might expect to find the rose, is, as Cirlot notes, "the place where Nature is subdued, ordered, selected and enclosed. Hence, it is a symbol of consciousness." As such, the garden provides a direct contrast to the violent, uncontrolled impulses of the unconscious; and Blake's poem, with its garden world, is a psychological portrayal of the harm one fears can be inflicted when the unconscious impulses represented by the worm are not restrained but instead break through to the surface and range about unbridled.

The garden is also a symbol for paradise, beauty, innocence, fruitfulness, and the female. If these associations with the rose, worm, and garden lead us to think of Eve, the Serpent, and the Garden of Eden, this is so precisely because the account of the Fall in Genesis contains the same archetypal imagery as Blake's poem. Like Genesis "The Sick Rose" depicts a fall from innocence to experience. Both the poem and the biblical story trace the movement from a happy state (the purity of the rose, or the bliss of Eden) to some mysterious, possibly forbidden action (the "dark secret love" of the worm, or the seduction by the serpent). In both cases this movement ends in sorrow and suffering (the sickness of the rose, or the expulsion from Eden). Indeed, Blake may well have known that many biblical commentators described the Fall as a kind of illness or corruption infecting all humankind.

In a poem so charged with figurative language it is prudent to ask whether the word "destroy" in the last line of "The Sick Rose" should be taken only in its literal sense of physical ruination. Perhaps we ought to consider the metaphorical implications of the word as well, focusing on the idea of spiritual or emotional decay. But how, we might then ask, could joy and life be destroyed by love? After all, isn't sexual love deemed one of the greatest human pleasures, and don't we seek the comfort that love in all its forms brings?

To these questions proponents of the moral-philosophical approach to literature would reply that "The Sick Rose" teaches a great deal about the complexity of love and about the good and bad in all aspects of human experience. As its name suggests, the moral-philosophical approach concerns itself with the lessons that can be derived from a text. Its basic premise is that the larger function of literature is to teach morality and probe philosophical issues. From this point of view "The Sick Rose" might be said to reveal that any emotional relationship, particularly one that involves love, has the potential to wound as well as give joy. Not all people who love find their generosity and feeling requited in kind. Sometimes lovers take more than they offer, and in their selfishness leave others, like the rose, sick at heart.

A moral-philosophical analysis of "The Sick Rose," combined with the biographical-historical approach, would also reveal that it is part of a group of poems, the *Songs of Innocence and of Experience,* which Blake published in 1794, having already issued the *Songs of Innocence* separately in 1789. The naïve emotions and desires of children are the subject of the *Songs of Innocence.* The harsher and more painful realities of the human condition are the essence of the *Songs of Experience,* among which "The Sick Rose" is found. A number of poems from the *Songs of Innocence* have a counterpart in the *Songs of Experience,* but the heartache of experience has made the world of the earlier book one of unremitting darkness, cruelty, bondage, poverty, and despair.

It is often customary to prefer innocence to experience, as the story of the Fall, with its emphasis on humanity's prelapsarian goodness, makes clear. Blake, however, welcomed the realm of experience. The title page to his book reads: "SONGS OF INNOCENCE AND OF EXPERIENCE Shewing the Two Contrary States of the Human Soul." In Blake's own highly developed though idiosyncratic philosophy, both of these "States of the Human Soul" are necessary in order for humanity to come to terms with the world and to understand life wisely and well. "Without Contraries is no Progression," he wrote in *The Marriage of Heaven and Hell.* "Attraction and Repulsion, Reason and Energy, Love and Hate, are necessary to Human existence." If people choose to remain in a state of innocence, they are always children, always subservient to those in positions of authority. Only by way of experience can the state of higher innocence and imagination that Blake calls Eden be achieved. If people do not take on responsibility, they can never effect change. If they do not experience suffering and disappointment, as does the rose, they may never find deeper and more abiding forms of freedom and love.

The critical interpretations that we have advanced—formalistic, psychological, archetypal, and moral-philosophical—illuminate different aspects of "The Sick Rose." These approaches help reveal that Blake has infused his brief and deceptively simple poem with a multitude of implications about the world of Experience, the world in which we live. The rich language and symbolic imagery of the poem, we have discovered, touch in many ways on life and death, good and evil, sexual experience, and the loss of innocence, beauty, and joy. Yet we would not want to limit the meanings of "The Sick Rose" too precisely nor claim that it is "about" one thing or idea. Indeed, this narrowing of perspective is impossible, for Blake's poem contains that remarkable but elusive quality that W. B. Yeats found in symbolic art: "a signature of some unanalysable imaginative essence."

At this point, however, we may be tempted to ask whether everything we find in these poems is really there or is instead a product of our own imaginations. How do we know that the poet meant to do and say all these things? Would some of the ideas we bring up surprise the poet who wrote the poem, and would the value of these observations therefore be suspect? Finally, we might ask if such intensive analysis ruins the beauty and emotional pleasure we gain from casually reading and enjoying a poem.

These are important questions. To them it might be replied that any critical interpretation is defensible when it is consistent with the details of a literary work. If the thoughts we have are grounded in the poem and tell us something about it we did not see before, then that reading is valid and contributes to our knowledge. Sometimes, however, we hesitate to probe deeply because criticism seems to be an unnatural, academic response to an instinctive and spontaneous act of creation. The impression of ease and assurance found in much good poetry leads us to think that the writer, in a sustained burst of inspiration, composed effortlessly and rapidly, producing a complete poem in one sitting. But if we study the revisions made by poets in drafts of their own works, it soon becomes clear that a great deal of labor goes into recasting and polishing those verses so that the poem is as perfect and evocative as the poet can make it. Often it may require many months or even years to write a poem that, as Yeats declares in "Adam's Curse," must "seem like a moment's thought." It may be surprising to learn, for example, that "In a Station of the Metro," the two-line poem by Ezra Pound quoted in our Introduction, took a year to achieve fruition. Pound relates:

> I wrote a thirty-line poem, and destroyed it because it was what we call work "of second intensity." Six months later I made a poem half that length; a year later I made the following *hokku*-like sentence:
>
> The apparition of these faces in the crowd:
> Petals, on a wet, black bough.

Pertinent to the question of whether a poet is aware of everything we find in a work are the comments of T. S. Eliot in "The Music of Poetry":

> A poem may appear to mean very different things to different readers, and all of these meanings may be different from what the author

thought he meant. For instance, the author may have been writing some peculiar personal experience, which he saw quite unrelated to anything outside; yet for the reader the poem may become the expression of a general situation, as well as some private experience of his own. The reader's interpretation may differ from the author's and be equally valid—it may even be better. There may be much more in a poem than the author was aware of. The different interpretations may all be partial formulations of one thing; the ambiguities may be due to the fact that the poem means more, not less, than ordinary speech can communicate.

When setting out to write a poem that will yield this kind of interpretive richness, poets do not generally have in mind a finished text they are merely transferring to paper. Most often poets are feeling their own way toward the development of an idea, image, melody, or emotion until it achieves completed form in a poem. In "The Figure a Poem Makes" Frost writes:

> The figure a poem makes. It begins in delight and ends in wisdom. . . . It begins in delight, it inclines to the impulse, it assumes direction with the first line laid down, it runs a course of lucky events, and ends in a clarification of life—not necessarily a great clarification, such as sects and cults are founded on, but in a momentary stay against confusion.

The "course of lucky events" a poem runs is a combination of conscious and unconscious impulses. These consist of the poet's technical skills (of which the writer is very much aware) and of instinctive responses (the origin and meanings of which the writer is largely unaware). When we analyze a poem we participate in this creative process. We are discovering for ourselves some of the motivations —both conscious and unconscious—that go into the making and reading of a poem. This enterprise need not be heartless and mechanical. We might again remind ourselves, as T. S. Eliot suggests, that "criticism is as inevitable as breathing, and that we should be none the worse for articulating what passes in our minds when we read a book [or a poem] and feel an emotion about it." The critical approaches we have discussed are, in truth, a means of enhancing not only our appreciation of poetry but also our understanding of the world around us and, ultimately, of the deep, fascinating world within us.

Anonymous

SUMER IS ICUMEN IN

Sumer is icumen in.
Lhudé sing cuccu.
Groweth sed and bloweth med
And springth the wudé nu.
5   Sing cuccu.

Awe bleteth after lomb.
Lhouth after calve cu.
Bulluc sterteth, bucke verteth.
Murie sing cuccu.
10 Cuccu, cuccu,
Wel singes thu cuccu.
Ne swik thu naver nu.

Sing cuccu nu. Sing cuccu.
Sing cuccu. Sing cuccu nu.

1 Sumer is icumen: Spring has come *2 Lhude:* Loudly *3 Groweth sed:* Seed grows *bloweth med:* meadow flowers bloom *4 wude nu:* wood now *6 Awe:* Ewe *7 Lhouth after calve cu:* cow lows for calf *8 Sterteth:* Starts *verteth:* breaks wind *9 Murie:* Merrily *12 Ne swik thu naver:* Do not ever stop

DISCUSSION TOPICS

1. Although the title would suggest that this is a poem about summer, with what season does the poem seem more closely associated?
2. What do the various images of plants and animals all have in common?
3. In some medieval manuscripts this poem has a Latin stanza about Easter. Why is that an appropriate juxtaposition with the lines in English?

WRITING TOPIC

Compare this medieval lyric with Ezra Pound's "Ancient Music." Has Pound's parody successfully captured the spirit of the original?

Anonymous

WESTERN WIND

Western wind, when will thou blow?
The small rain down can rain.
Christ, that my love were in my arms,
And I in my bed again.

DISCUSSION TOPICS

1. How does this poem make you feel? How does it evoke those feelings?
2. Which would you say are the most effective lines in the poem?
3. What pictures or images does the poem seem to call forth in your mind?

4. What is the situation suggested by the poem? Who is the speaker of these lines? Where is the speaker speaking them and to whom?
5. "Western Wind" is an anonymous poem of the Middle Ages. Why do you think this very brief and very old poem has retained its universal appeal over so many centuries?
6. How would the meaning of the poem be changed if the question mark came at the end of the second line, as it does in some versions?

Anonymous

SIR PATRICK SPENS

The king sits in Dumferling toune,
   Drinking the blue-reid wine:
"O whar will I get guid sailor,
   To sail this schip of mine?"

5 Up and spak an eldern knicht,
   Sat at the kings richt kne:
"Sir Patrick Spens is the best sailor
   That sails upon the se."

The king has written a braid letter,
10   And signd it wi' his hand,
And sent it to Sir Patrick Spens,
   Was walking on the sand.

The first line that Sir Patrick red,
   A loud lauch lauched he;
15 The next line that Sir Patrick red,
   The teir blinded his ee.

"O wha is this has don this deid,
   This ill deid don to me,
To send me out this time o' the yeir,
20   To sail upon the se?

"Mak haste, mak haste, my mirry men all,
   Our guid schip sails the morne."
"O say na sae, my master deir,
   For I feir a deadlie storme.

25 "Late, late yestreen I saw the new moone,
   Wi' the auld moone in hir arme,
And I feir, I feir, my deir master,
   That we will cum to harme."

337

O our Scots nobles wer richt laith
30   To weet their cork-heiled schoone;
Bot lang owre a' the play wer playd,
    Thair hats they swam aboone.

O lang, lang may their ladies sit,
    Wi' thair fans into their hand,
35   Or eir they se Sir Patrick Spens
    Cum sailing to the land.

O lang, lang may the ladies stand,
    Wi' thair gold kems in their hair,
Waiting for thair ain deir lords,
40   For they'll se thame na mair.

Haf owre, half owre to Aberdour,
    It's fiftie fadom deip,
And thair lies guid Sir Patrick Spens,
    Wi' the Scots lords at his feit.

---

5 *eldern:* elderly   9 *braid:* broad, long   14 *lauch:* laugh   16 *ee:* eye   17 *wha:* who
23 *na sae:* not so   25 *yestreen:* yesterday evening   26 *auld:* old   29 *richt laith:* very loath
30 *weet:* wet   *schoone:* shoes   31 *owre a':* before   32 *aboone:* above   35 *Or eir:* Ere ever
38 *kems:* combs   39 *ain:* own   41 *Haf owre:* Halfway over

DISCUSSION TOPICS

1. Ballads are folk songs that tell stories, sometimes based on fact, sometimes on legend. What story does the ballad "Sir Patrick Spens" tell?
2. How is contrast used in the ballad to create a sense of drama or of irony? What other devices increase tension in the poem?
3. How is the situation in which Sir Patrick Spens finds himself symbolic for all people, not only those who live by the sea?
4. What social conflicts are present in this ballad? How does the anonymous author make us aware of them?

Anonymous

LORD RANDAL

"O where hae ye been, Lord Randal, my son?
O where hae ye been, my handsome young man?"
"I hae been to the wild wood; mother, make my bed soon,
For I'm weary wi' hunting, and fain wald lie down."

5 "Where gat ye your dinner, Lord Randal, my son?
   Where gat ye your dinner, my handsome young man?"
   "I dined wi' my true-love; mother, make my bed soon,
   For I'm weary wi' hunting, and fain wald lie down."

   "What gat ye to your dinner, Lord Randal, my son?
10 What gat ye to your dinner, my handsome young man?"
   "I gat eels boiled in broo; mother, make my bed soon,
   For I'm weary wi' hunting, and fain wald lie down."

   "What became of your bloodhounds, Lord Randal, my son?
   What became of your bloodhounds, my handsome young man?"
15 "O they swelld and they died; mother, make my bed soon,
   For I'm weary wi' hunting, and fain wald lie down."

   "O I fear ye are poisoned, Lord Randal, my son!
   O I fear ye are poisoned, my handsome young man!"
   "Oh yes! I am poisoned; mother, make my bed soon,
20 For I'm sick at the heart, and I fain wald lie down."

1 *hae:* have   4 *fain wald:* gladly would   5 *gat:* got   11 *broo:* broth

DISCUSSION TOPICS

1. Many ballads tell their stories indirectly and with understatement. For example, what does Lord Randal mean when he asks his mother to "make my bed soon," or when he says he is "weary wi' hunting, and fain would lie down"? What story does the ballad "Lord Randal" tell?
2. What is the function of the repetition in "Lord Randal"?
3. Imagine that "Lord Randal" or any of the other ballads in this section was a news story and not a poem. How would the description of these events differ in a newspaper account? In what ways might they be similar? Why don't ballads simply report the facts of a story?

Anonymous

THE THREE RAVENS

   There were three ravens sat on a tree,
      Downe a downe, hay downe, hay downe
   There were three ravens sat on a tree,
      With a downe.
5 There were three ravens sat on a tree,
   They were as blacke as they might be.
      With a downe derrie, derrie, derrie, downe, downe.

339

The one of them said to his mate,
"Where shall we our breakfast take?"

10 "Downe in yonder greene field,
There lies a knight slain under his shield.

"His hounds they lie downe at his feete,
So well they can their master keepe.

"His haukes they flie so eagerly,
15 There's no fowle dare him come nie."

Downe there comes a fallow doe,
As great with yong as she might goe.

She lift up his bloudy hed,
And kist his wounds that were so red.

20 She got him up upon her backe,
And carried him to earthen lake.

She buried him before the prime,
She was dead herselfe ere even-song time.

God send every gentleman,
25 Such haukes, such hounds, and such a leman.

14 *eagerly:* fiercely   21 *lake:* pit   22 *prime:* prayers recited at the first hour of day   23 *even-song:* prayers recited shortly before sunset   25 *leman:* mistress, beloved

DISCUSSION TOPICS

1. What story does "The Three Ravens" tell? What is the effect of having the ravens tell a part of the story?
2. Does the ballad succeed in creating sympathy for the fallen knight? Why or why not?
3. How are the actions of the doe to be interpreted? What suggests that the doe is not to be taken literally as an animal but, instead, symbolically?
4. The black raven has long been considered a symbol of evil. Are the birds in this ballad purely malevolent? How would you characterize the view of nature depicted here?

Anonymous

THE TWA CORBIES

As I was walking all alane,
I herd twa corbies making a mane;
The tane unto the t'other say,
"Where sall we gang and dine to-day?"

5   "In behint yon auld fail dyke,
I wot there lies a new slain knight;
And naebody kens that he lies there,
But his hawk, his hound, and lady fair.

"His hound is to the hunting gane,
10   His hawk to fetch the wild-fowl hame,
His lady's ta'en another mate,
So we may make our dinner sweet.

"Ye'll sit on his white hause-bane,
And I'll pike out his bonny blue een;
15   Wi ae lock o his gowden hair
We'll theek our nest when it grows bare.

"Mony a one for him makes mane,
But nane sall ken where he is gane;
Oer his white banes when they are bare,
20   The wind sall blaw for evermair."

Twa Corbies: Two Ravens   1 *alane:* alone   2 *mane:* moan   3 *the tane:* the one   4 *sall we gang:* shall we go   5 *auld fail dyke:* old turf wall   6 *wot:* know   7 *naebody kens:* nobody knows   9 *gane:* gone   10 *hame:* home   13 *hause-bane:* neck bone   14 *een:* eyes   15 *Wi ae lock:* With a lock   *gowden:* golden   16 *theek:* thatch   17 *Mony:* Many   18 *nane:* none

DISCUSSION TOPICS

1. How does reading "The Twa Corbies" affect your reading of "The Three Ravens"? How would you describe the moods of the two poems? Which do you find more effective, and why?
2. What moral or philosophical values are implicit in "The Three Ravens" and "The Twa Corbies"?
3. What thematic tensions are set up by the contrast in feelings between the humans and the birds?

Anonymous

THE DEMON LOVER

"O where have you been, my long, long love,
    This long seven years and mair?"
"O I'm come to seek my former vows
    Ye granted me before."

5   "O hold your tongue of your former vows,
    For they will breed sad strife;
O hold your tongue of your former vows,
    For I am become a wife."

He turned him right and round about,
10   And the tear blinded his ee:
"I wad never hae trodden on Irish ground,
    If it had not been for thee.

"I might hae had a king's daughter,
    Far, far beyond the sea;
15 I might have had a king's daughter,
    Had it not been for love o thee."

"If ye might hae had a king's daughter,
    Yer sel ye had to blame;
Ye might hae had taken the king's daughter,
20   For ye kend that I was nane.

"If I was to leave my husband dear,
    And my two babes also,
O what have you to take me to,
    If with you I should go?"

25 "I hae seven ships upon the sea—
    The eighth brought me to land—
With four-and-twenty bold mariners,
    And music on every hand."

She has taken up her two little babes,
30   Kissed them baith cheek and chin:
"O fair ye weel, my ain two babes,
    For I'll never see you again."

She set her foot upon the ship,
    No mariners could she behold:
35 But the sails were o the taffetie,
    And the masts o the beaten gold.

She had not sailed a league, a league,
  A league but barely three,
When dismal grew his countenance,
40   And drumlie grew his ee.

They had not sailed a league, a league,
  A league but barely three,
Until she espied his cloven foot,
  And she wept right bitterlie.

45 "O hold your tongue of your weeping," says he,
  "Of your weeping now let me be;
I will shew you how the lilies grow
  On the banks of Italy."

"O what hills are yon, yon pleasant hills,
50   That the sun shines so sweetly on?"
"O yon are the hills of heaven," he said,
  "Where you will never win."

"O whaten a mountin is yon," she said,
  "All so dreary wi frost and snow?"
55 "O yon is the mountain of hell," he cried,
  "Where you and I will go."

He strack the tap-mast wi his hand,
  The fore-mast wi his knee,
And he brake that gallant ship in twain,
60   And sank her in the sea.

2 *mair:* more   10 *ee:* eye   11 *wad never hae:* would never have   18 *sel:* self   20 *kend:* knew
nane: none   30 *baith:* both   31 *ain:* own   40 *drumlie:* troubled, gloomy   53 *whaten:* what
sort   57 *tap-mast:* top-mast

DISCUSSION TOPICS

1. What story does this ballad tell?
2. What hints in the ballad foreshadow the revelation that the lover is a "demon"?
3. What does this ballad seem to say about the nature of temptation? What would you say is the moral of this story?
4. Does the moral message of "The Demon Lover" have masculine sexist overtones? Explain why you think it either does or does not. To whom is the poem's message addressed?
5. How might Freud's concepts of the id, ego, and superego be applied in a psychological interpretation of this poem? What, for example, in the poem would represent the drives of the id, the restraints of the superego?

6. The idea of a "demon lover" seems itself to be archetypal. What other mythic or archetypal elements do you find in the poem?

WRITING TOPIC

What similarities and differences can you find between the heroines of Bowen's "The Demon Lover" and of the anonymous ballad? Are there other important similarities or differences?

SIR THOMAS WYATT (1503?–1542) Highly accomplished lyric poet. With Henry Howard, Earl of Surrey, he introduced the sonnet from Italy into England.

THEY FLEE FROM ME

They flee from me, that sometime did me seek,
With naked foot stalking in my chamber.
I have seen them gentle, tame, and meek,
That now are wild, and do not remember
5   That sometime they put themself in danger
To take bread at my hand; and now they range
Busily seeking with a continual change.

Thankèd be fortune, it hath been otherwise
Twenty times better; but once in special,
10   In thin array, after a pleasant guise,
When her loose gown from her shoulders did fall,
And she me caught in her arms long and small,
Therewithall sweetly did me kiss
And softly said, "Dear heart, how like you this?"

15   It was no dream; I lay broad waking.
But all is turnèd, through my gentleness,
Into a strange fashion of forsaking;
And I have leave to go, of her goodness,
And she also to use newfangleness.
20   But since that I so kindly am servèd,
I fain would know what she hath deservèd.

10 *guise:* practice, custom   12 *small:* slender   17 *forsaking:* abandoning, denying   19 *use newfangleness:* practice fashionable inconstancy   20 *kindly:* according to one's nature, properly; also benevolently, as in the modern sense

DISCUSSION TOPICS

1. "They Flee from Me" is set against a background of intrigues and assignations in the Tudor court, the workings of which Wyatt knew firsthand. What has taken place between the speaker and his lady? How much of what has occurred remains unexplained, and why?
2. How might the speaker's responses to these events be described psychologically? Why does he say, "It was no dream"?
3. Some evidence suggests that in the court of Henry VIII there may have been a series of conventions, inherited from the Middle Ages and now called by the term "courtly love," which governed behavior by focusing on the ennobling power of love, gentility, and fidelity to one's beloved, even in the case of illicit affairs. From a sociological point of view, how are such idealizations treated in Wyatt's poem?
4. Animal imagery plays a significant role in "They Flee from Me." What do such images suggest about the speaker's attitude toward his world and experiences?

EDMUND SPENSER (1552?–1599) One of the major poets in the English language. He is best known as author of *The Faerie Queene,* an allegorical epic in the famed stanza form that he invented.

AMORETTI 15

> Ye tradeful merchants that with weary toil,
>   Do seek most precious things to make your gain;
>   And both the Indias of their treasures spoil,
>   What needeth you to seek so far in vain?
> 5   For lo, my love doth in her self contain
>   All this world's riches that may far be found:
>   If sapphires, lo her eyes be sapphires plain;
>   If rubies, lo her lips be rubies sound;
>   If pearls, her teeth be pearls both pure and round;
> 10   If ivory, her forehead ivory ween;
>   If gold, her locks are finest gold on ground;
>   If silver, her fair hands are silver sheen.
> But that which fairest is, but few behold:
>   Her mind adorn'd with virtues manifold.

Amoretti: "little loves," "little love poems"   3 *Indias:* the East and West Indies   7 *plain:* perfect
10 *ween:* think   11 *on ground:* on earth   12 *silver sheen:* shining silver

DISCUSSION TOPICS

1. Who is the speaker addressing in this sonnet? (Notice that all of the metaphorical language in the poem depends on the opening lines.)
2. How are the poem's images appropriate for a period of history often called the "age of discovery"?
3. What characteristics of the lady are described in this sonnet? What does the poet most praise, and why?
4. In some respects the poem resembles a logical proposition. How do the language and syntax suggest logical statement or proof?

CHRISTOPHER MARLOWE (1564–1593) English playwright *(Dr. Faustus)* and poet. He developed for stage use his "mighty line," blank verse combined with powerful rhetoric.

THE PASSIONATE SHEPHERD TO HIS LOVE

Come live with me, and be my love,
And we will all the pleasures prove
That valleys, groves, hills, and fields,
Woods, or steepy mountain yields.

5 And we will sit upon the rocks,
Seeing the shepherds feed their flocks
By shallow rivers, to whose falls
Melodious birds sing madrigals.

10 And I will make thee beds of roses,
And a thousand fragrant posies;
A cap of flowers, and a kirtle,
Embroidered all with leaves of myrtle;

A gown made of the finest wool
Which from our pretty lambs we pull;
15 Fair-lined slippers for the cold,
With buckles of the purest gold;

A belt of straw and ivy-buds,
With coral clasps and amber studs;
And if these pleasures may thee move,
20 Come live with me, and be my love.

346

The shepherds' swains shall dance and sing
For thy delight each May morning,
If these delights thy mind may move,
Then live with me, and be my love.

2 *prove:* test, experience   11 *kirtle;* skirt

DISCUSSION TOPICS

1. "The Passionate Shepherd to His Love" contains a vision of an idealized pastoral world. According to the shepherd, what is that world like?
2. How is the season of the year significant to the poem's meaning?
3. In what ways is the archetypal image of the earthly paradise related to this portrayal of pastoral existence? (Compare Marvell's "The Garden.")
4. Like many poems addressed to young ladies, this one is a proposition. What does the young shepherd want from his "love"? What does he offer her in return? (Read Ralegh's "The Nymph's Reply" for her answer.)

WALTER RALEGH (1552–1618) A "Renaissance man," courtier, poet, colonizer, soldier, and more. Although Ralegh was older than Marlowe, his poem is placed here after Marlowe's because it answers Marlowe's. It was not the only answer, but is the best known.

THE NYMPH'S REPLY

If all the world and love were young,
And truth in every shepherd's tongue,
These pretty pleasures might me move
To live with thee and be thy love.

5   Time drives the flocks from field to fold
When rivers rage and rocks grow cold,
And Philomel becometh dumb;
The rest complains of cares to come.

The flowers do fade, and wanton fields
10   To wayward winter reckoning yields;
A honey tongue, a heart of gall,
Is fancy's spring, but sorrow's fall.

Thy gowns, thy shoes, thy beds of roses,
Thy cap, thy kirtle, and thy posies
15 Soon break, soon wither, soon forgotten,—
In folly ripe, in reason rotten.

Thy belt of straw and ivy buds,
Thy coral clasps and amber studs,
All these in me no means can move
20 To come to thee and be thy love.

But could youth last and love still breed,
Had joys no date nor age no need,
Then these delights my mind might move
To live with thee and be thy love.

7 *Philomel:* the nightingale   *dumb:* silent   9 *wanton:* luxuriant   14 *kirtle:* skirt   22 *date:*
termination

DISCUSSION TOPICS

1. Notice how Ralegh's poem "echoes" Marlowe's, not only in specific words and phrases but in meter, rhythm, and rhyme scheme. What effects do these "echoes" have on your readings of both poems?
2. What changes do you detect in Ralegh's poem? For example, how has the tone changed? What is the significance of the change of seasons?
3. Ralegh's "Nymph" offers not only a reply to Marlowe's shepherd but an argument of her own. From a rhetorical point of view, how does the first word of the poem lend force to her counterargument? In the same vein, how do certain words—for example, "rage," "cold," "dumb," and "fade"—strengthen her position?
4. If Marlowe's shepherd may be said to represent Freud's pleasure principle, what Freudian principle might Ralegh's nymph personify? Put another way, whose is the voice of innocence, whose the voice of experience?
5. What moral and philosophical considerations do the nymph's objections raise?

WILLIAM SHAKESPEARE (1564–1616) England's supreme poet and playwright, both a child of his times and a poet of all times. He wrote his sonnets at the height of the Elizabethan interest in the form; the songs of his plays are excellent poems in their own right.

SONNET 18

Shall I compare thee to a summer's day?
Thou art more lovely and more temperate:
Rough winds do shake the darling buds of May,
And summer's lease hath all too short a date.
5   Sometime too hot the eye of heaven shines,
And often is his gold complexion dimmed;
And every fair from fair sometime declines,
By chance or nature's changing course untrimmed;
But thy eternal summer shall not fade,
10 Nor lose possession of that fair thou ow'st;
Nor shall death brag thou wander'st in his shade,
When in eternal lines to time thou grow'st.
     So long as men can breathe, or eyes can see,
     So long lives this, and this gives life to thee.

DISCUSSION TOPICS

1. This is one of Shakespeare's best-known sonnets. Notice how the question in the opening line announces his subject—a comparison. In how many ways does Shakespeare find his love superior to "a summer's day"?
2. Do you think the poet is being serious or playful in this poem? Can he be both at once? What is the function of the final rhymed couplet?
3. Shakespearean sonnets all follow more or less the same pattern. The fourteen lines are divided into three groups of four lines (quatrains), with alternating lines rhyming, and a final indented rhymed couplet. How is the "argument" of this sonnet arranged within this pattern?
4. How will the lover addressed in the poem conquer time so that "thy eternal summer shall not fade"?
5. Why is summer an apt season for the comparisons developed in this sonnet?

SONNET 55

Not marble nor the gilded monuments
Of princes shall outlive this pow'rful rime,
But you shall shine more bright in these contents
Than unswept stone, besmeared with sluttish time.
5   When wasteful war shall statues overturn,
And broils root out the work of masonry,
Nor Mars his sword nor war's quick fire shall burn
The living record of your memory.
'Gainst death and all oblivious enmity

10   Shall you pace forth; your praise shall still find room
       Even in the eyes of all posterity
       That wear this world out to the ending doom.
           So, till the judgment that yourself arise,
           You live in this, and dwell in lovers' eyes.

6 *broils:* battles, tumults   7 *Nor:* Neither   *Mars his sword:* Mars's sword   9 *all oblivious en-*
mity: enmity that causes oblivion or that is entirely oblivious to all things (a number of other meanings
aare possible)   13 *judgment that:* Judgment Day when

DISCUSSION TOPICS

1. In this sonnet Shakespeare develops further the thought expressed in the final
   couplet of Sonnet 18. What key images or comparisons does he employ? How
   are these images related to the theme of time? Why do you suppose the poem
   emphasizes marble and stone monuments?
2. What image is developed in each of the quatrains? How are they related to one
   another?
3. What is the function of the closing couplet?
4. In what ways is Shakespeare himself the subject of these two poems, Sonnets
   18 and 55?
5. What psychological or spiritual needs does art or poetry seem to fulfill in
   Sonnets 18 and 55?

SONNET 73

       That time of year thou mayst in me behold
       When yellow leaves, or none, or few, do hang
       Upon those boughs which shake against the cold,
       Bare ruin'd choirs, where late the sweet birds sang.
5   In me thou see'st the twilight of such day
       As after sunset fadeth in the west,
       Which by and by black night doth take away,
       Death's second self, that seals up all in rest.
       In me thou see'st the glowing of such fire
10   That on the ashes of his youth doth lie,
       As the death-bed whereon it must expire
       Consum'd with that which it was nourish'd by.
           This thou perceivest, which makes thy love more strong,
           To love that well which thou must leave ere long.

4 *choirs:* the area of a church where services are sung

DISCUSSION TOPICS

1. To what time of year or season does the sonnet refer? How is that related to the theme of the poem?
2. Each quatrain has a dominant image or metaphor. What are the three metaphors and how are they related to each other and the poem's theme?
3. What are some of the ways Shakespeare uses parallel structure in this sonnet?
4. How is the poem's concluding couplet (especially the word "that" in line 14) to be interpreted?
5. To what different kinds of love does the poem apply?

SONNET 129

Th' expense of spirit in a waste of shame
Is lust in action; and till action, lust
Is perjur'd, murd'rous, bloody, full of blame,
Savage, extreme, rude, cruel, not to trust;
5 Enjoy'd no sooner but despisèd straight;
Past reason hunted, and no sooner had,
Past reason hated, as a swallowed bait
On purpose laid to make the taker mad;
Mad in pursuit, and in possession so;
10 Had, having; and in quest to have, extreme;
A bliss in proof—and prov'd, a very woe;
Before, a joy propos'd; behind, a dream.
    All this the world well knows; yet none knows well
    To shun the heaven that leads men to this hell.

---

1 *expense:* expenditure   *spirit:* energy, vital power, soul   4 *rude:* brutal   *not to trust:* not to be trusted   6 *Past reason:* Beyond reason   11 *in proof:* while being experienced

DISCUSSION TOPICS

1. What is the subject of this sonnet?
2. Much of the language and many of the poem's images suggest a series of contrasts—"Enjoy'd no sooner but despised straight." What two things are being contrasted?
3. How do the rhythms, pauses, sounds, repetitions, and sentence structure of Sonnet 129 help to suggest the nature of lust?
4. Which of Freud's divisions of the human psyche is this poem describing: the ego, superego, or id?
5. What does the poem's speaker conclude about lust and love?

SONNET 130

My mistress' eyes are nothing like the sun;
Coral is far more red than her lips' red;
If snow be white, why then her breasts are dun;
If hairs be wires, black wires grow on her head.
5 I have seen roses damasked, red and white,
But no such roses see I in her cheeks,
And in some perfumes is there more delight
Than in the breath that from my mistress reeks.
I love to hear her speak, yet well I know
10 That music hath a far more pleasing sound.
I grant I never saw a goddess go;
My mistress when she walks treads on the ground.
    And yet by heav'n I think my love as rare
    As any she belied with false compare.

3 *dun:* dull grayish-brown   5 *damasked:* pink; variegated, as in a pattern mingling colors   8 *reeks:* breathes forth (not necessarily with the pejorative meaning *reek* now holds)   11 *go:* walk 14 *any she belied:* any woman misrepresented   *compare:* comparison

DISCUSSION TOPICS

1. The comparisons Shakespeare uses in Sonnet 130 were familiar enough to his readers to be considered clichés even then. What point is he trying to make by cataloging these familiar images?
2. What is the poet's attitude toward his mistress? Is he making fun of *her* or of exaggerated poetic comparisons or *hyperbole?* How can you tell?
3. Compare this sonnet with Spenser's *Amoretti 15* ("Ye Tradeful Merchants That with Weary Toil"). What happens in this poem to the conventions Spenser employed?
4. How does Shakespeare divide his "argument" up among the three quatrains and couplet in this poem? Compare and contrast the structure of the preceding sonnets.

FEAR NO MORE THE HEAT O' TH' SUN

Fear no more the heat o' th' sun;
Nor the furious winter's rages;
Thou thy worldly task hast done,
Home art gone, and ta'en thy wages.
5 Golden lads and girls all must,
As chimney-sweepers, come to dust.

Fear no more the frown o' th' great;
Thou art past the tyrant's stroke;
Care no more to clothe and eat;
10   To thee the reed is as the oak.
The scepter, learning, physic, must
All follow this and come to dust.

Fear no more the lightning-flash.
Nor th' all-dreaded thunder-stone.
15   Fear not slander, censure rash.
Thou hast finish'd joy and moan.
All lovers young, all lovers must
Consign to thee and come to dust.

No exorciser harm thee.
20   Nor no witchcraft charm thee.
Ghost unlaid forbear thee.
Nothing ill come near thee.
Quiet consummation have,
And renowned be thy grave.

"Fear No More . . .": Thinking that Imogen, the play's heroine, is dead, her friends sing these words over her body in *Cymbeline* IV.ii.258–281.   11 *physic:* medicine, medical knowledge   14 *thunder-stone:* thunderbolt   18 *Consign to thee:* accept the same terms as you, sign the same contract with you

DISCUSSION TOPICS

1. From a philosophical perspective, what thoughts and emotions are involved when one is faced with the sudden death of a young person?
2. In what ways are these ideas reinforced by the formal qualities of this dirge? Consider, for example, the effects of words and images such as "furious winter's rages," "worldly task," "home," "golden lads and girls," "thunder-stone," and "quiet consummation." How does repetition contribute to the sense of the song?

WRITING TOPICS

1. Compare the attitude toward death suggested here with Hamlet's soliloquy "To be or not to be."
2. Compare the way the theme of death and the young is treated in this song with one of the following: Hopkins, "Spring and Fall"; Housman, "With Rue My Heart Is Laden"; Ransom, "Bells for John Whiteside's Daughter"; and Thomas, "A Refusal to Mourn." See also Katherine Anne Porter's short story "The Grave."

FULL FATHOM FIVE

> Full fathom five thy father lies;
>   Of his bones are coral made;
> Those are pearls that were his eyes:
>   Nothing of him that doth fade
> 5   But doth suffer a sea-change
> Into something rich and strange.
> Sea-nymphs hourly ring his knell.
> Hark! now I hear them,—ding, dong, bell.

1 *father:* The spirit Ariel sings this song when he tells Ferdinand that his father has perished in a storm at sea in *The Tempest* I.ii.399–407.

DISCUSSION TOPICS

1. What does the term "sea-change" mean in this song?
2. How do the archetypal characteristics associated with the sea play a part in the song's effect? (Compare the ballads "Sir Patrick Spens" and "The Demon Lover.")
3. What philosophical view of death is expressed in "Full Fathom Five"?
4. What does the song suggest about the themes of death and transformation, permanence and change, and the way art itself is born?

MICHAEL DRAYTON (1563–1631) Prolific Renaissance poet. He wrote pastorals, lyrics, satires, historical poems. His best-known work, *Ideas Mirrour,* is a series of sonnets. The poem which follows is Number 61 in that sequence.

> Since there's no help, come let us kiss and part;
> Nay, I have done, you get no more of me,
> And I am glad, yea glad with all my heart
> That thus so cleanly I myself can free;
> 5   Shake hands forever, cancel all our vows,
> And when we meet at any time again,
> Be it not seen in either of our brows
> That we one jot of former love retain.
> Now at the last gasp of love's latest breath,
> 10 When, his pulse failing, passion speechless lies,
> When faith is kneeling by his bed of death,
> And innocence is closing up his eyes;
> Now if thou wouldst, when all have given him over,
> From death to life thou mightst him yet recover.

DISCUSSION TOPICS

1. What judgment does the speaker make about his love affair at the outset of the poem? Why and how does his opinion change?
2. Using the formalistic approach, discuss the ways in which this sonnet develops its contrasts in content and tone. Consider also shifts in diction, imagery, and feeling. How does personification function in the poem?

WRITING TOPIC

Compare this sonnet with Larkin's "Love, We Must Part Now." What similarities and differences in structure, content, and tone do you find?

JOHN DONNE (1572–1631) Author of two widely different kinds of poetry: the playful, bawdy, worldly verse of the young rake; and the serious religious work worthy of the Dean of St. Paul's, London. In both kinds his special style gave rise to what was later to be called the Metaphysical school of poets.

GO AND CATCH A FALLING STAR

     Go and catch a falling star,
       Get with child a mandrake root,
     Tell me where all past years are,
       Or who cleft the devil's foot,
5   Teach me to hear mermaids singing,
     Or to keep off envy's stinging,
        And find
        What wind
     Serves to advance an honest mind.

10   If thou be'st born to strange sights,
       Things invisible to see,
     Ride ten thousand days and nights
       Till age snow white hairs on thee,
     Thou, when thou return'st, wilt tell me
15   All strange wonders that befell thee,
        And swear
        No where
     Lives a woman true and fair.

     If thou find'st one, let me know;
20   Such a pilgrimage were sweet.

Yet do not, I would not go,
   Though at next door we might meet;
Though she were true when you met her,
And last till you write your letter,
25   Yet she
      Will be
False, ere I come, to two or three.

---

2 mandrake root: The forked root of the mandrake was thought to resemble the human shape and was believed to promote conception.

DISCUSSION TOPICS

1. Where does Donne's speaker finally reveal the subject of his poem? Why do you think he waits?
2. What is the speaker's attitude toward women? Does he expect to be taken seriously and literally? To whom is he speaking?
3. Why do you suppose Donne's speaker feels this way about women?
4. Make a catalog of the poem's images. What do they all seem to have in common?
5. How do the meter and rhyme-scheme help convey the poem's tone?
6. What other examples of the relationship between language and meaning, sound and sense, are there?

THE SUN RISING

    Busy old fool, unruly sun,
     Why dost thou thus,
Through windows, and through curtains call on us?
Must to thy motions lovers' seasons run?
5   Saucy pedantic wretch, go chide
     Late school boys, and sour prentices,
  Go tell court-huntsmen, that the King will ride,
   Call country ants to harvest offices;
Love, all alike, no season knows, nor clime,
10 Nor hours, days, months, which are the rags of time.

    Thy beams, so reverend, and strong
     Why shouldst thou think?
I could eclipse and cloud them with a wink,

But that I would not lose her sight so long:
15   If her eyes have not blinded thine,
       Look, and tomorrow late, tell me,
    Whether both th' Indias of spice and mine
    Be where thou left'st them, or lie here with me.
    Ask for those kings whom thou saw'st yesterday,
20   And thou shalt hear, All here in one bed lay.

      She is all states, and all princes, I,
       Nothing else is.
    Princes do but play us; compared to this,
    All honor's mimic; all wealth alchemy.
25   Thou, sun, art half as happy as we,
       In that the world's contracted thus;
    Thine age asks ease, and since thy duties be
    To warm the world, that's done in warming us.
    Shine here to us, and thou art everywhere;
30   This bed thy center is, these walls, thy sphere.

6 *prentices:* apprentices   8 *country ants:* farm workers   *offices:* chores   17 *both th' Indias:* The East Indies were a source of spices, the West Indies of gold *(mine).*   24 *alchemy:* false   30 *sphere:* The Ptolemaic system placed the earth at the center of the universe; the sun, planets, and fixed stars were set in (or, some said, on the surface of) transparent spheres that revolved around the earth.

DISCUSSION TOPICS

1. Why is the speaker in this poem addressing the sun? What does the sunrise symbolize to lovers?
2. Donne's poetry is famous for its difficult sentence structure. Construct your own prose paraphrase of the poem. What is its "argument"?
3. Identify some of the ways the speaker differentiates himself and his beloved from others. What do his distinctions and images convey about his attitude toward the rest of the world?
4. How is time a significant philosophical concept in the poem?
5. The medieval concept of *macrocosm* ("great world") and *microcosm* ("little world"), still current in Donne's day, is based on a belief in universal correspondences between things great and small. This view of existence encouraged physical and spiritual analogies to be drawn between different objects or among an individual, the state, and the cosmos. For instance, the workings of the body, in which the heart and limbs must function in harmony, might be compared to the workings of the body politic (or state) in which the king and his subjects must also act in harmony. How does the speaker turn the idea of the macrocosm and microcosm to his advantage in "The Sun Rising"?

THE FLEA

Mark but this flea, and mark in this.
How little that which thou deniest me is;
Me it sucked first, and now sucks thee,
And in this flea our two bloods mingled be;
5   Thou know'st that this cannot be said
A sin, or shame, or loss of maidenhead,
    Yet this enjoys before it woo,
      And pampered swells with one blood made of two,
    And this, alas, is more than we would do.

10   Oh stay, three lives in one flea spare.
Where we almost, nay more than married, are.
This flea is you and I, and this
Our marriage bed and marriage temple is;
Though parents grudge, and you, we are met,
15   And cloistered in these living walls of jet,
    Though use make you apt to kill me
    Let not to that, self-murder added be,
    And sacrilege, three sins in killing three.

Cruel and sudden, hast thou since
20   Purpled thy nail, in blood of innocence?
Wherein could this flea guilty be,
Except in that drop which it sucked from thee?
Yet thou triumph'st, and say'st that thou
Find'st not thy self nor me the weaker now;
25   'Tis true, then learn how false tears be;
    Just so much honor, when thou yield'st to me,
    Will waste, as this flea's death took life from thee.

---

4 *two bloods mingled:* a reference to the Aristotelian idea that sexual intercourse involved the mingling of bloods   15 *jet:* black; an inexpensive black stone   16 *use:* custom, habit

DISCUSSION TOPICS

1. A flea would seem to be a most unusual focal point for a seduction. How does the speaker build his argument around the flea in each of the three stanzas? Does he succeed in proving his case?
2. Visualize the dramatic scene described by the poem. What are the actions and responses of both the speaker and the woman?
3. The second stanza contains a series of comparisons between the lovers and religious images. How do these analogies function, and what do they contribute to the poem?

WRITING TOPIC

Compare "The Flea" with Marlowe's "The Passionate Shepherd to His Love," Herrick's "To the Virgins, to Make Much of Time," and Marvell's "To His Coy Mistress." In what ways does each of these poems illustrate the *carpe diem* motif, which calls on the listener to "seize the day" before it is too late?

A VALEDICTION: FORBIDDING MOURNING

As virtuous men pass mildly away,
   And whisper to their souls to go:
Whilst some of their sad friends do say,
   The breath goes now, and some say, No;

5 So let us melt, and make no noise,
   No tear-floods, nor sigh-tempests move;
'Twere profanation of our joys
   To tell the laity our love.

Moving of th' earth brings harms and fears,
10   Men reckon what it did and meant;
But trepidation of the spheres,
   Though greater far, is innocent.

Dull sublunary lovers' love,
   Whose soul is sense, cannot admit
15 Absence, because it doth remove
   Those things which elemented it.

But we're by love so much refined
   That ourselves know not what it is,
Inter-assurèd of the mind,
20   Care less, eyes, lips, hands to miss.

Our two souls therefore, which are one,
   Though I must go, endure not yet
A breach, but an expansion,
   Like gold to airy thinness beat.

25 If they be two, they are two so
   As stiff twin compasses are two;
Thy soul, the fixed foot, makes no show
   To move, but doth if th' other do.

And though it in the centre sit,
30   Yet when the other far doth roam,
It leans, and hearkens after it,
   And grows erect as that comes home.

Such wilt thou be to me who must,
　　Like th' other foot, obliquely run;
35　Thy firmness makes my circle just,
　　And makes me end where I begun.

8 *laity:* the ordinary people, as opposed to the clergy　9 *moving of the earth:* an earthquake
11 *trepidation of the spheres:* According to Ptolemaic astronomy, a trembling or oscillating motion was
ascribed to the celestial spheres by medieval and Renaissance astronomers. The speaker states that
although this motion in the heavens is far greater than the "moving of the earth," it is not thought
to be so harmful or ominous as the earthquakes of which people are aware.　12 *innocent:* harmless
13 *sublunary:* beneath the moon, earthly　14 *soul is sense:* dependent on physical gratification
16 *elemented:* composed

DISCUSSION TOPICS

1. What is the meaning of the word "Valediction" in the poem's title?
2. Who are the "virtuous men" referred to in the first stanza? What do they have
   to do with the theme of the poem?
3. What is the purpose of the speaker's reference to "the laity"?
4. What consolations does the speaker offer his beloved when he must leave?
5. A *metaphysical conceit* is a concept or metaphor developed in surprising ways and
   sometimes at length, so that the reader comes to see unexpected connections
   among ideas, things, or actions not usually associated with one another. What
   conceit is developed in the last three stanzas of the poem? Is it appropriate for
   describing the two lovers?
6. The circle has long been a symbol for perfection, infinity, and eternity. How
   are these meanings significant for the lovers of this poem?

WRITING TOPIC

How can the attitudes toward earthly and heavenly love in "A Valediction: Forbidding Mourning" be compared to those expressed in "The Sun Rising," "The
Flea," and "Holy Sonnet 14"?

HOLY SONNET 10: DEATH, BE NOT PROUD

Death, be not proud, though some have callèd thee
Mighty and dreadful, for thou art not so;
For those whom thou think'st thou dost overthrow
Die not, poor death, nor yet canst thou kill me.
5　From rest and sleep, which but thy pictures be,
Much pleasure, then from thee much more must flow,
And soonest our best men with thee do go,
Rest of their bones, and soul's delivery.
Thou art slave to fate, chance, kings, and desperate men,

10   And dost with poison, war, and sickness dwell,
      And poppy, or charms can make us sleep as well,
      And better than thy stroke; why swell'st thou then?
      One short sleep past, we wake eternally,
      And death shall be no more; death, thou shalt die.

12 *swell'st:* swell up with pride

DISCUSSION TOPICS

1. What is Donne's attitude toward death in this poem?
2. How do two figures of speech used in this sonnet—paradox and personification —signify a victory over "Death"? What other devices does Donne use to diminish the awesomeness of death?
3. What does "Death, Be Not Proud" reveal about the psychological needs that religion or belief in God can help to fulfill? (Compare Shakespeare's "Fear No More the Heat o' th' Sun.")

HOLY SONNET 14: BATTER MY HEART, THREE-PERSONED GOD

      Batter my heart, three-personed God; for You
      As yet but knock, breathe, shine, and seek to mend;
      That I may rise, and stand, o'erthrow me, and bend
      Your force, to break, blow, burn, and make me new.
5   I, like an usurped town to another due,
      Labor to admit You, but oh! to no end;
      Reason, Your viceroy in me, me should defend,
      But is captived and proves weak or untrue.
      Yet dearly I love You, and would be lovèd fain,
10   But am betrothed unto Your enemy.
      Divorce me, untie, or break that knot again,
      Take me to You, imprison me, for I
      Except You enthrall me, never shall be free;
      Nor ever chaste, except You ravish me.

9 *would be lovèd fain:* would gladly be loved

DISCUSSION TOPICS

1. Whom is Donne addressing in this poem? What is his tone?
2. What are the key images in the poem? To what does Donne compare himself in the simile in line 5? In line 9 a somewhat different metaphor is suggested

by words like "betrothed" and "divorced." How does Donne join these images together in the final lines of the poem?

3. How does Donne employ parallel structure to reinforce his meaning in lines 2 and 4?

4. A well-established Christian convention speaks of the marriage of the soul to God. How does Donne use this metaphor in "Holy Sonnet 14"?

5. Like "Death, Be Not Proud," this sonnet is rich in paradoxical statements. What conception of the relationship between the speaker and God emerges from these paradoxes? Is this portrait of God in any way unexpected or disturbing?

6. What does the poem's imagery suggest about the relationship between violence and sexuality? Do these seem like appropriate images in this theological context?

7. Does the speaker in "Holy Sonnet 14" seem to suffer from a guilt complex?

ROBERT HERRICK (1591–1674) One of the Cavaliers or "sons of Ben," those who followed not John Donne but Ben Jonson, and developed a polished, urbane style.

UPON JULIA'S CLOTHES

Whenas in silks my Julia goes,
Then, then, methinks, how sweetly flows
The liquefaction of her clothes.
Next, when I cast my eyes and see
5   That brave vibration each way free,
Oh, how that glittering taketh me!

1 *goes:* walks   5 *brave:* fine, splendid

DISCUSSION TOPICS

1. What is the tone of this poem?
2. What exactly is the poet describing?
3. Notice that the poem makes two statements. Where does the second statement begin? What word signals the shift?
4. To what is the poet referring in line 5: "That brave vibration each way free"?
5. How do the meter and rhythm of the poem help to convey tone and meaning?
6. Which words in the poem are the most sensual, actually seeming to merge sound and sense? (Look especially at lines 3, 5, and 6.)

DELIGHT IN DISORDER

A sweet disorder in the dress
Kindles in clothes a wantonness.
A lawn about the shoulders thrown
Into a fine distraction;
5   An erring lace, which here and there
Enthralls the crimson stomacher;
A cuff neglectful, and thereby
Ribbons to flow confusedly;
A winning wave, deserving note,
10   In the tempestuous petticoat;
A careless shoestring, in whose tie
I see a wild civility;
Do more bewitch me than when art
Is too precise in every part.

3 *lawn:* fine linen   5 *erring:* wandering   6 *stomacher:* ornamented covering for the breasts and abdomen

DISCUSSION TOPICS

1. Why do you think the poet finds "delight" in the "disorder" of his mistress's clothing? What signal would this young lady be sending?
2. Look up the word "wantonness" in the *Oxford English Dictionary.* What meanings would have applied in Herrick's day? How important is this one word to the poem's total effect? What are some of the other key thematic words in the poem?
3. Compare and contrast Herrick's blending of sound and sense in this poem and in "Upon Julia's Clothes." What similarities and differences do you find?
4. How might the delights that the poet finds in Julia's clothes and in "sweet disorder" be relevant to the art of poetry?

TO THE VIRGINS, TO MAKE MUCH OF TIME

Gather ye rose-buds while ye may,
    Old time is still a-flying;
And this same flower that smiles today,
    Tomorrow will be dying.

5 The glorious lamp of heaven, the sun,
  The higher he's a-getting,
The sooner will his race be run,
  And nearer he's to setting.

That age is best, which is the first,
10 When youth and blood are warmer;
But being spent, the worse and worst
  Times still succeed the former.

Then be not coy, but use your time,
  And while ye may, go marry;
15 For having lost but once your prime,
  You may forever tarry.

DISCUSSION TOPICS

1. This poem is a warning or admonition. To whom is it addressed? What is the poet's "message"?
2. A well-known adage from the Latin poet Horace advises *carpe diem* ("seize the day"). How does Herrick's poem illustrate this theme?
3. Why does the poet use the image of young girls gathering "rose-buds" to express his theme? What do rose-buds and flowers symbolize? What other images and symbols does the poem employ?
4. What philosophical position does the poem state with respect to time and human existence?

WRITING TOPIC

Compare and contrast the *carpe diem* theme in "To the Virgins" and in Marvell's "To His Coy Mistress." Pay particular attention to the intentions of the two speakers.

GEORGE HERBERT (1593–1633) Anglican priest. He was author of religious verse, often in the style of the metaphysical poets as in the use of quaint, ingenious imagery and extravagant conceits.

THE COLLAR

 I struck the board, and cried, "No more.
  I will abroad.
 What? shall I ever sigh and pine?
My lines and life are free; free as the road,
5 Loose as the wind, as large as store.

Shall I be still in suit?
Have I no harvest but a thorn
To let me blood, and not restore
What I have lost with cordial fruit?
10   Sure there was wine
Before my sighs did dry it: there was corn
Before my tears did drown it.
Is the year only lost to me?
Have I no bays to crown it?
15   No flowers, no garlands gay? all blasted?
All wasted?
Not so, my heart: but there is fruit,
And thou hast hands.
Recover all thy sigh-blown age
20   On double pleasures: leave thy cold dispute
Of what is fit, and not. Forsake thy cage,
Thy rope of sands,
Which petty thoughts have made, and made to thee
Good cable, to enforce and draw,
25   And be thy law,
While thou didst wink and wouldst not see.
Away, take heed:
I will abroad.
Call in thy death's-head there: tie up thy fears.
30   He that forbears
To suit and serve his need,
Deserves his load."
But as I raved and grew more fierce and wild
At every word,
35   Methought I heard one calling, *Child!*
And I replied, *My Lord.*

---

1 *board:* table   5 *store:* abundance, plenty   6 *suit:* in attendance, awaiting a favor or gift from someone   9 *cordial:* restorative   14 *bays:* laurel wreath, used to crown a poet   22 *rope of sands:* A rope made of sand would have no power to bind anyone, while "good cable" (line 24) would.   26 *wink:* close your eyes   29 *death's-head:* a skull that served as a *memento mori* or a reminder of death

DISCUSSION TOPICS

1. What devices does Herbert employ to help convey the spiritual struggle of "The Collar"? How might the denotations and connotations, as well as puns, suggested by the word "collar" be applied to an interpretation of the poem?

2. How can "The Collar" be seen initially as a revolt against moral and religious restrictions? How is this rebellion resolved? What are the implications of that resolution with respect to notions of responsibility, self-discipline, and obedience to God?
3. "The Collar" is imbued with symbols of fertility and sterility, life and death, fullness and emptiness. How are these contrasts symbolic of the speaker's spiritual dilemma?

EASTER-WINGS

Lord, who createdst man in wealth and store,
  Though foolishly he lost the same,
    Decaying more and more
     Till he became.
5   Most poor:

      With thee
     Oh let me rise
    As larks, harmoniously,
  And sing this day thy victories:
10 Then shall the fall further the flight in me.

My tender age in sorrow did begin:
  And still with sicknesses and shame
    Thou didst so punish sin,
     That I became
15   Most thin.

      With thee
     Let me combine.
    And feel thy victory:
  For, if I imp my wing on thine,
20 Affliction shall advance the flight in me.

1 *store:* plenty, abundance   19 *imp:* from falconry, to graft feathers on a damaged wing

DISCUSSION TOPICS

1. In all the early editions of "Easter-Wings" the poem is printed vertically, as it is here. How does the form of the poem reflect its content? Compare "r-p-o-p-h-e-s-s-a-g-r" by E. E. Cummings and "Women" by May Swenson.
2. What philosophical and religious beliefs concerning humankind, sin, and God are set forth in "Easter-Wings"? Consider especially the contrasts developed throughout the poem.

3. How do the facts that wings are symbolic of spirituality and that birds are symbolic of souls help to account for the imagery of Herbert's poem? (Consider other images of birds in works such as Marvell's "The Garden," Keats's "Ode to a Nightingale," Whitman's "Out of the Cradle Endlessly Rocking," Yeats's "Sailing to Byzantium," and Katherine Anne Porter's story "The Grave.")

LOVE (III)

Love bade me welcome: yet my soul drew back,
    Guilty of dust and sin.
But quick-eyed Love, observing me grow slack
    From my first entrance in,
5   Drew nearer to me, sweetly questioning
    If I lacked anything.

"A guest," I answered, "worthy to be here":
    Love said, "You shall be he."
"I, the unkind, ungrateful? Ah, my dear,
10   I cannot look on thee."
Love took my hand, and smiling did reply,
    "Who made the eyes but I?"

"Truth, Lord; but I have marred them; let my shame
    Go where it doth deserve."
15 "And know you not," says Love, "who bore the blame?"
    "My dear, then I will serve."
"You must sit down," says Love, "and taste my meat."
    So I did sit and eat.

3 *slack:* hesitant

DISCUSSION TOPICS

1. What kind of love is Herbert writing about in this poem?
2. Both Love and the poet speak the lines of dialogue in this poem. What dramatic setting is the poet imagining?
3. How does the poem illustrate the Christian idea, "God is love"?
4. How are the Gospel accounts of the Last Supper transformed into a metaphysical conceit in this poem?
5. Some of the language in the first stanza seems to connote a physical or even sexual union. (Look especially at lines 3 through 6.) Is this sexual imagery at odds with the poem's theme? (Compare the imagery of Donne's Holy Sonnet 14.)

WRITING TOPIC

Show how Herbert's "Love (III)" and "The Collar" may be said to depict similar religious experiences, themes, and concerns.

JOHN MILTON (1608–1674) Classically schooled and widely learned, in a sense the last of England's Renaissance poets. He was an officeholder in the Puritan Commonwealth. His greatest works, including *Paradise Lost,* were done only after the Restoration and his blindness.

HOW SOON HATH TIME

How soon hath Time, the subtle thief of youth,
    Stoln on his wing my three and twentieth year!
    My hasting days fly on with full career,
    But my late spring no bud or blossom show'th.
5 Perhaps my semblance might deceive the truth,
    That I to manhood am arrived so near,
    And inward ripeness doth much less appear,
    That some more timely-happy spirits endu'th.

Yet be it less or more, or soon or slow,
10   It shall be still in strictest measure even
    To that same lot, however mean or high,
Toward which Time leads me, and the will of Heaven;
    All is, if I have grace to use it so,
    As ever in my great Taskmaster's eye.

---

5 *semblance:* appearance   8 *endu'th:* endoweth   10 *still:* always   *even:* equal

DISCUSSION TOPICS

1. Using the formalist approach, discuss how the diction and images of "How Soon Hath Time" convey the sense of potential not yet achieved. In what ways does the turn in the ninth line suggest an answer to the dilemma posed in the preceding octave?
2. How should the word "All" in line 13, and therefore the final couplet, be interpreted?

WHEN I CONSIDER HOW MY LIGHT IS SPENT

When I consider how my light is spent
   Ere half my days, in this dark world and wide,
   And that one talent which is death to hide,
   Lodged with me useless, though my soul more bent
5   To serve therewith my Maker, and present
   My true account, lest he returning chide;
   "Doth God exact day-labor, light denied?"
   I fondly ask; but Patience to prevent

That murmur, soon replies, "God doth not need
10   Either man's work or his own gifts; who best
   Bear his mild yoke, they serve him best. His state
   Is kingly. Thousands at his bidding speed
   And post o'er land and ocean without rest:
   They also serve who only stand and wait."

8 *fondly:* foolishly   *prevent:* anticipate or forestall (an objection or action)   9 *soon:* immediately

DISCUSSION TOPICS

1. Milton became totally blind in 1651, at the age of 43. How does his affliction account for the tone, imagery, and content of this sonnet?
2. What symbolic overtones are associated with the word "light"? How are they important in this poem?
3. From a moral and philosophical point of view, how does this sonnet depict a process through which the speaker comes to a different perception of himself and his relationship with God? Compare this change with the shifts in perspective that occur in Herbert's "The Collar" and "Love (III)."

WRITING TOPIC

Read the parable of the talents in Matthew 25:14–30. How does the biblical text bear on the situation described in this sonnet?

ANNE BRADSTREET (1612–1672) New England Puritan; first noteworthy American poet; wife of Simon Bradstreet, Governor of Massachusetts Bay Colony. Her considerable body of verse was influenced by Spenser, Donne, and Herbert, among others. Her poems deal with domestic life and religious subject matter.

TO MY DEAR AND LOVING HUSBAND

If ever two were one, then surely we.
If ever man were loved by wife, then thee;
If ever wife was happy in a man,
Compare with me, ye women, if you can.
5   I prize thy love more than whole mines of gold,
Or all the riches that the East doth hold.
My love is such that rivers cannot quench,
Nor aught but love from thee give recompense.
Thy love is such I can no way repay,
10   The heavens reward thee manifold, I pray.
Then while we live, in love let's so persever
That when we live no more, we may live ever.

DISCUSSION TOPICS

1. Do you feel that Bradstreet is too sentimental in this poem? Why or why not?
2. What formal devices does Bradstreet employ to express her love for her husband? Consider the repetition of key words and image clusters.
3. How is the limitation expressed in line 9 resolved in the course of the poem? What different kinds of love are being explored here?
4. Compare "To My Dear and Loving Husband" with Spenser's *Amoretti 15* ("Ye Tradeful Merchants That with Weary Toil") and Donne's "A Valediction: Forbidding Mourning." What similarities and differences emerge when these poems are viewed together? How is a comparison with Donne particularly instructive in illuminating the characteristics of the plain style used by poets such as Bradstreet and Herbert?

RICHARD LOVELACE (1618–1657) Cavalier poet, soldier, supporter of Charles I against the Puritans.

TO LUCASTA, ON GOING TO THE WARS

Tell me not, sweet, I am unkind,
    That from the nunnery
Of thy chaste breast and quiet mind
    To war and arms I fly.

5   True, a new mistress now I chase,
    The first foe in the field;
And with a stronger faith embrace
    A sword, a horse, a shield.

Yet this inconstancy is such
10   As thou too shalt adore;
     I could not love thee, dear, so much,
        Loved I not Honour more.

DISCUSSION TOPICS

1. What is the tone of this poem? What seems to be the poet's attitude toward war? How old do you imagine the speaker is?
2. What is the meaning of "nunnery" in line 2? In what ways are Lucasta's "chaste breast and quiet mind" a "nunnery" to the speaker?
3. Who is the speaker's "new mistress" in line 5? What other words in the second stanza and the rest of the poem complete the metaphorical contrast between the speaker's two mistresses?
4. What two values or virtues are contrasted in the poem? What is the relationship between them? Which, according to the poet, takes precedence?

ANDREW MARVELL (1621–1678) Milton's assistant in the Commonwealth government; after the Restoration a member of Parliament. Notwithstanding strong Puritan biases in his personal life, his poems reflect a wide range of philosophical and religious points of view. His work has had considerable Influence on twentieth-century criticism and poetry.

TO HIS COY MISTRESS

        Had we but world enough and time,
     This coyness, lady, were no crime.
     We would sit down, and think which way
     To walk, and pass our long love's day.
5   Thou by the Indian Ganges' side
     Shouldst rubies find; I by the tide
     Of Humber would complain. I would
     Love you ten years before the Flood;
     And you should, if you please, refuse
10   Till the conversion of the Jews.
     My vegetable love should grow
     Vaster than empires, and more slow.
     An hundred years should go to praise
     Thine eyes, and on thy forehead gaze;
15   Two hundred to adore each breast;
     But thirty thousand to the rest:
     An age at least to every part,

And the last age should show your heart.
For, lady, you deserve this state;
20   Nor would I love at lower rate.
        But at my back I always hear
Time's wingèd chariot hurrying near;
And yonder all before us lie
Deserts of vast eternity.
25   Thy beauty shall no more be found,
Nor, in thy marble vault, shall sound
My echoing song. Then worms shall try
That long preserved virginity:
And your quaint honour turn to dust;
30   And into ashes all my lust.
The grave's a fine and private place,
But none, I think, do there embrace.
        Now, therefore, while the youthful hue
Sits on thy skin like morning dew,
35   And while thy willing soul transpires
At every pore with instant fires,
Now let us sport us while we may;
And now, like amorous birds of prey,
Rather at once our time devour
40   Than languish in his slow-chapped power.
Let us roll all our strength and all
Our sweetness up into one ball;
And tear our pleasures with rough strife
Thorough the iron gates of life.
45   Thus, though we cannot make our sun
Stand still, yet we will make him run.

2 *coyness:* reserve, modesty   7 *Humber:* a small river that flows through Hull, Marvell's hometown
complain: compose plaintive songs about suffering in love   10 *conversion of the Jews:* an event pro-
phesied to occur just before Judgment Day   11 *vegetable love:* characterized by slow growth only; a
reference to the doctrine of the three souls, in which the "vegetative" soul of plants is lower than the
"sensitive" soul of animals and the "rational" soul of man   19 *state:* existence, high status, pomp
29 *quaint:* fashionable, fastidious, dainty, odd, proud, haughty (The word can also refer to the female
genitalia.)   35 *transpires:* breathes forth   36 *instant:* urgent   40 *slow-chapped:* slow-jawed
44 *Thorough:* through

DISCUSSION TOPICS

1. Whom is the speaker in the poem addressing? What dramatic situation or
   context does the poem assume?
2. What is the tone of the poem? How does Marvell employ images and figures
   of speech to establish tone or mood?

3. Why do you think Marvell introduces the "Indian Ganges" and "Humber" rivers? What point is he making? How are these references related to the others in the rest of the first verse paragraph?

4. The three verse paragraphs of the poem present an argument or proposition. What is the speaker's position? What evidence does he bring forward to strengthen his case? Which words signal the logical development of his argument?

5. What use does "To His Coy Mistress" make of the *carpe diem* theme? (Compare Herrick's "To the Virgins . . . ," question 2.)

6. One of the most significant mythic themes in literature focuses attention on the power of time. Why should this be a compelling issue in "To His Coy Mistress"? Make an inventory of Marvell's references, both direct and figurative, to time. What kinds of images does he employ to describe time?

7. "To His Coy Mistress" contains some rather suggestive sexual imagery. Which words, phrases, and images have possible sexual connotations? (Did you notice, for example, the sexual meaning of the word "quaint" in line 29?)

8. Although "To His Coy Mistress" may appear to many readers to be nothing more than a very glib sexual advance, the speaker's arguments are built on a firm philosophical foundation. Describe in your own words the view of human existence advanced in the poem.

9. What universal human concerns does the poem express? What basic human urges might be said to motivate the speaker?

WRITING TOPIC

Along the lines of Ralegh's "Nymph's Reply" to Marlowe's "The Passionate Shepherd to His Love," write a reply for Marvell's Coy Mistress.

THE GARDEN

I

How vainly men themselves amaze
To win the palm, the oak, or bays;
And their uncessant labours see
Crowned from some single herb or tree,
5   Whose short and narrow-vergèd shade
Does prudently their toils upbraid;
While all flowers and all trees do close
To weave the garlands of repose!

II

Fair Quiet, have I found thee here,
10   And Innocence, thy sister dear!
Mistaken long, I sought you then

In busy companies of men.
Your sacred plants, if here below,
Only among the plants will grow.
15   Society is all but rude
To this delicious solitude.

III

No white nor red was ever seen
So amorous as this lovely green.
Fond lovers, cruel as their flame,
20   Cut in these trees their mistress' name:
Little, alas, they know or heed
How far these beauties hers exceed!
Fair trees! wheres'e'er your barks I wound,
No name shall but your own be found.

IV

25   When we have run our passion's heat,
Love hither makes his best retreat.
The gods, that mortal beauty chase,
Still in a tree did end their race.
Apollo hunted Daphne so,
30   Only that she might laurel grow;
And Pan did after Syrinx speed,
Not as a nymph, but for a reed.

V

What wondrous life in this I lead!
Ripe apples drop about my head;
35   The luscious clusters of the vine
Upon my mouth do crush their wine;
The nectarine and curious peach
Into my hands themselves do reach;
Stumbling on melons as I pass,
40   Ensnared with flowers, I fall on grass.

VI

Meanwhile the mind, from pleasure less,
Withdraws into its happiness:
The mind, that ocean where each kind
Does straight its own resemblance find;
45   Yet it creates, transcending these,
Far other worlds, and other seas;
Annihilating all that's made
To a green thought in a green shade.

VII

Here at the fountain's sliding foot,
50 Or at some fruit-tree's mossy root.
Casting the body's vest aside,
My soul into the boughs does glide:
There like a bird it sits and sings,
Then whets and combs its silver wings;
55 And, till prepared for longer flight,
Waves in its plumes the various light.

VIII

Such was that happy garden-state
While man there walked without a mate:
After a place so pure and sweet,
60 What other help could yet be meet?
But 'twas beyond a mortal's share
To wander solitary there:
Two Paradises 'twere in one,
To live in Paradise alone.

IX

65 How well the skilful gardener drew
Of flowers and herbs this dial new,
Where, from above, the milder sun
Does through a fragrant zodiac run;
And, as it works, the industrious bee
70 Computes its time as well as we.
How could such sweet and wholesome hours
Be reckoned but with herbs and flowers?

1 *amaze:* bewilder, puzzle   2 *the palm, the oak, or bays:* awards for military, civic, and poetic achievement   5 *narrow vergèd:* narrowly encompassed   7 *close:* unite   15 *rude:* uncivil, uncultivated   16 *To:* Compared to   19 *Fond:* Infatuated, foolish   25 *heat:* race   29–32 *Apollo . . . Daphne:* In Book I of Ovid's *Metamorphoses,* Daphne eludes her pursuer, Apollo, by turning into a laurel tree, and Syrinx evades Pan by changing into a reed.   37 *curious:* excellent, exquisite   41–42 *Meanwhile . . . happiness:* The mind withdraws from the lesser pleasure of the senses into the greater pleasure of its own happiness.   44 *resemblance:* an allusion to the popular notion that all terrestrial things have their counterpart in the ocean   47 *Annihilating:* reducing   51 *vest:* vestment, garment   54 *whets:* preens   56 *various:* varied in color   60 *meet:* fitting   66 *dial:* sun dial

DISCUSSION TOPICS

1. In what ways does Marvell's poem promote the argument that the garden is the most desirable state of existence? From the moral and philosophical points of

view, for instance, consider which aspects of daily life the speaker rejects in the first three stanzas and how he diminishes their worth.

2. Discuss the reasons that humankind has always been attracted to the idea of paradise. Why are such places always lost or remote from the world as we know it? Compare Marvell's pastoral images with those in poems such as Marlowe's "The Passionate Shepherd to His Love," Coleridge's "Kubla Khan," Yeats's "The Lake Isle of Innisfree," and Corrington's "Pastoral."

3. Discuss the significance of the masculine/feminine tension in the poem, particularly in stanzas III and VIII.

THOMAS GRAY (1716–1771) Professor at Cambridge. He was a quiet, genial author who was both a classicist and pre-Romantic.

ODE ON THE DEATH OF A FAVORITE CAT, DROWNED IN A TUB OF GOLD FISHES

'Twas on a lofty vase's side,
Where China's gayest art had dy'd
   The azure flowers, that blow;
Demurest of the tabby kind,
5   The pensive Selima reclin'd,
   Gazed on the lake below.

Her conscious tail her joy declar'd;
The fair round face, the snowy beard,
   The velvet of her paws,
10   Her coat, that with the tortoise vies,
Her ears of jet, and emerald eyes,
   She saw; and purr'd applause.

Still had she gaz'd; but 'midst the tide
Two angel forms were seen to glide,
15   The Genii of the stream:
Their scaly armour's Tyrian hue
Thro' richest purple to the view
   Betray'd a golden gleam.

The hapless Nymph with wonder saw:
20   A whisker first and then a claw,
   With many an ardent wish,
She stretch'd in vain to reach the prize.
What female heart can gold despise?
   What Cat's averse to fish?

25 Presumptuous Maid! with looks intent
    Again she stretch'd, again she bent,
      Nor knew the gulf between.
    (Malignant Fate sat by, and smil'd)
    The slipp'ry verge her feet beguil'd,
30   She tumbled headlong in.

    Eight times emerging from the flood
    She mew'd to ev'ry wat'ry God,
      Some speedy aid to send.
    No Dolphin came, no Nereid stirr'd:
35 Nor cruel Tom, nor Susan heard.
      A Fav'rite has no friend!

    From hence, ye Beauties, undeceiv'd,
    Know, one false step is ne'er retriev'd,
      And be with caution bold.
40 Not all that tempts your wand'ring eyes
    And heedless hearts, is lawful prize;
      Nor all, that glisters, gold.

Ode: composed at the request of his friend and fellow writer Horace Walpole, whose cat had recently drowned   3 *blow:* bloom   15 *Genii:* guardian spirits   16 *Tyrian:* Purple dye came in ancient times from the Phoenician city of Tyre.   34 *Nereid:* sea nymph   35 *Tom, nor Susan:* servants

DISCUSSION TOPICS

1. What is the tone of this poem? How would you read it aloud?
2. Describe the "story" told by the poem. How does Gray's cat come to grief?
3. The ode is conventionally a serious lyric poem, in exalted style, sometimes written for a special occasion and usually on some topic of import. What happens when Gray turns to this form in depicting Selima's fate? How does the poem achieve its "mock heroic" effect? What words and phrases tend to give the subject "mock" elevation or distinction? Are the rhythm and meter suited to "heroic" verse?
4. What is the thinly disguised satiric target for Gray's wit? Is he really making fun of some poor cat, or is he perhaps aiming his barbs elsewhere? What words and phrases reveal his satiric intentions?

ELEGY WRITTEN IN A COUNTRY CHURCHYARD

    The curfew tolls the knell of parting day,
    The lowing herd wind slowly o'er the lea,
    The ploughman homeward plods his weary way,
    And leaves the world to darkness and to me.

5   Now fades the glimmering landscape on the sight,
And all the air a solemn stillness holds,
Save where the beetle wheels his droning flight,
And drowsy tinklings lull the distant folds;

Save that from yonder ivy-mantled tower
10   The moping owl does to the moon complain
Of such, as wandering near her secret bower,
Molest her ancient solitary reign.

Beneath those rugged elms, that yew-tree's shade,
Where heaves the turf in many a moldering heap,
15   Each in his narrow cell forever laid,
The rude forefathers of the hamlet sleep.

The breezy call of incense-breathing morn,
The swallow twittering from the straw-built shed,
The cock's shrill clarion, or the echoing horn,
20   No more shall rouse them from their lowly bed.

For them no more the blazing hearth shall burn,
Or busy housewife ply her evening care;
No children run to lisp their sire's return,
Or climb his knees the envied kiss to share.

25   Oft did the harvest to their sickle yield;
Their furrow oft the stubborn glebe has broke;
How jocund did they drive their team afield!
How bowed the woods beneath their sturdy stroke!

Let not Ambition mock their useful toil,
30   Their homely joys, and destiny obscure;
Nor Grandeur hear with a disdainful smile
The short and simple annals of the poor.

The boast of heraldry, the pomp of power,
And all that beauty, all that wealth e'er gave,
35   Awaits alike the inevitable hour:
The paths of glory lead but to the grave.

Nor you, ye proud, impute to these the fault,
If Memory o'er their tomb no trophies raise,
Where through the long-drawn aisle and fretted vault
40   The pealing anthem swells the note of praise.

Can storied urn or animated bust
Back to its mansion call the fleeting breath?
Can Honour's voice provoke the silent dust,
Or Flattery soothe the dull cold ear of Death?

45 Perhaps in this neglected spot is laid
Some heart once pregnant with celestial fire;
Hands that the rod of empire might have swayed,
Or waked to ecstasy the living lyre.

But Knowledge to their eyes her ample page,
50 Rich with the spoils of time, did ne'er unroll;
Chill Penury repressed their noble rage,
And froze the genial current of the soul.

Full many a gem of purest ray serene,
The dark unfathomed caves of ocean bear;
55 Full many a flower is born to blush unseen,
And waste its sweetness on the desert air.

Some village Hampden, that with dauntless breast
The little tyrant of his fields withstood;
Some mute inglorious Milton here may rest,
60 Some Cromwell, guiltless of his country's blood.

The applause of listening senates to command,
The threats of pain and ruin to despise,
To scatter plenty o'er a smiling land,
And read their history in a nation's eyes

65 Their lot forbade; nor circumscribed alone
Their growing virtues, but their crimes confined;
Forbade to wade through slaughter to a throne,
And shut the gates of mercy on mankind;

The struggling pangs of conscious truth to hide,
70 To quench the blushes of ingenuous shame,
Or heap the shrine of Luxury and Pride
With incense kindled at the Muse's flame.

Far from the madding crowd's ignoble strife,
Their sober wishes never learned to stray;
75 Along the cool sequestered vale of life
They kept the noiseless tenor of their way.

Yet even these bones from insult to protect,
Some frail memorial still erected nigh,
With uncouth rhymes and shapeless sculpture decked,
80 Implores the passing tribute of a sigh.

Their name, their years, spelt by the unlettered Muse,
The place of fame and elegy supply;
And many a holy text around she strews,
That teach the rustic moralist to die.

85 For who, to dumb Forgetfulness a prey,
    This pleasing anxious being e'er resigned,
    Left the warm precincts of the cheerful day,
    Nor cast one longing lingering look behind?

    On some fond breast the parting soul relies,
90 Some pious drops the closing eye requires;
    Even from the tomb the voice of Nature cries,
    Even in our ashes live their wonted fires.

    For thee, who mindful of the unhonoured dead
    Dost in these lines their artless tale relate,
95 If chance, by lonely contemplation led,
    Some kindred spirit shall inquire thy fate,

    Haply some hoary-headed swain may say,
    "Oft have we seen him at the peep of dawn
    Brushing with hasty steps the dews away
100 To meet the sun upon the upland lawn.

    "There at the foot of yonder nodding beech
    That wreathes its old fantastic roots so high,
    His listless length at noontide would he stretch,
    And pore upon the brook that babbles by.

105 "Hard by yon wood, now smiling as in scorn,
    Muttering his wayward fancies he would rove;
    Now drooping, woeful-wan, like one forlorn,
    Or crazed with care, or crossed in hopeless love.

    "One morn I missed him on the customed hill,
110 Along the heath, and near his favorite tree;
    Another came; nor yet beside the rill,
    Nor up the lawn, nor at the wood was he;

    "The next, with dirges due, in sad array,
    Slow through the church-way path we saw him borne.
115 Approach and read (for thou canst read) the lay,
    Graved on the stone beneath yon agèd thorn."

THE EPITAPH

    Here rests his head upon the lap of earth
    A youth to Fortune and to Fame unknown;
    Fair Science frowned not on his humble birth,
120 *And Melancholy marked him for her own.*

Large was his bounty, and his soul sincere;
Heaven did a recompense as largely send:
He gave to Misery all he had, a tear;
He gained from Heaven ('twas all he wished) a friend.

125   *No farther seek his merits to disclose,*
       Or draw his frailties from their dread abode,
       (There they alike in trembling hope repose)
       The bosom of his Father and his God.

Elegy: From the Greek word *elegia,* a "lament," the elegy is one of the oldest forms of lyric. In classical and Christian verse it combines with pastoral and rural scenes to suggest themes of grief, death, and renewal. Contemplative and melancholy in tone, an elegy mourns the death of an individual and often the idea or ideal that person represents. An elegy may also lament the passing of a way of life or the painful aspects of human existence, while its conclusion offers some form of consolation for these sorrows.   16 *rude:* uneducated, simple   19 *horn:* the hunter's horn   26 *glebe:* soil   33 *heraldry:* title or rank, nobility   35 *Awaits:* The subject of this verb is "hour."   38 *trophies:* monuments or memorials   39 *fretted:* carved or decorated with interlacing patterns   41 *storied urn:* an urn decorated with various scenes or inscribed with a memorial record of the deceased *animated:* lifelike, as if breathing   42 *its mansion:* the body   43 *provoke:* call forth   57 *Hampden:* John Hampden (1594–1643) was an English statesman celebrated for his resistance to the tyrannical demands of Charles I.   60 *Cromwell:* Oliver Cromwell (1599–1658) was the Puritan statesman and military leader who was active in the overthrow and execution of Charles I. Responsible for brutal campaigns against Royalists in Ireland, he was often accused of tyranny during his reign as lord protector of England, Scotland, and Ireland (1653–1658).   73 *madding:* behaving madly   79 *uncouth:* unlearned, not refined   97 *Haply:* perchance   116 *Graved:* engraved   119 *Science:* knowledge

DISCUSSION TOPICS

1. How do the formal qualities of Gray's poem convey an elegiac atmosphere? (Note the use of aural and visual imagery and personification, as well as onomatapoeia, alliteration, consonance, and assonance.) What symbols of death and mortality are present here?

2. How are silence and solitude important characteristics in this elegy?

3. What do the contrasts developed between the rich and poor throughout this poem entail in moral and sociological terms? What is the speaker's attitude with respect to the class distinctions he sees in society?

4. What is the function of the epitaph at the end of the poem?

WILLIAM BLAKE (1757–1827) English mystic and visionary, poet, painter, and engraver.

THE LAMB

    Little Lamb, who made thee?
    Dost thou know who made thee?
Gave thee life & bid thee feed,
By the stream & o'er the mead;
5   Gave thee clothing of delight,
Softest clothing wooly bright;
Gave thee such a tender voice,
Making all the vales rejoice!
    Little Lamb who made thee?
10   Dost thou know who made thee?

    Little Lamb I'll tell thee,
    Little Lamb I'll tell thee!
He is calléd by thy name,
For he calls himself a Lamb:
15   He is meek & he is mild,
He became a little child:
I a child & thou a lamb,
We are calléd by his name.
    Little Lamb God bless thee.
20   Little Lamb God bless thee.

DISCUSSION TOPICS

1. What symbolic meanings may be attached to the image of the lamb in this poem?
2. What feelings are evoked when you read "The Lamb"? How does Blake's manipulation of language bring out these feelings? (Notice not only the meter and rhyme but also the words and sentence structure.)
3. What are the key words in the poem? Where do they appear?
4. What philosophical view of God and His creation does the poem offer?

THE TYGER

Tyger, Tyger, burning bright
In the forests of the night,
What immortal hand or eye
Could frame thy fearful symmetry?

5   In what distant deeps or skies
Burnt the fire of thine eyes?
On what wings dare he aspire?
What the hand, dare seize the fire?

And what shoulder, and what art,
10 Could twist the sinews of thy heart?
And when thy heart began to beat,
What dread hand? and what dread feet?

What the hammer? what the chain?
In what furnace was thy brain?
15 What the anvil? what dread grasp
Dare its deadly terrors clasp?

When the stars threw down their spears,
And watered heaven with their tears,
Did he smile his work to see?
20 Did he who made the Lamb make thee?

Tyger, Tyger, burning bright
In the forests of the night,
What immortal hand or eye
Dare frame thy fearful symmetry?

DISCUSSION TOPICS

1. In 1794 Blake combined his *Songs of Innocence* (which he had published in 1789) with his *Songs of Experience.* Why is it appropriate that "The Tyger" was included among the *Songs of Experience* whereas "The Lamb" was in *Songs of Innocence?*
2. What does a comparison of the archetypal qualities of "The Lamb" and "The Tyger" reveal?
3. What does Blake imply about the nature of God and the universe when he asks, in lines 19–20 of "The Tyger," "Did he smile his work to see? / Did he who made the lamb make thee?" Consider also the fact that the full title of Blake's book of poems is *Songs of Innocence and of Experience Shewing the Two Contrary States of the Human Soul.*
4. Compare the language and sentence patterns of "The Tyger" with those of "The Lamb." What significant differences do you find? Note Blake's use of questions in both poems. Why are there no answers in "The Tyger"?

AH, SUN-FLOWER!

Ah, Sun-flower! weary of time,
Who countest the steps of the Sun,
Seeking after that sweet golden clime
Where the traveller's journey is done;

5   Where the Youth pined away with desire,
And the pale Virgin shrouded in snow,
Arise from their graves, and aspire
Where my Sun-flower wishes to go.

DISCUSSION TOPIC

How does the symbolism of "Ah, Sun-flower" underscore the distinctions between the flower's present state and the existence that it, the Youth, and the Virgin are seeking?

LONDON

I wander through each chartered street,
Near where the chartered Thames does flow,
And mark in every face I meet
Marks of weakness, marks of woe.

5   In every cry of every Man,
In every Infant's cry of fear,
In every voice, in every ban,
The mind-forged manacles I hear.

How the Chimney-sweeper's cry
10   Every blackening Church appals;
And the hapless Soldier's sigh
Runs in blood down Palace walls.

But most through midnight streets I hear
How the youthful Harlot's curse
15   Blasts the new born Infant's tear,
And blights with plagues the Marriage hearse.

1 *chartered:* guaranteed certain liberties, rights, and privileges; but also with the meaning of "rented" or "hired out," so that all London, including the Thames River, is in effect private property 7 *ban:* public proclamation, denunciation, or prohibition; a curse expressing anger; also a play on "marriage banns," the Church's announcement of an impending marriage 16 *hearse:* a bier or coffin, as well as the vehicle for carrying the coffin during funerals

DISCUSSION TOPICS

1. How do the formal devices in this poem convey the impression of pain and suffering in Blake's London?
2. "The youthful Harlot's curse" of line 14 is often interpreted as venereal disease, which blinds the infant after birth. How does this information contribute

to our understanding of Blake's metaphor in this final stanza of the poem? Why is this curse so important to the speaker?

3. How might "London" be read from a sociological perspective as a reflection of Blake's animosity toward a repressive government and society that he hoped would be overturned as the spirit of the French Revolution spread through the rest of Europe?

ROBERT BURNS (1759–1796) Scots poet whose subject matter often marks him as a Romantic, but whose satire reminds us that he lived and died within the eighteenth century. The same poet wrote "Auld Lang Syne."

TO A MOUSE

ON TURNING HER UP IN HER NEST, WITH THE PLOUGH, NOVEMBER, 1785

Wee, sleeket, cowran, timorous beastie,
Oh what a panic's in thy breastie!
Thou need na start awa sae hasty,
      Wi' bickering brattle!
5 I wad be laith to rin an' chase thee,
      Wi' murdering pattle!

I'm truly sorry Man's dominion
Has broken Nature's social union,
An' justifies that ill opinion,
10   Which makes thee startle,
At me, thy poor, earth-born companion,
      An' fellow-mortal!

I doubt na, whyles, but thou may thieve;
What then? poor beastie, thou maun live!
15 A daimen-icker in a thrave
      'S a sma' request:
I'll get a blessin wi' the lave,
      And never miss't!

Thy wee-bit housie, too, in ruin!
20 It's silly wa's the win's are strewin!
An' naething, now, to big a new ane,
      O' foggage green!
An' bleak December's winds ensuin,
      Baith snell an' keen!

25   Thou saw the fields laid bare an' wast,
An' weary winter comin fast,
An' cozie here, beneath the blast,
          Thou thought to dwell,
Till crash! the cruel coulter passed
30   Out thro' thy cell.

That wee-bit heap o' leaves an' stibble,
Has cost thee monie a weary nibble!
Now thou's turned out, for a' thy trouble,
          But house or hald,
35   To thole the winter's sleety dribble,
            And cranreuch cauld!

But, mousie, thou art no thy-lane,
In proving foresight may be vain:
The best laid schemes o' mice an' men,
40   Gang aft agley,
An' lea'e us nought but grief an' pain,
            For promised joy!

Still, thou art blest, compared wi' me!
The present only toucheth thee:
45   But och! I backward cast my e'e,
          On prospects drear!
And forward, tho' I canna see,
           I guess and fear!

1 *sleeket:* sleek   3 *na:* not   *awa sae:* away so   4 *bickering brattle:* rapid scamper   5 *laith:* loath 6 *pattle:* ploughstaff, spade   13 *whyles:* sometimes   14 *maun:* must   15 *A . . . thrave:* An occasional ear in twenty-four sheaves   16 *sma:* small   17 *lave:* remainder   20 *silly wa's:* feeble walls   *win's:* winds   21 *big:* build   *ane:* one   22 *foggage:* moss   24 *Baith snell:* Both bitter 29 *coulter:* blade of a plough   31 *stibble:* stubble   32 *monie:* many   34 *But house or hald:* Without house or holding   35 *thole:* endure   36 *cranreuch:* hoar-frost   37 *no thy-lane:* not alone 40 *Gang aft agley:* Go often awry   41 *lea'e:* leave

DISCUSSION TOPICS

1. What economic and social themes are explored in this poem?
2. How does the Scottish dialect enhance the social and political message of the poem?
3. What kinds of suppositions are made when composing a poem to a mouse? What do these assumptions reveal about the bond between the Romantic poets and nature? Is the mouse the only victim in this poem?

WILLIAM WORDSWORTH (1770–1850) Chief of the earlier Romantics, collaborator with Coleridge. He was a poet who not only celebrated nature but also saw man as the crown of creation and the good life as his goal.

A SLUMBER DID MY SPIRIT SEAL

A slumber did my spirit seal;
  I had no human fears:
She seemed a thing that could not feel
  The touch of earthly years.

5　No motion has she now, no force;
  She neither hears nor sees;
Rolled round in earth's diurnal course,
  With rocks, and stones, and trees.

DISCUSSION TOPICS

1. How do irony and paradox function in this poem? Note particularly the tension between the first and second stanzas.
2. Compare the attitude toward death in this poem with that expressed in Donne's "Death, Be Not Proud."
3. Why does the speaker say: "I had no human fears"?

THE WORLD IS TOO MUCH WITH US

The world is too much with us; late and soon,
Getting and spending, we lay waste our powers:
Little we see in Nature that is ours;
We have given our hearts away, a sordid boon!
5　This sea that bares her bosom to the moon;
The winds that will be howling at all hours,
And are up-gathered now like sleeping flowers;
For this, for everything, we are out of tune;
It moves us not.—Great God! I'd rather be
10　A pagan suckled in a creed outworn;
So might I, standing on this pleasant lea,
Have glimpses that would make me less forlorn;
Have sight of Proteus rising from the sea;
Or hear old Triton blow his wreathèd horn.

---

4 *boon:* gift　　13 *Proteus:* a sea-god　　14 *Triton:* a god of the sea, often depicted blowing on a conch shell

DISCUSSION TOPICS

1. Against what kind of existence and sense of loss does this poem protest? How might it be used to illustrate philosophical beliefs held by Wordsworth and other Romantics about the detrimental effects of urban and industrial society on the human spirit? What alternatives to this dilemma does Wordsworth's poem offer?
2. How do the formal devices of "The World Is Too Much with Us" heighten the sense of wasteful, materialistic destructiveness that the speaker deplores?
3. How do the archetypal images used here—such as the sea, moon, winds, and flowers—strengthen the theme of the poem?

LONDON, 1802

> Milton! thou shouldst be living at this hour:
> England hath need of thee: she is a fen
> Of stagnant waters: altar, sword, and pen,
> Fireside, the heroic wealth of hall and bower,
> 5 Have forfeited their ancient English dower
> Of inward happiness. We are selfish men;
> Oh! raise us up, return to us again;
> And give us manners, virtue, freedom, power.
> Thy soul was like a Star, and dwelt apart;
> 10 Thou hadst a voice whose sound was like the sea:
> Pure as the naked heavens, majestic, free,
> So didst thou travel on life's common way,
> In cheerful godliness; and yet thy heart
> The lowliest duties on herself did lay.

DISCUSSION TOPICS

1. What is Wordsworth's theme? Why do you suppose he addresses Milton? How might Milton be of assistance?
2. What is the form of this poem? (Compare "Nuns Fret Not at Their Convent's Narrow Room," which follows.)
3. How does "London, 1802" convey the poet's concern with the moral and social conditions of his day? What does the poem indicate has been lost, and what does it argue should be regained?

WRITING TOPIC

This poem is replete with figures of speech, for example, apostrophe, simile, metaphor, hyperbole, and metonymy. Identify these and explain how they are used to enhance the theme of the poem.

NUNS FRET NOT AT THEIR CONVENT'S NARROW ROOM

Nuns fret not at their convent's narrow room;
And hermits are contented with their cells;
And students with their pensive citadels;
Maids at the wheel, the weaver at his loom,
5   Sit blithe and happy; bees that soar for bloom,
High as the highest Peak of Furness-fells,
Will murmur by the hour in foxglove bells:
In truth the prison, unto which we doom
Ourselves, no prison is: and hence for me,
10   In sundry moods, 'twas pastime to be bound
Within the Sonnet's scanty plot of ground;
Pleased if some Souls (for such there needs must be)
Who have felt the weight of too much liberty,
Should find brief solace there, as I have found.

6 *Furness-fells:* the mountains in the Lake District of England, Wordsworth's home

DISCUSSION TOPICS

1. Where is the true subject of this poem introduced? What does it have to do with nuns and hermits?
2. Make a list of all the images and comparisons in the poem. How does each illustrate "solace" for "the weight of too much liberty"?
3. What larger themes are introduced by the idea of "too much liberty"?
4. What commentary does the poem offer on the relationship between life and poetry?

I WANDERED LONELY AS A CLOUD

I wandered lonely as a cloud
That floats on high o'er vales and hills,
When all at once I saw a crowd,
A host, of golden daffodils;
5   Beside the lake, beneath the trees,
Fluttering and dancing in the breeze.

Continuous as the stars that shine
And twinkle on the milky way,
They stretched in never-ending line

10 Along the margin of a bay:
    Ten thousand saw I at a glance.
    Tossing their heads in sprightly dance.

    The waves beside them danced; but they
    Outdid the sparkling waves in glee;
15 A poet could not but be gay,
    In such a jocund company;
    I gazed—and gazed—but little thought
    What wealth the show to me had brought:

    For oft, when on my couch I lie
20 In vacant or in pensive mood,
    They flash upon that inward eye
    Which is the bliss of solitude;
    And then my heart with pleasure fills,
    And dances with the daffodils.

DISCUSSION TOPICS

1. In the Preface to *Lyrical Ballads* (1800) Wordsworth sets forth the principles on which his poetry is written: "I have said that Poetry is the spontaneous overflow of powerful feelings: it takes its origin from emotion recollected in tranquillity: the emotion is contemplated till by a species of reaction the tranquillity gradually disappears, and an emotion, similar to that which was before the subject of contemplation, is gradually produced, and does itself actually exist in the mind. In this mood successful composition generally begins, and in a mood similar to this it is carried on." How are these principles reflected in this poem?
2. What relationships between the poet and nature are presented here?

SAMUEL TAYLOR COLERIDGE (1772–1834) Author of *The Rime of the Ancient Mariner*. He was even more important as a major source of modern literary criticism—a wellspring for his statements on poetry, the poet, imagination, and individual poets and playwrights.

THE EOLIAN HARP

COMPOSED AT CLEVEDON, SOMERSETSHIRE

My pensive Sara! thy soft cheek reclined
Thus on mine arm, most soothing sweet it is
To sit beside our Cot, our Cot o'ergrown

With white-flowered Jasmin, and the broad-leaved Myrtle,
5   (Meet emblems they of Innocence and Love!)
And watch the clouds, that late were rich with light,
Slow saddening round, and mark the star of eve
Serenely brilliant (such should Wisdom be)
Shine opposite! How exquisite the scents
10   Snatched from yon bean-field! and the world so hushed!
The stilly murmur of the distant Sea
Tells us of silence.
                    And that simplest Lute,
Placed length-ways in the clasping casement, hark!
How by the desultory breeze caressed,
15   Like some coy maid half yielding to her lover,
It pours such sweet upbraiding, as must needs
Tempt to repeat the wrong! And now, its strings
Boldlier swept, the long sequacious notes
Over delicious surges sink and rise,
20   Such a soft floating witchery of sound
As twilight Elfins make, when they at eve
Voyage on gentle gales from Fairy-Land,
Where Melodies round honey-dropping flowers,
Footless and wild, like birds of Paradise,
25   Nor pause, nor perch, hovering on untamed wing!
O! the one Life within us and abroad,
Which meets all motion and becomes its soul,
A light in sound, a sound-like power in light,
Rhythm in all thought, and joyance everywhere—
30   Methinks, it should have been impossible
Not to love all things in a world so filled;
Where the breeze warbles, and the mute still air
Is Music slumbering on her instrument.

      And thus, my Love! as on the midway slope
35   Of yonder hill I stretch my limbs at noon,
Whilst through my half-closed eyelids I behold
The sunbeams dance, like diamonds, on the main,
And tranquil muse upon tranquillity:
Full many a thought uncalled and undetained,
40   And many idle flitting phantasies,
Traverse my indolent and passive brain,
As wild and various as the random gales
That swell and flutter on this subject Lute!

      And what if all of animated nature
45   Be but organic Harps diversely framed,
That tremble into thought, as o'er them sweeps

Plastic and vast, one intellectual breeze.
At once the Soul of each, and God of all?

But thy more serious eye a mild reproof
50 Darts, O belovéd Woman! nor such thoughts
Dim and unhallowed dost thou not reject,
And biddest me walk humbly with my God.
Meek Daughter in the family of Christ!
Well hast thou said and holily dispraised
55 These shapings of the unregenerate mind;
Bubbles that glitter as they rise and break
On vain Philosophy's aye-babbling spring.
For never guiltless may I speak of him,
The Incomprehensible! save when with awe
60 I praise him, and with Faith that inly *feels;*
Who with his saving mercies healed me,
A sinful and most miserable man,
Wildered and dark, and gave me to possess
Peace, and this Cot, and thee, heart-honored Maid!

Eolian Harp: a harp, or lute, that produced a sound when the wind (or Aeolus, the god of the winds) passed through its strings. It was a symbol of poetic inspiration, or of the mind receptive to nature. 1 *Sara:* Sara Fricker, whom Coleridge married in 1795   3 *Cot:* cottage   5 *Meet:* Fitting, proper 19 *sequacious:* regularly following one another   25 *birds of Paradise:* found largely in New Guinea and noted for remarkable plumage. Because natives would remove the feet in preparing the skin, Europeans though that the birds dwelled only in the air and that they came from Paradise.   47 *Plastic:* capable of being molded, readily changing shape

DISCUSSION TOPICS

1. What is Coleridge's subject in "The Eolian Harp"? Consider the first two stanzas or verse paragraphs that set the scene and introduce both Sara and the lute. Pay close attention to the description of the way the "desultory breeze" plays on the wind harp. Now read carefully Coleridge's thoughts in the fourth stanza beginning at line 34. How does he enlarge his original image?

2. What complication does Coleridge introduce in the poem's final stanza? Why does Sara's "more serious eye" dart "a mild reproof"? What does Coleridge mean by phrases such as "unregenerate mind" and "vain Philosophy's aye-babbling spring"?

3. How does Coleridge attempt to resolve the conflict between his pantheism or natural religion and traditional Judeo-Christian theology?

4. Compare this poem with Shelley's "Ode to the West Wind," especially lines 57–61 in the latter poem.

KUBLA KHAN: OR, A VISION IN A DREAM

A FRAGMENT

In Xanadu did Kubla Khan
A stately pleasure-dome decree:
Where Alph, the sacred river, ran
Through caverns measureless to man
5   Down to a sunless sea.
So twice five miles of fertile ground
With walls and towers were girdled round:
And here were gardens bright with sinuous rills,
Where blossomed many an incense-bearing tree;
10 And here were forests ancient as the hills,
Enfolding sunny spots of greenery.

But oh! that deep romantic chasm which slanted
Down the green hill athwart a cedarn cover!
A savage place! as holy and enchanted
15 As e'er beneath a waning moon was haunted
By woman wailing for her demon-lover!
And from this chasm, with ceaseless turmoil seething,
As if this earth in fast thick pants were breathing,
A mighty fountain momently was forced:
20 Amid whose swift half-intermitted burst
Huge fragments vaulted like rebounding hail,
Or chaffy grain beneath the thresher's flail:
And 'mid these dancing rocks at once and ever
It flung up momently the sacred river.
25 Five miles meandering with a mazy motion
Through wood and dale the sacred river ran,
Then reached the caverns measureless to man,
And sank in tumult to a lifeless ocean:
And 'mid this tumult Kubla heard from far
30 Ancestral voices prophesying war!
      The shadow of the dome of pleasure
      Floated midway on the waves;
      Where was heard the mingled measure
      From the fountain and the caves.
35 It was a miracle of rare device,
A sunny pleasure-dome with caves of ice!

      A damsel with a dulcimer
      In a vision once I saw:
      It was an Abyssinian maid,

40   And on her dulcimer she played,
        Singing of Mount Abora.
        Could I revive within me,
        Her symphony and song,
        To such a deep delight 'twould win me,
45 That with music loud and long,
    I would build that dome in air,
    That sunny dome! those caves of ice!
    And all who heard should see them there,
    And all should cry, Beware! Beware!
50 His flashing eyes, his floating hair!
    Weave a circle round him thrice,
    And close your eyes with holy dread,
    For he on honey-dew hath fed,
    And drunk the milk of Paradise.

---

1 *Kubla Khan:* Kublai Khan (1216–1294), founder of the Mongol dynasty in China   3 *Alph:* The name may be suggested by the Greek river Alpheus, which was said to run underground.   13 *athwart:* across   *cedarn:* of cedar trees   19 *momently:* every moment   41 *Mount Abora:* As with the river Alph, the name is imaginary; it may allude to Mount Amara, which Milton mentions in *Paradise Lost,* IV, 280, as the site of a palace supposed by some to be Paradise.

DISCUSSION TOPICS

1. According to Coleridge, "Kubla Khan" is a "fragment" preserved from a vision the poet had while under the influence of opium, which had been prescribed for medicinal reasons. Although taking note of Coleridge's own statement, many readers have nonetheless considered "Kubla Khan" a complete work. If you had not been told this, would you consider the poem complete in itself?

2. What is the relationship between the first thirty-six lines and the final stanza? What does the "damsel with a dulcimer" represent?

3. What do you think Coleridge means when he says "I would build that dome in air"? In what respect is he, in fact, building in air by writing (or reciting) this poem?

4. Why should those who heard and saw him cry "Beware! Beware"? Is Coleridge suggesting that pefect poetic creation would result, magically, in a visible re-creation of his dream vision?

5. "Kubla Khan" abounds with archetypal images such as the river, fountain, sea, cavern, and garden. It is also rich in male and female imagery, much of it sexual. What do these images suggest about creativity, destruction, and the forces of the unconscious and imagination in the poem?

ON DONNE'S POETRY

With Donne, whose muse on dromedary trots,
Wreathe iron pokers into truelove knots;
Rhyme's sturdy cripple, fancy's maze and clue,
Wit's forge and fire-blast, meaning's press and screw.

GEORGE GORDON, LORD BYRON (1788–1824) Brilliant, talented, dissolute creator of the Byronic hero. He epitomized the rebellious aspects of romanticism even though much of his poetry is neoclassical in form and outlook.

THE DESTRUCTION OF SENNACHERIB

The Assyrian came down like the wolf on the fold,
And his cohorts were gleaming in purple and gold;
And the sheen of their spears was like stars on the sea,
When the blue wave rolls nightly on deep Galilee.

5   Like the leaves of the forest when summer is green,
That host with their banners at sunset were seen:
Like the leaves of the forest when autumn hath blown,
That host on the morrow lay withered and strown.

For the Angel of Death spread his wings on the blast,
10   And breathed in the face of the foe as he passed;
And the eyes of the sleepers waxed deadly and chill,
And their hearts but once heaved—and for ever grew still!

And there lay the steed with his nostril all wide,
But through it there rolled not the breath of his pride;
15   And the foam of his gasping lay white on the turf,
And cold as the spray of the rock-beating surf.

And there lay the rider distorted and pale,
With the dew on his brow, and the rust on his mail;
And the tents were all silent, the banners alone,
20   The lances unlifted, the trumpet unblown.

And the widows of Ashur are loud in their wail,
And the idols are broke in the temple of Baal;
And the might of the Gentile, unsmote by the sword,
Hath melted like snow in the glance of the Lord!

Sennacherib: king of Assyria from 704–681 BC   21 *Ashur:* the religious capital of ancient Assyria
22 *Baal:* a god worshipped by many ancient Semitic nations.

DISCUSSION TOPIC

What is the dominant meter of this poem, and how does it contribute to the poem's effect on you?

SHE WALKS IN BEAUTY

1

She walks in beauty, like the night
  Of cloudless climes and starry skies;
And all that's best of dark and bright
  Meet in her aspect and her eyes:
5 Thus mellowed to that tender light
  Which heaven to gaudy day denies.

2

One shade the more, one ray the less,
  Had half impaired the nameless grace
Which waves in every raven tress,
10   Or softly lightens o'er her face;
Where thoughts serenely sweet express
  How pure, how dear their dwelling place.

3

And on that cheek, and o'er that brow,
  So soft, so calm, yet eloquent,
15 The smiles that win, the tints that glow,
  But tell of days in goodness spent,
A mind at peace with all below,
  A heart whose love is innocent!

DISCUSSION TOPICS

1. What mood does Byron create in this poem? What images does he use to create it? Which are the poem's most effective words?
2. Compare and contrast Byron's version of feminine beauty with those of Herrick in "Upon Julia's Clothes" and "Delight in Disorder" and in Swenson's "Women." What characteristics of Byron's poem stand out as essentially "Romantic"? Which of these visions do you prefer, and why?

Percy Bysshe Shelley (1792–1822) High-minded, radical idealist; supreme lyricist. Like his friend Byron, he was a Romantic rebel against tyranny and injustice and an apostle of liberty in body and spirit.

ODE TO THE WEST WIND

I

O wild west wind, thou breath of autumn's being,
Thou from whose unseen presence the leaves dead
Are driven like ghosts from an enchanter fleeing,

Yellow, and black, and pale, and hectic red,
5   Pestilence-stricken multitudes! O thou
Who chariotest to their dark wintry bed

The wingèd seeds, where they lie cold and low,
Each like a corpse within its grave, until
Thine azure sister of the spring shall blow

10   Her clarion o'er the dreaming earth, and fill
(Driving sweet buds like flocks to feed in air)
With living hues and odours plain and hill:

Wild spirit, which art moving everywhere;
Destroyer and preserver; hear, O hear!

II

15   Thou on whose stream, 'mid the steep sky's commotion,
Loose clouds like earth's decaying leaves are shed,
Shook from the tangled boughs of heaven and ocean,

Angels of rain and lightning: there are spread
On the blue surface of thine airy surge,
20   Like the bright hair uplifted from the head

Of some fierce Maenad, even from the dim verge
Of the horizon to the zenith's height,
The locks of the approaching storm. Thou dirge

Of the dying year, to which this closing night
25   Will be the dome of a vast sepulchre,
Vaulted with all thy congregated might

Of vapours, from whose solid atmosphere
Black rain, and fire, and hail will burst: O hear!

III

     Thou who didst waken from his summer dreams
30   The blue Mediterranean, where he lay,
     Lulled by the coil of his crystalline streams,

     Beside a pumice isle in Baiae's bay,
     And saw in sleep old palaces and towers
     Quivering within the wave's intenser day,

35   All overgrown with azure moss and flowers
     So sweet, the sense faints picturing them! Thou
     For whose path the Atlantic's level powers

     Cleave themselves into chasms, while far below
     The sea-blooms and the oozy woods which wear
40   The sapless foliage of the ocean, know

     Thy voice, and suddenly grow gray with fear,
     And tremble and despoil themselves: O hear!

IV

     If I were a dead leaf thou mightest bear;
     If I were a swift cloud to fly with thee;
45   A wave to pant beneath thy power, and share

     The impulse of thy strength, only less free
     Than thou, O uncontrollable! if even
     I were as in my boyhood, and could be

     The comrade of thy wanderings over heaven,
50   As then, when to outstrip thy skiey speed
     Scarce seemed a vision; I would ne'er have striven

     As thus with thee in prayer in my sore need.
     O! lift me as a wave, a leaf, a cloud!
     I fall upon the thorns of life! I bleed!

55   A heavy weight of hours has chained and bowed
     One too like thee: tameless, and swift, and proud.

V

     Make me thy lyre, even as the forest is:
     What if my leaves are falling like its own?
     The tumult of thy mighty harmonies

60 Will take from both a deep autumnal tone,
Sweet though in sadness. Be thou, spirit fierce,
My spirit! Be thou me, impetuous one!

Drive my dead thoughts over the universe,
Like withered leaves, to quicken a new birth;
65 And, by the incantation of this verse,

Scatter, as from an unextinguished hearth
Ashes and sparks, my words among mankind!
Be through my lips to unawakened earth

The trumpet of a prophecy! O wind,
70 If winter comes, can spring be far behind?

---

4 *hectic:* the fever accompanying consumption, or tuberculosis   9 *Thine . . . sister:* The wind that
brings in spring   10 *clarion:* horn   18 *Angels:* messengers, as in the original Greek   21
Maenad: in the Greek myths, a woman who participated in the nocturnal, orgiastic rites in honor of
Dionysus, god of wine   32 *Baiae's bay:* Located on the west coast of the Gulf of Pozzuoli, near
Naples, Baia was the site of many luxurious Roman villas.   57 *lyre:* the Eolian Harp, the strings of
which sounded as the winds passed through them. (See Coleridge's "The Eolian Harp.")

DISCUSSION TOPICS

1. Shelley wrote of the "Ode to the West Wind": "This poem was conceived and
   chiefly written in a wood that skirts the [River] Arno, near Florence, and on
   a day when that tempestuous wind, whose temperature is at once mild and
   animating, was collecting the vapors that pour down the autumnal rains. They
   began, as I foresaw, at sunset with a violent tempest of hail and rain, attended
   by the magnificent thunder and lightning peculiar to the Cisalpine regions." In
   what ways does Shelley's poem portray—yet differ from—his prose description? What do these differences reveal about the nature of poetry?
2. Why does the poet request, in Stanza V, "Make me thy lyre"?
3. How can the "Ode to the West Wind" be seen in philosophical and moral terms
   as the embodiment of Shelley's revolutionary attitudes and of his conviction
   that the poet can serve as a prophet for reform?
4. Unlike some of Shelley's poems, this ode is tightly structured. What are some
   of the formal characteristics that contribute to this structure?

JOHN KEATS (1795–1821) The great poet of the second generation of English Romantics, author of five or six of the best odes in English, a fine sonneteer, a master of
imagistic narration in poems like *The Eve of St. Agnes* and *Lamia.* He died of
tuberculosis at the age of 25.

ON FIRST LOOKING INTO CHAPMAN'S HOMER

Much have I travelled in the realms of gold
    And many goodly states and kingdoms seen;
    Round many western islands have I been
Which bards in fealty to Apollo hold.
5   Oft of one wide expanse had I been told
    That deep-browed Homer ruled as his demesne;
    Yet never did I breathe its pure serene
Till I heard Chapman speak out loud and bold:
Then felt I like some watcher of the skies
10   When a new planet swims into his ken;
Or like stout Cortez when with eagle eyes
    He stared at the Pacific—and all his men
Looked at each other with a wild surmise—
    Silent, upon a peak in Darien.

Chapman's Homer: The Elizabethan poet George Chapman (c. 1559–1634) produced his translations of the *Iliad* and *Odyssey* between 1598 and 1615. Keats wrote this sonnet in only an hour or two, making some corrections later, after he had stayed awake all night reading Chapman's *Homer* with a friend. 4 *fealty:* fidelity owed to a lord   *Apollo:* the god of poetry and music   6 *demesne:* domain 7 *serene:* clear and fine air   11 *Cortez:* It was actually Balboa, not Cortez, who first sighted the Pacific Ocean in 1513, from Darien, in Panama.

DISCUSSION TOPICS:

1. What mood is Keats trying to convey in this poem?
2. What has reading Chapman's translation of Homer meant to Keats?
3. How does he convey his feelings through the poem's imagery? Which are the key images and comparisons?
4. What is the significance of the word "Silent" in the poem's final line?

WHEN I HAVE FEARS THAT I MAY CEASE TO BE

When I have fears that I may cease to be
    Before my pen has gleaned my teeming brain,
Before high-pilèd books, in charactery,
    Hold like rich garners the full-ripened grain;
5   When I behold, upon the night's starred face,
    Huge cloudy symbols of a high romance,
And think that I may never live to trace
    Their shadows, with the magic hand of chance;

And when I feel, fair creature of an hour,
10   That I shall never look upon thee more,
Never have relish in the fairy power
        Of unreflecting love—then on the shore
Of the wide world I stand alone, and think
Till love and fame to nothingness do sink.

3 *charactery:* written or printed letters   11 *fairy:* enchanted, magical   12 *unreflecting:* not thought
upon, spontaneous

DISCUSSION TOPICS

1. What does the young Keats fear? In what ways are his fears both personal and universal?
2. This sonnet, like many others, presents a kind of "logical" proposition. What word signals the first part of that proposition? In which lines of the poem does Keats repeat that word?
3. Compare Keats's use of the sonnet form here to Shakespeare's, especially in Sonnet 73. What similarities do you find in the structure? How has Keats altered the rhythm of the final couplet?
4. What is the relationship between "love" and "fame," not only in the final line but throughout the poem?
5. What is the mood created by the poem's final three lines?

LA BELLE DAME SANS MERCI

A BALLAD

O what can ail thee, knight-at-arms,
    Alone and palely loitering?
The sedge has withered from the lake,
    And no birds sing.

5   O what can ail thee, knight-at-arms,
    So haggard and so woe-begone?
The squirrel's granary is full,
    And the harvest's done.

I see a lily on thy brow
10   With anguish moist and fever dew;
And on thy cheek a fading rose
    Fast withereth too.

"I met a lady in the meads,
　　Full beautiful—a faery's child,
15　Her hair was long, her foot was light,
　　And her eyes were wild.

"I made a garland for her head,
　　And bracelets too, and fragrant zone;
She looked at me as she did love,
20　　And made sweet moan.

"I set her on my pacing steed,
　　And nothing else saw all day long,
For sideways would she lean, and sing
　　A faery's song.

25　"She found me roots of relish sweet,
　　And honey wild, and manna dew;
And sure in language strange she said—
　　'I love thee true!'

"She took me to her elfin grot,
30　　And there she wept and sighed full sore,
And there I shut her wild wild eyes
　　With kisses four.

"And there she lullèd me asleep,
　　And there I dreamed—ah! woe betide!
35　The latest dream I ever dreamed
　　On the cold hill side.

"I saw pale kings, and princes too,
　　Pale warriors, death-pale were they all;
Who cried—'La Belle Dame sans merci
40　　Hath thee in thrall!'

"I saw their starved lips in the gloam,
　　With horrid warning gapèd wide,
And I awoke, and found me here,
　　On the cold hill side.

45　"And this is why I sojourn here,
　　Alone and palely loitering,
Though the sedge has withered from the lake,
　　And no birds sing."

La Belle Dame sans Merci: "The Beautiful Lady Without Pity." The phrase comes from a poem by the fifteenth-century French poet Alain Chartier.　18 *zone:* a belt of flowers　29 *grot:* grotto　35 *latest:* last

DISCUSSION TOPICS

1. Who—or what—is "the beautiful Lady without pity"?
2. What do you think has happened to the "Knight at arms" and to the other "Pale warriors" he encounters? Have you ever experienced anything at all comparable to the ailment he seems to be suffering from?
3. Why does Keats mention that "the squirrel's granary is full / And the harvest's done"?
4. Where does the Lady take the Knight? What are the archetypal implications of this place, the time of year, and the number of kisses he uses to "shut her wild wild eyes"?
5. Considered from the Freudian viewpoint, what is the significance of the sexual imagery in the poem? In what ways does the poem go beyond the sexual implications to suggest other meanings?

WRITING TOPICS

1. Compare Keats's poem with "The Demon Lover" (the poem and the story).
2. Compare and contrast the Lady with such other archetypal females as Mrs. Grimes (in Anderson's "Death in the Woods") and Emily Grierson (in Faulkner's "A Rose for Emily").

ODE TO A NIGHTINGALE

My heart aches, and a drowsy numbness pains
   My sense, as though of hemlock I had drunk,
Or emptied some dull opiate to the drains
   One minute past, and Lethe-wards had sunk:
5 'Tis not through envy of thy happy lot,
   But being too happy in thy happiness—
      That thou, light-wingèd dryad of the trees,
      In some melodious plot
Of beechen green, and shadows numberless,
10   Singest of summer in full-throated ease.

O for a draught of vintage! that hath been
   Cooled a long age in the deep-delvèd earth,
Tasting of Flora and the country green,
   Dance, and Provençal song, and sun-burnt mirth!
15 O for a beaker full of the warm South,
   Full of the true, the blushful Hippocrene,
      With beaded bubbles winking at the brim,
      And purple-stainèd mouth;
That I might drink, and leave the world unseen,
20   And with thee fade away into the forest dim:

Fade far away, dissolve, and quite forget
   What thou among the leaves hast never known,
The weariness, the fever, and the fret
   Here, where men sit and hear each other groan;
25 Where palsy shakes a few, sad, last gray hairs,
   Where youth grows pale, and spectre-thin, and dies;
      Where but to think is to be full of sorrow
         And leaden-eyed despairs,
   Where beauty cannot keep her lustrous eyes,
30   Or new love pine at them beyond to-morrow.

Away! away! for I will fly to thee,
   Not charioted by Bacchus and his pards,
But on the viewless wings of poesy,
   Though the dull brain perplexes and retards:
35 Already with thee! tender is the night,
   And haply the Queen-Moon is on her throne,
      Clustered around by all her starry Fays;
         But here there is no light,
Save what from heaven is with the breezes blown
40   Through verdurous glooms and winding mossy ways.

I cannot see what flowers are at my feet,
   Nor what soft incense hangs upon the boughs,
But, in embalmèd darkness, guess each sweet
   Wherewith the seasonable month endows
45 The grass, the thicket, and the fruit-tree wild;
   White hawthorn, and the pastoral eglantine;
      Fast-fading violets covered up in leaves;
         And mid-May's eldest child,
   The coming musk-rose, full of dewy wine,
50   The murmurous haunt of flies on summer eves.

Darkling I listen; and for many a time
   I have been half in love with easeful death,
Called him soft names in many a musèd rhyme,
   To take into the air my quiet breath;
55 Now more than ever seems it rich to die,
   To cease upon the midnight with no pain,
      While thou art pouring forth thy soul abroad
         In such an ecstasy!
   Still wouldst thou sing, and I have ears in vain—
60   To thy high requiem become a sod.

Thou wast not born for death, immortal bird!
No hungry generations tread thee down;
The voice I hear this passing night was heard
In ancient days by emperor and clown:
65 Perhaps the self-same song that found a path
Through the sad heart of Ruth, when, sick for home,
She stood in tears amid the alien corn;
The same that oft-times hath
Charmed magic casements, opening on the foam
70 Of perilous seas, in faery lands forlorn.

Forlorn! the very word is like a bell
To toll me back from thee to my sole self!
Adieu! the fancy cannot cheat so well
As she is famed to do, deceiving elf.
75 Adieu! adieu! thy plaintive anthem fades
Past the near meadows, over the still stream,
Up the hill-side; and now 'tis buried deep
In the next valley-glades:
Was it a vision, or a waking dream?
80 Fled is that music:—Do I wake or sleep?

2 *hemlock:* a drug distilled from the poisonous hemlock plant   3 *drains:* dregs   4 *Lethe-wards:* toward the river Lethe, in the underworld, the waters that brought loss of memory to those who drank from it   7 *dryad:* a nymph inhabiting a tree   13 *Flora:* Roman goddess of fertility and flowers; also the flowers themselves   14 *Provençal song:* the love songs composed by the troubadours, medieval poets from the southern region of France called Provence   16 *Hippocrene:* a fountain on Mt. Helicon, and sacred to the Muses. Its waters were thought to inspire poets.   32 *Bacchus and his pards:* the god of wine whose chariot was drawn by leopards   33 *viewless:* invisible   37 *fays:* fairies   43 *embalmèd:* fragrant, perfumed   51 *Darkling:* in darkness   53 *musèd:* thought-out, meditated on   66 *Ruth:* the biblical heroine who left her own land and sought food in the cornfields of her kinsman, Boaz (see Ruth 2)   73 *fancy:* the imaginative process

DISCUSSION TOPICS

1. What does the nightingale represent to Keats? Consider especially the imagery of stanzas 1, 2, 6, and 7. How do the symbolic meanings of the nightingale change as the poem progresses?
2. The poet obviously identifies with the bird. How does he propose to join the nightingale? Why do you think he desires such a union?
3. What is the significance of the references to sleep and dreaming throughout the poem and especially in the closing stanza?

4. Keats and others in his family suffered from consumption (tuberculosis), a disease that often left them, as the name implies, weakened (literally consumed) and bedridden. How does this fact affect your reading of the poem?
5. What does a psychological reading of this poem suggest about the relationship between love and death?

WRITING TOPIC

Poets often use birds as symbols of poetic inspiration. Compare and contrast Keats's nightingale with Whitman's mockingbird in "Out of the Cradle Endlessly Rocking" and Yeats's golden bird in "Sailing to Byzantium."

ODE ON A GRECIAN URN

Thou still unravished bride of quietness!
    Thou foster-child of silence and slow time,
Sylvan historian, who canst thus express
    A flowery tale more sweetly than our rhyme:
5 What leaf-fringed legend haunts about thy shape
    Of deities or mortals, or of both,
        In Tempe or the dales of Arcady?
    What men or gods are these? What maidens loath?
What mad pursuit? What struggle to escape?
10   What pipes and timbrels? What wild ecstasy?

Heard melodies are sweet, but those unheard
    Are sweeter; therefore, ye soft pipes, play on;
Not to the sensual ear, but, more endeared,
    Pipe to the spirit ditties of no tone:
15 Fair youth, beneath the trees, thou canst not leave
    Thy song, nor ever can those trees be bare;
        Bold lover, never, never canst thou kiss,
    Though winning near the goal—yet, do not grieve;
She cannot fade, though thou hast not thy bliss,
20   Forever wilt thou love, and she be fair!

Ah, happy, happy boughs! that cannot shed
    Your leaves, nor ever bid the spring adieu;
And, happy melodist, unwearièd,
    Forever piping songs forever new;
25 More happy love! more happy, happy love!
    Forever warm and still to be enjoyed,
        Forever panting and forever young;

All breathing human passion far above,
That leaves a heart high-sorrowful and cloyed,
30   A burning forehead, and a parching tongue.

Who are these coming to the sacrifice?
To what green altar, O mysterious priest,
Lead'st thou that heifer lowing at the skies,
And all her silken flanks with garlands dressed?
35 What little town by river or sea-shore,
Or mountain-built with peaceful citadel,
Is emptied of its folk, this pious morn?
And, little town, thy streets for evermore
Will silent be; and not a soul to tell
40   Why thou art desolate, can e'er return.

O Attic shape! Fair attitude! with brede
Of marble men and maidens overwrought,
With forest branches and the trodden weed;
Thou, silent form! dost tease us out of thought
45 As doth eternity: cold pastoral!
When old age shall this generation waste,
Thou shalt remain, in midst of other woe
Than ours, a friend to man, to whom thou say'st,
"Beauty is truth, truth beauty,"—that is all
50   Ye know on earth, and all ye need to know.

---

3 *Sylvan:* of or characteristic of woods and forests   7 *Tempe:* a valley in Greece. Its lush vegetation made it especially beautiful.   *dales of Arcady:* the valleys of Arcadia were celebrated as a pastoral ideal 13 *sensual ear:* the ear attuned to physical sensations   41 *Attic:* Greek, or having the qualities associated with classical Athenian art   *with brede:* decorated, as if plaited, with an interwoven pattern

DISCUSSION TOPICS

1. Keats employs several metaphors in the opening lines of this ode. Do you find them appropriate? For example, when he addresses the urn as a "bride," in what sense is it the "unravished" bride of "quietness"? What different meanings do you see in the phrase "still unravished"? Or how is it the "foster-child" of Silence and Time? Who would its real "parents" be?
2. What is the function of the series of unanswered questions in the first stanza?
3. The second and third stanzas of the ode contain a particularly clear expression of a central theme of the poem. What is that theme?
4. Why does Keats call the urn a "Cold Pastoral"? Why a "friend to man"?
5. Why does "human passion" in the third stanza leave "a heart high-sorrowful and cloy'd, / A burning forehead and a parching tongue"?

WRITING TOPIC

How do you interpret the message of the urn, "Beauty is truth, truth beauty"?
When only the words "Beauty is truth, truth beauty" are enclosed in quotation
marks (as they are here) what is the artistic and thematic effect on the poem? What
is the effect when there are no quotation marks or when the entire last two lines
appear within quotation marks (as they do in some editions of the poem)?

TO AUTUMN

    Season of mists and mellow fruitfulness,
        Close bosom-friend of the maturing sun;
    Conspiring with him how to load and bless
        With fruit the vines that round the thatch-eaves run;
5   To bend with apples the mossed cottage-trees,
        And fill all fruit with ripeness to the core;
            To swell the gourd, and plump the hazel shells
        With a sweet kernel; to set budding more,
    And still more, later flowers for the bees,
10   Until they think warm days will never cease,
            For summer has o'er-brimmed their clammy cells.

    Who hath not seen thee oft amid thy store?
        Sometimes whoever seeks abroad may find
    Thee sitting careless on a granary floor,
15   Thy hair soft-lifted by the winnowing wind;
    Or on a half-reaped furrow sound asleep,
        Drowsed with the fumes of poppies, while thy hook
            Spares the next swath and all its twinèd flowers:
    And sometime like a gleaner thou dost keep
20   Steady thy laden head across a brook;
        Or by a cider-press, with patient look,
            Thou watchest the last oozings hours by hours.

    Where are the songs of spring? Ay, where are they?
        Think not of them, thou hast thy music too,—
25   While barrèd clouds bloom the soft-dying day,
        And touch the stubble-plains with rosy hue;
    Then in a wailful choir the small gnats mourn
        Among the river sallows, borne aloft
            Or sinking as the light wind lives or dies;
30   And full-grown lambs loud bleat from hilly bourn;
        Hedge-crickets sing; and now with treble soft
    The red-breast whistles from a garden-croft;
            And gathering swallows twitter in the skies.

11 *clammy:* moist, sticky   12 *store:* abundance   14 *careless:* without cares   15 *winnowing:* separating or fanning out chaff from grain by means of wind   17 *hook:* sickle   28 *sallows:* willows
30 *bourn:* boundary, area of land   32 *garden-croft:* small piece of land near a house

DISCUSSION TOPICS

1. What is the prevailing mood of Keats's ode "To Autumn"? What aspects of the
   autumn season has Keats chosen to emphasize that mood?
2. Why do you suppose he introduces the reference to spring in the poem's final
   stanza?
3. What archetypal associations does the autumn season evoke? How has Keats
   emphasized those associations in his poem?
4. Which of the other three seasons does Keats mention by name? Which does
   he omit? How do you account for this omission? Is that season referred to in
   other ways?
5. What effect does Keats achieve by his personification of autumn? Pay close
   attention to his description of autumn's behavior in stanza 2.

WRITING TOPIC

Which of these odes ("Ode to a Nightingale," "Ode on a Grecian Urn," or "To
Autumn") do you think is Keats's best? Explain the reasons for your selection.

Rᴀʟᴘʜ Wᴀʟᴅᴏ Eᴍᴇʀsᴏɴ (1803–1882) Unitarian minister (who resigned from his pas-
torate), philosopher, poet. He was one of America's most important men of letters.

CONCORD HYMN

> *Sung at the Completion of the Battle Monument,*
> *July 4, 1837*

By the rude bridge that arched the flood,
    Their flag to April's breeze unfurled,
Here once the embattled farmers stood
    And fired the shot heard round the world.

5   The foe long since in silence slept;
    Alike the conqueror silent sleeps;
And Time the ruined bridge has swept
    Down the dark stream which seaward creeps.

On this green bank, by this soft stream,
10   We set to-day a votive stone;
That memory may their deed redeem,
        When, like our sires, our sons are gone.

        Spirit, that made those heroes dare
            To die, and leave their children free,
15   Bid Time and Nature gently spare
            The shaft we raise to them and thee.

Title and epigraph: Emerson's poem was distributed during the dedication of the monument commemorating the battles of Lexington and Concord (Massachusetts) on April 19, 1775.   10 *votive:* carried out, dedicated, or erected in fulfillment of a vow; expressive of a wish or vow

DISCUSSION TOPICS

1. Emerson calls his poem a "hymn." Why? (Check the meaning of "hymn" in your dictionary.)
2. Who were "the embattled farmers" and why was their "shot heard round the world"?
3. To whom is the poem addressed—and why does the address come only at the poem's end?
4. Compare this poem with Melville's "Shiloh." Note especially the difference in tone. Also note that Melville calls his poem "A Requiem." What is the difference between a hymn and a requiem?

DAYS

        Daughters of Time, the hypocritic Days,
        Muffled and dumb like barefoot dervishes,
        And marching single in an endless file,
        Bring diadems and faggots in their hands.
5   To each they offer gifts after his will
        Bread, kingdoms, stars, and sky that holds them all.
        I, in my pleachèd garden, watched the pomp,
        Forgot my morning wishes, hastily
        Took a few herbs and apples, and the Day
10   Turned and departed silent. I, too late,
        Under her solemn fillet saw the scorn.

2 *dervishes:* Moslem ascetics   4 *diadems and faggots:* crowns and sticks   7 *pleachèd:* shaded with interlaced branches   11 *fillet:* headband

410

DISCUSSION TOPICS

1. Why are the days described as "hypocritic"?
2. What contrast does the speaker suggest among "Bread, kingdoms, stars, and sky," on the one hand, and "a few herbs and apples," on the other?
3. How can we account for the day's "scorn" in the final line?

WRITING TOPIC

Compare and contrast the treatment of the *carpe diem* theme in Emerson's poem and Marvell's "To His Coy Mistress." Note particularly the ways in which the two poets personify time.

SEASHORE

I heard or seemed to hear the chiding Sea
Say, Pilgrim, why so late and slow to come?
Am I not always here, thy summer home?
Is not my voice thy music, morn and eve?
5   My breath thy healthful climate in the heats,
My touch thy antidote, my bay thy bath?
Was ever building like my terraces?
Was ever couch magnificent as mine?
Lie on the warm rock-ledges, and there learn
10   A little hut suffices like a town.
I make your sculptured architecture vain,
Vain beside mine. I drive my wedges home,
And carve the coastwise mountain into caves.
Lo! here is Rome and Nineveh and Thebes,
15   Karnak and Pyramid and Giant's Stairs
Half piled or prostrate; and my newest slab
Older than all thy race.

           Behold the Sea,
The opaline, the plentiful and strong,
Yet beautiful as is the rose in June,
20   Fresh as the trickling rainbow of July;
Sea full of food, the nourisher of kinds,
Purger of earth, and medicine of men;
Creating a sweet climate by my breath,
Washing out harms and griefs from memory,
25   And, in my mathematic ebb and flow,
Giving a hint of that which changes not.
Rich are the sea-gods:—who gives gifts but they?
They grope the sea for pearls, but more than pearls:

They pluck Force thence, and give it to the wise.
30　For every wave is wealth to Dædalus,
　　Wealth to the cunning artist who can work
　　This matchless strength. Where shall he find, O waves!
　　A load your Atlas shoulders cannot lift?

　　　I with my hammer pounding evermore
35　The rocky coast, smite Andes into dust,
　　Strewing my bed, and, in another age,
　　Rebuild a continent of better men.
　　Then I unbar the doors: my paths lead out
　　The exodus of nations: I disperse
40　Men to all shores that front the hoary main.

　　　I too have arts and sorceries;
　　Illusion dwells forever with the wave.
　　I know what spells are laid. Leave me to deal
　　With credulous and imaginative man;
45　For, though he scoop my water in his palm,
　　A few rods off he deems it gems and clouds.
　　Planting strange fruits and sunshine on the shore,
　　I make some coast alluring, some lone isle,
　　To distant men, who must go there, or die.

14 *Rome, Nineveh, Thebes:* all famous ancient cities　　15 *Karnak:* a village of central Egypt that contains many remains from the pharaohs　　*Giant's Stairs:* the Giant's Causeway off the coast of northern Ireland. It contains thousands of basalt pillars, some as much as 20 feet high, which form three platforms.　　30 *Dædalus:* the celebrated inventor, artist, and craftsman of Greek mythology. (See the annotation to Auden's "Musée des Beaux Arts.")

DISCUSSION TOPICS

1. Who is the speaker—or, more accurately, who are the speakers in this poem? Who is being spoken to?
2. What are the "arts and sorceries" in line 41? How do they relate to "credulous and imaginative men"?
3. What are the archetypal implications of this poem—and why do you think Emerson titled it "Seashore" rather than "Sea"?

EDGAR ALLAN POE (1809–1849) Poet, storyteller, critic, editor. He wrote highly influential critical articles and reviews, saw poetry as "the rhythmical creation of Beauty," and held that a poem should be no more than 100 lines in length to achieve fullest effect.

SONNET—TO SCIENCE

Science! true daughter of Old Time thou art!
  Who alterest all things with thy peering eyes.
Why preyest thou thus upon the poet's heart,
  Vulture, whose wings are dull realities?
5 How should he love thee? or how deem thee wise,
  Who wouldst not leave him in his wandering
To seek for treasure in the jewelled skies,
  Albeit he soared with an undaunted wing?
Hast thou not dragged Diana from her car?
10 And driven the Hamadryad from the wood
To seek a shelter in some happier star?
  Hast thou not torn the Naiad from her flood,
The Elfin from the green grass, and from me
The summer dream beneath the tamarind tree?

9 *Diana:* the virgin goddess of the moon and virginity   *car:* chariot   10 *Hamadryad:* a tree-nymph
12 *Naiad:* a nymph inhabiting springs, rivers, and lakes   14 *tamarind:* a large, fragrant tree, originally from the Orient

DISCUSSION TOPICS

1. What is the poet's attitude toward science?
2. Why is science the "true daughter of Old Time"?
3. How does "Time" in this poem compare with time in Emerson's "Days"?
4. Why do you think Poe chose not to name a more familiar tree in the last line?
5. The entire poem hinges on questions. Are they merely rhetorical questions—
   or is the speaker really seeking answers?

TO HELEN

Helen, thy beauty is to me
  Like those Nicean barks of yore,
That gently, o'er a perfumed sea,
  The weary, way-worn wanderer bore
5 To his own native shore.

On desperate seas long wont to roam,
  Thy hyacinth hair, thy classic face,
Thy Naiad airs have brought me home
  To the glory that was Greece,
10 And the grandeur that was Rome.

413

      Lo! in yon brilliant window-niche
        How statue-like I see thee stand,
    The agate lamp within thy hand!
        Ah, Psyche, from the regions which
15   Are Holy-Land!

2 *Nicean:* possibly one of the several places called Nicaea, or perhaps an adjective meaning "victorious" (from the Greek *Niké,* victory)   7 *hyacinth:* wavy, perhaps black   8 *Naiad:* a nymph associated with springs, rivers, and lakes   14 *Psyche:* In the *Golden Ass,* Apuleius tells the story of Psyche, a princess so beautiful that men worshipped her instead of Venus. In anger the goddess sent her son, Cupid, to punish Psyche, but he fell in love with her. *Psyche* is also the Greek word for "soul."

DISCUSSION TOPICS

1. This poem is packed with historical and mythological allusion. Yet Poe said that the poem celebrates the mother of a schoolmate. Does he intend the allusions to form a kind of metaphorical shorthand for his feelings about his subject? That is, does classical beauty—whether of Nicean boats or Naiads—define the person or aura of Mrs. Jane Stith Stannard of Richmond, Virginia, by association better than by description? Or do you think that Poe assumes too much about the reader's acquaintance with mythology?
2. Why are the "regions" of the allusions "Holy-Land" to the speaker?
3. Who is the "weary, way-worn wanderer"? Could the epithet possibly suggest Odysseus trying to get home after the Trojan War, or perhaps any quester, including the seeker after the classical ideal or even ideal beauty? What is the effect of the alliteration of the three words?
4. When "To Helen" originally appeared in 1831, lines 9–10 read: "To the beauty of fair Greece, / And the grandeur of old Rome." In 1843, Poe revised these lines to their present form. What difference does the change make? What subtle distinction is suggested by Greece's "glory" and Rome's "grandeur"?

ULALUME—A BALLAD

    The skies they were ashen and sober;
        The leaves they were crispéd and sere—
        The leaves they were withering and sere:
    It was night, in the lonesome October
5   Of my most immemorial year:
    It was hard by the dim lake of Auber,
        In the misty mid region of Weir—
    It was down by the dank tarn of Auber,
        In the ghoul-haunted woodland of Weir.

10   Here once, through an alley Titanic,
       Of cypress, I roamed with my Soul—
       Of cypress, with Psyche, my Soul.
   These were days when my heart was volcanic
       As the scoriac rivers that roll—
15   As the lavas that restlessly roll
   Their sulphurous currents down Yaanek
       In the ultimate climes of the Pole—
   That groan as they roll down Mount Yaanek
       In the realms of the Boreal Pole.

20   Our talk had been serious and sober,
       But our thoughts they were palsied and sere—
       Our memories were treacherous and sere;
   For we knew not the month was October,
       And we marked not the night of the year
25   (Ah, night of all nights in the year!)—
   We noted not the dim lake of Auber
       (Though once we had journeyed down here)—
   We remembered not the dank tarn of Auber,
       Nor the ghoul-haunted woodland of Weir.

30   And now, as the night was senescent
       And star-dials pointed to morn—
       As the star-dials hinted of morn—
   At the end of our path a liquescent
       And nebulous lustre was born,
35   Out of which a miraculous crescent
       Arose with a duplicate horn—
   Astarte's bediamonded crescent
       Distinct with its duplicate horn.

   And I said: "She is warmer than Dian;
40   She rolls through an ether of sighs—
       She revels in a region of sighs.
   She has seen that the tears are not dry on
       These cheeks, where the worm never dies,
   And has come past the stars of the Lion,
45   To point us the path to the skies—
       To the Lethean peace of the skies—
   Come up, in despite of the Lion,
       To shine on us with her bright eyes—
   Come up through the lair of the Lion,
50   With love in her luminous eyes."

   But Psyche, uplifting her finger,
       Said: "Sadly this star I mistrust—

Her pallor I strangely mistrust:
Ah, hasten!—ah, let us not linger!
55   Ah, fly!—let us fly!—for we must."
In terror she spoke, letting sink her
      Wings till they trailed in the dust—
In agony sobbed, letting sink her
      Plumes till they trailed in the dust—
60   Till they sorrowfully trailed in the dust.

I replied: "This is nothing but dreaming:
      Let us on by this tremulous light!
      Let us bathe in this crystalline light!
Its Sibyllic splendor is beaming
65   With Hope and in Beauty to-night:—
      See!—it flickers up the sky through the night!
Ah, we safely may trust to its gleaming,
      And be sure it will lead us aright—
We surely may trust to a gleaming,
70   That cannot but guide us aright,
      Since it flickers up to Heaven through the night."

Thus I pacified Psyche and kissed her,
      And tempted her out of her gloom—
      And conquered her scruples and gloom;
75 And we passed to the end of the vista,
      But were stopped by the door of a tomb—
      By the door of a legended tomb;
And I said: "What is written, sweet sister,
      On the door of this legended tomb?"
80   She replied: "Ulalume—Ulalume!—
      'Tis the vault of thy lost Ulalume!"

Then my heart it grew ashen and sober
      As the leaves that were crispéd and sere—
      As the leaves that were withering and sere;
85 And I cried: "It was surely October
      On *this* very night of last year
      That I journeyed—I journeyed down here!—
      That I brought a dread burden down here—
      On this night of all nights in the year,
90   Ah, what demon hath tempted me here?
Well I know, now, this dim lake of Auber—
      This misty mid region of Weir—
Well I know, now, this dank tarn of Auber,
      This ghoul-haunted woodland of Weir."

95 Said we, then—the two, then: "Ah, can it
   Have been that the woodlandish ghouls—
   The pitiful, the merciful ghouls—
  To bar up our way and to ban it
  From the secret that lies in these wolds—
100 From the thing that lies hidden in these wolds—
  Have drawn up the spectre of a planet
  From the limbo of lunary souls—
  This sinfully scintillant planet
  From the Hell of the planetary souls?"

6 *Auber:* poetic place name 7 *Weir:* poetic place name (*cf.* "weird") 10 *Titanic:* enormous, as in the pre-Olympian Greek gods 14 *scoriac:* like molten or slaggy lava 16 *Yaanek:* imaginary volcano 19 *Boreal:* North 37 *Astarte:* Phoenician goddess of fertility, described here as moon goddess 39 *Dian:* Diana, Roman goddess of the moon, renowned for chastity 44 *Lion:* constellation Leo 46 *Lethean:* in classical mythology, Lethe is the river of peaceful oblivion and forgetfulness for those who drink of its waters. 64 *Sibyllic:* mysteriously prophetic, as in "Sibyl," one of several prophetesses in Greek and Roman mythology 103 *scintillant:* refulgent or shining

DISCUSSION TOPICS

1. What if the name of the narrator's lost lover were something other than "Ulalume"—for example, "Cindy," "Debbie," or (as in another Poe poem about a dead sweetheart) "Annabel Lee"?
2. What insights into this weird poem might be provided through a psychoanalytic concept of sexual imagery (e. g., "flying") and the Freudian "death wish"?

ALFRED, LORD TENNYSON (1809–1892) One of England's greatest poets laureate, author of much poetry of steadily high quality over a long period of time. Strongly influenced by death of his friend Arthur Hallam, he raised questions about science, evolution, and immortality that seem at least as relevant to a troubled twentieth century as they must have seemed to his own age.

ULYSSES

 It little profits that an idle king,
By this still hearth, among these barren crags,
Matched with an agèd wife, I mete and dole
Unequal laws unto a savage race,
5 That hoard, and sleep, and feed, and know not me.
I cannot rest from travel; I will drink

Life to the lees. All times I have enjoyed
Greatly, have suffered greatly, both with those
That loved me, and alone; on shore, and when
10   Through scudding drifts the rainy Hyades
Vexed the dim sea. I am become a name;
For always roaming with a hungry heart
Much have I seen and known—cities of men,
And manners, climates, councils, governments,
15   Myself not least, but honored of them all—
And drunk delight of battle with my peers,
Far on the ringing plains of windy Troy.
I am a part of all that I have met;
Yet all experience is an arch wherethrough
20   Gleams that untraveled world, whose margin fades
Forever and forever when I move.
How dull it is to pause, to make an end,
To rust unburnished, not to shine in use!
As though to breathe were life! Life piled on life
25   Were all too little, and of one to me
Little remains: but every hour is saved
From that eternal silence, something more,
A bringer of new things; and vile it were
For some three suns to store and hoard myself,
30   And this gray spirit yearning in desire
To follow knowledge like a sinking star,
Beyond the utmost bound of human thought.
     This is my son, mine own Telemachus,
To whom I leave the scepter and the isle—
35   Well-loved of me, discerning to fulfill
This labor, by slow prudence to make mild
A rugged people, and through soft degrees
Subdue them to the useful and the good.
Most blameless is he, centered in the sphere
40   Of common duties, decent not to fail
In offices of tenderness, and pay
Meet adoration to my household gods,
When I am gone. He works his work, I mine.
     There lies the port; the vessel puffs her sail;
45   There gloom the dark broad seas. My mariners,
Souls that have toiled, and wrought, and thought with me,—
That ever with a frolic welcome took
The thunder and the sunshine, and opposed
Free hearts, free foreheads,—you and I are old;
50   Old age hath yet his honor and his toil.
Death closes all; but something ere the end,

Some work of noble note, may yet be done,
Not unbecoming men that strove with Gods.
The lights begin to twinkle from the rocks;
55 The long day wanes; the slow moon climbs; the deep
Moans round with many voices. Come, my friends,
'Tis not too late to seek a newer world.
Push off, and sitting well in order smite
The sounding furrows; for my purpose holds
60 To sail beyond the sunset, and the baths
Of all the western stars, until I die.
It may be that the gulfs will wash us down;
It may be we shall touch the Happy Isles,
And see the great Achilles, whom we knew.
65 Though much is taken, much abides; and though
We are not now that strength which in old days
Moved earth and heaven; that which we are, we are;
One equal temper of heroic hearts,
Made weak by time and fate, but strong in will
70 To strive, to seek, to find, and not to yield.

Ulysses: The hero of Homer's *Odyssey,* Ulysses fought for 10 years in the Trojan War and then wandered for 10 more years before his return home to his kingdom in Ithaca.   3 *mete and dole:* measure and give out   4 *unequal:* not affecting all people in the same way   10 *scudding drifts:* driving showers *Hyades:* a group of stars whose rising was thought to promise rain   17 *Troy:* the city destroyed by the Greeks after 10 years' fighting in order to avenge Paris's abduction of Helen   33 *Telemachus:* The accent is on the second syllable.   42 *Meet:* proper, fitting   63 *Happy Isles:* In Greek mythology the Happy Isles (Elysium) were the resting place of the blessed after death.   64 *Achilles:* the greatest of the Greek warriors during the Trojan War

DISCUSSION TOPICS

1. What does a close formalistic reading reveal about the kind of individual Tennyson's Ulysses is? Pay special attention to the images and diction Ulysses employs when describing his responsibilities as king and his delight in experiencing the world.

2. Using the biographical approach, consider the fact that Tennyson wrote "Ulysses" shortly after the death of his dearest friend, Arthur Hallam: "It gives the feeling," Tennyson said, "of going forward and braving the struggle of life."

3. Even without the use of biographical data, a careful reading of the poem reveals that Ulysses is concerned with more than merely physical adventure. Find evidence within the text to support this statement.

4. Some readers have felt that Tennyson's Ulysses is as much a product of Victorian disillusionment as he is a reflection of Homer's hero in *The Odyssey.* What do you think Ulysses means when he says, "I am become a name" (line 11)?

What attitude toward his son Telemachus does he reveal in the remark, "He works his work, I mine" (line 43)? When Ulysses says, "How dull it is to pause, to make an end, / To rust unburnished, not to shine in use!" (lines 22–23), he sums up his attitude toward an earlier heroic age. What kind of world does the poem suggest will replace the world of the heroes? (Compare Marlowe's disillusionment in Conrad's *Heart of Darkness.*)

ROBERT BROWNING (1812–1889) Inadequate at first as a dramatist, later found his place in the dramatic monologue. He was also a lyricist and storyteller of significant ability, often in experimental and widely varying techniques. He was noted for his use of realistic psychology and speech. Much of this Englishman's work is set on the Continent, especially in Italy.

SOLILOQUY OF THE SPANISH CLOISTER

<blockquote>

Gr-r-r—there go, my heart's abhorrence!
   Water your damned flower-pots, do!
If hate killed men, Brother Lawrence,
   God's blood, would not mine kill you!
5 What? your myrtle-bush wants trimming?
   Oh, that rose has prior claims—
Needs its leaden vase filled brimming?
   Hell dry you up with its flames!

At the meal we sit together:
10   *Salve tibi!* I must hear
Wise talk of the kind of weather,
   Sort of season, time of year:
Not a plenteous cork-crop: scarcely
   Dare we hope oak-galls, I doubt:
15 *What's the Latin name for "parsley"?*
   What's the Greek name for Swine's Snout?

Whew! We'll have our platter burnished,
   Laid with care on our own shelf!
With a fire-new spoon we're furnished,
20   And a goblet for ourself,
Rinsed like something sacrificial
   Ere 'tis fit to touch our chaps—
Marked with L. for our initial!
   (He-he! There his lily snaps!)

</blockquote>

25 *Saint,* forsooth! While brown Dolores
    Squats outside the Convent bank
With Sanchicha, telling stories,
    Steeping tresses in the tank,
Blue-black, lustrous, thick like horse-hairs,
30   —Can't I see his dead eye glow,
Bright as 'twere a Barbary corsair's?
    (That is, if he'd let it show!)

When he finishes refection,
    Knife and fork he never lays
35 Cross-wise, to my recollection,
    As do I, in Jesu's praise.
I the Trinity illustrate,
    Drinking watered orange-pulp—
In three sips the Arian frustrate;
40   While he drains his at one gulp.

Oh, those melons! If he's able
    We're to have a feast! so nice!
One goes to the Abbot's table,
    All of us get each a slice.
45 How go on your flowers? None double?
    Not one fruit-sort can you spy?
Strange!—And I, too, at such trouble
    Keep them close-nipped on the sly!

There's a great text in Galatians,
50   Once you trip on it, entails
Twenty-nine distinct damnations,
    One sure, if another fails:
If I trip him just a-dying,
    Sure of heaven as sure can be,
55 Spin him round and send him flying
    Off to hell, a Manichee!

Or, my scrofulous French novel
    On gray paper with blunt type!
Simply glance at it, you grovel
60   Hand and foot in Belial's gripe:
If I double down its pages
    At the woeful sixteenth print,
When he gathers his greengages,
    Ope a sieve and slip it in't?

65 Or, there's Satan! one might venture
    Pledge one's soul to him, yet leave

Such a flaw in the indenture
    As he'd miss till, past retrieve,
Blasted lay that rose-acacia
70   We're so proud of! *Hy, Zy, Hine . . .*
    'St, there's Vespers! *Plena gratiá,*
        Ave, Virgo! Gr-r-r—you swine!

10 *Salve tibi:* Hail to you   14 *oak-galls:* outgrowths produced by insects on oak trees; used in tanning, dyeing, or making ink   31 *Barbary corsair's:* Pirates from the Barbary Coast in North Africa often preyed on Christian vessels.   32 *refection:* a meal   39 *Arian:* The heretical followers of Arius (c. AD 250–336) rejected the doctrine of the Trinity.   49 *Galatians:* No specific text in Galatians has been found to contain "twenty-nine distinct damnations," though Galatians 5:19–21, which lists seventeen "works of the flesh," is often cited in commentaries on the poem. The speaker may also have in mind twenty-nine damnations incurred for misinterpreting a text of Galatians.   56 *Manichee:* The dualistic philosophy of the Persian Mani (AD 216–276) was denounced by the Church as heretical, and the term Manichaeism came to denote any dualistic Christian heresy.   57 *scrofulous:* diseased, hence morally corrupt   60 *Belial's gripe:* Satan's grip   63 *greengages:* a kind of plum   71–72 *Plena gratiá,/Ave, Virgo:* Hail, Virgin, Full of Grace.

DISCUSSION TOPICS

1. Whom do you think the speaker is addressing in this poem?
2. What formal qualities contribute to the sense of drama in the poem? Describe the different tones of voice, facial expressions, and gestures that the speaker assumes as he mocks Brother Lawrence.
3. This dramatic monologue reveals Browning's interest in psychology. What does it show of rationalization, projection, repression, the libido?

PORPHYRIA'S LOVER

The rain set early in tonight,
    The sullen wind was soon awake,
It tore the elm-tops down for spite,
    And did its worst to vex the lake:
5   I listened with heart fit to break.
When glided in Porphyria; straight
    She shut the cold out and the storm,
And kneeled and made the cheerless grate
    Blaze up, and all the cottage warm;
10   Which done, she rose, and from her form
Withdrew the dripping cloak and shawl,
    And laid her soiled gloves by, untied

Her hat and let the damp hair fall,
   And, last, she sat down by my side
15 And called me. When no voice replied,
She put my arm about her waist,
   And made her smooth white shoulder bare
And all her yellow hair displaced,
   And, stooping, made my cheek lie there,
20 And spread, o'er all, her yellow hair,
Murmuring how she loved me—she
   Too weak, for all her heart's endeavor,
To set its struggling passion free
   From pride, and vainer ties dissever,
25 And give herself to me forever.
But passion sometimes would prevail,
   Nor could tonight's gay feast restrain
A sudden thought of one so pale
   For love of her, and all in vain:
30 So, she was come through wind and rain.
Be sure I looked up at her eyes
   Happy and proud; at last I knew
Porphyria worshipped me; surprise
   Made my heart swell, and still it grew
35 While I debated what to do.
That moment she was mine, mine, fair,
   Perfectly pure and good: I found
A thing to do, and all her hair
   In one long yellow string I wound
40 Three times her little throat around,
And strangled her. No pain felt she;
   I am quite sure she felt no pain.
As a shut bud that holds a bee,
   I warily oped her lids: again
45 Laughed the blue eyes without a stain.
And I untightened next the tress
   About her neck; her cheek once more
Blushed bright beneath my burning kiss:
   I propped her head up as before,
50 Only, this time my shoulder bore
Her head, which droops upon it still:
   The smiling rosy little head,
So glad it has its utmost will,
   That all it scorned at once is fled,
55 And I, its love, am gained instead!

Porphyria's love: she guessed not how
  Her darling one wish would be heard.
And thus we sit together now,
  And all night long we have not stirred,
60 And yet God has not said a word!

DISCUSSION TOPICS

1. Visualize the details of the setting that the speaker reveals in his monologue. What is the importance of the position of Porphyria's head?
2. What does the weather imagery suggest?
3. What line of logical (or psychological) thinking brought the speaker to his decision ("I found / A thing to do . . .")?
4. Pay careful attention to the tone—or shifting tones—of voice of the speaker. How must the reader interpret the speaker's state of mind by hearing imagined speech?

MY LAST DUCHESS

FERRARA

That's my last Duchess painted on the wall,
Looking as if she were alive. I call
That piece a wonder, now: Frà Pandolf's hands
Worked busily a day, and there she stands.
5 Will't please you sit and look at her? I said
"Frà Pandolf" by design, for never read
Strangers like you that pictured countenance,
The depth and passion of its earnest glance,
But to myself they turned (since none puts by
10 The curtain I have drawn for you, but I)
And seemed as they would ask me, if they durst,
How such a glance came there; so, not the first
Are you to turn and ask thus. Sir, 'twas not
Her husband's presence only, called that spot
15 Of joy into the Duchess' cheek: perhaps
Frà Pandolf chanced to say "Her mantle laps
Over my lady's wrist too much," or "Paint
Must never hope to reproduce the faint
Half-flush that dies along her throat": such stuff
20 Was courtesy, she thought, and cause enough

For calling up that spot of joy. She had
A heart—how shall I say?—too soon made glad,
Too easily impressed; she liked whate'er
She looked on, and her looks went everywhere.
25 Sir, 'twas all one! My favor at her breast,
The dropping of the daylight in the West,
The bough of cherries some officious fool
Broke in the orchard for her, the white mule
She rode with round the terrace—all and each
30 Would draw from her alike the approving speech,
Or blush, at least. She thanked men—good! but thanked
Somehow—I know not how—as if she ranked
My gift of a nine-hundred-years-old name
With anybody's gift. Who'd stoop to blame
35 This sort of trifling? Even had you skill
In speech—(which I have not)—to make your will
Quite clear to such an one, and say, "Just this
Or that in you disgusts me; here you miss,
Or there exceed the mark"—and if she let
40 Herself be lessoned so, nor plainly set
Her wits to yours, forsooth, and made excuse
—E'en then would be some stooping; and I choose
Never to stoop. Oh sir, she smiled, no doubt,
Whene'er I passed her; but who passed without
45 Much the same smile? This grew; I gave commands;
Then all smiles stopped together. There she stands
As if alive. Will't please you rise? We'll meet
The company below, then. I repeat,
The Count your master's known munificence
50 Is ample warrant that no just pretense
Of mine for dowry will be disallowed;
Though his fair daughter's self, as I avowed
At starting, is my object. Nay, we'll go
Together down, sir. Notice Neptune, though,
55 Taming a sea horse, thought a rarity,
Which Claus of Innsbruck cast in bronze for me!

Ferrara: Browning's poem seems to allude to the life of Alfonso II, Duke of Ferrara, in northern Italy. His first wife, married to him when she was 14, died 3 years later in 1561 and was rumored to be a victim of poisoning. Through the offices of an agent (to whom the duke may be speaking in the poem), Alfonso married the sister of the Count of Tyrol in 1565.   3 *Frà Pandolf:* Brother Pandolf, an imaginary painter   25 *favor:* an article worn by one's beloved as a sign of affection   50 *pretense:* claim   54 *Neptune:* the god of the sea, often depicted with sea horses   56 *Claus of Innsbruck:* an imaginary sculptor. The capital of Tyrol, a province of Austria, is Innsbruck.

DISCUSSION TOPICS

1. Who is the speaker in this poem? To whom is he speaking? (Look at line 49.) What is the setting or dramatic situation?
2. What were the duchess's faults, according to the speaker?
3. What kind of man is the speaker?
4. From what psychological problems does the speaker seem to suffer?
5. Do you trust the speaker's account of the duchess and her "failings"? How does Browning reveal another more favorable interpretation of the duchess's behavior through the speaker's own biased account? Point to specific remarks made by the speaker that seem to suggest his view may be biased or distorted.
6. When they hear this poem read aloud, many listeners fail to notice that it is written in rhymed couplets. How does Browning disguise the poem's rhyme and meter? How does this technique enhance the poem's effect?

WRITING TOPIC

Imagine that you are the agent for the count referred to in line 49 and must write a letter to him concerning your meeting in Ferrara. How would you describe the duke? What advice would you give the Count concerning the marriage of his daughter?

HERMAN MELVILLE (1819–1891) Author of *Moby-Dick,* one of America's contributions to world literature, as well as of other important works, such as *Billy Budd* and *Benito Cereno,* where a mythopoeic imagination and a Calvinistic melancholy turn his prose into poetry.

SHILOH

A · REQUIEM
(APRIL 1862)

 Skimming lightly, wheeling still,
  The swallows fly low
 Over the field in clouded days,
  The forest-field of Shiloh—
5 Over the field where April rain
 Solaced the parched one stretched in pain
 Through the pause of night
 That followed the Sunday fight
  Around the church of Shiloh—
10 The church so lone, the log-built one,

426

That echoed to many a parting groan
    And natural prayer
    Of dying foemen mingled there—
Foemen at morn, but friends at eve—
15   Fame or country least their care:
(What like a bullet can undeceive!)
    But now they lie low,
While over them the swallows skim,
    And all is hushed at Shiloh.

Shiloh: One of the bloodiest battles of the Civil War was fought near Shiloh Church in southwest Tennessee on April 6–7, 1862.

DISCUSSION TOPICS

1. Why do you think Melville calls this poem "A Requiem"? Would "elegy" or "ode" be equally appropriate?
2. What clarification is achieved by the bullet in line 16?
3. What effect is gained by beginning and ending the poem with the flight of swallows? Does Melville thereby imply some relationship of nature to human violence? How does this implication relate to the theme and the tone of his poem?

WRITING TOPIC

Compare "Shiloh" with other poems such as Lovelace's "To Lucasta," Hardy's "Drummer Hodge," and Owen's "Dulce et Decorum Est."

WALT WHITMAN (1819–1892) "Son of Manhattan," whose free verse, realistic imagery, and unorthodox subject matter—science, sex, the workaday world—combined with an intense patriotism and mystical sense of democracy to reshape American poetry. His *Leaves of Grass,* first published in 1855, grew in a series of editions.

ONE'S-SELF I SING

One's-Self I sing, a simple separate person,
Yet utter the word Democratic, the word En-Masse.

Of physiology from top to toe I sing,
Not physiognomy alone nor brain alone is worthy for the Muse, I
5   say the Form complete is worthier far,
The Female equally with the Male I sing.

Of Life immense in passion, pulse, and power,
Cheerful, for freest action form'd under the laws divine,
The Modern Man I sing.

I HEAR AMERICA SINGING

I hear America singing, the varied carols I hear,
Those of mechanics, each one singing his as it should be blithe
    and strong,
The carpenter singing his as he measures his plank or beam,
The mason singing his as he makes ready for work, or leaves off
    work,
The boatman singing what belongs to him in his boat, the deckhand
5   singing on the steamboat deck,
The shoemaker singing as he sits on his bench, the hatter singing
    as he stands,
The wood-cutter's song, the ploughboy's on his way in the morning,
    or at noon intermission or at sundown,
The delicious singing of the mother, or of the young wife at work,
    or of the girl sewing or washing,
Each singing what belongs to him or her and to none else,
The day what belongs to the day—at night the party of young fellows,
10   robust, friendly,
Singing with open mouths their strong melodious songs.

OUT OF THE CRADLE ENDLESSLY ROCKING

Out of the cradle endlessly rocking,
Out of the mocking-bird's throat, the musical shuttle,
Out of the Ninth-month midnight,
Over the sterile sands and the fields beyond, where the child
    leaving his bed wander'd alone, bareheaded, barefoot,
5 Down from the shower'd halo,
Up from the mystic play of shadows twining and twisting as if
    they were alive,
Out from the patches of briers and blackberries,
From the memories of the bird that chanted to me,
From your memories sad brother, from the fitful risings and fall-
    ings I heard,
From under that yellow half-moon late-risen and swollen as if with
10   tears,

From those beginning notes of yearning and love there in the
    mist,
From the thousand responses of my heart never to cease,
From the myriad thence-arous'd words,
From the word stronger and more delicious than any,
15   From such as now they start the scene revisiting,
As a flock, twittering, rising, or overhead passing,
Borne hither, ere all eludes me, hurriedly,
A man, yet by these tears a little boy again,
Throwing myself on the sand, confronting the waves,
20   I, chanter of pains and joys, uniter of here and hereafter,
Taking all hints to use them, but swiftly leaping beyond them,
A reminiscence sing.

Once Paumanok,
When the lilac-scent was in the air and Fifth-month grass was
    growing,
25   Up this seashore in some briers,
Two feather'd guests from Alabama, two together,
And their nest, and four light-green eggs spotted with brown,
And every day the he-bird to and fro near at hand,
And every day the she-bird crouch'd on her nest, silent, with
    bright eyes,
And every day I, a curious boy, never too close, never disturbing
30   them,
Cautiously peering, absorbing, translating.

Shine! shine! shine!
Pour down your warmth, great sun!
While we bask, we two together.

35   *Two together!*
Winds blow south, or winds blow north,
Day come white, or night come black,
Home, or rivers and mountains from home,
Singing all time, minding no time,
40   *While we two keep together.*

Till of a sudden,
May-be kill'd, unknown to her mate,
One forenoon the she-bird crouch'd not on the nest,
Nor return'd that afternoon, nor the next,
45   Nor ever appear'd again.

And thenceforward all summer in the sound of the sea,
And at night under the full of the moon in calmer weather,

Over the hoarse surging of the sea,
Or flitting from brier to brier by day,
50   I saw, I heard at intervals the remaining one, the he-bird.
The solitary guest from Alabama.

Blow! blow! blow!
Blow up sea-winds along Paumanok's shore;
I wait and I wait till you blow my mate to me.

55   Yes, when the stars glisten'd,
All night long on the prong of a moss-scallop'd stake,
Down almost amid the slapping waves,
Sat the lone singer wonderful causing tears.

He call'd on his mate,
60   He pour'd forth the meanings which I of all men know.

Yes my brother I know,
The rest might not, but I have treasur'd every note,
For more than once dimly down to the beach gliding,
Silent, avoiding the moonbeams, blending myself with the shadows,
Recalling now the obscure shapes, the echoes, the sounds and
65   sights after their sorts,
The white arms out in the breakers tirelessly tossing,
I, with bare feet, a child, the wind wafting my hair,
Listen'd long and long.

Listen'd to keep, to sing, now translating the notes,
70   Following you my brother.

Soothe! soothe! soothe!
Close on its wave soothes the wave behind,
And again another behind embracing and lapping, every one close,
But my love soothes not me, not me.

75   *Low hangs the moon, it rose late,*
It is lagging—O I think it is heavy with love, with love.

O madly the sea pushes upon the land,
With love, with love.

O night! do I not see my love fluttering out among the breakers?
80   *What is that little black thing I see there in the white?*

Loud! loud! loud!
Loud I call to you, my love!
High and clear I shoot my voice over the waves,
Surely you must know who is here, is here,
85   *You must know who I am, my love.*

Low-hanging moon!
What is that dusky spot in your brown yellow?
O it is the shape, the shape of my mate!
O moon do not keep her from me any longer.

90   *Land! land! O land!*
Whichever way I turn, O I think you could give me my mate
     back again if you only would,
For I am almost sure I see her dimly whichever way I look.

O rising stars!
Perhaps the one I want so much will rise, will rise with some
     of you.

95   *O throat! O trembling throat!*
Sound clearer through the atmosphere!
Pierce the woods, the earth,
Somewhere listening to catch you must be the one I want.

Shake out carols!
100   *Solitary here, the night's carols!*
Carols of lonesome love! death's carols!
Carols under that lagging, yellow, waning moon!
O under that moon where she droops almost down into the sea!
O reckless despairing carols.

105   *But soft! sink low!*
Soft! let me just murmur,
And do you wait a moment you husky-nois'd sea,
For somewhere I believe I heard my mate responding to me,
So faint, I must be still, be still to listen,
But not altogether still, for then she might not come immediately
110   *to me.*

Hither my love!
Here I am! here!
With this just-sustain'd note I announce myself to you,
This gentle call is for you my love, for you.

115   *Do not be decoy'd elsewhere,*
That is the whistle of the wind, it is not my voice,
That is the fluttering, the fluttering of the spray,
Those are the shadows of leaves.

O darkness! O in vain!
120   *O I am very sick and sorrowful.*

O brown halo in the sky near the moon, drooping upon the sea!
O troubled reflection in the sea!

O throat! O throbbing heart!
And I singing uselessly, uselessly all the night.

125 *O past! O happy life! O songs of joy!*
In the air, in the woods, over fields,
Loved! loved! loved! loved! loved!
But my mate no more, no more with me!
We two together no more.

130 The aria sinking,
All else continuing, the stars shining,
The winds blowing, the notes of the bird continuous echoing,
With angry moans the fierce old mother incessantly moaning,
On the sands of Paumanok's shore gray and rustling,
The yellow half-moon enlarged, sagging down, drooping, the face
135   of the sea almost touching,
The boy ecstatic, with his bare feet the waves, with his hair the
    atmosphere dallying,
The love in the heart long pent, now loose, now at last tumultu-
    ously bursting,
The aria's meaning, the ears, the soul, swiftly depositing,
The strange tears down the cheeks coursing,
140 The colloquy there, the trio, each uttering,
The undertone, the savage old mother incessantly crying,
To the boy's soul's questions sullenly timing, some drown'd secret
    hissing,
To the outsetting bard.

Demon or bird! (said the boy's soul,)
145 Is it indeed toward your mate you sing? or is it really to me?
For I, that was a child, my tongue's use sleeping, now I have
    heard you,

Now in a moment I know what I am for, I awake,
And already a thousand singers, a thousand songs, clearer, louder
    and more sorrowful than yours,
A thousand warbling echoes have started to life within me, never
    to die.

150 O you singer solitary, singing by yourself, projecting me,
O solitary me listening, never more shall I cease perpetuating
    you,
Never more shall I escape, never more the reverberations,
Never more the cries of unsatisfied love be absent from me,
Never again leave me to be the peaceful child I was before what
    there in the night,
155 By the sea under the yellow and sagging moon,

The messenger there arous'd, the fire, the sweet hell within,
The unknown want, the destiny of me.

O give me the clew! (it lurks in the night here somewhere,)
O if I am to have so much, let me have more!

160   A word then, (for I will conquer it,)
The word final, superior to all,
Subtle, sent up—what is it?—I listen;
Are you whispering it, and have been all the time, you sea-
     waves?
Is that it from your liquid rims and wet sands?

165   Whereto answering, the sea,
Delaying not, hurrying not,
Whisper'd me through the night, and very plainly before day-
     break,
Lisp'd to me the low and delicious word death,
And again death, death, death, death,
Hissing melodious, neither like the bird nor like my arous'd child's
170   heart,
But edging near as privately for me rustling at my feet,
Creeping thence steadily up to my ears and laving me softly all
     over,
Death, death, death, death, death.

Which I do not forget,
175   But fuse the song of my dusky demon and brother,
That he sang to me in the moonlight on Paumanok's gray beach,
With the thousand responsive songs at random,
My own songs awaked from that hour,
And with them the key, the word up from the waves,
180   The word of the sweetest song and all songs,
That strong and delicious word which, creeping to my feet,
(Or like some old crone rocking the cradle, swathed in sweet
     garments, bending aside,)
The sea whisper'd me.

3 *Ninth-month:* the Quaker designation for September   23 *Paumanok:* the Indian name for Long
Island, where Whitman was born   144 *Demon:* spirit (not demon in its contemporary negative sense)

DISCUSSION TOPICS

1. This poem obviously tells a story; briefly summarize its plot.
2. What is the "cradle endlessly rocking"? Who is the "fierce old mother"? What
   archetypal significance do these images have?

3. Why does Whitman use italics for part of the poem?
4. Why is a mockingbird a particularly appropriate bird to use as a symbol?
5. In what ways is this poem about both the making of a poet and the making of poetry? What line or lines specifically establish this symbolic connection?
6. What is the "strong and delicious word" in line 181?

CAVALRY CROSSING A FORD

A line in long array where they wind betwixt green islands,
They take a serpentine course, their arms flash in the sun—hark
    to the musical clank,
Behold the silvery river, in it the splashing horses loitering stop to
    drink,
Behold the brown-faced men, each group, each person a picture,
    the negligent rest on the saddles,
Some emerge on the opposite bank, others are just entering the
5   ford—while,
Scarlet and blue and snowy white,
The guidon flags flutter gayly in the wind.

DISCUSSION TOPICS

1. The poem's rhythm is characteristic of Whitman. It is in free verse, the unit of which is the line with timing based on the poet's and the reader's breath. In reading the poem aloud, you will pause naturally somewhere midway in the line. How does such a rhythm seem to accentuate the kind of picture and attendant feeling Whitman seems to desire?
2. How do alliteration and assonance contribute to the picture and feeling?
3. Does the poem gain or lose by the succession of references to unit, then smaller group, and finally, "each person a picture"?
4. Although this is a war poem, it is neither grim nor morbid (contrast it with Melville's "Shiloh"). What keeps it from being so?

TO A LOCOMOTIVE IN WINTER

Thee for my recitative,
Thee in the driving storm even as now, the snow, the winter-day
    declining,
Thee in thy panoply, thy measur'd dual throbbing and thy beat
    convulsive,
Thy black cylindric body, golden brass and silvery steel,
Thy ponderous side-bars, parallel and connecting rods, gyrating,
5   shuttling at thy sides,

Thy metrical, now swelling pant and roar, now tapering in the
distance,
Thy great protruding head-light fix'd in front,
Thy long, pale, floating vapor-pennants, tinged with delicate
purple,
The dense and murky clouds out-belching from thy smoke-stack,
Thy knitted frame, thy springs and valves, the tremulous twinkle
10   of thy wheels,
Thy train of cars behind, obedient, merrily following,
Through gale or calm, now swift, now slack, yet steadily careering;
Type of the modern—emblem of motion and power—pulse of
the continent,
For once come serve the Muse and merge in verse, even as here
I see thee,
15   With storm and buffeting gusts of wind and falling snow,
By day thy warning ringing bell to sound its notes,
By night thy silent signal lamps to swing.

Fierce-throated beauty!
Roll through my chant with all thy lawless music, thy swinging
lamps at night,
Thy madly-whistled laughter, echoing, rumbling like an earth-
20   quake, rousing all,
Law of thyself complete, thine own track firmly holding,
(No sweetness debonair of tearful harp or glib piano thine,)
Thy trills of shrieks by rocks and hills return'd,
Launch'd o'er the prairies wide, across the lakes,
25   To the free skies unpent and glad and strong.

DISCUSSION TOPIC

Compare this poem with Emily Dickinson's "I like to see it lap the miles." Why
do you think that both of these poets celebrate the locomotive? What similar
technical innovation might a late twentieth-century poet celebrate?

MATTHEW ARNOLD (1822–1888) British "apostle of culture"—educator, critic, poet;
traveled and lectured in America. His poetry often captures a sense of loneliness
and isolation that speaks to twentieth-century existential man. His criticism has
contributed helpful insight into literature and society, as well as famous phrases—
"sweetness and light," "Hebraism and Hellenism," "touchstones," "culture and
anarchy."

DOVER BEACH

The sea is calm tonight,
The tide is full, the moon lies fair
Upon the straits;—on the French coast the light
Gleams and is gone; the cliffs of England stand,
5   Glimmering and vast, out in the tranquil bay.
Come to the window, sweet is the night-air!
Only, from the long line of spray
Where the sea meets the moon-blanched land,
Listen! you hear the grating roar
10   Of pebbles which the waves draw back, and fling,
At their return, up the high strand,
Begin, and cease, and then again begin,
With tremulous cadence slow, and bring
The eternal note of sadness in.

15   Sophocles long ago
Heard it on the Aegean, and it brought
Into his mind the turbid ebb and flow
Of human misery; we
Find also in the sound a thought,
20   Hearing it by this distant northern sea.

The Sea of Faith
Was once, too, at the full, and round earth's shore
Lay like the folds of a bright girdle furled.
But now I only hear
25   Its melancholy, long, withdrawing roar,
Retreating, to the breath
Of the night-wind, down the vast edges drear
And naked shingles of the world.

Ah, love, let us be true
30   To one another! for the world, which seems
To lie before us like a land of dreams,
So various, so beautiful, so new,
Hath really neither joy, nor love, nor light,
Nor certitude, nor peace, nor help for pain;
35   And we are here as on a darkling plain
Swept with confused alarms of struggle and flight,
Where ignorant armies clash by night.

---

3 *French coast:* The French coast is approximately 20 miles away from the white chalk cliffs of Dover, a port and seaside resort on the English Channel. 15–18 *Sophocles:* most probably an allusion to his *Antigone* (lines 583–591)   23 *girdle:* a cloth belt or sash worn around the waist   28 *shingles:* beaches covered with loose pebbles   35 *darkling* in darkness

DISCUSSION TOPICS

1. What is the central theme of "Dover Beach"? How do such formal devices as meter, onomatopoeia, and alliteration create the scene and convey the theme of the poem?
2. Why does the speaker seem so troubled? Is he expressing personal or cosmic woe? What is the force of his allusion to Sophocles?
3. What is the cultural and philosophical context of Arnold's reference to The Sea of Faith"? Do the problems of our own time evoke a response similar to his?
4. Whom is the speaker addressing when he cries, "Ah, love, let us be true / To one another!"?

EMILY DICKINSON (1830–1886) Ranks alongside Whitman as the greatest American lyric poet. Most of her works were published posthumously and have steadily grown in popularity and critical esteem in this century. Her seemingly simple verses, epigrammatic style, and startling imagery often mask deep insight and stark realism.

SUCCESS IS COUNTED SWEETEST

Success is counted sweetest
By those who ne'er succeed.
To comprehend a nectar
Requires sorest need.

5   Not one of all the purple Host
Who took the Flag today
Can tell the definition
So clear of Victory

As he defeated—dying—
10   On whose forbidden ear
The distant strains of triumph
Burst agonized and clear!

DISCUSSION TOPIC

What specific examples from your own life can you substitute for the military examples in stanzas two and three?

IF I SHOULDN'T BE ALIVE

If I shouldn't be alive
When the Robins come,
Give the one in Red Cravat,
A Memorial crumb.

5   If I couldn't thank you,
Being fast asleep,
You will know I'm trying
With my Granite lip!

DISCUSSION TOPICS

1. Dickinson has been called "the Poet of Surprise." How—and where exactly—does she achieve "surprise" in this poem?
2. What is the multiple meaning of "Granite lip"?

I TASTE A LIQUOR NEVER BREWED

I taste a liquor never brewed—
From Tankards scooped in Pearl—
Not all the Vats upon the Rhine
Yield such an Alcohol!

5   Inebriate of Air—am I—
And Debauchee of Dew—
Reeling—thro endless summer days—
From inns of Molten Blue—

When "Landlords" turn the drunken Bee
10   Out of the Foxglove's door—
When Butterflies—renounce their "drams"—
I shall but drink the more!

Till Seraphs swing their snowy Hats—
And Saints—to windows run—
15   To see the little Tippler
Leaning against the—Sun—

3 *Rhine:* the Rhine River, which passes through Switzerland, Germany, and the Netherlands
13 *Seraphs:* or seraphim; described in Isaiah 6:2 as six-winged celestial beings standing above the throne of God; also the highest order of angels

DISCUSSION TOPICS

1. What, exactly, is the kind of drunkenness described by the poet? Have you ever felt like this? Explain.
2. Justify the progressive pattern of Dickinson's successive images. What links them? Is there a meaningful order of images?
3. Why are the seemingly breathless punctuation and syntax appropriate for tone, theme, and form?
4. How would a set of abstract terms change the essence of the poem?
5. In a variant text of this poem, line 3 reads "Not all the Frankfort berries" (the grapes that grow in the wine country around Frankfort in Germany) and line 16 reads "From Manzanilla come" (Manzanilla, a Cuban port, once shipped large quantities of rum). Which set of lines do you prefer and why?

THERE'S A CERTAIN SLANT OF LIGHT

There's a certain Slant of light,
Winter Afternoons—
That oppresses, like the Heft
Of Cathedral Tunes—

5   Heavenly Hurt, it gives us—
We can find no scar,
But internal difference,
Where the Meanings, are—

None may teach it—Any—
10   'Tis the Seal Despair—
An imperial affliction
Sent us of the Air—

When it comes, the Landscape listens—
Shadows—hold their breath—
15   When it goes, 'tis like the Distance
On the look of Death—

DISCUSSION TOPICS

1. Personifications abound in this short poem. List them, and visualize each of them. How do these impersonal persons help to present the mood and the feelings of the speaker?
2. Why should a "cathedral tune" have "heft"? What is the "hurt"? Why should it be "heavenly"?
3. Contrast this poem with "I Taste a Liquor Never Brewed," beginning with tone and how it is achieved.

A BIRD CAME DOWN THE WALK

A Bird came down the Walk—
He did not know I saw—
He bit an Angleworm in halves
And ate the fellow, raw,

5   And then he drank a Dew
From a convenient Grass—
And then hopped sidewise to the Wall
To let a Beetle pass—

He glanced with rapid eyes
10   That hurried all around—
They looked like frightened Beads, I thought—
He stirred his Velvet Head

Like one in danger, Cautious,
I offered him a Crumb
15   And he unrolled his feathers
And rowed him softer home—

Than Oars divide the Ocean,
Too silver for a seam—
Or Butterflies, off Banks of Noon
20   Leap, plashless as they swim.

DISCUSSION TOPICS

1. To experience this poem, we must appreciate how lines 3 and 4 relate to the rest of the poem. How does the character of the bird differ in these lines from that described through his actions in the second stanza—and in the final stanza?
2. Where is the pun in the second stanza?
3. What do you think Dickinson is trying to tell us about this bird in particular —and Nature in general?
4. Why is the word "plashless" (instead of "splashless") especially appropriate in the last line?

AFTER GREAT PAIN, A FORMAL FEELING COMES

After great pain, a formal feeling comes—
The Nerves sit ceremonious, like Tombs—
The stiff Heart questions was it He, that bore,
And Yesterday, or Centuries before?

5   The Feet, mechanical, go round—
       Of Ground, or Air, or Ought—
       A Wooden way
       Regardless grown,
       A Quartz contentment, like a stone—

       This is the Hour of Lead—
10   Remembered, if outlived,
       As Freezing persons, recollect the Snow—
       First—Chill—then Stupor—then the letting go—

DISCUSSION TOPIC

This poem may be read as a response to a loss, perhaps the death of someone. Shakespeare's Sonnet 73 ("That time of year . . .") may be read as a statement about anticipated loss or bereavement. Which poem seems more poignant to you? Why? Which images in each poem most effectively capture the feelings? Do the poets make it easy enough for the reader to identify with the experience of the poem? Why, or why not?

I LIKE TO SEE IT LAP THE MILES

       I like to see it lap the Miles—
       And lick the Valleys up—
       And stop to feed itself at Tanks—
       And then—prodigious step

5   Around a Pile of Mountains—
       And supercilious peer
       In Shanties—by the sides of Roads—
       And then a Quarry pare

       To fit its Ribs
10   And crawl between
       Complaining all the while
       In horrid—hooting stanza—
       Then chase itself down Hill—

       And neigh like Boanerges—
15   Then—punctual as a Star
       Stop—docile and omnipotent
       At its own stable door—

14 *Boanerges:* "The sons of thunder," the surname given to James and John by Christ in Mark 3:17

DISCUSSION TOPICS

1. What is "it"?

2. What is the speaker's attitude toward and response to the object described? How would you characterize the tone of the poem?

3. The Industrial Revolution and its accompanying technology are sometimes seen as the antithesis of the poetic spirit. Why is that not so in this poem?

BECAUSE I COULD NOT STOP FOR DEATH

Because I could not stop for Death—
He kindly stopped for me—
The Carriage held but just Ourselves—
And Immortality.

5　We slowly drove—He knew no haste
And I had put away
My labor and my leisure too,
For His Civility—

We passed the School, where Children strove
10　At Recess—in the Ring—
We passed the Fields of Gazing Grain—
We passed the Setting Sun—

Or rather—He passed Us—
The Dews drew quivering and chill—
15　For only Gossamer, my Gown—
My Tippet—only Tulle—

We paused before a House that seemed
A Swelling of the Ground—
The Roof was scarcely visible—
20　The Cornice—in the Ground—

Since then—'tis Centuries—and yet
Feels shorter than the Day
I first surmised the Horses' Heads
Were toward Eternity—

16 *Tippet:* scarf　*Tulle:* a fine netting

DISCUSSION TOPICS

1. It is said that one of the characteristics of great poetry is its capacity to sublimate —to refine and even make beautiful—such terrifying aspects of reality as death. How does Dickinson manage to achieve this kind of sublimation in "Because

I Could Not Stop for Death"? Specifically, how is Death characterized in the poem?
2. What evidence, if any, is there in the poem that the speaker would have preferred not to die, or die so soon?
3. Why does the poet mention "Children," "Grain," and "Setting Sun" in the third stanza? What are the symbolic—even archetypal—implications of "Grain" and "Sun"?
4. How—and where—does Dickinson achieve "surprise" in this poem?

A NARROW FELLOW IN THE GRASS

A narrow Fellow in the Grass
Occasionally rides—
You may have met Him—did you not
His notice sudden is—

5   The Grass divides as with a Comb—
A spotted shaft is seen—
And then it closes at your feet
And opens further on—

He likes a Boggy Acre
10   A Floor too cool for Corn—
Yet when a Boy, and Barefoot—
I more than once at Noon

Have passed, I thought, a Whip lash
Unbraiding in the Sun
15   When stooping to secure it
It wrinkled, and was gone—

Several of Nature's People
I know, and they know me—
I feel for them a transport
20   Of cordiality—

But never met this Fellow
Attended, or alone
Without a tighter breathing
And Zero at the Bone—

DISCUSSION TOPIC

Who—or what—is this "Fellow," literally and symbolically (or archetypally, if you prefer)? What is the difference between him and the rest of "Nature's People"? Have you ever experienced a feeling like that described in the last stanza? What were the circumstances?

I NEVER SAW A MOOR

I never saw a Moor—
I never saw the Sea—
Yet know I how the Heather looks
And what a Billow be.

5   I never spoke with God
Nor visited in Heaven—
Yet certain am I of the spot
As if the Checks were given—

8 *Checks:* railway tickets

A ROUTE OF EVANESCENCE

A Route of Evanescence
With a revolving Wheel—
A Resonance of Emerald—
A Rush of Cochineal—
5   And every Blossom on the Bush
Adjusts its tumbled Head—
The mail from Tunis, probably,
An easy Morning's Ride—

4 *Cochineal:* a bright red dye

DISCUSSION TOPIC

Just as Dickinson shows a locomotive, a robin, and a snake in new and surprising ways, so here she takes a familiar phenomenon and through her poetic genius transforms it into something quite extraordinary. What, in fact, is she describing here?

APPARENTLY WITH NO SURPRISE

Apparently with no surprise
To any happy Flower
The Frost beheads it at its play—
In accidental power—

5   The blonde Assassin passes on—
      The Sun proceeds unmoved
      To measure off another Day
      For an Approving God.

DISCUSSION TOPICS

1. What views of the world of nature, even of the universe, are embodied in this poem and in "A Bird Came Down the Walk"?
2. There is a notable pun in this poem. Try to find it (reading the poem aloud will help).
3. Who—or what—is the "blonde Assassin" in line 5? What figure of speech is this?
4. How can the Sun "proceed" without being "moved" in line 6? What is Dickinson doing with the language here?

THOMAS HARDY (1840–1928) English novelist and poet; cosmic ironist. He was naturalistic in his attitudes toward life, but sympathetic toward people trying to work out their problems in a frequently hostile or at best an indifferent world.

HAP

      If but some vengeful god would call to me
      From up the sky, and laugh: "Thou suffering thing,
      Know that thy sorrow is my ecstasy,
      That thy love's loss is my hate's profiting!"

5   Then would I bear it, clench myself, and die,
      Steeled by the sense of ire unmerited;
      Half-eased in that a Powerfuller than I
      Had willed and meted me the tears I shed.

      But not so. How arrives it joy lies slain,
10   And why unblooms the best hope ever sown?
      —Crass Casualty obstructs the sun and rain,
      And dicing Time for gladness casts a moan. . . .
      These purblind Doomsters had as readily strown
      Blisses about my pilgrimage as pain.

Hap: chance or accident (like *Casualty,* in line 11)   13 *Doomsters:* judges

445

DISCUSSION TOPICS

1. What view of a human being's place in the universe does Hardy offer?
2. How does the sestet (last six lines) correct the propositions offered in the octave (first eight lines)?

NEUTRAL TONES

We stood by a pond that winter day,
And the sun was white, as though chidden of God,
And a few leaves lay on the starving sod;
    —They had fallen from an ash, and were gray.

5   Your eyes on me were as eyes that rove
Over tedious riddles of years ago;
And some words played between us to and fro
    On which lost the more by our love.

The smile on your mouth was the deadest thing
10   Alive enough to have strength to die;
And a grin of bitterness swept thereby
    Like an ominous bird a-wing. . . .

Since then, keen lessons that love deceives,
And wrings with wrong, have shaped to me
15   Your face, and the God-curst sun, and a tree,
    And a pond edged with grayish leaves.

DISCUSSION TOPICS

1. How does the landscape of "Neutral Tones" provide a setting for the emotions the speaker is describing?
2. In what ways is this poem similar to Arnold's "Dover Beach"? In what ways is it different?
3. How does the attitude toward love in this poem compare with that in other love poems you have read, for example, by Donne, Shakespeare, or Housman?

DRUMMER HODGE

They throw in Drummer Hodge, to rest
    Uncoffined—just as found:
His landmark is a kopje-crest
    That breaks the veldt around;
5   And foreign constellations west
    Each night above his mound.

Young Hodge the Drummer never knew—
   Fresh from his Wessex home—
The meaning of the broad Karoo,
10   The Bush, the dusty loam,
And why uprose to nightly view
   Strange stars amid the gloam.

Yet portion of that unknown plain
   Will Hodge forever be;
15 His homely Northern breast and brain
   Grow to some Southern tree,
And strange-eyed constellations reign
   His stars eternally.

1 *Drummer Hodge:* an English soldier killed in the Boer War (1899–1902) against the Dutch colonists in South Africa   3 *kopje:* Afrikaans for "small hill"   4 *veldt:* grassland, plain   5 *foreign constellations:* Groups of stars in the southern hemisphere would be unfamiliar to the Englishman Hodge. *west:* move westward   8 *Wessex:* Hardy's name for the area of southwest England   9 *Karoo:* elevated plateau of South Africa   10 *Bush:* uncleared land, covered with shrubs

DISCUSSION TOPICS

1. How would you describe the tone of this poem?
2. Compare Lovelace's "To Lucasta" and Owen's "Dulce et Decorum Est." What differences can you find in "Drummer Hodge"?
3. Discuss the similarity between Hardy's "strange-eyed constellations" and Crane's "high cold star on a winter's night" in "The Open Boat."

THE MAN HE KILLED

   "Had he and I but met
   By some old ancient inn,
We should have sat us down to wet
   Right many a nipperkin!

5   "But ranged as infantry,
   And staring face to face,
I shot at him as he at me,
   And killed him in his place.

   "I shot him dead because—
10   Because he was my foe,
Just so: my foe of course he was;
   That's clear enough; although

"He thought he'd 'list, perhaps,
Off-hand like—just as I—
15 Was out of work—had sold his traps—
No other reason why.

"Yes; quaint and curious war is!
You shoot a fellow down
You'd treat if met where any bar is,
20 Or help to half-a-crown."

4 *nipperkin:* a cup containing half a pint or less   13 *'list:* enlist   15 *traps:* belongings (trappings)
20 *half a crown:* A crown was a British coin worth five shillings.

DISCUSSION TOPIC

"The Man He Killed" is another of Hardy's war poems. How does the colloquial and even convivial tone of this poem point up the irony of war?

THE CONVERGENCE OF THE TWAIN

LINES ON THE LOSS OF THE "TITANIC"

I

In a solitude of the sea
Deep from human vanity,
And the Pride of Life that planned her, stilly couches she.

II

Steel chambers, late the pyres
5 Of her salamandrine fires,
Cold currents thrid, and turn to rhythmic tidal lyres.

III

Over the mirrors meant
To glass the opulent
The sea-worm crawls—grotesque, slimed, dumb, indifferent.

IV

10 Jewels in joy designed
To ravish the sensuous mind
Lie lightless, all their sparkles bleared and black and blind.

V

Dim moon-eyed fishes near
Gaze at the gilded gear
15 And query: "What does this vaingloriousness down here?" . . .

VI

Well: while was fashioning
This creature of cleaving wing,
The Immanent Will that stirs and urges everything

VII

Prepared a sinister mate
20 For her—so gaily great—
A Shape of Ice, for the time far and dissociate.

VIII

And as the smart ship grew
In stature, grace, and hue,
In shadowy silent distance grew the Iceberg too.

IX

25 Alien they seemed to be:
No mortal eye could see
The intimate welding of their later history,

X

Or sign that they were bent
By paths coincident
30 On being anon twin halves of one august event,

XI

Till the Spinner of the Years
Said "Now!" And each one hears,
And consummation comes, and jars two hemispheres.

Titanic: On April 15, 1912, the luxurious *Titanic,* presumed to be unsinkable, went down on her maiden voyage after striking an iceberg. Of the 2244 passengers on board, 1513 perished. 5 *Salamandrine:* Salamanders were said to live in, or be able to withstand, fire. 6 *thrid:* thread

DISCUSSION TOPICS

1. What is the "Immanent Will" of line 18? How does it act and why?
2. What philosophical view of historical events emerges in this poem?
3. What is the central metaphor of the poem? How does it enhance the theme of "convergence"?

GERARD MANLEY HOPKINS (1844–1889) Jesuit priest, teacher, nonprofessional poet. His works were published posthumously, but like those of Emily Dickinson, they have had both critical acclaim and steady influence. His style and technique resemble those of John Donne and Old English poetry.

SPRING

Nothing is so beautiful as spring—
    When weeds, in wheels, shoot long and lovely and lush;
    Thrush's eggs look little low heavens, and thrush
Through the echoing timber does so rinse and wring
5   The ear, it strikes like lightnings to hear him sing;
    The glassy peartree leaves and blooms, they brush
    The descending blue; that blue is all in a rush
With richness; the racing lambs too have fair their fling.

What is all this juice and all this joy?
10   A strain of the earth's sweet being in the beginning
In Eden garden.—Have, get, before it cloy,
    Before it cloud, Christ, lord, and sour with sinning,
Innocent mind and Mayday in girl and boy,
    Most, O maid's child, thy choice and worthy the winning.

DISCUSSION TOPICS

1. Hopkins was a brilliant poetic innovator and stylist, as witnessed by this poem especially. What traditional poetic form is he using here, and what notable modifications does he make?
2. Count the number of alliterations in this poem. What is their effect on the reader?
3. What is the tone of the poem—and where does this tone change? What word, particularly, is the key to this change?
4. What is the archetypal appropriateness of Hopkins's choice of seasons?

GOD'S GRANDEUR

The world is charged with the grandeur of God.
    It will flame out, like shining from shook foil;
    It gathers to a greatness, like the ooze of oil
Crushed. Why do men then now not reck his rod?
5   Generations have trod, have trod, have trod;
    And all is seared with trade; bleared, smeared with toil;
    And wears man's smudge and shares man's smell: the soil
Is bare now, nor can foot feel, being shod.

And for all this, nature is never spent;
10   There lives the dearest freshness deep down things;
And though the last lights off the black West went
      Oh, morning, at the brown brink eastward, springs—
Because the Holy Ghost over the bent
      World broods with warm breast and with ah! bright wings.

---

2 *shook foil:* In a letter to the poet Robert Bridges, Hopkins wrote: "Shaken goldfoil gives off broad glares like sheet lightning . . . a sort of fork lightning too."   4 *reck:* take heed of

DISCUSSION TOPICS

1. This poem is a particularly good example of Hopkins's delight in sound effects. What are some of these effects, and how does Hopkins direct our reading by means of them?
2. What are the multiple meanings of words like "charged" and "rod" and "spent"?
3. Hopkins develops a complex series of interrelated metaphors in this sonnet. How many of these can you discern?
4. Why is it particularly appropriate that Hopkins concludes the poem with his references to "warm breast" and "bright wings"?

THE WINDHOVER

TO CHRIST OUR LORD

I caught this morning morning's minion, king-
      dom of daylight's dauphin, dapple-dawn-drawn Falcon, in his riding
Of the rolling level underneath him steady air, and striding
High there, how he rung upon the rein of a wimpling wing
5   In his ecstasy! then off, off forth on swing,
      As a skate's heel sweeps smooth on a bow-bend: the hurl and gliding
Rebuffed the big wind. My heart in hiding
Stirred for a bird,—the achieve of, the mastery of the thing!

Brute beauty and valour and act, oh, air, pride, plume, here
10   Buckle! AND the fire that breaks from thee then, a billion
Times told lovelier, more dangerous, O my chevalier!

      No wonder of it: shéer plód makes plough down sillion
Shine, and blue-bleak embers, ah my dear,
      Fall, gall themselves, and gash gold-vermilion.

Windhover: a name given to the kestrel, a small falcon, because it hovers in midair against the wind
4 *rung upon the rein:* A horse is "rung on the rein" when it is held by a long rein and made to circle
tthe trainer. A hawk "rings" when it rises in a spiraling motion.   *wimpling:* rippling   12 *sil-lion:* furrow

DISCUSSION TOPICS

1. "The Windhover" illustrates very well some of Hopkins's ideas about poetic meter. He departs from conventional ways of counting metrical feet by means of a fixed number of stressed and unstressed syllables, with only a limited number of allowed variations or substitutions. In many of his poems he achieves more flexible metrical patterns akin to musical notation that he referred to as "sprung rhythm." His rhythmic effects usually depend on a fixed number of beats or accented syllables and various combinations of unaccented or "slack" syllables. He also experimented with rising and falling rhythms. For example, "The Windhover" has a falling rhythm: five major stresses per line, with the stress coming on the first syllable of each foot. To achieve the "sprung" effect, Hopkins sometimes introduces one or more slack syllables which he calls "out-riders"—extra syllables that are not counted as part of the meter. In a manu-script version of the poem, Hopkins scanned the first two lines as follows, with "outriders" marked by curved lines:

   I cáught this mórning mórning's mínion, kíng-
        dom of dáylight's dáuphin, dápple-dawn-drawn fálcon in his ríding

Some of Hopkins's other poetic devices also contribute to his metrical effects —alliteration, hyphenated words, grammatical and syntactic interruptions. The result is a unique blending of sound and meaning. After reading the poem aloud in order to hear the effect of Hopkins's music, see how many of these devices you can identify in "The Windhover."

2. Why do you think Hopkins dedicated the poem "To Christ Our Lord"? What relationship do you see between the bird and Christ?

3. Whom is the poet addressing as "O my chevalier"? What do you think he means by the word "chevalier"?

PIED BEAUTY

> Glory be to God for dappled things—
>   For skies of couple-colour as a brinded cow;
>   For rose-moles all in stipple upon trout that swim;
>   Fresh-firecoal chestnut-falls; finches' wings;
> 5   Landscape plotted and pieced—fold, fallow, and plough;
>   And áll trádes, their gear and tackle and trim.

> All things counter, original, spare, strange;
>   Whatever is fickle, freckled (who knows how?)
>   With swift, slow; sweet, sour; adazzle, dim;
> 10   He fathers-forth whose beauty is past change:
>   Praise him.

Pied: parti-colored, containing two or more colors   2 *brinded:* brindled, streaked   6 *trim:* equipment   7 *counter:* contrary, opposite

SPRING AND FALL

TO A YOUNG CHILD

> Márgarét, áre you gríeving
> Over Goldengrove unleaving?
> Leáves, líke the things of man, you
> With your fresh thoughts care for, can you?
> 5   Áh! ás the heart grows older
> It will come to such sights colder
> By and by, nor spare a sigh
> Though worlds of wanwood leafmeal lie;
> And yet you *will* weep and know why.
> 10   Now no matter, child, the name:
> Sórrow's spríngs áre the same.
> Nor mouth had, no nor mind, expressed
> What heart heard of, ghost guessed:
> It ís the blight man was born for,
> 15   It is Margaret you mourn for.

13 *ghost:* spirit

DISCUSSION TOPICS

1. Hopkins frequently plays with words, inventing some, occasionally using Old English or even French. In this poem both "wanwood" and "leafmeal" are invented compounds. How do these inventions enrich the poem?
2. In lines 3 and 4 Hopkins breaks up the normal order of English syntax. What effect does this manipulation of grammar have on the poem?
3. What extended meanings does the poet attach to the words "Goldengrove unleaving"?
4. What is "the blight man was born for"?

A. E. HOUSMAN (1859–1936) University professor and classics scholar at London and Cambridge. His pessimism and somberness are comparable to Hardy's, but his tone is modulated by a wry geniality and romantic nostalgia: ". . . of my threescore years and ten, / Twenty will not come again. . . ."

WHEN I WAS ONE-AND-TWENTY

    When I was one-and-twenty
      I heard a wise man say,
    "Give crowns and pounds and guineas
      But not your heart away;
5   Give pearls away and rubies
      But keep your fancy free."
    But I was one-and-twenty,
      No use to talk to me.

    When I was one-and-twenty
10   I heard him say again,
    "The heart out of the bosom
      Was never given in vain;
    'Tis paid with sighs a plenty
      And sold for endless rue."
15   And I am two-and-twenty,
      And oh, 'tis true, 'tis true.

TO AN ATHLETE DYING YOUNG

    The time you won your town the race
    We chaired you through the market-place;
    Man and boy stood cheering by,
    And home we brought you shoulder-high.

5   To-day, the road all runners come,
    Shoulder-high we bring you home,
    And set you at your threshold down,
    Townsman of a stiller town.

    Smart lad, to slip betimes away
10   From fields where glory does not stay
    And early though the laurel grows
    It withers quicker than the rose.

    Eyes the shady night has shut
    Cannot see the record cut,
15   And silence sounds no worse than cheers
    After earth has stopped the ears.

Now you will not swell the rout
Of lads that wore their honours out,
Runners whom renown outran
20 And the name died before the man.

So set, before its echoes fade,
The fleet foot on the sill of shade,
And hold to the low lintel up
The still-defended challenge-cup.

25 And round that early-laurelled head
Will flock to gaze the strengthless dead
And find unwithered on its curls
The garland briefer than a girl's.

DISCUSSION TOPICS

1. Is the tone of the poem tragic? Why or why not?
2. Why does the poet address the athlete as "Smart lad"?
3. In what ways may Housman's poem apply to contemporary sports heroes?

IS MY TEAM PLOUGHING

"Is my team ploughing,
    That I was used to drive
And hear the harness jingle
    When I was man alive?"

5 Ay, the horses trample,
    The harness jingles now;
No change though you lie under
    The land you used to plough.

"Is football playing
10   Along the river shore,
With lads to chase the leather,
    Now I stand up no more?"

Ay, the ball is flying,
    The lads play heart and soul;
15 The goal stands up, the keeper
    Stands up to keep the goal.

"Is my girl happy,
    That I thought hard to leave,
And has she tired of weeping
20   As she lies down at eve?"

Ay, she lies down lightly,
    She lies not down to weep:
Your girl is well contented.
    Be still, my lad, and sleep.

25 "Is my friend hearty,
    Now I am thin and pine,
And has he found to sleep in
    A better bed than mine?"

Yes, lad, I lie easy,
30   I lie as lads would choose;
I cheer a dead man's sweetheart,
    Never ask me whose.

DISCUSSION TOPIC

Like most of Housman's poems, this one deals with the theme of death—but what keeps it from being morbid?

WITH RUE MY HEART IS LADEN

With rue my heart is laden
    For golden friends I had,
For many a rose-lipt maiden
    And many a lightfoot lad.

5 By brooks too broad for leaping
    The lightfoot boys are laid;
The rose-lipt girls are sleeping
    In fields where roses fade.

DISCUSSION TOPICS

1. Why are the "brooks too broad for leaping"?
2. Why is Housman's use of the rose image especially appropriate? How can you tell the image is also a symbol?

"TERENCE, THIS IS STUPID STUFF"

"Terence, this is stupid stuff:
You eat your victuals fast enough;
There can't be much amiss, 'tis clear,
To see the rate you drink your beer.

5   But oh, good Lord, the verse you make,
It gives a chap the belly-ache.
The cow, the old cow, she is dead;
It sleeps well, the hornéd head:
We poor lads, 'tis our turn now
10   To hear such tunes as killed the cow.
Pretty friendship 'tis to rhyme
Your friends to death before their time
Moping melancholy mad:
Come, pipe a tune to dance to, lad."

15   Why, if 'tis dancing you would be,
There's brisker pipes than poetry.
Say, for what were hop-yards meant,
Or why was Burton built on Trent?
Oh many a peer of England brews
20   Livelier liquor than the Muse,
And malt does more than Milton can
To justify God's ways to man.
Ale, man, ale's the stuff to drink
For fellows whom it hurts to think:
25   Look into the pewter pot
To see the world as the world's not.
And faith, 'tis pleasant till 'tis past:
The mischief is that 'twill not last.
Oh I have been to Ludlow fair
30   And left my necktie God knows where,
And carried half-way home, or near,
Pints and quarts of Ludlow beer:
Then the world seemed none so bad,
And I myself a sterling lad;
35   And down in lovely muck I've lain,
Happy till I woke again.
Then I saw the morning sky:
Heigho, the tale was all a lie;
The world, it was the old world yet,
40   I was I, my things were wet,
And nothing now remained to do
But begin the game anew.

      Therefore, since the world has still
Much good, but much less good than ill,
45   And while the sun and moon endure
Luck's a chance, but trouble's sure,
I'd face it as a wise man would,
And train for ill and not for good.

'Tis true, the stuff I bring for sale
50　Is not so brisk a brew as ale:
Out of a stem that scored the hand
I wrung it in a weary land.
But take it: if the smack is sour,
The better for the embittered hour;
55　It should do good to heart and head
When your soul is in my soul's stead;
And I will friend you, if I may,
In the dark and cloudy day.

There was a king reigned in the East:
60　There, when kings will sit to feast,
They get their fill before they think
With poisoned meat and poisoned drink.
He gathered all that springs to birth
From the many-venomed earth;
65　First a little, thence to more,
He sampled all her killing store;
And easy, smiling, seasoned sound,
Sate the king when healths went round.
They put arsenic in his meat
70　And stared aghast to watch him eat;
They poured strychnine in his cup
And shook to see him drink it up:
They shook, they stared as white's their shirt:
Them it was their poison hurt.
75　—I tell the tale that I heard told.
Mithridates, he died old.

Terence: A Shropshire Lad, the volume in which this poem and the four preceding it appeared, was
originally titled The Poems of Terence Hearsay.　18 Burton . . .: Burton-upon-Trent is a town renowned
for its breweries.　22 Milton: At the beginning of Paradise Lost, Milton seeks the aid of the "Heaven'ly Muse" so that he can "justify the ways of God to men."　29 Ludlow: a market town in
Shropshire　76 Mithridates: Mithridates VI (d. 63 BC), king of Pontus, was said to have become
immune to poison by taking small doses gradually.

DISCUSSION TOPICS

1. Why is the first stanza enclosed in quotation marks?
2. What is the "stupid stuff"?
3. What "brisker pipes than poetry" does Terence mention in the second stanza?
   What is wrong with these "brisker pipes"?
4. Terence's "Therefore" at the beginning of the third stanza implies a logical
   shift. Can you reconstruct his argument in your own words?

5. Like most good poets, Housman is an inveterate punster. Note, for example, the word "stem" in line 51. How many possible meanings does this word have in the context of the poem?
6. What is the purpose of the poet's last stanza or verse paragraph? Why does Terence mention Mithridates?

WILLIAM BUTLER YEATS (1865–1939) Irish poet and more—mystic, producer of plays, participant in the Irish Renaissance, senator, public man of affairs—but steadily a poet, so that now he is in the first rank of poets in English in this century. His system of symbolism and power of imagery compare with Blake's.

THE LAKE ISLE OF INNISFREE

I will arise and go now, and go to Innisfree,
And a small cabin build there, of clay and wattles made:
Nine bean-rows will I have there, a hive for the honeybee,
And live alone in the bee-loud glade.

5   And I shall have some peace there, for peace comes dropping slow,
Dropping from the veils of the morning to where the cricket sings;
There midnight's all a glimmer, and noon a purple glow,
And evening full of the linnet's wings.

I will arise and go now, for always night and day
10   I hear lake water lapping with low sounds by the shore;
While I stand on the roadway, or on the pavements grey,
I hear it in the deep heart's core.

1 *Innisfree:* a small island in Lough Gill, near Yeats's beloved Sligo, in the west of Ireland
2 *wattles:* poles intertwined with sticks and vines

DISCUSSION TOPIC

Do you have your own personal version of "Innisfree"? What form does it take —what images or cluster of images in your own "deep heart's core"?

NO SECOND TROY

Why should I blame her that she filled my days
With misery, or that she would of late
Have taught to ignorant men most violent ways,
Or hurled the little streets upon the great,

5   Had they but courage equal to desire?
What could have made her peaceful with a mind
That nobleness made simple as a fire,
With beauty like a tightened bow, a kind
That is not natural in an age like this,
10   Being high and solitary and most stern?
Why, what could she have done, being what she is?
Was there another Troy for her to burn?

Troy: the city destroyed by the Greeks after 10 years of fighting to avenge the abduction of Helen by the Trojan prince Paris   1 *her:* Maud Gonne, the woman whom Yeats loved in vain for many years, is symbolized by Helen of Troy in his poetry.   3 *violent ways:* Maud Gonne was a revolutionary in the Irish movement for independence from England.

DISCUSSION TOPIC

What does Yeats's poem suggest about the nature of beauty, desire, and destruction? Compare "Leda and the Swan."

THE WILD SWANS AT COOLE

The trees are in their autumn beauty,
The woodland paths are dry,
Under the October twilight the water
Mirrors a still sky;
5   Upon the brimming water among the stones
Are nine-and-fifty swans.

The nineteenth autumn has come upon me
Since I first made my count;
I saw, before I had well finished,
10   All suddenly mount
And scatter wheeling in great broken rings
Upon their clamorous wings.

I have looked upon those brilliant creatures,
And now my heart is sore.
15   All's changed since I, hearing at twilight,
The first time on this shore,
The bell-beat of their wings above my head,
Trod with a lighter tread.

Unwearied still, lover by lover,
20   They paddle in the cold
Companionable streams or climb the air;

Their hearts have not grown old;
Passion or conquest, wander where they will,
Attend upon them still.

25 But now they drift on the still water,
Mysterious, beautiful;
Among what rushes will they build,
By what lake's edge or pool
Delight men's eyes when I awake some day
30 To find they have flown away?

Coole: Coole Park, in western Ireland, was the estate of Yeats's friend and patron, Lady Gregory.
8 *my count:* Yeats's visit to Coole Park in the summer of 1897 marked a turning point in his life.

DISCUSSION TOPICS

1. How does this poem explore the passage of time within the framework of humankind's relationship to nature?
2. When Yeats first published "The Wild Swans at Coole," the final stanza (in the version printed here) came directly after the second one. What are the effects of Yeats's change?
3. What is the symbolic—even archetypal—appropriateness of Yeats's use of the swans in this poem? What if these birds were geese or ducks instead?

EASTER 1916

I have met them at close of day
Coming with vivid faces
From counter or desk among grey
Eighteenth-century houses.
5 I have passed with a nod of the head
Or polite meaningless words,
Or have lingered awhile and said
Polite meaningless words,
And thought before I had done
10 Of a mocking tale or a gibe
To please a companion
Around the fire at the club,
Being certain that they and I
But lived where motley is worn:
15 All changed, changed utterly:
A terrible beauty is born.

That woman's days were spent
In ignorant good-will,
Her nights in argument
20 Until her voice grew shrill.
What voice more sweet than hers
When, young and beautiful,
She rode to harriers?
This man had kept a school
25 And rode our wingèd horse;
This other his helper and friend
Was coming into his force;
He might have won fame in the end,
So sensitive his nature seemed,
30 So daring and sweet his thought.
This other man I had dreamed
A drunken, vainglorious lout.
He had done most bitter wrong
To some who are near my heart,
35 Yet I number him in the song;
He, too, has resigned his part
In the casual comedy;
He, too, has been changed in his turn,
Transformed utterly:
40 A terrible beauty is born.

Hearts with one purpose alone
Through summer and winter seem
Enchanted to a stone
To trouble the living stream.
45 The horse that comes from the road,
The rider, the birds that range
From cloud to tumbling cloud,
Minute by minute they change;
A shadow of cloud on the stream
50 Changes minute by minute;
A horse-hoof slides on the brim,
And a horse plashes within it;
The long-legged moor-hens dive,
And hens to moor-cocks call;
55 Minute by minute they live:
The stone's in the midst of all.

Too long a sacrifice
Can make a stone of the heart.

O when may it suffice?
60 That is Heaven's part, our part
To murmur name upon name,
As a mother names her child
When sleep at last has come
On limbs that had run wild.
65 What is it but nightfall?
No, no, not night but death;
Was it needless death after all?
For England may keep faith
For all that is done and said.
70 We know their dream; enough
To know they dreamed and are dead;
And what if excess of love
Bewildered them till they died?
I write it out in a verse—
75 MacDonagh and MacBride
And Connolly and Pearse
Now and in time to be,
Wherever green is worn,
Are changed, changed utterly:
80 A terrible beauty is born.
            September 25, 1916

1 *them:* the rebels   17 *That woman's days:* Constance Gore-Booth (1868–1927), an Irish nationalist, writer, and one of the commanders during the rebellion; convicted of treason, but death sentence was commuted   24 *This man:* Patrick Henry Pearse (1879–1916); a schoolmaster, writer, poet, and commander of the insurgent forces during the rebellion; executed for treason   25 *wingèd horse:* Pegasus, a symbol for poetic inspiration   26 *This other:* Thomas MacDonagh (1878–1916), a poet, playwright and close friend of Pearse; executed as one of the leaders of the uprising   31 *This other man:* Major John MacBride (1865–1916), also executed for participating in the rebellion; married Yeats's great love, Maud Gonne, in 1903, separated from her in 1905   76 *Connolly:* James Connolly (1870–1916), socialist and labor organizer, wounded in the rebellion and later executed

DISCUSSION TOPIC

The poem refers to the Easter Rebellion of April 24, 1916, in which Irish rebels attempted to take Dublin by force and declare Ireland independent from England. The insurgents received little support, however, and after a week of fighting surrendered to the British. Fifteen of the rebel leaders—among them the men cited in the poem—were tried and executed in May. What does "Easter 1916" suggest about the poet's role in revolutions? Compare Shelley's "Ode to the West Wind" and Auden's "On the Death of W. B. Yeats."

THE SECOND COMING

Turning and turning in the widening gyre
The falcon cannot hear the falconer;
Things fall apart; the centre cannot hold;
Mere anarchy is loosed upon the world,
5   The blood-dimmed tide is loosed, and everywhere
The ceremony of innocence is drowned;
The best lack all conviction, while the worst
Are full of passionate intensity.

Surely some revelation is at hand;
10   Surely the Second Coming is at hand.
The Second Coming! Hardly are those words out
When a vast image out of *Spiritus Mundi*
Troubles my sight: somewhere in sands of the desert
A shape with lion body and the head of a man
15   A gaze blank and pitiless as the sun,
Is moving its slow thighs, while all about it
Reel shadows of the indignant desert birds.
The darkness drops again; but now I know
That twenty centuries of stony sleep
20   Were vexed to nightmare by a rocking cradle,
And what rough beast, its hour come round at last,
Slouches towards Bethlehem to be born?

The Second Coming: In Matthew 24, Christ prophesies "the coming of the Son of man," a time of tribulation and upheaval in nature.   1 *gyre:* the spiral-like flight of the falcon away from its master. Yeats used the figure of two interpenetrating cones (or gyres) in his personal philosophy to represent the cyclical movement in history from one era to another. When one of the gyres reaches its widest point of expansion, the age comes to an end and another age begins at the narrowest point of the other gyre. Each of these cycles lasts 2000 years (see line 19); then the new and contrasting cycle evolves. 12 *Spiritus Mundi:* the spirit, or soul, of the universe; Yeats's term for the "general storehouse of images" that the subconscious mind can receive   14 *A shape:* The Sphinx   19 *twenty centuries:* the cycle preceding the Christian era   20 *cradle:* the cradle of the Christ-child

DISCUSSION TOPICS

1. What mythical and archetypal elements does Yeats bring to his depiction of the second coming?
2. As indicated by the concept of the interlocking gyres, Yeats conceived of history as moving through contrasting cycles. What contrasts to Christianity are suggested here?
3. What similarities do you see between this poem and Arnold's "Dover Beach"?

SAILING TO BYZANTIUM

I

That is no country for old men. The young
In one another's arms, birds in the trees
—Those dying generations—at their song,
The salmon-falls, the mackerel-crowded seas,
5   Fish, flesh, or fowl, commend all summer long
Whatever is begotten, born, and dies.
Caught in that sensual music all neglect
Monuments of unageing intellect.

II

An aged man is but a paltry thing,
10 A tattered coat upon a stick, unless
Soul clap its hands and sing, and louder sing
For every tatter in its mortal dress,
Nor is there singing school but studying
Monuments of its own magnificence;
15 And therefore I have sailed the seas and come
To the holy city of Byzantium.

III

O sages standing in God's holy fire
As in the gold mosaic of a wall,
Come from the holy fire, perne in a gyre,
20 And be the singing-masters of my soul.
Consume my heart away; sick with desire
And fastened to a dying animal
It knows not what it is; and gather me
Into the artifice of eternity.

IV

25 Once out of nature I shall never take
My bodily form from any natural thing,
But such a form as Grecian goldsmiths make
Of hammered gold and gold enamelling
To keep a drowsy Emperor awake;
30 Or set upon a golden bough to sing
To lords and ladies of Byzantium
Of what is past, or passing, or to come.

Byzantium: later Constantinople (AD 330) and currently Istanbul, the seat of the Eastern Orthodox Church; renowned for its wealth, intellectual vitality, and artistic treasures   19 *perne in a gyre:* A "pern" (or "pirn"), as Yeats elsewhere notes, is the spool on which thread is wound. "To perne" is to make the spinning motion of such a spool. For the significance of the *gyre* in Yeats's thought, see the note on line 1 of "The Second Coming."   27 *such a form:* Yeats writes in *October Blast*, "I have read somewhere that in the Emperor's palace at Byzantium was a tree made of gold and silver, and artificial birds that sang."

DISCUSSION TOPICS

1. From both philosophical and psychological points of view, discuss the kind of journey involved in "Sailing to Byzantium."
2. What contrasts does Yeats develop between "That . . . country" (Ireland, and, by extension, any physical place) and the city of Byzantium? What formalistic devices underscore these differences?
3. What relationship between the worlds of art and nature does Yeats envision in this poem?

WRITING TOPIC

Compare this poem with Keats's "Ode on a Grecian Urn," with particular reference to the tension between the world of nature and the world of art.

LEDA AND THE SWAN

A sudden blow: the great wings beating still
Above the staggering girl, her thighs caressed
By the dark webs, her nape caught in his bill,
He holds her helpless breast upon his breast.

5   How can those terrified vague fingers push
The feathered glory from her loosening thighs?
And how can body, laid in that white rush,
But feel the strange heart beating where it lies?

A shudder in the loins engenders there
10   The broken wall, the burning roof and tower
And Agamemnon dead.
               Being so caught up,
So mastered by the brute blood of the air,
Did she put on his knowledge with his power
Before the indifferent beak could let her drop?

Leda: After being raped by Zeus, who had taken the form of a swan, Leda bore two eggs. From one of these came Helen, later the wife of Menelaus; from the other came Clytemnestra, later the wife of Agamemnon, Menelaus's brother. The abduction of Helen by Paris brought about the destruction of Troy (see line 10). When Agamemnon, the Greek king and commander-in-chief, returned home from the Trojan War, he was murdered by Clytemnestra.

DISCUSSION TOPICS

1. Discuss the ways in which "Leda and the Swan" suggests interrelationships between passion, sexuality, creation, and destruction.
2. What happens to the poem if we know that Yeats saw the union of Zeus and Leda as the pagan counterpart to the Immaculate Conception?
3. What is the form of this poem? Why does Yeats divide the octave and the sestet as he does?

EDWIN ARLINGTON ROBINSON (1869–1935) New Englander, creator of the imaginary "Tilbury Town." He wrote longer poems, too, including an Arthurian trilogy. His work is distinguished by somber tone and colloquial language. He won the Pulitzer prize in 1921.

MR. FLOOD'S PARTY

Old Eben Flood, climbing alone one night
Over the hill between the town below
And the forsaken upland hermitage
That held as much as he should ever know
5   On earth again of home, paused warily.
The road was his with not a native near;
And Eben, having leisure, said aloud,
For no man else in Tilbury Town to hear:

"Well, Mr. Flood, we have the harvest moon
10 Again, and we may not have many more;
The bird is on the wing, the poet says,
And you and I have said it here before.
Drink to the bird." He raised up to the light
The jug that he had gone so far to fill,
15 And answered huskily: "Well, Mr. Flood,
Since you propose it, I believe I will."

Alone, as if enduring to the end
A valiant armor of scarred hopes outworn,
He stood there in the middle of the road
20 Like Roland's ghost winding a silent horn.
Below him, in the town among the trees,
Where friends of other days had honored him,
A phantom salutation of the dead
Rang thinly till old Eben's eyes were dim.

467

25   Then, as a mother lays her sleeping child
      Down tenderly, fearing it may awake,
      He set the jug down slowly at his feet
      With trembling care, knowing that most things break;
      And only when assured that on firm earth
30   It stood, as the uncertain lives of men
      Assuredly did not, he paced away,
      And with his hand extended paused again:

      "Well, Mr. Flood, we have not met like this
      In a long time; and many a change has come
35   To both of us, I fear, since last it was
      We had a drop together. Welcome home!"
      Convivially returning with himself,
      Again he raised the jug up to the light;
      And with an acquiescent quaver said:
40   "Well, Mr. Flood, if you insist, I might.

      "Only a very little, Mr. Flood—
      For auld lang syne. No more, sir; that will do."
      So, for the time, apparently it did,
      And Eben evidently thought so too;
45   For soon amid the silver loneliness
      Of night he lifted up his voice and sang,
      Secure, with only two moons listening,
      Until the whole harmonious landscape rang—

      "For auld lang syne." The weary throat gave out,
50   The last word wavered; and the song being done,
      He raised again the jug regretfully
      And shook his head, and was again alone.
      There was not much that was ahead of him,
      And there was nothing in the town below—
55   Where strangers would have shut the many doors
      That many friends had opened long ago.

8 *Tilbury Town:* the fictional counterpart to Gardiner, Maine, where Robinson grew up   9 *harvest moon:* the full moon that appears nearest the autumnal equinox; so called because farmers could continue to harvest crops by its bright light   20 *Roland:* the hero of the medieval French epic *The Song of Roland.* Ambushed by enemy Saracen forces, Roland pridefully refuses to sound his horn and summon aid from King Charlemagne until all his men have perished. Mortally wounded, he then blows his horn and dies.

DISCUSSION TOPICS

1. Besides the allusion to Roland, there are other literary references in the poem
   —for example, "the bird is on the wing" (from *The Rubáiyát of Omar Khayyám*) and "auld lang syne" (from the poem by Robert Burns). How do these allusions enhance the theme of the poem?
2. What does "A valiant armor of scarred hopes outworn" (line 18) reveal about Mr. Flood's character?

WRITING TOPIC

Like Tennyson's "Ulysses" and Yeats's "Sailing to Byzantium," this poem deals with the theme of aging. Compare and contrast the ways in which these three poems treat the universal human problem of growing old.

MINIVER CHEEVY

Miniver Cheevy, child of scorn,
   Grew lean while he assailed the seasons;
He wept that he was ever born,
   And he had reasons.

5 Miniver loved the days of old
   When swords were bright and steeds were prancing;
The vision of a warrior bold
   Would set him dancing.

Miniver sighed for what was not,
10   And dreamed, and rested from his labors;
He dreamed of Thebes and Camelot,
   And Priam's neighbors.

Miniver mourned the ripe renown
   That made so many a name so fragrant:
15 He mourned Romance, now on the town,
   And Art, a vagrant.

Miniver loved the Medici,
   Albeit he had never seen one;
He would have sinned incessantly
20   Could he have been one.

Miniver cursed the commonplace
   And eyed a khaki suit with loathing;
He missed the mediaeval grace
   Of iron clothing.

25   Miniver scorned the gold he sought,
       But sore annoyed was he without it;
    Miniver thought, and thought, and thought,
       And thought about it.

    Miniver Cheevy, born too late,
30   Scratched his head and kept on thinking:
    Miniver coughed, and called it fate,
       And kept on drinking.

11 *Thebes:* One of the great cities of ancient Greece, Thebes figured prominently in a number of myths (see *Oedipus the King*).   *Camelot:* the legendary seat of King Arthur and his knights   12 *Priam:* the king of Troy during the Trojan War   15 *Romance:* the literary genre derived from lengthy medieval tales of chivalry and love   17 *Medici:* the powerful and wealthy family that ruled Florence and exerted great influence throughout Italy and Europe from the fifteenth to the early eighteenth centuries. Their members included merchants, bankers, popes, aristocrats, and patrons of the arts.

DISCUSSION TOPIC

What formal devices does Robinson use to gain a comic effect in this poem? Contrast the devices used in "Mr. Flood's Party" to get the opposite effect. Pay special attention to meter, time, and Robinson's play on words. For example, what do the names "Eben Flood" and "Miniver Cheevy" suggest?

RICHARD CORY

    Whenever Richard Cory went down town,
    We people on the pavement looked at him.
    He was a gentleman from sole to crown,
    Clean favored, and imperially slim.

5   And he was always quietly arrayed,
    And he was always human when he talked;
    But still he fluttered pulses when he said,
    "Good-morning," and he glittered when he walked.

    And he was rich—yes, richer than a king—
10   And admirably schooled in every grace:
    In fine, we thought that he was everything
    To make us wish that we were in his place.

    And so we worked, and waited for the light,
    And went without the meat, and cursed the bread;
15   And Richard Cory, one calm summer night,
    Went home and put a bullet through his head.

DISCUSSION TOPIC

In "Mr. Flood's Party," "Miniver Cheevy," and "Richard Cory," the names of all three characters are symbolic. Besides the name, what other devices in "Richard Cory" reinforce the theme of kingship?

ROBERT FROST (1874–1963) The first poet to be invited to read at an American presidential inauguration (John F. Kennedy's). As with E. A. Robinson, acclaim came late, but is now assured. His range is wide, from simple playfulness to gothic verse tales; his voice is never strident, often genial, always disciplined, masking a tough inner core that hints of stoicism amid naturalism.

THE ROAD NOT TAKEN

Two roads diverged in a yellow wood
And sorry I could not travel both
And be one traveler, long I stood
And looked down one as far as I could
5   To where it bent in the undergrowth;

Then took the other, as just as fair,
And having perhaps the better claim,
Because it was grassy and wanted wear;
Though as for that the passing there
10 Had worn them really about the same,

And both that morning equally lay
In leaves no step had trodden black.
Oh, I kept the first for another day!
Yet knowing how way leads on to way,
15 I doubted if I should ever come back.

I shall be telling this with a sigh
Somewhere ages and ages hence:
Two roads diverged in a wood, and I—
I took the one less traveled by,
20 And that has made all the difference.

DISCUSSION TOPICS

1. "Road" has a common symbolic meaning—for example, "the road of life," "the road to the poorhouse" or the "road to success." Do you think that Frost's "roads" are invested with some such significance? If so, how would you explain that significance?

2. As formal strategy, the speaker first suggests that the two roads are different but rather quickly says they are really alike. Is this a paradox?
3. Why does Frost title his poem "The Road Not Taken" instead of "The Road Taken"?

"OUT, OUT—"

The buzz saw snarled and rattled in the yard
And made dust and dropped stove-length sticks of wood,
Sweet-scented stuff when the breeze drew across it.
And from there those that lifted eyes could count
5   Five mountain ranges one behind the other
Under the sunset far into Vermont.
And the saw snarled and rattled, snarled and rattled,
As it ran light, or had to bear a load.
And nothing happened: day was all but done.
10   Call it a day, I wish they might have said
To please the boy by giving him the half hour
That a boy counts so much when saved from work.
His sister stood beside them in her apron
To tell them "Supper." At the word, the saw,
15   As if to prove saws knew what supper meant,
Leaped out at the boy's hand, or seemed to leap—
He must have given the hand. However it was,
Neither refused the meeting. But the hand!
The boy's first outcry was a rueful laugh,
20   As he swung toward them holding up the hand
Half in appeal, but half as if to keep
The life from spilling. Then the boy saw all—
Since he was old enough to know, big boy
Doing a man's work, though a child at heart—
25   He saw all spoiled. "Don't let him cut my hand off—
The doctor, when he comes. Don't let him, sister!"
So. But the hand was gone already.
The doctor put him in the dark of ether.
He lay and puffed his lips out with his breath.
30   And then—the watcher at his pulse took fright.
No one believed. They listened at his heart.
Little—less—nothing!—and that ended it.
No more to build on there. And they, since they
Were not the one dead, turned to their affairs.

"Out, Out—": taken from Shakespeare's *Macbeth*, V.v. 23–24: "Out, Out, brief candle! / Life's but a walking shadow. . . ."

DISCUSSION TOPICS

1. How may the theme of Frost's poem be related to the famous soliloquy from *Macbeth?*
2. What are the philosophical—as well as social and psychological—implications of the last two lines of this poem?

FIRE AND ICE

Some say the world will end in fire;
Some say in ice.
From what I've tasted of desire
I hold with those who favor fire.
5   But if it had to perish twice,
I think I know enough of hate
To know that for destruction ice
Is also great
And would suffice.

DISCUSSION TOPIC

What are the psychological—as well as the moral and philosophical—implications of Frost's poem? Why do you think he tends to "favor fire" over ice? Which do you think is more destructive?

STOPPING BY WOODS ON A SNOWY EVENING

Whose woods these are I think I know.
His house is in the village though;
He will not see me stopping here
To watch his woods fill up with snow.

5   My little horse must think it queer
To stop without a farmhouse near
Between the woods and frozen lake
The darkest evening of the year.

He gives his harness bells a shake
10   To ask if there is some mistake.
The only other sound's the sweep
Of easy wind and downy flake.

The woods are lovely, dark and deep,
But I have promises to keep,
15   And miles to go before I sleep,
And miles to go before I sleep.

DISCUSSION TOPICS

1. What are the dominant meter and the rhyme scheme in this poem? Why do you think Frost elected to use this pattern? What is the meaning of the last line, and how does that line differ substantially from the penultimate line?
2. Why do you think some critics have found a Freudian "death wish" in this poem?
3. What is the function of the horse?
4. Despite its apparent simplicity, Frost said that this poem "contains all I ever knew." What do you think he meant?

ACQUAINTED WITH THE NIGHT

I have been one acquainted with the night.
I have walked out in rain—and back in rain.
I have outwalked the furthest city light.

I have looked down the saddest city lane.
5   I have passed by the watchman on his beat
And dropped my eyes, unwilling to explain.

I have stood still and stopped the sound of feet
When far away an interrupted cry
Came over houses from another street,

10   But not to call me back or say good-by;
And further still at an unearthly height,
One luminary clock against the sky

Proclaimed the time was neither wrong nor right.
I have been one acquainted with the night.

DISCUSSION TOPICS

1. The "night," as well as other kinds of "darkness," often suggests death, mystery, the unconscious. How do these references apply to this poem?
2. What kind of journey, literal or symbolic, does the poem suggest?
3. What kind of time does "One luminary clock" tell?

DESIGN

I found a dimpled spider, fat and white,
On a white heal-all, holding up a moth
Like a white piece of rigid satin cloth—
Assorted characters of death and blight
5   Mixed ready to begin the morning right,

Like the ingredients of a witches' broth—
A snow-drop spider, a flower like froth,
And dead wings carried like a paper kite.

What had that flower to do with being white,
10   The wayside blue and innocent heal-all?
What brought the kindred spider to that height,
Then steered the white moth thither in the night?
What but design of darkness to appall?—
If design govern in a thing so small.

DISCUSSION TOPICS

1. Frost's poem is obviously a Petrarchan sonnet. In what ways does Frost follow the traditional rules for this kind of poem in both the thematic statement and the form of "Design"?
2. Although the "heal-all" (a low-growing plant reputed to have healing qualities) is normally light blue or violet in color, this "heal-all" is white. How does this mutation relate to Frost's theme?
3. What are the multiple symbolic associations of "white satin"? Why is this cloth "rigid" in "Design"?
4. Why does Frost use a dash following his question mark at the end of line 13?

WRITING TOPIC

Compare Frost's view of nature in "Design" with such other views as those presented in Dickinson's "Apparently with No Surprise," Hardy's "Convergence of the Twain," Hopkins's "God's Grandeur," Crane's "The Open Boat," and London's "The Red One."

WALLACE STEVENS (1879–1955) American lawyer and insurance executive whose interest and ability in poetry increased with his age, his first book, *Harmonium*, coming not until he was 44. He had a strong interest in imagery and the world of imagination.

SUNDAY MORNING

I

Complacencies of the peignoir, and late
Coffee and oranges in a sunny chair,
And the green freedom of a cockatoo
Upon a rug mingle to dissipate
5   The holy hush of ancient sacrifice.

She dreams a little, and she feels the dark
Encroachment of that old catastrophe,
As a calm darkens among water-lights.
The pungent oranges and bright, green wings
10   Seem things in some procession of the dead,
Winding across wide water, without sound.
The day is like wide water, without sound,
Stilled for the passing of her dreaming feet
Over the seas, to silent Palestine,
15   Dominion of the blood and sepulchre.

II

Why should she give her bounty to the dead?
What is divinity if it can come
Only in silent shadows and in dreams?
Shall she not find in comforts of the sun,
20   In pungent fruit and bright, green wings, or else
In any balm or beauty of the earth,
Things to be cherished like the thought of heaven?
Divinity must live within herself:
Passions of rain, or moods in falling snow;
25   Grievings in loneliness, or unsubdued
Elations when the forest blooms; gusty
Emotions on wet roads on autumn nights;
All pleasures and all pains, remembering
The bough of summer and the winter branch.
30   These are the measures destined for her soul.

III

Jove in the clouds had his inhuman birth.
No mother suckled him, no sweet land gave
Large-mannered motions to his mythy mind.
He moved among us, as a muttering king,
35   Magnificent, would move among his hinds,
Until our blood, commingling, virginal,
With heaven, brought such requital to desire
The very hinds discerned it, in a star.
Shall our blood fail? Or shall it come to be
40   The blood of paradise? And shall the earth
Seem all of paradise that we shall know?
The sky will be much friendlier then than now,
A part of labor and a part of pain,
And next in glory to enduring love,
45   Not this dividing and indifferent blue.

476

IV

She says, "I am content when wakened birds,
Before they fly, test the reality
Of misty fields, by their sweet questionings;
But when the birds are gone, and their warm fields
50 Return no more, where, then, is paradise?"
There is not any haunt of prophecy,
Nor any old chimera of the grave,
Neither the golden underground, nor isle
Melodious, where spirits gat them home,
55 Nor visionary south, nor cloudy palm
Remote on heaven's hill, that has endured
As April's green endures; or will endure
Like her remembrance of awakened birds,
Or her desire for June and evening, tipped
60 By the consummation of the swallow's wings.

V

She says, "But in contentment I still feel
The need of some imperishable bliss."
Death is the mother of beauty; hence from her,
Alone, shall come fulfilment to our dreams
65 And our desires. Although she strews the leaves
Of sure obliteration on our paths,
The path sick sorrow took, the many paths
Where triumph rang its brassy phrase, or love
Whispered a little out of tenderness,
70 She makes the willow shiver in the sun
For maidens who were wont to sit and gaze
Upon the grass, relinquished to their feet.
She causes boys to pile new plums and pears
On disregarded plate. The maidens taste
75 And stray impassioned in the littering leaves.

VI

Is there no change of death in paradise?
Does ripe fruit never fall? Or do the boughs
Hang always heavy in that perfect sky,
Unchanging, yet so like our perishing earth,
80 With rivers like our own that seek for seas
They never find, the same receding shores
That never touch with inarticulate pang?
Why set the pear upon those river-banks
Or spice the shores with odors of the plum?

477

85   Alas, that they should wear our colors there,
        The silken weavings of our afternoons,
        And pick the strings of our insipid lutes!
        Death is the mother of beauty, mystical,
        Within whose burning bosom we devise
90   Our earthly mothers waiting, sleeplessly.

VII

        Supple and turbulent, a ring of men
        Shall chant in orgy on a summer morn
        Their boisterous devotion to the sun,
        Not as a god, but as a god might be,
95   Naked among them, like a savage source.
        Their chant shall be a chant of paradise,
        Out of their blood, returning to the sky;
        And in their chant shall enter, voice by voice,
        The windy lake wherein their lord delights,
100   The trees, like serafin, and echoing hills,
        That choir among themselves long afterward.
        They shall know well the heavenly fellowship
        Of men that perish and of summer morn.
        And whence they came and whither they shall go
105   The dew upon their feet shall manifest.

VIII

        She hears, upon that water without sound,
        A voice that cries, "The tomb in Palestine
        Is not the porch of spirits lingering.
        It is the grave of Jesus, where he lay."
110   We live in an old chaos of the sun.
        Or old dependency of day and night,
        Or island solitude, unsponsored, free,
        Of that wide water, inescapable.
        Deer walk upon our mountains, and the quail
115   Whistle about us their spontaneous cries;
        Sweet berries ripen in the wilderness;
        And, in the isolation of the sky,
        At evening, casual flocks of pigeons make
        Ambiguous undulations as they sink,
120   Downward to darkness, on extended wings.

---

7 *old catastrophe:* the Crucifixion   31 *Jove:* the king of the gods   35 *hinds:* household or farm servants   39 *star:* the star of Bethlehem   54 *gat them:* got themselves   71 *wont:* accustomed

74 *disregarded plate:* In his *Letters,* Stevens explained, "Plate is used in the sense of so-called family plate. Disregarded refers to the disuse into which things fall that have been possessed for a long time. I mean therefore that death releases and renews. What the old have come to disregard, the young inherit and make use of." 92 *orgy:* a rite or ceremony 100 *serafin:* In Isaiah 6:2, the seraphs are six-winged beings hovering above the throne of God; they are also the highest order of angels.

DISCUSSION TOPICS

1. The poetry of Wallace Stevens is not so difficult as it first appears to be if we can get a glimpse of the scene it is depicting, or if we can place it in the context of other already familiar poems. Consider "Sunday Morning," for example, in moral-philosophical terms as a quest to find beauty, joy, and meaning in our seemingly brief existence. (Consider further the implications if one questions the existence of a higher being or of eternal life in heaven.) What possibilities for succeeding in this quest are presented in "Sunday Morning"? How is the poem's title significant in this regard?
2. How is death the "mother of beauty"?
3. How important is the highly sensuous, even slightly exotic setting for the lady's meditation and her recurring protests?
4. Why should Sunday morning particularly evoke her increasingly poignant demands?
5. Do you think she is at last reconciled to the futility of a conventional religious explanation of life and a possible hereafter?
6. Can you identify the respondent to the lady's protests?
7. What are the philosophical implications of the metaphor in the last line?

THIRTEEN WAYS OF LOOKING AT A BLACKBIRD

I

Among twenty snowy mountains,
The only moving thing
Was the eye of the blackbird.

II

I was of three minds,
5   Like a tree
In which there are three blackbirds.

III

The blackbird whirled in the autumn winds.
It was a small part of the pantomime.

IV

A man and a woman
10   Are one.
A man and a woman and a blackbird
Are one.

V

I do not know which to prefer,
The beauty of inflections
15   Or the beauty of innuendos,
The blackbird whistling
Or just after.

VI

Icicles filled the long window
With barbaric glass.
20   The shadow of the blackbird
Crossed it, to and fro.
The mood
Traced in the shadow
An indecipherable cause.

VII

25   O thin men of Haddam,
Why do you imagine golden birds?
Do you not see how the blackbird
Walks around the feet
Of the women about you?

VIII

30   I know noble accents
And lucid, inescapable rhythms;
But I know, too,
That the blackbird is involved
In what I know.

IX

35   When the blackbird flew out of sight,
It marked the edge
Of one of many circles.

X

At the sight of blackbirds
Flying in a green light,
40   Even the bawds of euphony
Would cry out sharply.

XI

He rode over Connecticut
In a glass coach.
Once, a fear pierced him,
45   In that he mistook
The shadow of his equipage
For blackbirds.

XII

The river is moving.
The blackbird must be flying.

XIII

50   It was evening all afternoon.
It was snowing
And it was going to snow.
The blackbird sat
In the cedar-limbs.

25 *Haddam:* a town in Connecticut

DISCUSSION TOPICS

1. What does the poem appear to say about the ways people view reality? How do the "thin men of Haddam" or the "bawds of euphony" or the man who "rode over Connecticut / In a glass coach" distort "things as they are" (Stevens's description of reality in another poem)?
2. Compare the stanzas of this poem with other imagistic poems like Williams's "The Red Wheelbarrow" and Pound's "In a Station of the Metro." What essential differences do you detect between Stevens's poem and the other two?

ANECDOTE OF THE JAR

> I placed a jar in Tennessee,
> And round it was, upon a hill.
> It made the slovenly wilderness
> Surround that hill.
>
> 5   The wilderness rose up to it,
> And sprawled around, no longer wild.
> The jar was round upon the ground
> And tall and of a port in air.
>
> It took dominion everywhere.
> 10   The jar was gray and bare.
> It did not give of bird or bush,
> Like nothing else in Tennessee.

DISCUSSION TOPICS

1. What is the relationship between the jar and its surroundings in Tennessee?
2. Compare Stevens's "jar" with Keats's "urn." What do these two famous artifacts tell us about the relationship between art and nature?

A HIGH-TONED OLD CHRISTIAN WOMAN

> Poetry is the supreme fiction, madame.
> Take the moral law and make a nave of it
> And from the nave build haunted heaven. Thus,
> The conscience is converted into palms,
> 5   Like windy citherns hankering for hymns.
> We agree in principle. That's clear. But take
> The opposing law and make a peristyle,
> And from the peristyle project a masque
> Beyond the planets. Thus, our bawdiness,
> 10   Unpurged by epitaph, indulged at last,
> Is equally converted into palms,
> Squiggling like saxophones. And palm for palm,
> Madame, we are where we began. Allow,
> Therefore, that in the planetary scene
> 15   Your disaffected flagellants, well-stuffed,
> Smacking their muzzy bellies in parade,
> Proud of such novelties of the sublime,
> Such tink and tank and tunk-a-tunk-tunk,
> May, merely may, madame, whip from themselves

20 A jovial hullabaloo among the spheres.
  This will make widows wince. But fictive things
  Wink as they will. Wink most when widows wince.

2 *nave:* the central part of a church 5 *citherns:* guitarlike instruments first made in the Middle Ages and extremely popular during the sixteenth and seventeenth centuries 7 *peristyle:* a colonnade surrounding a building or courtyard; also the space enclosed by the columns 8 *masque:* masquerade ball 15 *flagellants:* religious devotees who whip themselves

DISCUSSION TOPICS

1. What is suggested about the substance of religion and faith by the words "Poetry is the supreme fiction, madame"?
2. What formal devices—particularly rhythms, sounds, and contrasting images—capture the poem's spirit of playful iconoclasm?
3. Why do "fictive things / Wink as they will"?

THE EMPEROR OF ICE-CREAM

  Call the roller of big cigars,
  The muscular one, and bid him whip
  In kitchen cups concupiscent curds.
  Let the wenches dawdle in such dress
5 As they are used to wear, and let the boys
  Bring flowers in last month's newspapers.
  Let be be finale of seem.
  The only emperor is the emperor of ice-cream.

  Take from the dresser of deal,
10 Lacking the three glass knobs, that sheet
  On which she embroidered fantails once
  And spread it so as to cover her face.
  If her horny feet protrude, they come
  To show how cold she is, and dumb.
15 Let the lamp affix its beam.
  The only emperor is the emperor of ice-cream.

9 *deal:* fir or pine, used in making cheap furniture.

DISCUSSION TOPICS

1. This patently whimsical poem becomes accessible as we realize that it dramatizes the wake for an old woman who has just died. Why should the speaker call for festivities in the presence of the unattractive corpse?

2. Speculate on the possible identity of the proposed presiding presence, a sort of master of the revels—"the roller of big cigars, / The muscular one." What are "concupiscent curds"?
3. What is the meaning of the line "Let be be finale of seem"?
4. Does this poem's view of death essentially concur with the view expressed in "Sunday Morning"? Why—or why not?

WILLIAM CARLOS WILLIAMS (1883–1963) American medical doctor who also wrote prose and poetry, the latter often reflecting the Imagist style and using to good effect the homely and common. His *Paterson* is an epic about the New Jersey city.

THE RED WHEELBARROW

so much depends
upon

a red wheel
barrow

5   glazed with rain
water

beside the white
chickens

DISCUSSION TOPICS

1. Like many modern poems, "The Red Wheelbarrow" has no conventional meter or rhyme, yet it clearly has a formal pattern. How does the poet achieve this pattern?
2. There is only one metaphor in this poem. Where (or what) is it?
3. How does the poem convey a sense of tension?
4. Why does "so much depend upon . . ."?

BY THE ROAD TO THE CONTAGIOUS HOSPITAL

(*FROM* SPRING AND ALL)

By the road to the contagious hospital
under the surge of the blue
mottled clouds driven from the

northeast—a cold wind. Beyond, the
5   waste of broad, muddy fields
brown with dried weeds, standing and fallen

patches of standing water
the scattering of tall trees

All along the road the reddish
10   purplish, forked, upstanding, twiggy
stuff of bushes and small trees
with dead, brown leaves under them
leafless vines—

Lifeless in appearance, sluggish
15   dazed spring approaches—

They enter the new world naked,
cold, uncertain of all
save that they enter. All about them
the cold, familiar wind—

20   Now the grass, tomorrow
the stiff curl of wildcarrot leaf

One by one objects are defined—
It quickens: clarity, outline of leaf

But now the stark dignity of
25   entrance—Still, the profound change
has come upon them: rooted they
grip down and begin to awaken

DISCUSSION TOPICS

1. How does the pattern of natural imagery in this poem suggest that the poem is also about human life? What is the theme of the poem?
2. "One by one objects are defined" (line 22) might be read as the topic sentence for the poem considered as a paragraph. How do Williams's details throughout the poem develop that sentence?
3. Why does Williams not use a period at the end of his verse paragraph?

THIS IS JUST TO SAY

I have eaten
the plums
that were in
the icebox

5   and which
       you were probably
       saving
       for breakfast

       Forgive me
10   they were delicious
       so sweet
       and so cold

THE DANCE

       In Brueghel's great picture, The Kermess,
       the dancers go round, they go round and
       around, the squeal and the blare and the
       tweedle of bagpipes, a bugle and fiddles
5   tipping their bellies (round as the thick-
       sided glasses whose wash they impound)
       their hips and their bellies off balance
       to turn them. Kicking and rolling about
       the Fair Grounds, swinging their butts, those
10   shanks must be sound to bear up under such
       rollicking measures, prance as they dance
       in Breughel's great picture, the Kermess.

1 *The Kermess: The Peasant Dance* (1568), by the Flemish painter Pieter Brueghel, hangs in the Kunsthis-toriches Museum in Vienna. A *kermess* ("church mass") is an exuberant outdoor fair and festival held by Flemish peasants on the feast day of a local saint.

DISCUSSION TOPIC

How does this poem convey the whirling motion of peasants at a kermess?

D. H. Lawrence (1885–1930) One of those who see their work banned before praised. He was a poetic novelist and short story writer whose ideas of love and marriage shook his British world so that he exiled himself to live and die abroad but whose richly symbolic art has subsequently led critics to acclaim him as the greatest English novelist of the twentieth century.

SNAKE

A snake came to my water-trough
On a hot, hot day, and I in pyjamas for the heat,
To drink there.

In the deep, strange-scented shade of the great dark carobtree
5   I came down the steps with my pitcher
And must wait, must stand and wait, for there he was at the trough
     before me.

He reached down from a fissure in the earth-wall in the gloom
And trailed his yellow-brown slackness soft-bellied down, over the
     edge of the stone trough
And rested his throat upon the stone bottom,
10   And where the water had dripped from the tap, in a small clearness,
He sipped with his straight mouth,
Softly drank through his straight gums, into his slack long body,
Silently.

Someone was before me at my water-trough,
15   And I, like a second comer, waiting.
He lighted his head from his drinking, as cattle do,
And looked at me vaguely, as drinking cattle do,
And flickered his two-forked tongue from his lips, and mused a moment,
And stooped and drank a little more,
20   Being earth-brown, earth-golden from the burning bowels of the earth
On the day of Sicilian July, with Etna smoking.

The voice of my education said to me
He must be killed,
For in Sicily the black, black snakes are innocent, the gold are
     venomous.

25   And voices in me said, If you were a man
You would take a stick and break him now, and finish him off.
But must I confess how I liked him,
How glad I was he had come like a guest in quiet, to drink at my
     water-trough
And depart peaceful, pacified, and thankless,
30   Into the burning bowels of this earth?

Was it cowardice, that I dared not kill him?
Was it perversity, that I longed to talk to him?
Was it humility, to feel so honoured?
I felt so honoured.

35   And yet those voices:
If you were not afraid, you would kill him!

And truly I was afraid, I was most afraid,
But even so, honoured still more
That he should seek my hospitality
40   From out the dark door of the secret earth.

He drank enough
And lifted his head, dreamily, as one who has drunken,
And flickered his tongue like a forked night on the air, so black,
Seeming to lick his lips,
45   And looked around like a god, unseeing, into the air,
And slowly turned his head,
And slowly, very slowly, as if thrice adream,
Proceeded to draw his slow length curving round
And climb again the broken bank of my wall-face.

50   And as he put his head into that dreadful hole,
And as he slowly drew up, snake-easing his shoulders, and entered
      farther,
A sort of horror, a sort of protest against his withdrawing into that
      horrid black hole,
Deliberately going into the blackness, and slowly drawing himself
      after,
Overcame me now his back was turned.

55   I looked round, I put down my pitcher,
I picked up a clumsy log
And threw it at the water-trough with a clatter.
I think it did not hit him,
But suddenly that part of him that was left behind convulsed in
      undignified haste,
60   Writhed like lightning, and was gone
Into the black hole, the earth-lipped fissure in the wall-front,
At which, in the intense still noon, I stared with fascination.

And immediately I regretted it.
I thought how paltry, how vulgar, what a mean act!
65   I despised myself and the voices of my accursed human education.

And I thought of the albatross,
And I wished he would come back, my snake.

For he seemed to me again like a king,
Like a king in exile, uncrowned in the underworld,
70   Now due to be crowned again.

And so, I missed my chance with one of the lords
Of life.
And I have something to expiate;
A pettiness.

DISCUSSION TOPICS

1. As you may have noted, a number of selections in this anthology involve snakes. As you consider the interrelationships, bear in mind the mythic and symbolic possibilities. Compare Lawrence's poem to the opening chapters of Genesis. Who was king of the underworld?
2. Why does the poet say "I despised myself and the voices of my accursed human education"? What is the "pettiness" that he has to expiate?

EZRA POUND (1885–1972) Learned and influential modernist American poet with close ties to artists in England and on the Continent. He was among the expatriates who achieved a second "American Renaissance" between 1912 and 1940. He edited T. S. Eliot's *The Waste Land,* for which effort Eliot called him "the better craftsman." Pound led the campaigns for imagism and vorticism. He received the Bollingen prize for his *Pisan Cantos* in 1949.

A PACT

I make a pact with you, Walt Whitman—
I have detested you long enough.
I come to you as a grown child
Who has had a pig-headed father;
5   I am old enough now to make friends.
It was you that broke the new wood,
Now is a time for carving.
We have one sap and one root—
Let there be commerce between us.

DISCUSSION TOPIC

What aesthetic and psychological tensions between Pound and Whitman are suggested in "A Pact"? How does the poem recall Whitman's own verse and themes? Compare Ginsberg's "A Supermarket in California."

ALBA

As cool as the pale wet leaves
                        of lily-of-the-valley
She lay beside me in the dawn.

Alba: the word for "dawn" in Provençal, the Romance language of the medieval troubadours of France, whom Pound intensively studied and extensively translated.

DISCUSSION TOPIC

Although the poem (a haiku) is brief, what symbolic richness and dramatic complexity does it suggest?

ANCIENT MUSIC

Winter is icumen in,
Lhude sing Goddamm,
Raineth drop and staineth slop,
And how the wind doth ramm!
5   Sing: Goddamm.
Skiddeth bus and sloppeth us,
An ague hath my ham.
Freezeth river, turneth liver,
          Damn you, sing: Goddamm.
10   Goddamm, Goddamm, 'tis why I am, Goddamm,
          So 'gainst the winter's balm.
Sing goddamm, damm, sing Goddamm,
Sing goddamm, sing goddamm, DAMM.

DISCUSSION TOPIC

"Ancient Music" looks back to the medieval lyric "Sumer Is Icumen In." What has Pound done with the older song, which offered a pastoral context and rapturous response to an English summer, by transposing it into a grouse about winter and an urban context? Does he gain anything rhetorically by retaining the inflections of Middle English (*icumen* for *come, lhude* for *loud,* and the *-eth* ending for the verbs)?

ROBINSON JEFFERS (1887–1962) American poet, translator. His early education in the classics contributed to both the style and content of his poetry, which combines classical beauty and control with colloquial American speech. His themes and subjects are frequently modern reworkings of classical myths.

TO THE STONE-CUTTERS

Stone-cutters fighting time with marble, you foredefeated
Challengers of oblivion
Eat cynical earnings, knowing rock splits, records fall down,
The square-limbed Roman letters
5   Scale in the thaws, wear in the rain.
      The poet as well
Builds his monument mockingly;
For man will be blotted out, the blithe earth die, the brave sun
Die blind, his heart blackening:
Yet stones have stood for a thousand years, and pained thoughts found
10   The honey peace in old poems.

DISCUSSION TOPICS

1. What is the philosophical attitude of the poet here—and what is his tone?
2. Compare "To the Stone Cutters" with Shakespeare's "Sonnet 55," Keats's "Ode on a Grecian Urn," and Emerson's "Concord Hymn." How does each poet treat the passage of time and the longevity of art?

MARIANNE MOORE (1887–1972) Influential leader in modern poetic techniques and editor of *The Dial,* famous literary magazine. She was an ardent fan of the old Brooklyn Dodgers baseball team.

POETRY

I too, dislike it: there are things that are important beyond all this fiddle.
    Reading it, however, with a perfect contempt for it, one discovers that
        there is in
    it after all, a place for the genuine.
      Hands that can grasp, eyes
5   that can dilate, hair that can rise
          if it must, these things are important not because a

high sounding interpretation can be put upon them but because they are
    useful; when they become so derivative as to become unintelligible, the

same thing may be said for all of us—that we
10   do not admire what
we cannot understand. The bat,
holding on upside down or in quest of something to

eat, elephants pushing, a wild horse taking a roll, a tireless wolf under
a tree, the immovable critic twinkling his skin like a horse that feels a
flea, the base-
15   ball fan, the statistician—case after case
could be cited did
one wish it; nor is it valid
to discriminate against "business documents and

school-books"; all these phenomena are important. One must make a
distinction
however: when dragged into prominence by half poets, the result is not
20   poetry,
nor till the autocrats among us can be
"literalists of
the imagination"—above
insolence and triviality and can present

25   for inspection, imaginary gardens with real toads in them, shall we have
it. In the meantime, if you demand on one hand, in defiance of their
opinion—
the raw material of poetry in
all its rawness and
that which is, on the other hand,
30   genuine then you are interested in poetry.

DISCUSSION TOPICS

1. What views of poetry are expressed in this poem? How does its form bear on
its content? Compare MacLeish's "Ars Poetica" and Auden's "In Memory of
W. B. Yeats."
2. The phrase "imaginary gardens with real toads in them" has become quite
famous. What do you think Moore means by this phrase?

T. S. Eliot (1888–1965) American poet and critic who became a British citizen in
1927. He was employed in banking and publishing, while working out his own
poetic *métier* and shaping modernist Anglo-American poetry, literary theory, and
verse drama. He had a reservoir of culture of the past with affinities for the English
Metaphysical poets, the French Symbolists, oral rhythms, and intellectual, highly
allusive poetry. He won the Nobel prize in 1948.

THE LOVE SONG OF J. ALFRED PRUFROCK

S'io credesse che mia risposta fosse
A persona che mai tornasse al mondo,
Questa fiamma staria senza più scosse.
Ma per ciò che giammai di questo fondo
Non tornò vivo alcun, s'i'odo il vero,
Senza tema d'infamia ti rispondo.

Let us go then, you and I,
When the evening is spread out against the sky
Like a patient etherised upon a table;
Let us go, through certain half-deserted streets,
5   The muttering retreats
Of restless nights in one-night cheap hotels
And sawdust restaurants with oyster-shells:
Streets that follow like a tedious argument
Of insidious intent
10   To lead you to an overwhelming question . . .
Oh, do not ask, "What is it?"
Let us go and make our visit.

In the room the women come and go
Talking of Michelangelo.

15   The yellow fog that rubs its back upon the window-panes,
The yellow smoke that rubs its muzzle on the window-panes
Licked its tongue into the corners of the evening,
Lingered upon the pools that stand in drains,
Let fall upon its back the soot that falls from chimneys,
20   Slipped by the terrace, made a sudden leap,
And seeing that it was a soft October night,
Curled once about the house, and fell asleep.

And indeed there will be time
For the yellow smoke that slides along the street,
25   Rubbing its back upon the window-panes;
There will be time, there will be time
To prepare a face to meet the faces that you meet;
There will be time to murder and create,
And time for all the works and days of hands
30   That lift and drop a question on your plate;
Time for you and time for me,
And time yet for a hundred indecisions,
And for a hundred visions and revisions,
Before the taking of a toast and tea.

35   In the room the women come and go
    Talking of Michelangelo.

      And indeed there will be time
    To wonder, "Do I dare?" and, "Do I dare?"
    Time to turn back and descend the stair,
40   With a bald spot in the middle of my hair—
    (They will say: "How his hair is growing thin!")
    My morning coat, my collar mounting firmly to the chin,
    My necktie rich and modest, but asserted by a simple pin—
    (They will say: "But how his arms and legs are thin!")
45   Do I dare
    Disturb the universe?
    In a minute there is time
    For decisions and revisions which a minute will reverse.

      For I have known them all already, known them all:—
50   Have known the evenings, mornings, afternoons,
    I have measured out my life with coffee spoons;
    I know the voices dying with a dying fall
    Beneath the music from a farther room.
      So how should I presume?

55   And I have known the eyes already, known them all:—
    The eyes that fix you in a formulated phrase,
    And when I am formulated, sprawling on a pin,
    When I am pinned and wriggling on the wall,
    Then how should I begin
60   To spit out all the butt-ends of my days and ways?
      And how should I presume?

      And I have known the arms already, known them all—
    Arms that are braceleted and white and bare
    (But in the lamplight, downed with light brown hair!)
65   Is it perfume from a dress
    That makes me so digress?
    Arms that lie along a table, or wrap about a shawl.
      And should I then presume?
      And how should I begin?

        •   •   •   •   •

70   Shall I say, I have gone at dusk through narrow streets
    And watched the smoke that rises from the pipes
    Of lonely men in shirt-sleeves, leaning out of windows? . . .

        •   •   •   •   •

      I should have been a pair of ragged claws
    Scuttling across the floors of silent seas.

75 And the afternoon, the evening, sleeps so peacefully!
Smoothed by long fingers,
Asleep . . . tired . . . or it malingers,
Stretched on the floor, here beside you and me.
Should I, after tea and cakes and ices,
80 Have the strength to force the moment to its crisis?
But though I have wept and fasted, wept and prayed,
Though I have seen my head (grown slightly bald) brought in upon
           a platter,
I am no prophet—and here's no great matter;
I have seen the moment of my greatness flicker,
85 And I have seen the eternal Footman hold my coat, and snicker,
And in short, I was afraid.

       And would it have been worth it, after all,
After the cups, the marmalade, the tea,
Among the porcelain, among some talk of you and me,
90 Would it have been worth while,
To have bitten off the matter with a smile,
To have squeezed the universe into a ball
To roll it toward some overwhelming question,
To say: "I am Lazarus, come from the dead,
95 Come back to tell you all, I shall tell you all"—
If one, settling a pillow by her head,
      Should say: "That is not what I meant at all.
      That is not it, at all."
      And would it have been worth it, after all,
100 Would it have been worth while,
After the sunsets and the dooryards and the sprinkled streets,
After the novels, after the teacups, after the skirts that trail along the
           floor—
And this, and so much more?—
It is impossible to say just what I mean!
105 But as if a magic lantern threw the nerves in patterns on a screen:
Would it have been worth while
If one, settling a pillow or throwing off a shawl,
And turning toward the window, should say:
      That is not it at all,
110   That is not what I meant, at all."

           • • • • •

No! I am not Prince Hamlet, nor was meant to be;
Am an attendant lord, one that will do
To swell a progress, start a scene or two,
Advise the prince; no doubt, an easy tool,
115 Deferential, glad to be of use,

Politic, cautious, and meticulous;
Full of high sentence, but a bit obtuse;
At times, indeed, almost ridiculous—
Almost, at times, the Fool.

120   I grow old . . . I grow old . . .
I shall wear the bottoms of my trousers rolled.

Shall I part my hair behind? Do I dare to eat a peach?
I shall wear white flannel trousers, and walk upon the beach.
I have heard the mermaids singing, each to each.

125   I do not think that they will sing to me.

I have seen them riding seaward on the waves
Combing the white hair of the waves blown back
When the wind blows the water white and black.

We have lingered in the chambers of the sea
130 By sea-girls wreathed with seaweed red and brown
Till human voices wake us, and we drown.

S'io credesse . . . respondo: These lines come from Dante's *Inferno* (XXVII. 61–66). Dante has encountered in hell the shade of a still proud Guido da Montefeltro undergoing torment as an evil counselor in life and has asked for his story. Guido, consumed in flame that shakes as he speaks, answers Dante: "If I believed that my answer were to one who could return to the world, this flame would shake no more. But since, if I hear truth, no one ever returned alive from this pit, I answer you without fear of infamy." 14 *Michelangelo:* Michelangelo Buonarroti (1475–1564), great Italian painter, sculptor, architect, and poet 82 *My head . . . brought in upon a platter:* John the Baptist was beheaded by King Herod at the insistence of his stepdaughter, Salome, to whom the head was brought upon a platter. Presumably, John's head was thickly covered with hair. 85 *the eternal Footman:* death 92–93 *squeezed the universe . . . question:* Compare the courageous vision of lovers defeating time in lines 41–46 of Marvell's "To His Coy Mistress." 94 *Lazarus:* Both of the biblical stories about men named Lazarus seem relevant to the context, for both emphasize the motif of death and rebirth. See Luke 16 and John 11. 111 *Prince Hamlet:* praised by Ophelia as "The courtier's, soldier's, scholar's eye, tongue, sword, / Th'expectancy and rose of the fair state, / The glass of fashion and the mould of form, / Th'observed of all observers . . ." (*Hamlet*, III.i.151–154) 119 *the Fool:* the king's jester, a character in such Elizabethan tragedies as Shakespeare's *King Lear*, in which, however, the Fool utters profound wisdom behind apparent nonsense

DISCUSSION TOPICS

1. The dramatic monologue, as revived by Eliot and Pound from the nineteenth-century models of Tennyson and especially Browning, features a *persona* or *mask*—a fictional character—who creates his own drama as he speaks or meditates. We know that Prufrock is the character speaking in Eliot's poem, but who is the "you" in line 1?
2. What kind of love song is this?
3. What is the setting for the poem—and how does this setting seem to intensify Prufrock's sense of dilemma?

4. What seems to be the basis for Prufrock's fear of women? Is that fear related to other fears—of decisive action, of exploring profound issues about life's meaning, of standing apart from the crowd?
5. Why are the women "Talking of Michelangelo"?
6. What is the purpose of Prufrock's allusions to such heroic figures as John the Baptist and Hamlet?
7. What insect is the basis for his metaphor beginning at line 57?
8. Discuss the archetypal and Freudian significance of Prufrock's reference to mermaids in line 124 and after.

WRITING TOPIC

Compare and contrast the treatment of love in Eliot's poem and Marvell's "To His Coy Mistress."

JOHN CROWE RANSOM (1888–1974) Student, later teacher, at Vanderbilt, where he helped found and lead a group, with a Southern, agrarian bent, called the Fugitives, from which, in part, evolved a new school of criticism and literature, a movement that has had a strong influence on the shape of literature and the kind of teaching it now gets. He was later affiliated with Kenyon College and the *Kenyon Review.*

BELLS FOR JOHN WHITESIDE'S DAUGHTER

There was such speed in her little body,
And such lightness in her footfall,
It is no wonder that her brown study
Astonishes us all.

5   Her wars were bruited in our high window.
We looked among orchard trees and beyond,
Where she took arms against her shadow,
Or harried unto the pond

The lazy geese, like a snow cloud
10   Dripping their snow on the green grass,
Tricking and stopping, sleepy and proud,
Who cried in goose, Alas,

For the tireless heart within the little
Lady with rod that made them rise
15   From their noon apple-dreams, and scuttle
Goose-fashion under the skies!

But now go the bells, and we are ready;
In one house we are sternly stopped
To say we are vexed at her brown study,
20   Lying so primly propped.

3 *brown study:* idle reverie   5 *bruited:* heard because of the noise and clamor   8 *harried:* made raids

DISCUSSION TOPICS

1. What is "her brown study" and why does it astonish us?
2. What relationship does the poem suggest between the speaker and John White-side's daughter? How does Ransom convey that relationship?
3. Why does the speaker refer to the geese? What do they add to the poem?

PIAZZA PIECE

—I am a gentleman in a dustcoat trying
To make you hear. Your ears are soft and small
And listen to an old man not at all,
They want the young men's whispering and sighing.
5   But see the roses on your trellis dying
And hear the spectral singing of the moon;
For I must have my lovely lady soon,
I am a gentleman in a dustcoat trying.

—I am a lady young in beauty waiting
10   Until my truelove comes, and then we kiss.
But what grey man among the vines is this
Whose words are dry and faint as in a dream?
Back from my trellis, Sir, before I scream!
I am a lady young in beauty waiting.

DISCUSSION TOPICS

1. How does Ransom exploit the conventional division between octave and sestet in an unusual fashion in this sonnet?
2. Who are the speakers in the poem?

ARCHIBALD MACLEISH (1892–1982) Lawyer, editor, Librarian of Congress, Assistant Secretary of State, Harvard professor. He was the author of radio plays and *J.B.* and of poetry, some of it reflecting the interests and techniques of expatriates, especially Eliot.

ARS POETICA

A poem should be palpable and mute
As a globed fruit,

Dumb
As old medallions to the thumb,

5   Silent as the sleeve-worn stone
Of casement ledges where the moss has grown—

A poem should be wordless
As the flight of birds.

          • • •

A poem should be motionless in time
10   As the moon climbs,

Leaving, as the moon releases
Twig by twig the night-entangled trees,

Leaving, as the moon behind the winter leaves,
Memory by memory the mind—

15   A poem should be motionless in time
As the moon climbs.

          • • •

A poem should be equal to:
Not true.

For all the history of grief
20   An empty doorway and a maple leaf.

For love
The leaning grasses and two lights above the sea—

A poem should not mean
But be.

Ars poetica: the art of poetry; sometimes, a systematic "poetics."

DISCUSSION TOPICS

1. Through what formal devices does "Ars Poetica" affirm that good literature is not "about" experience but is itself a form of experience?
2. Do you think MacLeish has adequately defined the province of poetry? What might be added—or subtracted?

THE END OF THE WORLD

Quite unexpectedly as Vasserot
The armless ambidextrian was lighting
A match between his great and second toe
And Ralph the lion was engaged in biting
5   The neck of Madame Sossman while the drum
Pointed, and Teeny was about to cough
In waltz-time swinging Jocko by the thumb—
Quite unexpectedly the top blew off:

And there, there overhead, there, there, hung over
10 Those thousands of white faces, those dazed eyes,
There in the starless dark, the poise, the hover,
There with vast wings across the canceled skies,
There in the sudden blackness, the black pall
Of nothing, nothing, nothing—nothing at all.

WILFRED OWEN (1893–1918) English poet of great promise, killed in action in World War I, shortly after the cessation of hostilities. His reaction against the waste of war was cast in experimental forms that looked ahead to the 1920s he never saw.

DULCE ET DECORUM EST

Bent double, like old beggars under sacks,
Knock-kneed, coughing like hags, we cursed through sludge,
Till on the haunting flares we turned our backs,
And towards our distant rest began to trudge.
5   Men marched asleep. Many had lost their boots,
But limped on, blood-shod. All went lame, all blind;
Drunk with fatigue; deaf even to the hoots
Of gas-shells dropping softly behind.

Gas! GAS! Quick, boys!—An ecstasy of fumbling,
10 Fitting the clumsy helmets just in time,
But someone still was yelling out and stumbling
And flound'ring like a man in fire or lime.
Dim through the misty panes and thick green light,
As under a green sea, I saw him drowning.

15 In all my dreams before my helpless sight
He plunges at me, guttering, choking, drowning.

500

If in some smothering dreams, you too could pace
Behind the wagon that we flung him in,
And watch the white eyes writhing in his face,
20   His hanging face, like a devil's sick of sin,
If you could hear, at every jolt, the blood
Come gargling from the froth-corrupted lungs
Bitter as the cud
Of vile, incurable sores on innocent tongues,—
25   My friend, you would not tell with such high zest
To children ardent for some desperate glory,
The old Lie: *Dulce et decorum est*
Pro patria mori.

27–28 *Dulce . . . mori:* Sweet and fitting it is to die for the fatherland (from Horace's *Odes*).

DISCUSSION TOPICS

1. This powerful antiwar poem contains a number of graphic similes. Discuss their appropriateness. What is especially ironic about those in the first two lines?
2. Explain the irony in the title of the poem.
3. Compare the sentiments in this poem with those in Lovelace's "To Lucasta, on Going to the Wars."
4. How would someone like Patrick Henry respond to the ideas in this poem?

E. E. CUMMINGS (1894–1962) American poet who fractured syntax, broke conventions of punctuation and typography, to startle and tease the reader into perceiving a precise image and responding to the poem's full experience. He was a devotee of the classics but a romanticist in attitude.

BUFFALO BILL'S

Buffalo Bill's
defunct
            who used to
            ride a watersmooth-silver
5   stallion
and break onetwothreefourfive pigeonsjustlikethat
                                                    Jesus

he was a handsome man
                        and what i want to know is
10   how do you like your blueeyed boy
Mister Death

DISCUSSION TOPICS

1. Although Cummings often summons traditional poetic techniques, his verse usually abandons standard spelling, punctuation, diction, syntax, grammar, and typography. How do such departures from established usage bring out effects that otherwise would be lost?
2. How is a contrast between the vitality of life and the finality of death achieved in "Buffalo Bill's"? Compare Housman's "To an Athlete Dying Young" and Ransom's "Bells for John Whiteside's Daughter."
3. In the last line of the poem, what does Cummings gain by personifying Death? Compare Donne's "Death, Be Not Proud" and Ransom's "Piazza Piece," as well as Chaucer's "The Pardoner's Tale" and Poe's "Masque of Red Death."

THE CAMBRIDGE LADIES WHO LIVE IN FURNISHED SOULS

> the Cambridge ladies who live in furnished souls
> are unbeautiful and have comfortable minds
> (also, with the church's protestant blessings
> daughters, unscented shapeless spirited)
> 5   they believe in Christ and Longfellow, both dead,
> are invariably interested in so many things—
> at the present writing one still finds
> delighted fingers knitting for the is it Poles?
> perhaps. While permanent faces coyly bandy
> 10   scandal of Mrs. N and Professor D
> . . . . the Cambridge ladies do not care, above
> Cambridge if sometimes in its box of
> sky lavender and cornerless the
> moon rattles like a fragment of angry candy

DISCUSSION TOPICS

1. What image of the Cambridge ladies is projected here? Why does the speaker feel toward them as he does, and how does he make his feelings known? Compare Stevens's "A High-Toned Old Christian Woman."
2. In the Introduction to *New Poems,* Cummings writes: "Life, for most people, simply isn't." How does "Cambridge Ladies" illustrate this contention?
3. What is the purpose of Cummings's allusion to Christ and Longfellow?

R - P - O - P - H - E - S - S - A - G - R

<pre>
                    r-p-o-p-h-e-s-s-a-g-r
                who
        a)s w(e loo)k
        upnowgath
5   PPEGORHRASS
                        eringint(o-'
        aThe):l
            eA
                !p:
10   S   a
                    (r
        rIvInG   .gRrEaPsPhOs)
                            to
        rea(be)rran(com)gi(e)ngly
15   ,grasshopper;
</pre>

DISCUSSION TOPICS

1. How does the arrangement of this poem on the page suggest the nature of its subject? How does it compare as "visual poetry" with Williams's "A Red Wheelbarrow"?
2. Why does line 15 end with a semicolon rather than with a period?

ANYONE LIVED IN A PRETTY HOW TOWN

anyone lived in a pretty how town
(with up so floating many bells down)
spring summer autumn winter
he sang his didn't he danced his did.

5 Women and men (both little and small)
cared for anyone not at all
they sowed their isn't they reaped their same
sun moon stars rain

children guessed (but only a few
10 and down they forgot as up they grew
autumn winter spring summer)
that noone loved him more by more

when by now and tree by leaf
she laughed his joy she cried his grief
15 bird by snow and stir by still
anyone's any was all to her

someones married their everyones
laughed their cryings and did their dance
(sleep wake hope and then) they
20 said their nevers they slept their dream

stars rain sun moon
(and only the snow can begin to explain
how children are apt to forget to remember
with up so floating many bells down)

25 one day anyone died i guess
(and noone stooped to kiss his face)
busy folk buried them side by side
little by little and was by was

all by all and deep by deep
30 and more by more they dream their sleep
noone and anyone earth by april
wish by spirit and if by yes.

Women and men (both dong and ding)
summer autumn winter spring
35 reaped their sowing and went their came
sun moon stars rain

DISCUSSION TOPICS

1. How does Cummings distinguish by using a system of contrasts between the mundane, anonymous, meaningless life of the townspeople and the celebrated, committed life of "anyone" and "noone"? In what ways do the language, grammatical functions and relationships, and syntax of the poem reinforce the contrast?

2. "Anyone lived in a pretty how town" is imbued with archetypal imagery—the seasons, elements, cycles of innocence and experience and birth and death are strongly felt throughout the poem. What does the presence of such images contribute to the portrayal of the people in this town?

JEAN TOOMER (1894–1967) Along with Langston Hughes and Countee Cullen, he was a leader of the Harlem Renaissance of the 1920s. His novel *Cane* (1923) was an important experimental modernist work. He is now perceived as a major black American writer.

NOVEMBER COTTON FLOWER

Boll-weevil's coming, and the winter's cold,
Made cotton-stalks look rusty, seasons old,
And cotton, scarce as any southern snow,
Was vanishing; the branch, so pinched and slow,
Failed in its function as the autumn rake;
Drouth fighting soil had caused the soil to take
All water from the streams; dead birds were found
In wells a hundred feet below the ground—
Such was the season when the flower bloomed.
Old folks were startled, and it soon assumed
Significance. Superstition saw
Something it had never seen before:
Brown eyes that loved without a trace of fear,
Beauty so sudden for that time of year.

5

10

DISCUSSION TOPICS

1. Why is the appearance of a cotton flower in November so astonishing?
2. What thematic function do the poem's opening lines depicting the late autumn landscape serve?
3. What is the form of "November Cotton Flower"? What are the structural and thematic relationships between the first eight lines (octave) and the final six (sestet)?
4. Why does the November flower assume "Significance" for the "old folks" who were startled by its appearance? What part does "Superstition" play in their response?
5. What do you think is the meaning of the final couplet? How do these lines change your reading of the entire poem? What does the November cotton flower symbolize?

REAPERS

Black reapers with the sound of steel on stones
Are sharpening scythes. I see them place the hones
In their hip-pockets as a thing that's done,
And start their silent swinging, one by one.
Black horses drive a mower through the weeds,
And there, a field rat, startled, squealing bleeds,
His belly close to ground. I see the blade,
Blood-stained, continue cutting weeds and shade.

5

505

DISCUSSION TOPICS

1. What is your initial response to this poem? What seems to be its subject?
2. How does Toomer manage to suggest a deeper level of meaning beneath the literal one? Which words seem loaded with symbolic significance?
3. What archetypal associations do "reapers" have in many cultures? (Think of the "grim reaper.") How do those associations affect your reading of the poem?
4. What or who might the field rat represent? What does the death of the field rat suggest about the relationship between humanity and nature? (Compare Burns's "To a Mouse.")
5. Compare Toomer's handling of the natural setting in "Reapers" and in "November Cotton Flower." How does each poem use nature to comment on the human condition?

HART CRANE (1899–1932) American poet whose brief but brilliant career linked the modernism of Pound and Eliot to the mystical affirmation of Whitman in passionate, sometimes lavish language. Oppressed by doubts about himself and America, he died by jumping overboard at sea. He was the author of *White Buildings* (1926) and *The Bridge* (1930).

AT MELVILLE'S TOMB

Often beneath the wave, wide from this ledge
The dice of drowned men's bones he saw bequeath
An embassy. Their numbers as he watched,
Beat on the dusty shore and were obscured.

5   And wrecks passed without sound of bells,
The calyx of death's bounty giving back
A scattered chapter, livid hieroglyph,
The portent wound in corridors of shells.

Then in the circuit calm of one vast coil,
10   Its lashings charmed and malice reconciled,
Frosted eyes there were that lifted altars;
And silent answers crept across the stars.

Compass, quadrant and sextant contrive
No farther tides . . . High in the azure steeps
15   Monody shall not wake the mariner.
This fabulous shadow only the sea keeps.

3 *embassy:* message   6 *calyx:* chalice; also cup of a flower   15 *monody:* an ode or a lament for another person's death sung by a single voice

DISCUSSION TOPICS

1. How and why might some of the difficulties raised by Crane's poetic technique be linked to an emphasis on the process of interpretation itself? Compare the last sentence of Stephen Crane's short story "The Open Boat."
2. How do the sea and the men buried beneath it take on symbolic overtones, particularly if we recall that the ocean is an archetype for the unconscious, death and rebirth, and spiritual mystery? Compare "Sir Patrick Spens," Emerson's "Seashore," and Whitman's "Out of the Cradle Endlessly Rocking."
3. By title and content, Crane's poem announces its mode as elegy—a tribute to Melville, the dead poet who pursued in *Moby-Dick* and his other romances of the sea the answers behind the agonizing ambiguities of the universe. But as is usual in an elegy, the writer of the tribute must consider his own role as poet. In this case, how does Crane express Melville's aspiration and achievement even as he implies that he shares them?

VOYAGES

I

Above the fresh ruffles of the surf
Bright striped urchins flay each other with sand.
They have contrived a conquest for shell shucks,
And their fingers crumble fragments of baked weed
5   Gaily digging and scattering.

And in answer to their treble interjections
The sun beats lightning on the waves,
The waves fold thunder on the sand;
And could they hear me I would tell them:

10   O brilliant kids, frisk with your dog,
Fondle your shells and sticks, bleached
By time and the elements; but there is a line
You must not cross nor ever trust beyond it
Spry cordage of your bodies to caresses
15   Too lichen-faithful from too wide a breast.
The bottom of the sea is cruel.

DISCUSSION TOPICS

1. How does this poem shape a series of similarities and contrasts between the scene of the urchins at play and the speaker's perception of the sea's nature?

507

2. Why would the speaker try to warn the children that "there is a line / You must not cross"? What archetypal significance for both children and the sea does the poem suggest? Might the meeting place of sand and sea be the threshold of myth?

Langston Hughes (1902–1967) Black American poet of wide-ranging experience, from class poet in high school to truck farming, work on ocean-going ships, a stay in Mexico, Parisian night clubs, and always back to writing. He turned out a rich profusion of poetry, plays, musicals and opera, short and long fiction, history, and folklore, in over forty volumes.

THE NEGRO SPEAKS OF RIVERS

> I've known rivers:
> I've known rivers ancient as the world and older than the
>   flow of human blood in human veins.
>
> My soul has grown deep like the rivers.
>
> I bathed in the Euphrates when dawns were young.
> 5   I built my hut near the Congo and it lulled me to sleep.
> I looked upon the Nile and raised the pyramids above it.
> I heard the singing of the Mississippi when Abe Lincoln
>   went down to New Orleans, and I've seen its muddy
>   bosom turn all golden in the sunset.
>
> I've known rivers:
> Ancient, dusky rivers.
>
> 10   My soul has grown deep like the rivers.

DISCUSSION TOPICS

1. What happens in this poem when Hughes juxtaposes "The Negro" and "Rivers"? What special relationship do they have with each other?
2. Rivers have strong archetypal associations for all human cultures. What do the rivers in this poem stand for? What is the special significance of each of the rivers Hughes names for black people?
3. What symbolic meanings does the idea of rivers assume in the poem?
4. How does Hughes's repetition of "I" affect your response to the poem?
5. Compare Hughes's rhythms with those of Whitman. How does Hughes employ rhythm to reflect meaning? Why do you think some of the lines are short, some long, and some in between?

HARLEM

What happens to a dream deferred?

Does it dry up
like a raisin in the sun?
Or fester like a sore—
5   And then run?
Does it stink like rotten meat?
Or crust and sugar over—
like a syrupy sweet?

Maybe it just sags
10   like a heavy load.

Or does it explode?

DISCUSSION TOPICS

1. How did you react to reading this poem? What seemed to you its most effective quality?
2. How many direct statements are there in this poem? What is the effect of the series of questions?
3. Lines 2 through 10 are a series of similes. Explain their appropriateness. What is the implied simile in line 11? Why do you think Hughes left it incomplete?
4. What symbolic significance attaches to the name "Harlem"? How does Hughes invoke that significance?

STEVIE SMITH (1902–1971) English poet who illustrated her own writing. Her verse is deceptively simple, even childlike, often masking agonizing as well as serious subjects.

NOT WAVING BUT DROWNING

Nobody heard him, the dead man,
But still he lay moaning:
I was much further out than you thought
And not waving but drowning.

5   Poor chap, he always loved larking
And now he's dead
It must have been too cold for him his heart gave way,
They said.

Oh, no no no, it was too cold always
10   (Still the dead one lay moaning)
I was much too far out all my life
And not waving but drowning.

DISCUSSION TOPICS

1. Smith uses the key phrase in this poem as its title. What point does that phrase make about human relationships?
2. Who is saying the lines in the second stanza? How do these lines reinforce the point made in the first and last stanzas? Do "they" understand what was happening to the dead man?
3. How does the final stanza add a further dimension of meaning to the poem?
4. What emotions does the poem's matter-of-fact tone mask? Is this a successful way to evoke a response from readers?
5. What are the symbolic and archetypal suggestions of drowning?
6. What does the poem seem to be saying about human society?

RICHARD EBERHART (1904–   ) A native of Minnesota, educated at the University of Minnesota, Dartmouth, and Cambridge University. A sometime business executive, he is the recipient of prizes for poetry, has an honorary Doctor of Letters from Dartmouth, and is a poet-in-residence and lecturer at many schools and colleges.

THE GROUNDHOG

In June, amid the golden fields,
I saw a groundhog lying dead.
Dead lay he, my senses shook,
And mind outshot our naked frailty.
5   There lowly in the vigorous summer
His form began its senseless change,
And made my senses waver dim
Seeing nature ferocious in him.
Inspecting close his maggots' might
10   And seething cauldron of his being,
Half with loathing, half with a strange love,
I poked him with an angry stick.
The fever arose, became a flame
And Vigor circumscribed the skies,
15   Immense energy in the sun,

And through my frame a sunless trembling.
My stick had done nor good nor harm.
Then stood I silent in the day
Watching the object, as before;
20 And kept my reverence for knowledge
Trying for control, to be still,
To quell the passion of the blood;
Until I had bent down on my knees
Praying for joy in the sight of decay.
25 And so I left; and I returned
In Autumn strict of eye, to see
The sap gone out of the groundhog,
But the bony sodden hulk remained.
But the year had lost its meaning,
30 And in intellectual chains
I lost both love and loathing,
Mured up in the wall of wisdom.
Another summer took the fields again
Massive and burning, full of life,
35 But when I chanced upon the spot
There was only a little hair left,
And bones bleaching in the sunlight
Beautiful as architecture;
I watched them like a geometer,
40 And cut a walking stick from a birch.
It has been three years, now.
There is no sign of the groundhog.
I stood there in the whirling summer,
My hand capped a withered heart,
45 And thought of China and of Greece,
Of Alexander in his tent;
Of Montaigne in his tower,
Of Saint Theresa in her wild lament.

46 *Alexander:* Alexander the Great (356–323 BC), the Macedonian king and general who conquered much of Asia   47 *Montaigne:* Michel de Montaigne (1533–1592), the French writer known for his *Essays,* which focused not only on the outside world but also on the thoughts of the author himself   48 *Saint Theresa:* One of the most important saints of the Roman Catholic Church, Teresa of Avila (1515–1582) was the author of a number of religious works and mystical tracts.

DISCUSSION TOPICS

1. Why does the speaker keep returning to the place where the groundhog has died? What changes does he undergo?

511

2. Compare "The Groundhog" with "Shakespeare's "Full Fathom Five," Wordsworth's "A Slumber Did My Spirit Seal," Hopkins's "Spring and Fall," as well as the two stories "Death in the Woods" by Anderson and "The Grave" by Porter. See also the graveyard scenes in Act V of Shakespeare's *Hamlet.* What do such comparisons reveal about philosophical and emotional attempts to come to terms with death and mortality?
3. The first two lines of the poem are conventional iambic tetrameter. What effect does Eberhart achieve by the inverted syntax and abrupt change of meter in line 3? Do the shifts accentuate the meaning and dramatic force of the poem's "plot"?

W. H. Auden (1907–1973) Englishman turned American, professor in American colleges and at Oxford. He was influenced by Eliot, Hopkins, Owen, as well as poetry in Old English. Like Eliot, he persistently probed the spiritual fragmentation of Western civilization.

MUSÉE DES BEAUX ARTS

About suffering they were never wrong,
The Old Masters: how well they understood
Its human position; how it takes place
While someone else is eating or opening a window or just walking
    dully along;
5 How, when the aged are reverently, passionately waiting
For the miraculous birth, there always must be
Children who did not specially want it to happen, skating
On a pond at the edge of the wood:
They never forgot
10 That even the dreadful martyrdom must run its course
Anyhow in a corner, some untidy spot
Where the dogs go on with their doggy life and the torturer's horse
Scratches its innocent behind on a tree.

In Brueghel's *Icarus,* for instance: how everything turns away
15 Quite leisurely from the disaster; the ploughman may
Have heard the splash, the forsaken cry,
But for him it was not an important failure; the sun shone
As it had to on the white legs disappearing into the green
Water; and the expensive delicate ship that must have seen
20 Something amazing, a boy falling out of the sky,
Had somewhere to get to and sailed calmly on.

Musée des Beaux Arts: Museum of Fine Arts   14 *Brueghel's Icarus:* In Greek mythology, the inventor Daedalus escapes from the island of Crete with his son, Icarus, by fashioning two pairs of wings made of feathers joined together by wax. Although warned by his father not to stray too near the sun because its heat would melt the wax, Icarus is swept away by the joy of flight and goes too high. His wings dissolve, and he plunges into the sea. Pieter Brueghel's *Landscape with the Fall of Icarus* (c. 1558), which hangs in the Royal Museum of Fine Arts in Brussels, shows a landscape peopled by a ploughman and others, all of whom ignore the pair of white legs sticking out of the water in the right-hand corner of the painting.

DISCUSSION TOPICS

1. Why, according to Auden, were the Old Masters "never wrong"?
2. How does Brueghel's painting illustrate the meaning of the poem?

IN MEMORY OF W. B. YEATS

1

He disappeared in the dead of winter:
The brooks were frozen, the airports almost deserted,
The snow disfigured the public statues;
The mercury sank in the mouth of the dying day.
5   O all the instruments agree
The day of his death was a dark cold day.

Far from his illness
The wolves ran on through the evergreen forests,
The peasant river was untempted by the fashionable quays;
10   By mourning tongues
The death of the poet was kept from his poems.

But for him it was his last afternoon as himself,
An afternoon of nurses and rumours;
The provinces of his body revolted,
15   The squares of his mind were empty,
Silence invaded the suburbs,
The current of his feeling failed: he became his admirers.

Now he is scattered among a hundred cities
And wholly given over to unfamiliar affections;
20   To find his happiness in another kind of wood
And be punished under a foreign code of conscience.
The words of a dead man
Are modified in the guts of the living.

But in the importance and noise of tomorrow
25 When the brokers are roaring like beasts on the floor of the Bourse,
And the poor have the sufferings to which they are fairly accustomed,
And each in the cell of himself is almost convinced of his freedom;
A few thousand will think of this day
As one thinks of a day when one did something slightly unusual.
30 O all the instruments agree
The day of his death was a dark cold day.

2

You were silly like us: your gift survived it all;
The parish of rich women, physical decay,
Yourself; mad Ireland hurt you into poetry.
35 Now Ireland has her madness and her weather still,
For poetry makes nothing happen: it survives
In the valley of its saying where executives
Would never want to tamper; it flows south
From ranches of isolation and the busy griefs,
40 Raw towns that we believe and die in; it survives,
A way of happening, a mouth.

3

Earth, receive an honoured guest;
William Yeats is laid to rest:
Let the Irish vessel lie
45 Emptied of its poetry.

Time that is intolerant
Of the brave and innocent,
And indifferent in a week
To a beautiful physique,

50 Worships language and forgives
Everyone by whom it lives;
Pardons cowardice, conceit,
Lays its honours at their feet.

Time that with this strange excuse
55 Pardoned Kipling and his views,
And will pardon Paul Claudel,
Pardons him for writing well.

In the nightmare of the dark
All the dogs of Europe bark,
60 And the living nations wait,
Each sequestered in its hate;

Intellectual disgrace
Stares from every human face,
And the seas of pity lie
65   Locked and frozen in each eye.

Follow, poet, follow right
To the bottom of the night,
With your unconstraining voice
Still persuade us to rejoice;

70   With the farming of a verse
Make a vineyard of the curse,
Sing of human unsuccess
In a rapture of distress;

In the deserts of the heart
75   Let the healing fountain start,
In the prison of his days
Teach the free man how to praise.

Yeats: died on January 28, 1939, in France   25 *Bourse:* French for "stock exchange"   46–57: Auden deleted the three stanzas contained in these lines when he published his *Collected Shorter Poems* in 1966.   55 *Kipling:* Rudyard Kipling (1865–1936), the English author who was often accused of supporting imperialism   56 *Paul Claudel:* the French diplomat, playwright, and poet (1868–1955), whose ardent catholicism and conservative views were objectionable to many people 58 *nightmare:* the impending horror of World War II

DISCUSSION TOPICS

1. As we have noted in connection with Hart Crane's "At Melville's Tomb," an *elegy* is a lament for the dead, usually an individual and quite often another poet. (You may wish to look at the commentary on Gray's "Elegy Written in a Country Churchyard.") In what ways does the poem's tripartite structure bring forth different dimensions of the meaning of the poet's death and extend the theme beyond a concern with death alone?
2. What is the relationship between society and the poet in this elegy?
3. How do season and landscape function symbolically in this lyric?
4. What exactly do you think Auden means by the remark "poetry makes nothing happen"? Consider the poems you have read by Yeats. Do you think Auden's remark is applicable? How does it apply to the work of other poets—to literature in general?

THE UNKNOWN CITIZEN

(TO JS/07/M/378
THIS MARBLE MONUMENT
IS ERECTED BY THE STATE)

He was found by the Bureau of Statistics to be
One against whom there was no official complaint,
And all the reports on his conduct agree
That, in the modern sense of an old-fashioned word, he was a saint,
5   For in everything he did he served the Greater Community.
Except for the War till the day he retired
He worked in a factory and never got fired,
But satisfied his employers, Fudge Motors Inc.
Yet he wasn't a scab or odd in his views,
10   For his Union reports that he paid his dues,
(Our report on his Union shows it was sound)
And our Social Psychology workers found
That he was popular with his mates and liked a drink.
The Press are convinced that he bought a paper every day
15   And that his reactions to advertisements were normal in every way.
Policies taken out in his name prove that he was fully insured,
And his Health-card shows he was once in hospital but left it cured.
Both Producers Research and High-Grade Living declare
He was fully sensible to the advantages of the Installment Plan
20   And had everything necessary to the Modern Man,
A phonograph, a radio, a car and a frigidaire.
Our researchers into Public Opinion are content
That he held the proper opinions for the time of year;
When there was peace, he was for peace; when there was war, he
       went.
25   He was married and added five children to the population,
Which our Eugenist says was the right number for a parent of his
       generation,
And our teachers report that he never interfered with their education.
Was he free? Was he happy? The question is absurd:
Had anything been wrong, we should certainly have heard.

DISCUSSION TOPICS

1. What is Auden's theme in this poem? Is it closer to Huxley's *Brave New World* or to Orwell's *1984?*
2. The poem is clearly dated by line 21. What items would you add (or modify) to bring the poem up to the present age?

Theodore Roethke (1908–1963) Born in Michigan; educated at the University of Michigan and Harvard; taught in colleges and universities—finally and long at the University of Washington. He received many honors and awards such as the Pulitzer, Bollingen, Guggenheim, and Fulbright.

MY PAPA'S WALTZ

The whiskey on your breath
Could make a small boy dizzy;
But I hung on like death:
Such waltzing was not easy.

5 We romped until the pans
Slid from the kitchen shelf;
My mother's countenance
Could not unfrown itself.

The hand that held my wrist
10 Was battered on one knuckle;
At every step you missed
My right ear scraped a buckle.

You beat time on my head
With a palm caked hard by dirt,
15 Then waltzed me off to bed
Still clinging to your shirt.

DISCUSSION TOPICS

1. How do the rhythms and images of "My Papa's Waltz" suggest the motion of the dance in the little boy's home? Compare "The Dance" by Williams.
2. What do the details of this scene indicate about the boy's perception of his father? What kind of man do you think his father was?

THE WAKING

I wake to sleep, and take my waking slow.
I feel my fate in what I cannot fear.
I learn by going where I have to go.

We think by feeling. What is there to know?
5 I hear my being dance from ear to ear.
I wake to sleep, and take my waking slow.

517

Of those so close beside me, which are you?
God bless the Ground! I shall walk softly there,
And learn by going where I have to go.

10   Light takes the Tree; but who can tell us how?
The lowly worm climbs up a winding stair;
I wake to sleep, and take my waking slow.

Great Nature has another thing to do
To you and me; so take the lively air,
15   And, lovely, learn by going where to go.

This shaking keeps me steady. I should know.
What falls away is always. And is near.
I wake to sleep, and take my waking slow.
I learn by going where I have to go.

DISCUSSION TOPICS

1. "The Waking" borrows a verse form of Italian and French origin called the *villanelle.* It contains nineteen lines and uses only two rhymes in six stanzas consisting of five tercets and a quatrain. Certain lines of the villanelle are repeated in accordance with the following pattern in which *a'* and *a"* stand for the first and third lines of the initial tercet: a'ba" aba' aba" aba' aba" aba'a". "Do Not Go Gentle into That Good Night" by Dylan Thomas is also a *villanelle.* What effects does Roethke achieve by using the *villanelle* form?
2. What kind of relationship between the speaker and nature is experienced here? How does the speaker "learn by going where I have to go"? Compare Frost's "Stopping by Woods."

ELIZABETH BISHOP (1911–1979) American poet, short story writer and translator. Having traveled widely, Bishop established geography and travel as dominant themes in her work. Her poetry is characterized by sharp, clear observations of physical detail, precise language, and subtle irony. She was awarded the Pulitzer prize in 1956 for *Poems North & South; A Cold Spring* (1955).

THE FISH

I caught a tremendous fish
and held him beside the boat
half out of water, with my hook
fast in a corner of his mouth.

5   He didn't fight.
He hadn't fought at all.
He hung a grunting weight,
battered and venerable
and homely. Here and there
10   his brown skin hung in strips
like ancient wallpaper,
and its pattern of darker brown
was like wallpaper:
shapes like full-blown roses
15   stained and lost through age.
He was speckled with barnacles,
fine rosettes of lime,
and infested
with tiny white sea-lice,
20   and underneath two or three
rags of green weed hung down.
While his gills were breathing in
the terrible oxygen
—the frightening gills,
25   fresh and crisp with blood,
that can cut so badly—
I thought of the coarse white flesh
packed in like feathers,
the big bones and the little bones,
30   the dramatic reds and blacks
of his shiny entrails,
and the pink swim-bladder
like a big peony.
I looked into his eyes
35   which were far larger than mine
but shallower, and yellowed,
the irises backed and packed
with tarnished tinfoil
seen through the lenses
40   of old scratched isinglass.
They shifted a little, but not
to return my stare.
—It was more like the tipping
of an object toward the light.
45   I admired his sullen face,
the mechanism of his jaw,
and then I saw
that from his lower lip
—if you could call it a lip—

50   grim, wet, and weaponlike,
      hung five old pieces of fish-line,
      or four and a wire leader
      with the swivel still attached,
      with all their five big hooks
55   grown firmly in his mouth.
      A green line, frayed at the end
      where he broke it, two heavier lines,
      and a fine black thread
      still crimped from the strain and snap
60   when it broke and he got away.
      Like medals with their ribbons
      frayed and wavering,
      a five-haired beard of wisdom
      trailing from his aching jaw.
65   I stared and stared
      and victory filled up
      the little rented boat,
      from the pool of bilge
      where oil had spread a rainbow
70   around the rusted engine
      to the bailer rusted orange,
      the sun-cracked thwarts,
      the oarlocks on their strings,
      the gunnels—until everything
75   was rainbow, rainbow, rainbow!
      And I let the fish go.

DISCUSSION TOPICS

1. In Bishop's poem "At the Fishhouses," the speaker describes herself as "a believer in total immersion." How does "The Fish" immerse the reader in the experience of the fisherman?
2. Why does the speaker let the fish go?
3. What is the victory that "filled up / the little rented boat" (lines 66 and 67)?

MURIEL RUKEYSER (1913–1980) American poet, born in New York City, educated at Vassar College and Columbia University. Known for her experiments with form and her poems of social protest, she has called herself a "she-poet," but in seeking deeper knowledge of the inner self she has transcended such narrow categories.

MYTH

Long afterward, Oedipus, old and blinded, walked the
roads.   He smelled a familiar smell.   It was
the Sphinx.   Oedipus said, "I want to ask one question.
Why didn't I recognize my mother?"   "You gave the
5   wrong answer," said the Sphinx.   "But that was what
made everything possible," said Oedipus.   "No," she said.
"When I asked, What walks on four legs in the morning,
two at noon, and three in the evening, you answered,
Man.   You didn't say anything about woman."
10   "When you say Man," said Oedipus, "you include women
too. Everyone knows that."   She said, "That's what
you think."

DISCUSSION TOPICS

1. How do the structure and appearance of this poem on the page affect your
   response to it? Even though it looks more like prose than poetry, are there
   certain elements or qualities that mark it as poetry?
2. Why do you think Rukeyser approaches a contemporary issue—equality for
   women—through an ancient myth? Is there a hint that the issue is of ancient
   origin?
3. How does Rukeyser use tone and style to help close the distance between the
   modern issue and the ancient myth? Is her technique effective?

WILLIAM STAFFORD (1914–   ) Native of Kansas; educated at the Universities of
Kansas and Iowa; conscientious objector assigned to work in civilian public service
camps during World War II. He began a long teaching career at Lewis and
Clark College and thus associated with poets of the West and Northwest since
1948.

A SOUND FROM THE EARTH

Somewhere, I think in Dakota,
they found the leg bones—just the
big leg bones—of several hundred
buffalo, in a gravel pit.

5   Near there, a hole in a cliff
has been hollowed so that
the prevailing wind

thrums a note so low and persistent
that bowls of water placed in that
10   cave will tremble to foam.

The grandfather of Crazy Horse
lived there, they say, at the last,
and his voice like the thrum of the hills
made winter come as he sang, "Boy,
15   where was your buffalo medicine?
I say you were not brave enough, Boy.
I say Crazy Horse was too cautious."

Then the sound he cried out for his grandson
made that thin Agency soup that they
20   put before him tremble. The whole
earthen bowl churned into foam.

DISCUSSION TOPICS

1. What is the significance of the poem's title?
2. The key word in this poem is "foam." Notice where it appears. How does Stafford link the first two stanzas to the final two through this word? What is the significance of the fact that the foam in the final stanza appears in a bowl of "thin Agency soup"? To what agency is Stafford referring?
3. What explanation does the poem offer for the pit filled with the "big leg bones" of buffalo in Dakota?
4. What relationship between the gravel pit and Crazy Horse is suggested?
5. Why does his grandfather say, "Crazy Horse was too cautious"?
6. This poem may require several readings before all the subtle relationships are clear to you. Stafford himself said, "Poetry is the kind of thing you have to see from the corner of your eye. You can be too well prepared for poetry. . . . It's like a very faint star. If you look straight at it you can't see it, but if you look a little to one side it is there." What does a sideways look at the dead buffalo and Crazy Horse reveal in this poem?

RANDALL JARRELL (1914–1965) Born in Nashville, educated at Vanderbilt and Princeton; magazine editor; college and university teacher of English. He was a poet, critic, and novelist.

THE DEATH OF THE BALL TURRET GUNNER

From my mother's sleep I fell into the State,
And I hunched in its belly till my wet fur froze.
Six miles from earth, loosed from its dream of life,
I woke to black flak and the nightmare fighters.
5   When I died they washed me out of the turret with a hose.

Ball Turret: As Jarrell himself describes it, "A ball turret was a plexiglass sphere set into the belly of a B-17 or B-24, and inhabited by two .50 caliber machine-guns and one man, a short small man. When this gunner tracked with his machine-guns a fighter attacking his bomber from below, he revolved with the turret; hunched upside-down in his little sphere, he looked like the foetus in the womb. The fighters which attacked him were armed with cannon firing explosive shells. The hose was a steam hose."

DISCUSSION TOPICS

1. What impresses you most about this poem?
2. What image or metaphor does Jarrell employ, especially in the first two lines? What do the words "mother's sleep," "belly," and "wet fur" suggest? Does Jarrell continue the metaphor in the rest of the poem?
3. How does the poem's imagery join birth and death? In what ways is that union symbolic? What other symbolic associations are there in the poem?
4. In what ways is the fifth and final line the key to the poem's effect?

LA BELLE AU BOIS DORMANT

She lies, her head beneath her knees,
In their old trunk; and no one comes—
No porter, even, with a check
Or forceps for her hard delivery.
5   The trains pant outside; and she coils breathlessly
Inside his wish and is not waked.

She is sleeping but, alas! not beautiful.
Travelers doze around; are borne away;
And the thorns clamber up her stony veins.
10   She is irreparable; and yet a state
Asks for her absently, and citizens
Drown for an instant in her papery eyes.

Yet where is the hunter black enough to storm
Her opening limbs, or shudder like a fish
15   Into the severed maelstrom of her skull?

The blood fondles her outrageous mouth;
The lives flourish in her life, to alienate
Their provinces from her outranging smile.

What wish, what keen pain has enchanted her
20 To this cold period, the end of pain,
Wishes, enchantment: this suspending sleep?
She waits here to be waked—as he has waited
For her to wake, for her to wake—
Her lips set in their slack conclusive smile.

DISCUSSION TOPICS

1. What has happened to the young woman of this poem? Where is she, and what kind of sleep is she undergoing?
2. How does the old nursery tale of "Sleeping Beauty" and her long sleep before a brave young prince comes to awaken her echo in this poem? In what ways do the imagery, language, and tone of "La Belle au Bois Dormant" diverge from those of the tale?
3. There is, to be sure, some explicit sexual imagery. Do you find also some Freudian symbolism?
4. The nursery tale evokes the archetypal theme of death and rebirth, perhaps a hint of a fertility motif. Does Jarrell mean us to recall such archetypal features as a short cut to irony?

JOHN BERRYMAN (1914–1972) Critic, essayist, biographer of Stephen Crane, and author of *Homage to Mistress Bradstreet* (1956), a long poem on the struggles of the seventeenth-century Puritan poet Anne Bradstreet. His *Dream Songs* won the Pulitzer prize in 1965. His experimental verse, with its complex syntax, shifting rhythms, and constantly changing diction, often chronicles the poet's own troubled life and anxieties. He committed suicide by leaping from a bridge in St. Paul, Minnesota.

LIFE, FRIENDS, IS BORING

Life, friends, is boring. We must not say so.
After all, the sky flashes, the great sea yearns,
we ourselves flash and yearn,
and moreover my mother told me as a boy
5 (repeatingly) 'Ever to confess you're bored
means you have no

524

Inner Resources.' I conclude now I have no
inner resources, because I am heavy bored.
Peoples bore me,
10   literature bores me, especially great literature,
Henry bores me, with his plights & gripes
as bad as achilles,

who loves people and valiant art, which bores me.
And the tranquil hills, & gin, look like a drag
15   and somehow a dog
has taken itself & its tail considerably away
into mountains or sea or sky, leaving
behind: me, wag.

11 *Henry:* the central character of *The Dream Songs,* who often reflects aspects of the author's own life.
Berryman writes that *The Dream Songs* "is essentially about an imaginary character (not the poet, not
me) named Henry, a white American in early middle age sometimes in blackface, who has suffered
an irreversible loss and talks about himself sometimes in the first person, sometimes in the third,
sometimes even in the second; . . ."   12 *achilles:* In the *Iliad,* and especially in later versions of the
Troy legend, Achilles, the greatest of the Greek warriors, is portrayed as sulking and complaining about
the unjust treatment he receives from the commander-in-chief, Agamemnon. He refuses to fight against
the Trojans until his friend is killed.

DISCUSSION TOPICS

1. Why do you think the narrator in this poem finds life boring? Why is his attitude
   considered unseemly?
2. This poem was one of Berryman's *Dream Songs,* the central character of which
   was "Henry" (see note for line 11). What appears to be the relationship
   between Henry and the narrator? Are they the same? Is the narrator the poet
   Berryman?
3. What are some of the things Berryman does with language to keep his poem
   from boring the reader?
4. How do the different meanings of the word "wag" come into play at the end
   of the poem?
5. What kinds of things contribute to the boredom mentioned in the poem? Are
   there large archetypal or mythic themes here? Why does the poet mention
   "achilles"? And why has he used a lower case "a" instead of a capital in the
   name?

DYLAN THOMAS (1914–1953) Keatsian in style and manner, energetic and vivid in his
imagery. He was a Welshman whose voice brought many to enjoy poetry and who
brought many voices together to sound with each other in his play *Under Milk
Wood.* He died in New York, where he had been giving readings.

A REFUSAL TO MOURN THE DEATH, BY FIRE, OF A CHILD IN LONDON

Never until the mankind making
Bird beast and flower
Fathering and all humbling darkness
Tells with silence the last light breaking
5   And the still hour
Is come of the sea tumbling in harness

And I must enter again the round
Zion of the water bead
And the synagogue of the ear of corn
10   Shall I let pray the shadow of a sound
Or sow my salt seed
In the least valley of sackcloth to mourn

The majesty and burning of the child's death.
I shall not murder
15   The mankind of her going with a grave truth
Nor blaspheme down the stations of the breath
With any further
Elegy of innocence and youth.

Deep with the first dead lies London's daughter,
20   Robed in the long friends,
The grains beyond age, the dark veins of her mother
Secret by the unmourning water
Of the riding Thames.
After the first death, there is no other.

DISCUSSION TOPICS

1. Why do you think Thomas titled his poem "A Refusal to Mourn . . ."?
2. The sentence structure of Thomas's poetry is often fractured or disjointed. What effect does that have on your reading of this poem?
3. What are some of the ways Thomas creates the poem's music and rhythm? (Notice particularly his repetition of similar sounds.)
4. How do archetypal themes of creation, death, and rebirth inform this poem? In what ways are these aspects of nature tied into the child's fate? Why does the last line state: "After the first death, there is no other"?
5. Poems about the death of a child are rather common. Compare this poem with Ransom's "Bells for John Whiteside's Daughter." What similarities and differences do you discover? How do these poems enable us to sublimate the experience of death? How is this process of sublimation different in the case of a child's death?

DO NOT GO GENTLE INTO THAT GOOD NIGHT

Do not go gentle into that good night,
Old age should burn and rave at close of day;
Rage, rage against the dying of the light.

Though wise men at their end know dark is right,
5   Because their words had forked no lightning they
Do not go gentle into that good night.

Good men, the last wave by, crying how bright
Their frail deeds might have danced in a green bay,
Rage, rage against the dying of the light.

10   Wild men who caught and sang the sun in flight,
And learn, too late, they grieved it on its way,
Do not go gentle into that good night.

Grave men, near death, who see with blinding sight
Blind eyes could blaze like meteors and be gay,
15   Rage, rage against the dying of the light.

And you, my father, there on the sad height,
Curse, bless, me now with your fierce tears, I pray.
Do not go gentle into that good night.
Rage, rage against the dying of the light.

DISCUSSION TOPIC

Like "The Waking" by Roethke, "Do Not Go Gentle into That Good Night" is
a *villanelle.* (See the discussion of Roethke's poem.) How do the characteristics of
the *villanelle* combine with Thomas's distinctive poetic voice to increase the force
of the exhortation that "Old age should burn and rave at close of day"?

GWENDOLYN BROOKS (1917–   ) Chicago-reared poet, writer of short and long
fiction; college teacher. She has been a winner of awards and prizes, including the
1950 Pulitzer prize and a Guggenheim.

THE RITES FOR COUSIN VIT

Carried her unprotesting out the door.
Kicked back the casket-stand. But it can't hold her,
That stuff and satin aiming to enfold her,
The lid's contrition nor the bolts before.

5   Oh oh. Too much. Too much. Even now, surmise,
She rises in the sunshine. There she goes,
Back to the bars she knew and the repose
In love-rooms and the things in people's eyes.
Too vital and too squeaking. Must emerge.
10   Even now she does the snake-hips with a hiss,
Slops the bad wine across her shantung, talks
Of pregnancy, guitars and bridgework, walks
In parks or alleys, comes haply on the verge
Of happiness, haply hysterics. Is.

14 *haply:* by accident, perhaps

DISCUSSION TOPICS

1. How does this poem, like so many of the poems in this anthology, find a means of superseding the disheartening effects that the death of a loved one brings? What are the psychological needs and benefits of such a victory?
2. How does the last word of the poem capture the essence of the woman it praises?

WE REAL COOL

The Pool Players.
Seven at the Golden Shovel.

We real cool. We
Left school. We

Lurk late. We
Strike straight. We

Sing sin. We
Thin gin. We

Jazz June. We
Die soon.

DISCUSSION TOPICS

1. Like much American writing, "We Real Cool" requires us to *hear* the colloquial voice. How does the language of the streets and the pool hall convey a kind of exactness that a more formal language would fail at?

528

2. Can we see a kind of group biography behind the clipped syntax? Besides an intricate internal rhyme, what other poetic devices has Brooks implanted to solidify a desired effect?
3. How does the final stanza escape sentimentality?

MAY SWENSON (1919–   ) American poet, short-story writer, teacher, translator. Born and educated in Utah, she has been a teacher and poet-in-residence at several universities.

WOMEN

Women   Or they
   should be   should be
     pedestals   little horses
       moving   those wooden
         pedestals   sweet
           moving   oldfashioned
         to the   painted
        motions   rocking
         of men   horses

      the gladdest things in the toyroom

       The   feelingly
       pegs   and then
     of their   unfeelingly
      ears   To be
    so familiar   joyfully
   and dear   ridden
  to the trusting   rockingly
fists   ridden until
To be chafed   the restored

egos dismount and the legs stride away

Immobile   willing
  sweetlipped   to be set
   sturdy   into motion
    and smiling   Women
     women   should be
       should always   pedestals
        be waiting   to men

DISCUSSION TOPICS

1. In a pattern poem, the shape of the words on the page is usually related in some way to the poem's meaning. (Compare Herbert's "Easter-Wings" and Cummings's "r-p-o-p-h-e-s-s-a-g-r.") What relationship do you see between the pattern and the meaning of this poem?
2. How should the poem's lines and stanzas be put together? (Read the poem aloud, and notice the use of capital letters.)
3. What is the symbolic relationship between "pedestals" and "rocking horses"? Notice the poem says women should *be* pedestals, not be *on* pedestals. What difference does that make?
4. What social attitudes does this poem hold up to scrutiny? How does it subvert these views?
5. What sexual imagery do you find in the poem?

RICHARD WILBUR (1921–   ) Born in New York City, educated at Amherst and Harvard. He is poet, translator, editor, teacher at Harvard, Wellesley, Wesleyan. He won the Guggenheim and other prizes, and was a cultural representative for the State Department on trip to Russia.

GRACE

"The young lambs bound as to the tabor's sound." They toss and toss; it is as if it were the earth that flung them, not themselves. It is the pitch of graceful agility when we think that.—G. M. HOPKINS, Notebooks

So active they seem passive, little sheep
Please, and Nijinsky's out-the-window leap
And marvelous midair pause please too
A taste for blithe brute reflex; flesh made word
5   Is grace's revenue.

One is tickled, again, by the dining-car waiter's absurd
Acrobacy—tipfingered tray like a wind-besting bird
Plumblines his swinging shoes, the sole things sure
In the shaken train; but this is all done for food,
10   Is habitude, if not pure

Hebetude. It is a graph of a theme that flings
The dancer kneeling on nothing into the wings,
And Nijinsky hadn't the words to make the laws
For learning to loiter in air; he "merely" said,
15   "I merely leap and pause."

530

Lambs are constrained to bound. Consider instead
The intricate neural grace in Hamlet's head;
A grace not barbarous implies a choice
Of courses, not in a lingo of leaps-in-air
20 But in such a waiting voice

As one would expect to hear in the talk of Flaubert.
Piety makes for awkwardness, and where
Balance is not urgent, what one utters
May be puzzled and perfect, and we respect
25 *Some* scholars' stutters.

Even fraction-of-a-second action is not wrecked
By a graceful still reserve. To be unchecked
Is needful then: choose, challenge, jump, poise, run. . . .
Nevertheless, the praiseful, graceful soldier
30 Shouldn't be fired by his gun.

"The young lambs . . .": The epigraph refers to Wordsworth's "Ode: Intimations of Immortality."
2 *Nijinsky:* Vaslav Nijinsky (1890–1950), the Russian-born choreographer and ballet dancer celebrated
for his leaps and ability seemingly to remain suspended high in the air   21 *Flaubert:* Gustave Flaubert
(1821–1880), the French writer known for his painstaking method of writing, concern for exactitude,
and intricate sentence structure

DISCUSSION TOPICS

1. How do the formal qualities of this poem, as well as its content, constitute an
   exercise in grace? What do the various kinds of wordplay such as paradoxes and
   puns contribute to the theme of grace in art and nature? What are the several
   meanings of the word "grace" itself?
2. Compare "Grace" with the poems by Hopkins printed previously, particularly
   "The Windhover." In what ways does the spirit of Hopkins inform Wilbur's
   poem?
3. How is the "intricate neural grace in Hamlet's head" different from the kinds
   of grace depicted in the first three stanzas?

JUGGLER

A ball will bounce, but less and less. It's not
A light-hearted thing, resents its own resilience.
Falling is what it loves, and the earth falls
So in our hearts from brilliance,
5 Settles and is forgot.
It takes a sky-blue juggler with five red balls

531

To shake our gravity up. Whee, in the air
The balls roll round, wheel on his wheeling hands,
Learning the ways of lightness, alter to spheres
10   Grazing his finger ends,
Cling to their courses there,
Swinging a small heaven about his ears.

But a heaven is easier made of nothing at all
Than the earth regained, and still and sole within
15   The spin of worlds, with a gesture sure and noble
He reels that heaven in,
Landing it ball by ball,
And trades it all for a broom, a plate, a table.

Oh, on his toe the table is turning, the broom's
20   Balancing up on his nose, and the plate whirls
On the tip of the broom! Damn, what a show, we cry:
The boys stamp, and the girls
Shriek, and the drum booms
And all come down, and he bows and says good-bye.

25   If the juggler is tired now, if the broom stands
In the dust again, if the table starts to drop
Through the daily dark again, and though the plate
Lies flat on the table top,
For him we batter our hands
30   Who has won for once over the world's weight.

DISCUSSION TOPIC

Who is the juggler—and why do we "batter our hands" for him? Compare this poem with Wilbur's "Grace," as well as with the concept of "difficult balance" in the next poem, "Love Calls Us to the Things of This World."

LOVE CALLS US TO THE THINGS OF THIS WORLD

The eyes open to a cry of pulleys,
And spirited from sleep, the astounded soul
Hangs for a moment bodiless and simple
As false dawn.
5   Outside the open window
The morning air is all awash with angels.

Some are in bed-sheets, some are in blouses,
Some are in smocks: but truly there they are.
Now they are rising together in calm swells
10 Of halcyon feeling, filling whatever they wear
With the deep joy of their impersonal breathing;

Now they are flying in place, conveying
The terrible speed of their omnipresence, moving

And staying like white water; and now of a sudden
15 They swoon down into so rapt a quiet
That nobody seems to be there.
                              The soul shrinks

From all that it is about to remember,
From the punctual rape of every blessed day,
20 And cries,
            "Oh, let there be nothing on earth but laundry,
Nothing but rosy hands in the rising steam
And clear dances done in the sight of heaven."

Yet, as the sun acknowledges
25 With a warm look the world's hunks and colors,
The soul descends once more in bitter love
To accept the waking body, saying now
In a changed voice as the man yawns and rises,

"Bring them down from their ruddy gallows;
30 Let there be clean linen for the backs of thieves;
Let lovers go fresh and sweet to be undone,
And the heaviest nuns walk in a pure floating
Of dark habits,
                keeping their difficult balance."

DISCUSSION TOPICS

1. What is the dominant metaphor in this poem? Why is the morning air "all awash with angels"?
2. Why does the soul shrink in line 17?
3. What is the "bitter love" mentioned in line 26?
4. Who—or what—is speaking in the final stanza?
5. Why is the balance mentioned in the last line "difficult"?
6. Wilbur clearly delights in wordplay. How does this play enhance this poem especially? (How many puns can you spot in the poem?)
7. Why do you think love calls us to things of this world?

A GRASSHOPPER

But for a brief
Moment, a poised minute,
He paused on the chicory-leaf;
Yet within it

5   The sprung perch
Had time to absorb the shock,
Narrow its pitch and lurch,
Cease to rock.

A quiet spread
10   Over the neighbor ground;
No flower swayed its head
For yards around;

The wind shrank
Away with a swallowed hiss;
15   Caught in a widening, blank
Parenthesis,

Cry upon cry
Faltered and faded out;
Everything seemed to die.
20   Oh, without doubt

Peace like a plague
Had gone to the world's verge,
But that an aimless, vague
Grasshopper-urge

25   Leapt him aloft,
Giving the leaf a kick,
Starting the grasses' soft
Chafe and tick,

So that the sleeping
30   Crickets resumed their chimes,
And all things wakened, keeping
Their several times.

In gay release
The whole field did what it did,
35   Peaceful now that its peace
Lay busily hid.

DISCUSSION TOPIC

Like other New England poets such as Emily Dickinson and Robert Frost, Wilbur often uses some common natural phenomenon as a metaphor for some philosophical insight. What is the philosophical import of this poem? How does Wilbur's grasshopper differ essentially from E. E. Cummings's?

PHILIP LARKIN (1922–   ) Native of Coventry in Warwickshire, Oxford-educated, librarian at University of Hull since 1943. In college he was a member of a group rebelling against grandiloquence in poetry and arguing for the matter-of-fact, conversational tone reflected in his own poems.

THE DANCER

> *Butterfly*
> *Or falling leaf,*
> *Which ought I to imitate*
> *In my dancing?*

5 And if she were to admit
  The world weaved by her feet
  Is leafless, is incomplete?
  And if she abandoned it,
  Broke the pivoted dance,
10 Set loose the audience?
  Then would the moon go raving,
  The moon, the anchorless
  Moon go swerving
  Down at the earth for a catastrophic kiss.

DISCUSSION TOPICS

1. What is the relationship between the italicized lines and the rest of the poem?
2. How does Larkin develop the image of the dance as a metaphor for an ordered universe?

LOVE, WE MUST PART NOW

  Love, we must part now: do not let it be
  Calamitous and bitter. In the past
  There has been too much moonlight and self-pity:

Let us have done with it: for now at last
5   Never has sun more boldly paced the sky,
Never were hearts more eager to be free,
To kick down worlds, lash forests; you and I
No longer hold them; we are husks, that see
The grain going forward to a different use.

10   There is regret. Always, there is regret.
But it is better that our lives unloose,
As two tall ships, wind-mastered, wet with light,
Break from an estuary with their courses set,
And waving part, and waving drop from sight.

DISCUSSION TOPICS

1. What is the theme of this poem?
2. What images does the poet use in the poem? How are they appropriate to the theme?
3. How does Larkin achieve a contemporary voice in this rather traditional love sonnet?
4. Compare Larkin's poem with Drayton's Sonnet Number 61 in *Ideas Mirrour*.

LINES ON A YOUNG LADY'S PHOTOGRAPH ALBUM

At last you yielded up the album, which,
Once open, sent me distracted. All your ages
Matt and glossy on the thick black pages!
Too much confectionery, too rich:
5   I choke on such nutritious images.

My swivel eye hungers from pose to pose—
In pigtails, clutching a reluctant cat;
Or furred yourself, a sweet girl-graduate;
Or lifting a heavy-headed rose
10   Beneath a trellis, or in a trilby hat

(Faintly disturbing, that, in several ways)—
From every side you strike at my control,
Not least through these disquieting chaps who loll
At ease about your earlier days:
15   Not quite your class, I'd say, dear, on the whole.

But o, photography! as no art is,
Faithful and disappointing! that records

536

  Dull days as dull, and hold-it smiles as frauds,
  And will not censor blemishes
20 Like washing-lines, and Hall's-Distemper boards,

  But shows the cat as disinclined, and shades
  A chin as doubled when it is, what grace
  Your candour thus confers upon her face!
  How overwhelmingly persuades
25 That this is a real girl in a real place,

  In every sense empirically true!
  Or is it just *the past?* Those flowers, that gate,
  These misty parks and motors, lacerate
  Simply by being over; you
30 Contract my heart by looking out of date.

  Yes, true; but in the end, surely, we cry
  Not only at exclusion, but because
  It leaves us free to cry. We know *what was*
  Won't call on us to justify
35 Our grief, however hard we yowl across

  The gap from eye to page. So I am left
  To mourn (without a chance of consequence)
  You, balanced on a bike against a fence;
  To wonder if you'd spot the theft
40 Of this one of you bathing; to condense,

  In short, a past that no one now can share,
  No matter whose your future; calm and dry,
  It holds you like a heaven, and you lie
  Unvariably lovely there,
45 Smaller and clearer as the years go by.

DISCUSSION TOPICS

1. Who is the speaker in this poem? What is the dramatic situation? (Have you ever had a similar experience, looking at old photographs of someone else's past?)
2. What is the speaker mourning in the next to last stanza? Is there a suggestion of death? Whose?
3. What role does photography play in the speaker's lament? How is photography important to the poem's meaning? How is photography, "as no art is, / Faithful and disappointing"?
4. What relationship between the speaker's present and the young lady's past does the poem explore?
5. What seems to be the poem's dominant theme?

6. Compare Larkin's "Lines on a Young Lady's Photograph Album" with Keats's "Ode on a Grecian Urn." How are the poems similar? In what ways are they dissimilar?

AS BAD AS A MILE

Watching the shied core
Striking the basket, skidding across the floor,
Shows less and less of luck, and more and more

Of failure spreading back up the arm
5   Earlier and earlier, the unraised hand calm,
The apple unbitten in the palm.

DISCUSSION TOPICS

1. What do you think is the tone of this poem?
2. Where does Larkin get the title? Why do you think he changes the familiar expression from "as good as a mile" to "as *bad* as a mile"?
3. What philosophical point of view does the poem seem to express? What comment does the poem make on the notion of original sin?

Louis Simpson (1923–   ) College professor, combat veteran of World War II. He combines surrealistic techniques and everyday subject matter to produce philosophical poetry.

A STORY ABOUT CHICKEN SOUP

In my grandmother's house there was always chicken soup.
And talk of the old country—mud and boards,
Poverty,
The snow falling down the necks of lovers.

5   Now and then, out of her savings
She sent them a dowry. Imagine
The rice-powdered faces!
And the smell of the bride, like chicken soup.

But the Germans killed them.
10   I know it's in bad taste to say it,
But it's true. The Germans killed them all.

In the ruins of Berchtesgaden
A child with yellow hair
Ran out of a doorway.

A German girl-child—
Cuckoo, all skin and bones—
Not even enough to make chicken soup.
She sat by the stream and smiled.

Then as we splashed in the sun
20   She laughed at us.
We had killed her mechanical brothers,
So we forgave her.

The sun is shining.
The shadows of the lovers have disappeared.
25   They are all eyes; they have some demand on me—
They want me to be more serious than I want to be.

They want me to stick in their mudhole
Where no one is elegant.
They want me to wear old clothes,
30   They want me to be poor, to sleep in a room with many others—

Not to walk in the painted sunshine
To a summer house,
But to live in the tragic world forever.

12 *Berchtesgaden:* a resort in the Bavarian Alps. Near it was Hitler's residence, the Berghof.

DISCUSSION TOPICS

1. What responses to the experiences of World War II are portrayed in this poem?
2. What are the effects of the poem's tripartite structure? How is its title significant?
3. What psychological conflicts are present here, particularly in the third section?

DENISE LEVERTOV (1923–   ) Poet, teacher. Born in England, she came to the United States in 1948. Her *Collected Earlier Poems Nineteen Forty to Nineteen Sixty* appeared in 1979.

SUNDAY AFTERNOON

> After the First Communion
> and the banquet of mangoes and
> bridal cake, the young daughters
> of the coffee merchant lay down
> 5 for a long siesta, and their white dresses
> lay beside them in quietness
> and the white veils floated
> in their dreams as the flies buzzed.
> But as the afternoon
> 10 burned to a close they rose
> and ran about the neighborhood
> among the halfbuilt villas
> alive, alive, kicking a basketball, wearing
> other new dresses, of bloodred velvet.

DISCUSSION TOPICS

1. What is the dramatic setting of this poem?
2. What are the relationships between morning and afternoon in the poem and how are these significant?
3. What are the symbolic implications of the colors "white" and "bloodred" used to describe the dresses? Which other words also seem to have symbolic implications?
4. Notice the formal arrangement of the poem? In what ways does it resemble a sonnet?

MAXINE KUMIN (1925–   ) American poet, professor. She has written in several styles about a wide variety of subjects, but her later poems have focused on the natural rhythms of rural life experienced on her New Hampshire farm.

HOW IT GOES ON

> Today I trade my last unwise
> ewe lamb, the one who won't leave home,
> for two cords of stove-length oak
> and wait on the old enclosed
> 5 front porch to make the swap.
> November sun revives the thick
> trapped buzz of horseflies. The siren

for noon and forest fires blows
a sliding scale. The lamb of woe
10   looks in at me through glass
on the last day of her life.

Geranium scraps from the window box
trail from her mouth, burdock burrs
are stickered to her fleece like chicken pox,
15   under her tail stub, permanent smears.

I think of how it goes on,
this dark particular bent of our hungers:
the way wire eats into a tree
year after year on the pasture's perimeter,
20   keeping the milk cows penned
until they grow too old to freshen;
of how the last wild horses were scoured
from canyons in Idaho, roped, thrown,
their nostrils twisted shut with wire
25   to keep them down, the mares aborting,
days later, all of them carted to town.

I think of how it will be
In January, nights so cold
the pond ice cracks like target practice,
30   daylight glue-colored, sleet falling,
my yellow horse slick with the ball-bearing
sleet, raising up from his dingy browse
out of boredom and habit
to strip bark from the fenced-in trees;
35   of February, month of the hard palate,
the split wood running out,
worms working in the flour bin.

The lamb, whose time has come, goes off
in the cab of the dump truck, tied to the seat
40   with baling twine, durable enough
to bear her to the knife and rafter.

O lambs! The whole wolf-world sits down to eat
and cleans its muzzle after.

DISCUSSION TOPICS

1. What seems to be the dominant emotion in this poem? In what way is that
   emotion related to the poem's title, "How It Goes On"? Trace the ways in
   which the title makes itself felt throughout the poem?

2. Which words used in the description of the lamb suggest that the poem is about something more than the sale of a farm animal for slaughter? What symbolic associations does the poet evoke by using a "lamb"? (Compare Blake's "The Lamb.")
3. What do you think this poem is about? What is its "theme"? See how many different meanings you can discover in the poet's presentation of this very common experience, including psychological conflicts, archetypal and religious symbolism, and social commentary.

ROBERT CREELEY (1926–   ) Educated in this country (Harvard, Black Mountain College in North Carolina, New Mexico), but widely traveled, both during World War II (Burma) and otherwise, having lived in France, Spain, Canada, Guatemala. He has been a professor in a number of colleges and universities.

KORE

As I was walking
   I came upon
chance walking
   the same road upon.

5 As I sat down
   by chance to move
later
   if and as I might,

light the wood was,
10   light and green,
and what I saw
   before I had not seen.

It was a lady
   accompanied
15 by goat men
   leading her.

Her hair held earth.
   Her eyes were dark.
A double flute
20   made her move.

"O love,
   where are you
leading
   me now?"

Kore: Greek for "maiden," often identified with Persephone, daughter of Demeter   15 *goat men:* Satyrs were half-man, half-goat.   19 *double flute:* The god Pan is often shown with a flute.

DISCUSSION TOPICS

1. What do you think the poet intends the "lady" in "Kore" to represent?
2. In what ways does she resemble the lady in Keats's "La Belle Dame sans Merci"?
3. What is the answer to the question in the last stanza?

JUST FRIENDS

Out of the table endlessly rocking,
sea-shells, and firm,
I saw a face appear
which called me dear.

To be loved is half the battle
I thought.
To be
is to be better than is not.

Now when you are old what will you say?
You don't say,
she said.
That was on a Thursday.

Friday night I left
and haven't been back since.
Everything is water
if you look long enough.

DISCUSSION TOPICS

1. What do you think is the tone of this poem? What does the title "Just Friends" suggest?
2. There are several allusions in the poem. The opening lines recall Whitman; the second stanza brings Hamlet's famous soliloquy to mind. How does Creeley

alter the originals? What effects do these allusions have on your experience of the poem?

3. What might the poet-speaker mean by the final two lines? Do those lines have an effect on the poem's tone?

ALLEN GINSBERG (1926–   ) Best-known work, *Howl* (1956), describes the alienated "Beat Generation" of post-World War II, to whom he became pop hero and cult leader.

A SUPERMARKET IN CALIFORNIA

What thoughts I have of you tonight, Walt Whitman, for I walked down the sidestreets under the trees with a headache self-conscious looking at the full moon.

In my hungry fatigue, and shopping for images, I went into the neon fruit supermarket, dreaming of your enumerations!

What peaches and what penumbras! Whole families shopping at night! Aisles full of husbands! Wives in the avocados, babies in the tomatoes!—and you, Garcia Lorca, what were you doing down by the watermelons?

I saw you, Walt Whitman, childless, lonely old grubber, poking among the meats in the refrigerator and eyeing the grocery boys.

I heard you asking questions of each: Who killed the pork chops? What
5   price bananas? Are you my Angel?

I wandered in and out of the brilliant stacks of cans following you, and followed in my imagination by the store detective.

We strode down the open corridors together in our solitary fancy tasting artichokes, possessing every frozen delicacy, and never passing the cashier.

Where are we going, Walt Whitman? The doors close in an hour. Which way does your beard point tonight?

(I touch your book and dream of our odyssey in the supermarket and feel absurd.)

Will we walk all night through solitary streets? The trees add shade to
10   shade, lights out in the houses, we'll both be lonely.

Will we stroll dreaming of the lost America of love past blue automobiles in driveways, home to our silent cottage?

Ah, dear father, graybeard, lonely old courage-teacher, what America did you have when Charon quit poling his ferry and you got out on a smoking bank and stood watching the boat disappear on the black waters of Lethe?

3 *Garcia Lorca:* Spanish poet and playwright (1899–1936)   12 *Charon:* in Greek mythology, the boatman who ferried dead souls to the underworld   *Lethe:* a river in the underworld. Drinking its waters caused forgetfulness.

DISCUSSION TOPICS

1. Ginsberg's poem is both a parody and a celebration of Walt Whitman. What devices and techniques of Whitman's poetry does Ginsberg specifically evoke? (You may want to look back to some of the Whitman selections.)
2. How do you respond to Ginsberg's blending of humor, irony, and adulation? Do you think this blending works? Why do you suppose Ginsberg introduces humor and irony in a poem of celebration?
3. What is the significance in modern America of evoking Whitman's spirit for a visit to a supermarket? In what ways can this visit be seen as symbolic?

W. S. MERWIN (1927–   ) Princeton-educated and widely traveled. He studied under Robert Graves and was awarded the Pulitzer prize. His poetry is often compressed and unsentimental, with mythic dimensions.

PROTEUS

By the splashed cave I found him. Not
(As I had expected) patently delusive
In a shape sea-monstrous, terrible though sleeping,
To scare all comers, nor as that bronze-thewed
5   Old king of Pharos with staring locks,
But under a gray rock, resting his eyes
From futurity, from the blinding crystal
Of that morning sea, his face flicked with a wisp
Of senile beard, a frail somnolent old man.

10   Who would harness the sea-beast
To the extravagant burden of his question
Must find him thus dreaming of his daughters,
Of porpoises and horses; then pitiless
Of an old man's complaints, unawed
15   At what fierce beasts are roused under his grasp,
Between the brutal ignorance of his hands
Must seize and hold him till the beast stands again
Manlike but docile, the neck bowed to answer.

I had heard in seven wise cities
20 Of the last shape of his wisdom: when he,
Giver of winds, father as some said
Of the triple nightmare, from the mouth of a man
Would loose the much-whistled wind of prophecy.
The nothing into which a man leans forward
25 Is mother of all restiveness, drawing
The body prone to falling into no
Repose at last but the repose of falling.

Wherefore I had brought foot to his island
In the dead of dawn, had picked my way
30 Among the creaking cypresses, the anonymous
Granite sepulchres; wherefore, beyond these,
I seized him now by sleeping throat and heel.
What were my life, unless I might be stone
To grasp him like the grave, though wisdom change
35 From supposition to savage supposition;
Unless the rigor of mortal hands seemed deathly?

I was a sepulchre to his pleadings,
Stone to his arguments, to his threats;
When he leapt in a bull's rage
40 By horn and tail I held him; I became
A mad bull's shadow, and would not leave him;
As a battling ram he rose in my hands;
My arms were locked horns that would not leave his horns;
I was the cleft stick and the claws of birds
45 When he was a serpent between my fingers.

Wild as heaven erupting into a child
He burst under my fists into a lion;
By mane and foot I grappled him;
Closer to him than his own strength I strained
50 And held him longer. The sun had fought
Almost to noon when I felt the beast's sinews
Fail, the beast's bristles fall smooth
Again to the skin of a man. I loosed him then.
The head he turned toward me wore a face of mine.

55 Here was no wisdom but my own silence
Echoed as from a mirror; no marine
Oracular stare but my own eyes
Blinded and drowned in their reflections;
No voice came but a voice we shared, saying,

60   "You prevail always, but, deathly, I am with you
        Always." I am he, by grace of no wisdom,
        Who to no end battles the foolish shapes
        Of his own death by the insatiate sea.

Proteus: a sea-god who lived on the island of Pharos and who could change his shape at will

DISCUSSION TOPICS

1. Why has the speaker come to this island in search of Proteus? What do you think he is seeking?
2. In what images is his battle with the sea-god described, and why do these seem to be especially appropriate? What are the effects of this struggle on the speaker both during the conflict and after the god has submitted?
3. In *The Archetypes and the Collective Unconscious,* C. G. Jung explains the archetypal "wise old man": the spiritual figure—often gifted with magical powers and capable of taking on animal as well as human form—who leads a person to accomplish something that, because of some internal or external obstacle, cannot be achieved alone and who "thus represents knowledge, reflection, insight, wisdom, cleverness and intuition. . . ." Concerning our perception of spiritual archetypes in dreams and literature, Jung adds: "Man conquers not only nature, but spirit also, without realizing what he is doing. To the man of enlightened intellect it seems like the correction of a fallacy when he recognizes that what he took to be spirits is simply the human spirit and ultimately his own spirit." How do these comments relate to "Proteus" and enhance your understanding of the poem?

GALWAY KINNELL (1927–   ) Pulitzer prize-winning poet and teacher educated at Princeton and Rochester. His work is inspired mainly by Whitman and to some extent by William Carlos Williams.

THE RIVER THAT IS EAST

1

Buoys begin clanging like churches
And peter out. Sunk to the gunwhales
In their shapes tugs push upstream.
A carfloat booms down, sweeping past

5   Illusory suns that blaze in puddles
On the shores where it rained, past the Navy Yard,
Under the Williamsburg Bridge
That hangs facedown from its strings
Over which the Jamaica Local crawls,
10   Through white-winged gulls which shriek
And flap from the water and sideslip in
Over the chaos of illusions, dangling
Limp red hands, and screaming as they touch.

2

A boy swings his legs from the pier,
15   His days go by, tugs and carfloats go by,
Each prow pushing a whitecap. On his deathbed
Kane remembered the abrupt, missed Grail
Called Rosebud, Gatsby must have thought back
On his days digging clams in Little Girl Bay
20   In Minnesota, Nick fished in dreamy Michigan,
Gant had his memories, Griffeths, those
Who went baying after the immaterial
And whiffed its strange dazzle in a blonde
In a canary convertible, who died
25   Thinking of the Huck Finns of themselves
On the old afternoons, themselves like this boy
Swinging his legs, who sees the *Ile de France*
Come in, and wonders if in some stateroom
There is not a sick-hearted heiress sitting
30   Drink in hand, saying to herself his name.

3

A man stands on the pier.
He has long since stopped wishing his heart were full
Or his life dear to him.
He watches the snowfall hitting the dirty water.
35   He thinks: Beautiful. Beautiful.
If I were a gull I would be one with white wings,
I would fly out over the water, explode, and
Be beautiful snow hitting the dirty water.

4

And thou, River of Tomorrow, flowing . . .
40   We stand on the shore, which is mist beneath us,
And regard the onflowing river. Sometimes
It seems the river stops and the shore

Flows into the past. Nevertheless, its leaked promises
Hopping in the bloodstream, we strain for the future,
45 Sometimes even glimpse it, a vague, scummed thing
We dare not recognize, and peer again
At the cabled shroud out of which it came,
We who have no roots but the shifts of our pain,
No flowering but our own strange lives.

50 What is this river but the one
Which drags the things we love,
Processions of debris like floating lamps,
Towards the radiance in which they go out?

No, it is the River that is East, known once
55 From a high window in Brooklyn, in agony—river
On which a door locked to the water floats,
A window sash paned with brown water, a whisky crate,
Barrel staves, sun spokes, feathers of the birds,
A breadcrust, a rat, spittle, butts, and peels,
60 The immaculate stream, heavy, and swinging home again.

9 *Jamaica Local:* New York commuter line   17 *Kane:* title character in Orson Welles's film *Citizen Kane* (1941)   18 *Rosebud:* Kane's childhood snowsled, the enigmatic last word he speaks before dying   18 *Gatsby:* title character of F. Scott Fitzgerald's *The Great Gatsby* (1926)   19 *Nick:* Nick Adams, Hemingway's alter ego in a number of early stories set in Michigan   20 *Gant:* Eugene Gant, protagonist of Thomas Wolfe's *Look Homeward, Angel* (1929)   21 *Griffeths:* Clyde Griffiths, antihero of Theodore Dreiser's *An American Tragedy* (1925)   27 *Ile de France:* famous luxury liner

DISCUSSION TOPICS

1. The East River separates Brooklyn from Manhattan Island. What clues does the poet offer that it is something more than an actual river in this poem?
2. The man in stanza 3 is separated from the boy in stanza 1 by a series of allusions, mostly literary. How is our appreciation of the poem enhanced or enlarged by our understanding of these allusions?
3. Why do you think the speaker mentions gulls in stanzas 1 and 3? What is the relationship between the gulls in these two stanzas, and how do they relate to the central theme of the poem?
4. What is the central theme of the poem?
5. What relationship do you see between Kinnell's "things we love" (line 51) and "the Things of This World" in Wilbur's "Love Calls Us to the Things of This World"?
6. In what ways is Kinnell's "immaculate stream" archetypal? Why does he call the poem "The River That Is East" rather than simply the East River?

THOMAS KINSELLA (1928–   ) Irish poet, professor of English. He has lived in the United States since 1965. He has said that his principal aim is "to elicit order from significant experience, with a view to acceptance on the basis of some kind of understanding."

GIRL ON A SWING

My touch has little force:
Her infant body falls.
Her lips lightly purse
With panic and delight
5   And fly up to kiss
The years' brimming glass;
To drink; to sag sweetly
When I drop from sight.

DISCUSSION TOPICS

1. What is your reaction to this poem? What is most interesting about it?
2. Notice the meter and rhythm of the short lines. How is the form related to the content? (It may help to say the poem aloud.) Pay particular attention to the use of alliteration, assonance, and consonance (see the glossary).
3. What is the imagined situation of the poem? Who might the speaker be? Who is the "girl on a swing"?

ST. PAUL'S ROCKS: 16 FEBRUARY 1832

A cluster of rocks far from the trade routes
a thousand miles from any other land
they appear abruptly in the ocean,
low lying, so hidden in driving mists
5   they are seldom sighted, and then briefly,
white and glittering against the eternal grey.

Despite the lack of any vegetation
they have succeeded in establishing
symbiosis with the surrounding water.
10   Colonies of birds eat the abundant fish;
moths feed on the feathers; lice and beetles
live in the dung; countless spiders
prey on these scavangers; in the crevices
a race of crabs lives on the eggs and young.

15   In squalor and killing and parasitic things
life takes its first hold.
Later the noble accident: the seed, dropped
in some exhausted excrement, or bobbing
like a matted skull into an inlet.

St. Paul's Rocks: a cluster of islets in the mid-Atlantic, visited by Charles Darwin on February 16, 1832, during the voyage of the Beagle. Darwin's observation that the rocks were not volcanic in origin enabled him to map geological changes in the elevation of landmasses. Because of information such as this, he was able to determine that these changes took place over periods of time, as is the case with processes of biological evolution.

DISCUSSION TOPICS

1. What is the meaning of "symbiosis"? How is this word central to an understanding of the poem?
2. The language of this poem sounds at times rather scientific or like an objective description. What poetic devices intrude just often enough to turn this language into poetry? What, if anything, do you think differentiates the language of poetry from that of science?
3. What is the view of life expressed in the poem, particularly in the final stanza?
4. How might the views about evolution expressed here be as troubling to us as Darwin's views were to our Victorian ancestors?

ANNE SEXTON (1928–1975) American poet who studied under Robert Lowell. Her poetry possesses marked narrative and autobiographical elements. She has said that poetry "should be a shock" and "almost hurt."

THE STARRY NIGHT

> That does not keep me from having a terrible
> need of—shall I say the word—religion. Then
> I go out at night to paint the stars.
>
> VINCENT VAN GOGH in a letter to his brother

The town does not exist
except where one black-haired tree slips
up like a drowned woman into the hot sky.
The town is silent. The night boils with eleven stars.
5   Oh starry starry night! This is how
I want to die.

It moves. They are all alive.
Even the moon bulges in its orange irons
to push children, like a god, from its eye.
10   The old unseen serpent swallows up the stars.
Oh starry starry night! This is how
I want to die:

into that rushing beast of the night,
sucked up by that great dragon, to split
15   from my life with no flag,
no belly,
no cry.

Starry Night: painted by Vincent Van Gogh in 1888. The letter to his brother Theo was written in
September 1888.

DISCUSSION TOPICS

1. What emotion do you find expressed in this poem?
2. What do you think the speaker means by the phrase, "This is how / I want to die" in stanza 1? How is your understanding of this line enlarged in stanzas 2 and 3?
3. How does it affect your understanding of this poem to know that the poet Anne Sexton committed suicide?

WRITING TOPIC

How might this poem be interpreted in the light of Freud's comments on the death wish, the unconscious urge to return to an inanimate or quiescent state of being? (Compare Whitman's "Out of the Cradle Endlessly Rocking," Keats's "Ode to a Nightingale," Frost's "Stopping by Woods," and Hughes's "A Dream of Horses.")

ADRIENNE RICH (1929–   ) Radcliffe College graduate, influenced first by Frost and Yeats, later by William Carlos Williams and Robert Lowell. She often presents a feminist point of view about human relationships.

STORM WARNINGS

The glass has been falling all the afternoon,
And knowing better than the instrument
What winds are walking overhead, what zone

Of gray unrest is moving across the land,
5   I leave the book upon a pillowed chair
And walk from window to closed window, watching
Boughs strain against the sky

And think again, as often when the air
Moves inward toward a silent core of waiting,
10   How with a single purpose time has traveled
By secret currents of the undiscerned
Into this polar realm. Weather abroad
And weather in the heart alike come on
Regardless of prediction.

15   Between foreseeing and averting change
Lies all the mastery of elements
Which clocks and weatherglasses cannot alter.
Time in the hand is not control of time,
Nor shattered fragments of an instrument
20   A proof against the wind; the wind will rise,
We can only close the shutters.

I draw the curtains as the sky goes black
And set a match to candles sheathed in glass
Against the keyhole draught, the insistent whine
25   Of weather through the unsealed aperture.
This is our sole defense against the season;
These are the things that we have learned to do
Who live in troubled regions.

1 *glass:* barometer

DISCUSSION TOPICS

1. What is the dominant metaphor in this poem?
2. How does Rich lead the reader to metaphysical observations by means of this metaphor?
3. In which specific lines does she alert the reader to the symbolic meanings of the dominant metaphor?
4. What point is Rich making in the third stanza? Why do you think she introduces the idea of "time"?
5. How do you interpret the final stanza? To what "troubled regions" do you think the poem is referring?

MOURNING PICTURE

The picture was painted by Edwin Romanzo Elmer
(1850–1923) as a memorial to his daughter Effie.
In the poem, it is the dead girl who speaks.

They have carried the mahogany chair and the cane rocker
out under the lilac bush,
and my father and mother darkly sit there, in black clothes.
Our clapboard house stands fast on its hill,
5   my doll lies in her wicker pram
gazing at western Massachusetts.
This was our world.
I could remake each shaft of grass
feeling its rasp on my fingers,
10   draw out the map of every lilac leaf
or the net of veins on my father's
grief-tranced hand.

Out of my head, half-bursting,
still filling, the dream condenses—
15   shadows, crystals, ceilings, meadows, globes of dew.
Under the dull green of the lilacs, out in the light
carving each spoke of the pram, the turned porch-pillars,
under high early-summer clouds,
I am Effie, visible and invisible,
20   remembering and remembered.

They will move from the house,
give the toys and pets away.
Mute and rigid with loss my mother
will ride the train to Baptist Corner,
25   the silk-spool will run bare.
I tell you, the thread that bound us lies
faint as a web in the dew.
Should I make you, world, again,
could I give back the leaf its skeleton, the air
30   its early-summer cloud, the house
its noonday presence, shadowless,
and leave *this* out? I am Effie, you were my dream.

DISCUSSION TOPICS

1. What is the significance of the refrain, "I am Effie," in lines 19 and 32?
2. What is the effect of having the dead girl speak the lines of the poem? To whom
   or what is she speaking? What seems to be her message?

3. What is the tone of the poem?
4. What is the meaning of the title, "Mourning Picture"?
5. Why does Rich tell the reader that the poem is based on a painting? (Compare the relationship between poetry and pictures in this poem and in Larkin's "Lines on a Young Lady's Photograph Album.)

PAULA BECKER TO CLARA WESTHOFF

Paula Becker 1876–1907
Clara Westhoff 1878–1954

became friends at Worpswede, an artists' colony near
Bremen, Germany, summer 1899. In January 1900, spent
a half-year together in Paris, where Paula painted and Clara
studied sculpture with Rodin. In August they returned to
Worpswede, and spent the next winter together in Berlin.
In 1901, Clara married the poet Rainer Maria Rilke: soon
after, Paula married the painter Otto Modersohn. She died
in a hemorrhage after childbirth, murmuring, *What a pity!*

The autumn feels slowed down,
summer still holds on here, even the light
seems to last longer than it should
or maybe I'm using it to the thin edge.
5   The moon rolls in the air. I didn't want this child.
You're the only one I've told.
I want a child maybe, someday, but not now.
Otto has a calm, complacent way
of following me with his eyes, as if to say
10   Soon you'll have your hands full!
And yes, I will; this child will be mine
not his, the failures, if I fail,
will be all mine. We're not good, Clara,
at learning to prevent these things,
15   and once we have a child, it *is* ours.
But lately, I feel beyond Otto or anyone.
I know now the kind of work I have to do.
It takes such energy! I have the feeling I'm
moving somewhere, patiently, impatiently,
20   in my loneliness. I'm looking everywhere in nature
for new forms, old forms in new places,
the planes of an antique mouth, let's say, among the leaves.
I know and do not know
what I am searching for.
25   Remember those months in the studio together,

555

you up to your strong forearms in wet clay,
I trying to make something of the strange impressions
assailing me—the Japanese
flowers and birds on silk, the drunks
30 sheltering in the Louvre, that river-light,
those faces. . . . Did we know exactly
why we were there? Paris unnerved you,
you found it too much, yet you went on
with your work . . . and later we met there again,
35 both married then, and I thought you and Rilke
both seemed unnerved. I felt a kind of joylessness
between you. Of course he and I
have had our difficulties. Maybe I was jealous
of him, to begin with, taking you from me,
40 maybe I married Otto to fill up
my loneliness for you.
Rainer, of course, *knows* more than Otto knows:
he believes in women. But he feeds on us,
like all of them. His whole life, his art
45 is protected by women. Which of us could say that?
Which of us, Clara, hasn't had to take that leap
out beyond our being women
to save our work? or is it to save ourselves?
Marriage is lonelier than solitude.
50 Do you know: I was dreaming I had died
giving birth to the child.
I couldn't paint or speak or even move.
My child—I think—survived me. But what was funny
in the dream was, Rainer had written my requiem—
55 a long, beautiful poem, and calling me his friend.
I was *your* friend
but in the dream you didn't say a word.
In the dream his poem was like a letter
to someone who has no right
60 to be there but must be treated gently, like a guest
who comes on the wrong day. Clara, why don't I dream of you?
That photo of the two of us—I have it still,
you and I looking hard into each other
and my painting behind us. How we used to work
65 side by side! And how I've worked since then
trying to create according to our plan
that we'd bring, against all odds, our full power
to every subject. Hold back nothing
because we were women. Clara, our strength still lies
70 in the things we used to talk about:

how life and death take one another's hands,
the struggle for truth, our old pledge against guilt.
And now I feel dawn and the coming day.
I love waking in my studio, seeing my pictures
75   come alive in the light. Sometimes I feel
it is myself that kicks inside me,
myself I must give suck to, love . . .
I wish we could have done this for each other
all our lives, but we can't . . .
80   They say a pregnant woman
dreams of her own death. But life and death
take one another's hands. Clara, I feel so full
of work, the life I see ahead, and love
for you, who of all people
85   however badly I say this
will hear all I say and cannot say.

DISCUSSION TOPICS

1. In the epigraph, the lines that precede the poem itself, Rich gives us some essential biographical information about the two women in her poem. What does the poem's title tell us? In what way is the poem ironic? (Look, e.g., at lines 50–54.)
2. Describe the conflict between the demands of Paula Becker's marriage and her art. What resolution to that conflict does the poem present?
3. What do you think Paula Becker means when she says, "Marriage is lonelier than solitude" (line 49)?
4. What is the nature of the relationship between Paula Becker and Clara Westhoff? What change has taken place in their relationship since their marriages?
5. What is the dominant theme of the poem?

WRITING TOPIC

Analyze the image of women presented in this poem. Consider the roles of friendship, marriage, and creativity (artistic and biological). (You may want to compare and contrast this poem with others such as Bradstreet's "To My Dear and Loving Husband" and May Swenson's "Women.")

Thom Gunn (1929–   ) Poet, editor. Born in England, he was educated at Cambridge and became a member of the English university "Movement" decrying Romantic and modernist excesses in poetry. In the 1950s he moved to the United States and settled in the San Francisco area, where he has taught and worked as a freelance writer.

ON THE MOVE

The blue jay scuffling in the bushes follows
Some hidden purpose, and the gust of birds
That spurts across the field, the wheeling swallows,
Has nested in the trees and undergrowth.
5   Seeking their instinct, or their poise, or both,
One moves with an uncertain violence
Under the dust thrown by a baffled sense
Or the dull thunder of approximate words.

On motorcycles, up the road, they come:
10   Small, black, as flies hanging in heat, the Boys,
Until the distance throws them forth, their hum
Bulges to thunder held by calf and thigh.
In goggles, donned impersonality,
In gleaming jackets trophied with the dust,
15   They strap in doubt—by hiding it, robust—
And almost hear a meaning in their noise.

Exact conclusion of their hardiness
Has no shape yet, but from known whereabouts
They ride, direction where the tires press.
20   They scare a flight of birds across the field:
Much that is natural, to the will must yield.
Men manufacture both machine and soul,
And use what they imperfectly control
To dare a future from the taken routes.

25   It is a part solution, after all.
One is not necessarily discord
On earth; or damned because, half animal,
One lacks direct instinct, because one wakes
Afloat on movement that divides and breaks.
30   One joins the movement in a valueless world,
Choosing it, till, both hurler and the hurled,
One moves as well, always toward, toward.

A minute holds them, who have come to go:
The self-defined, astride the created will
35   They burst away; the towns they travel through
Are home for neither bird nor holiness,
For birds and saints complete their purposes.
At worst, one is in motion; and at best,
Reaching no absolute, in which to rest,
40   One is always nearer by not keeping still.
                                California

DISCUSSION TOPICS

1. Why do you think Thom Gunn calls this poem "On the Move"? To what kind of motion is he referring?
2. What is the relationship between the birds and the bikers? How does the existence chosen by the bikers merge with and yet diverge from the natural world depicted in the poem? (Look carefully at the third stanza.)
3. What philosophical statement about the nature of life and human existence does the poem make?
4. Formally the poem is very restrained, even consciously prosaic. What effect does this have on your response? What poetic techniques does Gunn employ?

TED HUGHES (1930–   ) Poet Laureate of England, husband to the late Sylvia Plath. The subject matter of his poems includes violence, brutal acts, and predators. The horse and birds of prey are among his favorite symbols.

A DREAM OF HORSES

We were born grooms, in stable-straw we sleep still,
All our wealth horse-dung and the combings of horses,
And all we can talk about is what horses ail.

Out of the night that gulfed beyond the palace-gate
5   There shook hooves and hooves and hooves of horses:
Our horses battered their stalls; their eyes jerked white.

And we ran out, mice in our pockets and straw in our hair,
Into darkness that was avalanching to horses
And a quake of hooves. Our lantern's little orange flare

10   Made a round mask of our each sleep-dazed face,
Bodiless, or else bodied by horses
That whinnied and bit and cannoned the world from its place.

The tall palace was so white, the moon was so round,
Everything else this plunging of horses
15   To the rim of our eyes that strove for the shapes of the sound.

We crouched at our lantern, our bodies drank the din,
And we longed for a death trampled by such horses
As every grain of the earth had hooves and mane.

We must have fallen like drunkards into a dream
20   Of listening, lulled by the thunder of the horses.
We awoke stiff; broad day had come.

Out through the gate the unprinted desert stretched
To stone and scorpion; our stable-horses
Lay in their straw, in a hag-sweat, listless and wretched.

25 Now let us, tied, be quartered by these poor horses,
If but doomsday's flames be great horses,
The forever itself a circling of the hooves of horses.

DISCUSSION TOPICS

1. To whom does the "we" in the poem seem to refer?
2. What words and images reinforce the poem's title, "A Dream of Horses"? In what ways is the poem dreamlike?
3. What archetypal qualities do the dream horses in the poem have? How do the "stable-horses" differ from the dream horses?
4. Does the poem express a death wish? (Consider lines 17 and 25–27.) What is the relationship between horses and death, horses and life, horses and night?
5. What formal devices in the poem seem to control—even bridle or rein in—the archetypal energy represented by the horses?

GEOFFREY HILL (1932–   ) One of the foremost English poets writing in the second half of the twentieth century. Hill is an essayist and translator as well as a poet. His complex, meticulously crafted poems embody a passionate concern with tradition, Christian ritual, and religious belief. They also embrace mythic themes of violence, powerful emotion, loss, and sacrifice.

LACHRIMAE COACTAE

Crucified Lord, however much I burn
to be enamoured of your paradise,
knowing what ceases and what will not cease,
frightened of hell, not knowing where to turn,

5   I fall between harsh grace and hurtful scorn.
You are the crucified who crucifies,
self-withdrawn even from your own device,
your trim-plugged body, wreath of rakish thorn.

What grips me then, or what does my soul grasp?
10 If I grasp nothing what is there to break?
You are beyond me, innermost true light,

uttermost exile for no exile's sake,
king of our earth not caring to unclasp
its void embrace, the semblance of your quiet.

Lachrimae Coactae: The title means "forced tears" or "uncontrollable tears."

DISCUSSION TOPICS

1. What relationship between the speaker and Christ is depicted here? Compare Donne's "Holy Sonnet 14: Batter My Heart, Three Personed God." What similarities and differences do you find between these two poems?
2. What kinds of paradox are presented in "Lachrimae Coactae"? Why should they be a part of religious experience?

LACHRIMAE AMANTIS

What is there in my heart that you should sue
so fiercely for its love? What kind of care
brings you as though a stranger to my door
through the long night and in the icy dew

5   seeking the heart that will not harbour you,
that keeps itself religiously secure?
At this dark solstice filled with frost and fire
your passion's ancient wounds must bleed anew.

So many nights the angel of my house
10 has fed such urgent comfort through a dream,
whispered 'your lord is coming, he is close'

that I have drowsed half-faithful for a time
bathed in pure tones of promise and remorse:
'tomorrow I shall wake to welcome him.'

DISCUSSION TOPICS

1. The title means "the tears of the lover." To what lover does the poem refer? What does such love entail? Compare Herbert, "Love (III)."
2. In Mark 13:35–37, the Gospel states:

   Watch ye therefore: for ye know not when the master of the house cometh, at even, or at midnight, or at the cockcrowing, or in the morning: Lest coming suddenly he find you sleeping. And what I say unto you I say unto all, Watch.

   How might this biblical passage be linked to Hill's poem?

Sylvia Plath (1932–1963) Brilliant but unstable poet obsessed with death, isolation, and entrapment. She writes of her fears with horrifying clarity. Her last poems deal with the chaos of human experience and with violence and terror.

MIRROR

I am silver and exact. I have no preconceptions.
Whatever I see I swallow immediately
Just as it is, unmisted by love or dislike.
I am not cruel, only truthful—
5   The eye of a little god, four-cornered.
Most of the time I meditate on the opposite wall.
It is pink, with speckles. I have looked at it so long
I think it is a part of my heart. But it flickers.
Faces and darkness separate us over and over.

10   Now I am a lake. A woman bends over me,
Searching my reaches for what she really is.
Then she turns to those liars, the candles or the moon.
I see her back, and reflect it faithfully.
She rewards me with tears and an agitation of hands.
15   I am important to her. She comes and goes.
Each morning it is her face that replaces the darkness.
In me she has drowned a young girl, and in me an old woman
Rises toward her day after day, like a terrible fish.

DISCUSSION TOPICS

1. What is your initial reaction to "Mirror"? What characteristics of the poem do you think are most effective?
2. The subject of this poem is fairly obvious. The title gives it away. But there are a few lines that ask for a more complex reading. How do you interpret the phrase, "The eye of a little god"? Why are "candles or the moon" liars?
3. How does Plath modify her imagery in the second stanza? Why do you think she uses the image of "a terrible fish"? How does that image fit into the rest of the stanza?
4. What underlying theme do you detect in the poem? How does Plath draw this theme from the description of a mirror observing its owner?

DADDY

You do not do, you do not do
Any more, black shoe
In which I have lived like a foot
For thirty years, poor and white,
5   Barely daring to breathe or Achoo.

Daddy, I have had to kill you.
You died before I had time——
Marble-heavy, a bag full of God,
Ghastly statue with one grey toe
10   Big as a Frisco seal

And a head in the freakish Atlantic
Where it pours bean green over blue
In the waters off beautiful Nauset.
I used to pray to recover you.
15   Ach, du.

In the German tongue, in the Polish town
Scraped flat by the roller
Of wars, wars, wars.
But the name of the town is common.
20   My Polack friend

Says there are a dozen or two.
So I never could tell where you
Put your foot, your root,
I never could talk to you.
25   The tongue stuck in my jaw.

It stuck in a barb wire snare.
Ich, ich, ich, ich,
I could hardly speak.
I thought every German was you.
30   And the language obscene

An engine, an engine
Chuffing me off like a Jew.
A Jew to Dachau, Auschwitz, Belsen.
I began to talk like a Jew.
35   I think I may well be a Jew.

The snows of the Tyrol, the clear beer of Vienna
Are not very pure or true.
With my gypsy ancestress and my weird luck
And my Taroc pack and my Taroc pack
40   I may be a bit of a Jew.

I have always been scared of *you,*
With your Luftwaffe, your gobbledygoo.
And your neat moustache
And your Aryan eye, bright blue.
45 Panzer-man, panzer-man, O You——

Not God but a swastika
So black no sky could squeak through.
Every woman adores a Fascist,
The boot in the face, the brute
50 Brute heart of a brute like you.

You stand at the blackboard, daddy,
In the picture I have of you,
A cleft in your chin instead of your foot
But no less a devil for that, no not
55 Any less the black man who

Bit my pretty red heart in two.
I was ten when they buried you.
At twenty I tried to die
And get back, back, back to you.
60 I thought even the bones would do.

But they pulled me out of the sack,
And they stuck me together with glue.
And then I knew what to do.
I made a model of you,
65 A man in black with a Meinkampf look

And a love of the rack and the screw.
And I said I do, I do.
So daddy, I'm finally through.
The black telephone's off at the root,
70 The voices just can't worm through.

If I've killed one man, I've killed two——
The vampire who said he was you
And drank my blood for a year,
Seven years, if you want to know.
75 Daddy, you can lie back now.

There's a stake in your fat black heart
And the villagers never liked you.
They are dancing and stamping on you.
They always *knew* it was you.
80 Daddy, daddy, you bastard, I'm through.

564

13 *Nauset:* Nauset Harbor, off Cape Cod in Massachusetts   15 *Ach, du:* Ah, you (German)
27 *Ich:* I (German)   33 *Dachau, Auschwitz, Belsen:* extermination camps for Jews and others during
World War II   36 *Tyrol:* a resort center in Austria   39 *Taroc pack:* Tarot cards used primarily in
fortune-telling   42 *Luftwaffe:* the German Air Force   44 *Aryan:* During the Nazi era Germans
who claimed racial purity traced their origins back to Aryan ancestors.   45 *Panzerman:* Panzer units
were mechanized divisions of the German army used for quick strikes.   65 *Meinkampf:* Hitler's
autobiography was titled *Mein Kampf* ("my struggle").

DISCUSSION TOPICS

1. What has happened to the speaker's father? What emotions does she feel about
   the death of her father?
2. How does "Daddy" convey the speaker's ambivalence toward her father? What
   images of the speaker and her father surface during the course of the poem?
3. Why would the speaker label her father a Nazi and herself a Jew? Why do you
   think she says "Every woman adores a fascist"?
4. What are the implications of her remarks in lines 6 and 71: "Daddy, I have had
   to kill you" and "If I've killed one man, I've killed two"? Who is the "vampire"
   in line 72?
5. What do you think a Freudian critic would say about the relationship between
   the speaker and her father? How has that relationship affected her life?

JOHN WILLIAM CORRINGTON (1932–   ) Reared in Louisiana, educated at Centenary
and Rice, and at Sussex. He is a professor, novelist, editor, poet, lawyer, and
screenwriter.

PASTORAL

            in the fields
            where larks emoted
            where tender summer
            groomed green children
5   and the miraculous sea
                              wove
            its breath among parvenu
            leaves

            tiny cattle strolled in
10   the circle of a wooden
            bell
            along a stream wound
            silver through rare trees

—my god
15 farmer surakawa gasped
the breath of armageddon
on his neck
and turned to see
a brook leap into steam
20 cattle tumble
their delicate legs
snapped like hoofed matchsticks
leaves puff white to sift
on fields of glass
25 as larks burst into flame

and on the august horizon
the city being eaten by a sun

DISCUSSION TOPICS

1. What is the subject of "Pastoral"? What city is "being eaten by a sun"? What one word gives the poem its location?
2. What is the tone of the poem? Is it effective? What is your emotional response?
3. Some of the poem's images, especially in the second stanza, have a terrible beauty. How does Corrington use these images to recall the pastoral tradition and yet diverge from it? (Compare Marlowe's "The Passionate Shepherd to His Love.")

ETHERIDGE KNIGHT (1933–   ) Korean War veteran, wounded in action. His poems are frequently about black heroes and martyrs. He served six years in prison for robbery.

HARD ROCK RETURNS TO PRISON FROM THE HOSPITAL FOR THE CRIMINAL INSANE

Hard Rock was "known not to take no shit
From nobody," and he had the scars to prove it:
Split purple lips, lumped ears, welts above
His yellow eyes, and one long scar that cut
5 Across his temple and plowed through a thick
Canopy of kinky hair.

The WORD was that Hard Rock wasn't a mean nigger
Anymore, that the doctors had bored a hole in his head,
Cut out part of his brain, and shot electricity

10 Through the rest. When they brought Hard Rock back,
  Handcuffed and chained, he was turned loose,
  Like a freshly gelded stallion, to try his new status.
  And we all waited and watched, like indians at a corral,
  To see if the WORD was true.

15 As we waited we wrapped ourselves in the cloak
  Of his exploits: "Man, the last time, it took eight
  Screws to put him in the Hole." "Yeah, remember when he
  Smacked the captain with his dinner tray?" "He set
  The record for time in the Hole—67 straight days!"
20 "Ol Hard Rock! man, that's one crazy nigger."
  And then the jewel of a myth that Hard Rock had once bit
  A screw on the thumb and poisoned him with syphilitic spit.

  The testing came, to see if Hard Rock was really tame.
  A hillbilly called him a black son of a bitch
25 And didn't lose his teeth, a screw who knew Hard Rock
  From before shook him down and barked in his face.
  And Hard Rock did *nothing*. Just grinned and looked silly,
  His eyes empty like knot holes in a fence.

  And even after we discovered that it took Hard Rock
30 Exactly 3 minutes to tell you his first name,
  We told ourselves that he had just wised up,
  Was being cool; but we could not fool ourselves for long,
  And we turned away, our eyes on the ground. Crushed.
  He had been our Destroyer, the doer of things
35 We dreamed of doing but could not bring ourselves to do,
  The fears of years, like a biting whip,
  Had cut grooves too deeply across our backs.

DISCUSSION TOPICS

1. What is your initial response to this poem? Do you have an emotional reaction? What kind? How does Knight's use of dialect influence your response?
2. What seems to be the theme? Is the poem about society, about individuals? What does the poem say to you about the human condition? Is it significant that Hard Rock is a black man?
3. What kind of man is Hard Rock? Is he a "hero"? Explain your answer.

CHARLES SIMIC (1938–) Born in Belgrade, Yugoslavia; emigrated to the United States in 1950. He has won numerous awards as a poet and translator. His poems embrace the elemental forces of nature and the ancient, primitive wellsprings of human experience.

FOREST

My time is coming. Once again
My trees will swing their heavy bells.

My termites, my roots and streams
Will stitch their chill into the heart of man
5   Laying out my most ancient trail.

I speak of the north, of its pull
Stuck in my mouth like a bit.

Whoever looks now in the palm of his hand
Will notice the imprints of strange flowers
10   I have preserved in my rocks.

I will bare bones to tell fortunes by,
Snow with tracks of all the fabled highwaymen.
Ladies and gentlemen, you will hear a star
Dead a million years, in the throat of a bird.

15   The human body will be revealed for what it is—
A cluster of roots
Pulling in every direction.

There'll be plenty of time
When an acorn grows out of your ear
20   To accustom yourself to my ways,
To carve yourself a hermit's toothpick.

DISCUSSION TOPICS

1. What poetic devices does Simic use to draw the reader into the world of the poem?
2. Who or what is speaking? What relationship does the poem suggest between nature and human beings?
3. In what ways does the forest become a web that contains strands of the entire universe?
4. How do you interpret the reference to "a hermit's toothpick" in the final line?

John Digby (1938–   ) Poet and artist. Born in London, he left school at 15 and spent 5 years as a keeper at London Zoo. Subsequently, he moved to the United States.

SHORTER BIOGRAPHY OF A SAINT
CIRCA 20TH CENTURY

Usually on Monday evenings
In his grandmother's house
Under the back stairs
A group of taxi-drivers drove nails
5   Into his head
They were handsomely paid
But nevertheless complained rather bitterly
For his stuffed rabbits kept shouting
Vile obscenities in their ears

10   Every Tuesday after lunch
Rather than waste time sleeping in the deep-freeze
He blew into a bunch of roses
Producing a delicate shade of blue
His neighbours clapping enthusiastically but with sullen faces

15   He once wrote
Tobacco-tins dropped from over a height of three hundred feet
Create music not appreciated by western ears
He considered the statement a little pompous
And later stated
20   Tobacco-tins thrown into the air
Above the height of three hundred feet
Silently explode into vague music
Disturbing clouds and confusing birds

After twenty years of lecturing on oreology
25   To tailors' dummies retired race horses
He exchanged his clockwork goat
For a dozen plastic pokers to beat the sky
And retired to Hove

There
30   To while away his time
He did a little evening work
Inflating punctured footballs for pensioned gardeners

On most mornings before four o'clock
Spring Summer Winter
35   He rolled under his bed
Spending not less than an hour
Spelling his name backwards to disorientate the minutes

Autumn
He kept to his room
40   For he considered it the dangerous season
Slapping health back into his grandfather's corpse
Staggering around the house with empty wine bottles

DISCUSSION TOPICS

1. What is the effect of the contrast between Digby's matter-of-fact diction and the unexpected incidents and images of the poem?
2. What seems to be the tone? Did you find the poem humorous?
3. What use does Digby make of the absurd? (Compare Ionesco's one-act play, "The Gap.")
4. The Middle Ages produced many books recounting the lives, deeds, and miracles of saints. How does Digby bring that traditional genre into the modern era? What is saintlike in the character Digby describes?

WRITING TOPIC

Compare and contrast this poem with Auden's "The Unknown Citizen." What similarities and differences do you find?

SEAMUS HEANEY (1939–   ) Irish poet and critic. His poems deal with recollections of Irish country life, contemporary politics, and mythological and archaeological subjects.

ANTAEUS

When I lie on the ground
I rise flushed as a rose in the morning.
In fights I arrange a fall on the ring
    To rub myself with sand

5   That is operative
As an elixir. I cannot be weaned
Off the earth's long contour, her river-veins.
    Down here in my cave

    Girdered with root and rock
10   I am cradled in the dark that wombed me
And nurtured in every artery
    Like a small hillock.

570

Let each new hero come
Seeking the golden apples and Atlas.
15 He must wrestle with me before he pass
Into that realm of fame

Among sky-born and royal:
He may well throw me and renew my birth
But let him not plan, lifting me off the earth,
20 My elevation, my fall.

Antaeus: In the Greek myths the giant Antaeus was the son of the sea-god Poseidon and the Earth (Gaea). Since his parentage enabled him to renew his strength each time he made contact with the earth, he challenged all visitors to his land to a wrestling match and killed them. He was finally overcome by Hercules, who held him in the air and crushed him with a bear hug.   14 *the golden apples and Atlas:* The golden apples, which grew in a grove near the end of the earth, were guarded by a dragon and the Hesperides, who were, according to some accounts, the daughters of the titan Atlas. It was in the course of seeking the apples as one of his twelve labors that Hercules was challenged by Antaeus.

HERCULES AND ANTAEUS

Sky-born and royal,
snake-choker, dung-heaver,
his mind big with golden apples,
his future hung with trophies,

5 Hercules has the measure
of resistance and black powers
feeding off the territory.
Antaeus, the mould-hugger,

is weaned at last:
10 a fall was a renewal
but now he is raised up—
the challenger's intelligence

is a spur of light,
a blue prong graiping him
15 out of his element
into a dream of loss

and origins—the cradling dark,
the river-veins, the secret gullies
of his strength,
20 the hatching grounds

571

of cave and souterrain,
he has bequeathed it all
to elegists. Balor will die
and Byrthnoth and Sitting Bull.

25 Hercules lifts his arms
in a remorseless V,
his triumph unassailed
by the powers he has shaken

and lifts and banks Antaeus
30 high as a profiled ridge,
a sleeping giant,
pap for the dispossessed.

1 *Sky-born and royal:* Hercules was the child of Zeus, the king of the gods, and Alcmene.   2
snake-choker: As an infant, Hercules strangled two serpents that Hera, the queen of the gods, had sent
to kill him.   *dung-heaver:* In another of his twelve labors Hercules had to remove the vast heaps of
dung that lay in the stables of Augeas.   14 *graiping:* grasping or gripping. A *graip* is a three- or
four-pronged fork used to lift manure or litter.   23 *Balor:* in Celtic mythology a warrior giant whose
single eye, when opened, would destroy the enemy   24 *Byrthnoth:* the heroic warrior who led the
ill-fated English troops at the Battle of Maldon in 991   *Sitting Bull:* the Sioux Indian Chief (d. 1890)
who defeated Custer at the Battle of the Little Bighorn

DISCUSSION TOPIC

After reading both poems by Heaney, discuss the themes of the two poems. Are
the themes related? Why do you think the poet uses the mythological figure of
Antaeus to develop his themes? What does Hercules represent in the second
poem?

DONALD **D. K**UMMINGS (1940–   ) University professor, scholar, winner of American Poets prize at Indiana University in 1969. In addition to compiling a critical
reference guide to Walt Whitman, he has published widely in poetry magazines and
professional journals.

THE CONTEST BETWEEN HARMONY
AND INVENTION

Wallace Stevens invented a man,
a woman and a moving river,
a blackbird;
the latter, of course, may be looked upon as a crow.

5   Meanwhile I am spending twenty-seven years in drawing
a breath; a crow
has hidden in it,
as wetness hides in water.

And am observing: the crow—as though the color
10   of the darkness were moving, or folding
up like a wing.

I think
back: a knobby burlap bag of a woman
boiling rags in a pot,
15   an old man coughing up honey-colored phlegm,
a cold brown fried crow wing clinging
waxlike
to an icebox plate,
a river, as though the river is moving.

20   A crow and the ways of looking at a crow
are one.

I say that a crow is a blackbird.

I have invented Wallace Stevens.

DISCUSSION TOPIC

How is Kummings responding to Stevens's "Thirteen Ways of Looking at a Black-bird"? What is implied in saying: "I have invented Wallace Stevens"?

LOUISE GLÜCK (1943–   ) Born in New York City. She has published three volumes of poems, *Firstborn* (1968), *The House on Marshland* (1975), and *Descending Figure* (1980).

GRETEL IN DARKNESS

This is the world we wanted.
All who would have seen us dead
are dead. I hear the witch's cry
break in the moonlight through a sheet
5   of sugar: God rewards.
Her tongue shrivels into gas. . . .

       Now, far from women's arms
and memory of women, in our father's hut
we sleep, are never hungry.

10   Why do I not forget?
My father bars the door, bars harm
from this house, and it is years.

No one remembers. Even you, my brother,
summer afternoons you look at me as though
15   you meant to leave,
as though it never happened.
But I killed for you. I see armed firs,
the spires of that gleaming kiln—

Nights I turn to you to hold me
20   but you are not there.
Am I alone? Spies
hiss in the stillness, Hansel,
we are there still and it is real, real,
that black forest and the fire in earnest.

DISCUSSION TOPICS

1. What happens to the fairy-tale of "Hansel and Gretel" in this version of the story? How does point of view color the tale?
2. What kinds of emotional conflict is Gretel describing? In what ways is the darkness of the title symbolic?

MICHAEL C. BLUMENTHAL (1949–   ) Attorney, editor, television producer, professor, winner of many poetry awards, including the grand prize from the Associated Writing Programs. A fellow of Yaddo as well as at the Bread Loaf Writer's Conference, he has published two volumes of poetry: *Sympathetic Magic* (1983), which won the Walter Mark Award from the Poets of America, and *Days We Would Rather Know* (1984).

THE WOMAN INSIDE

There is a woman
inside me.
She is not beautiful
or divine,
5   but when I turn
in my sleep, restless
with other worlds,
she is always there—
placing a lilac

10   in my hand, gesturing
to the earth where
it all begins and
all ends. She knows
there are cruel men
15   everywhere, and angels
in unlikely places.
She knows the darkness
is only a passage
between light and light,
20   that the wisteria
climbing the house
are real, and lust
only tenderness gone wild
in the wrong field.
25   She is the one who is
always fertile in times
of barrenness, the one
with the silver hair
carrying a candle
30   through the long tunnel.
She is Halcyone,
calming the waters
after all my deaths;
she is Eurydice,
35   refusing to fade
when I look behind me.
She is the one
who wakes
with her arms around me
40   when I wake
alone.

34 *Eurydice:* In Greek mythology, she is permitted to follow her husband Orpheus out of Hades on the condition that he refrain from looking back at her—but he does look back and Eurydice is doomed to return to the underworld.

DISCUSSION TOPICS

1. What is the sex of the narrator? How do you know?
2. What do the qualities of "the woman inside" suggest about her nature? With what archetype of C. G. Jung's would you associate her? Of what women in other poems, stories, and plays does she remind you?
3. Why is Eurydice an appropriate mythological image for this woman?

JUNGIANS & FREUDIANS
AT THE JOSEPH CAMPBELL LECTURE

The Jungians are all wearing purple
and are fat, believers
in the archetypal pancake. The Freudians
wear dark gray and are thin
5   from all their *Lieben und Arbeiten.*
Phallic and yonic is how the afternoon goes,
myth and icon, serpent and mother earth.
And if Dali's drooped clocks are merely
a joke about time, for the Freudians
10   there's a menopausal tinge to that sagging hour.
And if the serpent in the grass is just
another word for love, to the Jungians
there's a rebirth waiting in the slipped skin,
a worm in the apple.

15   But in the end, it's all in good fun,
and everyone leaves happy—
The Jungians crying Freudian tears
into their lavender garments,
the Freudians purple with laughter
20   in their dark gray suits,
everyone delighted and friendly
over Jungian wine and Freudian doughnuts
in the pale, white room.

Joseph Campbell: outstanding contemporary scholar in field of myth and archetypes 5 *Lieben und Arbeiten:* Loves and Works   6 *Phallic and yonic:* Male and female sexual symbols   8 *Dali's:* Salvador Dali (1904–   ), famous surrealist painter

CAROLYN FORCHÉ (1950–   ) American poet-teacher. Her interest in other cultures and in the relationship between past and present is evident in the two poems used here.

THE VISITOR

In Spanish he whispers there is no time left.
It is the sound of scythes arcing in wheat,
the ache of some field song in Salvador.

The wind along the prison, cautious
as Francisco's hands on the inside, touching
the walls as he walks, it is his wife's breath
slipping into his cell each night while he
imagines his hand to be hers. It is a small country.

There is nothing one man will not do to another.
1979

DISCUSSION TOPICS

1. Who is the "visitor" in this poem? Is it the poet only?
2. What forms does the whisper of the first line take, and how are these metamorphoses significant in conveying an impression of El Salvador?
3. Why does the speaker say "It is a small country"?

THE COLONEL

WHAT YOU HAVE HEARD is true. I was in his house. His wife carried a tray of coffee and sugar. His daughter filed her nails, his son went out for the night. There were daily papers, pet dogs, a pistol on the cushion beside him. The moon swung bare on its black cord over the house. On the television was a cop show. It was in English. Broken bottles were embedded in the walls around the house to scoop the kneecaps from a man's legs or cut his hands to lace. On the windows there were gratings like those in liquor stores. We had dinner, rack of lamb, good wine, a gold bell was on the table for calling the maid. The maid brought green mangoes, salt, a type of bread. I was asked how I enjoyed the country. There was a brief commercial in Spanish. His wife took everything away. There was some talk then of how difficult it had become to govern. The parrot said hello on the terrace. The colonel told it to shut up, and pushed himself from the table. My friend said to me with his eyes: say nothing. The colonel returned with a sack used to bring groceries home. He spilled many human ears on the table. They were like dried peach halves. There is no other way to say this. He took one of them in his hands, shook it in our faces, dropped it into a water glass. It came alive there. I am tired of fooling around he said. As for the rights of anyone, tell your people they can go fuck themselves. He swept the ears to the floor with his arm and held the last of his wine in the air. Something for your poetry, no? he said. Some of the ears on the floor caught this scrap of his voice. Some of the ears on the floor were pressed to the ground.

May 1978

DISCUSSION TOPICS

1. A prose poem conveys many of the aspects of formal verse, such as rhythm, imagery, and attention to sound patterns, but it captures these qualities in the freer form of a prose paragraph. What poetic attributes emerge in this description? How would the effect of the poem be changed had the poet used conventional poetic form or even free verse?
2. How do the details related here provide a portrait of the colonel? Consider not only the man himself but also his surroundings.
3. In Forché's volume of poems *The Country Between Us* (1981), "The Colonel" directly follows "The Visitor." In what ways is this arrangement significant?

GARY SOTO (1952–   ) Chicano poet-teacher, winner of the United States Award of the International Poetry Forum in 1976. His poems often focus on individual rather than collective pain.

GRACIELA

    Wedding night
    Graciela bled lightly—
    But enough to stain his thighs—
    And left an alphabet
5   Of teeth marks on his arm.
    At this, he was happy.
    They drank mescal
    In bed like the rich
    And smoked cigarettes.
10 She asleep
    And the bottle empty, he hid
    A few coins in her left shoe,
    Earrings in the right.
    They worked long hours
15 Hoeing crooked rows of maize.
    Evenings she wove rugs
    And embroidered curtains
    To market in Taxco.
    In short they lived well.
20 However in the seventh month
    With child, her belly
    Rising like a portion of the sun,
    Something knotted inside her.
    The ribs ached. A fever climbed.

25   Manuel summoned the Partera
    And though she burned pepper,
    And tied belts around
    The stretched belly,
    The child did not ease out.
30   Days later she turned
    Onto her belly
    And between her legs
    Unraveled a spine of blood.

18 *Taxco:* Taxco de Alarcón, a city in the south of Mexico.   25 *Partera:* midwife

DISCUSSION TOPICS

1. The name Graciela comes from the word "grace." In what ways might this derivation be significant in reading the story of these two lovers?
2. Why does the image of blood recur at the beginning and end of the poem? Compare Poe's "The Masque of the Red Death." What symbolic qualities does blood have in Poe's tale and this poem?

ROBERT SWIFT (1954–   ) Poet, journalist, copywriter. He studied creative writing at Centenary College of Louisiana and has published two collections of poems, *Green Meadows* (1980) and *Polarities* (1981).

ALTER EGOS

    Two embroidered birds on silk
    Made in China long ago
    Perch on embroidered tree limbs
    In bamboo frames on the wall.
    One has long legs and a beak for fish,
    The other has claws and keen eyes.
    They face each other, unaware
    That they share the same sky on the wall.

    The fisher has patience he learned from lagoons,
    He looks through reflections on shallow light
    To see minnows shine in the sun.
    He strikes while standing very still,
    Then eats until they fill him,
    And then he glides back home.

The hunter is wind in a storm as it blows,
He strikes by descent to his shadow below
On the prey that has seen its last light.
He knows the sound of a rabbit's cry
And the taste of its trembling fear.
He sleeps among stones in the clouds.

The two methods vary
But they're both birds of prey
And they both fill a space on the wall.
But the wall
Is just part
Of the house.

DISCUSSION TOPICS

1. What is the significance of the poem's title?
2. Compare this poem with Dickinson's "A Bird Came Down the Walk" and Frost's "Design."

WRITING TOPIC

First argue that Swift's poem is more concerned with similarities than with differences. Then reverse your line of argument and pursue the possibility that he is emphasizing differences rather than similarities. Which seems more valid and why? How does your argument fit the last stanza?

BOXES AND CHEESE

You're in a car
On a street
And the light up above you is red.
You wait for the color to change.
The green light comes on
And you go.
Conditioning is such a subtle thing,
One wonders where it ends.

Reading Drama

It is helpful to say at the outset what the root meaning of the word *drama* is.

It is "to do." That is, drama is doing, acting; it is what Northrop Frye has called "words acted in front of a spectator."

That is what it was when the ancient Greeks enacted plays two and a half millennia ago, when self-righteous Oedipus shouted accusations against Teiresias. That is what it was when English actors tossed Mak the sheepstealer in a blanket some five or six centuries ago and when Noah's wife kicked Noah's shins in medieval plays. That is what it was when Hamlet plunged his sword into Polonius, Laertes, and Claudius in the early seventeenth century. And that is what it is when Rosencrantz and Guildenstern toss coins that come up the same way eighty-nine times and more in a modern absurdist play.

Drama is action. It is conflict. It is dialogue that "dramatizes" the action and conflict—often internal as much as physical and external. The dialogue may soar to lyrical heights of romantic fancy, as in Romeo's words:

But soft! what light through yonder window breaks?
It is the east, and Juliet is the sun!

Or the words may capture the emotions of a distraught Ophelia as she tries to articulate the sense of loss when she believes her Hamlet to be insane:

O what a noble mind is here o'erthrown!
The courtier's, soldier's, scholar's eye, tongue, sword,
The expectancy and rose of the fair state,
The glass of fashion and the mould of form,
The observed of all observers, quite, quite down,
And I of ladies most deject and wretched,
That sucked the honey of his music vows,
Now see that noble and most sovereign reason
Like sweet bells jangled, out of tune and harsh,
That unmatched form and feature of blown youth
Blasted with ecstasy; O woe is me
To have seen what I have seen, see what I see!

The dialogue may dramatize the pathos of self-blinded Oedipus as he reaches out for his sister-daughters:

But my two girls, my poor unhappy daughters,
Who never knew what it was to eat a meal
Away from their father's side, but had their share

581

Of every little thing I had myself. . . .
Please look after them. And I beg this favor now,
Let me lay my hands on them and weep with them.
Please, my lord,
Please, noble heart. If I could touch them now
I should think they were with me, as if I could see them.
[Enter Antigone and Ismene]
What is that?
Oh you gods; is it my darlings that I hear
Sobbing? Has Creon taken pity on me
And sent my darlings, sent my children to me?
Am I right?

There is also the dialogue of high wit in a comedy of manners:

> LADY BRACKNELL: Algernon is an extremely, I may almost say an ostenta-
> tiously, eligible young man. He has nothing, but he looks everything. What
> more can one desire?
>
> JACK: It pains me very much to have to speak frankly to you, Lady Bracknell,
> about your nephew, but the fact is that I do not approve at all of his moral
> character. I suspect him of being untruthful.
>
> LADY BRACKNELL: Untruthful! My nephew Algernon? Impossible! He is an
> Oxonian.

And it is more: the intensity of poetry and the scope of fiction, the development of characters who show and tell us what they are without a narrator's media-
tion, the sweep of philosophical and moral concerns or of the battlefield at Agin-
court, the farce of tossing slop jars.

It has been all of this for over two thousand years of Western tradition, as
we can see from Aristotle's *Poetics* and the plays that have come down to us from
his era and earlier. He saw what we still recognize as "drama": the imitation of
an action. This was the foremost of his six "formative elements," and we still have
the other five also, though different translations and different interpretations suggest various meanings of some of them to us. Those other five are often given in
simple terms as character (moral bent), thought (intellect), diction, music, and
spectacle. It is not difficult to see the relevance of all of these in modern plays, even
though the meanings of at least two of them, character and thought, are not so
simple as those words might suggest. Nevertheless, we know that ethics, the
manner of thought processes, the ways of expressing oneself were important to
Aristotle, as they are to us, just as music and scenery and lighting are.

Aristotle thus dealt consciously with formal and structural matters, like the
unity and completeness of action, and the peripeties, or reversals, action may have;
with the psychological and moral aspects of characters; and with the nuances of
their speech. In a sense he dealt with some other highly important matters almost
incidentally, like the mythic elements of the stories. He knew, as all Greek audiences knew—it was as simple as breathing the air of Athens—that their plays dealt

582

with gods, with the heroes of their past, with the myths and history that shaped their culture at least from the time of Homer. They may not have used the word *archetype,* Greek though it is, but they recognized their "chief symbols"—the wise old man Teiresias, the libidinous forces in the bacchic women, the terrible mother Clytemnestra, the dark shadow-side of the otherwise good and solicitous Oedipus, the overly repressive superego of Hippolytus. They needed no Jung or Freud to give technical names to these deep psychic forces. Myth, viable as well as vital, was the stuff of their daily, conscious lives.

In short, the drama of the Greeks early went to the heart of the matter, and the earliest of the supreme critics soon came to articulate his insights in formulas that have provided critics ever since with germinal ideas—what we now call formalist or psychological or mythic criticism. We can explore these concepts more fully in their dramatic implications after we read a modern tragedy that lends itself well to study from "modern" points of view—and from Aristotle's. That tragedy, that "imitation of a serious action that is serious [and] complete," with appropriate magnitude and language, is John Millington Synge's *Riders to the Sea.*

RIDERS TO THE SEA

Characters

MAURYA (an old woman)
BARTLEY (her son)
CATHLEEN (her daughter)
NORA (a younger daughter)
MEN AND WOMEN

Scene: *An Island off the West of Ireland.*

[*Cottage kitchen, with nets, oil-skins, spinning wheel, some new boards standing by the wall, etc. Cathleen, a girl of about twenty, finishes kneading cake, and puts it down in the pot-oven by the fire; then wipes her hands, and begins to spin at the wheel. Nora, a young girl, puts her head in at the door.*]

NORA (*in a low voice*).   Where is she?

CATHLEEN.   She's lying down, God help her, and may be sleeping, if she's able.

[*Nora comes in softly, and takes a bundle from under her shawl.*]

CATHLEEN (*spinning the wheel rapidly*).   What is it you have?

NORA.   The young priest is after bringing them. It's a shirt and a plain stocking were got off a drowned man in Donegal.

[*Cathleen stops her wheel with a sudden movement, and leans out to listen.*]

NORA.   We're to find out if it's Michael's they are, some time herself will be down looking by the sea.

CATHLEEN.   How would they be Michael's, Nora. How would he go the length of that way to the far north?

NORA.   The young priest says he's known the like of it. "If it's Michael's they are," says he, "you can tell herself he's got a clean burial by the grace of God, and if they're not his, let no one say a word about them, for she'll be getting her death," says he, "with crying and lamenting."

[*The door which Nora half closed is blown open by a gust of wind.*]

CATHLEEN (*looking out anxiously*).   Did you ask him would he stop Bartley going this day with the horses to the Galway fair?

NORA.   "I won't stop him," says he, "but let you not be afraid. Herself does be saying prayers half through the night, and the Almighty God won't leave her destitute," says he, "with no son living."

CATHLEEN.   Is the sea bad by the white rocks, Nora?

NORA.   Middling bad, God help us. There's a great roaring in the west, and it's worse it'll be getting when the tide's turned to the wind.

[*She goes over to the table with the bundle.*]

Shall I open it now?

CATHLEEN.   Maybe she'd wake up on us, and come in before we'd done. (*Coming to the table*). It's a long time we'll be, and the two of us crying.

NORA (*goes to the inner door and listens*).   She's moving about on the bed. She'll be coming in a minute.

CATHLEEN.   Give me the ladder, and I'll put them up in the turf-loft, the way she won't know of them at all, and maybe when the tide turns she'll be going down to see would he be floating from the east.

[*They put the ladder against the gable of the chimney; Cathleen goes up a few steps and hides the bundle in the turf-loft. Maurya comes from the inner room.*]

MAURYA (*looking up at Cathleen and speaking querulously*).   Isn't it turf enough you have for this day and evening?

CATHLEEN.   There's a cake baking at the fire for a short space (*throwing down the turf*) and Bartley will want it when the tide turns if he goes to Connemara.

[*Nora picks up the turf and puts it round the pot-oven.*]

MAURYA (*sitting down on a stool at the fire*).   He won't go this day with the wind rising from the south and west. He won't go this day, for the young priest will stop him surely.

584

NORA. He'll not stop him, mother, and I heard Eamon Simon and Stephen Pheety and Colum Shawn saying he would go.

MAURYA. Where is he itself?

NORA. He went down to see would there be another boat sailing in the week, and I'm thinking it won't be long till he's here now, for the tide's turning at the green head, and the hooker's tacking from the east.

CATHLEEN. I hear some one passing the big stones.

NORA (*looking out*). He's coming now, and he in a hurry.

BARTLEY (*comes in and looks round the room. Speaking sadly and quietly*). Where is the bit of new rope, Cathleen, was bought in Connemara?

CATHLEEN (*coming down*). Give it to him, Nora; it's on a nail by the white boards. I hung it up this morning, for the pig with the black feet was eating it.

NORA (*giving him a rope*). Is that it, Bartley?

MAURYA. You'd do right to leave that rope, Bartley, hanging by the boards. (*Bartley takes the rope.*) It will be wanting in this place, I'm telling you, if Michael is washed up to-morrow morning, or the next morning, or any morning in the week, for it's a deep grave we'll make him by the grace of God.

BARTLEY (*beginning to work with the rope*). I've no halter the way I can ride down on the mare, and I must go now quickly. This is the one boat going for two weeks or beyond it, and the fair will be a good fair for horses I heard them saying below.

MAURYA. It's a hard thing they'll be saying below if the body is washed up and there's no man in it to make the coffin, and I after giving a big price for the finest white boards you'd find in Connemara.

[*She looks round at the boards.*]

BARTLEY. How would it be washed up, and we after looking each day for nine days, and a strong wind blowing a while back from the west and south?

MAURYA. If it wasn't found itself, that wind is raising the sea, and there was a star up against the moon, and it rising in the night. If it was a hundred horses, or a thousand horses you had itself, what is the price of a thousand horses against a son where there is one son only?

BARTLEY (*working at the halter, to Cathleen*). Let you go down each day, and see the sheep aren't jumping in on the rye, and if the jobber comes you can sell the pig with the black feet if there is a good price going.

MAURYA. How would the like of her get a good price for a pig?

BARTLEY (*to Cathleen*). If the west wind holds with the last bit of the moon let you and Nora get up weed enough for another cock for the kelp. It's hard set we'll be from this day with no one in it but one man to work.

MAURYA. It's hard set we'll be surely the day you're drownd'd with the rest. What way will I live and the girls with me, and I an old woman looking for the grave?

[*Bartley lays down the halter, takes off his old coat, and puts on a newer one of the same flannel.*]

BARTLEY (*to Nora*).   Is she coming to the pier?

NORA (*looking out*).   She's passing the green head and letting fall her sails.

BARTLEY (*getting his purse and tobacco*).   I'll have half an hour to go down, and you'll see me coming again in two days, or in three days, or maybe in four days if the wind is bad.

MAURYA (*turning round to the fire, and putting her shawl over her head*).   Isn't it a hard and cruel man won't hear a word from an old woman, and she holding him from the sea?

CATHLEEN.   It's the life of a young man to be going on the sea, and who would listen to an old woman with one thing and she saying it over?

BARTLEY (*taking the halter*).   I must go now quickly. I'll ride down on the red mare, and the gray pony'll run behind me. . . . The blessing of God on you.

[*He goes out.*]

MAURYA (*crying out as he is in the door*).   He's gone now, God spare us, and we'll not see him again. He's gone now, and when the black night is falling I'll have no son left me in the world.

CATHLEEN.   Why wouldn't you give him your blessing and he looking round in the door? Isn't it sorrow enough is on every one in this house without your sending him out with an unlucky word behind him, and a hard word in his ear?

[*Maurya takes up the tongs and begins raking the fire aimlessly without looking round.*]

NORA (*turning towards her*).   You're taking away the turf from the cake.

CATHLEEN (*crying out*).   The Son of God forgive us, Nora, we're after forgetting his bit of bread.

[*She comes over to the fire.*]

NORA.   And it's destroyed he'll be going till dark night, and he after eating nothing since the sun went up.

CATHLEEN (*turning the cake out of the oven*).   It's destroyed he'll be, surely. There's no sense left on any person in a house where an old woman will be talking for ever.

[*Maurya sways herself on her stool.*]

CATHLEEN (*cutting off some of the bread and rolling it in a cloth; to Maurya*).   Let you go down now to the spring well and give him this and he passing. You'll see him then and the dark word will be broken, and you can say "God speed you," the way he'll be easy in his mind.

MAURYA (*taking the bread*).   Will I be in it as soon as himself?

CATHLEEN.   If you go now quickly.

MAURYA (*standing up unsteadily*).   It's hard set I am to walk.

CATHLEEN (*looking at her anxiously*).   Give her the stick, Nora, or maybe she'll slip on the big stones.

NORA.   What stick?

CATHLEEN.   The stick Michael brought from Connemara.

MAURYA (*taking a stick Nora gives her*).   In the big world the old people do be leaving things after them for their sons and children, but in this place it is the young men do be leaving things behind for them that do be old.

[*She goes out slowly. Nora goes over to the ladder.*]

CATHLEEN.   Wait, Nora, maybe she'd turn back quickly. She's that sorry, God help her, you wouldn't know the thing she'd do.

NORA.   Is she gone round by the bush?

CATHLEEN (*looking out*).   She's gone now. Throw it down quickly, for the Lord knows when she'll be out of it again.

NORA (*getting the bundle from the loft*).   The young priest said he'd be passing to-morrow, and we might go down and speak to him below if it's Michael's they are surely.

CATHLEEN (*taking the bundle*).   Did he say what way they were found?

NORA (*coming down*).   "There were two men," says he, "and they rowing round with poteen before the cocks crowed, and the oar of one of them caught the body, and they passing the black cliffs of the north."

CATHLEEN (*trying to open the bundle*).   Give me a knife, Nora, the string's perished with the salt water, and there's a black knot on it you wouldn't loosen in a week.

NORA (*giving her a knife*).   I've heard tell it was a long way to Donegal.

CATHLEEN (*cutting the string*).   It is surely. There was a man in here a while ago —the man sold us that knife—and he said if you set off walking from the rocks beyond, it would be seven days you'd be in Donegal.

NORA.   And what time would a man take, and he floating?

[*Cathleen opens the bundle and takes out a bit of a stocking. They look at them eagerly.*]

CATHLEEN (*in a low voice*).   The Lord spare us, Nora! isn't it a queer hard thing to say if it's his they are surely?

NORA.   I'll get his shirt off the hook the way we can put the one flannel on the other. (*She looks through some clothes hanging in the corner.*) It's not with them, Cathleen, and where will it be?

CATHLEEN.   I'm thinking Bartley put it on him in the morning, for his own shirt was heavy with the salt in it (*pointing to the corner*). There's a bit of a sleeve was of the same stuff. Give me that and it will do.

[*Nora brings it to her and they compare the flannel.*]

CATHLEEN.   It's the same stuff, Nora; but if it is itself aren't there great rolls of it in the shops of Galway, and isn't it many another man may have a shirt of it as well as Michael himself?

NORA (*who has taken up the stocking and counted the stitches, crying out*).   It's Michael, Cathleen, it's Michael; God spare his soul, and what will herself say when she hears this story, and Bartley on the sea?

CATHLEEN (*taking the stocking*).   It's a plain stocking.

NORA.   It's the second one of the third pair I knitted, and I put up three score stitches, and I dropped four of them.

CATHLEEN (*counts the stitches*).   It's that number is in it (*crying out*). Ah, Nora, isn't it a bitter thing to think of him floating that way to the far north, and no one to keen him but the black hags that do be flying on the sea?

NORA (*swinging herself round, and throwing out her arms on the clothes*).   And isn't it a pitiful thing when there is nothing left of a man who was a great rower and fisher, but a bit of an old shirt and a plain stocking?

CATHLEEN (*after an instant*).   Tell me is herself coming, Nora? I hear a little sound on the path.

NORA (*looking out*).   She is, Cathleen. She's coming up to the door.

CATHLEEN.   Put these things away before she'll come in. Maybe it's easier she'll be after giving her blessing to Bartley, and we won't let on we've heard anything the time he's on the sea.

NORA (*helping Cathleen to close the bundle*).   We'll put them here in the corner.

[*They put them into a hole in the chimney corner. Cathleen goes back to the spinning-wheel.*]

NORA.   Will she see it was crying I was?

CATHLEEN.   Keep your back to the door the way the light'll not be on you.

[*Nora sits down at the chimney corner, with her back to the door. Maurya comes in very slowly, without looking at the girls, and goes over to her stool at the other side of the fire. The cloth with the bread is still in her hand. The girls look at each other, and Nora points to the bundle of bread.*]

CATHLEEN (*after spinning for a moment*).   You didn't give him his bit of bread?

[*Maurya begins to keen softly, without turning round.*]

CATHLEEN.   Did you see him riding down?

[*Maurya goes on keening.*]

CATHLEEN (*a little impatiently*).   God forgive you; isn't it a better thing to raise your voice and tell what you seen, than to be making lamentation for a thing that's done? Did you see Bartley, I'm saying to you.

588

MAURYA (*with a weak voice*). My heart's broken from this day.

CATHLEEN (*as before*). Did you see Bartley?

MAURYA. I seen the fearfulest thing.

CATHLEEN (*leaves her wheel and looks out*). God forgive you; he's riding the mare now over the green head, and the gray pony behind him.

MAURYA (*starts, so that her shawl falls back from her head and shows her white tossed hair. With a frightened voice*). The gray pony behind him.

CATHLEEN (*coming to the fire*). What is it ails you, at all?

MAURYA (*speaking very slowly*). I've seen the fearfulest thing any person has seen, since the day Bride Dara seen the dead man with the child in his arms.

CATHLEEN AND NORA. Uah.

[*They crouch down in front of the old woman at the fire.*]

NORA. Tell us what it is you seen.

MAURYA. I went down to the spring well, and I stood there saying a prayer to myself. Then Bartley came along, and he riding on the red mare with the gray pony behind him. (*She puts up her hands, as if to hide something from her eyes.*) The Son of God spare us, Nora!

CATHLEEN. What is it you seen.

MAURYA. I seen Michael himself.

CATHLEEN (*speaking softly*). You did not, mother; It wasn't Michael you seen, for his body is after being found in the far north, and he's got a clean burial by the grace of God.

MAURYA (*a little defiantly*). I'm after seeing him this day, and he riding and galloping. Bartley came first on the red mare; and I tried to say "God speed you," but something choked the words in my throat. He went by quickly; and "the blessing of God on you," says he, and I could say nothing. I looked up then, and I crying, at the gray pony, and there was Michael upon it—with fine clothes on him, and new shoes on his feet.

CATHLEEN (*begins to keen*). It's destroyed we are from this day. It's destroyed, surely.

NORA. Didn't the young priest say the Almighty God wouldn't leave her destitute with no son living?

MAURYA (*in a low voice, but clearly*). It's little the like of him knows of the sea. . . . Bartley will be lost now, and let you call in Eamon and make me a good coffin out of the white boards, for I won't live after them. I've had a husband, and a husband's father, and six sons in this house—six fine men, though it was a hard birth I had with every one of them and they coming to the world—and some of them were found and some of them were not found, but they're gone now the lot of them. . . . There were Stephen, and Shawn, were lost in the great wind, and found after in the Bay of Gregory of the Golden Mouth, and carried up the two of them on the one plank, and in by that door.

[*She pauses for a moment, the girls start as if they heard something through the door that is half open behind them.*]

NORA (*in a whisper*).   Did you hear that, Cathleen? Did you hear a noise in the north-east?

CATHLEEN (*in a whisper*).   There's some one after crying out by the seashore.

MAURYA (*continues without hearing anything*).   There was Sheamus and his father, and his own father again, were lost in a dark night, and not a stick or sign was seen of them when the sun went up. There was Patch after was drowned out of a curagh that turned over. I was sitting here with Bartley, and he a baby, lying on my two knees, and I seen two women, and three women, and four women coming in, and they crossing themselves, and not saying a word. I looked out then, and there were men coming after them, and they holding a thing in the half of a red sail, and water dripping out of it—it was a dry day, Nora—and leaving a track to the door.

[*She pauses again with her hand stretched out towards the door. It opens softly and old women begin to come in, crossing themselves on the threshold, and kneeling down in front of the stage with red petticoats over their heads.*]

MAURYA (*half in a dream, to Cathleen*).   Is it Patch, or Michael, or what is it at all?

CATHLEEN.   Michael is after being found in the far north, and when he is found there how could he be here in this place?

MAURYA.   There does be a power of young men floating round in the sea, and what way would they know if it was Michael they had, or another man like him, for when a man is nine days in the sea, and the wind blowing, it's hard set his own mother would be to say what man was it.

CATHLEEN.   It's Michael, God spare him, for they're after sending us a bit of his clothes from the far north.

[*She reaches out and hands Maurya the clothes that belonged to Michael. Maurya stands up slowly and takes them in her hands. Nora looks out.*]

NORA.   They're carrying a thing among them and there's water dripping out of it and leaving a track by the big stones.

CATHLEEN (*in a whisper to the women who have come in*).   Is it Bartley it is?

ONE OF THE WOMEN.   It is surely, God rest his soul.

[*Two younger women come in and pull out the table. Then men carry in the body of Bartley, laid on a plank, with a bit of a sail over it, and lay it on the table.*]

CATHLEEN (*to the women, as they are doing so*).   What way was he drowned?

ONE OF THE WOMEN.   The gray pony knocked him into the sea, and he was washed out where there is a great surf on the white rocks.

[*Maurya has gone over and knelt down at the head of the table. The women are keening softly and swaying themselves with a slow movement. Cathleen and Nora kneel at the other end of the table. The men kneel near the door.*]

MAURYA (*raising her head and speaking as if she did not see the people around her*). They're all gone now, and there isn't anything more the sea can do to me. . . . I'll have no call now to be up crying and praying when the wind breaks from the south, and you can hear the surf is in the east, and the surf is in the west, making a great stir with the two noises, and they hitting one on the other. I'll have no call now to be going down and getting Holy Water in the dark nights after Samhain, and I won't care what way the sea is when the other women will be keening. (*To Nora.*) Give me the Holy Water, Nora, there's a small sup still on the dresser.

[*Nora gives it to her.*]

MAURYA (*drops Michael's clothes across Bartley's feet, and sprinkles the Holy Water over him*).   It isn't that I haven't prayed for you, Bartley, to the Almighty God. It isn't that I haven't said prayers in the dark night till you wouldn't know what I'd be saying; but it's a great rest I'll have now, and it's time surely. It's a great rest I'll have now, and great sleeping in the long nights after Samhain, if it's only a bit of wet flour we do have to eat, and maybe a fish that would be stinking.

[*She kneels down again, crossing herself, and saying prayers under her breath.*]

CATHLEEN (*to an old man*).   Maybe yourself and Eamon would make a coffin when the sun rises. We have fine white boards herself bought, God help her, thinking Michael would be found, and I have a new cake you can eat while you'll be working.

THE OLD MAN (*looking at the boards*).   Are there nails with them?

CATHLEEN.   There are not, Colum; we didn't think of the nails.

ANOTHER MAN.   It's a great wonder she wouldn't think of the nails, and all the coffins she's seen made already.

CATHLEEN.   It's getting old she is, and broken.

[*Maurya stands up again very slowly and spreads out the pieces of Michael's clothes beside the body, sprinkling them with the last of the Holy Water.*]

NORA (*in a whisper to Cathleen*).   She's quiet now and easy; but the day Michael was drowned you could hear her crying out from this to the spring well. It's fonder she was of Michael, and would any one have thought that?

CATHLEEN (*slowly and clearly*).   An old woman will be soon tired with anything she will do, and isn't it nine days herself is after crying and keening, and making great sorrow in the house?

MAURYA (*puts the empty cup mouth downwards on the table, and lays her hands together on Bartley's feet*).   They're all together this time, and the end is come. May the Almighty God have mercy on Bartley's soul, and on Michael's soul, and on the souls of Sheamus and Patch, and Stephen and Shawn (*bending her head*); and may He have mercy on my soul, Nora, and on the soul of every one is left living in the world.

[*She pauses, and the keen rises a little more loudly from the women, then sinks away.*]

MAURYA (*continuing*).   Michael has a clean burial in the far north, by the grace of the Almighty God. Bartley will have a fine coffin out of the white boards, and a deep grave surely. What more can we want than that? No man at all can be living for ever, and we must be satisfied.

[*She kneels down again and the curtain falls slowly.*]

Aristotle's six formative elements, once again, are action *(mythos),* character *(ethos),* thought *(dianoia),* diction *(lexis),* music *(melos),* and spectacle *(opsis).* Aristotle discussed much more than these elements in the *Poetics,* but they are especially helpful because they encompass so much of what is the nature of drama as an art form. Let us continue, then, with these in mind as we pursue multiple critical approaches to drama generally and *Riders to the Sea* specifically.

Some argue that in Synge's play there is no "action," in spite of its intense and powerful portrayal of life on a rocky island; this may be so if "action" means the external confrontation of protagonists and antagonists. But to say that this play is not Aristotelian on that ground would strike others as a slim argument. Whether or not its action is Aristotelian, the play is surely a "serious imitation," at least of a family's life at a moment of crisis. Furthermore, there is a movement within the personality of Maurya (the central character) to a mental and emotional stance at the end of the play that differs from her stance at the beginning (Aristotle's *anagnorisis,* or discovery). There is suffering or pathos, as described in the *Poetics,* just as there is hope dashed and as there are fears realized (Aristotle's peripeties). Those who do not see the play as Aristotelian will also note that the central figure is no king or queen, no god or hero, figures whom Aristotle assumed to be appropriate as protagonists. But the central figure, Maurya, is larger than life without losing her realism. She cannot be charged with hubris, the overweening pride discussed by Aristotle; but there is a hint of hubris in the play when her son Bartley does tempt his fate by going to Galway fair with the horses. That tempting of fate takes us closer to the real conflict within the play. Notwithstanding the hint of conflict between Maurya and Bartley, we must observe that she and her family are in conflict not with each other but with forces of nature, with a fate beyond their comprehension. They are doomed as are all human beings, who are all riders to the sea. Taken together, these several elements come close to being the first three of Aristotle's list—action, character, and thought. It is easier to see evidence of the other three—spectacle in the color and stark contrasts of stage properties and movement and music not in instruments or song (though the play has been turned into an opera by Ralph Vaughn Williams), but in the magnificent lilting rhythm that Synge uses in the play and the language itself, which will merit further attention in subsequent discussion.

In other words, it is easy to see much of the subject matter of the six elements manifesting itself in this modern "Aristotelian" play. But let us move on now to what may be an even richer critical approach: the mythic and archetypal appeal of the drama. The sea, to take a major instance, has long been one of the clear forces of the earth, and early mythmakers tried to understand and contend with that force. They gave it names like Neptune and Poseidon, and they made Odysseus contend with it in those parts of his story related to Scylla and Charybdis and to Aeolus, the lord of the winds, the forces of which drove Odysseus's vessel in a storm. As Shelley recognized in his "Ode to the West Wind," the uncontrollable forces of wind and sea lend themselves easily to being archetypes ("chief symbols") for human beings who try to cope with powers. It is hardly surprising that Synge pits these simple persons against such forces to show the human being's dilemma in this swirling cosmos.

If sea and wind are threatening forces, the rocky island that bears these persons up amid these forces provides scant shelter and sustenance for them. The island too is an archetype, and compares with the open boat in Crane's story of that name. Both the island and the dinghy suggest the tenuous grasp of humankind on life. One remembers the correspondent's laconic comment about the bathtub-size of the boat; the island seems hardly more. It is not hard to extrapolate from these two microcosms to all humankind on spaceship Earth, whirling around a small sun in one galaxy of many. The boat/island metaphor suggests a related metaphor or archetype, that of the journey to experience, to knowledge and insight. That is what the correspondent gains, and that is what Maurya gains too (Aristotle's *anagnorisis*), but the knowledge that she and her like gain is at best a dismal acceptance of that which cannot be changed. She and the correspondent can only "interpret" what sea, wind, and shore mean to us, although that is much indeed.

Maurya remains, however, a strong figure who gains her own tragic victory. She is like other Great Mother archetypes who breed and nurture the race in spite of pain. She is the Mater Dolorosa, the bowed head of the Pietà. She is the old woman in "A Death in the Woods." She is the black servant Dilsey in *The Sound and the Fury,* of whom Faulkner said, "They endured." That plural reference ("they") to Dilsey has relevance for us here. It reminds us that Dilsey is not just herself but a race, and perhaps more than "a" race: perhaps she is all enduring races. Like Dilsey, Maurya is a matriarchal figure who endures. Or, to return to classical parallels for a moment, she is Niobe ("all tears," said Hamlet), who challenged the gods and consequently lost all her children (at least in some versions), first her sons, then her daughters. In utter grief, Niobe was finally turned to stone, still weeping. There she retains her fixed state of mourning, like Maurya, the epitome of a mother's losses at the hands of forces beyond her control.

This parallel to a classical myth may be something more than accidental or incidental, for Synge may have had several classical parallels in mind. It is notable that in the first stage direction we are presented a spinning wheel, and shortly thereafter daughter Cathleen is spinning as her sister Nora enters. Cathleen and Nora later cut the cords binding the clothes that they then recognize as those of Michael, their drowned brother. The spinning wheel, the cord, and the confirmation of Michael's death in that symbolic cutting remind us of the three Fates of classic myth: Clotho, who spun the thread of a person's life; Lachesis, who measured out its length; and Atropos, who cut it. Although the parallel is not perfect (two sisters, three Fates), it is clearly possible. Further, the third woman, Maurya, bears a name quite similar to the Greek name for Fate, *Moira.* In this role, these characters also remind us of the two women knitting black wool at the beginning of Marlow's fateful journey in *Heart of Darkness.*

This drawing of parallels is not mere symbol-hunting, and we need not know whether Synge was conscious of them. The point is that much of the enduring power of Synge's play derives from major concerns in human history—motherhood, death and loss, the forces of nature, the sense that our lives at best are only partially under our control.

That is why this tragedy, brief though it is, has its own kind of scope. Aristotle indicated that a tragedy should have magnitude, and this play surely is less in size than *Hamlet* or even the brief classical tragedies. But the largeness of the major symbols provides the basis for the extrapolation to all humankind, mentioned earlier. Because of the elemental powers these symbols represent, the play has sufficient magnitude and depth to arouse the emotions of pity and fear, the stimulation of which, Aristotle said, would make the members of the audience experience a *catharsis,* or cleansing.

At least one more classical parallel helps to show the continuity of this play with its tradition: the chorus of women who come in near the end of the play. Like various choruses in classical theater (the bereaved mothers in Euripides's *The Suppliants* is a direct parallel), they represent the community that shares in this experience. Not quite archetypes, perhaps, they nevertheless have a symbolic role. They extend in an obvious way the pathos of one family to the whole island and beyond, even to us. We can find other parallels. T. S. Eliot, for example, was also to use the device of the chorus in modern theater. In *Murder in the Cathedral,* a play with an ethos quite different from that of Synge, the chorus of townswomen represents Canterbury and, again, all human beings who try to understand how their lives intersect with transcendent forces and realities. So here with these women of Aran, and when next a person drowns off the island's rocky coast, Maurya, Cathleen, and Nora will join in the chorus of keening women.

Thus far our critical approaches to *Riders to the Sea* have mostly been Aristotelian and mythic or archetypal. But we have just noted that the island is one of the Arans, off the western coast of Ireland and near Galway, mentioned in the play.

594

Knowing this information brings us to some other critical approaches, such as the biographical and historical. For example, we know that Synge went to the Arans at the suggestion of William Butler Yeats, making several trips to study the people and the scene, to hear their language, and ultimately, to write. Since Synge described his sojourns in *The Aran Islands,* we know that the play's setting is real and factually perceived. Its sense of elemental life is something that a biography of Synge would present to us. He saw the rocks, the barrenness, the dangerous surf, and he heard tales of drownings and coffins. Indeed, the starkness of the play compares with that of scenes in the documentary film *Man of Aran,* made in 1934 by Robert Flaherty, who acknowledged Synge's influence. As in the instance of Stephen Crane's "The Open Boat," great art often is an imaginative work founded on some form of direct experience, so it is with Synge's play.

Beyond the physical reality thus evoked, Synge also uses the religious ambiance of the islanders. Traditionally conscious of their Roman Catholic culture, the Irish people of this work are like those in the works of other Irishmen like Sean O'Casey and James Joyce. Some of the characters in the works of these writers merely acquiesce in the acceptance of the traditional faith, as Nora and Cathleen seem to accept the words of their priest. In other characters, we can see a sense of frustration, even of revolt coming through. In *Riders to the Sea* it seems that we have something of both, for the acceptance of divine benevolence alluded to early in the play has only an ironic relevance by the end. In this sense, the religious milieu is part of a cultural or sociological approach to the play, not just a theological one. These several approaches evolve finally into a philosophical approach as we sense not a benevolent God at the end but a dispassionate universe that controls the fates of these persons. It may be significant that one of the play's scriptural echoes is just as negative as the classical myths mentioned earlier. It comes when Maurya reports seeing Bartley riding away on a red mare with a gray pony behind him. What frightens her is that on the gray pony sits the dead Michael. That Bartley rides to death after his mother sees such a vision reminds us of a passage in Revelation 6:8—

> And I looked, and behold a pale horse: and
> his name that sat on him was Death.

It is an ominous image, as it is in the title of Katharine Anne Porter's well-known novella *Pale Horse, Pale Rider.*

Yet all is not bleak, as we have observed: Maurya does endure. There has been keening before. That there will be keening again, a ritual reenactment of the world's grief, is a kind of victory after all. That victory is celebrated by appropriate language, a point that brings us to still another interpretive approach, the linguistic or stylistic, and compares with Aristotle's *lexis.* For the perpetuating of life is caught up in a celebratory language, one appropriate to ritual and a cyclical series of events. Clearly Synge tried to make that language rich and vibrant, with a distinct rhythmic quality. It is *lexis* and *melos* together, transmuted from the Gaelic that Synge actually heard on the Arans into a dialectal English that has its own poetry.

595

The rhythms are everywhere, in Bartley's speech, in the conversation of the daughters, most especially in Maurya's great final speeches. At first she seems only crushed: "They're all gone now, and there isn't anything more the sea can do to me." But here too is insight (*anagnorisis*), and the simple rhythms catch it up: "it's a great rest I'll have now, and it's time surely." Her final sentence—"No man at all can be living for ever, and we must be satisfied"—compares with that at the end of *Oedipus*. It is tragic, but a tragic victory caught in the rhythm and meaning of words.

Much of what has been said already applies to a formalistic approach—the language, rhythm, and symbols of drama contribute to the form of a play, just as they do to the forms of poems and stories. A play, however, stresses action, as Aristotle noted, and its components are often related to conflict. Thus action, with its complication, crisis, and resolution, offers in many plays a form that can be sketched in a triangular or pyramidal shape. Similarly, Aristotle's peripety points to reversals in the movement of a play, to turns, whether they be upward or downward. In *Riders to the Sea* we have virtually all of these forms, and have sufficiently hinted at them if we have not always elaborated on them. However, we may note further that aspect of form to which the word *tension,* as a modern critical term, seems especially to apply, along with irony and paradox. There is in this play, as in most, a pattern of tension, a pull between opposites that must be ultimately reconciled. Specifically, there is tension between the ominous expectation that Michael's drowned body will be found and the knowledge that a body has already been found. There is the tension between the hope that after all there will be no finding of his body (with the possibility that he is alive) and the knowledge that bodies show up far away. There is the tension that the clothes may or may not provide confirmation. There is the tension between the realization that Bartley is challenging his fate and the awareness that ultimately he can only lose. With the discovery of Michael's body, with the symbolic as well as the actual cutting of the bindings on the clothes, and with Bartley's drowning, all the tensions are successively resolved in the action of the play. Parallel with these is the irony that there is a hint of conflict between Maurya and her last remaining son, for as he leaves she gives him not her blessing but only an "unlucky" and a "dark" word. This "word" points to the ultimate paradox. Maurya, this Great Mother archetype, this quintessential mother, sends her last son to death, doing what all mothers do: They give life to children so that the children may die, riding to the sea.

In that paradox is the ultimate form—the essential meaning—of the play.

We wish to address one final approach to the reading of the plays in this collection. We have an anomaly whenever plays are to be read. We began our commentary by noting that drama is *doing,* and that drama is "words acted in front of a spectator." Yet now we are about to embark upon the reading of plays, not the acting of them.

The read play, it has been said, is really a poem. That might be a bit of verbal trickery, but clearly the response that the readers make to a play is analogous to what we do when we read a story or a poem. All the actions, the intonations, the very props and stage lighting must exist in the reader's theater of the mind. To respond to the spirit of the play when it is read, not acted, we must yield to that spirit, and must become actor, director, and lighting technician. We must interpret, as they would, so as to experience the play. Thus the readers of *Oedipus* must sense the stately pace of the words and must move with the choreography and chants of the chorus. Then we will experience the ancient Greeks' sense that these characters are larger than daily life, fit personages to wrestle with gods and with eternal questions of destiny.

Conversely, how can we fully enjoy the farce of *Lysistrata* and some portions of *The Marriage Proposal, The Gap,* and *Rosencrantz and Guildenstern Are Dead* without first working into the mood for high silliness? There is no audience laughter to support our smiles; there is not even the sound-track laughter that modern television supplies so that the viewer, watching alone perhaps, senses the communal activity that laughter usually connotes. Instead, we must be responsive to the play of words, must visualize a character's concern about frustrated sexuality and characters confusing their own identities, and must supply the timing in the delivery of speeches. In such ways we place ourselves directly into the play, as actor, director, and technician, and experience the play from multiple points of view. The rewards of reading comedy are not identical with those of viewing, but they are real rewards.

If reading comedies, or plays with comic elements, brings its own rewards, then perhaps even more so is this true of reading plays like *Hamlet* and *Death of a Salesman.* The read play is a poem. Surely the poetry of *Hamlet* is evidence of that assertion. But it is not just poetry in the limited sense of meter and imagery and heightened language. *Hamlet* is the poetry of thought, of philosophical debate, of theological conflict, of the depths of psychology. *Hamlet* as a read play gives the reader opportunity to appreciate slowly, even deliberately, both the words and the thoughts. When the Romantic critics said that Shakespeare should be read and not acted, they went too far: Shakespeare himself would not have agreed. But they had some truth too. Reading a play of depth enables us to appreciate and ponder in a way that seeing the play enacted might not do—at least not on a first viewing. *Rosencrantz and Guildenstern,* comical and farcical though it is, offers depths as well, and its ironies and existential dilemmas call forth a response to those elements in Shakespeare's earlier creation, on which this play is based. We may laugh—but we must be a bit unsettled at the same time. Although Willie Loman the salesman and the other characters of *Death of a Salesman* might not call up the greatness of Shakespeare's creations, they too and the themes they suggest are sufficient for us to think with and to feel with. We may visualize their doings and mentally hear their sayings—and for a moment put down the book and think about them. As viewers, we cannot stop stage action in that way.

So drama is doing, and we must never forget that. But drama can be read, and can offer its special tautness and structures and conventions to the reader. Let us respond in the special ways demanded by the read play.

SOPHOCLES (495–406 B.C.) This ancient Greek perceived and described with terrible clarity in *Oedipus the King* how chance, religious fatalism, and human weakness combine to destroy a basically good man. In doing this, he set the pattern for writers of tragedy from his own day to ours, and there is scarcely a question that contemporary drama poses that is not anticipated in *Oedipus*—for example, the reduction of man to an automaton and the essential absurdity (that is, unreasonableness) of evil.

OEDIPUS THE KING

Translated and edited by Peter D. Arnott

Characters

PRIEST
OEDIPUS *King of Thebes*
CREON *brother of* JOCASTA
CHORUS *of Theban elders*
TEIRESIAS *a blind prophet*
JOCASTA *wife of* OEDIPUS
FIRST MESSENGER
HERDSMAN
SECOND MESSENGER
ANTIGONE *and* ISMENE *daughters of* OEDIPUS *and* JOCASTA (*nonspeaking parts*)
Citizens of Thebes, Attendants

Scene: *Before the palace of* OEDIPUS *in Thebes.*

[*A crowd of Theban citizens—priests, young men and children—kneel in supplication before the palace, wearing wreaths and carrying branches. Enter* OEDIPUS *from the palace to address them.*]

OEDIPUS   My children, in whom old Cadmus is reborn,
   Why have you come with wreathed boughs in your hands
   To sit before me as petitioners?
   The town is full of smoke from altar-fires
   And voices crying, and appeals to heaven.
   I thought it, children, less than just to hear
   Your cause at second-hand, but come in person—
   I, Oedipus, a name that all men know.
   Speak up, old man; for you are qualified
   To be their spokesman. What is in your minds?   10

1 *Cadmus:* legendary founder of Thebes. He killed the dragon guarding the site and sowed its teeth in the ground. From them sprang up armed men who fought each other. All were killed except five, who became the ancestors of the Thebans.   2 *wreathed boughs:* branches entwined with wool, the customary symbol of supplication

598

Are you afraid? In need? Be sure I am ready
To do all I can. I should truly be hard-hearted
To have no pity on such prayers as these.

PRIEST   Why, Oedipus, my country's lord and master,
You see us, of all ages, sitting here
Before your altars—some too young to fly
Far from the nest, and others bent with age,
Priests—I of Zeus—and these, who represent
Our youth. The rest sit with their boughs
In the city squares, at both of Pallas' shrines,   20
And where Ismenus' ashes tell the future.
The storm, as you can see, has hit our land
Too hard; she can no longer raise her head
Above the waves of this new sea of blood.
A blight is on the blossoms of the field,
A blight is on the pastured herds, on wives
In childbed; and the curse of heaven, plague,
Has struck, and runs like wildfire through the city,
Emptying Cadmus' house, while black Death reaps
The harvest of our tears and lamentations.   30
Not that we see you as a god, these boys
And I, who sit here at your feet for favors,
But as one pre-eminent in life's affairs
And in man's dealings with the powers above.
For it was you who came to Cadmus' town
And freed us from the monster who enslaved us
With her song, relying on your wits, and knowing
No more than we. Some god was at your side,
As men believe, when you delivered us.
So now, great Oedipus, giant among men,   40
We beg you, all of us who come in prayer,
Find us some remedy—a whisper heard
From heaven, or any human way you know.
In men proved by experience we see
A living promise, both in word and deed.
Greatest of men, give our city back its pride!
Look to your name! This country now remembers
Your former zeal, and hails you as her savior.
Never leave us with a memory of your reign
As one that raised and let us fall again,   50

18 *Zeus:* king of the gods   20 *Pallas:* Athena, goddess of wisdom   21 *Ismenus:* river near Thebes.
Here the reference is to the prophetic shrine of Apollo by the river, where divination by burnt offerings
was practised.   36 *the monster . . . her song:* the Sphinx and the riddle

But lift our city up, and keep it safe.
You came to make us happy years ago,
Good omens; show you are the same man still.
If you continue in your present power
Better a land with citizens than empty.
For city walls without their men are nothing,
Or empty ships, when once the crew has gone.

OED.   Poor children, I already know too well
The desires that bring you here. Yes, I have seen
Your sufferings; but suffer as you may,   60
There is not one of you who knows my pain.
Your griefs are private, every man here mourns
For himself, and for no other; but my heart grieves
At once for the state, and for myself, and you.
So do not think you rouse me from my sleep.
Let me tell you, I have wept, yes, many tears,
And sent my mind exploring every path.
My anxious thought found but one hope of cure
On which I acted—sent Creon, Menoeceus' son,
My own wife's brother, to Apollo's shrine   70
At Delphi, with commission to enquire
What I could say or do to save this town.
Now I am counting the days, and growing anxious
To know what he is doing. It is strange
He should delay so long beyond his time.
But when he comes, I shall be no true man
If I fail to take the course the god has shown us.

PRIEST   Well said, and timely! My friends are signaling
This very moment that Creon is in sight.

OED.   O Lord Apollo, let him bring us news   80
Glad as his face, to give our town good fortune.

PRIEST   I think he brings us comfort; otherwise
He would not wear so thick a crown of laurel.

[*Enter* CREON]

OED.   We shall soon know, he is close enough to hear us.
Prince, brother of my house, Menoeceus' son,
What is the news you bring us from the god?

CREON   Good news! Our sorrows, heavy as they are,
With proper care may yet end happily.

---

70 *Apollo's shrine at Delphi:* most famous and prosperous of Greek oracular shrines, believed to stand
at the geographical center of the earth   83 *crown of laurel:* leaves from Apollo's sacred tree

OED. What is the oracle? So far you have said nothing
  To raise my spirits or to dampen them.   90

CREON If you wish to have it here and now, in public,
  I am ready to speak; if not, to go inside.

OED. Speak before all. The sorrows of my people
  I count of greater weight than life itself.

CREON Then, by your leave, I speak as I was told.
  Phoebus commands us, in plain terms, to rid
  Our land of some pollution, nourished here,
  He says, and not to keep a thing past cure.

OED. How shall we purge ourselves? What stain is this?

CREON By banishing a man, or taking life   100
  For life, since murder brought this storm on us.

OED. Who is the man whose fate the god reveals?

CREON Our country once had Laius for its king,
  My lord, before you came to guide this city.

OED. I have been told as much; I never saw him.

CREON Laius was murdered. Phoebus tells us plainly
  To find his murderers and punish them.

OED. Where on earth are they? An ancient crime,
  A scent grown cold; where shall we find it now?

CREON Here, in this land, he said; seek it and we   110
  Shall find; seek not, and it shall be hidden.

OED. And where did Laius meet his bloody end?
  In the country? The palace? Traveling abroad?

CREON He left us on a visit, as he said,
  To Delphi, and he never came back home.

OED. Could no-one tell you? Had he no companion,
  No witness, who could give you facts to work on?

CREON All were killed but one, who ran away in fright,
  And will swear to only one thing that he saw.

OED. What was that? One thing might give the clue to more   120
  If we had some encouragement, some small beginning.

CREON He said they met with bandits; it was not
  By one man's hands that Laius died, but many.

OED. What bandit would have taken such a risk
  Unless he were bribed—by someone here, in Thebes?

96 *Phoebus:* Apollo

CREON It was suspected; but then our troubles came
  And there was no-one to avenge dead Laius.

OED. It must have been great trouble, that could make you
  Leave the death of royalty unsolved!

CREON The Sphinx, whose riddles made us turn our minds   130
  To things at home, and abandon mysteries.

OED. Then I shall start afresh, and once again
  Find secrets out. Apollo and you too
  Have rightly taken up the dead man's cause.
  You will see me working with you, as is just,
  To avenge the land, and give the god his due.
  It is not on some far-distant friend's behalf
  But on my own, that I shall purge this stain.
  The man whose hand killed Laius might some time
  Feel a desire to do the same to me,   140
  And so by avenging him I protect myself.
  Waste no more time, my children, take away
  Your branches and your wreaths, and leave my steps.
  Have Cadmus' people summoned here and tell them
  I will see to everything. We shall be happy now,
  God helping us, or be forever damned.

[*Exeunt* OEDIPUS *and* CREON]

PRIEST Let us arise, my sons. He promises
  The favors that we first came here to ask.
  May Phoebus who has sent this oracle
  Come to save Thebes, and cure us of the plague!   150

[*Exeunt. Enter* CHORUS *of Theban elders*]

CHORUS Sweet voice of Zeus, what word do you bring
  From golden Pytho to glorious Thebes?
  I am heart-shaken, torn on the rack of fear.
  Apollo, Healer, to whom men cry,
  I tremble before you; what will it please you
  To send us? Some new visitation?
  Or something out of the past, come due
  In fullness of time? Tell me, Voice undying,
  The child of golden Hope.

  Daughter of Zeus, to you first I cry,   160
  Immortal Athena; and then her sister

152 *Pytho:* Delphi

602

Artemis, guardian of our land, enthroned
In honor in our assemblies; Apollo,
Heavenly archer, now shine on us all three,
Champions strong against death; if ever
In time gone by you stood between Thebes
And threatened disaster, turning the fire
Of pestilence from us, come now!

For my sorrows have grown past counting.
The plague is on all our people, and wit   170
Can devise no armor. No more the good earth
Brings forth its crops; women groan in their barren labors,
And you may see, like flying birds,
Souls speeding, one by one,
To join the sunset god; their flight
Is faster than the racing flame.

Thebes dies a new death each moment; her children
Lie in the dust, death's agents, and no-one
Spares them a tear; their wives and gray-haired mothers
Flock screaming to the altars, and pray for their own lives.   180
Above the counterpoint of tears
There rings out clear the healing chant.
Show us, golden child of Zeus,
The smiling face of comfort!

Grim Death is marching on us, not now with clashing shields
But blasts of fiery breath, and the cry goes up around him.
Turn him away from us, drive him from our land!
Come, fair wind, and blow him away
To the vasty halls of the western ocean
Or the Thracian seas, where sailors fear to go.   190
For if night has left any harm undone
Day treads on its heels to finish the work.
Zeus our Father, lord of the bright lightning,
Come with your thunder and destroy!

And we pray Apollo the archer to string his golden bow
And send invincible arrows to fight for us in the field,
And Artemis' blazing torches, that she carries
To light her way through the Lycian mountains.
On the god with gold-bound hair I call,

162 *Artemis:* goddess of childbirth and of wild things   190 *Thracian:* seas off the northeast coast of
Greece, notoriously treacherous. Ares, god of war, was regarded as having his home in this wild region.
198 *Lycian mountains:* in Asia Minor

603

Bacchus, whose name we have made our own,   200
Who comes with a cry of maidens dancing.
Bright comforter, bring the joyous light
Of your torch, stand with us against our foe,
The rogue-god, whom his brothers shun!

[*Enter* OEDIPUS]

OED.   You pray; now for answer. If you are prepared
  To accept what I say, and be your own physician,
  Cure may be yours, and respite from your pain.
  I must speak as a stranger to your story, one
  Unacquainted with the facts; I could not press
  My enquiries far alone, without some clue.   210
  But now I am a Theban among Thebans
  And make this proclamation to the sons
  Of Cadmus: if anyone among you knows
  Who murdered Laius, son of Labdacus,
  I order him to make a full disclosure.
  If he should fear to implicate himself
  By confessing, why, nothing unpleasant will happen;
  He will leave the land unharmed, and that is all.
  If anybody knows another guilty—
  An alien perhaps—then let him not keep silent.   220
  He will earn a reward and my gratitude besides.
  But if you refuse to talk; if anyone
  Is frightened into shielding self or friend,
  Pay good attention to the consequences.
  As lord and master of this land of Thebes
  I declare this man, whoever he may be
  An outlaw; order you to break off speech
  With him, to excommunicate him from your prayers
  And sacrifices, to deny him holy water,
  To drive him from your doors, remembering   230
  That this is our pollution, which the god
  This day revealed to me in oracles.
  In this I show myself on heaven's side,
  One with the murdered man. My solemn curse
  Is on the killer, whether he is hiding
  In lonely guilt or has accomplices.
  May he reap the harm he sowed, and die unblest.
  And what is more, I pray that if this man

---

200 *Bacchus:* Dionysus, god of wine, traditionally born in Thebes from the union of Zeus and a mortal woman, Semele

Should live among my household with my knowledge,
The curse I swore just now should fall on me.   240
I lay the responsibility on you,
For my sake, and the gods', and for our country
Turned to a stricken, god-forsaken waste.
For even if heaven had not shown its hand
Fitness alone forbade such negligence
When one so noble, and your king, had died.
You should have held enquiries. Now since I
Have fallen heir to the power which once was his,
Sleep in his bed, and take his bride to wife,
And since, if he had not been disappointed   250
In his succession, we two would have had
A bond between us, children of one mother,
But as it was, his fortune struck him down,
For all these reasons, I shall fight for him
As I would for my own father, leave no stone
Unturned to find the man who shed his blood
In honor of the son of Labdacus,
Of Polydorus, Cadmus, and Agenor.
For those who disobey my words I pray
The gods to send no harvest to their fields,   260
Their wives no children, but to let them die
In present misery, or worse to come.
But as for you, the rest of Cadmus' children,
Who think as I do, may our ally, Right,
And all the gods be with you evermore.

CHORUS   You put me on my oath and I must speak.
I did not kill him, nor can I point to the man
Who did. It was for Phoebus, who sent the question,
To answer it, and find the murderer.

OED.   What you say is fair enough, but no man living   270
Can force the gods to speak when they do not want to.

CHORUS   By your leave, a second best occurs to me. . . .

OED.   Second or third best, do not keep it from us!

CHORUS   I know Teiresias has powers of vision
Second only to Phoebus. A man who asked of him,
My lord, might find his questions answered.

OED.   Another thing that I have not neglected.
On Creon's bidding I have sent men twice
To bring him; it is strange he is not yet come.

CHORUS   We have nothing else but vague and ancient rumors.   280

OED.   What are they? I must examine every story.

CHORUS   He is said to have been killed by men on the road.

OED.   Yes, so I hear; but no-one knows who did it.

CHORUS   If he has any fear in him, a curse
  Such as you swore will bring him out of hiding.

OED.   Words will not scare a man when actions do not.

CHORUS   But here is one to convict him. They are bringing
  The prophet here at last, the man of god,
  The only one who has the truth born in him.

[*Enter* TEIRESIAS, *led by a boy*]

OED.   Teiresias, all things are known to you,   290
  Open and secret, things of heaven and earth.
  Blind though you are, you sense how terrible
  A plague is on us; and in you, great prophet,
  We find our only means of self-defence.
  We sent—perhaps my messengers have told you—
  To Phoebus; he replied, by one way only
  Could Thebes secure deliverance from the plague,
  By hunting down the murderers of Laius
  And killing them or driving them abroad.
  So grudge us nothing of your bird-cry lore   300
  Or any means of prophecy you know.
  Come, save the city; save yourself and me,
  And heal the foulness spread by Laius' blood.
  We are in your hands. Man knows no finer task
  Than helping friends with all his might and means.

TEIRESIAS.   How terrible is wisdom when it turns
  Against you! All of this I know, but let it
  Slip from my mind, or I should not have come here.

OED.   What is it? Why have you come in so black a mood?

TEIR.   Send me home. It will be easiest for each of us   310
  To bear his own burden to the end, believe me.

OED.   A fine way to talk! You do your motherland
  No kindness by withholding information.

TEIR.   When I see you opening your mouth at the wrong moment
  I take care to avoid a like mistake.

OED.   By heaven, if you know something, do not turn away!
  You see us all on our knees imploring you.

300 *bird-cry lore:* Omens were commonly deduced from the flight of birds.

TEIR.   Yes, for you all know nothing. I shall never
  Reveal my sorrows—not to call them yours.

OED.   What do you say? You know and will not talk?   320
  Do you mean to turn traitor and betray the state?

TEIR.   I wish to cause no pain—to either of us.
  So why ask useless questions? My lips are sealed.

OED.   Why, you old reprobate, you could provoke
  A stone to anger! Will you never speak?
  Can nothing touch you? Is there no end to this?

TEIR.   You blame my temper, but you fail to recognize
  Your own working in you; no, you criticize me!

OED.   And who would not be angry when he hears you
  Talking like this, and holding Thebes in contempt?   330

TEIR.   These things will happen, if I speak or not.

OED.   Then if they must, it is your duty to tell me.

TEIR.   This discussion is at an end. Now, if you like,
  You may be as angry as your heart knows how.

OED.   Then in my anger I will spare you none
  Of my suspicions. This is what I think;
  You helped contrive the plot—no, did it all
  Except the actual killing. If you had
  Your eyesight I should say you did that too.

TEIR.   Indeed? Then listen to what I say. Obey
  Your own pronouncement, and from this day on   340
  Speak not to me or any man here present.
  You are the curse, the defiler of this land.

OED.   You dare fling this at me? Have you no fear?
  Where can you hope for safety after this?

TEIR.   I am safe enough. My strength is in my truth.

OED.   Who put you up to this? No skill of yours!

TEIR.   You did—by forcing me to speak against my will.

OED.   What was it? Say it again, I must be sure.

TEIR.   Did you not understand? Or are you tempting me?

OED.   I have not quite grasped it. Tell it me again.   350

TEIR.   You hunt a murderer; it is yourself.

OED.   You will pay for uttering such slanders twice.

TEIR.   Shall I say something else, to make you angrier still?

OED.   Say what you like, it is a waste of breath.

TEIR.   You have been living in unimagined shame
With your nearest, blind to your own degradation.

OED.   How long do you think such taunts will go unpunished?

TEIR.   For ever, if there is any strength in truth.

OED.   In truth, but not in you. You have no strength,
Failing in sight, in hearing, and in mind.

TEIR.   And you are a fool to say such things to me,   360
Things that the world will soon hurl back at you!

OED.   You live in the dark; you are incapable
Of hurting me or any man with eyes.

TEIR.   Your destiny is not to fall by me.
That is Apollo's task, and he is capable.

OED.   Who is behind this? You? Or is it Creon?

TEIR.   Your ruin comes not from Creon, but yourself.

OED.   Oh wealth! Oh monarchy! Talent which outruns
Its rivals in the cutthroat game of life,   370
How envy dogs your steps, and with what strength,
When tempted by the power the city gave
Into my hands, a gift, and never asked for,
The man I trusted, Creon, my earliest friend,
Yearns to depose me, plots behind my back,
Makes accomplices of conjurers like this
Who sells his tricks to the highest bidder, who looks
Only for profits, and in his art is blind.
Let us hear where you have proved yourself a seer!
Why did you not, when the Singing Bitch was here,   380
Utter one word to set your people free?
For this was not a riddle to be solved
By the first-comer; it cried out for divination.
You were tried and found wanting; neither birds
Nor voices from heaven could help you. Then I came,
I, ignorant Oedipus, and put a stop to her
By using my wits, no lessons from the birds!
And it is I you try to depose, assuming
That you will have a place by Creon's throne.
You and your mastermind will repent your zeal   390
To purge this land. You are old, by the look of you;
If not, you would have learnt the price of boldness.

CHORUS   It seems to me that this man's words were spoken
In anger, Oedipus, and so were yours.

380 *Singing Bitch:* the Sphinx

608

This is not what we need; we ask to know
How we can best obey the oracle.

TEIR.   King though you are, the right of speech must be
The same for all. Here, I am my own master.
I live in Apollo's service, not in yours,
And have no need of Creon to endorse me.   400
Listen to me; you taunt me with my blindness,
But you have eyes, and do not see your sorrows,
Or where you live, or what is in your house.
Do you know whose son you are? You are abhorrent
To your kin on earth and under it, and do not know.
One day your mother's and your father's curse,
A two-tongued lash, will run you out of Thebes,
And you who see so well will then be blind.
What place will not give shelter to your cries?
What corner of Cithairon will not ring with them,   410
When you have understood the marriage song which brought you
From prosperous voyage to uneasy harbor?
And a throng of sorrows that you cannot guess
Will drag you down and level you with those
You have begotten, and your proper self.
So go your way; heap mockery and insult
On Creon and my message; you will be crushed
More miserably than any man on earth.

OED.   Am I to listen to such things from him
Without protest? Out of my sight this instant! Leave my house!   420
Go back where you came from, and be damned!

TEIR.   I would never have come here, if you had not called me.

OED.   If I had known you would rave like this, it would have been
A long time before I asked you to my house.

TEIR.   I am what I am. I pass for a fool to you,
But as sane enough for the parents who begot you.

OED.   Who were they? Wait! What is my father's name?

TEIR.   This day will give you parents and destroy you.

OED.   All the time you talk in riddles, mysteries.

TEIR.   And who can decipher riddles better than you?   430

OED.   Yes, laugh at that! There you will find my greatness!

TEIR.   And it is just this luck that has destroyed you.

OED.   I saved the city; nothing else can matter.

---

410 *Cithairon:* mountain near Thebes where Oedipus was exposed

TEIR.   Very well then, I shall go. Boy, take me home.

OED.   Yes, let him take you. Here you are in the way,
    A hindrance; out of sight is out of mind.

TEIR.   I will go when my errand is done. I do not fear
    Your frown. There is no way that you can harm me.
    Listen to me: the man you have sought so long,
    Threatening, issuing your proclamations   440
    About the death of Laius—he is here,
    Passing for an alien, but soon to be revealed
    A Theban born; and he will find no pleasure
    In this turn of fortune. He who now has eyes
    Will be blind, who now is rich, a beggar,
    And wander abroad with a stick to find his way.
    He will be revealed as father and as brother
    Of the children in his home, as son and husband
    Of the woman who bore him, his father's murderer
    And successor to his bed. Now go away   450
    And think about these things; and if you find I lie
    Then you can say that I am no true prophet.

[*Exeunt* TEIRESIAS *and* OEDIPUS]

CHORUS   Who is the man denounced
    By the voice of god from the Delphian rock?
    Who is the man with bloody hands
    Guilty of horrors the tongue cannot name?
    It is time for him to run
    Faster of foot than the horses of the storm,
    For the Son of Zeus is leaping upon him
    With fire and lightning, and at his side   460
    The Fates, remorseless avengers.

    Fresh from Parnassus' snows
    The call blazes forth: the hunt is up!
    Search every place for the unknown man!
    He doubles among the wild woods for cover,
    From hole to hole in the hills,
    A rogue bull running a lost race, trying
    To shake off the sentence ringing in his ears
    Pronounced by the shrine at earth's center, forever
    Haunting him, goading him on.   470

---

462 *Parnassus:* mountain near Delphi celebrated as the home of Apollo and the Muses, and also as the
haunt of Dionysus

The wise man with his birds and omens
Leaves me troubled and afraid,
Unable to believe or disbelieve.
What can I say? I fly from hope to fear.
Dark is the present, dark the days to come.
There is no quarrel that I know of
Now or in the past between
Labdacus' house and the son of Polybus,
Nothing that I could use as proof
Against Oedipus' reputation   480
In avenging Labdacus' line, and solving
The riddle of Laius' death.

To Zeus and Apollo all things are known,
They see the doings of mankind.
But who is to say that a human prophet
Knows any more of the future than I?
Though some men, I know, are wiser than others.
But I shall never join with his accusers
Until they have made good their charge.
We saw his wisdom tried and tested   490
When he fought the girl with wings.
Thebes took him then to her heart, and I
Will never name him guilty.

[*Enter* CREON]

CREON   Citizens, I hear that Oedipus our king
Lays monstrous charges against me, and am here
In indignation. If in the present crisis
He thinks I have injured him in any way
By word or action calculated to harm him,
I would rather die before my time is up
Than bear this stigma. Such malicious slander   500
Touches me on more than one tender spot.
What hurts me most is this—to have my friends
And you and my city brand me as a traitor.

CHORUS   This insult was probably spoken under stress,
In anger, not with deliberate intent.

CREON   And what about the taunt that the seer was coerced
Into lying by my design? Who started it?

CHORUS   It was said—I do not know how seriously.

491 *the girl with wings:* the Sphinx

CREON   Did he lay this charge against me steady-eyed?   510
   Did he sound as if he knew what he was saying?

CHORUS   I know nothing about it. I do not look at what
   My masters do. Here he comes himself, from the palace.
   [*Enter* Oedipus]

OED.   You! And what brings you here? Can you put on
   So bold a face, to visit your victim's house,
   Shown up for what you are, a murderer
   Openly plotting to rob me of my crown?
   In heaven's name, what did you take me for?
   A fool? A coward? to entertain such schemes?
   Do you think I would let you work behind my back
   Unnoticed, or not take precautions once I knew?   520
   Then is it not senseless, this attempt of yours
   To bid for the throne alone and unsupported?
   It takes men and money to make a revolution.

CREON   Wait! You have said your say; it is now your turn
   To listen. Learn the facts and then pass judgment.

OED.   Smooth talker! But I have no inclination
   To learn from you, my bitter enemy.

CREON   One thing let me say, before we go any further. . . .

OED.   One thing you must never say—that you are honest!   530

CREON   If you think there is any virtue in stubbornness
   Devoid of reason, you have little sense.

OED.   If you think you can wrong one of your family
   and get away unpunished, you are mad.

CREON   Justly said, I grant you. But give me some idea,
   What injury do you say that I have done you?

OED   Did you suggest it would be advisable
   To bring the prophet here, or did you not?

CREON   I did; and I am still of the same opinion.

OED.   And how many years ago was it that Laius . . .

CREON   That Laius what? I cannot follow you.   540

OED.   Was lost to his people by an act of violence.

CREON   That would take us a long way back into the past.

OED.   And was the prophet practicing in those days?

CREON   As skillfully as today, with equal honor.

OED.   And did he then make any mention of me?

CREON   Not at any time when I was there to hear him.

OED.   But did you not investigate the murder?

612

CREON   We were bound to, of course, but discovered nothing.

OED.   And why did this know-all not tell his story then?

CREON   I prefer not to talk about things I do not know.   550

OED.   You know one thing well enough that you could tell me.

CREON   What is it? If I know, I shall keep nothing back.

OED.   This: if you had not put your heads together
  We should never have heard about my killing Laius.

CREON   If he says so, you know best. Now let me ask
  And you must answer as I answered you.

OED.   Ask what you like. I am innocent of murder.

CREON   Come now; are not you married to my sister?

OED.   A question to which I can hardly answer no.

CREON   And you rule the country with her, equally?   560

OED.   I give her everything that she could wish for.

CREON   Do I, the third, not rank with both of you?

OED.   You do; which makes your treachery the worse.

CREON   Not if you reason with yourself as I do.
  First ask yourself this question: would any man
  Be king in constant fear, when he could live
  In peace and quiet, and have no less power?
  I want to be a king in everything
  But name—and I have no desire for that,
  Nor has any man who knows what is good for him.   570
  As it is, I am carefree. You give me all I want,
  But as king I should have many tiresome obligations.
  Then why should I find monarchy more desirable
  Than power and influence without the trouble?
  So far I have not been misguided enough
  To hanker after dishonorable gains.
  As it is, all wish me well and greet me kindly,
  And people with suits to you call first on me
  For there are all their chances of success.
  So why should I give up one life for the other?   580
  No man with any sense would stoop to treason.
  I have no love for such ideas, nor would I
  Associate with any man who did.
  Do you look for proof of this? Then go to Delphi
  And ask if I quoted the oracle correctly.
  And another thing; if you find that I have made
  A plot with the prophet, there will be two voices
  To sentence me to death—yours and my own.

But do not convict me out of mere suspicion!   590
It is hardly just to label good men bad
Or bad men good, according to your whim.
Mark my words: the man who drops an honest friend
Cuts out his heart, the thing he loves the best.
But you will learn this sure enough in time,
For time alone can tell an honest man
While one day is enough to show a villain.

CHORUS   Good advice, my lord, for one who keeps a watch
  For pitfalls. Hasty thoughts are dangerous.

OED.   When conspirators make haste to set plots moving
  I must make haste myself to counteract them.   600
  If I waited and did nothing it would mean
  Success for him and ruin for myself.

CREON   Then what do you want? My banishment from Thebes?

OED.   No, not your banishment. I want your death!

CREON   There speaks a man who will not listen to reason.

OED.   No, you must show the world what comes of envy!

CREON   I think you must be mad.

OED.   And I think sane.

CREON   Then hear me sensibly.

OED.   Hear you, a traitor?

CREON   Suppose you are wrong?

OED.   Kings must still be obeyed.

CREON   Kings, but not tyrants.

OED.   City, oh my city!   610

CREON   My city also. I have rights here too.

CHORUS   Stop this, my lords. I can see Jocasta coming
  From the palace just in time. Let her advise you,
  Put your quarrel aside and be friends again.

[*Enter* JOCASTA]

JOCASTA   Have you both gone out of your minds? What is the sense
  Of bandying insults? Are you not ashamed
  To start a private feud, when Thebes is ailing?
  Come inside. And Creon, you must go back home.
  Do not make a mortal grievance out of nothing.

CREON   Sister, your husband Oedipus thinks fit   620
  To make me suffer one way or the other—
  To drive me into banishment or kill me.

614

OED.   Exactly. I have caught him plotting mischief—
　　A criminal attempt on the royal person.

CREON   May heaven's anger strike me dead this minute
　　If I have done anything to deserve this charge!

JOC.   In the gods' name, Oedipus, believe what he says!
　　If not from respect of the oath he has sworn,
　　For the sake of your wife and everyone here!

CHORUS   Listen to reason, my lord;　　　　　　　　　　630
　　I beg you, be guided by us.

OED.   You ask for a favor; what is it?

CHORUS   He has been no fool in the past;
　　He is strong in his oath; respect him.

OED.   Do you know what it is you ask?

CHORUS   I do.

OED.　　　　　　Then explain yourselves; what do you mean?

CHORUS   Your friend has invoked a curse on his head.
　　Do not brand him traitor on rumor alone.

OED.   You must know, by asking this
　　You are asking my exile or death.　　　　　　　　640

CHORUS   No, by the Sun, the first among gods!
　　May I die the death that men fear most,
　　Shunned, unclean in the sight of heaven,
　　If I have such thoughts in my mind.
　　But my heart is heavy at our country's dying
　　If you add new troubles to her present load.

OED.   Let him go then; but I am signing my own death warrant
　　Or condemning myself to exile and disgrace.
　　Your voice has moved me where his oath could not.
　　As for him, wherever he may go, I hate him.　　　650

CREON   Now we have seen you—wild when you lose your temper,
　　And yielding with bad grace. Such a nature as yours
　　Is its own worst enemy, and so it should be.

OED.   Get out, and leave me in peace.

CREON　　　　　　　　　　　　　I am going.
　　They know I am honest, though you will not see it.

[Exit]

CHORUS   Now quickly, my lady, take him inside.

JOC.   Not before I know what has happened.

CHORUS There were words, a vague suspicion,
  False, but injustice stings.

JOC. On both sides?

CHORUS   Yes.

JOC.   What was said?   660

CHORUS Our country has troubles enough.
  Better let sleeping dogs lie.

OED. You meant well enough, but see where it leads you,
  Checking me, blunting the edge of my anger.

CHORUS I have said it before and say it again:
  Men would think that my wits had wandered,
  Would think me insane, to abandon you.
  Our beloved country was sinking fast
  Till you took the helm; and now you may prove
  Our guide and salvation again.   670

JOC. Tell me as well, my lord, in heaven's name,
  What can have set such fury working in you?

OED. I will tell you; you are more to me than they are.
  It is Creon, and the way he is plotting against me.

JOC. Go on, and tell me how this quarrel started.

OED. He says that I am Laius' murderer.

JOC. Does he speak from knowledge or from hearsay only?

OED. Neither; he sent a mischief-making prophet.
  He is taking care to keep his own mouth clean.

JOC. You can relieve your mind of all such fears.   680
  Listen, and learn from me: no human being
  Is gifted with the art of prophecy.
  Once an oracle came to Laius—I will not say
  From Apollo himself, but from his ministers—
  To say a child would be born to him and me
  By whose hand it was fated he should die.
  And Laius, as rumor goes, was killed by bandits,
  From another land, at a place where three roads meet.
  And as for our son, before he was in this world
  Three days, Laius pinned his ankles together   690
  And had him abandoned on the trackless mountain.
  So in this case Apollo's purpose failed—
  That the child should kill his father, or that Laius
  Should be murdered by his son, the fear that haunted him.
  So much for oracles which map our future!

Then take no notice of such things; whatever the god
Finds needful, he will show without assistance.

OED.   Oh wife, the confusion that is in my heart,
The fearful apprehension, since I heard you speak!

JOC.   What is it? What have I said to startle you?   700

OED.   I thought I heard you telling me that Laius
Was murdered at a place where three roads meet.

JOC.   Such was the story. People tell it still.

OED.   What country was it where the thing was done?

JOC.   In the land called Phocis, at the meeting-point
Of the roads from Delphi and from Daulia.

OED.   And how many years have gone by since it happened?

JOC.   It was just before you first appeared in Thebes
To rule us; that is when we heard of it.

OED.   Oh Zeus, what have you planned to do with me?   710

JOC.   Oedipus, what is it? Why has this upset you?

OED.   Do not ask me yet; but tell me about Laius.
What did he look like? How far gone in years?

JOC.   A tall man, with his hair just turning gray,
To look at, not so different from you.

OED.   Oh, what have I done? I think that I have laid
A dreadful curse on myself and never knew it!

JOC.   What are you saying? It frightens me to look at you.

OED.   I am terrified the prophet sees too well.
I shall know better if you tell me one thing more.   720

JOC.   You frighten me; but ask and I will tell you.

OED.   Did he ride with a handful of men, or with a band
Of armed retainers, as a chieftain should?

JOC.   There were five in all—a herald one of them,
And a single carriage in which Laius rode.

OED.   Oh, now I see it all. Jocasta, answer me,
Who was the man who told you what had happened?

JOC.   A servant—the only one who returned alive.

OED.   Is he with us? Is he in our household now?

JOC.   No, he is not. When he came back and found   730
You ruling here in Thebes and Laius dead
He wrung me by the hand and begged me send him
Into the country where we graze our sheep

As far as possible from the sight of Thebes.
I let him go away; slave though he was
He could have asked far more and had it granted.

OED.   I want him here, as fast as he can come.

JOC.   That can be seen to. What is in your mind?

OED.   I fear I have already said
More than I should; that is why I want to see him.   740

JOC.   He shall come then; but I too have a right
To know what lies heavy on your heart, my lord.

OED.   I shall keep nothing from you, now my apprehension
Has gone so far. Who else should I confide in
Unless in you, when this crisis is upon me?
My father's name was Polybus of Corinth,
My mother a Dorian, Merope. In that city
I lived as first in honor, till one day
There happened something—worth surprise perhaps,
But not such anger as it roused in me.   750
A man at dinner, too far gone in wine,
Jeered in his cups, I was my father's bastard.
It preyed on my mind; and I restrained myself
That day as best I could, but in the morning
Went questioning my parents. They were angry
At such a taunt, and the man who let it fly,
So on their part I was satisfied; but still
The slander rankled as it spread and grew.
And so I went, without my parents' knowledge,
On a journey to Delphi. Phoebus sent me away   760
No wiser than I came, but something else
He showed me, sad and strange and terrible:
That I was doomed to mate with my own mother,
Bring an abhorrent brood into the world;
That I should kill the father who begat me.
When I heard, I fled from Corinth, ever since
Marking its whereabouts only by the stars,
To find some place where I should never see
This evil oracle's calamities fulfilled,
And in my travels reached that very place   770
Where, as you tell me, Laius met his death.
Wife, I shall tell the truth: I was on my way
And had nearly come to the joining of the roads
When there met me, from the opposite direction,

747 *Dorian:* one of the oldest Greek tribes; Oedipus says this with some pride.

A herald, and a man in a horse-drawn carriage
Exactly as you described. The fellow in front
And the old man tried to push me out of the way.
I lost my temper, hit out at the one
Who jostled me, the driver; when the old man saw it,
He watched me, from the carriage, coming past   780
And brought his double goad down on my head—
But took it back with interest! One swift blow
From the good staff in my hand, and over he went
Clean out of the chariot, sprawling on his back,
And I killed every man in sight. If this stranger
Should turn out to have anything to do with Laius,
Who is more wretched than this man before you,
And who could be more hateful to the gods,
A man no citizen, no stranger even,
May take into his house or speak with him   790
But drive him from their doors; and this, this curse
Was laid on me by no-one but myself.
And now my hands, by which he met his death,
Defile his bed. Am I not evil? Am I not
Foul through and through, when I must go to exile
And in that exile never see my people,
Or set foot in my homeland—for if I do
I must marry my mother, murder Polybus,
The father who gave me life and livelihood.
Then if you saw in Oedipus the prey   800
Of some tormenting power, would you be wrong?
Never, oh never, pure and awful gods,
Let me see that day; no, let me rather vanish
Out of the sight of men, before I see
This dreadful visitation come upon me.

CHORUS   This is fearful, my lord; but do not give up hope
Until you have questioned the man who saw it done.

OED.   Yes, that is all the hope I have left me now,
To wait the coming of this man, our shepherd.

JOC.   And when he comes, what would you have from him?   810

OED.   I will tell you. If I find his story tallies
With yours, then it will mean that I am safe.

JOC.   And what is so important in my story?

OED.   You said that Laius, as he told the tale,
Was killed by robbers. If he stands by this,
That there were more than one, I did not kill him;
You could not make one man a company.

But if he names one solitary traveler
There is no more doubt; the deed swings back to me.

JOC.   You can be sure that this is what he said.   820
He cannot go back on it, all the city heard him.
I was not the only one. But even supposing
We find he tells a different tale today,
My lord, he can never show that Laius' death
Ran true to prophecy. Phoebus expressly said
That he was doomed to die at my child's hands;
But that unhappy babe went to his death
Before he did; then how could he have killed him?
So when it comes to oracles, after this
I shall keep both eyes fixed firmly on the front.   830

OED.   You speak good sense. But all the same, send someone
To bring the peasant here; do as I say.

JOC.   I will send at once. Come now, let us go home.
Would I ever fail to do anything you wanted?

[*Exeunt*]

CHORUS   I pray that this may crown my every day,
In all my words and deeds to walk
Pure-hearted, in proper fear;
For thus we are commanded from on high
By laws created in the shining heavens,
Who know no other father but Olympus,   840
In their birth owing nothing to mortals
Nor sleeping though forgotten; great the god
Within them, and he grows not old.

Out of insolence is born the tyrant,
Insolence grown fat in vain
On things immoderate, unfit.
For a man who has mounted to the highest places
Must fall to meet his destiny below
Where there can be no help, no footing.
But honest ambition let us keep,   850
For thus the state is served; O Lord Apollo
Guide and strengthen me all my days.

But I pray that the man whose hands and tongue
Are arrogant, careless of retribution,

840 *Olympus:* mountain home of the gods

620

Who blasphemes in the holy places,
May fall upon evil days, the reward
Of the sin of self-conceit.
If he goes the wrong way to gain his ends,
And follows unholy courses, laying
Profaning hands on things he should not touch,   860
Could any man boast his life was safe
From the arrows of angry heaven?
But when such things as these are held in honor
Why should I sing the praises of the gods?

No longer shall I visit with my prayers
The inviolate shrine at the center of the world,
Or Abae's temple, or Olympia,
If the prophecy should fail to come to pass
As spoken, for all the world to see.
O Zeus, if you are rightly called   870
The Almighty, the ruler of mankind,
Look to these things; and let them not escape
Your power eternal; for the oracles
Once told of Laius are forgotten, slighted;
Apollo is divested of his glory
And man turns his face away from heaven.

[*Enter* JOCASTA]

JOC.   Elders of Thebes, I have a mind to pay
   A visit to the holy shrines, with gifts
   Of incense and wreathed branches in my hands.
   For Oedipus has let his mind succumb   880
   To all manner of fears, and will not judge the present
   By what has gone before, like a sensible man,
   But is the prey of every fearful rumor.
   There is nothing more that I can say to help him,
   And so I bring offerings to you, Apollo—
   The nearest to us—and request this favor:
   Show us how we can find a clean way out,
   For now we are afraid to see him frightened,
   Like sailors who see panic in their steersman.

866 *the inviolate . . . world:* Delphi; see n. on l. 70   867 *Abae:* near Thebes, site of temple and oracle
of Apollo   *Olympia:* home of the temple of Zeus and the famous Olympic Games   876 *And
man . . . heaven:* a fair description of the growing agnosticism of Sophocles' own time

[*Enter* Messenger]

MESSENGER   Could you tell me, my friends, where a man might find   890
  The palace of King Oedipus—better still,
  Where the king himself is, if you happen to know?

CHORUS   This is his house, and the king is indoors.
  This lady is the mother of his children.

MESS.   May heaven bless Oedipus' honored queen
  Her whole life long with every happiness!

JOC.   Stranger, I wish you the same; so fair a greeting
  Deserves no less. But tell us why you come.
  What have you to ask of us, or tell us?

MESS.   Good news for your house, my lady, and your husband!   900

JOC.   What news is this? Who sent you here to us?

MESS.   I come from Corinth; what I have to tell
  Will please you, no doubt; but there is sadness too.

JOC.   Pleasure and pain at once? What is this message?

MESS.   The people living in the Isthmian land
  Will have him for their king; so goes the story.

JOC.   Why? Is old Polybus no longer king?

MESS.   No, death has claimed him. He is in his grave.

JOC.   What are you saying? Oedipus' father dead?

MESS.   If I am lying, may I die myself!   910

JOC.   Maid, run away and tell this to your master
  As fast as you can. Oh gods, where are
  Your oracles now? This is the man that Oedipus
  Has shunned for years, for fear of killing him,
  And now he is dead, and Oedipus never touched him!

[*Enter* OEDIPUS]

OED.   Jocasta, dearest wife, why have you sent
  For me, and called me from the palace?

JOC.   Listen to this man here, and learn from his words
  To what these holy oracles have come!

OED.   This man? Who is he? What has he to say?   920

JOC.   From Corinth; his message is that Polybus,
  Your father, lives no longer—he is dead!

OED.   What? Stranger, let me have it from your mouth.

905 *Isthmian land:* Corinth, situated on the narrow neck of land that joins the two parts of Greece

MESS. If this is where I must begin my message,
  I assure you, Polybus is dead and gone.

OED. Did it happen by foul play? Or was he sick?

MESS. When a man is old his life hangs by a thread.

OED. Poor Polybus. He died of illness, then?

MESS. That and old age. He had lived a long life.

OED. Oh, wife, why should we ever spare a glance   930
  For the shrine of Delphi, or the birds that scream
  Above our heads? On their showing, I was doomed
  To be my father's murderer; but he
  Is dead and buried, and here am I, who never
  Laid hand on sword. Unless perhaps he died
  Through pining for me; thus I could have killed him.
  But as they stand, the oracles have gone
  To join him underground, and they are worthless!

JOC. Did I not tell you so a long while since?

OED. You did, but I was led astray through fear.   940

JOC. Then do not take them any more to heart.

OED. But my mother's bed . . . how should I not fear that?

JOC. What has a man to fear, when life is ruled
  By chance, and the future is unknowable?
  The best way is to take life as it comes.
  So have no fear of marriage with your mother.
  Many men before this time have dreamt that they
  Have shared their mother's bed. The man to whom
  These things are nothing lives the easiest life.

OED. It would be well enough to talk in such a way   950
  If my mother were not living. As she is,
  Though your words make sense, I have good cause to fear.

JOC. But your father's death is a ray of light in darkness.

OED. A bright one; but I fear the living woman.

MESS. Who is this woman that you are afraid of?

OED. Merope, old man, the wife of Polybus.

MESS. And what is there in her to make you afraid?

OED. A terrifying oracle from heaven.

MESS. May it be told? Or are you sworn to silence?

OED. Why should it not? Apollo told me once   960
  That I was doomed to marry with my mother
  And shed my father's blood with these my hands.
  And that is why I put my home in Corinth

Behind me—for the best, but all the same
There is nothing so sweet as the sight of parents' faces.

MESS. Was it for fear of this you left our city?

OED. It was; and to avoid my father's murder.

MESS. Then had I better not remove your fear,
My lord, since I am here with friendly purpose?

OED. If so you would deserve reward, and have it. 970

MESS. Indeed, this was my principal reason for coming,
To do myself some good when you came home.

OED. I shall never come. I must not see my parents.

MESS. My son, I see you are making a mistake—

OED. What do you mean, old man? In god's name tell me.

MESS. —if you shrink from going home because of this.

OED. I am terrified of proving Phoebus true.

MESS. Of the guilt and shame that will come to you through your parents?

OED. You have it, old man; that fear is always with me.

MESS. Then let me tell you that these fears are groundless! 980

OED. How can they be, if I were born their son?

MESS. Because there is none of Polybus' blood in you.

OED. Are you telling me that he was not my father?

MESS. No more than I—one thing we had in common.

OED. What could he have in common with a nobody?

MESS. Why, I am not your father, and neither was he.

OED. But then . . . he called me son . . . what made him do it?

MESS. He took you as a present from my hands.

OED. He had such love . . . for an adopted son?

MESS. He had no sons of his own; this moved his heart. 990

OED. You gave me to him—had you bought me?
Found me?

MESS. I found you, in the wild woods of Cithairon.

OED. What led your wanderings to such a place?

MESS. I was in charge of sheep there, on the mountain.

OED. A shepherd, going from place to place for hire?

MESS. But your preserver at that time, my son.

OED. Why? What was the matter with me when you found me?

MESS. Your ankles are best witnesses of that.

OED   Oh, why do you have to talk of that old trouble?

MESS.   They were pinned together, and I cut you loose.   1000

OED.   A shameful mark I carried from my cradle.

MESS.   And from this chance you took the name you bear.

OED.   Who did this to me? My father or my mother?

MESS.   The man who gave you me knows; I do not.

OED.   You took me from someone else? You did not find me?

MESS.   No, another shepherd passed you on to me.

OED.   Who was this man? Can you identify him?

MESS.   We knew him, I think, as one of Laius' people.

OED.   You mean the king who used to rule this country?

MESS.   The very same. This man was Laius' herdsman.   1010

OED.   And is he still alive for me to see him?

MESS.   You in this country would best know of that.

OED.   My people, is there anyone here present
Who knows the herdsman he is talking of,
Who has seen him in the country or the town?
Come, tell me; it is time to solve this riddle.

CHORUS   I think he means no other than the man
You already want to see. Jocasta here
Would be best qualified to tell you that.

OED.   My lady, do you know the man we mean—   1020
The man we just sent for; is he speaking of him?

JOC.   Why ask who he means? Do not bother with it.
This story is not worth thinking of; it is nothing.

OED.   No, that can never be. I have the clues
Here in my hand. I must find out my birth.

JOC.   No, by the gods! If you care for your own safety
Ask no more questions. I have suffered enough.

OED.   Take courage. If my mother was a slave, and hers,
And hers, before her, you are still pure-born.

JOC.   Listen, please listen to me! Do not do this!   1030

OED.   No-one could stop me finding out the truth.

JOC.   It is for your sake; I advise you for the best.

OED.   If this is your best, I have no patience with it.

JOC.   I pray you may never find out who you are.

OED.   Go, somebody, and fetch the herdsman here.
Leave her to glory in her wealthy birth!

JOC.   Accursed! Accursed! I have no other name
     To call you; you will never hear me again.

[*Exit*]

CHORUS   What can have made her leave you, Oedipus,
     In this burst of frantic grief? I have a fear   1040
     That from her silence there will break a storm.

OED.   Let break what will! As for my parentage,
     Humble though it may be, I want to know it.
     She is a woman, with a woman's pride,
     And is ashamed, no doubt, of my low birth.
     But I proclaim myself the child of Luck,
     My benefactress; this is no dishonor.
     Yes, Luck is my mother, and the months, my cousins,
     Saw me first humble and then saw me great.
     With such a parentage I could not be false   1050
     To myself again, or let this secret rest.

CHORUS   If I am any judge of the future,
     If my mind does not play me false,
     Cithairon, tomorrow at the full moon's rising,
     By Olympus, you will need no second telling
     That Oedipus boasts of your kinship, hailing you
     As nurse and mother.
     And we shall be there with dances in your honor
     Because you have found favor in our king's sight.
     Apollo, hear us when we pray,   1060
     And bless our good intentions!

     Which of the nymphs, the long-lived ones,
     Lay with the mountain-wanderer Pan
     To bring you to birth? Or was it Loxias?
     He is a god who loves the upland pastures.
     Or was it Cyllene's lord, or the god
     Of the Bacchanals, dwelling
     High in the hilltops, who received you,
     A new-born treasure, from the arms of a nymph
     Of Helicon, the favorite   1070
     Companions of his pleasure?

1063 *Pan:* primitive nature deity, half man, half goat   1064 *Loxias:* Apollo   1066 *Cyllene's lord:*
Hermes, the messenger god, born on Mount Cyllene   1067 *Bacchanals:* frenzied women who
worshipped Dionysus   1070 *Helicon:* mountain sacred to Apollo and the Muses

[*Enter attendants with* HERDSMAN]

OED.   Elders, if I, who never saw the man,
  May make a guess, I think I see the herdsman
  We have sought so long; he is well advanced in years—
  This answers the description—and besides
  I recognize the men escorting him
  As servants of my own. But you may well
  Have the advantage of me, if you have seen him before;

CHORUS   I know him, no mistake. He worked for Laius,
  As honest a shepherd as you could hope to find.   1080

OED.   First let me hear from you, my Corinthian friend.
  Is this your man?

MESS.   The one you see before you.

OED.   Come here, old man, and look me in the face.
  Answer my questions. You once worked for Laius?

HERDSMAN   I did; and I was palace-bred, not bought.

OED.   In what employment? How did you spend your time?

HERDS.   For the best part of my life I watched the flocks.

OED.   What part of the country did you mostly work in?

HERDS.   Sometimes Cithairon, sometimes round about.

OED.   Have you seen this man in those parts, to your knowledge?   1090

HERDS.   Who? Doing what? What man are you talking about?

OED.   This man in front of you. Have you ever met him?

HERDS.   Not to remember off-hand. I cannot say.

MESS.   Small wonder, master. But let me refresh
  His failing memory. I have no doubt
  That he recalls the time we spent together
  In the country round Cithairon. He had two flocks,
  And I, his mate, had one. Three years we did this,
  For six months at a time, from spring to fall.
  Then, for the winter, I used to drive my flocks   1100
  Home to my fold, he his to that of Laius.
  Did it happen as I say, or did it not?

HERDS.   Yes, true; but it was many years ago.

MESS.   Now tell me: do you remember giving me
  A boy for me to bring up as my own?

HERDS.   What now? What has put that question in your head?

MESS.   That child, my friend, is the man you see before you.

627

HERDS. Curse you! Do not say another word!

OED. Old man, do not reprove him. Your words stand
In greater need of admonition than his. 1110

HERDS. And where do I offend, most noble master?

OED. In not telling of the boy he asks about.

HERDS. This meddler does not know what he is saying.

OED. If you will not speak to oblige me I must make you.

HERDS. No, no, for god's sake; you would not hurt an old man?

OED. Quickly, somebody, tie his arms behind him.

HERDS. Unhappy man, what more do you want to know?

OED. This child he talks of; did you give it him?

HERDS. I did; and I wish that day had been my last.

OED. It will come to that, unless you tell the truth. 1120

HERDS. I shall do myself more harm by telling you.

OED. It seems he is determined to waste our time.

HERDS. No, no! I told you once, I gave it him.

OED. Where did you get it? Your home or another's?

HERDS. It was not mine. Somebody gave it me.

OED. Who? Which one of my people? Where does he live?

HERDS. No, master, in heaven's name, ask no more questions.

OED. You are a dead man if I have to ask again.

HERDS. It was a child of the house of Laius.

OED. A slave? Or one of his own family? 1130

HERDS. I am near to saying what should not be said.

OED. And I to hearing; but it must be heard.

HERDS. They said it was Laius' son. But go inside
And ask your wife; for she could tell you all.

OED. You mean she gave it you?

HERDS.   She did, my lord.

OED. But why?

HERDS.   For me to make away with it.

OED. Her child!

HERDS.   She feared an evil prophecy.

OED. What was it?

HERDS.   That the son should kill his father.

OED. Then why did you give him up to this old man?

HERDS.   For pity, master, thinking he would take   1140
   The child home, out of Thebes; but he preserved him
   For a fate worse than any other. If you are truly
   The man he says, then know you were born accursed.

[Exit]

OED.   Oh, oh, then everything has come out true.
   Light, I shall not look on you again.
   I have been born where I should not be born,
   I have married where I should not marry,
   I have killed whom I should not kill; now all is clear.

[Exit]

CHORUS   You that are born into this world,
   I count you in your lives as nothing worth.   1150
   What man has ever won for himself
   More of happiness than this,
   To seem, and having seemed, to pass?
   For Oedipus, when I look at you
   And the fate which fell upon you, can I
   Call any human being happy?

   Zeus knows, his arrow went straight to its mark
   And all of life's blessings became his prize.
   He killed the girl with the crooked claws,
   The riddle-monger, and stood up among us   1160
   A tower of strength to drive death from our land,
   For which we called you our king, paid you honors
   The greatest we knew; in the proud land
   Of Thebes you were lord and master.

   Now who has a sadder tale to tell?
   A life turned upside down,
   The door flung wide to misfortune,
   The hounds of fate let loose.
   Oh Oedipus, famous Oedipus,
   The same ample shelter sufficed   1170
   For father and son, a bed for the mating.
   How could the furrows your father sowed
   Have endured you so long in silence?

   Time sees all, and has found you out
   Despite yourself, passing sentence
   On the marriage that is no marriage,
   Where begetter is one with begotten.

Laius' child, oh Laius' child,
Better if I had not seen you,
For when all is said, he that gave me new life   1180
Has taken all my joy in living.

[*Enter* SECOND MESSENGER]

MESS.   Ancestral and most honorable lords,
Such things you will see and hear of; such a weight
Of grief is yours, if like true sons of Thebes
You still care for the sons of Labdacus.
I think there is no river wide enough
To wash this palace clean, so many are
The horrors it hides, or soon will bring to light,
Done willfully, from choice; no sufferings
Hurt more than those we bring upon ourselves.   1190

CHORUS   Those that we know already claim their weight
Of tears. What more have you to add to these?

MESS.   A tale which can be very briefly told
And heard: our royal lady Jocasta is dead.

CHORUS   Oh miserable queen; what was the cause?

MESS.   By her own hand. The worst of what has happened
You shall be spared, you were not there to see it.
But you shall hear as much as I recall
About the sufferings of the wretched queen.
Past caring what she did, she rushed inside   1200
The hall, and made straight for her marriage bed,
Head in hands, and fingers tearing at her hair.
Once in the room she slammed the doors behind her
And called on Laius rotting in his grave,
Remembering a once begotten child
By whom the father should die, and leave the mother
To bear his son's cursed children; she bewailed
The bed where she had borne a double brood,
Husband by husband, children by her child,
And then she died—I cannot tell you how,   1210
For Oedipus burst on us with a cry
And we had no chance to watch her agonies.
We had eyes for none but him, as he ran from one
To another, demanding a sword, and where
He might find his wife—his mother, not his wife,
The womb that gave him and his children birth.
In his frenzy he was guided by some power
More than human—not by any of us who stood there.

With a dreadful cry, as though a hand had pointed,
He sprang at the double doors, forced back the bolts   1220
Till the sockets gave, and ran into the room.
And there inside we saw the woman hanging,
Her body swinging in a twist of rope.
When he saw, a shuddering cry welled up inside him;
He cut the noose that held her; when she lay
Cold on the ground, we saw a ghastly sight.
He tore away the golden brooches from
Her dress, that she had used as ornaments,
And lifted them, and plunged them in his eyes   1230
With words like these: "You shall not see again
Such horrors as I did, saw done to me,
But stare in darkness on forbidden faces,
Meet those I longed to find, and pass them by."
And to this tune he raised his hands and struck
His eyes again and again; with every blow
Blood spurted down his cheeks. It did not fall
In slow and sluggish drops, but all at once
Black blood came pouring like a shower of hail.
This storm has broken on two people's heads,
Not one alone; both man and wife have suffered.   1240
Till now, the happiness they inherited
Was happiness indeed; and now, today,
Tears, ruin, death, disgrace, as many ills
As there are names for them; not one is lacking.

CHORUS How is he now? Is he in peace from pain?

MESS.   He shouts for the doors to be opened, for every man
In Thebes to see his father's murderer,
His mother's—heaven forbid I speak that word.
He means to cast himself from Thebes, to stay
In this house no more, a self-inflicted curse.   1250
But his strength is gone; he needs someone to guide
His steps, the pain is more than he can bear.
And this too he will show you. See, the doors
Are opening, and soon you will see a sight
To move your tears, though you recoil from it.

[Enter OEDIPUS, blind]

CHORUS Oh sufferings dreadful to see,
Most dreadful of all that ever
Greeted my eyes. Wretched king,
What insanity possessed you?
What demon, in one colossal spring   1260

631

Pounced on your ill-fated life?
Unhappy king,
I cannot even look you in the face,
Though there are still many questions to be asked,
Many things left unsaid, much remaining to be seen,
You fill me with such shuddering.

OED. Oh, oh, the pain, the pain!
Where do my poor legs take me?
Where do the wild winds scatter my words?
Oh, my fate, where have you leapt with me?   1270

CHORUS To a dreadful place that must not be named,
To a place unfit for the eyes of man.

OED. Oh, this fog,
This horrible darkness all around me,
Unspeakable visitation
Blown by an evil wind; I am powerless.
Oh, when I remember my sorrows
I feel again the points in my eyes.

CHORUS No wonder; in such sorrows you must have
Evils redoubled to endure and mourn.   1280

OED. Oh, my friend,
You are my faithful servant still,
Blind Oedipus' patient nurse.
I know you are here, I can feel your presence.
Although I am in the darkness
I can recognize your voice.

CHORUS Oh man of wrath, how could you bring yourself
To blind your eyes? What demon drove you on?

OED. It was Apollo, my friends, Apollo
Who contrived my ruin, who worked my fall.   1290
But no-one blinded my eyes
But myself, in my own grief.
What use are eyes to me, who could never
See anything pleasant again?

CHORUS Yes, it was as you say.

OED. What is there left for me to see,
To love? Who still has a kindly word,
My friends, for me?
Take me away from this land, my friends,
Take me with all the speed you may,   1300
For Oedipus is no more,
Contaminated, cursed,
Unclean in heaven's sight.

632

CHORUS Knowledge and pain; they hurt you equally.
I wish your path and mine had never crossed.

OED. Cursed be the man who struck the cruel chains
From my feet as I lay abandoned,
And saved me from death, gave me back
To the world of the living—why?
If I had died then, I should never   1310
Have grieved myself or my loved ones so.

CHORUS I too would have had it so.

OED. I would not have shed my father's blood
Or heard men call me my mother's husband.
And now I am
God-shunned, the son of a mother defiled,
Have taken my turn in my mother's bed.
If there is any sorrow
Greater than all others
It belongs to Oedipus.   1320

CHORUS I cannot praise your judgment. You would be
Far better dead than living still and blind.

OED. Do not tell me I am wrong. What I have done
Is best as it is. Give me no more advice.
If I had sight, I know not with what eyes
I would have looked upon my father, when
I walked among the dead, or my sad mother,
For sins so great cannot be paid by hanging.
Or do you think the sight of children born
As mine were born could give me any joy?   1330
No, never to these eyes of mine again,
Nor the proud wall of our city, nor the holy
Statues of our gods; these I, ten times accursed,
I, who was noblest of the sons of Thebes,
Have set behind me by my own command
That all cast out the sinner, the man revealed
By heaven as unclean, as Laius' son.
And tainted thus for all the world to see
How could I look my people in the face?
I could not. If I could have stopped my ears,   1340
My fount of hearing, I would not have rested
Till I had made a prison of this body
Barred against sight and sound. How happy the mind
That can so live, beyond the reach of suffering.
Cithairon, why did you shelter me? Why did you not

633

Kill me there, where you found me, so that I might never
Show to mankind the secret of my birth?
Oh Polybus, Corinth, the ancestral home
Men called my father's; oh, how fair of face
Was I, your child, and how corrupt beneath!   1350
For now I am found evil, evil born.
Those three roads, and the hidden clump of trees,
The wood, the narrow place where three paths met,
Who drank from my own hands the father's blood.
And so, my own blood; do you still remember
The things you saw me do? Then I came here
To do other things besides. Oh marriage, marriage,
You gave me birth, and after I was born
Bore children to your child, and brought to light
Sons, fathers, brothers in a web of incest,   1360
Than which men know nothing more abominable.
But what is sin to do is sin to speak of.
For heaven's love, hide me in some wilderness,
Or strike me dead, or throw me in the sea,
Where you will never set eyes on me again.
Come, do not shrink from touching my poor body.
Please; do not be afraid. My sufferings
Are all my own, no-one will be infected.

CHORUS   No. Here is Creon, in time to listen to you,
Ready to act or advise. Now you are gone   1370
He is the only one we have to turn to.

OED.   Oh, what words can I find to say to him?
What proof of my good faith? I have been found
An arrant traitor to him in the past.

[*Enter* CREON *with attendants*]

CREON   Oedipus, I have not come to jeer at you
Or throw your past misconduct in your face.

[*To the* CHORUS]

As for you, if you have no sense of decency
To a fellow man, at least have some respect
For holy sunlight, giver of warmth and life.
Do not leave this pollution uncovered, an offence   1380
To earth, to light, to the pure rain from heaven.
Take him indoors as quickly as you can.
Propriety forbids he should be made
A public spectacle. These things are for his family.

OED.   Listen: since you have removed my apprehension
And behave so nobly to a man so low
Grant me this favor—for your good, not for mine.

CREON   What is it you are so anxious to have me do?

OED.   Lose no more time; drive me away from Thebes
To some place where nobody will know my name.   1390

CREON   Believe me, I would have done so; but first I wanted
To find out from the god what I should do.

OED.   The will of the god is clear enough already.
Kill the parricide, the sinner; and that am I.

CREON   So he said. But all the same, now things have gone
So far, it is better that we seek clear guidance.

OED.   You will go to the god? For a poor wretch like myself?

CREON   I will. Perhaps you will believe him this time.

OED.   I do. And I will urge your duties on you.
The woman inside—bury her as you would wish   1400
To be buried yourself. It is right, she is your sister.
But as for me, never sentence my father's city
To have me within its walls, as long as I live,
But leave me to the hills, to my Cithairon
As men now call It—destined for my grave
By my father and mother when they were alive.
They tried to kill me; let me die the way they wanted.
But I am sure of one thing: no disease,
Nothing can kill me now. I would not have been saved
From death, unless it were for some strange destiny.   1410
But let my destiny go where it will.
As for my children—Creon, do not trouble yourself
About my sons. They are men, they can never lack
A livelihood, wherever they may be.
But my two girls, my poor unhappy daughters,
Who never knew what it was to eat a meal
Away from their father's side, but had their share
Of every little thing I had myself. . . .
Please look after them. And I beg this favor now,   1420
Let me lay my hands on them and weep with them.
Please, my lord,
Please, noble heart. If I could touch them now
I should think they were with me, as if I could see them.

[*Enter* ANTIGONE *and* ISMENE]

    What is that?
Oh you gods; is it my darlings that I hear
Sobbing? Has Creon taken pity on me
And sent my darlings, sent my children to me?
Am I right?

CREON Yes, I had them brought to you; I knew
They would delight you as they always have done.   1430

OED. Bless you for your trouble. May you find
A kinder fate than what has come to me.
Where are you now, my children? Over here:
Come to these hands of mine, your brother's hands,
Whose offices have made your father's eyes
That were once so bright, to see as they see now.
For the truth is out; your father, stupid, blind,
Begot you in the womb where he was born.
Sight have I none, but tears I have for you
When I think of how you will be forced to live   1440
At men's hands in the bitter days to come.
What gathering of the folk will you attend,
What festival that will not send you home
In tears, instead of making holiday?
And when the time has come for you to marry,
Show me the man, my children, bold enough
To take upon his own head such disgrace,
The stain that you and your brothers will inherit.
What sorrow is not ours? Your father killed
His father, sowed his seed in her   1450
Where he was sown as seed, and did beget you
In the selfsame place where he was once begotten.
That is how men will talk. Then who will marry you?
No-one, my children. Marriage is not for you.
You must be barren till your lives are done.
Son of Menoeceus, you are the only father
These girls have left, for we, their parents,
Are both of us gone. So do not let them wander
Beggared and husbandless. They are your kin.
And do not level them with my misfortunes   1460
But pity them. You see how young they are.
You are the only friend they have in the world.
Touch me, kind heart, in token of your promise.
Children, if you were old enough to understand,
There is much I could say to help you. As it is,

Pray after me—to live with moderation
And better fortune than your father did.

CREON   Your time is up. Dry your tears and go indoors.

OED.   It is hard, but I must obey.

CREON   There must be moderation in all things.

OED.   I shall go on one condition.

CREON   Tell me what it is.   1470

OED.   Send me away from Thebes to live.

CREON   That is for the gods to say.

OED.   They will be glad to see me gone.

CREON   Then your wish will soon be granted.

OED.   You agree then?

CREON   When I do not know, I do not speak.

OED.   Take me away, it is time.

CREON   Come along. Leave your children here.

OED.   Never part us!

CREON   Do not ask to have everything your way.
Your time for giving orders is over.

[*Exeunt*]

CHORUS   People of this city, look, this man is Oedipus,
Who guessed the famous riddle, who rose to greatness,
Envy of all in the city who saw his good fortune.
And now what a fearful storm of disaster has struck him.   1480
That is why we wait until we see the final day,
Not calling anybody happy who is mortal
Until he has passed the last milestone without calamity.

DISCUSSION TOPICS

1. What do you think is the theme of this play? How important are the questions Oedipus and the others ask the oracles and the gods?
2. According to Aristotle, the tragic hero must be a noble character who has some significant character defect or "tragic flaw." What is Oedipus's tragic flaw?
3. Is Oedipus's destiny controlled by fate or by his tragic flaw? Does he help to bring about his own downfall or is he the innocent victim of the gods? How would a modern psychologist analyze Oedipus's behavior?
4. What are Creon's attitudes toward Oedipus, both early and late in the play? How does Creon view his own station in life? What virtues does he represent?

As Creon is portrayed here, is there any hint of a flaw in his character that might make him a tragic figure in a different version of the play?

5. Teiresias is the prototypical wise old man. Which other characters in the play share something of that role?

6. Aristotle refers several times to *Oedipus the King* in his discussion of tragedy in the *Poetics*. One of his key points is that tragedy should bring about an emotional catharsis in the viewer, a purging through pity and fear that is not provided by everyday existence. Do you think *Oedipus* does this? (Ask yourself this question again after you have read *Hamlet* and *Death of a Salesman*.)

7. Discuss some of the implications of Sophocles's use of the imagery of blindness and insight. This imagery is, of course, ironic. How many other kinds of irony are there in the play?

8. Account for Jocasta's silence from line 954 to line 1022 on pp. 623–625. What gestures and stage action must be executed by the person playing her role during those lines? Why?

WRITING TOPICS

1. Analyze the exchange between Oedipus and Teiresias as a dramatic epitome of the hero's tragic fall.

2. Study the device of questions and answers, at first partial answers, as a device for giving the play its informing structure. Especially account for the revelation about Laius's having been killed where three roads meet, a revelation that comes halfway through the play.

3. When Sigmund Freud described the Oedipus complex, he had in mind the audience's response to this play over the centuries more than Oedipus's own "Oedipus complex," since Oedipus, of course, did not know until years later that he had killed his father and married his mother. But even so, there is some evidence that Sophocles worked into the play what we have since come to call the *Oedipus complex*. Trace that evidence.

ARISTOPHANES (C. 448–C. 380 B.C.) Greatest of ancient Greek comedy writers. His plays chiefly satirize social life, trendy philosophies and literature, and Athenian foreign policy. Other works include *The Clouds, The Birds,* and *The Frogs.*

LYSISTRATA

Translated by Donald Sutherland

Characters

LYSISTRATA
KALONIKE ⎱ Athenian women
MYRRHINA ⎰
LAMPITO, a Spartan woman
CHORUS OF OLD MEN
CHORUS OF WOMEN
ATHENIAN COMMISSIONER
OLD MARKET-WOMEN
CINESIAS, an Athenian, husband of Myrrhina
SPARTAN HERALD
SPARTAN AMBASSADORS
ATHENIAN AMBASSADORS

[*A street in Athens before daylight*]

LYSISTRATA If anyone had asked them to a festival
of Aphrodite or of Bacchus or of Pan,
you couldn't get through Athens for the tambourines,
but now there's not one solitary woman here.
Except my next-door neighbor. Here she's coming out.
Hello, Kalonike.

KALONIKE   Hello, Lysistrata.
What are you so upset about? Don't scowl so, dear.
You're less attractive when you knit your brows and glare.

LYSISTRATA I know, Kalonike, but I am smoldering
with indignation at the way we women act.
Men think we are so gifted for all sorts of crime
that we will stop at nothing—

KALONIKE   Well, we are, by Zeus!

LYSISTRATA —but when it comes to an appointment here with me
to plot and plan for something really serious
they lie in bed and do not come.

KALONIKE   They'll come, my dear.
You know what trouble women have in going out:

639

one of us will be wrapped up in her husband still,
another waking up the maid, or with a child
to put to sleep, or give its bath, or feed its pap.

LYSISTRATA   But they had other more important things to do
than those.

KALONIKE   What ever is it, dear Lysistrata?
What have you called us women all together for?
How much of a thing is it?

LYSISTRATA   Very big.

KALONIKE   And thick?

LYSISTRATA   Oh very thick indeed.

KALONIKE   Then *how* can we be late?

LYSISTRATA   That's not the way it is. Or we would all be here.
But it is something I have figured out myself
and turned and tossed upon for many a sleepless night.

KALONIKE   It must be something slick you've turned and tossed
upon!

LYSISTRATA   So slick that the survival of all Greece depends
upon the women.

KALONIKE   On the women? In that case
poor Greece has next to nothing to depend upon.

LYSISTRATA   Since now it's we who must decide affairs of state:
either there is to be no Spartan left alive—

KALONIKE   A very good thing too, if none were left, by Zeus!

LYSISTRATA   —and every living soul in Thebes to be destroyed—

KALONIKE   Except the eels! Spare the delicious eels of Thebes!

LYSISTRATA   —and as for Athens—I can't bring myself to say
the like of that for us. But just think what I mean!
Yet if the women meet here as I told them to
from Sparta, Thebes, and all of their allies,
and we of Athens, all together we'll save Greece.

KALONIKE   What reasonable thing could women ever do,
or glorious, we who sit around all prettied up
in flowers and scandalous saffron-yellow gowns,
groomed and draped to the ground in oriental stuffs
and fancy pumps?

LYSISTRATA   And those are just the very things
I count upon to save us—wicked saffron gowns,
perfumes and pumps and rouge and sheer transparent frocks.

KALONIKE   But what use can they be?

LYSISTRATA   So no man in our time
   will raise a spear against another man again—

KALONIKE   I'll get a dress dyed saffron-yellow, come what may!

LYSISTRATA   —nor touch a shield—

KALONIKE   I'll slip into the sheerest gown!

LYSISTRATA   —nor so much as a dagger—

KALONIKE   I'll buy a pair of pumps!

LYSISTRATA   So don't you think the women should be here by now?

KALONIKE   I don't. They should have *flown* and got here long ago.

LYSISTRATA   You'll see, my dear. They will, like good Athenians,
   do everything too late. But from the coastal towns
   no woman is here either, nor from Salamis.

KALONIKE   I'm certain those from Salamis have crossed the strait:
   they're always straddling *something* at this time of night.

LYSISTRATA   Not even those I was expecting would be first
   to get here, from Acharnaea, from so close to town,
   not even they are here.

KALONIKE   But one of them, I know,
   is under way, and three sheets to the wind, by now.
   But look—some women are approaching over there.

LYSISTRATA   And over here are some, coming this way—

KALONIKE   Phew! Phew!
   Where are they from?

LYSISTRATA   Down by the marshes.

KALONIKE   Yes, by Zeus!
   It smells as if the bottoms had been all churned up!

[*Enter* MYRRHINA, *and others.*]

MYRRHINA   Hello Lysistrata. Are we a little late?
   What's that? Why don't you speak?

LYSISTRATA   I don't think much of you,
   Myrrhina, coming to this business only now.

MYRRHINA   Well, I could hardly find my girdle in the dark.
   If it's so urgent, tell us what it is. We're here.

KALONIKE   Oh no. Let's wait for just a little while until
   the delegates from Sparta and from Thebes arrive.

LYSISTRATA   You show much better judgment.

[*Enter* LAMPITO, *and others.*]

Here comes Lampito!

LYSISTRATA   Well, darling Lampito! My dearest Spartan friend!
  How very sweet, how beautiful you look! That fresh
  complexion! How magnificent your figure is!
  Enough to crush a bull!

LAMPITO   Ah shorely think Ah could.
  Ah take mah exacise. Ah jump and thump mah butt.

KALONIKE   And really, what a handsome set of tits you have!

LAMPITO   You feel me ovah lahk a cow of sacrafahce!

LYSISTRATA   And this other young thing—where ever is *she* from?

LAMPITO   She's prominent, Ah sweah, in Thebes—a delegate
  ample enough.

LYSISTRATA   By Zeus, she represent Thebes well,
  having so trim a ploughland.

KALONIKE   Yes, by Zeus, she does!
  There's not a weed of all her field she hasn't plucked.

LYSISTRATA   And who's the other girl?

LAMPITO   Theah's nothing small, Ah sweah,
  or tahght about her folks in Corinth.

KALONIKE   No, by Zeus!—
  to judge by this side of her, nothing small or tight.

LAMPITO   But who has called togethah such a regiment
  of all us women?

LYSISTRATA   Here I am. I did.

LAMPITO   Speak up,
  just tell us what you want.

KALONIKE   Oh yes, by Zeus, my dear,
  do let us know what the important business is!

LYSISTRATA   Let me explain it, then. And yet . . . before I do . . .
  I have one little question.

KALONIKE   Anything you like.

LYSISTRATA   Don't you all miss the fathers of your little ones,
  your husbands who have gone away to war? I'm sure
  you all have husbands in the armies far from home.

KALONIKE   Mine's been away five months in Thrace—a general's
  guard,
  posted to see his general does not desert.

MYRRHINA   And mine has been away in Pylos seven whole months.

642

LAMPITO   And mahn, though he does get back home on leave sometahms,
  no soonah has he come than he is gone again.

LYSISTRATA   No lovers either. Not a sign of one is left.
  For since our eastern allies have deserted us
  they haven't sent a single six-inch substitute
  to serve as leatherware replacement for our men.
  Would you be willing, then, if I thought out a scheme,
  to join with me to end the war?

KALONIKE   Indeed I would,
  even if I had to pawn this very wrap-around
  and drink up all the money in one day, I would!

MYRRHINA   And so would I, even if I had to see myself
  split like a flounder, and give half of me away!

LAMPITO   And so would Ah! Ah'd climb up Mount Taygetos
  if Ah just had a chance of seeing peace from theah!

LYSISTRATA   Then I will tell you. I may now divulge my plan.
  Women of Greece!—if we intend to force the men
  to make a peace, we must abstain . . .

KALONIKE   From what? Speak out!

LYSISTRATA   But will you do it?

KALONIKE   We will, though death should be the price!

LYSISTRATA   Well then, we must abstain utterly from the prick.
  Why do you turn your backs? Where are you off to now?
  And you—why pout and make such faces, shake your heads?
  Why has your color changed? Why do you shed those tears?
  Will you do it or will you not? Why hesitate?

KALONIKE   I will not do it. Never. Let the war go on!

MYRRHINA   Neither will I. By Zeus, no! Let the war go on!

LYSISTRATA   How can you say so, Madam Flounder, when just now
  you were declaiming you would split yourself in half?

KALONIKE   Anything else you like, anything! If I must
  I'll gladly walk through fire. That, rather than the prick!
  Because there's nothing like it, dear Lysistrata.

LYSISTRATA   How about you?

MYRRHINA   I too would gladly walk through fire.

LYSISTRATA   Oh the complete depravity of our whole sex!
  It is no wonder tragedies are made of us,
  we have such unrelenting unity of mind!
  But you, my friend from Sparta, dear, if you alone
  stand by me, only you, we still might save the cause.
  Vote on my side!

LAMPITO　　　　　　They'ah hahd conditions, mahty hahd,
to sleep without so much as the fo'skin of one . . .
but all the same . . . well . . . yes. We need peace just as bad.

LYSISTRATA　Oh dearest friend!—the one real woman of them all!

KALONIKE　And if we really should abstain from what you say—
which Heaven forbid!—do you suppose on that account
that peace might come to be?

LYSISTRATA　　　　　　　　I'm absolutely sure.
If we should sit around, rouged and with skins well creamed,
with nothing on but a transparent negligé,
and come up to them with our deltas plucked quite smooth,
and, once our men get stiff and want to come to grips,
we do not yield to them at all but just hold off,
they'll make a truce in no time. There's no doubt of that.

LAMPITO　We say in Spahta that when Menelaos saw
Helen's ba'e apples he just tossed away his swo'd.

KALONIKE　And what, please, if our husbands just toss *us* away?

LYSISTRATA　Well, you have heard the good old saying: Know Thyself.

KALONIKE　It isn't worth the candle. I hate cheap substitutes.
But what if they should seize and drag us by brute force
into the bedroom?

LYSISTRATA　　　　Hang onto the doors!

KALONIKE　　　　　　　　　　　And if—
they beat us?

LYSISTRATA　Then you must give in, but nastily,
and do it badly. There's no fun in it by force.
And then, just keep them straining. They will give it up
in no time—don't you worry. For never will a man
enjoy himself unless the woman coincides.

KALONIKE　If both of you are for this plan, then so are we.

LAMPITO　And we of Spahta shall persuade ouah men to keep
the peace sinceahly and with honah in all ways,
but how could anyone pe'suade the vulgah mob
of Athens not to deviate from discipline?

LYSISTRATA　Don't worry, we'll persuade our men. They'll keep the peace.

LAMPITO　They won't, so long as they have battleships afloat
and endless money sto'ed up in the Pahthenon.

LYSISTRATA　But that too has been carefully provided for:
we shall take over the Acropolis today.
The oldest women have their orders to do that:

while *we* meet here, *they* go as if to sacrifice
up there, but really seizing the Acropolis.

LAMPITO   All should go well. What you say theah is very smaht.

LYSISTRATA   In that case, Lampito, what are we waiting for?
Let's take an oath, to bind us indissolubly.

LAMPITO   Well, just you show us what the oath is. Then we'll sweah.

LYSISTRATA   You're right. Where is that lady cop?

[*To the armed* LADY COP *looking around for a* LADY COP]

What do you think
you're looking for? Put down your shield in front of us,
there, on its back, and someone get some scraps of gut.

KALONIKE   Lysistrata, what in the world do you intend
to make us take an oath on?

LYSISTRATA   What? Why, on a shield,
just as they tell me some insurgents in a play
by Aeschylus once did, with a sheep's blood and guts.

KALONIKE   Oh don't, Lysistrata, don't swear upon a *shield,*
not if the oath has anything to do with peace!

LYSISTRATA   Well then, what *will* we swear on? Maybe we should get
a white horse somewhere, like the Amazons, and cut
some bits of gut from it.

KALONIKE   *Where* would we get a horse?

LYSISTRATA   But what kind of an oath *is* suitable for us?

KALONIKE   By Zeus, I'll tell you if you like. First we put down
a big black drinking-cup, face up, and then we let
the neck of a good jug of wine bleed into it,
and take a solemn oath to—add no water in.

LAMPITO   Bah Zeus, Ah jest can't tell you how Ah lahk that oath!

LYSISTRATA   Someone go get a cup and winejug from inside.

[KALONIKE *goes and is back in a flash.*]

KALONIKE   My dears, my dearest dears—how's *this* for pottery?
You feel good right away, just laying hold of it.

LYSISTRATA   Well, set it down, and lay your right hand on this pig.
O goddess of Persuasion, and O Loving-cup,
accept this victim's blood! Be gracious unto us.

KALONIKE   It's not anaemic, and flows clear. Those are good signs.

LAMPITO   What an aroma, too! Bah Castah, it *is* sweet!

KALONIKE   My dears, if you don't mind—I'll be the first to swear.

LYSISTRATA   By Aphrodite, no! If you had drawn first place
by lot—but now let all lay hands upon the cup.
Yes, Lampito—and now, let one of you repeat
for all of you what I shall say. You will be sworn
by every word she says, and bound to keep this oath:
No lover and no husband and no man on earth—

KALONIKE   No lover and no husband and no man on earth—

LYSISTRATA   *shall e'er approach me with his penis up.* Repeat.

KALONIKE   Shall e'er approach me with his penis up. Oh dear,
my knees are buckling under me, Lysistrata!

LYSISTRATA   *and I shall lead an unlaid life alone at home,*

KALONIKE   and I shall lead an unlaid life alone at home,

LYSISTRATA   *wearing a saffron gown and groomed and beautified*

KALONIKE   wearing a saffron gown and groomed and beautified

LYSISTRATA   *so that my husband will be all on fire for me*

KALONIKE   so that my husband will be all on fire for me

LYSISTRATA   *but I will never willingly give in to him*

KALONIKE   but I will never willingly give in to him

LYSISTRATA   *and if he tries to force me to against my will*

KALONIKE   and if he tries to force me to against my will

LYSISTRATA   *I'll do it badly and not wiggle in response*

KALONIKE   I'll do it badly and not wiggle in response

LYSISTRATA   *nor toward the ceiling will I lift my Persian pumps*

KALONIKE   nor toward the ceiling will I lift my Persian pumps

LYSISTRATA   *nor crouch down as the lions on cheese-graters do*

KALONIKE   nor crouch down as the lions on cheese-graters do

LYSISTRATA   *and if I keep my promise, may I drink of this—*

KALONIKE   and if I keep my promise, may I drink of this—

LYSISTRATA   *but if I break it, then may water fill the cup!*

KALONIKE   but if I break it, then may water fill the cup!

LYSISTRATA   Do you all swear to this with her?

ALL   We do, by Zeus!

LYSISTRATA   I'll consecrate our oath now.

KALONIKE   Share alike, my dear,
so we'll be friendly to each other from the start.

LAMPITO   What was that screaming?

LYSISTRATA   That's what I was telling you:
  the women have already seized the Parthenon
  and the Acropolis. But now, dear Lampito,
  return to Sparta and set things in order there—
  but leave these friends of yours as hostages with us—
  And let *us* join the others in the citadel
  and help them bar the gates.

KALONIKE   But don't you think the men
  will rally to the rescue of the citadel,
  attacking us at once?

LYSISTRATA   They don't worry me much:
  they'll never bring against us threats or fire enough
  to force open the gates, except upon our terms.

KALONIKE   Never by Aphrodite! Or we'd lose our name
  for being battle-axes and unbearable!

[*Exeunt. The scene changes to the Propylaea of the Acropolis. A chorus of very old men struggles slowly
in, carrying logs and firepots.*]

ONE OLD MAN   Lead on! O Drakës, step by step, although your
                              shoulder's aching
                    and under this green olive log's great weight
                         your back be breaking!

ANOTHER   Eh, life is long but always has
                    more surprises for us!
            Now who'd have thought we'd live to hear
                    this, O Strymodorus?—

            The wives we fed and looked upon
            as helpless liabilities
            now dare to occupy the Parthenon,
            our whole Acropolis, for once they seize
            the Propylaea, straightway
            they lock and bar the gateway.

CHORUS   Let's rush to the Acropolis with due precipitation
  and lay these logs down circlewise, till presently we turn them
  into one mighty pyre to make a general cremation
  of all the women up there—eh! with our own hands we'll burn them,
  the leaders and the followers, without discrimination!

AN OLD MAN   They'll never have the laugh on me!
                    Though I may not look it,
            I rescued the Acropolis
                    when the Spartans took it
            about a hundred years ago.

647

We laid a siege that kept their king
six years unwashed, so when I made him throw
his armor off, for all his blustering,
in nothing but his shirt he
looked very very dirty.

CHORUS How strictly I besieged the man! These gates were all invested
with seventeen ranks of armored men all equally ferocious!
Shall women—by Euripides and all the gods detested—
not be restrained—with me on hand—from something so atrocious?
They shall!—or may our trophies won at Marathon be bested!
But we must go a long way yet
up that steep and winding road
before we reach the fortress where we want to get.
How shall we ever drag this load,
lacking pack-mules, way up there?
I can tell you that my shoulder has caved in beyond
repair!
Yet we must trudge ever higher,
ever blowing on the fire,
so its coals will still be glowing when we get where we
are going
Fooh! Fooh!
Whoo! I choke!
What a smoke!

Lord Herakles! How fierce it flies
out against me from the pot!
and like a rabid bitch it bites me in the eyes!
It's female fire, or it would not
scratch my poor old eyes like this.
Yet undaunted we must onward, up the high Acropolis
where Athena's temple stands
fallen into hostile hands.
O my comrades! shall we ever have a greater need to
save her?
Fooh! Fooh!
Whoo! I choke!
What a smoke!

FIRST OLD MAN Well, thank the gods, I see the fire is yet alive and
walking!

SECOND OLD MAN Why don't we set our lumber down right here in
handy batches,
then stick a branch of grape-vine in the pot until it catches

648

THIRD OLD MAN   and hurl ourselves against the gate with battering and
  shaking?

FIRST OLD MAN   And if the women won't unbar at such an ultimatum
  we'll set the gate on fire and then the smoke will suffocate 'em.

SECOND OLD MAN   Well, let's put down our load. Fooh fooh, what smoke!
  But blow as needed!

THIRD OLD MAN   Your ablest generals *these* days would not carry wood
  like *we* did.

SECOND OLD MAN   At last the lumber ceases grinding my poor back to
  pieces!

THIRD OLD MAN   These are your orders, Colonel Pot: wake up the coals
  and bid them
report here and present to me a torch lit up and flaring.

FIRST OLD MAN   O Victory, be with us! If you quell the women's daring
  we'll raise a splendid trophy of how you and we undid them!

[A CHORUS *of middle-aged women appears in the offing.*]

A WOMAN   I think that I perceive a smoke in which appears a flurry
  of sparks as of a lighted fire. Women, we'll have to hurry!

CHORUS OF WOMEN
            Oh fleetly fly, oh swiftly flit,
            my dears, e'er Kalykë be lit
            and with Kritylla swallowed up alive
                in flames which the gales dreadfully drive
                and deadly old men fiercely inflate!
        Yet one thing I'm afraid of: will I not arrive too late?
        for filling up my water-jug has been no easy matter
        what with the crowd at the spring in the dusk and the
                clamor and pottery clatter.
            Pushed as I was, jostled by slave-
            women and sluts marked with a brand
            yet with my jug firmly in hand
                here I have come, hoping to save
                my burning friends and brave,

            for certain windy, witless, old,
            and wheezy fools, so I was told,
        with wood some tons in weight crept up this path,
                not having in mind heating a bath
                but uttering threats, vowing they will
        consume those nasty women into cinders on grill!
        But O Athena! never may I see my friends igniting!

Nay!—let them save all the cities of Greece and their
     people from folly and fighting!
    Goddess whose crest flashes with gold,
    they were so bold taking your shrine
    only for this—Goddess who hold
    Athens—for *this* noble design
    braving the flames, calling on you
     to carry water too!

[*One of the old men urinates noisily.*]

CHORUS OF WOMEN   Be still! What was that noise? Aha! Oh, wicked and
   degraded!
Would any good religious men have ever done what *they* did?

CHORUS OF MEN   Just look! It's a surprise-attack! Oh, dear, we're being
   raided
by swarms of them below us when we've got a swarm above us!

CHORUS OF WOMEN   Why panic at the sight of us? This is not many of us.
We number tens of thousands but you've hardly seen a fraction.

CHORUS OF MEN   O Phaidrias, shall they talk so big and we not take some
   action?
Oh, should we not be bashing them and splintering our lumber?

[*The old men begin to strip for combat.*]

CHORUS OF WOMEN   Let us, too, set our pitchers down, so they will not
   encumber
our movements if these gentlemen should care to offer battle.

CHORUS OF MEN   Oh someone should have clipped their jaws—twice,
   thrice, until they rattle—
(as once the poet put it)—then we wouldn't hear their prating.

CHORUS OF WOMEN   Well, here's your chance. Won't someone hit me?
   Here I stand, just waiting!
No other bitch will ever grab your balls, the way I'll treat you!

CHORUS OF MEN   Shut up—or I will drub you so old age will never reach
   you!

CHORUS OF WOMEN   Won't anyone step and lay one finger on Stratyllis?

CHORUS OF MEN   And if we pulverize her with our knuckles, will you kill
   us?

CHORUS OF WOMEN   No, only chew your lungs out and your innards and
   your eyes, sir.

CHORUS OF MEN   How clever is Euripides! There is no poet wiser:
he says indeed that women are the worst of living creatures.

CHORUS OF WOMEN   Now is the time, Rhodippe: let us raise our brimming pitchers.

CHORUS OF MEN   Why come up here with water, you, the gods' abomination?

CHORUS OF WOMEN   And why come here with fire, you tomb? To give yourself cremation?

CHORUS OF MEN   To set your friends alight upon a pyre erected for them.

CHORUS OF WOMEN   And so we brought our water-jugs. Upon your pyre we'll pour them.

CHORUS OF MEN   *You'll* put my fire out?

CHORUS OF WOMEN   Any time! You'll see there's nothing to it.

CHORUS OF MEN   I think I'll grill you right away, with just this torch to do it!

CHORUS OF WOMEN   Have you some dusting-powder? Here's your wedding-bath all ready.

CHORUS OF MEN   *You'll* bathe me, garbage that you are?

CHORUS OF WOMEN   Yes, bridegroom, just hold steady!

CHORUS OF MEN   Friends, you have heard her insolence—

CHORUS OF WOMEN   I'm free-born, not your slave, sir.

CHORUS OF MEN   I'll have this noise of yours restrained—

CHORUS OF WOMEN   Court's out—so be less grave, sir.

CHORUS OF MEN   Why don't you set her hair on fire?

CHORUS OF WOMEN   Oh, Water, be of service!

CHORUS OF MEN   Oh woe is me!

CHORUS OF WOMEN   Was it too hot?

CHORUS OF MEN   Oh, stop! What *is* this? Hot? Oh no!

CHORUS OF WOMEN   I'm watering you to make you grow.

CHORUS OF MEN   I'm withered from this chill I got!

CHORUS OF WOMEN   You've got a fire, so warm yourself. You're trembling: are you nervous?

[*Enter a* COMMISSIONER, *escorted by four Scythian policemen with bows and quivers slung on their backs.*]

COMMISSIONER   Has the extravagance of women broken out
   into full fury, with their banging tambourines
   and constant wailings for their oriental gods,
   and on the roof-tops their Adonis festival,
   which I could hear myself from the Assembly once?
   For while Demostratos—that numbskull—had the floor,

urging an expedition against Sicily,
his wife was dancing and we heard her crying out
"Weep for Adonis!"—so the expedition failed
with such an omen. When the same Demostratos
was urging that we levy troops from our allies
his wife was on the roof again, a little drunk:
"Weep for Adonis! Beat your breast!" says she. At that,
he gets more bellicose, that god-Damn-ox-tratos.
To this has the incontinence of women come!

CHORUS OF MEN   You haven't *yet* heard how outrageous they can be!
With other acts of violence, these women here
have showered us from their jugs, so now we are reduced
to shaking out our shirts as if we'd pissed in them.

COMMISSIONER   Well, by the God of Waters, what do you expect?
When we ourselves conspire with them in waywardness
and give them good examples of perversity
such wicked notions naturally sprout in them.
We go into a shop and say something like this:
"Goldsmith, about that necklace you repaired: last night
my wife was dancing, when the peg that bolts the catch
fell from its hole. I have to sail for Salamis,
but if you have the time, by all means try to come
towards evening, and put in the peg she needs."
Another man says to a cobbler who is young
and has no child's-play of a prick, "Cobbler," he says,
"her sandal-strap is pinching my wife's little toe,
which is quite delicate. So please come by at noon
and stretch it for her so it has a wider play."
Such things as that result of course in things like this:
when I, as a Commissioner, have made a deal
to fit the fleet with oars and need the money now,
I'm locked out by these women from the very gates.
But it's no use just standing here. Bring on the bars,
so I can keep these women in their proper place.
What are *you* gaping at, you poor unfortunate?
Where are *you* looking? Only seeing if a bar
is open yet downtown? Come, drive these crowbars in
under the gates on that side, pry away, and I
will pry away on this.

[LYSISTRATA *comes out.*]

LYSISTRATA   No need to pry at all.
I'm coming out, of my own will. What use are bars?
It isn't bolts and bars we need so much as brains.

652

COMMISSIONER   Really, you dirty slut? Where is that officer?
Arrest her, and tie both her hands behind her back.

LYSISTRATA   By Artemis, just let him lift a hand at me
and, public officer or not, you'll hear him howl.

COMMISSIONER   You let her scare you? Grab her round the middle, you.
Then *you* go help him and between you get her tied.

[KALONIKE *comes out.*]

KALONIKE   By Artemis, if you just lay one hand on her
I have a mind to trample the shit out of you.

COMMISSIONER   It's out already! Look! Now where's the other one?
Tie up *that* woman first. She babbles, with it all.

[*Myrrhina comes out.*]

MYRRHINA   By Hecatë, if you just lay a hand on her
you'll soon ask for a cup—to get your swellings down!

[*The policeman dashes behind the* COMMISSIONER *and clings to him for protection.*]

COMMISSIONER   What happened? Where's that bowman, now? Hold onto
her!

[*He moves quickly away downhill.*]

I'll see that none of you can get away through here!

LYSISTRATA   By Artemis, you come near her and I'll bereave
your head of every hair! You'll weep for each one, too.

COMMISSIONER   What a calamity! This one has failed me too.
But never must we let ourselves be overcome
by women. All together now, O Scythians!—
let's march against them in formation!

LYSISTRATA   You'll find out
that inside there we have four companies
of fighting women perfectly equipped for war.

COMMISSIONER   Charge! Turn their flanks, O Scythians! and tie their
hands!

LYSISTRATA   O allies—comrades—women! Sally forth and fight!
O vegetable vendors, O green-grocery-
grain-garlic-bread-bean-dealers and inn-keepers all!

[*A group of fierce* OLD MARKET-WOMEN, *carrying baskets of vegetables, spindles, etc. emerges. There is a volley of vegetables. The Scythians are soon routed.*]

Come pull them, push them, smite them, smash them into bits!
Rail and abuse them in the strongest words you know!
Halt, Halt! Retire in order! We'll forego the spoils!

COMMISSIONER [*tragically, like say Xerxes*]   Oh what reverses have my
bowmen undergone!

LYSISTRATA   But what did you imagine? Did you think you came
against a pack of slaves? Perhaps you didn't know
that women can be resolute?

COMMISSIONER   I know they can—
above all when they spot a bar across the way.

CHORUS OF MEN   Commissioner of Athens, you are spending words
unduly,
to argue with these animals, who only roar the louder,
or don't you know they showered us so coldly and so cruelly,
and in our undershirts at that, and furnished us no powder?

CHORUS OF WOMEN   But beating up your neighbor is inevitably
bringing
a beating on yourself, sir, with your own eyes black and bloody.
I'd rather sit securely like a little girl demurely
not stirring up a single straw nor harming anybody,
So long as no one robs my hive and rouses me to stinging.

CHORUS OF MEN   How shall we ever tame these brutes? We cannot
tolerate
the situation further, so we must investigate
this occurrence and find
with what purpose in mind
they profane the Acropolis, seize it, and lock
the approach to this huge and prohibited rock,
to our holiest ground!
Cross-examine them! Never believe one word
they tell you—refute them, confound them!
We must get to the bottom of things like this
and the circumstances around them.

COMMISSIONER   Yes indeed! and I want to know first one thing:
just *why* you committed this treason,
barricading the fortress with locks and bars—
I insist on knowing the reason.

LYSISTRATA   To protect all the money up there from you—
you'll have nothing to fight for without it.

COMMISSIONER   You think it is *money* we're fighting for?

LYSISTRATA   All the troubles we have are about it.
It was so Peisander and those in power
     of his kind could embezzle the treasure
that they cooked up emergencies all the time.
     Well, let them, if such is their pleasure,
but they'll never get into this money again,
     though you men should elect them to spend it.

COMMISSIONER   And just what will *you* do with it?

LYSISTRATA   Can you ask?
     Of course we shall superintend it.

COMMISSIONER   You will superintend the treasury, *you!?*

LYSISTRATA   And why should it strike you so funny?
     when we manage our houses in everything
          and it's we who look after your money.

COMMISSIONER   But it's not the same thing!

LYSISTRATA   Why not?

COMMISSIONER   It's **war**,
     and *this* money must pay the expenses.

LYSISTRATA   To begin with, you needn't be waging war.

COMMISSIONER   To survive, we don't need our defenses?

LYSISTRATA   You'll survive: we shall save you.

COMMISSIONER   Who? You?

LYSISTRATA   Yes, we.

COMMISSIONER   You absolutely disgust me.

LYSISTRATA   You may like it or not, but you *shall* be saved.

COMMISSIONER   I protest!

LYSISTRATA   If you care to, but, trust me,
     this has got to be done all the same.

COMMISSIONER   It has?
     It's illegal, unjust, and outrageous!

LYSISTRATA   We must save you, sir.

COMMISSIONER   Yes? And if I refuse?

LYSISTRATA   You will much the more grimly engage us.

COMMISSIONER   And whence does it happen that war and peace
     are fit matters for women to mention?

LYSISTRATA   I will gladly explain—

COMMISSIONER   And be quick, or else
     you'll be howling!

LYSISTRATA   Now, just pay attention
  and keep your hands to yourself, if you can!

COMMISSIONER   But I can't. You can't think how I suffer
  from holding them back in my anger!

AN OLD WOMAN   Sir—
  if you don't you will have it much rougher.

COMMISSIONER   You may croak that remark to yourself, you hag!
            Will *you* do the explaining?

LYSISTRATA   I'll do it.
  Heretofore we women in time of war
          have endured very patiently through it,
  putting up with whatever you men might do,
          for never a peep would you let us
  deliver on your unstatesmanly acts
          no matter how much they upset us,
  but we knew very well, while we sat at home,
          when you'd handled a big issue poorly,
  and we'd ask you then, with a pretty smile
          though our heart would be grieving us sorely,
  "And what were the terms for a truce, my dear,
          you drew up in assembly this morning?"
  "And what's it to you?" says our husband, "Shut up!"
          —so, as ever, at this gentle warning
  I of course would discreetly shut up.

KALONIKE   Not me!
          You can bet I would never be quiet!

COMMISSIONER   I'll bet, if you weren't, you were beaten up.

LYSISTRATA   *I'd* shut up, and I do not deny it,
  but when plan after plan was decided on,
          so bad we could scarcely believe it,
  I would say "This last is so mindless, dear,
          I cannot think how you achieve it!"
  And then he would say, with a dirty look,
          "Just you think what your spindle is for, dear,
  or your head will be spinning for days on end—
          let the *men* attend to the war, dear."

COMMISSIONER   By Zeus, *he* had the right idea!

LYSISTRATA   You fool!
          Right ideas were quite out of the question,
  when your reckless policies failed, and yet
  we never could make a suggestion.
  And lately we heard you say so yourselves:
          in the streets there'd be someone lamenting:

"There's not one man in the country now!"
    —and we heard many others assenting.
After that, we conferred through our deputies
    and agreed, having briefly debated,
to act in common to save all Greece
    at once—for why should we have waited?
So now, when we women are talking sense,
    if you'll only agree to be quiet
and to listen to us as we did to you,
    you'll be very much edified by it.

COMMISSIONER   *You* will edify *us!* I protest!

LYSISTRATA   Shut up!

COMMISSIONER   *I'm* to shut up and listen, you scum, you?!
Sooner death! And a veil on your head at that!

LYSISTRATA   We'll fix that. It may really become you:
do accept this veil as a present from me.
Drape it modestly—so—round your head, do you see?
And now—*not* a word more, sir.

KALONIKE   Do accept this dear little wool-basket, too!
Hitch your girdle and card! Here are beans you may chew
the way all of the nicest Athenians do—
and the *women* will see to the war, sir!

CHORUS OF WOMEN   Oh women, set your jugs aside and keep a closer
   distance:
our friends may need from us as well some resolute assistance.

Since never shall I weary of the stepping of the dance
nor will my knees of treading, for these ladies I'll advance
    anywhere they may lead,
    and they're daring indeed,
they have wit, a fine figure, and boldness of heart,
they are prudent and charming, efficient and smart,
    patriotic and brave!

But, O manliest grandmothers, onward now!
    And you matronly nettles, don't waver!
but continue to bristle and rage, my dears,
    for you've still got the wind in your favor!

[*The* CHORUS OF WOMEN *and the* OLD MARKET-WOMEN *join.*]

LYSISTRATA   But if only the spirit of tender Love
    and the power of sweet Aphrodite

were to breathe down over our breasts and thighs
 an attraction both melting and mighty,
and infuse a pleasanter rigor in men,
 raising only their cudgels of passion,
then I think we'd be known throughout all of Greece
 as makers of peace and good fashion.

COMMISSIONER Having done just what?

LYSISTRATA   Well, first of all
 we shall certainly make it unlawful
to go madly to market in armor.

AN OLD MARKET-WOMAN Yes!
 By dear Aphrodite, it's awful!

LYSISTRATA For now, in the midst of the pottery-stalls
 and the greens and the beans and the garlic,
men go charging all over the market-place
 in full armor and beetling and warlike.

COMMISSIONER They must do as their valor impels them to!

LYSISTRATA But it makes a man only look funny
 to be wearing a shield with a Gorgon's head
 and be wanting sardines for less money.

OLD MARKET-WOMEN Well, I saw a huge cavalry-captain once
 on a stallion that scarcely could hold him,
pouring into his helmet of bronze a pint
 of pea-soup an old woman had sold him.
And a Thracian who, brandishing shield and spear
 like some savage Euripides staged once,
when he'd frightened a vendor of figs to death,
 gobbled up all her ripest and aged ones.

COMMISSIONER And how, on the international scale,
 can you straighten out the enormous
confusion among all the states of Greece?

LYSISTRATA Very easily.

COMMISSIONER   How? Do inform us.

LYSISTRATA When our skein's in a tangle we take it thus
 on our spindles, or haven't you seen us?—
one on this side and one on the other side,
 and we work out the tangles between us.
And that is the way we'll undo this war,
 by exchanging ambassadors, whether
you like it or not, one from either side,
 and we'll work out the tangles together.

COMMISSIONER Do you really think that with wools and skeins
     and just being able to spin you
can end these momentous affairs, you fools?

LYSISTRATA With any intelligence in you
you statesmen would govern as we work wool,
     and in everything Athens would profit.

COMMISSIONER How so? Do tell.

LYSISTRATA First, you take raw fleece
     and you wash the beshittedness off it:
just so, you should first lay the city out
     on a washboard and beat out the rotters
and pluck out the sharpers like burrs, and when
     you find tight knots of schemers and plotters
who are out for key offices, card them loose,
     but best tear off their heads in addition.
Then into one basket together card
     all those of a good disposition
be they citizens, resident aliens, friends,
     an ally or an absolute stranger,
even people in debt to the commonwealth,
     you can mix them all in with no danger.
And the cities which Athens has colonized—
     by Zeus, you should try to conceive them
as so many shreddings and tufts of wool
     that are scattered about and not leave them
to lie around loose, but from all of them
     draw the threads in here, and collect them
into one big ball and then weave a coat
     for the people, to warm and protect them.

COMMISSIONER Now, isn't this awful? They treat the state
     like wool to be beaten and carded,
who have nothing at all to do with war!

LYSISTRATA Yes we do, you damnable hard-head!
We have none of your honors but we have more
     than double your sufferings by it.
First of all, we bear sons whom you send to war.

COMMISSIONER Don't bring up our old sorrows! Be quiet!

LYSISTRATA And now, when we ought to enjoy ourselves,
     making much of our prime and our beauty,
we are sleeping alone because all the men
     are away on their soldierly duty.
But never mind *us*—when young girls grow old
     in their bedrooms with no men to share them.

659

COMMISSIONER   You seem to forget that men, too, grow old.

LYSISTRATA   By Zeus, but you cannot compare them!
  When a man gets back, though he be quite gray,
      he can wed a young girl in a minute,
  but the season of woman is very short:
      she must take what she can while she's in it.
  And you know she must, for when it's past,
      although you're not awfully astute, you're
  aware that no man will marry her then
      and she sits staring into the future.

COMMISSIONER   But he who can raise an erection still—

LYSISTRATA   Is there some good reason you don't drop dead?
  We'll sell you a coffin if you but will.
  Here's a string of onions to crown your head
  and I'll make a honey-cake large and round
  you can feed to Cerberus underground!

FIRST OLD MARKET-WOMAN   Accept these few fillets of leek from me!

SECOND OLD MARKET-WOMAN   Let me offer you these for your garland,
    sir!

LYSISTRATA   What now? Do you want something else you see?
  Listen! Charon's calling his passenger—
  will you catch the ferry or still delay
  when his other dead want to sail away?

COMMISSIONER   Is it not downright monstrous to treat *me* like this?
  By Zeus, I'll go right now to the Commissioners
  and show myself in evidence, just as I am!

[*He begins to withdraw with dignity and his four Scythian policemen.*]

LYSISTRATA   Will you accuse us of not giving you a wake?
  But your departed spirit will receive from us
  burnt offerings in due form, two days from now at dawn!

[LYSISTRATA *with the other women goes into the Acropolis. The* COMMISSIONER *etc. have left. The male chorus and the mixed female chorus are alone.*]

CHORUS OF MEN   No man now dare fall to drowsing, if he wishes to stay
    free!
  Men, let's strip and grid ourselves for this eventuality!

      To me this all begins to have a smell
      of bigger things and larger things as well:
      most of all I sniff a tyranny afoot. I'm much afraid

660

certain secret agents of the Spartans may have come,
    meeting under cover here, in Cleisthenes's home,
instigating those damned women by deceit to make a raid
    upon our treasury and that great sum
    the city paid my pension from.

Sinister events already!—think of lecturing the state,
women as they are, and prattling on of things like shields of bronze,
even trying hard to get us reconciled to those we hate—
those of Sparta, to be trusted like a lean wolf when it yawns!
All of this is just a pretext, men, for a dictatorship—
but to me they shall not dictate! Watch and ward! A sword I'll hide
underneath a branch of myrtle; through the agora I'll slip,
following Aristogeiton, backing the tyrannicide!

[*The* OLD MEN *pair off to imitate the gestures of the famous group statue of the tyrannicides Harmodius and Aristogeiton.*]

Thus I'll take my stand beside him! Now my rage is goaded raw
    I'm as like as not to clip this damned old woman on the jaw!
CHORUS OF WOMEN Your own mother will not know you when you
    come home, if you do!
Let us first, though, lay our things down, O my dear old friends and
    true.

For now, O fellow-citizens, we would
    consider what will do our city good.
Well I may, because it bred me up in wealth and elegance:
    letting me at seven help with the embroidering
    of Athena's mantle, and at ten with offering
cakes and flowers. When I was grown and beautiful I had my
    chance
    to bear her baskets, at my neck a string
    of figs, and proud as anything.

Must I not, then, give my city any good advice I can?
Need you hold the fact against me that I was not born a man,
when I offer better methods than the present ones, and when
I've a share in this economy, for I contribute men?
But, you sad old codgers, *yours* is forfeited on many scores:
you have drawn upon our treasure dating from the Persian wars,
what they call grampatrimony, and you've paid no taxes back.
Worse, you've run it nearly bankrupt, and the prospect's pretty black.
Have you anything to answer? Say you were within the law
and I'll take this rawhide boot and clip you one across the jaw!

CHORUS OF MEN   Greater insolence than ever!—
                that's the method that she calls
                "better"—if you would believe her.
But this threat must be prevented! Every man with both his balls
must make ready—take our shirts off, for a man must reek of male
outright—not wrapped up in leafage like an omelet for sale!

        Forward and barefoot: we'll do it again
        to the death, just as when we resisted
        tyranny out at Leipsydrion, when
        we really existed!

        Now or never we must grow
        young again and, sprouting wings
        over all our bodies, throw
        off this heaviness age brings!

  For if any of us give them even just a little hold
nothing will be safe from their tenacious grasp. They are so bold
they will soon build ships of war and, with exorbitant intent,
send such navies out against us as Queen Artemisia sent.
But if they attack with horse, our knights we might as well delete:
nothing rides so well as woman, with so marvelous a seat,
never slipping at the gallop. Just look at those Amazons
in that picture in the Stoa, from their horses bringing bronze
axes down on men. We'd better grab *these* members of the sex
one and all, arrest them, get some wooden collars on their necks!

CHORUS OF WOMEN   By the gods, if you chagrin me
                or annoy me, if you dare,
                I'll turn loose the sow that's in me
till you rouse the town to help you with the way I've done your hair!
Let us too make ready, women, and our garments quickly doff
so we'll smell like women angered fit to bite our fingers off!

        Now I am ready: let one of the men
        come against me, and *he'll* never hanker
        after a black bean or garlic again:
        no woman smells ranker!

        Say a single unkind word,
        I'll pursue you till you drop,
        as the beetle did the bird.
        My revenge will never stop!

Yet you will not worry me so long as Lampito's alive
and my noble friends in Thebes and other cities still survive.
You'll not overpower us, even passing seven decrees or eight,
you, poor brute, whom everyone and everybody's neighbors hate.
Only yesterday I gave a party, honoring Hecatë,
but when I invited in the neighbor's child to come and play,
such a pretty thing from Thebes, as nice and quiet as you please,
just an eel, they said she couldn't, on account of your decrees.
You'll go on forever passing such decrees without a check
till somebody takes you firmly by the leg and breaks your neck!

[LYSISTRATA *comes out. The* CHORUS OF WOMEN *addresses her in the manner of tragedy.*]

Oh Queen of this our enterprise and all our hopes,
wherefore in baleful brooding hast thou issued forth?

LYSISTRATA   The deeds of wicked women and the female mind
discourage me and set me pacing up and down.

CHORUS OF WOMEN   What's that? What's that you say?

LYSISTRATA   The truth, alas, the truth!

CHORUS OF WOMEN   What is it that's so dreadful? Tell it to your
friends.

LYSISTRATA   A shameful thing to tell and heavy not to tell.

CHORUS OF WOMEN   Oh, never hide from me misfortune that is ours!

LYSISTRATA   To put it briefly as I can, we are in heat.

CHORUS OF WOMEN   Oh Zeus!

LYSISTRATA   Why call on Zeus? This is the way
things are.
At least it seems I am no longer capable
of keeping them from men. They are deserting me.
This morning I caught one of them digging away
to make a tunnel to Pan's grotto down the slope,
another letting herself down the parapet
with rope and pulley, and another climbing down
its sheerest face, and yesterday was one I found
sitting upon a sparrow with a mind to fly
down to some well-equipped whoremaster's place in town.
Just as she swooped I pulled her backward by the hair.
They think of every far-fetched excuse they can
for going home. And here comes one deserter now.
You there, where are you running?

FIRST WOMAN   I want to go home,
because I left some fine Milesian wools at home
that must be riddled now with moths.

LYSISTRATA   Oh, damn your moths!
  Go back inside.

FIRST WOMAN   But I shall come back right away,
  just time enough to stretch them out upon my bed.

LYSISTRATA   Stretch nothing out, and don't you go away at all.

FIRST WOMAN   But shall I let my wools be ruined?

LYSISTRATA   If you must.

SECOND WOMAN   Oh miserable me! I sorrow for the flax
  I left at home unbeaten and unstripped!

LYSISTRATA   One more—
  wanting to leave for stalks of flax she hasn't stripped.
  Come back here!

SECOND WOMAN   But, by Artemis, I only want
  to strip my flax. Then I'll come right back here again.

LYSISTRATA   Strip me no strippings! If you start this kind of thing
  some other woman soon will want to do the same.

THIRD WOMAN   O lady Artemis, hold back this birth until
  I can get safe to some unconsecrated place!

LYSISTRATA   What is this raving?

THIRD WOMAN   I'm about to have a child.

LYSISTRATA   But you weren't pregnant yesterday.

THIRD WOMAN   I am today.
  Oh, send me home this instant, dear Lysistrata,
  so I can find a midwife.

LYSISTRATA   What strange tale is this?
  What is this hard thing you have here?

THIRD WOMAN   The child is male.

LYSISTRATA   By Aphrodite, no! You obviously have
  some hollow thing of bronze. I'll find out what it is.
  You silly thing!—you have Athena's helmet here—
  and claiming to be pregnant!

THIRD WOMAN   So I am, by Zeus!

LYSISTRATA   In that case, what's the helmet for?

THIRD WOMAN   So if the pains
  came on me while I'm still up here, I might give birth
  inside the helmet, as I've seen the pigeons do.

LYSISTRATA   What an excuse! The case is obvious. Wait here.
  I want to show this bouncing baby helmet off.

[*She passes the huge helmet around the* CHORUS OF WOMEN.]

SECOND WOMAN   But I can't even sleep in the Acropolis,
   not for an instant since I saw the sacred snake!

FOURTH WOMAN   The owls are what are killing *me*. How can I sleep
   with their eternal whit-to-whoo-to-whit-to-whoo?

LYSISTRATA   You're crazy! Will you stop this hocus-pocus now?
   No doubt you miss your husbands: don't you think that they
   are missing us as much? I'm sure the nights they pass
   are just as hard. But, gallant comrades, do bear up,
   and face these gruelling hardships yet a little while.
   There is an oracle that says we'll win, if we
   only will stick together. Here's the oracle.

CHORUS OF WOMAN   Oh, read us what it says!

LYSISTRATA   Keep silence, then and hear:
   "Now when to one high place are gathered the fluttering swallows,
   Fleeing the Hawk and the Cock however hotly it follows,
   Then will their miseries end, and that which is over be under:
   Thundering Zeus will decide.

A WOMAN   Will *we* lie on top now, I wonder?

LYSISTRATA   *But if the Swallows go fighting each other and springing and winging*
   Out of the holy and high sanctuary, then people will never
   Say there was any more dissolute bitch of a bird whatsoever.

A WOMAN   The oracle is clear, by Zeus!

LYSISTRATA   By *all* the gods!
   So let us not renounce the hardships we endure.
   But let us go back in. Indeed, my dearest friends,
   it would be shameful to betray the oracle.

[*Exeunt into the Acropolis.*]

CHORUS OF MEN   Let me tell you a story I heard one day
         when I was a child:
   There was once a young fellow Melanion by name
   who refused to get married and ran away
         to the wild.
         To the mountains he came
         and inhabited there
         in a grove
         and hunted the hare
         both early and late
         with nets that he wove
         and also a hound

665

and he never came home again, such was his hate,
    all women he found
    so nasty, and we
    quite wisely agree.
  Let us kiss you, dear old dears!

CHORUS OF WOMEN With no onions, you'll shed tears!

CHORUS OF MEN I mean, lift my leg and *kick.*

CHORUS OF WOMEN My, you wear your thicket thick!

CHORUS OF MEN Great Myronides was rough
    at the front and black enough
    in the ass to scare his foes.
      Just ask anyone who knows:
      it's with hair that wars are won—
      take for instance Phormion.

CHORUS OF WOMEN Let me tell you a story in answer to
    Melanion's case.
  There is now a man, Timon, who wanders around
  in the wilderness, hiding his face from view
      in a place
    where the brambles abound   ·
    so he looks like a chip
      off a Fur-
    y, curling his lip.
    Now Timon retired
    in hatred and pure
    contempt of all men
  and he cursed them in words that were truly inspired
    again and again
    but women he found
    delightful and sound.
  Would you like your jaw repaired?

CHORUS OF MEN Thank you, no. You've got me scared.

CHORUS OF WOMEN Let me jump and kick it though.

CHORUS OF MEN You will let your man-sack show.

CHORUS OF WOMEN All the same you wouldn't see,
    old and gray as I may be,
    any superfluity
      of unbarbered hair on me;
      it is plucked and more, you scamp,
      since I singe it with a lamp!

[*Enter* LYSISTRATA *on the wall.*]

LYSISTRATA Women, O women, come here quickly, here to me!

WOMEN Whatever is it? Tell me! What's the shouting for?

LYSISTRATA I see a man approaching, shaken and possessed,
 seized and inspired by Aphrodite's power.
 O thou, of Cyprus, Paphos, and Cythera, queen!
 continue straight along this way you have begun!

A WOMAN Whoever he is, where is he?

LYSISTRATA   Near Demeter's shrine.

A WOMAN Why yes, by Zeus, he is. Who ever can he be?

LYSISTRATA Well, look at him. Do any of you know him?

MYRRHINA   Yes.
 I do. He's my own husband, too, Cinesias.

LYSISTRATA Then it's your duty now to turn him on a spit,
 cajole him and make love to him and not make love,
 to offer everything, short of those things of which
 the wine-cup knows.

MYRRHINA   I'll do it, don't you fear.

LYSISTRATA   And I
 will help you tantalize him. I will stay up here
 and help you roast him slowly. But now, disappear!

[*Enter* CINESIAS.]

CINESIAS Oh how unfortunate I am, gripped by what spasms,
 stretched tight like being tortured on a wheel!

LYSISTRATA Who's there? Who has got this far past the sentries?

CINESIAS   I.

LYSISTRATA A man?

CINESIAS   A man, for sure.

LYSISTRATA   Then clear away from here.

CINESIAS Who're you, to throw me out?

LYSISTRATA   The look-out for the day.

CINESIAS Then, for the gods' sake, call Myrrhina out for me.

LYSISTRATA You don't say! Call Myrrhina out! And who are you?

CINESIAS Her husband. I'm Cinesias Paionides.

LYSISTRATA Well, my dear man, hello! Your name is not unknown
 among us here and not without a certain fame,
 because your wife has it forever on her lips.

She can't pick up an egg or quince but she must say:
Cinesias would enjoy it so!

CINESIAS   How wonderful!

LYSISTRATA By Aphrodite, yes. And if we chance to talk
of husbands, your wife interrupts and says the rest
are nothing much compared to her Cinesias.

CINESIAS Go call her.

LYSISTRATA   Will you give me something if I do?

CINESIAS Indeed I will, by Zeus, if it is what you want.
I can but offer what I have, and I have this.

LYSISTRATA Wait there. I will go down and call her.

CINESIAS   Hurry up!
because I find no charm whatever left in life
since she departed from the house. I get depressed
whenever I go into it, and everything
seems lonely to me now, and when I eat my food
I find no taste in it at all—because I'm stiff.

MYRRHINA [*offstage*] I love him, how I love him! But he doesn't want
my love! [*on wall*] So what's the use of calling me to him?

CINESIAS My sweet little Myrrhina, why do you act like that?
Come down here.

MYRRHINA   There? By Zeus, I certainly will not.

CINESIAS Won't you come down, Myrrhina, when I'm calling you?

MYRRHINA Not when you call me without needing anything.

CINESIAS Not needing anything? I'm desperate with need.

MYRRHINA I'm going now.

CINESIAS   Oh no! No, don't go yet! At least
you'll listen to the baby. Call your mammy, you.

BABY Mammy mammy mammy!

CINESIAS What's wrong with you? Have you no pity on your child
when it is six days now since he was washed or nursed?

MYRRHINA Oh, *I* have pity. But his father takes no care
of him.

CINESIAS Come down, you flighty creature, for the child.

MYRRHINA Oh, what it is to be a mother! I'll come down,
for what else can I do?

[Myrrhina *exits to reenter below.*]

CINESIAS   It seems to me she's grown
much younger, and her eyes have a more tender look.

668

Even her being angry with me and her scorn
are just the things that pain me with the more desire.

MYRRHINA   Come let me kiss you, dear sweet little baby mine,
with such a horrid father. Mammy loves you, though.

CINESIAS   But why are you so mean? Why do you listen to
those other women, giving me such pain?—And you,
you're suffering yourself.

MYRRHINA   Take your hands off of me!

CINESIAS   But everything we have at home, my things and yours,
you're letting go to pieces.

MYRRHINA   Little do I care!

CINESIAS   Little you care even if your weaving's pecked apart
and carried off by chickens?

MYRRHINA [*bravely*]   Little I care, by Zeus!

CINESIAS   You have neglected Aphrodite's rituals
for such a long time now. Won't you come back again?

MYRRHINA   Not I, unless you men negotiate a truce
and make an end of war.

CINESIAS   Well, if it's so decreed,
we will do even that.

MYRRHINA   Well, if it's so decreed,
I will come home again. Not now. I've sworn I won't.

CINESIAS   All right, all right. But now lie down with me once more.

MYRRHINA   No! No!—yet I don't say I'm not in love with you.

CINESIAS   You love me? Then why not lie down, Myrrhina dear?

MYRRHINA   Don't be ridiculous! Not right before the child!

CINESIAS   By Zeus, of course not. Manes, carry him back home.
There now. You see the baby isn't in your way.
Won't you lie down?

MYRRHINA   But *where,* you rogue, just where
is one to do it?

CINESIAS   Where? Pan's grotto's a fine place.

MYRRHINA   But how could I come back to the Acropolis
in proper purity?

CINESIAS   Well, there's a spring below
the grotto—you can very nicely bathe in that.

[*Ekkyklema or inset-scene with grotto*]

MYRRHINA   And then I'm under oath. What if I break my vows?

CINESIAS   Let me bear all the blame. Don't worry about your oath.

MYRRHINA   Wait here, and I'll go get a cot for us.

CINESIAS   No no,
   the ground will do.

MYRRHINA   No, by Apollo! Though you *are*
   so horrid, I can't have you lying on the ground. [*Leaves.*]

CINESIAS   You know, the woman loves me—*that's* as plain as day.

MYRRHINA   There. Get yourself in bed and I'll take off my clothes.
   Oh, what a nuisance! I must go and get a mat.

CINESIAS   What for? I don't need one.

MYRRHINA   Oh yes, by Artemis!
   On the bare cords? How ghastly!

CINESIAS   Let me kiss you now.

MYRRHINA   Oh, very well.

CINESIAS   Wow! Hurry, hurry and come back.

[MYRRHINA *leaves. A long wait.*]

MYRRHINA   Here is the mat. Lie down now, while I get undressed.
   Oh, what a nuisance! You don't have a pillow, dear.

CINESIAS   But I don't need one, not one bit!

MYRRHINA   By Zeus, *I* do! [*Leaves.*]

CINESIAS   Poor prick, the service around here is terrible!

MYRRHINA   Sit up, my dear, jump up! Now I've got everything.

CINESIAS   Indeed you have. And now, my golden girl, come here.

MYRRHINA   I'm just untying my brassiere. Now don't forget:
   about that treaty—you won't disappoint me, dear?

CINESIAS   By Zeus, no! On my life!

MYRRHINA   You have no blanket, dear.

CINESIAS   By Zeus, I do not need one. I just want to screw.

MYRRHINA   Don't worry, dear, you will. I'll be back right away.

[*Leaves.*]

CINESIAS   This number, with her bedding, means to murder me.

MYRRHINA   Now raise yourself upright.

CINESIAS   But *this* is upright now!

MYRRHINA   Wouldn't you like some perfume?

CINESIAS   By Apollo, no!

MYRRHINA   By Aphrodite, yes! You must—like it or not. [*Leaves.*]

CINESIAS   Lord Zeus! Just let the perfume spill! That's all I ask!

670

MYRRHINA Hold out your hand. Take some of this and rub it on.

CINESIAS This perfume, by Apollo, isn't sweet at all.
It smells a bit of stalling—not of wedding nights!

MYRRHINA I brought the *Rhodian* perfume! How absurd of me!

CINESIAS It's fine! Let's keep it.

MYRRHINA You *will* have your little joke.

[*Leaves.*]

CINESIAS Just let me at the man who first distilled perfumes!

MYRRHINA Try this, in the long vial.

CINESIAS I've got one like it, dear.
But don't be tedious. Lie down. And please don't bring
anything more.

MYRRHINA [*going*] That's what I'll do, by Artemis!
I'm taking off my shoes. But dearest, don't forget
you're going to vote for peace.

CINESIAS I will consider it.
She has destroyed me, murdered me, that woman has!
On top of which she's got me skinned and gone away!
        What shall I do? Oh, whom shall I screw,
        cheated of dear Myrrhina, the first
        beauty of all, a creature divine?
        How shall I tend this infant of mine?
        Find me a pimp: it has to be nursed!

CHORUS OF MEN [*in tragic style, as if to Prometheus or Andromeda bound*]
        In what dire woe, how heavy-hearted
        I see thee languishing, outsmarted!
            I pity thee, alas I do.
        What kidney could endure such pain,
        what spirit could, what balls, what back,
        what loins, what sacroiliac,
        if they came under such a strain
        and never had a morning screw?

CINESIAS O Zeus! the twinges! Oh, the twitches!

CHORUS OF MEN And this is what she did to you,
        that vilest, hatefullest of bitches!

CINESIAS Oh nay, by Zeus, she's dear and sweet!

CHORUS OF MEN How can she be? She's vile, O Zeus, she's vile!
        Oh treat her, Zeus, like so much wheat—
        O God of Weather, hear my prayer—
        and raise a whirlwind's mighty blast

671

to roll her up into a pile
and carry her into the sky
far up and up and then at last
drop her and land her suddenly
astride that pointed penis there!

[*The ekkyklema turns, closing the inset-scene. Enter, from opposite
sides, a* SPARTAN *and an Athenian official.*]

SPARTAN   Wheah is the Senate-house of the Athenians?
  Ah wish to see the chaihman. Ah have news of him.

ATHENIAN   And who are you? Are you a Satyr or a man?

SPARTAN   Ah am a herald, mah young friend, yes, by the gods,
  and Ah have come from Sparta to negotiate.

ATHENIAN   And yet you come here with a spear under your arm?

SPARTAN   Not Ah, bah Zeus, not Ah!

ATHENIAN   Why do you turn around?
  Why throw your cloak out so in front? Has the long trip
  given you a swelling?

SPARTAN   Ah do think the man is queah!

ATHENIAN   But you have an erection, oh you reprobate!

SPARTAN   Bah Zeus, Ah've no sech thing! And don't you fool around!

ATHENIAN   And what have you got there?

SPARTAN   A Spahtan scroll-stick, suh.

ATHENIAN   Well, if it is, *this* is a Spartan scroll-stick, too.
  But look, I know what's up: you can tell *me* the truth.
  Just how are things with you in Sparta: tell me that.

SPARTAN   Theah is uprising in all Spahta. Ouah allies
  are all erect as well. We need ouah milkin'-pails.

ATHENIAN   From where has this great scourge of frenzy fallen on you?
  From Pan?

SPARTAN   No, Ah think Lampito began it all,
  and then, the othah women throughout Spahta joined
  togethah, just lahk at a signal of a race,
  and fought theah husbands off and drove them from theah cunts.

ATHENIAN   So, how're you getting on?

SPARTAN   We suffah. Through the town
  we walk bent ovah as if we were carrying
  lamps in the wind. The women will not let us touch
  even theah berries, till we all with one acco'd
  have made a peace among the cities of all Greece.

672

ATHENIAN   This is an international conspiracy
launched by the women! Now I comprehend it all!
Return at once to Sparta. Tell them they must send
ambassadors fully empowered to make peace.
And our Assembly will elect ambassadors
from our side, when I say so, showing them this prick.

SPARTAN   Ah'll run! Ah'll flah! Fo all you say is excellent!

CHORUS OF MEN   No wild beast is more impossible than woman is to fight,
nor is fire, nor has the panther such unbridled appetite!

CHORUS OF WOMEN   Well you know it, yet you go on warring with me
without end,
when you might, you cross-grained creature, have me as a trusty
friend.

CHORUS OF MEN   Listen: I will never cease from hating women till I die!

CHORUS OF WOMEN   Any time you like. But meanwhile is there any reason
why
I should let you stand there naked, looking so ridiculous?
I am only coming near you, now, to slip your coat on, thus.

CHORUS OF MEN   That was very civil of you, very kind to treat me so,
when in such uncivil rage I took it off a while ago.

CHORUS OF WOMEN   Now you're looking like a man again, and not
ridiculous.
If you hadn't hurt my feelings, I would not have made a fuss,
I would even have removed that little beast that's in your eye.

CHORUS OF MEN   *That* is what was hurting me! Well, won't you take my
ring to pry
back my eyelid? Rake the beast out. When you have it, let me see,
for some time now it's been at my eye and irritating me.

CHORUS OF WOMEN   Very well, I will—though you were *born* an irritable
man.
What a monster of a gnat, by Zeus! Look at it if you can.
Don't you see it? It's a native of great marshes, can't you tell?

CHORUS OF MEN   Much obliged, by Zeus! The brute's been digging at me
like a well!
So that now you have removed it, streams of tears come welling out.

CHORUS OF WOMEN   I will dry them. You're the meanest man alive,
beyond a doubt,
yet I will, and kiss you, too.

CHORUS OF MEN   Don't kiss me!

CHORUS OF WOMEN   If you will or not!

CHORUS OF MEN   Damn you! Oh, what wheedling flatterers you all are,
        born and bred!
That old proverb is quite right and not inelegantly said:
"There's no living *with* the bitches and, without them, even *less*"—
so I might as well make peace with you; and from now on, I guess,
I'll do nothing mean to you and, from you, suffer nothing wrong.
So let's draw our ranks together now and start a little song:
        For a change, we're not preparing
        any mean remark or daring
        aimed at any man in town,
    but the very opposite: we plan to do and say
    only good to everyone,
    when the ills we have already are sufficient anyway.
        Any man or woman who
        wants a little money, oh
        say three minas, maybe two,
        kindly let us know.
        What we have is right in here.
        (Notice we have purses, too!)
        And if ever peace appear,
        He who takes our loan today
            never need repay.
        We are having guests for supper,
        allies asked in by our upper
        classes to improve the town.
    There's pea-soup, and I had killed a sucking-pig of mine:
    I shall see it is well done,
    so you will be tasting something very succulent and fine.
        Come to see us, then, tonight
        early, just as soon as you
        have a bath and dress up right:
        bring your children, too.
        Enter boldly, never mind
        asking anyone in sight.
        Go straight in and you will find
        you are quite at home there, but
        all the doors are shut.

And here come the Spartan ambassadors,
            dragging beards that are really the biggest I
have ever beheld, and around their thighs
            they are wearing some sort of a pig-sty.
    Oh men of Sparta, let me bid you welcome first,
    and then you tell us how you are and why you come.

SPARTAN   What need is theah to speak to you in many words?
Fo you may see youahself in what a fix we come.

CHORUS OF MEN   Too bad! Your situation has become
terribly hard and seems to be at fever-pitch.

SPARTAN   Unutterably so! And what is theah to say?
Let someone bring us peace on any tuhms he will!

CHORUS OF MEN   And here I see some natives of Athenian soil,
holding their cloaks far off their bellies, like the best
wrestlers, who sicken at the touch of cloth. It seems
that overtraining may bring on this strange disease.

ATHENIAN   Will someone tell us where to find Lysistrata?
We're men, and here we are, in this capacity.

CHORUS OF MEN   This symptom and that other one sound much alike.
Toward morning I expect convulsions do occur?

ATHENIAN   By Zeus, we are exhausted with just doing that,
so, if somebody doesn't reconcile us quick,
there's nothing for it; we'll be screwing Cleisthenes.

CHORUS OF MEN   Be careful—put your cloaks on, or you might be seen
by some young blade who knocks the phalluses off herms.

ATHENIAN   By Zeus, an excellent idea!

SPARTAN [*having overheard*]   Yes, bah the gods!
It altogethah is. Quick, let's put on our cloaks.

[*Both groups cover quick and then recognize each other with full diplomatic pomp.*]

ATHENIAN   Greetings, O men of Sparta! [*to his group*] We have been
disgraced!

SPARTAN [*to one of his group*]   Mah dearest fellah, what a dreadful thing for
us,
if these Athenians had seen ouah wo'st defeat!

ATHENIAN   Come now, O Spartans: one must specify each point.
Why have you come here?

SPARTAN   To negotiate a peace.
We ah ambassadahs.

ATHENIAN   Well put. And so are we.
Therefore, why do we not call in Lysistrata,
she who alone might get us to agree on terms?

SPARTAN   Call her or any man, even a Lysistratus!

CHORUS OF MEN   But you will have no need, it seems, to call her now,
for here she is. She heard you and is coming out.

CHORUS OF MEN *and* CHORUS OF WOMEN   All hail, O manliest woman
    of all!
            It is time for you now to be turning
    into something still better, more dreadful, mean,
            unapproachable, charming, discerning,
    for here are the foremost nations of Greece,
            bewitched by your spells like a lover,
    who have come to you, bringing you all their claims,
            and to *you* turning everything over.

LYSISTRATA   The work's not difficult, if one can catch them now
    while they're excited and not making passes at
    each other. I will soon find out. Where's *HARMONY?*

[*A naked maid, perhaps wearing a large ribbon reading HARMONY, appears from inside.*]

        Go take the Spartans first, and lead them over here,
    not with a rough hand nor an overbearing one,
    nor, as our husbands used to do this, clumsily,
    but like a woman, in our most familiar style:
    If he won't give his hand, then lead him by the prick.
    And now, go bring me those Athenians as well,
    leading them by whatever they will offer you.
    O men of Sparta, stand right here, close by my side,
    and *you* stand over there, and listen to my words.
    I am a woman, yes, but there is mind in me.
    In native judgment I am not so badly off,
    and, having heard my father and my elders talk
    often enough, I have some cultivation, too.
    And so, I want to take and scold you, on both sides,
    as you deserve, for though you use a lustral urn
    in common at the altars, like blood-relatives,
    when at Olympia, Delphi, or Thermopylae—
    how many others I might name if I took time!—
    yet, with barbarian hordes of enemies at hand,
    it is Greek men, it is Greek cities, you destroy.
    That is one argument so far, and it is done.

ATHENIAN   My prick is skinned alive—that's what's destroying *me.*

LYSISTRATA   Now, men of Sparta—for I shall address you first—
    do you not know that once one of your kings came here
    and as a suppliant of the Athenians
    sat by our altars, death-pale in his purple robe,
    and begged us for an army? For Messenē then
    oppressed you, and an earthquake from the gods as well.
    Then Cimon went, taking four thousand infantry,

676

and saved the whole of Lacedaemon for your state.
That is the way Athenians once treated you;
you ravage their land now, which once received you well.

ATHENIAN   By Zeus, these men are in the wrong, Lysistrata!

SPARTAN [*with his eyes on* Harmony]   We'ah wrong . . . What an
   unutterably lovely ass!

LYSISTRATA   Do you suppose I'm letting you Athenians off?
   Do you not know that once the Spartans in their turn,
   when you were wearing the hide-skirts of slavery,
   came with their spears and slew many Thessalians,
   many companions and allies of Hippias?
   They were the only ones who fought for you that day,
   freed you from tyranny and, for the skirt of hide,
   gave back your people the wool mantle of free men.

SPARTAN   Ah nevah saw a woman broadah—in her views.

ATHENIAN   And I have never seen a lovelier little nook.

LYSISTRATA   So why, when you have done each other so much good,
   go on fighting with no end of malevolence?
   Why don't you make a peace? Tell me, what's in your way?

SPARTAN   Whah, *we* ah willin', if *they* will give up to us
   that very temptin' cuhve.   [*of* Harmony, *as hereafter*]

LYSISTRATA   What curve, my friend?

SPARTAN   The bay
   of Pylos, which we've wanted and felt out so long.

ATHENIAN   No, by Poseidon, you will not get into that!

LYSISTRATA   Good friend, do let them have it.

ATHENIAN   No! What other town
   can we manipulate so well?

LYSISTRATA   Ask them for one.

ATHENIAN   Damn, let me think! Now first suppose you cede to us
   that bristling tip of land, Echinos, behind which
   the gulf of Malia recedes, and those long walls,
   the legs on which Megara reaches to the sea.

SPARTAN   No, mah deah man, not *everything,* bah Castah, no!

LYSISTRATA   Oh, give them up. Why quarrel for a pair of legs?

ATHENIAN   I'd like to strip and get to plowing right away.

SPARTAN   And *Ah* would lahk to push manuah, still earliah.

LYSISTRATA   When you have made a peace, then you will do all that.
   But if you want to do it, first deliberate,
   go and inform your allies and consult with them.

677

ATHENIAN   Oh, damn our allies, my good woman! We are stiff.
   Will all of our allies not stand resolved with us—
   namely, to screw?

SPARTAN   And so will ouahs, Ah'll guarantee.

ATHENIAN   Our mercenaries, even, will agree with us.

LYSISTRATA   Excellent. Now to get you washed and purified
   so you may enter the Acropolis, where we
   women will entertain you out of our supplies.
   You will exchange your pledges there and vows for peace.
   And after that each one of you will take his wife,
   departing then for home.

ATHENIAN   Let's go in right away.

SPARTAN   Lead on, ma'am, anywheah you lahk.

ATHENIAN   Yes, and be quick.

[*Exeunt into Acropolis*]

CHORUS OF MEN *and* CHORUS OF WOMEN
            All the rich embroideries, the
            scarves, the gold accessories, the
            trailing gowns, the robes I own
      I begrudge to no man: let him take what things he will
      for his children or a grown
   daughter who must dress for the procession up Athena's hill.
            Freely of my present stocks
            I invite you all to take.
            There are here no seals nor locks
            very hard to break.
            Search through every bag and box,
            look—you will find nothing there
            if your eyesight isn't fine—
            sharper far than mine!

            Are there any of you needing
            food for all the slaves you're feeding,
            all your little children, too?
      I have wheat in tiny grains for you, the finest sort,
      and I also offer you
   plenty of the handsome strapping grains that slaves get by the quart.
            So let any of the poor
            visit me with bag or sack
            which my slave will fill with more
            wheat than they can pack,
            giving each his ample share.

678

Might I add that at my door
I have watch-dogs?—so beware.
Come too close by day or night,
you will find they bite.

[*Voice of drunken* ATHENIANS *from inside*]

FIRST ATHENIAN   Open the door! [*shoves the porter aside*]
                                          And will you get out of my way?

[*A second drunken* ATHENIAN *follows. The first sees the chorus.*]

   What are you sitting *there* for? Shall I, with this torch,
burn you alive? [*drops character*]
                        How vulgar! Oh, how commonplace!
I can not do it!

[*Starts back in. The second* ATHENIAN *stops him and remonstrates
with him in a whisper. The first turns and addresses the audience.*]

                                    Well, if it really must be done
to please you, we shall face it and go through with it.

CHORUS OF MEN *and* CHORUS OF WOMEN
   And *we* shall face it and go through with it with you.

FIRST ATHENIAN [*in character again, extravagantly*]
   Clear out of here! Or you'll be wailing for your hair!

[CHORUS OF WOMEN *scours away in mock terror.*]

   Clear out of here! so that the Spartans can come out
and have no trouble leaving, after they have dined.

[CHORUS OF MEN *scours away in mock terror.*]

SECOND ATHENIAN   I never saw a drinking-party like this one:
   even the Spartans were quite charming, and of course
   we make the cleverest company, when in our cups.

FIRST ATHENIAN   You're right, because when sober we are not quite sane.
   If I can only talk the Athenians into it,
   we'll always go on any embassy quite drunk,
   for now, going to Sparta sober, we're so quick
   to look around and see what trouble we can make
   that we don't listen to a single word they say—
   instead we think we hear them say what they do not—
   and none of our reports on anything agree.
   But just now everything was pleasant. If a man

got singing words belonging to another song,
we all applauded and swore falsely it was fine!
But here are those same people coming back again
to the same spot! Go and be damned, the pack of you!

[*The* CHORUS, *having thrown off their masks, put on other cloaks, and rushed back on stage, stays put.*]

SECOND ATHENIAN   Yes, damn them, Zeus! Just when the party's coming
  out!

[*The party comes rolling out.*]

A SPARTAN [*to another*]
  Mah very chahmin friend, will you take up youah flutes?
  Ah'll dance the dipody and sing a lovely song
  of us and the Athenians, of both at once!

FIRST ATHENIAN [*as pleasantly as he can*]
  Oh yes, take up your little reeds, by all the gods:
  I very much enjoy seeing you people dance.

SPARTAN   Memory, come,
          come inspiah thah young
          votaries to song,
          come inspiah theah dance!

[*other* SPARTANS *join*]
          Bring thah daughtah, bring the sweet
              Muse, of well she knows
          us and the Athenians,
              how at Ahtemisium
          they in godlike onslaught rose
          hahd against the Puhsian fleet,
              drove it to defeat!
          Well she knows the Spartan waws,
              how Leonidas
              in the deadly pass
          led us on lahk baws
          whettin' shahp theah tusks, how sweat
          on ouah cheeks in thick foam flowahed,
          off ouah legs show thick it showahed,
              fo the Puhsian men were mo'
          than the sands along the sho'.
          Goddess, huntress, Ahtemis,
          slayeh of the beasts, descend:
          vuhgin goddess, come to this
          feast of truce to bind us fast

680

so ouah peace may nevah end.
Now let friendship, love, and wealth
come with ouah acco'd at last.
May we stop ouah villainous
wahly foxy stealth!
    Come, O huntress, heah to us,
    heah, O vuhgin, neah to us!

LYSISTRATA   Come, now that all the rest has been so well arranged,
you Spartans take these women home; these others, you.
Let husband stand beside his wife, and let each wife
stand by her husband: then, when we have danced a dance
to thank the gods for our good fortune, let's take care
hereafter not to make the same mistakes again.

ATHENIAN   Bring on the chorus! Invite the three Graces to follow,
and then call on Artemis, call her twin brother,
the leader of choruses, healer Apollo!

CHORUS [*joins*]   Pray for their friendliest favor, the one and the other.
Call Dionysus, his tender eyes casting
flame in the midst of his Maenads ecstatic with dancing.
    Call upon Zeus, the resplendent in fire,
    call on his wife, rich in honor and ire,
call on the powers who possess everlasting
memory, call them to aid,
call them to witness the kindly, entrancing
peace Aphrodite has made!
    Alalai!
    Bound, and leap high! Alalai!
    Cry, as for victory, cry
    Alalai!

LYSISTRATA   Sing us a new song, Spartans, capping our new song.

SPARTANS   Leave thah favohed mountain's height,
Spahtan Muse, come celebrate
Amyclae's lord with us and great
Athena housed in bronze;
praise Tyndareus' paih of sons,
gods who pass the days in spoht
wheah the cold Eurotas runs.

[*general dancing*]

    Now to tread the dance,
    now to tread it light,
    praising Spahta, wheah you find

love of singing quickened bah the pounding beat
   of dancing feet,
when ouah guhls lahk foals cavoht
wheah the cold Eurotas runs,
when they fleetly bound and prance
   till theah haih unfilleted shakes in the wind,
as of Maenads brandishin'
ahvied wands and revelin',
   Leda's daughtah, puah and faiah,
leads the holy dances theah.

FULL CHORUS [*as everyone leaves dancing*]
So come bind up youah haih with youah hand,
   with youah feet make a bound
lahk a deeah; of the chorus clap out
   an encouragin' sound,
singin' praise of the temple of bronze
   housin' her we adaw:
sing the praise of Athena: the goddess unvanquished in waw!

DISCUSSION TOPICS

1. Why do you think Donald Sutherland, the present translator of *Lysistrata,* has made the Spartans talk like American Southerners? (British translations often have them speaking Scots or a provincial dialect.)

2. Do you find the obscenity in the play more erotic or more comic? Explain your answer. "Obscenity" was part and parcel of Greek Old Comedy. What makes it an especially appropriate device or weapon to use against war? What are some of Aristophanes' other comic weapons? What are some of the other objects of his satire besides war? How does the play function in a larger context as a celebration of the life force as a weapon against the forces of death?

3. What do you think a modern feminist critic would say about Aristophanes's portrayal of women in the play?

4. In *Oedipus the King,* Teiresias is the archetypal wise old man. What are the sources of wisdom in this play? Which characters or groups of characters have that role?

5. Greek drama had choreography or patterned movement for the chorus. But in *Lysistrata* as presented here, the final dance is an important symbol for the whole play. Why is this so? Compare the appearance of the maid in the role of "Harmony" near the end of the play.

WRITING TOPIC

Select one or two choral passages in each of the Greek plays given here that seem to you especially important for presenting major themes in the plays. Show how the choruses function for Sophocles and for Aristophanes.

WILLIAM SHAKESPEARE (1564–1616) Actor, poet, playwright. Although he aspired to be a gentleman-poet, as in *Venus and Adonis,* it was the drama he wrote to earn his livelihood from the sixteenth- and seventeenth-century London stage that won him enduring fame.

HAMLET

Characters

CLAUDIUS, King of Denmark
HAMLET, son to the former, and nephew to the present King
POLONIUS, lord chamberlain
HORATIO, friend to Hamlet
LAERTES, son to Polonius
VOLTEMAND ⎫
CORNELIUS ⎟
ROSENCRANTZ ⎬ courtiers
GUILDENSTERN ⎟
OSRIC ⎭
A Gentleman
A Priest
MARCELLUS ⎫ officers
BERNARDO ⎭
FRANCISCO, a soldier
REYNALDO, servant to Polonius
PLAYERS
Two Clowns, gravediggers
FORTINBRAS, prince of Norway
A Captain
ENGLISH AMBASSADORS
GERTRUDE, Queen of Denmark, and mother to Hamlet
OPHELIA, daughter to Polonius
Lords, Ladies, Officers, Soldiers, Sailors, Messengers, and other Attendants
Ghost of Hamlet's Father

[*Scene: Denmark*]

ACT I

Scene I.

Elsinore. A Platform before the Castle.

[*Enter two* SENTINELS—*first,* FRANCISCO, *who paces up and down at his post; then* BERNARDO, *who approaches him.*]

BERNARDO   Who's there?

FRANCISCO   Nay, answer me. Stand and unfold yourself.

BERNARDO   Long live the King!

FRANCISCO   Bernardo?

BERNARDO   He.   5

FRANCISCO   You come most carefully upon your hour.

BERNARDO   'Tis now struck twelve. Get thee to bed, Francisco.

FRANCISCO   For this relief much thanks. 'Tis bitter cold,
   And I am sick at heart.

BERNARDO   Have you had quiet guard?

FRANCISCO   Not a mouse stirring.   10

BERNARDO   Well, good night.
   If you do meet Horatio and Marcellus,
   The rivals of my watch, bid them make haste.

[*Enter* HORATIO *and* MARCELLUS.]

FRANCISCO   I think I hear them. Stand, ho! Who is there?

HORATIO   Friends to this ground.

MARCELLUS   And liegemen to the Dane.   15

FRANCISCO   Give you good night.

MARCELLUS   O, farewell, honest soldier.
   Who hath reliev'd you?

FRANCISCO   Bernardo hath my place.
   Give you good night.

[*Exit.*]

MARCELLUS   Holla, Bernardo!

BERNARDO   Say—
   What, is Horatio there?

HORATIO   A piece of him.

BERNARDO   Welcome, Horatio. Welcome, good Marcellus.   20

MARCELLUS   What, has this thing appear'd again to-night?

BERNARDO   I have seen nothing.

2 *unfold:* identify   6 *carefully:* punctually   9 *sick at heart:* depressed   13 *rivals:* partners
15 *ground:* Denmark; *the Dane:* newly crowned Claudius

MARCELLUS   Horatio says 'tis but our fantasy,
    And will not let belief take hold of him
    Touching this dreaded sight, twice seen of us.   25
    Therefore I have entreated him along,
    With us to watch the minutes of this night,
    That, if again this apparition come,
    He may approve our eyes and speak to it.

HORATIO   Tush, tush, 'twill not appear.

BERNARDO   Sit down awhile,   30
    And let us once again assail your ears,
    That are so fortified against our story,
    What we two nights have seen.

HORATIO   Well, sit we down,
    And let us hear Bernardo speak of this.

BERNARDO   Last night of all,   35
    When yond same star that's westward from the pole
    Had made his course t' illume that part of heaven
    Where now it burns, Marcellus and myself,
    The bell then beating one—

[*Enter* GHOST.]

MARCELLUS   Peace! break thee off! Look where it comes again!   40

BERNARDO   In the same figure, like the King that's dead.

MARCELLUS   Thou art a scholar; speak to it, Horatio.

BERNARDO   Looks it not like the King? Mark it, Horatio.

HORATIO   Most like. It harrows me with fear and wonder.

BERNARDO   It would be spoke to.

MARCELLUS   Question it, Horatio.   45

HORATIO   What art thou that usurp'st this time of night
    Together with that fair and warlike form
    In which the majesty of buried Denmark
    Did sometimes march? By heaven I charge thee speak!

MARCELLUS   It is offended.

BERNARDO   See, it stalks away!   50

HORATIO   Stay! Speak, speak! I charge thee speak!

[*Exit* GHOST.]

23 *fantasy:* imagination   25 *of us:* by us   29 *approve our eyes:* agree that we have indeed seen what
we have told him we have seen   44 *harrows:* distresses   49 *sometimes:* formerly

MARCELLUS 'Tis gone and will not answer.

BERNARDO How now, Horatio? You tremble and look pale.
Is not this something more than fantasy?
What think you on't?   55

HORATIO Before my God, I might not this believe
Without the sensible and true avouch
Of mine own eyes.

MARCELLUS   Is it not like the King?

HORATIO As thou art to thyself.
Such was the very armour he had on   60
When he th' ambitious Norway combated.
So frown'd he once when, in an angry parle,
He smote the sledded Polacks on the ice.
'Tis strange.

MARCELLUS Thus twice before, and jump at this dead hour,   65
With martial stalk hath he gone by our watch.

HORATIO In what particular thought to work I know not;
But, in the gross and scope of my opinion,
This bodes some strange eruptions to our state.

MARCELLUS Good now, sit down, and tell me he that knows,   70
Why this same strict and most observant watch
So nightly toils the subject of the land,
And why such daily cast of brazen cannon
And foreign mart for implements of war;
Why such impress of shipwrights, whose sore task   75
Does not divide the Sunday from the week.
What might be toward, that this sweaty haste
Doth make the night joint-labourer with the day?
Who is't that can inform me?

HORATIO   That can I.
At least, the whisper goes so. Our last king,   80
Whose image even but now appear'd to us,
Was, as you know, by Fortinbras of Norway,
Thereto prick'd on by a most emulate pride,
Dar'd to the combat; in which our valiant Hamlet
(For so this side of our known world esteem'd him)   85
Did slay this Fortinbras; who, by a seal'd compact,
Well ratified by law and heraldry,

62 _angry parle:_ loud negotiations   65 _jump:_ exactly   74 _foreign mart:_ dealing with foreign markets
75 _impress:_ conscription   77 _might be toward:_ might be about to happen

686

Did forfeit, with his life, all those his lands
Which he stood seiz'd of, to the conqueror;
Against the which a moiety competent   90
Was gaged by our king; which had return'd
To the inheritance of Fortinbras,
Had he been vanquisher, as, by the same comart
And carriage of the article design'd,
His fell to Hamlet. Now, sir, young Fortinbras,   95
Of unimproved mettle hot and full,
Hath in the skirts of Norway, here and there,
Shark'd up a list of lawless resolutes,
For food and diet, to some enterprise
That hath a stomach in't; which is no other,   100
As it doth well appear unto our state,
But to recover of us, by strong hand
And terms compulsatory, those foresaid lands
So by his father lost; and this, I take it,
Is the main motive of our preparations,   105
The source of this our watch, and the chief head
Of this post-haste and romage in the land.

BERNARDO   I think it be no other but e'en so.
  Well may it sort that this portentous figure
  Comes armed through our watch, so like the King   110
  That was and is the question of these wars.

HORATIO   A mote it is to trouble the mind's eye.
  In the most high and palmy state of Rome,
  A little ere the mightiest Julius fell,
  The graves stood tenantless, and the sheeted dead   115
  Did squeak and gibber in the Roman streets;
  As stars with trains of fire, and dews of blood,
  Disasters in the sun; and the moist star
  Upon whose influence Neptune's empire stands
  Was sick almost to doomsday with eclipse.   120
  And even the like precurse of fierce events,
  As harbingers preceding still the fates
  And prologue to the omen coming on,
  Have heaven and earth together demonstrated
  Unto our climature and countrymen.   125

---

90 *moiety competent:* a sufficient portion   91 *gaged:* pledged   93 *comart:* bargain agreed upon
98 *Shark'd up:* took any war-willing, desperate men, as allegedly sharks indiscriminately gather their
prey   100 *a stomach:* valor   106 *head:* motive   107 *romage:* feverish activity   118 *moist star:*
the moon   122 *harbingers:* officers who precede the king to make arrangements for his care; here
forerunners of disaster   123 *omen:* terrible happening   125 *climature:* region

[*Enter* GHOST *again.*]

But soft! behold! Lo, where it comes again!
I'll cross it, though it blast me.—Stay, illusion!

[*Spreads his arms*]

If thou hast any sound, or use of voice,
Speak to me.
If there be any good thing to be done,   130
That may to thee do ease, and grace to me,
Speak to me.
If thou art privy to thy country's fate,
Which happily foreknowing may avoid,
O, speak!   135
Or if thou hast uphoarded in thy life
Extorted treasure in the womb of earth
(For which, they say, you spirits oft walk in death),

[*The cock crows.*]

Speak of it! Stay, and speak!—Stop it, Marcellus!
MARCELLUS   Shall I strike at it with my partisan?   140
HORATIO   Do, if it will not stand.
BERNARDO   'Tis here!
HORATIO   'Tis here!
MARCELLUS   'Tis gone!

[*Exit* GHOST.]

We do it wrong, being so majestical,
To offer it the show of violence;
For it is as the air, invulnerable,   145
And our vain blows malicious mockery.
BERNARDO   It was about to speak, when the cock crew.
HORATIO   And then it started, like a guilty thing
Upon a fearful summons. I have heard
The cock, that is the trumpet to the morn,   150
Doth with his lofty and shrill-sounding throat
Awake the god of day; and at his warning,
Whether in sea or fire, in earth or air,
Th' extravagant and erring spirit hies

126 *soft:* hush!   127 *blast:* destroy   131 *to thee do ease, and grace to me:* bring the ghost relief without disgracing Horatio   140 *partisan:* a shafted weapon with a broad blade   154 *extravagant and erring:* wandering out-of-bounds; *hies:* hastens

To his confine; and of the truth herein   155
This present object made probation.

MARCELLUS   It faded on the crowing of the cock.
Some say that ever, 'gainst that season comes
Wherein our Saviour's birth is celebrated,
The bird of dawning singeth all night long;   160
And then, they say, no spirit dare stir abroad,
The nights are wholesome, then no planets strike,
No fairy takes, nor witch hath power to charm,
So hallow'd and so gracious is the time.

HORATIO   So have I heard and do in part believe it.   165
But look, the morn, in russet mantle clad,
Walks o'er the dew of yon high eastward hill.
Break we our watch up; and by my advice
Let us impart what we have seen to-night
Unto young Hamlet; for, upon my life,   170
This spirit, dumb to us, will speak to him.
Do you consent we shall acquaint him with it,
As needful in our loves, fitting our duty?

MARCELLUS   Let's do't, I pray; and I this morning know
Where we shall find him most conveniently.   175

[*Exeunt.*]

Scene II.

Elsinore. A Room of State in the Castle.

[*Flourish. Enter* CLAUDIUS, KING *of Denmark,* GERTRUDE *the* QUEEN, HAMLET, POLONIUS, LAERTES, *and his sister* OPHELIA, VOLTEMAND, CORNELIUS, LORDS *Attendant.*]

KING   Though yet of Hamlet our dear brother's death
The memory be green, and that it us befitted
To bear our hearts in grief, and our whole kingdom
To be contracted in one brow of woe,
Yet so far hath discretion fought with nature   5
That we with wisest sorrow think on him
Together with remembrance of ourselves.
Therefore our sometime sister, now our queen,
Th' imperial jointress to this warlike state,

---

156 *made probation:* offered proof   158 *'gainst:* immediately preceding   162 *wholesome:* healthful
in every respect; *strike:* exert harmful influence   163 *takes:* puts under a spell   165 *in part believe
it:* some I believe   *Scene II:* morning of the same day   2 *us:* all Danes   5 *discretion:* moderation
6 *wisest sorrow:* sorrow held in check   9 *jointress:* co-inheritor

Have we, as 'twere with a defeated joy,   10
With an auspicious, and a dropping eye,
With mirth in funeral, and with dirge in marriage,
In equal scale weighing delight and dole,
Taken to wife; nor have we herein barr'd
Your better wisdoms, which have freely gone   15
With this affair along. For all, our thanks.
Now follows, that you know, young Fortinbras,
Holding a weak supposal of our worth,
Or thinking by our late dear brother's death
Our state to be disjoint and out of frame,   20
Colleagued with this dream of his advantage,
He hath not fail'd to pester us with message
Importing the surrender of those lands
Lost by his father, with all bands of law,
To our most valiant brother. So much for him.   25
Now for ourself and for this time of meeting.
Thus much the business is: we have here writ
To Norway, uncle of young Fortinbras,
Who, impotent and bedrid, scarcely hears
Of this his nephew's purpose, to suppress   30
His further gait herein, in that the levies,
The lists, and full proportions are all made
Out of his subject; and we here dispatch
You, good Cornelius, and you, Voltemand,
For bearers of this greeting to old Norway,   35
Giving to you no further personal power
To business with the King, more than the scope
Of these dilated articles allow. [*Gives a paper*]
Farewell, and let your haste commend your duty.

CORNELIUS, VOLTEMAND   In that, and all things, will we show our
   duty.   40

KING   We doubt it nothing. Heartily farewell.

[*Exeunt* VOLTEMAND *and* CORNELIUS.]

And now, Laertes, what's the news with you?
You told us of some suit. What is't, Laertes?
You cannot speak of reason to the Dane
And lose your voice. What wouldst thou beg, Laertes,   45

11 *auspicious . . . dropping:* cheerful . . . weeping   18 *a weak supposal of our worth:* an underestimate
of my ability to rule   21 *Colleagued . . . advantage:* produced a dream of superiority   24 *bands:*
sanctions   38 *dilated:* fully expressed   40 *will we show our duty:* we will do what we are ordered
to do

690

That shall not be my offer, not thy asking?
The head is not more native to the heart,
The hand more instrumental to the mouth,
Than is the throne of Denmark to thy father.
What wouldst thou have, Laertes?

LAERTES   My dread lord,   50
Your leave and favour to return to France;
From whence though willingly I came to Denmark
To show my duty in your coronation,
Yet now I must confess, that duty done,
My thoughts and wishes bend again toward France   55
And bow them to your gracious leave and pardon.

KING   Have you your father's leave? What says Polonius?

POLONIUS   He hath, my lord, wrung from me my slow leave
By laboursome petition, and at last
Upon his will I seal'd my hard consent.   60
I do beseech you give him leave to go.

KING   Take thy fair hour, Laertes. Time be thine,
And thy best graces spend it at thy will!
But now, my cousin Hamlet, and my son—

HAMLET [Aside]   A little more than kin, and less than kind!   65

KING   How is it that the clouds still hang on you?

HAMLET   Not so, my lord. I am too much i' th' sun.

QUEEN   Good Hamlet, cast thy nighted colour off,
And let thine eye look like a friend on Denmark.
Do not for ever with thy vailed lids   70
Seek for thy noble father in the dust.
Thou know'st 'tis common. All that lives must die,
Passing through nature to eternity.

HAMLET   Ay, madam, it is common.

QUEEN   If it be,
Why seems it so particular with thee?   75

HAMLET   Seems, madam? Nay, it is. I know not "seems."
'Tis not alone my inky cloak, good mother,
Nor customary suits of solemn black,
Nor windy suspiration of forc'd breath,
No, nor the fruitful river in the eye,   80
Nor the dejected haviour of the visage,

---

51 *leave and favour:* generous permission   56 *leave and pardon:* permission to go back   62 *fair hour:* youth   63 *graces:* qualities   64 *cousin:* kinsman   67 *too much i' th' sun:* in the unwanted forefront of affairs   69 *Denmark:* the King of Denmark   70 *vailed:* downcast

Together with all forms, moods, shapes of grief,
That can denote me truly. These indeed seem,
For they are actions that a man might play;
But I have that within which passeth show—   85
These but the trappings and the suits of woe.

KING   'Tis sweet and commendable in your nature, Hamlet,
To give these mourning duties to your father;
But you must know, your father lost a father;
That father lost, lost his, and the survivor bound   90
In filial obligation for some term
To do obsequious sorrow. But to persever
In obstinate condolement is a course
Of impious stubbornness. 'Tis unmanly grief;
It shows a will most incorrect to heaven,   95
A heart unfortified, a mind impatient,
An understanding simple and unschool'd;
For what we know must be, and is as common
As any the most vulgar thing to sense,
Why should we in our peevish opposition   100
Take it to heart? Fie! 'tis a fault to heaven,
A fault against the dead, a fault to nature,
To reason most absurd, whose common theme
Is death of fathers, and who still hath cried,
From the first corse till he that died to-day,   105
"This must be so." We pray you throw to earth
This unprevailing woe, and think of us
As of a father; for let the world take note
You are the most immediate to our throne,
And with no less nobility of love   110
Than that which dearest father bears his son
Do I impart toward you. For your intent
In going back to school in Wittenberg,
It is most retrograde to our desire;
And we beseech you, bend you to remain   115
Here in the cheer and comfort of our eye,
Our chiefest courtier, cousin, and our son.

QUEEN   Let not thy mother lose her prayers, Hamlet.
I pray thee stay with us, go not to Wittenberg.

HAMLET   I shall in all my best obey you, madam.   120

KING   Why, 'tis a loving and a fair reply.
Be as ourself in Denmark. Madam, come.
This gentle and unforc'd accord of Hamlet
Sits smiling to my heart; in grace whereof,
No jocund health that Denmark drinks to-day   125

But the great cannon to the clouds shall tell,
And the King's rouse the heaven shall bruit again,
Respeaking earthly thunder. Come away.

[*Flourish. Exeunt all but* HAMLET.]

HAMLET   O that this too too solid flesh would melt,
Thaw, and resolve itself into a dew!   130
Or that the Everlasting had not fix'd
His canon 'gainst self-slaughter! O God! God!
How weary, stale, flat, and unprofitable
Seem to me all the uses of this world!
Fie on't! ah, fie! 'Tis an unweeded garden   135
That grows to seed; things rank and gross in nature
Possess it merely. That it should come to this!
But two months dead! Nay, not so much, not two.
So excellent a king, that was to this
Hyperion to a satyr; so loving to my mother   140
That he might not beteem the winds of heaven
Visit her face too roughly. Heaven and earth!
Must I remember? Why, she would hang on him
As if increase of appetite had grown
By what it fed on; and yet, within a month—   145
Let me not think on't! Frailty, thy name is woman!—
A little month, or ere those shoes were old
With which she followed my poor father's body
Like Niobe, all tears—why she, even she
(O God! a beast that wants discourse of reason   150
Would have mourn'd longer) married with my uncle;
My father's brother, but no more like my father
Than I to Hercules. Within a month,
Ere yet the salt of most unrighteous tears
Had left the flushing in her galled eyes,   155
She married. O, most wicked speed, to post
With such dexterity to incestuous sheets!
It is not, nor it cannot come to good.
But break, my heart, for I must hold my tongue!

[*Enter* HORATIO, MARCELLUS, *and* BERNARDO.]

HORATIO   Hail to your lordship!
HAMLET   I am glad to see you well.   160
Horatio!—or I do forget myself.

---

137 *merely:* completely   140 *Hyperion to a satyr:* the sun god to a creature half human and half goat
141 *beteem:* allow   150 *wants:* lacks   155 *galled:* irritated

HORATIO   The same, my lord, and your poor servant ever.

HAMLET   Sir, my good friend—I'll change that name with you.
And what make you from Wittenberg, Horatio?
Marcellus?   165

MARCELLUS   My good lord!

HAMLET   I am very glad to see you.—[*To* BERNARDO] Good even, sir.—
But what, in faith, make you from Wittenberg?

HORATIO   A truant disposition, good my lord.

HAMLET   I would not hear your enemy say so,   170
Nor shall you do my ear that violence
To make it truster of your own report
Against yourself. I know you are no truant.
But what is your affair in Elsinore?
We'll teach you to drink deep ere you depart.   175

HORATIO   My lord, I came to see your father's funeral.

HAMLET   I prithee do not mock me, fellow student.
I think it was my mother's wedding.

HORATIO   Indeed, my lord, it followed hard upon.

HAMLET   Thrift, thrift, Horatio! The funeral bak'd meats   180
Did coldly furnish forth the marriage tables.
Would I had met my dearest foe in heaven
Or ever I had seen that day, Horatio!
My father—methinks I see my father.

HORATIO   O, where, my lord?

HAMLET   In my mind's eye, Horatio.   185

HORATIO   I saw him once. He was a goodly king.

HAMLET   He was a man, take him for all in all.
I shall not look upon his like again.

HORATIO   My lord, I think I saw him yesternight.

HAMLET   Saw? who?   190

HORATIO   My lord, the King your father.

HAMLET   The King my father?

HORATIO   Season your admiration for a while
With an attent ear, till I may deliver,
Upon the witness of these gentlemen,
This marvel to you.

---

175 *to drink deep:* to exchange many toasts   182 *dearest foe:* worst enemy   186 *goodly:* good-
looking or handsome   192 *Season your admiration:* control your wonderment

HAMLET	For God's love let me hear!	195

HORATIO Two nights together had these gentlemen
　(Marcellus and Bernardo) on their watch
　In the dead vast and middle of the night
　Been thus encount'red. A figure like your father,
　Armed at point exactly, cap-a-pe,　　　　　　　　　　200
　Appears before them and with solemn march
　Goes slow and stately by them. Thrice he walk'd
　By their oppress'd and fear-surprised eyes,
　Within his truncheon's length; whilst they distill'd
　Almost to jelly with the act of fear,　　　　　　　　205
　Stand dumb and speak not to him. This to me
　In dreadful secrecy impart they did,
　And I with them the third night kept the watch;
　Where, as they had deliver'd, both in time,
　Form of the thing, each word made true and good,　　210
　The apparition comes. I knew your father.
　These hands are not more like.

HAMLET　　　　　　　　　But where was this?

MARCELLUS My lord, upon the platform where we watch'd.

HAMLET Did you not speak to it?

HORATIO　　　　　　　　　My lord, I did;
　But answer made it none. Yet once methought　　　215
　It lifted up it head and did address
　Itself to motion, like as it would speak;
　But even then the morning cock crew loud,
　And at the sound it shrunk in haste away
　And vanish'd from our sight.

HAMLET　　　　　　　　　'Tis very strange.　　　　220

HORATIO As I do live, my honour'd lord, 'tis true;
　And we did think it writ down in our duty
　To let you know of it.

HAMLET Indeed, indeed, sirs. But this troubles me.
　Hold you the watch to-night?

BOTH [MARCELLUS and BERNARDO] We do, my lord.　　225

HAMLET Arm'd, say you?

BOTH Arm'd, my lord.

---

198 *the dead vast:* unlimited darkness　　200 *at point . . . cap-a-pe:* completely, from head to foot
204 *truncheon's length:* the distance represented by a short baton　　216 *it head:* its head

HAMLET   From top to toe?

BOTH   My lord, from head to foot.

HAMLET   Then saw you not his face?

HORATIO   O, yes, my lord! He wore his beaver up.   230

HAMLET   What, look'd he frowningly?

HORATIO   A countenance more in sorrow than in anger.

HAMLET   Pale or red?

HORATIO   Nay, very pale.

HAMLET   And fix'd his eyes upon you?

HORATIO   Most constantly.

HAMLET   I would I had been there.   235

HORATIO   It would have much amaz'd you.

HAMLET   Very like, very like. Stay'd it long?

HORATIO   While one with moderate haste might tell a hundred.

BOTH   Longer, longer.

HORATIO   Not when I saw't.

HAMLET   His beard was grizzled—no?   240

HORATIO   It was, as I have seen it in his life,
  A sable silver'd.

HAMLET   I will watch to-night.
  Perchance 'twill walk again.

HORATIO   I warr'nt it will.

HAMLET   If it assume my noble father's person,
  I'll speak to it, though hell itself should gape   245
  And bid me hold my peace. I pray you all,
  If you have hitherto conceal'd this sight,
  Let it be tenable in your silence still;
  And whatsoever else shall hap to-night,
  Give it an understanding but no tongue.   250
  I will requite your loves. So, fare you well.
  Upon the platform, 'twixt eleven and twelve,
  I'll visit you.

ALL   Our duty to your honour.

HAMLET   Your loves, as mine to you. Farewell.

[*Exeunt all but* HAMLET.]

230 *beaver:* visor   238 *tell:* count   244 *assume:* put on

My father's spirit—in arms? All is not well. 255
I doubt some foul play. Would the night were come!
Till then sit still, my soul. Foul deeds will rise,
Though all the earth o'erwhelm them, to men's eyes.

[*Exit.*]

Scene III.

Elsinore. A Room in the House of POLONIUS.

[*Enter* LAERTES *and* OPHELIA.]

LAERTES My necessaries are embark'd. Farewell.
　And, sister, as the winds give benefit
　And convoy is assistant, do not sleep,
　But let me hear from you.

OPHELIA　　　　　　　　Do you doubt that?

LAERTES For Hamlet, and the trifling of his favour, 5
　Hold it a fashion, and a toy in blood;
　A violet in the youth of primy nature,
　Forward, not permanent—sweet, not lasting,
　The perfume and suppliance of a minute;
　No more.

OPHELIA No more but so?

LAERTES　　　　　　　Think it no more. 10
　For nature crescent does not grow alone
　In thews and bulk; but as this temple waxes
　The inward service of the mind and soul
　Grows wide withal. Perhaps he loves you now,
　And now no soil nor cautel doth besmirch 15
　The virtue of his will; but you must fear,
　His greatness weigh'd, his will is not his own;
　For he himself is subject to his birth.
　He may not, as unvalued persons do,
　Carve for himself, for on his choice depends 20
　The safety and health of this whole state,
　And therefore must his choice be circumscrib'd
　Unto the voice and yielding of that body
　Whereof he is the head. Then if he says he loves you,

256 *I doubt some foul play:* I suspect some sort of crime has been committed　*Scene III:* afternoon of
the same day　3 *convoy:* mail service　9 *perfume and suppliance of a minute:* fragrance pleasant now
but soon gone　11 *nature crescent:* nature moving toward dominance　15 *cautel:* deceit　23 *voice
and yielding:* assent

It fits your wisdom so far to believe it   25
As he in his particular act and place
May give his saying deed; which is no further
Than the main voice of Denmark goes withal.
Then weigh what loss your honour may sustain
If with too credent ear you list his songs,   30
Or lose your heart, or your chaste treasure open
To his unmast'red importunity.
Fear it, Ophelia, fear it, my dear sister,
And keep you in the rear of your affection,
Out of the shot and danger of desire.   35
The chariest maid is prodigal enough
If she unmask her beauty to the moon.
Virtue itself scapes not calumnious strokes.
The canker galls the infants of the spring
Too oft before their buttons be disclos'd,   40
And in the morn and liquid dew of youth
Contagious blastments are most imminent.
Be wary then; best safety lies in fear.
Youth to itself rebels, though none else near.

OPHELIA   I shall th' effect of this good lesson keep   45
As watchman to my heart. But, good my brother,
Do not as some ungracious pastors do,
Show me the steep and thorny way to heaven,
Whiles, like a puff'd and reckless libertine,
Himself the primrose path of dalliance treads   50
And recks not his own rede.

LAERTES   O, fear me not!

[*Enter* POLONIUS.]

I stay too long. But here my father comes.
A double blessing is a double grace;
Occasion smiles upon a second leave.

POLONIUS   Yet here, Laertes? Aboard, aboard, for shame!   55
The wind sits in the shoulder of your sail,
And you are stay'd for. There—my blessing with thee!
And these few precepts in thy memory
Look thou character. Give thy thoughts no tongue,
Nor any unproportion'd thought his act.   60

---

30 *credent:* easily believing   36 *chariest:* most modest, most careful   37 *to the moon:* to the man in the moon?   39 *infants of the spring:* early flowers   59 *character:* write down

Be thou familiar, but by no means vulgar:
Those friends thou hast, and their adoption tried,
Grapple them unto thy soul with hoops of steel;
But do not dull thy palm with entertainment
Of each new-hatch'd, unfledg'd comrade. Beware   65
Of entrance to a quarrel; but being in,
Bear't that th' opposed may beware of thee.
Give every man thine ear, but few thy voice;
Take each man's censure, but reserve thy judgment.
Costly thy habit as thy purse can buy,   70
But not express'd in fancy; rich, not gaudy;
For the apparel oft proclaims the man,
And they in France of the best rank and station
Are most select and generous, chief in that.
Neither a borrower nor a lender be;   75
For loan oft loses both itself and friend,
And borrowing dulls the edge of husbandry.
This above all—to thine own self be true,
And it must follow, as the night the day,
Thou canst not then be false to any man.   80
Farewell. My blessing season this in thee!

LAERTES Most humbly do I take my leave, my lord.

POLONIUS The time invites you. Go, your servants tend.

LAERTES Farewell, Ophelia, and remember well
  What I have said to you.

OPHELIA   'Tis in my memory lock'd,   85
  And you yourself shall keep the key of it.

LAERTES Farewell.

[*Exit.*]

POLONIUS What is't, Ophelia, he hath said to you?

OPHELIA So please you, something touching the Lord Hamlet.

POLONIUS Marry, well bethought!   90
  'Tis told me he hath very oft of late
  Given private time to you, and you yourself
  Have of your audience been most free and bounteous.
  If it be so—as so 'tis put on me,
  And that in way of caution—I must tell you   95
  You do not understand yourself so clearly
  As it behooves my daughter and your honour.
  What is between you? Give me up the truth.

OPHELIA   He hath, my lord, of late made many tenders
    Of his affection to me.   100

POLONIUS   Affection? Pooh! You speak like a green girl,
    Unsifted in such perilous circumstance.
    Do you believe his tenders, as you call them?

OPHELIA   I do not know, my lord, what I should think.

POLONIUS   Marry, I will teach you! Think yourself a baby   105
    That you have ta'en these tenders for true pay,
    Which are not sterling. Tender yourself more dearly,
    Or (not to crack the wind of the poor phrase,
    Running it thus) you'll tender me a fool.

OPHELIA   My lord, he hath importun'd me with love   110
    In honourable fashion.

POLONIUS   Ay, fashion you may call it. Go to, go to!

OPHELIA   And hath given countenance to his speech, my lord,
    With almost all the holy vows of heaven.

POLONIUS   Ay, springes to catch woodcocks! I do know.   115
    When the blood burns, how prodigal the soul
    Lends the tongue vows. These blazes, daughter,
    Giving more light than heat, extinct in both
    Even in their promise, as it is a-making,
    You must not take for fire. From this time   120
    Be something scanter of your maiden presence.
    Set your entreatments at a higher rate
    Than a command to parley. For Lord Hamlet,
    Believe so much in him, that he is young,
    And with a larger tether may he walk   125
    Than may be given you. In few, Ophelia,
    Do not believe his vows; for they are brokers,
    Not of that dye which their investments show,
    But mere implorators of unholy suits,
    Breathing like sanctified and pious bawds,   130
    The better to beguile. This is for all:
    I would not, in plain terms, from this time forth
    Have you so slander any moment leisure
    As to give words or talk with the Lord Hamlet.
    Look to't, I charge you. Come your ways.   135

OPHELIA   I shall obey, my lord.

[*Exeunt.*]

---

99 *tenders:* assurances   108 *crack the wind of a poor phrase:* overdo or ride to wheezing a bad pun
109 *you'll tender me a fool:* you'll present me with an illegitimate grandchild · 115 *springes:* traps
125 *larger tether:* more leeway to make love   127 *brokers:* cheaters

Scene IV.

Elsinore. The Platform before the Castle.

[*Enter* HAMLET, HORATIO, *and* MARCELLUS.]

HAMLET   The air bites shrewdly; it is very cold.

HORATIO   It is a nipping and an eager air.

HAMLET   What hour now?

HORATIO   I think it lacks of twelve.

MARCELLUS   No, it is struck.

HORATIO   Indeed! I heard it not. It then draws near the season   5
  Wherein the spirit held his wont to walk.

[*A flourish of trumpets, and two pieces go off.*]

  What does this mean, my lord?

HAMLET   The King doth wake to-night and takes his rouse,
  Keeps wassail, and the swagg'ring upspring reels,
  And, as he drains his draughts of Rhenish down,   10
  The kettledrum and trumpet thus bray out
  The triumph of his pledge.

HORATIO   Is it a custom?

HAMLET   Ay, marry, is't;
  But to my mind, though I am native here
  And to the manner born, it is a custom   15
  More honour'd in the breach than the observance.
  This heavy-headed revel east and west
  Makes us traduc'd and tax'd of other nations;
  They clip us drunkards and with swinish phrase
  Soil our addition; and indeed it takes   20
  From our achievements, though perform'd at height,
  The pith and marrow of our attribute.
  So oft it chances in particular men
  That, for some vicious mole of nature in them,
  As in their birth,—wherein they are not guilty,   25
  Since nature cannot choose his origin,—
  By the o'ergrowth of some complexion,
  Oft breaking down the pales and forts of reason,
  Or by some habit that too much o'erleavens

Scene IV: after midnight, about 24 hours later than Scene I   9 *swagg'ring upspring:* a lively dance
12 *the triumph of his pledge:* the lusty feat of swigging down at one gulp liquor drunk as a toast
19 *clip:* name   20 *Soil our addition:* blemish our reputation   24 *mole:* flaw, blemish

The form of plausive manners, that these men 30
Carrying, I say, the stamp of one defect,
Being nature's livery, or fortune's star,
Their virtues else—be they as pure as grace,
As infinite as man may undergo—
Shall in the general censure take corruption 35
From that particular fault. The dram of e'il
Doth all the noble substance often dout
To his own scandal.

[*Enter* GHOST.]

HORATIO   Look, my lord, it comes!

HAMLET   Angels and ministers of grace defend us!
Be thou a spirit of health or goblin damn'd, 40
Bring with thee airs from heaven or blasts from hell,
Be thy intents wicked or charitable,
Thou com'st in such a questionable shape
That I will speak to thee. I'll call thee Hamlet,
King, father, royal Dane. O, answer me! 45
Let me not burst in ignorance, but tell
Why thy canoniz'd bones, hearsed in death,
Have burst their cerements; why the sepulchre
Wherein we saw thee quietly inurn'd,
Hath op'd his ponderous and marble jaws 50
To cast thee up again. What may this mean
That thou, dead corse, again in complete steel,
Revisits thus the glimpses of the moon,
Making night hideous, and we fools of nature
So horridly to shake our disposition 55
With thoughts beyond the reaches of our souls?
Say, why is this? wherefore? What should we do?

[GHOST *beckons* HAMLET.]

HORATIO   It beckons you to go away with it,
As if it some impartment did desire
To you alone.

MARCELLUS   Look with what courteous action 60
It waves you to a more removed ground.
But do not go with it!

---

35 *dout:* extinguish   43 *questionable shape:* in a shape to be questioned   47 *canoniz'd:* given church-approved burial service; *hearsed:* entombed   59 *impartment:* communication

HORATIO   No, by no means!

HAMLET   It will not speak. Then will I follow it.

HORATIO   Do not, my lord!

HAMLET   Why, what should be the fear?
  I do not set my life at a pin's fee;   65
  And for my soul, what can it do to that,
  Being a thing immortal as itself?
  It waves me forth again. I'll follow it.

HORATIO   What if it tempt you toward the flood, my lord,
  Or to the dreadful summit of the cliff   70
  That beetles o'er his base into the sea,
  And there assume some other, horrible form
  Which might deprive your sovereignty of reason
  And draw you into madness? Think of it.
  The very place puts toys of desperation,   75
  Without more motive, into every brain
  That looks so many fathoms to the sea
  And hears it roar beneath.

HAMLET   It waves me still.
  Go on. I'll follow thee.

MARCELLUS   You shall not go, my lord.

HAMLET   Hold off your hands!   80

HORATIO   Be rul'd. You shall not go.

HAMLET   My fate cries out
  And makes each petty artery in this body
  As hardy as the Nemean lion's nerve.

[GHOST *beckons.*]

  Still am I call'd. Unhand me, gentlemen.
  By heaven, I'll make a ghost of him that lets me!—   85
  I say, away!—Go on. I'll follow thee.

[*Exeunt* GHOST *and* HAMLET.]

HORATIO   He waxes desperate with imagination.

MARCELLUS   Let's follow. 'Tis not fit thus to obey him.

HORATIO   Have after. To what issue will this come?

MARCELLUS   Something is rotten in the state of Denmark.

---

65 *a pin's fee:* the value of a pin   81 *My fate cries out:* my destiny is calling   83 *Nemean lion's nerve:*
One of the twelve labors of Hercules was to kill the lion of Nemea.   85 *lets me:* hinders me

HORATIO   Heaven will direct it.

MARCELLUS   Nay, let's follow him.

[*Exeunt.*]

Scene V.

Elsinore. The Castle. Another Part of the Fortifications.

[*Enter* GHOST *and* HAMLET.]

HAMLET   Whither wilt thou lead me? Speak! I'll go no further.

GHOST   Mark me.

HAMLET   I will.

GHOST   My hour is almost come,
  When I to sulph'rous and tormenting flames
  Must render up myself.

HAMLET   Alas, poor ghost!

GHOST   Pity me not, but lend thy serious hearing   5
  To what I shall unfold.

HAMLET   Speak. I am bound to hear.

GHOST   So art thou to revenge, when thou shalt hear.

HAMLET   What?

GHOST   I am thy father's spirit,
  Doom'd for a certain term to walk the night,   10
  And for the day confin'd to fast in fires,
  Till the foul crimes done in my days of nature
  Are burnt and purg'd away. But that I am forbid
  To tell the secrets of my prison house,
  I could a tale unfold whose lightest word   15
  Would harrow up thy soul, freeze thy young blood,
  Make thy two eyes, like stars, start from their spheres,
  Thy knotted and combined locks to part,
  And each particular hair to stand on end
  Like quills upon the fretful porpentine.   20
  But this eternal blazon must not be
  To ears of flesh and blood. List, list, O, list!
  If thou didst ever thy dear father love—

HAMLET   O God!

GHOST   Revenge his foul and most unnatural murther.   25

---

6 *bound:* eager   11 *fast:* do penance   20 *porpentine:* porcupine   21 *blazon:* revelation

HAMLET   Murther?

GHOST   Murther most foul, as in the best it is;
But this most foul, strange, and unnatural.

HAMLET   Haste me to know't, that I, with wings as swift
As meditation or the thoughts of love,   30
May sweep to my revenge.

GHOST   I find thee apt;
And duller shouldst thou be than the fat weed
That rots itself in ease on Lethe wharf,
Wouldst thou not stir in this. Now, Hamlet, hear.
'Tis given out that, sleeping in my orchard,   35
A serpent stung me. So the whole ear of Denmark
Is by a forged process of my death
Rankly abus'd. But know, thou noble youth,
The serpent that did sting thy father's life
Now wears his crown.

HAMLET   O my prophetic soul!   40
My uncle?

GHOST   Ay, that incestuous, that adulterate beast,
With witchcraft of his wit, with traitorous gifts—
O wicked wit and gifts, that have the power
So to seduce!—won to his shameful lust   45
The will of my most seeming-virtuous queen.
O Hamlet, what a falling-off was there,
From me, whose love was of that dignity
That it went hand in hand even with the vow
I made to her in marriage, and to decline   50
Upon a wretch whose natural gifts were poor
To those of mine!
But virtue, as it never will be mov'd,
Though lewdness court it in a shape of heaven,
So lust, though to a radiant angel link'd,   55
Will sate itself in a celestial bed
And prey on garbage.
But soft! methinks I scent the morning air.
Brief let me be. Sleeping within my orchard,
My custom always of the afternoon,   60
Upon my secure hour thy uncle stole,
With juice of cursed hebona in a vial,
And in the porches of my ears did pour

---

33 *Lethe:* river of oblivion in Hades   35 *orchard:* garden area   37 *forged process:* falsified report
40 *O my prophetic soul!:* O how right my intuitions!   62 *hebona:* sap of the ebony tree

The leperous distilment; whose effect
Holds such an enmity with blood of man   65
That swift as quicksilver it courses through
The natural gates and alleys of the body,
And with a sudden vigour it doth posset
And curd, like eager droppings into milk,
The thin and wholesome blood. So did it mine;   70
And a most instant tetter bark'd about,
Most lazar-like, with vile and loathsome crust
All my smooth body.
Thus was I, sleeping, by a brother's hand
Of life, of crown, of queen, at once dispatch'd;   75
Cut off even in the blossoms of my sin,
Unhous'led, disappointed, unanel'd,
No reck'ning made, but sent to my account
With all my imperfections on my head.

HAMLET O, horrible! O, horrible! most horrible!   80

GHOST If thou hast nature in thee, bear it not.
Let not the royal bed of Denmark be
A couch for luxury and damned incest.
But, howsoever thou pursuest this act,
Taint not thy mind, nor let thy soul contrive   85
Against thy mother aught. Leave her to heaven,
And to those thorns that in her bosom lodge
To prick and sting her. Fare thee well at once.
The glowworm shows the matin to be near
And gins to pale his uneffectual fire.   90
Adieu, adieu, adieu! Remember me.

[*Exit.*]

HAMLET O all you host of heaven! O earth! What else?
And shall I couple hell? Hold, hold, my heart!
And you, my sinews, grow not instant old,
But bear me stiffly up. Remember thee?   95
Ay, thou poor ghost, while memory holds a seat
In this distracted globe. Remember thee?
Yea, from the table of my memory
I'll wipe away all trivial fond records,
All saws of books, all forms, all pressures past   100

68 *posset:* coagulate   71 *tetter bark'd about:* eczema made the skin resemble the rough bark of a tree
77 *Unhous'led, disappointed, unanel'd:* unconfessed, unready, not having received extreme unction
83 *luxury:* lechery   93 *shall I couple hell?:* shall I conspire with hell?   97 *distracted globe:* confused
head   100 *saws:* wise sayings

706

That youth and observation copied there,
And thy commandment all alone shall live
Within the book and volume of my brain,
Unmix'd with baser matter. Yes, by heaven!
O most pernicious woman!   105
O villain, villain, smiling, damned villain!
My tables! Meet it is I set it down
That one may smile, and smile, and be a villain;
At least I am sure it may be so in Denmark.

[*Writes*]

So, uncle, there you are. Now to my word: 110
It is "Adieu, adieu! Remember me."
I have sworn't.

HORATIO [*Within*]   My lord, my lord!

[*Enter* HORATIO *and* MARCELLUS.]

MARCELLUS   Lord Hamlet!

HORATIO   Heaven secure him!

HAMLET   So be it!

MARCELLUS   Illo, ho, ho, my lord!   115

HAMLET   Hillo, ho, ho, boy! Come, bird, come.

MARCELLUS   How is't, my noble lord?

HORATIO   What news, my lord?

HAMLET   O, wonderful!

HORATIO   Good my lord, tell it.

HAMLET   No, you will reveal it.

HORATIO   Not I, my lord, by heaven!

MARCELLUS   Nor I, my lord.   120

HAMLET   How say you then? Would heart of man once think it?
But you'll be secret?

BOTH   Ay, by heaven, my lord.

HAMLET   There's ne'er a villain dwelling in all Denmark
But he's an arrant knave.

HORATIO   There needs no ghost, my lord, come from the grave   125
To tell us this.

HAMLET   Why, right! You are in the right!

107 *My tables!:* my notebooks   116 *Hillo . . . bird:* falconer's cry

707

And so, without more circumstance at all,
I hold it fit that we shake hands and part;
You, as your business and desire shall point you,
For every man hath business and desire,   130
Such as it is; and for my own poor part,
Look you, I'll go pray.

HORATIO   These are but wild and whirling words, my lord.

HAMLET   I am sorry they offend you, heartily;
Yes, faith, heartily.

HORATIO   There's no offence, my lord.   135

HAMLET   Yes, by Saint Patrick, but there is, Horatio,
And much offence too. Touching this vision here,
It is an honest ghost, that let me tell you.
For your desire to know what is between us,
O'ermaster't as you may. And now, good friends,   140
As you are friends, scholars, and soldiers,
Give me one poor request.

HORATIO   What is't, my lord? We will.

HAMLET   Never make known what you have seen to-night.

BOTH   My lord, we will not.

HAMLET   Nay, but swear't.

HORATIO   In faith,   145
My lord, not I.

MARCELLUS   Nor I, my lord—in faith.

HAMLET   Upon my sword.

MARCELLUS   We have sworn, my lord, already.

HAMLET   Indeed, upon my sword, indeed.

[GHOST *cries under the stage.*]

Ghost   Swear.

HAMLET   Aha boy, say'st thou so? Are thou there, truepenny?   150
Come on! You hear this fellow in the cellarage.
Consent to swear.

HORATIO   Propose the oath, my lord.

HAMLET   Never to speak of this that you have seen.
Swear by my sword.

---

127 *circumstance:* ceremony   138 *an honest ghost:* above-board, nondemonic ghost   147 *Upon my sword:* on the cross formed by the hilt   150 *truepenny:* good old boy

GHOST [*Beneath*] Swear.   155

HAMLET *Hic et ubique?* Then we'll shift our ground.
Come hither, gentlemen,
And lay your hands again upon my sword.
Swear by my sword.
Never to speak of this that you have heard.   160

GHOST [*Beneath*] Swear by his sword.

HAMLET Well said, old mole! Canst work i' th' earth so fast?
A worthy pioner! Once more remove, good friends.

HORATIO O day and night, but this is wondrous strange!

HAMLET And therefore as a stranger give it welcome.   165
There are more things in heaven and earth, Horatio,
Than are dreamt of in your philosophy.
But come!
Here, as before, never, so help you mercy,
How strange or odd soe'er I bear myself   170
(As I perchance hereafter shall think meet
To put an antic disposition on),
That you, at such times seeing me, never shall,
With arms encumb'red thus, or this headshake,
Or by pronouncing of some doubtful phrase,   175
As "Well, well, we know," or "We could, an if we would,"
Or "If we list to speak," or "There be, an if they might,"
Or such ambiguous giving out, to note
That you know aught of me—this not to do,
So grace and mercy at your most need help you,   180
Swear.

GHOST [*Beneath*] Swear.

[*They swear.*]

HAMLET Rest, rest, perturbed spirit! So, gentlemen,
With all my love I do commend me to you;
And what so poor a man as Hamlet is   185
May do t' express his love and friending to you,
God willing, shall not lack. Let us go in together;
And still your fingers on your lips, I pray.
The time is out of joint. O cursed spite

156 *Hic et ubique?:* here and everywhere   163 *pioner:* a digger in the earth   167 *philosophy:*
scientific attitude   172 *antic:* whimsical, feigning madness   174 *encumb'red:* folded   177 *list:*
chose   189 *spite:* imposition

That ever I was born to set it right!   190
Nay, come, let's go together.

[*Exeunt.*]

ACT II

Scene I.

Elsinore. A Room in the House of POLONIUS.

[*Enter* POLONIUS *and* REYNALDO.]

POLONIUS   Give him this money and these notes, Reynaldo.

REYNALDO   I will, my lord.

POLONIUS   You shall do marvell's wisely, good Reynaldo,
Before you visit him, to make inquire
Of his behaviour.

REYNALDO   My lord, I did intend it.   5

POLONIUS   Marry, well said, very well said. Look you, sir,
Enquire me first what Danskers are in Paris;
And how, and who, what means, and where they keep,
What company, at what expense; and finding
By this encompassment and drift of question   10
That they do know my son, come you more nearer
Than your particular demands will touch it.
Take you, as 'twere, some distant knowledge of him;
As thus, "I know his father and his friends,
And in part him." Do you mark this, Reynaldo?   15

REYNALDO   Ay, very well, my lord.

POLONIUS   "And in part him, but," you may say, "not well.
But if't be he I mean, he's very wild
Addicted so and so"; and there put on him
What forgeries you please; marry, none so rank   20
As may dishonour him—take heed of that;
But, sir, such wanton, wild, and usual slips
As are companions noted and most known
To youth and liberty.

REYNALDO   As gaming, my lord.

POLONIUS   Ay, or drinking, fencing, swearing, quarrelling,   25
Drabbing. You may go so far.

REYNALDO   My lord, that would dishonour him.

---

3 *marvell's:* extraordinarily   20 *forgeries:* false accusations   26 *Drabbing:* whoring

POLONIUS   Faith, no, as you may season it in the charge.
  You must not put another scandal on him,
  That he is open to incontinency.   30
  That's not my meaning. But breathe his faults so quaintly
  That they may seem the taints of liberty,
  The flash and outbreak of a fiery mind,
  A savageness in unreclaimed blood,
  Of general assault.

REYNALDO   But, my good lord—   35

POLONIUS   Wherefore should you do this?

REYNALDO   Ay, my lord,
  I would know that.

POLONIUS   Marry, sir, here's my drift,
  And I believe it is a fetch of warrant.
  You laying these slight sullies on my son
  As 'twere a thing a little soil'd i' th' working,   40
  Mark you,
  Your party in converse, him you would sound,
  Having ever seen in the prenominate crimes
  The youth you breathe of guilty, be assur'd
  He closes with you in this consequence: 45
  "Good sir," or so, or "friend," or "gentleman"—
  According to the phrase or the addition
  Of man and country—

REYNALDO   Very good, my lord.

POLONIUS   And then, sir, does 'a this—'a does—
  What was I about to say? By the mass, I was about to say something!   50
  Where did I leave?

REYNALDO   At "closes in the consequence," at "friend or so,"
  and "gentleman."

POLONIUS   At "closes in the consequence"—Ay, marry!
  He closes thus: "I know the gentleman.   55
  I saw him yesterday, or t'other day,
  Or then, or then, with such or such; and, as you say,
  There was 'a gaming; there o'ertook in's rouse;
  There falling out at tennis"; or perchance,
  "I saw him enter such a house of sale,"   60
  Videlicet, a brothel, or so forth.
  See you now—

---

31 *quaintly:* artfully   34 *unreclaimed:* untamed   35 *Of general assault:* of common occurrence
38 *a fetch of warrant:* fully justified   43 *prenominate:* aforementioned   45 *closes with:* goes along
with   58 *o'ertook in's rouse:* done in by overdrinking   61 *Videlicet:* that is, or namely

Your bait of falsehood takes this carp of truth;
And thus do we of wisdom and of reach,
With windlasses and with assays of bias   65
By indirections find directions out.
So, by my former lecture and advice,
Shall you my son. You have me, have you not?

REYNALDO   My lord, I have.

POLONIUS   God b' wi' ye, fare ye well!

[*Going.*]

REYNALDO   Good my lord!   70

POLONIUS   Observe his inclination in yourself.

REYNALDO   I shall, my lord.

POLONIUS   And let him ply his music.

REYNALDO   Well, my lord.

POLONIUS   Farewell!

[*Exit* REYNALDO.]

[*Enter* OPHELIA.]

                    How now, Ophelia? What's the matter?

OPHELIA   O my lord, my lord, I have been so affrighted!   75

POLONIUS   With what, i' th' name of God?

OPHELIA   My lord, as I was sewing in my closet,
Lord Hamlet, with his doublet all unbrac'd,
No hat upon his head, his stockings foul'd,
Ungart'red, and down-gyved to his ankle;   80
Pale as his shirt, his knees knocking each other,
And with a look so piteous in purport
As if he had been loosed out of hell
To speak of horrors—he comes before me.

POLONIUS   Mad for thy love?

OPHELIA   My lord, I do not know,   85
But truly I do fear it.

POLONIUS   What said he?

OPHELIA   He took me by the wrist and held me hard;
Then goes he to the length of all his arm,
And, with his other hand thus o'er his brow,

---

65 *windlasses . . . bias:* roundabout methods and indirect attempts   68 *you have me:* you understand
me   78 *unbrac'd:* unlaced   80 *down-gyved:* drooping   85 *Mad:* insane

He falls to such perusal of my face   90
As he would draw it. Long stay'd he so.
At last, a little shaking of mine arm,
And thrice his head thus waving up and down,
He rais'd a sigh so piteous and profound
As it did seem to shatter all his bulk   95
And end his being. That done, he lets me go.
And with his head over his shoulder turn'd
He seem'd to find his way without his eyes,
For out o'doors he went without their help
And to the last bended their light on me.   100

POLONIUS   Come, go with me. I will go seek the King.
This is the very ecstasy of love,
Whose violent property fordoes itself
And leads the will to desperate undertakings
As oft as any passion under heaven   105
That does afflict our natures. I am sorry.
What, have you given him any hard words of late?

OPHELIA   No, my good lord; but, as you did command,
I did repel his letters and denied
His access to me.

POLONIUS   That hath made him mad.   110
I am sorry that with better heed and judgment
I had not quoted him. I fear'd he did but trifle
And meant to wrack thee; but beshrew my jealousy!
By heaven, it is as proper to our age
To cast beyond ourselves in our opinions   115
As it is common for the younger sort
To lack discretion. Come, go we to the King.
This must be known; which, being kept close, might move
More grief to hide than hate to utter love.
Come.   120

[*Exeunt.*]

Scene II.

Elsinore. A Room in the Castle.

[*Flourish. Enter* KING, QUEEN, ROSENCRANTZ, GUILDENSTERN, *and others.*]

KING   Welcome, dear Rosencrantz and Guildenstern.
Moreover that we much did long to see you,

102 *ecstasy:* height   112 *quoted:* credited   113 *wrack:* ruin; *beshrew,* curse   118 *close:* concealed

The need we have to use you did provoke
Our hasty sending. Something have you heard
Of Hamlet's transformation. So I call it,   5
Sith nor th' exterior nor the inward man
Resembles that it was. What it should be,
More than his father's death, that thus hath put him
So much from th' understanding of himself,
I cannot dream of. I entreat you both   10
That, being of so young days brought up with him,
And since so neighbour'd to his youth and haviour,
That you vouchsafe your rest here in our court
Some little time; so by your companies
To draw him on to pleasures, and to gather   15
So much as from occasion you may glean,
Whether aught to us unknown afflicts him thus
That, open'd, lies within our remedy.

QUEEN   Good gentlemen, he hath much talk'd of you,
And sure I am two men there are not living   20
To whom he more adheres. If it will please you
To show us so much gentry and good will
As to expend your time with us awhile
For the supply and profit of our hope,
Your visitation shall receive such thanks   25
As fits a king's remembrance.

ROSENCRANTZ   Both your Majesties
Might, by the sovereign power you have of us,
Put your dread pleasures more into command
Than to entreaty.

GUILDENSTERN   But we both obey,
And here give up ourselves, in the full bent,   30
To lay our service at your feet,
To be commanded.

KING   Thanks, Rosencrantz and gentle Guildenstern.

QUEEN   Thanks, Guildenstern and gentle Rosencrantz.
And I beseech you instantly to visit   35
My too much changed son.—Go, some of you,
And bring these gentlemen where Hamlet is.

13 *vouchsafe your rest:* agree to stay   22 *gentry:* gentle manliness   24 *supply and profit:* realization
and advancement

GUILDENSTERN Heavens make our presence and our practices
  Pleasant and helpful to him!

QUEEN   Ay, amen!

[*Exeunt* ROSENCRANTZ *and* GUILDENSTERN *with some attendants.*]

[*Enter* POLONIUS.]

POLONIUS Th' ambassadors from Norway, my good lord,   40
  Are joyfully return'd.

KING Thou still hast been the father of good news.

POLONIUS Have I, my lord? Assure you, my good liege,
  I hold my duty as I hold my soul,
  Both to my God and to my gracious king;   45
  And I do think—or else this brain of mine
  Hunts not the trail of policy so sure
  As it hath us'd to do—that I have found
  The very cause of Hamlet's lunacy.

KING O, speak of that! That do I long to hear.   50

POLONIUS Give first admittance to th' ambassadors.
  My news shall be the fruit to that great feast.

KING Thyself do grace to them, and bring them in.

[*Exit* POLONIUS.]

  He tells me, my dear Gertrude, he hath found
  The head and source of all your son's distemper.   55

QUEEN I doubt it is no other but the main,
  His father's death and our o'erhasty marriage.

KING Well, we shall sift him.

[*Enter* POLONIUS, VOLTEMAND, *and* CORNELIUS.]

               Welcome, my good friends.
  Say, Voltemand, what from our brother Norway?

VOLTEMAND Most fair return of greetings and desires.   60
  Upon our first, he sent out to suppress
  His nephew's levies; which to him appear'd
  To be a preparation 'gainst the Polack,
  But better look'd into, he truly found
  It was against your Highness; whereat griev'd,   65

47 *policy:* statecraft   56 *doubt:* suspect

That so his sickness, age, and impotence
Was falsely borne in hand, sends out arrests
On Fortinbras; which he, in brief, obeys,
Receives rebuke from Norway, and, in fine,
Makes vow before his uncle never more   70
To give th' assay of arms against your Majesty.
Whereon old Norway, overcome with joy,
Gives him three thousand crowns in annual fee
And his commission to employ those soldiers,
So levied as before, against the Polack;   75
With an entreaty, herein further shown,

[*Gives a paper*]

That it might please you to give quiet pass
Through your dominions for this enterprise,
On such regards of safety and allowance
As therein are set down.

KING   It likes us well;   80
And at our more consider'd time we'll read,
Answer, and think upon this business.
Meantime we thank you for your well-took labour.
Go to your rest; at night we'll feast together.
Most welcome home!

[*Exeunt Ambassadors.*]

POLONIUS   This business is well ended.   85
My liege, and madam, to expostulate
What majesty should be, what duty is,
Why day is day, night night, and time is time,
Were nothing but to waste night, day, and time.
Therefore, since brevity is the soul of wit,   90
And tediousness the limbs and outward flourishes,
I will be brief. Your noble son is mad.
Mad call I it; for, to define true madness,
What is't but to be nothing else but mad?
But let that go.

QUEEN   More matter, with less art.   95

POLONIUS   Madam, I swear I use no art at all.
That he is mad, 'tis true: 'tis true 'tis pity;
And pity 'tis 'tis true. A foolish figure!

67 *borne in hand:* acted upon   80 *likes:* pleases   86 *expostulate:* describe   90 *wit:* wisdom

But farewell it, for I will use no art.
Mad let us grant him then. And now remains   100
That we find out the cause of this effect—
Or rather say, the cause of this defect,
For this effect defective comes by cause.
Thus it remains, and the remainder thus.
Perpend.   105
I have a daughter (have while she is mine),
Who in her duty and obedience, mark,
Hath given me this. Now gather, and surmise.

[Reads the letter]

"To the celestial, and my soul's idol,
The most beautified Ophelia."—   110
   That's an ill phrase, a vile phrase; "beautified" is a vile phrase. But you
   shall hear. Thus:

[Reads]

"In her excellent white bosom, these, &c."

QUEEN   Came this from Hamlet to her?

POLONIUS   Good madam, stay awhile. I will be faithful.   115

[Reads]

"Doubt thou the stars are fire;
   Doubt that the sun doth move;
 Doubt truth to be a liar;
   But never doubt I love.
O dear Ophelia, I am ill at these numbers;   120
I have not art to reckon my groans; but that I
love thee best, O most best, believe it. Adieu.
Thine evermore, most dear lady, whilst this
              machine is to him, HAMLET."
This, in obedience, hath my daughter shown me;   125
And more above, hath his solicitings,
As they fell out by time, by means, and place,
All given to mine ear.

KING   But how hath she
Receiv'd his love?

POLONIUS   What do you think of me?

---

105 *Perpend:* listen carefully   124 *machine:* body   126 *above:* besides

KING   As of a man faithful and honourable.   130

POLONIUS   I would fain prove so. But what might you think,
When I had seen this hot love on the wing
(As I perceiv'd it, I must tell you that,
Before my daughter told me), what might you,
Or my dear Majesty your queen here, think,   135
If I had play'd the desk or table book,
Or given my heart a winking, mute and dumb,
Or look'd upon this love with idle sight?
What might you think? No, I went round to work
And my young mistress thus I did bespeak: 140
"Lord Hamlet is a prince, out of thy star.
This must not be." And then I prescripts gave her,
That she should lock herself from his resort,
Admit no messengers, receive no tokens.
Which done, she took the fruits of my advice,   145
And he, repulsed, a short tale to make,
Fell into a sadness, then into a fast,
Thence to a watch, thence into a weakness,
Thence to a lightness, and, by this declension,
Into the madness wherein now he raves,   150
And all we mourn for.

KING   Do you think 'tis this?

QUEEN   It may be, very like.

POLONIUS   Hath there been such a time—I would fain know that—
That I have positively said " 'Tis so,"
When it prov'd otherwise?

KING   Not that I know.   155

POLONIUS [*Points to his head and shoulder*]
Take this from this, if this be otherwise.
If circumstances lead me, I will find
Where truth is hid, though it were hid indeed
Within the centre.

KING   How may we try it further?

POLONIUS   You know sometimes he walks four hours together   160
Here in the lobby.

QUEEN   So he does indeed.

POLONIUS   At such a time I'll loose my daughter to him.
Be you and I behind an arras then.

---

136 *play'd the desk or table book:* filed the matter away   141 *out of thy star:* not included in your destiny
148 *watch:* wakefulness   149 *declension:* decline

Mark the encounter. If he love her not,
And be not from his reason fall'n thereon,   165
Let me be no assistant for a state,
But keep a farm and carters.

KING   We will try it.

[*Enter* HAMLET, *reading on a book.*]

QUEEN   But look where sadly the poor wretch comes reading.

POLONIUS   Away, I do beseech you, both away!
I'll board him presently. O, give me leave.   170

[*Exeunt* KING *and* QUEEN, *with attendants.*]

How does my good Lord Hamlet?

HAMLET   Well, God-a-mercy.

POLONIUS   Do you know me, my lord?

HAMLET   Excellent well. You are a fishmonger.

POLONIUS   Not I, my lord.   175

HAMLET   Then I would you were so honest a man.

POLONIUS   Honest, my lord?

HAMLET   Ay, sir. To be honest, as this world goes, is to be one man pick'd
out of ten thousand.

POLONIUS   That's very true, my lord.   180

HAMLET   For if the sun breed maggots in a dead dog, being a god kissing
carrion—Have you a daughter?

POLONIUS   I have, my lord.

HAMLET   Let her not walk i' th' sun. Conception is a blessing, but not as
your daughter may conceive. Friend, look to't.   185

POLONIUS [*Aside*]   How say you by that? Still harping on my daughter. Yet
he knew me not at first. He said I was a fishmonger. He is far gone, far
gone! And truly in my youth I suff'red much extremity for love—very
near this. I'll speak to him again.—What do you read, my lord?

HAMLET   Words, words, words.   190

POLONIUS   What is the matter, my lord?

HAMLET   Between who?

POLONIUS   I mean, the matter that you read, my lord.

170 *board:* accost   174 *fishmonger:* procurer   186 *How say you by that?:* What did I tell you!

HAMLET Slanders, sir; for the satirical rogue says here that old men have
grey beards; that their faces are wrinkled; their eyes purging thick amber   195
and plum-tree gum; and that they have a plentiful lack of wit, together
with most weak hams. All which, sir, though I most powerfully and
potently believe, yet I hold it not honesty to have it thus set down; for
you yourself, sir, should be old as I am if, like a crab, you could go
backward.

POLONIUS [*Aside*] Though this be madness, yet there is method in't.—Will   200
you walk out of the air, my lord?

HAMLET Into my grave?

POLONIUS Indeed, that is out o' th' air. [*Aside*] How pregnant sometimes
his replies are! a happiness that often madness hits on, which reason and
sanity could not so prosperously be delivered of. I will leave him and   205
suddenly contrive the means of meeting between him and my daughter.
—My honourable lord, I will most humbly take my leave of you.

HAMLET You cannot, sir, take from me anything that I will more willingly
part withal—except my life, except my life, except my life.

[*Enter* ROSENCRANTZ *and* GUILDENSTERN.]

POLONIUS Fare you well, my lord.   210

HAMLET These tedious old fools!

POLONIUS You go to seek the Lord Hamlet. There he is.

ROSENCRANTZ [*To* POLONIUS] God save you sir!

[*Exit* POLONIUS.]

GUILDENSTERN My honour'd lord!

ROSENCRANTZ My most dear lord!   215

HAMLET My excellent good friends! How dost thou, Guildenstern? Ah,
Rosencrantz! Good lads, how do ye both?

ROSENCRANTZ As the indifferent children of the earth.

GUILDENSTERN Happy in that we are not overhappy. On Fortune's cap we
are not the very button.   220

HAMLET Nor the soles of her shoe?

ROSENCRANTZ Neither, my lord.

HAMLET Then you live about her waist, or in the middle of her favours?

GUILDENSTERN Faith, her privates we.

HAMLET In the secret parts of Fortune? O, most true! she is a strumpet.
What news?   225

218 *indifferent children:* ordinary persons

ROSENCRANTZ   None, my lord, but that the world's grown honest.

HAMLET   Then is doomsday near! But your news is not true. Let me question more in particular. What have you, my good friends, deserved at the hands of Fortune that she sends you to prison hither?

GUILDENSTERN   Prison, my lord?   230

HAMLET   Denmark's a prison.

ROSENCRANTZ   Then is the world one.

HAMLET   A goodly one; in which there are many confines, wards, and dungeons, Denmark being one o' th' worst.

ROSENCRANTZ   We think not so, my lord.   235

HAMLET   Why, then 'tis none to you; for there is nothing either good or bad but thinking makes it so. To me it is a prison.

ROSENCRANTZ   Why, then your ambition makes it one. 'Tis too narrow for your mind.

HAMLET   O God, I could be bounded in a nutshell and count myself a king   240
of infinite space, were it not that I had bad dreams.

GUILDENSTERN   Which dreams indeed are ambition; for the very substance of the ambitious is merely the shadow of a dream.

HAMLET   A dream itself is but a shadow.

ROSENCRANTZ   Truly, and I hold ambition of so airy and light a quality that   245
it is but a shadow's shadow.

HAMLET   Then are our beggars bodies, and our monarchs and outstretch'd heroes the beggars' shadows. Shall we to th' court? for, by my fay, I cannot reason.

BOTH   We'll wait upon you.   250

HAMLET   No such matter! I will not sort you with the rest of my servants; for, to speak to you like an honest man, I am most dreadfully attended. But in the beaten way of friendship, what make you at Elsinore?

ROSENCRANTZ   To visit you, my lord; no other occasion.

HAMLET   Beggar that I am, I am even poor in thanks; but I thank you; and   255
sure, dear friends, my thanks are too dear a halfpenny. Were you not sent for? Is it your own inclining? Is it a free visitation? Come, deal justly with me. Come, come! Nay, speak.

GUILDENSTERN   What should we say, my lord?

HAMLET   Why, anything—but to th' purpose. You were sent for; and there   260
is a kind of confession in your looks, which your modesties have not craft enough to colour. I know the good King and Queen have sent for you.

256 *too dear a halfpenny:* not worth a halfpenny

ROSENCRANTZ   To what end, my lord?

HAMLET   That you must teach me. But let me conjure you by the rights of
our fellowship, by the consonancy of our youth, by the obligation of our   265
ever-preserved love, and by what more dear a better proposer could
charge you withal, be even and direct with me, whether you were sent
for or no.

ROSENCRANTZ [*Aside to* GUILDENSTERN]   What say you?

HAMLET   [*Aside*]   Nay then, I have an eye of you.—If you love me, hold   270
not off.

GUILDENSTERN   My lord, we were sent for.

HAMLET   I will tell you why. So shall my anticipation prevent your discovery, and your secrecy to the King and Queen moult no feather. I have
of late—but wherefore I know not—lost all my mirth, forgone all cus-   275
tom of exercises; and indeed, it goes so heavily with my disposition that
this goodly frame, the earth, seems to me a sterile promontory; this most
excellent canopy, the air, look you, this brave o'erhanging firmament,
this majestical roof fretted with golden fire—why, it appeareth no other
thing to me than a foul and pestilent congregation of vapours. What a   280
piece of work is a man! how noble in reason! how infinite in faculties!
in form and moving how express and admirable! in action how like an
angel! in apprehension how like a god! the beauty of the world, the
paragon of animals! And yet to me what is this quintessence of dust? Man
delights not me—no, nor woman neither, though by your smiling you   285
seem to say so.

ROSENCRANTZ   My lord, there was no such stuff in my thoughts.

HAMLET   Why did you laugh then, when I said "Man delights not me"?

ROSENCRANTZ   To think, my lord, if you delight not in man, what lenten
entertainment the players shall receive from you. We coted them on the   290
way, and hither are they coming to offer you service.

HAMLET   He that plays the king shall be welcome—his Majesty shall have
tribute of me; the adventurous knight shall use his foil and target; the
lover shall not sigh gratis; the humorous man shall end his part in peace;
the clown shall make those laugh whose lungs are tickle o' th' sere; and   295
the lady shall say her mind freely, or the blank verse shall halt for't. What
players are they?

ROSENCRANTZ   Even those you were wont to take such delight in, the
tragedians of the city.

HAMLET   How chances it they travel? Their residence, both in reputation   300
and profit, was better both ways.

273 *prevent:* forestall; *discovery:* disclosure   278 *brave:* magnificent   289 *lenten:* spare
290 *coted:* passed   295 *tickle o' th' sere:* easily amused

ROSENCRANTZ I think their inhibition comes by the means of the late innovation.

HAMLET Do they hold the same estimation they did when I was in the city? Are they so follow'd? 305

ROSENCRANTZ No indeed are they not.

HAMLET How comes it? Do they grow rusty?

ROSENCRANTZ Nay, their endeavour keeps in the wonted pace; but there is, sir, an eyrie of children, little eyases, that cry out on the top of question and are most tyrannically clapp'd for't. These are now the 310 fashion, and so berattle the common stages (so they call them) that many wearing rapiers are afraid of goosequills and dare scarce come thither.

HAMLET What, are they children? Who maintains 'em? How are they escoted? Will they pursue the quality no longer than they can sing? Will they not say afterwards, if they should grow themselves to common 315 players (as it is most like, if their means are no better), their writers do them wrong to make them exclaim against their own succession?

ROSENCRANTZ Faith, there has been much to do on both sides; and the nation holds it no sin to tarre them to controversy. There was, for a while, no money bid for argument unless the poet and the player went 320 to cuffs in the question.

HAMLET Is't possible?

GUILDENSTERN O, there has been much throwing about of brains.

HAMLET Do the boys carry it away?

ROSENCRANTZ Ay, that they do, my lord—Hercules and his load too. 325

HAMLET It is not very strange; for my uncle is King of Denmark, and those that would make mows at him while my father lived give twenty, forty, fifty, a hundred ducats apiece for his picture in little. 'Sblood, there is something in this more than natural, if philosophy could find it out.

[*Flourish for the players.*]

GUILDENSTERN There are the players. 330

HAMLET Gentlemen, you are welcome to Elsinore. Your hands, come! Th' appurtenance of welcome is fashion and ceremony. Let me comply with you in this garb, lest my extent to the players (which I tell you must show

---

302 *inhibition . . . innovation:* plan to go on the road is attributable to changes in styles of dramatic presentation 309 *eyrie . . . eyases:* covey . . . baby hawks 310 *tyrannically:* loudly 311 *berattle the common stages:* berate (make fun of) adult actors 311–312 *many wearing rapiers . . . goosequills:* armed adults . . . pens (used to make fun of "common stages" and those who attended them) 314 *escoted:* financed; *pursue the quality . . . sing?:* continue to act until their voices change? 319 *tarre:* egg on 327 *make mows:* make faces

fairly outwards) should more appear like entertainment than yours. You   335
are welcome. But my uncle-father and aunt-mother are deceiv'd.

GUILDENSTERN   In what, my dear lord?

HAMLET   I am but mad north-north-west. When the wind is southerly I
know a hawk from a handsaw.

[*Enter* POLONIUS.]

POLONIUS   Well be with you, gentlemen!

HAMLET   Hark you, Guildenstern—and you too—at each ear a hearer!   340
That great baby you see there is not yet out of his swaddling clouts.

ROSENCRANTZ   Happily he's the second time come to them; for they say
an old man is twice a child.

HAMLET   I will prophesy he comes to tell me of the players. Mark it.—You
say right, sir; a Monday morning; 'twas so indeed.   345

POLONIUS   My lord, I have news to tell you.

HAMLET   My lord, I have news to tell you. When Roscius was an actor in
Rome—

POLONIUS   The actors are come hither, my lord.

HAMLET   Buzz, buzz!   350

POLONIUS   Upon my honour—

HAMLET   Then came each actor on his ass—

POLONIUS   The best actors in the world, either for tragedy, comedy, history, pastoral, pastoral-comical, historical-pastoral, tragical-historical,
tragical-comical-historical-pastoral; scene individable, or poem unlim-   355
ited. Seneca cannot be too heavy, nor Plautus too light. For the law of
writ and the liberty, these are the only men.

HAMLET   O Jephthah, judge of Israel, what a treasure hadst thou!

POLONIUS   What treasure had he, my lord?

HAMLET   Why,   360

"One fair daughter, and no more,
The which he loved passing well."

POLONIUS [*Aside*]   Still on my daughter.

HAMLET   Am I not i' th' right, old Jephthah?

356–357 *law of writ and the liberty:* for strict observance of the rules

POLONIUS   If you call me Jephthah, my lord, I have a daughter that I love   365
passing well.

HAMLET   Nay, that follows not.

POLONIUS   What follows then, my lord?

HAMLET   Why,

"As by lot, Got wot,"   370

and then, you know,

"It came to pass, as most like it was."

The first row of the pious chanson will show you more; for look where
my abridgment comes.

[*Enter four or five players.*]

You are welcome, masters; welcome, all.—I am glad to see thee well.   375
—Welcome, good friends.—O, my old friend? Why, thy face is valanc'd
since I saw thee last. Com'st thou to beard me in Denmark?—What, my
young lady and mistress? By'r Lady, your ladyship is nearer to heaven
than when I saw you last by the altitude of a chopine. Pray God your
voice, like a piece of uncurrent gold, be not crack'd within the ring.   380
—Masters, you are all welcome. We'll e'en to't like French falconers, fly
at anything we see. We'll have a speech straight. Come, give us a taste
of your quality. Come, a passionate speech.

1. PLAYER   What speech, my good lord?

HAMLET   I heard thee speak me a speech once, but it was never acted; or   385
if it was, not above once; for the play, I remember, pleas'd not the
million, 'twas caviar to the general; but it was (as I receiv'd it, and others,
whose judgments in such matters cried in the top of mine) an excellent
play, well digested in the scenes, set down with as much modesty as
cunning. I remember one said there were no sallets in the lines to make   390
the matter savoury, nor no matter in the phrase that might indict the
author of affectation; but call'd it an honest method, as wholesome as
sweet, and by very much more handsome than fine. One speech in't I
chiefly lov'd. 'Twas Aeneas' tale to Dido, and thereabout of it especially
where he speaks of Priam's slaughter. If it live in your memory, begin   395
at this line—let me see, let me see:

373 *row . . . chanson:* stanza . . . song; *abridgment:* interruption   376 *valanc'd:* bearded   378 *young lady,* boy who played the rôle of a young woman in the play—standard Elizabethan practice   379 *chopine:* short stilt   380 *not crack'd within the ring:* not made worthless as a cracked coin; Hamlet prays the boy's voice has not changed   387 *caviar to the general:* gourmet food to the great masses, hence an unappreciated delicacy   389–390 *modesty . . . cunning:* artistic control . . . skill; *sallets:* salads   392 *honest:* unaffected   394 *Dido:* mythological Queen of Carthage   395 *Priam's slaughter:* Trojan king's death

"The rugged Pyrrhus, like th' Hyrcanian beast—"

'Tis not so; it begins with Pyrrhus:

"The rugged Pyrrhus, he whose sable arms,
Black as his purpose, did the night resemble   400
When he lay couched in the ominous horse,
Hath now this dread and black complexion smear'd
With heraldry more dismal. Head to foot
Now is he total gules, horridly trick'd
With blood of fathers, mothers, daughters, sons,   405
Bak'd and impasted with the parching streets,
That lend a tyrannous and a damned light
To their lord's murther. Roasted in wrath and fire,
And thus o'ersized with coagulate gore,
With eyes like carbuncles, the hellish Pyrrhus   410
Old grandsire Priam seeks."

So, proceed you.

POLONIUS 'Fore God, my lord, well spoken, with good accent and good
  discretion.

1. PLAYER   "Anon he finds him,   415
  Striking too short at Greeks. His antique sword,
  Rebellious to his arm, lies where it falls,
  Repugnant to command. Unequal match'd,
  Pyrrhus at Priam drives, in rage strikes wide;
  But with the whiff and wind of his fell sword   420
  Th' unnerved father falls. Then senseless Ilium,
  Seeming to feel this blow, with flaming top
  Stoops to his base, and with a hideous crash
  Takes prisoner Pyrrhus' ear. For lo! his sword,
  Which was declining on the milky head   425
  Of reverend Priam, seem'd i' th' air to stick.
  So, as a painted tyrant, Pyrrhus stood,
  And, like a neutral to his will and matter,
  Did nothing.
  But, as we often see, against some storm,   430
  A silence in the heavens, the rack stand still,
  The bold winds speechless, and the orb below
  As hush as death—anon the dreadful thunder
  Doth rend the region; so, after Pyrrhus' pause,
  Aroused vengeance sets him new awork;   435

397 *Hyrcanian beast:* Hyrcania, a province of the Ancient Persian empire   404 *gules . . . trick'd:*
red . . . adorned   409 *o'ersized:* glazed   418 *repugnant:* refusing

And never did the Cyclops' hammers fall
On Mars's armour, forg'd for proof eterne,
With less remorse than Pyrrhus' bleeding sword
Now falls on Priam.
Out, out, thou strumpet Fortune! All you Gods,   440
In general synod take away her power;
Break all the spokes and fellies from her wheel,
And bowl the round nave down the hill of heaven,
As low as to the fiends!''

POLONIUS   This is too long.   445

HAMLET   It shall to the barber's, with your beard.—Prithee say on. He's
for a jig or a tale of bawdry, or he sleeps. Say on; come to Hecuba.

1. PLAYER   "But who, O who, had seen the mobled queen—"

HAMLET   "The mobled queen"?

POLONIUS   That's good! "Mobled queen" is good.   450

1. PLAYER   "Run barefoot up and down, threat'ning the flames
With bisson rheum; a clout upon that head
Where late the diadem stood, and for a robe,
About her lank and all o'erteemed loins,
A blanket, in the alarm of fear caught up—   455
Who this had seen, with tongue in venom steep'd
'Gainst Fortune's state would treason have pronounc'd.
But if the gods themselves did see her then,
When she saw Pyrrhus make malicious sport
In mincing with his sword her husband's limbs,   460
The instant burst of clamour that she made
(Unless things mortal move them not at all)
Would have made milch the burning eyes of heaven
And passion in the gods."

POLONIUS   Look, whe'r he has not turn'd his colour, and has tears in's eyes.   465
Prithee no more!

HAMLET   'Tis well. I'll have thee speak out the rest of this soon.—Good my
lord, will you see the players well bestow'd? Do you hear? Let them be
well us'd; for they are the abstract and brief chronicles of the time. After
your death you were better have a bad epitaph than their ill report while   470
you live.

POLONIUS   My lord, I will use them according to their desert.

HAMLET   God's bodkins, man, much better! Use every man after his desert,
and who should scape whipping? Use them after your own honour and

---

447 *jig:* short, comic exchange   448 *mobled:* muffled   452 *bisson rheum . . . clout:* blinding tears
. . . a cloth   454 *o'erteemed loins:* loins worn out by excessive child-bearing

dignity. The less they deserve, the more merit is in your bounty. Take   475
them in.

POLONIUS   Come, sirs.

HAMLET   Follow him, friends. We'll hear a play to-morrow.

[*Exeunt* POLONIUS *and* PLAYERS *except the* FIRST.]

Dost thou hear me, old friend? Can you play "The Murther of Gonzago"?

1. PLAYER   Ay, my lord.   480

HAMLET   We'll ha't to-morrow night. You could, for a need, study a speech
of some dozen or sixteen lines which I would set down and insert in't,
could you not?

1. PLAYER   Ay, my lord.

HAMLET   Very well. Follow that lord—and look you mock him not.   485

[*Exit* FIRST PLAYER.]

My good friends, I'll leave you till night. You are welcome to Elsinore.

ROSENCRANTZ   Good my lord!

HAMLET   Ay, so, God b' wi' ye!

[*Exeunt* ROSENCRANTZ *and* GUILDENSTERN.]

Now I am alone.
O, what a rogue and peasant slave am I!   490
Is it not monstrous that this player here,
But in a fiction, in a dream of passion,
Could force his soul so to his own conceit
That, from her working, all his visage wann'd,
Tears in his eyes, distraction in's aspect,
A broken voice, and his whole function suiting   495
With forms to his conceit? And all for nothing!
For Hecuba!
What's Hecuba to him, or he to Hecuba,
That he should weep for her? What would he do,   500
Had he the motive and the cue for passion
That I have? He would drown the stage with tears
And cleave the general ear with horrid speech;
Make mad the guilty and appal the free,
Confound the ignorant, and amaze indeed   505
The very faculties of eyes and ears.
Yet I,

A dull and muddy-mettled rascal, peak
Like John-a-dreams, unpregnant of my cause,
And can say nothing! No, not for a king,   510
Upon whose property and most dear life
A damn'd defeat was made. Am I a coward?
Who calls me villain? breaks my pate across?
Plucks off my beard and blows it in my face?
Tweaks me by th' nose? gives me the lie i' th' throat   515
As deep as to the lungs? Who does me this, ha?
'Swounds, I should take it! for it cannot be
But I am pigeon-liver'd and lack gall
To make oppression bitter, or ere this
I should have fatted all the region kites,   520
With this slave's offal. Bloody, bawdy villain!
Remorseless, treacherous, lecherous, kindless villain!
O, vengeance!
Why, what an ass am I! This is most brave,
That I, the son of a dear father murther'd,   525
Prompted to my revenge by heaven and hell,
Must (like a whore) unpack my heart with words
And fall a-cursing like a very drab,
A scullion!
Fie upon't! foh! About, my brain! Hum, I have heard   530
That guilty creatures, sitting at a play,
Have by the very cunning of the scene
Been struck so to the soul that presently
They have proclaim'd their malefactions;
For murther, though it have no tongue, will speak   535
With most miraculous organ. I'll have these players
Play something like the murther of my father
Before mine uncle. I'll observe his looks;
I'll tent him to the quick. If he but blench,
I know my course. The spirit that I have seen   540
May be a devil; and the devil hath power
T' assume a pleasing shape; yea, and perhaps
Out of my weakness and my melancholy,
As he is very potent with such spirits,
Abuses me to damn me. I'll have grounds   545
More relative than this. The play's the thing
Wherein I'll catch the conscience of the King.

[*Exit.*]

530 *about:* get to work   532 *cunning:* skill   539 *tent:* watch intently

ACT III

Scene I.

Elsinore. A Room in the Castle

[*Enter* KING, QUEEN, POLONIUS, OPHELIA, ROSENCRANTZ, GUILDENSTERN, *and* LORDS.]

KING   And can you by no drift of circumstance
  Get from him why he puts on this confusion,
  Grating so harshly all his days of quiet
  With turbulent and dangerous lunacy?

ROSENCRANTZ   He does confess he feels himself distracted,   5
  But from what cause he will by no means speak.

GUILDENSTERN   Nor do we find him forward to be sounded,
  But with a crafty madness keeps aloof
  When we would bring him on to some confession
  Of his true state.

QUEEN   Did he receive you well?   10

ROSENCRANTZ   Most like a gentleman.

GUILDENSTERN   But with much forcing of his disposition.

ROSENCRANTZ   Niggard of question, but of our demands
  Most free in his reply.

QUEEN   Did you assay him
  To any pastime?   15

ROSENCRANTZ   Madam, it so fell out that certain players
  We o'erraught on the way. Of these we told him,
  And there did seem in him a kind of joy
  To hear of it. They are here about the court,
  And, as I think, they have already order   20
  This night to play before him.

POLONIUS   'Tis most true;
  And he beseech'd me to entreat your Majesties
  To hear and see the matter.

KING   With all my heart, and it doth much content me
  To hear him so inclin'd.   25
  Good gentlemen, give him a further edge
  And drive his purpose on to these delights.

ROSENCRANTZ   We shall, my lord.

[*Exeunt* ROSENCRANTZ *and* GUILDENSTERN.]

---

1 *by no drift of circumstance:* by no trick of questioning   2 *puts on this confusion:* dresses in madness
13 *demands:* questions   17 *o'erraught:* overtook

KING   Sweet Gertrude, leave us too;
For we have closely sent for Hamlet hither,
That he, as 'twere by accident, may here   30
Affront Ophelia.
Her father and myself (lawful espials)
Will so bestow ourselves that, seeing unseen,
We may of their encounter frankly judge
And gather by him, as he is behav'd,   35
If't be th' affliction of his love, or no,
That thus he suffers for.

QUEEN   I shall obey you;
And for your part, Ophelia, I do wish
That your good beauties be the happy cause
Of Hamlet's wildness. So shall I hope your virtues   40
Will bring him to his wonted way again,
To both your honours.

OPHELIA   Madam, I wish it may.

[*Exit* QUEEN.]

POLONIUS   Ophelia, walk you here.—Gracious, so please you,
We will bestow ourselves.—[*To* OPHELIA] Read on this book,
That show of such an exercise may colour   45
Your loneliness.—We are oft to blame in this,
'Tis too much prov'd, that with devotion's visage
And pious action we do sugar o'er
The devil himself.

KING [*Aside*]   O, 'tis too true!
How smart a lash that speech doth give my conscience!   50
The harlot's cheek, beautied with plast'ring art,
Is not more ugly to the thing that helps it
Than is my deed to my most painted word.
O heavy burthen!

POLONIUS   I hear him coming. Let's withdraw, my lord.   55

[*Exeunt* KING *and* POLONIUS.]

[*Enter* HAMLET.]

HAMLET   To be, or not to be—that is the question:
Whether 'tis nobler in the mind to suffer
The slings and arrows of outrageous fortune

29 *closely:* privately   31 *affront:* meet   32 *espials:* eavesdroppers

Or to take arms against a sea of troubles,
And by opposing end them. To die—to sleep— 60
No more; and by a sleep to say we end
The heartache, and the thousand natural shocks
That flesh is heir to. 'Tis a consummation
Devoutly to be wish'd. To die—to sleep.
To sleep—perchance to dream: ay, there's the rub! 65
For in that sleep of death what dreams may come
When we have shuffled off this mortal coil,
Must give us pause. There's the respect
That makes calamity of so long life.
For who would bear the whips and scorns of time, 70
Th' oppressor's wrong, the proud man's contumely,
The pangs of despis'd love, the law's delay,
The insolence of office, and the spurns
That patient merit of th' unworthy takes,
When he himself might his quietus make 75
With a bare bodkin? Who would these fardels bear,
To grunt and sweat under a weary life,
But that the dread of something after death—
The undiscover'd country, from whose bourn
No traveller returns—puzzles the will, 80
And makes us rather bear those ills we have
Than fly to others that we know not of?
Thus conscience does make cowards of us all,
And thus the native hue of resolution
Is sicklied o'er with the pale cast of thought, 85
And enterprises of great pith and moment
With this regard their currents turn awry
And lose the name of action.—Soft you now.
The fair Ophelia!—Nymph, in thy orisons
Be all my sins rememb'red.

OPHELIA   Good my lord, 90
How does your honour for this many a day?

HAMLET   I humbly thank you; well, well, well.

OPHELIA   My lord, I have remembrances of yours
That I have longed long to re-deliver.
I pray you, now receive them.

HAMLET   No, not I! 95
I never gave you aught.

---

76 *bodkin:* needle—or perhaps dagger; *fardels:* burdens   79 *bourn:* borders   89 *orisons:* prayers

OPHELIA   My honour'd lord, you know right well you did,
And with them words of so sweet breath compos'd
As made the things more rich. Their perfume lost,
Take these again; for to the noble mind   100
Rich gifts wax poor when givers prove unkind.
There, my lord.

HAMLET   Ha, ha! Are you honest?

OPHELIA   My lord?

HAMLET   Are you fair?   105

OPHELIA   What means your lordship?

HAMLET   That if you be honest and fair, your honesty should admit no
discourse to your beauty.

OPHELIA   Could beauty, my lord, have better commerce than with
honesty?   110

HAMLET   Ay, truly; for the power of beauty will sooner transform honesty
from what it is to a bawd than the force of honesty can translate beauty
into his likeness. This was sometime a paradox, but now the time gives
it proof. I did love you once.

OPHELIA   Indeed, my lord, you made me believe so.   115

HAMLET   You should not have believ'd me; for virtue cannot so inoculate
our old stock but we shall relish of it. I loved you not.

OPHELIA   I was the more deceived.

HAMLET   Get thee to a nunnery! Why wouldst thou be a breeder of sin-
ners? I am myself indifferent honest, but yet I could accuse me of such   120
things that it were better my mother had not borne me. I am very proud,
revengeful, ambitious; with more offences at my beck than I have
thoughts to put them in, imagination to give them shape, or time to act
them in. What should such fellows as I do, crawling between earth and
heaven? We are arrant knaves all; believe none of us. Go thy ways to   125
a nunnery. Where's your father?

OPHELIA   At home, my lord.

HAMLET   Let the doors be shut upon him, that he may play the fool nowhere but in's own house. Farewell.

OPHELIA   O, help him, you sweet heavens!   130

HAMLET   If thou dost marry, I'll give thee this plague for thy dowry: be
thou as chaste as ice, as pure as snow, thou shalt not escape calumny. Get
thee to a nunnery. Go, farewell. Or if thou wilt needs marry, marry a

103 *honest:* virginal   116–117 *inoculate our old stock:* produce a change in our store   131 *plague:*
black reputation

733

fool; for wise men know well enough what monsters you make of them.
To a nunnery, go; and quickly too. Farewell.   135

OPHELIA   O heavenly powers, restore him!

HAMLET   I have heard of your paintings too, well enough. God hath given
you one face, and you make yourselves another. You jig, you amble, and
you lisp; you nickname God's creatures and make your wantonness your
ignorance. Go to, I'll no more on't! it hath made me mad. I say, we will   140
have no moe marriages. Those that are married already—all but one—
shall live; the rest shall keep as they are. To a nunnery, go.

[*Exit.*]

OPHELIA   O, what a noble mind is here o'erthrown!
The courtier's, scholar's, soldier's, eye, tongue, sword,
Th' expectancy and rose of the fair state,   145
The glass of fashion and the mould of form,
Th' observ'd of all observers—quite, quite down!
And I, of ladies most deject and wretched,
That suck'd the honey of his music vows,
Now see that noble and most sovereign reason,   150
Like sweet bells jangled, out of tune and harsh;
That unmatch'd form and feature of blown youth
Blasted with ecstasy. O, woe is me
T' have seen what I have seen, see what I see!

[*Enter* KING *and* POLONIUS.]

KING   Love? his affections do not that way tend;   155
Nor what he spake, though it lack'd form a little,
Was not like madness. There's something in his soul
O'er which his melancholy sits on brood;
And I do doubt the hatch and the disclose
Will be some danger; which for to prevent,   160
I have in quick determination
Thus set it down: he shall with speed to England
For the demand of our neglected tribute.
Haply the seas, and countries different,
With variable objects, shall expel   165
This something-settled matter in his heart,
Whereon his brains still beating puts him thus
From fashion of himself. What think you on't?

134 *monsters:* cuckolds   137 *paintings:* rougings   139–140 *make your wantonness your ignorance:*
blame your licentiousness on innocence   152 *blown:* full-blown   153 *ecstasy:* insanity
159 *doubt:* fear   163 *our neglected tribute:* their unpaid debt

POLONIUS   It shall do well. But yet do I believe
    The origin and commencement of his grief   170
    Sprung from neglected love.—How now, Ophelia?
    You need not tell us what Lord Hamlet said.
    We heard it all.—My lord, do as you please;
    But if you hold it fit, after the play
    Let his queen mother all alone entreat him   175
    To show his grief. Let her be round with him;
    And I'll be plac'd, so please you, in the ear
    Of all their conference. If she find him not,
    To England send him; or confine him where
    Your wisdom best shall think.

KING   It shall be so.   180
    Madness in great ones must not unwatch'd go.

[*Exeunt.*]

Scene II.

Elsinore. A Hall in the Castle.

[*Enter* HAMLET *and three of the* PLAYERS.]

HAMLET   Speak the speech, I pray you, as I pronounc'd it to you, trippingly
on the tongue. But if you mouth it, as many of our players do, I had as
lief the town crier spoke my lines. Nor do not saw the air too much with
your hand, thus, but use all gently; for in the very torrent, tempest, and
(as I may say) whirlwind of your passion, you must acquire and beget   5
a temperance that may give it smoothness. O, it offends me to the soul
to hear a robustious periwig-pated fellow tear a passion to tatters, to very
rags, to split the ears of the groundlings, who (for the most part) are
capable of nothing but inexplicable dumb shows and noise. I would have
such a fellow whipp'd for o'erdoing Termagant. It out-herods Herod.   10
Pray you avoid it.

PLAYER   I warrant your honour.

HAMLET   Be not too tame neither; but let your own discretion be your
tutor. Suit the action to the word, the word to the action; with this special
observance, that you o'erstep not the modesty of nature: for anything   15
so overdone is from the purpose of playing, whose end, both at the first
and now, was and is, to hold, as 'twere, the mirror up to nature; to show
virtue her own feature, scorn her own image, and the very age and body
of the time his form and pressure. Now this overdone, or come tardy
off, though it make the unskilful laugh, cannot but make the judicious   20

10 *Termagant . . . Herod:* noisy stage roles   19 *pressure:* impression   20 *unskilful:* those lacking
taste

grieve; the censure of the which one must in your allowance o'erweigh a whole theatre of others. O, there be players that I have seen play, and heard others praise, and that highly (not to speak it profanely), that, neither having the accent of Christians, nor the gait of Christian, pagan, nor man, have so strutted and bellowed that I have thought some of   25
Nature's journeymen had made men, and not made them well, they imitated humanity so abominably.

PLAYER   I hope we have reform'd that indifferently with us, sir.

HAMLET   O, reform it altogether! And let those that play your clowns speak no more than is set down for them. For there be of them that will   30
themselves laugh, to set on some quantity of barren spectators to laugh too, though in the mean time some necessary question of the play be then to be considered. That's villanous and shows a most pitiful ambition in the fool that uses it. Go make you ready.

[*Exeunt* PLAYERS.]

[*Enter* POLONIUS, ROSENCRANTZ, *and* GUILDENSTERN.]

How now, my lord? Will the King hear this piece of work?   35

POLONIUS   And the Queen too, and that presently.

HAMLET   Bid the players make haste. [*Exit* POLONIUS.] Will you two help to hasten them?

BOTH   We will, my lord.

[*Exeunt they two.*]

HAMLET   What, ho, Horatio!   40

[*Enter* HORATIO.]

HORATIO   Here, sweet lord, at your service.

HAMLET   Horatio, thou art e'en as just a man
As e'er my conversation cop'd withal.

HORATIO   O, my dear lord!

HAMLET   Nay, do not think I flatter;
For what advancement may I hope from thee,   45
That no revenue hast but thy good spirits
To feed and clothe thee? Why should the poor be flatter'd?
No, let the candied tongue lick absurd pomp,
And crook the pregnant hinges of the knee

---

21 *the censure of the which one:* the judgment of one astute playgoer   28 *indifferently:* passably
36 *presently:* immediately   42 *just:* well-balanced   43 *cop'd withal:* had to do with

Where thrift may follow fawning. Dost thou hear?   50
Since my dear soul was mistress of her choice
And could of men distinguish, her election
Hath seal'd thee for herself. For thou hast been
As one, in suff'ring all, that suffers nothing;
A man that Fortune's buffets and rewards   55
Hast ta'en with thanks; and blest are those
Whose blood and judgment are so well commingled
That they are not a pipe for Fortune's finger
To sound what stop she please. Give me that man
That is not passion's slave, and I will wear him   60
In my heart's core, ay, in my heart of heart,
As I do thee. Something too much of this!
There is a play to-night before the King.
One scene of it comes near the circumstance,
Which I have told thee, of my father's death.   65
I prithee, when thou seest that act afoot,
Even with the very comment of thy soul
Observe my uncle. If his occulted guilt
Do not itself unkennel in one speech,
It is a damned ghost that we have seen,   70
And my imaginations are as foul
As Vulcan's stithy. Give him heedful note;
For I mine eyes will rivet to his face,
And after we will both our judgments join
In censure of his seeming.

HORATIO   Well, my lord.   75
If he steal aught the whilst this play is playing,
And scape detecting, I will pay the theft.

[*Sound a flourish. Enter Trumpets and Kettledrums. Danish march. Enter* KING, QUEEN,
POLONIUS, OPHELIA, ROSENCRANTZ, GUILDENSTERN, *and other* LORDS *attendant, with the*
GUARD *carrying torches.*]

HAMLET   They are coming to the play. I must be idle.
Get you a place.

KING   How fares our cousin Hamlet?   80

HAMLET   Excellent, i' faith; of the chameleon's dish. I eat the air, promise-
cramm'd. You cannot feed capons so.

KING   I have nothing with this answer, Hamlet.
These words are not mine.

50 *thrift:* reward   78 *idle:* mad   81 *chameleon's dish:* air

737

HAMLET   No, nor mine now. [*To* POLONIUS] My lord, you play'd once i'   85
th' university, you say?

POLONIUS   That did I, my lord, and was accounted a good actor.

HAMLET   What did you enact?

POLONIUS   I did enact Julius Caesar; I was kill'd i' th' Capitol; Brutus kill'd
me.   90

HAMLET   It was a brute part of him to kill so capital a calf there. Be the
players ready?

ROSENCRANTZ   Ay, my lord. They stay upon your patience.

QUEEN   Come hither, my dear Hamlet, sit by me.

HAMLET   No, good mother. Here's metal more attractive.   95

POLONIUS [*To the* KING]   O, ho! do you mark that?

HAMLET   Lady, shall I lie in your lap?

[*Sits down at* OPHELIA'S *feet.*]

OPHELIA   No, my lord.

HAMLET   I mean, my head upon your lap?

OPHELIA   Ay, my lord.   100

HAMLET   Do you think I meant country matters?

OPHELIA   I think nothing, my lord.

HAMLET   That's a fair thought to lie between maids' legs.

OPHELIA   What is, my lord?

HAMLET   Nothing.   105

OPHELIA   You are merry, my lord.

HAMLET   Who, I?

OPHELIA   Ay, my lord.

HAMLET   O God, your only jig-maker! What should a man do but be
merry? For look you how cheerfully my mother looks, and my father   110
died within 's two hours.

OPHELIA   Nay, 'tis twice two months, my lord.

HAMLET   So long? Nay then, let the devil wear black, for I'll have a suit
of sables. O heavens! die two months ago, and not forgotten yet? Then
there's hope a great man's memory may outlive his life half a year. But,   115
by'r Lady, he must build churches then; or else shall he suffer not
thinking on, with the hobby-horse, whose epitaph is "For O, for O, the
hobby-horse is forgot!"

109 *jig-maker:* comic song writer   116–117 *suffer not thinking on:* risk not being remembered

[Hautboys play. The dumb show enters.]

Enter a KING *and a* QUEEN *very lovingly; the* QUEEN *embracing him, and he her. She kneels, and makes show of protestation unto him. He takes her up, and declines his head upon her neck. He lays him down upon a bank of flowers. She, seeing him asleep, leaves him. Anon comes in a fellow, takes off his crown, kisses it, pours poison in the sleeper's ears, and leaves him. The* QUEEN *returns, finds the* KING *dead, and makes passionate action. The* POISONER *with some three or four* MUTES, *come in again, seem to condole with her. The dead body is carried away. The* POISONER *woos the* QUEEN *with gifts; she seems harsh and unwilling awhile, but in the end accepts his love.*

[Exeunt.]

OPHELIA   What means this, my lord?

HAMLET   Marry, this is miching malhecho; it means mischief.   120

OPHELIA   Belike this show imports the argument of the play.

[Enter PROLOGUE]

HAMLET   We shall know by this fellow. The players cannot keep counsel;
   they'll tell all.

OPHELIA   Will he tell us what this show meant?

HAMLET   Ay, or any show that you'll show him. Be not you asham'd to   125
   show, he'll not shame to tell you what it means.

OPHELIA   You are naught, you are naught! I'll mark the play.

PROLOGUE   For us, and for our tragedy,
   Here stooping to your clemency,
   We beg your hearing patiently.   130

[Exit.]

HAMLET   Is this a prologue, or the posy of a ring?

OPHELIA   'Tis brief, my lord.

HAMLET   As a woman's love.

[Enter two PLAYERS *as* KING *and* QUEEN.]

PLAYER KING   Full thirty times hath Phoebus' cart gone round
   Neptune's salt wash and Tellus' orbed ground,   135
   And thirty dozen moons with borrowed sheen
   About the world have times twelve thirties been,
   Since love our hearts, and Hymen did our hands,
   Unite comutual in most sacred bands.

---

120 *miching malhecho:* underhanded crime   122 *keep counsel:* keep a secret   127 *naught:* naughty
131 *posy . . . ring:* poem inscribed in a ring   134 *Phoebus' cart:* the sun's chariot   135 *Neptune's salt wash:* the ocean; *Tellus' orbed ground:* the earth   138 *Hymen:* god of marriage

PLAYER QUEEN   So many journeys may the sun and moon   140
  Make us again count o'er ere love be done!
  But woe is me! you are so sick of late,
  So far from cheer and from your former state,
  That I distrust you. Yet, though I distrust,
  Discomfort you, my lord, it nothing must;   145
  For women's fear and love holds quantity,
  In neither aught, or in extremity.
  Now what my love is, proof hath made you know;
  And as my love is siz'd, my fear is so.
  Where love is great, the littlest doubts are fear;   150
  Where little fears grow great, great love grows there.

PLAYER KING   Faith, I must leave thee, love, and shortly too;
  My operant powers their functions leave to do.
  And thou shalt live in this fair world behind,
  Honour'd, belov'd, and haply one as kind   155
  For husband shalt thou—

PLAYER QUEEN   O, confound the rest!
  Such love must needs be treason in my breast.
  In second husband let me be accurst!
  None wed the second but who kill'd the first.

HAMLET [*Aside*]   Wormwood, wormwood!   160

PLAYER QUEEN   The instances that second marriage move
  Are base respects of thrift, but none of love.
  A second time I kill my husband dead
  When second husband kisses me in bed.

PLAYER KING   I do believe you think what now you speak;   165
  But what we do determine oft we break.
  Purpose is but the slave to memory,
  Of violent birth, but poor validity;
  Which now, like fruit unripe, sticks on the tree,
  But fall unshaken when they mellow be.   170
  Most necessary 'tis that we forget
  To pay ourselves what to ourselves is debt.
  What to ourselves in passion we propose,
  The passion ending, doth the purpose lose.
  The violence of either grief or joy   175
  Their own enactures with themselves destroy.
  Where joy most revels, grief doth most lament;
  Grief joys, joy grieves, on slender accident.

144 *distrust you:* am concerned about you   153 *operant powers:* vital force   156 *O, confound the rest!:*
The Player Queen says she doesn't even want to hear about second husbands.

This world is not for aye, nor 'tis not strange
That even our loves should with our fortunes change;   180
For 'tis a question left us yet to prove,
Whether love lead fortune, or else fortune love.
The great man down, you mark his favourite flies,
The poor advanc'd makes friends of enemies;
And hitherto doth love on fortune tend,   185
For who not needs shall never lack a friend,
And who in want a hollow friend doth try,
Directly seasons him his enemy.
But, orderly to end where I begun,
Our wills and fates do so contrary run   190
That our devices still are overthrown;
Our thoughts are ours, their ends none of our own.
So think thou wilt no second husband wed;
But die thy thoughts when thy first lord is dead.

PLAYER QUEEN   Nor earth to me give food, nor heaven light,   195
Sport and repose lock from me day and night,
To desperation turn my trust and hope,
An anchor's cheer in prison be my scope,
Each opposite that blanks the face of joy
Meet what I would have well, and it destroy,   200
Both here and hence pursue me lasting strife,
If, once a widow, ever I be wife!

HAMLET   If she should break it now!

PLAYER KING   'Tis deeply sworn. Sweet, leave me here awhile.
My spirits grow dull, and fain I would beguile   205
The tedious day with sleep.

PLAYER QUEEN   Sleep rock thy brain,

[*He sleeps.*]

And never come mischance between us twain!

[*Exit.*]

HAMLET   Madam, how like you this play?

QUEEN   The lady doth protest too much, methinks.

HAMLET   O, but she'll keep her word.   210

KING   Have you heard the argument? Is there no offence in't?

HAMLET   No, no! They do but jest, poison in jest; no offence i' th' world.

KING   What do you call the play?

HAMLET "The Mousetrap." Marry, how? Tropically. This play is the image of a murther done in Vienna. Gonzago is the duke's name; his wife, Baptista. You shall see anon. 'Tis a knavish piece of work; but what o' that? Your Majesty, and we that have free souls, it touches us not. Let the gall'd jade winch; our withers are unwrung. 215

[*Enter* LUCIANUS.]

This is one Lucianus, nephew to the King.

OPHELIA You are as good as a chorus, my lord. 220

HAMLET I could interpret between you and your love, if I could see the puppets dallying.

OPHELIA You are keen, my lord, you are keen.

HAMLET It would cost you a groaning to take off my edge.

OPHELIA Still better, and worse. 225

HAMLET So you must take your husbands.—Begin, murtherer. Pox, leave thy damnable faces, and begin! Come, the croaking raven doth bellow for revenge.

LUCIANUS Thoughts black, hands apt, drugs fit, and time agreeing;
Confederate season, else no creature seeing; 230
Thou mixture rank, of midnight weeds collected,
With Hecate's ban thrice blasted, thrice infected,
Thy natural magic and dire property
On wholesome life usurp immediately.

[*Pours the poison in his ears.*]

HAMLET He poisons him i' th' garden for's estate. His name's Gonzago. 235
The story is extant, and written in very choice Italian. You shall see anon how the murtherer gets the love of Gonzago's wife.

OPHELIA The King rises.

HAMLET What, frighted with false fire?

QUEEN How fares my lord? 240

POLONIUS Give o'er the play.

KING Give me some light! Away!

ALL Lights, lights, lights!

[*Exeunt all but* HAMLET *and* HORATIO.]

---

214 *Tropically:* figuratively   218 *gall'd jade winch; our withers are unwrung:* the sore horse may wince, but this neck is not rubbed raw.   222 *puppets:* Hamlet refers to Ophelia and some supposed secret lover   230 *Confederate season:* right moment   232 *ban:* curse

HAMLET   Why, let the strucken deer go weep,
      The hart ungalled play;   245
      For some must watch, while some must sleep:
      Thus runs the world away.
Would not this, sir, and a forest of feathers—
If the rest of my fortunes turn Turk with me—
With two Provincial roses on my raz'd shoes,   250
Get me a fellowship in a cry of players, sir?

HORATIO   Half a share.

HAMLET   A whole one I!
      For thou dost know, O Damon dear,
      This realm dismantled was   255
      Of Jove himself; and now reigns here
      A very, very—pajock.

HORATIO   You might have rhym'd.

HAMLET   O good Horatio, I'll take the ghost's word for a thousand pound!
   Didst perceive?   260

HORATIO   Very well, my lord.

HAMLET   Upon the talk of the poisoning?

HORATIO   I did very well note him.

HAMLET   Aha! Come, some music! Come, the recorders!
   For if the King like not the comedy,   265
   Why then, belike he likes it not, perdy.
   Come, some music!

[*Enter* ROSENCRANTZ *and* GUILDENSTERN.]

GUILDENSTERN   Good my lord, vouchsafe me a word with you.

HAMLET   Sir, a whole history.

GUILDENSTERN   The King, sir—   270

HAMLET   Ay, sir, what of him?

GUILDENSTERN   Is in his retirement, marvellous distemper'd.

HAMLET   With drink, sir?

GUILDENSTERN   No, my lord; rather with choler.

HAMLET   Your wisdom should show itself more richer to signify this to the   275
   doctor; for for me to put him to his purgation would perhaps plunge him
   into far more choler.

GUILDENSTERN   Good my lord, put your discourse into some frame, and
   start not so wildly from my affair.

---

249 *turn Turk:* play false   257 *pajock:* peacock   264 *recorders:* musical instruments   274 *choler:*
bile

HAMLET   I am tame, sir; pronounce.   280

GUILDENSTERN   The Queen, your mother, in most great affliction of spirit
hath sent me to you.

HAMLET   You are welcome.

GUILDENSTERN   Nay, good my lord, this courtesy is not of the right breed.
If it shall please you to make me a wholesome answer, I will do your   285
mother's commandment; if not, your pardon and my return shall be the
end of my business.

HAMLET   Sir, I cannot.

GUILDENSTERN   What, my lord?

HAMLET   Make you a wholesome answer; my wit's diseas'd. But, sir, such   290
answer as I can make, you shall command; or rather, as you say, my
mother. Therefore no more, but to the matter! My mother, you
say—

ROSENCRANTZ   Then thus she says: your behavior hath struck her into
amazement and admiration.   295

HAMLET   O wonderful son, that can so stonish a mother! But is there no
sequel at the heels of this mother's admiration? Impart.

ROSENCRANTZ   She desires to speak with you in her closet ere you go to
bed.

HAMLET   We shall obey, were she ten times our mother. Have you any   300
further trade with us?

ROSENCRANTZ   My lord, you once did love me.

HAMLET   And do still, by these pickers and stealers!

ROSENCRANTZ   Good my lord, what is your cause of distemper? You do
surely bar the door upon your own liberty, if you deny your griefs to   305
your friend.

HAMLET   Sir, I lack advancement.

ROSENCRANTZ   How can that be, when you have the voice of the King
himself for your succession in Denmark?

HAMLET   Aye, sir, but "while the grass grows"—the proverb is something   310
musty.

[*Enter the* PLAYERS *with recorders.*]

O, the recorders! Let me see one. To withdraw with you—why do you
go about to recover the wind of me, as if you would drive me into a
toil?

---

295 *amazement and admiration:* bewilderment and wonder   298 *closet:* bedroom   303 *pickers and*
stealers: two hands   305 *liberty:* freedom of action   311 *musty:* lacking in frankness
312–313 *go about to recover the wind of me:* try to discover my purposes   314 *toil:* trap

GUILDENSTERN O my lord, if my duty be too bold, my love is too unman- 315
nerly.

HAMLET I do not well understand that. Will you play upon this pipe?

GUILDENSTERN My lord, I cannot.

HAMLET I pray you.

GUILDENSTERN Believe me, I cannot. 320

HAMLET I do beseech you.

GUILDENSTERN I know no touch of it, my lord.

HAMLET It is as easy as lying. Govern these ventages with your fingers and
thumbs, give it breath with your mouth, and it will discourse most
eloquent music. Look you, these are the stops. 325

GUILDENSTERN But these cannot I command to any utt'rance of harmony.
I have not the skill.

HAMLET Why, look you now, how unworthy a thing you make of me! You
would play upon me; you would seem to know my stops; you would
pluck out the heart of my mystery; you would sound me from my lowest 330
note to the top of my compass; and there is much music, excellent voice,
in this little organ, yet cannot you make it speak. 'Sblood, do you think
I am easier to be play'd on than a pipe? Call me what instrument you
will, though you can fret me, you cannot play upon me.

[*Enter* POLONIUS.]

God bless you, sir! 335

POLONIUS My lord, the Queen would speak with you, and presently.

HAMLET Do you see yonder cloud that's almost in shape of a camel?

POLONIUS By th' mass, and 'tis like a camel indeed.

HAMLET Methinks it is like a weasel.

POLONIUS It is back'd like a weasel. 340

HAMLET Or like a whale.

POLONIUS Very like a whale.

HAMLET Then will I come to my mother by-and-by.—They fool me to the
top of my bent.
—I will come by-and-by. 345

POLONIUS I will say so.

[*Exit.*]

323 *ventages:* holes, or stops, in the instrument   334 *fret:* bar of wire or wood to guide fingering
345 *by-and-by:* at once

HAMLET "By-and-by" is easily said.—Leave me, friends.

[*Exeunt all but* HAMLET.]

'Tis now the very witching time of night,
When churchyards yawn, and hell itself breathes out
Contagion to this world. Now could I drink hot blood   350
And do such bitter business as the day
Would quake to look on. Soft! now to my mother!
O heart, lose not thy nature; let not ever
The soul of Nero enter this firm bosom.
Let me be cruel, not unnatural;   355
I will speak daggers to her, but use none.
My tongue and soul in this be hypocrites—
How in my words somever she be shent,
To give them seals never, my soul, consent!

Scene III.

A Room in the Castle.

[*Enter* KING, ROSENCRANTZ, *and* GUILDENSTERN.]

KING I like him not, nor stands it safe with us
To let his madness range. Therefore prepare you;
I your commission will forthwith dispatch,
And he to England shall along with you.
The terms of our estate may not endure   5
Hazard so near us as doth hourly grow
Out of his lunacies.

GUILDENSTERN   We will ourselves provide.
Most holy and religious fear it is
To keep those many many bodies safe
That live and feed upon your Majesty.   10

ROSENCRANTZ The single and peculiar life is bound
With all the strength and armour of the mind
To keep itself from noyance; but much more
That spirit upon whose weal depends and rests
The lives of many. The cesse of majesty   15
Dies not alone, but like a gulf doth draw
What's near it with it. It is a massy wheel,
Fix'd on the summit of the highest mount,

358 *shent:* castigated   3 *dispatch:* prepare   11 *peculiar:* individual   13 *noyance:* harm
15 *cesse:* demise

To whose huge spokes ten thousand lesser things
Are mortis'd and adjoin'd; which when it falls,
Each small annexment, petty consequence,
Attends the boist'rous ruin. Never alone
Did the king sigh, but with a general groan.

KING Arm you, I pray you, to this speedy voyage;   25
For we will fetters put upon this fear,
Which now goes too free-footed.

BOTH   We will haste us.

[*Exeunt* GENTLEMEN.]

[*Enter* POLONIUS.]

POLONIUS My lord, he's going to his mother's closet.
Behind the arras I'll convey myself
To hear the process. I'll warrant she'll tax him home;
And, as you said, and wisely was it said,   30
'Tis meet that some more audience than a mother,
Since nature makes them partial, should o'erhear
The speech, of vantage. Fare you well, my liege.
I'll call upon you ere you go to bed
And tell you what I know.

KING   Thanks, dear my lord.   35

[*Exit* POLONIUS.]

O, my offence is rank, it smells to heaven;
It hath the primal eldest curse upon't,
A brother's murther! Pray can I not,
Though inclination be as sharp as will.
My stronger guilt defeats my strong intent,   40
And, like a man to double business bound,
I stand in pause where I shall first begin,
And both neglect. What if this cursed hand
Were thicker than itself with brother's blood.
Is there not rain enough in the sweet heavens   45
To wash it white as snow? Whereto serves mercy
But to confront the visage of offence?
And what's in prayer but this twofold force,
To be forestalled ere we come to fall,
Or pardon'd being down? Then I'll look up;   50
My fault is past. But, O, what form of prayer

24 *arm you:* make ready   29 *tax him home:* scold him thoroughly

Can serve my turn? "Forgive me my foul murther"?
That cannot be; since I am still possess'd
Of those effects for which I did the murther—
My crown, mine own ambition, and my queen. 55
May one be pardon'd and retain th' offence?
In the corrupted currents of this world
Offence's gilded hand may shove by justice,
And oft 'tis seen the wicked prize itself
Buys out the law; but 'tis not so above. 60
There is no shuffling; there the action lies
In his true nature, and we ourselves compell'd,
Even to the teeth and forehead of our faults,
To give in evidence. What then? What rests?
Try what repentance can. What can it not? 65
Yet what can it when one cannot repent?
O wretched state! O bosom black as death!
O limed soul, that, struggling to be free,
Art more engag'd! Help, angels! Make assay.
Bow, stubborn knees; and heart with strings of steel, 70
Be soft as sinews of the new-born babe!
All may be well.

[*He kneels.*]

[*Enter* HAMLET.]

HAMLET Now might I do it pat, now he is praying;
And now I'll do't. And so he goes to heaven,
And so am I reveng'd. That would be scann'd. 75
A villain kills my father; and for that,
I, his sole son, do this same villain send
To heaven.
Why, this is hire and salary, not revenge!
He took my father grossly, full of bread, 80
With all his crimes broad blown, as flush as May;
And how his audit stands, who knows save heaven?
But in our circumstances and course of thought,
'Tis heavy with him; and am I then reveng'd,
To take him in the purging of his soul, 85
When he is fit and season'd for his passage?
No.
Up, sword, and know thou a more horrid hent.

73 *pat:* easily   75 *scann'd:* examined   80 *full of bread:* filled with earthly satisfactions   82 *his audit:* judgment of him   83 *our circumstance:* our restricted, human point of view   88 *hent:* moment

When he is drunk asleep; or in his rage;
Or in th' incestuous pleasure of his bed;   90
At gaming, swearing, or about some act
That has no relish of salvation in't—
Then trip him, that his heels may kick at heaven,
And that his soul may be as damn'd and black
As hell, whereto it goes. My mother stays.   95
This physic but prolongs thy sickly days.

[*Exit.*]

KING [*Rises*]   My words fly up, my thoughts remain below.
  Words without thoughts never to heaven go.

[*Exit.*]

Scene IV.

The QUEEN's *Closet.*

[*Enter* QUEEN *and* POLONIUS.]

POLONIUS   He will come straight. Look you lay home to him.
  Tell him his pranks have been too broad to bear with,
  And that your Grace hath screen'd and stood between
  Much heat and him. I'll silence me even here.
  Pray you be round with him.   5

HAMLET [*Within*]   Mother, mother, mother!

QUEEN   I'll warrant you; fear me not. Withdraw; I hear him coming.

[POLONIUS *hides behind the arras.*]

[*Enter* HAMLET.]

HAMLET   Now, mother, what's the matter?

QUEEN   Hamlet, thou hast thy father much offended.

HAMLET   Mother, you have my father much offended.   10

QUEEN   Come, come, you answer with an idle tongue.

HAMLET   Go, go, you question with a wicked tongue.

QUEEN   Why, how now, Hamlet?

HAMLET   What's the matter now?

QUEEN   Have you forgot me?

96 *physic:* purgation   2 *broad:* free-wheeling

HAMLET   No, by the rood, not so!
  You are the Queen, your husband's brother's wife,   15
  And (would it were not so!) you are my mother.

QUEEN   Nay, then I'll set those to you that can speak.

HAMLET   Come, come, and sit you down. You shall not budge!
  You go not till I set you up a glass
  Where you may see the inmost part of you.   20

QUEEN   What wilt thou do? Thou wilt not murther me?
  Help, help, ho!

POLONIUS [Behind]   What, ho! help, help, help!

HAMLET [Draws]   How now? a rat? Dead for a ducat, dead!

[Makes a pass through the arras and kills POLONIUS.]

POLONIUS [Behind]   O, I am slain!

QUEEN   O me, what hast thou done?   25

HAMLET   Nay, I know not. Is it the King?

QUEEN   O, what a rash and bloody deed is this!

HAMLET   A bloody deed—almost as bad, good mother,
  As kill a king, and marry with his brother.

QUEEN   As kill a king?

HAMLET   Ay, lady, it was my word.   30

[Lifts up the arras and sees POLONIUS]

  Thou wretched, rash, intruding fool, farewell!
  I took thee for thy better. Take thy fortune.
  Thou find'st to be too busy is some danger.
  Leave wringing of your hands. Peace! sit you down
  And let me wring your heart; for so I shall   35
  If it be made of penetrable stuff;
  If damned custom have not braz'd it so
  That it is proof and bulwark against sense.

QUEEN   What have I done that thou dar'st wag thy tongue
  In noise so rude against me?

HAMLET   Such an act   40
  That blurs the grace and blush of modesty;
  Calls virtue hypocrite; takes off the rose
  From the fair forehead of an innocent love,
  And sets a blister there; makes marriage vows

33 *too busy:* too much a busybody   40 *Such an act:* hasty marriage   44 *blister:* brand

As false as dicers' oaths. O, such a deed   45
As from the body of contraction plucks
The very soul, and sweet religion makes
A rhapsody of words! Heaven's face doth glow;
Yea, this solidity and compound mass,
With tristful visage; as against the doom,   50
Is thought-sick at the act.

QUEEN   Ay me, what act,
   That roars so loud and thunders in the index?

HAMLET Look here upon this picture, and on this,
   The counterfeit presentment of two brothers.
   See what a grace was seated on this brow;   55
   Hyperion's curls; the front of Jove himself;
   An eye like Mars, to threaten and command;
   A station like the herald Mercury
   New lighted on a heaven-kissing hill:
   A combination and a form indeed   60
   Where every god did seem to set his seal
   To give the world assurance of a man.
   This was your husband. Look you now what follows.
   Here is your husband, like a mildew'd ear
   Blasting his wholesome brother. Have you eyes?   65
   Could you on this fair mountain leave to feed,
   And batten on this moor? Ha! have you eyes?
   You cannot call it love; for at your age
   The heydey in the blood is tame, it's humble,
   And waits upon the judgment; and what judgment   70
   Would step from this to this? Sense sure you have,
   Else could you not have motion; but sure that sense
   Is apoplex'd; for madness would not err,
   Nor sense to ecstasy was ne'er so thrall'd
   But it reserv'd some quantity of choice   75
   To serve in such a difference. What devil was't
   That thus hath cozen'd you at hoodman-blind?
   Eyes without feeling, feeling without sight,
   Ears without hands or eyes, smelling sans all,
   Or but a sickly part of one true sense   80
   Could not so mope.
   O shame! where is thy blush? Rebellious hell,
   If thou canst mutine in a matron's bones,

---

46 *contraction:* marriage vows   48 *glow:* blush with shame   52 *index:* table of contents
58 *station:* posture   67 *batten:* gorge   74 *ecstasy:* madness   77 *cozen'd:* fooled   79 *sans:*
without   81 *so mope:* be so insensitive

To flaming youth let virtue be as wax
And melt in her own fire. Proclaim no shame   85
When the compulsive ardour gives the charge,
Since frost itself as actively doth burn,
And reason panders will.

QUEEN   O Hamlet, speak no more!
Thou turn'st mine eyes into my very soul,
And there I see such black and grained spots   90
As will not leave their tinct.

HAMLET   Nay, but to live
In the rank sweat of an enseamed bed,
Stew'd in corruption, honeying and making love
Over the nasty sty!

QUEEN   O, speak to me no more!
These words like daggers enter in mine ears.   95
No more, sweet Hamlet!

HAMLET   A murtherer and villain!
A slave that is not twentieth part the tithe
Of your precedent lord; a vice of kings;
A cutpurse of the empire and the rule,
That from a shelf the precious diadem stole   100
And put it in his pocket!

QUEEN   No more!

[*Enter the* GHOST *in his nightgown.*]

HAMLET   A king of shreds and patches!—
Save me and hover o'er me with your wings,
You heavenly guards! What would your gracious figure?

QUEEN   Alas, he's mad!   105

HAMLET   Do you not come your tardy son to chide,
That, laps'd in time and passion, lets go by
Th' important acting of your dread command?
O, say!

GHOST   Do not forget. This visitation   110
Is but to whet thy almost blunted purpose.
But look, amazement on thy mother sits.
O, step between her and her fighting soul!
Conceit in weakest bodies strongest works.
Speak to her, Hamlet.

88 *reason panders will:* reason becomes a slave to ardor   92 *enseamed:* greasy   102 *shreds and patches:* disreputable appearance

HAMLET How is it with you, lady? 115

QUEEN Alas, how is't with you,
  That you do bend your eye on vacancy,
  And with th' incorporal air do hold discourse?
  Forth at your eyes your spirits wildly peep;
  And, as the sleeping soldiers in th' alarm, 120
  Your bedded hairs, like life in excrements,
  Start up and stand on end. O gentle son,
  Upon the heat and flame of thy distemper
  Sprinkle cool patience! Whereon do you look?

HAMLET On him, on him! Look you how pale he glares! 125
  His form and cause conjoin'd, preaching to stones,
  Would make them capable.—Do not look upon me,
  Lest with this piteous action you convert
  My stern effects. Then what I have to do
  Will want true colour—tears perchance for blood. 130

QUEEN To whom do you speak this?

HAMLET Do you see nothing there?

QUEEN Nothing at all; yet all that is I see.

HAMLET Nor did you nothing hear?

QUEEN No, nothing but ourselves.

HAMLET Why, look you there! Look how it steals away!
  My father, in his habit as he liv'd! 135
  Look where he goes even now out at the portal!

[*Exit* GHOST.]

QUEEN This is the very coinage of your brain.
  This bodiless creation ecstasy
  Is very cunning in.

HAMLET Ecstasy?
  My pulse as yours doth temperately keep time 140
  And makes as healthful music. It is not madness
  That I have utt'red. Bring me to the test,
  And I the matter will reword; which madness
  Would gambol from. Mother, for love of grace,
  Lay not that flattering unction to your soul, 145
  That not your trespass but my madness speaks.
  It will but skin and film the ulcerous place,
  Whiles rank corruption, mining all within,
  Infects unseen. Confess yourself to heaven;

---

121 *bedded:* groomed; *excrements:* outgrowths   144 *gambol from:* skip away from

Repent what's past; avoid what is to come; 150
And do not spread the compost on the weeds
To make them ranker. Forgive me this my virtue;
For in the fatness of these pursy times
Virtue itself of vice must pardon beg—
Yea, curb and woo for leave to do him good. 155

QUEEN O Hamlet, thou hast cleft my heart in twain.

HAMLET O, throw away the worser part of it,
And live the purer with the other half.
Good night—but go not to my uncle's bed.
Assume a virtue, if you have it not. 160
That monster, custom, who all sense doth eat
Of habits evil, is angel yet in this,
That to the use of actions fair and good
He likewise gives a frock or livery,
That aptly is put on. Refrain to-night, 165
And that shall lend a kind of easiness
To the next abstinence; the next more easy;
For use almost can change the stamp of nature,
And either [master] the devil, or throw him out
With wondrous potency. Once more, good night; 170
And when you are desirous to be blest,
I'll blessing beg of you.—For this same lord,
I do repent; but heaven hath pleas'd it so,
To punish me with this, and this with me,
That I must be their scourge and minister. 175
I will bestow him, and will answer well
The death I gave him. So again, good night.
I must be cruel, only to be kind;
Thus bad begins, and worse remains behind.
One word more, good lady.

QUEEN   What shall I do? 180

HAMLET Not this, by no means, that I bid you do:
Let the bloat King tempt you again to bed;
Pinch wanton on your cheek; call you his mouse;
And let him, for a pair of reechy kisses,
Or paddling in your neck with his damn'd fingers, 185
Make you to ravel all this matter out,
That I essentially am not in madness,
But mad in craft. 'Twere good you let him know;
For who that's but a queen, fair, sober, wise,

153 *pursy:* over-fat   172 *this same lord:* Polonius   182 *bloat:* swollen with drink   184 *reechy:* slobbery

Would from a paddock, from a bat, a gib,   190
Such dear concernings hide? Who would do so?
No, in despite of sense and secrecy,
Unpeg the basket on the house's top,
Let the birds fly, and like the famous ape,
To try conclusions, in the basket creep   195
And break your own neck down.

QUEEN   Be thou assur'd, if words be made of breath,
And breath of life, I have no life to breathe
What thou hast said to me.

HAMLET   I must to England; you know that?

QUEEN   Alack,   200
I had forgot! 'Tis so concluded on.

HAMLET   There's letters seal'd; and my two schoolfellows,
Whom I will trust as I will adders fang'd,
They bear the mandate; they must sweep my way
And marshal me to knavery. Let it work;   205
For 'tis the sport to have the enginer
Hoist with his own petar; and 't shall go hard
But I will delve one yard below their mines
And blow them at the moon. O, 'tis most sweet
When in one line two crafts directly meet.   210
This man shall set me packing.
I'll lug the guts into the neighbour room.—
Mother, good night.—Indeed, this counsellor
Is now most still, most secret, and most grave,
Who was in life a foolish prating knave.   215
Come, sir, to draw toward an end with you.
Good night, mother.

[*Exit the* QUEEN. *Then exit* HAMLET, *tugging in* POLONIUS.]

ACT IV

Scene I.

Elsinore. A Room in the Castle

[*Enter* KING *and* QUEEN, *with* ROSENCRANTZ *and* GUILDENSTERN.]

KING   There's matter in these sighs. These profound heaves
You must translate; 'tis fit we understand them.
Where is your son?

---

190 *gib:* tomcat   196 *down:* by the fall   207 *Hoist with his own petar:* blown up with his own bomb

QUEEN   Bestow this place on us a little while.

[*Exeunt* ROSENCRANTZ *and* GUILDENSTERN.]

   Ah; mine own lord, what have I seen tonight!   5
KING   What, Gertrude? How does Hamlet?
QUEEN   Mad as the sea and wind when both contend
   Which is the mightier. In his lawless fit,
   Behind the arras hearing something stir,
   Whips out his rapier, cries "A rat, a rat!"   10
   And in this brainish apprehension kills
   The unseen good old man.
KING   O heavy deed!
   It had been so with us, had we been there.
   His liberty is full of threats to all—
   To you yourself, to us, to every one.   15
   Alas, how shall this bloody deed be answer'd?
   It will be laid to us, whose providence
   Should have kept short, restrain'd, and out of haunt
   This mad young man. But so much was our love
   We would not understand what was most fit,   20
   But, like the owner of a foul disease,
   To keep it from divulging, let it feed
   Even on the pith of life. Where is he gone?
QUEEN   To draw apart the body he hath kill'd;
   O'er whom his very madness, like some ore   25
   Among a mineral of metals base,
   Shows itself pure. He weeps for what is done.
KING   O Gertrude, come away!
   The sun no sooner shall the mountains touch
   But we will ship him hence; and this vile deed   30
   We must with all our majesty and skill
   Both countenance and excuse. Ho, Guildenstern!

[*Enter* ROSENCRANTZ *and* GUILDENSTERN.]

   Friends both, go join you with some further aid.
   Hamlet in madness hath Polonius slain,
   And from his mother's closet hath he dragg'd him.   35
   Go seek him out; speak fair, and bring the body
   Into the chapel. I pray you haste in this.

[*Exeunt* ROSENCRANTZ *and* GUILDENSTERN.]

---

11 *brainish apprehension:* demented notion   17 *providence:* foresight   18 *short:* on a short leash;
out of haunt: away from others   25 *ore:* precious metal   26 *mineral:* mine

Come, Gertrude, we'll call up our wisest friends
And let them know both what we mean to do
And what's untimely done. (So haply slander—)   40
Whose whisper o'er the world's diameter,
As level as the cannon to his blank,
Transports his pois'ned shot—may miss our name
And hit the woundless air.—O, come away!
My soul is full of discord and dismay.   45

[*Exeunt.*]

Scene II.

Elsinore. A Passage in the Castle.

[*Enter* HAMLET.]

HAMLET   Safely stow'd.

GENTLEMEN [*Within*]   Hamlet! Lord Hamlet!

HAMLET   But soft! What noise? Who calls on Hamlet? O, here they come.

[*Enter* ROSENCRANTZ *and* GUILDENSTERN.]

ROSENCRANTZ   What have you done, my lord, with the dead body?

HAMLET   Compounded it with dust, whereto 'tis kin.   5

ROSENCRANTZ   Tell us where 'tis, that we may take it thence
   And bear it to the chapel.

HAMLET   Do not believe it.

ROSENCRANTZ   Believe what?

HAMLET   That I can keep your counsel, and not mine own. Besides, to be   10
   demanded of a sponge, what replication should be made by the son of
   a king?

ROSENCRANTZ   Take you me for a sponge, my lord?

HAMLET   Ay, sir; that soaks up the King's countenance, his rewards, his
   authorities. But such officers do the King best service in the end. He   15
   keeps them, like an ape, in the corner of his jaw; first mouth'd, to be
   last swallowed. When he needs what you have glean'd, it is but squeezing you and, sponge, you shall be dry again.

ROSENCRANTZ   I understand you not, my lord.

HAMLET   I am glad of it. A knavish speech sleeps in a foolish ear.   20

ROSENCRANTZ   My lord, you must tell us where the body is and go with
   us to the King.

---

42 *level:* accurate aim; *blank:* target   10 *counsel:* secrets   11 *replication,* formal reply

HAMLET   The body is with the King, but the King is not with the body. The
   King is a thing—

GUILDENSTERN   A thing, my lord?   25

HAMLET   Of nothing. Bring me to him. Hide fox, and all after.

[*Exeunt.*]

Scene III.

Elsinore. A Room in the Castle.

[*Enter* KING.]

KING   I have sent to seek him and to find the body.
   How dangerous is it that this man goes loose!
   Yet must not we put the strong law on him.
   He's lov'd of the distracted multitude,
   Who like not in their judgment, but their eyes;   5
   And where 'tis so, th' offender's scourge is weigh'd,
   But never the offence. To bear all smooth and even,
   This sudden sending him away must seem
   Deliberate pause. Diseases desperate grown
   By desperate appliance are reliev'd,   10
   Or not at all.

[*Enter* ROSENCRANTZ.]

                   How now? What hath befall'n?

ROSENCRANTZ   Where the dead body is bestow'd, my lord,
   We cannot get from him.

KING   But where is he?

ROSENCRANTZ   Without, my lord; guarded, to know your pleasure.

KING   Bring him before us.

ROSENCRANTZ   Ho, Guildenstern! Bring in my lord.   15

[*Enter* HAMLET *and* GUILDENSTERN *with* ATTENDANTS.]

KING   Now, Hamlet, where's Polonius?

HAMLET   At supper.

KING   At supper? Where?

---

22 *Hide fox:* probably a reference to a game like hide-and-seek   4 *distracted:* fooled   7 *bear:*
manage   9 *Deliberate pause:* the result of thoughtful deliberation

HAMLET   Not where he eats, but where he is eaten. A certain convocation
   of politic worms are e'en at him. Your worm is your only emperor for   20
   diet. We fat all creatures else to fat us, and we fat ourselves for maggots.
   Your fat king and your lean beggar is but variable service—two dishes,
   but to one table. That's the end.

KING   Alas, alas!

HAMLET   A man may fish with the worm that hath eat of a king, and eat   25
   of the fish that hath fed of that worm.

KING   What dost thou mean by this?

HAMLET   Nothing but to show you how a king may go a progress through
   the guts of a beggar.

KING   Where is Polonius?   30

HAMLET   In heaven. Send thither to see. If your messenger find him not
   there, seek him i' th' other place yourself. But indeed, if you find him
   not within this month, you shall nose him as you go up the stairs into
   the lobby.

KING   Go seek him there. [*To* ATTENDANTS.]

HAMLET   He will stay till you come.   35

[*Exeunt* ATTENDANTS.]

KING   Hamlet, this deed, for thine especial safety,—
   Which we do tender as we dearly grieve
   For that which thou hast done,—must send thee hence
   With fiery quickness. Therefore, prepare thyself.
   The bark is ready and the wind at help,   40
   Th' associates tend, and everything is bent
   For England.

HAMLET   For England?

KING   Ay, Hamlet.

HAMLET   Good.

KING   So is it, if thou knew'st our purposes.

HAMLET   I see a cherub that sees them. But come, for England! Farewell,
   dear mother.

KING   Thy loving father, Hamlet.   45

HAMLET   My mother! Father and mother is man and wife; man and wife
   is one flesh; and so, my mother. Come, for England!

[*Exit.*]

28 *a progress:* royal visits to estates of noblemen   44 *I see a cherub:* I see as a cherub

KING Follow him at foot; tempt him with speed aboard.
   Delay it not; I'll have him hence to-night.
   Away! for everything is seal'd and done   50
   That else leans on th' affair. Pray you make haste.

[*Exeunt* ROSENCRANTZ *and* GUILDENSTERN.]

   And, England, if my love thou hold'st at aught,—
   As my great power thereof may give thee sense,
   Since yet thy cicatrice looks raw and red
   After the Danish sword, and thy free awe   55
   Pays homage to us,—thou mayst not coldly set
   Our sovereign process, which imports at full,
   By letters congruing to that effect,
   The present death of Hamlet. Do it, England;
   For like the hectic in my blood he rages,   60
   And thou must cure me. Till I know 'tis done,
   Howe'er my haps, my joys were ne'er begun.

[*Exit.*]

Scene IV.

Near Elsinore.

[*Enter* FORTINBRAS *with his* ARMY *over the stage.*]

FORTINBRAS Go, Captain, from me greet the Danish king.
   Tell him that by his license Fortinbras
   Craves the conveyance of a promis'd march
   Over his kingdom. You know the rendezvous.
   If that his Majesty would aught with us,   5
   We shall express our duty in his eye;
   And let him know so.
CAPTAIN   I will do't, my lord.
FORTINBRAS Go softly on.

[*Exeunt all but the* CAPTAIN.]

[*Enter* HAMLET, ROSENCRANTZ, GUILDENSTERN, *and others.*]

HAMLET Good sir, whose powers are these?
CAPTAIN They are of Norway, sir.   10

---

48 *tempt him:* coax him   51 *leans on:* pertains to   56 *coldly set:* be indifferent to   57 *process:* command   58 *congruing:* informing   60 *the hectic:* constant fever   62 *haps:* fortune   3 *conveyance:* escort

HAMLET   How purpos'd, sir, I pray you?

CAPTAIN   Against some part of Poland.

HAMLET   Who commands them, sir?

CAPTAIN   The nephew to old Norway, Fortinbras.

HAMLET   Goes it against the main of Poland, sir,   15
Or for some frontier?

CAPTAIN   Truly to speak, and with no addition,
We go to gain a little patch of ground
That hath in it no profit but the name.
To pay five ducats, five, I would not farm it;   20
Nor will it yield to Norway or the Pole
A ranker rate, should it be sold in fee.

HAMLET   Why, then the Polack never will defend it.

CAPTAIN   Yes, it is already garrison'd.

HAMLET   Two thousand souls and twenty thousand ducats   25
Will not debate the question of this straw.
This is th' imposthume of much wealth and peace,
That inward breaks, and shows no cause without
Why the man dies.—I humbly thank you, sir.

CAPTAIN   God b' wi' you, sir.   30

[*Exit.*]

ROSENCRANTZ   Will't please you go, my lord?

HAMLET   I'll be with you straight. Go a little before.

[*Exeunt all but* HAMLET.]

How all occasions do inform against me
And spur my dull revenge! What is a man,
If his chief good and market of his time   35
Be but to sleep and feed? A beast, no more.
Sure he that made us with such large discourse,
Looking before and after, gave us not
That capability and godlike reason
To fust in us unus'd. Now, whether it be   40
Bestial oblivion, or some craven scruple
Of thinking too precisely on th' event,—
A thought which, quarter'd, hath but one part wisdom
And ever three parts coward,—I do not know

20 *farm:* lease   22 *a ranker rate:* a higher return; *in fee:* outright   27 *imposthume:* abscess
35 *market of his time:* wager for his time   40 *fust:* become moldy

Why yet I live to say "This thing's to do,"   45
Sith I have cause, and will, and strength, and means
To do't. Examples gross as earth exhort me.
Witness this army of such mass and charge,
Led by a delicate and tender prince,
Whose spirit, with divine ambition puff'd,   50
Makes mouths at the invisible event,
Exposing what is mortal and unsure
To all that fortune, death, and danger dare,
Even for an eggshell. Rightly to be great
Is not to stir without great argument,   55
But greatly to find quarrel in a straw
When honour's at the stake. How stand I then,
That have a father kill'd, a mother stain'd,
Excitements of my reason and my blood,
And let all sleep, while to my shame I see   60
The imminent death of twenty thousand men
That for a fantasy and trick of fame
Go to their graves like beds, fight for a plot
Whereon the numbers cannot try the cause,
Which is not tomb enough and continent   65
To hide the slain? O, from this time forth,
My thoughts be bloody, or be nothing worth!

[*Exit.*]

Scene V.

Elsinore. A Room in the Castle.

[*Enter* HORATIO, QUEEN, *and a* GENTLEMAN.]

QUEEN   I will not speak with her.

GENTLEMAN   She is importunate, indeed distract.
  Her mood will needs be pitied.

QUEEN   What would she have?

GENTLEMAN   She speaks much of her father; says she hears
  There's tricks i' th' world, and hems, and beats her heart;   5
  Spurns enviously at straws; speaks things in doubt,
  That carry but half sense. Her speech is nothing,
  Yet the unshaped use of it doth move
  The hearers to collection; they aim at it,

62 *a fantasy:* caprice; *trick:* trifle   65 *continent:* able to contain   6 *spurns enviously at straws:* takes
offense over small things   9 *collection:* combined interpretations

And botch the words up fit to their own thoughts; 10
Which, as her winks and nods and gestures yield them,
Indeed would make one think there might be thought,
Though nothing sure, yet much unhappily.

HORATIO 'Twere good she were spoken with; for she may strew
Dangerous conjectures in ill-breeding minds. 15

QUEEN Let her come in.

[Exit Gentleman.]

[Aside] To my sick soul (as sin's true nature is)
Each toy seems prologue to some great amiss.
So full of artless jealousy is guilt
It spills itself in fearing to be spilt. 20

[Enter OPHELIA *distracted.]*

OPHELIA Where is the beauteous Majesty of Denmark?

QUEEN How now, Ophelia?

OPHELIA *[Sings]* How should I your true-love know
From another one?
By his cockle hat and staff 25
And his sandal shoon.

QUEEN Alas, sweet lady, what imports this song?

OPHELIA Say you? Nay, pray you mark.
[Sings] He is dead and gone, lady,
He is dead and gone; 30
At his head a grass-green turf,
At his heels a stone.
O, ho!

QUEEN Nay, but Ophelia—

OPHELIA Pray you mark. 35
[Sings] White his shroud as the mountain snow—

[Enter KING.*]*

QUEEN Alas, look here, my lord!

OPHELIA *[Sings]* Larded all with sweet flowers;
Which bewept to the grave did not go
With true-love showers. 40

KING How do you, pretty lady?

10 *botch:* patch   15 *ill-breeding:* evilly imagining   18 *toy:* trifle   20 *spills:* destroys

763

OPHELIA Well, God dild you! They say the owl was a baker's daughter.
Lord, we know what we are, but know not what we may be. God be at
your table!

KING Conceit upon her father.

OPHELIA Pray let's have no words of this; but when they ask you what it   45
means, say you this:
[*Sings*]   To-morrow is Saint Valentine's day
          All in the morning betime,
          And I a maid at your window,
            To be your Valentine.   50
          Then up he rose and donn'd his clo'es
            And dupp'd the chamber door,
          Let in the maid, that out a maid
            Never departed more.

KING Pretty Ophelia!   55

OPHELIA Indeed, la, without an oath, I'll make an end on't!
[*Sings*]   By Gis and by Saint Charity,
            Alack, and fie for shame!
          Young men will do't if they come to't.
            By Cock, they are to blame.   60
          Quoth she, "Before you tumbled me,
            You promis'd me to wed."
  He answers:
          "So would I 'a' done, by yonder sun,
            An thou hadst not come to my bed."   65

KING How long hath she been thus?

OPHELIA I hope all will be well. We must be patient; but I cannot choose
but weep to think they would lay him i' th' cold ground. My brother
shall know of it; and so I thank you for your good counsel. Come, my
coach! Good night, ladies, good night. Sweet ladies, good night, good
night.   70

[*Exit.*]

KING Follow her close; give her good watch, I pray you.

[*Exit* HORATIO.]

  O, this is the poison of deep grief; it springs
  All from her father's death. O Gertrude, Gertrude,
  When sorrows come, they come not single spies,

---

42 *God dild you:* God be good to you   44 *Conceit upon:* suggested by thoughts of her father
52 *dupp'd:* opened   57 *By Gis:* by Jesus   60 *by Cock:* by God   61 *tumbled:* had intercourse with

But in battalions! First, her father slain;   75
Next, your son gone, and he most violent author
Of his own just remove; the people muddied,
Thick and unwholesome in their thoughts and whispers
For good Polonius' death, and we have done but greenly
In hugger-mugger to inter him; poor Ophelia   80
Divided from herself and her fair judgment,
Without the which we are pictures or mere beasts;
Last, and as much containing as all these,
Her brother is in secret come from France;
Feeds on his wonder, keeps himself in clouds,   85
And wants not buzzers to infect his ear
With pestilent speeches of his father's death,
Wherein necessity, of matter beggar'd,
Will nothing stick our person to arraign
In ear and ear. O my dear Gertrude, this,   90
Like to a murd'ring piece, in many places
Gives me superfluous death.

[*A noise within.*]

QUEEN   Alack, what noise is this?

KING   Where are my Switzers? Let them guard the door.

[*Enter a* MESSENGER.]

What is the matter?

MESSENGER   Save yourself, my lord:
The ocean, overpeering of his list,   95
Eats not the flats with more impetuous haste
Than young Laertes, in a riotous head,
O'erbears your officers. The rabble call him lord;
And, as the world were now but to begin,
Antiquity forgot, custom not known,   100
The ratifiers and props of every word,
They cry "Choose we! Laertes shall be king!"
Caps, hands, and tongues applaud it to the clouds,
"Laertes shall be king! Laertes king!"

[*A noise within.*]

---

77 *muddied:* muddled   79 *greenly:* too innocently   80 *in hugger-mugger:* without respectful ceremony   85 *wonder:* speculation   86 *buzzers:* irresponsible gossipers   89 *stick:* hesitate
93 *Switzers:* Swiss guards   95 *overpeering of his list:* surging over its high-water mark

QUEEN   How cheerfully on the false trail they cry!   105
  O, this is counter, you false Danish dogs!

KING   The doors are broke.

[*Enter* LAERTES *with others.*]

LAERTES   Where is this king?—Sirs, stand you all without.

ALL   No, let's come in!

LAERTES   I pray you give me leave.   110

ALL   We will, we will!

LAERTES · I thank you. Keep the door. [*Exeunt Followers.*] O thou vile king,
  Give me my father!

QUEEN   Calmly, good Laertes.

LAERTES   That drop of blood that's calm proclaims me bastard;
  Cries cuckold to my father; brands the harlot   115
  Even here between the chaste unsmirched brows
  Of my true mother.

KING   What is the cause, Laertes,
  That thy rebellion looks so giantlike?
  Let him go, Gertrude. Do not fear our person.
  There's such divinity doth hedge a king   120
  That treason can but peep to what it would,
  Acts little of his will. Tell me, Laertes,
  Why thou art thus incens'd. Let him go, Gertrude.
  Speak, man.

LAERTES   Where is my father?

KING   Dead.

QUEEN   But not by him!   125

KING   Let him demand his fill.

LAERTES   How came he dead? I'll not be juggled with:
  To hell, allegiance! vows, to the blackest devil!
  Conscience and grace, to the profoundest pit!
  I dare damnation. To this point I stand,   130
  That both the worlds I give to negligence,
  Let come what comes; only I'll be reveng'd
  Most throughly for my father.

KING   Who shall stay you?

LAERTES   My will, not all the world!
  And for my means, I'll husband them so well   135
  They shall go far with little.

---

106 *counter:* following the wrong scent   121 *peep to:* look from afar

766

KING   Good Laertes,
  If you desire to know the certainty
  Of your dear father's death, is't writ in your revenge
  That swoopstake you will draw both friend and foe,
  Winner and loser?   140

LAERTES   None but his enemies.

KING   Will you know them then?

LAERTES   To his good friends thus wide I'll ope my arms
  And, like the kind life-rend'ring pelican,
  Repast them with my blood.

KING   Why, now you speak
  Like a good child and a true gentleman.   145
  That I am guiltless of your father's death,
  And am most sensibly in grief for it,
  It shall as level to your judgment pierce
  As day does to your eye.
          [A noise within] "Let her come in!"

LAERTES   How, now? What noise is that?   150

[Enter OPHELIA.]

  O heat, dry up my brains! Tears seven times salt
  Burn out the sense and virtue of mine eye!
  By heaven, thy madness shall be paid by weight
  Till our scale turn the beam. O rose of May!
  Dear maid, kind sister, sweet Ophelia!   155
  O heavens! is't possible a young maid's wits
  Should be as mortal as an old man's life?
  Nature is fine in love, and where 'tis fine,
  It sends some precious instance of itself
  After the thing it loves.   160

OPHELIA [Sings]
  They bore him barefac'd on the bier
      (Hey non nony, nony, hey nony)
  And in his grave rain'd many a tear.
  Fare you well, my dove!

LAERTES   Hadst thou thy wits, and didst persuade revenge   165
  It could not move thus.

139 swoopstake: in one fell swoop   143 pelican: The female pelican was thought to feed her young
with her own blood.   148 as . . . pierce: aim so accurately as to convince without question

OPHELIA   You must sing "A-down a-down, and you call him a-down-a." O, how the wheel becomes it! It is the false steward, that stole his master's daughter.

LAERTES   This nothing's more than matter.

OPHELIA   There's rosemary, that's for remembrance. Pray you, love, remember. And there is pansies, that's for thoughts.   170

LAERTES   A document in madness! Thoughts and remembrance fitted.

OPHELIA   [*to* CLAUDIUS] There's fennel for you, and columbines. [*to* GERTRUDE] There's rue for you, and here's some for me. We may call it herb of grace o' Sundays. O, you must wear your rue with a difference! There's a daisy. I would give you some violets, but they wither'd all   175
when my father died. They say he made a good end.
[*Sings*] For bonny sweet Robin is all my joy.

LAERTES   Thought and affliction, passion, hell itself,
She turns to favour and to prettiness.

OPHELIA [*Sings*]

And will he not come again?   180
And will he not come again?
   No, no, he is dead;
   Go to thy deathbed;
He never will come again.

His beard was as white as snow,   185
All flaxen was his poll.
   He is gone, he is gone,
   And we cast away moan.
God 'a' mercy on his soul!

And of all Christian souls, I pray God. God b' wi' you.   190

[*Exit.*]

LAERTES   Do you see this, O God?

KING   Laertes, I must commune with your grief,
Or you deny me right. Go but apart,
Make choice of whom your wisest friends you will,
And they shall hear and judge 'twixt you and me.   195
If by direct or by collateral hand
They find us touch'd, we will our kingdom give,
Our crown, our life, and all that we call ours,

---

167 *wheel:* spinning wheel   168 *this nothing's more than matter:* this meaninglessness carries more effect than sane speech would   196 *collateral:* indirect

To you in satisfaction; but if not,
Be you content to lend your patience to us,   200
And we shall jointly labour with your soul
To give it due content.

LAERTES   Let this be so.
His means of death, his obscure funeral—
No trophy, sword, nor hatchment o'er his bones,
No noble rite nor formal ostentation,—   205
Cry to be heard, as 'twere from heaven to earth,
That I must call't in question.

KING   So you shall;
And where th' offence is let the great axe fall.
I pray you go with me.

[*Exeunt.*]

Scene VI.

Elsinore. Another Room in the Castle.

[*Enter* HORATIO *and an* ATTENDANT.]

HORATIO   What are they that would speak with me?

SERVANT   Seafaring men, sir. They say they have letters for you.

HORATIO   Let them come in.

[*Exit* ATTENDANT]

I do not know from what part of the world
I should be greeted, if not from Lord Hamlet.   5

[*Enter* SAILORS.]

SAILOR   God bless you, sir.

HORATIO   Let him bless thee too.

SAILOR   'A shall, sir, an't please him. There's a letter for you, sir,—it comes
   from th' ambassador that was bound for England—if your name be
   Horatio, as I am let to know it is.   10

HORATIO [*Reads the letter*]   "Horatio, when thou shalt have overlook'd this,
   give these fellows some means to the King. They have letters for him.
   Ere we were two days old at sea, a pirate of very warlike appointment
   gave us chase. Finding ourselves too slow of sail, we put on a compelled
   valour, and in the grapple I boarded them. On the instant they got clear   15

204 *hatchment:* gravestone   208 *the great axe:* vengeance

of our ship; so I alone became their prisoner. They have dealt with me
like thieves of mercy; but they knew what they did: I am to do a good
turn for them. Let the King have the letters I have sent, and repair thou
to me with as much speed as thou wouldest fly death. I have words to
speak in thine ear will make thee dumb; yet are they much too light for   20
the bore of the matter. These good fellows will bring thee where I am.
Rosencrantz and Guildenstern hold their course for England. Of them
I have much to tell thee. Farewell.
　　　He that thou knowest thine,

　　　　　　　　　　　　　　　　　　　　　　　　　Hamlet."

Come, I will give you way for these your letters,   25
And do't the speedier that you may direct me
To him from whom you brought them.

[*Exeunt.*]

Scene VII.

Elsinore. Another Room in the Castle.

[*Enter* KING *and* LAERTES.]

KING　Now must your conscience my acquittance seal,
　　And you must put me in your heart for friend,
　　Sith you have heard, and with a knowing ear,
　　That he which hath your noble father slain
　　Pursued my life.

LAERTES　　　　　　It well appears. But tell me   5
　　Why you proceeded not against these feats
　　So crimeful and so capital in nature,
　　As by your safety, wisdom, all things else,
　　You mainly were stirr'd up.

KING　　　　　　　　　　O, for two special reasons,
　　Which may to you, perhaps, seem much unsinew'd,   10
　　But yet to me they are strong. The Queen his mother
　　Lives almost by his looks; and for myself,—
　　My virtue or my plague, be it either which,—
　　She's so conjunctive to my life and soul
　　That, as the star moves not but in his sphere,   15
　　I could not but by her. The other motive
　　Why to a public count I might not go
　　Is the great love the general gender bear him,
　　Who, dipping all his faults in their affection,
　　Would, like the spring that turneth wood to stone,   20

10 *much unsinew'd:* without strength　　18 *general gender:* ordinary citizens

Convert his gyves to graces; so that my arrows,
Too slightly timber'd for so loud a wind,
Would have reverted to my bow again,
And not where I had aim'd them.

LAERTES   And so have I a noble father lost;   25
A sister driven into desp'rate terms,
Whose worth, if praises may go back again,
Stood challenger on mount of all the age
For her perfections. But my revenge will come.

KING   Break not your sleeps for that. You must not think   30
That we are made of stuff so flat and dull
That we can let our beard be shook with danger,
And think it pastime. You shortly shall hear more.
I lov'd your father, and we love ourself,
And that, I hope, will teach you to imagine—   35

[*Enter a* MESSENGER *with letters.*]

How now? What news?

MESSENGER   Letters, my lord, from Hamlet:
This to your Majesty; this to the Queen.

KING   From Hamlet? Who brought them?

MESSENGER   Sailors, my lord, they say; I saw them not.
They were given me by Claudio; he receiv'd them   40
Of him that brought them.

KING   Laertes, you shall hear them.
Leave us.

[*Exit* MESSENGER.]

[*Reads*] "High and Mighty,—You shall know I am set naked on your
kingdom. To-morrow shall I beg leave to see your kingly eyes; when I
shall (first asking your pardon thereunto) recount the occasion of my
sudden and more strange return. Hamlet."   45

What should this mean? Are all the rest come back?
Or is it some abuse, and no such thing?

LAERTES   Know you the hand?

KING   'Tis Hamlet's character, "Naked!"
And in a postscript here, he says "alone."
Can you advise me?   50

21 *gyves:* fetters   42 *naked:* destitute   47 *abuse:* trick

LAERTES   I am lost in it, my lord. But let him come!
   It warms the very sickness in my heart
   That I shall live and tell him to his teeth,
   "Thus didest thou."

KING   If it be so, Laertes
   (As how should it be so? how otherwise?),   55
   Will you be rul'd by me?

LAERTES   Ay, my lord,
   So you will not o'errule me to a peace.

KING   To thine own peace. If he be now return'd,
   As checking at his voyage, and that he means
   No more to undertake it, I will work him   60
   To an exploit now ripe in my device,
   Under the which he shall not choose but fall;
   And for his death no wind of blame shall breathe,
   But even his mother shall uncharge the practice
   And call it accident.

LAERTES   My lord, I will be rul'd;   65
   The rather, if you could devise it so
   That I might be the organ.

KING   It falls right.
   You have been talk'd of since your travel much,
   And that in Hamlet's hearing, for a quality
   Wherein they say you shine. Your sum of parts   70
   Did not together pluck such envy from him
   As did that one; and that, in my regard,
   Of the unworthiest siege.

LAERTES   What part is that, my lord?

KING   A very riband in the cap of youth—
   Yet needful too; for youth no less becomes   75
   The light and careless livery that it wears
   Than settled age his sables and his weeds,
   Importing health and graveness. Two months since
   Here was a gentleman of Normandy.
   I have seen myself, and serv'd against, the French,   80
   And they can well on horseback; but this gallant
   Had witchcraft in't. He grew unto his seat,
   And to such wondrous doing brought his horse
   As had he been incorps'd and demi-natur'd

---

64 *uncharge the practice:* accept what happens   73 *siege:* rank   77 *weeds:* clothes   84 *incorps'd and demi-natur'd:* a part of the horse and thus a kind of half-man, half-horse

With the brave beast. So far he topp'd my thought   85
That I, in forgery of shapes and tricks,
Come short of what he did.

LAERTES   A Norman was't?

KING   A Norman.

LAERTES   Upon my life, Lamound.

KING   The very same.

LAERTES   I know him well. He is the brooch indeed   90
And gem of all the nation.

KING   He made confession of you;
And gave you such a masterly report
For art and exercise in your defence,
And for your rapier most especially,   95
That he cried out 'twould be a sight indeed
If one could match you. The scrimers of their nation
He swore had neither motion, guard, nor eye,
If you oppos'd them. Sir, this report of his
Did Hamlet so envenom with his envy   100
That he could nothing do but wish and beg
Your sudden coming o'er to play with you.
Now, out of this—

LAERTES   What out of this, my lord?

KING   Laertes, was your father dear to you?
Or are you like the painting of a sorrow,   105
A face without a heart?

LAERTES   Why ask you this?

KING   Not that I think you did not love your father;
But that I know love is begun by time,
And that I see, in passages of proof,
Time qualifies the spark and fire of it.   110
There lives within the very flame of love
A kind of wick or snuff that will abate it;
And nothing is at a like goodness still;
For goodness, growing to a plurisy,
Dies in his own too-much. That we would do,   115
We should do when we would; for this "would" changes,
And hath abatements and delays as many
As there are tongues, are hands, are accidents;
And then this "should" is like a spendthrift sigh,

---

90 *brooch:* ornament   97 *scrimers:* fencers   110 *qualifies:* moderate   114 *plurisy:* overabundance

That hurts by easing. But to the quick o' th' ulcer!   120
Hamlet comes back. What would you undertake
To show yourself your father's son in deed
More than in words?

LAERTES   To cut his throat i' th' church!

KING   No place indeed should murther sanctuarize;
Revenge should have no bounds. But, good Laertes,   125
Will you do this? Keep close within your chamber.
Hamlet return'd shall know you are come home.
We'll put on those shall praise your excellence
And set a double varnish on the fame
The Frenchman gave you; bring you in fine together   130
And wager on your heads. He, being remiss,
Most generous, and free from all contriving,
Will not peruse the foils; so that with ease,
Or with a little shuffling, you may choose
A sword unbated, and, in a pass of practice,   135
Requite him for your father.

LAERTES   I will do't!
And for that purpose I'll anoint my sword.
I bought an unction of a mountebank,
So mortal that, but dip a knife in it,
Where it draws blood no cataplasm so rare,   140
Collected from all simples that have virtue
Under the moon, can save the thing from death
That is but scratch'd withal. I'll touch my point
With this contagion, that, if I gall him slightly,
It may be death.   145

KING   Let's further think of this,
Weigh what convenience both of time and means
May fit us to our shape. If this should fail,
And that our drift look through our bad performance,
'Twere better not assay'd. Therefore this project
Should have a back or second, that might hold   150
If this did blast in proof. Soft! let me see.
We'll make a solemn wager on your cunnings—
I ha't!
When in your motion you are hot and dry—
As make your bouts more violent to that end—   155
And that he calls for drink, I'll have prepar'd him

131 *remiss:* easygoing   134 *shuffling:* trickery   139 *mountebank:* medicine man   140 *cataplasm:*
poultice   144 *gall:* break the skin   151 *blast in proof:* blow up when tested

A chalice for the nonce; whereon but sipping,
If he by chance escape your venom'd stuck,
Our purpose may hold there.—But stay, what noise?

[*Enter* QUEEN.]

How now, sweet queen? 160

QUEEN   One woe doth tread upon another's heel,
So fast they follow. Your sister's drown'd, Laertes.

LAERTES   Drown'd! O, where?

QUEEN   There is a willow grows aslant a brook,
That shows his hoar leaves in the glassy stream. 165
There with fantastic garlands did she come
Of crowflowers, nettles, daisies, and long purples
That liberal shepherds give a grosser name,
But our cold maids do dead men's fingers call them.
There on the pendent boughs her coronet weeds 170
Clamb'ring to hang, an envious sliver broke,
When down her weedy trophies and herself
Fell in the weeping brook. Her clothes spread wide
And, mermaid-like, awhile they bore her up;
Which time she chaunted snatches of old tunes, 175
As one incapable of her own distress,
Or like a creature native and indued
Unto that element; but long it could not be
Till that her garments, heavy with their drink,
Pull'd the poor wretch from her melodious lay 180
To muddy death.

LAERTES   Alas, then she is drown'd?

QUEEN   Drown'd, drown'd.

LAERTES   Too much of water hast thou, poor Ophelia,
And therefore I forbid my tears; but yet
It is our trick; nature her custom holds, 185
Let shame say what it will. When these are gone,
The woman will be out. Adieu, my lord.
I have a speech of fire, that fain would blaze
But that this folly douts it.

[*Exit.*]

157 *for the nonce:* for the occasion   158 *stuck:* thrust   167 *long purples:* orchids   168 *liberal:*
licentious   171 *envious:* malicious   176 *incapable:* unwitting   187 *woman:* coward   189 *folly*
douts: weeping douses

KING   Let's follow, Gertrude.
How much I had to do to calm his rage!   190
Now fear I this will give it start again;
Therefore let's follow.

[*Exeunt.*]

ACT V

Scene I.

Elsinore. A Churchyard.

[*Enter two* CLOWNS *with spades and pickaxes.*]

CLOWN   Is she to be buried in Christian burial when she wilfully seeks her
own salvation?

OTHER   I tell thee she is; therefore make her grave straight. The crowner
hath sate on her, and finds it Christian burial.

CLOWN   How can that be, unless she drown'd herself in her own
defence?   5

OTHER   Why, 'tis found so.

CLOWN   It must be *se offendendo;* it cannot be else. For here lies the point:
if I drown myself wittingly, it argues an act; and an act hath three
branches—it is to act, to do, and to perform; argal, she drown'd herself
wittingly.   10

OTHER   Nay, but hear you, Goodman Delver!

CLOWN   Give me leave. Here lies the water; good. Here stands the man;
good. If the man go to this water and drown himself, it is, will he nill
he, he goes—mark you that. But if the water come to him and drown
him, he drowns not himself. Argal, he that is not guilty of his own death   15
shortens not his own life.

OTHER   But is this law?

CLOWN   Ay, marry, is't—crowner's quest law.

OTHER   Will you ha' the truth an't? If this had not been a gentlewoman,
she should have been buried out o' Christian burial.   20

CLOWN   Why, there thou say'st! And the more pity that great folk should
have count'nance in this world to drown or hang themselves more than
their even-Christen. Come, my spade! There is no ancient gentlemen
but gard'ners, ditchers, and grave-makers. They hold up Adam's profession.   25

Clowns: rustics   3 *crowner:* coroner   7 *se offendendo:* self-offense, a mistake for *se defendendo,*
self-defense   9 *argal:* therefore, for *ergo*   13 *will he nill he:* willy-nilly   18 *quest:* inquest
23 *even-Christen:* fellow Christians

OTHER Was he a gentleman?

CLOWN 'A was the first that ever bore arms.

OTHER Why, he had none.

CLOWN What, art a heathen? How dost thou understand the Scripture? The Scripture says Adam digg'd. Could he dig without arms? I'll put 30 another question to thee. If thou answerest me not to the purpose, confess thyself—

OTHER Go to!

CLOWN What is he that builds stronger than either the mason, the ship-wright, or the carpenter? 35

OTHER The gallows-maker; for that frame outlives a thousand tenants.

CLOWN I like thy wit well, in good faith. The gallows does well. But how does it well? It does well to those that do ill. Now, thou dost ill to say that gallows is built stronger than the church. Argal, the gallows may do well to thee. To't again, come! 40

OTHER Who builds stronger than a mason, a shipwright, or a carpenter?

CLOWN Ay, tell me that, and unyoke.

OTHER Marry, now I can tell!

CLOWN To't.

OTHER Mass, I cannot tell. 45

[*Enter* HAMLET *and* HORATIO *afar off.*]

CLOWN Cudgel thy brains no more about it, for your dull ass will not mend his pace with beating; and when you are ask'd this question next, say "a grave-maker." The houses he makes lasts till doomsday. Go, get thee to Yaughan; fetch me a stoup of liquor.

[*Exit* SECOND CLOWN.]

[CLOWN *digs and sings.*]

In youth when I did love, did love 50
  Methought it was very sweet;
To contract—O—the time for—a—my behove,
O, methought there—a—was nothing—a—meet.

HAMLET Has this fellow no feeling of his business, that he sings at grave- 55 making?

HORATIO Custom hath made it in him a property of easiness.

43 *unyoke:* unharness   45 *Mass:* By the Mass   49 *Yaughan:* John; *stoup:* large mug   52 *contract* . . . *behove:* to shorten time to my benefit

777

HAMLET 'Tis e'en so. The hand of little employment hath the daintier sense.

CLOWN [*Sings*]

But age with his stealing steps   60
Hath clawed me in his clutch,
And hath shipped me intil the land,
As if I had never been such.

[*Throws up a skull.*]

HAMLET That skull had a tongue in it, and could sing once. How the knave jowls it to the ground, as if 'twere Cain's jawbone, that did the first   65
murther! This might be the pate of a politician, which this ass now o'erreaches; one that would circumvent God, might it not?

HORATIO It might, my lord.

HAMLET Or of a courtier, which could say "Good morrow, sweet lord! How dost thou, good lord?" This might be my Lord Such-a-one, that   70
prais'd my Lord Such-a-one's horse when he meant to beg it—might it not?

HORATIO Ay, my lord.

HAMLET Why, e'en so! and now my Lady Worm's, chapless, and knock'd about the mazzard with a sexton's spade. Here's fine revolution, an we   75
had the trick to see't. Did these bones cost no more the breeding but to play at loggets with 'em? Mine ache to think o't.

CLOWN [*Sings*]

A pickaxe and a spade, a spade,
For and a shrouding sheet;
O, a pit of clay for to be made   80
For such a guest is meet.

[*Throws up another skull.*]

HAMLET There's another. Why may not that be the skull of a lawyer? Where be his quidits now, his quillets, his cases, his tenures, and his tricks? Why does he suffer this rude knave now to knock him about the sconce with a dirty shovel, and will not tell him of his action of battery?   85
Hum! This fellow might be in's time a great buyer of land, with his statutes, his recognizances, his fines, his double vouchers, his recoveries. Is this the fine of his fines, and the recovery of his recoveries, to have

61 *clawed:* grabbed   62 *intil:* into   65 *jowls:* tosses   67 *o'erreaches:* acts superior to   74 *chapless:* without a lower jaw   75 *mazzard:* head   77 *loggets:* a game played with small pieces of wood   83 *quiddits . . . quillets:* tricky definitions . . . quibbles   85 *sconce:* pate   88 *fine:* end, result

his fine pate full of fine dirt? Will his vouchers vouch him no more of
his purchases, and double ones too, than the length and breadth of a pair   90
of indentures? The very conveyances of his lands will scarcely lie in this
box; and must th' inheritor himself have no more, ha?

HORATIO   Not a jot more, my lord.

HAMLET   Is not parchment made of sheepskins?

HORATIO   Ay, my lord, and of calveskins too.   95

HAMLET   They are sheep and calves which seek out assurance in that. I will
speak to this fellow. Whose grave's this, sirrah?

CLOWN   Mine, sir.
[Sings]   O, a pit of clay for to be made
                For such a guest is meet.   100

HAMLET   I think it be thine indeed for thou liest in't.

CLOWN   You lie out on't, sir, and therefore 'tis not yours. For my part, I
do not lie in't, yet it is mine.

HAMLET   Thou dost lie in't, to be in't and say it is thine. 'Tis for the dead,
not for the quick; therefore thou liest.   105

CLOWN   'Tis a quick lie, sir; 'twill away again from me to you.

HAMLET   What man dost thou dig it for?

CLOWN   For no man, sir.

HAMLET   What woman then?

CLOWN   For none neither.   110

HAMLET   Who is to be buried in't?

CLOWN   One that was a woman, sir; but, rest her soul, she's dead.

HAMLET   How absolute the knave is! We must speak by the card, or equiv-
ocation will undo us. By the Lord, Horatio, this three years I have taken
note of it, the age is grown so picked that the toe of the peasant comes   115
so near the heel of the courtier he galls his kibe.—How long has thou
been a grave-maker?

CLOWN   Of all the days i' th' year, I came to't that day that our last king
Hamlet overcame Fortinbras.

HAMLET   How long is that since?   120

CLOWN   Cannot you tell that? Every fool can tell that. It was the very day
that young Hamlet was born—he that is mad, and sent into England.

HAMLET   Ay, marry, why was he sent into England?

---

91 *indentures:* contracts   105 *quick:* alive   113 *by the card:* accurately   115 *so picked:* so refined
116 *galls his kibe:* rubs raw the chilblains on his heel

CLOWN   Why, because 'a was mad. 'A shall recover his wits there; or, if 'a do not, 'tis no great matter there.   125

HAMLET   Why?

CLOWN   'Twill not be seen in him there. There the men are as mad as he.

HAMLET   How came he mad?

CLOWN   Very strangely, they say.

HAMLET   How strangely?   130

CLOWN   Faith, e'en with losing his wits.

HAMLET   Upon what ground?

CLOWN   Why, here in Denmark. I have been sexton here, man and boy, thirty years.

HAMLET   How long will a man lie i' th' earth ere he rot?   135

CLOWN   Faith, if 'a be not rotten before 'a die (as we have many pocky corses now-a-days that will scarce hold the laying in), 'a will last you some eight year or nine year. A tanner will last you nine year.

HAMLET   Why he more than another?

CLOWN   Why, sir, his hide is so tann'd with his trade that 'a will keep out   140
water a great while; and your water is a sore decayer of your whoreson dead body. Here's a skull now. This skull hath lien you i' th' earth three-and-twenty years.

HAMLET   Whose was it?

CLOWN   A whoreson mad fellow's it was. Whose do you think it was?   145

HAMLET   Nay, I know not.

CLOWN   A pestilence on him for a mad rogue! 'A pour'd a flagon of Rhenish on my head once. This same skull, sir, was Yorick's skull, the King's jester.

HAMLET   This?   150

CLOWN   E'en that.

HAMLET   Let me see. [*Takes the skull*] Alas, poor Yorick! I knew him, Horatio. A fellow of infinite jest, of most excellent fancy. He hath borne me on his back a thousand times. And now how abhorred in my imagination it is! My gorge rises at it. Here hung those lips that I have kiss'd   155
I know not how oft. Where be your gibes now? your gambols? your songs? your flashes of merriment that were wont to set the table on a roar? Not one now, to mock your own grinning? Quite chapfall'n? Now get you to my lady's chamber, and tell her, let her paint an inch thick, to this favour she must come. Make her laugh at that. Prithee, Horatio,   160
tell me one thing.

HORATIO   What's that, my lord?

HAMLET Dost thou think Alexander look'd o' this fashion i' th' earth?

HORATIO E'en so.

HAMLET And smelt so? Pah!   165

[*Puts down the skull.*]

HORATIO E'en so, my lord.

HAMLET To what base uses we may return, Horatio! Why may not imagination trace the noble dust of Alexander till he find it stopping a bunghole?

HORATIO 'Twere to consider too curiously, to consider so.   170

HAMLET No, faith, not a jot; but to follow him thither with modesty enough, and likelihood to lead it; as thus: Alexander died, Alexander was buried, Alexander returneth into dust; the dust is earth; of earth we make loam; and why of that loam (whereto he was converted) might they not stop a beer barrel?   175
Imperious Cæsar, dead and turn'd to clay,
Might stop a hole to keep the wind away.
O, that that earth which kept the world in awe
Should patch a wall t' expel the winter's flaw!
But soft! but soft! aside! Here comes the King—   180

[*Enter* PRIESTS *with a coffin in funeral procession,* KING, QUEEN, LAERTES, *with* LORDS *attendant.*]

The Queen, the courtiers. Who is this they follow?
And with such maimed rites? This doth betoken
The corse they follow did with desp'rate hand
Fordo it own life. 'Twas of some estate.
Couch we awhile, and mark.   185

[*Retires with* HORATIO.]

LAERTES What ceremony else?

HAMLET That is Laertes,
A very noble youth. Mark.

LAERTES What ceremony else?

PRIEST Her obsequies have been as far enlarg'd   190
As we have warranty. Her death was doubtful;
And, but that great command o'ersways the order,
She should in ground unsanctified have lodg'd
Till the last trumpet. For charitable prayers,

---

170 *curiously:* closely   171 *modesty:* moderation   179 *flaw:* wind   182 *maimed:* incomplete

Shards, flints, and pebbles should be thrown on her. 195
Yet here she is allow'd her virgin crants,
Her maiden strewments, and the bringing home
Of bell and burial.

LAERTES   Must there no more be done?

PRIEST   No more be done.
We should profane the service of the dead 200
To sing a requiem and such a rest to her
As to peace-parted souls.

LAERTES   Lay her i' th' earth;
And from her fair and unpolluted flesh
May violets spring! I tell thee, churlish priest,
A minist'ring angel shall my sister be 205
When thou liest howling.

HAMLET   What, the fair Ophelia?

QUEEN   Sweets to the sweet! Farewell.

[Scatters flowers]

I hop'd thou shouldst have been my Hamlet's wife;
I thought thy bride-bed to have deck'd, sweet maid,
And not have strew'd thy grave.

LAERTES   O, treble woe 210
Fall ten times treble on that cursed head
Whose wicked deed thy most ingenious sense
Depriv'd thee of! Hold off the earth awhile,
Till I have caught her once more in mine arms.

[Leaps in the grave]

Now pile your dust upon the quick and dead 215
Till of this flat mountain you have made
T' o'ertop old Pelion or the skyish head
Of blue Olympus.

HAMLET *[Comes forward]*   What is he whose grief
Bears such an emphasis? whose phrase of sorrow
Conjures the wand'ring stars, and makes them stand 220
Like wonder-wounded hearers? This is I,
Hamlet the Dane.

195 *shards:* pieces of broken pottery   196 *crants:* garland   212 *ingenious sense:* keen intellect
217 *Pelion:* a high mountain   220 *conjures:* affects

[*Leaps in after* LAERTES.]

LAERTES   The devil take thy soul!

[*Grapples with him.*]

HAMLET   Thou pray'st not well.
  I prithee take thy fingers from my throat;
  For, though I am not splenitive and rash,   225
  Yet have I in me something dangerous,
  Which let thy wisdom fear. Hold off thy hand!

KING   Pluck them asunder.

QUEEN   Hamlet, Hamlet!

ALL   Gentlemen!

HORATIO   Good my lord, be quiet.

[*The* ATTENDANTS *part them, and they come out of the grave.*]

HAMLET   Why, I will fight with him upon this theme   230
  Until my eyelids will no longer wag.

QUEEN   O my son, what theme?

HAMLET   I lov'd Ophelia. Forty thousand brothers
  Could not (with all their quantity of love)
  Make up my sum. What wilt thou do for her?   235

KING   O, he is mad, Laertes.

QUEEN   For love of God, forbear him!

HAMLET   'Swounds, show me what thou't do.
  Woo't weep? woo't fight? woo't fast? woo't tear thyself?
  Woo't drink up esill? eat a crocodile?   240
  I'll do't. Dost thou come here to whine?
  To outface me with leaping in her grave?
  Be buried quick with her, and so will I.
  And if thou prate of mountains, let them throw
  Millions of acres on us, till our ground,   245
  Singeing his pate against the burning zone,
  Make Ossa like a wart! Nay, an thou'lt mouth,
  I'll rant as well as thou.

QUEEN   This is mere madness;
  And thus a while the fit will work on him.

---

225 *splenitive:* easily angered   240 *esill:* vinegar   246 *burning zone:* celestial area bounded by the
Tropics of Cancer and Capricorn   248 *mere:* utter

Anon, as patient as the female dove   250
When that her golden couplets are disclos'd,
His silence will sit drooping.

HAMLET   Hear you, sir!
What is the reason that you use me thus?
I lov'd you ever. But it is no matter.
Let Hercules himself do what he may,   255
The cat will mew, and dog will have his day.

[*Exit.*]

KING   I pray thee, good Horatio, wait upon him.

[*Exit* HORATIO.]

(*To* LAERTES) Strengthen your patience in our last night's speech.
We'll put the matter to the present push.—
Good Gertrude, set some watch over your son.—   260
This grave shall have a living monument.
An hour of quiet shortly shall we see;
Till then in patience our proceeding be.

[*Exeunt.*]

Scene II.

Elsinore. A Hall in the Castle.

[*Enter* HAMLET *and* HORATIO.] ·

HAMLET   So much for this, sir; now shall you see the other.
You do remember all the circumstance?

HORATIO   Remember it, my lord!

HAMLET   Sir, in my heart there was a kind of fighting
That would not let me sleep. Methought I lay   5
Worse than the mutines in the bilboes. Rashly—
And prais'd be rashness for it; let us know,
Our indiscretion sometime serves us well
When our deep plots do pall; and that should learn us
There's a divinity that shapes our ends,   10
Rough-hew them how we will—

HORATIO   That is most certain.

_____

259 *to the present push:* into immediate action   6 *mutines:* mutineers; *bilboes:* irons   7 *rashness:*
unreasoned action   9 *deep plots:* carefully planned actions; *pall:* lose force

HAMLET   Up from my cabin,
  My sea-gown scarf'd about me, in the dark
  Grop'd I to find out them; had my desire,
  Finger'd their packet, and in fine withdrew   15
  To mine own room again; making so bold
  (My fears forgetting manners) to unseal
  Their grand commission; where I found, Horatio
  (O royal knavery!), an exact command,
  Larded with many several sorts of reasons,   20
  Importing Denmark's health, and England's too,
  With, hoo! such bugs and goblins in my life—
  That, on the supervise, no leisure bated,
  No, not to stay the grinding of the axe,
  My head should be struck off.

HORATIO   Is't possible?   25

HAMLET   Here's the commission; read it at more leisure.
  But wilt thou hear me how I did proceed?

HORATIO   I beseech you.

HAMLET   Being thus benetted round with villanies,
  Or I could make a prologue to my brains,   30
  They had begun the play. I sat me down;
  Devis'd a new commission; wrote it fair.
  I once did hold it, as our statists do,
  A baseness to write fair, and labour'd much
  How to forget that learning; but, sir, now   35
  It did me yeoman's service. Wilt thou know
  Th' effect of what I wrote?

HORATIO   Ay, good my lord.

HAMLET   An earnest conjuration from the King,
  As England was his faithful tributary,
  As love between them like the palm might flourish,   40
  As peace should still her wheaten garland wear
  And stand a comma 'tween their amities,
  And many such-like as's of great charge,
  That, on the view and knowing of these contents,
  Without debatement further, more or less,   45
  He should the bearers put to sudden death,
  Not shriving time allow'd.

HORATIO   How was this seal'd?

15 *finger'd:* stole   22 *bugs:* bugbears   23 *on the supervise:* on the reading of the document
30 *or:* ere   37 *effect:* gist   47 *shriving time:* time for confession and absolution

HAMLET Why, even in that was heaven ordinant.
I had my father's signet in my purse,
Which was the model of that Danish seal;   50
Folded the writ up in the form of th' other,
Subscrib'd it, gave't th' impression, plac'd it safely,
The changeling never known. Now, the next day
Was our sea-fight; and what to this was sequent
Thou know'st already.   55

HORATIO So Guildenstern and Rosencrantz go to't.

HAMLET Why, man, they did make love to this employment!
They are not near my conscience; their defeat
Does by their own insinuation grow.
'Tis dangerous when the baser nature comes   60
Between the pass and fell incensed points
Of mighty opposites.

HORATIO   Why, what a king is this!

HAMLET Does it not, thinks't thee, stand me now upon
He that hath kill'd my king, and whor'd my mother;
Popp'd in between th' election and my hopes;   65
Thrown out his angle for my proper life,
And with such coz'nage—is't not perfect conscience
To quit him with this arm? And is't not to be damn'd
To let this canker of our nature come
In further evil?   70

HORATIO It must be shortly known to him from England
What is the issue of the business there.

HAMLET It will be short; the interim is mine,
And a man's life's no more than to say "one."
But I am very sorry, good Horatio,   75
That to Laertes I forgot myself;
For by the image of my cause I see
The portraiture of his. I'll court his favours.
But sure the bravery of his grief did put me
Into a tow'ring passion.

HORATIO   Peace! Who comes here?   80

[*Enter young* OSRIC, *a courtier.*]

OSRIC Your lordship is right welcome back to Denmark.

HAMLET I humbly thank you, sir. [*Aside to* HORATIO] Dost know this
    waterfly?

---

48 *ordinant:* helpful   58 *defeat:* destruction   59 *their own insinuation:* their own efforts to become
involved in the plot   61 *fell:* fierce   82 *waterfly:* gorgeous, flitty creature

HORATIO [*Aside to* HAMLET]   No, my good lord.

HAMLET [*Aside to* HORATIO]   Thy state is the more gracious; for 'tis a vice to   85
know him. He hath much land, and fertile. Let a beast be lord of beasts,
and his crib shall stand at the king's mess. 'Tis a chough; but, as I say,
spacious in the possession of dirt.

OSRIC   Sweet lord, if your lordship were at leisure, I should impart a thing
to you from his Majesty.   90

HAMLET   I will receive it, sir, with all diligence of spirit. Put your bonnet
to his right use. 'Tis for the head.

OSRIC   I thank your lordship, it is very hot.

HAMLET   No, believe me, 'tis very cold; the wind is northerly.

OSRIC   It is indifferent cold, my lord, indeed.   95

HAMLET   But yet methinks it is very sultry and hot for my complexion.

OSRIC   Exceedingly, my lord; it is very sultry, as 'twere—I cannot tell how.
But, my lord, his Majesty bade me signify to you that he has laid a great
wager on your head. Sir, this is the matter—

HAMLET   I beseech you remember.   100

[HAMLET *moves him to put on his hat.*]

OSRIC   Nay, good my lord; for mine ease, in good faith. Sir, here is newly
come to court Laertes; believe me, an absolute gentleman, full of most
excellent differences, of very soft society and great showing. Indeed, to
speak feelingly of him, he is the card or calendar of gentry; for you shall
find in him the continent of what part a gentleman would see.   105

HAMLET   Sir, his definement suffers no perdition in you; though, I know,
to divide him inventorially would dozy th' arithmetic of memory, and
yet but yaw neither in respect of his quick sail. But, in the verity of
extolment, I take him to be a soul of great article, and his infusion of
such dearth and rareness as, to make true diction of him, his semblable   110
is his mirror, and who else would trace him, his umbrage, nothing
more.

OSRIC   Your lordship speaks most infallibly of him.

HAMLET   The concernancy, sir? Why do we wrap the gentleman in our
more rawer breath?   115

OSRIC   Sir?

88 *chough:* jackdaw   105 *differences:* superiorities   107 *dozy:* confuse   108 *yaw:* steer badly
109 *his infusion:* his natural quality   110 *semblable:* seeming   111 *umbrage:* shadow

HORATIO [*Aside to* HAMLET] Is't not possible to understand in another
tongue? You will do't, sir, really.

HAMLET What imports the nomination of this gentleman?

OSRIC Of Laertes?

HORATIO [*Aside*] His purse is empty already. All's golden words are
spent.   120

HAMLET Of him, sir.

OSRIC I know you are not ignorant—

HAMLET I would you did, sir; yet, in faith, if you did, it would not much
approve me. Well, sir?

OSRIC You are not ignorant of what excellence Laertes is—   125

HAMLET I dare not confess that, lest I should compare with him in excellence; but to know a man well were to know himself.

OSRIC I mean, sir, for his weapon; but in the imputation laid on him by
them, in his meed he's unfellowed.

HAMLET What's his weapon?   130

OSRIC Rapier and dagger.

HAMLET That's two of his weapons—but well.

OSRIC The King, sir, hath wager'd with him six Barbary horses; against the
which he has impon'd, as I take it, six French rapiers and poniards, with
their assigns, as girdle, hangers, and so. Three of the carriages, in faith, 135
are very dear to fancy, very responsive to the hilts, most delicate carriages, and of very liberal conceit.

HAMLET What call you the carriages?

HORATIO [*Aside to* HAMLET] I knew you must be edified by the margent
ere you had done.   140

OSRIC The carriages, sir, are the hangers.

HAMLET The phrase would be more germane to the matter if we could
carry cannon by our sides. I would it might be hangers till then. But on!
Six Barbary horses against six French swords, their assigns, and three
liberal-conceited carriages: that's the French bet against the Danish.   145
Why is this all impon'd, as you call it?

OSRIC The King, sir, hath laid that, in a dozen passes between yourself and
him, he shall not exceed you three hits; he hath laid on twelve for nine,
and it would come to immediate trial if your lordship would vouchsafe
the answer.   150

---

129 *meed:* competence; *unfellowed:* nobody can equal   134 *impon'd:* put up   137 *liberal conceit:*
handsomely designed   139 *edified by the margent:* impressed by the marginal note

HAMLET   How if I answer no?

OSRIC   I mean, my lord, the opposition of your person in trial.

HAMLET   Sir, I will walk here in the hall. If it please his Majesty, it is the breathing time of day with me. Let the foils be brought, the gentleman willing, and the King hold his purpose, I will win for him if I can; if not, 155 I will gain nothing but my shame and the odd hits.

OSRIC   Shall I redeliver you e'en so?

HAMLET   To this effect, sir, after what flourish your nature will.

OSRIC   I commend my duty to your lordship.

HAMLET   Yours, yours. [*Exit Osric.*] He does well to commend it himself; 160 there are no tongues else for's turn.

HORATIO   This lapwing runs away with the shell on his head.

HAMLET   He did comply with his dug before he suck'd it. Thus has he, and many more of the same bevy that I know the drossy age dotes on, only got the tune of the time and outward habit of encounter—a kind of yesty 165 collection, which carries them through and through the most fann'd and winnowed opinions; and do but blow them to their trial—the bubbles are out.

[*Enter a* LORD.]

LORD   My lord, his Majesty commended him to you by young Osric, who brings back to him, that you attend him in the hall. He sends to know 170 if your pleasure hold to play with Laertes, or that you will take longer time.

HAMLET   I am constant to my purposes; they follow the King's pleasure. If his fitness speaks, mine is ready; now or whensoever, provided I be so able as now. 175

LORD   The King and Queen and all are coming down.

HAMLET   In happy time.

LORD   The Queen desires you to use some gentle entertainment to Laertes before you fall to play.

HAMLET   She well instructs me. 180

[*Exit* LORD.]

154 *breathing time:* time for physical exercise   163 *comply . . . dug:* bow politely to his mother's nipple
164 *drossy:* degenerate   165 *yesty:* frothy   166–167 *fann'd and winnowed:* sophisticated to the
point of absurdity   178 *entertainment:* cordiality; *fall to play:* start the fencing

HORATIO   You will lose this wager, my lord.

HAMLET   I do not think so. Since he went into France I have been in
continual practice. I shall win at the odds. But thou wouldst not think
how ill all's here about my heart. But it is no matter.

HORATIO   Nay, good my lord—   185

HAMLET   It is but foolery; but it is such a kind of gaingiving as would
perhaps trouble a woman.

HORATIO   If your mind dislike anything, obey it. I will forestall their repair
hither and say you are not fit.

HAMLET   Not a whit, we defy augury; there's a special providence in the   190
fall of a sparrow. If it be now, 'tis not to come; if it be not to come, it
will be now; if it be not now, yet it will come: the readiness is all. Since
no man knows aught of what he leaves, what is't to leave betimes? Let
be.

[*Enter* KING, QUEEN, LAERTES, OSRIC, *and* LORDS, *with other* ATTENDANTS *with foils and
gauntlets. A table and flagons of wine on it.*]

KING   Come, Hamlet, come, and take this hand from me.   195

[*The* KING *puts* LAERTES' *hand into* HAMLET'S.]

HAMLET   Give me your pardon, sir. I have done you wrong;
But pardon't, as you are a gentleman.
This presence knows,
And you must needs have heard, how I am punish'd
With sore distraction. What I have done   200
That might your nature, honour, and exception
Roughly awake, I here proclaim was madness.
Was't Hamlet wrong'd Laertes? Never Hamlet.
If Hamlet from himself be ta'en away,
And when he's not himself does wrong Laertes,   205
Then Hamlet does it not, Hamlet denies it.
Who does it, then? His madness. If't be so,
Hamlet is of the faction that is wrong'd;
His madness is poor Hamlet's enemy.
Sir, in this audience,   210
Let my disclaiming from a purpos'd evil
Free me so far in your most generous thoughts
That I have shot my arrow o'er the house
And hurt my brother.

---

186 *gaingiving:* misgiving   198 *This presence:* the King and Queen   201 *exception:* resentment
211 *purpos'd evil:* intended harm   212 *Free:* Absolve

LAERTES   I am satisfied in nature,
  Whose motive in this case should stir me most   215
  To my revenge. But in my terms of honour
  I stand aloof, and will no reconcilement
  Till by some elder masters of known honour
  I have a voice and precedent of peace
  To keep my name ungor'd. But till that time   220
  I do receive your offer'd love like love,
  And will not wrong it.

HAMLET   I embrace it freely,
  And will this brother's wager frankly play.
  Give us the foils. Come on.

LAERTES   Come, one for me.

HAMLET   I'll be your foil, Laertes. In mine ignorance   225
  Your skill shall, like a star i' th' darkest night
  Stick fiery off indeed.

LAERTES   You mock me, sir.

HAMLET   No, by this hand.

KING   Give them the foils, young Osric. Cousin Hamlet,
  You know the wager?

HAMLET   Very well, my lord.   230
  Your Grace has laid the odds o' th' weaker side.

KING   I do not fear it, I have seen you both;
  But since he is better'd, we have therefore odds.

LAERTES   This is too heavy; let me see another.

HAMLET   This likes me well. These foils have all a length?   235

[*Prepare to play.*]

OSRIC   Ay, my good lord.

KING   Set me the stoups of wine upon that table.
  If Hamlet give the first or second hit,
  Or quit in answer of the third exchange,
  Let all the battlements their ordnance fire;   240
  The King shall drink to Hamlet's better breath,
  And in the cup an union shall he throw
  Richer than that which four successive kings
  In Denmark's crown have worn. Give me the cups;
  And let the kettle to the trumpet speak,   245

218 *elder masters:* authorities   220 *name ungor'd:* reputation uninjured   223 *frankly:* without constraint   237 *stoups:* large mugs   242 *an union:* a large, perfect pearl   245 *kettle:* kettledrum

The trumpet to the cannoneer without,
The cannons to the heavens, the heaven to earth,
"Now the King drinks to Hamlet." Come, begin.
And you the judges, bear a wary eye.

HAMLET   Come on, sir.

LAERTES   Come, my lord.

[*They play.*]

HAMLET   One.

LAERTES   No.

HAMLET   Judgment!   250

OSRIC   A hit, a very palpable hit.

LAERTES   Well, again!

KING   Stay, give me drink. Hamlet, this pearl is thine;
Here's to thy health.

[*Drum; trumpets sound; a piece goes off within.*]

                    Give him the cup.

HAMLET   I'll play this bout first; set it by awhile.   255
Come. [*They play.*] Another hit. What say you?

LAERTES   A touch, a touch; I do confess't.

KING   Our son shall win.

QUEEN   He's fat, and scant of breath.
Here, Hamlet, take my napkin, rub thy brows.
The Queen carouses to thy fortune, Hamlet.   260

HAMLET   Good madam!

KING   Gertrude, do not drink.

QUEEN   I will, my lord; I pray you pardon me.

[*Drinks.*]

KING [*Aside*]   It is the poison'd cup; it is too late.

HAMLET   I dare not drink yet, madam; by-and-by.

QUEEN   Come, let me wipe thy face.   265

LAERTES   My lord, I'll hit him now.

KING   I do not think't.

LAERTES [*Aside*]   And yet it is almost against my conscience.

258 *fat:* soft, sweaty   260 *carouses:* drink a toast

HAMLET   Come for the third, Laertes! You but dally.
  I pray you pass with your best violence;
  I am afeard you make a wanton of me.   270

LAERTES   Say you so? Come on.

[*Play.*]

OSRIC   Nothing neither way.

LAERTES   Have at you now!

[LAERTES *wounds* HAMLET; *then, in scuffling, they change rapiers and* HAMLET *wounds* LAERTES.]

KING   Part them! They are incens'd.

HAMLET   Nay come! again!

[*The* QUEEN *falls.*]

OSRIC   Look to the Queen there, ho!

HORATIO   They bleed on both sides. How is it, my lord?   275

OSRIC   How is't, Laertes?

LAERTES   Why, as a woodcock to mine own springe, Osric.
  I am justly kill'd with mine own treachery.

HAMLET   How does the Queen?

KING   She sounds to see them bleed.

QUEEN   No, no! the drink, the drink! O my dear Hamlet!   280
  The drink, the drink! I am poison'd.

[*Dies.*]

HAMLET   O villany! Ho! let the door be lock'd. Treachery! Seek it out.

[LAERTES *falls.*]

LAERTES   It is here, Hamlet. Hamlet, thou art slain;
  No med'cine in the world can do thee good.
  In thee there is not half an hour of life.   285
  The treacherous instrument is in thy hand,
  Unbated and envenom'd. The foul practice
  Hath turn'd itself on me. Lo, here I lie,
  Never to rise again. Thy mother's poison'd.
  I can no more. The King, the King's to blame.   290

---

270 make a wanton of me: treat me too carelessly   *277 springe:* snare   *279 sounds:* swoons

HAMLET   The point envenom'd too?
  Then, venom, to thy work.

[*Hurts the* KING.]

ALL   Treason! treason!

KING   O, yet defend me, friends! I am but hurt.

HAMLET   Here, thou incestuous, murd'rous, damned Dane,   295
  Drink off this potion! Is thy union here?
  Follow my mother.

[KING *dies.*]

LAERTES   He is justly serv'd.
  It is a poison temper'd by himself.
  Exchange forgiveness with me, noble Hamlet.
  Mine and my father's death come not upon thee,   300
  Nor thine on me!

[*Dies.*]

HAMLET   Heaven make thee free of it! I follow thee.
  I am dead, Horatio. Wretched queen, adieu!
  You that look pale and tremble at this chance,
  That are but mutes or audience to this act,
  Had I but time (as this fell sergeant, Death,   305
  Is strict in his arrest) O, I could tell you—
  But let it be. Horatio, I am dead;
  Thou liv'st; report me and my cause aright
  To the unsatisfied.

HORATIO   Never believe it.   310
  I am more an antique Roman than a Dane.
  Here's yet some liquor left.

HAMLET   As th'art a man,
  Give me the cup. Let go! By heaven, I'll ha't.
  O good Horatio, what a wounded name
  (Things standing thus unknown) shall live behind me!   315
  If thou didst ever hold me in thy heart,
  Absent thee from felicity awhile,
  And in this harsh world draw thy breath in pain,
  To tell my story.

[*March afar off, and shot within*]

305 *mutes or audiences:* silent witnesses   306 *fell:* cruel   310 *the unsatisfied:* the uninformed

What warlike noise is this?

OSRIC   Young Fortinbras, with conquest come from Poland,   320
  To the ambassadors of England gives
  This warlike volley.

HAMLET   O, I die, Horatio!
  The potent poison quite o'ercrows my spirit.
  I cannot live to hear the news from England,
  But I do prophesy th' election lights   325
  On Fortinbras. He has my dying voice.
  So tell him, with th' occurrents, more and less,
  Which have solicited—the rest is silence.

[*Dies.*]

HORATIO   Now cracks a noble heart. Good night, sweet prince,
  And flights of angels sing thee to thy rest!   330

[*March within*]

  Why does the drum come hither?

[*Enter* FORTINBRAS *and* ENGLISH AMBASSADORS, with DRUM, COLOURS, and ATTEND-
ANTS.]

FORTINBRAS   Where is this sight?

HORATIO   What is it you would see?
  If aught of woe or wonder, cease your search.

FORTINBRAS   This quarry cries on havoc. O proud Death,
  What feast is toward in thine eternal cell
  That thou so many princes at a shot   335
  So bloodily hast struck?

AMBASSADOR   The sight is dismal;
  And our affairs from England come too late.
  The ears are senseless that should give us hearing
  To tell him his commandment is fulfill'd,   340
  That Rosencrantz and Guildenstern are dead.
  Where should we have our thanks?

HORATIO   Not from his mouth,
  Had it th' ability of life to thank you.
  He never gave commandment for their death.
  But since, so jump upon this bloody question,   345
  You from the Polack wars, and you from England,
  Are here arriv'd, give order that these bodies

323 *o'ercrows:* triumphs over   326 *voice:* vote   334 *havoc:* massacre   345 *so jump:* so opportunely

High on a stage be placed to the view;
And let me speak to th' yet unknowing world
How these things came about. So shall you hear   350
Of carnal, bloody, and unnatural acts;
Of accidental judgments, casual slaughters;
Of deaths put on by cunning and forc'd cause;
And, in this upshot, purposes mistook
Fall'n on th'inventors' heads. All this can I   355
Truly deliver.

FORTINBRAS   Let us haste to hear it,
And call the noblest to the audience.
For me, with sorrow I embrace my fortune.
I have some rights of memory in this kingdom,
Which now to claim my vantage doth invite me.   360

HORATIO   Of that I shall have also cause to speak,
And from his mouth whose voice will draw on more.
But let this same be presently perform'd,
Even while men's minds are wild, lest more mischance
On plots and errors happen.

FORTINBRAS   Let four captains   365
Bear Hamlet like a soldier to the stage;
For he was likely, had he been put on,
To have prov'd most royally; and for his passage
The soldiers' music and the rites of war
Speak loudly for him.   370
Take up the bodies. Such a sight as this
Becomes the field, but here shows much amiss.
Go, bid the soldiers shoot.

[*Exeunt marching, after the which a peal of ordnance are shot off.*]

DISCUSSION TOPICS

1. Critics have often complained that Hamlet delays taking action in the play. Is
   that a valid criticism? Does the play give us any explanation for his delay?
   Read Hamlet's five soliloquies. Does Hamlet himself give us some insight into
   this question of delay?
2. Some of the other characters in the play function as foils or reflectors, mirror-
   ing different facets of Hamlet's own personality. Which aspects of his character are reflected by Horatio, Laertes, Fortinbras? Are there other foils?
3. Claudius is not a total villain, although he is Hamlet's antagonist—that is, his
   opposite in the action of the play. Find evidence in the play that Shakespeare
   sees Claudius as a person who is devoid of neither kingship, nor leadership
   abilities, nor a moral sense.

4. Polonius's advice to his son Laertes in Act I, scene iii, is often quoted with approval. To what extent is this speech ironical in the context of the play?

5. In Act II, scene ii, Hamlet exclaims "The play's the thing/Wherein I'll catch the conscience of the King." Discuss the many functions of the play within the play and the players in *Hamlet*.

6. Study the exchange between Hamlet and Ophelia, III.i. Why do you think he asks her "Are you honest?" Why does he tell her "Get thee to a nunnery"? Why does he ask her "Where's your father?" What is the significance of the relationship between Hamlet and Ophelia to the rest of the play? What Jungian archetypes are suggested by a study of Ophelia's character and Hamlet's responses to her?

7. Why doesn't Hamlet kill Claudius when he has the opportunity in Act III, scene iii? Why does he kill Polonius in Act III, scene iv?

8. Among the play's imagistic patterns is one that includes animals, traps, and decay. How does that imagery contribute to the themes of the play? What are some of the central themes?

9. Unlike Oedipus, who rushes boldly, although blindly, toward his tragic fate, Hamlet is a reluctant hero. In the first act he says:

The time is out of joint. O cursed spite
That ever I was born to set it right!

How then would you interpret his remarks to Horatio in the play's final act:

There's a special providence in the fall of a sparrow. If it be now, 'tis not to come; if it be not to come, it will be now; if it be not now; yet it will come: the readiness is all.

What insight do these lines give us into Hamlet's character? Do you think they indicate a significant change in him?

10. Some modern interpreters find evidence of the Oedipus complex in Hamlet. What passages in Hamlet's speeches and what actions contribute to this interpretation? Consider the complexity of Hamlet's relationships with his mother, father, and stepfather.

WRITING TOPICS

1. Compare and contrast Oedipus and Hamlet as tragic heroes.
2. Compare and contrast Teiresias and Polonius.
3. One of the universal themes that make the play *Hamlet* appeal to succeeding generations is that the character Hamlet embodies a sense of loneliness, the essential loneliness of a human being in the universe. Find evidence in his statements and in his relationships with others to justify this interpretation.
4. Both *Hamlet* and *Oedipus* employ the archetypal theme of the sacrificial king or the scapegoat. Compare and contrast the ways in which this archetype is dramatized in the two plays.

Henrik Ibsen (1828–1906) Norwegian dramatist and father of modern drama. His plays often emphasize ideas and social comment, but his great strength is with the presentation of character. His later plays develop strategies for revealing the submerged and often unacknowledged qualities of the central characters.

HEDDA GABLER

Translated by Edmund Gosse and William Archer

Characters

GEORGE TESMAN.
HEDDA TESMAN, *his wife.*
MISS JULIANA TESMAN, *his aunt.*
MRS. ELVSTED.
JUDGE BRACK.
EILERT LÖVBORG.
BERTA, *servant at the Tesmans'.*

The scene of the action is TESMAN'S *villa, in the west end of Christiania.*

ACT I

Scene: A spacious, handsome, and tastefully furnished drawing-room, decorated in dark colors. In the back, a wide doorway with curtains drawn back, leading into a smaller room decorated in the same style as the drawing-room. In the right-hand wall of the front room, a folding door leading out to the hall. In the opposite wall, on the left, a glass door, also with curtains drawn back. Through the panes can be seen part of a veranda outside, and trees covered with autumn foliage. An oval table, with a cover on it, and surrounded by chairs, stands well forward. In front, by the wall on the right, a wide stove of dark porcelain, a high-backed arm-chair, a cushioned foot-rest, and two footstools. A settee, with a small round table in front of it, fills the upper right-hand corner. In front, on the left, a little way from the wall, a sofa. Farther back than the glass door, a piano. On either side of the doorway at the back a whatnot with terra-cotta and majolica ornaments.—Against the back wall of the inner room a sofa, with a table, and one or two chairs. Over the sofa hangs the portrait of a handsome elderly man in a general's uniform. Over the table a hanging lamp, with an opal glass shade.—A number of bouquets are arranged about the drawing-room, in vases and glasses. Others lie upon the tables. The floors in both rooms are covered with thick carpets.—Morning light. The sun shines in through the glass door.

(MISS JULIANA TESMAN, *with her bonnet on and carrying a parasol, comes in from the hall, followed by Berta, who carries a bouquet wrapped in paper.* MISS TESMAN *is a comely and pleasant-looking lady of about sixty-five. She is nicely but simply dressed in a gray walking-costume.* BERTA *is a middle-aged woman of plain and rather countrified appearance.*)

MISS TESMAN (*steps close to the door, listens, and says softly*)   Upon my word, I don't believe they are stirring yet!

BERTA (*also softly*) I told you so, Miss. Remember how late the steamboat got in last night. And then, when they got home!—good Lord, what a lot the young mistress had to unpack before she could get to bed.

MISS TESMAN Well, well—let them have their sleep out. But let us see that they get a good breath of the fresh morning air when they do appear. (*She goes to the glass door and throws it open*)

BERTA (*beside the table, at a loss what to do with the bouquet in her hand*) I declare there isn't a bit of room left. I think I'll put it down here, Miss. (*She places it on the piano*)

MISS TESMAN So you've got a new mistress now, my dear Berta. Heaven knows it was a wrench to me to part with you.

BERTA (*on the point of weeping*) And do you think it wasn't hard for me too, Miss? After all the blessed years I've been with you and Miss Rina.

MISS TESMAN We must make the best of it, Berta. There was nothing else to be done. George can't do without you, you see—he absolutely can't. He has had you to look after him ever since he was a little boy.

BERTA Ah, but, Miss Julia, I can't help thinking of Miss Rina lying helpless at home there, poor thing. And with only that new girl, too! She'll never learn to take proper care of an invalid.

MISS TESMAN Oh, I shall manage to train her. And of course, you know, I shall take most of it upon myself. You needn't be uneasy about my poor sister, my dear Berta.

BERTA Well, but there's another thing, Miss. I'm so mortally afraid I shan't be able to suit the young mistress.

MISS TESMAN Oh, well—just at first there may be one or two things——

BERTA Most like she'll be terrible grand in her ways.

MISS TESMAN Well, you can't wonder at that—General Gabler's daughter! Think of the sort of life she was accustomed to in her father's time. Don't you remember how we used to see her riding down the road along with the General? In that long black habit—and with feathers in her hat?

BERTA Yes, indeed—I remember well enough—! But good Lord, I should never have dreamt in those days that she and Master George would make a match of it.

MISS TESMAN Nor I.—But, by-the-bye, Berta—while I think of it: in future you mustn't say Master George. You must say Dr. Tesman.

BERTA Yes, the young mistress spoke of that too—last night—the moment they set foot in the house. Is it true, then, Miss?

MISS TESMAN Yes, indeed it is. Only think, Berta—some foreign university has made him a doctor—while he has been abroad, you understand. I hadn't heard a word about it, until he told me himself upon the pier.

BERTA Well, well, he's clever enough for anything, he is. But I didn't think he'd have gone in for doctoring people too.

MISS TESMAN   No, no, it's not that sort of doctor he is. (*Nods significantly*) But let me tell you, we may have to call him something still grander before long.

BERTA   You don't say so! What can that be, Miss?

MISS TESMAN (*smiling*)   H'm—wouldn't you like to know! (*With emotion*) Ah, dear, dear—if my poor brother could only look up from his grave now, and see what his little boy has grown into! (*Looks around*) But bless me, Berta—why have you done this? Taken the chintz covers off all the furniture?

BERTA   The mistress told me to. She can't abide covers on the chairs, she says.

MISS TESMAN   Are they going to make this their everyday sitting-room then?

BERTA   Yes, that's what I understood—from the mistress. Master George—the doctor—he said nothing.

(GEORGE TESMAN *comes from the right into the inner room, humming to himself, and carrying an unstrapped empty portmanteau. He is a middle-sized, young-looking man of thirty-three, rather stout, with a round, open, cheerful face, fair hair and beard. He wears spectacles, and is somewhat carelessly dressed in comfortable indoor clothes.*)

MISS TESMAN   Good morning, good morning, George.

TESMAN (*in the doorway between the rooms*)   Aunt Julia! Dear Aunt Julia! (*Goes up to her and shakes hands warmly*) Come all this way—so early! Eh?

MISS TESMAN   Why of course I had to come and see how you were getting on.

TESMAN   In spite of your having had no proper night's rest?

MISS TESMAN   Oh, that makes no difference to me.

TESMAN   Well, I suppose you got home all right from the pier? Eh?

MISS TESMAN   Yes, quite safely, thank goodness. Judge Brack was good enough to see me right to my door.

TESMAN   We were so sorry we couldn't give you a seat in the carriage. But you saw what a pile of boxes Hedda had to bring with her.

MISS TESMAN   Yes, she had certainly plenty of boxes.

BERTA (*to Tesman*)   Shall I go in and see if there's anything I can do for the mistress?

TESMAN   No, thank you, Berta—you needn't. She said she would ring if she wanted anything.

BERTA (*going towards the right*)   Very well.

TESMAN   But look here—take this portmanteau with you.

BERTA (*taking it*)   I'll put it in the attic.

(*She goes out by the hall door*)

TESMAN   Fancy, Aunty—I had the whole of that portmanteau chock full of copies of documents. You wouldn't believe how much I have picked up from all the

800

archives I have been examining—curious old details that no one has had any idea of——

MISS TESMAN   Yes, you don't seem to have wasted your time on your wedding trip, George.

TESMAN   No, that I haven't. But do take off your bonnet, Aunty. Look here! Let me untie the strings—eh?

MISS TESMAN (*while he does so*)   Well, well—this is just as if you were still at home with us.

TESMAN (*with the bonnet in his hand, looks at it from all sides*)   Why, what a gorgeous bonnet you've been investing in!

MISS TESMAN   I bought it on Hedda's account.

TESMAN   On Hedda's account? Eh?

MISS TESMAN   Yes, so that Hedda needn't be ashamed of me if we happened to go out together.

TESMAN (*patting her cheek*)   You always think of everything, Aunt Julia. (*Lays the bonnet on a chair beside the table*) And now, look here—suppose we sit comfortably on the sofa and have a little chat, till Hedda comes.

(*They seat themselves. She places her parasol in the corner of the sofa*)

MISS TESMAN (*takes both his hands and looks at him*)   What a delight it is to have you again, as large as life, before my very eyes, George! My George—my poor brother's own boy!

TESMAN   And it's a delight for me, too, to see you again, Aunt Julia! You, who have been father and mother in one to me.

MISS TESMAN   Oh, yes, I know you will always keep a place in your heart for your old aunts.

TESMAN   And what about Aunt Rina? No improvement—eh?

MISS TESMAN   Oh, no—we can scarcely look for any improvement in her case, poor thing. There she lies, helpless, as she has lain for all these years. But heaven grant I may not lose her yet awhile! For if I did, I don't know what I should make of my life, George—especially now that I haven't you to look after any more.

TESMAN (*patting her back*)   There, there, there——!

MISS TESMAN (*suddenly changing her tone*)   And to think that here you a married man, George!—And that you should be the one to carry off Hedda Gabler—the beautiful Hedda Gabler! Only think of it—she, that was so beset with admirers!

TESMAN (*hums a little and smiles complacently*)   Yes, I fancy I have several good friends about town who would like to stand in my shoes—eh?

MISS TESMAN   And then this fine long wedding-tour you have had! More than five—nearly six months——

TESMAN Well, for me it has been a sort of tour of research as well. I have had to do so much grubbing among old records—and to read no end of books too, Auntie.

MISS TESMAN Oh, yes, I suppose so. (*More confidentially, and lowering her voice a little*) But listen now, George—have you nothing—nothing special to tell me?

TESMAN As to our journey?

MISS TESMAN Yes.

TESMAN No, I don't know of anything except what I have told you in my letters. I had a doctor's degree conferred on me—but that I told you yesterday.

MISS TESMAN Yes, yes, you did. But what I mean is—haven't you any—any—expectations——?

TESMAN Expectations?

MISS TESMAN Why, you know, George—I'm your old auntie!

TESMAN Why, of course I have expectations.

MISS TESMAN Ah!

TESMAN I have every expectation of being a professor one of these days.

MISS TESMAN Oh, yes, a professor——

TESMAN Indeed, I may say I am certain of it. But my dear Auntie—you know all about that already!

MISS TESMAN (*laughing to herself*) Yes, of course I do. You are quite right there. (*Changing the subject*) But we were talking about your journey. It must have cost a great deal of money, George?

TESMAN Well, you see—my handsome traveling-scholarship went a good way.

MISS TESMAN But I can't understand how you can have made it go far enough for two.

TESMAN No, that's not so easy to understand—eh?

MISS TESMAN And especially traveling with a lady—they tell me that makes it ever so much more expensive.

TESMAN Yes, of course—it makes it a little more expensive. But Hedda had to have this trip, Auntie! She really had to. Nothing else would have done.

MISS TESMAN No, no, I suppose not. A wedding-tour seems to be quite indispensable nowadays.—But tell me now—have you gone thoroughly over the house yet?

TESMAN Yes, you may be sure I have. I have been afoot ever since daylight.

MISS TESMAN And what do you think of it all?

TESMAN I'm delighted! Quite delighted! Only I can't think what we are to do with the two empty rooms between this inner parlor and Hedda's bedroom.

MISS TESMAN (*laughing*) Oh, my dear George, I dare say you may find some use for them—in the course of time.

TESMAN   Why of course you are quite right, Aunt Julia! You mean as my library increases—eh?

MISS TESMAN   Yes, quite so, my dear boy. It was your library I was thinking of.

TESMAN   I am specially pleased on Hedda's account. Often and often, before we were engaged, she said that she would never care to live anywhere but in Secretary Falk's villa.

MISS TESMAN   Yes, it was lucky that this very house should come into the market, just after you had started.

TESMAN   Yes, Aunt Julia, the luck was on our side, wasn't it—eh?

MISS TESMAN   But the expense, my dear George! You will find it very expensive, all this.

TESMAN (*looks at her, a little cast down*)   Yes, I suppose I shall, Aunt!

MISS TESMAN   Oh, frightfully!

TESMAN   How much do you think? In round numbers?—Eh?

MISS TESMAN   Oh, I can't even guess until all the accounts come in.

TESMAN   Well, fortunately, Judge Brack has secured the most favorable terms for me,—so he said in a letter to Hedda.

MISS TESMAN   Yes, don't be uneasy, my dear boy.—Besides, I have given security for the furniture and all the carpets.

TESMAN   Security? You? My dear Aunt Julia—what sort of security could you give?

MISS TESMAN   I have given a mortgage on our annuity.

TESMAN (*jumps up*)   What! On your—and Aunt Rina's annuity!

MISS TESMAN   Yes, I knew of no other plan, you see.

TESMAN (*placing himself before her*)   Have you gone out of your senses, Auntie! Your annuity—it's all that you and Aunt Rina have to live upon.

MISS TESMAN   Well, well, don't get so excited about it. It's only a matter of form you know—Judge Brack assured me of that. It was he that was kind enough to arrange the whole affair for me. A mere matter of form, he said.

TESMAN   Yes, that may be all very well. But nevertheless——

MISS TESMAN   You will have your own salary to depend upon now. And, good heavens, even if we did have to pay up a little——! To eke things out a bit at the start——! Why, it would be nothing but a pleasure to us.

TESMAN   Oh, Auntie—will you never be tired of making sacrifices for me!

MISS TESMAN (*rises and lays her hands on his shoulders*)   Have I had any other happiness in this world except to smooth your way for you, my dear boy? You, who have had neither father nor mother to depend on. And now we have reached the goal, George! Things have looked black enough for us, sometimes; but, thank heaven, now you have nothing to fear.

TESMAN   Yes, it is really marvelous how everything has turned out for the best.

MISS TESMAN   And the people who opposed you—who wanted to bar the way for you—now you have them at your feet. They have fallen, George. Your most dangerous rival—his fall was the worst.—And now he has to lie on the bed he has made for himself—poor misguided creature.

TESMAN   Have you heard anything of Eilert? Since I went away, I mean.

MISS TESMAN   Only that he is said to have published a new book.

TESMAN   What! Eilert Lövborg! Recently—eh?

MISS TESMAN   Yes, so they say. Heaven knows whether it can be worth anything! Ah, when your new book appears—that will be another story, George! What is it to be about?

TESMAN   It will deal with the domestic industries of Brabant during the Middle Ages.

MISS TESMAN   Fancy—to be able to write on such a subject as that!

TESMAN   However, it may be some time before the book is ready. I have all these collections to arrange first, you see.

MISS TESMAN   Yes, collecting and arranging—no one can beat you at that. There you are my poor brother's own son.

TESMAN   I am looking forward eagerly to setting to work at it; especially now that I have my own delightful home to work in.

MISS TESMAN   And, most of all, now that you have got the wife of your heart, my dear George.

TESMAN (*embracing her*)   Oh, yes, yes, Aunt Julia. Hedda—she is the best part of all! (*Looks toward the doorway*) I believe I hear her coming—eh?

(HEDDA *enters from the left through the inner room. She is a woman of nine-and-twenty. Her face and figure show refinement and distinction. Her complexion is pale and opaque. Her steel-gray eyes express a cold, unruffled repose. Her hair is of an agreeable medium brown, but not particularly abundant. She is dressed in a tasteful, somewhat loose-fitting morning-gown.*)

MISS TESMAN (*going to meet Hedda*)   Good morning, my dear Hedda! Good morning, and a hearty welcome.

HEDDA (*holds out her hand*)   Good morning, dear Miss Tesman! So early a call! That is kind of you.

MISS TESMAN (*with some embarrassment*)   Well—has the bride slept well in her new home?

HEDDA   Oh yes, thanks. Passably.

TESMAN (*laughing*)   Passably! Come, that's good, Hedda! You were sleeping like a stone when I got up.

HEDDA   Fortunately. Of course one has always to accustom one's self to new surroundings, Miss Tesman—little by little. (*Looking towards the left*) Oh—there the servant has gone and opened the veranda door, and let in a whole flood of sunshine.

MISS TESMAN (*going towards the door*) Well, then, we will shut it.

HEDDA No, no, not that! Tesman, please draw the curtains. That will give a softer light.

TESMAN (*at the door*) All right—all right. There now, Hedda, now you have both shade and fresh air.

HEDDA Yes, fresh air we certainly must have, with all these stacks of flowers— But—won't you sit down, Miss Tesman?

MISS TESMAN No, thank you. Now that I have seen that everything is all right here—thank heaven!—I must be getting home again. My sister is lying longing for me, poor thing.

TESMAN Give her my very best love, Auntie; and say I shall look in and see her later in the day.

MISS TESMAN Yes, yes, I'll be sure to tell her. But by-the-bye, George—(*feeling in her dress pocket*)—I have almost forgotten—I have something for you here.

TESMAN What is it, Auntie? Eh?

MISS TESMAN (*produces a flat parcel wrapped in newspaper and hands it to him*) Look here, my dear boy.

TESMAN (*opening the parcel*) Well, I declare!—Have you really saved them for me, Aunt Julia! Hedda! Isn't this touching—eh?

HEDDA (*beside the whatnot on the right*) Well, what is it?

TESMAN My old morning-shoes! My slippers.

HEDDA Indeed. I remember you often spoke of them while we were abroad.

TESMAN Yes, I missed them terribly. (*Goes up to her*) Now you shall see them, Hedda!

HEDDA (*going towards the stove*) Thanks, I really don't care about it.

TESMAN (*following her*) Only think—ill as she was, Aunt Rina embroidered these for me. Oh you can't think how many associations cling to them.

HEDDA (*at the table*) Scarcely for me.

MISS TESMAN Of course not for Hedda, George.

TESMAN Well, but now that she belongs to the family; I thought——

HEDDA (*interrupting*) We shall never get on with this servant, Tesman.

MISS TESMAN Not get on with Berta?

TESMAN Why, dear, what puts that in your head? Eh?

HEDDA (*pointing*) Look there! She has left her old bonnet lying about on a chair.

TESMAN (*in consternation, drops the slippers on the floor*) Why, Hedda——

HEDDA Just fancy, if any one should come in and see it!

TESMAN   But Hedda—that's Aunt Julia's bonnet.

HEDDA   Is it!

MISS TESMAN (*taking up the bonnet*)   Yes, indeed it's mine. And, what's more, it's not old, Madame Hedda.

HEDDA   I really did not look closely at it, Miss Tesman.

MISS TESMAN (*trying on the bonnet*)   Let me tell you it's the first time I have worn it—the very first time.

TESMAN   And a very nice bonnet it is too—quite a beauty!

MISS TESMAN   Oh, it's no such great things, George. (*Looks around her*) My parasol——? Ah, here. (*Takes it*) For this is mine too—(*mutters*)—not Berta's.

TESMAN   A new bonnet and a new parasol! Only think, Hedda!

HEDDA   Very handsome indeed.

TESMAN   Yes, isn't it? But Aunty, take a good look at Hedda before you go! See how handsome she is!

MISS TESMAN   Oh, my dear boy, there's nothing new in that. Hedda was always lovely. (*She nods and goes towards the right*)

TESMAN (*following*)   Yes, but have you noticed what splendid condition she is in? How she has filled out on the journey?

HEDDA (*crossing the room*)   Oh, do be quiet——!

MISS TESMAN (*who has stopped and turned*)   Filled out?

TESMAN   Of course you don't notice it so much now that she has that dress on. But I, who can see——

HEDDA (*at the glass door, impatiently*)   Oh, you can't see anything.

TESMAN   It must be the mountain air in the Tyrol——

HEDDA (*curtly, interrupting*)   I am exactly as I was when I started.

TESMAN   So you insist; but I'm quite certain you are not. Don't you agree with me, Aunty?

MISS TESMAN (*who has been gazing at her with folded hands*)   Hedda is lovely— lovely—lovely. (*Goes up to her, takes her head between both hands, draws it downwards, and kisses her hair*) God bless and preserve Hedda Tesman—for George's sake.

HEDDA (*gently freeing herself*)   Oh—! Let me go.

MISS TESMAN (*in quiet emotion*)   I shall not let a day pass without coming to see you.

TESMAN   No you won't, will you, Auntie? Eh?

MISS TESMAN   Good-bye—good-bye!

(*She goes out by the hall door.* TESMAN *accompanies her. The door remains half open.* TESMAN *can be heard repeating his message to Aunt Rina and his thanks for the slippers.*

806

In the meantime, HEDDA *walks about the room raising her arms and clenching her hands as if in desperation. Then she flings back the curtains from the glass door, and stands there looking out.*

Presently TESMAN *returns and closes the door behind him.*)

TESMAN (*picks up the slippers from the floor*) What are you looking at, Hedda?

HEDDA (*once more calm and mistress of herself*) I am only looking at the leaves. They are so yellow—so withered.

TESMAN (*wraps up the slippers and lays them on the table*) Well you see, we are well into September now.

HEDDA (*again restless*) Yes, to think of it!—Already in—in September.

TESMAN Don't you think Aunt Julia's manner was strange, dear? Almost solemn? Can you imagine what was the matter with her? Eh?

HEDDA I scarcely know her, you see. Is she often like that?

TESMAN No, not as she was today.

HEDDA (*leaving the glass door*) Do you think she was annoyed about the bonnet?

TESMAN Oh, scarcely at all. Perhaps a little, just at the moment——

HEDDA But what an idea, to pitch her bonnet about in the drawing-room! No one does that sort of thing.

TESMAN Well you may be sure Aunt Julia won't do it again.

HEDDA In any case, I shall manage to make my peace with her.

TESMAN Yes, my dear, good Hedda, if you only would.

HEDDA When you call this afternoon, you might invite her to spend the evening here.

TESMAN Yes, that I will. And there's one thing more you can do that would delight her heart.

HEDDA What is it?

TESMAN If you could only prevail on yourself to say *du*[1] to her. For my sake, Hedda? Eh?

HEDDA No, no, Tesman—you really mustn't ask that of me. I have told you so already. I shall try to call her "Aunt"; and you must be satisfied with that.

TESMAN Well, well. Only I think now that you belong to the family, you——

HEDDA H'm—I can't in the least see why——

(*She goes up towards the middle doorway*)

TESMAN (*after a pause*) Is there anything the matter with you, Hedda? Eh?

HEDDA I'm only looking at my old piano. It doesn't go at all well with all the other things.

---

1 *Du:* thou; Tesman means, "If you could persuade yourself to *tutoyer* her."

TESMAN   The first time I draw my salary, we'll see about exchanging it.

HEDDA   No, no—no exchanging. I don't want to part with it. Suppose we put it there in the inner room, and then get another here in its place. When it's convenient, I mean.

TESMAN (*a little taken aback*)   Yes—of course we could do that.

HEDDA (*takes up the bouquet from the piano*)   These flowers were not here last night when we arrived.

TESMAN   Aunt Julia must have brought them for you.

HEDDA (*examining the bouquet*)   A visiting-card. (*Takes it out and reads*) "Shall return later in the day." Can you guess whose card it is?

TESMAN   No. Whose? Eh?

HEDDA   The name is "Mrs. Elvsted."

TESMAN   Is it really? Sheriff Elvsted's wife? Miss Rysing that was.

HEDDA   Exactly. The girl with the irritating hair, that she was always showing off. An old flame of yours, I've been told.

TESMAN (*laughing*)   Oh, that didn't last long; and it was before I knew you, Hedda. But fancy her being in town!

HEDDA   It's odd that she should call upon us. I have scarcely seen her since we left school.

TESMAN   I haven't seen her either for—heaven knows how long. I wonder how she can endure to live in such an out-of-the-way hole—eh?

HEDDA (*after a moment's thought says suddenly*)   Tell me, Tesman—isn't it somewhere near there that he—that—Eilert Lövborg is living?

TESMAN   Yes, he is somewhere in that part of the country.

(BERTA *enters by the hall door*)

BERTA   That lady, ma'am, that brought some flowers a little while ago, is here again. (*Pointing*) The flowers you have in your hand, ma'am.

HEDDA   Ah, is she? Well, please show her in.

(BERTA *opens the door for* MRS. ELVSTED, *and goes out herself.*—MRS. ELVSTED *is a woman of fragile figure, with pretty, soft features. Her eyes are light blue, large, round, and somewhat prominent, with a startled, inquiring expression. Her hair is remarkably light, almost flaxen, and unusually abundant and wavy. She is a couple of years younger than* HEDDA. *She wears a dark visiting dress, tasteful, but not quite in the latest fashion.*)

HEDDA (*receives her warmly*)   How do you do, my dear Mrs. Elvsted? It's delightful to see you again.

MRS. ELVSTED (*nervously, struggling fo. self-control*)   Yes, it's a very long time since we met.

TESMAN (*gives her his hand*) And we too—eh?

HEDDA Thanks for your lovely flowers——

MRS. ELVSTED Oh, not at all——I would have come straight here yesterday afternoon; but I heard that you were away——

TESMAN Have you just come to town? Eh?

MRS. ELVSTED I arrived yesterday, about midday. Oh, I was quite in despair when I heard that you were not at home.

HEDDA In despair! How so?

TESMAN Why, my dear Mrs. Rysing—I mean Mrs. Elvsted——

HEDDA I hope that you are not in any trouble?

MRS. ELVSTED Yes, I am. And I don't know another living creature here that I can turn to.

HEDDA (*laying the bouquet on the table*) Come—let us sit here on the sofa——

MRS. ELVSTED Oh, I am too restless to sit down.

HEDDA Oh no, you're not. Come here. (*She draws* MRS. ELVSTED *down upon the sofa and sits at her side*)

TESMAN Well? What is it, Mrs. Elvsted?

HEDDA Has anything particular happened to you at home?

MRS. ELVSTED Yes—and no. Oh—I am so anxious you should not misunderstand me——

HEDDA Then your best plan is to tell us the whole story, Mrs. Elvsted.

TESMAN I suppose that's what you have come for—eh?

MRS. ELVSTED Yes, yes—of course it is. Well then, I must tell you—if you don't already know—that Eilert Lövborg is in town, too.

HEDDA Lövborg——!

TESMAN What! Has Eilert Lövborg come back? Fancy that, Hedda!

HEDDA Well, well—I hear it.

MRS. ELVSTED He has been here a week already. Just fancy—a whole week! In this terrible town, alone! With so many temptations on all sides.

HEDDA But my dear Mrs. Elvsted—how does he concern you so much?

MRS. ELVSTED (*looks at her with a startled air, and says rapidly*) He was the children's tutor.

HEDDA Your children's?

MRS. ELVSTED. My husband's. I have none.

HEDDA Your step-children's, then?

MRS. ELVSTED Yes.

TESMAN (*somewhat hesitatingly*) Then was he—I don't know how to express it— was he—regular enough in his habits to be fit for the post? Eh?

MRS. ELVSTED For the last two years his conduct has been irreproachable.

TESMAN Has it indeed? Fancy that, Hedda!

HEDDA I hear it.

MRS. ELVSTED Perfectly irreproachable. I assure you! In every respect. But all the same—now that I know he is here—in this great town—and with a large sum of money in his hands—I can't help being in mortal fear for him.

TESMAN Why did he not remain where he was? With you and your husband? Eh?

MRS. ELVSTED After his book was published he was too restless and unsettled to remain with us.

TESMAN Yes, by-the-bye, Aunt Julia told me he had published a new book.

MRS. ELVSTED Yes, a big book, dealing with the march of civilization—in broad outline, as it were. It came out about a fortnight ago. And since it has sold so well, and been so much read—and made such a sensation——

TESMAN Has it indeed? It must be something he has had lying by since his better days.

MRS. ELVSTED Long ago, you mean?

TESMAN Yes.

MRS. ELVSTED No, he has written it all since he has been with us—within the last year.

TESMAN Isn't that good news, Hedda? Think of that.

MRS. ELVSTED Ah, yes, if only it would last!

HEDDA Have you seen him here in town?

MRS. ELVSTED No, not yet. I have had the greatest difficulty in finding out his address. But this morning I discovered it at last.

HEDDA (*looks searchingly at her*) Do you know, it seems to me a little odd of your husband—h'm——

MRS. ELVSTED (*starting nervously*) Of my husband. What?

HEDDA That he should send you to town on such an errand—that he does not come himself and look after his friend.

MRS. ELVSTED Oh no, no—my husband has no time. And besides, I—I had some shopping to do.

HEDDA (*with a slight smile*) Ah, that is a different matter.

MRS. ELVSTED (*rising quickly and uneasily*) And now I beg and implore you, Mr. Tesman—receive Eilert Lövborg kindly if he comes to you! And that he is sure to do. You see you were such great friends in the old days. And then you are interested in the same studies—the same branch of science—so far as I can understand.

TESMAN We used to be, at any rate.

MRS. ELVSTED That is why I beg so earnestly that you—you too—will keep a sharp eye upon him. Oh, you will promise me that, Mr. Tesman—won't you?

TESMAN With the greatest of pleasure, Mrs. Rysing——

HEDDA Elvsted.

TESMAN I assure you I shall do all I possibly can for Eilert. You may rely upon me.

MRS. ELVSTED Oh, how very, very kind of you! (*Presses his hands*) Thanks, thanks, thanks! (*Frightened*) You see, my husband is very fond of him!

HEDDA (*rising*) You ought to write to him, Tesman. Perhaps he may not care to come to you of his own accord.

TESMAN Well, perhaps it would be the right thing to do, Hedda? Eh?

HEDDA And the sooner the better. Why not at once?

MRS. ELVSTED (*imploringly*) Oh, if you only would!

TESMAN I'll write this moment. Have you his address, Mrs.—Mrs. Elvsted?

MRS. ELVSTED Yes. (*Takes a slip of paper from her pocket, and hands it to him*) Here it is.

TESMAN Good, good. Then I'll go in——(*Looks about him*) By-the-bye,—my slippers? Oh, here. (*Takes the packet, and is about to go*)

HEDDA Be sure you write him a cordial, friendly letter. And a good long one too.

TESMAN Yes, I will.

MRS. ELVSTED But please, please don't say a word to show that I have suggested it.

TESMAN No, how could you think I would? Eh?

(*He goes out to the right, through the inner room*)

HEDDA (*goes up to Mrs. Elvsted, smiles, and says in a low voice*) There. We have killed two birds with one stone.

MRS. ELVSTED What do you mean?

HEDDA Could you not see that I wanted him to go?

MRS. ELVSTED Yes, to write the letter——

HEDDA And that I might speak to you alone.

MRS. ELVSTED (*confused*) About the same thing?

HEDDA Precisely.

MRS. ELVSTED (*apprehensively*) But there is nothing more, Mrs. Tesman! Absolutely nothing!

HEDDA Oh, yes, but there is. There is a great deal more—I can see that. Sit here —and we'll have a cozy, confidential chat. (*She forces* MRS. ELVSTED *to sit in the easy-chair beside the stove, and seats herself on one of the footstools*)

MRS. ELVSTED (*anxiously, looking at her watch*)   But, my dear Mrs. Tesman—I was really on the point of going.

HEDDA   Oh, you can't be in such a hurry.—Well? Now tell me something about your life at home.

MRS. ELVSTED   Oh, that is just what I care least to speak about.

HEDDA   But to me, dear——? Why, weren't we schoolfellows?

MRS. ELVSTED   Yes, but you were in the class above me. Oh, how dreadfully afraid of you I was then!

HEDDA   Afraid of me?

MRS. ELVSTED   *Yes,* dreadfully. For when we met on the stairs you used always to pull my hair.

HEDDA   Did I, really?

MRS. ELVSTED   Yes, and once you said you would burn it off my head.

HEDDA   Oh, that was all nonsense, of course.

MRS. ELVSTED   Yes, but I was so silly in those days.—And since then, too—we have drifted so far—far apart from each other. Our circles have been so entirely different.

HEDDA   Well then, we must try to drift together again. Now listen! At school we said *du* to each other; and we called each other by our Christian names——

MRS. ELVSTED   No, I am sure you must be mistaken.

HEDDA   No, not at all! I can remember quite distinctly. So now we are going to renew our old friendship. (*Draws the footstool closer to* MRS. ELVSTED) There now! (*Kisses her cheek*) You must say *du* to me and call me Hedda.

MRS. ELVSTED (*presses and pats her hands*)   Oh, how good and kind you are! I am not used to such kindness.

HEDDA   There, there, there! And I shall say *du* to you, as in the old days, and call you my dear Thora.

MRS. ELVSTED   My name is Thea.

HEDDA   Why, of course! I meant Thea. (*Looks at her compassionately*) So you are not accustomed to goodness and kindness, Thea? Not in your own home?

MRS. ELVSTED   Oh, if I only had a home! But I haven't any; I have never had a home.

HEDDA (*looks at her for a moment*)   I almost suspected as much.

MRS. ELVSTED (*gazing helplessly before her*)   Yes—yes—yes.

HEDDA   I don't quite remember—was it not as housekeeper that you first went to Mr. Elvsted's?

MRS. ELVSTED   I really went as governess. But his wife—his late wife—was an invalid,—and rarely left her room. So I had to look after the housekeeping as well.

HEDDA   And then—at last—you became mistress of the house.

MRS. ELVSTED (*sadly*) Yes, I did.

HEDDA Let me see—about how long ago was that?

MRS. ELVSTED My marriage?

HEDDA Yes.

MRS. ELVSTED Five years ago.

HEDDA To be sure; it must be that.

MRS. ELVSTED Oh, those five years——! Or at all events the last two or three of them! Oh, if you[2] could only imagine——

HEDDA (*giving her a little slap on the hand*) De? Fie, Thea!

MRS. ELVSTED Yes, yes, I will try——Well if—you could only imagine and understand——

HEDDA (*lightly*) Eilert Lövborg has been in your neighborhood about three years, hasn't he?

MRS. ELVSTED (*looks at her doubtfully*) Eilert Lövborg? Yes—he has.

HEDDA Had you known him before, in town here?

MRS. ELVSTED Scarcely at all. I mean—I knew him by name of course.

HEDDA But you saw a good deal of him in the country?

MRS. ELVSTED Yes, he came to us every day. You see, he gave the children lessons; for in the long run I couldn't manage it all myself.

HEDDA No, that's clear.—And your husband——? I suppose he is often away from home?

MRS. ELVSTED Yes. Being sheriff, you know, he has to travel about a good deal in his district.

HEDDA (*leaning against the arm of the chair*) Thea—my poor, sweet Thea—now you must tell me everything—exactly as it stands.

MRS. ELVSTED Well, then, you must question me.

HEDDA What sort of a man is your husband, Thea? I mean—you know—in everyday life. Is he kind to you?

MRS. ELVSTED (*evasively*) I am sure he means well in everything.

HEDDA I should think he must be altogether too old for you. There is at least twenty years' difference between you, is there not?

MRS. ELVSTED (*irritably*) Yes, that is true, too. Everything about him is repellent to me! We have not a thought in common. We have no single point of sympathy —he and I.

HEDDA But is he not fond of you all the same? In his own way?

---

2 Mrs. Elvsted here uses the formal pronoun *De,* whereupon Hedda rebukes her. In her next speech Mrs. Elvsted says *du.*

MRS. ELVSTED   Oh, I really don't know. I think he regards me simply as a useful property. And then it doesn't cost much to keep me. I am not expensive.

HEDDA   That is stupid of you.

MRS. ELVSTED (*shakes her head*)   It cannot be otherwise—not with him. I don't think he really cares for any one but himself—and perhaps a little for the children.

HEDDA   And for Eilert Lövborg, Thea.

MRS. ELVSTED (*looking at her*)   For Eilert Lövborg? What puts that into your head?

HEDDA   Well, my dear—I should say, when he sends you after him all the way to town——(*Smiling almost imperceptibly*) And besides, you said so yourself, to Tesman.

MRS. ELVSTED (*with a little nervous twitch*)   Did I? Yes, I suppose I did. (*Vehemently, but not loudly*) No—I may just as well make a clean breast of it at once! For it must all come out in any case.

HEDDA   Why, my dear Thea——?

MRS. ELVSTED   Well, to make a long story short: My husband did not know that I was coming.

HEDDA   What! Your husband didn't know it!

MRS. ELVSTED   No, of course not. For that matter, he was away from home himself—he was traveling. Oh, I could bear it no longer, Hedda! I couldn't indeed —so utterly alone as I should have been in future.

HEDDA   Well? And then?

MRS. ELVSTED   So I put together some of my things—what I needed most—as quietly as possible. And then I left the house.

HEDDA   Without a word?

MRS. ELVSTED   Yes—and took the train straight to town.

HEDDA   Why, my dear, good Thea—to think of you daring to do it!

MRS. ELVSTED (*rises and moves about the room*)   What else could I possibly do?

HEDDA   But what do you think your husband will say when you go home again?

MRS. ELVSTED (*at the table, looks at her*)   Back to him?

HEDDA   Of course.

MRS. ELVSTED   I shall never go back to him again.

HEDDA (*rising and going towards her*)   Then you have left your home—for good and all?

MRS. ELVSTED   Yes. There was nothing else to be done.

HEDDA   But then—to take flight so openly.

MRS. ELVSTED   Oh, it's impossible to keep things of that sort secret.

HEDDA   But what do you think people will say of you, Thea?

814

MRS. ELVSTED   They may say what they like for aught *I* care. (*Seats herself wearily and sadly on the sofa*) I have done nothing but what I had to do.

HEDDA (*after a short silence*)   And what are your plans now? What do you think of doing?

MRS. ELVSTED   I don't know yet. I only know this, that I must live here, where Eilert Lövborg is—if I am to live at all.

HEDDA (*takes a chair from the table, seats herself beside her, and strokes her hands*) My dear Thea—how did this—this friendship—between you and Eilert Lövborg come about?

MRS. ELVSTED   Oh, it grew up gradually. I gained a sort of influence over him.

HEDDA   Indeed?

MRS. ELVSTED   He gave up his old habits. Not because I asked him to, for I never dared do that. But of course he saw how repulsive they were to me; and so he dropped them.

HEDDA (*concealing an involuntary smile of scorn*)   Then you have reclaimed him— as the saying goes—my little Thea.

MRS. ELVSTED   So he says himself, at any rate. And he, on his side, has made a real human being of me—taught me to think, and to understand so many things.

HEDDA   Did he give you lessons too, then?

MRS. ELVSTED   No, not exactly lessons. But he talked to me—talked about such an infinity of things. And then came the lovely, happy time when I began to share in his work—when he allowed me to help him!

HEDDA   Oh, he did, did he?

MRS. ELVSTED   Yes! He never wrote anything without my assistance.

HEDDA   You were two good comrades, in fact?

MRS. ELVSTED (*eagerly*)   Comrades! Yes, fancy, Hedda—that is the very word he used!—Oh, I ought to feel perfectly happy; and yet I cannot; for I don't know how long it will last.

HEDDA   Are you no surer of him that that?

MRS. ELVSTED (*gloomily*)   A woman's shadow stands between Eilert Lövborg and me.

HEDDA (*looks at her anxiously*)   Who can that be?

MRS. ELVSTED   I don't know. Some one he knew in his—in his past. Some one he has never been able wholly to forget.

HEDDA   What has he told you—about this?

MRS. ELVSTED   He has only once—quite vaguely—alluded to it.

HEDDA   Well! And what did he say?

MRS. ELVSTED   He said that when they parted, she threatened to shoot him with a pistol.

HEDDA (*with cold composure*)   Oh, nonsense! No one does that sort of thing here.

MRS. ELVSTED   No. And that is why I think it must have been that red-haired singing woman whom he once——

HEDDA   Yes, very likely.

MRS. ELVSTED   For I remember they used to say of her that she carried loaded firearms.

HEDDA   Oh—then of course it must have been she.

MRS. ELVSTED (*wringing her hands*)   And now just fancy, Hedda—I hear that this singing-woman—that she is in town again! Oh, I don't know what to do——

HEDDA (*glancing towards the inner room*)   Hush! Here comes Tesman. (*Rises and whispers*) Thea—all this must remain between you and me.

MRS. ELVSTED (*springing up*)   Oh, yes, yes! for heaven's sake——!

(GEORGE TESMAN, *with a letter in his hand, comes from the right through the inner room.*)

TESMAN   There now—the epistle is finished.

HEDDA   That's right. And now Mrs. Elvsted is just going. Wait a moment—I'll go with you to the garden gate.

TESMAN   Do you think Berta could post the letter, Hedda dear?

HEDDA (*takes it*)   I will tell her to.

(BERTA *enters from the hall*)

BERTA   Judge Brack wishes to know if Mrs. Tesman will receive him.

HEDDA   Yes, ask Judge Brack to come in. And look here—put this letter in the post.

BERTA (*taking the letter*)   Yes, ma'am.

(*She opens the door for* JUDGE BRACK *and goes out herself.* BRACK *is a man of forty-five; thick-set, but well-built and elastic in his movements. His face is roundish with an aristocratic profile. His hair is short, still almost black, and carefully dressed. His eyes are lively and sparkling. His eyebrows thick. His moustaches are also thick, with short-cut ends. He wears a well-cut walking-suit, a little too youthful for his age. He uses an eye-glass, which he now and then lets drop.*)

JUDGE BRACK (*with his hat in his hand, bowing*)   May one venture to call so early in the day?

HEDDA   Of course one may.

TESMAN (*presses his hand*)   You are welcome at any time. (*Introducing him*) Judge Brack—Miss Rysing——

HEDDA   Oh——!

BRACK (*bowing*)   Ah—delighted——

HEDDA (*looks at him and laughs*)   It's nice to have a look at you by daylight, Judge!

BRACK   Do you find me—altered?

HEDDA   A little younger, I think.

BRACK   Thank you so much.

TESMAN   But what do you think of Hedda—eh? Doesn't she look flourishing? She has actually——

HEDDA   Oh, do leave me alone. You haven't thanked Judge Brack for all the trouble he has taken——

BRACK   Oh, nonsense—it was a pleasure to me——

HEDDA   Yes, you are a friend indeed. But here stands Thea all impatience to be off—so *au revoir* Judge. I shall be back again presently.

(*Mutual salutations.* MRS. ELVSTED *and* HEDDA *go out by the hall door*)

BRACK   Well,—is your wife tolerably satisfied——

TESMAN   Yes, we can't thank you sufficiently. Of course she talks a little re-arrangement here and there; and one or two things are still wanting. We shall have to buy some additional trifles.

BRACK   Indeed!

TESMAN   But we won't trouble you about these things. Hedda says she herself will look after what is wanting.——Shan't we sit down? Eh?

BRACK   Thanks, for a moment. (*Seats himself beside the table*) There is something I wanted to speak to you about, my dear Tesman.

TESMAN   Indeed? Ah, I understand! (*Seating himself*) I suppose it's the serious part of the frolic that is coming now. Eh?

BRACK   Oh, the money question is not so very pressing; though, for that matter, I wish we had gone a little more economically to work.

TESMAN   But that would never have done, you know! Think of Hedda, my dear fellow! You, who know her so well——. I couldn't possibly ask her to put up with a shabby style of living!

BRACK   No, no—that is just the difficulty.

TESMAN   And then—fortunately—it can't be long before I receive my appointment.

BRACK   Well, you see—such things are often apt to hang fire for a time.

TESMAN   Have you heard anything definite? Eh?

BRACK   Nothing exactly definite—— (*Interrupting himself*) But, by-the-bye—I have one piece of news for you.

TESMAN   Well?

BRACK   Your old friend, Eilert Lövborg, has returned to town.

TESMAN   I know that already.

BRACK   Indeed! How did you learn it?

TESMAN From that lady who went out with Hedda.

BRACK Really? What was her name? I didn't quite catch it.

TESMAN Mrs. Elvsted.

BRACK Aha—Sheriff Elvsted's wife? Of course—he has been living up in their regions.

TESMAN And fancy—I'm delighted to hear that he is quite a reformed character!

BRACK So they say.

TESMAN And then he has published a new book—eh?

BRACK Yes, indeed he has.

TESMAN And I hear it has made some sensation!

BRACK Quite an unusual sensation.

TESMAN Fancy—isn't that good news! A man of such extraordinary talents—— I felt so grieved to think that he had gone irretrievably to ruin.

BRACK That was what everybody thought.

TESMAN But I cannot imagine what he will take to now! How in the world will he be able to make his living? Eh?

(*During the last words,* HEDDA *has entered by the hall door*)

HEDDA (*to* BRACK, *laughing with a touch of scorn*) Tesman is forever worrying about how people are to make their living.

TESMAN Well, you see, dear—we were talking about poor Eilert Lövborg.

HEDDA (*glancing at him rapidly*) Oh, indeed? (*Seats herself in the arm-chair beside the stove and asks indifferently*) What is the matter with him?

TESMAN Well—no doubt he has run through all his property long ago; and he can scarcely write a new book every year—eh? So I really can't see what is to become of him.

BRACK Perhaps I can give you some information on that point.

TESMAN Indeed!

BRACK You must remember that his relations have a good deal of influence.

TESMAN Oh, his relations, unfortunately, have entirely washed their hands of him.

BRACK At one time they called him the hope of the family.

TESMAN At one time, yes! But he has put an end to all that.

HEDDA Who knows? (*With a slight smile*) I hear they have reclaimed him up at Sheriff Elvsted's——

BRACK And then this book that he has published——

TESMAN Well, well, I hope to goodness they may find something for him to do. I have just written to him. I asked him to come and see us this evening, Hedda dear.

BRACK But, my dear fellow, you are booked for my bachelors' party this evening. You promised on the pier last night.

HEDDA Had you forgotten, Tesman?

TESMAN Yes, I had utterly forgotten.

BRACK But it doesn't matter, for you may be sure he won't come.

TESMAN What makes you think that? Eh?

BRACK (*with a little hesitation, rising and resting his hands on the back of his chair*) My dear Tesman—and you too, Mrs. Tesman—I think I ought not to keep you in the dark about something that—that——

TESMAN That concerns Eilert——?

BRACK Both you and him.

TESMAN Well, my dear Judge, out with it.

BRACK You must be prepared to find your appointment deferred longer than you desired or expected.

TESMAN (*jumping up uneasily*) Is there some hitch about it? Eh?

BRACK The nomination may perhaps be made conditional on the result of a competition——

TESMAN Competition! Think of that, Hedda!

HEDDA (*leans farther back in the chair*) Aha—aha!

TESMAN But who can my competitor be? Surely not——?

BRACK Yes, precisely—Eilert Lövborg.

TESMAN (*clasping his hands*) No, no—it's quite inconceivable! Quite impossible! Eh?

BRACK H'm—that is what it may come to, all the same.

TESMAN Well but, Judge Brack—it would show the most incredible lack of consideration for me. (*Gesticulates with his arms*) For—just think—I'm a married man. We have been married on the strength of these prospects, Hedda and I; and run deep into debt; and borrowed money from Aunt Julia too. Good heavens, they had as good as promised me the appointment. Eh?

BRACK Well, well, well—no doubt you will get it in the end; only after a contest.

HEDDA (*immovable in her arm-chair*) Fancy, Tesman, there will be a sort of sporting interest in that.

TESMAN Why, my dearest Hedda, how can you be so indifferent about it?

HEDDA (*as before*) I am not at all indifferent. I am most eager to see who wins.

BRACK In any case, Mrs. Tesman, it is best that you should know how matters stand. I mean—before you set about the little purchases I hear you are threatening.

HEDDA This can make no difference.

BRACK Indeed! Then I have no more to say. Good-bye! (*To* TESMAN) I shall look in on my way back from my afternoon walk, and take you home with me.

TESMAN Oh, yes, yes—your news has quite upset me.

HEDDA (*reclining, holds out her hand*) Good-bye, Judge; and be sure you call in the afternoon.

BRACK Many thanks. Good-bye, good-bye!

TESMAN (*accompanying him to the door*) Good-bye, my dear Judge! You must really excuse me——

(JUDGE BRACK *goes out by the hall door*)

TESMAN (*crosses the room*) Oh, Hedda—one should never rush into adventures. Eh?

HEDDA (*looks at him, smiling*) Do you do that?

TESMAN Yes, dear—there is no denying—it was adventurous to go and marry and set up house upon mere expectations.

HEDDA Perhaps you are right there.

TESMAN Well—at all events, we have our delightful home, Hedda! Fancy, the home we both dreamed of—the home we were in love with, I may almost say. Eh?

HEDDA (*rising slowly and wearily*) It was part of our compact that we were to go into society—to keep open house.

TESMAN Yes, if you only knew how I had been looking forward to it! Fancy—to see you as hostess—in a select circle? Eh? Well, well, well—for the present we shall have to get on without society, Hedda—only to invite Aunt Julia now and then.—Oh, I intended you to lead such an utterly different life, dear——!

HEDDA Of course I cannot have my man in livery just yet.

TESMAN Oh no, unfortunately. It would be out of the question for us to keep a footman, you know.

HEDDA And the saddle-horse I was to have had——

TESMAN (*aghast*) The saddle-horse!

HEDDA ——I suppose I must not think of that now.

TESMAN Good heavens, no!—that's as clear as daylight.

HEDDA (*goes up the room*) Well, I shall have one thing at least to kill time with in the meanwhile.

TESMAN (*beaming*) Oh, thank heaven for that! What is it, Hedda? Eh?

HEDDA (*in the middle doorway, looks at him with covert scorn*) My pistols, George.

TESMAN (*in alarm*) Your pistols!

HEDDA (*with cold eyes*) General Gabler's pistols. (*She goes out through the inner room, to the left*)

TESMAN (*rushes up to the middle doorway and calls after her*) No, for heaven's sake, Hedda darling—don't touch those dangerous things! For my sake, Hedda! Eh?

ACT II

Scene: The room at the TESMANS' *as in the first act, except that the piano has been removed, and an elegant little writing-table with bookshelves put in its place. A smaller table stands near the sofa at the left. Most of the bouquets have been taken away.* MRS. ELVSTED'S *bouquet is upon the large table in front.—It is afternoon.*

(HEDDA, *dressed to receive callers, is alone in the room. She stands by the open glass door, loading a revolver. The fellow to it lies in an open pistol-case on the writing-table.*)

HEDDA (*looks down the garden, and calls*) So you are here again, Judge!

BRACK (*is heard calling from a distance*) As you see, Mrs. Tesman!

HEDDA (*raises the pistol and points*) Now I'll shoot you, Judge Brack!

BRACK (*calling unseen*) No, no, no! Don't stand aiming at me!

HEDDA This is what comes of sneaking in by the back way.[1] (*She fires*)

BRACK (*nearer*) Are you out of your senses——!

HEDDA Dear me—did I happen to hit you?

BRACK (*still outside*) I wish you would let these pranks alone!

HEDDA Come in then, Judge.

(JUDGE BRACK, *dressed as though for a men's party, enters by the glass door. He carries a light overcoat over his arm.*)

BRACK What the deuce—haven't you tired of that sport, yet? What are you shooting at?

HEDDA Oh, I am only firing in the air.

BRACK (*gently takes the pistol out of her hand*) Allow me, madam! (*Looks at it*) Ah —I know this pistol well! (*Looks around*) Where is the case? Ah, here it is. (*Lays the pistol in it, and shuts it*) Now we won't play at that game any more today.

HEDDA Then what in heaven's name would you have me do with myself?

BRACK Have you had no visitors?

HEDDA (*closing the glass door*) Not one. I suppose all our set are still out of town.

BRACK And is Tesman not at home either?

HEDDA (*at the writing-table, putting the pistol-case in a drawer which she shuts*) No. He rushed off to his aunt's directly after lunch; he didn't expect you so early.

BRACK H'm—how stupid of me not to have thought of that!

HEDDA (*turning her head to look at him*) Why stupid?

BRACK Because if I had thought of it I should have come a little—earlier.

1 Bagueje means both "back ways" and "underhand courses."

HEDDA (*crossing the room*)   Then you would have found no one to receive you; for I have been in my room changing my dress ever since lunch.

BRACK   And is there no sort of little chink that we could hold a parley through?

HEDDA   You have forgotten to arrange one.

BRACK   That was another piece of stupidity.

HEDDA   Well, we must just settle down here—and wait. Tesman is not likely to be back for some time yet.

BRACK   Never mind; I shall not be impatient.

(HEDDA *seats herself in the corner of the sofa.* BRACK *lays his overcoat over the back of the nearest chair, and sits down, but keeps his hat in his hand. A short silence. They look at each other.*)

HEDDA   Well?

BRACK (*in the same tone*)   Well?

HEDDA   I spoke first.

BRACK (*bending a little forward*)   Come, let us have a cozy little chat, Mrs. Hedda.

HEDDA (*leaning further back in the sofa*)   Does it not seem like a whole eternity since our last talk? Of course I don't count those few words yesterday evening and this morning.

BRACK   You mean since our last confidential talk? Our last tête-à-tête?

HEDDA   Well, yes—since you put it so.

BRACK   Not a day has passed but I have wished that you were home again.

HEDDA   And I have done nothing but wish the same thing.

BRACK   You? Really, Mrs. Hedda? And I thought you had been enjoying your tour so much!

HEDDA   Oh, yes, you may be sure of that!

BRACK   But Tesman's letters spoke of nothing but happiness.

HEDDA   Oh, Tesman! You see, he thinks nothing so delightful as grubbing in libraries and making copies of old parchments, or whatever you call them.

BRACK (*with a spice of malice*)   Well, that is his vocation in life—or part of it at any rate.

HEDDA   Yes, of course; and no doubt when it's your vocation—— But *I!* Oh, my dear Mr. Brack, how mortally bored I have been.

BRACK (*sympathetically*)   Do you really say so? In downright earnest?

HEDDA   Yes, you can surely understand it——! To go for six whole months without meeting a soul that knew anything of our circle, or could talk about the things we are interested in.

BRACK   Yes, yes—I too should feel that a deprivation.

HEDDA   And then, what I found most intolerable of all——

BRACK   Well?

HEDDA   ——was being everlastingly in the company of—one and the same person——

BRACK (*with a nod of assent*)   Morning, noon, and night, yes—at all possible times and seasons.

HEDDA   I said "everlastingly."

BRACK   Just so. But I should have thought, with our excellent Tesman, one could——

HEDDA   Tesman is—a specialist, my dear Judge.

BRACK   Undeniably.

HEDDA   And specialists are not at all amusing to travel with. Not in the long run at any rate.

BRACK   Not even—the specialist one happens to love?

HEDDA   Faugh—don't use that sickening word!

BRACK (*taken aback*)   What do you say, Mrs. Hedda?

HEDDA (*half laughing, half irritated*)   You should just try it! To hear of nothing but the history of civilization, morning, noon, and night——

BRACK   Everlastingly.

HEDDA   Yes, yes, yes! And then all this about the domestic industry of the Middle Ages——! That's the most disgusting part of it!

BRACK (*looks searchingly at her*)   But tell me—in that case, how am I to understand your——? H'm——

HEDDA   My accepting George Tesman, you mean?

BRACK   Well, let us put it so.

HEDDA   Good heavens, do you see anything so wonderful in that?

BRACK   Yes and no—Mrs. Hedda.

HEDDA   I had positively danced myself tired, my dear Judge. My day was done—— (*With a slight shudder*) Oh no—I won't say that; nor think it either!

BRACK   You have assuredly no reason to.

HEDDA   Oh, reasons—— (*Watching him closely*) And George Tesman—after all, you must admit that he is correctness itself.

BRACK   His correctness and respectability are beyond all question.

HEDDA   And I don't see anything absolutely ridiculous about him.—Do you?

BRACK   Ridiculous? N—no—I shouldn't exactly say so——

HEDDA   Well—and his powers of research, at all events, are untiring.—I see no reason why he should not one day come to the front, after all.

BRACK (*looks at her hesitatingly*)   I thought that you, like every one else, expected him to attain the highest distinction.

HEDDA (*with an expression of fatigue*) Yes, so I did.—And then, since he was bent, at all hazards, on being allowed to provide for me—I really don't know why I should not have accepted his offer?

BRACK No—if you look at it in that light——

HEDDA It was more than my other adorers were prepared to do for me, my dear Judge.

BRACK (*laughing*) Well, I can't answer for all the rest; but as for myself, you know quite well that I have always entertained a—a certain respect for the marriage tie—for marriage as an institution, Mrs. Hedda.

HEDDA (*jestingly*) Oh, I assure you I have never cherished any hopes with respect to you.

BRACK All I require is a pleasant and intimate interior, where I can make myself useful in every way, and am free to come and go as—as a trusted friend——

HEDDA Of the master of the house, do you mean?

BRACK (*bowing*) Frankly—of the mistress first of all; but of course of the master, too, in the second place. Such a triangular friendship—if I may call it so—is really a great convenience for all parties, let me tell you.

HEDDA Yes, I have many a time longed for some one to make a third on our travels. Oh—those railway-carriage tête-à-têtes——!

BRACK Fortunately your wedding journey is over now.

HEDDA (*shaking her head*) Not by a long—long way. I have only arrived at a station on the line.

BRACK Well, then the passengers jump out and move about a little, Mrs. Hedda.

HEDDA I never jump out.

BRACK Really?

HEDDA No—because there is always some one standing by to——

BRACK (*laughing*) To look at your ankles, do you mean?

HEDDA Precisely.

BRACK Well but, dear me——

HEDDA (*with a gesture of repulsion*) I won't have it. I would rather keep my seat where I happen to be—and continue the tête-à-tête.

BRACK But suppose a third person were to jump in and join the couple.

HEDDA Ah—that is quite another matter!

BRACK A trusted, sympathetic friend——

HEDDA ——with a fund of conversation on all sorts of lively topics——

BRACK ——and not the least bit of a specialist!

HEDDA (*with an audible sigh*) Yes, that would be a relief indeed.

824

BRACK (*hears the front door open, and glances in that direction*)   The triangle is completed.

HEDDA (*half aloud*)   And on goes the train.

(GEORGE TESMAN, *in a gray walking-suit, with a soft felt hat, enters from the hall. He has a number of unbound books under his arm and in his pockets.*)

TESMAN (*goes up to the table beside the corner settee*)   Ouf—what a load for a warm day—all these books. (*Lays them on the table*) I'm positively perspiring, Hedda. Hallo—are you there already, my dear Judge? Eh? Berta didn't tell me.

BRACK (*rising*)   I came in through the garden.

HEDDA   What books have you got there?

TESMAN (*stands looking them through*)   Some new books on my special subjects— quite indispensable to me.

HEDDA   Your special subjects?

BRACK   Yes, books on his special subjects, Mrs. Tesman. (*Brack and Hedda exchange a confidential smile*)

HEDDA   Do you need still more books on your special subjects?

TESMAN   Yes, my dear Hedda, one can never have too many of them. Of course one must keep up with all that is written and published.

HEDDA   Yes, I suppose one must.

TESMAN (*searching among his books*)   And look here—I have got hold of Eilert Lövborg's new book too. (*Offering it to her*) Perhaps you would like to glance through it, Hedda? Eh?

HEDDA   No, thank you. Or rather—afterwards perhaps.

TESMAN   I looked into it a little on the way home.

BRACK   Well, what do you think of it—as a specialist?

TESMAN   I think it shows quite remarkable soundness of judgment. He never wrote like that before. (*Putting the books together*) Now I shall take all these into my study. I'm longing to cut the leaves——! And then I must change my clothes. (*To* BRACK) I suppose we needn't start just yet? Eh?

BRACK   Oh, dear no—there is not the slightest hurry.

TESMAN   Well then, I will take my time. (*Is going with his books, but stops in the doorway and turns*) By-the-bye, Hedda—Aunt Julia is not coming this evening.

HEDDA   Not coming? Is it that affair of the bonnet that keeps her away?

TESMAN   Oh, not at all. How could you think such a thing of Aunt Julia? Just fancy——! The fact is, Aunt Rina is very ill.

HEDDA   She always is.

TESMAN   Yes, but today she is much worse than usual, poor dear.

HEDDA Oh, then it's only natural that her sister should remain with her. I must bear my disappointment.

TESMAN And you can't imagine, dear, how delighted Aunt Julia seemed to be —because you had come home looking so flourishing!

HEDDA (*half aloud, rising*) Oh, those everlasting aunts!

TESMAN What?

HEDDA (*going to the glass door*) Nothing.

TESMAN Oh, all right.

(*He goes through the inner room, out to the right*)

BRACK What bonnet were you talking about?

HEDDA Oh, it was a little episode with Miss Tesman this morning. She had laid down her bonnet on the chair there—(*Looks at him and smiles*)—and I pretended to think it was the servant's.

BRACK (*shaking his head*) Now my dear Mrs. Hedda, how could you do such a thing? To that excellent old lady, too!

HEDDA (*nervously crossing the room*) Well, you see—these impulses come over me all of a sudden; and I cannot resist them. (*Throws herself down in the easy-chair by the stove*) Oh, I don't know how to explain it.

BRACK (*behind the easy-chair*) You are not really happy—that is at the bottom of it.

HEDDA (*looking straight before her*) I know of no reason why I should be—happy. Perhaps you can give me one?

BRACK Well—amongst other things, because you have got exactly the home you had set your heart on.

HEDDA (*looks up at him and laughs*) Do you too believe in that legend?

BRACK Is there nothing in it, then?

HEDDA Oh, yes, there is something in it.

BRACK Well?

HEDDA There is this in it, that I made use of Tesman to see me home from evening parties last summer——

BRACK I, unfortunately, had to go quite a different way.

HEDDA That's true. I know you were going a different way last summer.

BRACK (*laughing*) Oh fie, Mrs. Hedda! Well, then—you and Tesman——?

HEDDA Well, we happened to pass here one evening; Tesman, poor fellow, was writhing in the agony of having to find conversation; so I took pity on the learned man——

BRACK (*smiles doubtfully*) You took pity? H'm——

HEDDA   Yes, I really did. And so—to help him out of his torment—I happened to say, in pure thoughtlessness, that I should like to live in this villa.

BRACK   No more than that?

HEDDA   Not that evening.

BRACK   But afterwards?

HEDDA   Yes, my thoughtlessness had consequences, my dear Judge.

BRACK   Unfortunately that too often happens, Mrs. Hedda.

HEDDA   Thanks! So you see it was this enthusiasm for Secretary Falk's villa that first constituted a bond of sympathy between George Tesman and me. From that came our engagement and our marriage, and our wedding journey, and all the rest of it. Well, well, my dear Judge—as you make your bed so you must lie, I could almost say.

BRACK   This is exquisite! And you really cared not a rap about it all the time.

HEDDA   No, heaven knows I didn't.

BRACK   But now? Now that we have made it so homelike for you?

HEDDA   Ugh—the rooms all seem to smell of lavender and dried love-leaves.— But perhaps it's Aunt Julia that has brought that scent with her.

BRACK (*laughingly*)   No, I think it must be a legacy from the late Mrs. Secretary Falk.

HEDDA   Yes, there is an odor of mortality about it. It reminds me of a bouquet —the day after the ball. (*Clasps her hands behind her head, leans back in her chair and looks at him*) Oh, my dear Judge—you cannot imagine how horribly I shall bore myself here.

BRACK   Why should not you, too, find some sort of vocation in life, Mrs. Hedda?

HEDDA   A vocation—that should attract me?

BRACK   If possible, of course.

HEDDA   Heaven knows what sort of a vocation that could be. I often wonder whether——(*Breaking off*) But that would never do either.

BRACK   Who can tell? Let me hear what it is.

HEDDA   Whether I might not get Tesman to go into politics, I mean.

BRACK (*laughing*)   Tesman? No, really now, political life is not the thing for him —not at all in his line.

HEDDA   No, I daresay not.—But if I could get him into it all the same?

BRACK   Why—what satisfaction could you find in that? If he is not fitted for that sort of thing, why should you want to drive him into it?

HEDDA   Because I am bored, I tell you! (*After a pause*) So you think it quite out of the question that Tesman should ever get into the ministry?

BRACK   H'm—you see, my dear Mrs. Hedda—to get into the ministry, he would have to be a tolerably rich man.

HEDDA (*rising impatiently*) Yes, there we have it! It is this genteel poverty I have managed to drop into——! (*Crosses the room*) That is what makes life so pitiable! So utterly ludicrous!—For that's what it is.

BRACK Now *I* should say the fault lay elsewhere.

HEDDA Where, then?

BRACK You have never gone through any really stimulating experience.

HEDDA Anything serious, you mean?

BRACK Yes, you may call it so. But now you may perhaps have one in store.

HEDDA (*tossing her head*) Oh, you're thinking of the annoyances about this wretched professorship! But that must be Tesman's own affair. I assure you I shall not waste a thought upon it.

BRACK No, no, I daresay not. But suppose now that what people call—in elegant language—a solemn responsibility were to come upon you? (*Smiling*) A new responsibility, Mrs. Hedda?

HEDDA (*angrily*) Be quiet! Nothing of that sort will ever happen!

BRACK (*warily*) We will speak of this again a year hence—at the very outside.

HEDDA (*curtly*) I have no turn for anything of the sort, Judge Brack. No responsibilities for me!

BRACK Are you so unlike the generality of women as to have no turn for duties which——?

HEDDA (*beside the glass door*) Oh, be quiet, I tell you!—I often think there is only one thing in the world I have any turn for.

BRACK (*drawing near to her*) And what is that, if I may ask?

HEDDA (*stands looking out*) Boring myself to death. Now you know it. (*Turns, looks towards the inner room, and laughs*) Yes, as I thought! Here comes the Professor.

BRACK (*softly, in a tone of warning*) Come, come, come, Mrs. Hedda!

(GEORGE TESMAN, *dressed for the party, with his gloves and hat in his hand, enters from the right through the inner room*)

TESMAN Hedda, has no message come from Eilert Lövborg? Eh?

HEDDA No.

TESMAN Then you'll see he'll be here presently.

BRACK Do you really think he will come?

TESMAN Yes, I am almost sure of it. For what you were telling us this morning must have been a mere floating rumor.

BRACK You think so?

TESMAN At any rate, Aunt Julia said she did not believe for a moment that he would ever stand in my way again. Fancy that!

BRACK Well then, that's all right.

TESMAN (*placing his hat and gloves on a chair on the right*)   Yes, but you must really let me wait for him as long as possible.

BRACK   We have plenty of time yet. None of my guests will arrive before seven or half-past.

TESMAN   Then meanwhile we can keep Hedda company, and see what happens. Eh?

HEDDA (*placing* BRACK'S *hat and overcoat upon the corner settee*)   And at the worst Mr. Lövborg can remain here with me.

BRACK (*offering to take his things*)   Oh, allow me, Mrs. Tesman!—What do you mean by "At the worst"?

HEDDA   If he won't go with you and Tesman.

TESMAN (*looks dubiously at her*)   But, Hedda dear—do you think it would quite do for him to remain with you? Eh? Remember, Aunt Julia can't come.

HEDDA   No, but Mrs. Elvsted is coming. We three can have a cup of tea together.

TESMAN   Oh, yes, that will be all right.

BRACK (*smiling*)   And that would perhaps be the safest plan for him.

HEDDA   Why so?

BRACK   Well, you know, Mrs. Tesman, how you used to gird at my little bachelor parties. You declared they were adapted only for men of the strictest principles.

HEDDA   But no doubt Mr. Lövborg's principles are strict enough now. A converted sinner——

(BERTA *appears at the hall door*)

BERTA   There's a gentleman asking if you are at home, ma'am——

HEDDA   Well, show him in.

TESMAN (*softly*)   I'm sure it is he! Fancy that!

(EILERT LÖVBORG *enters from the hall. He is slim and lean; of the same age as* TESMAN, *but looks older and somewhat worn-out. His hair and beard are of a blackish brown, his face long and pale, but with patches of color on the cheekbones. He is dressed in a well-cut black visiting suit, quite new. He has dark gloves and a silk hat. He stops near the door, and makes a rapid bow, seeming somewhat embarrassed.*)

TESMAN (*goes up to him and shakes him warmly by the hand*)   Well, my dear Eilert —so at last we meet again!

EILERT LÖVBORG (*speaks in a subdued voice*)   Thanks for your letter, Tesman. (*Approaching* HEDDA)   Will you too shake hands with me, Mrs. Tesman?

HEDDA (*taking his hand*)   I am glad to see you, Mr. Lövborg. (*With a motion of her hand*)   I don't know whether you two gentlemen——?

LÖVBORG (*bowing slightly*)   Judge Brack, I think.

BRACK (*doing likewise*) Oh, yes,—in the old days——

TESMAN (*to* LÖVBORG, *with his hands on his shoulders*) And now you must make yourself entirely at home, Eilert! Mustn't he, Hedda?—For I hear you are going to settle in town again? Eh?

LÖVBORG Yes, I am.

TESMAN Quite right, quite right. Let me tell you, I have got hold of your new book; but I haven't had time to read it yet.

LÖVBORG You may spare yourself the trouble.

TESMAN Why so?

LÖVBORG Because there is very little in it.

TESMAN Just fancy—how can you say so?

BRACK But it has been much praised, I hear.

LÖVBORG That was what I wanted; so I put nothing into the book but what everyone would agree with.

BRACK Very wise of you.

TESMAN Well but, my dear Eilert——!

LÖVBORG For now I mean to win myself a position again—to make a fresh start.

TESMAN (*a little embarrassed*) Ah, that is what you wish to do? Eh?

LÖVBORG (*smiling, lays down his hat, and draws a packet, wrapped in paper, from his coat pocket*) But when this one appears, George Tesman, you will have to read it. For this is the real book—the book I have put my true self into.

TESMAN Indeed? And what is it?

LÖVBORG It is the continuation.

TESMAN The continuation? Of what?

LÖVBORG Of the book.

TESMAN Of the new book?

LÖVBORG Of course.

TESMAN Why, my dear Eilert—does it not come down to our own days?

LÖVBORG Yes, it does; and this one deals with the future.

TESMAN With the future! But, good heavens, we know nothing of the future!

LÖVBORG No; but there is a thing or two to be said about it all the same. (*Opens the packet*) Look here——

TESMAN Why, that's not your handwriting.

LÖVBORG I dictated it. (*Turning over the pages*) It falls into two sections. The first deals with the civilizing forces of the future. And here is the second—(*running through the pages towards the end*)—forecasting the probable line of development.

TESMAN How odd now! I should never have thought of writing anything of that sort.

HEDDA (*at the glass door, drumming on the pane*)   H'm—I daresay not.

LÖVBORG (*replacing the manuscript in its paper and laying the packet on the table*)   I brought it, thinking I might read you a little of it this evening.

TESMAN   That was very good of you, Eilert. But this evening——? (*Looking at Brack*) I don't quite see how we can manage it——

LÖVBORG   Well then, some other time. There is no hurry.

BRACK   I must tell you, Mr. Lövborg—there is a little gathering at my house this evening—mainly in honor of Tesman, you know——

LÖVBORG (*looking for his hat*)   Oh—then I won't detain you——

BRACK   No, but listen—will you not do me the favor of joining us?

LÖVBORG (*curtly and decidedly*)   No, I can't—thank you very much.

BRACK   Oh, nonsense—do! We shall be quite a select little circle. And I assure you we shall have a "lively time" as Mrs. Hed—as Mrs. Tesman says.

LÖVBORG   I have no doubt of it. But nevertheless——

BRACK   And then you might bring your manuscript with you, and read it to Tesman at my house. I could give you a room to yourselves.

TESMAN   Yes, think of that, Eilert,—why shouldn't you? Eh?

HEDDA (*interposing*)   But, Tesman, if Mr. Lövborg would really rather not! I am sure Mr. Lövborg is much more inclined to remain here and have supper with me.

LÖVBORG (*looking at her*)   With you, Mrs. Tesman?

HEDDA   And with Mrs. Elvsted.

LÖVBORG   Ah—— (*Lightly*) I saw her for a moment this morning.

HEDDA   Did you? Well, she is coming this evening. So you see you are almost bound to remain, Mr. Lövborg, or she will have no one to see her home.

LÖVBORG   That's true. Many thanks, Mrs. Tesman—in that case I will remain.

HEDDA   Then I have one or two orders to give the servant——

(*She goes to the hall door and rings.* BERTA *enters.* HEDDA *talks to her in a whisper, and points towards the inner room.* BERTA *nods and goes out again.*)

TESMAN (*at the same time, to* LÖVBORG)   Tell me, Eilert—is it this new subject— the future—that you are going to lecture about?

LÖVBORG   Yes.

TESMAN   They told me at the bookseller's, that you are going to deliver a course of lectures this autumn.

LÖVBORG   That is my intention. I hope you won't take it ill, Tesman.

TESMAN   Oh no, not in the least! But——?

LÖVBORG   I can quite understand that it must be disagreeable to you.

TESMAN (*cast down*)   Oh, I can't expect you, out of consideration for me, to——

LÖVBORG   But I shall wait till you have received your appointment.

TESMAN Will you wait? Yes, but—yes, but—are you not going to compete with me? Eh?

LÖVBORG No; it is only the moral victory I care for.

TESMAN Why, bless me—then Aunt Julia was right after all! Oh yes—I knew it! Hedda! Just fancy—Eilert Lövborg is not going to stand in our way!

HEDDA (*curtly*) Our way? Pray leave me out of the question.

(*She goes up towards the inner room, where* BERTA *is placing a tray with decanters and glasses on the table.* HEDDA *nods approval, and comes forward again.* BERTA *goes out.*)

TESMAN (*at the same time*) And you, Judge Brack—what do you say to this? Eh?

BRACK Well, I say that a moral victory—h'm—may be all very fine——

TESMAN Yes, certainly. But all the same——

HEDDA (*looking at Tesman with a cold smile*) You stand there looking as if you were thunderstruck——

TESMAN Yes—so I am—I almost think——

BRACK Don't you see, Mrs. Tesman, a thunderstorm has just passed over?

HEDDA (*pointing towards the inner room*) Will you not take a glass of cold punch, gentlemen?

BRACK (*looking at his watch*) A stirrup-cup? Yes, it wouldn't come amiss.

TESMAN A capital idea, Hedda! Just the thing! Now that the weight has been taken off my mind——

HEDDA Will you not join them, Mr. Lövborg?

LÖVBORG (*with a gesture of refusal*) No, thank you. Nothing for me.

BRACK Why, bless me—cold punch is surely not poison.

LÖVBORG Perhaps not for everyone.

HEDDA I will keep Mr. Lövborg company in the meantime.

TESMAN Yes, yes, Hedda dear, do.

(*He and* BRACK *go into the inner room, seat themselves, drink punch, smoke cigarettes, and carry on a lively conversation during what follows.* EILERT LÖVBORG *remains beside the stove.* HEDDA *goes to the writing-table.*)

HEDDA (*raising her voice a little*) Do you care to look at some photographs, Mr. Lövborg? You know Tesman and I made a tour in the Tyrol on our way home?

(*She takes up an album, and places it on the table beside the sofa, in the farther corner of which she seats herself.* EILERT LÖVBORG *approaches, stops, and looks at her. Then he takes a chair and seats himself at her left, with his back towards the inner room.*)

HEDDA (*opening the album*) Do you see this range of mountains, Mr. Lövborg? It's the Ortler group. Tesman has written the name underneath. Here it is: "The Ortler group near Meran."

LÖVBORG (*who has never taken his eyes off her, says softly and slowly*) Hedda— Gabler!

HEDDA (*glancing hastily at him*) Ah, hush!

LÖVBORG (*repeats softly*) Hedda Gabler!

HEDDA (*looking at the album*) That was my name in the old days—when we two knew each other.

LÖVBORG And I must teach myself never to say Hedda Gabler again—never, as long as I live.

HEDDA (*still turning over the pages*) Yes, you must. And I think you ought to practice in time. The sooner the better, I should say.

LÖVBORG (*in a tone of indignation*) Hedda Gabler married? And married to— George Tesman!

HEDDA Yes—so the world goes.

LÖVBORG Oh, Hedda, Hedda—how could you[2] throw yourself away!

HEDDA (*looks sharply at him*) What? I can't allow this!

LÖVBORG What do you mean?

(TESMAN *comes into the room and goes toward the sofa*)

HEDDA (*hears him coming and says in an indifferent tone*) And this is a view from the Val d'Ampezzo, Mr. Lövborg. Just look at these peaks! (*Looks affectionately up at* TESMAN) What's the name of these curious peaks, dear?

TESMAN Let me see? Oh, those are the Dolomites.

HEDDA Yes, that's it!—Those are the Dolomites, Mr. Lövborg.

TESMAN Hedda dear,—I only wanted to ask whether I shouldn't bring you a little punch after all? For yourself at any rate—eh?

HEDDA Yes, do, please; and perhaps a few biscuits.

TESMAN No cigarettes?

HEDDA No.

TESMAN Very well.

(*He goes into the inner room and out to the right.* BRACK *sits in the inner room, and keeps an eye from time to time on* HEDDA *and* LÖVBORG.)

LÖVBORG (*softly, as before*) Answer me, Hedda—how could you go and do this?

HEDDA (*apparently absorbed in the album*) If you continue to say *du* to me I won't talk to you.

LÖVBORG May I not say *du* when we are alone?

---

2 He uses the familiar *du*.

HEDDA No. You may think it; but you mustn't say it.

LÖVBORG Ah, I understand. It is an offense against George Tesman, whom you[3]
—love.

HEDDA (*glances at him and smiles*) Love? What an idea!

LÖVBORG You don't love him then!

HEDDA But I won't hear of any sort of unfaithfulness! Remember that.

LÖVBORG Hedda—answer me one thing——

HEDDA Hush!

(TESMAN *enters with a small tray from the inner room*)

TESMAN Here you are! Isn't this tempting? (*He puts the tray on the table*)

HEDDA Why do you bring it yourself?

TESMAN (*filling the glasses*) Because I think it's such fun to wait upon you, Hedda.

HEDDA But you have poured out two glasses. Mr. Lövborg said he wouldn't
have any——

TESMAN No, but Mrs. Elvsted will soon be here, won't she?

HEDDA Yes, by-the-bye—Mrs. Elvsted——

TESMAN Had you forgotten her? Eh?

HEDDA We were so absorbed in these photographs. (*Shows him a picture*) Do you
remember this little village?

TESMAN Oh, it's that one just below the Brenner Pass. It was there we passed
the night——

HEDDA ——and met that lively party of tourists.

TESMAN Yes, that was the place. Fancy—if we could only have had you with us,
Eilert! Eh? (*He returns to the inner room and sits beside* BRACK)

LÖVBORG Answer me this one thing, Hedda——

HEDDA Well?

LÖVBORG Was there no love in your friendship for me either? Not a spark—not
a tinge of love in it?

HEDDA I wonder if there was? To me it seems as though we were two good
comrades—two thoroughly intimate friends. (*Smilingly*) You especially were
frankness itself.

LÖVBORG It was you that made me so.

HEDDA As I look back upon it all, I think there was really something beautiful,
something fascinating—something daring—in—in that secret intimacy—that comradeship which no living creature so much as dreamed of.

3 From this point onward Lövborg uses the formal *De*.

LÖVBORG   Yes, yes, Hedda! Was there not?—When I used to come to your father's in the afternoon—and the General sat over at the window reading his papers—with his back towards us——

HEDDA   And we two on the corner sofa——

LÖVBORG   Always with the same illustrated paper before us——

HEDDA   For want of an album, yes.

LÖVBORG   Yes, Hedda, and when I made my confessions to you—told you about myself, things that at that time no one else knew! There I would sit and tell you of my escapades—my days and nights of devilment. Oh, Hedda—what was the power in you that forced me to confess these things?

HEDDA   Do you think it was any power in me?

LÖVBORG   How else can I explain it? And all those—those roundabout questions you used to put to me——

HEDDA   Which you understood so particularly well——

LÖVBORG   How could you sit and question me like that? Question me quite frankly——

HEDDA   In roundabout terms, please observe.

LÖVBORG   Yes, but frankly nevertheless. Cross-question me about—all that sort of thing?

HEDDA   And how could you answer, Mr. Lövborg?

LÖVBORG   Yes, that is just what I can't understand—in looking back upon it. But tell me now, Hedda—was there not love at the bottom of our friendship? On your side, did you not feel as though you might purge my stains away if I made you my confessor? Was it not so?

HEDDA   No, not quite.

LÖVBORG   What was your motive, then?

HEDDA   Do you think it quite incomprehensible that a young girl—when it can be done—without any one knowing——

LÖVBORG   Well?

HEDDA   ——should be glad to have a peep, now and then, into a world which——

LÖVBORG   Which——?

HEDDA   ——which she is forbidden to know anything about?

LÖVBORG   So that was it?

HEDDA   Partly. Partly—I almost think.

LÖVBORG   Comradeship in the thirst for life. But why should not that, at any rate, have continued?

HEDDA   The fault was yours.

LÖVBORG   It was you that broke with me.

HEDDA Yes, when our friendship threatened to develop into something more serious. Shame upon you, Eilert Lövborg! How could you think of wronging your —your frank comrade?

LÖVBORG (*clenching his hands*) Oh, why did you not carry out your threat? Why did you not shoot me down?

HEDDA Because I have such a dread of scandal.

LÖVBORG Yes, Hedda, you are a coward at heart.

HEDDA A terrible coward. (*Changing her tone*) But it was a lucky thing for you. And now you have found ample consolation at the Elvsteds'.

LÖVBORG I know what Thea has confided to you.

HEDDA And perhaps you have confided to her something about us?

LÖVBORG Not a word. She is too stupid to understand anything of that sort.

HEDDA Stupid?

LÖVBORG She is stupid about matters of that sort.

HEDDA And I am cowardly. (*Bends over towards him, without looking him in the face, and says more softly*) But now I will confide something to you.

LÖVBORG (*eagerly*) Well?

HEDDA The fact that I dared not shoot you down——

LÖVBORG Yes!

HEDDA ——that was not my most arrant cowardice—that evening.

LÖVBORG (*looks at her a moment, understands, and whispers passionately*) Oh, Hedda! Hedda Gabler! Now I begin to see a hidden reason beneath our comradeship! You[4] and I——! After all, then, it was your craving for life——

HEDDA (*softly, with a sharp glance*) Take care! Believe nothing of the sort!

(*Twilight has begun to fall. The hall door is opened from without by* BERTA.)

HEDDA (*closes the album with a bang and calls smilingly*) Ah, at last! My darling Thea,—come along!

(MRS. ELVSTED *enters from the hall. She is in evening dress. The door is closed behind her.*)

HEDDA (*on the sofa, stretches out her arms towards her*) My sweet Thea—you can't think how I have been longing for you!

(MRS. ELVSTED, *in passing, exchanges slight salutations with the gentlemen in the inner room, then goes up to the table and gives* HEDDA *her hands.* EILERT LÖVBORG *has risen. He and* MRS. ELVSTED *greet each other with a silent nod.*)

MRS. ELVSTED Ought I to go in and talk to your husband for a moment?

HEDDA Oh, not at all. Leave those two alone. They will soon be going.

---

4 In this speech he once more says *du*. Hedda addresses him throughout as *De*.

MRS. ELVSTED   Are they going out?

HEDDA   Yes, to a supper-party.

MRS. ELVSTED (*quickly, to* LÖVBORG)   Not you?

LÖVBORG   No.

HEDDA   Mr. Lövborg remains with us.

MRS. ELVSTED (*takes a chair and is about to seat herself at his side*)   Oh, how nice it is here!

HEDDA   No, thank you, my little Thea! Not there! You'll be good enough to come over here to me. I will sit between you.

MRS. ELVSTED   Yes, just as you please.

(*She goes around the table and seats herself on the sofa on* HEDDA'S *right. Lövborg reseats himself on his chair.*)

LÖVBORG (*after a short pause, to* HEDDA)   Is not she lovely to look at?

HEDDA (*lightly stroking her hair*)   Only to look at?

LÖVBORG   Yes. For we two—she and I—we are two real comrades. We have absolute faith in each other; so we can sit and talk with perfect frankness——

HEDDA   Not roundabout, Mr. Lövborg?

LÖVBORG   Well——

MRS. ELVSTED (*softly clinging close to* HEDDA)   Oh, how happy I am, Hedda; for, only think, he says I have inspired him too.

HEDDA (*looks at her with a smile*)   Ah! Does he say that, dear?

LÖVBORG   And then she is so brave, Mrs. Tesman!

MRS. ELVSTED   Good heavens—am I brave?

LÖVBORG   Exceedingly—where your comrade is concerned.

HEDDA   Ah, yes—courage! If one only had that!

LÖVBORG   What then? What do you mean?

HEDDA   Then life would perhaps be livable, after all. (*With a sudden change of tone*) But now, my dearest Thea, you really must have a glass of cold punch.

MRS. ELVSTED   No, thanks—I never take anything of that kind.

HEDDA   Well then, you, Mr. Lövborg.

LÖVBORG   Nor I, thank you.

MRS. ELVSTED   No, he doesn't either.

HEDDA (*looks fixedly at him*)   But if I say you shall?

LÖVBORG   It would be no use.

HEDDA (*laughing*)   Then I, poor creature, have no sort of power over you?

LÖVBORG   Not in that respect.

HEDDA   But seriously, I think you ought to—for your own sake.

MRS. ELVSTED   Why, Hedda——!

LÖVBORG   How so?

HEDDA   Or rather on account of other people.

LÖVBORG   Indeed?

HEDDA   Otherwise people might be apt to suspect that—in your heart of hearts —you did not feel quite secure—quite confident of yourself.

MRS. ELVSTED (*softly*)   Oh please, Hedda——

LÖVBORG   People may suspect what they like—for the present.

MRS. ELVSTED (*joyfully*)   Yes, let them!

HEDDA   I saw it plainly in Judge Brack's face a moment ago.

LÖVBORG   What did you see?

HEDDA   His contemptuous smile, when you dared not go with them into the inner room.

LÖVBORG   Dared not? Of course I preferred to stop here and talk to you.

MRS. ELVSTED   What could be more natural, Hedda?

HEDDA   But the Judge could not guess that. And I saw, too, the way he smiled and glanced at Tesman when you dared not accept his invitation to this wretched little supper-party of his.

LÖVBORG   Dared not! Do you say I dared not?

HEDDA   *I* don't say so. But that was how Judge Brack understood it.

LÖVBORG   Well, let him.

HEDDA   Then you are not going with them?

LÖVBORG   I will stay here with you and Thea.

MRS. ELVSTED   Yes, Hedda—how can you doubt that?

HEDDA (*smiles and nods approvingly to* LÖVBORG)   Firm as a rock! Faithful to your principles, now and forever! Ah, that is how a man should be! (*Turns to* MRS. ELVSTED *and caresses her*) Well now, what did I tell you, when you came to us this morning in such a state of distraction——

LÖVBORG (*surprised*)   Distraction!

MRS. ELVSTED (*terrified*)   Hedda—oh Hedda——!

HEDDA   You can see for yourself; you haven't the slightest reason to be in such mortal terror——(*Interrupting herself*) There! Now we can all three enjoy ourselves!

LÖVBORG (*who has given a start*)   Ah—what is all this, Mrs. Tesman?

MRS. ELVSTED   Oh my God, Hedda! What are you saying? What are you doing?

HEDDA   Don't get excited! That horrid Judge Brack is sitting watching you.

LÖVBORG So she was in mortal terror! On my account!

MRS. ELVSTED (*softly and piteously*) Oh, Hedda—now you have ruined everything!

LÖVBORG (*looks fixedly at her for a moment. His face is distorted.*) So that was my comrade's frank confidence in me?

MRS. ELVSTED (*imploringly*) Oh, my dearest friend—only let me tell you——

LÖVBORG (*takes one of the glasses of punch, raises it to his lips, and says in a low, husky voice*) Your health, Thea!

(*He empties the glass, puts it down, and takes the second*)

MRS. ELVSTED (*softly*) Oh, Hedda, Hedda—how could you do this?

HEDDA *I* do it? *I?* Are you crazy?

LÖVBORG Here's to your health too, Mrs. Tesman. Thanks for the truth. Hurrah for the truth!

(*He empties the glass and is about to refill it*)

HEDDA (*lays her hand on his arm*) Come, come—no more for the present. Remember you are going out to supper.

MRS. ELVSTED No, no, no!

HEDDA Hush! They are sitting watching you.

LÖVBORG (*putting down the glass*) Now, Thea—tell me the truth——

MRS. ELVSTED Yes.

LÖVBORG Did your husband know that you had come after me?

MRS. ELVSTED (*wringing her hands*) Oh, Hedda—do you hear what he is asking?

LÖVBORG Was it arranged between you and him that you were to come to town and look after me? Perhaps it was the Sheriff himself that urged you to come? Aha, my dear—no doubt he wanted my help in his office! Or was it at the card-table that he missed me?

MRS. ELVSTED (*softly, in agony*) Oh, Lövborg, Lövborg——!

LÖVBORG (*seizes a glass and is on the point of filling it*) Here's a glass for the old Sheriff too!

HEDDA (*preventing him*) No more just now. Remember you have to read your manuscript to Tesman.

LÖVBORG (*calmly, putting down the glass*) It was stupid of me—all this, Thea—to take it in this way, I mean. Don't be angry with me, my dear, dear comrade. You shall see—both you and the others—that if I was fallen once—now I have risen again! Thanks to you, Thea.

MRS. ELVSTED (*radiant with joy*) Oh, heaven be praised——!

[BRACK *has in the meantime looked at his watch. He and* TESMAN *rise and come into the drawing-room.*]

BRACK (*takes his hat and overcoat*) Well, Mrs. Tesman, our time has come.

HEDDA I suppose it has.

LÖVBORG (*rising*) Mine too, Judge Brack.

MRS. ELVSTED (*softly and imploringly*) Oh, Lövborg, don't do it!

HEDDA (*pinching her arm*) They can hear you!

MRS. ELVSTED (*with a suppressed shriek*) Ow!

LÖVBORG (*to Brack*) You were good enough to invite me.

BRACK Well, are you coming after all?

LÖVBORG Yes, many thanks.

BRACK I'm delighted——

LÖVBORG (*to* TESMAN, *putting the parcel of MS. in his pocket*) I should like to show you one or two things before I send it to the printers.

TESMAN Fancy—that will be delightful. But, Hedda dear, how is Mrs. Elvsted to get home? Eh?

HEDDA Oh, that can be managed somehow.

LÖVBORG (*looking towards the ladies*) Mrs. Elvsted? Of course, I'll come again and fetch her. (*Approaching*) At ten or thereabouts, Mrs. Tesman? Will that do?

HEDDA Certainly. That will do capitally.

TESMAN Well, then, that's all right. But you must not expect me so early, Hedda.

HEDDA Oh, you may stop as long—as long as ever you please.

MRS. ELVSTED (*trying to conceal her anxiety*) Well then, Mr. Lövborg—I shall remain here until you come.

LÖVBORG (*with his hat in his hand*) Pray do, Mrs. Elvsted.

BRACK And now off goes the excursion train, gentlemen! I hope we shall have a lively time, as a certain fair lady puts it.

HEDDA Ah, if only the fair lady could be present unseen——!

BRACK Why unseen?

HEDDA In order to hear a little of your liveliness at first hand, Judge Brack.

BRACK (*laughingly*) I should not advise the fair lady to try it.

TESMAN (*also laughing*) Come, you're a nice one Hedda! Fancy that!

BRACK Well, good-bye, good-bye, ladies.

LÖVBORG (*bowing*) About ten o'clock, then.

(BRACK, LÖVBORG, *and* TESMAN *go out by the hall door. At the same time* BERTA *enters from the inner room with a lighted lamp, which she places on the dining-room table; she goes out by the way she came.*)

MRS. ELVSTED (*who has risen and is wandering restlessly about the room*) Hedda—Hedda—what will come of all this?

HEDDA At ten o'clock—he will be here. I can see him already—with vine-leaves in his hair—flushed and fearless——

MRS. ELVSTED Oh, I hope he may.

HEDDA And then, you see—then he will have regained control over himself. Then he will be a free man for all his days.

MRS. ELVSTED Oh God!—if he would only come as you see him now!

HEDDA He will come as I see him—so, and not otherwise! (*Rises and approaches* THEA) You may doubt him as long as you please; I believe in him. And now we will try——

MRS. ELVSTED You have some hidden motive in this, Hedda!

HEDDA Yes, I have. I want for once in my life to have power to mold a human destiny.

MRS. ELVSTED Have you not the power?

HEDDA I have not—and have never had it.

MRS. ELVSTED Not your husband's?

HEDDA Do you think that is worth the trouble? Oh, if you could only understand how poor I am. And fate has made you so rich! (*Clasps her passionately in her arms*) I think I must burn your hair off, after all.

MRS. ELVSTED Let me go! Let me go! I am afraid of you, Hedda!

BERTA (*in the middle doorway*) Tea is laid in the dining room, ma'am.

HEDDA Very well. We are coming.

MRS. ELVSTED No, no, no! I would rather go home alone! At once!

HEDDA Nonsense? First you shall have a cup of tea, you little stupid. And then —at ten o'clock—Eilert Lövborg will be here—with vine-leaves in his hair.

(*She drags* MRS. ELVSTED *almost by force towards the middle doorway.*)

ACT III

Scene: The room at the TESMANS'. *The curtains are drawn over the middle doorway, and also over the glass door. The lamp, half turned down, and with a shade over it, is burning on the table. In the stove, the door of which stands open, there has been a fire, which is now nearly burnt out.*

[MRS. ELVSTED, *wrapped in a large shawl, and with her feet upon a foot-rest, sits close to the stove, sunk back in the arm-chair.* HEDDA, *fully dressed, lies sleeping upon the sofa, with a sofa-blanket over her.*]

MRS. ELVSTED (*after a pause, suddenly sits up in her chair, and listens eagerly. Then she sinks back again wearily, moaning to herself.*) Not yet!—Oh God—oh God—not yet!

(BERTA *slips in by the hall door. She has a letter in her hand.*)

MRS. ELVSTED (*turns and whispers eagerly*)   Well—has anyone come?

BERTA (*softly*)   Yes, a girl has brought this letter.

MRS. ELVSTED (*quickly, holding out her hand*)   A letter! Give it to me!

BERTA   No, it's for Dr. Tesman, ma'am.

MRS. ELVSTED   Oh, indeed.

BERTA   It was Miss Tesman's servant that brought it. I'll lay it here on the table.

MRS. ELVSTED   Yes, do.

BERTA (*laying down the letter*)   I think I had better put out the lamp. It's smoking.

MRS. ELVSTED   Yes, put it out. It must soon be daylight now.

BERTA (*putting out the lamp*)   It is daylight already, ma'am.

MRS. ELVSTED   Yes, broad day! And no one come back yet——!

BERTA   Lord bless you, ma'am! I guessed how it would be.

MRS. ELVSTED   You guessed?

BERTA   Yes, when I saw that a certain person had come back to town—and that he went off with them. For we've heard enough about that gentleman before now.

MRS. ELVSTED   Don't speak so loud. You will waken Mrs. Tesman.

BERTA (*looks towards the sofa and sighs*)   No, no—let her sleep, poor thing, Shan't I put some wood on the fire?

MRS. ELVSTED   Thanks, not for me.

BERTA   Oh, very well.

(*She goes softly out by the hall door*)

HEDDA (*is awakened by the shutting of the door, and looks up*)   What's that——?

MRS. ELVSTED   It was only the servant——

HEDDA (*looking about her*)   Oh, we're here——! Yes, now I remember. (*Sits erect upon the sofa, stretches herself, and rubs her eyes*) What o'clock is it, Thea?

MRS. ELVSTED (*looks at her watch*)   It's past seven.

HEDDA   When did Tesman come home?

MRS. ELVSTED   He has not come.

HEDDA   Not come home yet?

MRS. ELVSTED (*rising*)   No one has come.

HEDDA   Think of our watching and waiting here till four in the morning——

MRS. ELVSTED (*wringing her hands*)   And how I watched and waited for him!

HEDDA (*yawns, and says with her hand before her mouth*)   Well, well—we might have spared ourselves the trouble.

MRS. ELVSTED   Did you get a little sleep?

HEDDA   Oh yes; I believe I have slept pretty well. Have you not?

MRS. ELVSTED   Not for a moment. I couldn't, Hedda!—not to save my life.

HEDDA (*rises and goes towards her*)   There, there, there! There's nothing to be so alarmed about. I understand quite well what has happened.

MRS. ELVSTED   Well, what do you think? Won't you tell me?

HEDDA   Why, of course it has been a very late affair at Judge Brack's——

MRS. ELVSTED   Yes, yes, that is clear enough. But all the same——

HEDDA   And then, you see, Tesman hasn't cared to come home and ring us up in the middle of the night. (*Laughing*) Perhaps he wasn't inclined to show himself either—immediately after a jollification.

MRS. ELVSTED   But in that case—where can he have gone?

HEDDA   Of course he has gone to his aunts' and slept there. They have his old room ready for him.

MRS. ELVSTED   No, he can't be with them; for a letter has just come for him from Miss Tesman. There it lies.

HEDDA   Indeed? (*Looks at the address*) Why yes, it's addressed in Aunt Julia's own hand. Well then, he has remained at Judge Brack's. And as for Eilert Lövborg— he is sitting, with vine-leaves in his hair, reading his manuscript.

MRS. ELVSTED   Oh Hedda, you are just saying things you don't believe a bit.

HEDDA   You really are a little blockhead, Thea.

MRS. ELVSTED   Oh yes, I suppose I am.

HEDDA   And how mortally tired you look.

MRS. ELVSTED   Yes, I am mortally tired.

HEDDA   Well then, you must do as I tell you. You must go into my room and lie down for a little while.

MRS. ELVSTED   Oh no, no—I shouldn't be able to sleep.

HEDDA   I am sure you would.

MRS. ELVSTED   Well, but your husband is certain to come soon now; and then I want to know at once——

HEDDA   I shall take care to let you know when he comes.

MRS. ELVSTED   Do you promise me, Hedda?

HEDDA   Yes, rely upon me. Just you go in and have a sleep in the meantime.

MRS. ELVSTED   Thanks; then I'll try to.

(*She goes off through the inner room*)

843

(HEDDA *goes up to the glass door and draws back the curtains. The broad daylight streams into the room. Then she takes a little hand-glass from the writing-table, looks at herself in it, and arranges her hair. Next she goes to the hall door and presses the bell-button.*

BERTA *presently appears at the hall door.*)

BERTA   Did you want anything, ma'am?

HEDDA   Yes; you must put some more wood in the stove. I am shivering.

BERTA   Bless me—I'll make up the fire at once. (*She rakes the embers together and lays a piece of wood upon them; then stops and listens*) That was a ring at the front door, ma'am.

HEDDA   Then go to the door. I will look after the fire.

BERTA   It'll soon burn up. (*She goes out by the hall door*)

(HEDDA *kneels on the foot-rest and lays some more pieces of wood in the stove. After a short pause,* GEORGE TESMAN *enters from the hall. He looks tired and rather serious. He steals on tiptoe towards the middle doorway and is about to slip through the curtains.*)

HEDDA (*at the stove, without looking up*)   Good morning.

TESMAN (*turns*)   Hedda! (*Approaching her*) Good heavens—are you up so early? Eh?

HEDDA   Yes, I am up very early this morning.

TESMAN   And I never doubted you were still sound asleep! Fancy that, Hedda!

HEDDA   Don't speak so loud. Mrs. Elvsted is resting in my room.

TESMAN   Has Mrs. Elvsted been here all night?

HEDDA   Yes, since no one came to fetch her.

TESMAN   Ah, to be sure.

HEDDA (*closes the door of the stove and rises*)   Well, did you enjoy yourself at Judge Brack's?

TESMAN   Have you been anxious about me? Eh?

HEDDA   No, I should never think of being anxious. But I asked if you had enjoyed yourself.

TESMAN   Oh yes,—for once in a way. Especially the beginning of the evening; for then Eilert read me part of his book. We arrived more than an hour too early —fancy that! And Brack had all sorts of arrangements to make—so Eilert read to me.

HEDDA (*seating herself by the table on the right*)   Well? Tell me, then——

TESMAN (*sitting on a footstool near the stove*)   Oh Hedda, you can't conceive what a book that is going to be! I believe it is one of the most remarkable things that have ever been written. Fancy that!

HEDDA   Yes, yes; I don't care about that——

844

TESMAN   I must make a confession to you, Hedda. When he had finished reading —a horrid feeling came over me.

HEDDA   A horrid feeling?

TESMAN   I felt jealous of Eilert for having had it in him to write such a book. Only think, Hedda!

HEDDA   Yes, yes, I am thinking!

TESMAN   And then how pitiful to think that he—with all his gifts—should be irreclaimable after all.

HEDDA   I suppose you mean that he has more courage than the rest?

TESMAN   No, not at all—I mean that he is incapable of taking his pleasures in moderation.

HEDDA   And what came of it all—in the end?

TESMAN   Well, to tell the truth, I think it might best be described as an orgy, Hedda.

HEDDA   Had he vine-leaves in his hair?

TESMAN   Vine-leaves? No, I saw nothing of the sort. But he made a long, rambling speech in honor of the woman who had inspired him in his work—that was the phrase he used.

HEDDA   Did he name her?

TESMAN   No, he didn't; but I can't help thinking he meant Mrs. Elvsted. You may be sure he did.

HEDDA   Well—where did you part from him?

TESMAN   On the way to town. We broke up—the last of us at any rate—all together; and Brack came with us to get a breath of fresh air. And then, you see, we agreed to take Eilert home; for he had had far more than was good for him.

HEDDA   I daresay.

TESMAN   But now comes the strange part of it, Hedda; or, I should rather say, the melancholy part of it. I declare I am almost ashamed—on Eilert's account— to tell you——

HEDDA   Oh, go on——

TESMAN   Well, as we were getting near town, you see, I happened to drop a little behind the others. Only for a minute or two—fancy that!

HEDDA   Yes, yes, yes, but——?

TESMAN   And then, as I hurried after them—what do you think I found by the wayside? Eh?

HEDDA   Oh, how should I know!

TESMAN   You mustn't speak of it to a soul, Hedda! Do you hear! Promise me, for Eilert's sake. (*Draws a parcel, wrapped in paper, from his coat pocket*) Fancy, dear —I found this.

HEDDA   Is not that the parcel he had with him yesterday?

TESMAN   Yes, it is the whole of his precious, irreplaceable manuscript! And he had gone and lost it, and knew nothing about it. Only fancy, Hedda! So deplorably——

HEDDA   But why did you not give him back the parcel at once?

TESMAN   I didn't dare to—in the state he was then in——

HEDDA   Did you not tell any of the others that you had found it?

TESMAN   Oh, far from it. You can surely understand that, for Eilert's sake, I wouldn't do that.

HEDDA   So no one knows that Eilert Lövborg's manuscript is in your possession?

TESMAN   No. And no one must know it.

HEDDA   Then what did you say to him afterwards?

TESMAN   I didn't talk to him again at all; for when we got in among the streets, he and two or three of the others gave us the slip and disappeared. Fancy that!

HEDDA   Indeed! They must have taken him home then.

TESMAN   Yes, so it would appear. And Brack, too, left us.

HEDDA   And what have you been doing with yourself since?

TESMAN   Well, I and some of the others went home with one of the party, a jolly fellow, and took our morning coffee with him; or perhaps I should rather call it our night coffee—eh? But now, when I have rested a little, and given Eilert, poor fellow, time to have his sleep out, I must take this back to him.

HEDDA (*holds out her hand for the packet*)   No—don't give it to him! Not in such a hurry, I mean. Let me read it first.

TESMAN   No, my dearest Hedda, I mustn't, I really mustn't.

HEDDA   You must not?

TESMAN   No—for you can imagine what a state of despair he will be in when he awakens and misses the manuscript. He has no copy of it, you know! He told me so.

HEDDA (*looking searchingly at him*)   Can such a thing not be reproduced? Written over again?

TESMAN   No, I don't think that would be possible. For the inspiration, you see——

HEDDA   Yes, yes—I suppose it depends on that. (*Lightly*) But, by-the-bye—here is a letter for you.

TESMAN   Fancy——!

HEDDA (*handing it to him*)   It came early this morning.

TESMAN   It's from Aunt Julia! What can it be? (*He lays the packet on the other footstool, opens the letter, runs his eye through it, and jumps up*) Oh, Hedda—she says that poor Aunt Rina is dying!

HEDDA   Well, we were prepared for that.

TESMAN   And that if I want to see her again, I must make haste. I'll run in to them at once.

HEDDA (*suppressing a smile*)   Will you run?

TESMAN   Oh, dearest Hedda—if you could only make up your mind to come with me! Just think!

HEDDA (*rises and says wearily, repelling the idea*)   No, no, don't ask me. I will not look upon sickness and death. I loathe all sorts of ugliness.

TESMAN   Well, well, then——! (*Bustling around*) My hat—My overcoat——? Oh, in the hall—I do hope I mayn't come too late, Hedda! Eh?

HEDDA   Oh, if you run——

(BERTA *appears at the hall door.*)

BERTA   Judge Brack is at the door, and wishes to know if he may come in.

TESMAN   At this time! No, I can't possibly see him.

HEDDA   But I can. (*To* BERTA) Ask Judge Brack to come in. (BERTA *goes out*)

HEDDA (*quickly whispering*)   The parcel, Tesman! (*She snatches it up from the stool*)

TESMAN   Yes, give it to me!

HEDDA   No, no, I will keep it till you come back.

(*She goes to the writing-table and places it in the bookcase.* TESMAN *stands in a flurry of haste, and cannot get his gloves on.*
JUDGE BRACK *enters from the hall.*)

HEDDA (*nodding to him*)   You are an early bird, I must say.

BRACK   Yes, don't you think so? (*To Tesman*) Are you on the move, too?

TESMAN   Yes, I must rush off to my aunts'. Fancy—the invalid one is lying at death's door, poor creature.

BRACK   Dear me, is she indeed? Then on no account let me detain you. At such a critical moment——

TESMAN   Yes, I must really rush—Good-bye! Good-bye! (*He hastens out by the hall door*)

HEDDA (*approaching*)   You seem to have made a particularly lively night of it at your rooms, Judge Brack.

BRACK   I assure you I have not had my clothes off, Mrs. Hedda.

HEDDA   Not you, either?

BRACK   No, as you may see. But what has Tesman been telling you of the night's adventures?

HEDDA   Oh, some tiresome story. Only that they went and had coffee somewhere or other.

BRACK I have heard about that coffee-party already. Eilert Lövborg was not with them, I fancy?

HEDDA No, they had taken him home before that.

BRACK Tesman, too?

HEDDA No, but some of the others, he said.

BRACK (*smiling*) George Tesman is really an ingenuous creature, Mrs. Hedda.

HEDDA Yes, heaven knows he is. Then is there something behind all this?

BRACK Yes, perhaps there may be.

HEDDA Well then, sit down, my dear Judge, and tell your story in comfort.

(*She seats herself to the left of the table.* BRACK *sits near her, at the long side of the table.*)

HEDDA Now then?

BRACK I had special reasons for keeping track of my guests—or rather of some of my guests—last night.

HEDDA Of Eilert Lövborg among the rest, perhaps?

BRACK Frankly, yes.

HEDDA Now you make me really curious——

BRACK Do you know where he and one or two of the others finished the night, Mrs. Hedda?

HEDDA If it is not quite unmentionable, tell me.

BRACK Oh no, it's not at all unmentionable. Well, they put in an appearance at a particularly animated soirée.

HEDDA Of the lively kind?

BRACK Of the very liveliest——

HEDDA Tell me more of this, Judge Brack——

BRACK Lövborg, as well as the others, had been invited in advance. I knew all about it. But he had declined the invitation; for now, as you know, he has become a new man.

HEDDA Up at the Elvsteds', yes. But he went after all, then?

BRACK Well, you see, Mrs. Hedda—unhappily the spirit moved him at my rooms last evening——

HEDDA Yes, I hear he found inspiration.

BRACK Pretty violent inspiration. Well, I fancy that altered his purpose; for we men folk are unfortunately not always so firm in our principles as we ought to be.

HEDDA Oh, I am sure you are an exception, Judge Brack. But as to Lövborg——?

BRACK To make a long story short—he landed at last in Mademoiselle Diana's rooms.

848

HEDDA   Mademoiselle Diana's?

BRACK   It was Mademoiselle Diana that was giving the soirée, to a select circle of her admirers and her lady friends.

HEDDA   Is she a red-haired woman?

BRACK   Precisely.

HEDDA   A sort of a—singer?

BRACK   Oh yes—in her leisure moments. And moreover a mighty huntress—of men—Mrs. Hedda. You have no doubt heard of her. Eilert Lövborg was one of her most enthusiastic protectors—in the days of his glory.

HEDDA   And how did all this end?

BRACK   Far from amicably, it appears. After a most tender meeting, they seem to have come to blows——

HEDDA   Lövborg and she?

BRACK   Yes. He accused her or her friends of having robbed him. He declared that his pocket-book had disappeared—and other things as well. In short, he seems to have made a furious disturbance.

HEDDA   And what came of it all?

BRACK   It came to a general scrimmage, in which the ladies as well as the gentlemen took part. Fortunately the police at last appeared on the scene.

HEDDA   The police too?

BRACK   Yes. I fancy it will prove a costly frolic for Eilert Lövborg, crazy being that he is.

HEDDA   How so?

BRACK   He seems to have made a violent resistance—to have hit one of the constables on the head and torn the coat off his back. So they had to march him off to the police station with the rest.

HEDDA   How have you learnt all this?

BRACK   From the police themselves.

HEDDA   (*gazing straight before her*)   So that is what happened. Then he had no vine-leaves in his hair.

BRACK   Vine-leaves, Mrs. Hedda?

HEDDA   (*changing her tone*)   But tell me now, Judge—what is your real reason for tracking out Eilert Lövborg's movements so carefully?

BRACK   In the first place, it could not be entirely indifferent to me if it should appear in the police-court that he came straight from my house.

HEDDA   Will the matter come into court, then?

BRACK   Of course. However, I should scarcely have troubled so much about that. But I thought that, as a friend of the family, it was my duty to supply you and Tesman with a full account of his nocturnal exploits.

HEDDA   Why so, Judge Brack?

BRACK   Why, because I have a shrewd suspicion that he intends to use you as a sort of blind.

HEDDA   Oh, how can you think such a thing!

BRACK   Good heavens, Mrs. Hedda—we have eyes in our head. Mark my words! This Mrs. Elvsted will be in no hurry to leave town again.

HEDDA   Well, even if there should be anything between them, I suppose there are plenty of other places where they could meet.

BRACK   Not a single home. Henceforth, as before, every respectable house will be closed against Eilert Lövborg.

HEDDA   And so ought mine to be, you mean?

BRACK   Yes. I confess it would be more than painful to me if this personage were to be made free of your house. How superfluous, how intrusive, he would be, if he were to force his way into——

HEDDA   ——into the triangle?

BRACK   Precisely. It would simply mean that I should find myself homeless.

HEDDA (*looks at him with a smile*)   So you want to be the one cock in the basket —that is your aim.

BRACK (*nods slowly and lowers his voice*)   Yes, that is my aim. And for that I will fight—with every weapon I can command.

HEDDA (*her smile vanishing*)   I see you are a dangerous person—when it comes to the point.

BRACK   Do you think so?

HEDDA   I am beginning to think so. And I am exceedingly glad to think—that you have no sort of hold over me.

BRACK (*laughing equivocally*)   Well, well, Mrs. Hedda—perhaps you are right there. If I had, who knows what I might be capable of?

HEDDA   Come, come now, Judge Brack. That sounds almost like a threat.

BRACK (*rising*)   Oh, not at all! The triangle, you know, ought, if possible, to be spontaneously constructed.

HEDDA   There I agree with you.

BRACK   Well, now I have said all I had to say; and I had better be getting back to town. Good-bye, Mrs. Hedda. (*He goes towards the glass door*)

HEDDA (*rising*)   Are you going through the garden?

BRACK   Yes, it's a short cut for me.

HEDDA   And then it is the back way, too.

BRACK   Quite so. I have no objection to back ways. They may be piquant enough at times.

HEDDA   When there is ball practice going on, you mean?

BRACK (*in the doorway, laughing to her*)   Oh, people don't shoot their tame poultry, I fancy.

HEDDA (*also laughing*)   Oh no, when there is only one cock in the basket——

(*They exchange laughing nods of farewell. He goes. She closes the door behind him.*
HEDDA, *who has become quite serious, stands for a moment looking out. Presently she goes and peeps through the curtain over the middle doorway. Then she goes to the writing-table, takes* LÖVBORG'S *packet out of the bookcase, and is on the point of looking through its contents.* BERTA *is heard speaking loudly in the hall.* HEDDA *turns and listens. Then she hastily locks up the packet in the drawer, and lays the key on the inkstand.*

EILERT LÖVBORG, *with his great coat on and his hat in his hand, tears open the hall door. He looks somewhat confused and irritated.*)

LÖVBORG (*looking towards the hall*) And I tell you I must and will come in! There!

(*He closes the door, turns and sees* HEDDA, *at once regains his self-control, and bows*)

HEDDA (*at the writing table*)   Well, Mr. Lövborg, this is rather a late hour to call for Thea.

LÖVBORG   You mean rather an early hour to call on you. Pray pardon me.

HEDDA   How do you know that she is still here?

LÖVBORG   They told me at her lodgings that she had been out all night.

HEDDA (*going to the oval table*)   Did you notice anything about the people of the house when they said that?

LÖVBORG (*looks inquiringly at her*)   Notice anything about them?

HEDDA   I mean, did they seem to think it odd?

LÖVBORG (*suddenly understanding*)   Oh yes, of course! I am dragging her down with me! However, I didn't notice anything.—I suppose Tesman is not up yet?

HEDDA   No—I think not——

LÖVBORG   When did he come home?

HEDDA   Very late.

LÖVBORG   Did he tell you anything?

HEDDA   Yes, I gathered that you had had an exceedingly jolly evening at Judge Brack's.

LÖVBORG   Nothing more?

HEDDA   I don't think so. However, I was so dreadfully sleepy——

(MRS. ELVSTED *enters through the curtains of the middle doorway*)

MRS. ELVSTED (*going towards him*)   Ah, Lövborg! At last——!

LÖVBORG   Yes, at last. And too late!

MRS. ELVSTED (*looks anxiously at him*)   What is too late?

LÖVBORG   Everything is too late now. It is all over with me.

MRS. ELVSTED   Oh no, no—don't say that.

LÖVBORG   You will say the same when you hear——

MRS. ELVSTED   I won't hear anything!

HEDDA   Perhaps you would prefer to talk to her alone! If so, I will leave you.

LÖVBORG   No, stay—you too. I beg you to stay.

MRS. ELVSTED   Yes, but I won't hear anything, I tell you.

LÖVBORG   It is not last night's adventures that I want to talk about.

MRS. ELVSTED   What is it then——?

LÖVBORG   I want to say that now our ways must part.

MRS. ELVSTED   Part!

HEDDA (*involuntarily*)   I knew it!

LÖVBORG   You can be of no more service to me, Thea.

MRS. ELVSTED   How can you stand there and say that! No more service to you! Am I not to help you now, as before? Are we not to go on working together?

LÖVBORG   Henceforward I shall do no work.

MRS. ELVSTED (*despairingly*)   Then what am I to do with my life?

LÖVBORG   You must try to live your life as if you had never known me.

MRS. ELVSTED   But you know I cannot do that!

LÖVBORG   Try if you cannot, Thea. You must go home again——

MRS. ELVSTED (*in vehement protest*)   Never in this world! Where you are, there will I be also! I will not let myself be driven away like this! I will remain here! I will be with you when the book appears.

HEDDA (*half aloud, in suspense*)   Ah yes—the book!

LÖVBORG (*looks at her*)   My book and Thea's; for that is what it is.

MRS. ELVSTED   Yes, I feel that it is. And that is why I have a right to be with you when it appears! I will see with my own eyes how respect and honor pour in upon you afresh. And the happiness—the happiness—oh, I must share it with you!

LÖVBORG   Thea—our book will never appear.

HEDDA   Ah!

MRS. ELVSTED   Never appear!

LÖVBORG   Can never appear.

MRS. ELVSTED (*in agonized foreboding*)   Lövborg—what have you done with the manuscript?

HEDDA (*looks anxiously at him*)   Yes, the manuscript——?

MRS. ELVSTED   Where is it?

LÖVBORG   Oh Thea—don't ask me about it!

852

MRS. ELVSTED   Yes, yes, I will know. I demand to be told at once.

LÖVBORG   The manuscript— Well then—I have torn the manuscript into a thousand pieces.

MRS. ELVSTED (*shrieks*)   Oh no, no——!

HEDDA (*involuntarily*)   But that's not——

LÖVBORG (*looks at her*)   Not true, you think?

HEDDA (*collecting herself*)   Oh well, of course—since you say so. But it sounded so improbable——

LÖVBORG   It is true, all the same.

MRS. ELVSTED (*wringing her hands*)   Oh God—oh God, Hedda—torn his own work to pieces!

LÖVBORG   I have torn my own life to pieces. So why should I not tear my life-work too——?

MRS. ELVSTED   And you did this last night?

LÖVBORG   Yes, I tell you! Tore it into a thousand pieces and scattered them on the fiord—far out. There there is cool sea-water at any rate—let them drift upon it—drift with the current and the wind. And then presently they will sink—deeper and deeper—as I shall, Thea.

MRS. ELVSTED   Do you know, Lövborg, that what you have done with the book —I shall think of it to my dying day as though you had killed a little child.

LÖVBORG   Yes, you are right. It is a sort of child-murder.

MRS. ELVSTED   How could you, then——! Did not the child belong to me too?

HEDDA (*almost inaudibly*)   Ah, the child——

MRS. ELVSTED (*breathing heavily*)   It is all over then. Well, well, now I will go, Hedda.

HEDDA   But you are not going away from town?

MRS. ELVSTED   Oh, I don't know what I shall do. I see nothing but darkness before me. (*She goes out by the hall door*)

HEDDA (*stands waiting for a moment*)   So you are not going to see her home, Mr. Lövborg?

LÖVBORG   I? Through the streets? Would you have people see her walking with me?

HEDDA   Of course I don't know what else may have happened last night. But is it so utterly irretrievable?

LÖVBORG   It will not end with last night—I know that perfectly well. And the thing is that now I have no taste for that sort of life either. I won't begin it anew. She has broken my courage and my power of braving life out.

HEDDA (*looking straight before her*)   So that pretty little fool has had her fingers in a man's destiny. (*Looks at him*) But all the same, how could you treat her so heartlessly?

LÖVBORG   Oh, don't say that it was heartless!

HEDDA   To go and destroy what has filled her whole soul for months and years! You do not call that heartless!

LÖVBORG   To you I can tell the truth, Hedda.

HEDDA   The truth?

LÖVBORG   First promise me—give me your word—that what I now confide to you Thea shall never know.

HEDDA   I give you my word.

LÖVBORG   Good. Then let me tell you that what I said just now was untrue.

HEDDA   About the manuscript?

LÖVBORG   Yes. I have not torn it to pieces—nor thrown it into the fiord.

HEDDA   No, n— But—where is it then?

LÖVBORG   I have destroyed it none the less—utterly destroyed it, Hedda!

HEDDA   I don't understand.

LÖVBORG   Thea said that what I had done seemed to her like a child-murder.

HEDDA   Yes, so she said.

LÖVBORG   But to kill his child—that is not the worst thing a father can do to it.

HEDDA   Not the worst?

LÖVBORG   No. I wanted to spare Thea from hearing the worst.

HEDDA   Then what is the worst?

LÖVBORG   Suppose now, Hedda, that a man—in the small hours of the morning —came home to his child's mother after a night of riot and debauchery, and said: "Listen—I have been here and there—in this place and in that. And I have taken our child with me—to this place and to that. And I have lost the child—utterly lost it. The devil knows into what hands it may have fallen—who may have had their clutches on it."

HEDDA   Well—but when all is said and done, you know—that was only a book——

LÖVBORG   Thea's pure soul was in that book.

HEDDA   Yes, so I understand.

LÖVBORG   And you can understand, too, that for her and me together no future is possible.

HEDDA   What path do you mean to take then?

LÖVBORG   None. I will only try to make an end of it all—the sooner the better.

HEDDA (a step nearer to him)   Eilert Lövborg—listen to me. Will you not try to —to do it beautifully?

LÖVBORG   Beautifully? (*Smiling*) With vine-leaves in my hair, as you used to dream in the old days——?

HEDDA   No, no. I have lost my faith in the vine-leaves. But beautifully, nevertheless! For once in a way!—Good-bye! You must go now—and do not come here any more.

LÖVBORG   Good-bye, Mrs. Tesman. And give George Tesman my love. (*He is on the point of going*)

HEDDA   No, wait! I must give you a memento to take with you.

(*She goes to the writing-table and opens the drawer and the pistol-case; then returns to* LÖVBORG *with one of the pistols*)

LÖVBORG (*looks at her*)   This? Is this the memento?

HEDDA (*nodding slowly*)   Do you recognize it? It was aimed at you once.

LÖVBORG   You should have used it then.

HEDDA   Take it—and do you use it now.

LÖVBORG (*puts the pistol in his breast pocket*)   Thanks!

HEDDA   And beautifully, Eilert Lövborg. Promise me that!

LÖVBORG   Good-bye, Hedda Gabler. (*He goes out by the hall door*)

(HEDDA *listens for a moment at the door. Then she goes up to the writing-table, takes out the packet of manuscript, peeps under the cover, draws a few of the sheets half out, and looks at them. Next she goes over and seats herself in the armchair beside the stove, with the packet in her lap. Presently she opens the stove door, and then the packet.*)

HEDDA (*throws one of the quires into the fire and whispers to herself*)   Now I am burning your child, Thea!—Burning it, curly-locks! (*Throwing one or two more quires into the stove*) Your child and Eilert Lövborg's. (*Throws the rest in*) I am burning —I am burning your child.

ACT IV

Scene: The same rooms at the TESMANS'. *It is evening. The drawing-room is in darkness. The back room is lighted by the hanging lamp over the table. The curtains over the glass door are drawn close.*

(HEDDA, *dressed in black, walks to and fro in the dark room. Then she goes into the back room and disappears for a moment to the left. She is heard to strike a few chords on the piano. Presently she comes in sight again, and returns to the drawing-room.*

BERTA *enters from the right, through the inner room, with a lighted lamp, which she places on the table in front of the corner settee in the drawing-room. Her eyes are red with weeping, and she has black ribbons in her cap. She goes quietly and circumspectly out to the right.*

HEDDA *goes up to the glass door, lifts the curtain a little aside, and looks out into the darkness.*

Shortly afterwards, MISS TESMAN, *in mourning, with a bonnet and veil on, comes in from the hall.* HEDDA *goes towards her and holds out her hand.*)

MISS TESMAN   Yes, Hedda, here I am, in mourning and forlorn; for now my poor sister has at last found peace.

HEDDA   I have heard the news already, as you see. Tesman sent me a card.

MISS TESMAN   Yes, he promised me he would. But nevertheless I thought that to Hedda—here in the house of life—I ought myself to bring the tidings of death.

HEDDA   That was very kind of you.

MISS TESMAN   Ah, Rina ought not to have left us just now. This is not the time for Hedda's house to be a house of mourning.

HEDDA (*changing the subject*)   She died quite peacefully, did she not, Miss Tesman?

MISS TESMAN   Oh, her end was so calm, so beautiful. And then she had the unspeakable happiness of seeing George once more—and bidding him good-bye. —Has he come home yet?

HEDDA   No. He wrote that he might be detained. But won't you sit down?

MISS TESMAN   No thank you, my dear, dear Hedda. I should like to, but I have so much to do. I must prepare my dear one for her rest as well as I can. She shall go to her grave looking her best.

HEDDA   Can I not help you in any way?

MISS TESMAN   Oh, you must not think of it! Hedda Tesman must have no hand in such mournful work. Nor let her thoughts dwell on it either—not at this time.

HEDDA   One is not always mistress of one's thoughts——

MISS TESMAN (*continuing*)   Ah yes, it is the way of the world. At home we shall be sewing a shroud; and here there will soon be sewing too, I suppose—but of another sort, thank God!

(GEORGE TESMAN *enters by the hall door*)

HEDDA   Ah, you have come at last!

TESMAN   You here, Aunt Julia? With Hedda? Fancy that!

MISS TESMAN   I was just going, my dear boy. Well, have you done all you promised?

TESMAN   No; I'm really afraid I have forgotten half of it. I must come to you again tomorrow. Today my brain is all in a whirl. I can't keep my thoughts together.

MISS TESMAN   Why, my dear George, you mustn't take it in this way.

TESMAN   Mustn't——? How do you mean?

MISS TESMAN   Even in your sorrow you must rejoice, as I do—rejoice that she is at rest.

TESMAN   Oh yes, yes—you are thinking of Aunt Rina.

HEDDA   You will feel lonely now, Miss Tesman.

MISS TESMAN   Just at first, yes. But that will not last very long, I hope. I daresay I shall soon find an occupant for poor Rina's little room.

TESMAN   Indeed? Who do you think will take it? Eh?

MISS TESMAN   Oh, there's always some poor invalid or other in want of nursing, unfortunately.

HEDDA   Would you really take such a burden upon you again?

MISS TESMAN   A burden! Heaven forgive you, child—it has been no burden to me.

HEDDA   But suppose you had a total stranger on your hands——

MISS TESMAN   Oh, one soon makes friends with sick folk; and it's such an absolute necessity for me to have someone to live for. Well, heaven be praised, there may soon be something in this house, too, to keep an old aunt busy.

HEDDA   Oh, don't trouble about anything here.

TESMAN   Yes, just fancy what a nice time we three might have together, if——?

HEDDA   If——?

TESMAN   (*uneasily*)   Oh, nothing. It will all come right. Let us hope so—eh?

MISS TESMAN   Well, well, I daresay you two want to talk to each other. (*Smiling*) And perhaps Hedda may have something to tell you too, George. Good-bye! I must go home to Rina. (*Turning at the door*) How strange it is to think that now Rina is with me and with my poor brother as well!

TESMAN   Yes, fancy that, Aunt Julia! Eh?

(*Miss* TESMAN *goes out by the hall door*)

HEDDA (*follows* TESMAN *coldly and searchingly with her eyes*)   I almost believe your Aunt Rina's death affects you more than it does your Aunt Julia.

TESMAN   Oh, it's not that alone. It's Eilert I am so terribly uneasy about.

HEDDA (*quickly*)   Is there anything new about him?

TESMAN   I looked in at his rooms this afternoon, intending to tell him the manuscript was in safe keeping.

HEDDA   Well, did you not find him?

TESMAN   No. He wasn't at home. But afterwards I met Mrs. Elvsted, and she told me that he had been here early this morning.

HEDDA   Yes, directly after you had gone.

TESMAN   And he said that he had torn his manuscript to pieces—eh?

HEDDA   Yes, so he declared.

TESMAN Why, good heavens, he must have been completely out of his mind! And I suppose you thought it best not to give it back to him, Hedda?

HEDDA No, he did not get it.

TESMAN But of course you told him that we had it?

HEDDA No. (*Quickly*) Did you tell Mrs. Elvsted?

TESMAN No; I thought I had better not. But you ought to have told him. Fancy, if, in desperation, he should go and do himself some injury! Let me have the manuscript, Hedda! I will take it to him at once. Where is it?

HEDDA (*cold and immovable, leaning on the armchair*) I have not got it.

TESMAN Have not got it? What in the world do you mean?

HEDDA I have burnt it—every line of it.

TESMAN (*with a violent movement of terror*) Burnt! Burnt Eilert's manuscript!

HEDDA Don't scream so. The servant might hear you.

TESMAN Burnt! Why, good God——! No, no, no! It's impossible!

HEDDA It is so, nevertheless.

TESMAN Do you know what you have done, Hedda? It's unlawful appropriation of lost property. Fancy that! Just ask Judge Brack, and he'll tell you what it is.

HEDDA I advise you not to speak of it—either to Judge Brack, or to any one else.

TESMAN But how could you do anything so unheard-of? What put it into your head? What possessed you? Answer me that—eh?

HEDDA (*suppressing an almost imperceptible smile*) I did it for your sake, George.

TESMAN For my sake!

HEDDA This morning, when you told me about what he had read to you——

TESMAN Yes, yes—what then?

HEDDA You acknowledged that you envied him his work.

TESMAN Oh, of course I didn't mean that literally.

HEDDA No matter—I could not bear the idea that any one should throw you into the shade.

TESMAN (*in an outburst of mingled doubt and joy*) Hedda! Oh, is this true? But—but—I never knew you to show your love like that before. Fancy that!

HEDDA Well, I may as well tell you that—just at this time—— (*Impatiently, breaking off*) No, no; you can ask Aunt Julia. She will tell you, fast enough.

TESMAN Oh, I almost think I understand you, Hedda! (*Clasps his hands together*) Great heavens! do you really mean it! Eh?

HEDDA Don't shout so. The servant might hear.

TESMAN (*laughing in irrepressible glee*) The servant! Why, how absurd you are, Hedda. It's only my old Berta! Why, I'll tell Berta myself.

HEDDA (*clenching her hands together in desperation*) Oh, it is killing me,—it is killing me, all this!

TESMAN What is, Hedda? Eh?

HEDDA (*coldly, controlling herself*) All this—absurdity—George.

TESMAN Absurdity! Do you see anything absurd in my being overjoyed at the news! But after all perhaps I had better not say anything to Berta.

HEDDA Oh—why not that too?

TESMAN No, no, not yet! But I must certainly tell Aunt Julia. And then that you have begun to call me George too! Fancy that! Oh, Aunt Julia will be so happy —so happy.

HEDDA When she hears that I have burnt Eilert Lövborg's manuscript—for your sake?

TESMAN No, by-the-bye—that affair of the manuscript—of course nobody must know about that. But that you love me so much, Hedda—Aunt Julia must really share my joy in that! I wonder, now, whether this sort of thing is usual in young wives? Eh?

HEDDA I think you had better ask Aunt Julia that question too.

TESMAN I will indeed, some time or other. (*Looks uneasy and downcast again*) And yet the manuscript—the manuscript! Good God! it is terrible to think what will become of poor Eilert now.

(MRS. ELVSTED, *dressed as in the first act, with hat and cloak, enters by the hall door*)

MRS. ELVSTED (*greets them hurriedly, and says in evident agitation*) Oh, dear Hedda, forgive my coming again.

HEDDA What is the matter with you, Thea?

TESMAN Something about Eilert Lövborg again—eh?

MRS. ELVSTED Yes! I am dreadfully afraid some misfortune has happened to him.

HEDDA (*seizes her arm*) Ah,—do you think so?

TESMAN Why, good Lord—what makes you think that, Mrs. Elvsted?

MRS. ELVSTED I heard them talking of him at my boarding-house—just as I came in. Oh, the most incredible rumors are afloat about him to-day.

TESMAN Yes, fancy, so I heard too! And I can bear witness that he went straight home to bed last night. Fancy that!

HEDDA Well, what did they say at the boarding-house?

MRS. ELVSTED Oh, I couldn't make out anything clearly. Either they knew nothing definite, or else—— They stopped talking when they saw me; and I did not dare to ask.

TESMAN (*moving about uneasily*) We must hope—we must hope that you misunderstood them, Mrs. Elvsted.

MRS. ELVSTED   No, no; I am sure it was of him they were talking. And I heard something about the hospital or——

TESMAN   The hospital?

HEDDA   No—surely that cannot be!

MRS. ELVSTED   Oh, I was in such mortal terror! I went to his lodgings and asked for him there.

HEDDA   You could make up your mind to that, Thea!

MRS. ELVSTED   What else could I do? I really could bear the suspense no longer.

TESMAN   But you didn't find him either—eh?

MRS. ELVSTED   No. And the people knew nothing about him. He hadn't been home since yesterday afternoon, they said.

TESMAN   Yesterday! Fancy, how could they say that?

MRS. ELVSTED   Oh, I am sure something terrible must have happened to him.

TESMAN   Hedda dear—how would it be if I were to go and make inquiries——?

HEDDA   No, no—don't you mix yourself up in this affair.

(JUDGE BRACK, *with his hat in his hand, enters by the hall door, which* BERTA *opens, and closes behind him. He looks grave and bows in silence.*)

TESMAN   Oh, is that you, my dear Judge? Eh?

BRACK   Yes. It was imperative I should see you this evening.

TESMAN   I can see you have heard the news about Aunt Rina.

BRACK   Yes, that among other things.

TESMAN   Isn't it sad—eh?

BRACK   Well, my dear Tesman, that depends on how you look at it.

TESMAN (*looks doubtfully at him*)   Has anything else happened?

BRACK   Yes.

HEDDA (*in suspense*)   Anything sad, Judge Brack?

BRACK   That, too, depends on how you look at it, Mrs. Tesman.

MRS. ELVSTED (*unable to restrain her anxiety*)   Oh! it is something about Eilert Lövborg!

BRACK (*with a glance at her*)   What makes you think that, Madam? Perhaps you have already heard something——?

MRS. ELVSTED (*in confusion*)   No, nothing at all, but——

TESMAN   Oh, for heaven's sake, tell us!

BRACK (*shrugging his shoulders*)   Well, I regret to say Eilert Lövborg has been taken to the hospital. He is lying at the point of death.

MRS. ELVSTED (*shrieks*) Oh God! Oh God——

TESMAN To the hospital! And at the point of death.

HEDDA (*involuntarily*) So soon then——

MRS. ELVSTED (*wailing*) And we parted in anger, Hedda!

HEDDA (*whispers*) Thea—Thea—be careful!

MRS. ELVSTED (*not heeding her*) I must go to him! I must see him alive!

BRACK It is useless, Madam. No one will be admitted.

MRS. ELVSTED Oh, at least tell me what has happened to him? What is it?

TESMAN You don't mean to say that he has himself—— Eh?

HEDDA Yes, I am sure he has.

TESMAN Hedda, how can you——?

BRACK (*keeping his eyes fixed upon her*) Unfortunately you have guessed quite correctly, Mrs. Tesman.

MRS. ELVSTED Oh, how horrible!

TESMAN Himself, then! Fancy that!

HEDDA Shot himself!

BRACK Rightly guessed again, Mrs. Tesman.

MRS. ELVSTED (*with an effort at self-control*) When did it happen, Mr. Brack?

BRACK This afternoon—between three and four.

TESMAN But, good Lord, where did he do it? Eh?

BRACK (*with some hesitation*) Where? Well—I suppose at his lodgings.

MRS. ELVSTED No, that cannot be; for I was there between six and seven.

BRACK Well, then, somewhere else. I don't know exactly. I only know that he was found——. He had shot himself—in the breast.

MRS. ELVSTED Oh, how terrible! That he should die like that!

HEDDA (*to Brack*) Was it in the breast?

BRACK Yes—as I told you.

HEDDA Not in the temple?

BRACK In the breast, Mrs. Tesman.

HEDDA Well, well—the breast is a good place, too.

BRACK How do you mean, Mrs. Tesman?

HEDDA (*evasively*) Oh, nothing—nothing.

TESMAN And the wound is dangerous, you say—eh?

BRACK Absolutely mortal. The end has probably come by this time.

MRS. ELVSTED Yes, yes, I feel it. The end! The end! Oh, Hedda——!

TESMAN But tell me, how have you learnt all this?

BRACK (*curtly*)   Through one of the police. A man I had some business with.

HEDDA (*in a clear voice*)   At last a deed worth doing!

TESMAN (*terrified*)   Good heavens, Hedda; what are you saying?

HEDDA   I say there is beauty in this.

BRACK   H'm, Mrs. Tesman——

TESMAN   Beauty! Fancy that!

MRS. ELVSTED   Oh, Hedda, how can you talk of beauty in such an act!

HEDDA   Eilert Lövborg has himself made up his account with life. He has had the courage to do—the one right thing.

MRS. ELVSTED   No, you must never think that was how it happened! It must have been in delirium that he did it.

TESMAN   In despair!

HEDDA   That he did not. I am certain of that.

MRS. ELVSTED   Yes, yes! In delirium! Just as when he tore up our manuscript.

BRACK (*starting*)   The manuscript? Has he torn that up?

MRS. ELVSTED   Yes, last night.

TESMAN (*whispers softly*)   Oh, Hedda, we shall never get over this.

BRACK   H'm, very extraordinary.

TESMAN (*moving about the room*)   To think of Eilert going out of the world in this way! And not leaving behind him the book that would have immortalized his name——

MRS. ELVSTED   Oh, if only it could be put together again!

TESMAN   Yes, if it only could! I don't know what I would not give——

MRS. ELVSTED   Perhaps it can, Mr. Tesman.

TESMAN   What do you mean?

MRS. ELVSTED (*searches in the pocket of her dress*)   Look here. I have kept all the loose notes he used to dictate from.

HEDDA (*a step forward*)   Ah——!

TESMAN   You have kept them, Mrs. Elvsted! Eh?

MRS. ELVSTED   Yes, I have them here. I put them in my pocket when I left home. Here they still are——

TESMAN   Oh, do let me see them!

MRS. ELVSTED (*hands him a bundle of papers*)   But they are in such disorder—all mixed up.

TESMAN   Fancy, if we could make something out of them, after all! Perhaps if we two put our heads together——

MRS. ELVSTED   Oh, yes, at least let us try——

862

TESMAN   We will manage it! We must! I will dedicate my life to this task.

HEDDA   You, George! Your life?

TESMAN   Yes, or rather all the time I can spare. My own collections must wait in the meantime. Hedda—you understand, eh? I owe this to Eilert's memory.

HEDDA   Perhaps.

TESMAN   And so, my dear Mrs. Elvsted, we will give our whole minds to it. There is no use in brooding over what can't be undone—eh? We must try to control our grief as much as possible, and——

MRS. ELVSTED   Yes, yes, Mr. Tesman, I will do the best I can.

TESMAN   Well then, come here. I can't rest until we have looked through the notes. Where shall we sit? Here? No, in there, in the back room. Excuse me, my dear Judge. Come with me, Mrs. Elvsted.

MRS. ELVSTED   Oh, if only it were possible!

(TESMAN *and* MRS. ELVSTED *go into the back room. She takes off her hat and cloak. They both sit at the table under the hanging lamp, and are soon deep in an eager examination of the papers.* HEDDA *crosses to the stove and sits in the armchair. Presently* BRACK *goes up to her.*)

HEDDA (*in a low voice*)   Oh, what a sense of freedom it gives one, this act of Eilert Lövborg's.

BRACK   Freedom, Mrs. Hedda? Well, of course, it is a release for him——

HEDDA   I mean for me. It gives me a sense of freedom to know that a deed of deliberate courage is still possible in this world,—a deed of spontaneous beauty.

BRACK (*smiling*)   H'm—my dear Mrs. Hedda——

HEDDA   Oh, I know what you are going to say. For you are a kind of a specialist too, like—you know!

BRACK (*looking hard at her*)   Eilert Lövborg was more to you than perhaps you are willing to admit to yourself. Am I wrong?

HEDDA   I don't answer such questions. I only know Eilert Lövborg has had the courage to live his life after his own fashion. And then—the last great act, with its beauty! Ah! that he should have the will and the strength to turn away from the banquet of life—so early.

BRACK   I am sorry, Mrs. Hedda,—but I fear I must dispel an amiable illusion.

HEDDA   Illusion.

BRACK   Which could not have lasted long in any case.

HEDDA   What do you mean?

BRACK   Eilert Lövborg did not shoot himself voluntarily.

HEDDA   Not voluntarily?

BRACK   No. The thing did not happen exactly as I told it.

HEDDA (*in suspense*)   Have you concealed something? What is it?

BRACK   For poor Mrs. Elvsted's sake I idealized the facts a little.

HEDDA   What are the facts?

BRACK   First, that he is already dead.

HEDDA   At the hospital?

BRACK   Yes—without regaining consciousness.

HEDDA   What more have you concealed?

BRACK   This—the event did not happen at his lodgings.

HEDDA   Oh, that can make no difference.

BRACK   Perhaps it may. For I must tell you—Eilert Lövborg was found shot in —in Mademoiselle Diana's boudoir.

HEDDA (*makes a motion as if to rise, but sinks back again*)   That is impossible, Judge Brack! He cannot have been there again today.

BRACK   He was there this afternoon. He went there, he said, to demand the return of something which they had taken from him. Talked wildly about a lost child——

HEDDA   Ah—so that was why——

BRACK   I thought probably he meant his manuscript; but now I hear he destroyed that himself. So I suppose it must have been his pocketbook.

HEDDA   Yes, no doubt. And there—there he was found?

BRACK   Yes, there. With a pistol in his breast-pocket, discharged. The ball had lodged in a vital part.

HEDDA   In the breast—yes.

BRACK   No—in the bowels.

HEDDA (*looks up at him with an expression of loathing*)   That too! Oh, what curse is it that makes everything I touch turn ludicrous and mean?

BRACK   There is one point more, Mrs. Hedda—another disagreeable feature in the affair.

HEDDA   And what is that?

BRACK   The pistol he carried——

HEDDA (*breathless*)   Well? What of it?

BRACK   He must have stolen it.

HEDDA (*leaps up*)   Stolen it! That is not true! He did not steal it!

BRACK   No other explanation is possible. He must have stolen it—— Hush!

(TESMAN *and* MRS. ELVSTED *have risen from the table in the back room, and come into the drawing room*)

TESMAN (*with the papers in both his hands*)   Hedda dear, it is almost impossible to see under that lamp. Think of that!

HEDDA   Yes, I am thinking.

TESMAN   Would you mind our sitting at your writing-table—eh?

HEDDA   If you like. (*Quickly*) No, wait! Let me clear it first!

TESMAN   Oh, you needn't trouble, Hedda. There is plenty of room.

HEDDA   No, no; let me clear it, I say! I will take these things in and put them on the piano. There!

(*She has drawn out an object, covered with sheet music, from under the bookcase, places several other pieces of music upon it, and carries the whole into the inner room, to the left. TESMAN lays the scraps of paper on the writing-table, and moves the lamp there from the corner table. HEDDA returns.*)

HEDDA (*behind* MRS. ELVSTED'S *chair, gently ruffling her hair*)   Well, my sweet Thea,—how goes it with Eilert Lövborg's monument?

MRS. ELVSTED (*looks dispiritedly up at her*)   Oh, it will be terribly hard to put in order.

TESMAN   We must manage it. I am determined. And arranging other people's papers is just the work for me.

(HEDDA *goes over to the stove, and seats herself on one of the foot-stools.* BRACK *stands over her, leaning on the armchair*)

HEDDA (*whispers*)   What did you say about the pistol?

BRACK (*softly*)   That he must have stolen it.

HEDDA   Why stolen it?

BRACK   Because every other explanation ought to be impossible, Mrs. Hedda.

HEDDA   Indeed?

BRACK (*glances at her*)   Of course Eilert Lövborg was here this morning. Was he not?

HEDDA   Yes.

BRACK   Were you alone with him?

HEDDA   Part of the time.

BRACK   Did you not leave the room whilst he was here?

HEDDA   No.

BRACK   Try to recollect. Were you not out of the room a moment?

HEDDA   Yes, perhaps just a moment—out in the hall.

BRACK   And where was your pistol-case during that time?

HEDDA   I had it locked up in——

BRACK   Well, Mrs. Hedda?

HEDDA   The case stood there on the writing-table.

BRACK   Have you looked since, to see whether both the pistols are there?

HEDDA   No.

BRACK   Well, you need not. I saw the pistol found in Lövborg's pocket, and I knew it at once as the one I had seen yesterday—and before, too.

HEDDA   Have you it with you?

BRACK   No; the police have it.

HEDDA   What will the police do with it?

BRACK   Search till they find the owner.

HEDDA   Do you think they will succeed?

BRACK   (*bends over her and whispers*)   No, Hedda Gabler—not so long as I say nothing.

HEDDA   (*looks frightened at him*)   And if you do not say nothing,—what then?

BRACK   (*shrugs his shoulders*)   There is always the possibility that the pistol was stolen.

HEDDA   (*firmly*)   Death rather than that.

BRACK   (*smiling*)   People say such things—but they don't do them.

HEDDA   (*without replying*)   And supposing the pistol was stolen, and the owner is discovered? What then?

BRACK   Well, Hedda—then comes the scandal.

HEDDA   The scandal!

BRACK   Yes, the scandal—of which you are mortally afraid. You will, of course, be brought before the court—both you and Mademoiselle Diana. She will have to explain how the thing happened—whether it was an accidental shot or murder. Did the pistol go off as he was trying to take it out of his pocket, to threaten her with? Or did she tear the pistol out of his hand, shoot him, and push it back into his pocket? That would be quite like her; for she is an able-bodied young person, this same Mademoiselle Diana.

HEDDA   But *I* have nothing to do with all this repulsive business.

BRACK   No. But you will have to answer the question: Why did you give Eilert Lövborg the pistol? And what conclusions will people draw from the fact that you did give it to him?

HEDDA   (*lets her head sink*)   That is true. I did not think of that.

BRACK   Well, fortunately, there is no danger, so long as I say nothing.

HEDDA   (*looks up at him*)   So I am in your power, Judge Brack. You have me at your beck and call, from this time forward.

BRACK   (*whispers softly*)   Dearest Hedda—believe me—I shall not abuse my advantage.

HEDDA   I am in your power none the less. Subject to your will and your demands. A slave, a slave then! (*Rises impetuously*) No, I cannot endure the thought of that! Never!

866

BRACK (*looks half-mockingly at her*) People generally get used to the inevitable.

HEDDA (*returns his look*) Yes, perhaps. (*She crosses to the writing-table. Suppressing an involuntary smile, she imitates* TESMAN'S *intonations.*) Well? Are you getting on, George? Eh?

TESMAN Heaven knows, dear. In any case it will be the work of months.

HEDDA (*as before*) Fancy that! (*Passes her hands softly through* MRS. ELVSTED'S *hair*) Doesn't it seem strange to you, Thea? Here are you sitting with Tesman—just as you used to sit with Eilert Lövborg?

MRS. ELVSTED Ah, if I could only inspire your husband in the same way.

HEDDA Oh, that will come too—in time.

TESMAN Yes, do you know, Hedda—I really think I begin to feel something of the sort. But won't you go and sit with Brack again?

HEDDA Is there nothing I can do to help you two?

TESMAN No, nothing in the world. (*Turning his head*) I trust to you to keep Hedda company, my dear Brack.

BRACK (*with a glance at* HEDDA) With the very greatest of pleasure.

HEDDA Thanks. But I am tired this evening. I will go in and lie down a little on the sofa.

TESMAN Yes, do dear—eh?

(HEDDA *goes into the back room and draws the curtains. A short pause. Suddenly she is heard playing a wild dance on the piano.*)

MRS. ELVSTED (*starts from her chair*) Oh—what is that?

TESMAN (*runs to the doorway*) Why, my dearest Hedda—don't play dance music tonight! Just think of Aunt Rina! And of Eilert too!

HEDDA (*puts her head out between the curtains*) And of Aunt Julia. And of all the rest of them.—After this, I will be quiet. (*Closes the curtains again*)

TESMAN (*at the writing-table*) It's not good for her to see us at this distressing work. I'll tell you what, Mrs. Elvsted,—you shall take the empty room at Aunt Julia's, and then I will come over in the evenings, and we can sit and work there —eh?

HEDDA (*in the inner room*) I hear what you are saying, Tesman. But how am *I* to get through the evenings out here?

TESMAN (*turning over the papers*) Oh, I dare say Judge Brack will be so kind as to look in now and then, even though I am out.

BRACK (*in the armchair, calls out gaily*) Every blessed evening, with all the pleasure in life, Mrs. Tesman! We shall get on capitally together, we two!

HEDDA (*speaking loud and clear*) Yes, don't you flatter yourself we will, Judge Brack? Now that you are the one cock in the basket——

867

(*A shot is heard within.* TESMAN, MRS. ELVSTED, *and* BRACK *leap to their feet.*)

TESMAN Oh, now she is playing with those pistols again.

(*He throws back the curtains and runs in, followed by* MRS. ELVSTED. HEDDA *lies stretched on the sofa, lifeless. Confusion and cries.* BERTA *enters in alarm from the right.*)

TESMAN (*shrieks to* BRACK) Shot herself! Shot herself in the temple! Fancy that!

BRACK (*half-fainting in the armchair*) Good God!—people don't do such things.

DISCUSSION TOPICS

1. The play *Hedda Gabler* has a number of scenes that can be especially effective when acted out on stage. One of the most outstanding is Hedda's burning of the manuscript. Which other scenes do you think would give a director and cast special opportunities to present character, or to build tension, or to reveal themes? As a reader rather than a viewer, how do you see these scenes in the "theater of your mind"?

2. Hedda, like the woman in Chekhov's *The Marriage Proposal*, is faced (before her marriage to George Tesman) with the possibility of being unmarried well after the proper matrimonial age. How do the social milieu and the era of the play's setting contribute to Hedda's actions? What economic factors enter into the action of the play itself?

3. Summarize Hedda's attitude toward each of the other women in the play. Are the attitudes different in any respect? How does Ibsen use these attitudes to help us understand Hedda?

4. What are Hedda's relationships with the various men in the play? Again, are they different from one person to the other, or much the same? What do these relationships reveal about Hedda?

5. What do we know of Hedda's parents? What does that knowledge contribute to our interpretation of Hedda? Why is the father's portrait important? And why are his pistols a recurrent device in the play?

6. What evidence is there that Hedda suffers from a confused sense of her own identity? Why does she have difficulty coping with motherhood, both in general and specifically with her own pregnancy? Does she have lesbian tendencies?

7. What characteristics does Thea share with the archetypal good mother? What is Ibsen's dramatic purpose in endowing her with these characteristics?

8. Eilert represents for Hedda the romantic side of life, the world of excitement, energy, beauty. Seek out those passages that seem to develop this notion and seem to fit the concept of the libido or the Freudian concepts of the id and the pleasure principle. How, for example, is Dionysus (Bacchus) an element of the play's symbolism?

9. In what ways—social pressures, characters, conscience—does the superego or morality principle manifest itself in this play?

10. What are Tesman's speech mannerisms? What does Ibsen tell us about his character through those speech patterns?

11. If you were the director of a staging of *Hedda Gabler,* what kind of physical build would you want in the person who acts the role of Judge Brack? How would you have him talk? Walk? What does the imagery associated with him suggest?

12. The plot structure of this play follows what is fairly common in traditional full length plays—a rising or complicating action, a crisis or turn, and a falling action or resolution. What are the early complications in the play? What specific actions or revelations in Act IV lead, detail by detail, to Hedda's suicide? At the end of Act III, two actions by Hedda are effective on stage —giving Eilert one of the pistols and burning the manuscript. Which action is more important in precipitating the falling action of Act IV?

Anton Chekhov (1860–1904) Russian dramatist and short story writer. His most famous dramas include *Three Sisters, The Cherry Orchard, The Sea Gull,* and *Uncle Vanya.* He also wrote popular farces. *The Proposal* (or *The Marriage Proposal*) was written in 1888.

THE MARRIAGE PROPOSAL

Translated by Irina Prishvin and X. J. Kennedy

Characters

STEPAN STEPANOVICH CHUBUKOV, a rich landowner.
IVAN VASSILEVICH LOMOV, a younger man, neighbor of Chubukov. Although he is in excellent health, he imagines himself to be ailing.
NATALIA STEPANOVNA, Chubukov's unmarried daughter, twenty-five years old.

Scene: The main room in Chubukov's mansion. Lomov enters in a tuxedo and white gloves.

CHUBUKOV (*rising to greet him*): Why, Lomov, you of all people! (*Pumps Lomov's hand.*) You're a sight for sore eyes, young fellow—how are you?

LOMOV: Oh, no use complaining. And you?

CHUBUKOV: We're still alive, my poor old daughter and me. Why haven't you been to see us? Pull up a chair. But what's this? What are you doing in that get-up? Look at you! Tuxedo, black tie, gloves, et cetera. What's happened? Are you going to be somebody's pall-bearer?

LOMOV (*sitting*): No, no, nothing like that. I've dressed to come and see you.

CHUBUKOV (*incredulously*): To see *me?* Then why the special get-up, old friend? You look like a caterer on New Year's Eve.

LOMOV: You see, it's like this. (*He leans closer.*) I've come, Stepan Stepanovich, to ask a favor of you. Oh, I know you've helped me often in the past, but this is different. You see—oh, I'm so nervous I'm shaking. Excuse me, Stepan Stepanovich, I'll just drink a little water. (*Pours himself some water from a pitcher and gulps, gargling it.*)

CHUBUKOV (*to himself*): Why, the sly dog, he's come to ask for a loan. Should I give it to him? Not a chance! (*Aloud.*) Well, what can I do for you, old friend?

LOMOV: I'll tell you, old neighbor—forgive me, I don't mean you're *old.* I mean —oh, Lord, now I'm all mixed up. What I mean is, you're the only one that can help me. Oh, I know I'm a pitiful worm, I don't deserve it—

CHUBUKOV: Don't deserve what? For God's sake, quit beating around the bush. Spit it out, man, spit it out!

LOMOV: Very well. I'll spit it *right* out. I've come—I've come to ask you for Natalia's hand in marriage.

CHUBUKOV: Ivan Vassilevich, are you serious? Say that again—I don't trust these old ears.

LOMOV: I hereby request the hand. . . .

CHUBUKOV (*butting in*): Son-in-law! Sweet boy! Et cetera! (*Jumping up and giving him a bear-hug.*) For years—years!—I've been waiting for this moment. I always said it would make sense for you and Natalia to tie the knot, seeing as our two properties abut. I'm so glad I could cry! (*Dabs a tear.*) God bless your marriage bed, have a whole army of children. Why am I standing here blithering? What news! You could knock me over with a feather. I've got to call Natalia.

LOMOV: Oh dear. Tell me, Stepan Stepanovich, what do you think she'll say? Will she have me?

CHUBUKOV: Have you? How could she possibly say no to a handsome, good-looking, et cetera? Why, she's crazy about you. Don't go away! I'll run and fetch her. (*He exits.*)

LOMOV: Ugh, it's cold in here. I'm shaking like a leaf. I've got butterflies in my stomach as if I was going to take a final examination. Decisive, that's what I've got to be. Don't dare think. Think too long, keep waiting for the perfect woman, wait for true love to come along, and I'll never get married at all. Brrrr, it's like an ice-box. Natalia Stepanovna is a good housekeeper, she was always on the honor roll at school, and as for looks—well, I've seen worse. What more could anybody want? I'm so scared there's a buzzing in my ears. (*Gulps more water.*) Anyway, I absolutely have got to get married. Here I am, thirty-five—a dangerous age. If I don't get married now, I never will. Besides, I should settle down, quit running around, take better care of myself. This heart murmur of mine. The palpitations. I'm always getting excited and blowing up. One of these days I might keel right over. See, even now I can't hold my hand steady. And there's that twitch in my right eyebrow again. Trying to sleep at night, that's the worst. Every time I start to drop off—yow! pain shoots through my left side and wakes me up again. Ouch! It travels to my shoulder. It makes for my head. I have to jump out of bed like a crazy man and run around the room. I work the thing off and lie back down. I no sooner go back to sleep than—yow! there it goes again! Sometimes it hits me twenty times a night.

NATALIA (*entering*): Oh. It's you. Papa told me there was a buyer here, come to pick up his goods. Hello, Ivan Vassilevich.

LOMOV (*rising*): How—how are you, Natalia?

NATALIA: Don't mind my apron. We've been shelling peas. Where have you been keeping yourself? Sit down. (*They sit.*) Will you have lunch?

LOMOV: No thanks, I'm full.

NATALIA: Smoke if you like. There are matches on the table. Nice weather we've been having. Better than yesterday, I mean—all that rain. Our men couldn't cut hay. How is it going at your place? How many stacks have you finished? The day before yesterday I got anxious to see it all done, so I had a whole field cut, and now I could just kick myself, because the hay got rained on and now it will probably rot. I should have let them wait. Say, why are you wearing that tuxedo? You look great in it. Come on, tell me, why are you all dressed up? Is there a party?

LOMOV (*agitatedly*):   Well you see it's this way, my dear Natalia Stepanovna. To make a long story short I've made up my mind to ask you to listen to me. Now perhaps this will come as a surprise to you, perhaps you won't like the idea at first, and you'll be angry. Anyway. . . . (*Aside.*) Damn! it's cold in here!

NATALIA: What's the matter with you? (*Pause, while Lomov sits silently squirming.*) Will you please explain yourself?

LOMOV: All right. I'll come to the point. You remember, Natalia Stepanovna, that ever since you and I were children, I've been proud to consider myself a friend of your family. My aunt that's now dead, and her husband—you know, the ones that left me their estate—always thought the world of your father and your mother when she was alive. In business, the Lomovs and the Chubukovs have always been thick as thieves, and I believe they think a lot of each other. And after all, my land borders yours. Why, my White Ox Meadows run right up to your birch woods, and. . . .

NATALIA: Excuse me, did you say *your* White Ox Meadows?

LOMOV: That's right. *My* meadows.

NATALIA: What do you mean? The White Ox Meadows are ours, not yours.

LOMOV: Now just hold on a minute, Natalia Stepanovna. You know they're mine, and they always will be.

NATALIA: Well, that's news to me! What gives you the right to claim our meadows?

LOMOV: What gives *me* . . . ? See here now, it's the White Ox Meadows I'm talking about—the ones in between your birch woods and the swamp.

NATALIA: That's what I thought you meant. They're ours.

LOMOV: I'm sorry to have to put you straight, Natalia Stepanovna, but they're mine just as plain as the nose on your face.

NATALIA: You're out of your mind. Since when have they been yours?

LOMOV: Since when? Since as long as my family goes back. Since as long as I can remember.

NATALIA: Stop talking nonsense, Ivan Vassilevich.

LOMOV: You can look at the deed, my dear Natalia. It's true there was once an argument over those meadows, but now that's all past and the whole town knows they're mine. Why are you arguing? Listen, here's how it was—my aunt's grandmother let your great-grandfather's peasants graze their oxen on those meadows, rent free, for as long as they'd make bricks for her. Forty years went by, and your great-grandfather's peasants got so used to working those meadows, they forgot and thought they owned them, when the truth was. . . .

NATALIA: No, no, that wasn't how it was at all. My grandfather and his father took a survey of that land, and they claimed it all the way to the swamp, which means the White Ox Meadows are ours. There's nothing to argue about. You're just being difficult.

LOMOV: The deed, Natalia Stepanovna, I can show you the deed!

NATALIA: You must be joking. For three hundred years that land has been in our family, and now you come along and say it isn't ours. What sort of fool do you take me for? It's not that those meadows are worth anything, really—maybe three, four hundred rubles—it's just that I can't stand cheating. I won't be cheated. I won't!

LOMOV: (*losing his temper*): Will you calm down and listen to me? Your great-grandfather's peasants baked my aunt's grandmother's bricks, and my aunt's grandmother, out of the goodness of her heart. . . .

NATALIA: I don't care about your aunt's grandmother's bricks! The meadows belong to us and that's final!

LOMOV: They're *my* meadows.

NATALIA: They're ours! You can talk till you're blue in the face, you can go home and put on fifteen tuxedoes if you like, but you can't change a thing—those meadows are ours, ours, ours! I don't want anything of yours, and you're not going to get anything of mine!

LOMOV: The meadows mean nothing to me, Natalia Stepanovna. I'm simply defending what belongs to me. You can take the meadows, if it'll make you happy —I'll make you a gift of them.

NATALIA: *You?* Give them to *me?* I'm the one that ought to do the giving. I must say, Ivan Vassilevich, you're certainly acting strangely. Up till now I've always thought of you as a good neighbor, a true friend. Why, only last year didn't we lend you our only threshing machine even though it meant we couldn't thresh our own wheat till November? And now here you are treating us like a band of gypsies trying to rob you. Making me a present of my own family's land! What a neighbor you are! You've got a lot of nerve, if you ask me.

LOMOV: What do you take me for, a swindler? I've never tried to take anybody else's land in my life, and I'm not going to stand for your accusations. (*Hurries to the pitcher, pours more water, and gulps.*) The White Ox Meadows are mine!

NATALIA: That's a lie! They're ours!

LOMOV: They're mine. Mine, mine, I say!

NATALIA: Never! I'll show you—I'll send my men to mow those meadows before sundown!

LOMOV: What's that you said?

NATALIA: You'll see. My mowers will be out there in five minutes, swinging their scythes.

LOMOV: I'll take a shotgun to them!

NATALIA: Just you try it!

LOMOV (*clapping a hand to his heart*): The White Ox Meadows are mine! Understand? Mine!

NATALIA: Keep your voice down. When you're in your own house you can rant and rave and roar yourself hoarse, but when you're in my house you can talk like a human being.

LOMOV: If it wasn't for these stabbing pains in my side and my splitting headache, I'd give you a roar that would blow your ears out. (*Shouts.*) The White Ox Meadows are mine!

NATALIA: Ours!

LOMOV: Mine!

NATALIA: Ours!

LOMOV: Mine! Mine!

CHUBUKOV (*entering*): Here, here, what's all the shouting about?

NATALIA: Papa, will you please explain to this gentleman who the White Ox Meadows belong to, us or him?

CHUBUKOV (*to Lomov*): Why, they're ours, my friend, as you well know.

LOMOV: Now see here, Stepan Stepanovich, will you listen to reason? My aunt's grandmother let your grandfather's peasants use those meadows for free, temporarily. The peasants used that land for forty years and started thinking it was their own. But after the Emancipation. . . .

CHUBUKOV: Oh come on now, old friend, aren't you forgetting something? The reason the peasants didn't pay rent to your aunt's grandmother was that nobody was sure the meadows belonged to her, and there was a big fuss, et cetera. But today, why even the pigs and goats know that that land is Chubukov's. I guess you haven't looked at the deed lately.

LOMOV: I—I can prove to you those meadows are mine.

CHUBUKOV: You'll have a hard time proving that.

LOMOV: I can show it to you in black and white.

CHUBUKOV: Well then what are you shouting for? Do you think you can have my meadows just by shouting for 'em? I'm not out to get anything of yours, and you're not going to get what's mine. If you're going to make a big fuss about those meadows, I'd sooner give 'em to the peasants than I'd give 'em to you. Got that straight, et cetera?

LOMOV: Now wait a minute. Since when do you think you can steal somebody else's land and give it to your stinking peasants?

CHUBUKOV: Leave that for me to decide. And you'd better get another thing clear, young fellow—I'm not used to anybody marching into my own house and bawling me out, et cetera. Not to mention the fact that I'm twice as old as you, and have a right to a little respect, et cetera. So you can just talk to me calmly, without flying off the handle.

LOMOV: You think I'm still just a little boy you can twist around your finger. First you say my land is yours and then you expect me to lie back and be calm about it. Call yourself a neighbor? You're no neighbor, you're a landshark.

CHUBUKOV: How was that again?

NATALIA: The mowers, Papa! Send the mowers out to cut the meadows, now!

CHUBUKOV: Young man, would you mind repeating what you just called me?

NATALIA: The White Ox Meadows are ours, and so they'll stay! He won't get 'em! Never, never!

LOMOV: We'll see about that. I'm going to my lawyer. We'll let the judge decide.

CHUBUKOV: Go ahead and see your lawyer, a lot I care. I know your kind—never happy unless you're suing somebody. You little weasel, your family always did have a weakness for lawyers, the whole damned crew of you.

LOMOV: Keep your filthy mouth off of my family. The Lomovs have always been fine upstanding citizens. Not one of us ever got put in jail for embezzling, like your father.

CHUBUKOV: Every last one of you Lomovs has been cuckoo in the head.

NATALIA: That's right, every last one!

CHUBUKOV: Why, your grandfather was a well-known lush, et cetera, and your youngest aunt ran away with an architect. Fact is fact.

LOMOV: A hunchback, your mother was. (*Grabs his chest.*) O God, the pain is stabbing me! I'm seeing flashes! Help! Give me water!

CHUBUKOV: And your old man was a vodka-soak that ate himself fat as a tick.

NATALIA: And your aunt was the high priestess of dirty gossip!

LOMOV: My left foot is paralyzed. And you're a schemer. Ah, ah, my heart! The whole town knows that on election day you were going around buying votes. I can see shooting-stars! My hat, where's my hat?

NATALIA: It's a low trick you've tried to play on us, you crook.

CHUBUKOV: Cheap double-crosser.

LOMOV: Here's my hat. My heart. . . . Which way is the door? I think I'm dying. My foot's turned to stone. (*Staggers toward the door.*)

CHUBUKOV (*following him*): Well, don't set your big stone foot in my house again!

NATALIA: Go on, take us to court, see if we care!

[Lomov goes out.]

CHUBUKOV: To hell with him! (*Paces up and down in agitation.*)

NATALIA: That snake-in-the-grass. Oh, Papa, we can't even trust our neighbors any more.

CHUBUKOV: That skunk. That overdressed scarecrow. Et cetera.

NATALIA: That monster! Makes a pass at our land and then shoots off his mouth at us.

CHUBUKOV: And on top of all that, that silly jackass had the nerve to make a proposal, et cetera. Can you imagine?

NATALIA: A—proposal? What kind of proposal?

CHUBUKOV: Why, he came over here to propose to you.

NATALIA: To propose? To *me?* Why didn't you tell me that before?

CHUBUKOV: Sure, why do you think he got all decked out in his monkey-suit? That underdone sausage, that—that ghost of a turnip!

NATALIA: But—but—to *propose* to me! (*She gives a wail of anguish and plops herself into a chair.*) Bring him back, oh, Papa, bring him back! Bring him back—right now—here!

CHUBUKOV: Bring back who?

NATALIA: Hurry up, I'm telling you, will you hurry? I'm going to be sick! Don't let him get away! (*Whimpers and beats fists against her chair hysterically.*)

CHUBUKOV: What's the matter with you? (*Claps a hand to his head.*) Now, if this isn't a fine kettle of fish! I could hang myself, I could put a bullet through my head. Her last chance, he was, and I went and ruined it.

NATALIA: I'll die! Go, go, bring him back!

CHUBUKOV: All right, all right. I'm going! Just don't howl like that! (*He dashes out.*)

NATALIA (*still moaning*): What have they done to me? Bring him back! Bring him back!

[A pause. Then Chubukov dashes in.]

CHUBUKOV: He's coming right away, damn him. You can talk to him yourself, I'm not going to.

NATALIA (*wails*): Just bring him in!

CHUBUKOV (*shouting*): Hold on, will you? I tell you he's coming. Lord, what agony it is to have a grown daughter! I could slash my throat. By heaven, I'm going to! To think of it! Here we insulted the man, called him names, threw him out, and it's all your fault.

NATALIA: *My* fault? It was yours!

CHUBUKOV: *Your* fault, you, you—(*Lomov appears at the door.*) All right, here he is, *you* talk to him.

[Lomov enters as if exhausted.]

LOMOV: These awful palpitations in my chest . . . Oh, my leg has gone dead! There's this pain in my side . . .

NATALIA: Now, Ivan Vassilevich, you'll just have to forgive us, we didn't know what we were saying. Why, now I remember perfectly—the White Ox Meadows are yours.

LOMOV: My heart—it's jumping so! Of course they're my meadows. Oh dear, now *both* my brows are twitching!

NATALIA: Just calm yourself. Come over here and sit down next to me. (*They sit, side by side.*) Oh, we were so wrong! We got carried away. The meadows are yours, really.

LOMOV: I—I don't give a hoot about the land. It was the principle of the thing!

NATALIA: I always knew you were a man of principle. Now do let's talk about something else.

LOMOV: Anyhow, I can prove it. My aunt's grandmother let your grandfather's peasants use the land because they supplied her with bricks. . . .

NATALIA: Oh, let's forget about all that! (*To herself.*) How am I going to get him off those meadows and on to the right track? (*Aloud.*) Are you going to go hunting this year?

LOMOV: I guess I'll do a little grouse-shooting after the hay is in. And oh, Natalia Stepanovna, did you hear about the bad luck I had? You know my dog Kuska? Well, he's gone lame.

NATALIA: The poor old pooch, what happened to him?

LOMOV: I don't know. Must have twisted a leg in a rabbit hole or maybe another dog took a bite of him. (*Sighs.*) My number one dog, he is. Not to mention what he cost me. Why, do you know, I gave Mironov a hundred and twenty-five rubles for him.

NATALIA: You were robbed, Ivan Vassilevich.

LOMOV: Do you think so? I call that a bargain. There's no dog like him.

NATALIA: Well, Papa gave eighty-five rubles for our Puksa, and Puksa is a better dog than Kuska any day.

LOMOV: Puksa? Better than Kuska? Are you crazy? (*Laughs.*) What a notion! Puksa better than Kuska!

NATALIA: Why, of course he's better. Puksa isn't full-grown yet, it's true, but when it comes to brains and breeding, even Count Volchanyetsky hasn't got a better dog.

LOMOV: Please excuse me, Natalia Stepanovna, but isn't there something you're leaving out? Puksa has an overshot jaw, and a dog with an overshot jaw can't ever amount to anything.

NATALIA: Oh, sure, he has an overshot jaw, has he? That's news to me!

LOMOV: Now, Natalia, I know all about these things, and I swear to you his lower jaw is a good inch shorter than his upper.

NATALIA (*sarcastically*):   And I suppose you got him down and measured him with a tape measure?

LOMOV: That's just what I did. He can run, all right, but when it comes to hunting, he'll never get anywhere. He'll snap at a rabbit and it will just slip out.

NATALIA: Now, look. In the first place, our Puksa is a thoroughbred, the son of Chisels and Harness. Your Kuska—what's he? Such a mixture there's no telling what he is. He's old and ugly as a worn-out nag.

LOMOV: Are you out of your mind? He's mature, it's true, but I wouldn't take five of your Puksas for him. I wouldn't dream of it! Kuska is a real dog, but as for your Puksa—why, this whole discussion is just plain silly. Any dog's as good as Puksa. Twenty-five rubles for him would be highway robbery.

NATALIA: Ivan Vassilevich, some perverse spirit has got into you. First you pretend you own the White Ox Meadows and now you claim Kuska is a better dog than Puksa. I just don't have any use for liars like you, because you know perfectly well that Puksa is a hundred times the dog your flea-ridden old Kuska is. Why are you arguing?

LOMOV: You think I'm blind? You think I'm a fool? Won't you admit your Puksa has an overshot jaw?

NATALIA: That's not true.

LOMOV: It's true!

NATALIA: It isn't!

LOMOV: Lady, why are you shouting at me?

NATALIA: And why are you talking a lot of rot? High time you put a bullet through your old Kuska and put him out of his misery. And you say he's better than Puksa!

LOMOV: Please. I can't go on arguing. I'm having palpitations.

NATALIA: Isn't that always the way! Hunters that talk the most are the ones that know the least!

LOMOV: Lady, will you please be quiet? My heart is pounding. It's going to explode. (*Shouts.*) For God's sake, shut up!

NATALIA: Not on your life. I'll keep right on talking until you admit that Puksa is a hundred times better than your Kuska.

LOMOV: A hundred times worse! I wish he was dead, your Puksa. Oh, my head! My shoulder! My eyebrows!

NATALIA: As for your mangy old Kuska, he's half dead already.

LOMOV (*practically in tears*):   Shut your mouth! My heart is blowing up!

NATALIA: I will not shut up.

CHUBUKOV (*entering*):   What's the matter now?

NATALIA: Papa, give us your word of honor, which is the better dog, his Kuska or our Puksa?

878

LOMOV: Stepan Stepanovich, tell me the truth—does your Puksa have an over-shot jaw or doesn't he? Yes or no?

CHUBUKOV: So what if he does? Who cares? He's still the best dog in the district, et cetera.

LOMOV: But isn't my Kuska better? Now, honestly, isn't he?

CHUBUKOV: Don't get yourself in an uproar. All right, I'll admit your Kuska has his points. He's well bred, fast on his feet, has nice ribs, et cetera. But if the truth has to be told, that dog has two things wrong with him. He's old as the hills and his muzzle's too short.

LOMOV: His muzzle's too short? Ah, ah, my heart! Will you look at the facts? Remember that hunt over at Marusinsky's? My Kuska ran neck-and-neck with the Count's best dog, while your Puksa was a whole mile in the rear!

CHUBUKOV: That was only because the Count's huntsman hit him with a whip.

LOMOV: Yes, and for good reason. All the other dogs took off after the fox, and your Puksa started chasing a sheep.

CHUBUKOV: Listen, you, I'm going to lose my temper if you don't stop arguing. The huntsman gave Puksa a crack on the nose just because some people are always jealous of other people's dogs. That's how it is, that's how *you* are. You see some dog that's better than yours and right away you start finding things wrong with him —this, that, and the other thing, et cetera. Oh, don't tell *me* about that hunt. I remember how it went.

LOMOV: Yes, and so do I.

CHUBUKOV (*mimicking him*): "Yes, and so do I." What can *you* remember? You had such a jag on at the time.

LOMOV: My—my heart! My foot's turning to stone again. I can't feel . . .

NATALIA (*mimicking him*): "My heart, my foot!" Call yourself a hunter? You couldn't catch a cockroach on a kitchen sink, let alone a fox. "My heart! My foot!"

CHUBUKOV: Some hunter you are! You ought to be home taking your blood pressure, not gallivanting around trying to catch dumb animals. The only reason you go hunting is to drink and give people a hard time about their dogs. Oh, let's get off this subject before I lose my temper and give you a poke, et cetera. I hate to tell you, boy, but as a hunter you aren't worth beans.

LOMOV: And you? You think *you're* a hunter? The only reason you go hunting is to flatter the Count and pull shady deals and connive—oh, oh, my heart! You're a conniver, that's what you are!

CHUBUKOV: Who, me, a conniver? (*Shouts.*) Shut up!

LOMOV: Conniver!

CHUBUKOV: Babyface! Sassy puppy!

LOMOV: Old rat! Old slippery Jesuit!

CHUBUKOV: Shut up before I fill you full of buckshot like a partridge!

LOMOV: The whole town knows—oh, my heart!—how your dying wife used to beat you up. Oh, my foot! My eyebrows! Here come those shooting-stars again. I'm going to keel over. I'm falling. . . . (*He staggers about.*)

CHUBUKOV: Yeah, the whole town knows how your housekeeper bosses you. How she won't let you out at night.

LOMOV: Oh, oh, my heart's exploded! My shoulder—where's my shoulder?—can't find my shoulder. Shooting-stars. I'm passing out. . . . (*He sinks into a chair.*) A doctor, I've got to have a doctor. (*Swoons and goes limp.*)

CHUBUKOV: You worm. You ninny. You make me sick to my stomach. (*Gulps water.*)

NATALIA: Call yourself a hunter? You can't tell one end of a horse from the other. Papa—what's wrong with him? Look, look! (*Shrieks.*) He's dead!

CHUBUKOV: I'm going to throw up. Give me room!

NATALIA: He's gone! (*Tugs Lomov's sleeve.*) Ivan Vassilevich, Ivan Vassilevich, wake up! Don't run out on me! It's no use! He's dead! (*Drops into a chair.*) Doctor! Doctor!

CHUBUKOV: Is something the matter?

NATALIA (*wailing*): He's dead, dead, dead, that's all!

CHUBUKOV: Who is? (*Stares at Lomov.*) Good Lord, I do believe he is. Good Lord. Should we call a doctor? House calls are twenty rubles. Let's try some water. (*Presses a glass of water to Lomov's lips.*) Drink up, old friend. He won't drink. Must be dead. Oh, if this isn't my rotten luck. Why don't I just blow my brains out, et cetera? I ought to have cut my throat ten years ago. What am I waiting for? Hand me a knife, give me a gun! (*Lomov stirs.*) Wait a minute. I think he's coming to. Here, drink this water. That's a good boy.

LOMOV: Shooting-stars . . . everything's foggy . . . where am I?

CHUBUKOV: Go on, get married, and then you can go to hell. She says yes! (*He places Lomov's hand in Natalia's.*) She says yes, she'll marry you, et cetera. I give you my blessing. Just get married and get out of my hair, the two of you!

LOMOV: Huh? What? (*He stands up.*) Who says yes to me?

CHUBUKOV: She does! Well, what are you waiting for? Pucker up and kiss her, damn it!

NATALIA (*wailing*): He isn't dead! Yes, yes, I'm willing!

CHUBUKOV: Quick, seal it with a kiss!

LOMOV: What's that? Kiss who? (*They kiss.*) Oh, that feels rather good. Excuse me, what's all this about? Oh yes, now I remember. My heart . . . the shooting-stars . . . Natalia Stepanovna, I'm so happy. (*Kisses her hand.*) But my foot feels like pins and needles.

NATALIA: And I'm happy too.

CHUBUKOV: Whew! what a weight off my back!

NATALIA: Maybe now you'll admit that Kuska is worse than Puksa?

LOMOV: Better!

NATALIA: Worse!

CHUBUKOV: This marriage is off to a great start. Let's have some champagne.

LOMOV: He's better!

NATALIA: Worse! Worse, worse, worse!

CHUBUKOV (*calling offstage to his servants*):   Champagne! Bring champagne! Champagne!

CURTAIN

DISCUSSION TOPICS:

1. What adaptations, if any, do you see as necessary if this play were to be done for television?
2. What pace seems best for the delivery of the speeches in this play? Should the pace noticeably change at some points, or remain much the same throughout? Explain your decisions.
3. Entrances and exits are minimal in this short work, and there are very few characters. But a play must have physical activity and movement on stage if it is to be visually effective. What actions are clearly called for in the course of this play? What would you add beyond what the lines clearly indicate so as to make on-stage action effective?
4. What stage properties would you see as helpful or necessary to stage this play?
5. Chekhov seems to suggest that this little slice of life before marriage is quite like many slices of life in marriage. How does he make this suggestion? Does it seem to be a positive or negative commentary on marriage, or something else again?
6. Trying to limit yourself to the information provided in the text of the play or clearly implied by it, what is the socioeconomic milieu or social class of these three characters? What do we know about the state of their workers and servants? Is there any significant difference between the socioeconomic condition or social class of these characters and their forebears?

Susan Glaspell (1882–1948) American dramatist, founder of Provincetown Players. Her play *Alison's House,* based on the life of Emily Dickinson, won the Pulitzer prize in 1930. *Trifles* is the dramatic version of her short story "A Jury of Her Peers."

TRIFLES

Characters

Sheriff
County Attorney
Mr. Hale
Mrs. Hale
Mrs. Peters

Scene

The kitchen in the now abandoned farm-house of John Wright, a gloomy kitchen, and left without having been put in order—unwashed pans under the sink, a loaf of bread outside the bread-box, a dish-towel on the table—other signs of incompleted work. At the rear the outer door opens and the SHERIFF *comes in followed by the* COUNTY ATTORNEY *and* HALE. *The* SHERIFF *and* HALE *are men in middle life, the* COUNTY ATTORNEY *is a young man; all are much bundled up and go at once to the stove. They are followed by the two women—the Sheriff's wife first; she is a slight wiry woman, with a thin nervous face.* MRS. HALE *is larger and would ordinarily be called more comfortable looking, but she is disturbed now and looks fearfully about as she enters. The women have come in slowly, and stand close together near the door.*

COUNTY ATTORNEY (*rubbing his hands*)   This feels good. Come up to the fire, ladies.

MRS. PETERS (*after taking a step forward*)   I'm not—cold.

SHERIFF (*unbuttoning his overcoat and stepping away from the stove as if to mark the beginning of official business*)   Now, Mr. Hale, before we move things about, you explain to Mr. Henderson just what you saw when you came here yesterday morning.

COUNTY ATTORNEY   By the way, has anything been moved? Are things just as you left them yesterday?

SHERIFF (*looking about*)   It's just the same. When it dropped below zero last night I thought I'd better send Frank out this morning to make a fire for us—no use getting pneumonia with a big case on, but I told him not to touch anything except the stove—and you know Frank.

COUNTY ATTORNEY   Somebody should have been left here yesterday.

SHERIFF   Oh—yesterday. When I had to send Frank to Morris Center for that man who went crazy—I want you to know I had my hands full yesterday. I knew

882

you could get back from Omaha by to-day and as long as I went over everything here myself—

COUNTY ATTORNEY   Well, Mr. Hale, tell just what happened when you came here yesterday morning.

HALE   Harry and I had started to town with a load of potatoes. We came along the road from my place and as I got here I said, "I'm going to see if I can't get John Wright to go in with me on a party telephone." I spoke to Wright about it once before and he put me off, saying folks talked too much anyway, and all he asked was peace and quiet—I guess you know about how much he talked himself; but I thought maybe if I went to the house and talked about it before his wife, though I said to Harry that I didn't know as what his wife wanted made much difference to John—

COUNTY ATTORNEY   Let's talk about that later, Mr. Hale. I do want to talk about that, but tell now just what happened when you got to the house.

HALE   I didn't hear or see anything; I knocked at the door, and still it was all quiet inside. I knew they must be up, it was past eight o'clock. So I knocked again, and I thought I heard somebody say "Come in." I wasn't sure, I'm not sure yet, but I opened the door—this door (*indicating the door by which the two women are still standing*) and there in that rocker—(*pointing to it*) sat Mrs. Wright. (*They all look at the rocker.*)

COUNTY ATTORNEY   What—was she doing?

HALE   She was rockin' back and forth. She had her apron in her hand and was kind of—pleating it.

COUNTY ATTORNEY   And how did she—look?

HALE   Well, she looked queer.

COUNTY ATTORNEY   How do you mean—queer?

HALE   Well, as if she didn't know what she was going to do next. And kind of done up.

COUNTY ATTORNEY   How did she seem to feel about your coming?

HALE   Why, I don't think she minded—one way or other. She didn't pay much attention. I said, "How do, Mrs. Wright, it's cold, ain't it?" And she said "Is it?" —and went on kind of pleating at her apron. Well, I was surprised; she didn't ask me to come up to the stove, or to set down, but just sat there, not even looking at me, so I said, "I want to see John." And then she—laughed. I guess you would call it a laugh. I thought of Harry and the team outside, so I said a little sharp: "Can't I see John?" "No," she says, kind o' dull like. "Ain't he home?" says I. "Yes," says she, "he's home." "Then why can't I see him?" I asked her, out of patience. " 'Cause he's dead," says she. *"Dead?"* says I. She just nodded her head, not getting a bit excited, but rockin' back and forth. "Why—where is he?" says I, not knowing what to say. She just pointed upstairs—like that (*himself pointing to the room above*). I got up, with the idea of going up there. I walked from there to here—then I says, "Why, what did he die of?" "He died of a rope around his neck," says she, and just went on pleatin' at her apron. Well, I went out and called Harry. I thought I might—need help. We went upstairs and there he was lyin'—

COUNTY ATTORNEY I think I'd rather have you go into that upstairs, where you can point it all out. Just go on now with the rest of the story.

HALE Well, my first thought was to get that rope off. It looked . . . (*Stops, his face twitches.*) . . . but Harry, he went up to him, and he said, "No, he's dead all right, and we'd better not touch anything." So we went back down stairs. She was still sitting that same way. "Has anybody been notified?" I asked. "No," says she, unconcerned. "Who did this, Mrs. Wright?" said Harry. He said it business-like —and she stopped pleatin' of her apron. "I don't know," she says. "You don't *know?*" says Harry. "No," says she. "Weren't you sleepin' in the bed with him?" says Harry. "Yes," says she, "but I was on the inside." "Somebody slipped a rope round his neck and strangled him and you didn't wake up?" says Harry. "I didn't wake up," she said after him. We must 'a looked as if we didn't see how that could be, for after a minute she said, "I sleep sound." Harry was going to ask her more questions, but I said maybe we ought to let her tell her story first to the coroner, or the sheriff, so Harry went fast as he could to Rivers' place, where there's a telephone.

COUNTY ATTORNEY And what did Mrs. Wright do when she knew that you had gone for the coroner?

HALE She moved from that chair to this over here . . . (*Pointing to a small chair in the corner.*) . . . and just sat there with her hands held together and looking down. I got a feeling that I ought to make some conversation, so I said I had come in to see if John wanted to put in a telephone, and at that she started to laugh, and then she stopped and looked at me—scared. (*The* COUNTY ATTORNEY, *who has had his notebook out, makes a note.*) I dunno, maybe it wasn't scared. I wouldn't like to say it was. Soon Harry got back, and then Dr. Lloyd came, and you, Mr. Peters, and so I guess that's all I know that you don't.

COUNTY ATTORNEY (*looking around*) I guess we'll go upstairs first—and then out to the barn and around there. (*To the* SHERIFF.) You're convinced that there was nothing important here—nothing that would point to any motive?

SHERIFF Nothing here but kitchen things. (*The* COUNTY ATTORNEY, *after again looking around the kitchen, opens the door of a cupboard closet. He gets up on a chair and looks on a shelf. Pulls his hand away, sticky.*)

COUNTY ATTORNEY Here's a nice mess.

(*The women draw nearer.*)

MRS. PETERS (*to the other woman*) Oh, her fruit; it did freeze. (*To the Lawyer.*) She worried about that when it turned so cold. She said the fire'd go out and her jars would break.

SHERIFF Well, can you beat the women! Held for murder and worryin' about her preserves.

COUNTY ATTORNEY   I guess before we're through she may have something more serious than preserves to worry about.

HALE   Well, women are used to worrying over trifles.

(The two women move a little closer together.)

COUNTY ATTORNEY *(with the gallantry of a young politician)*   And yet, for all their worries, what would we do without the ladies? *(The women do not unbend. He goes to the sink, takes a dipperful of water from the pail and, pouring it into a basin, washes his hands. Starts to wipe them on the roller-towel, turns it for a cleaner place.)* Dirty towels! *(Kicks his foot against the pans under the sink.)* Not much of a housekeeper, would you say, ladies?

MRS. HALE *(stiffly)*   There's a great deal of work to be done on a farm.

COUNTY ATTORNEY   To be sure. And yet . . . *(With a little bow to her.)* . . . I know there are some Dickson county farmhouses which do not have such roller towels.

(He gives it a pull to expose its full length again.)

MRS. HALE   Those towels get dirty awful quick. Men's hands aren't always as clean as they might be.

COUNTY ATTORNEY   Ah, loyal to your sex, I see. But you and Mrs. Wright were neighbors. I suppose you were friends, too.

MRS. HALE *(shaking her head)*   I've not seen much of her of late years. I've not been in this house—it's more than a year.

COUNTY ATTORNEY   And why was that? You didn't like her?

MRS. HALE   I like her all well enough. Farmers' wives have their hands full, Mr. Henderson. And then—

COUNTY ATTORNEY   Yes—?

MRS. HALE *(looking about)*   It never seemed a very cheerful place.

COUNTY ATTORNEY   No—it's not cheerful. I shouldn't say she had the home-making instinct.

MRS. HALE   Well, I don't know as Wright had, either.

COUNTY ATTORNEY   You mean that they didn't get on very well?

MRS. HALE   No, I don't mean anything. But I don't think a place'd be any cheerful for John Wright's being in it.

COUNTY ATTORNEY   I'd like to talk more of that a little later. I want to get the lay of things upstairs now.

(He goes to the left, where three steps lead to a stair door.)

SHERIFF   I suppose anything Mrs. Peters does'll be all right. She was to take in some clothes for her, you know, and a few little things. We left in such a hurry yesterday.

885

COUNTY ATTORNEY   Yes, but I would like to see what you take, Mrs. Peters, and keep an eye out for anything that might be of use to us.

MRS. PETERS   Yes, Mr. Henderson.

(*The women listen to the men's steps on the stairs, then look about the kitchen.*)

MRS. HALE   I'd hate to have men coming into my kitchen, snooping around and criticizing.

(*She arranges the pans under sink which the Lawyer had shoved out of place.*)

MRS. PETERS   Of course it's no more than their duty.

MRS. HALE   Duty's all right, but I guess that deputy sheriff that came out to make the fire might have got a little of his own. (*Gives the roller towel a pull.*) Wish I'd thought of that sooner. Seems mean to talk about her for not having things slicked up when she had to come away in such a hurry.

MRS. PETERS (*who has gone to a small table in the left rear corner of the room, and lifted one end of a towel that covers a pan*)   She had bread set.

(*Stands still.*)

MRS. HALE (*eyes fixed on a loaf of bread beside the bread-box, which is on a low shelf at the other side of the room. Moves slowly toward it.*)   She was going to put this in there. (*Picks up loaf, then abruptly drops it. In a manner of returning to familiar things.*) It's a shame about her fruit. I wonder if it's all gone. (*Gets up on the chair and looks.*) I think there's some here that's all right, Mrs. Peters. Yes—here; (*Holding it toward the window.*) this is cherries, too. (*Looking again.*) I declare I believe that's the only one. (*Gets down, bottle in her hand. Goes to the sink and wipes it off on the outside.*) She'll feel awful bad after all her hard work in the hot weather. I remember the afternoon I put up my cherries last summer.

(*She puts the bottle on the big kitchen table, center of the room, front table. With a sigh, is about to sit down in the rocking-chair. Before she is seated realizes what chair it is; with a slow look at it, steps back. The chair which she has touched rocks back and forth.*)

MRS. PETERS   Well, I must get those things from the front room closet. (*She goes to the door at the right, but after looking into the other room, steps back.*) You coming with me, Mrs. Hale? You could help me carry them.

(*They go in the other room; reappear,* MRS. PETERS *carrying a dress and skirt,* MRS. HALE *following with a pair of shoes.*)

MRS. PETERS   My, it's cold in there.

(*She puts the cloth on the big table, and hurries to the stove.*)

MRS. HALE (*examining the skirt*)   Wright was close. I think maybe that's why she kept so much to herself. She didn't even belong to the Ladies' Aid. I suppose she

886

felt she couldn't do her part, and then you don't enjoy things when you feel shabby. She used to wear pretty clothes and be lively, when she was Minnie Foster, one of the town girls singing in the choir. But that—oh, that was thirty years ago. This all you was to take in?

MRS. PETERS She said she wanted an apron. Funny thing to want, for there isn't much to get you dirty in jail, goodness knows. But I suppose just to make her feel more natural. She said they was in the top drawer in this cupboard. Yes, here. And then her little shawl that always hung behind the door. (*Opens stair door and looks.*) Yes, here it is.

(*Quickly shuts door leading upstairs.*)

MRS. HALE (*abruptly moving toward her*) Mrs. Peters?

MRS. PETERS Yes, Mrs. Hale?

MRS. HALE Do you think she did it?

MRS. PETERS (*in a frightened voice*) Oh, I don't know.

MRS. HALE Well, I don't think she did. Asking for an apron and her little shawl. Worrying about her fruit.

MRS. PETERS (*starts to speak, glances up, where footsteps are heard in the room above. In a low voice*) Mr. Peters says it looks bad for her. Mr. Henderson is awful sarcastic in a speech and he'll make fun of her sayin' she didn't wake up.

MRS. HALE Well, I guess John Wright didn't wake when they was slipping that rope under his neck.

MRS. PETERS No, it's strange. It must have been done awful crafty and still. They say it was such a—funny way to kill a man, rigging it all up like that.

MRS. HALE That's just what Mr. Hale said. There was a gun in the house. He says that's what he can't understand.

MRS. PETERS Mr. Henderson said coming out that what was needed for the case was a motive; something to show anger, or—sudden feeling.

MRS. HALE (*who is standing by the table*) Well, I don't see any signs of anger around here. (*She puts her hand on the dish towel which lies on the table, stands looking down at table, one half of which is clean, the other half messy.*) It's wiped here. (*Makes a move as if to finish work, then turns and looks at loaf of bread outside the bread-box. Drops towel. In that voice of coming back to familiar things.*) Wonder how they are finding things upstairs? I hope she had it a little more red-up up there. You know, it seems kind of *sneaking.* Locking her up in town and then coming out here and trying to get her own house to turn against her!

MRS. PETERS But, Mrs. Hale, the law is the law.

MRS. HALE I s'pose 'tis. (*Unbuttoning her coat.*) Better loosen up your things, Mrs. Peters. You won't feel them when you go out.

(MRS. PETERS *takes off her fur tippet, goes to hang it on hook at back of room, stands looking at the under part of the small corner table.*)

MRS. PETERS   She was piecing a quilt. (*She brings the large sewing basket and they look at the bright pieces.*)

MRS. HALE   It's log cabin pattern. Pretty, isn't it? I wonder if she was goin' to quilt it or just knot it?

(*Footsteps have been heard coming down the stairs. The* SHERIFF *enters, followed by* HALE *and the* COUNTY ATTORNEY.)

SHERIFF   They wonder if she was going to quilt it or just knot it.

(*The men laugh, the women look abashed.*)

COUNTY ATTORNEY (*rubbing his hands over the stove*)   Frank's fire didn't do much up there, did it? Well, let's go out to the barn and get that cleared up.

(*The men go outside.*)

MRS. HALE (*resentfully*)   I don't know as there's anything so strange, our takin' up our time with little things while we're waiting for them to get the evidence. (*She sits down at the big table smoothing out a block with decision.*) I don't see as it's anything to laugh about.

MRS. PETERS (*apologetically*)   Of course they've got awful important things on their minds.

(*Pulls up a chair and joins* MRS. HALE *at the table.*)

MRS. HALE (*examining another block*)   Mrs. Peters, look at this one. Here, this is the one she was working on, and look at the sewing! All the rest of it has been so nice and even. And look at this! It's all over the place! Why, it looks as if she didn't know what she was about!

(*After she has said this they look at each other, then start to glance back at the door. After an instant* MRS. HALE *has pulled at a knot and ripped the sewing.*)

MRS. PETERS   Oh, what are you doing, Mrs. Hale?

MRS. HALE (*mildly*)   Just pulling out a stitch or two that's not sewed very good. (*Threading a needle.*) Bad sewing always made me fidgety.

MRS. PETERS (*nervously*)   I don't think we ought to touch things.

MRS. HALE   I'll just finish up this end. (*Suddenly stopping and leaning forward.*) Mrs. Peters?

MRS. PETERS   Yes, Mrs. Hale?

MRS. HALE   What do you suppose she was so nervous about?

MRS. PETERS   Oh—I don't know. I don't know as she was nervous. I sometimes sew awful queer when I'm just tired. (MRS. HALE *starts to say something, looks at* MRS.

PETERS, *then goes on sewing.*) Well, I must get these things wrapped up. They may be through sooner than we think. (*Putting apron and other things together.*) I wonder where I can find a piece of paper, and string.

MRS. HALE   In that cupboard, maybe.

MRS. PETERS (*looking in cupboard*)   Why, here's a bird-cage. (*Holds it up.*) Did she have a bird, Mrs. Hale?

MRS. HALE   Why, I don't know whether she did or not—I've not been here for so long. There was a man around last year selling canaries cheap, but I don't know as she took one; maybe she did. She used to sing real pretty herself.

MRS. PETERS (*glancing around*)   Seems funny to think of a bird here. But she must have had one, or why should she have a cage? I wonder what happened to it?

MRS. HALE   I s'pose maybe the cat got it.

MRS. PETERS   No, she didn't have a cat. She's got that feeling some people have about cats—being afraid of them. My cat got in her room and she was real upset and asked me to take it out.

MRS. HALE   My sister Bessie was like that. Queer, ain't it?

MRS. PETERS (*examining the cage*)   Why, look at this door. It's broke. One hinge is pulled apart.

MRS. HALE (*looking too*)   Looks as if some one must have been rough with it.

MRS. PETERS   Why, yes.

(*She brings the cage forward and puts it on the table.*)

MRS. HALE   I wish if they're going to find any evidence they'd be about it. I don't like this place.

MRS. PETERS   But I'm awful glad you came with me, Mrs. Hale. It would be lonesome for me sitting here alone.

MRS. HALE   It would, wouldn't it? (*Dropping her sewing.*) But I tell you what I do wish, Mrs. Peters. I wish I had come over some times when *she* was here. I— (*Looking around the room.*)—wish I had.

MRS. PETERS   But of course you were awful busy, Mrs. Hale—your house and your children.

MRS. HALE   I could've come. I stayed away because it weren't cheerful—and that's why I ought to have come. I—I've never liked this place. Maybe because it's down in a hollow and you don't see the road. I dunno what it is, but it's a lonesome place and always was. I wish I had come over to see Minnie Foster sometimes. I can see now—

(*Shakes her head.*)

MRS. PETERS   Well, you mustn't reproach yourself, Mrs. Hale. Somehow we just don't see how it is with other folks until—something comes up.

MRS. HALE   Not having children makes less work—but it makes a quiet house, and Wright out to work all day, and no company when he did come in. Did you know John Wright, Mrs. Peters?

MRS. PETERS   Not to know him; I've seen him in town. They say he was a good man.

MRS. HALE   Yes—good; he didn't drink, and kept his word as well as most, I guess, and paid his debts. But he was a hard man, Mrs. Peters. Just to pass the time of day with him. (*Shivers.*) Like a raw wind that gets to the bone. (*Pauses, her eye falling on the cage.*) I should think she would 'a wanted a bird. But what do you suppose went with it?

MRS. PETERS   I don't know, unless it got sick and died.

(*She reaches over and swings the broken door, swings it again, both women watch it.*)

MRS. HALE   You weren't raised round here, were you? (MRS. PETERS *shakes her head.*) You didn't know—her?

MRS. PETERS   Not till they brought her yesterday.

MRS. HALE   She—come to think of it, she was kind of like a bird herself—real sweet and pretty, but kind of timid and—fluttery. How—she—did—change. (*Silence; then as if struck by a happy thought and relieved to get back to everyday things.*) Tell you what, Mrs. Peters, why don't you take the quilt in with you? It might take up her mind.

MRS. PETERS   Why, I think that's a real nice idea, Mrs. Hale. There couldn't possibly be any objection to it, could there? Now, just what would I take? I wonder if her patches are in here—and her things.

(*They look in the sewing basket.*)

MRS. HALE   Here's some red. I expect this has got sewing things in it. (*Brings out a fancy box.*) What a pretty box. Looks like something somebody would give you. Maybe her scissors are in here. (*Opens box. Suddenly puts her hand to her nose.*) Why—(MRS. PETERS *bends nearer, then turns her face away.*) There's something wrapped up in this piece of silk.

MRS. PETERS   Why, this isn't her scissors.

MRS. HALE (*lifting the silk*)   Oh, Mrs. Peters—it's—

(MRS. PETERS *bends closer.*)

MRS. PETERS   It's the bird.

MRS. HALE (*jumping up*)   But, Mrs. Peters—look at it. Its neck! Look at its neck! It's all—other side to.

MRS. PETERS   Somebody—wrung—its neck.

890

(*Their eyes meet. A look of growing comprehension, of horror. Steps are heard outside.* MRS. HALE *slips box under quilt pieces, and sinks into her chair. Enter* SHERIFF *and* COUNTY ATTORNEY. MRS. PETERS *rises.*)

COUNTY ATTORNEY (*as one turning from serious things to little pleasantries*)   Well, ladies, have you decided whether she was going to quilt it or knot it?

MRS. PETERS   We think she was going to—knot it.

COUNTY ATTORNEY   Well, that's interesting, I'm sure. (*Seeing the birdcage.*) Has the bird flown?

MRS. HALE (*putting more quilt pieces over the box*)   We think the—cat got it.

COUNTY ATTORNEY (*preoccupied*)   Is there a cat?

(MRS. HALE *glances in a quick covert way at* MRS. PETERS.)

MRS. PETERS   Well, not now. They're superstitious, you know. They leave.

COUNTY ATTORNEY (*to* SHERIFF PETERS, *continuing an interrupted conversation*) No sign at all of any one having come from the outside. Their own rope. Now let's go up again and go over it piece by piece. (*They start upstairs.*) It would have to have been some one who knew just the—

(MRS. PETERS *sits down. The two women sit there not looking at one another, but as if peering into something and at the same time holding back. When they talk now it is in the manner of feeling their way over strange ground, as if afraid of what they are saying, but as if they can not help saying it.*)

MRS. HALE   She liked the bird. She was going to bury it in that pretty box.

MRS. PETERS (*in a whisper*)   When I was a girl—my kitten—there was a boy took a hatchet, and before my eyes—and before I could get there—(*Covers her face an instant.*) If they hadn't held me back I would have—(*Catches herself, looks upstairs where steps are heard, falters weakly*)—hurt him.

MRS. HALE (*with a slow look around her*)   I wonder how it would seem never to have had any children around. (*Pause.*) No, Wright wouldn't like the bird—a thing that sang. She used to sing. He killed that, too.

MRS. PETERS (*moving uneasily*)   We don't know who killed the bird.

MRS. HALE   I knew John Wright.

MRS. PETERS   It was an awful thing was done in this house that night, Mrs. Hale. Killing a man while he slept, slipping a rope around his neck that choked the life out of him.

MRS. HALE   His neck. Choked the life out of him.

(*Her hand goes out and rests on the bird-cage.*)

MRS. PETERS (*with rising voice*)   We don't know who killed him. We don't know.

MRS. HALE (*her own feeling not interrupted*) If there'd been years and years of nothing, then a bird to sing to you, it would be awful—still, after the bird was still.

MRS. PETERS (*something within her speaking*) I know what stillness is. When we homesteaded in Dakota, and my first baby died—after he was two years old, and me with no other then—

MRS. HALE (*moving*) How soon do you suppose they'll be through, looking for the evidence?

MRS. PETERS I know what stillness is. (*Pulling herself back.*) The law has got to punish crime, Mrs. Hale.

MRS. HALE (*not as if answering that*) I wish you'd seen Minnie Foster when she wore a white dress with blue ribbons and stood up there in the choir and sang. (*A look around the room.*) Oh, I *wish* I'd come over here once in a while. That was a crime! That was a crime! Who's going to punish that?

MRS. PETERS (*looking upstairs*) We mustn't—take on.

MRS. HALE I might have known she needed help! I know how things can be— for women. I tell you, it's queer, Mrs. Peters. We live close together and we live far apart. We all go through the same things—it's all just a different kind of the same thing. (*Brushes her eyes, noticing the bottle of fruit, reaches out for it.*) If I was you I wouldn't tell her her fruit was gone. Tell her it *ain't.* Tell her it's all right. Take this in to prove it to her. She—she may never know whether it was broke or not.

MRS. PETERS (*takes the bottle, looks about for something to wrap it in; takes petticoat from the clothes brought from the other room, very nervously begins winding this around the bottle. In a false voice*) My, it's a good thing the men couldn't hear us. Wouldn't they just laugh. Getting all stirred up over a little thing like a—dead canary. As if that could have anything to do with—with—wouldn't they *laugh!*

(*The men are heard coming down stairs.*)

MRS. HALE (*under her breath*) Maybe they would—maybe they wouldn't.

COUNTY ATTORNEY No, Peters, it's all perfectly clear except a reason for doing it. But you know juries when it comes to women. If there was some definite thing. Something to show—something to make a story about—a thing that would connect up with this strange way of doing it.

(*The women's eyes meet for an instant. Enter* HALE *from outer door.*)

HALE Well, I've got the team around. Pretty cold out there.

COUNTY ATTORNEY I'm going to stay here a while by myself. (*To the* SHERIFF.) You can send Frank out for me, can't you? I want to go over everything. I'm not satisfied that we can't do better.

SHERIFF Do you want to see what Mrs. Peters is going to take in?

(*The Lawyer goes to the table, picks up the apron, laughs.*)

COUNTY ATTORNEY Oh, I guess they're not very dangerous things the ladies have picked out. (*Moves a few things about, disturbing the quilt pieces which cover the box. Steps back.*) No, Mrs. Peters doesn't need supervising. For that matter, a sheriff's wife is married to the law. Ever think of it that way, Mrs. Peters?

MRS. PETERS Not—just that way.

SHERIFF (*chuckling*) Married to the law. (*Moves toward the other room.*) I just want you to come in here a minute, George. We ought to take a look at these windows.

COUNTY ATTORNEY (*scoffingly*) Oh, windows!

SHERIFF We'll be right out, Mr. Hale.

(HALE *goes outside. The* SHERIFF *follows the* COUNTY ATTORNEY *into the other room. Then* MRS. HALE *rises, hands tight together, looking intensely at* MRS. PETERS, *whose eyes makes a slow turn, finally meeting* MRS. HALE'S. *A moment* MRS. HALE *holds her, then her own eyes point the way to where the box is concealed. Suddenly* MRS. PETERS *throws back quilt pieces and tries to put the box in the bag she is wearing. It is too big. She opens box, starts to take bird out, cannot touch it, goes to pieces, stands there helpless. Sound of a knob turning in the other room.* MRS. HALE *snatches the box and puts it in the pocket of her big coat. Enter* COUNTY ATTORNEY *and* SHERIFF.)

COUNTY ATTORNEY (*facetiously*) Well, Henry, at least we found out that she was not going to quilt it. She was going to—what is it you call it, ladies?

MRS. HALE (*her hand against her pocket*) We call it—knot it. Mr. Henderson.

(*Curtain*)

DISCUSSION TOPICS

1. Assuming that Mrs. Wright is indicted for murder and that you are her attorney, how would you defend her?
2. Why do Mrs. Hale and Mrs. Peters come to sympathize so strongly with Mrs. Wright?
3. Explain the symbolic value of the dead bird and the cage.
4. Why do the men fail to see the clues so evident to the women?

WRITING TOPIC

Comment on *Trifles* as an effective, understated protest against male-dominated society.

EUGENE IONESCO (1912–   ) Rumanian-born French dramatist, whose name is virtually synonymous with the Theater of the Absurd. His view of life as essentially absurd has produced in him a pessimism that marks many of his best plays, among which are *The Leader, The Lesson, Rhinoceros,* and *Exit the King.*

THE GAP

Translated by Rosette Lamont

Characters

THE FRIEND
THE ACADEMICIAN
THE ACADEMICIAN'S WIFE
THE MAID

Scene: *A rich bourgeois living room with artistic pretensions. One or two sofas, a number of armchairs, among which, a green,* Régence *style one, right in the middle of the room. The walls are covered with framed diplomas. One can make out, written in heavy script at the top of a particularly large one, "Doctor Honoris causa." This is followed by an almost illegible Latin inscription. Another equally impressive diploma states: "Doctorat honoris causa," again followed by a long, illegible text. There is an abundance of smaller diplomas, each of which bears a clearly written "doctorate."*

A door to the right of the audience.

As the curtain rises, one can see THE ACADEMICIAN'S WIFE *dressed in a rather crumpled robe. She has obviously just gotten out of bed, and has not had time to dress.* THE FRIEND *faces her. He is well dressed: hat, umbrella in hand, stiff collar, black jacket and striped trousers, shiny black shoes.*

THE WIFE   Dear friend, tell me all.

THE FRIEND   I don't know what to say.

THE WIFE   I know.

THE FRIEND   I heard the news last night. I did not want to call you. At the same time I couldn't wait any longer. Please forgive me for coming so early with such terrible news.

THE WIFE   He didn't make it! How terrible! We were still hoping. . . .

THE FRIEND   It's hard, I know. He still had a chance. Not much of one. We had to expect it.

THE WIFE   I didn't expect it. He was always so successful. He could always manage somehow, at the last moment.

THE FRIEND   In that state of exhaustion. You shouldn't have let him!

THE WIFE   What can we do, what can we do! . . . How awful!

THE FRIEND   Come on, dear friend, be brave. That's life.

THE WIFE   I feel faint: I'm going to faint. (*She falls in one of the armchairs.*)

THE FRIEND (*holding her, gently slapping her cheeks and hands*).   I shouldn't have blurted it out like that. I'm sorry.

THE WIFE   No, you were right to do so. I had to find out somehow or other.

THE FRIEND   I should have prepared you, carefully.

THE WIFE   I've got to be strong. I can't help thinking of him, the wretched man. I hope they won't put it in the papers. Can we count on the journalists' discretion?

THE FRIEND   Close your door. Don't answer the telephone. It will still get around. You could go to the country. In a couple of months, when you are better, you'll come back, you'll go on with your life. People forget such things.

THE WIFE   People won't forget so fast. That's all they were waiting for. Some friends will feel sorry, but the others, the others. . . . (THE ACADEMICIAN *comes in, fully dressed: uniform, chest covered with decorations, his sword on his side.*)

THE ACADEMICIAN   Up so early, my dear? (*To* THE FRIEND) You've come early too. What's happening? Do you have the final results?

THE WIFE   What a disgrace!

THE FRIEND   You mustn't crush him like this, dear friend. (*To* THE ACADEMICIAN) You have failed.

THE ACADEMICIAN   Are you quite sure?

THE FRIEND   You should never have tried to pass the baccalaureate examination.

THE ACADEMICIAN   They failed me. The rats! How dare they do this to me!

THE FRIEND   The marks were posted late in the evening.

THE ACADEMICIAN   Perhaps it was difficult to make them out in the dark. How could you read them?

THE FRIEND   They had set up spotlights.

THE ACADEMICIAN   They're doing everything to ruin me.

THE FRIEND   I passed by in the morning; the marks were still up.

THE ACADEMICIAN   You could have bribed the concierge into pulling them down.

THE FRIEND   That's exactly what I did. Unfortunately the police were there. Your name heads the list of those who failed. Everyone's standing in line to get a look. There's an awful crush.

THE ACADEMICIAN   Who's there? The parents of the candidates?

THE FRIEND   Not only they.

THE WIFE   All your rivals, all your colleagues must be there. All those you attacked in the press for ignorance: your undergraduates, your graduate students, all those who failed when you were chairman of the board of examiners.

THE ACADEMICIAN   I am discredited! But I won't let them. There must be some mistake.

THE FRIEND   I saw the examiners. I spoke with them. They gave me your marks. Zero in mathematics.

THE ACADEMICIAN   I had no scientific training.

THE FRIEND   Zero in Greek, zero in Latin.

THE WIFE (*to her husband*).   You, a humanist, the spokesman for humanism, the author of that famous treatise "The Defense of Poesy and Humanism."

THE ACADEMICIAN   I beg your pardon, but my book concerns itself with twentieth century humanism. (*To* THE FRIEND) What about composition? What grade did I get in composition?

THE FRIEND   Nine hundred. You have nine hundred points.

THE ACADEMICIAN   That's perfect. My average must be all the way up.

THE FRIEND   Unfortunately not. They're marking on the basis of two thousand. The passing grade is one thousand.

THE ACADEMICIAN   They must have changed the regulations.

THE WIFE   They didn't change them just for you. You have a frightful persecution complex.

THE ACADEMICIAN   I tell you they changed them.

THE FRIEND   They went back to the old ones, back to the time of Napoleon.

THE ACADEMICIAN   Utterly outmoded. Besides, when did they make those changes? It isn't legal. I'm chairman of the Baccalaureate Commission of the Ministry of Public Education. They didn't consult me, and they cannot make any changes without my approval. I'm going to expose them. I'm going to bring government charges against them.

THE WIFE   Darling, you don't know what you're doing. You're in your dotage. Don't you recall handing in your resignation just before taking the examination so that no one could doubt the complete objectivity of the board of examiners?

THE ACADEMICIAN   I'll take it back.

THE WIFE   You should never have taken that test. I warned you. After all, it's not as if you needed it. But you have to collect all the honors, don't you? You're never satisfied. What did you need this diploma for? Now all is lost. You have your Doctorate, your Master's, your high school diploma, your elementary school certificate, and even the first part of the baccalaureate.

THE ACADEMICIAN   There was a gap.

THE WIFE   No one suspected it.

THE ACADEMICIAN   But *I* knew it. Others might have found out. I went to the office of the Registrar and asked for a transcript of my record. They said to me: "Certainly Professor, Mr. President, Your Excellency. . . ." Then they looked up my file, and the Chief Registrar came back looking embarrassed, most embarrassed indeed. He said: "There's something peculiar, very peculiar. You have your Master's, certainly, but it's no longer valid." I asked him why, of course. He answered: "There's a gap behind your Master's. I don't know how it happened. You must have registered and been accepted at the University without having passed the second part of the baccalaureate examination."

THE FRIEND   And then?

THE WIFE   Your Master's degree is no longer valid?

THE ACADEMICIAN   No, not quite. It's suspended. "The duplicate you are asking for will be delivered to you upon completion of the baccalaureate. Of course you will pass the examination with no trouble." That's what I was told, so you see now that I had to take it.

THE FRIEND   Your husband, dear friend, wanted to fill the gap. He's a conscientious person.

THE WIFE   It's clear you don't know him as I do. That's not it at all. He wants fame, honors. He never has enough. What does one diploma more or less matter? No one notices them anyway, but he sneaks in at night, on tiptoe, into the living room, just to look at them, and count them.

THE ACADEMICIAN   What else can I do when I have insomnia?

THE FRIEND   The questions asked at the baccalaureate are usually known in advance. You were admirably situated to get this particular information. You could also have sent in a replacement to take the test for you. One of your students, perhaps. Or if you wanted to take the test without people realizing that you already knew the questions, you could have sent your maid to the black market, where one can buy them.

THE ACADEMICIAN   I don't understand how I could have failed in my composition. I filled three sheets of paper. I treated the subject fully, taking into account the historical background. I interpreted the situation accurately . . . at least plausibly. I didn't deserve a bad grade.

THE FRIEND   Do you recall the subject?

THE ACADEMICIAN   Hum . . . let's see. . . .

THE FRIEND   He doesn't even remember what he discussed.

THE ACADEMICIAN   I do . . . wait . . . hum.

THE FRIEND   The subject to be treated was the following: "Discuss the influence of Renaissance painters on novelists of the Third Republic." I have here a photostatic copy of your examination paper. Here is what you wrote.

THE ACADEMICIAN (*grabbing the photostat and reading*).   "The trial of Benjamin. After Benjamin was tried and acquitted, the assessors holding a different opinion from that of the President murdered him, and condemned Benjamin to the suspension of his civic rights, imposing on him a fine of nine hundred francs. . . ."

THE FRIEND   That's where the nine hundred points come from.

THE ACADEMICIAN   "Benjamin appealed his case . . . Benjamin appealed his case. . . ." I can't make out the rest. I've always had bad handwriting. I ought to have taken a typewriter along with me.

THE WIFE   Horrible handwriting, scribbling and crossing out; ink spots didn't help you much.

THE ACADEMICIAN (*goes on with his reading after having retrieved the text his wife had pulled out of his hand*). "Benjamin appealed his case. Flanked by policemen dressed in zouave uniforms . . . in zouave uniforms. . . ." It's getting dark. I can't see the rest. . . . I don't have my glasses.

THE WIFE   What you've written has nothing to do with the subject.

THE FRIEND   Your wife's quite right, friend. It has nothing to do with the subject.

THE ACADEMICIAN   Yes, it has. Indirectly.

THE FRIEND   Not even indirectly.

THE ACADEMICIAN   Perhaps I chose the second question.

THE FRIEND   There was only one.

THE ACADEMICIAN   Even if there was only that one, I treated another quite adequately. I went to the end of the story. I stressed the important points, explaining the motivations of the characters, highlighting their behavior. I explained the mystery, making it plain and clear. There was even a conclusion at the end. I can't make out the rest. (*To* THE FRIEND) Can you read it?

THE FRIEND   It's illegible. I don't have my glasses either.

THE WIFE (*taking the text*).   It's illegible and I have excellent eyes. You pretended to write. Mere scribbling.

THE ACADEMICIAN   That's not true. I've even provided a conclusion. It's clearly marked here in heavy print: "Conclusion or sanction . . . Conclusion or sanction. . . ." They can't get away with it. I'll have this examination rendered null and void.

THE WIFE   Since you treated the wrong subject, and treated it badly, setting down only titles, and writing nothing in between, the mark you received is justified. You'd lose your case.

THE FRIEND   You'd most certainly lose. Drop it. Take a vacation.

THE ACADEMICIAN   You're always on the side of the Others.

THE WIFE   After all, these professors know what they're doing. They haven't been granted their rank for nothing. They passed examinations, received serious training. They know the rules of composition.

THE ACADEMICIAN   Who was on the board of examiners?

THE FRIEND   For Mathematics, a movie star. For Greek, one of the Beatles. For Latin, the champion of the automobile race, and many others.

THE ACADEMICIAN   But these people aren't any more qualified than I am. And for composition?

THE FRIEND   A woman, a secretary in the editorial division of the review *Yesterday, the Day Before Yesterday, and Today.*

898

THE ACADEMICIAN   Now I know. This wretch gave me a poor grade out of spite because I never joined her political party. It's an act of vengeance. But I have ways and means of rendering the examination null and void. I'm going to call the President.

THE WIFE   Don't! You'll make yourself look even more ridiculous. (*To* THE FRIEND) Please try to restrain him. He listens to you more than to me. (THE FRIEND *shrugs his shoulders, unable to cope with the situation.* THE WIFE *turns to her husband, who has just lifted the receiver off the hook.*) Don't call!

THE ACADEMICIAN (*On the telephone*)   Hello, John? It is I . . . What? . . . What did you say? . . . But, listen, my dear friend . . . but, listen to me . . . Hello! Hello! (*Puts down the receiver.*)

THE FRIEND   What did he say?

THE ACADEMICIAN   He said . . . He said . . . , "I don't want to talk to you. My mummy won't let me make friends with boys at the bottom of the class." Then he hung up on me.

THE WIFE   You should have expected it. All is lost. How could you do this to me? How could you do this to me?

THE ACADEMICIAN   Think of it! I lectured at the Sorbonne, at Oxford, at American universities. Ten thousand theses have been written on my work; hundreds of critics have analyzed it. I hold an *honoris causa* doctorate from Amsterdam as well as a secret university Chair with the Duchy of Luxembourg. I received the Nobel Prize three times. The King of Sweden himself was amazed by my erudition. A doctorate *honoris causa, honoris causa* . . . and I failed the baccalaureate examination!

THE WIFE   Everyone will laugh at us! (THE ACADEMICIAN *takes off his sword and breaks it on his knee.*)

THE FRIEND (*picking up the two pieces*).   I wish to preserve these in memory of our ancient glory.

(THE ACADEMICIAN *meanwhile in a fit of rage is tearing down his decorations, throwing them on the floor, and stepping on them.*)

THE WIFE (*trying to salvage the remains*).   Don't do this! Don't! That's all we've got left.

[*Curtain.*]

DISCUSSION TOPICS

1. Discuss the symbolic function of the many references to diplomas, medals, decorations, citations, prizes, and badges. As external, and here worthless, acknowledgments of academic distinction, how do they reflect on the academic world at large?

2. In the play the "gap" is the missing baccalaureate degree. But if at another level the gap is a necessary part in the creation of a meaningful world, what does the play suggest about values? Religion? Moral order?
3. Identify the members of the board of examiners. How do they constitute a commentary on the question of whether or not the world has meaning?
4. In absurdist drama, language, like characters and events, can sometimes be used to show the absence of sense. In this context, discuss the passages on the Academician's composition.

WRITING TOPICS

1. Contrast the absurdist "hero" of *The Gap* with such traditional heroes as Oedipus and Hamlet.
2. Analyze and compare and contrast the following as symbols for cosmic significances: the gap in the world of education, the open boat in Crane's story, and the island in Synge's play.

ARTHUR MILLER (1915–   ) American dramatist and Pulitzer prize winner. His *Death of a Salesman* and *A View from the Bridge,* in demonstrating how the so-called "little man" may suffer a catastrophe, have added new dimensions to the ideas of tragedy and tragic hero.

DEATH OF A SALESMAN

CERTAIN PRIVATE CONVERSATIONS IN TWO ACTS AND A REQUIEM

Characters

WILLY LOMAN
LINDA, HIS WIFE
BIFF   ⎫
       ⎬ HIS SONS
HAPPY   ⎭
BERNARD
THE WOMAN
CHARLEY
UNCLE BEN
HOWARD WAGNER
JENNY
STANLEY
MISS FORSYTHE
LETTA

The action takes place in WILLY LOMAN's *house and yard and in various places he visits in the New York and Boston of today.*

Throughout the play, in the stage directions, left and right mean stage left and stage right.

ACT I

A melody is heard, played upon a flute. It is small and fine, telling of grass and trees and the horizon. The curtain rises.

Before us is the Salesman's house. We are aware of towering, angular shapes behind it, surrounding it on all sides. Only the blue light of the sky falls upon the house and forestage; the surrounding area shows an angry glow of orange. As more light appears, we see a solid vault of apartment houses around the small, fragile-seeming home. An air of the dream clings to the place, a dream rising out of reality. The kitchen at center seems actual enough, for there is a kitchen table with three chairs, and a refrigerator. But no other fixtures are seen. At the back of the kitchen there is a draped entrance, which leads to the living-room. To the right of the kitchen, on a level raised two feet, is a bedroom furnished only with a brass bedstead and a straight chair. On a shelf over the bed a silver athletic trophy stands. A window opens onto the apartment house at the side.

Behind the kitchen, on a level raised six and a half feet, is the boys' bedroom, at present barely

901

visible. *Two beds are dimly seen, and at the back of the room a dormer window. (This bedroom is above the unseen living-room.) At the left a stairway curves up to it from the kitchen.*

The entire setting is wholly or, in some places, partially transparent. The roof-line of the house is one-dimensional; under and over it we see the apartment buildings. Before the house lies an apron, curving beyond the forestage into the orchestra. This forward area serves as the back yard as well as the locale of all WILLY*'s imaginings and of his city scenes. Whenever the action is in the present the actors observe the imaginary wall-lines, entering the house only through its door at the left. But in the scenes of the past these boundaries are broken, and characters enter or leave a room by stepping "through" a wall onto the forestage.*

From the right, WILLY LOMAN, *the Salesman, enters, carrying two large sample cases. The flute plays on. He hears but is not aware of it. He is past sixty years of age, dressed quietly. Even as he crosses the stage to the doorway of the house, his exhaustion is apparent. He unlocks the door, comes into the kitchen, and thankfully lets his burden down, feeling the soreness of his palms. A word-sigh escapes his lips—it might be "Oh, boy, oh, boy." He closes the door, then carries his cases out into the living-room, through the draped kitchen doorway.*

LINDA, *his wife, has stirred in her bed at the right. She gets out and puts on a robe, listening. Most often jovial, she has developed an iron repression of her expectations to* WILLY*'s behavior—she more than loves him, she admires him, as though his mercurial nature, his temper, his massive dreams and little cruelties, served her only as sharp reminders of the turbulent longings within him, longings which she shares but lacks the temperament to utter and follow to their end.*

LINDA (*hearing* WILLY *outside the bedroom, calls with some trepidation*) Willy!

WILLY It's all right. I came back.

LINDA Why? What happened? (*Slight pause.*) Did something happen, Willy?

WILLY No, nothing happened.

LINDA You didn't smash the car, did you?

WILLY (*with casual irritation*) I said nothing happened. Didn't you hear me?

LINDA Don't you feel well?

WILLY I am tired to the death. (*The flute has faded away. He sits on the bed beside her, a little numb.*) I couldn't make it. I just couldn't make it, Linda.

LINDA (*very carefully, delicately*) Where were you all day? You look terrible.

WILLY I got as far as a little above Yonkers. I stopped for a cup of coffee. Maybe it was the coffee.

LINDA What?

WILLY (*after a pause*) I suddenly couldn't drive any more. The car kept going off onto the shoulder, y'know?

LINDA (*helpfully*) Oh. Maybe it was the steering again. I don't think Angelo knows the Studebaker.

WILLY No, it's me, it's me. Suddenly I realize I'm goin' sixty miles an hour and I don't remember the last five minutes. I'm—I can't seem to—keep my mind to it.

LINDA Maybe it's your glasses. You never went for your new glasses.

WILLY No, I see everything. I came back ten miles an hour. It took me nearly four hours from Yonkers.

LINDA (*resigned*) Well, you'll just have to take a rest, Willy, you can't continue this way.

WILLY I just got back from Florida.

LINDA But you didn't rest your mind. Your mind is overactive, and the mind is what counts, dear.

WILLY I'll start out in the morning. Maybe I'll feel better in the morning. (*She is taking off his shoes.*) These goddam arch supports are killing me.

LINDA Take an aspirin. Should I get you an aspirin? It'll soothe you.

WILLY (*with wonder*) I was driving along, you understand? And I was fine. I was even observing the scenery. You can imagine, me looking at scenery, on the road every week of my life. But it's so beautiful up there, Linda, the trees are so thick, and the sun is warm. I opened the windshield and just let the warm air bathe over me. And then all of a sudden I'm goin' off the road! I'm tellin' ya, I absolutely forgot I was driving. If I'd've gone the other way over the white line I might've killed somebody. So I went on again—and five minutes later I'm dreamin' again, and I nearly—(*He presses two fingers against his eyes.*) I have such thoughts, I have such strange thoughts.

LINDA Willy, dear. Talk to them again. There's no reason why you can't work in New York.

WILLY They don't need me in New York. I'm the New England man. I'm vital in New England.

LINDA But you're sixty years old. They can't expect you to keep traveling every week.

WILLY I'll have to send a wire to Portland. I'm supposed to see Brown and Morrison tomorrow morning at ten o'clock to show the line. Goddammit, I could sell them! (*He starts putting on his jacket.*)

LINDA (*taking the jacket from him*) Why don't you go down to the place tomorrow and tell Howard you've simply got to work in New York? You're too accommodating, dear.

WILLY If old man Wagner was alive I'd a been in charge of New York now! That man was a prince, he was a masterful man. But that boy of his, that Howard, he don't appreciate. When I went north the first time, the Wagner Company didn't know where New England was!

LINDA Why don't you tell those things to Howard, dear?

WILLY (*encouraged*) I will, I definitely will. Is there any cheese?

LINDA I'll make you a sandwich.

WILLY No, go to sleep. I'll take some milk. I'll be up right away. The boys in?

LINDA They're sleeping. Happy took Biff on a date tonight.

WILLY (*interested*) That so?

LINDA It was so nice to see them shaving together, one behind the other, in the bathroom. And going out together. You notice? The whole house smells of shaving lotion.

WILLY Figure it out. Work a lifetime to pay off a house. You finally own it, and there's nobody to live in it.

LINDA Well, dear, life is a casting off. It's always that way.

WILLY No, no, some people—some people accomplish something. Did Biff say anything after I went this morning?

LINDA You shouldn't have criticized him, Willy, especially after he just got off the train. You mustn't lose your temper with him.

WILLY When the hell did I lose my temper? I simply asked him if he was making any money. Is that a criticism?

LINDA But, dear, how could he make any money?

WILLY (*worried and angered*) There's such an undercurrent in him. He became a moody man. Did he apologize when I left this morning?

LINDA He was crestfallen, Willy. You know how he admires you. I think if he finds himself, then you'll both be happier and not fight any more.

WILLY How can he find himself on a farm? Is that a life? A farmhand? In the beginning, when he was young, I thought, well, a young man, it's good for him to tramp around, take a lot of different jobs. But it's more than ten years now and he has yet to make thirty-five dollars a week!

LINDA He's finding himself, Willy.

WILLY Not finding yourself at the age of thirty-four is a disgrace!

LINDA Shh!

WILLY The trouble is he's lazy, goodammit!

LINDA Willy, please!

WILLY Biff is a lazy bum!

LINDA They're sleeping. Get something to eat. Go on down.

WILLY Why did he come home? I would like to know what brought him home.

LINDA I don't know. I think he's still lost, Willy. I think he's very lost.

WILLY Biff Loman is lost. In the greatest country in the world a young man with such—personal attractiveness, gets lost. And such a hard worker. There's one thing about Biff—he's not lazy.

LINDA Never.

WILLY (*with pity and resolve*) I'll see him in the morning; I'll have a nice talk with him. I'll get him a job selling. He could be big in no time. My God! Remember how they used to follow him around in high school? When he smiled at one of them their faces lit up. When he walked down the street . . . (*He loses himself in reminiscences.*)

LINDA (*trying to bring him out of it*)   Willy, dear, I got a new kind of American-type cheese today. It's whipped.

WILLY   Why do you get American when I like Swiss?

LINDA   I just thought you'd like a change—

WILLY   I don't want a change! I want Swiss cheese. Why am I always being contradicted?

LINDA (*with a covering laugh*)   I thought it would be a surprise.

WILLY   Why don't you open a window in here, for God's sake?

LINDA (*with infinite patience*)   They're all open, dear.

WILLY   The way they boxed us in here. Bricks and windows, windows and bricks.

LINDA   We should've bought the land next door.

WILLY   The street is lined with cars. There's not a breath of fresh air in the neighborhood. The grass don't grow any more, you can't raise a carrot in the back yard. They should've had a law against apartment houses. Remember those two beautiful elm trees out there? When I and Biff hung the swing between them?

LINDA   Yeah, like being a million miles from the city.

WILLY   They should've arrested the builder for cutting those down. They massacred the neighborhood. (*Lost.*) More and more I think of those days, Linda. This time of year it was lilac and wisteria. And then the peonies would come out, and the daffodils. What fragrance in this room!

LINDA   Well, after all, people had to move somewhere.

WILLY   No, there's more people now.

LINDA   I don't think there's more people. I think—

WILLY   There's more people! That's what's ruining this country! Population is getting out of control. The competition is maddening! Smell the stink from that apartment house! And another one on the other side . . . How can they whip cheese?

(*On* WILLY's *last line,* BIFF *and* HAPPY *raise themselves up in their beds, listening.*)

LINDA   Go down, try it. And be quiet.

WILLY (*turning to* LINDA, *guiltily*)   You're not worried about me, are you, sweetheart?

BIFF   What's the matter?

HAPPY   Listen!

LINDA   You've got too much on the ball to worry about.

WILLY   You're my foundation and my support, Linda.

LINDA   Just try to relax, dear. You make mountains out of molehills.

WILLY   I won't fight with him any more. If he wants to go back to Texas, let him go.

LINDA   He'll find his way.

WILLY   Sure. Certain men just don't get started till later in life. Like Thomas Edison, I think. Or B. F. Goodrich. One of them was deaf. (*He starts for the bedroom doorway.*) I'll put my money on Biff.

LINDA   And Willy—if it's warm Sunday we'll drive in the country. And we'll open the windshield, and take lunch.

WILLY   No, the windshields don't open on the new cars.

LINDA   But you opened it today.

WILLY   Me? I didn't. (*He stops.*) Now isn't that peculiar! Isn't that a remarkable —(*He breaks off in amazement and fright as the flute is heard distantly.*)

LINDA   What, darling?

WILLY   That is the most remarkable thing.

LINDA   What, dear?

WILLY   I was thinking of the Chevvy. (*Slight pause.*) Nineteen twenty-eight . . . when I had that red Chevvy—(*Breaks off.*) That funny? I coulda sworn I was driving that Chevvy today.

LINDA   Well, that's nothing. Something must've reminded you.

WILLY   Remarkable. Ts. Remember those days? The way Biff used to simonize that car? The dealer refused to believe there was eighty thousand miles on it. (*He shakes his head.*) Heh! (*To Linda.*) Close your eyes, I'll be right up. (*He walks out of the bedroom.*)

HAPPY (*to* BIFF)   Jesus, maybe he smashed up the car again!

LINDA (*calling after* WILLY)   Be careful on the stairs, dear! The cheese is on the middle shelf! (*She turns, goes over to the bed, takes his jacket, and goes out of the bedroom.*)

(*Light has risen on the boys' room. Unseen,* WILLY *is heard talking to himself, "Eighty thousand miles," and a little laugh.* BIFF *gets out of bed, comes downstage a bit, and stands attentively,* BIFF *is two years older than his brother* HAPPY, *well built, but in these days bears a worn air and seems less self-assured. He has succeeded less, and his dreams are stronger and less acceptable than* HAPPY's. HAPPY *is tall, powerfully made. Sexuality is like a visible color on him, or a scent that many women have discovered. He, like his brother, is lost, but in a different way, for he has never allowed himself to turn his face toward defeat and is thus more confused and hard-skinned, although seemingly more content.*)

HAPPY (*getting out of bed*)   He's going to get his license taken away if he keeps that up. I'm getting nervous about him, y'know, Biff?

BIFF   His eyes are going.

906

HAPPY   No, I've driven with him. He sees all right. He just doesn't keep his mind on it. I drove into the city with him last week. He stops at a green light and then it turns red and he goes. (*He laughs.*)

BIFF   Maybe he's color-blind.

HAPPY   Pop? Why he's got the finest eye for color in the business. You know that.

BIFF (*sitting down on his bed*)   I'm going to sleep.

HAPPY   You're not still sour on Dad, are you, Biff?

BIFF   He's all right, I guess.

WILLY (*underneath them, in the livingroom*)   Yes, sir, eighty thousand miles—eighty-two thousand!

BIFF   You smoking?

HAPPY (*holding out a pack of cigarettes*)   Want one?

BIFF (*taking a cigarette*)   I can never sleep when I smell it.

WILLY   What a simonizing job, heh!

HAPPY (*with deep sentiment*)   Funny, Biff, y'know? Us sleeping in here again? The old beds. (*He pats his bed affectionately.*) All the talk that went across those two beds, huh? Our whole lives.

BIFF   Yeah. Lotta dreams and plans.

HAPPY (*with a deep and masculine laugh*)   About five hundred women would like to know what was said in this room. (*They share a soft laugh.*)

BIFF   Remember that big Betsy something—what the hell was her name—over on Bushwick Avenue?

HAPPY (*combing his hair*)   With the collie dog!

BIFF   That's the one. I got you in there, remember?

HAPPY   Yeah, that was my first time—I think. Boy, there was a pig! (*They laugh, almost crudely.*) You taught me everything I know about women. Don't forget that.

BIFF   I bet you forgot how bashful you used to be. Especially with girls.

HAPPY   Oh, I still am, Biff.

BIFF   Oh, go on.

HAPPY   I just control it, that's all. I think I got less bashful and you got more so. What happened, Biff? Where's the old humor, the old confidence? (*He shakes* BIFF's *knee.* BIFF *gets up and moves restlessly about the room.*) What's the matter?

BIFF   Why does Dad mock me all the time?

HAPPY   He's not mocking you, he—

BIFF   Everything I say there's a twist of mockery on his face. I can't get near him.

HAPPY   He just wants you to make good, that's all. I wanted to talk to you about Dad for a long time, Biff. Something's—happening to him. He—talks to himself.

BIFF   I noticed that this morning. But he always mumbled.

HAPPY   But not so noticeable. It got so embarrassing I sent him to Florida. And you know something? Most of the time he's talking to you.

BIFF   What's he say about me?

HAPPY   I can't make it out.

BIFF   What's he say about me?

HAPPY   I think the fact that you're not settled, that you're still kind of up in the air . . .

BIFF   There's one or two other things depressing him, Happy.

HAPPY   What do you mean?

BIFF   Never mind. Just don't lay it all to me.

HAPPY   But I think if you just got started—I mean—is there any future for you out there?

BIFF   I tell ya, Hap, I don't know what the future is. I don't know—what I'm supposed to want.

HAPPY   What do you mean?

BIFF   Well, I spent six or seven years after high school trying to work myself up. Shipping clerk, salesman, business of one kind or another. And it's a measly manner of existence. To get on that subway on the hot mornings in summer. To devote your whole life to keeping stock, or making phone calls, or selling or buying. To suffer fifty weeks of the year for the sake of a two-week vacation, when all you really desire is to be outdoors, with your shirt off. And always to have to get ahead of the next fella. And still—that's how you build a future.

HAPPY   Well, you really enjoy it on a farm? Are you content out there?

BIFF   (*with rising agitation*)   Hap, I've had twenty or thirty different kinds of jobs since I left home before the war, and it always turns out the same. I just realized it lately. In Nebraska when I herded cattle, and the Dakotas, and Arizona, and now in Texas. It's why I came home now, I guess, because I realized it. This farm I work on, it's spring there now, see? And they've got about fifteen new colts. There's nothing more inspiring or—beautiful than the sight of a mare and a new colt. And it's cool there now, see? Texas is cool now, and it's spring. And whenever spring comes to where I am, I suddenly get the feeling, my God, I'm not gettin' anywhere! What the hell am I doing, playing around with horses, twenty-eight dollars a week! I'm thirty-four years old, I oughta be makin' my future. That's when I come running home. And now, I get here, and I don't know what to do with myself. (*After a pause.*) I've always made a point of not wasting my life, and everytime I come back here I know that all I've done is to waste my life.

HAPPY   You're a poet, you know that, Biff? You're a—you're an idealist!

BIFF   No, I'm mixed up very bad. Maybe I oughta get married. Maybe I oughta get stuck into something. Maybe that's my trouble. I'm like a boy. I'm not married,

I'm not in business, I just—I'm like a boy. Are you content, Hap? You're a success, aren't you? Are you content?

HAPPY   Hell, no!

BIFF   Why? You're making money, aren't you?

HAPPY (*moving about with energy, expressiveness*)   All I can do now is wait for the merchandise manager to die. And suppose I get to be merchandise manager? He's a good friend of mine, and he just built a terrific estate on Long Island. And he lived there about two months and sold it, and now he's building another one. He can't enjoy it once it's finished. And I know that's just what I would do. I don't know what the hell I'm workin' for. Sometimes I sit in my apartment—all alone. And I think of the rent I'm paying. And it's crazy. But then, it's what I always wanted. My own apartment, a car, and plenty of women. And still, goddammit, I'm lonely.

BIFF (*with enthusiasm*)   Listen, why don't you come out West with me?

HAPPY   You and I, heh?

BIFF   Sure, maybe we could buy a ranch. Raise cattle, use our muscles. Men built like we are should be working out in the open.

HAPPY (*avidly*)   The Loman Brothers, heh?

BIFF (*with vast affection*)   Sure, we'd be known all over the counties!

HAPPY (*enthralled*)   That's what I dream about, Biff. Sometimes I want to just rip my clothes off in the middle of the store and outbox that goddam merchandise manager. I mean I can outbox, outrun, and outlift anybody in that store, and I have to take orders from those common, petty sons-of-bitches till I can't stand it any more.

BIFF   I'm tellin' you, kid, if you were with me I'd be happy out there.

HAPPY (*enthused*)   See, Biff, everybody around me is so false that I'm constantly lowering my ideals . . .

BIFF   Baby, together we'd stand up for one another, we'd have someone to trust.

HAPPY   If I were around you—

BIFF   Hap, the trouble is we weren't brought up to grub for money. I don't know how to do it.

HAPPY   Neither can I!

BIFF   Then let's go!

HAPPY   The only thing is—what can you make out there?

BIFF   But look at your friend. Builds an estate and then hasn't the peace of mind to live in it.

HAPPY   Yeah, but when he walks into the store the waves part in front of him. That's fifty-two thousand dollars a year coming through the revolving door, and I got more in my pinky finger than he's got in his head.

BIFF   Yeah, but you just said—

HAPPY I gotta show some of those pompous, self-important executives over there that Hap Loman can make the grade. I want to walk into the store the way he walks in. Then I'll go with you, Biff. We'll be together yet, I swear. But take those two we had tonight. Now weren't they gorgeous creatures?

BIFF Yeah, yeah, most gorgeous I've had in years.

HAPPY I get that any time I want, Biff. Whenever I feel disgusted. The only trouble is, it gets like bowling or something. I just keep knockin' them over and it doesn't mean anything. You still run around a lot?

BIFF Naa. I'd like to find a girl—steady, somebody with substance.

HAPPY That's what I long for.

BIFF Go on! You'd never come home.

HAPPY I would! Somebody with character, with resistance! Like Mom, y'know? You're gonna call me a bastard when I tell you this. That girl Charlotte I was with tonight is engaged to be married in five weeks. (*He tries on his new hat.*)

BIFF No kiddin'!

HAPPY Sure, the guy's in line for the vice-presidency of the store. I don't know what gets into me, maybe I just have an overdeveloped sense of competition or something, but I went and ruined her, and furthermore I can't get rid of her. And he's the third executive I've done that to. Isn't that a crummy characteristic? And to top it all, I go to their weddings! (*Indignantly, but laughing.*) Like I'm not supposed to take bribes. Manufacturers offer me a hundred-dollar bill now and then to throw an order their way. You know how honest I am, but it's like this girl, see. I hate myself for it. Because I don't want the girl, and, still, I take it and —I love it!

BIFF Let's go to sleep.

HAPPY I guess we didn't settle anything, heh?

BIFF I just got one idea that I think I'm going to try.

HAPPY What's that?

BIFF Remember Bill Oliver?

HAPPY Sure, Oliver is very big now. You want to work for him again?

BIFF No, but when I quit he said something to me. He put his arm on my shoulder, and he said, "Biff, if you ever need anything, come to me."

HAPPY I remember that. That sounds good.

BIFF I think I'll go to see him. If I could get ten thousand or even seven or eight thousand dollars I could buy a beautiful ranch.

HAPPY I bet he'd back you. 'Cause he thought highly of you, Biff. I mean, they all do. You're well liked, Biff. That's why I say to come back here, and we both have the apartment. And I'm tellin' you, Biff, any babe you want . . .

BIFF No, with a ranch I could do the work I like and still be something. I just wonder though. I wonder if Oliver still thinks I stole that carton of basketballs.

HAPPY Oh, he probably forgot that long ago. It's almost ten years. You're too sensitive. Anyway, he didn't really fire you.

BIFF Well, I think he was going to. I think that's why I quit. I was never sure whether he knew or not. I know he thought the world of me, though. I was the only one he'd let lock up the place.

WILLY (*below*) You gonna wash the engine, Biff?

HAPPY Shh!

(BIFF *looks at* HAPPY, *who is gazing down, listening.* WILLY *is mumbling in the parlor.*)

HAPPY You hear that?

(*They listen.* WILLY *laughs warmly.*)

BIFF (*growing angry*) Doesn't he know Mom can hear that?

WILLY Don't get your sweater dirty, Biff!

(*A look of pain crosses* BIFF's *face.*)

HAPPY Isn't that terrible? Don't leave again, will you? You'll find a job here. You gotta stick around. I don't know what to do about him, it's getting embarrassing.

WILLY What a simonizing job!

BIFF Mom's hearing that!

WILLY No kiddin', Biff, you got a date? Wonderful!

HAPPY Go on to sleep. But talk to him in the morning, will you?

BIFF (*reluctantly getting into bed*) With her in the house. Brother!

HAPPY (*getting into bed*) I wish you'd have a good talk with him.

(*The light on their room begins to fade.*)

BIFF (*to himself in bed*) That selfish, stupid . . .

HAPPY Sh . . . Sleep, Biff.

(*Their light is out. Well before they have finished speaking,* WILLY's *form is dimly seen below in the darkened kitchen. He opens the refrigerator, searches in there, and takes out a bottle of milk. The apartment houses are fading out, and the entire house and surroundings become covered with leaves. Music insinuates itself as the leaves appear.*)

WILLY Just wanna be careful with those girls, Biff, that's all. Don't make any promises. No promises of any kind. Because a girl, y'know, they always believe what you tell 'em, and you're very young, Biff, you're too young to be talking seriously to girls.

(*Light rises on the kitchen.* WILLY, *talking, shuts the refrigerator door and comes downstage to the kitchen table. He pours milk into a glass. He is totally immersed in himself, smiling faintly.*)

WILLY Too young entirely, Biff. You want to watch your schooling first. Then when you're all set, there'll be plenty of girls for a boy like you. (*He smiles broadly at a kitchen chair.*) That so? The girls pay for you? (*He laughs.*) Boy, you must really be makin' a hit.

(WILLY *is gradually addressing—physically—a point offstage, speaking through the wall of the kitchen, and his voice has been rising in volume to that of a normal conversation.*)

WILLY I been wondering why you polish the car so careful. Ha! Don't leave the hubcaps, boys. Get the chamois to the hubcaps. Happy, use newspaper on the windows, it's the easiest thing. Show him how to do it, Biff! You see, Happy? Pad it up, use it like a pad. That's it, that's it, good work. You're doin' all right, Hap. (*He pauses, then nods in approbation for a few seconds, then looks upward.*) Biff, first thing we gotta do when we get time is clip that big branch over the house. Afraid it's gonna fall in a storm and hit the roof. Tell you what. We get a rope and sling her around, and then we climb up there with a couple of saws and take her down. Soon as you finish the car, boys, I wanna see ya. I got a surprise for you, boys.

BIFF (*offstage*) Whatta ya got, Dad?

WILLY No, you finish first. Never leave a job till you're finished—remember that. (*Looking toward the "big trees."*) Biff, up in Albany I saw a beautiful hammock. I think I'll buy it next trip, and we'll hang it right between those two elms. Wouldn't that be something? Just swingin' there under those branches. Boy, that would be . . . (YOUNG BIFF *and* YOUNG HAPPY *appear from the direction* WILLY *was addressing.* HAPPY *carries rags and a pail of water.* BIFF, *wearing a sweater with a block "S," carries a football.*)

BIFF (*pointing in the direction of the car offstage*) How's that, Pop, professional?

WILLY Terrific. Terrific job, boys. Good work, Biff.

HAPPY Where's the surprise, Pop?

WILLY In the back seat of the car.

HAPPY Boy! (*He runs off.*)

BIFF What is it, Dad? Tell me, what'd you buy?

WILLY (*laughing, cuffs him*) Never mind, something I want you to have.

BIFF (*turns and starts off*) What is it, Hap?

HAPPY (*offstage*) It's a punching bag!

BIFF Oh, Pop!

WILLY It's got Gene Tunney's signature on it!

(HAPPY *runs onstage with a punching bag.*)

BIFF Gee, how'd you know we wanted a punching bag?

WILLY Well, it's the finest thing for the timing.

912

HAPPY (*lies down on his back and pedals with his feet*)   I'm losing weight, you notice, Pop?

WILLY (*to* HAPPY)   Jumping rope is good too.

BIFF   Did you see the new football I got?

WILLY (*examining the ball*)   Where'd you get a new ball?

BIFF   The coach told me to practice my passing.

WILLY   That so? And he gave you the ball, heh?

BIFF   Well, I borrowed it from the locker room. (*He laughs confidentially.*)

WILLY (*laughing with him at the theft*)   I want you to return that.

HAPPY   I told you he wouldn't like it!

BIFF (*angrily*)   Well, I'm bringing it back!

WILLY (*stopping the incipient argument, to* HAPPY)   Sure, he's gotta practice with a regulation ball, doesn't he? (*To* BIFF.) Coach'll probably congratulate you on your initiative!

BIFF   Oh, he keeps congratulating my initiative all the time, Pop.

WILLY   That's because he likes you. If somebody else took that ball there'd be an uproar. So what's the report, boys, what's the report?

BIFF   Where'd you go this time, Dad? Gee we were lonesome for you.

WILLY (*pleased, puts an arm around each boy and they come down to the apron*)   Lonesome, heh?

BIFF   Missed you every minute.

WILLY   Don't say? Tell you a secret, boys. Don't breathe it to a soul. Someday I'll have my own business, and I'll never have to leave home any more.

HAPPY   Like Uncle Charley, heh?

WILLY   Bigger than Uncle Charley! Because Charley is not—liked. He's liked, but he's not—well liked.

BIFF   Where'd you go this time, Dad?

WILLY   Well, I got on the road, and I went north to Providence. Met the Mayor.

BIFF   The Mayor of Providence!

WILLY   He was sitting in the hotel lobby.

BIFF   What'd he say?

WILLY   He said, "Morning!" And I said, "You got a fine city here, Mayor," And then he had coffee with me. And then I went to Waterbury. Waterbury is a fine city. Big clock city, the famous Waterbury clock. Sold a nice bill there. And then Boston—Boston is the cradle of the Revolution. A fine city. And a couple of other towns in Mass., and on to Portland and Bangor and straight home!

BIFF   Gee, I'd love to go with you sometime, Dad.

WILLY   Soon as summer comes.

HAPPY Promise?

WILLY You and Hap and I, and I'll show you all the towns. America is full of beautiful towns and fine, upstanding people. And they know me, boys, they know me up and down New England. The finest people. And when I bring you fellas up, there'll be open sesame for all of us, 'cause one thing, boys: I have friends. I can park my car in any street in New England, and the cops protect it like their own. This summer, heh?

BIFF AND HAPPY (*together*) Yeah! You bet!

WILLY We'll take our bathing suits.

HAPPY We'll carry your bags, Pop!

WILLY Oh, won't that be something! Me comin' into the Boston stores with you boys carryin' my bags. What a sensation!

(BIFF *is prancing around, practicing passing the ball.*)

WILLY You nervous, Biff, about the game?

BIFF Not if you're gonna be there.

WILLY What do they say about you in school, now that they made you captain?

HAPPY There's a crowd of girls behind him everytime the classes change.

BIFF (*taking* WILLY'*s hand*) This Saturday, Pop, this Saturday—just for you, I'm going to break through for a touchdown.

HAPPY You're supposed to pass.

BIFF I'm takin' one play for Pop. You watch me, Pop, and when I take off my helmet, that means I'm breakin' out. Then you watch me crash through that line!

WILLY (*kisses* BIFF) Oh, wait'll I tell this in Boston!

(BERNARD *enters in knickers. He is younger than* BIFF, *earnest and loyal, a worried boy.*)

BERNARD Biff, where are you? You're supposed to study with me today.

WILLY Hey, looka Bernard. What're you lookin' so anemic about, Bernard?

BERNARD He's gotta study, Uncle Willy. He's got Regents next week.

HAPPY (*tauntingly, spinning* BERNARD *around*) Let's box, Bernard!

BERNARD Biff! (*He gets away from* HAPPY.) Listen, Biff, I heard Mr. Birnbaum say that if you don't start studyin' math he's gonna flunk you, and you won't graduate. I heard him!

WILLY You better study with him, Biff. Go ahead now.

BERNARD I heard him!

BIFF Oh, Pop, you didn't see my sneakers! (*He holds up a foot for* WILLY *to look at.*)

WILLY Hey, that's a beautiful job of printing.

BERNARD (*wiping his glasses*) Just because he printed University of Virginia on his sneakers doesn't mean they've got to graduate him, Uncle Willy!

WILLY (*angrily*) What're you talking about? With scholarships to three universities they're gonna flunk him?

BERNARD But I heard Mr. Birnbaum say—

WILLY Don't be a pest, Bernard! (*To his boys.*) What an anemic!

BERNARD Okay, I'm waiting for you in my house, Biff.

(*Bernard goes off.* THE LOMANS *laugh.*)

WILLY Bernard is not well liked, is he?

BIFF He's liked, but he's not well liked.

HAPPY That's right, Pop.

WILLY That's just what I mean. Bernard can get the best marks in school, y'understand, but when he gets out in the business world, y'understand, you are going to be five times ahead of him. That's why I thank Almighty God you're both built like Adonises. Because the man who makes an appearance in the business world, the man who creates personal interest, is the man who gets ahead. Be liked and you will never want. You take me, for instance. I never have to wait in line to see a buyer. "Willy Loman is here!" That's all they have to know, and I go right through.

BIFF Did you knock them dead, Pop?

WILLY Knocked 'em cold in Providence, slaughtered 'em in Boston.

HAPPY (*on his back, pedaling again*) I'm losing weight, you notice, Pop?

(LINDA *enters, as of old, a ribbon in her hair, carrying a basket of washing.*)

LINDA (*with youthful energy*) Hello, dear!

WILLY Sweetheart!

LINDA How'd the Chevvy run?

WILLY Chevrolet, Linda, is the greatest car ever built. (*To the boys.*) Since when do you let your mother carry wash up the stairs?

BIFF Grab hold there, boy!

HAPPY Where to, Mom?

LINDA Hang them up on the line. And you better go down to your friends, Biff. The cellar is full of boys. They don't know what to do with themselves.

BIFF Ah, when Pop comes home they can wait!

WILLY (*laughs appreciatively*) You better go down and tell them what to do, Biff.

BIFF I think I'll have them sweep out the furnace room.

WILLY Good work, Biff.

BIFF (*goes through wall-line of kitchen to doorway at back and calls down*) Fellas! Everybody sweep out the furnace room! I'll be right down!

VOICES All right! Okay, Biff.

BIFF George and Sam and Frank, come out back! We're hangin' up the wash! Come on, Hap, on the double! (*He and* HAPPY *carry out the basket.*)

LINDA The way they obey him!

WILLY Well, that's training, the training. I'm tellin' you, I was sellin' thousands and thousands, but I had to come home.

LINDA Oh, the whole block'll be at that game. Did you sell anything?

WILLY I did five hundred gross in Providence and seven hundred gross in Boston.

LINDA No! Wait a minute, I've got a pencil. (*She pulls pencil and paper out of her apron pocket.*) That makes your commission . . . Two hundred—my God! Two hundred and twelve dollars!

WILLY Well, I didn't figure it yet, but . . .

LINDA How much did you do?

WILLY Well, I—I did—about a hundred and eighty gross in Providence. Well, no—it came to—roughly two hundred gross on the whole trip.

LINDA (*without hesitation*) Two hundred gross. That's . . . (*She figures.*)

WILLY The trouble was that three of the stores were half closed for inventory in Boston. Otherwise I woulda broke records.

LINDA Well, it makes seventy dollars and some pennies. That's very good.

WILLY What do we owe?

LINDA Well, on the first there's sixteen dollars on the refrigerator—

WILLY Why sixteen?

LINDA Well, the fan belt broke, so it was a dollar eighty.

WILLY But it's brand new.

LINDA Well, the man said that's the way it is. Till they work themselves in, y'know.

(*They move through the wall-line into the kitchen.*)

WILLY I hope we didn't get stuck on that machine.

LINDA They got the biggest ads of any of them!

WILLY I know, it's a fine machine. What else?

LINDA Well, there's nine-sixty for the washing machine. And for the vacuum cleaner there's three and a half due on the fifteenth. Then the roof, you got twenty-one dollars remaining.

WILLY It don't leak, does it?

LINDA   No, they did a wonderful job. Then you owe Frank for the carburetor.

WILLY   I'm not going to pay that man! That goddam Chevrolet, they ought to prohibit the manufacture of that car!

LINDA   Well, you owe him three and a half. And odds and ends, comes to around a hundred and twenty dollars by the fifteenth.

WILLY   A hundred and twenty dollars! My God, if business don't pick up I don't know what I'm gonna do!

LINDA   Well, next week you'll do better.

WILLY   Oh, I'll knock 'em dead next week. I'll go to Hartford. I'm very well liked in Hartford. You know, the trouble is, Linda, people don't seem to take to me.

(*They move onto the forestage.*)

LINDA   Oh, don't be foolish.

WILLY   I know it when I walk in. They seem to laugh at me.

LINDA   Why? Why would they laugh at you? Don't talk that way, Willy.

(WILLY *moves to the edge of the stage.* LINDA *goes into the kitchen and starts to darn stockings.*)

WILLY   I don't know the reason for it, but they just pass me by. I'm not noticed.

LINDA   But you're doing wonderful, dear. You're making seventy to a hundred dollars a week.

WILLY   But I gotta be at it ten, twelve hours a day. Other men—I don't know—they do it easier. I don't know why—I can't stop myself—I talk too much. A man oughta come in with a few words. One thing about Charley. He's a man of few words, and they respect him.

LINDA   You don't talk too much, you're just lively.

WILLY (*smiling*)   Well, I figure, what the hell, life is short, a couple of jokes. (*To himself.*) I joke too much! (*The smile goes.*)

LINDA   Why? You're—

WILLY   I'm fat. I'm very—foolish to look at, Linda. I didn't tell you, but Christmas time I happened to be calling on F. H. Stewarts, and a salesman I know, as I was going in to see the buyer I heard him say something about—walrus. And I—I cracked him right across the face. I won't take that. I simply will not take that. But they do laugh at me. I know that.

LINDA   Darling . . .

WILLY   I gotta overcome it. I know I gotta overcome it. I'm not dressing to advantage, maybe.

LINDA   Willy, darling, you're the handsomest man in the world—

WILLY   Oh, no, Linda.

LINDA   To me you are. (*Slight pause.*) The handsomest.

917

(*From the darkness is heard the laughter of a woman.* WILLY *doesn't turn to it, but it continues through* LINDA's *lines.*)

LINDA   And the boys, Willy. Few men are idolized by their children the way you are.

(*Music is heard as behind a scrim, to the left of the house,* THE WOMAN, *dimly seen, is dressing.*)

WILLY (*with great feeling*)   You're the best there is, Linda, you're a pal, you know that? On the road—on the road I want to grab you sometimes and just kiss the life outa you.

(*The laughter is loud now, and he moves into a brightening area at the left, where* THE WOMAN *has come from behind the scrim and is standing, putting on her hat, looking into a "mirror" and laughing.*)

WILLY   Cause I get so lonely—especially when business is bad and there's nobody to talk to. I get the feeling that I'll never sell anything again, that I won't make a living for you, or a business, a business for the boys. (*He talks through* THE WOMAN's *subsiding laughter;* THE WOMAN *primps at the "mirror."*) There's so much I want to make for—

THE WOMAN   Me? You didn't make me, Willy. I picked you.

WILLY (*pleased*)   You picked me?

THE WOMAN (*who is quite proper-looking,* WILLY's *age*)   I did. I've been sitting at that desk watching all the salesmen go by, day in, day out. But you've got such a sense of humor, and we do have such a good time together, don't we?

WILLY   Sure, sure. (*He takes her in his arms.*) Why do you have to go now?

THE WOMAN   It's two o'clock . . .

WILLY   No, come on in! (*He pulls her.*)

THE WOMAN   . . . my sisters'll be scandalized. When'll you be back?

WILLY   Oh, two weeks about. Will you come up again?

THE WOMAN   Sure thing. You do make me laugh. It's good for me. (*She squeezes his arm, kisses him.*) And I think you're a wonderful man.

WILLY   You picked me, heh?

THE WOMAN   Sure. Because you're so sweet. And such a kidder.

WILLY   Well, I'll see you next time I'm in Boston.

THE WOMAN   I'll put you right through to the buyers.

WILLY (*slapping her bottom*)   Right. Well, bottoms up!

THE WOMAN (*slaps him gently and laughs*)   You just kill me, Willy. (*He suddenly grabs her and kisses her roughly.*) You kill me. And thanks for the stockings. I love a lot of stockings. Well, good night.

918

WILLY   Good night. And keep your pores open!

THE WOMAN   Oh, Willy!

(THE WOMAN *bursts out laughing, and* LINDA'*s laughter blends in.* THE WOMAN *disappears into the dark. Now the area at the kitchen table brightens.* LINDA *is sitting where she was at the kitchen table, but now is mending a pair of her silk stockings.*)

LINDA   You are, Willy. The handsomest man. You've got no reason to feel that—

WILLY (*coming out of* THE WOMAN'*s dimming area and going over to* LINDA)   I'll make it all up to you, Linda, I'll—

LINDA   There's nothing to make up, dear. You're doing fine, better than—

WILLY (*noticing her mending*)   What's that?

LINDA   Just mending my stockings. They're so expensive—

WILLY (*angrily, taking them from her*)   I won't have you mending stockings in this house! Now throw them out!

(LINDA *puts the stockings in her pocket.*)

BERNARD (*entering on the run*)   Where is he? If he doesn't study!

WILLY (*moving to the forestage, with great agitation*)   You'll give him the answers!

BERNARD   I do, but I can't on a Regents! That's a state exam! They're liable to arrest me!

WILLY   Where is he? I'll whip him, I'll whip him!

LINDA   And he'd better give back that football, Willy, it's not nice.

WILLY   Biff! Where is he? Why is he taking everything?

LINDA   He's too rough with the girls, Willy. All the mothers are afraid of him!

WILLY   I'll whip him!

BERNARD   He's driving the car without a license!

(THE WOMAN'*s laugh is heard.*)

WILLY   Shut up!

LINDA   All the mothers—

WILLY   Shut up!

BERNARD (*backing quietly away and out*)   Mr. Birnbaum says he's stuck up.

WILLY   Get outa here!

BERNARD   If he doesn't buckle down he'll flunk math! (*He goes off*).

LINDA   He's right, Willy, you've gotta—

WILLY (*exploding at her*)   There's nothing the matter with him! You want him to be a worm like Bernard? He's got spirit, personality . . .

(As he speaks, LINDA, *almost in tears, exits into the living-room.* WILLY *is alone in the kitchen, wilting and staring. The leaves are gone. It is night again, and the apartment houses look down from behind.)*

WILLY   Loaded with it. Loaded! What is he stealing? He's giving it back, isn't he? Why is he stealing? What did I tell him? I never in my life told him anything but decent things.

*(*HAPPY *in pajamas has come down the stairs;* WILLY *suddenly becomes aware of* HAPPY'*s presence.)*

HAPPY   Let's go now, come on.

WILLY *(sitting down at the kitchen table)*   Huh! Why did she have to wash the floors herself? Everytime she waxes the floors she keels over. She knows that!

HAPPY   Shh! Take it easy. What brought you back tonight?

WILLY   I got an awful scare. Nearly hit a kid in Yonkers. God! Why didn't I go to Alaska with my brother Ben that time! Ben! That man was a genius, that man was success incarnate! What a mistake! He begged me to go.

HAPPY   Well, there's no use in—

WILLY   You guys! There was a man started with the clothes on his back and ended up with diamond mines!

HAPPY   Boy, someday I'd like to know how he did it.

WILLY   What's the mystery? The man knew what he wanted and went out and got it! Walked into a jungle, and comes out, the age of twenty-one, and he's rich! The world is an oyster, but you don't crack it open on a mattress!

HAPPY   Pop, I told you I'm gonna retire you for life.

WILLY   You'll retire me for life on seventy goddam dollars a week? And your women and your car and your apartment, and you'll retire me for life! Christ's sake, I couldn't get past Yonkers today! Where are you guys, where are you? The woods are burning! I can't drive a car!

*(*CHARLEY *has appeared in the doorway. He is a large man, slow of speech, laconic, immovable. In all he says, despite what he says, there is pity, and, now trepidation. He has a robe over pajamas, slippers on his feet. He enters the kitchen.)*

CHARLEY   Everything all right?

HAPPY   Yeah, Charley, everything's . . .

WILLY   What's the matter?

CHARLEY   I heard some noise. I thought something happened. Can't we do something about the walls? You sneeze in here, and in my house hats blow off.

HAPPY   Let's go to bed, Dad. Come on.

920

(CHARLEY *signals to* HAPPY *to go.*)

WILLY   You go ahead, I'm not tired at the moment.

HAPPY (*to* WILLY)   Take it easy, huh? (*He exits.*)

WILLY   What're you doin' up?

CHARLEY (*sitting down at the kitchen table opposite* WILLY)   Couldn't sleep good. I had a heartburn.

WILLY   Well, you don't know how to eat.

CHARLEY   I eat with my mouth.

WILLY   No, you're ignorant. You gotta know about vitamins and things like that.

CHARLEY   Come on, let's shoot. Tire you out a little.

WILLY (*hesitantly*)   All right. You got cards?

CHARLEY (*taking a deck from his pocket*)   Yeah, I got them. Someplace. What is it with those vitamins?

WILLY (*dealing*)   They build up your bones. Chemistry.

CHARLEY   Yeah, but there's no bones in a heartburn.

WILLY   What are you talkin' about? Do you know the first thing about it?

CHARLEY   Don't get insulted.

WILLY   Don't talk about something you don't know anything about.

(*They are playing. Pause.*)

CHARLEY   What're you doin' home?

WILLY   A little trouble with the car.

CHARLEY   Oh. (*Pause.*) I'd like to take a trip to California.

WILLY   Don't say.

CHARLEY   You want a job?

WILLY   I got a job, I told you that. (*After a slight pause.*) What the hell are you offering me a job for?

CHARLEY   Don't get insulted.

WILLY   Don't insult me.

CHARLEY   I don't see no sense in it. You don't have to go on this way.

WILLY   I got a good job. (*Slight pause.*) What do you keep comin' in here for?

CHARLEY   You want me to go?

WILLY (*after a pause, withering*)   I can't understand it. He's going back to Texas again. What the hell is that?

CHARLEY   Let him go.

WILLY   I got nothin' to give him, Charley, I'm clean, I'm clean.

CHARLEY   He won't starve. None a them starve. Forget about him.

WILLY Then what have I got to remember?

CHARLEY You take it too hard. To hell with it. When a deposit bottle is broken you don't get your nickel back.

WILLY That's easy enough for you to say.

CHARLEY That ain't easy for me to say.

WILLY Did you see the ceiling I put up in the living-room?

CHARLEY Yeah, that's a piece of work. To put up a ceiling is a mystery to me. How do you do it?

WILLY What's the difference?

CHARLEY Well, talk about it.

WILLY You gonna put up a ceiling?

CHARLEY How could I put up a ceiling?

WILLY Then what the hell are you bothering me for?

CHARLEY You're insulted again.

WILLY A man who can't handle tools is not a man. You're disgusting.

CHARLEY Don't call me disgusting, Willy.

(UNCLE BEN, *carrying a valise and an umbrella, enters the forestage from around the right corner of the house. He is a stolid man, in his sixties, with a mustache and an authoritative air. He is utterly certain of his destiny, and there is an aura of far places about him. He enters exactly as* WILLY *speaks.*)

WILLY I'm getting awfully tired, Ben.

(BEN's *music is heard.* BEN *looks around at everything.*)

CHARLEY Good, keep playing; you'll sleep better. Did you call me Ben?

(BEN *looks at his watch.*)

WILLY That's funny. For a second there you reminded me of my brother Ben.

BEN I only have a few minutes. (*He strolls, inspecting the place.* WILLY *and* CHARLEY *continue playing.*)

CHARLEY You never heard from him again, heh? Since that time?

WILLY Didn't Linda tell you? Couple of weeks ago we got a letter from his wife in Africa. He died.

CHARLEY That so.

BEN (*chuckling*) So this is Brooklyn, eh?

CHARLEY Maybe you're in for some of his money.

WILLY Naa, he had seven sons. There's just one opportunity I had with that man . . .

BEN I must make a train, William. There are several properties I'm looking at in Alaska.

WILLY Sure, sure! If I'd gone with him to Alaska that time, everything would've been totally different.

CHARLEY Go on, you'd froze to death up there.

WILLY What're you talking about?

BEN Opportunity is tremendous in Alaska, William. Surprised you're not up there.

WILLY Sure, tremendous.

CHARLEY Heh?

WILLY There was the only man I ever met who knew the answers.

CHARLEY Who?

BEN How are you all?

WILLY (*taking a pot, smiling*) Fine, fine.

CHARLEY Pretty sharp tonight.

BEN Is Mother living with you?

WILLY No, she died a long time ago.

CHARLEY Who?

BEN That's too bad. Fine specimen of a lady, Mother.

WILLY (*to* CHARLEY) Heh?

BEN I'd hoped to see the old girl.

CHARLEY Who died?

BEN Heard anything from Father, have you?

WILLY (*unnerved*) What do you mean, who died?

CHARLEY (*taking a pot*) What're you talkin' about?

BEN (*looking at his watch*) William, it's half-past eight!

WILLY (*as though to dispel his confusion he angrily stops* CHARLEY'*s hand*) That's my build!

CHARLEY I put the ace—

WILLY If you don't know how to play the game I'm not gonna throw my money away on you!

CHARLEY (*rising*) It was my ace, for God's sake!

WILLY I'm through, I'm through!

BEN When did Mother die?

WILLY Long ago. Since the beginning you never knew how to play cards.

CHARLEY (*picks up the cards and goes to the door*) All right! Next time I'll bring a deck with five aces.

WILLY   I don't play that kind of game!

CHARLEY (*turning to him*)   You ought to be ashamed of yourself!

WILLY   Yeah?

CHARLEY   Yeah! (*He goes out.*)

WILLY (*slamming the door after him*)   Ignoramus!

BEN (*as* WILLY *comes toward him through the wall-line of the kitchen*)   So you're William.

WILLY (*shaking* BEN's *hand*)   Ben! I've been waiting for you so long! What's the answer? How did you do it?

BEN   Oh, there's a story in that.

(LINDA *enters the forestage, as of old, carrying the wash basket.*)

LINDA   Is this Ben?

BEN (*gallantly*)   How do you do, my dear.

LINDA   Where've you been all these years? Willy's always wondered why you—

WILLY (*pulling* BEN *away from her impatiently*)   Where is Dad? Didn't you follow him? How did you get started?

BEN   Well, I don't know how much you remember.

WILLY   Well, I was just a baby, of course, only three or four years old—

BEN   Three years and eleven months.

WILLY   What a memory, Ben!

BEN   I have many enterprises, William, and I have never kept books.

WILLY   I remember I was sitting under the wagon in—was it Nebraska?

BEN   It was South Dakota, and I gave you a bunch of wild flowers.

WILLY   I remember you walking away down some open road.

BEN (*laughing*)   I was going to find Father in Alaska.

WILLY   Where is he?

BEN   At that age I had a very faulty view of geography, William. I discovered after a few days that I was heading due south, so instead of Alaska, I ended up in Africa.

LINDA   Africa!

WILLY   The Gold Coast!

BEN   Principally diamond mines.

LINDA   Diamond mines!

BEN   Yes, my dear. But I've only a few minutes—

WILLY   No! Boys! Boys! (YOUNG BIFF *and* HAPPY *appear.*) Listen to this. This is your Uncle Ben, a great man! Tell my boys, Ben!

924

BEN   Why, boys, when I was seventeen I walked into the jungle, and when I was twenty-one I walked out. (*He laughs.*) And by God I was rich.

WILLY (*to the boys*)   You see what I been talking about? The greatest things can happen!

BEN (*glancing at his watch*)   I have an appointment in Ketchikan Tuesday week.

WILLY   No, Ben! Please tell about Dad. I want my boys to hear. I want them to know the kind of stock they spring from. All I remember is a man with a big beard, and I was in Mamma's lap, sitting around a fire, and some kind of high music.

BEN   His flute. He played the flute.

WILLY   Sure, the flute, that's right!

(*New music is heard, a high, rollicking tune.*)

BEN   Father was a very great and a very wild-hearted man. We would start in Boston, and he'd toss the whole family into the wagon, and then he'd drive the team right across the country; through Ohio, and Indiana, Michigan, Illinois, and all the Western states. And we'd stop in the towns and sell the flutes that he'd made on the way. Great inventor, Father. With one gadget he made more in a week than a man like you could make in a lifetime.

WILLY   That's just the way I'm bringing them up, Ben—rugged, well liked, all-around.

BEN   Yeah? (*To* BIFF.) Hit that, boy—hard as you can. (*He pounds his stomach.*)

BIFF   Oh, no, sir!

BEN (*taking boxing stance*),   Come on, get to me! (*He laughs.*)

WILLY   Go to it, Biff! Go ahead, show him!

BIFF   Okay! (*He cocks his fists and starts in.*)

LINDA (*to* WILLY)   Why must he fight, dear?

BEN (*sparring with* BIFF)   Good boy! Good boy!

WILLY   How's that, Ben, heh?

HAPPY   Give him the left, Biff!

LINDA   Why are you fighting?

BEN   Good boy! (*Suddenly comes in, trips* BIFF, *and stands over him, the point of his umbrella poised over* BIFF's *eye.*)

LINDA   Look, out, Biff!

BIFF   Gee!

BEN (*patting* BIFF's *knee*)   Never fight fair with a stranger, boy. You'll never get out of the jungle that way. (*Taking* LINDA's *hand and bowing.*) It was an honor and a pleasure to meet you, Linda.

LINDA (*withdrawing her hand coldly, frightened*)   Have a nice—trip.

BEN (*to* WILLY) And good luck with your—what do you do?

WILLY Selling.

BEN Yes. Well . . . (*He raises his hand in farewell to all.*)

WILLY No, Ben, I don't want you to think . . . (*He takes* BEN*'s arm to show him.*) It's Brooklyn, I know, but we hunt too.

BEN Really, now.

WILLY Oh, sure, there's snakes and rabbits and—that's why I moved out here. Why, Biff can fell any one of these trees in no time! Boys! Go right over to where they're building the apartment house and get some sand. We're gonna rebuild the entire front stoop right now! Watch this, Ben!

BIFF Yes, sir! On the double, Hap!

HAPPY (*as he and* BIFF *run off*) I lost weight, Pop, you notice?

(CHARLEY *enters in knickers, even before the boys are gone.*)

CHARLEY Listen, if they steal any more from that building the watchman'll put the cops on them!

LINDA (*to* WILLY) Don't let Biff . . .

(BEN *laughs lustily.*)

WILLY You shoulda seen the lumber they brought home last week. At least a dozen six-by-tens worth all kinds a money.

CHARLEY Listen, if that watchman—

WILLY I gave them hell, understand. But I got a couple of fearless characters there.

CHARLEY Willy, the jails are full of fearless characters.

BEN (*clapping* WILLY *on the back, with a laugh at* CHARLEY) And the stock exchange, friend!

WILLY (*joining in* BEN*'s laughter*) Where are the rest of your pants?

CHARLEY My wife bought them.

WILLY Now all you need is a golf club and you can go upstairs and go to sleep. (*To* BEN.) Great athlete! Between him and his son Bernard they can't hammer a nail!

BERNARD (*rushing in*) The watchman's chasing Biff!

WILLY (*angrily*) Shut up! He's not stealing anything!

LINDA (*alarmed, hurrying off left*) Where is he? Biff, dear! (*She exits.*)

WILLY (*moving toward the left, away from* BEN) There's nothing wrong. What's the matter with you?

BEN Nervy boy. Good!

WILLY (*laughing*) Oh, nerves of iron, that Biff!

CHARLEY Don't know what it is. My New England man comes back and he's bleedin', they murdered him up there.

WILLY It's contacts, Charley, I got important contacts!

CHARLEY (*sarcastically*) Glad to hear it, Willy. Come in later, we'll shoot a little casino. I'll take some of your Portland money. (*He laughs at* WILLY *and exits.*)

WILLY (*turning to* BEN) Business is bad, it's murderous. But not for me, of course.

BEN I'll stop by on my way back to Africa.

WILLY (*longingly*) Can't you stay a few days? You're just what I need, Ben, because I—I have a fine position here, but I—well, Dad left when I was such a baby and I never had a chance to talk to him and I still feel—kind of temporary about myself.

BEN I'll be late for my train.

(*They are at opposite ends of the stage.*)

WILLY Ben, my boys—can't we talk? They'd go into the jaws of hell for me, see, but I—

BEN William, you're being first-rate with your boys. Outstanding, manly chaps!

WILLY (*hanging on to his words*) Oh, Ben, that's good to hear! Because sometimes I'm afraid that I'm not teaching them the right kind of—Ben, how should I teach them?

BEN (*giving great weight to each word, and with a certain vicious audacity*) William, when I walked into the jungle, I was seventeen. When I walked out I was twenty-one. And, by God, I was rich! (*He goes off into darkness around the right corner of the house.*)

WILLY . . . was rich! That's just the spirit I want to imbue them with! To walk into a jungle! I was right! I was right! I was right!

(BEN *is gone, but* WILLY *is still speaking to him as* LINDA, *in nightgown and robe, enters the kitchen, glances around for* WILLY, *then goes to the door of the house, looks out and sees him. Comes down to his left. He looks at her.*)

LINDA Willy, dear? Willy?

WILLY I was right!

LINDA Did you have some cheese? (*He can't answer.*) It's very late, darling. Come to bed, heh?

WILLY (*looking straight up*) Gotta break your neck to see a star in this yard.

LINDA You coming in?

WILLY Whatever happened to that diamond watch fob? Remember? When Ben came from Africa that time? Didn't he give me a watch fob with a diamond in it?

LINDA   You pawned it, dear. Twelve, thirteen years ago. For Biff's radio correspondence course.

WILLY   Gee, that was a beautiful thing. I'll take a walk.

LINDA   But you're in your slippers.

WILLY (*starting to go around the house at the left*)   I was right! I was! (*Half to* LINDA, *as he goes, shaking his head.*) What a man! There was a man worth talking to. I was right!

LINDA (*calling after* WILLY)   But in your slippers, Willy!

(WILLY *is almost gone when* BIFF, *in his pajamas, comes down the stairs and enters the kitchen.*)

BIFF   What is he doing out there?

LINDA   Sh!

BIFF   God Almighty, Mom, how long has he been doing this?

LINDA   Don't, he'll hear you.

BIFF   What the hell is the matter with him?

LINDA   It'll pass by morning.

BIFF   Shouldn't we do anything?

LINDA   Oh, my dear, you should do a lot of things, but there's nothing to do, so go to sleep.

(HAPPY *comes down the stairs and sits on the steps.*)

HAPPY   I never heard him so loud, Mom.

LINDA   Well, come around more often; you'll hear him. (*She sits down at the table and mends the lining of* WILLY'*s jacket.*)

BIFF   Why didn't you ever write me about this, Mom?

LINDA   How would I write to you? For over three months you had no address.

BIFF   I was on the move. But you know I thought of you all the time. You know that, don't you, pal?

LINDA   I know, dear, I know. But he likes to have a letter. Just to know that there's still a possibility for better things.

BIFF   He's not like this all the time, is he?

LINDA   It's when you come home he's always the worst.

BIFF   When I come home?

LINDA   When you write you're coming, he's all smiles, and talks about the future, and—he's just wonderful. And then the closer you seem to come, the more shaky he gets, and then, by the time you get here, he's arguing, and he seems angry at you. I think it's just that maybe he can't bring himself to—to open up to you. Why are you so hateful to each other? Why is that?

928

BIFF (*evasively*) I'm not hateful, Mom.

LINDA But you no sooner come in the door than you're fighting!

BIFF I don't know why. I mean to change. I'm tryin', Mom, you understand?

LINDA Are you home to stay now?

BIFF I don't know. I want to look around, see what's doin'.

LINDA Biff, you can't look around all your life, can you?

BIFF I just can't take hold, Mom. I can't take hold of some kind of a life.

LINDA Biff, a man is not a bird, to come and go with the springtime.

BIFF Your hair . . . (*He touches her hair.*) Your hair got so gray.

LINDA Oh, it's been gray since you were in high school. I just stopped dyeing it, that's all.

BIFF Dye it again, will ya? I don't want my pal looking old. (*He smiles.*)

LINDA You're such a boy! You think you can go away for a year and . . . You've got to get it into your head now that one day you'll knock on this door and there'll be strange people here—

BIFF What are you talking about? You're not even sixty, Mom.

LINDA But what about your father?

BIFF (*lamely*) Well, I meant him too.

HAPPY He admires Pop.

LINDA Biff, dear, if you don't have any feeling for him, then you can't have any feeling for me.

BIFF Sure I can, Mom.

LINDA No. You can't come to see me, because I love him. (*With a threat, but only a threat, of tears.*) He's the dearest man in the world to me, and I won't have anyone making him feel unwanted and low and blue. You've got to make up your mind now, darling, there's no leeway any more. Either he's your father and you pay him that respect, or else you're not to come here. I know he's not easy to get along with—nobody knows that better than me—but . . .

WILLY (*from the left, with a laugh*) Hey, hey, Biffo!

BIFF (*starting to go out after* WILLY) What the hell is the matter with him? (HAPPY *stops him.*)

LINDA Don't—don't go near him!

BIFF Stop making excuses for him! He always, always wiped the floor with you. Never had an ounce of respect for you.

HAPPY He's always had respect for—

BIFF What the hell do you know about it?

HAPPY (*surlily*) Just don't call him crazy!

BIFF He's got no character—Charley wouldn't do this. Not in his own house— spewing out that vomit from his mind.

HAPPY   Charley never had to cope with what he's got to.

BIFF   People are worse off than Willy Loman. Believe me, I've seen them!

LINDA   Then make Charley your father, Biff. You can't do that, can you? I don't say he's a great man. Willy Loman never made a lot of money. His name was never in the paper. He's not the finest character that ever lived. But he's a human being, and a terrible thing is happening to him. So attention must be paid. He's not to be allowed to fall into his grave like an old dog. Attention, attention must be finally paid to such a person. You called him crazy—

BIFF   I didn't mean—

LINDA   No, a lot of people think he's lost his—balance. But you don't have to be very smart to know what his trouble is. The man is exhausted.

HAPPY   Sure!

LINDA   A small man can be just as exhausted as a great man. He works for a company thirty-six years this March, opens up unheard-of territories to their trade-mark, and now in his old age they take his salary away.

HAPPY (*indignantly*)   I didn't know that, Mom.

LINDA   You never asked, my dear! Now that you get your spending money someplace else you don't trouble your mind with him.

HAPPY   But I gave you money last—

LINDA   Christmas time, fifty dollars! To fix the hot water it cost ninety-seven fifty! For five weeks he's been on straight commission, like a beginner, an unknown!

BIFF   Those ungrateful bastards!

LINDA   Are they any worse than his sons? When he brought them business, when he was young, they were glad to see him. But now his old friends, the old buyers that loved him so and always found some order to hand him in a pinch—they're all dead, retired. He used to be able to make six, seven calls a day in Boston. Now he takes his valises out of the car and puts them back and takes them out again and he's exhausted. Instead of walking he talks now. He drives seven hundred miles, and when he gets there no one knows him any more, no one welcomes him. And what goes through a man's mind, driving seven hundred miles home without having earned a cent? Why shouldn't he talk to himself? Why? When he has to go to Charley and borrow fifty dollars a week and pretend to me that it's his pay? How long can that go on? How long? You see what I'm sitting here and waiting for? And you tell me he has no character? The man who never worked a day but for your benefit? When does he get the medal for that? Is this his reward—to turn around at the age of sixty-three and find his sons, who he loved better than his life, one a philandering bum—

HAPPY   Mom!

LINDA   That's all you are, my baby! (*To* BIFF.) And you! What happened to the love you had for him? You were such pals! How you used to talk to him on the phone every night! How lonely he was till he could come home to you!

BIFF   All right, Mom. I'll live here in my room, and I'll get a job. I'll keep away from him, that's all.

LINDA   No, Biff. You can't stay here and fight all the time.

BIFF   He threw me out of this house, remember that.

LINDA   Why did he do that? I never knew why.

BIFF   Because I know he's a fake and he doesn't like anybody around who knows!

LINDA   Why a fake? In what way? What do you mean?

BIFF   Just don't lay it all at my feet. It's between me and him—that's all I have to say. I'll chip in from now on. He'll settle for half my pay check. He'll be all right. I'm going to bed. (*He starts for the stairs.*)

LINDA   He won't be all right.

BIFF (*turning on the stairs, furiously*)   I hate this city and I'll stay here. Now what do you want?

LINDA   He's dying, Biff.

(HAPPY *turns quickly to her, shocked.*)

BIFF (*after a pause*)   Why is he dying?

LINDA   He's been trying to kill himself.

BIFF (*with great horror*)   How?

LINDA   I live from day to day.

BIFF   What're you talking about?

LINDA   Remember I wrote you that he smashed up the car again? In February?

BIFF   Well?

LINDA   The insurance inspector came. He said that they have evidence. That all these accidents in the last year—weren't—weren't—accidents.

HAPPY   How can they tell that? That's a lie.

LINDA   It seems there's a woman . . . (*She takes a breath as—*)

BIFF (*sharply but contained*)   What woman?

LINDA (*simultaneously*)   . . . and this woman . . .

LINDA   What?

BIFF   Nothing. Go ahead.

LINDA   What did you say?

BIFF   Nothing. I just said what woman?

HAPPY   What about her?

LINDA   Well, it seems she was walking down the road and saw his car. She says that he wasn't driving fast at all, and that he didn't skid. She says he came to that little bridge, and then deliberately smashed into the railing, and it was only the shallowness of the water that saved him.

931

BIFF Oh, no, he probably just fell asleep again.

LINDA I don't think he fell asleep.

BIFF Why not?

LINDA Last month . . . (*With great difficulty.*) Oh, boys, it's so hard to say a thing like this! He's just a big stupid man to you, but I tell you there's more good in him than in many other people. (*She chokes, wipes her eyes.*) I was looking for a fuse. The lights blew out, and I went down the cellar. And behind the fuse box—it happened to fall out—was a length of rubber pipe—just short.

HAPPY No kidding?

LINDA There's a little attachment on the end of it. I knew right away. And sure enough, on the bottom of the water heater there's a new little nipple on the gas pipe.

HAPPY (*angrily*) That—jerk.

BIFF Did you have it taken off?

LINDA I'm—I'm ashamed to. How can I mention it to him? Every day I go down and take away that little rubber pipe. But, when he comes home, I put it back where it was. How can I insult him that way? I don't know what to do. I live from day to day, boys. I tell you, I know every thought in his mind. It sounds so old-fashioned and silly, but I tell you he put his whole life into you and you've turned your backs on him. (*She is bent over in the chair, weeping, her face in her hands.*) Biff, I swear to God! Biff, his life is in your hands!

HAPPY (*to* BIFF) How do you like that damned fool!

BIFF (*kissing her*) All right, pal, all right. It's all settled now. I've been remiss. I know that, Mom. But now I'll stay, and I swear to you, I'll apply myself. (*Kneeling in front of her, in a fever of self-reproach.*) It's just—you see, Mom. I don't fit in business. Not that I won't try. I'll try, and I'll make good.

HAPPY Sure you will. The trouble with you in business was you never tried to please people.

BIFF I know, I—

HAPPY Like when you worked for Harrison's. Bob Harrison said you were tops, and then you go and do some damn fool thing like whistling whole songs in the elevator like a comedian.

BIFF (*against* HAPPY) So what? I like to whistle sometimes.

HAPPY You don't raise a guy to a responsible job who whistles in the elevator!

LINDA Well, don't argue about it now.

HAPPY Like when you'd go off and swim in the middle of the day instead of taking the line around.

BIFF (*his resentment rising*) Well, don't you run off? You take off sometimes, don't you? On a nice summer day?

HAPPY Yeah, but I cover myself!

LINDA   Boys!

HAPPY   If I'm going to take a fade the boss can call any number where I'm supposed to be and they'll swear to him that I just left. I'll tell you something that I hate to say, Biff, but in the business world some of them think you're crazy.

BIFF (*angered*)   Screw the business world!

HAPPY   All right, screw it! Great, but cover yourself!

LINDA   Hap, Hap!

BIFF   I don't care what they think! They've laughed at Dad for years, and you know why? Because we don't belong in this nut-house of a city! We should be mixing cement on some open plain, or—or carpenters. A carpenter is allowed to whistle!

(WILLY *walks in from the entrance of the house, at left.*)

WILLY   Even your grandfather was better than a carpenter. (*Pause. They watch him.*) You never grew up. Bernard does not whistle in the elevator, I assure you.

BIFF (*as though to laugh* WILLY *out of it*)   Yeah, but you do, Pop.

WILLY   I never in my life whistled in an elevator! And who in the business world thinks I'm crazy?

BIFF   I didn't mean it like that, Pop. Now don't make a whole thing out of it, will ya?

WILLY   Go back to the West! Be a carpenter, a cowboy, enjoy yourself!

LINDA   Willy, he was just saying—

WILLY   I heard what he said!

HAPPY (*trying to quiet* WILLY)   Hey, Pop, come on now . . .

WILLY (*continuing over* HAPPY*'s line*)   They laugh at me heh? Go to Filene's, go to the Hub, go to Slattery's, Boston. Call out the name Willy Loman and see what happens! Big shot!

BIFF   All right, Pop.

WILLY   Big!

BIFF   All right!

WILLY   Why do you always insult me?

BIFF   I didn't say a word. (*To* LINDA.) Did I say a word?

LINDA   He didn't say anything, Willy.

WILLY (*going to the doorway of the livingroom*)   All right, good night, good night.

LINDA   Willy, dear, he just decided . . .

WILLY (*to* BIFF)   If you get tired hanging around tomorrow, paint the ceiling I put up in the living-room.

BIFF   I'm leaving early tomorrow.

HAPPY   He's going to see Bill Oliver, Pop.

WILLY (*interestedly*)   Oliver? For what?

BIFF (*with reserve, but trying, trying*)   He always said he'd stake me. I'd like to go into business, so maybe I can take him up on it.

LINDA   Isn't that wonderful?

WILLY   Don't interrupt. What's wonderful about it? There's fifty men in the City of New York who'd stake him. (*To* BIFF.) Sporting goods?

BIFF   I guess so. I know something about it and—

WILLY   He knows something about it! You know sporting goods better than Spalding, for God's sake! How much is he giving you?

BIFF   I don't know, I didn't even see him yet, but—

WILLY   Then what're you talkin' about?

BIFF (*getting angry*)   Well, all I said was I'm gonna see him, that's all!

WILLY (*turning away*)   Ah, you're counting your chickens again.

BIFF (*starting left for the stairs*)   Oh, Jesus, I'm going to sleep!

WILLY (*calling after him*)   Don't curse in this house!

BIFF (*turning*)   Since when did you get so clean?

HAPPY (*trying to stop them*)   Wait a . . .

WILLY   Don't use that language to me! I won't have it!

HAPPY (*grabbing* BIFF, *shouts*)   Wait a minute! I got an idea. I got a feasible idea. Come here, Biff, let's talk this over now, let's talk some sense here. When I was down in Florida last time, I thought of a great idea to sell sporting goods. It just came back to me. You and I, Biff—we have a line, the Loman Line. We train a couple of weeks, and put on a couple of exhibitions, see?

WILLY   That's an idea!

HAPPY   Wait! We form two basketball teams, see? Two water-polo teams. We play each other. It's a million dollars' worth of publicity. Two brothers, see? The Loman Brothers. Displays in the Royal Palms—all the hotels. And banners over the ring and the basketball court: "Loman Brothers." Baby, we could sell sporting goods!

WILLY   That is a one-million-dollar idea!

LINDA   Marvelous!

BIFF   I'm in great shape as far as that's concerned.

HAPPY   And the beauty of it is, Biff, it wouldn't be like a business. We'd be out playin' ball again . . .

BIFF (*enthused*)   Yeah, that's . . .

WILLY   Million-dollar . . .

HAPPY   And you wouldn't get fed up with it, Biff. It'd be the family again. There'd be the old honor, and comradeship, and if you wanted to go off for a swim or somethin'—well, you'd do it! Without some smart cooky gettin' up ahead of you!

WILLY   Lick the world! You guys together could absolutely lick the civilized world.

BIFF   I'll see Oliver tomorrow. Hap, if we could work that out . . .

LINDA   Maybe things are beginning to—

WILLY (*wildly enthused, to* LINDA)   Stop interrupting! (*To* BIFF.) But don't wear sport jacket and slacks when you see Oliver.

BIFF   No, I'll—

WILLY   A business suit, and talk as little as possible, and don't crack any jokes.

BIFF   He did like me. Always liked me.

LINDA   He loved you!

WILLY (*to* LINDA)   Will you stop! (*To* BIFF.) Walk in very serious. You are not applying for a boy's job. Money is to pass. Be quiet, fine, and serious. Everybody likes a kidder, but nobody lends him money.

HAPPY   I'll try to get some myself, Biff. I'm sure I can.

WILLY   I see great things for you kids, I think your troubles are over. But remember, start big and you'll end big. Ask for fifteen. How much you gonna ask for?

BIFF   Gee, I don't know—

WILLY   And don't say "Gee." "Gee" is a boy's word. A man walking in for fifteen thousand dollars does not say "Gee!"

BIFF   Ten, I think, would be top though.

WILLY   Don't be so modest. You always started too low. Walk in with a big laugh. Don't look worried. Start off with a couple of your good stories to lighten things up. It's not what you say, it's how you say it—because personality always wins the day.

LINDA   Oliver always thought the highest of him—

WILLY   Will you let me talk?

BIFF   Don't yell at her, Pop, will ya?

WILLY (*angrily*)   I was talking, wasn't I?

BIFF   I don't like you yelling at her all the time, and I'm tellin' you, that's all.

WILLY   What're you, takin' over this house?

LINDA   Willy—

WILLY (*turning on her*)   Don't take his side all the time, goddammit!

BIFF (*furiously*)   Stop yelling at her!

WILLY (*suddenly pulling on his cheek, beaten down, guilt ridden*)   Give my best to Bill Oliver—he may remember me. (*He exits through the living-room doorway.*)

LINDA (*her voice subdued*)   What'd you have to start that for? (BIFF *turns away.*) You see how sweet he was as soon as you talked hopefully? (*She goes over to* BIFF.) Come up and say good night to him. Don't let him go to bed that way.

HAPPY   Come on, Biff, let's buck him up.

LINDA   Please, dear. Just say good night. It takes so little to make him happy. Come. (*She goes through the living-room doorway, calling upstairs from within the living-room.*) Your pajamas are hanging in the bathroom, Willy!

HAPPY (*looking toward where* LINDA *went out*)   What a woman! They broke the mold when they made her. You know that, Biff?

BIFF   He's off salary. My God, working on commission!

HAPPY   Well, let's face it: he's no hot-shot selling man. Except that sometimes, you have to admit, he's a sweet personality.

BIFF (*deciding*)   Lend me ten bucks, will ya? I want to buy some new ties.

HAPPY   I'll take you to a place I know. Beautiful stuff. Wear one of my striped shirts tomorrow.

BIFF   She got gray. Mom got awful old. Gee, I'm gonna go in to Oliver tomorrow and knock him for a—

HAPPY   Come on up. Tell that to Dad. Let's give him a whirl. Come on.

BIFF (*steamed up*)   You know, with ten thousand bucks, boy!

HAPPY (*as they go into the living-room*)   That's the talk, Biff, that's the first time I've heard the old confidence out of you! (*From within the living-room, fading off.*) You're gonna live with me, kid, and any babe you want just say the word . . . (*The last lines are hardly heard. They are mounting the stairs to their parents' bedroom.*)

LINDA (*entering her bedroom and addressing* WILLY, *who is in the bathroom. She is straightening the bed for him*)   Can you do anything about the shower? It drips.

WILLY (*from the bathroom*)   All of a sudden everything falls to pieces! Goddam plumbing, oughta be sued, those people. I hardly finished putting it in and the thing . . . (*His words rumble off.*)

LINDA   I'm just wondering if Oliver will remember him. You think he might?

WILLY (*coming out of the bathroom in his pajamas*)   Remember him? What's the matter with you, you crazy? If he'd've stayed with Oliver he'd be on top by now! Wait'll Oliver gets a look at him. You don't know the average caliber any more. The average young man today—(*he is getting into bed*)—is got a caliber of zero. Greatest thing in the world for him was to bum around.

(BIFF *and* HAPPY *enter the bedroom. Slight pause.*)

WILLY (*stops short, looking at* BIFF)   Glad to hear it, boy.

HAPPY   He wanted to say good night to you, sport.

WILLY (*to* BIFF) Yeah. Knock him dead, boy. What'd you want to tell me?

BIFF Just take it easy, Pop. Good night. (*He turns to go.*)

WILLY (*unable to resist*) And if anything falls off the desk while you're talking to him—like a package or something—don't you pick it up. They have office boys for that.

LINDA I'll make a big breakfast—

WILLY Will you let me finish? (*To* BIFF.) Tell him you were in the business in the West. Not farm work.

BIFF All right, Dad.

LINDA I think everything—

WILLY (*going right through her speech*) And don't undersell yourself. No less than fifteen thousand dollars.

BIFF (*unable to bear him*) Okay. Good night, Mom. (*He starts moving.*)

WILLY Because you got a greatness in you, Biff, remember that. You got all kinds a greatness . . . (*He lies back, exhausted.* BIFF *walks out.*)

LINDA (*calling after* BIFF) Sleep well, darling!

HAPPY I'm gonna get married, Mom. I wanted to tell you.

LINDA Go to sleep, dear.

HAPPY (*going*) I just wanted to tell you.

WILLY Keep up the good work. (HAPPY *exits.*) God . . . remember that Ebbets Field game? The championship of the city?

LINDA Just rest. Should I sing to you?

WILLY Yeah. Sing to me. (LINDA *hums a soft lullaby.*) When that team came out —he was the tallest, remember?

LINDA Oh, yes. And in gold.

(BIFF *enters the darkened kitchen, takes a cigarette, and leaves the house. He comes downstage into a golden pool of light. He smokes, staring at the night.*)

WILLY Like a young god. Hercules—something like that. And the sun, the sun all around him. Remember how he waved to me? Right up from the field, with the representatives of three colleges standing by? And the buyers I brought, and the cheers when he came out—Loman, Loman, Loman! God Almighty, he'll be great yet. A star like that, magnificent, can never really fade away!

(*The light on* WILLY *is fading. The gas heater begins to glow through the kitchen wall, near the stairs, a blue flame beneath red coils.*)

LINDA (*timidly*) Willy dear, what has he got against you?

WILLY I'm so tired. Don't talk any more.

(BIFF *slowly returns to the kitchen. He stops, stares toward the heater.*)

LINDA   Will you ask Howard to let you work in New York?

WILLY   First thing in the morning. Everything'll be all right.

(BIFF *reaches behind the heater and draws out a length of rubber tubing. He is horrified and turns his head toward* WILLY's *room, still dimly lit, from which the strains of* LINDA's *desperate but monotonous humming rise.*)

WILLY (*staring through the window into the moonlight*)   Gee, look at the moon moving between the buildings!

(BIFF *wraps the tubing around his hand and quickly goes up the stairs.*) CURTAIN

ACT II

Music is heard, gay and bright. The curtain rises as the music fades away. WILLY, *in shirt sleeves, is sitting at the kitchen table, sipping coffee, his hat in his lap.* LINDA *is filling his cup when she can.*

WILLY   Wonderful coffee. Meal in itself.

LINDA   Can I make you some eggs?

WILLY   No. Take a breath.

LINDA   You look so rested, dear.

WILLY   I slept like a dead one. First time in months. Imagine, sleeping till ten on a Tuesday morning. Boys left nice and early, heh?

LINDA   They were out of here by eight o'clock.

WILLY   Good work!

LINDA   It was so thrilling to see them leaving together. I can't get over the shaving lotion in this house!

WILLY (*smiling*)   Mmm—

LINDA   Biff was very changed this morning. His whole attitude seemed to be hopeful. He couldn't wait to get downtown to see Oliver.

WILLY   He's heading for a change. There's no question, there simply are certain men that take longer to get—solidified. How did he dress?

LINDA   His blue suit. He's so handsome in that suit. He could be a—anything in that suit!

(WILLY *gets up from the table.* LINDA *holds his jacket for him.*)

WILLY   There's no question, no question at all. Gee, on the way home tonight I'd like to buy some seeds.

LINDA (*laughing*)   That'd be wonderful. But not enough sun gets back there. Nothing'll grow any more.

WILLY   You wait, kid, before it's all over we're gonna get a little place out in the country, and I'll raise some vegetables, a couple of chickens . . .

LINDA   You'll do it yet, dear.

(WILLY *walks out of his jacket.* LINDA *follows him.*)

WILLY   And they'll get married, and come for a weekend. I'd build a little guest house. 'Cause I got so many fine tools, all I'd need would be a little lumber and some peace of mind.

LINDA (*joyfully*)   I sewed the lining . . .

WILLY   I could build two guest houses, so they'd both come. Did he decide how much he's going to ask Oliver for?

LINDA (*getting him into the jacket*)   He didn't mention it, but I imagine ten or fifteen thousand. You going to talk to Howard today?

WILLY   Yeah. I'll put it to him straight and simple. He'll just have to take me off the road.

LINDA   And Willy, don't forget to ask for a little advance, because we've got the insurance premium. It's the grace period now.

WILLY   That's a hundred . . . ?

LINDA   A hundred and eight, sixty-eight. Because we're a little short again.

WILLY   Why are we short?

LINDA   Well, you had the motor job on the car . . .

WILLY   That goddam Studebaker!

LINDA   And you got one more payment on the refrigerator . . .

WILLY   But it just broke again!

LINDA   Well, it's old, dear.

WILLY   I told you we should've bought a well-advertised machine. Charley bought a General Electric and it's twenty years old and it's still good, that son-of-a-bitch.

LINDA   But, Willy—

WILLY   Whoever heard of a Hastings refrigerator? Once in my life I would like to own something outright before it's broken! I'm always in a race with the junkyard! I just finished paying for the car and it's on its last legs. The refrigerator consumes belts like a goddam maniac. They time those things. They time them so when you finally paid for them, they're used up.

LINDA (*buttoning up his jacket as he unbuttons it*)   All told, about two hundred dollars would carry us, dear. But that includes the last payment on the mortgage. After this payment, Willy, the house belongs to us.

WILLY   It's twenty-five years!

LINDA   Biff was nine years old when we bought it.

WILLY   Well, that's a great thing. To weather a twenty-five year mortgage is—

LINDA   It's an accomplishment.

WILLY   All the cement, the lumber, the reconstruction I put in this house! There ain't a crack to be found in it any more.

LINDA   Well, it served its purpose.

WILLY   What purpose? Some stranger'll come along, move in, and raise a family . . . (*He starts to go.*) Good-by, I'm late.

LINDA (*suddenly remembering*)   Oh, I forgot! You're supposed to meet them for dinner.

WILLY   Me?

LINDA   At Frank's Chop House on Forty-eighth near Sixth Avenue.

WILLY   Is that so! How about you?

LINDA   No, just the three of you. They're gonna blow you to a big meal!

WILLY   Don't say! Who thought of that?

LINDA   Biff came to me this morning, Willy, and he said, "Tell Dad, we want to blow him to a big meal." Be there six o'clock. You and your two boys are going to have dinner.

WILLY   Gee whiz! That's really somethin'. I'm gonna knock Howard for a loop, kid. I'll get an advance, and I'll come home with a New York job. Goddammit, now I'm gonna do it!

LINDA   Oh, that's the spirit, Willy!

WILLY   I will never get behind a wheel the rest of my life!

LINDA   It's changing, Willy, I can feel it changing!

WILLY   Beyond a question. G'by, I'm late. (*He starts to go again.*)

LINDA (*calling after him as she runs to the kitchen table for a handkerchief*)   You got your glasses?

WILLY (*feels for them, then comes back in*)   Yeah, yeah, got my glasses.

LINDA (*giving him the handkerchief*)   And a handkerchief.

WILLY   Yeah, handkerchief.

LINDA   And your saccharine?

WILLY   Yeah, my saccharine.

LINDA   Be careful on the subway stairs.

(*She kisses him, and a silk stocking is seen hanging from her hand.* WILLY *notices it.*)

WILLY   Will you stop mending stockings? At least while I'm in the house. It gets me nervous. I can't tell you. Please.

(LINDA *hides the stocking in her hand as she follows* WILLY *across the forestage in front of the house.*)

LINDA   Remember, Frank's Chop House.

WILLY (*passing the apron*)   Maybe beets would grow out there.

LINDA (*laughing*)   But you tried so many times.

WILLY   Yeah. Well, don't work hard today. (*He disappears around the right corner of the house.*)

LINDA   Be careful!

(*As* WILLY *vanishes,* LINDA *waves to him. Suddenly the phone rings. She runs across the stage and into the kitchen and lifts it.*)

LINDA   Hello? Oh, Biff! I'm so glad you called, I just . . . Yes, sure, I just told him. Yes, he'll be there for dinner at six o'clock, I didn't forget. Listen, I was just dying to tell you. You know that little rubber pipe I told you about? That he connected to the gas heater? I finally decided to go down the cellar this morning and take it away and destroy it. But it's gone! Imagine? He took it away himself, it isn't there! (*She listens.*) When? Oh, then you took it. Oh—nothing, it's just that I'd hoped he'd taken it away himself. Oh, I'm not worried, darling, because this morning he left in such high spirits, it was like the old days! I'm not afraid any more. Did Mr. Oliver see you? . . . Well, you wait there then. And make a nice impression on him, darling. Just don't perspire too much before you see him. And have a nice time with Dad. He may have big news too! . . . That's right, a New York job. And be sweet to him tonight, dear. Be loving to him. Because he's only a little boat looking for a harbor. (*She is trembling with sorrow and joy.*) Oh, that's wonderful, Biff, you'll save his life. Thanks, darling. Just put your arm around him when he comes into the restaurant. Give him a smile. That's the boy . . . Good-by, dear. . . . You got your comb? . . . That's fine. Good-by, Biff dear.

(*In the middle of her speech,* HOWARD WAGNER, *thirty-six, wheels on a small typewriter table on which is a wire-recording machine and proceeds to plug it in. This is on the left forestage. Light slowly fades on* LINDA *as it rises on* HOWARD. HOWARD *is intent on threading the machine and only glances over his shoulder as* WILLY *appears.*)

WILLY   Pst! Pst!

HOWARD   Hello, Willy, come in.

WILLY   Like to have a little talk with you, Howard.

HOWARD   Sorry to keep you waiting. I'll be with you in a minute.

WILLY   What's that, Howard?

HOWARD   Didn't you ever see one of these? Wire recorder.

WILLY   Oh. Can we talk a minute?

HOWARD   Records things. Just got delivery yesterday. Been driving me crazy, the most terrific machine I ever saw in my life. I was up all night with it.

941

WILLY   What do you do with it?

HOWARD   I bought it for dictation, but you can do anything with it. Listen to this. I had it home last night. Listen to what I picked up. The first one is my daughter. Get this. (*He flicks the switch and "Roll out the Barrel" is heard being whistled.*) Listen to that kid whistle.

WILLY   That is lifelike, isn't it?

HOWARD   Seven years old. Get that tone.

WILLY   Ts, ts. Like to ask a little favor if you . . .

(*The whistling breaks off, and the voice of* HOWARD'S DAUGHTER *is heard.*)

HIS DAUGHTER   "Now you, Daddy."

HOWARD   She's crazy for me! (*Again the same song is whistled.*) That's me! Ha! (*He winks.*)

WILLY   You're very good!

(*The whistling breaks off again. The machine runs silent for a moment.*)

HOWARD   Sh! Get this now, this is my son.

HIS SON   "The capital of Alabama is Montgomery; the capital of Arizona is Phoenix; the capital of Arkansas is Little Rock; the capital of California is Sacramento . . ." (*And on, and on.*)

HOWARD (*holding up five fingers*)   Five years old, Willy!

WILLY   He'll make an announcer some day!

HIS SON (*continuing*)   "The capital . . ."

HOWARD   Get that—alphabetical order! (*The machine breaks off suddenly.*) Wait a minute. The maid kicked the plug out.

WILLY   It certainly is a—

HOWARD   Sh, for God's sake!

HIS SON   "It's nine o'clock, Bulova watch time. So I have to go to sleep."

WILLY   That really is—

HOWARD   Wait a minute! The next is my wife.

(*They wait.*)

HOWARD'S VOICE   "Go on, say something." (*Pause.*) "Well, you gonna talk?"

HIS WIFE   "I can't think of anything."

HOWARD'S VOICE   "Well, talk—it's turning."

HIS WIFE (*shyly, beaten*)   "Hello." (*Silence.*) "Oh, Howard, I can't talk into this . . ."

HOWARD (*snapping the machine off*)   That was my wife.

WILLY   That is a wonderful machine. Can we—

HOWARD   I tell you, Willy, I'm gonna take my camera, and my bandsaw, and all my hobbies, and out they go. This is the most fascinating relaxation I ever found.

WILLY   I think I'll get one myself.

HOWARD   Sure, they're only a hundred and a half. You can't do without it. Supposing you wanna hear Jack Benny, see? But you can't be at home at that hour. So you tell the maid to turn the radio on when Jack Benny comes on, and this automatically goes on with the radio . . .

WILLY   And when you come home you . . .

HOWARD   You can come home twelve o'clock, one o'clock, any time you like, and you get yourself a Coke and sit yourself down, throw the switch, and there's Jack Benny's program in the middle of the night!

WILLY   I'm definitely going to get one. Because lots of time I'm on the road, and I think to myself, what I must be missing on the radio!

HOWARD   Don't you have a radio in the car?

WILLY   Well, yeah, but who ever thinks of turning it on?

HOWARD   Say, aren't you supposed to be in Boston?

WILLY   That's what I want to talk to you about, Howard. You got a minute? (*He draws a chair in from the wing.*)

HOWARD   What happened? What're you doing here?

WILLY   Well . . .

HOWARD   You didn't crack up again, did you?

WILLY   Oh, no. No . . .

HOWARD   Geez, you had me worried there for a minute. What's the trouble?

WILLY   Well, tell you the truth, Howard. I've come to the decision that I'd rather not travel any more.

HOWARD   Not travel! Well, what'll you do?

WILLY   Remember, Christmas time, when you had the party here? You said you'd try to think of some spot for me here in town.

HOWARD   With us?

WILLY   Well, sure.

HOWARD   Oh, yeah, yeah. I remember. Well, I couldn't think of anything for you, Willy.

WILLY   I tell ya, Howard. The kids are all grown up, y'know. I don't need much any more. If I could take home—well, sixty-five dollars a week, I could swing it.

HOWARD   Yeah, but Willy, see I—

943

WILLY   I tell ya why, Howard. Speaking frankly and between the two of us, y'know—I'm just a little tired.

HOWARD   Oh, I could understand that, Willy. But you're a road man, Willy, and we do a road business. We've only got a half-dozen salesmen on the floor here.

WILLY   God knows, Howard, I never asked a favor of any man. But I was with the firm when your father used to carry you in here in his arms.

HOWARD   I know that, Willy, but—

WILLY   Your father came to me the day you were born and asked me what I thought of the name of Howard, may he rest in peace.

HOWARD   I appreciate that, Willy, but there just is no spot here for you. If I had a spot I'd slam you right in, but I just don't have a single solitary spot.

(*He looks for his lighter.* WILLY *has picked it up and gives it to him. Pause.*)

WILLY (*with increasing anger*)   Howard, all I need to set my table is fifty dollars a week.

HOWARD   But where am I going to put you, kid?

WILLY   Look, it isn't a question of whether I can sell merchandise, is it?

HOWARD   No, but it's a business, kid, and everybody's gotta pull his own weight.

WILLY (*desperately*)   Just let me tell you a story, Howard—

HOWARD   'Cause you gotta admit, business is business.

WILLY (*angrily*)   Business is definitely business, but just listen for a minute. You don't understand this. When I was a boy—eighteen, nineteen—I was already on the road. And there was a question in my mind as to whether selling had a future for me. Because in those days I had a yearning to go to Alaska. See, there were three gold strikes in one month in Alaska, and I felt like going out. Just for the ride, you might say.

HOWARD (*barely interested*)   Don't say.

WILLY   Oh, yeah, my father lived many years in Alaska. He was an adventurous man. We've got quite a little streak of self-reliance in our family. I thought I'd go out with my older brother and try to locate him, and maybe settle in the North with the old man. And I was almost decided to go, when I met a salesman in the Parker House. His name was Dave Singleman. And he was eighty-four years old, and he'd drummed merchandise in thirty-one states. And old Dave, he'd go up to his room, y'understand, put on his green velvet slippers—I'll never forget—and pick up his phone and call the buyers, and without ever leaving his room, at the age of eighty-four, he made his living. And when I saw that, I realized that selling was the greatest career a man could want. 'Cause what could be more satisfying than to be able to go, at the age of eighty-four, into twenty or thirty different cities, and pick up a phone, and be remembered and loved and helped by so many different people? Do you know? when he died—and by the way he died the death of a salesman, in his green velvet slippers in the smoker of the New York, New

944

Haven and Hartford, going into Boston—when he died, hundreds of salesmen and buyers were at his funeral. Things were sad on a lotta trains for months after that. (*He stands up.* HOWARD *has not looked at him.*) In those days there was personality in it, Howard. There was respect, and comradeship, and gratitude in it. Today, it's all cut and dried, and there's no chance for bringing friendship to bear—or personality. You see what I mean? They don't know me any more.

HOWARD (*moving away, to the right*) That's just the thing, Willy.

WILLY If I had forty dollars a week—that's all I'd need. Forty dollars, Howard.

HOWARD Kid. I can't take blood from a stone, I—

WILLY (*desperation is on him now*) Howard, the year Al Smith was nominated, your father came to me and—

HOWARD (*starting to go off*) I've got to see some people, kid.

WILLY (*stopping him*) I'm talking about your father! There were promises made across this desk! You mustn't tell me you've got people to see—I put thirty-four years into this firm, Howard, and now I can't pay my insurance! You can't eat the orange and throw the peel away—a man is not a piece of fruit! (*After a pause.*) Now pay attention. Your father—in 1928 I had a big year. I averaged a hundred and seventy dollars a week in commissions.

HOWARD (*impatiently*) Now, Willy, you never averaged—

WILLY (*banging his hand on the desk*) I averaged a hundred and seventy dollars a week in the year of 1928! And your father came to me—or rather, I was in the office here—it was right over this desk—and he put his hand on my shoulder—

HOWARD (*getting up*) You'll have to excuse me, Willy, I gotta see some people. Pull yourself together. (*Going out.*) I'll be back in a little while.

(*On* HOWARD'*s exit, the light on his chair grows very bright and strange.*)

WILLY Pull myself together! What the hell did I say to him? My God, I was yelling at him! How could I! (WILLY *breaks off, staring at the light, which occupies the chair, animating it. He approaches this chair, standing across the desk from it.*) Frank, Frank, don't you remember what you told me that time? How you put your hand on my shoulder, and Frank . . .

(*He leans on the desk and as he speaks the dead man's name he accidentally switches on the recorder, and instantly—*)

HOWARD'S SON ". . . of New York is Albany. The capital of Ohio is Cincinnati, the capital of Rhode Island is . . ." (*The recitation continues.*)

WILLY (*leaping away with fright, shouting*) Ha! Howard! Howard! Howard!

HOWARD (*rushing in*) What happened?

WILLY (*pointing at the machine, which continues nasally, childishly, with the capital cities*) Shut it off! Shut it off!

945

HOWARD (*pulling the plug out*) Look, Willy . . .

WILLY (*pressing his hands to his eyes*) I gotta get myself some coffee. I'll get some coffee . . .

(WILLY *starts to walk out.* HOWARD *stops him.*)

HOWARD (*rolling up the cord*) Willy, look . . .

WILLY I'll go to Boston.

HOWARD Willy, you can't go to Boston for us.

WILLY Why can't I go?

HOWARD I don't want you to represent us. I've been meaning to tell you for a long time now.

WILLY Howard, are you firing me?

HOWARD I think you need a good long rest, Willy.

WILLY Howard—

HOWARD And when you feel better, come back, and we'll see if we can work something out.

WILLY But I gotta earn money, Howard. I'm in no position to—

HOWARD Where are your sons? Why don't your sons give you a hand?

WILLY They're working on a very big deal.

HOWARD This is no time for false pride, Willy. You go to your sons and you tell them that you're tired. You've got two great boys, haven't you?

WILLY Oh, no question, no question, but in the meantime . . .

HOWARD Then that's that, heh?

WILLY All right, I'll go to Boston tomorrow.

HOWARD No, no.

WILLY I can't throw myself on my sons. I'm not a cripple!

HOWARD Look, kid, I'm busy this morning.

WILLY (*grasping* HOWARD's *arm*) Howard, you've got to let me go to Boston!

HOWARD (*hard, keeping himself under control*) I've got a line of people to see this morning. Sit down, take five minutes, and pull yourself together, and then go home, will ya? I need the office, Willy. (*He starts to go, turns, remembering the recorder, starts to push off the table holding the recorder.*) Oh, yeah. Whenever you can this week, stop by and drop off the samples. You'll feel better, Willy, and then come back and we'll talk. Pull yourself together, kid, there's people outside.

946

(HOWARD *exits, pushing the table off left.* WILLY *stares into space, exhausted. Now the music is heard* —BEN's *music—first distantly, then closer, closer. As* WILLY *speaks,* BEN *enters from the right. He carries valise and umbrella.*)

WILLY Oh, Ben, how did you do it? What is the answer? Did you wind up the Alaska deal already?

BEN Doesn't take much time if you know what you're doing. Just a short business trip. Boarding ship in an hour. Wanted to say good-by.

WILLY Ben, I've got to talk to you.

BEN (*glancing at his watch*) Haven't the time, William.

WILLY (*crossing the apron to* BEN) Ben, nothing's working out. I don't know what to do.

BEN Now, look here, William. I've bought timberland in Alaska and I need a man to look after things for me.

WILLY God, timberland! Me and my boys in those grand outdoors.

BEN You've a new continent at your doorstep, William. Get out of these cities, they're full of talk and time payments and courts of law. Screw on your fists and you can fight for a fortune up there.

WILLY Yes, yes! Linda, Linda!

(LINDA *enters as of old, with the wash.*)

LINDA Oh, you're back?

BEN I haven't much time.

WILLY No, wait! Linda, he's got a proposition for me in Alaska.

LINDA But you've got—(*To* BEN.) He's got a beautiful job here.

WILLY But in Alaska, kid, I could—

LINDA You're doing well enough, Willy!

BEN (*to* LINDA) Enough for what, my dear?

LINDA (*frightened of* BEN *and angry at him*) Don't say those things to him! Enough to be happy right here, right now. (*To* WILLY, *while* BEN *laughs.*) Why must everybody conquer the world? You're well liked, and the boys love you, and someday—(*to* BEN)—why, old man Wagner told him just the other day that if he keeps it up he'll be a member of the firm, didn't he, Willy?

WILLY Sure, sure. I am building something with this firm, Ben, and if a man is building something he must be on the right track, mustn't he?

BEN What are you building? Lay your hand on it. Where is it?

WILLY (*hesitantly*) That's true, Linda, there's nothing.

LINDA Why? (*To* BEN.) There's a man eighty-four years old—

WILLY   That's right, Ben, that's right. When I look at that man I say, what is there to worry about?

BEN   Bah!

WILLY   It's true, Ben. All he has to do is go into any city, pick up the phone, and he's making his living and you know why?

BEN (*picking up his valise*)   I've got to go.

WILLY (*holding* BEN *back*)   Look at this boy!

(BIFF, *in his high school sweater, enters carrying suitcase.* HAPPY *carries* BIFF'*s shoulder guards, gold helmet, and football pants.*)

WILLY   Without a penny to his name, three great universities are begging for him, and from there the sky's the limit, because it's not what you do, Ben. It's who you know and the smile on your face! It's contacts, Ben, contacts! The whole wealth of Alaska passes over the lunch table at the Commodore Hotel, and that's the wonder, the wonder of this country, that a man can end with diamonds here on the basis of being liked! (*He turns to* BIFF.) And that's why when you get out on that field today it's important. Because thousands of people will be rooting for you and loving you. (*To* BEN, *who has again begun to leave.*) And Ben! when he walks into a business office his name will sound out like a bell and all the doors will open to him! I've seen it, Ben, I've seen it a thousand times! You can't feel it with your hand like timber, but it's there!

BEN   Good-by, William.

WILLY   Ben, am I right? Don't you think I'm right? I value your advice.

BEN   There's a new continent at your doorstep, William. You could walk out rich. Rich! (*He is gone.*)

WILLY   We'll do it here, Ben! You hear me? We're gonna do it here!

(YOUNG BERNARD *rushes in. The gay music of the boys is heard.*)

BERNARD   Oh, gee, I was afraid you left already!

WILLY   Why? What time is it?

BERNARD   It's half-past one!

WILLY   Well, come on, everybody! Ebbets Field next stop! Where's the pennants? (*He rushes through the wall-line of the kitchen and out into the living-room.*)

LINDA (*to* BIFF)   Did you pack fresh underwear?

BIFF (*who has been limbering up*)   I want to go!

BERNARD   Biff, I'm carrying your helmet, ain't I?

HAPPY   No, I'm carrying the helmet.

BERNARD   Oh, Biff, you promised me.

HAPPY   I'm carrying the helmet.

BERNARD   How am I going to get in the locker room?

LINDA   Let him carry the shoulder guards. (*She puts her coat and hat on in the kitchen.*)

BERNARD   Can I, Biff? 'Cause I told everybody I'm going to be in the locker room.

HAPPY   In Ebbets Field it's the clubhouse.

BERNARD   I meant the clubhouse. Biff!

HAPPY   Biff!

BIFF (*grandly, after a slight pause*)   Let him carry the shoulder guards.

HAPPY (*as he gives* BERNARD *the shoulder guards*)   Stay close to us now.

(WILLY *rushes in with the pennants.*)

WILLY (*handing them out*)   Everybody wave when Biff comes out on the field. (HAPPY *and* BERNARD *run off.*) You set now, boy?

(*The music has died away.*)

BIFF   Ready to go, Pop. Every muscle is ready.

WILLY (*at the edge of the apron*)   You realize what this means?

BIFF   That's right, Pop.

WILLY (*feeling* BIFF*'s muscles*)   You're comin' home this afternoon captain of the All-Scholastic Championship Team of the City of New York.

BIFF   I got it, Pop. And remember, pal, when I take off my helmet, that touchdown is for you.

WILLY   Let's go! (*He is starting out, with his arm around* BIFF, *when* CHARLEY *enters, as of old, in knickers.*) I got no room for you, Charley.

CHARLEY   Room? For what?

WILLY   In the car.

CHARLEY   You goin' for a ride? I wanted to shoot some casino.

WILLY (*furiously*)   Casino! (*Incredulously.*) Don't you realize what today is?

LINDA   Oh, he knows, Willy. He's just kidding you.

WILLY   That's nothing to kid about!

CHARLEY   No, Linda, what's goin' on?

LINDA   He's playing in Ebbets Field.

CHARLEY   Baseball in this weather?

WILLY   Don't talk to him. Come on, come on! (*He is pushing them out.*)

CHARLEY   Wait a minute, didn't you hear the news?

WILLY   What?

949

CHARLEY   Don't you listen to the radio? Ebbets Field just blew up.

WILLY   You go to hell! (CHARLEY *laughs. Pushing them out.*) Come on, come on! We're late.

CHARLEY (*as they go*)   Knock a homer, Biff, knock a homer!

WILLY (*the last to leave, turning to* CHARLEY)   I don't think that was funny, Charley. This is the greatest day of his life.

CHARLEY   Willy, when are you going to grow up?

WILLY   Yeah, heh? When this game is over, Charley, you'll be laughing out of the other side of your face. They'll be calling him another Red Grange. Twenty-five thousand a year.

CHARLEY (*kidding*)   Is that so?

WILLY   Yeah, that's so.

CHARLEY   Well, then, I'm sorry, Willy. But tell me something.

WILLY   What?

CHARLEY   Who is Red Grange?

WILLY   Put up your hands. Goddam you, put up your hands!

(CHARLEY, *chuckling, shakes his head and walks away, around the left corner of the stage.* WILLY *follows him. The music rises to a mocking frenzy.*)

WILLY   Who the hell do you think you are, better than everybody else? You don't know everything, you big, ignorant, stupid . . . Put up your hands!

(*Light rises, on the right side of the forestage, on a small table in the reception room of* CHARLEY's *office. Traffic sounds are heard.* BERNARD, *now mature, sits whistling to himself. A pair of tennis rackets and an overnight bag are on the floor beside him.*)

WILLY (*offstage*)   What are you walking away for? Don't walk away! If you're going to say something say it to my face! I know you laugh at me behind my back. You'll laugh out of the other side of your goddam face after this game. Touchdown! Touchdown! Eighty thousand people! Touchdown! Right between the goal posts.

(BERNARD *is a quiet, earnest, but self-assured young man.* WILLY's *voice is coming from right upstage now.* BERNARD *lowers his feet off the table and listens.* JENNY, *his father's secretary, enters.*)

JENNY (*distressed*)   Say, Bernard, will you go out in the hall?

BERNARD   What is that noise? Who is it?

JENNY   Mr. Loman. He just got off the elevator.

BERNARD (*getting up*)   Who's he arguing with?

JENNY   Nobody. There's nobody with him. I can't deal with him any more, and your father gets all upset everytime he comes. I've got a lot of typing to do, and your father's waiting to sign it. Will you see him?

WILLY (*entering*) Touchdown! Touch—(*He sees* JENNY.) Jenny, Jenny, good to see you. How're ya? Workin'? Or still honest?

JENNY Fine. How've you been feeling?

WILLY Not much any more, Jenny. Ha, ha! (*He is surprised to see the rackets.*)

BERNARD Hello, Uncle Willy.

WILLY (*almost shocked*) Bernard! Well, look who's here! (*He comes quickly, guiltily, to* BERNARD *and warmly shakes his hand.*)

BERNARD How are you? Good to see you.

WILLY What are you doing here?

BERNARD Oh, just stopped by to see Pop. Get off my feet till my train leaves. I'm going to Washington in a few minutes.

WILLY Is he in?

BERNARD Yes, he's in his office with the accountant. Sit down.

WILLY (*sitting down*) What're you going to do in Washington?

BERNARD Oh, just a case I've got there, Willy.

WILLY That so? (*Indicating the rackets.*) You going to play tennis there?

BERNARD I'm staying with a friend who's got a court.

WILLY Don't say. His own tennis court. Must be fine people, I bet.

BERNARD They are, very nice. Dad tells me Biff's in town.

WILLY (*with a big smile*) Yeah, Biff's in. Working on a very big deal, Bernard.

BERNARD What's Biff doing?

WILLY Well, he's been doing very big things in the West. But he decided to establish himself here. Very big. We're having dinner. Did I hear your wife had a boy?

BERNARD That's right. Our second.

WILLY Two boys! What do you know!

BERNARD What kind of a deal has Biff got?

WILLY Well, Bill Oliver—very big sporting goods man—he wants Biff very badly. Called him in from the West. Long distance, carte blanche, special deliveries. Your friends have their own private tennis court?

BERNARD You still with the old firm, Willy?

WILLY (*after a pause*) I'm—I'm overjoyed to see how you made the grade, Bernard, overjoyed. It's an encouraging thing to see a young man really—really —Looks very good for Biff—very—(*He breaks off, then.*) Bernard—(*He is so full of emotion, he breaks off again.*)

BERNARD What is it, Willy?

WILLY (*small and alone*) What—what's the secret?

BERNARD   What secret?

WILLY   How—how did you? Why didn't he ever catch on?

BERNARD   I wouldn't know that, Willy.

WILLY (*confidentially, desperately*)   You were his friend, his boyhood friend. There's something I don't understand about it. His life ended after that Ebbets Field game. From the age of seventeen nothing good ever happened to him.

BERNARD   He never trained himself for anything.

WILLY   But he did, he did. After high school he took so many correspondence courses. Radio mechanics; television; God knows what, and never made the slightest mark.

BERNARD (*taking off his glasses*)   Willy, do you want to talk candidly?

WILLY (*rising, faces* BERNARD)   I regard you as a very brilliant man, Bernard. I value your advice.

BERNARD   Oh, the hell with the advice, Willy. I couldn't advise you. There's just one thing I've always wanted to ask you. When he was supposed to graduate, and the math teacher flunked him—

WILLY   Oh, that son-of-a-bitch ruined his life.

BERNARD   Yeah, but, Willy, all he had to do was go to summer school and make up that subject.

WILLY   That's right, that's right.

BERNARD   Did you tell him not to go to summer school?

WILLY   Me? I begged him to go. I ordered him to go!

BERNARD   Then why wouldn't he go?

WILLY   Why? Why! Bernard, that question has been trailing me like a ghost for the last fifteen years. He flunked the subject, and laid down and died like a hammer hit him!

BERNARD   Take it easy, kid.

WILLY   Let me talk to you—I got nobody to talk to. Bernard, Bernard, was it my fault? Y'see? It keeps going around in my mind, maybe I did something to him. I got nothing to give him.

BERNARD   Don't take it so hard.

WILLY   Why did he lay down? What is the story there? You were his friend!

BERNARD   Willy, I remember, it was June, and our grades came out. And he'd flunked math.

WILLY   That son-of-a-bitch!

BERNARD   No, it wasn't right then. Biff just got very angry, I remember, and he was ready to enroll in summer school.

WILLY (*surprised*)   He was?

952

BERNARD   He wasn't beaten by it at all. But then, Willy, he disappeared from the block for almost a month. And I got the idea that he'd gone up to New England to see you. Did he have a talk with you then?

(WILLY *stares in silence.*)

BERNARD   Willy?

WILLY (*with a strong edge of resentment in his voice*)   Yeah, he came to Boston. What about it?

BERNARD   Well, just that when he came back—I'll never forget this, it always mystifies me. Because I'd thought so well of Biff, even though he'd always taken advantage of me. I loved him, Willy, y'know? And he came back after that month and took his sneakers—remember those sneakers with "University of Virginia" printed on them? He was so proud of those, wore them every day. And he took them down in the cellar, and burned them up in the furnace. We had a fist fight. It lasted at least half an hour. Just the two of us, punching each other down the cellar, and crying right through it. I've often thought of how strange it was that I knew he'd given up his life. What happened in Boston, Willy?

(WILLY *looks at him as at an intruder.*)

BERNARD   I just bring it up because you asked me.

WILLY (*angrily*)   Nothing. What do you mean, "What happened?" What's that got to do with anything?

BERNARD   Well, don't get sore.

WILLY   What are you trying to do, blame it on me? If a boy lays down is that my fault?

BERNARD   Now, Willy, don't get—

WILLY   Well, don't—don't talk to me that way! What does that mean, "What happened?"

(CHARLEY *enters. He is in his vest, and he carries a bottle of bourbon.*)

CHARLEY   Hey, you're going to miss that train. (*He waves the bottle.*)

BERNARD   Yeah, I'm going. (*He takes the bottle.*) Thanks, Pop. (*He picks up his rackets and bag.*) Good-by, Willy, and don't worry about it. You know, "If at first you don't succeed . . ."

WILLY   Yes, I believe in that.

BERNARD   But sometimes, Willy, it's better for a man just to walk away.

WILLY   Walk away?

BERNARD   That's right.

WILLY   But if you can't walk away?

BERNARD (*after a slight pause*) I guess that's when it's tough. (*Extending his hand.*) Good-by, Willy.

WILLY (*shaking* BERNARD's *hand*) Good-by, boy.

CHARLEY (*an arm on* BERNARD's *shoulder*) How do you like this kid? Gonna argue a case in front of the Supreme Court.

BERNARD (*protesting*) Pop!

WILLY (*genuinely shocked, pained, and happy*) No! The Supreme Court!

BERNARD I gotta run. 'By, Dad!

CHARLEY Knock 'em dead, Bernard!

(BERNARD *goes off.*)

WILLY (*as* CHARLEY *takes out his wallet*) The Supreme Court! And he didn't even mention it!

CHARLEY (*counting out money on the desk*) He don't have to—he's gonna do it.

WILLY And you never told him what to do, did you? You never took any special interest in him.

CHARLEY My salvation is that I never took any interest in anything. There's some money—fifty dollars. I got an accountant inside.

WILLY Charley, look . . . (*With difficulty.*) I got my insurance to pay. If you can manage it—I need a hundred and ten dollars.

(CHARLEY *doesn't reply for a moment; merely stops moving*).

WILLY I'd draw it from my bank but Linda would know, and I . . .

CHARLEY Sit down, Willy.

WILLY (*moving toward the chair*) I'm keeping an account of everything, remember. I'll pay every penny back. (*He sits.*)

CHARLEY Now listen to me, Willy.

WILLY I want you to know I appreciate . . .

CHARLEY (*sitting down on the table*) Willy, what're you doin'? What the hell is goin' on in your head?

WILLY Why? I'm simply . . .

CHARLEY I offered you a job. You can make fifty dollars a week. And I won't send you on the road.

WILLY I've got a job.

CHARLEY Without pay? What kind of job is a job without pay? (*He rises.*) Now, look, kid, enough is enough. I'm no genius but I know when I'm being insulted.

WILLY Insulted!

CHARLEY Why don't you want to work for me?

WILLY   What's the matter with you? I've got a job.

CHARLEY   Then what're you walkin' in here every week for?

WILLY (*getting up*)   Well, if you don't want me to walk in here—

CHARLEY   I am offering you a job.

WILLY   I don't want your goddam job!

CHARLEY   When the hell are you going to grow up?

WILLY (*furiously*)   You big ignoramus, if you say that to me again I'll rap you one! I don't care how big you are! (*He's ready to fight.*)

(*Pause.*)

CHARLEY (*kindly, going to him*)   How much do you need, Willy?

WILLY   Charley, I'm strapped. I'm strapped. I don't know what to do. I was just fired.

CHARLEY   Howard fired you?

WILLY   That snotnose. Imagine that? I named him. I named him Howard.

CHARLEY   Willy, when're you gonna realize that them things don't mean anything? You named him Howard, but you can't sell that. The only thing you got in this world is what you can sell. And the funny thing is that you're a salesman, and you don't know that.

WILLY   I've always tried to think otherwise, I guess. I always felt that if a man was impressive, and well liked, that nothing—

CHARLEY   Why must everybody like you? Who liked J. P. Morgan? Was he impressive? In a Turkish bath he'd look like a butcher. But with his pockets on he was very well liked. Now listen, Willy, I know you don't like me, and nobody can say I'm in love with you, but I'll give you a job because—just for the hell of it, put it that way. Now what do you say?

WILLY   I—I just can't work for you, Charley.

CHARLEY   What're you, jealous of me?

WILLY   I can't work for you, that's all, don't ask me why.

CHARLEY (*angered, takes out more bills*)   You been jealous of me all your life, you damned fool! Here, pay your insurance. (*He puts the money in* WILLY's *hand.*)

WILLY   I'm keeping strict accounts.

CHARLEY   I've got some work to do. Take care of yourself. And pay your insurance.

WILLY (*moving to the right*)   Funny, y'know? After all the highways, and the trains, and the appointments, and the years, you end up worth more dead than alive.

CHARLEY   Willy, nobody's worth nothin' dead. (*After a slight pause.*) Did you hear what I said?

955

(WILLY *stands still, dreaming.*)

CHARLEY Willy!

WILLY Apologize to Bernard for me when you see him. I didn't mean to argue with him. He's a fine boy. They're all fine boys, and they'll end up big—all of them. Someday they'll all play tennis together. Wish me luck, Charley. He saw Bill Oliver today.

CHARLEY Good luck.

WILLY (*on the verge of tears*) Charley, you're the only friend I got. Isn't that a remarkable thing? (*He goes out.*)

CHARLEY Jesus!

(CHARLEY *stares after him a moment and follows. All light blacks out. Suddenly raucous music is heard, and a red glow rises behind the screen at right.* STANLEY, *a young waiter, appears, carrying a table, followed by* HAPPY, *who is carrying two chairs.*)

STANLEY (*putting the table down*) That's all right, Mr. Loman, I can handle it myself. (*He turns and takes the chairs from* HAPPY *and places them at the table.*)

HAPPY (*glancing around*) Oh, this is better.

STANLEY Sure, in the front there you're in the middle of all kinds a noise. Whenever you got a party, Mr. Loman, you just tell me and I'll put you back here. Y'know, there's a lotta people they don't like it private, because when they go out they like to see a lotta action around them because they're sick and tired to stay in the house by theirself. But I know you, you ain't from Hackensack. You know what I mean?

HAPPY (*sitting down*) So how's it coming, Stanley?

STANLEY Ah, it's a dog's life. I only wish during the war they'd a took me in the Army. I coulda been dead by now.

HAPPY My brother's back, Stanley.

STANLEY Oh, he come back, heh? From the Far West.

HAPPY Yeah, big cattle man, my brother, so treat him right. And my father's coming too.

STANLEY Oh, your father too!

HAPPY You got a couple of nice lobsters?

STANLEY Hundred per cent, big.

HAPPY I want them with the claws.

STANLEY Don't worry, I don't give you no mice. (HAPPY *laughs.*) How about some wine? It'll put a head on the meal.

HAPPY No. You remember, Stanley, that recipe I brought you from overseas? With the champagne in it?

956

STANLEY   Oh, yeah, sure. I still got it tacked up yet in the kitchen. But that'll have to cost a buck apiece anyways.

HAPPY   That's all right.

STANLEY   What'd you, hit a number or somethin'?

HAPPY   No, it's a little celebration. My brother is—I think he pulled off a big deal today. I think we're going into business together.

STANLEY   Great! That's the best for you. Because a family business, you know what I mean?—that's the best.

HAPPY   That's what I think.

STANLEY   'Cause what's the difference? Somebody steals? It's in the family. Know what I mean? (*Sotto voce.*) Like this bartender here. The boss is goin' crazy what kinda leak he's got in the cash register. You put it in but it don't come out.

HAPPY (*raising his head*)   Sh!

STANLEY   What?

HAPPY   You notice I wasn't lookin' right or left, was I?

STANLEY   No.

HAPPY   And my eyes are closed.

STANLEY   So what's the—?

HAPPY   Strudel's comin'.

STANLEY (*catching on, looks around*)   Ah, no, there's no—

(*He breaks off as a furred, lavishly dressed* GIRL *enters and sits at the next table. Both follow her with their eyes.*)

STANLEY   Geez, how'd ya know?

HAPPY   I got radar or something. (*Staring directly at her profile.*) Oooooooo . . . Stanley.

STANLEY   I think that's for you, Mr. Loman.

HAPPY   Look at that mouth. Oh, God. And the binoculars.

STANLEY   Geez, you got a life, Mr. Loman.

HAPPY   Wait on her.

STANLEY (*going to* THE GIRL*'s table*)   Would you like a menu, ma'am?

GIRL   I'm expecting someone, but I'd like a—

HAPPY   Why don't you bring her—excuse me, miss, do you mind? I sell champagne, and I'd like you to try my brand. Bring her a champagne, Stanley.

GIRL   That's awfully nice of you.

HAPPY   Don't mention it. It's all company money. (*He laughs.*)

GIRL   That's a charming product to be selling, isn't it?

HAPPY   Oh, gets to be like everything else. Selling is selling, y'know.

GIRL   I suppose.

HAPPY   You don't happen to sell, do you?

GIRL   No, I don't sell.

HAPPY   Would you object to a compliment from a stranger? You ought to be on a magazine cover.

GIRL (*looking at him a little archly*)   I have been.

(STANLEY *comes in with a glass of champagne.*)

HAPPY   What'd I say before, Stanley? You see? She's a cover girl.

STANLEY   Oh, I could see, I could see.

HAPPY (*to* THE GIRL)   What magazine?

GIRL   Oh, a lot of them. (*She takes the drink.*) Thank you.

HAPPY   You know what they say in France, don't you? "Champagne is the drink of the complexion"—Hya, Biff!

(BIFF *has entered and sits with* HAPPY.)

BIFF   Hello, kid. Sorry I'm late.

HAPPY   I just got here. Uh, Miss—?

GIRL   Forsythe.

HAPPY   Miss Forsythe, this is my brother.

BIFF   Is Dad here?

HAPPY   His name is Biff. You might've heard of him. Great football player.

GIRL   Really? What team?

HAPPY   Are you familiar with football?

GIRL   No, I'm afraid I'm not.

HAPPY   Biff is quarterback with the New York Giants.

GIRL   Well, that is nice, isn't it? (*She drinks.*)

HAPPY   Good health.

GIRL   I'm happy to meet you.

HAPPY   That's my name. Hap. It's really Harold, but at West Point they called me Happy.

GIRL (*now really impressed*)   Oh, I see. How do you do? (*She turns her profile.*)

BIFF   Isn't Dad coming?

HAPPY   You want her?

BIFF   Oh, I could never make that.

HAPPY   I remember the time that idea would never come into your head. Where's the old confidence, Biff?

958

BIFF I just saw Oliver—

HAPPY Wait a minute. I've got to see that old confidence again. Do you want her? She's on call.

BIFF Oh, no. (*He turns to look at* THE GIRL.)

HAPPY I'm telling you. Watch this. (*Turning to* THE GIRL.) Honey? (*She turns to him.*) Are you busy?

GIRL Well, I am . . . but I could make a phone call.

HAPPY Do that, will you, honey? And see if you can get a friend. We'll be here for a while. Biff is one of the greatest football players in the country.

GIRL (*standing up*) Well, I'm certainly happy to meet you.

HAPPY Come back soon.

GIRL I'll try.

HAPPY Don't try, honey, try hard.

(THE GIRL *exits.* STANLEY *follows, shaking his head in bewildered admiration.*)

HAPPY Isn't that a shame now? A beautiful girl like that? That's why I can't get married. There's not a good woman in a thousand. New York is loaded with them, kid!

BIFF Hap, look—

HAPPY I told you she was on call!

BIFF (*strangely unnerved*) Cut it out, will ya? I want to say something to you.

HAPPY Did you see Oliver?

BIFF I saw him all right. Now look, I want to tell Dad a couple of things and I want you to help me.

HAPPY What? Is he going to back you?

BIFF Are you crazy? You're out of your goddam head, you know that?

HAPPY Why? What happened?

BIFF (*breathlessly*) I did a terrible thing today, Hap. It's been the strangest day I ever went through. I'm all numb, I swear.

HAPPY You mean he wouldn't see you?

BIFF Well, I waited six hours for him, see? All day. Kept sending my name in. Even tried to date his secretary so she'd get me to him, but no soap.

HAPPY Because you're not showin' the old confidence, Biff. He remembered you, didn't he?

BIFF (*stopping* HAPPY *with a gesture*) Finally, about five o'clock, he comes out. Didn't remember who I was or anything. I felt like such an idiot, Hap.

HAPPY Did you tell him my Florida idea?

BIFF He walked away. I saw him for one minute. I got so mad I could've torn the walls down! How the hell did I ever get the idea I was a salesman there? I even

959

believed myself that I'd been a salesman for him! And then he gave me one look and—I realized what a ridiculous lie my whole life has been! We've been talking in a dream for fifteen years. I was a shipping clerk.

HAPPY   What'd you do?

BIFF (*with great tension and wonder*).   Well, he left, see. And the secretary went out. I was all alone in the waiting-room. I don't know what came over me, Hap. The next thing I know I'm in his office—paneled walls, everything. I can't explain it. I—Hap, I took his fountain pen.

HAPPY   Geez, did he catch you?

BIFF   I ran out. I ran down all eleven flights. I ran and ran and ran.

HAPPY   That was an awful dumb—what'd you do that for?

BIFF (*agonized*)   I don't know, I just—wanted to take something, I don't know. You gotta help me, Hap, I'm gonna tell Pop.

HAPPY   You crazy? What for?

BIFF   Hap, he's got to understand that I'm not the man somebody lends that kind of money to. He thinks I've been spiting him all these years and it's eating him up.

HAPPY   That's just it. You tell him something nice.

BIFF   I can't.

HAPPY   Say you got a lunch date with Oliver tomorrow.

BIFF   So what do I do tomorrow?

HAPPY   You leave the house tomorrow and come back at night and say Oliver is thinking it over. And he thinks it over for a couple of weeks, and gradually it fades away and nobody's the worse.

BIFF   But it'll go on forever!

HAPPY   Dad is never so happy as when he's looking forward to something!

(WILLY *enters.*)

HAPPY   Hello, scout!

WILLY   Gee, I haven't been here in years!

(STANLEY *has followed* WILLY *in and sets a chair for him.* STANLEY *starts off but* HAPPY *stops him.*)

HAPPY   Stanley!

(STANLEY *stands by, waiting for an order.*)

BIFF (*going to* WILLY *with guilt, as to an invalid*)   Sit down, Pop. You want a drink?

WILLY   Sure, I don't mind.

BIFF   Let's get a load on.

WILLY   You look worried.

BIFF   N-no. (*To* STANLEY.) Scotch all around. Make it doubles.

STANLEY   Doubles, right. (*He goes.*)

WILLY   You had a couple already, didn't you?

BIFF   Just a couple, yeah.

WILLY   Well, what happened, boy? (*Nodding affirmatively, with a smile.*) Everything go all right?

BIFF (*takes a breath, then reaches out and grasps* WILLY'*s hand*)   Pal . . . (*He is smiling bravely, and* WILLY *is smiling too.*) I had an experience today.

HAPPY   Terrific, Pop.

WILLY   That so? What happened?

BIFF (*high, slightly alcoholic, above the earth*)   I'm going to tell you everything from first to last. It's been a strange day. (*Silence. He looks around, composes himself as best he can, but his breath keeps breaking the rhythm of his voice.*) I had to wait quite a while for him, and—

WILLY   Oliver?

BIFF   Yeah, Oliver. All day, as a matter of cold fact. And a lot of—instances—facts, Pop, facts about my life came back to me. Who was it, Pop? Who ever said I was a salesman with Oliver?

WILLY   Well, you were.

BIFF   No, Dad, I was a shipping clerk.

WILLY   But you were practically—

BIFF (*with determination*)   Dad, I don't know who said it first, but I was never a salesman for Bill Oliver.

WILLY   What're you talking about?

BIFF   Let's hold on to the facts tonight, Pop. We're not going to get anywhere bullin' around. I was a shipping clerk.

WILLY (*angrily*)   All right, now listen to me—

BIFF   Why don't you let me finish?

WILLY   I'm not interested in stories about the past or any crap of that kind because the woods are burning, boys, you understand? There's a big blaze going on all around. I was fired today.

BIFF (*shocked*)   How could you be?

WILLY   I was fired, and I'm looking for a little good news to tell your mother, because the woman has waited and the woman has suffered. The gist of it is that I haven't got a story left in my head, Biff. So don't give me a lecture about facts and aspects. I am not interested. Now what've you got to say to me?

(STANLEY *enters with three drinks. They wait until he leaves.*)

WILLY Did you see Oliver?

BIFF Jesus, Dad!

WILLY You mean you didn't go up there?

HAPPY Sure he went up there.

BIFF I did. I—saw him. How could they fire you?

WILLY (*on the edge of his chair*) What kind of a welcome did he give you?

BIFF He won't even let you work on commission?

WILLY I'm out! (*Driving.*) So tell me, he gave you a warm welcome?

HAPPY Sure, Pop, sure!

BIFF (*driven*) Well, it was kind of—

WILLY I was wondering if he'd remember you. (*To* HAPPY.) Imagine, man doesn't see him for ten, twelve years and gives him that kind of a welcome!

HAPPY Damn right!

BIFF (*trying to return to the offensive*) Pop, look—

WILLY You know why he remembered you, don't you? Because you impressed him in those days.

BIFF Let's talk quietly and get this down to the facts, huh?

WILLY (*as though* BIFF *had been interrupting*) Well, what happened? It's great news, Biff. Did he take you into his office or'd you talk in the waiting-room?

BIFF Well, he came in, see, and—

WILLY (*with a big smile*) What'd he say? Betcha he threw his arm around you.

BIFF Well, he kinda—

WILLY He's a fine man. (*To* HAPPY.) Very hard man to see, y'know.

HAPPY (*agreeing*) Oh, I know.

WILLY (*to* BIFF) Is that where you had the drinks?

BIFF Yeah, he gave me a couple of—no, no!

HAPPY (*cutting in*) He told him my Florida idea.

WILLY Don't interrupt. (*To* BIFF.) How'd he react to the Florida idea?

BIFF Dad, will you give me a minute to explain?

WILLY I've been waiting for you to explain since I sat down here! What happened? He took you into his office and what?

BIFF Well—I talked. And—and he listened, see.

WILLY Famous for the way he listens, y'know. What was his answer?

BIFF His answer was—(*He breaks off, suddenly angry.*) Dad, you're not letting me tell you what I want to tell you!

WILLY (*accusing, angered*) You didn't see him, did you?

962

BIFF I did see him!

WILLY What'd you insult him or something? You insulted him, didn't you?

BIFF Listen, will you let me out of it, will you just let me out of it!

HAPPY What the hell!

WILLY Tell me what happened!

BIFF (*to* HAPPY) I can't talk to him!

(*A single trumpet note jars the ear. The light of green leaves stains the house, which holds the air of night and a dream.* YOUNG BERNARD *enters and knocks on the door of the house.*)

YOUNG BERNARD (*frantically*) Mrs. Loman, Mrs. Loman!

HAPPY Tell him what happened!

BIFF (*to* HAPPY) Shut up and leave me alone!

WILLY No, no! You had to go and flunk math!

BIFF What math? What're you talking about?

YOUNG BERNARD Mrs. Loman, Mrs. Loman!

(LINDA *appears in the house, as of old.*)

WILLY (*wildly*) Math, math, math!

BIFF Take it easy, Pop!

YOUNG BERNARD Mrs. Loman!

WILLY (*furiously*) If you hadn't flunked you'd've been set by now!

BIFF Now, look, I'm gonna tell you what happened, and you're going to listen to me.

YOUNG BERNARD Mrs. Loman!

BIFF I waited six hours—

HAPPY What the hell are you saying?

BIFF I kept sending in my name but he wouldn't see me. So finally he . . . (*He continues unheard as light fades low on the restaurant.*)

YOUNG BERNARD Biff flunked math!

LINDA No!

YOUNG BERNARD Birnbaum flunked him! They won't graduate him!

LINDA But they have to. He's gotta go to the university. Where is he? Biff! Biff!

YOUNG BERNARD No, he left. He went to Grand Central.

LINDA Grand—You mean he went to Boston!

YOUNG BERNARD Is Uncle Willy in Boston?

LINDA Oh, maybe Willy can talk to the teacher. Oh, the poor, poor boy!

(*Light on house area snaps out.*)

BIFF (*at the table, now audible, holding up a gold fountain pen*) . . . so I'm washed up with Oliver, you understand? Are you listening to me?

WILLY (*at a loss*) Yeah, sure. If you hadn't flunked—

BIFF Flunked what? What're you talking about?

WILLY Don't blame everything on me! I didn't flunk math—you did! What pen?

HAPPY That was awful dumb, Biff, a pen like that is worth—

WILLY (*seeing the pen for the first time*) You took Oliver's pen?

BIFF (*weakening*) Dad, I just explained it to you.

WILLY You stole Bill Oliver's fountain pen!

BIFF I didn't exactly steal it! That's just what I've been explaining to you!

HAPPY He had it in his hand and just then Oliver walked in, so he got nervous and stuck it in his pocket!

WILLY My God, Biff!

BIFF I never intended to do it, Dad!

OPERATOR'S VOICE Standish Arms, good evening!

WILLY (*shouting*) I'm not in my room!

BIFF (*frightened*) Dad, what's the matter? (*He and* HAPPY *stand up.*)

OPERATOR Ringing Mr. Loman for you!

WILLY I'm not there, stop it!

BIFF (*horrified, gets down on one knee before* WILLY) Dad, I'll make good, I'll make good. (WILLY *tries to get to his feet.* BIFF *holds him down.*) Sit down now.

WILLY No, you're no good, you're no good for anything.

BIFF I am, Dad, I'll find something else, you understand? Now don't worry about anything. (*He holds up* WILLY's *face.*) Talk to me, Dad.

OPERATOR Mr. Loman does not answer. Shall I page him?

WILLY (*attempting to stand, as though to rush and silence the* OPERATOR) No, no, no!

HAPPY He'll strike something, Pop.

WILLY No, no . . .

BIFF (*desperately, standing over* WILLY) Pop, listen to me! I'm telling you something good. Oliver talked to his partner about the Florida idea. You listening? He —he talked to his partner, and he came to me . . . I'm going to be all right, you hear? Dad, listen to me, he said it was just a question of the amount!

WILLY Then you . . . got it?

HAPPY He's gonna be terrific, Pop!

WILLY (*trying to stand*) Then you got it, haven't you? You got it! You got it!

BIFF (*agonized, holds* WILLY *down*) No, no. Look, Pop. I'm supposed to have lunch with them tomorrow. I'm just telling you this so you'll know that I can still make an impression, Pop. And I'll make good somewhere, but I can't go tomorrow, see?

WILLY Why not? You simply—

BIFF But the pen, Pop!

WILLY You give it to him and tell him it was an oversight!

HAPPY Sure, have lunch tomorrow!

BIFF I can't say that—

WILLY You were doing a crossword puzzle and accidentally used his pen!

BIFF Listen, kid, I took those balls years ago, now I walk in with his fountain pen? That clinches it, don't you see? I can't face him like that! I'll try elsewhere.

PAGE'S VOICE Paging Mr. Loman!

WILLY Don't you want to be anything?

BIFF Pop, how can I go back?

WILLY You don't want to be anything, is that what's behind it?

BIFF (*now angry at* WILLY *for not crediting his sympathy*) Don't take it that way! You think it was easy walking into that office after what I'd done to him? A team of horses couldn't have dragged me back to Bill Oliver!

WILLY Then why'd you go?

BIFF Why did I go? Why did I go! Look at you! Look at what's become of you!

(*Off left,* THE WOMAN *laughs.*)

WILLY Biff, you're going to go to that lunch tomorrow, or—

BIFF I can't go. I've got no appointment!

HAPPY Biff, for . . . !

WILLY Are you spiting me?

BIFF Don't take it that way! Goddammit!

WILLY (*strikes* BIFF *and falters away from the table*) You rotten little louse! Are you spiting me?

THE WOMAN Someone's at the door, Willy!

BIFF I'm no good, can't you see what I am?

HAPPY (*separating them*) Hey, you're in a restaurant! Now cut it out, both of you! (THE GIRLS *enter.*) Hello, girls, sit down.

(THE WOMAN *laughs, off left.*)

MISS FORSYTHE I guess we might as well. This is Letta.

THE WOMAN Willy, are you going to wake up?

965

BIFF (*ignoring* WILLY) How're ya, miss, sit down. What do you drink?

MISS FORSYTHE Letta might not be able to stay long.

LETTA I gotta get up very early tomorrow. I got jury duty. I'm so excited! Were you fellows ever on a jury?

BIFF No, but I been in front of them! (THE GIRLS *laugh.*) This is my father.

LETTA Isn't he cute? Sit down with us, Pop.

HAPPY Sit him down, Biff!

BIFF (*going to him*) Come on, slugger, drink us under the table. To hell with it! Come on, sit down, pal.

(*On* BIFF'*s last insistence,* WILLY *is about to sit.*)

THE WOMAN (*now urgently*) Willy, are you going to answer the door!

(THE WOMAN'*s call pulls* WILLY *back. He starts right, befuddled.*)

BIFF Hey, where are you going?

WILLY Open the door.

BIFF The door?

WILLY The washroom . . . the door . . . where's the door?

BIFF (*leading* WILLY *to the left*) Just go straight down.

(WILLY *moves left.*)

THE WOMAN Willy, Willy, are you going to get up, get up, get up, get up?

(WILLY *exists left.*)

LETTA I think it's sweet you bring your daddy along.

MISS FORSYTHE Oh, he isn't really your father!

BIFF (*at left, turning to her resentfully*) Miss Forsythe, you've just seen a prince walk by. A fine, troubled prince. A hard-working, unappreciated prince. A pal, you understand? A good companion. Always for his boys.

LETTA That's so sweet.

HAPPY Well, girls, what's the program? We're wasting time. Come on, Biff. Gather round. Where would you like to go?

BIFF Why don't you do something for him?

HAPPY Me!

BIFF Don't you give a damn for him, Hap?

HAPPY What're you talking about? I'm the one who—

BIFF I sense it, you don't give a good goddam about him. (*He takes the rolled-up hose from his pocket and puts it on the table in front of* HAPPY.) Look what I found in the cellar, for Christ's sake. How can you bear to let it go on?

HAPPY Me? Who goes away? Who runs off and—

BIFF Yeah, but he doesn't mean anything to you. You could help him—I can't! Don't you understand what I'm talking about? He's going to kill himself, don't you know that?

HAPPY Don't I know it! Me!

BIFF Hap, help him! Jesus . . . help him . . . Help me, help me, I can't bear to look at his face! (*Ready to weep, he hurries out, up right.*)

HAPPY (*starting after him*) Where are you going?

MISS FORSYTHE What's he so mad about?

HAPPY Come on, girls, we'll catch up with him.

MISS FORSYTHE (*as* HAPPY *pushes her out*) Say, I don't like that temper of his!

HAPPY He's just a little overstrung, he'll be all right!

WILLY (*off left, as* THE WOMAN *laughs*) Don't answer! Don't answer!

LETTA Don't you want to tell your father—

HAPPY No, that's not my father. He's just a guy. Come on, we'll catch Biff, and, honey, we're going to paint this town! Stanley, where's the check! Hey, Stanley!

(*They exit.* STANLEY *looks toward left.*)

STANLEY (*calling to* HAPPY *indignantly*) Mr. Loman! Mr. Loman!

(STANLEY *picks up a chair and follows them off. Knocking is heard off left.* THE WOMAN *enters, laughing.* WILLY *follows her. She is in a black slip; he is buttoning his shirt. Raw, sensuous music accompanies their speech.*)

WILLY Will you stop laughing? Will you stop?

THE WOMAN Aren't you going to answer the door? He'll wake the whole hotel.

WILLY I'm not expecting anybody.

THE WOMAN Whyn't you have another drink, honey, and stop being so damn self-centered?

WILLY I'm so lonely.

THE WOMAN You know you ruined me, Willy? From now on, whenever you come to the office, I'll see that you go right through to the buyers. No waiting at my desk any more, Willy. You ruined me.

WILLY That's nice of you to say that.

THE WOMAN Gee, you are self-centered! Why so sad? You are the saddest self-centeredest soul I ever did see-saw. (*She laughs. He kisses her.*) Come on inside, drummer boy. It's silly to be dressing in the middle of the night. (*As knocking is heard.*) Aren't you going to answer the door?

WILLY They're knocking on the wrong door.

THE WOMAN But I felt the knocking. And he heard us talking in here. Maybe the hotel's on fire!

WILLY (*his terror rising*) It's a mistake.

THE WOMAN Then tell him to go away!

WILLY There's nobody there.

THE WOMAN It's getting on my nerves, Willy. There's somebody standing out there and it's getting on my nerves!

WILLY (*pushing her away from him*) All right, stay in the bathroom here, and don't come out. I think there's a law in Massachusetts about it, so don't come out. It may be that new room clerk. He looked very mean. So don't come out. It's a mistake, there's no fire.

(*The knocking is heard again. He takes a few steps away from her, and she vanishes into the wing. The light follows him, and now he is facing* YOUNG BIFF, *who carries a suitcase.* BIFF *steps toward him. The music is gone.*)

BIFF Why didn't you answer?

WILLY Biff! What are you doing in Boston?

BIFF Why didn't you answer? I've been knocking for five minutes, I called you on the phone—

WILLY I just heard you. I was in the bathroom and had the door shut. Did anything happen home?

BIFF Dad—I let you down.

WILLY What do you mean?

BIFF Dad . . .

WILLY Biffo, what's this about? (*Putting his arm around* BIFF.) Come on, let's go downstairs and get you a malted.

BIFF Dad, I flunked math.

WILLY Not for the term?

BIFF The term. I haven't got enough credits to graduate.

WILLY You mean to say Bernard wouldn't give you the answers?

BIFF He did, he tried, but I only got a sixty-one.

WILLY And they wouldn't give you four points?

BIFF Birnbaum refused absolutely. I begged him, Pop, but he won't give me those points. You gotta talk to him before they close the school. Because if he saw the kind of man you are, and you just talked to him in your way, I'm sure he'd come through for me. The class came right before practice, see, and I didn't go enough. Would you talk to him? He'd like you, Pop. You know the way you could talk.

WILLY You're on. We'll drive right back.

968

BIFF   Oh, Dad, good work! I'm sure he'll change it for you!

WILLY   Go downstairs and tell the clerk I'm checkin' out. Go right down.

BIFF   Yes, sir! See, the reason he hates me, Pop—one day he was late for class so I got up at the blackboard and imitated him. I crossed my eyes and talked with a lithp.

WILLY (*laughing*)   You did? The kids like it?

BIFF   They nearly died laughing!

WILLY   Yeah? What'd you do?

BIFF   The thquare root of thixthy twee is . . . (WILLY *bursts out laughing;* BIFF *joins him.*) And in the middle of it he walked in!

(WILLY *laughs and* THE WOMAN *joins in offstage.*)

WILLY (*without hesitation*)   Hurry downstairs and—

BIFF   Somebody in there?

WILLY   No, that was next door.

(THE WOMAN *laughs offstage.*)

BIFF   Somebody got in your bathroom!

WILLY   No, it's the next room, there's a party—

THE WOMAN (*enters, laughing. She lisps this.*)   Can I come in? There's something in the bathtub, Willy, and it's moving!

(WILLY *looks at* BIFF, *who is staring open-mouthed and horrified at* THE WOMAN.)

WILLY   Ah—you better go back to your room. They must be finished painting by now. They're painting her room so I let her take a shower here. Go back, go back . . . (*He pushes her.*)

THE WOMAN (*resisting*)   But I've got to get dressed, Willy, I can't—

WILLY   Get out of here! Go back, go back . . . (*Suddenly striving for the ordinary.*) This is Miss Francis, Biff, she's a buyer. They're painting her room. Go back, Miss Francis, go back . . .

THE WOMAN   But my clothes, I can't go out naked in the hall!

WILLY (*pushing her offstage*)   Get outa here! Go back, go back!

(BIFF *slowly sits down on his suitcase as the argument continues offstage.*)

THE WOMAN   Where's my stockings? You promised me stockings, Willy!

WILLY   I have no stockings here!

THE WOMAN   You had two boxes of size nine sheers for me, and I want them!

WILLY   Here, for God's sake, will you get outa here!

THE WOMAN (*enters holding a box of stockings*)   I just hope there's nobody in the hall. That's all I hope. (*To* BIFF.) Are you football or baseball?

BIFF   Football.

THE WOMAN (*angry, humiliated*)   That's me too. G'night. (*She snatches her clothes from* WILLY, *and walks out.*)

WILLY (*after a pause*)   Well, better get going. I want to get to the school first thing in the morning. Get my suits out of the closet. I'll get my valise. (BIFF *doesn't move.*) What's the matter? (BIFF *remains motionless, tears falling.*) She's a buyer. Buys for J. H. Simmons. She lives down the hall—they're painting. You don't imagine —(*He breaks off. After a pause.*) Now listen, pal, she's just a buyer. She sees merchandise in her room and they have to keep it looking just so . . . (*Pause. Assuming command.*) All right, get my suits. (BIFF *doesn't move.*) Now stop crying and do as I say. I gave you an order. Biff, I gave you an order! Is that what you do when I give you an order? How dare you cry! (*Putting his arm around* BIFF.) Now look, Biff, when you grow up you'll understand about these things. You mustn't—you mustn't overemphasize a thing like this. I'll see Birnbaum first thing in the morning.

BIFF   Never mind.

WILLY (*getting down beside* BIFF)   Never mind! He's going to give you those points. I'll see to it.

BIFF   He wouldn't listen to you.

WILLY   He certainly will listen to me. You need those points for the U. of Virginia.

BIFF   I'm not going there.

WILLY   Heh? If I can't get him to change that mark you'll make it up in summer school. You've got all summer to—

BIFF (*his weeping breaking from him*)   Dad . . .

WILLY (*infected by it*)   Oh, my boy . . .

BIFF   Dad . . .

WILLY   She's nothing to me, Biff. I was lonely, I was terribly lonely.

BIFF   You—you gave her Mama's stockings! (*His tears break through and he rises to go.*)

WILLY (*grabbing for* BIFF)   I gave you an order!

BIFF   Don't touch me, you—liar!

WILLY   Apologize for that!

BIFF   You fake! You phony little fake! You fake! (*Overcome, he turns quickly and weeping fully goes out with his suitcase.* WILLY *is left on the floor on his knees.*)

WILLY   I gave you an order! Biff, come back here or I'll beat you! Come back here! I'll whip you!

(STANLEY *comes quickly in from the right and stands in front of* WILLY.)

WILLY (*shouts at* STANLEY) I gave you an order . . .

STANLEY Hey, let's pick it up, pick it up. Mr. Loman. (*He helps* WILLY *to his feet.*) Your boys left with the chippies. They said they'll see you home.

(*A second waiter watches some distance away.*)

WILLY But we were supposed to have dinner together.

(*Music is heard,* WILLY*'s theme.*)

STANLEY Can you make it?

WILLY I'll—sure, I can make it. (*Suddenly concerned about his clothes.*) Do I—I look all right?

STANLEY Sure, you look all right. (*He flicks a speck off* WILLY*'s lapel.*)

WILLY Here—here's a dollar.

STANLEY Oh, your son paid me. It's all right.

WILLY (*putting it in* STANLEY*'s hand*) No, take it. You're a good boy.

STANLEY Oh, no, you don't have to . . .

WILLY Here—here's some more, I don't need it any more. (*After a slight pause.*) Tell me—is there a seed store in the neighborhood?

STANLEY Seeds? You mean like to plant?

(*As* WILLY *turns,* STANLEY *slips the money back into his jacket pocket.*)

WILLY Yes. Carrots, peas . . .

STANLEY Well, there's hardware stores on Sixth Avenue, but it may be too late now.

WILLY (*anxiously*) Oh, I'd better hurry. I've got to get some seeds. (*He starts off to the right.*) I've got to get some seeds, right away. Nothing's planted. I don't have a thing in the ground.

(WILLY *hurries out as the light goes down.* STANLEY *moves over to the right after him, watches him off. The other waiter has been staring at* WILLY.)

STANLEY (*to the waiter*) Well, whatta you looking at?

(*The waiter picks up the chairs and moves off right.* STANLEY *takes the table and follows him. The light fades on this area. There is a long pause, the sound of the flute coming over. The light gradually rises on the kitchen, which is empty.* HAPPY *appears at the door of the house, followed by* BIFF. HAPPY *is carrying a large bunch of long-stemmed roses. He enters the kitchen, looks around for* LINDA. *Not seeing her, he turns to* BIFF, *who is just outside the house door, and makes a gesture with his hands, indicating "Not here, I guess." He looks into the living-room and freezes. Inside,* LINDA, *unseen, is seated,* WILLY's *coat on her lap. She rises ominously and quietly and moves toward* HAPPY, *who backs up into the kitchen, afraid.*)

HAPPY Hey, what're you doing up? (LINDA *says nothing but moves toward him implacably.*) Where's Pop? (*He keeps backing to the right, and now* LINDA *is in full view in the doorway to the living-room.*) Is he sleeping?

LINDA Where were you?

HAPPY (*trying to laugh it off*) We met two girls, Mom, very fine types. Here, we brought you some flowers. (*Offering them to her.*) Put them in your room, Ma.

(*She knocks them to the floor at* BIFF's *feet. He has now come inside and closed the door behind him. She stares at* BIFF, *silent.*)

HAPPY Now what'd you do that for? Mom, I want you to have some flowers—

LINDA (*cutting* HAPPY *off, violently to* BIFF) Don't you care whether he lives or dies?

HAPPY (*going to the stairs*) Come upstairs, Biff.

BIFF (*with a flare of disgust, to* HAPPY) Go away from me! (*To* LINDA.) What do you mean, lives or dies? Nobody's dying around here, pal.

LINDA Get out of my sight! Get out of here!

BIFF I wanna see the boss.

LINDA You're not going near him!

BIFF Where is he? (*He moves into the living-room and* LINDA *follows.*)

LINDA (*shouting after* BIFF) You invite him for dinner. He looks forward to it all day—(BIFF *appears in his parents' bedroom, looks around, and exits*)—and then you desert him there. There's no stranger you'd do that to!

HAPPY Why? He had a swell time with us. Listen, when I—(LINDA *comes back into the kitchen*)—desert him I hope I don't outlive the day!

LINDA Get out of here!

HAPPY Now look, Mom . . .

LINDA Did you have to go to women tonight? You and your lousy rotten whores!

(BIFF *re-enters the kitchen.*)

HAPPY Mom, all we did was follow Biff around trying to cheer him up! (*To* BIFF.) Boy, what a night you gave me!

LINDA Get out of here, both of you, and don't come back! I don't want you tormenting him any more. Go on now, get your things together! (*To* BIFF.) You can sleep in his apartment. (*She starts to pick up the flowers and stops herself.*) Pick up this stuff, I'm not your maid any more. Pick it up, you bum, you!

(HAPPY *turns his back to her in refusal.* BIFF *slowly moves over and gets down on his knees, picking up the flowers.*)

LINDA   You're a pair of animals! Not one, not another living soul would have had the cruelty to walk out on that man in a restaurant!

BIFF (*not looking at her*)   Is that what he said?

LINDA   He didn't have to say anything. He was so humiliated he nearly limped when he came in.

HAPPY   But, Mom, he had a great time with us—

BIFF (*cutting him off violently*)   Shut up!

(*Without another word,* HAPPY *goes upstairs.*)

LINDA   You! You didn't even go in to see if he was all right!

BIFF (*still on the floor in front of* LINDA, *the flowers in his hand; with self-loathing*) No. Didn't. Didn't do a damned thing. How do you like that, heh? Left him babbling in a toilet.

LINDA   You louse. You . . .

BIFF   Now you hit it on the nose! (*He gets up, throws the flowers in the wastebasket.*) The scum of the earth, and you're looking at him!

LINDA   Get out of here!

BIFF   I gotta talk to the boss, Mom. Where is he?

LINDA   You're not going near him. Get out of this house!

BIFF (*with absolute assurance, determination*)   No. We're gonna have an abrupt conversation, him and me.

LINDA   You're not talking to him!

(*Hammering is heard from outside the house, off right.* BIFF *turns toward the noise.*)

LINDA (*suddenly pleading*)   Will you please leave him alone?

BIFF   What's he doing out there?

LINDA   He's planting the garden!

BIFF (*quietly*)   Now? Oh, my God!

(BIFF *moves outside,* LINDA *following. The light dies down on them and comes up on the center of the apron as* WILLY *walks into it. He is carrying a flashlight, a hoe, and a handful of seed packets. He raps the top of the hoe sharply to fix it firmly, and then moves to the left, measuring off the distance with his foot. He holds the flashlight to look at the seed packets, reading off the instructions. He is in the blue of night.*)

WILLY   Carrots . . . quarter-inch apart. Rows . . . one-foot rows. (*He measures it off.*) One foot. (*He puts down a package and measures off.*) Beets. (*He puts down another package and measures again.*) Lettuce. (*He reads the package, puts it down.*) One foot

—(*He breaks off as* BEN *appears at the right and moves slowly down to him.*) What a proposition, ts, ts. Terrific, terrific. 'Cause she's suffered, Ben, the woman has suffered. You understand me? A man can't go out the way he came in, Ben, a man has got to add up to something. You can't, you can't—(*Ben moves toward him as though to interrupt.*) You gotta consider, now. Don't answer so quick. Remember, it's a guaranteed twenty-thousand-dollar proposition. Now look, Ben, I want you to go through the ins and outs of this thing with me. I've got nobody to talk to, Ben, and the woman has suffered, you hear me?

BEN (*standing still, considering*) What's the proposition?

WILLY It's twenty thousand dollars on the barrelhead. Guaranteed, gilt-edged, you understand?

BEN You don't want to make a fool of yourself. They might not honor the policy.

WILLY How can they dare refuse? Didn't I work like a coolie to meet every premium on the nose? And now they don't pay off? Impossible!

BEN It's called a cowardly thing, William.

WILLY Why? Does it take more guts to stand here the rest of my life ringing up a zero?

BEN (*yielding*) That's a point, William. (*He moves, thinking, turns.*) And twenty thousand—that *is* something one can feel with the hand, it is there.

WILLY (*now assured, with rising power*) Oh, Ben, that's the whole beauty of it! I see it like a diamond, shining in the dark, hard and rough, that I can pick up and touch in my hand. Not like—like an appointment! This would not be another damned-fool appointment, Ben, and it changes all the aspects. Because he thinks I'm nothing, see, and so he spites me. But the funeral—(*Straightening up.*) Ben, that funeral will be massive! They'll come from Maine, Massachusetts, Vermont, New Hampshire! All the old-timers with the strange license plates—that boy will be thunderstruck, Ben, because he never realized—I am known! Rhode Island, New York, New Jersey—I am known, Ben, and he'll see it with his eyes once and for all. He'll see what I am, Ben! He's in for a shock, that boy!

BEN (*coming down to the edge of the garden*) He'll call you a coward.

WILLY (*suddenly fearful*) No, that would be terrible.

BEN Yes. And a damned fool.

WILLY No, no, he mustn't, I won't have that! (*He is broken and desperate.*)

BEN He'll hate you, William.

(*The gay music of the boys is heard.*)

WILLY Oh, Ben, how do we get back to all the great times? Used to be so full of light, and comradeship, the sleigh-riding in winter, and the ruddiness on his cheeks. And always some kind of good news coming up, always something nice coming up ahead. And never even let me carry the valises in the house, and simonizing, simonizing that little red car! Why, why can't I give him something and not have him hate me?

BEN   Let me think about it. (*He glances at his watch.*) I still have a little time. Remarkable proposition, but you've got to be sure you're not making a fool of yourself.

(BEN *drifts off upstage and goes out of sight.* BIFF *comes down from the left*).

WILLY (*suddenly conscious of* BIFF, *turns and looks up at him, then begins picking up the packages of seeds in confusion*)   Where the hell is that seed? (*Indignantly.*) You can't see nothing out here! They boxed in the whole goddam neighborhood!

BIFF   There are people all around here. Don't you realize that?

WILLY   I'm busy. Don't bother me.

BIFF (*taking the hoe from* WILLY)   I'm saying good-by to you, Pop. (WILLY *looks at him, silent, unable to move.*) I'm not coming back any more.

WILLY   You're not going to see Oliver tomorrow?

BIFF   I've got no appointment, Dad.

WILLY   He put his arm around you, and you've got no appointment?

BIFF   Pop, get this now, will you? Everytime I've left it's been a fight that sent me out of here. Today I realized something about myself and I tried to explain it to you and I—I think I'm just not smart enough to make any sense out of it for you. To hell with whose fault it is or anything like that. (*He takes* WILLY's *arm.*) Let's just wrap it up, heh? Come on in, we'll tell Mom. (*He gently tries to pull* WILLY *to left.*)

WILLY (*frozen, immobile, with guilt in his voice*)   No, I don't want to see her.

BIFF   Come on! (*He pulls again, and* WILLY *tries to pull away.*)

WILLY (*highly nervous*)   No, no, I don't want to see her.

BIFF (*tries to look into* WILLY's *face, as if to find the answer there*) Why don't you want to see her?

WILLY (*more harshly now*)   Don't bother me, will you?

BIFF   What do you mean, you don't want to see her? You don't want them calling you yellow, do you? This isn't your fault; it's me, I'm a bum. Now come inside! (WILLY *strains to get away.*) Did you hear what I said to you?

(WILLY *pulls away and quickly goes by himself into the house,* BIFF *follows.*)

LINDA (*to* WILLY)   Did you plant, dear?

BIFF (*at the door, to* LINDA)   All right, we had it out. I'm going and I'm not writing any more.

LINDA (*going to* WILLY *in the kitchen*)   I think that's the best way, dear. 'Cause there's no use drawing it out, you'll just never get along.

(WILLY *doesn't respond.*)

BIFF People ask where I am and what I'm doing, you don't know, and you don't care. That way it'll be off your mind and you can start brightening up again. All right? That clears it, doesn't it? (WILLY *is silent, and* BIFF *goes to him.*) You gonna wish me luck, scout? (*He extends his hand.*) What do you say?

LINDA Shake his hand, Willy.

WILLY (*turning to her, seething with hurt*) There's no necessity to mention the pen at all, y'know.

BIFF (*gently*) I've got no appointment, Dad.

WILLY (*erupting fiercely*) He put his arm around . . .?

BIFF Dad, you're never going to see what I am, so what's the use of arguing? If I strike oil I'll send you a check. Meantime forget I'm alive.

WILLY (*to* LINDA) Spite, see?

BIFF Shake hands, Dad.

WILLY Not my hand.

BIFF I was hoping not to go this way.

WILLY Well, this is the way you're going. Good-by.

(BIFF *looks at him a moment, then turns sharply and goes to the stairs.*)

WILLY (*stops him with*) May you rot in hell if you leave this house!

BIFF (*turning*) Exactly what is it that you want from me?

WILLY I want you to know, on the train, in the mountains, in the valleys, wherever you go, that you cut down your life for spite!

BIFF No, no.

WILLY Spite, spite, is the word of your undoing! And when you're down and out, remember what did it. When you're rotting somewhere beside the railroad tracks, remember, and don't you dare blame it on me!

BIFF I'm not blaming it on you!

WILLY I won't take the rap for this, you hear?

(HAPPY *comes down the stairs and stands on the bottom step, watching.*)

BIFF That's just what I'm telling you!

WILLY (*sinking into a chair at the table, with full accusation*) You're trying to put a knife in me—don't think I don't know what you're doing!

BIFF All right, phony! Then let's lay it on the line. (*He whips the rubber tube out of his pocket and puts it on the table.*)

HAPPY You crazy—

LINDA Biff! (*She moves to grab the hose, but* BIFF *holds it down with his hand.*)

976

BIFF   Leave it there! Don't move it!

WILLY (*not looking at it*)   What is that?

BIFF   You know goddam well what that is.

WILLY (*caged, wanting to escape*)   I never saw that.

BIFF   You saw it. The mice didn't bring it into the cellar! What is this supposed to do, make a hero out of you? This supposed to make me sorry for you?

WILLY   Never heard of it.

BIFF   There'll be no pity for you, you hear it? No pity!

WILLY (*to* LINDA)   You hear the spite!

BIFF   No, you're going to hear the truth—what you are and what I am!

LINDA   Stop it!

WILLY   Spite!

HAPPY (*coming down toward* BIFF)   You cut it now!

BIFF (*to* HAPPY)   The man don't know who we are! The man is gonna know! (*To* WILLY.) We never told the truth for ten minutes in this house!

HAPPY   We always told the truth!

BIFF (*turning on him*)   You big blow, are you the assistant buyer? You're one of the two assistants to the assistant, aren't you?

HAPPY   Well, I'm practically—

BIFF   You're practically full of it! We all are! And I'm through with it. (*To* WILLY.) Now hear this, Willy, this is me.

WILLY   I know you!

BIFF   You know why I had no address for three months? I stole a suit in Kansas City and I was in jail. (*To* LINDA, *who is sobbing.*) Stop crying. I'm through with it.

(LINDA *turns away from them, her hands covering her face.*)

WILLY   I suppose that's my fault!

BIFF   I stole myself out of every good job since high school!

WILLY   And whose fault is that?

BIFF   And I never got anywhere because you blew me so full of hot air I could never stand taking orders from anybody! That's whose fault it is!

WILLY   I hear that!

LINDA   Don't, Biff!

BIFF   It's goddam time you heard that! I had to be boss big shot in two weeks, and I'm through with it!

WILLY   Then hang yourself! For spite, hang yourself!

BIFF No! Nobody's hanging himself, Willy! I ran down eleven flights with a pen in my hand today. And suddenly I stopped, you hear me? And in the middle of that office building, do you hear this? I stopped in the middle of that building and I saw—the sky. I saw the things that I love in this world. The work and the food and time to sit and smoke. And I looked at the pen and said to myself, what the hell am I grabbing this for? Why am I trying to become what I don't want to be? What am I doing in an office, making a contemptuous, begging fool of myself, when all I want is out there, waiting for me the minute I say I know who I am! Why can't I say that, Willy? (*He tries to make* WILLY *face him, but* WILLY *pulls away and moves to the left.*)

WILLY (*with hatred, threateningly*) The door of your life is wide open!

BIFF Pop! I'm a dime a dozen, and so are you!

WILLY (*turning on him now in an uncontrolled outburst*) I am not a dime a dozen! I am Willy Loman, and you are Biff Loman!

(BIFF *starts for* WILLY, *but is blocked by* HAPPY. *In his fury,* BIFF *seems on the verge of attacking his father.*)

BIFF I am not a leader of men, Willy, and neither are you. You were never anything but a hard-working drummer who landed in the ash can like all the rest of them! I'm one dollar an hour, Willy! I tried seven states and couldn't raise it. A buck an hour! Do you gather my meaning? I'm not bringing home any prizes any more, and you're going to stop waiting for me to bring them home!

WILLY (*directly to* BIFF) You vengeful, spiteful mutt!

(BIFF *breaks from* HAPPY. WILLY, *in fright, starts up the stairs.* BIFF *grabs him.*)

BIFF (*at the peak of his fury*) Pop, I'm nothing! I'm nothing, Pop. Can't you understand that? There's no spite in it any more. I'm just what I am, that's all.

(BIFF's *fury has spent itself, and he breaks down, sobbing, holding on to* WILLY, *who dumbly fumbles for* BIFF's *face.*)

WILLY (*astonished*) What're you doing? What're you doing? (*To* LINDA.) Why is he crying?

BIFF (*crying, broken*) Will you let me go, for Christ's sake? Will you take that phony dream and burn it before something happens? (*Struggling to contain himself, he pulls away and moves to the stairs.*) I'll go in the morning. Put him—put him to bed. (*Exhausted,* BIFF *moves up the stairs to his room.*)

WILLY (*after a long pause, astonished, elevated*) Isn't that—isn't that remarkable? Biff—he likes me!

LINDA He loves you, Willy!

HAPPY (*deeply moved*) Always did, Pop.

WILLY Oh, Biff! (*Staring wildly.*) He cried! Cried to me. (*He is choking with his love, and now cries out his promise.*) That boy—that boy is going to be magnificent!

978

(BEN *appears in the light just outside the kitchen.*)

BEN Yes, outstanding, with twenty thousand behind him.

LINDA (*sensing the racing of his mind, fearfully, carefully*) Now come to bed, Willy. It's all settled now.

WILLY (*finding it difficult not to rush out of the house*) Yes, we'll sleep. Come on. Go to sleep, Hap.

BEN And it does take a great kind of a man to crack the jungle.

(*In accents of dread,* BEN's *idyllic music starts up.*)

HAPPY (*his arm around* LINDA) I'm getting married, Pop, don't forget it. I'm changing everything. I'm gonna run that department before the year is up. You'll see, Mom. (*He kisses her.*)

BEN The jungle is dark but full of diamonds, Willy.

(WILLY *turns, moves, listening to* BEN.)

LINDA Be good. You're both good boys, just act that way, that's all.

HAPPY 'Night, Pop. (*He goes upstairs.*)

LINDA (*to* WILLY) Come, dear.

BEN (*with greater force*) One must go in to fetch a diamond out.

WILLY (*to* LINDA, *as he moves slowly along the edge of the kitchen, toward the door*) I just want to get settled down, Linda. Let me sit alone for a little.

LINDA (*almost uttering her fear*) I want you upstairs.

WILLY (*taking her in his arms*) In a few minutes, Linda. I couldn't sleep right now. Go on, you look awful tired. (*He kisses her.*)

BEN Not like an appointment at all. A diamond is rough and hard to the touch.

WILLY Go on now. I'll be right up.

LINDA I think this is the only way, Willy.

WILLY Sure, it's the best thing.

BEN Best thing!

WILLY The only way. Everything is gonna be—go on, kid, get to bed. You look so tired.

LINDA Come right up.

WILLY Two minutes.

(LINDA *goes into the living-room, then reappears in her bedroom.* WILLY *moves just outside the kitchen door.*)

WILLY Loves me. (*Wonderingly.*) Always loved me. Isn't that a remarkable thing? Ben, he'll worship me for it!

BEN (*with promise*) It's dark there, but full of diamonds.

WILLY Can you imagine that magnificence with twenty thousand dollars in his pocket?

LINDA (*calling from her room*) Willy! Come up!

WILLY (*calling into the kitchen*) Yes! Yes. Coming! It's very smart, you realize that, don't you, sweetheart? Even Ben sees it. I gotta go, baby. 'By! 'By! (*Going over to* BEN, *almost dancing.*) Imagine? When the mail comes he'll be ahead of Bernard again!

BEN A perfect proposition all around.

WILLY Did you see how he cried to me? Oh, if I could kiss him, Ben!

BEN Time, William, time!

WILLY Oh, Ben, I always knew one way or another we were gonna make it, Biff and I!

BEN (*looking at his watch*) The boat. We'll be late. (*He moves slowly off into the darkness.*)

WILLY (*elegiacally, turning to the house*) Now when you kick off, boy, I want a seventy-yard boot, and get right down the field under the ball, and when you hit, hit low and hit hard, because it's important, boy. (*He swings around and faces the audience.*) There's all kinds of important people in the stands, and the first thing you know . . . (*Suddenly realizing he is alone.*) Ben! Ben, where do I . . .? (*He makes a sudden movement of search.*) Ben, how do I . . . ?

LINDA (*calling*) Willy, you coming up?

WILLY (*uttering a gasp of fear, whirling about as if to quiet her*) Sh! (*He turns around as if to find his way; sounds, faces, voices, seem to be swarming in upon him and he flicks at them, crying*) Sh! Sh! (*Suddenly music, faint and high, stops him. It rises in intensity, almost to an unbearable scream. He goes up and down on his toes, and rushes off around the house.*) Shhh!

LINDA Willy?

(*There is no answer.* LINDA *waits.* BIFF *gets up off his bed. He is still in his clothes.* HAPPY *sits up.* BIFF *stands listening.*)

LINDA (*with real fear*) Willy, answer me! Willy!

(*There is the sound of a car starting and moving away at full speed.*)

LINDA No!

BIFF (*rushing down the stairs*) Pop!

(*As the car speeds off, the music crashes down in a frenzy of sound, which becomes the soft pulsation of a single cello string.* BIFF *slowly returns to his bedroom. He and* HAPPY *gravely don their jackets.* LINDA *slowly walks out of her room. The music has developed into a dead march. The leaves of day are appearing over everything.* CHARLEY *and* BERNARD, *somberly dressed, appear and knock on the kitchen door.* BIFF *and* HAPPY *slowly descend the stairs to the kitchen as* CHARLEY *and* BERNARD *enter. All stop a moment when* LINDA, *in clothes of mourning, bearing a little bunch of roses, comes through the draped doorway into the kitchen. She goes to* CHARLEY *and takes his arm. Now all move toward the audience, through the wall-line of the kitchen. At the limit of the apron,* LINDA *lays down the flowers, kneels, and sits back on her heels. All stare down at the grave.*)

Requiem

CHARLEY   It's getting dark, Linda.

(LINDA *doesn't react. She stares at the grave.*)

BIFF   How about it, Mom? Better get some rest, heh? They'll be closing the gate soon.

(LINDA *makes no move. Pause.*)

HAPPY (*deeply angered*)   He had no right to do that. There was no necessity for it. We would've helped him.

CHARLEY (*grunting*)   Hmmm.

BIFF   Come along, Mom.

LINDA   Why didn't anybody come?

CHARLEY   It was a very nice funeral.

LINDA   But where are all the people he knew? Maybe they blame him.

CHARLEY   Naa. It's a rough world, Linda. They wouldn't blame him.

LINDA   I can't understand it. At this time especially. First time in thirty-five years we were just about free and clear. He only needed a little salary. He was even finished with the dentist.

CHARLEY   No man only needs a little salary.

LINDA   I can't understand it.

BIFF   There were a lot of nice days. When he'd come home from a trip; or on Sundays, making the stoop; finishing the cellar; putting on the new porch; when he built the extra bathroom; and put up the garage. You know something, Charley, there's more of him in that front stoop than in all the sales he ever made.

CHARLEY   Yeah. He was a happy man with a batch of cement.

LINDA   He was so wonderful with his hands.

BIFF   He had the wrong dreams. All, all, wrong.

HAPPY (*almost ready to fight* BIFF)   Don't say that!

BIFF   He never knew who he was.

CHARLEY (*stopping* HAPPY's *movement and reply. To* BIFF)   Nobody dast blame this man. You don't understand: Willy was a salesman. And for a salesman, there is no rock bottom to the life. He don't put a bolt to a nut, he don't tell you the law or give you medicine. He's a man way out there in the blue, riding on a smile and a shoeshine. And when they start not smiling back—that's an earthquake. And then you get yourself a couple of spots on your hat, and you're finished. Nobody dast blame this man. A salesman is got to dream, boy. It comes with the territory.

BIFF Charley, the man didn't know who he was.

HAPPY (*infuriated*) Don't say that!

BIFF Why don't you come with me, Happy?

HAPPY I'm not licked that easily. I'm staying right in this city, and I'm gonna beat this racket! (*He looks at* BIFF, *his chin set.*) The Loman Brothers!

BIFF I know who I am, kid.

HAPPY All right, boy. I'm gonna show you and everybody else that Willy Loman did not die in vain. He had a good dream. It's the only dream you can have—to come out number-one man. He fought it out here, and this is where I'm gonna win it for him.

BIFF (*with a hopeless glance at* HAPPY, *bends toward his mother*) Let's go, Mom.

LINDA I'll be with you in a minute. Go on, Charley. (*He hesitates.*) I want to, just for a minute. I never had a chance to say good-by.

(CHARLEY *moves away, followed by* HAPPY. BIFF *remains a slight distance up and left of* LINDA. *She sits there, summoning herself. The flute begins, not far away, playing behind her speech.*)

LINDA Forgive me, dear. I can't cry. I don't know what it is, but I can't cry. I don't understand it. Why did you ever do that? Help me, Willy, I can't cry. It seems to me that you're just on another trip. I keep expecting you. Willy, dear, I can't cry. Why did you do it? I search and search and I search, and I can't understand it, Willy. I made the last payment on the house today. Today, dear. And there'll be nobody home. (*A sob rises in her throat.*) We're free and clear. (*Sobbing more fully, released.*) We're free. (BIFF *comes slowly toward her.*) We're free . . . We're free . . .

(BIFF *lifts her to her feet and moves out up right with her in his arms.* LINDA *sobs quietly.* BERNARD *and* CHARLEY *come together and follow them, followed by* HAPPY. *Only the music of the flute is left on the darkening stage as over the house the hard towers of the apartment buildings rise into sharp focus, and—*)

THE CURTAIN FALLS

DISCUSSION TOPICS

1. Several of the names in the play apparently have symbolic significance. What are they?
2. Arthur Miller was well aware that Aristotle required a tragic hero to be an elevated, noble character. Nevertheless, in *Death of a Salesman* he attempted to

982

portray the tragedy of the common man. Do you feel that Willy Loman is a suitably tragic figure?

3. To what extent is Willy Loman responsible for his own tragedy? What is his tragic flaw?

4. Willy Loman's mind recurrently slips from the present into the past. What is the thematic function of these lapses?

5. What does Willy's brother Ben represent to him? Is Ben an archetypal figure?

6. Why is Willy so concerned to get seeds planted in his garden?

7. How is the play a commentary on the American Dream and its extended meanings?

8. Many tragedies, including *Oedipus the King* and *Hamlet,* are plays about truth and the gaps between appearance and reality. How is this theme presented in *Death of a Salesman?* The Requiem scene at the end of the play portrays a recognition of truth *(anagnorisis)* for some of the characters. Which ones seem to have grown through their experiences in the play? Which seem to remain deluded?

9. Willy presents a very complex mixture of the three principles Freud delineated —the morality, the reality, and the pleasure principles. Find instances of each of these in his actions and his musings, and discuss how they impinge on one another.

LONNE ELDER III (1931–   ) Georgia-born playwright; attended Yale School of Drama. A former waiter, dockworker, and professional gambler, he lived for several years in New York City. His plays have won a number of awards; he has also written for television and film.

CEREMONIES IN DARK OLD MEN

Characters

MR. RUSSELL B. PARKER
MR. WILLIAM JENKINS
THEOPOLIS PARKER
BOBBY PARKER
ADELE ELOISE PARKER
BLUE HAVEN
Young Girl

ACT ONE

Early spring, about 4:30 in the afternoon, now.

A small, poverty-stricken barbershop on 126th Street between Seventh and Lenox avenues, Harlem, U.S.A.

There is only one barber's throne in this barbershop. There is a not too lengthy mirror along the wall, and a high, broad shelf in the immediate area of the throne. There are two decks of shelves of equal width projecting just below the main shelf. These shelves are covered by small, sliding panels. On the far left corner of the shop is the street door, and on the far right corner is a door leading to a back room. Just to the right of the door, flush against the wall, is a card table and two chairs. Farther right is a clothes rack. Against the wall to the far left of the shop, near the door, are four chairs lined up uniformly.

The back room is like any back room in a poverty-stricken barbershop. It has an old refrigerator, an even older antique-type desk, and a medium-size bed. On the far right is a short flight of stairs leading up. A unique thing about this room: a door to stairs coming up from a small basement.

The action of the play takes place in the barbershop and the back room.

Scene One

As the curtain rises, MR. RUSSELL B. PARKER *is seated in the single barber's throne, reading the* Daily News. *He is in his early or middle fifties. He rises nervously, moves to the window, and peers out, his right hand over his eyebrows. He returns to the chair and continues to read. After checking his watch, he rises again and moves to the window for another look. Finally he sees the right person coming and moves to the door to open it.* MR. WILLIAM JENKINS *enters: early fifties, well dressed in a complete suit of clothes, and carrying a newspaper under his arm.*

MR. PARKER   Where have you been?

MR. JENKINS   Whatcha mean? You know where I was.

MR. PARKER   You want to play the game or not?

MR. JENKINS   That's what I came here for.

MR. PARKER (*Slides open a panel in the counter.*)   I wanted to get in at least three games before Adele got home, but this way we'll be lucky if we get in one.

MR. JENKINS   Stop complaining and get the board out—I'll beat you, and that will be that.

MR. PARKER   I can do without your bragging. (*Pulls out a checkerboard and a small can, quickly places them on the table, then shakes up the can.*) Close your eyes and take a man.

MR. JENKINS (*Closing his eyes.*)   You never learn. (*Reaches into the can and pulls out a checker.*) It's red.

MR. PARKER   All right, I get the black. (*Sits at the table and rushes to set up his men.*) Get your men down, Jenkins!

MR. JENKINS (*sits.*)   Aw, man, take it easy, the checkers ain't gon' run away! (*Setting his men up.*) If you could play the game I wouldn't mind it—but you can't play! —Your move.

MR. PARKER   I'll start here—I just don't want Adele to catch us here playing checkers. She gave me and the boys a notice last week that we had to get jobs or get out of the house.

MR. JENKINS   Don't you think it's about time you got a job? In the five years I've been knowing you, I can count the heads of hair you done cut in this shop on one hand.

MR. PARKER   This shop is gon' work yet; I know it can. Just give me one more year and you'll see . . . Going out to get a job ain't gon' solve nothing—all it's gon' do is create a lot of bad feelings with everybody. I can't work! I don't know how to! (*Moves checker.*)

MR. JENKINS   I bet if all your children were living far from you like mine, you'd know how to. That's one thing I don't understand about you, Parker. How long do you expect your daughter to go on supporting you and those two boys?

MR. PARKER   I don't expect that! I just want some time until I can straighten things out. My dear Doris understood that. She understood me like a book. (*Makes another move.*)

MR. JENKINS   You mean to tell me your wife enjoyed working for you?

MR. PARKER   Of course she didn't, but she never worried me. You been married, Jenkins: you know what happens to a man when a woman worries him all the time, and that's what Adele been doing, worrying my head off! (*Makes another move.*)

MR. JENKINS   Whatcha gon' do about it?

MR. PARKER   I'm gon' get tough, evil and bad. That's the only sign a woman gets from a man. (*Makes move.*)

985

(THEOPOLIS PARKER *enters briskly from street. He is in his twenties, of medium height, and has a lean, solid physique. His younger brother* BOBBY *follows, carrying a huge paper bag whose contents are heavy and fragile.*)

THEO That's the way I like to hear you talk, Pop, but she's gon' be walking through that door soon, and I wants to see how tough you gon' be.

MR. PARKER Leave me alone, boy.

THEO Pop, we got six more days. You got to do something!

MR. PARKER I'll do it when the time comes.

THEO Pop, the time is *now.*

MR. PARKER And right now I am playing a game of checkers with Mr. Jenkins, so leave me alone!

THEO All right—don't say I didn't warn you when she locks us out of the house!

(THEO *and* BOBBY *rush through the back room.* BOBBY *places the brown bag in the old refrigerator as they dart up the stairs leading to the apartment.* PARKER *makes another move.*)

MR. PARKER *You're trapped, Jenkins!*

(*Pause.*)

MR. JENKINS (*Pondering.*) Hmmmmmm . . . It looks that way, don't it?

MR. PARKER (*Moves to the door.*) While you're moaning over the board, I'll just make a little check to see if Adele is coming . . . Don't cheat now! (*He backs toward the window, watching that his adversary does not cheat. He quickly looks out the window.*) Uh-uh! It's Adele! She's in the middle of the block, talking to Miss Thomas! (*Rushes to take out a towel and spreads it over the checkerboard.*) Come on, man! (*Drags* MR. JENKINS *by the arm toward the back room.*)

MR. JENKINS *What are you doing, Parker!*

MR. PARKER You gon' have to hide out in the back room, 'cause if Adele comes in here and sees you, she'll think that we been playing checkers all day!

MR. JENKINS I don't care about that!

MR. PARKER You want to finish the game, don't you?

MR. JENKINS Yeah, but—

MR. PARKER All you have to do, Jenks, is lay low for a minute, that's all. She'll stop in and ask me something about getting a job, I'll tell her I got a good line on one, and then she'll go on upstairs. There won't be nobody left here but you and me. Whatcha say, Jenks?

MR. JENKINS (*Pause.*) All right, I'll do it. I don't like it, but I'll do it, and you better not mention this to nobody, you hear!

MR. PARKER Not a single soul in this world will know but you and me.

MR. JENKINS (*Moves just inside the room and stands.*)   This is the most ridiculous thing I ever heard of, hiding in somebody's back room just to finish up a checker game.

MR. PARKER   Stop fighting it, man!

MR. JENKINS   All right!

MR. PARKER   Not there!

MR. JENKINS   What in the hell is it now!

MR. PARKER   *You've got to get under the bed!*

MR. JENKINS   No, I'm not gettin' under nobody's bed!

MR. PARKER   Now look . . . Adele never goes through the front way. She comes through the shop and the back room, up the basement stairs to the apartment. Now you want her to catch you hiding in there, looking like a fool?

MR. JENKINS   No, I can take myself out of here and go home!

MR. PARKER (*Pushes* JENKINS *over to the table and uncovers the checkerboard.*)   Look at this! Now you just take a good look at this board! (*Releases him.*)

MR. JENKINS   I'm looking, so what?

MR. PARKER   *So what?* I got you and you know it! There ain't no way in the world you'll ever get out of that little trap I got you in. *And it's your move.* How many years we been playing against each other?

MR. JENKINS   Three.

MR. PARKER   Never won a game from you in all that time, have I?

MR. JENKINS   That ain't the half of it. You ain't gon' win one either.

MR. PARKER   Now that I finally got you, that's easy talk, comin' from a running man. All right, go on. Run. (*Moves away.*)

MR. JENKINS   Go on, hell! All I gotta do is put my king here, give you this jump here, move this man over there, and you're dead!

MR. PARKER (*Turns to him.*)   Try me then. Try me, or are you scared at last I'm gon' beat you?

MR. JENKINS   I can't do it now, there ain't enough time!

MR. PARKER (*Strutting like a sport.*)   Run, rabbit, run . . .

MR. JENKINS   All right! I'll get under the bed. But I swear, Parker, I'm gon' beat you silly! (*They move into the back room.*)

MR. PARKER   Hurry it up then. We ain't got much time.

(*As* MR. PARKER *struggles to help* MR. JENKINS *get under the bed in the back room,* ADELE *comes in from the street. She is in her late twenties, well dressed in conventional New York office attire. She is carrying a smart-looking handbag and a manila envelope. She stops near the table on which checkerboard is hidden under towel.* MR. PARKER *enters from the back room.*)

MR. PARKER   Hi, honey.

987

(*She doesn't answer, instead busies herself putting minor things in order.*)

ADELE   You looked for work today?

MR. PARKER   All morning . . .

(*Pause.*)

ADELE   No luck in the morning, and so you played checkers all afternoon.

MR. PARKER   No, I've been working on a few ideas of mine. My birthday comes up the tenth of the month, and I plan to celebrate it with an idea to shake up this whole neighborhood, and then I'm gon' really go to the country!

ADELE   Don't go to the country—go to work, huh? (*Moves toward back room.*) Oh, God, I'm tired!

MR. PARKER (*Rushing to get her away from bed.*)   Come on and let me take you upstairs. I know you must've had yourself a real tough day at the office . . . and you can forget about cooking supper and all of that stuff.

ADELE (*Breaks away, moves back into shop toward counter.*)   Thank you, but I've already given myself the privilege of not cooking your supper tonight.

MR. PARKER   You did?

ADELE   The way I figure it, you should have my dinner waiting for me.

MR. PARKER   But I don't know how to cook.

ADELE (*Turns sharply.*)   You can learn.

MR. PARKER   Now look, Adele, if you got something on your mind, say it, 'cause you know damn well I ain't doin' no cooking.

ADELE (*Pause.*)   All right, I will. A thought came to me today as it does every day, and I'm damn tired of thinking about it—

MR. PARKER   What?

ADELE   —and that is, I've been down at that motor-license bureau so long, sometimes I forget the reasons I ever took the job in the first place.

MR. PARKER   Now look, everybody knows you quit college and came home to help your mama out. Everybody knows it! What you want me to do? Write some prayers to you?

(*The two boys enter the back room from upstairs.*)

ADELE   I just want you to get a job!

(*The boys step into shop and stand apart from each other.*)

BOBBY   Hey, Adele.

ADELE   Well! From what cave did you fellows crawl out of? I didn't know you hung around barbershops . . . Want a haircut, boys?

988

THEO   For your information, this is the first time we been in this barbershop today. We been upstairs thinking.

ADELE   With what?

THEO   With our *minds,* baby!

ADELE   If the two of you found that house upstairs so attractive to keep you in it all day, then I can think of only three things: the telephone, the bed, and the kitchen.

BOBBY   The kitchen, that's it: we been washing dishes all day!

ADELE   I don't like that, Bobby!

THEO   And I don't like your attitude!

ADELE   Do you like it when I go out of here every morning to work?

THEO   There you go again with that same old tired talk: work! Mama understood about us, I don't know why you gotta give everybody a hard time . . .

ADELE   That was one of Mama's troubles: understanding everybody.

THEO   Now don't start that junk with me!

ADELE   I have got to start that, *Mr. Theopolis Parker!*

MR. PARKER   Hold on now, there's no need for all this . . . Can't we settle this later on, Adele . . .

ADELE   We settle it now. You got six days left, so you gotta do something, and quick. I got a man coming here tomorrow to change the locks on the door. So for the little time you have left, you'll have to come by me to enter this house.

THEO   Who gives you the right to do that?

ADELE   Me, Adele Eloise Parker, black, over twenty-one, and the only working person in this house!

(*Pause.*)

I am not going to let the three of you drive me into the grave the way you did Mama. And if you really want to know how I feel about that, I'll tell you: Mama killed herself because there was no kind of order in this house. There was nothing but her old-fashion love for a bum like you, Theo—and this one (*points to* BOBBY) who's got nothing better to do with his time but to shoplift every time he walks into a department store. And you, Daddy, you and those fanciful stories you're always ready to tell, and all the talk of the good old days when you were the big vaudeville star, of hitting the numbers big. How? How, Daddy? The money you spent on the numbers you got from Mama . . . In a way, you let Mama make a bum out of you—you let her kill herself!

MR. PARKER   That's a terrible thing to say, Adele, and I'm not going to let you put that off on me!

ADELE   But the fact remains that in the seven years you've been in this barber-shop you haven't earned enough money to buy two hot dogs! Most of your time is spent playing checkers with that damn Mr. Jenkins.

THEO (*Breaks in.*)   Why don't you get married or something! We don't need you —Pop is here, it's HIS HOUSE!

ADELE   You're lucky I don't get married and—

THEO   Nobody wants you, baby!

ADELE (*Theo's remark stops her for a moment. She resettles herself.*)   All right, you just let someone ask me, and I'll leave you with *Pop,* to starve with Pop. Or, there's another way: why don't the three of you just leave right now and try making it on your own? Why don't we try that!

MR. PARKER   What about my shop?

ADELE   Since I'm the one that has to pay the extra forty dollars a month for you to keep this place, there's going to be no more shop. It was a bad investment and the whole of Harlem knows it!

MR. PARKER (*Grabbing her by the arm, in desperation.*)   I'm fifty-four years old!

ADELE (*Pulling away.*)   Don't touch me!

MR. PARKER   You go ahead and do what you want, but I'm not leaving this shop! (*Crosses away from her.*)

ADELE   Can't you understand, Father? I can't go on forever supporting three grown men! *That ain't right!*

(*Long pause.*)

MR. PARKER (*Shaken by her remarks.*)   No, it's not right—it's not right at all.

ADELE   —It's going to be *you* or *me.*

BOBBY (*After a pause.*)   I'll do what I can, Adele.

ADELE   You'll do *more* than you can.

BOBBY   I'll do more than I can.

ADELE   Is that all right by you, Mr. Theopolis?

THEO   Yes.

(*Pause.*)

ADELE   That's fine. Out of this house tomorrow morning—before I leave here, or with me—suit your choice. And don't look so mournful (*gathers up her belongings at the shelf*), smile. You're going to be happier than you think, earning a living for a change. (*Moves briskly through the back room and up the stairs.*)

BOBBY   You do look pretty bad, Theo. A job might be just the thing for you.

(MR. JENKINS *comes rushing from the bed into the shop.*)

MR. PARKER Jenkins! I plumb forgot—

MR. JENKINS I let you make a fool out of me, Parker!

MR. PARKER We can still play!

MR. JENKINS (*Gathering his jacket and coat.*) We can't play nothing, I'm going home where I belong!

MR. PARKER Okay, okay, I'll come over to your place tonight.

MR. JENKINS That's the only way. I ain't gon' have my feelings hurt by that daughter of yours.

MR. PARKER I'll see you tonight—about eight.

MR. JENKINS (*At the door.*) And, Parker, tell me something?

MR. PARKER Yeah, what, Jenks?

MR. JENKINS Are you positively sure Adele is your daughter?

MR. PARKER Get out of here! (MR. JENKINS *rushes out.*) Now what made him ask a silly question like that?

THEO I think he was trying to tell you that you ain't supposed to be taking all that stuff from Adele.

BOBBY Yeah, Pop, he's right.

(MR. PARKER *starts putting his checker set together.*)

THEO (*To* BOBBY.) I don't know what you talking about—you had your chance a few minutes ago, but all you did was poke your eyes at me and nod your head like a fool.

BOBBY I don't see why you gotta make such a big thing out of her taking charge. Somebody's gotta do it. I think she's right!

THEO I know what she's up to. She wants us to get jobs so she can fix up the house like she always wanted it, and then it's gon' happen.

BOBBY What's that?

THEO She gon' get married to some konkhead out on the Avenue, and then she gon' throw us out the door.

BOBBY She wouldn't do that.

THEO She wouldn't, huh? Put yourself in her place. She's busting thirty wide open. *Thirty years old*—that's a lot of years for a broad that's not married.

BOBBY I never thought of it that way . . .

THEO (*In half confidence.*) And you know something else, Pop? I sneaked and peeped at her bank book, and you know what she got saved?

MR. PARKER and BOBBY (*Simultaneously, turning their heads.*) How much!?

THEO Two thousand two hundred and sixty-five dollars!

BOBBY   WHAT!!!

MR. PARKER   I don't believe it!

THEO   You better—and don't let her hand you that stuff about how she been sacrificing all these years for the house. The only way she could've saved up that kind of money was by staying right here!

MR. PARKER   Well, I'll be damned—two thousand dollars!

THEO   She better watch out is all I gotta say, 'cause I know some guys out there on that Avenue who don't do nothing but sit around all day figuring out ways to beat working girls out of their savings.

MR. PARKER   You oughta know, 'cause you're one of them yourself. The way I figure it, Theo, anybody that can handle you the way she did a few minutes ago can very well take care of themselves. (*He occupies himself putting checkers and board away and cleaning up.*)

THEO   That's mighty big talk coming from you, after the way she treated you.

MR. PARKER   Lay off me, boy.

THEO   You going out to look for a job?

MR. PARKER   I'm giving it some serious thought.

THEO   Well, I'm not. I ain't wasting myself on no low, dirty, dead-end job. I got my paintings to think about.

BOBBY   Do you really think you're some kind of painter or something?

THEO   You've seen them.

BOBBY   Yeah, but how would I know?

THEO   (*Rushes into the back room, takes paintings from behind the refrigerator.*)   All right, look at 'em.

BOBBY   Don't bring that stuff in here to me—show it to Pop!

(THEO *holds up two ghastly, inept paintings to his brother.* MR. PARKER, *sweeping the floor, pays no attention.*)

THEO   Look at it! Now tell me what you see.

BOBBY   Nothing.

THEO   You've got to see something—even an idiot has impressions.

BOBBY   I ain't no idiot.

THEO   All right, fool then.

BOBBY   Now look, you better stop throwing them words "fool" and "idiot" at me any time you feel like it. I'm gon' be one more fool, and then my fist is gonna land right upside your head!

THEO   Take it easy now—I tell you what: try to see something.

BOBBY   Try?

THEO Yeah, close your eyes and really try.

BOBBY (*Closes his eyes.*) Okay, I'm trying, but I don't know how I'm gon' see anything with my eyes closed!

THEO Well, open them!

BOBBY They open.

THEO Now tell me what you see.

BOBBY I see paint.

THEO I know you see paint, stupid.

BOBBY (*Slaps him ferociously across the face.*) Now I told you about that! Every time you call me out of my name, you get hit!

THEO You'll never understand!

BOBBY All I know is that a picture is supposed to be pretty, but I'm sorry, that mess you got there is downright ugly!

THEO You're hopeless.—You understand this, don't you, Pop? (*Holding the painting for him to see.*)

MR. PARKER (*Not looking at the painting.*) Don't ask me—I don't know nothing about no painting.

THEO You were an artist once.

MR. PARKER That was a different kind.

THEO Didn't you ever go out on the stage with a new thing inside of you? One of them nights when you just didn't want to do that ol' soft-shoe routine? You knew you had to do it—after all, it was your job—but when you did it, you gave it a little bite here, a little acid there, and still, with all that, they laughed at you anyway. Didn't that ever happen to you?

MR. PARKER More than once . . . But you're BSn', boy, and you know it. You been something new every year since you quit school. First you was going to be a racing-car driver, then a airplane pilot, then a office big shot, and now it's a painter. As smart a boy as you is, you should've stayed in school, but who do you think you're fooling with them pictures?—It all boils down to one thing: you don't want to work. But I'll tell you something, Theo: time done run out on you. Adele's not playing, so you might as well put all that junk and paint away.

THEO Who the hell is Adele? You're my father, you're the man of the house.

MR. PARKER True, and that's what I intend to be, but until I get a job, I'm gon' play it cool.

THEO You're going to let her push you out into the streets to hustle up a job. You're an old man. You ain't used to working, it might kill you.

MR. PARKER Yeah, but what kind of leg do I have to stand on if she puts me out in the street?

THEO She's bluffing!

MR. PARKER   A buddy of mine who was in this same kind of fix told me exactly what you just said. Well, the last time I saw him, he was standing on the corner of Eighth Avenue and 125th Street at four o'clock in the morning, twenty-degree weather, in nothing but his drawers, mumbling to himself, "I could've sworn she was bluffing!"

THEO   Hey, Pop! Let me put it to you this way: if none of us come up with anything in that two-week deadline she gave us—none of us, you hear me?

MR. PARKER   I hear you and that's just about all.

THEO   Don't you get the point? That's three of us—you, me, and Bobby. What she gon' do? Throw the three of us out in the street? I tell you, she ain't gon' do that!

MR. PARKER   If you want to take that chance, that's your business, but don't try to make me take it with you. Anyway, it ain't right that she has to work for three grown men. It just ain't right.

THEO   Mama did it for you.

MR. PARKER (*Sharply.*)   That was different. She was my wife. She knew things about me you will never know. We oughtn' talk about her at all.

THEO   I'm sorry, Pop, but ever since Mama's funeral I've been thinking. Mama was the hardest-working person I ever knew, and it killed her! Is that what I'm supposed to do? No, that's not it, I know it's not. You know what I've been doing? I've been talking to some people, to a very important person right here in Harlem, and I told him about this big idea of mine—

MR. PARKER   You're loaded with ideas, boy—*bad ideas!* (*Puts broom away.*)

THEO   WHY DON'T YOU LISTEN TO WHAT I HAVE TO SAY!

MR. PARKER   Listen to you for what? Another con game you got up your sleeve because your sister's got fed up with you lying around this house all day while she's knocking herself out. You're pulling the same damn thing on me you did with those ugly paintings of yours a few minutes ago.

THEO   Okay, I can't paint. So I was jiving, but now I got something I really want to do—something I got to do!

MR. PARKER   If you're making a point, Theo, you've gotta be smarter than you're doing to get it through to me.

THEO (*Goes to back room, opens refrigerator, and takes out brown-paper bag, then comes back into the shop.*)   Pop, I got something here to show how smart I really am. (*Lifts an old jug out of the bag.*) Check this out, Pop! Check it out!

MR. PARKER   What is it?

THEO   Whiskey—corn whiskey—you want some?

MR. PARKER (*Hovers.*)   Well, I'll try a little bit of it out, but we better not let Adele see us.

THEO (*Starts unscrewing cork from jug.*) That girl sure puts a scare in you, Pop, and I remember when you wouldn't take no stuff off Mama, Adele, or nobody.

MR. PARKER God is the only person I fear.

THEO (*Stops unscrewing the jug.*) God! Damn, you're all alike!

MR. PARKER What are you talking about, boy?

THEO You, the way Mama was—ask you any question you can't answer, and you throw that Bible stuff at us.

MR. PARKER I don't get you.

THEO For instance, let me ask you about the black man's oppressions, and you'll tell me about some small nation in the East rising one day to rule the world. Ask you about pain and dying, and you say, "God wills it." . . . Fear?—and you'll tell me about Daniel, and how Daniel wasn't scared of them lions. Am I right or wrong?

MR. PARKER It's all in the book and you can't dispute it.

THEO You wanta bet? If that nation in the East ever do rise, how can I be sure they won't be worse than the jokers we got running things now?—Nobody but nobody wills me to pain and dying, not if I can do something about it. That goes for John, Peter, Mary, J.C., the whole bunch of 'em! And as for ol' Daniel: sure, Daniel didn't care nothing about them lions—*but them lions didn't give a damn about him either! They tore him into a million pieces!*

MR. PARKER That's a lie! That's an ungodly, unholy lie! (*Takes his Bible from the shelf.*) And I'll prove it!

THEO What lie?

MR. PARKER (*Moving from the counter, thumbing through Bible.*) You and those bastard ideas of yours. Here, here it is! (*Reading from Bible.*) "And when he came near unto the den to Daniel, he cried with a pained voice; The King spoke and said to Daniel: 'O Daniel, servant of the living God, is thy God, whom thou servest continually, able to deliver thee from the lions?' Then said Daniel unto the King: 'O King, live forever! My God hath sent his angel, and hath shut the lions' mouths, and they have not hurt me; for as much as before him innocence was found in me, and also before thee, O King, have I done no hurt.' Then was the King exceeding glad, and commanded that they should take Daniel up out of the den. So Daniel was taken up out of the den, and no manner of hurt was found upon him, because he trusted his God!!!" (*Slams the book closed, triumphant.*)

THEO Hollywood, Pop, Hollywood!

MR. PARKER Damn you! How I ever brought something like you into this world, I'll never know! You're no damn good! Sin! That's who your belief is! Sin and corruption! With you, it's nothing but women! Whiskey! Women! Whiskey! (*While he is carrying on, Theo pours out a glass of corn and puts it in Mr. Parker's hand.*) Women! Whiskey! (*Takes a taste.*) Whisk— Where did you get this from? (*Sits on throne.*)

THEO (*Slapping* BOBBY'S *hand.*) I knew you'd get the message, Pop—I just knew it!

MR. PARKER Why, boy, this is the greatest corn I ever tasted!

BOBBY And Theo puts that stuff together like he was born to be a whiskey maker!

MR. PARKER Where did you learn to make corn like this?

THEO Don't you remember? You taught me.

MR. PARKER By George, I did! Why, you weren't no more'n nine years old—

THEO Eight. Let's have another one. (*Pours another for* PARKER.) Drink up. Here's to ol' Daniel. You got to admit one thing—he had a whole lot of heart!

MR. PARKER (*Drinks up and puts his hand out again.*) Another one, please . . .

THEO (*Pouring.*) Anything you say, Pop! *You're the boss of this house!*

MR. PARKER Now that's the truth if you ever spoke it. (*Drinks up.*) Whew! This is good! (*Putting his glass out again, slightly tipsy.*)

THEO About this idea of mine, Pop: well, it's got something to do with this corn.

MR. PARKER (*Drinks up.*) Wow! Boy, people oughta pay you to make this stuff.

THEO Well, that's what I kinda had in mind. I tested some of it out the other day, and I was told this corn liquor could start a revolution—that is, if I wanted to start one. I let a preacher taste some, and he asked me to make him a whole keg for him.

MR. PARKER (*Pauses. Then, in a sudden change of mood.*) God! Damnit!

BOBBY What's wrong, Pop?

MR. PARKER I miss her, boy, I tell you, I miss her! Was it really God's will?

THEO Don't you believe that—*don't you ever believe that!*

MR. PARKER But I think, boy—I think hard!

THEO That's all right. We think hard too. We got it from you. Ain't that right, Bobby?

BOBBY Yeah.

MR. PARKER (*Pause.*) You know something? That woman was the first woman I ever got close to—your mama . . .

BOBBY *How old were you?*

MR. PARKER Twenty.

BOBBY Aw, come on, Pop!

MR. PARKER May God wipe me away from this earth . . .

THEO Twenty years old and you had never touched a woman? You must've been in bad shape.

MR. PARKER I'll tell you about it.

THEO   Here he goes with another one of his famous stories!

MR. PARKER   I can always go on upstairs, you know.

THEO   No, Pop, we want to hear it.

MR. PARKER   Well, I was working in this circus in Tampa, Florida—your mother's hometown. You remember Bob Shepard—well, we had this little dance routine of ours we used to do a sample of outside the tent. One day we was out there doing one of our numbers, when right in the middle of the number I spied this fine, foxy-looking thing, blinking her eyes at me. 'Course ol' Bob kept saying it was him she was looking at, but I knew it was *me*—'cause if there was one thing that was my specialty, it was a fine-looking woman.

THEO   You live twenty years of you life not getting anywhere near a woman, and all of a sudden they become *your specialty?*

MR. PARKER   Yeah, being that—

THEO   Being that you had never had a woman for all them terrible years, naturally it was on your mind all the time.

MR. PARKER   That's right.

THEO   And it being on your mind so much, you sorta became a specialist on women?

MR. PARKER   Right again.

THEO (*Laughs.*)   I don't know. But I guess you got a point there!

MR. PARKER   You want to hear this or not!?

BOBBY   Yeah, go on, Pop. *I'm* listening.

MR. PARKER   Well, while I was standing on the back of the platform, I motions to her with my hand to kinda move around to the side of the stand, so I could talk to 'er. She strolled 'round to the side, stood there for a while, and you know what? Ol' Bob wouldn't let me get a word in edgewise. But you know what she told him; she said Mister, you talk like a fool! (*All laugh.*)

BOBBY   That was Mama, all right.

MR. PARKER   So I asked her if she would like to meet me after the circus closed down. When I got off that night, sure enough, she was waiting for me. We walked up to the main section of town, off to the side of the road, 'cause we had a hard rain that day and the road was full of muddy little ponds. I got to talking to her and telling her funny stories and she would laugh—boy, I'm telling you that woman could laugh!

THEO   That was your technique, huh? Keep 'em laughing!

MR. PARKER   Believe it or not, it worked—'cause she let me kiss her. I kissed her under this big ol' pecan tree. She could kiss too. When that woman kissed me, somethin' grabbed me so hard and shook me so, I fell flat on my back into a big puddle of water! *And that woman killed herself laughing!*

997

(*Pause.*)

I married her two weeks later.

THEO   And then you started making up for lost time. I'm glad you did, Pop—
'cause if you hadn't, I wouldn't be here today.

MR. PARKER   If I know you, you'd have made some kind of arrangement.

BOBBY   What happened after that?

MR. PARKER   We just lived and had fun—and children too, that part you know
about. We lived bad and we lived good—and then my legs got wobbly, and my
feet got heavy, I lost my feeling, and everything just stayed as it was.

(*Pause.*)

I only wish I had been as good a haircutter as I was a dancer. Maybe she wouldn't
have had to work so hard. She might be living today.

THEO   Forget it, Pop—it's all in the gone by. Come on, you need another drink.
(*Pouring.*)

MR. PARKER   Get me to talking about them old days. It hurts, I tell you, it—

THEO   Pop, you have got to stop thinking about those things. We've got work
to do!

MR. PARKER   You said you had an idea . . .

THEO   Yes—you see, Pop, this idea has to do with Harlem. It has to do with the
preservation of Harlem. That's what it's all about. So I went to see this leader, and
I spoke to him about it. He thought it was great and said he would pay me to use
it!

MR. PARKER   Who wants to preserve this dump! Tear it down, is what I say!

THEO   But this is a different kind of preserving. Preserve it for black men—
preserve it for men like you, me, and Bobby. That's what it's all about.

MR. PARKER   That sounds good.

THEO   Of course I told this leader, I couldn't promise to do anything until I had
spoken to my father. I said, after straightening everything out with you I would
make arrangements for the two of you to meet.

MR. PARKER   Meet him for what?

THEO   For making money! For business! *This man knows how to put people in
business!*

MR. PARKER   All right, I'll meet him. What's his name?

THEO   —But first you gotta have a showdown with Adele and put her in her place
once and for all.

MR. PARKER   Now wait just a minute. You didn't say Adele would have anything
to do with this.

998

THEO   Pop, this man can't be dealing with men who let women rule them. Pop, you've got to tell that girl off or we can't call ourselves men!

MR. PARKER (*Pause.*)   All right. If she don't like it, that's too bad. Whatever you have in mind for us to do with this leader of yours, we'll do it.

THEO   Now that's the way I like to hear my old man talk! Take a drink, Pop! (*Starts popping his fingers and moves dancing about the room.*)

> We're gonna show 'em now
> We're gonna show 'em how
> All over
> This ol' Harlem Town!

(THEO *and* BOBBY *start making rhythmic scat sounds with their lips as they dance around the floor.*) —Come on, Pop, show us how you used to cut one of them things!

BOBBY (*Dancing.*)   This is how he did it!

THEO   Nawwww, that's not it. He did it like this!

MR. PARKER (*Rising.*)   No, no! Neither one of you got it! Speed up that riff a little bit . . . (*The two boys speed up the riff, singing, stomping their feet, clapping their hands. Humped over,* MR. PARKER *looks down on the floor concentrating.*) Faster! (*They speed it up more.*)

THEO   Come on now, Pop—let 'er loose!

MR. PARKER   Give me time . . .

BOBBY   Let that man have some time!

(MR. PARKER *breaks into his dance.*)

THEO   Come on, Pop, take it with you!

BOBBY   Work, Pop!

THEO   DOWNTOWN!

(MR. PARKER *does a coasting "camel walk."*)

BOBBY   NOW BRING IT ON BACK UPTOWN!

(MR. PARKER *really breaks loose: a rapid series of complicated dance steps.*)

THEO   YEAHHHHHHH!

BOBBY   That's what I'm talkin' about!

(ADELE *enters, stops at the entrance to the shop, observes the scene, bemused.* PARKER, *glimpsing her first, in one motion abruptly stops dancing and reaches for the broom.* BOBBY *looks for something to busy himself with.* THEO *just stares.*)

ADELE   Supper's ready, fellows!

Curtain

Scene Two

Six days later. Late afternoon.

BOBBY *is seated in the barber's throne, munching on a sandwich.* THEO *enters from the front of the shop.*

THEO   Did Pop get back yet?

(BOBBY *shrugs shoulders.*)

THEO   You eating again? Damn. (*Calling upstairs.*) Pop! (*No answer.* THEO *checks his watch, steps back into shop, looks through window, then crosses to* BOBBY *and snatches the sandwich from his mouth.*) You eat too damn much!

BOBBY   What the fuck you do that for?

THEO (*Handing the sandwich back.*)   'Cause you always got a mouth full of peanut butter and jelly!

BOBBY   I'm hungry! And let me tell you something: don't you *ever* snatch any food from my mouth again.

THEO   You'll hit me—you don't care nothing about your brother. One of these days, I'm gon' hit back.

BOBBY   *Nigger!* The day you swing your hand at me, you'll draw back a nub.

THEO   You see! That's exactly what I mean. Now when Blue gets here tonight, I don't want you talking like that, or else you gon' blow the whole deal.

BOBBY   I know how to act. I don't need no lessons from you.

THEO   Good. I got a job for you.

BOBBY   A job? Shit!

THEO   Don't get knocked out now—it ain't no real job. I just want you to jump over to Smith's on 125th Street and pick me up a portable typewriter.

BOBBY   Typewriter—for what?

THEO   Don't ask questions, just go and get it.

BOBBY   Them typewriters cost a lotta money.

THEO   You ain't gon' use money.

BOBBY   You mean—

THEO   —I mean you walk in there and take one.

BOBBY   Naw, you don't mean I walk into nowhere and take nothing!

THEO   Now, Bobby.

BOBBY   No!

THEO   Aw, come on, Bobby. You the one been bragging about how good you are, how you can walk into any store and get anything you wanted, provided it was not too heavy to carry out.

1000

BOBBY I ain't gon' do it!

THEO You know what day it is?

BOBBY Thursday.

THEO That's right. Thursday, May 10th.

BOBBY What's that suppose to mean, Thieves' Convention on 125th Street?

THEO It's Pop's birthday!

BOBBY I didn't know he was still having them.

THEO Well, let me tell you something: Adele remembered it and she's planning on busting into this shop tonight with a birthday cake to surprise him.

BOBBY She suppose to be throwing us out today. That don't make no sense with her buying him a birthday cake.

THEO He's been looking for work, I guess she changed her mind about him. Maybe it's gon' be just me and you that goes.

BOBBY (*Pause.*) What's he gon' type?

THEO Them lies he's always telling—like the one about how he met Mama. Pop can tell some of the greatest lies you ever heard of and you know how he's always talking about writing them down.

BOBBY Pop don't know nothing 'bout writing—specially no typewriting!

THEO (*Takes out his father's notebook.*) Oh no? take a look at this. (*Hands book to* BOBBY.) All he has to do is put it down on paper the way he tells it. Who knows, somebody might get interested in it for television or movies, and we can make ourselves some money, and besides, I kinda think he would get a real charge out of you thinking about him that way—don't you?

BOBBY (*Pause.*) Well, ain't no use in lettin' you go over there, gettin' yourself in jail with them old clumsy fingers of yours.

THEO Good boy, Bobby! (MR. PARKER *enters the shop.*) Hey, Pop! Did you get that thing straightened out with Adele yet?

MR. PARKER What?

THEO *Adele?*

MR. PARKER Oh, yeah, I'm gon' take care of that right away. (*Shoves* BOBBY *out of throne and sits.*)

THEO Where you been all day?

(BOBBY *moves into back room.*)

MR. PARKER Downtown, seeing about some jobs.

THEO You sure don't care much about yourself.

MR. PARKER I can agree with you on that, because lookin' for a job can really hurt a man. I was interviewed five times today, and I could've shot every last one of them interviewers—the white ones and the colored ones too. I don't know if I can take any more of this.

THEO Yeah, looking for a job can be very low-grading to a man, and it gets worse after you get the job. Anyway, I'm glad you got back here on time, or you would've missed your appointment. (*No response from* PARKER.) Now don't tell me you don't remember! The man, the man that's suppose to come here and tell you how life in Harlem can be profitable.

MR. PARKER (*Steps out of throne, edging toward back room.*) Oh, that.

THEO (*Following him.*) Oh, that—my foot! Today is the day we're suppose to come up with those jobs, and you ain't said one word to Adele about it—not one single word! All you do is waste your time looking for work! Now that don't make no sense at all, Pop, and you know it.

MR. PARKER Look, son. Let me go upstairs now and tell her about all the disappointments I suffered today, soften her up a bit, and then I'll come on back down here to meet your man. I promise, you won't have to worry about me going downtown any more—not after what I went through today. And I certainly ain't giving up my shop for nobody!

(*Exits upstairs.*)

THEO (*Turns to* BOBBY, *who's at the mirror.*) Now that's the way I like to hear my old man talk! Hey, baby, don't forget that thing. It's late, we ain't got much time.

BOBBY All right!

(*A jet-black-complexioned young man comes in. He is dressed all in blue and wears sunglasses. He carries a gold-top cane and a large salesman's valise. He stops just inside the door.*)

THEO Blue, baby!

BLUE Am I late?

THEO No, my father just walked in the door. He's upstairs now, but he'll be right back down in a few minutes. Let me take your things. (*Takes* BLUE'S *cane and valise.*) Sit down, man, while I fix you a drink. (*Places* BLUE'S *things on the table and moves into back room.* BOBBY *enters shop.*)

BLUE Hey, Bobby. How's the stores been treating you?

BOBBY I'm planning on retiring next year. (*Laughs.*)

THEO (*Returning with jug and two glasses. Moves to the table and pours.*) I was thinking, Blue—we can't let my old man know about our "piano brigade." I know he ain't going for that, but we can fix it where he will never know a thing.

BLUE You know your father better than I do. (*Takes a drink.*)

BOBBY What's the "piano brigade"?

THEO Blue here has the best thieves and store burglars in this part of town, and we plan to work on those businesses over on 125th Street until they run the insurance companies out of business.

BOBBY You mean breaking into people's stores at night and taking their stuff?

THEO That's right, but not the way you do it. We'll be organized, we'll be revolutionary.

BOBBY If the police catch you, they ain't gon' care what you is, and if Pop ever finds out, the police gon' seem like church girls! (*Slips out the front door.*)

THEO (*After him.*) You just remember that the only crime you'll ever commit is the one you get caught at!

(*Pause.*)

Which reminds me, Blue—I don't want Bobby to be a part of that "piano brigade."

BLUE If that's the way you want it, that's the way it shall be, Theo. How's your sister?

THEO You mean Adele?

BLUE You got a sister named Mary or something?

THEO What's this with Adele?

BLUE I want to know, how are you going to get along with her, selling bootleg whiskey in this place?

THEO This is not her place, it's my father's. And once he puts his okay on the deal, that's it. What kind of house do you think we're living in, where we gon' let some woman tell us what to do? Come here, let me show you something. (*Moves into back room.* BLUE *follows.*) How you like it—ain't it something?

BLUE (*Standing in doorway.*) It's a back room.

THEO Yeah, I know. But I have some great plans for reshaping it by knocking down this wall, and putting—

BLUE Like I said, it's a back room. All I wanta know is, will it do the job? It's a good room. You'll do great with that good-tasting corn of yours. You're going to be so busy here, you're going to grow to hate this place—you might not have any time for your love life, Theopolis!

THEO (*Laughing.*) Don't you worry about that—I can manage my sex life!

BLUE Sex! Who's talking about sex? You surprise me, Theo. Everyone's been telling me about how you got so much heart, how you so deep. I sit and talk to you about life, and you don't know the difference between sex and love.

THEO Is it that important?

BLUE Yes, it is, ol' buddy, if you want to hang out with me, and you do want to hang out with me, don't you?

THEO That depends—

BLUE It depends upon you knowing that sex's got nothing to do with anything but you and some woman laying up in some funky bed, pumping and sweating your life away all for one glad moment—you hear that, *one moment!*

1003

THEO   I'll take that moment!

BLUE   With every woman you've had?

THEO   One out of a hundred!

BLUE (*Laughing, and moving back into shop.*)   One out of a hundred! All that sweat! All that pumping and grinding for the sake of one little dead minute out of a hundred hours!

(MR. PARKER *comes in from upstairs.*)

THEO (*Pause. Stopping* PARKER.)   Pop, you know who this is?

MR. PARKER   I can't see him.

THEO   This is Blue!

MR. PARKER   Blue who?

THEO   The man I was telling you about . . . *Mr. Blue Haven.*

MR. PARKER (*Extends his hand to shake* BLUE'S.)   Please to make your acquaintance, Mr. Haven.

BLUE (*Shaking* MR. PARKER'S *hand.*)   Same to you, Mr. Parker.

THEO   You sure you don't know who Blue Haven is, Pop?

MR. PARKER   I'm sorry, but I truly don't know you, Mr. Haven. If you're a celebrity, you must accept my apology. You see, since I got out of the business, I don't read the *Variety* any more.

THEO   I'm not talking about a celebrity.

MR. PARKER   Oh, no?

THEO   He's the leader!

MR. PARKER   Ohhhhh!

THEO   Right here in Harlem.

MR. PARKER   Where else he gon' be but in Harlem? We got more leaders within ten square blocks of this barbershop than they got liars down in City Hall. That's why you dressed up that way, huh, boy? So people can pick you out of a crowded room?

THEO   Pop, this is serious!

MR. PARKER   All right, go on, don't get carried away—there are some things I don't catch on to right away, Mr. Blue.

THEO   Well, get to this: I got to thinking the other day when Adele busted in here shoving everybody around—I was thinking about this barbershop, and I said to myself: Pop's gon' lose this shop if he don't start making himself some money.

MR. PARKER   Now tell me something I don't know. (*Sits on throne.*)

THEO   Here I go. What would you say if I were to tell you that Blue here can make it possible for you to have a thriving business going on, right here in this shop, for twenty-four hours a day?

MR. PARKER   What is he—some kind of hair grower!

THEO   Even if you don't cut but one head of hair a week!

MR. PARKER   Do I look like a fool to you?

THEO (*Holds up his jug.*)   Selling this!

MR. PARKER (*Pause.*)   Well, well, well. I knew it was something like that. I didn't exactly know what it was, but I knew it was something. And I don't want to hear it!

THEO   Pop, you've always been a man to listen—even when you didn't agree, even when I was wrong, you listened! That's the kind of man you are! You—

MR. PARKER   Okay, okay, I'm listening!

THEO (*Pause.*)   Tell him who you are, Blue.

BLUE   I am the Prime Minister of the Harlem De-Colonization Association.

MR. PARKER (*Pause.*)   Some kind of organization?

BLUE   Yes.

MR. PARKER (*As an aside, almost under his breath.*)   They got all kinds of committees in Harlem. What was that name again, "De"?

THEO   De-Colo-ni-zation! Which means that Harlem is owned and operated by Mr. You-Know-Who. Let me get this stuff—we gon' show you something . . . (*Moves to the table and opens* BLUE'S *valise.*)

BLUE   We're dead serious about this project, Mr. Parker. I'd like you to look at this chart.

THEO   And you'll see, we're not fooling. (*Hurriedly pins charts taken from* BLUE'S *valise on wall out in the shop.*)

MR. PARKER (*Reading from center chart.*)   The Harlem De-Colonization Association, with Future Perspective for Bedford Stuyvesant. (*Turns to* BLUE.) All right, so you got an organization. What do you do? I've never heard of you.

BLUE   The only reason you've never heard of us is because we don't believe in picketing, demonstrating, rioting, and all that stuff. We always look like we're doing something that we ain't doing, but we are doing something—and in that way nobody gets hurt. Now you may think we're passive. To the contrary, we believe in direct action. We are doers, enterprisers, thinkers—and most of all, we're businessmen! Our aim is to drive Mr. You-Know-Who out of Harlem.

MR. PARKER   Who's this Mr. You-Know-Who?

THEO   Damn, Pop! The white man!

MR. PARKER   Oh, himmm!

BLUE   We like to use that name for our members in order to get away from the bad feelings we have whenever we use the word "white." We want our members to always be objective and in this way we shall move forward. Before we get through, there won't be a single Mr. You-Know-Who left in this part of town.

We're going to capture the imagination of the people of Harlem. And that's never been done before, you know.

MR. PARKER   Now, tell me how?

BLUE (*Standing before the charts, pointing with his cane.*)   You see this here. This is what we call a "brigade." And you see this yellow circle?

MR. PARKER   What's that for?

BLUE   My new and entertaining system for playing the numbers. You do play the numbers, Mr. Parker?

MR. PARKER   I do.

BLUE   You see, I have a lot of colors in this system and these colors are mixed up with a whole lot of numbers, and the idea is to catch the right number with the right color. The right number can be anything from one to a hundred, but in order to win, the color must always be black. The name of this game is called "Black Heaven." It's the color part that gives everybody all the fun in playing this game of mine.

MR. PARKER   Anybody ever catch it?

BLUE   Sure, but not until every number and every color has paid itself off. The one thing you'll find out about my whole operation: you can't lose. (*Pause for effect.*)

MR. PARKER   Keep talking.

BLUE   Now over here is the Red Square Circle Brigade, and this thing here is at the heart of my dream to create here in Harlem a symbolic life-force in the heart of the people.

MR. PARKER   You don't say . . .

BLUE   Put up that target, Theo. (THEO *hurriedly pins on wall a dart target with the face of a beefy, Southern-looking white man as bull's-eye.*)

MR. PARKER   Why, that's that ol' dirty sheriff from that little town in Mississippi!

BLUE (*Taking a dart from* THEO.)   That's right—we got a face on a target for every need. We got governors, mayors, backwood crackers, city crackers, Southern crackers, and Northern crackers. We got all kinds of faces on these targets that any good Harlemite would be willing to buy for the sake of slinging one of these darts in that bastard's throat! (*Throws dart, puncturing face on board.*)

MR. PARKER   Let me try it one time. (*Rising, takes dart from* BLUE *and slings it into the face on the target.*) Got him! (*A big laugh.*)

BLUE   It's like I said, Mr. Parker: the idea is to capture the imagination of the people!

MR. PARKER   You got more? Let me see more!

BLUE   Now this is our green circle—that's Theo and his corn liquor—for retail purposes will be called "Black Lightning." This whiskey of Theo's can make an everlasting contribution to this life-force I've been telling you about. I've tested this whiskey out in every neighborhood in Harlem, and everybody claimed it was the best they ever tasted this side of Washington, D.C. You see, we plan to supply every after-hours joint in this area, and this will run Mr. You-Know-Who and his bonded product out of Harlem.

THEO You see, Pop, this all depends on the barbershop being open night and day so the people can come and go as they please, to pick up their play for the day, to get a bottle of corn, and to take one of them targets home to the kiddies. They can walk in just as if they were getting a haircut. In fact, I told Blue that we can give a haircut as a bonus for anyone who buys two quarts.

MR. PARKER What am I suppose to say now?

THEO You're suppose to be daring. You're suppose to wake up to the times, Pop! These are urgent days—a man has to stand up and be counted!

MR. PARKER The police might have some counting of their own to do.

THEO Do you think I would bring you into something that was going to get us in trouble? Blue has an organization! Just like Mr. You-Know-Who. He's got members on the police force! In the city government, the state government.

BLUE Mr. Parker, if you have any reservations concerning the operation of my association, I'd be only too happy to have you come to my summer home, and I'll let you in on everything—especially our protective system against being caught doing this thing.

THEO Did you hear him, Pop, *he's got a summer home!*

MR. PARKER Aw, shut up, boy! Let me think! (*Turns to* BLUE.) So you want to use my place as a headquarters for Theo's corn, the colored numbers, and them targets?

BLUE Servicing the area of 125th to 145th, between the East and West rivers.

MR. PARKER (*Pause.*) I'm sorry, fellows, but I can't do it. (*Moves into back room.*)

THEO (*Following* MR. PARKER.) Why?

MR. PARKER It's not right.

THEO Not right! What are you talking about? Is it right that all that's out there for us is to go downtown and push one of them carts? I have done that, and I ain't gon' do it no more!

MR. PARKER That still don't make it right.

THEO I don't buy it! I'm going into this thing with Blue, with or without you!

MR. PARKER Go on, I don't care! You quit school, I couldn't stop you! I asked you to get a job, you wouldn't work! You have never paid any attention to any of my advice, and I don't expect you to start heeding me now!

THEO Remember what you said to me about them paintings, and being what I am—well, this is me! At last I've found what I can do, and it'll work—I know it will. Please, Pop, just—

MR. PARKER Stop begging, Theo. (*Crosses back into shop, looks at* BLUE.) Why?

BLUE I don't get you.

MR. PARKER What kind of boy are you that you went through so much pain to dream up this cockeyed, ridiculous plan of yours?

BLUE Mr. Parker, I was born about six blocks from here, and before I was ten I had the feeling I had been living for a hundred years. I got so old and tired I didn't know how to cry. Now you just think about that. But now I own a piece of this neighborhood. I don't have to worry about some bastard landlord or those credit crooks on 125th Street. Beautiful, black Blue—they have to worry about me! (*Reaches into his pocket and pulls out a stack of bills. Places them in* PARKER'S *hands.*) Can't you see, man—I'm here to put you in business! (MR. PARKER *runs his fingers through the money.*) Money, Mr. Parker—brand-new money . . .

(*After concentrated attention,* MR. PARKER *drops money on table and moves into back room.* THEO *hurriedly follows.* MR. PARKER *sits on bed, in deep thought.*)

THEO That's just to get us started. And if we can make a dent into Mr. You-Know-Who's going-ons in Harlem, nobody's going to think of us as crooks. We'll be heroes from 110th Street to Sugar Hill. And just think, Pop, you won't have to worry about jobs and all that. You'll have so much time for you and Mr. Jenkins to play checkers, your arms will drop off. You'll be able to sit as long as you want, and tell enough stories and lies to fit between the cover of a 500-page book. That's right! Remember you said you wanted to write all them stories down! Now you'll have time for it! You can dress up the way you used to. And the girls—remember how you used to be so tough with the girls before you got married? All that can come back to you, and some of that you never had. It's so easy! All you have to do is call Adele down those stairs and let her know that you're going into business and if she don't like it she can pack up and move out, because you're not going to let her drive you down because you're a man, and—

MR. PARKER All right! (*Moves back into shop, where* BLUE *is putting away his paraphernalia.*) I'll do it!

(*Pause.*)

I'll do it under one condition—

BLUE And that is?

MR. PARKER If my buddy Jenkins wants to buy into this deal, you'll let him.

BLUE Theo?

THEO It's all right.

MR. PARKER (*Extending his hand to* BLUE.) Then you got yourself some partners, Mr. Haven!

BLUE Welcome into the association, Mr. Parker.

MR. PARKER   Welcome into my barbershop!

THEO (*Jubilantly.*)   Yehhhhhhhhhh!

(BLUE *checks his watch.* ADELE *comes into the back room.*)

BLUE   Well, I have to check out now, but I'll stop over tomorrow and we will set the whole thing up just as you want it, Mr. Parker. See you later, Theo.

MR. PARKER (*To* BLUE *as he is walking out the front door.*)   You should stick around awhile and watch my polish!

THEO   Pop, don't you think it would be better if you would let me give the word to Adele?

MR. PARKER   No. If I'm going to run a crooked house, *I'm* going to run it, and that goes for you as well as her.

THEO   But, Pop, sometimes she kinda gets by you.

MR. PARKER   Boy, I have never done anything like this in my life, but since I've made up my mind to it, you have nothing to say—not a word. You have been moaning about me never making it so you can have a chance. Well, this time you can say I'm with you. But let me tell you something: I don't want no more lies from you, and no more conning me about painting, airplane piloting, or nothing. If being a crook is what you want to be, you're going to be the best crook in the world —even if you have to drink mud to prove it.

THEO (*Pause.*)   Okay, Pop.

MR. PARKER (*Moves toward back room.*)   Well, here goes nothing. Adele! (*Just as he calls,* ADELE *steps out of the back room, stopping him in his tracks.*)

ADELE   Yes, Father.

MR. PARKER   Oh, you're here already. Well, I want to talk to—well, I, er—

ADELE   What is it?

MR. PARKER (*Pause.*)   Nothing. I'll talk to you later. (*He spots* BOBBY *entering from the outside with a package wrapped in newspaper.*) What you got there?

BOBBY   Uh . . . uh . . . —fish!

MR. PARKER   Well, you better get them in the refrigerator before they stink on you.

THEO (*Going over to* BOBBY *and taking package from him.*)   No, no. Now, Bobby, I promised Pop we would never lie to him again. It ain't fish, Pop. We've got something for you. (*Puts the package on the table and starts unwrapping it. The two boys stand over the table, and as the typewriter is revealed, both turn to him.*)

THEO AND BOBBY   Happy Birthday!

MR. PARKER   Birthday? Birthday?

THEO AND BOBBY   Yes, Happy Birthday!

MR. PARKER   Now hold on just a minute!

BOBBY   What are we holding on for, Pop?

MR. PARKER (*Pause.*)   That's a good question, son. We're—we're holding on for a celebration! (*Laughs loudly.*) Thanks, fellows! But what am I going to do with a typewriter! I don't know nothing about no typing!

ADELE   I would like to know where they got the money to buy one!

THEO (*Ignoring her.*)   You know what you told me about writing down your stories—now you can write them down three times as fast!

MR. PARKER   But I don't know how to type!

THEO   With the money we're gonna be having, I can hire somebody to teach you!

ADELE   What money you going to have?

THEO   We're going into business, baby—right here in this barbershop!

MR. PARKER   Theo—

THEO (*Paying no attention.*)   We're going to sell bootleg whiskey, numbers, and—

ADELE   You're what!?

MR. PARKER   Theo—

THEO   You heard me, and if you don't like it you can pack your bags and leave!

ADELE   Leave? I pay the rent here!

THEO   No more! I pay it now!

MR. PARKER   Shut up, Theo!

THEO   We're going to show you something, girl. You think—

MR. PARKER   *I said shut up!*

ADELE   Is he telling the truth?

MR. PARKER   Yes, he is telling the truth.

ADELE   You mean to tell me you're going to turn this shop into a bootleg joint?

MR. PARKER   I'll turn it into anything I want to!

ADELE   Not while I'm still here!

MR. PARKER   The lease on this house has my signature, not yours!

ADELE   I'm not going to let you do this!

MR. PARKER   You got no choice, Adele. *You don't have a damn thing to say!*

ADELE (*Turns sharply to* THEO.)   You put him up to this!

MR. PARKER   Nobody puts me up to anything I don't want to do! These two boys have made it up in their minds they're not going to work for nobody but themselves, and the thought in my mind is *why should they!* I did like you said, I went downtown, and it's been a long time since I did that, but *you're* down there every day, and you oughta know by now that I am too old a man to ever dream I . . . could overcome the dirt and filth they got waiting for me down there. I'm surprised at you, that you would have so little care in you to shove me into the middle of that mob.

1010

ADELE You can talk about caring? What about Mama? She *died* working for you! Did you ever stop to think about that! In fact, *did you ever love her?* No!!!

MR. PARKER That's a lie!

ADELE I hope that one day you'll be able to do one good thing to drive that doubt out of my mind. *But this is not it!* You've let this hoodlum sell you his twisted ideas of making a short cut through life. But let me tell you something—this bastard is going to ruin you!

THEO (*Into her face.*) Start packing, baby!

ADELE (*Strikes him across the face.*) Don't you talk to me like that!

(*He raises his hand to strike her back.*)

MR. PARKER Drop your hand, boy! (THEO *does not respond.*) I said, drop your goddamn hand!

THEO She hit me!

MR. PARKER I don't care if she had broken your jaw. If you ever draw your hand back to hit this girl again—*as long as you* live! You better not be in my hand reach when you do, 'cause *I'll split your back in two!* (*To* ADELE.) We're going into business, Adele. I have come to that and I have come to it on my own. I am going to stop worrying once and for all whether I live naked in the cold or whether I die like an animal, unless I can live the best way I know how to. I am getting old and I oughta have some fun. I'm going to get me some money, and I'm going to spend it! I'm going to get drunk! I'm going to dance some more! *I'm getting old! I'm going to fall in love one more time before I die!* So get to that, girl, and if it's too much for you to bear, I wouldn't hold it against you if you walked away from here this very minute—

ADELE (*Opens the door to the back room to show him the birthday surprise she has for him.*) Happy birthday!

MR. PARKER (*Goes into the room and stands over table where birthday cake is.*) I guess I fooled all of you. Today is not my birthday. It never was. (*Moves up the stairs.*)

ADELE It's not going to work! You're going to cut your throat—you hear me! You're going to rip yourself into little pieces! (*Turns to* THEO.) It's not going to be the way you want it—because I know Mr. Blue Haven, and he is not a person to put your trust in. (THEO *turns his back on her, heads for the shop door.*) . . . I am talking to you!

THEO (*Stops and turns.*) Why don't you leave us alone. You're the one who said we had to go out and do something. Well, we did, but we're doing it our way. Me and Bobby, we're men—if we lived the way you wanted us to, we wouldn't have nothing but big fat veins popping out of our heads.

ADELE I'll see what kind of men you are every time a cop walks through that door, every time a stranger steps into this back room and you can't be too sure

1011

about him, and the day they drag your own father off and throw him into a jail cell.

THEO But, tell me, what else is there left for us to do. You tell me and I'll do it. You show me where I can go to spin the world around before it gets too late for somebody like Mama living fifty years just to die on 126th Street! *You tell me of a place where there are no old crippled vaudeville men!*

ADELE There is no such place.

(*Pause.*)

But you don't get so hung up about it you have to plunge a knife into your own body. You don't bury yourself here in this place; you climb up out of it! Now that's something for you to wonder about, boy.

THEO I wonder all the time—how you have lived here all your whole life on this street, and you haven't seen, heard, learned, or felt a thing in all those years. I wonder how you ever got to be such a damn fool!

Curtain

ACT TWO

Scene One

Two months later. It is about 9 P.M.
    As the curtain rises, the lights come up in the back room. BOBBY *is there, listening to a record of James Brown's "Money Won't Change You, But Time Will Take You On." As he is dancing out to the shop,* THEO *appears from the cellar, which has been enlarged by taking out a panel in the lower section of the wall and houses the whiskey-making operation.* THEO *brings in two boxes filled with bottles of corn whiskey and shoves them under the bed.*
    BOBBY *moves past* THEO *into the shop, carrying a target rolled up in his hand, and two darts. He is wearing a fancy sports shirt, new trousers, new keen-toed shoes, and a stingy, diddy-bop hat. He pins the target up on the wall of the shop. In the center of the target is the face of a well-known American racist.*

BOBBY (*Moves away from the target, aims and hurls the dart.*) That's for Pop! Huh! (*Throws another.*) And this is for me! Huh! (*Moves to the target to pull darts out.* THEO *cuts record off abruptly. A knock at the door.*)

THEO (*Calling out to* BOBBY *from the back room.*) Lock that door!

BOBBY Lock it yourself!

THEO (*With quick but measured steps moves toward front door.*) I'm not selling another bottle, target, or anything, till I get some help! (*Locks door in spite of persistent knocking.*) We're closed!

BOBBY I don't think Blue is gon' like you turning customers away. (*Sits in barber chair, lighting up cigar.*)

THEO   You can tell Blue I don't like standing over that stove all day, that I don't like him promising me helpers that don't show up. There are a lot of things I don't go for, like Pop taking off and not showing up for two days. I make this whiskey, I sell it, I keep books, I peddle numbers and those damn targets. *And I don't like you standing around here all day not lifting a finger to help me!*

BOBBY   (*Taking a big puff on his cigar.*)   I don't hear you.

THEO   Look at you—all decked out in your new togs. Look at me: I haven't been out of these dungarees since we opened this place up.

BOBBY   (*Jumps out of chair.*)   I don't wanta hear nothing! You do what you wanta do, and leave me alone!

THEO   What am I supposed to be, a work mule or something?

BOBBY   You're the one that's so smart—you can't answer your own stupid questions?

THEO   You done let Blue turn you against me, huh?

BOBBY   You ask the questions, and you gon' answer them—but for now, stop blowing your breath in my face!

THEO   You make me sick. (*Moves into back room. Sits on bed.*)

ADELE   (*Enters from upstairs, dressed in a smart Saks Fifth Avenue outfit.*)   Getting tired already, Theo?

THEO   No, just once in a while I'd like to have some time to see one of my women!

ADELE   You being the big industrialist and all that, I thought you had put girls off for a year or two!

THEO   Get away from me. (*Crosses to desk and sits.*)

ADELE   I must say, however—it is sure a good sight to see you so wrapped up in work. I never thought I'd live to see the day, but—

THEO   Don't you ever have anything good to say?

ADELE   I say what I think and feel. I'm honest.

THEO   Honest? You're just hot because Pop decided to do something my way for a change.

ADELE   That's a joke, when you haven't seen him for two whole days. Or, *do* you know where he has gone to practically every night since you opened up this little store.

THEO   He's out having a little sport for himself. What's wrong with that? He hasn't had any fun in a long time.

ADELE   Is fun all you can think of? When *my* father doesn't show up for two days, I worry.

THEO   You're not worried about nobody but yourself—I'm on to your game. You'd give anything in the world to go back just the way we were, because you liked the idea of us being dependent on you. Well, that's all done with, baby.

We're on our own. So don't worry yourself about Pop. When Blue gets here tonight with our money, he'll be here!

ADELE If my eyes and ears are clear, then I would say that Father isn't having the kind of money troubles these days that he must rush home for your pay day.

THEO What do you mean by that?

ADELE I mean that he has been dipping his hands into that little drawer of yours at least two or three times a week.

THEO You ain't telling nothing I don't know.

ADELE What about your friend Blue?

THEO I can handle him.

ADELE I hope so, since it is a known fact that he can be pretty evil when he thinks someone has done him wrong—and it happened once, in a bar uptown, he actually killed a man.

THEO You're lying. (*He moves quickly to shop entrance.*) Bobby, have you heard anything about Blue killing a man? (BOBBY, *seated in the barber's chair, looks at him, then turns away, not answering.* THEO *returns to the back room.*)

ADELE Asking him about it is not going to help you. Ask yourself a few questions and you will know that you are no better than Blue—because it is you two who are the leaders of those mysterious store raids on 125th Street, and your ace boy on those robberies is no one other than your brother, Bobby Parker!

THEO Bobby!

ADELE I don't know why that should surprise you, since he is known as the swiftest and coolest young thief in Harlem.

THEO I didn't know about Bobby—*who told you!*

ADELE As you well know by now, I've been getting around lately, and I meet people, and people like to have something to talk about, and you know something: this place is becoming the talk along every corner and bar on the Avenue!

THEO You're just trying to scare me.

ADELE I wish to God I was. (*Starts out.*)

THEO Where are you going?

ADELE (*Stops, turns abruptly.*) Out. Do you mind?

THEO *That's all you ever do!*

ADELE Yes, you're right.

THEO They tell me you're going with Wilmer Robinson?

ADELE Yes, that's true. (*Moving through shop toward door.* BOBBY *doesn't move from the barber's throne and buries his nose in a comic book.*)

THEO (*Following behind her.*) He's a snake.

ADELE No better or worse than someone like you or Blue.

THEO He'll bleed you for every dime you've got!

ADELE So what. He treats me like a woman, and that's more than I can say for any man in this house!

THEO He'll treat you like a woman until he's gotten everything he wants, and then he's gon' split your ass wide open!

ADELE (*Turns sharply at door.*) Theoooooooooooo!

(*Pause.*)

You talk like that to me because you don't know how to care for the fact that I am your sister.

THEO But why are you trying to break us up? Why?

ADELE I don't have to waste that kind of good time. I can wait for you to bust it up yourself. Good night! (*Slams the door behind herself.*)

(THEO *stands with a long, deep look in his eyes, then goes down cellar.* MR. PARKER *steps into the shop, all dapper, dressed up to a fare-thee-well, holding a gold-top cane in one hand and a book in the other.* BOBBY *stares at him, bewildered.*)

BOBBY What's that you got on?

MR. PARKER What does it look like?

BOBBY Nothing.

MR. PARKER You call this nothing!

BOBBY Nothing—I mean, I didn't mean nothing when I asked you that question.

MR. PARKER Where's Theo?

BOBBY In the back, working.

MR. PARKER Good! Shows he's got his mind stretched out for good and great things. (*Hangs up hat and puts away cane.*)

BOBBY He's been stretching his mind out to find out where you been.

MR. PARKER Where I been is none of his business, Blue is the man to think about. It's pay day, and I wanta know, where the hell is he! (*Checks his watch, taps* BOBBY, *indicating he should step down from chair.*)

BOBBY (*Hops down from chair.* PARKER *sits.*) Whatcha reading?

MR. PARKER A book I picked up yesterday. I figured since I'm in business I might as well read a businessman's book.

BOBBY Let me see it. (*Takes the book in his hand.*) The Thief's Journal, by Jean Gin-nett. (*Fingering through pages.*) Is it a good story?

MR. PARKER So far—

BOBBY (*Hands it back.*) What's it all about?

MR. PARKER A Frenchman who was a thief.

BOBBY Steal things?

MR. PARKER   Uh-huh.

BOBBY   Where did he get all that time to write a book?

MR. PARKER   Oh, he had the time all right, 'cause he spent most of it in jail.

BOBBY   Some thief!

MR. PARKER   The trouble with this bird is that he became a thief and then he became a thinker.

BOBBY   No shucking!

MR. PARKER   No shucking. But it is my logicalism that you've got to become a thinker and then you become a crook! Or else, why is it when you read up on some of these politicians' backgrounds you find they all went to one of them big law colleges? That's where you get your start!

BOBBY   Well, I be damned!

MR. PARKER   (*Jumps down out of the chair, moves briskly toward door.*)   Now where is Blue! He said he would be here nine-thirty on the nose! (*Opens the door and* JENKINS *comes in.*) Hey, Jenkins! What's up!

MR. JENKINS   That Blue fellow show up yet?

MR. PARKER   No, he didn't, and I'm gon' call him down about that too.

MR. JENKINS   It don't matter. I just want whatever money I got coming, and then I'm getting out of this racket.

MR. PARKER   Don't call it that, it's a committee!

MR. JENKINS   This committee ain't no committee. It ain't nothing but a racket, and I'm getting out of it!

MR. PARKER   You put your money into this thing, man. It ain't good business to walk out on an investment like that.

MR. JENKINS   I can, and that's what I'm doing before I find myself in jail! Man, this thing you got going here is the talk in every bar in this neighborhood.

MR. PARKER   There ain't nothing for you to be scared of, Jenkins. Blue guaranteed me against ever being caught by the police. Now that's all right by me, but I've got some plans of my own. When he gets here tonight, I'm gon' force him to make me one of the leaders in this group, and if he don't watch out, I just might take the whole operation over from him. I'll make you my right-hand man, and not only will you be getting more money, and I won't just guarantee you against getting caught, but I'll guarantee you against being scared!

MR. JENKINS   There's nothing you can say to make me change my mind. I shouldn't've let you talk me into this mess in the first place. I'm getting out, and that's it! (*Starts for the door.*) And if he gets back before I do, you hold my money for me! (*Exiting.*)

MR. PARKER (*Pursuing him to door.*)   Suit yourself, but you're cutting your own throat. This little set-up is the biggest thing to hit this neighborhood since the day I started dancing! (*Slams door.*) Fool! (*Takes off coat, hangs it up. Goes to mirror to primp.*)

1016

BOBBY   Going somewhere again?

MR. PARKER   Got myself a little date to get to if Blue ever gets here with our money—*and he better get here with our money!*

BOBBY   You been dating a lot lately—nighttime dates, and day ones too—and Theo's not happy about it. He says you don't stay here long enough to cut Yul Brynner's hair.

MR. PARKER   He can complain all he wants to. I'm the boss here, and he better not forget it. He's the one that's got some explaining to do: don't talk to nobody no more, don't go nowhere, looking like he's mad all the time . . . I've also noticed that he don't get along with you any more.

BOBBY   Well, Pop, that's another story.

MR. PARKER   Come on, boy, there's something on his mind, and you know what it is.

BOBBY (*Moving away.*)   Nothing, except he wants to tell me what to do all the time. But I've got some ideas of my own. I ain't no dumbbell; I just don't talk as much as he do. If I did, the people I talk to would know just as much as I do. I just want him to go his way, and I'll go mine.

MR. PARKER   There's more to it than that, and I wanta know what it is.

BOBBY   There's nothing.

MR. PARKER   Come on now, boy.

BOBBY   That's all, Pop!

MR. PARKER (*Grabs him.*)   It's not, and you better say something!

BOBBY   He—I don't know what to tell you, Pop. He just don't like the way things are going—with you, me—Adele. He got in a fight with her today and she told him about Blue killing a man.

MR. PARKER   Is it true?

BOBBY   Yeah. Blue killed this man one time for saying something about his woman, and this woman got a child by Blue but Blue never married her and so this man started signifying about it. Blue hit him, the man reached for a gun in his pocket, Blue took the gun from him, and the—man started running, but by that time Blue had fire in his eyes, and he shot the man three times.

MR. PARKER   Well . . .

BOBBY   Blue got only two years for it!

MR. PARKER   Two years, hunh? That's another thing I'm gon' throw in his face tonight if he tries to get smart with me. Ain't that something. Going around bumping people off, and getting away with it too! What do he think he is, white or something! (THEO *comes in and sits at desk.* MR. PARKER *checks his watch.*) I'm getting tired of this! (*Moves into back room.*) Where's that friend of yours!? I don't have to wait around this barbershop all night for him. It's been two months now, and I want my money! When I say be here at nine-thirty, I mean be here!

THEO (*Rising from desk.*) Where have you been, Pop?

MR. PARKER That's none of your business! Now where is that man with my money!

THEO Money is not your problem—you've been spending it all over town! And you've been taking it out of this desk!

MR. PARKER So? I borrowed a little.

THEO You call four hundred dollars a little! Now I've tried to fix these books so it don't show too big, and you better hope Blue don't notice it when he starts fingering through these pages tonight.

MR. PARKER To hell with Blue! It's been two months now, and he ain't shown us a dime!

THEO What are you doing with all that money, Pop?

MR. PARKER I don't have to answer to you! I'm the boss here. And another thing, there's a lot about Blue and this association I want to know about. I want a position! I don't have to sit around here every month or so, waiting for somebody to bring me *my* money.

THEO Money! Money! That's all you can think about!

MR. PARKER Well, look who's talking. You forget this was all your idea. Remember what I told you about starting something and sticking with it. What is it now, boy? The next thing you'll tell me is that you've decided to become a priest or something. What's the new plan, Theo?

THEO No new plans, Pop. I just don't want us to mess up. Don't you understand —things must be done right, or else we're going to get ourselves in jail. We have to be careful, we have to think about each other all the time. I didn't go into this business just for myself, I wasn't out to prove how wrong Adele was. I just thought the time had come for us to do something about all them years we laid around here letting Mama kill herself!

MR. PARKER I have told you a thousand times I don't wanta hear any talk about your mama. She's dead, damnit! So let it stay that way! (*Moves toward shop.*)

THEO All right, let's talk about Adele then.

MR. PARKER (*Stopping at steps.*) What about her?

THEO She's out of this house every night.

MR. PARKER Boy, you surprise me. What do you think she should do, work like a dog all day and then come to this house and bite her fingernails all night?

THEO She's got herself a boy friend too, and—

MR. PARKER (*Crossing to counter.*) Good! I got myself a girl friend, now that makes two of us!

THEO (*Following him.*) But he's—aw, what's the use. But I wish you'd stay in the shop more!

MR. PARKER   That's too bad. I have things to do. I don't worry about where you're going when you leave here.

THEO   I don't go anywhere and you know it. If I did, we wouldn't do an hour's business. *But we have been doing great business!* And you wanta know why? They love it! *Everybody* loves the way ol' Theo brews corn! Every after-hours joint is burning with it! And for us to do that kind of business, I've had to sweat myself down in this hole for something like sixteen hours a day for two whole months!

MR. PARKER   What do you want from me?

THEO   I just want you here in the shop with me, so at least we can pretend that this is a barbershop. A cop walked through that door today while I had three customers in here, and I had to put one of them in that chair and cut his hair!

MR. PARKER   How did you make out?

THEO   Pop, I don't need your jokes!

MR. PARKER   All right, don't get carried away. (*Goes to* THEO *and puts his arm around the boy's shoulders.*) I'll make it my business to stay here in the shop with you more.

THEO   And make Blue guarantee me some help.

MR. PARKER   You'll get that too. But you've got to admit one thing, though—you've always been a lazy boy. I didn't expect you to jump and all of a sudden act like John Henry!

THEO   I have never been lazy. I just didn't wanta break my back for the man!

MR. PARKER   Well, I can't blame you for that. I know, because I did it. I did it when they didn't pay me a single dime!

BOBBY   When was that?

MR. PARKER   When I was on the chain gang!

BOBBY   Now you know you ain't never been on no chain gang!

MR. PARKER   (*Holds up two fingers.*) Two months, that's all it was. Just two months.

BOBBY   Two months, my foot!

MR. PARKER   I swear to heaven I was. It was in 19-something, I was living in Jersey City, New Jersey . . . (*Crosses to throne and sits.*)

BOBBY   Here we go with another story!

MR. PARKER   That was just before I started working as a vaudeville man, and there was this ol' cousin of mine we used to call "Dub," and he had this job driving a trailer truck from Jersey City to Jacksonville, Florida. One day he asked me to come along with him for company. I weren't doing nothing at the time, and—

BOBBY   As usual.

MR. PARKER   I didn't say that! Anyway, we drove along. Everything was fine till we hit Macon, Georgia. We weren't doing a thing, but before we knew it this cracker police stopped us, claiming we'd ran through a red light. He was yelling and hollering and, boyyy, did I get mad—I was ready to get a hold of that cracker and work on his head until . . .

BOBBY   Until what?

MR. PARKER   Until they put us on the chain gang, and the chain gang they put us on was a chain gang and a half! I busted some rocks John Wayne couldn't've busted! I was a rock-busting fool! (*Rises and demonstrates how he swung the hammer.*) I would do it like this! I would hit the rock, and the hammer would bounce —bounce so hard it would take my hand up in the air with it—but I'd grab it with my left hand and bring it down like this: Hunh! (*Carried away by the rhythm of his story, he starts twisting his body to the swing of it.*) It would get so good to me, I'd say: Hunh! Yeah! Hunh! I'd say, Ooooooooooooweeeee! I'm wide open now! (*Swinging and twisting.*) Yeah, baby, I say, Hunh! Sooner or later that rock would crack! Old Dub ran into a rock one day that was hard as Theo's head. He couldn't bust that rock for nothing. He pumped and swung, but that rock would not move. So finally he said to the captain: "I'm sorry, Cap, but a elephant couldn't break this rock." Cap didn't wanna hear nothing. He said, "Well, Dub, I wanna tell you something —your lunch and your supper is in the middle of that rock." On the next swing of the hammer, Dub busted that rock into a thousand pieces! (*Laughs.*) I'm telling you, them crackers is mean. Don't let nobody tell you about no Communists, Chinese, or anything: there ain't nothing on this earth meaner and dirtier than an American-born cracker! We used to sleep in them long squad tents on the ground, and we was all hooked up to this one big long chain: the guards had orders to shoot at random in the dark if ever one of them chains would rattle. You couldn't even turn over in your sleep! (*Sits on throne.*)

BOBBY   A man can't help but turn over in his sleep!

MR. PARKER   Not on this chain gang you didn't. You turn over on this chain gang in your sleep and your behind was shot! But if you had to, you would have to wake up, announce that you was turning over, and then you go back to sleep!

BOBBY   What!

MR. PARKER   Just like this. (*Illustrating physically.*) "Number 4 turning over!" But that made all the chains on the other convicts rattle, so they had to turn over too and shout: "Number 5 turning over! Number 6 turning over! Number 7!"

THEO   Why don't you stop it!

MR. PARKER   I ain't lying!

BOBBY   Is that all?

MR. PARKER   Yeah, and I'm gon' get Adele to type that up on my typewriter! (*Goes to the window.*) Now where the hell is that Blue Haven!

MR. JENKINS (*Rushing in.*)   Did he show up yet?

MR. PARKER   Naw, and when he does, I'm—

MR. JENKINS   I told you I didn't trust that boy—who knows where he is! Well, I'm going out there and get him! (*Starts back out.*)

MR. PARKER (*Grabs him by the arm.*)   Now don't go out there messing with Blue, Jenkins! If there's anybody got a reason for being mad with him, it's me. Now take it easy. When he gets here, we'll all straighten him out. Come on, sit down and let me beat you a game one time. (*Takes board out quickly.*)

BOBBY   Tear him up, Pop!

MR. JENKINS (*Pause.*)   Okay, you're on. (*Moves toward* MR. PARKER *and the table.*) It's hopeless. I been playing your father for three solid years, and he has yet to beat me one game!

MR. PARKER   Yeah! But his luck done come to past!

MR. JENKINS   My luck ain't come to past, 'cause my luck is skill. (*Spelling the word out.*) S-K-I-L-L.

MR. PARKER (*Shakes up the can.*)   Come on now, Jenkins, let's play the game. Take one. (MR. JENKINS *pulls out a checker.*) You see there, you get the first move.

MR. JENKINS   You take me for a fool, Parker, and just for that I ain't gon' let you get a king.

MR. PARKER   Put your money where your lips is. I say I'm gon' win this game!

MR. JENKINS   I don't want your money, I'm just gon' beat you!

MR. PARKER   I got twenty dollars here to make a liar out of you! (*Slams down a twenty-dollar bill on the table.*) Now you doing all the bragging about how I never beat you, but I'm valiant enough to say that, from here on in, you can't win air, and I got twenty dollars up on the table to back it up.

MR. JENKINS   Oh, well, he ain't satisfied with me beating him all the time for sport. He wants me to take his money too.

MR. PARKER   But that's the difference.

MR. JENKINS   What kind of difference?

MR. PARKER   We're playing for money, and I don't think you can play under that kind of pressure. You do have twenty dollars, don't you?

MR. JENKINS   I don't know what you're laughing about, I always keep some money on me. (*Pulls out change purse and puts twenty dollars on the table.*) You get a little money in your pocket and you get carried away.

MR. PARKER   It's your move.

MR. JENKINS   Start you off over here in this corner.

MR. PARKER   Give you that little ol'fellow there.

MR. JENKINS   I'll take him.

MR. PARKER   I'll take this one.

MR. JENKINS   I'll give you this man here.

MR. PARKER   I'll jump him—so that you can have this one.

MR. JENKINS   I'll take him.

MR. PARKER   Give you this man here.

MR. JENKINS   All right. (*He moves.*)

MR. PARKER   I'll take this one. (*Series of grunts and groans as they exchange men.*) And I'll take these three. (*Jumping* MR. JENKINS'S *men and laughing loud.*) Boom! Boom! Boom! (*The game is now definitely in favor of* MR. PARKER. MR. JENKINS *is pondering over his situation. Relishing* MR. JENKINS'S *predicament:*) Study long, you study wrong. I'm afraid that's you, ol' buddy . . . I knew it, I knew it all the time —I used to ask myself: I wonder how ol' Jenks would play if he really had some pressure on him? You remember how the Dodgers used to raise hell every year until they met the Yankees in the World Series, and how under all that pressure they would crack up? (*Laughs.*) That pressure got him!

MR. JENKINS   Hush up, man. I'm trying to think!

MR. PARKER   I don't know what you could be thinking about, 'cause the rooster done came and wrote, skiddy biddy!

MR. JENKINS (*Finally makes a move.*)   There!

MR. PARKER (*In sing-song.*)   That's all—that's all . . . (*Makes another jump.*) Boom! Just like you say, Bobby—"tear him up!" (*Rears his head back in ecstatic laughter.*)

MR. JENKINS (*Makes a move.*)   It's your move.

MR. PARKER (*His laughter trails off sickly as he realizes that the game is now going his opponent's way.*)   Well, I see. I guess that kinda changes the color of the game . . . Let me see now . . .

MR. JENKINS (*Getting his revenge.*)   Why don't you laugh some more? I like the way you laugh, Parker.

MR. PARKER   Shut up, Jenkins. I'm thinking!

MR. JENKINS   Thinking? Thinking for what? The game is over! (*Now he is laughing hard.* MR. PARKER *ruefully makes his move.*) Uh-uh! Lights out! (*Still laughing, answers* PARKER'S *move.*) Game time, and you know it! Take your jump! (MR. PARKER *is forced to take his jump.* JENKINS *takes his opponent's last three men.*) I told you about laughing and bragging in my game! Boom! Boom! Boom!

MR. PARKER (*Rises abruptly from the table and dashes to coat rack.*)   DAMNIT!!!

MR. JENKINS   Where you going—ain't we gon' play some more?

MR. PARKER (*Putting on coat.*)   I don't wanta play you no more. You too damn lucky!

MR. JENKINS   Aw, come on, Parker. I don't want your money, I just want to play!

MR. PARKER   You won it, you keep it—I can *afford* it! But one of these days you're going to leave that voodoo root of yours home, and that's gonna be the day —you hear me, you sonofabitch!

BOBBY   Pop!

MR. PARKER   I don't want to hear nothing from you!

1022

MR. JENKINS (*Realizing that* PARKER *is really upset.*) It's only a game—and it don't have nothing to do with luck . . . But you keep trying, Parker, and one of these days you're going to beat me. And when you do, it won't have nothing to do with luck—it just might be the unluckiest and worst day of your life. You'll be champion checker player of the world. Meanwhile, I'm the champ, *and you're gonna have to live with it.*

MR. PARKER (*Smiling, grudgingly moves toward him with his hand extended.*) All right, Jenkins! You win this time, but I'm gon' beat you yet. I'm gon' whip your behind until it turns white!

BOBBY That's gon' be some strong whipping! (*There's a tap at the door.*) That must be Blue. (*Rushes to the door and opens it.*)

MR. PARKER About time. (BLUE *enters.*) Hey, boy, where have you been?

BLUE (*Moves in, carrying an attaché case.*) I got stuck with an emergency council meeting.

MR. PARKER What kind of council?

BLUE The council of the Association. I see you're sporting some new clothes there, Mr. P. You must be rolling in extra dough these days.

MR. PARKER Just a little something I picked up the other day. All right, where is the money, Blue?

BLUE You'll get your money, but first I want to see those books. (*Moves to the desk in the back room and starts going over the books. In the shop an uneasy silence prevails.* JENKINS, *out of nervousness, sets up the checkers for another game.*)

BLUE I see. (*Takes out pencil and pad and starts scribbling on a sheet of paper.*) Uh-huh. Uh-huh . . . (*Re-enters shop.*)

MR. PARKER Well?

BLUE Everything seems to be okay.

MR. PARKER Of course everything is all right. What did you expect? (*Angry, impatient.*) Now come on and give me my money.

BLUE Take it easy, Mr. Parker! (*Takes a white envelope from his case and passes it on to* PARKER.) Here's your money.

MR. PARKER Now this is what I like to see!

BLUE (*Passes some bills to* MR. JENKINS.) And you, Mr. Jenkins.

MR. JENKINS Thank you, young man. But from here on in, you can count me out of your operation.

BLUE What's the trouble?

MR. JENKINS No trouble at all. I just want to be out of it.

BLUE People and headaches—that's all I ever get from all the Mr. Jenkinses in this world!

MR. JENKINS Why don't you be quiet sometime, boy.

MR. PARKER I'm afraid he's telling you right, Blue.

BLUE *He's telling me that he is a damn idiot, who can get himself hurt!*

THEO Who's going to hurt him?

(*They all stare at* BLUE.)

BLUE (*Calming down.*) I'm sorry. I guess I'm working too hard these days. I got a call today from one of them "black committees" here in Harlem . . .

THEO What did they want?

BLUE They wanted to know what we did. They said they had heard of us, but they never see us—meaning they never see us picketing, demonstrating, and demanding something all the time.

MR. PARKER So?

BLUE They want us to demonstrate with them next Saturday, and I have decided to set up a demonstrating committee, with you in charge, Mr. Parker.

MR. PARKER You what!

BLUE You'd be looking good!

MR. PARKER You hear that! (*Cynical laughter.*) *I'd be looking good!* Count me out! When I demonstrate, it's for real!

BLUE You demonstrate in front of any store out there on that street, and you'll have a good sound reason for being there!

MR. PARKER I thought you said we was suppose to be different, and we was to drive out that Mr. You-Know-Somebody—well, ain't that what we doing? Two stores already done put up "going out of business" signs.

BLUE That's what we started this whole thing for, and that's what we're doing.

MR. PARKER I got some questions about that, too. I don't see nothing that we're doing that would cause a liquor store, a clothing store, and a radio store to just all of a sudden close down like that, unless we've been raiding and looting them at night or something like that.

(BOBBY *quickly moves out of the shop into the back room and exits upstairs.*)

BLUE It's the psychological thing that's doing it, man!

MR. PARKER Psychological? Boy, you ain't telling me everything, and anyway I wanta know who made this decision about picketing.

BLUE The council!

MR. PARKER Who is on this council?

BLUE You know we don't throw names around like that!

MR. PARKER I don't get all the mystery, Blue. This is my house, and you know everything about it from top to bottom. I got my whole family in this racket!

BLUE You're getting a good share of the money—ain't that enough?

MR. PARKER   Not when I'm dealing with you in the dark.

BLUE   You're asking for something, so stop beating around corners and tell me what it is you want!

MR. PARKER   All right! You been promising my boy some help for two months now, and he's still waiting. Now I want you to give him that help starting tomorrow, and I want you to put somebody in this shop who can cut hair to relieve me when I'm not here. And from here on in, I want to know everything that's to be known about this "de-colonization committee"—how it works, who's in it, who's running it—*and I want to be on that council you was talking about!*

BLUE   NO!

MR. PARKER   Then I can't cooperate with you any more!

BLUE   What does that mean?

MR. PARKER   It means we can call our little deal off, and you can take your junk out of here!

BLUE   Just like that?

MR. PARKER   Just any ol' way you want it. I take too many risks in this place, not to know where I stand.

BLUE   Mr. Parker—

MR. PARKER   All right, let me hear it and let me hear it quick!

BLUE   There is an opening on our council. It's a—

MR. PARKER   Just tell me what position is it!

BLUE   President.

MR. PARKER   President?

BLUE   The highest office on our council.

MR. PARKER   Boy, you're gonna have to get up real early to get by an old fox like me. A few minutes ago you offered me nothing, and now you say I can be president—that should even sound strange to *you!*

BLUE   There's nothing strange. A few minutes ago you weren't ready to throw me out of your place, but now *I've got no other choice!*

MR. PARKER (*Pointing his finger at him and laughing.*)   That's true! You don't! All right, I'll give you a break—I accept! Just let me know when the next meeting is. (*Checks watch and grabs his hat.*) Come on, Jenkins, let's get out of here! (*Starts out with* MR. JENKINS.)

THEO   Hey, Pop—you're going out there with all that money in your pocket.

MR. PARKER   Don't worry about it. I'm a grown man, I can take care of myself.

THEO   But what about our part of it?

MR. PARKER   Look, son, he held me up—I'm late already. You'll get yours when I get back.

THEO   But, Pop—

MR. PARKER   Good night, Theo! (*Bolts out the door, with* MR. JENKINS *following.*)

THEO (*Rushes to the door.*)   Pop, you better be careful! I'll be waiting for you! I don't care if it's till dawn!

BLUE   You're becoming a worrier, Theo!

(*Pause.*)

But that's the nature of all things . . . I'm forever soothing and pacifying someone. Sometimes I have to pacify myself. You don't think that president stuff is going to mean anything, do you? He had me up-tight, so what I did was to bring him closer to me so I would be definitely sure of letting him know less and having more control over him—and over you, too.

THEO   What do you mean by that?

BLUE   It didn't take me more than one glance into those books to know that he's been spending money out of the box. And to think—you didn't bother to tell me about it.

THEO   Why should I? I trust your intelligence.

BLUE   Please don't let him do it any more.

THEO   Why don't you hire your own cashier and bookkeeper? (*He goes into back room.*)

BLUE (*Following him.*)   That's an idea! What about Adele! Now that was a thought in the back of my mind, but I'm putting that away real quick. Seems this sweet, nice-girl sister of yours has took to partying with the good-time set and keeping company with a simple ass clown like Wilmer Robinson. No, that wouldn't work, would it? I'd have more trouble with her than I'm having with you. When a girl as intelligent as your sister, who all of a sudden gets into things, and hooked up to people who just don't go with her personality, that could mean trouble. To be honest with you, I didn't think this thing was going to work, but *it is working,* Theo! I've got three places just like this one, and another on the way. A man has to care about what he does. Don't you want to get out of this place?

THEO   Yes, but lately I've been getting the feeling that I'm gonna have to hurt someone.

BLUE   I see.

THEO   You think the old man was asking you those questions about stores closing down as a joke or something?

BLUE   He asks because he thinks, but he is still in the dark!

THEO   He was playing with you! And when my father holds something inside of him and plays with a man, he's getting meaner and more dangerous by the minute.

BLUE   I don't care what he was doing—he is messing with my work! He has gotten himself into a "thing" with one of the rottenest bitches on the Avenue, who

1026

happens to be tight with a nigger who is trying to fuck up my business. Now that's something you had better get straight: it's your turn to soothe and pacify!

THEO Why should I do anything for you when you lied to me and sent my brother out with that band of thieves of yours?

BLUE He said he needed the money, and I couldn't stop him.

THEO But I told you I didn't want that!

BLUE Let's face it, baby! Bobby's the greatest thief in the world! He's been prancing around stores and stealing all of his life! And I think that's something to bow down to—because he's black and in trouble, just like you and me. So don't ride me so hard, Theo! (*They cross back into shop. He picks up attaché case, preparing to leave.*)

THEO Blue! Now I don't care what kind of protection you got, but I say those store raids are dangerous and I don't want my brother on them, and I mean it!

BLUE When we first made our plans, you went along with it—you knew somebody had to do it. What makes you and your brother so special?

THEO Well, you better—

BLUE *To hell with you, Theo!* I could take this hand and make you dead! You are nothing but what I make you be!

THEO (*Pause.*) That just might be. But what if tomorrow this whole operation were to bust wide open in your face because of some goof-up by my father or sister —something that would be just too much for you to clean up. What would you do? Kill them?

BLUE (*Pause. Then calmly and deliberately.*) The other day I went up on the hill to see my little boy. I took him out for a ride and as we were moving along the streets he asked me where all the people were coming from. I said from work, going home, going to the store, and coming back from the store. Then we went out to watch the river and then he asked me about the water, the ships, the weeds —everything. That kid threw so many questions at me, I got dizzy—I wanted to hit him once to shut him up. He was just a little dark boy discovering for the first time that there are things in the world like stones and trees . . . It got late and dark, so I took him home and watched him fall asleep. Then I took his mother into my arms and put her into bed. I just laid there for a while, listening to her call me all kinds of dirty mother-fuckers. After she got that out of her system, I put my hands on her and before long our arms were locked at each other's shoulders and then my thighs moved slowly down between her thighs and then we started that sweet rolling until the both of us were screaming as if the last piece of love was dying forever. After that, we just laid there, talking soft up into the air. I would tell her she was the loveliest bitch that ever lived, and all of a sudden she was no longer calling me a dirty mother-fucker, she was calling me a sweet mother-fucker. It got quiet. I sat up on the edge of the bed with my head hanging long and deep, trying to push myself out of the room and back into it at one and the same time. She looked up at me and I got that same question all over again. Will you marry me and be the father of your son! I tried to move away from her, but she dug her fingernails into my shoulders. I struck her once, twice, and again and again—with this hand! And her face was a bloody mess! And I felt real bad about that. I said, I'll marry you, *Yes! Yes! Yes!*

(*Pause.*)

I put my clothes on and I walked out into the streets, trembling with the knowledge that now I have a little boy who I must walk through the park with every Sunday, who one day just may blow my head off—and an abiding wife who on a given evening may get herself caught in the bed of some other man, and I could be sealed in a dungeon until dead! I was found lying in a well of blood on the day I was born! But I have been kind! I have kissed babies for the simple reason they were babies! I'm going to get married to some bitch and that gets me to shaking all over! (*He moves close to* THEO.) The last time I trembled this way *I killed a man!* (*Quickly and rhythmically takes out a long, shiny switchblade knife. It pops open just at* THEO's *neck.* BLUE *holds it there for a moment, then withdraws and closes it. Puts it away. Then he collects his belongings, then calmly addresses* THEO.) Things are tight and cool on my end, Theo, and that's how you should keep it here. If not, everything gets messy and I find myself acting like a policeman, keeping order. I don't have the time for that kind of trick. (BLUE *exits.*)

THEO (*After a moment of silent thought, moves decisively to the back-room stairs and calls.*) Bobby! (BOBBY *comes downstairs.*)

THEO   I want you to stay away from those store raids, Bobby.

BOBBY   Not as long as I can get myself some extra money. (*Moving close to him.*) You didn't say nothing to me before, when I was stealing every other day and giving you half of everything I stole. You didn't think nothing that day you sent me for that typewriter!

THEO   I don't know what you're going to do from here on in, because I'm calling the whole affair off with Blue.

BOBBY   That won't stop me, and you know it!

THEO   What is it, Bobby—we used to be so close! Bobby, don't get too far away from me!

BOBBY (*Heatedly.*)   What do you want me to do? Stick around you all the time? Hell, I'm tired of you! I stick by you and I don't know what to do! I steal and that puts clothes on my back and money in my pockets! *That's* something to do! But I sit here with you all day just thinking about the next word I'm going to say— I'm not stupid! I sit here all day thinking about what I'm going to say to you. I stuck by you and I hoped for you because whatever you became, I was gonna become. I thought about that, and that ain't shit!

1028

(*He leaves the shop.* THEO *is alone with his troubled thoughts. Suddenly he rushes into back room, gets hat and shirt, puts them on, and goes out into the street.*)

MR. PARKER (*Stepping down into the back room from the apartment upstairs.*) Come on, girl! (*A very attractive, well-dressed* YOUNG GIRL *in her early twenties follows him into the shop.*)

MR. PARKER You wanted to see it. Well, here it is.

GIRL (*Looking about the place.*) So this is where you do your business. Like I keep asking you, Russell, what kind of business is it for you to make all that money you got?

MR. PARKER (*Heading toward the refrigerator in the back room.*) Come on in here, sweetheart. I'll fix us a drink!

GIRL (*Moves briskly after him.*) I asked you a question, Russell.

MR. PARKER (*Still ignoring her question, he takes a jug out of refrigerator and grabs two glasses.*) I'm going to make you a special drink, made from my own hands. It's called "Black Lightning."

GIRL (*Surveys the room as* PARKER *pours drink.*) That should be exciting.

MR. PARKER Here you go. (*Hands her the drink.*) *Toujours l'amour!*

GIRL (*Gasping from the drink.*) What the fuck is this! What *is* this, Russell?

MR. PARKER (*Patting her on the back.*) Knocks the tail off of you, don't it! But it gets smoother after the second swallow . . . Go on, drink up!

GIRL Okay. (*Tries it again and scowls. Moves away as he sits on bed.*)

MR. PARKER Now, did you think about what I asked you last night?

GIRL About getting married?

MR. PARKER Yes.

GIRL Why do you want to marry me, Russell?

MR. PARKER Because I love you, and I think you could make me happy.

GIRL Well, I don't believe you. When I asked you a question about your business, you deliberately ignored me. It was like you didn't trust me, and I thought that love and trust went together.

MR. PARKER I'm not so sure about that. My son Theo, I'm wild about him, but I wouldn't trust him no farther 'n I could throw a building.

GIRL I'm not your son!

MR. PARKER What is it you wanta know?

GIRL Where you gettin' all that money from?

MR. PARKER Oh, that. That's not for a girl to know, baby doll.

GIRL Then it's time for me to go. I'm not gettin' myself hooked up with no mystery man! (*Moves as if to leave.* PARKER *stops her, then pauses for a moment.*)

MR. PARKER All right, I'll tell you. I'm partners in a big business, which I'm the president of.

GIRL   Partners with who, Russell?

MR. PARKER   That's not important, baby.

GIRL   Partners with who, Russell.

MR. PARKER   Mr. Blue Haven.

GIRL   *Blue Haven!* Then it's crooked business.

MR. PARKER   Oh no, baby, it's nothing like that. It's real straight.

GIRL   What does that mean?

MR. PARKER   That what we're doing is right!

GIRL   Tell me about it, then.

MR. PARKER   I've said enough. Now let's leave it at that! (*Tries to embrace her.*)

GIRL (*Wards him off, sits on bed.*)   All you take me for is something to play with.

MR. PARKER   That's not true, I wanna marry you. (*Sits beside her.*)

GIRL   You say you want to marry me, but how do you expect me to think about marrying somebody who won't confide in me about what they're doing. How do I know I'm not letting myself in for trouble.

MR. PARKER (*Ponders for a moment, then rises.*)   All right, I'll tell you! We peddle a variety of products to the community and we sell things to people at a price they can't get nowhere else in this city. Yes, according to the law it's illegal, but we help our people, our own people. We take care of business and at the same time we make everybody happy. We take care of our people. Just like I been taking care of you.

GIRL   You take care of me? How? You've never given me more than ten dollars in cash since I've known you.

MR. PARKER   Well, I've got a big present for you coming right out of this pocket and I'm gon' take you downtown tomorrow and let you spend till the store runs out.

GIRL   Taking me to a store and giving me spending change makes me feel like a child and I don't like it and I'm not gonna stand for it any more.

MR. PARKER   Then take this and you do whatever you want with it.

GIRL (*Taking the money and putting it away.*)   Now don't get the idea I'm just in love with your money.

MR. PARKER   Now I want you to stop talking to me about money. I've got *plenty* of it! You've got to understand—I'm the most different man you ever met. I've been around this world, I danced before the King and Queen of England. I've seen and heard many a thing in my lifetime—and you know what: I'm putting it all down on paper—my story!

GIRL   Your story!

(MR. PARKER *moves into shop, gets notebook from behind one of the sliding panels. During his absence* GIRL *checks under the bed.*)

MR. PARKER (*Re-enters.*) Here it is, right here. (*Sits next to her on the bed, giving her the notebook.*)

GIRL (*Thumbing through the pages.*) You write things too?

MR. PARKER I certainly do—and I've been thinking about writing a poem about you.

GIRL A poem about me!

MR. PARKER (*Taking book from her and dropping it on floor.*) I'm gon' do it tonight before I go to sleep. (*He kisses her neck and reaches for the hem of her dress.*)

GIRL (*Breaking out of his embrace.*) No, Russell, not here!

MR. PARKER Why not?

GIRL Just because there's a bed wherever we go don't mean that we have to jump into it. You don't understand, Russell! You've got to start treating me the same as if I was your wife.

MR. PARKER *That's exactly what I'm trying to do!*

GIRL (*Rising.*) Don't yell at me!

MR. PARKER All right. I tell you what: I'm kinda tired, let's just lie down for a while and talk. I ain't gon' try nothing.

GIRL Russell—

MR. PARKER May the Lord smack me down this minute into hell—I swear I won't do nothing.

GIRL What are the three biggest lies men tell to women, Russell?

MR. PARKER I ain't just any man—I'm the man you gon' spend your life with.

GIRL Okay, Russell, we'll lie down, but you've got to keep your word. If I'm the girl you want to marry, you've got to learn to keep your word. (*They lie on bed. To her surprise,* PARKER *is motionless, seemingly drifting off to sleep. After a moment she takes the initiative and begins love-making. He responds, and once his passion has reached an aggressive peak she breaks off abruptly.*) Where do you get these things you sell to people?

MR. PARKER What are you talking about?

GIRL You know what I'm saying. I overheard you tell Mr. Jenkins you suspected your son was robbing stores.

MR. PARKER You heard no such thing!

GIRL (*Desperately.*) Where do they keep the stuff?

MR. PARKER Now, baby, you've got to relax and stop worrying about things like that! (*Pulls her by the shoulders. She does not resist.*) Come here. (*He pulls her down to the bed, takes her into his arms and kisses her, reaching again for the hem of her dress.*)

GIRL (*Struggling, but weakening to his ardor.*) Russell, you said you wouldn't do nothing!

MR. PARKER   I ain't! I just want to get a little closer to you!

GIRL   Russell, not here!

MR. PARKER   Just let me feel it a little bit!

GIRL   You swore to God, Russell! (THEO *comes in the front door and heads toward the back room.*)

MR. PARKER   I ain't gon' do nothing!

GIRL (*Hears* THEO.)   Russell! Russell! Somebody is out there!

MR. PARKER (*Jumps up quickly.* THEO *stands before him.*)   What are you doing here?

THEO   The question is, *what are you doing!*

MR. PARKER   I have been having a private talk with a good friend of mine. Now get out of here!

(GIRL *jumps up, moving past* MR. PARKER.)

MR. PARKER (*Stopping her.*)   Where are you going?

GIRL   Home!

MR. PARKER   Hold it now, honey!

GIRL   I never should have come here in the first place!

MR. PARKER   No, you're not going anywhere. This is my place and you don't have to run off because of this Peeping Tom!

THEO   Pop, it's time to give us our money.

MR. PARKER   You'll get your share tomorrow and not before!

THEO   I want it now before you give it all to that girl. Pop, cut that broad loose!

MR. PARKER   What was that?

THEO   I said, cut her loose! She don't need an old man like you, she's just pumping you for information. That bitch is a hustler!

MR. PARKER (*Slaps* THEO *with the back of his hand.*)   Bite your tongue!

GIRL   I think I better go, Russell. (*Heads for the front door.*)

MR. PARKER (*Following her.*)   Okay, but I'll be right with you as soon as I get things straight here. You will be waiting for me, won't you?

GIRL   Sure!

MR. PARKER   You run along now and I'll be right over there. (GIRL *exits.* PARKER *whirls back into shop.*) What do you think you're doing, boy?

THEO   Just be careful, Pop. Please be careful.

MR. PARKER   If there's anybody I got to be careful of, it's you! You lying selfish sonofabitch! You think I don't know about you and Blue running that gang of thieves—about you sending your own brother out there with them?

1032

THEO I didn't do that!

MR. PARKER If Bobby gets hurt out on them streets, I'm gonna kill you, boy! I'm gonna kill you. (*Hurriedly collects hat and coat.*)

THEO You're not worried about Bobby! All you can think of is the money you're rolling in. The clothes. And that stupid outfit you've got on.

(ADELE *comes in from the street, obviously distraught.*)

MR. PARKER What's wrong with you? Are you drunk? (*Moves in.* ADELE *doesn't answer, so he moves off.*)

THEO Of course she's drunk. What did you expect—did you think everything would stop and stand still while you were being reborn again!

MR. PARKER What do you want from me? Call this whole thing off? It was your idea, not mine! But now that I've got myself something—I'm not going to throw it away for nobody!

THEO But can't you see what's happening here?

MR. PARKER If she wants to be a drunken wench, let her! I'm not going to take the blame. And as for you—(*Fumbles in his coat pocket.*) If you want this money, you can take it from me—I can throw every dollar of it into the ocean if I want to! You can call me a fool too, but I'm a *burning fool!* I'm going to marry that little girl. She is not a whore! She is a woman! And I'm going to marry her! And if the two of you don't like it, you can kiss my ass! (*Bolts out into the street.*)

THEO You're not drunk. What happened?

ADELE (*Heading for the back room.*) What does it look like. Wilmer hit me.

THEO (*Following.*) Why?

ADELE (*Sits on bed.*) He caught me in Morgan's with a friend of his after I had lied about going bowling with the girls. He just walked in and started hitting me, over and over again. His friend just stood there pleading with him not to hit me, but he never did anything to stop him. I guess he figured, "Why should I risk getting myself killed over just another piece of ass?" I thought he was going to kill me but then Blue came in with some of his friends and they just grabbed him by the arms and took him away.

THEO Was Bobby with them?

ADELE I couldn't tell.

THEO Damnit! Everything gets fucked up!

ADELE It had to, because you don't think. If you're going to be a crook, you don't read a comic book for research, you don't recruit an old black man that's about to die!

THEO No matter what you do, he's gon' die anyway. This whole place was built for him to die in—so you bite, you scratch, you kick: you do anything to stay alive!

ADELE Yes, you bite! You scratch, you steal, you kick, and you get killed anyway! Just as I was doing, coming back here to help Momma.

THEO   Adele, I'm sick and tired of your talk about sacrifices. You were here because you had no other place to go. You just got scared too young and too soon.

ADELE   You're right. All I was doing was waiting for her to die so I could get on with what I thought I wanted to do with myself. But, God, *she took so long to die!* But then I found myself doing the same things she had done, taking care of three men, trying to shield them from the danger beyond that door, *but who the hell ever told every black woman she was some kind of goddamn savior!* Sure, this place was built for us to die in, but if we aren't very careful, Theo—that can actually happen. Good night. (*Heads for the stairs.*)

THEO   Adele—(*She stops in her tracks and turns.*) I've decided that there's going to be no more of Blue's business here. It's over. We're getting out.

ADELE (*After a long pause.*)   Theo, do you really mean it? (THEO *nods yes.*)

ADELE   What about Daddy?

THEO   He will have to live with it. This set-up can't move without me.

ADELE   And Bobby?

THEO   I'll take care of him.

ADELE   That's fine, Theo. We'll throw the old things into the river—and we'll try something new: I won't push and you won't call me a bitch! (*Goes upstairs.* THEO *picks up his father's notebook from the floor beside the bed. A knock at the door.*)

THEO   We're closed!

(*The knocking continues.*)

THEO   WE'RE CLOSED!

(*The knocking turns to banging and a voice calls out to* THEO. *He rushes to the door and opens.*)

THEO   I SAID WE'RE CLOSED! Oh, I'm sorry, Mr. Jenkins, I didn't know that was you . . . What are you doing here this time of night?

MR. JENKINS   I want to speak to Parker.

THEO   You know him—he's been keeping late hours lately . . .

MR. JENKINS   I'll wait for him.

THEO   Suit yourself, but don't you have to work tomorrow?

MR. JENKINS   I have something to tell him, and I'll wait if it takes all night.

THEO   In that case, you can tell me about it.

(ADELE *comes downstairs and stops on steps leading to shop, looking about confusedly. She has a deadly, almost blank look on her face.*)

THEO   What's wrong with you?

ADELE (*Pause.*)   Some—somebody just called me.

THEO   What did they call you about? (*She does not answer.* JENKINS *rises and seats her gently on bed.*) Didn't you hear me—what about? (*She still does not respond.*) WHAT IS IT, ADELE!!!

MR. JENKINS   THEO!!! (THEO *turns to* MR. JENKINS.) I think she probably just heard that your brother Bobby has been killed in a robbery by a night watchman.

THEO   Uh-uh, nawww, nawww, that's not true.

MR. JENKINS   Yes, it is, son.

ADELE   Yes.

THEO   No.

MR. JENKINS   Yes! (*Moves toward the shop door.*)

THEO   *I don't believe you!*

MR. JENKINS   I saw him, boy, I saw him. (*Dead silence as* MR. JENKINS *slowly moves toward the street exit.*)

THEO   You should've seen this dude I caught the other day on Thirty-second Street. He had on a bright purple suit, gray shirt, yellow tie, and his hair was processed with bright purple color. What a sight he was! But I have to say one thing for him—he was clean. (*The lights are slowly dimming.*) Used to be a time when a dude like that came in numbers, but you don't see too many of them nowadays. I have to say one thing for him—he was clean. You don't see too many like—he was clean. He was—he was clean—

Blackout

Scene Two

About two hours later, in the shop.

MR. PARKER *and* MR. JENKINS *enter the shop.* MR. PARKER *is drunk, and* MR. JENKINS *helps him walk and finally seats him on the barber's throne.*

MR. PARKER   Thank you, Jenkins. You are the greatest friend a man can have. They don't make 'em like you any more. You are one of the last of the great friends, Jenkins. Pardon me, Mister Jenkins. No more will I ever call you Jenks or Jenkins. From now on, it's Mister Jenkins!

MR. JENKINS   Thank you, but when I ran into Theo and Adele tonight, they said they had something important to say to you, and I think you oughta see them.

MR. PARKER   I know what they want. They want to tell me what an old fool I am.

MR. JENKINS   I don't think that's it, and you should go on upstairs and—

MR. PARKER   Never! Upstairs is for the people upstairs!

MR. JENKINS   Russell, I—

MR. PARKER I am downstairs people! You ever hear of downstairs people?

MR. JENKINS (*Pause.*) No.

MR. PARKER Well, they're the people to watch in this world.

MR. JENKINS If you say so.

MR. PARKER *Put your money on 'em!*

MR. JENKINS Come on, Mister Parker: why don't you lie down in the back room and—

MR. PARKER Oh! No—you don't think I'd have you come all the way over here just for me to go to bed, do you? I wouldn't do a thing like that to you, Jenkins. I'm busy—Mister Jenkins. Just stay with me for a little while . . . (*His tone changes.*) Why did that girl lock me out? She said she would be waiting for me, but she locked me out. Why did she do a thing like that? I give her everything —money, clothes, pay her rent. I even love her!

MR. JENKINS Russell—

MR. PARKER (*Rising precariously.*) Tell me something, Mister Jenkins—since you are my friend—why do you think she locked me out?

MR. JENKINS (*Steadying him.*) I don't know.

MR. PARKER I'll tell you why. I'm an old man, and all I've got is a few dollars in my pocket. Ain't that it?

MR. JENKINS I don't know . . . Good night, Parker. (*Starts out.*)

MR. PARKER (*Grabs his arm.*) You think a man was in that room with my girl?

MR. JENKINS *Yes!*

MR. PARKER *Goddamnit! Goddamnit!*

MR. JENKINS Russell—

MR. PARKER I don't believe it! When I love 'em, they stay loved!

MR. JENKINS Nobody's got that much love, man!

MR. PARKER (*Pause.*) No, no—you're wrong. My wife—my dear Doris had more love in her than life should've allowed. A hundred men couldn't have taken all that love.

MR. JENKINS We ain't talking about Doris, Russell.

MR. PARKER Aw, forget it! (*Crossing toward table.*) *Goddamnit!* You stumble around like an old black cow and you never get up again . . .

I have had my fun!
If I don't get well no more!
I have had my fun!
If I—

(PARKER *falls down.*) Get up, old bastard! Get up! (*Rises to his feet, aided by* JEN-KINS.) Get up and fall back down again. Come on, Mister Jenkins, let's play ourselves a game of checkers.

MR. JENKINS   I don't want to play no damn checkers.

MR. PARKER   Why do you curse my home, Mister Jenkins?

MR. JENKINS (*Pause.*)   I apologize for that.

MR. PARKER   Come on, have a game of checkers with your good friend. (*Sits at table.*)

MR. JENKINS (*Moves to the table.*)   All right, one game and then I'm going home.

MR. PARKER   One game.

MR. PARKER (*Pausing while* JENKINS *sits down.*)   I said a lot of dirty things to my children tonight—the kind of things you have to live a long time to overcome.

MR. JENKINS   I know exactly what you mean. (JENKINS *sets up jumps for* PARKER. PARKER *seems unaware of it. They play briefly.* PARKER *stops.*)

MR. PARKER   Theo is a good boy, and a smart one too, but he lets people push him around. That's because he's always trying to con somebody out of something —you know the kind: can't see for looking. And Bobby? He wouldn't hurt a flea. A lot of people think that boy is dumb, but just let somebody try to trick or fool him if they dare! (*Begins a series of checker jumps.*)

(*Pause.*)

Got a story for you.

MR. JENKINS   No stories tonight, Parker . . .

MR. PARKER   Mister Parker. (*The last move is made, the game is over. His conquest slowly sinks in. And* MR. PARKER *is at long last the victor. Rising from the table.*) Call me champ! (THEO *and* ADELE *enter shop from outside, and stand just inside the door.* PARKER *is laughing.*) You're beat! I beat you! I beat you! (MR. PARKER *throws his arm around* MR. JENKINS'S *waist and holds him from behind.*) . . . You fall down and you never get up! (*Still laughing.*) Fall down, old man! Fall down! (*Releases* JEN-KINS *upon seeing* ADELE *and* THEO.) You hear that, children, I beat him! I beat him! (*His laughter subsides as he realizes they are not responding to him. Guilt-ridden, he approaches* THEO, *looks at him intently, then reaches into his inside coat pocket and pulls out the money.*) Here, Theo, here's the money, here's all of it. Take it, it's yours. Go out and try to get happy, boy. (THEO *does not move or take the money from his father's outstretched hand. He turns to* ADELE. *Her face is almost a blank.*) WHY DON'T SOMEBODY SAY SOMETHING! (ADELE *attempts to speak but* PARKER *cuts her off.*) I know you have some trouble with me . . . (PARKER *spies the notebook in the throne, takes it in his hand, and approaches* ADELE.) You have a woman, you love her, you stop loving her, and sooner or later she ups and dies and you sit around behaving like you was a killer. I didn't have no more in me. I just didn't have no more in me!

(*Pause.*)

I know you don't believe I ever loved your mother, but it's here in this book—read it . . . (*She does not respond.*) You wanta read something, boy! (THEO *turns away.* PARKER *slowly crosses, hands the book to* MR. JENKINS, *and addresses his remarks to him.*) I got sour the day my legs got so trembly and sore on the stage of the Strand Theatre—I couldn't even walk out to take a proper bow. It was then I knew nobody would ever hire me to dance again. I just couldn't run downtown to meet the man the way she did—not after all those years of shuffling around like I was a dumb clown, with my feet hurting and aching the way they did, having my head patted as if I was some little pet animal: back of the bus, front of the train, grinning when I was bleeding to death! . . . After all of that I was going to ask for more by throwing myself into the low drag of some dusty old factory in Brooklyn. All I could do was to stay here in this shop with you, my good friend. And we acted out the ceremony of a game. And you, boy— (*Turns to* THEO.) . . . You and Blue with your ideas of overcoming the evil of white men. To an old man like me, it was nothing more than an ounce of time to end my dragging about this shop. All it did was to send me out into those streets to live a time—and I did live myself a time for a while. I did it amongst a bunch of murderers—all kinds of 'em—where at times it gets so bad till it seems that the only thing that's left is for you to go out there and kill somebody before they kill you. That's all—that's out there! (*Goes to* ADELE.) Adele, as for that girl that was here tonight, she's probably no good, but if at my age I was stupid enough to think that I could have stepped out of here and won that little girl, loved her, and moved through the rest of my days without killing anybody, that was a victory! (*Moves to center stage, stands silently, then does a little dance.*) Be a dancer—any kind of dancer you wanta be—but dance it! (*Tries out a difficult step, but can't quite make it.*) Uh-uhhh! Can't make that one no more. (*Continues to dance.*) Be a singer—sing any song you wanta sing, but sing! (*Stops in his tracks.*) *And you've got enough trouble to take you to the graveyard!*

(*Pause.*)

But think of all that life you had before they buried you. (*Breaks into a frantic dance, attempting steps that just cross him up. He stumbles about until he falls. Everyone in the room rushes to help him up.*) . . . I'm okay, I'm okay . . . (*He rises from the floor, slowly.*) I'm tired, I'm going to bed and by the time tomorrow comes around, let's see if we can't all throw it into the river. (*Moves into the back room, singing.*)

> I have had my fun!
> If I don't get well no more
> I have had my fun
> If I don't get well no more—

(*A thought strikes him. He turns and moves back to where* JENKINS *is standing at the entrance to the back room.*) Jenkins, you said that the day I beat you playing checkers, you said it could be the unluckiest day of my life. But after all that's happened today

—I'm straight—I feel just great! (*Moves to the stairs leading up, suddenly stops, turns and briskly moves back to the doorway leading to the shop.*) Say, where's Bobby?

Curtain

DISCUSSION TOPICS

1. The checker games are important throughout the play, and are in part the source of the title of the play, as we see in Mr. Parker's long speech near the end of the play. The games are similar to the coin tossing game in *Rosencrantz and Guildenstern Are Dead.* What does the string of defeats mean to Mr. Parker? How does the string suggest the themes of the play in relation to him and to other characters? If Mr. Parker is a loser, is Mr. Jenkins a winner? In *Rosencrantz and Guildenstern,* mathematical probability is significant. Why is the absence of mathematical probability in the checker games significant?

2. Mr. Parker is gradually seduced by a value system, just as Willy Loman is in *Death of a Salesman.* Examine those value systems and Parker's and Loman's reactions to them.

3. The comparison between Parker and Loman might be extended to other aspects of these two plays—the two pairs of sons, the mother figures, the motif of stealing, the search for the American Dream, and the contrasting content of the Requiem scene in the Miller play and that of the long speech by Mr. Parker near the end of *Ceremonies.* What conclusions can you draw from these parallels?

4. Theo's pattern of development is accentuated by several ironies. What are they?

5. Trace the similarities and differences between Adele and her dead mother.

6. Do you think Mr. Parker is a suitable tragic hero? What is his tragic flaw? In the *Poetics,* Aristotle says that the tragic hero is not evil but is guilty of an error in judgment. What errors of judgment are there in *Ceremonies?*

7. Parker and his three children are all involved in illegal or at least less than praiseworthy action. How does Elder preserve audience sympathy for these characters? Is Blue a sympathetic character?

8. There is a sense of inevitability in this play, something like the fated doom that informs *Oedipus the King* and *Riders to the Sea.* How does Elder build that sense of inevitability?

9. There are a number of rituals in the play: the games of checkers, Parker's stories from the past, even the song-and-dance routine and the speech patterns. How do these rituals function in the play?

10. The stories of Mr. Parker, especially the effort to write them down, suggest an attempt to transcend or transmute the circumstances of the lives of the characters. How successful is Parker in that attempt? To what extent are Parker's stories true? Does that matter?

11. What kinds of victory, if any, do you find in this play?

Tom Stoppard (1937–) Born in Czechoslovakia, educated in England. He has worked as a reviewer and journalist, turning later to fiction and drama. *Rosencrantz and Guildenstern Are Dead* was the first of a number of stage successes. His plays examine the human condition and are known for their wit and often dark humor.

ROSENCRANTZ AND GUILDENSTERN ARE DEAD

Characters

ROSENCRANTZ
GUILDENSTERN
THE PLAYER
ALFRED
TRAGEDIANS
HAMLET
OPHELIA
CLAUDIUS
GERTRUDE
POLONIUS
SOLDIER
HORATIO
COURTIERS, AMBASSADORS, SOLDIERS, AND ATTENDANTS
MUSICIANS

ACT I

[*Two* ELIZABETHANS *passing the time in a place without any visible character.*

They are well dressed—hats, cloaks, sticks and all.

Each of them has a large leather money bag.

GUILDENSTERN'*s bag is nearly empty.*

ROSENCRANTZ'*s bag is nearly full.*

The reason being: they are betting on the toss of a coin, in the following manner: GUILDENSTERN (*hereafter* "GUIL") *takes a coin out of his bag, spins it, letting it fall.* ROSENCRANTZ (*hereafter* "ROS") *studies it, announces it as "heads" (as it happens) and puts it into his own bag. Then they repeat the process. They have apparently been doing this for some time.*

The run of "heads" is impossible, yet ROS *betrays no surprise at all—he feels none. However, he is nice enough to feel a little embarrassed at taking so much money off his friend. Let that be his character note.*

GUIL *is well alive to the oddity of it. He is not worried about the money, but he is worried by the implications; aware but not going to panic about it—his character note.*

GUIL *sits.* ROS *stands (he does the moving, retrieving coins).* GUIL *spins.* ROS *studies coin.*]

ROS   Heads.

[*He picks it up and puts it in his bag. The process is repeated.*]

Heads.

[*Again*]

Heads.

[*Again*]

Heads.

[*Again*]

Heads.

GUIL [*flipping a coin*]   There is an art to the building up of suspense.

ROS   Heads.

GUIL [*flipping another*]   Though it can be done by luck alone.

ROS   Heads.

GUIL   If that's the word I'm after.

ROS [*raises his head at* GUIL]   Seventy-six—love.

[GUIL *gets up but has nowhere to go. He spins another coin over his shoulder without looking at it, his attention being directed at his environment or lack of it.*]

Heads.

GUIL   A weaker man might be moved to re-examine his faith, if in nothing else at least in the law of probability. [*He slips a coin over his shoulder as he goes to look upstage.*]

ROS   Heads.

[GUIL, *examining the confines of the stage, flips over two more coins as he does so, one by one of course,* ROS *announces each of them as "heads."*]

GUIL [*musing*]   The law of probability, it has been oddly asserted, is something to do with the proposition that if six monkeys [*he has surprised himself*] . . . if six monkeys were . . .

ROS   Game?

GUIL   Were they?

ROS   Are you?

GUIL [*understanding*] Game. [*Flips a coin.*] The law of averages, if I have got this right, means that if six monkeys were thrown up in the air for long enough they would land on their tails about as often as they would land on their—

ROS Heads. [*He picks up the coin.*]

GUIL Which even at first glance does not strike one as a particularly rewarding speculation, in either sense, even without the monkeys. I mean you wouldn't *bet* on it. I mean *I* would, but *you* wouldn't . . . [*As he flips a coin.*]

ROS Heads.

GUIL Would you? [*Flips a coin.*]

ROS Heads.

[*Repeat*]

Heads. [*He looks up at* GUIL—*embarrassed laugh.*] Getting a bit of a bore, isn't it?

GUIL [*coldly*] A bore?

ROS Well . . .

GUIL What about the suspense?

ROS [*innocently*] What suspense?

[*Small pause.*]

GUIL It must be the law of diminishing returns. . . . I feel the spell about to be broken. [*Energizing himself somewhat. He takes out a coin, spins it high, catches it, turns it over on to the back of his other hand, studies the coin—and tosses it to* ROS. *His energy deflates and he sits.*]

   Well, it was an even chance . . . if my calculations are correct.

ROS Eighty-five in a row—beaten the record!

GUIL Don't be absurd.

ROS Easily!

GUIL [*angry*] Is that *it,* then? Is that all?

ROS What?

GUIL A new record? Is that as far as you are prepared to go?

ROS Well . . .

GUIL No questions? Not even a pause?

ROS You spun them yourself.

GUIL Not a flicker of doubt?

ROS [*aggrieved, aggressive*] Well, I won—didn't I?

GUIL [*approaches him—quieter*] And if you'd lost? If they'd come down against you, eighty-five times, one after another, just like that?

ROS [*dumbly*] Eighty-five in a row? *Tails?*

1042

GUIL   Yes! What would you think?

ROS [*doubtfully*]   Well . . . [*Jocularly.*] Well, I'd have a good look at your coins for a start!

GUIL [*retiring*]   I'm relieved. At least we can still count on self-interest as a predictable factor. . . . I suppose it's the last to go. Your capacity for trust made me wonder if perhaps . . . you alone . . . [*He turns on him suddenly, reaches out a hand.*] Touch.

[ROS *clasps his hand.* GUIL *pulls him up to him.*]

GUIL [*more intensely*]   We have been spinning coins together since—[*He releases him almost as violently.*] This is not the first time we have spun coins!

ROS   Oh no—we've been spinning coins for as long as I remember.

GUIL   How long is that?

ROS   I forget. Mind you—eighty-five times!

GUIL   Yes?

ROS   It'll take some beating, I imagine.

GUIL   Is *that* what you imagine? Is that it? No *fear?*

ROS   Fear?

GUIL [*in fury—flings a coin on the ground*]   Fear! The crack that might flood your brain with light!

ROS   Heads. . . . [*He puts it in his bag.*]

[GUIL *sits despondently. He takes a coin, spins it, lets it fall between his feet. He looks at it, picks it up, throws it to* ROS, *who puts it in his bag.*

GUIL *takes another coin, spins it, catches it, turns it over on to his other hand, looks at it, and throws it to* ROS, *who puts it in his bag.*

GUIL *takes a third coin, spins it, catches it in his right hand, turns it over onto his left wrist, lobs it in the air, catches it with his left hand, raises his left leg, throws the coin up under it, catches it and turns it over on the top of his head, where it sits.* ROS *comes, looks at it, puts it in his bag.*]

ROS   I'm afraid—

GUIL   So am I.

ROS   I'm afraid it isn't your day.

GUIL   I'm afraid it is.

[*Small pause.*]

ROS   Eighty-nine.

GUIL   It must be indicative of something, besides the redistribution of wealth. [*He muses.*] List of possible explanations. One: I'm willing it. Inside where nothing shows, I am the essence of a man spinning double-headed coins, and betting against himself in private atonement for an unremembered past. [*He spins a coin at* ROS.]

ROS Heads.

GUIL Two: time has stopped dead, and the single experience of one coin being spun once has been repeated ninety times. . . . [*He flips a coin, looks at it, tosses it to* ROS.] On the whole, doubtful. Three: divine intervention, that is to say, a good turn from above concerning him, cf. children of Israel, or retribution from above concerning me, cf. Lot's wife. Four: a spectacular vindication of the principle that each individual coin spun individually [*he spins one*] is as likely to come down heads as tails and therefore should cause no surprise each individual time it does.

[*It does. He tosses it to* ROS.]

ROS I've never known anything like it!

GUIL And a syllogism: One, he has never known anything like it. Two, he has never known anything to write home about. Three, it is nothing to write home about. . . . Home . . . What's the first thing you remember?

ROS Oh, let's see. . . . The first thing that comes into my head, you mean?

GUIL No—the first thing you remember.

ROS Ah. [*Pause*] No, it's no good, it's gone. It was a long time ago.

GUIL [*patient but edged*] You don't get my meaning. What is the first thing after all the things you've forgotten?

ROS Oh I see. [*Pause.*] I've forgotten the question.

[GUIL *leaps up and paces.*]

GUIL Are you happy?

ROS What?

GUIL Content? At ease?

ROS I suppose so.

GUIL What are you going to do now?

ROS I don't know. What do you want to do?

GUIL I have no desires. None. [*He stops pacing dead.*] There was a messenger . . . that's right. We were sent for. [*He wheels at* ROS *and raps out*] Syllogism the second: One, probability is a factor which operates within natural forces. Two, probability is not operating as a factor. Three, we are now within un-, sub- or supernatural forces. Discuss. [ROS *is suitably startled. Acidly.*] Not too heatedly.

ROS I'm sorry I—What's the matter with you?

GUIL The scientific approach to the examination of phenomena is a defence against the pure emotion of fear. Keep tight hold and continue while there's time. Now—counter to the previous syllogism: tricky one, follow me carefully, it may

1044

prove a comfort. If we postulate, and we just have, that within un-, sub- or supernatural forces *the probability is* that the law of probability will not operate as a factor, then we must accept that the probability of the *first* part will not operate as a factor, in which case the law of probability *will* operate as a factor within un-, sub- or supernatural forces. And since it obviously hasn't been doing so, we can take it that we are not held within un-, sub- or supernatural forces after all; in all probability, that is. Which is a great relief to me personally. [*Small pause.*] Which is all very well, except that—[*He continues with tight hysteria, under control.*] We have been spinning coins together since I don't know when, and in all that time (if it *is* all that time) I don't suppose either of us was more than a couple of gold pieces up or down. I hope that doesn't sound surprising because its very unsurprisingness is something I am trying to keep hold of. The equanimity of your average tosser of coins depends upon a law, or rather a tendency, or let us say a probability, or at any rate a mathematically calculable chance, which ensures that he will not upset himself by losing too much nor upset his opponent by winning too often. This made for a kind of harmony and a kind of confidence. It related the fortuitous and the ordained into a reassuring union which we recognized as nature. The sun came up about as often as it went down, in the long run, and a coin showed heads about as often as it showed tails. Then a messenger arrived. We had been sent for. Nothing else happened. Ninety-two coins spun consecutively have come down heads ninety-two consecutive times . . . and for the last three minutes on the wind of a windless day I have heard the sound of drums and flute. . . .

ROS [*cutting his fingernails*]   Another curious scientific phenomenon is the fact that the fingernails grow after death, as does the beard.

GUIL   What?

ROS [*loud*]   Beard!

GUIL   But you're not dead.

ROS [*irritated*]   I didn't say they *started* to grow after death! [*Pause, calmer.*] The fingernails also grow before birth, though *not* the beard.

GUIL   *What?*

ROS [*shouts*]   Beard! What's the matter with you? [*Reflectively.*] The toenails, on the other hand, never grow at all.

GUIL [*bemused*]   The toenails never grow at all?

ROS   Do they? It's a funny thing—I cut my fingernails all the time, and every time I think to cut them, they need cutting. Now, for instance. And yet, I never, to the best of my knowledge, cut my toenails. They ought to be curled under my feet by now, but it doesn't happen. I never think about them. Perhaps I cut them absent-mindedly, when I'm thinking of something else.

GUIL [*tensed up by this rambling*]   Do you remember the first thing that happened today?

ROS [*promptly*]   I woke up, I suppose. [*Triggered.*] Oh—I've got it now—that man, a foreigner, he woke us up—

GUIL   A messenger. [*He relaxes, sits.*]

ROS   That's it—pale sky before dawn, a man standing on his saddle to bang on the shutters—shouts—What's all the row about?! Clear off!—But then he called our names. You remember that—this man woke us up.

GUIL   Yes.

ROS   We were sent for.

GUIL   Yes.

ROS   That's why we're here. [*He looks round, seems doubtful, then the explanation.*] Travelling.

GUIL   Yes.

ROS   [*dramatically*]   It was urgent—a matter of extreme urgency, a royal summons, his very words: official business and no questions asked—lights in the stable-yard, saddle up and off headlong and hotfoot across the land, our guides outstripped in breakneck pursuit of our duty! Fearful lest we come too late!!

[*Small pause.*]

GUIL   Too late for what?

ROS   How do I know? We haven't got there yet.

GUIL   Then what are we doing here, I ask myself.

ROS   You might well ask.

GUIL   We better get on.

ROS   You might well think.

GUIL   We better get on.

ROS   [*actively*]   Right [*Pause.*] On where?

GUIL   Forward.

ROS   [*forward to footlights*]   Ah. [*Hesitates.*] Which way do we—[*He turns round.*] Which way did we—?

GUIL   Practically starting from scratch. . . . An awakening, a man standing on his saddle to bang on the shutters, our names shouted in a certain dawn, a message, a summons . . . A new record for heads and tails. We have not been . . . picked out . . . simply to be abandoned . . . set loose to find our own way . . . We are entitled to some direction. . . . I would have thought.

ROS   [*alert, listening*]   I say—! I say—

GUIL   Yes?

ROS   I can hear—I thought I heard—music.

[GUIL *raises himself.*]

GUIL   Yes?

ROS   Like a band. [*He looks around, laughs embarrassedly, expiating himself.*] It sounded like—a band. Drums.

1046

GUIL   Yes.

ROS [*relaxes*]   It couldn't have been real.

GUIL   "The colours red, blue and green are real. The colour yellow is a mystical experience shared by everybody"—demolish.

ROS [*at edge of stage*]   It must have been thunder. Like drums . . .

[*By the end of the next speech, the band is faintly audible.*]

GUIL   A man breaking his journey between one place and another at a third place of no name, character, population or significance, sees a unicorn cross his path and disappear. That in itself is startling, but there are precedents for mystical encounters of various kinds, or to be less extreme, a choice of persuasions to put it down to fancy; until—"My God," says a second man, "I must be dreaming, I thought I saw a unicorn." At which point, a dimension is added that makes the experience as alarming as it will ever be. A third witness, you understand, adds no further dimension but only spreads it thinner, and a fourth thinner still, and the more witnesses there are the thinner it gets and the more reasonable it becomes until it is as thin as reality, the name we give to the common experience. . . . "Look, look!" recites the crowd. "A horse with an arrow in its forehead! It must have been mistaken for a deer."

ROS [*eagerly*]   I knew all along it was a band.

GUIL [*tiredly*]   He knew all along it was a band.

ROS   Here they come!

GUIL [*at the last moment before they enter—wistfully*]   I'm sorry it wasn't a unicorn. It would have been nice to have unicorns.

The TRAGEDIANS *are six in number, including a small* BOY [ALFRED]. *Two pull and push a cart piled with props and belongings. There is also a* DRUMMER, *a* HORN-PLAYER *and a* FLAUTIST. *The* SPOKESMAN ["*the* PLAYER"] *has no instrument. He brings up the rear and is the first to notice them.*

PLAYER   Halt!

[*The group turns and halts.*]

[*Joyously*] An audience!

[ROS *and* GUIL *half rise.*]

Don't move!

[*They sink back. He regards them fondly.*]

Perfect! A lucky thing we came along.

ROS   For us?

PLAYER   Let us hope so. But to meet two gentlemen on the road—we would not hope to meet them off it.

ROS   No?

PLAYER   Well met, in fact, and just in time.

ROS   Why's that?

PLAYER   Why, we grow rusty and you catch us at the very point of decadence—by this time tomorrow we might have forgotten everything we ever knew. That's a thought, isn't it? [*He laughs generously.*] We'd be back where we started—improvising.

ROS   Tumblers, are you?

PLAYER   We can give you a tumble if that's your taste, and times being what they are. . . . Otherwise, for a jingle of coin we can do you a selection of gory romances, full of fine cadence and corpses, pirated from the Italian; and it doesn't take much to make a jingle—even a single coin has music in it.

[*They all flourish and bow, raggedly.*]

Tragedians, at your command.

[ROS *and* GUIL *have got to their feet.*]

ROS   My name is Guildenstern, and this is Rosencrantz.

[GUIL *confers briefly with him.*]

[*Without embarrassment*] I'm sorry—*his* name's Guildenstern, and *I'm* Rosencrantz.

PLAYER   A pleasure. We've played to bigger, of course, but quality counts for something. I recognized you at once—

ROS   And who are we?

PLAYER   —as fellow artists.

ROS   I thought we were gentlemen.

PLAYER   For some of us it is performance, for others, patronage. They are two sides of the same coin, or, let us say, being as there are so many of us, the same side of two coins. [*Bows again.*] Don't clap too loudly—it's a very old world.

ROS   What is your line?

PLAYER   Tragedy, sir. Deaths and disclosures, universal and particular, denouements both unexpected and inexorable, transvestite melodrama on all levels including the suggestive. We transport you into a world of intrigue and illusion . . . clowns, if you like, murderers—we can do you ghosts and battles, on the skirmish level, heroes, villains, tormented lovers—set pieces in the poetic vein; we can do you rapiers or rape or both, by all means, faithless wives and ravished virgins—*flagrante delicto* at a price, but that comes under realism for which there are special terms. Getting warm, am I?

ROS [*doubtfully*]   Well, I don't know. . . .

PLAYER   It costs little to watch, and little more if you happen to get caught up in the action, if that's your taste and times being what they are.

ROS   What are they?

PLAYER   Indifferent.

ROS   Bad?

PLAYER   Wicked. Now what precisely is your pleasure? [*He turns to the* TRAGEDI-ANS.] Gentlemen, disport yourselves.

[*The* TRAGEDIANS *shuffle into some kind of line.*]

There! See anything you like?

ROS [*doubtful, innocent*]   What do they do?

PLAYER   Let your imagination run riot. They are beyond surprise.

ROS   And how much?

PLAYER   To take part?

ROS   To watch.

PLAYER   Watch what?

ROS   A private performance.

PLAYER   How private?

ROS   Well, there are only two of us. Is that enough?

PLAYER   For an audience, disappointing. For voyeurs, about average.

ROS   What's the difference?

PLAYER   Ten guilders.

ROS [*horrified*]   Ten *guilders!*

PLAYER   I mean eight.

ROS   Together?

PLAYER   Each. I don't think you understand—

ROS   What are you *saying?*

PLAYER   What am I saying—seven.

ROS   Where have you *been?*

PLAYER   Roundabout. A nest of children carries the custom of the town. Juvenile companies, they are the fashion. But they cannot match our repertoire . . . we'll stoop to anything if that's your bent. . . .

He regards ROS *meaningfully but* ROS *returns the stare blankly.*

ROS   They'll grow up.

PLAYER [*giving up*]   There's one born every minute. [*To* TRAGEDIANS] Onward!

[*The* TRAGEDIANS *start to resume their burdens and their journey.* GUIL *stirs himself at last.*]

GUIL   Where are you going?

PLAYER   Ha-alt!

[*They halt and turn.*]

Home, sir.

GUIL   Where from?

PLAYER   Home. We're travelling people. We take our chances where we find them.

GUIL   It was chance, then?

PLAYER   Chance?

GUIL   You found us.

PLAYER   Oh, yes.

GUIL   You were looking?

PLAYER   Oh no.

GUIL   Chance, then.

PLAYER   Or fate.

GUIL   Yours or ours?

PLAYER   It could hardly be one without the other.

GUIL   Fate, then.

PLAYER   Oh, yes. We have no control. Tonight we play to the court. Or the night after. Or to the tavern. Or not.

GUIL   Perhaps I can use my influence.

PLAYER   At the tavern?

GUIL   At the court. I would say I have some influence.

PLAYER   Would you say so?

GUIL   I have influence yet.

PLAYER   Yet what?

[GUIL *seizes the* PLAYER *violently.*]

GUIL   I have influence!

[*The* PLAYER *does not resist.* GUIL *loosens his hold.*]

[*More calmly.*] You said something—about getting caught up in the action—

PLAYER [*gaily freeing himself*]   I did!—I did!—You're quicker than your friend. . . . [*Confidently.*] Now for a handful of guilders I happen to have a private and uncut performance of *The Rape of the Sabine Women*—or rather woman, or rather Alfred—[*Over his shoulder.*] Get your skirt on, Alfred—

1050

[*The* BOY *starts struggling into a female robe.*]

. . . and for eight you can participate.

[GUIL *backs,* PLAYER *follows.*]

. . . taking either part.

[GUIL *backs.*]

. . . or both for ten.

[GUIL *tries to turn away,* PLAYER *holds his sleeve.*]

. . . with encores—

[GUIL *smashes the* PLAYER *across the face. The* PLAYER *recoils.* GUIL *stands trembling.*]

[*Resigned and quiet.*] Get your skirt off, Alfred . . .

[ALFRED *struggles out of his half-on robe.*]

GUIL [*shaking with rage and fright*] It could have been—it didn't have to be *obscene.* . . . It could have been—a bird out of season, dropping bright-feathered on my shoulder. . . . It could have been a tongueless dwarf standing by the road to point the way. . . . I was *prepared.* But it's this, is it? No enigma, no dignity, nothing classical, portentous, only this—a comic pornographer and a rabble of prostitutes. . . .

PLAYER [*acknowledging the description with a sweep of his hat, bowing; sadly*] You should have caught us in better times. We were purists then. [*Straightens up.*] On-ward.

[*The* PLAYERS *make to leave.*]

ROS [*his voice has changed: he has caught on*] Excuse me!
PLAYER: Ha-alt!

[*They halt.*]

A-al-l-fred!

[ALFRED *resumes the struggle. The* PLAYER *comes forward.*]

ROS You're not—ah—exclusively players, then?
PLAYER We're inclusively players, sir.
ROS So you give—exhibitions?
PLAYER Performances, sir.
ROS Yes, of course. There's more money in that, is there?

PLAYER There's more trade, sir.

ROS Times being what they are.

PLAYER Yes.

ROS Indifferent.

PLAYER Completely.

ROS You know I'd no idea—

PLAYER No.

ROS I mean, I've *heard* of—but I've never actually—

PLAYER No.

ROS I mean, what exactly do you *do?*

PLAYER We keep to our usual stuff, more or less, only inside out. We do on stage the things that are supposed to happen off. Which is a kind of integrity, if you look on every exit being an entrance somewhere else.

ROS [*nervy, loud*] Well, I'm not really the type of man who—no, but don't hurry off—sit down and tell us about some of the things people ask you to do—

[*The* PLAYER *turns away.*]

PLAYER On-ward!

ROS Just a minute!

[*They turn and look at him without expression.*]

Well, all right—I wouldn't mind seeing—just an idea of the kind of—[*Bravely.*] What will you do for that? [*And tosses a single coin on the ground between them.*]

[*The* PLAYER *spits at the coin, from where he stands.*

The TRAGEDIANS *demur, trying to get at the coin. He kicks and cuffs them back.*]

On!

[ALFRED *is still half in and out of his robe. The* PLAYER *cuffs him.*]

[*To* ALFRED] What are you playing at?

[ROS *is shamed into fury.*]

ROS Filth! Disgusting—I'll report you to the authorities—*perverts!* I know your game all right, it's all filth!

[*The* PLAYERS *are about to leave.* GUIL *has remained detached.*]

GUIL [*casually*] Do you like a bet?

[*The* TRAGEDIANS *turn and look interested. The* PLAYER *comes forward.*]

PLAYER What kind of bet did you have in mind?

[GUIL *walks half the distance towards the* PLAYER, *stops with his foot over the coin.*]

GUIL   Double or quits.

PLAYER   Well . . . heads.

[GUIL *raises his foot. The* PLAYER *bends. The* TRAGEDIANS *crowd round. Relief and congratulations. The* PLAYER *picks up the coin.* GUIL *throws him a second coin.*]

GUIL   Again?

[*Some of the* TRAGEDIANS *are for it, others against.*]

GUIL   Evens.

[*The* PLAYER *nods and tosses the coin.*]

GUIL   Heads.

[*It is. He picks it up.*]

Again.

[GUIL *spins coin.*]

PLAYER   Heads.

[*It is.* PLAYER *picks up coin. He has two coins again. He spins one.*]

GUIL   Heads.

[*It is.* GUIL *picks it up. Then tosses it immediately.*]

PLAYER [*fractional hesitation*]   Tails.

[*But it's heads.* GUIL *picks it up.* PLAYER *tosses down his last coin by way of paying up, and turns away.* GUIL *doesn't pick it up; he puts his foot on it.*]

GUIL   Heads.

PLAYER   No!

[*Pause. The* TRAGEDIANS *are against this.*]

[*Apologetically.*]   They don't like the odds.

GUIL [*lifts his foot, squats; picks up the coin still squatting; looks up*] You were right
—heads. [*Spins it, slaps his hand on it, on the floor.*] Heads I win.

PLAYER   No.

GUIL [*uncovers coin*]   Right again. [*Repeat.*] Heads I win.

PLAYER   No.

GUIL [*uncovers coin*]   And right again. [*Repeat.*] Heads I win.
PLAYER   No!

[*He turns away, the* TRAGEDIANS *with him.* GUIL *stands up, comes close.*]

GUIL   Would you believe it? [*Stands back, relaxes, smiles.*] Bet me the year of my birth doubled is an odd number.
PLAYER   *Your* birth—!
GUIL   If you don't trust me don't bet with me.
PLAYER   Would you trust *me?*
GUIL   *Bet* me then.
PLAYER   My birth?
GUIL   Odd numbers you win.
PLAYER   You're on—

[*The* TRAGEDIANS *have come forward, wide awake.*]

GUIL   Good. Year of your birth. Double it. Even numbers I win, odd numbers I lose.

[*Silence. An awful sigh as the* TRAGEDIANS *realize that any number doubled is even. Then a terrible row as they object. Then a terrible silence.*]

PLAYER   We have no money.

[GUIL *turns to him.*]

GUIL   Ah. Then what *have* you got?

[*The* PLAYER *silently brings* ALFRED *forward.* GUIL *regards* ALFRED *sadly.*]

Was it for this?
PLAYER   It's the best we've got.
GUIL [*looking up and around*]   Then the times are bad indeed.

[*The* PLAYER *starts to speak, protestation, but* GUIL *turns on him viciously.*]

The very *air* stinks.

[*The* PLAYER *moves back.* GUIL *moves down to the footlights and turns.*]

Come here, Alfred.

[ALFRED *moves down and stands, frightened and small.*]

[*Gently.*] Do you lose often?
ALFRED   Yes, sir.

GUIL   Then what could you have left to lose?
ALFRED   Nothing, sir.

[*Pause.* GUIL *regards him.*]

GUIL   Do you like being . . . an actor?
ALFRED   No, sir.

[GUIL *looks around, at the audience.*]

GUIL   You and I, Alfred—we could create a dramatic precedent here.

[*And* ALFRED, *who has been near tears, starts to sniffle.*]

Come, come, Alfred, this is no way to fill the theatres of Europe.

[*The* PLAYER *has moved down, to remonstrate with* ALFRED. GUIL *cuts him off again.*]

[*Viciously.*] Do you know any good plays?
PLAYER   Plays?
ROS [*coming forward, faltering shyly*]   Exhibitions. . . .
GUIL   I thought you said you were actors.
PLAYER [*dawning*]   Oh. Oh well, we are. We are. But there hasn't been much call—
GUIL   You lost. Well then—one of the Greeks, perhaps? You're familiar with the tragedies of antiquity, are you? The great homicidal classics? Matri, patri, fratri, sorrori, uxori and it goes without saying—
ROS   Saucy——
GUIL   —Suicidal—hm? Maidens aspiring to godheads——
ROS   And vice versa——
GUIL   Your kind of thing, is it?
PLAYER   Well, no. I can't say it is, really. We're more of the blood, love and rhetoric school.
GUIL   Well, I'll leave the choice to you, if there is anything to choose between them.
PLAYER   They're hardly divisible, sir—well, I can do you blood and love without the rhetoric, and I can do you blood and rhetoric without the love, and I can do you all three concurrent or consecutive, but I can't do you love and rhetoric without the blood. Blood is compulsory—they're all blood, you see.
GUIL   Is that what people want?
PLAYER   It's what we do. [*Small pause. He turns away.*]

[GUIL *touches* ALFRED *on the shoulder.*]

GUIL [*wry, gentle*]   Thank you: we'll let you know.

[*The* PLAYER *has moved upstage.* ALFRED *follows.*]

PLAYER [*to* TRAGEDIANS] Thirty-eight!

ROS [*moving across, fascinated and hopeful*] Position?

PLAYER Sir?

ROS One of your—tableaux?

PLAYER No, sir.

ROS Oh.

PLAYER [*to the* TRAGEDIANS, *now departing with their cart, already taking various props off it*] Entrances there and there [*indicating upstage*].

[*The* PLAYER *has not moved his position for his last four lines. He does not move now.* GUIL *waits.*]

GUIL Well . . . aren't you going to change into your costume?

PLAYER I never change out of it, sir.

GUIL Always in character.

PLAYER That's it.

[*Pause.*]

GUIL Aren't you going to—come *on?*

PLAYER I *am* on.

GUIL But if you *are* on, you can't *come* on. *Can* you?

PLAYER I *start* on.

GUIL But it hasn't *started.* Go on. We'll look out for you.

PLAYER I'll give you a wave.

[*He does not move. His immobility is now pointed, and getting awkward. Pause.* ROS *walks up to him till they are face to face.*]

ROS Excuse me.

[*Pause. The* PLAYER *lifts his downstage foot. It was covering* GUIL'S *coin.* ROS *puts his foot on the coin. Smiles.*]

Thank you.

[*The* PLAYER *turns and goes.* ROS *has bent for the coin.*]

GUIL [*moving out*] Come on.

ROS I say—that was lucky.

GUIL [*turning*] What?

ROS It was tails.

[*He tosses the coin to* GUIL *who catches it. Simultaneously—a lighting change sufficient to alter the exterior mood into interior, but nothing violent.*

And OPHELIA *runs on in some alarm, holding up her skirts—followed by* HAMLET.

OPHELIA *has been sewing and she holds the garment. They are both mute.* HAMLET, *with his doublet all unbraced, no hat upon his head, his stockings fouled, ungartered and downgyved to his ankle, pale as his shirt, his knees knocking each other . . . and with a look so piteous, he takes her by the wrist and holds her hard, then he goes to the length of his arm, and with his other hand over his brow, falls to such perusal of her face as he would draw it. . . . At last, with a little shaking of his arm, and thrice his head waving up and down, he raises a sigh so piteous and profound that it does seem to shatter all his bulk and end his being. That done he lets her go, and with his head over his shoulder turned, he goes out backwards without taking his eyes off her . . . she runs off in the opposite direction.*

ROS *and* GUIL *have frozen.* GUIL *unfreezes first. He jumps at* ROS.]

GUIL   Come on!

[*But a flourish—enter* CLAUDIUS *and* GERTRUDE, *attended.*]

CLAUDIUS   Welcome, dear Rosencrantz . . . [*he raises a hand at* GUIL *while* ROS *bows*—GUIL *bows late and hurriedly*] . . . and Guildenstern.

[*He raises a hand at* ROS *while* GUIL *bows to him*—ROS *is still straightening up from his previous bow and halfway up he bows down again. With his head down, he twists to look at* GUIL, *who is on the way up.*]

> Moreover that we did much long to see you.
> The need we have to use you did provoke
> Our hasty sending.

[ROS *and* GUIL *still adjusting their clothing for* CLAUDIUS'*s presence.*]

> Something have you heard
> Of Hamlet's transformation, so call it.
> Sith nor th' exterior nor the inward man
> Resembles that it was. What it should be,
> More than his father's death, that thus hath put him,
> So much from th'understanding of himself,
> I cannot dream of, I entreat you both
> That, being of so young days brought up with him
> And sith so neighboured to his youth and haviour
> That you vouchsafe your rest here in our court
> Some little time, so by your companies
> To draw him on to pleasures, and to gather
> So much as from occasion you may glean,
> Whether aught to us unknown afflicts him thus,
> That opened lies within our remedy.

GERTRUDE   Good [*fractional suspense*] gentlemen . . .

[*They both bow.*]

He hath much talked of you.
And sure I am, two men there is not living
To whom he more adheres. If it will please you
To show us so much gentry and goodwill
As to expand your time with us awhile
For the supply and profit of our hope,
Your visitation shall receive such thanks
As fits a king's remembrance.

ROS   Both your majesties
Might, by the sovereign power you have of us,
Put your dread pleasures more into command
Than to entreaty.

GUIL   But we both obey.
And here give up ourselves in the full bent
To lay our service freely at your feet,
To be commanded.

CLAUDIUS   Thanks, Rosencrantz [*turning to* ROS *who is caught unprepared, while* GUIL *bows*] and gentle Guildenstern [*turning to* GUIL *who is bent double*].

GERTRUDE [*correcting*]   Thanks, Guildenstern [*turning to* ROS, *who bows as* GUIL *checks upward movement to bow too—both bent double, squinting at each other*] . . . and gentle Rosencrantz [*turning to* GUIL, *both straightening up—*GUIL *checks again and bows again*].
And I beseech you instantly to visit
My too much changed son. Go, some of you,
And bring these gentlemen where Hamlet is.

[*Two* ATTENDANTS *exit backwards, indicating that* ROS *and* GUIL *should follow.*]

GUIL   Heaven make our presence and our practices
Pleasant and helpful to him.

GERTRUDE   Ay, amen!

[ROS *and* GUIL *move towards a downstage wing. Before they get there,* POLONIUS *enters. They stop and bow to him. He nods and hurries upstage to* CLAUDIUS. *They turn to look at him.*]

POLONIUS   The ambassadors from Norway, my good lord, are joyfully returned.

CLAUDIUS   Thou still hast been the father of good news.

POLONIUS   Have I, my lord? Assure you, my good liege,
I hold my duty as I hold my soul,
Both to my God and to my gracious King;
And I do think, or else this brain of mine
Hunts not the trail of policy so sure

As it hath used to do, that I have found
The very cause of Hamlet's lunacy. . . .

[*Exeunt—leaving* ROS *and* GUIL.]

ROS   I want to go home.

GUIL   Don't let them confuse you.

ROS   I'm out of my step here——

GUIL   We'll soon be home and high—dry and home—I'll——

ROS   It's all over my *depth*——

GUIL   —I'll hie you home and——

ROS   —out of my head——

GUIL   —dry you high and——

ROS [*cracking high*]   —over my step over my head body!—I tell you it's all stopping to a death, it's boding to a depth, stepping to a head, it's all heading to a dead stop——

GUIL [*the nursemaid*]   There! . . . and we'll soon be home and dry . . . and *high* and dry. . . . [*Rapidly.*] Has it ever happened to you that all of a sudden and for no reason at all you haven't the faintest idea how to spell the word—"wife"—or "house"—because when you write it down you just can't remember ever having seen those letters in that order before . . . ?

ROS   I remember——

GUIL   Yes?

ROS   I remember when there were no questions.

GUIL   There were always questions. To exchange one set for another is no great matter.

ROS   Answers, yes. There were answers to everything.

GUIL   You've forgotten.

ROS [*flaring*]   I haven't forgotten—how I used to remember my own name—and yours, oh *yes!* There were answers everywhere you *looked.* There was no question about it—people knew who I was and if they didn't they asked and I told them.

GUIL   You did, the trouble is, each of them is . . . plausible, without being instinctive. All your life you live so close to truth, it becomes a permanent blur in the corner of your eye, and when something nudges it into outline it is like being ambushed by a grotesque. A man standing in his saddle in the half-lit half-alive dawn banged on the shutters and called two names. He was just a hat and a cloak levitating in the grey plume of his own breath, but when he called we came. That much is certain—we came.

ROS   Well I can tell you I'm sick to death of it. I don't care one way or another, so why don't you make up your mind.

GUIL We can't afford anything quite so arbitrary. Nor did we come all this way for a christening. All *that*—preceded us. But we are comparatively fortunate; we might have been left to sift the whole field of human nomenclature, like two blind men looting a bazaar for their own portraits. . . . At least we are presented with alternatives.

ROS Well as from now——

GUIL —But not choice.

ROS You made me look ridiculous in there.

GUIL I looked just as ridiculous as you did.

ROS [*an anguished cry*] Consistency is all I ask!

GUIL [*low, wry rhetoric*] Give us this day our daily mask.

ROS [*a dying fall*] I want to go home. [*Moves.*] Which way did we come in? I've lost my sense of direction.

GUIL The only beginning is birth and the only end is death—if you can't count on that, what can you count on?

[*They connect again.*]

ROS We don't owe anything to anyone.

GUIL We've been caught up. Your smallest action sets off another somewhere else, and is set off by it. Keep an eye open, an ear cocked. Tread warily, follow instructions. We'll be all right.

ROS For how long?

GUIL Till events have played themselves out. There's a logic at work—it's all done for you, don't worry. Enjoy it. Relax. To be taken in hand and led, like being a child again, even without the innocence, a child—it's like being given a prize, an extra slice of childhood when you least expect it, as a prize for being good, or compensation for never having had one. . . . Do I contradict myself?

ROS I can't remember. . . . What have we got to go on?

GUIL We have been briefed. Hamlet's transformation. What do you recollect?

ROS Well, he's changed, hasn't he? The exterior and inward man fails to resemble——

GUIL Draw him on to pleasures—glean what afflicts him.

ROS Something more than his father's death——

GUIL He's always talking about us—there aren't two people living whom he dotes on more than us.

ROS We cheer him up—find out what's the matter——

GUIL Exactly, it's a matter of asking the right questions and giving away as little as we can. It's a game.

ROS And then we can go?

GUIL   And receive such thanks as fits a king's remembrance.

ROS   I like the sound of that. What do you think he means by remembrance?

GUIL   He doesn't forget his friends.

ROS   Would you care to estimate?

GUIL   Difficult to say, really—some kings tend to be amnesiac, others I suppose —the opposite, whatever that is. . . .

ROS   Yes—but——

GUIL   Elephantine . . . ?

ROS   Not how long—how much?

GUIL   *Retentive*—he's a very retentive king, a royal retainer. . . .

ROS   What are you playing at?

GUIL   Words, words. They're all we have to go on.

[*Pause.*]

ROS   Shouldn't we be doing something—constructive?

GUIL   What did you have in mind? . . . A short, blunt human pyramid . . . ?

ROS   We could go.

GUIL   Where?

ROS   After him.

GUIL   Why? They've got us placed now—if we start moving around, we'll all be chasing each other all night.

[*Hiatus.*]

ROS [*at footlights*]   How very intriguing! [*Turns*] I feel like a spectator—an appalling business. The only thing that makes it bearable is the irrational belief that somebody interesting will come on in a minute. . . .

GUIL   See anyone?

ROS   No. You?

GUIL   No. [*At footlights*] What a fine persecution—to be kept intrigued without ever quite being enlightened. . . . [*Pause*] We've had no practice.

ROS   We could play at questions.

GUIL   What good would that do?

ROS   Practice!

GUIL   Statement! One—love.

ROS   Cheating!

GUIL   How?

ROS   I hadn't started yet.

GUIL   Statement. Two—love.

ROS   Are you counting that?

GUIL   What?

ROS   Are you counting that?

GUIL   Foul! No repetitions. Three—love. First game to . . .

ROS   I'm not going to play if you're going to be like that.

GUIL   Whose serve?

ROS   Hah?

GUIL   Foul! No grunts. Love—one.

ROS   Whose go?

GUIL   Why?

ROS   Why not?

GUIL   What for?

ROS   Foul! No synonyms! One—all.

GUIL   What in God's name is going on?

ROS   Foul! No rhetoric. Two—one.

GUIL   What does it all add up to?

ROS   Can't you guess?

GUIL   Were you addressing me?

ROS   Is there anyone else?

GUIL   Who?

ROS   How would I know?

GUIL   Why do you ask?

ROS   Are you serious?

GUIL   Was that rhetoric?

ROS   No.

GUIL   Statement! Two—all. Game point.

ROS   What's the matter with you today?

GUIL   When?

ROS   What?

GUIL   Are you deaf?

ROS   Am I dead?

GUIL   Yes or no?

ROSR   Is there a choice?

GUIL   Is there a God?

ROS   Foul! No *non sequiturs,* three—two, one game all.

1062

GUIL [*seriously*] What's your name?

ROS What's yours?

GUIL I asked you first.

ROS Statement. One—love.

GUIL What's your name when you're at home?

ROS What's yours?

GUIL When I'm at home?

ROS Is it different at home?

GUIL What home?

ROS Haven't you got one?

GUIL Why do you ask?

ROS What are you driving at?

GUIL [*with emphasis*] What's your name?!

ROS Repetition. Two—love. Match point to me.

GUIL [*seizing him violently*] WHO DO YOU THINK YOU ARE?

ROS Rhetoric! Game and match! [*Pause*] Where's it going to end?

GUIL That's the question.

ROS It's *all* questions.

GUIL Do you think it matters?

ROS Doesn't it matter to you?

GUIL Why should it matter?

ROS What does it matter why?

GUIL [*teasing gently*] Doesn't it *matter* why it matters?

ROS [*rounding on him*] What's the *matter* with you?

[*Pause.*]

GUIL It doesn't matter.

ROS [*voice in the wilderness*] . . . What's the game?

GUIL What are the rules?

[*Enter* HAMLET *behind, crossing the stage, reading a book—as he is about to disappear* GUIL *notices him.*]

GUIL [*sharply*] Rosencrantz!

ROS [*jumps*] What!

[HAMLET *goes. Triumph dawns on them, they smile.*]

GUIL There! How was that?

ROS Clever!

GUIL   Natural?

ROS   Instinctive.

GUIL   Got it in your head?

ROS   I take my hat off to you.

GUIL   Shake hands.

[*They do.*]

ROS   Now I'll try you—Guil—!

GUIL   —Not yet—catch me unawares.

ROS   Right.

[*They separate. Pause. Aside to* GUIL.]

Ready?

GUIL [*explodes*]   Don't be stupid.

ROS   Sorry.

[*Pause.*]

GUIL [*snaps*]   Guildenstern!

ROS [*jumps*]   What?

[*He is immediately crestfallen,* GUIL *is disgusted.*]

GUIL   Consistency is all I ask!

ROS [*quietly*]   Immortality is all I seek. . . .

GUIL [*dying fall*]   Give us this day our daily week. . . .

[*Beat.*]

ROS   Who was that?

GUIL   Didn't you know him?

ROS   He didn't know me.

GUIL   He didn't see you.

ROS   I didn't see him.

GUIL   We shall see. I *hardly* knew him, he's changed.

ROS   You could see that?

GUIL   Transformed.

ROS   How do you know?

GUIL   Inside and out.

ROS   I see.

GUIL   He's not himself.

ROS   He's changed.

GUIL   I could see that.

[*Beat.*]

Glean what afflicts him.

ROS   Me?

GUIL   Him.

ROS   How?

GUIL   Question and answer. Old ways are the best ways.

ROS   He's afflicted.

GUIL   You question. I'll answer.

ROS   He's not himself, you know.

GUIL   I'm him, you see.

[*Beat.*]

ROS   Who am I then?

GUIL   You're yourself.

ROS   And he's you?

GUIL   Not a bit of it.

ROS   Are you afflicted?

GUIL   That's the idea. Are you ready?

ROS   Let's go back a bit.

GUIL   I'm afflicted.

ROS   I see.

GUIL   Glean what afflicts me.

ROS   Right.

GUIL   Question and answer.

ROS   How should I begin?

GUIL   Address me.

ROS   My dear Guildenstern!

GUIL [*quietly*]   You've forgotten—haven't you?

ROS   My dear Rosencrantz!

GUIL [*great control*]   I don't think you quite understand. What we are attempting is a hypothesis in which *I* answer for *him,* while *you* ask me questions.

ROS   Ah! Ready?

GUIL   You know what to do?

ROS   What?

GUIL   Are you stupid?

ROS   Pardon?

GUIL   Are you deaf?

ROS   Did you speak?

GUIL [*admonishing*]   Not now——

ROS   Statement.

GUIL [*shouts*]   Not now! [*Pause*] If I had any doubts, or rather hopes, they are dispelled. What could we possibly have in common except our situation? [*They separate and sit.*] Perhaps he'll come back this way.

ROS   Should we go?

GUIL   Why?

[*Pause.*]

ROS [*starts up. Snaps fingers*]   Oh! You mean—you pretend to be *him,* and I ask you questions!

GUIL [*dry*]   Very good.

ROS   You had me confused.

GUIL   I could see I had.

ROS   How should I begin?

GUIL   Address me.

[*They stand and face each other, posing.*]

ROS   My honoured Lord!

GUIL   My dear Rosencrantz!

[*Pause.*]

ROS   Am I pretending to be you, then?

GUIL   Certainly not. If you like. Shall we continue?

ROS   Question and answer.

GUIL   Right.

ROS   Right. My honoured lord!

GUIL   My dear fellow!

ROS   How are you?

GUIL   Afflicted!

ROS   Really? In what way?

GUIL Transformed.

ROS Inside or out?

GUIL Both.

ROS I see. [*Pause*] Not much new there.

GUIL Go into details. *Delve.* Probe the background, establish the situation.

ROS So—so your uncle is the king of Denmark?!

GUIL And my father before him.

ROS His father before him?

GUIL No, my father before him.

ROS But surely——

GUIL You might well ask.

ROS Let me get it straight. Your father was king. You were his only son. Your father dies. You are of age. Your uncle becomes king.

GUIL Yes.

ROS Unorthodox.

GUIL Undid me.

ROS Undeniable. Where were you?

GUIL In Germany.

ROS Usurpation, then.

GUIL He slipped in.

ROS Which reminds me.

GUIL Well, it would.

ROS I don't want to be personal.

GUIL It's common knowledge.

ROS Your mother's marriage.

GUIL He slipped in.

[*Beat.*]

ROS [*lugubriously*] His body was still warm.

GUIL So was hers.

ROS Extraordinary.

GUIL Indecent.

ROS Hasty.

GUIL Suspicious.

ROS It makes you think.

GUIL Don't think I haven't thought of it.

ROS And with her husband's brother.

GUIL They were close.

ROS She went to him——

GUIL —Too close——

ROS —for comfort.

GUIL It looks bad.

ROS It adds up.

GUIL Incest to adultery.

ROS Would you go so far?

GUIL Never.

ROS To sum up: your father, whom you love, dies, you are his heir, you come back to find that hardly was the corpse cold before his young brother popped onto his throne and into his sheets, thereby offending both legal and natural practice. Now why exactly are you behaving in this extraordinary manner?

GUIL I can't imagine! [*Pause*] But all that is well known, common property. Yet he sent for us. And we did come.

ROS [*alert, ear cocked*] I say! I heard music——

GUIL We're here.

ROS —Like a band—I thought I heard a band.

GUIL Rosencrantz . . .

ROS [*absently, still listening*] What?

[*Pause, short.*]

GUIL [*gently wry*] Guildenstern . . .

ROS [*irritated by the repetition*] *What?*

GUIL Don't you discriminate at all?

ROS [*turning dumbly*] Wha'?

[*Pause.*]

GUIL Go and see if he's there.

ROS Who?

GUIL There.

[ROS *goes to an upstage wing, looks, returns, formally making his report.*]

ROS Yes.

GUIL What is he doing?

1068

[ROS *repeats movement.*]

ROS   Talking.

GUIL   To himself?

[ROS *starts to move.* GUIL *cuts in impatiently.*]

Is he alone?

ROS   No.

GUIL   Then he's not talking to himself, is he?

ROS   Not *by* himself. . . . Coming this way, I think. [*Shiftily*] Should we go?

GUIL   Why? We're marked now.

[HAMLET *enters, backwards, talking, followed by* POLONIUS, *upstage,* ROS *and* GUIL *occupy the two downstage corners looking upstage.*]

HAMLET   . . . for you yourself, sir, should be as old as I am if like a crab you could go backward.

POLONIUS [*aside*]   Though this be madness, yet there is method in it. Will you walk out of the air, my lord?

HAMLET   Into my grave.

POLONIUS   Indeed, that's out of the air.

[HAMLET *crosses to upstage exit,* POLONIUS *asiding unintelligibly until——*]

My lord, I will take my leave of you.

HAMLET   You cannot take from me anything that I will more willingly part withal —except my life, except my life, except my life. . . .

POLONIUS [*crossing downstage*]   Fare you well, my lord. [*To* ROS] You go to seek Lord Hamlet? There he is.

ROS [*to* POLONIUS]   God save you sir.

[POLONIUS *goes.*]

GUIL [*calls upstage to* HAMLET]   My honoured lord!

ROS   My most dear lord!

[HAMLET *centred upstage, turns to them.*]

HAMLET   My excellent good friends! How dost thou Guildenstern? [*Coming downstage with an arm raised to* ROS, GUIL *meanwhile bowing to no greeting.* HAMLET *corrects himself. Still to* ROS] Ah Rosencrantz!

[*They laugh good-naturedly at the mistake. They all meet midstage, turn upstage to walk,* HAMLET *in the middle, arm over each shoulder.*]

HAMLET   Good lads how do you both?

BLACKOUT

ACT II

[HAMLET, ROS *and* GUIL *talking, the continuation of the previous scene. Their conversation, on the move, is indecipherable at first. The first intelligible line is* HAMLET'*s, coming at the end of a short speech—see Shakespeare Act II, scene ii.*]

HAMLET   S'blood, there is something in this more than natural, if philosophy could find it out.

[*A flourish from the* TRAGEDIANS' *band.*]

GUIL   There are the players.

HAMLET   Gentlemen, you are welcome to Elsinore. Your hands, come then. [*He takes their hands.*] The appurtenance of welcome is fashion and ceremony. Let me comply with you in this garb, lest my extent to the players (which I tell you must show fairly outwards) should more appear like entertainment than yours. You are welcome. [*About to leave.*] But my uncle-father and aunt-mother are deceived.

GUIL   In what, my dear lord?

HAMLET   I am but mad north north-west; when the wind is southerly I know a hawk from a handsaw.

[POLONIUS *enters as* GUIL *turns away.*]

POLONIUS   Well be with you gentlemen.

HAMLET [*to* ROS]   Mark you, Guildenstern [*uncertainly* to GUIL] and you too; at each ear a hearer. That great baby you see there is not yet out of his swaddling clouts. . . . [*He takes* ROS *upstage with him, talking together.*]

POLONIUS   My Lord! I have news to tell you.

HAMLET [*releasing* ROS *and mimicking*]   My lord, I have news to tell you. . . . When Roscius was an actor in Rome . . .

[ROS *comes downstage to rejoin* GUIL.]

POLONIUS [*as he follows* HAMLET *out*]   The actors are come hither my lord.

HAMLET   Buzz, buzz.

1070

[*Exeunt* HAMLET *and* POLONIUS.

ROS *and* GUIL *ponder. Each reluctant to speak first.*]

GUIL Hm?

ROS Yes?

GUIL What?

ROS I thought you . . .

GUIL No.

ROS Ah.

[*Pause.*]

GUIL I think we can say we made some headway.

ROS You think so?

GUIL I think we can say that.

ROS I think we can say he made us look ridiculous.

GUIL We played it close to the chest of course.

ROS [*derisively*] "Question and answer. Old ways are the best ways"! He was scoring off us all down the line.

GUIL He caught us on the wrong foot once or twice, perhaps, but I thought we gained some ground.

ROS [*simply*] He murdered us.

GUIL He might have had the edge.

ROS [*roused*] Twenty-seven—three, and you think he might have had the edge?! He *murdered* us.

GUIL What about our evasions?

ROS Oh, our evasions were lovely. "Were you sent for?" he says. "My lord, we were sent for. . . ." I didn't know where to put myself.

GUIL He had six rhetoricals—

ROS It was question and answer, all right. Twenty-seven questions he got out in ten minutes, and answered three. I was waiting for you to *delve*. "When is he going to start *delving?*" I asked myself.

GUIL —And two repetitions.

ROS Hardly a leading question between us.

GUIL We got his *symptoms,* didn't we?

ROS Half of what he said meant something else, and the other half didn't mean anything at all.

GUIL Thwarted ambition—a sense of grievance, that's my diagnosis.

ROS Six rhetorical and two repetition, leaving nineteen, of which we answered fifteen. And what did we get in return? He's depressed! . . . Denmark's a prison and he'd rather live in a nutshell; some shadow-play about the nature of ambition, which never got down to cases, and finally one direct question which might have led somewhere, and led in fact to his illuminating claim to tell a hawk from a handsaw.

[*Pause.*]

GUIL When the wind is southerly.

ROS And the weather's clear.

GUIL And when it isn't he can't.

ROS He's at the mercy of the elements. [*Licks his finger and holds it up—facing audience*] Is that southerly?

[*They stare at audience.*]

GUIL It doesn't *look* southerly. What made you think so?

ROS I didn't *say* I think so. It could be northerly for all I know.

GUIL I wouldn't have thought so.

ROS Well, if you're going to be dogmatic.

GUIL Wait a minute—we came from roughly south according to a rough map.

ROS I see. Well, which way did we come in? [GUIL *looks round vaguely.*] Roughly.

GUIL [*clears his throat*] In the morning the sun would be easterly. I think we can assume that.

ROS That it's morning?

GUIL If it is, and the sun is over *there* [*his right as he faces the audience*] for instance, *that* [*front*] would be northerly. On the other hand, if it is not morning and the sun is over *there* [*his left*] . . . *that* . . . [*lamely*] would *still* be northerly. [*Picking up*] To put it another way, if we came from down there [*front*] and it is morning, the sun would be up there [*his left*], and if it is actually over *there* [*his right*] and it's still morning, we must have come from up *there* [*behind him*], and if *that* is southerly [*his left*] and the sun is really over *there* [*front*], then it's the afternoon. However, if none of these is the case——

ROS Why don't you go and have a look?

GUIL Pragmatism?!—is that all you have to offer? You seem to have no conception of where we stand! You won't find the answer written down for you in the bowl of a compass—I can tell you that. [*Pause*] Besides, you can never tell this far north—it's probably dark out there.

ROS I merely suggest that the position of the sun, if it is out, would give you a rough idea of the time; alternatively, the clock, if it is going, would give you a rough idea of the position of the sun. I forget which you're trying to establish.

GUIL I'm trying to establish the direction of the wind.

ROS There isn't any wind. *Draught,* yes.

GUIL In that case, the origin. Trace it to its source and it might give us a rough idea of the way we came in—which might give us a rough idea of south, for further reference.

ROS It's coming up through the floor. [*He studies the floor.*] That can't be south, can it?

GUIL That's not a direction. Lick your toe and wave it around a bit.

ROS *considers the distance of his foot.*

ROS No, I think you'd have to lick it for me.

[*Pause.*]

GUIL I'm prepared to let the whole matter drop.

ROS Or I could lick yours, of course.

GUIL No thank you.

ROS I'll even wave it around for you.

GUIL [*down* ROS*'s throat*] What in God's name is the matter with you?

ROS Just being friendly.

GUIL [*retiring*] Somebody might come in. It's what we're counting on, after all. Ultimately.

[*Good pause.*]

ROS Perhaps they've all trampled each other to death in the rush. . . . Give them a shout. Something provocative. *Intrigue* them.

GUIL Wheels have been set in motion, and they have their own pace, to which we are . . . condemned. Each move is dictated by the previous one—that is the meaning of order. If we start being arbitrary it'll just be a shambles; at least, let us hope so. Because if we happened, just happened to discover, or even suspect, that our spontaneity was part of their order we'd know that we were lost. [*He sits.*] A Chinaman of the Tang Dynasty—and, by which definition, a philosopher — dreamed he was a butterfly, and from that moment he was never quite sure that he was not a butterfly dreaming it was a Chinese philosopher. Envy him; in his two-fold security.

[*A good pause.* ROS *leaps up and bellows at the audience.*]

ROS Fire!

[GUIL *jumps up.*]

GUIL   Where?

ROS   It's all right—I'm demonstrating the misuse of free speech. To prove that it exists. [*He regards the audience, that is the direction, with contempt—and other directions, then front again.*] Not a move. They should burn to death in their shoes. [*He takes out one of his coins. Spins it. Catches it. Looks at it. Replaces it.*]

GUIL   What was it?

ROS   What?

GUIL   Heads or tails?

ROS   Oh, I didn't look.

GUIL   Yes you did.

ROS   Oh, did I? [*He takes out a coin, studies it.*] Quite right—it rings a bell.

GUIL   What's the last thing you remember?

ROS   I don't wish to be reminded of it.

GUIL   We cross our bridges when we come to them and burn them behind us, with nothing to show for our progress except a memory of the smell of smoke, and a presumption that once our eyes watered.

[ROS *approaches him brightly, holding a coin between finger and thumb. He covers it with his other hand, draws his fists apart and holds them for* GUIL. GUIL *considers them. Indicates the left hand,* ROS *opens it to show it empty.*]

ROS   No.

[*Repeat process.* GUIL *indicates left hand again.* ROS *shows it empty.*]

Double bluff!

[*Repeat process*—GUIL *taps one hand, then the other hand, quickly.* ROS *inadvertently shows that both are empty.* ROS *laughs as* GUIL *turns upstage,* ROS *stops laughing, looks around his feet, pats his clothes, puzzled.*

POLONIUS *breaks that up by entering upstage followed by the* TRAGEDIANS *and* HAMLET.]

POLONIUS [*entering*]   Come sirs.

HAMLET   Follow him, friends. We'll hear a play tomorrow. [*Aside to the* PLAYER, *who is the last of the* TRAGEDIANS:] Dost thou hear me, old friend? Can you play *The Murder of Gonzago?*

PLAYER   Ay, my lord.

HAMLET   We'll ha't tomorrow night. You could for a need study a speech of some dozen or sixteen lines which I would set down and insert in't, could you not?

PLAYER   Ay, my lord.

HAMLET   Very well. Follow that lord, and look you mock him not.

[*The* PLAYER *crossing downstage, notes* ROS *and* GUIL. *Stops.* HAMLET *crossing downstage addresses them without pause.*]

HAMLET   My good friends, I'll leave you till tonight. You are welcome to Elsinore.

ROS   Good, my lord.

[HAMLET *goes.*]

GUIL   So you've caught up.

PLAYER [*coldly*]   Not yet, sir.

GUIL   Now mind your tongue, or we'll have it out and throw the rest of you away, like a nightingale at a Roman feast.

ROS   Took the very words out of my mouth.

GUIL   You'd be *lost* for words.

ROS   You'd be tongue-tied.

GUIL   Like a mute in a monologue.

ROS   Like a nightingale at a Roman feast.

GUIL   Your diction will go to pieces.

ROS   Your lines will be cut.

GUIL   To dumbshows.

ROS   And dramatic pauses.

GUIL   You'll never *find* your tongue.

ROS   Lick your lips.

GUIL   Taste your tears.

ROS   Your breakfast.

GUIL   You won't know the difference.

ROS   There won't be any.

GUIL   We'll take the very words out of your mouth.

ROS   So you've caught on.

GUIL   So you've caught up.

PLAYER [*tops*]   Not yet! [*Bitterly*] You left us.

GUIL   Ah! I'd forgotten—you performed a dramatic spectacle on the way. Yes, I'm sorry we had to miss it.

PLAYER [*bursts out*]   We can't look each other in the face! [*Pause, more in control*] You don't understand the humiliation of it—to be tricked out of the single assumption which makes our existence viable—that somebody is *watching.* . . . The plot was two corpses gone before we caught sight of ourselves, stripped naked in the middle of nowhere and pouring ourselves down a bottomless well.

ROS   Is *that* thirty-eight?

PLAYER [*lost*]   There we were—demented children mincing about in clothes that no one ever wore, speaking as no man ever spoke, swearing love in wigs and rhymed couplets, killing each other with wooden swords, hollow protestations of faith hurled after empty promises of vengeance—and every gesture, every pose, vanishing into the thin unpopulated air. We ransomed our dignity to the clouds, and the uncomprehending birds listened. [*He rounds on them.*] Don't you see?! We're *actors*—we're the opposite of people! [*They recoil nonplussed, his voice calms.*] Think in your head, *now,* think of the most . . . *private* . . . *secret* . . . *intimate* thing you have ever done secure in the knowledge of its privacy. . . . [*He gives them —and the audience—a good pause.* ROS *takes on a shifty look.*] Are you thinking of it? [*He strikes with his voice and his head.*] *Well, I saw you do it!*

[ROS *leaps up, dissembling madly.*]

ROS   You never! It's a lie! [*He catches himself with a giggle in a vacuum and sits down again.*]

PLAYER   We're actors. . . . We pledged our identities, secure in the conventions of our trade, that someone would be watching. And then, gradually, no one was. We were caught high and dry. It was not until the murderer's long soliloquy that we were able to look around: frozen as we were in profile, our eyes searched you out, first confidently, then hesitantly, then desperately as each patch of turf, each log, every exposed corner in every direction proved uninhabited, and all the while the murderous king addressed the horizon with his dreary interminable guilt. . . . Our heads began to move, wary as lizards, the corpse of unsullied Rosalinda peeped through his fingers, and the King faltered. Even then, habit and a stubborn trust that our audience spied upon us from behind the nearest bush, forced our bodies to blunder on long after they had emptied of meaning, until like runaway carts they dragged to a halt. No one came forward. No one shouted at us. The silence was unbreakable, it imposed itself upon us; it was obscene. We took off our crowns and swords and cloth of gold and moved silent on the road to Elsinore.

[*Silence. Then* GUIL *claps solo with slow measured irony.*]

GUIL   Brilliantly re-created—if these eyes could weep! . . . Rather strong on metaphor, mind you. No criticism—only a matter of taste. And so here you are — with a vengeance. That's a figure of speech . . . isn't it? Well let's say we're made up for it, for you may have no doubt whom to thank for your performance at the court.

ROS   We are counting on you to take him out of himself. You are the pleasures which we draw him on to—[*he escapes a fractional giggle but recovers immediately*] and by that I don't mean your usual filth; you can't treat royalty like people with normal perverted desires. They know nothing of that and you know nothing of them, to your mutual survival. So give him a good clean show suitable for all the family, or you can rest assured you'll be playing the tavern tonight.

GUIL   Or the night after.

ROS   Or not.

PLAYER   We already have an entry here. And always have had.

GUIL   You've played for him before?

PLAYER   Yes sir.

ROS   And what's *his* bent?

PLAYER   Classical.

ROS   Saucy!

GUIL   What will you play?

PLAYER   *The Murder of Gonzago.*

GUIL   Full of fine cadence and corpses.

PLAYER   Pirated from the Italian. . . .

ROS   What is it about?

PLAYER   It's about a King and Queen. . . .

GUIL   Escapism! What else?

PLAYER   Blood——

GUIL   —Love and rhetoric.

PLAYER   Yes. [*Going*]

GUIL   Where are you going?

PLAYER   I can come and go as I please.

GUIL   You're evidently a man who knows his way around.

PLAYER   I've been here before.

GUIL   We're still finding our feet.

PLAYER   I should concentrate on not losing your heads.

GUIL   Do you speak from knowledge?

PLAYER   Precedent.

GUIL   You've been here before.

PLAYER   And I know which way the wind is blowing.

GUIL   Operating on two levels, are we?! How clever! I expect it comes naturally to you, being in the business so to speak.

[*The* PLAYER's *grave face does not change. He makes to move off again.* GUIL *for the second time cuts him off.*]

The truth is, we value your company, for want of any other. We have been left so much to our own devices—after a while one welcomes the uncertainty of being left to other people's.

PLAYER   Uncertainty is the normal state. You're nobody special.

[*He makes to leave again.* GUIL *loses his cool.*]

GUIL   But for God's sake what are we supposed to *do?!*

PLAYER   Relax. Respond. That's what people do. You can't go through life questioning your situation at every turn.

GUIL   But we don't know what's going on, or what to do with ourselves. We don't know how to *act*.

PLAYER   Act natural. You know why you're here at least.

GUIL   We only know what we're told, and that's little enough. And for all we know it isn't even true.

PLAYER   For all anyone knows, nothing is. Everything has to be taken on trust; truth is only that which is taken to be true. It's the currency of living. There may be nothing behind it, but it doesn't make any difference so long as it is honoured. One acts on assumptions. What do you assume?

ROS   Hamlet is not himself, outside or in. We have to glean what afflicts him.

GUIL   He doesn't give much away.

PLAYER   Who does, nowadays?

GUIL   He's—melancholy.

PLAYER   Melancholy?

ROS   Mad.

PLAYER   How is he mad?

ROS   Ah. [*To* GUIL] How is he mad?

GUIL   More morose than mad, perhaps.

PLAYER   Melancholy.

GUIL   Moody.

ROS   He has moods.

PLAYER   Of moroseness?

GUIL   Madness. And yet.

ROS   Quite.

GUIL   For instance.

ROS   He talks to himself, which might be madness.

GUIL   If he didn't talk sense, which he does.

ROS   Which suggests the opposite.

PLAYER   Of what?

[*Small pause.*]

GUIL   I think I have it. A man talking sense to himself is no madder than a man talking nonsense not to himself.

ROS   Or just as mad.

GUIL   Or just as mad.

ROS   And he does both.
GUIL   So there you are.
ROS   Stark raving sane.

[*Pause.*]

PLAYER   Why?
GUIL   Ah. [*to* ROS] Why?
ROS   Exactly.
GUIL   Exactly what?
ROS   Exactly why.
GUIL   Exactly why *what?*
ROS   What?
GUIL   *Why?*
ROS   Why what, exactly?
GUIL   Why is he mad?!
ROS   *I* don't know!

[*Beat.*]

PLAYER   The old man thinks he's in love with his daughter.
ROS [*appalled*]   Good God! We're out of our depth here.
PLAYER   No, no, no—*he* hasn't got a daughter—the old man thinks he's in love with *his* daughter.
ROS   The old man is?
PLAYER   Hamlet, in love with the old man's daughter, the old man thinks.
ROS   Ha! It's beginning to make sense! Unrequited passion!

[*The* PLAYER *moves.*]

GUIL [*fascist.*]   Nobody leaves this room! [*Pause, lamely*] Without a *very* good reason.
PLAYER   Why not?
GUIL   All this strolling about is getting too arbitrary by half—I'm rapidly losing my grip. From now on reason will prevail.
PLAYER   I have lines to learn.
GUIL   Pass!

[*The* PLAYER *passes into one of the wings.* ROS *cups his hands and shouts into the opposite one.*]

ROS   Next!

[*But no one comes.*]

GUIL What do you expect?

ROS Something . . . someone . . . nothing.

[*They sit facing front.*]

Are you hungry?

GUIL No, are you?

ROS [*thinks*] No. You remember that coin?

GUIL No.

ROS I think I lost it.

GUIL What coin?

ROS I don't remember exactly.

[*Pause.*]

GUIL Oh, that coin . . . clever.

ROS I can't remember how I did it.

GUIL It probably comes natural to you.

ROS Yes, I've got a show-stopper there.

GUIL Do it again.

[*Slight pause.*]

ROS We can't afford it.

GUIL Yes, one must think of the future.

ROS It's the normal thing.

GUIL To have one. One is, after all, having it all the time . . . now . . . and now . . . and now. . . .

ROS It could go on for ever. Well, not for *ever,* I suppose. [*Pause*] Do you ever think of yourself as actually *dead,* lying in a box with a lid on it?

GUIL No.

ROS Nor do I, really. . . . It's silly to be depressed by it. I mean one thinks of it like being *alive* in a box, one keeps forgetting to take into account the fact that one is *dead* . . . which should make all the difference . . . shouldn't it? I mean, you'd never *know* you were in a box, would you? It would be just like being *asleep* in a box. Not that I'd like to sleep in a box, mind you, not without any air—you'd wake up dead, for a start, and then where would you be? Apart from inside a box. That's the bit I don't like, frankly. That's why I don't think of it. . . .

[GUIL *stirs restlessly, pulling his cloak round him.*]

Because you'd be helpless, wouldn't you? Stuffed in a box like that, I mean you'd be in there for ever. Even taking into account the fact that you're dead, it isn't a pleasant thought. *Especially* if you're dead, really . . . *ask* yourself, if I asked you straight off—I'm going to stuff you in this box now, would you rather be alive or dead? Naturally, you'd prefer to be alive. Life in a box is better than no life at all, I expect. You'd have a chance at least. You could lie there thinking—well, at least I'm not dead! In a minute someone's going to bang on the lid and tell me to come out. [*Banging the floor with his fists.*] "Hey you, whatsyername! Come out of there!"

GUIL [*jumps up savagely*]   You don't have to flog it to death!

[*Pause.*]

ROS   I wouldn't think about it if I were you. You'd only get depressed. [*Pause.*] Eternity is a terrible thought. I mean, where's it going to end? [*Pause, then brightly.*] Two early Christians chanced to meet in Heaven. "Saul of Tarsus yet!" cried one. "What are you doing here?!" . . . "Tarsus-Schmarsus," replied the other, "I'm Paul already." [*He stands up restlessly and flaps his arms.*] They don't care. We count for nothing. We could remain silent till we're green in the face, they wouldn't come.

GUIL   Blue, red.

ROS   A Christian, a Moslem and a Jew chanced to meet in a closed carriage. . . . "Silverstein!" cried the Jew. "Who's your friend?" . . . "His name's Abdullah," replied the Moslem, "but he's no friend of mine since he became a convert." [*He leaps up again, stamps his foot and shouts into the wings.*] All right, we know you're in there! Come out talking! [*Pause*] We have no control. None at all . . . [*He paces.*] Whatever became of the moment when one first knew about death? There must have been one, a moment, in childhood when it first occurred to you that you don't go on for ever. It must have been shattering—stamped into one's memory. And yet I can't remember it. It never occurred to me at all. What does one make of that? We must be born with an intuition of mortality. Before we know the words for it, before we know that there are words, out we come, bloodied and squalling with the knowledge that for all the compasses in the world, there's only one direction, and time is its only measure. [*He reflects, getting more desperate and rapid.*] A Hindu, a Buddhist and a lion-tamer chanced to meet, in a circus on the Indo-Chinese border. [*He breaks out.*] They're taking us for granted! Well, I won't stand for it. In future, notice will be taken. [*He wheels again to face into the wings.*] Keep out, then! I forbid anyone to enter! [*No one comes. Breathing heavily.*] That's better. . . .

[*Immediately, behind him a grand procession enters, principally* CLAUDIUS, GERTRUDE, POLONIUS *and* OPHELIA. CLAUDIUS *takes* ROS's *elbow as he passes and is immediately deep in conversation: the context is Shakespeare Act III, scene i.* GUIL *still faces front as* CLAUDIUS, ROS, *etc., pass upstage and turn.*]

GUIL   Death followed by eternity . . . the worst of both worlds. It *is* a terrible thought.

[*He turns upstage in time to take over the conversation with* CLAUDIUS. GERTRUDE *and* ROS *head downstage.*]

GERTRUDE Did he receive you well?

ROS Most like a gentleman.

GUIL [*returning in time to take it up*] But with much forcing of his disposition.

ROS [*a flat lie and he knows it and shows it, perhaps catching* GUIL'*s eye*]
Niggard of question, but of our demands most free in his reply.

GERTRUDE Did you assay him to any pastime?

ROS Madam, it so fell out that certain players
We o'erraught on the way; of these we told him
And there did seem in him a kind of joy
To hear of it. They are here about the court,
And, as I think, they have already order
This night to play before him.

POLONIUS Tis most true
And he beseeched me to entreat your Majesties
To hear and see the matter.

CLAUDIUS With all my heart, and it doth content me
To hear him so inclined.
Good gentlemen, give him a further edge
And drive his purpose into these delights.

ROS We shall, my lord

CLAUDIUS [*leading out procession*]
Sweet Gertrude, leave us, too.
For we have closely sent for Hamlet hither,
That he, as t'were by accident, may here
Affront Ophelia. . . .

[*Exeunt* CLAUDIUS *and* GERTRUDE.]

ROS [*peevish*] Never a moment's peace! In and out, on and off, they're coming at us from all sides.

GUIL You're never satisfied.

ROS Catching us on the trot. . . . Why can't *we* go by *them?*

GUIL What's the difference?

ROS I'm going.

[ROS *pulls his cloak round him.* GUIL *ignores him. Without confidence* ROS *heads upstage. He looks out and comes back quickly.*]

He's coming

GUIL What's he doing?

ROS Nothing.

GUIL   He must be doing something.

ROS   Walking.

GUIL   On his hands?

ROS   No, on his feet.

GUIL   Stark naked?

ROS   Fully dressed.

GUIL   Selling toffee apples?

ROS   Not that I noticed.

GUIL   You could be wrong?

ROS   I don't think so.

[*Pause.*]

GUIL   I can't for the life of me see how we're going to get into conversation.

[HAMLET *enters upstage, and pauses, weighing up the pros and cons of making his quietus.*

ROS *and* GUIL *watch him.*]

ROS   Nevertheless, I suppose one might say that this was a chance. . . . One might well . . . accost him. . . . Yes, it definitely looks like a chance to me. . . . Something on the lines of a direct informal approach . . . man to man . . . straight from the shoulder. . . . Now look here, what's it all about . . . sort of thing. Yes. Yes, this looks like one to be grabbed with both hands. I should say . . . if I were asked. . . . No point in looking at a gift horse till you see the whites of its eyes, etcetera. [*He has moved towards* HAMLET *but his nerve fails. He returns.*] We're overawed, that's our trouble. When it comes to the point we succumb to their personality. . . .

[OPHELIA *enters, with prayerbook, a religious procession of one.*]

HAMLET   Nymph, in thy orisons be all my sins remembered.

[*At his voice she has stopped for him, he catches her up.*]

OPHELIA   Good my lord, how does your honour for this many a day?

HAMLET   I humbly thank you—well, well, well.

[*They disappear talking into the wing.*]

ROS   It's like living in a public park!

GUIL   Very impressive. Yes, I thought your direct informal approach was going to stop this thing dead in its tracks there. If I might make a suggestion—shut up and sit down. Stop being perverse.

ROS [*near tears*]   I'm not going to stand for it!

[*A* FEMALE FIGURE, *ostensibly the* QUEEN, *enters.* ROS *marches up behind her, puts his hands over her eyes and says with a desperate frivolity.*]

ROS Guess who?!

PLAYER [*having appeared in a downstage corner*] Alfred!

[ROS *lets go, spins around. He has been holding* ALFRED, *in his robe and blond wig.* PLAYER *is in the downstage corner still.* ROS *comes down to that exit. The* PLAYER *does not budge. He and* ROS *stand toe to toe.*]

ROS Excuse me.

[*The* PLAYER *lifts his downstage foot.* ROS *bends to put his hand on the floor. The* PLAYER *lowers his foot.* ROS *screams and leaps away.*]

PLAYER [*gravely*] I beg your pardon.

GUIL [*to* ROS] What did he do?

PLAYER I put my foot down.

ROS My hand was on the floor!

GUIL You put your hand under his foot?

ROS I——

GUIL What for?

ROS I thought——[*Grabs* GUIL] Don't leave me!

[*He makes a break for an exit. A* TRAGEDIAN *dressed as a* KING *enters.* ROS *recoils, breaks for the opposite wing. Two cloaked* TRAGEDIANS *enter.* ROS *tries again but another* TRAGEDIAN *enters, and* ROS *retires to midstage. The* PLAYER *claps his hands matter-of-factly.*]

PLAYER Right! We haven't got much time.

GUIL What are you doing?

PLAYER Dress rehearsal. Now if you two wouldn't mind just moving back . . . there . . . good. . . . [*To* TRAGEDIANS] Everyone ready? And for goodness' sake, remember what we're doing. [*To* ROS *and* GUIL] We always use the same costumes more or less, and they forget what they are supposed to be *in* you see. . . . Stop picking your nose, Alfred. When Queens have to they do it by a cerebral process passed down in the blood. . . . Good. Silence! Off we go!

PLAYER-KING Full thirty times hath Phoebus' cart——

[PLAYER *jumps up angrily.*]

PLAYER No, no, no! Dumbshow first, your confounded majesty! [*To* ROS *and* GUIL] They're a bit out of practice, but they always pick up wonderfully for the deaths—it brings out the poetry in them.

GUIL How nice.

1084

PLAYER There's nothing more unconvincing than an unconvincing death.

GUIL I'm sure.

[PLAYER *claps his hands.*]

PLAYER Act One—moves now.

[*The mime. Soft music from a recorder.* PLAYER-KING *and* PLAYER-QUEEN *embrace. She kneels and makes a show of protestation to him. He takes her up, declining his head upon her neck. He lies down. She, seeing him asleep, leaves him.*]

GUIL What is the dumbshow for?

PLAYER Well, it's a device, really—it makes the action that follows more or less comprehensible; you understand, we are tied down to a language which makes up in obscurity what it lacks in style.

[*The mime (continued)—enter another. He takes off the* SLEEPER'*s crown, kisses it. He has brought in a small bottle of liquid. He pours the poison in the* SLEEPER'*s ear, and leaves him. The* SLEEPER *convulses heroically, dying.*]

ROS Who was that?

PLAYER The King's brother and uncle to the Prince.

GUIL Not exactly fraternal.

PLAYER Not exactly avuncular, as time goes on.

[*The* QUEEN *returns, makes passionate action, finding the* KING *dead. The* POISONER *comes in again, attended by two others (the two in cloaks). The* POISONER *seems to console with her. The dead body is carried away. The* POISONER *woos the* QUEEN *with gifts. She seems harsh awhile but in the end accepts his love. End of mime, at which point, the wail of a woman in torment and* OPHELIA *appears, wailing, closely followed by* HAMLET *in a hysterical state, shouting at her, circling her, both midstage.*]

HAMLET Go to. I'll no more on't; it hath made me mad!

[*She falls on her knees weeping.*]

I say we will have no more marriage! [*His voice drops to include the* TRAGEDIANS, *who have frozen.*] Those that are married already [*he leans close to the* PLAYER-QUEEN *and* POISONER, *speaking with quiet edge*] all but one shall live. [*He smiles briefly at them without mirth, and starts to back out, his parting shot rising again.*] The rest shall keep as they are. [*As he leaves,* OPHELIA *tottering upstage, he speaks into her ear a quick clipped sentence.*] To a nunnery, go.

[*He goes out.* OPHELIA *falls on to her knees upstage, her sobs barely audible. A slight silence.*]

PLAYER-KING Full thirty times hath Phoebus' cart——

[CLAUDIUS *enters with* POLONIUS *and goes over to* OPHELIA *and lifts her to her feet. The* TRAGEDIANS *jump back with heads inclined.*]

CLAUDIUS   Love? His affections do not that way tend.
Or what he spake, though it lacked form a little,
Was not like madness. There's something
In his soul o'er which his melancholy sits on
Brood, and I do doubt the hatch and the
Disclose will be some danger; which for to
Prevent I have in quick determination thus set
It down: he shall with speed to England . . .

[*Which carries the three of them*—CLAUDIUS, POLONIUS, OPHELIA—*out of sight. The* PLAYER *moves, clapping his hands for attention.*]

PLAYER   Gentlemen! [*They look at him.*] It doesn't seem to be coming. We are not getting it at all. [*To* GUIL] What did you think?

GUIL   What was I supposed to think?

PLAYER [*to* TRAGEDIANS]   You're not getting across!

[ROS *had gone halfway up to* OPHELIA; *he returns.*]

ROS   That didn't look like love to me.

GUIL   Starting from scratch again . . .

PLAYER [*to* TRAGEDIANS]   It was a *mess.*

ROS [*to* GUIL]   It's going to be chaos on the night.

GUIL   Keep back—we're spectators.

PLAYER   Act Two! Positions!

GUIL   Wasn't that the end?

PLAYER   Do you call that an ending?—with practically everyone on his feet? My goodness no—over your dead body.

GUIL   How am I supposed to take that?

PLAYER   Lying down. [*He laughs briefly and in a second has never laughed in his life.*] There's a design at work in all art—surely you know that? Events must play themselves out to aesthetic, moral and logical conclusion.

GUIL   And what's that, in this case?

PLAYER   It never varies—we aim at the point where everyone who is marked for death dies.

GUIL   Marked?

PLAYER   Between "just desserts" and "tragic irony" we are given quite a lot of scope for our particular talent. Generally speaking, things have gone about as far as they can possibly go when things have got about as bad as they reasonably get.

1086

[*He switches on a smile.*]

GUIL Who decides?

PLAYER [*switching off his smile*] *Decides?* It is *written.*

[*He turns away.* GUIL *grabs him and spins him back violently.*]

[*Unflustered.*] Now if you're going to be subtle, we'll miss each other in the dark. I'm referring to oral tradition. So to speak.

[GUIL *releases him.*]

We're tragedians, you see. We follow directions—there is no *choice* involved. The bad end unhappily, the good unluckily. That is what tragedy means. [*Calling*] Positions!

[*The* TRAGEDIANS *have taken up positions for the continuation of the mime: which in this case means a love scene, sexual and passionate, between the* QUEEN *and the* POISONER/KING.]

Player Go!

[*The lovers begin. The* PLAYER *contributes a breathless commentary for* ROS *and* GUIL.]

Having murdered his brother and wooed the widow—the poisoner mounts the throne! Here we see him and his queen give rein to their unbridled passion! She little knowing that the man she holds in her arms——!

ROS Oh, I say—here—really! You can't do that!

PLAYER Why not?

ROS Well, really—I mean, people want to be *entertained*—they don't come expecting sordid and gratuitous filth.

PLAYER You're wrong—they do! Murder, seduction and incest—what do you want—*jokes?*

ROS I want a good story, with a beginning, middle and end.

PLAYER [*to* GUIL] And you?

GUIL I'd prefer art to mirror life, if it's all the same to you.

PLAYER It's all the same to me, sir. [*To the grappling* LOVERS] All right, no need to indulge yourselves. [*They get up. To* GUIL] I come on in a minute. Lucianus, nephew to the king! [*Turns his attention to the* TRAGEDIANS.] Next!

[*They disport themselves to accommodate the next piece of mime, which consists of the* PLAYER *himself exhibiting an excitable anguish (choreographed, stylized) leading to an impassioned scene with the* QUEEN (*cf. "The Closet Scene," Shakespeare Act III, scene iv*) *and a very stylized reconstruction of a* POLONIUS *figure being stabbed behind the arras (the murdered* KING *to stand in for* POLONIUS) *while the* PLAYER *himself continues his breathless commentary for the benefit of* ROS *and* GUIL.]

PLAYER Lucianus, nephew to the king . . . usurped by his uncle and shattered by his mother's incestuous marriage . . . loses his reason . . . throwing the court into turmoil and disarray as he alternates between bitter melancholy and unrestricted lunacy . . . staggering from the suicidal [*a pose*] to the homicidal [*here he kills* "POLONIUS"] . . . he at last confronts his mother and in a scene of provocative ambiguity—[*a somewhat oedipal embrace*] begs her to repent and recant——[*He springs up, still talking.*] The King—[*he pushes forward the* POISONER/KING] tormented by guilt—haunted by fear—decides to despatch his nephew to England— and entrusts this undertaking to two smiling accomplices—friends—courtiers—to two spies——

[*He has swung round to bring together the* POISONER/KING *and the two cloaked* TRAGEDIANS; *the latter kneel and accept a scroll from the* KING.]

—giving them a letter to present to the English court——!
And so they depart—on board ship——

[*The two* SPIES *position themselves on either side of the* PLAYER, *and the three of them sway gently in unison, the motion of a boat; and then the* PLAYER *detaches himself.*]

—and they arrive——

[*One* SPY *shades his eyes at the horizon.*]

—and disembark—and present themselves before the English king——[*He wheels round.*] The English king——

[*An exchange of headgear creates the* ENGLISH KING *from the remaining player—that is, the* PLAYER *who played the original murdered king.*]

But where is the Prince? Where indeed? The plot has thickened—a twist of fate and cunning has put into their hands a letter that seals their deaths!

[*The two spies present their letter; the* ENGLISH KING *reads it and orders their deaths. They stand up as the* PLAYER *whips off their cloaks preparatory to execution.*]

Traitors hoist by their own petard?—or victims of the gods?—we shall never know!

[*The whole mime has been fluid and continuous but now* ROS *moves forward and brings it to a pause. What brings* ROS *forward is the fact that under their cloaks the two Spies are wearing coats identical to those worn by* ROS *and* GUIL, *whose coats are now covered by their cloaks.* ROS *approaches "his"* SPY *doubtfully. He does not quite understand why the coats are familiar.* ROS *stands close, touches the coat, thoughtfully. . . .*]

ROS   Well, if it isn't——! No, wait a minute, don't tell me—it's a long time since —where was it? Ah, this is taking me back to—when was it? I know you, don't I? I never forget a face—(*he looks into the* SPY'S *face*) . . . not that I know yours, that is. For a moment I thought—no, I don't know you, do I? Yes, I'm afraid you're quite wrong. You must have mistaken me for someone else.

1088

[GUIL *meanwhile has approached the other* SPY, *brow creased in thought.*]

PLAYER [*to* GUIL]   Are you familiar with this play?

GUIL   No.

PLAYER   A slaughterhouse—eight corpses all told. It brings out the best in us.

GUIL [*tense, progressively rattled during the whole mime and commentary*]   You!—What do *you* know about *death?*

PLAYER   It's what the actors do best. They have to exploit whatever talent is given to them, and their talent is dying. They can die heroically, comically, ironically, slowly, suddenly, disgustingly, charmingly, or from a great height. My own talent is more general. I extract significance from melodrama, a significance which it does not in fact contain; but occasionally, from out of this matter, there escapes a thin beam of light that, seen at the right angle, can crack the shell of mortality.

ROS   Is that all they can do—die?

PLAYER   No, no—they kill beautifully. In fact some of them kill even better than they die. The rest die better than they kill. They're a team.

ROS   Which ones are which?

PLAYER   There's not much in it.

GUIL [*fear, derision*]   Actors! The mechanics of cheap melodrama! That isn't *death!* [*More quietly.*] You scream and choke and sink to your knees, but it doesn't bring death home to anyone—it doesn't catch them unawares and start the whisper in their skulls that says—"One day you are going to die." [*He straightens up.*] You die so many times; how can you expect them to believe in your death?

PLAYER   On the contrary, it's the only kind they do believe. They're conditioned to it. I had an actor once who was condemned to hang for stealing a sheep—or a lamb, I forget which—so I got permission to have him hanged in the middle of a play—had to change the plot a bit but I thought it would be effective, you know —and you wouldn't believe it, he just *wasn't* convincing! It was impossible to suspend one's disbelief—and what with the audience jeering and throwing pea-nuts, the whole thing was a *disaster!*—he did nothing but cry all the time—right out of character—just stood there and cried. . . . Never again.

[*In good humour he has already turned back to the mime: the two* SPIES *awaiting execution at the hands of the* PLAYER, *who takes his dagger out of his belt.*]

Audiences know what to expect, and that is all that they are prepared to believe in. [*To the* SPIES] Show!

[*The* SPIES *die at some length, rather well.*

The light has begun to go, and it fades as they die, and as GUIL *speaks.*]

GUIL   No, no, no . . . you've got it all wrong . . . you can't act death. The *fact* of it is nothing to do with seeing it happen—it's not gasps and blood and falling about—that isn't what makes it death. It's just a man failing to reappear, that's all

1089

—now you see him, now you don't, that's the only thing that's real: here one minute and gone the next and never coming back—an exit, unobtrusive and unannounced, a disappearance gathering weight as it goes on, until, finally, it is heavy with death.

[*The two* SPIES *lie still, barely visible. The* PLAYER *comes forward and throws the* SPIES' *cloaks over their bodies.* ROS *starts to clap, slowly.*]

BLACKOUT.

[*A second of silence, then much noise. Shouts . . . "The King rises!" . . . "Give o'er the play!" . . . and cries for "Lights, lights, lights!"*

When the light comes, after a few seconds, it comes as a sunrise.

The stage is empty save for two cloaked figures sprawled on the ground in the approximate positions last held by the dead SPIES. *As the light grows, they are seen to be* ROS *and* GUIL, *and to be resting quite comfortably.* ROS *raises himself on his elbows and shades his eyes as he stares into the auditorium. Finally:*]

ROS That must be east, then. I think we can assume that.

GUIL I'm assuming nothing.

ROS No, it's all right. That's the sun. East.

GUIL [*looks up*] Where?

ROS I watched it come up.

GUIL No . . . it was light all the time, you see, and you opened your eyes very, very slowly. If you'd been facing back there you'd be swearing *that* was east.

ROS [*standing up*] You're a mass of prejudice.

GUIL I've been taken in before.

ROS [*looks out over the audience*] Rings a bell.

GUIL They're waiting to see what we're going to do.

ROS Good old east.

GUIL As soon as we make a move they'll come pouring in from every side, shouting obscure instructions, confusing us with ridiculous remarks, messing us about from here to breakfast and getting our names wrong.

[ROS *starts to protest but he has hardly opened his mouth before:*]

CLAUDIUS [*off stage—with urgency*] Ho, Guildenstern!

[GUIL *is still prone. Small pause*]

ROS AND GUIL You're wanted. . . .

1090

[GUIL *furiously leaps to his feet as* CLAUDIUS *and* GERTRUDE *enter. They are in some desperation.*]

CLAUDIUS   Friends both, go join you with some further aid: Hamlet in madness hath Polonius slain, and from his mother's closet hath he dragged him. Go seek him out; speak fair and bring the body into the chapel. I pray you haste in this. [*As he and* GERTRUDE *are hurrying out*] Come Gertrude, we'll call up our wisest friends and let them know both what we mean to do. . . .

[*They've gone.* ROS *and* GUIL *remain quite still.*]

GUIL   Well . . .
ROS   Quite . . .
GUIL   Well, well.
ROS   Quite, quite. [*Nods with spurious confidence*] Seek him out. [*Pause*] Etcetera.
GUIL   Quite.
ROS   Well. [*Small pause*] Well, that's a step in the right direction.
GUIL   You didn't like him?
ROS   Who?
GUIL   Good God, I hope more tears are shed for *us!* . . .
ROS   Well, it's *progress,* isn't it? Something positive. Seek him out. [*Looks round without moving his feet*] Where does one begin . . . ? [*Takes one step towards the wings and halts*]
GUIL   Well, that's a step in the right direction.
ROS   You think so? He could be anywhere.
GUIL   All right—you go that way, I'll go this way.
ROS   Right.

[*They walk towards opposite wings.* ROS *halts.*]

No.

[GUIL *halts.*]

You go this way—I'll go that way.
GUIL   All right.

[*They march towards each other, cross.* ROS *halts.*]

ROS   Wait a minute.

[GUIL *halts.*]

I think we should stick together. He might be violent.
GUIL   Good point. I'll come with you.

[GUIL *marches across to* ROS. *They turn to leave.* ROS *halts.*]

ROS No, I'll come with *you.*
GUIL Right.

[*They turn, march across to the opposite wing.* ROS *halts.*]

GUIL *halts.*

ROS I'll come with *you, my* way.
GUIL All right.

[*They turn again and march across.* ROS *halts.* GUIL *halts.*]

ROS I've just thought. If we both go, he could come *here.* That would be stupid, wouldn't it?
GUIL All right—I'll stay, you go.
ROS Right.

[GUIL *marches to midstage.*]

I say.

[GUIL *wheels and carries on marching back towards* ROS, *who starts marching downstage. They cross.* ROS *halts.*]

I've just thought.

[GUIL *halts.*]

We ought to stick together; he might be violent.
GUIL Good point.

[GUIL *marches down to join* ROS. *They stand still for a moment in their original positions.*]

Well, at last we're getting somewhere.

[*Pause*]

Of course, he might not come.
ROS [*airily*] Oh, he'll come.
GUIL We'd have some explaining to do.
ROS He'll come. [*Airily wanders upstage*] Don't worry—take my word for it— [*Looks out—is appalled*] He's coming!
GUIL What's he doing?
ROS Walking.
GUIL Alone?

1092

ROS   No.

GUIL   Not walking?

ROS   No.

GUIL   Who's with him?

ROS   The old man.

GUIL   Walking?

ROS   No.

GUIL   Ah. That's an opening if ever there was one. [*And is suddenly galvanized into action*] Let him walk into the trap!

ROS   What trap.

GUIL   You stand there! Don't let him pass!

[*He positions* ROS *with his back to one wing, facing* HAMLET'*s entrance.*

GUIL *positions himself next to* ROS, *a few feet away, so that they are covering one side of the stage, facing the opposite side.* GUIL *unfastens his belt.* ROS *does the same. They join the two belts, and hold them taut between them.* ROS'*s trousers slide slowly down.*

HAMLET *enters opposite, slowly, dragging* POLONIUS'*s body. He enters upstage, makes a small arc and leaves by the same side, a few feet downstage.*

ROS *and* GUIL, *holding the belts taut, stare at him in some bewilderment.*

HAMLET *leaves, dragging the body. They relax the strain on the belts.*]

ROS   That was close.

GUIL   There's a limit to what two people can do.

[*They undo the belts:* ROS *pulls up his trousers.*]

ROS [*worriedly—he walks a few paces towards* HAMLET'*s exit*]   He was dead.

GUIL   Of course he's dead!

ROS [*turns to* GUIL]   Properly.

GUIL [*angrily*]   Death's death, isn't it?

[ROS *falls silent. Pause.*]

Perhaps he'll come back this way.

[ROS *starts to take off his belt.*]

No, no, no!—if we can't learn by experience, what else have we got?

[ROS *desists.*]

[*Pause*]

ROS Give him a shout.

GUIL I thought we'd been into all that.

ROS [*shouts*] Hamlet!

GUIL Don't be absurd.

ROS [*shouts*] Lord Hamlet!

[HAMLET *enters.* ROS *is a little dismayed.*]

What have you done, my lord, with the dead body?

HAMLET Compounded it with dust, whereto 'tis kin.

ROS Tell us where 'tis, that we may take it thence and bear it to the chapel.

HAMLET Do not believe it.

ROS Believe what?

HAMLET That I can keep your counsel and not mine own. Besides, to be demanded of a sponge, what replication should be made by the son of a king?

ROS Take you me for a sponge, my lord?

HAMLET Ay, sir, that soaks up the King's countenance, his rewards, his authorities. But such officers do the King best service in the end. He keeps them, like an ape, in the corner of his jaw, first mouthed, to be last swallowed. When he needs what you have gleaned, it is but squeezing you and, sponge, you shall be dry again.

ROS I understand you not, my lord.

HAMLET I am glad of it: a knavish speech sleeps in a foolish ear.

ROS My lord, you must tell us where the body is and go with us to the King.

HAMLET The body is with the King, but the King is not with the body. The King is a thing——

GUIL A thing, my lord——?

HAMLET Of nothing. Bring me to him.

[HAMLET *moves resolutely towards one wing. They move with him, shepherding. Just before they reach the exit,* HAMLET, *apparently seeing* CLAUDIUS *approaching from off stage, bends low in a sweeping bow.* ROS *and* GUIL, *cued by* HAMLET, *also bow deeply—a sweeping ceremonial bow with their cloaks swept round them.* HAMLET, *however, continues the movement into an about-turn and walks off in the opposite direction.* ROS *and* GUIL, *with their heads low, do not notice.*

No one comes on. ROS *and* GUIL *squint upwards and find that they are bowing to nothing.*

CLAUDIUS *enters behind them. At first words they leap up and do a double-take.*]

CLAUDIUS How now? What hath befallen?

ROS Where the body is bestowed, my lord, we cannot get from him.

CLAUDIUS But where is he?

ROS [*fractional hesitation*] Without, my lord; guarded to know your pleasure.

CLAUDIUS [*moves*] Bring him before us.

[*This hits* ROS *between the eyes but only his eyes show it. Again his hesitation is fractional. And then with great deliberation he turns to* GUIL.]

ROS Ho! Bring in the lord.

[*Again there is a fractional moment in which* ROS *is smug,* GUIL *is trapped and betrayed.* GUIL *opens his mouth and closes it.*

The situation is saved: HAMLET, *escorted, is marched in just as* CLAUDIUS *leaves.* HAMLET *and his* ESCORT *cross the stage and go out, following* CLAUDIUS.

Lighting changes to Exterior.]

ROS [*moves to go*] All right, then?
GUIL [*does not move; thoughtfully*] And yet it doesn't seem enough; to have breathed such significance. Can that be all? And why us?—anybody would have done. And we have contributed nothing.
ROS It was a trying episode while it lasted, but they've done with us now.
GUIL Done what?
ROS I don't pretend to have understood. Frankly, I'm not very interested. If they won't tell us, that's their affair. [*He wanders upstage towards the exit.*] For my part, I'm only glad that that's the last we've seen of him—[*And he glances off stage and turns front, his face betraying the fact that* HAMLET *is there.*]
GUIL I knew it wasn't the end. . . .
ROS [*high*] What else?!
GUIL We're taking him to England. What's he doing?

[ROS *goes upstage and returns.*]

ROS Talking.
GUIL To himself?

[ROS *makes to go,* GUIL *cuts him off.*]

Is he alone?
ROS No, he's with a soldier.
GUIL Then he's not talking to himself, is he?
ROS Not *by* himself. . . . Should we go?
GUIL Where?
ROS Anywhere.
GUIL Why?

[ROS *puts up his head listening.*]

ROS There it is again. [*In anguish*] All I ask is a change of ground!
GUIL [*coda*] Give us this day our daily round. . . .

[HAMLET *enters behind them, talking with a soldier in arms.* ROS *and* GUIL *don't look round.*]

ROS   They'll have us hanging about till we're dead. At least. And the weather will change. [*Looks up*] The spring can't last for ever.

HAMLET   Good sir, whose powers are these?

SOLDIER   They are of Norway, sir.

HAMLET   How purposed sir, I pray you?

SOLDIER   Against some part of Poland.

HAMLET   Who commands them, sir?

SOLDIER   The nephew to old Norway, Fortinbras.

ROS   We'll be cold. The summer won't last.

GUIL   It's autumnal.

ROS [*examining the ground*]   No leaves.

GUIL   Autumnal—nothing to do with leaves. It is to do with a certain brownness at the edges of the day. . . . Brown is creeping up on us, take my word for it. . . . Russets and tangerine shades of old gold flushing the very outside edge of the senses . . . deep shining ochres, burnt umber and parchments of baked earth —reflecting on itself and through itself, filtering the light. At such times, perhaps, coincidentally, the leaves might fall, somewhere, by repute. Yesterday was blue, like smoke.

ROS [*head up, listening*]   I got it again then.

[*They listen—faintest sound of* TRAGEDIANS' *band.*]

HAMLET   I humbly thank you, sir.

SOLDIER   God by you, sir. [*Exit*]

[ROS *gets up quickly and goes to* HAMLET.]

ROS   Will it please you go, my lord?

HAMLET   I'll be with you straight. Go you a little before.

[HAMLET *turns to face upstage.* ROS *returns down.* GUIL *faces front, doesn't turn.*]

GUIL   Is he here?

ROS   Yes.

GUIL   What's he doing?

[ROS *looks over his shoulder.*]

ROS   Talking.

GUIL   To himself?

ROS   Yes.

[*Pause.* ROS *makes to leave.*]

ROS   He said we can go. Cross my heart.

GUIL   I like to know where I am. Even if I don't know where I am, I like to know *that.* If we go there's no knowing.

ROS   No knowing what?

GUIL   If we'll ever come back.

ROS   We don't want to come back.

GUIL   That may very well be true, but do we want to go?

ROS   We'll be free.

GUIL   I don't know. It's the same sky.

ROS   We've come this far.

[*He moves towards exit.* GUIL *follows him.*]

And besides, anything could happen yet.

[*They go.*]

BLACKOUT

ACT III

[*Opens in pitch darkness.*
Soft sea sounds.

After several seconds of nothing, a voice from the dark . . .]

GUIL   Are you there?

ROS   Where?

GUIL [*bitterly*]   A flying start. . . .

[*Pause*]

ROS   Is that you?

GUIL   Yes.

ROS   How do you know?

GUIL [*explosion*]   Oh-for-God's-sake!

ROS   We're not finished, then?

GUIL   Well, we're here, aren't we?

ROS   Are we? I can't see a thing.

GUIL   You can still *think,* can't you?

ROS   I think so.

GUIL   You can still *talk.*

ROS   What should I say?

GUIL   Don't bother. You can *feel,* can't you?

ROS   Ah! There's life in me yet!

GUIL   What are you feeling?

ROS   A leg. Yes, it feels like my leg.

GUIL   How does it feel?

ROS   Dead.

GUIL   Dead?

ROS [*panic*]   I can't feel a thing!

GUIL   Give it a pinch! [*Immediately he yelps.*]

ROS   Sorry.

GUIL   Well, that's cleared that up.

[*Longer pause: the sound builds a little and identifies itself—the sea. Ship timbers, wind in the rigging, and then shouts of sailors calling obscure but inescapably nautical instructions from all directions, far and near: A short list:*]

Hard a larboard!
Let go the stays!
Reef down me hearties!
Is that you, cox'n?
Hel-llo! Is that you?
Hard a port!
Easy as she goes!
Keep her steady on the lee!
Haul away, lads!
[*Snatches of sea shanty maybe.*]
Fly the jib!
Tops'l up, me maties!

[*When the point has been well made and more so.*]

ROS   We're on a boat. [*Pause.*] Dark, isn't?

GUIL   Not for night.

ROS   No, not for *night.*

GUIL   Dark for day.

[*Pause*]

ROS   Oh yes, it's dark for *day!*

GUIL   We must have gone north, of course.

ROS   Off course?

1098

GUIL   Land of the midnight sun, that is.
ROS   Of course.

[*Some sailor sounds.*

A lantern is lit upstage—in fact by HAMLET.

The stage lightens disproportionately—

Enough to see:

ROS *and* GUIL *sitting downstage.*

Vague shapes of rigging, etc., behind.]

I think it's getting light.
GUIL   Not for night.
ROS   This far north.
GUIL   Unless we're off course.
ROS   [*small pause*]   Of course.

[*A better light—Lantern? Moon? . . . Light. Revealing, among other things, three large man-sized casks on deck, upended, with lids. Spaced but in line. Behind and above—a gaudy striped umbrella, on a pole stuck into the deck, tilted so that we do not see behind it—one of those huge six-foot-diameter jobs. Still dim upstage.* ROS *and* GUIL *still facing front.*]

ROS   Yes, it's lighter than it was. It'll be night soon. This far north. [*Dolefully.*] I suppose we'll have to go to sleep. [*He yawns and stretches.*]
GUIL   Tired?
ROS   No . . . I don't think I'd take to it. Sleep all night, can't see a thing all day. . . . Those eskimos must have a quiet life.
GUIL   Where?
ROS   What?
GUIL   I thought you——[*Relapses*] I've lost all capacity for disbelief. I'm not sure that I could even rise to a little gentle scepticism.

[*Pause*]

ROS   Well, shall we stretch our legs?
GUIL   I don't feel like stretching my legs.
ROS   I'll stretch them for you, if you like.
GUIL   No.
ROSS   We could stretch each other's. That way we wouldn't have to go anywhere.
GUIL   [*pause*]   No, somebody might come in.
ROS   In where?
GUIL   Out here.

ROS   In out here?

GUIL   On deck.

[ROS *considers the floor: slaps it.*]

ROS   Nice bit of planking, that.

GUIL   Yes, I'm very fond of boats myself. I like the way they're—contained. You don't have to worry about which way to go, or whether to go at all—the question doesn't arise, because you're on a *boat,* aren't you? Boats are safe areas in the game of tag . . . the players will hold their positions until the music starts. . . . I think I'll spend most of my life on boats.

ROS   Very healthy.

[ROS *inhales with expectation, exhales with boredom.* GUIL *stands up and looks over the audience.*]

GUIL   One is free on a boat. For a time. Relatively.

ROS   What's it like?

GUIL   Rough.

[ROS *joins him. They look out over the audience.*]

ROS   I think I'm going to be sick.

[GUIL *licks a finger, holds it up experimentally.*]

GUIL   Other side, I think.

[ROS *goes upstage: Ideally a sort of upper deck joined to the downstage lower deck by short steps. The umbrella being on the upper deck.* ROS *pauses by the umbrella and looks behind it.* GUIL *meanwhile has been resuming his own theme—looking out over the audience—*]

Free to move, speak, extemporise, and yet. We have not been cut loose. Our truancy is defined by one fixed star, and our drift represents merely a slight change of angle to it; we may seize the moment, toss it around while the moments pass, a short dash here, an exploration there, but we are brought round full circle to face again the single immutable fact—that we, Rosencrantz and Guildenstern, bearing a letter from one king to another, are taking Hamlet to England.

[*By which time,* ROS *has returned, tiptoeing with great import, teeth clenched for secrecy, gets to* GUIL, *points surreptitiously behind him—and a tight whisper:*]

ROS   I say—*he's there!*

GUIL   [*unsurprised*]   What's he doing?

ROS   Sleeping.

GUIL   It's all right for him.

1100

ROS   What is?

GUIL   He can sleep.

ROS   It's all right for him.

GUIL   He's got us now.

ROS   He can sleep.

GUIL   It's all done for him.

ROS   He's got us.

GUIL   And we've got nothing. [*A cry.*] All I ask is our common due!

ROS   For those in peril on the sea. . . .

GUIL   Give us this day our daily cue.

[*Beat, pause. Sit. Long pause.*]

ROS [*after shifting, looking around*]   What now?

GUIL   What do you mean?

ROS   Well, nothing is happening.

GUIL   We're on a boat.

ROS   I'm aware of that.

GUIL [*angrily*]   Then what do you expect? [*Unhappily.*] We act on scraps of information . . . sifting half-remembered directions that we can hardly separate from instinct.

[ROS *puts a hand into his purse, then both hands behind his back, then holds his fists out.*

GUIL *taps one fist.*

ROS *opens it to show a coin.*

He gives it to GUIL.

He puts his hand back into his purse. Then both hands behind his back, then holds his fists out.

GUIL *taps one.*

ROS *opens it to show a coin. He gives it to* GUIL.

Repeat.

Repeat.

GUIL *getting tense. Desperate to lose.*

Repeat.

GUIL *taps a hand, changes his mind, taps the other, and* ROS *inadvertently reveals that he has a coin in both fists.*]

GUIL   You had money in both hands.

ROS [*embarrassed*]   Yes.

GUIL   Every time?

ROS   Yes.

GUIL   What's the point of that?

ROS [*pathetic*]   I wanted to make you happy.

[*Beat.*]

GUIL   How much did he give you?

ROS   Who?

GUIL   The King. He gave us some money.

ROS   How much did he give you?

GUIL   I asked you first.

ROS   I got the same as you.

GUIL   He wouldn't discriminate between us.

ROS   How much did you get?

GUIL   The same.

ROS   How do you know?

GUIL   You just told me—how do *you* know?

ROS   He wouldn't discriminate between us.

GUIL   Even if he could.

ROS   Which he never could.

GUIL   He couldn't even be sure of mixing us up.

ROS   Without mixing us up.

GUIL [*turning on him furiously*]   Why don't you say something original! No wonder the whole thing is so stagnant! You don't take me up on anything—you just repeat it in a different order.

ROS   I can't think of anything original. I'm only good in support.

GUIL   I'm sick of making the running.

ROS [*humbly*]   It must be your dominant personality. [*Almost in tears*] Oh, what's going to become of us!

[*And* GUIL *comforts him, all harshness gone.*]

GUIL   Don't cry . . . it's all right . . . there . . . there. I'll see we're all right.

ROS   But we've got nothing to go on, we're out on our own.

GUIL   We're on our way to England—we're taking Hamlet there.

ROS   What for?

GUIL   What for? Where have you been?

ROS   When? [*Pause.*] We won't know what to do when we get there.

GUIL   We take him to the King.

ROS   Will *he* be there?

1102

GUIL   No—the king of England.

ROS   He's expecting us?

GUIL   No.

ROS   He won't know what we're playing at. What are we going to *say?*

GUIL   We've got a letter. You remember the letter.

ROS   Do I?

GUIL   Everything is explained in the letter. We count on that.

ROS   Is that it, then?

GUIL   What?

ROS   We take Hamlet to the English king, we hand over the letter—what then?

GUIL   There may be something in the letter to keep us going a bit.

ROS   And if not?

GUIL   Then that's it—we're finished.

ROS   At a loose end?

GUIL   Yes.

[*Pause.*]

ROS   Are there likely to be loose ends? [*Pause.*] Who is the English king?

GUIL   That depends on when we get there.

ROS   What do you think it says?

GUIL   Oh . . . greetings. Expressions of loyalty. Asking of favours, calling in of debts. Obscure promises balanced by vague threats. . . . Diplomacy. Regards to the family.

ROS   And about Hamlet?

GUIL   Oh yes.

ROS   And us—the full background?

GUIL   I should say so.

[*Pause.*]

ROS   So we've got a letter which explains everything.

GUIL   You've got it.

[ROS *takes that literally. He starts to pat his pockets, etc.*]

What's the matter?

ROS   The letter.

GUIL   Have you got it?

ROS   [*rising fear*] Have I? [*Searches frantically.*] Where would I have put it?

GUIL   You can't have lost it.

ROS   I must have!

GUIL   That's odd—I thought he gave it to me.

[ROS *looks at him hopefully.*]

ROS Perhaps he did.

GUIL But you seemed so sure it was *you* who hadn't got it.

ROS [*high*] It *was* me who hadn't got it!

GUIL But if he gave it to me there's no reason why you should have had it in the first place, in which case I don't see what all the fuss is about you *not* having it.

ROS [*pause*] I admit it's confusing.

GUIL This is all getting rather undisciplined. . . . The boat, the night, the sense of isolation and uncertainty . . . all these induce a loosening of the concentration. We must not lose control. Tighten up. Now. Either you have lost the letter or you didn't have it to lose in the first place, in which case the King never gave it to you, in which case he gave it to me, in which case I would have put it into my inside top pocket, in which case [*calmly producing the letter*] . . . it will be . . . here. [*They smile at each other.*] We mustn't drop off like that again.

[*Pause.* ROS *takes the letter gently from him.*]

ROS Now that we have found it, why were we looking for it?

GUIL [*thinks*] We thought it was lost.

ROS Something else?

GUIL No.

[*Deflation.*]

ROS Now we've lost the tension.

GUIL What tension?

ROS What was the last thing I said before we wandered off?

GUIL When was that?

ROS [*helplessly*] I can't remember.

GUIL [*leaping up*] What a shambles! We're just not getting anywhere.

ROS [*mournfully*] Not even England. I don't believe in it anyway.

GUIL What?

ROS England.

GUIL Just a conspiracy of cartographers, you mean?

ROS I mean I don't believe it! [*Calmer.*] I have no image. I try to picture us arriving, a little harbour perhaps . . . roads . . . inhabitants to point the way . . . horses on the road . . . riding for a day or a fortnight and then a palace and the English king. . . . That would be the logical kind of thing. . . . But my mind remains a blank. No. We're slipping off the map.

GUIL Yes . . . yes. . . . [*Rallying.*] But you don't believe anything till it happens. And it *has* all happened. Hasn't it?

1104

ROS We drift down time, clutching at straws. But what good's a brick to a drowning man?

GUIL Don't give up, we can't be long now.

ROS We might as well be dead. Do you think death could possibly be a boat?

GUIL No, no, no ... Death is ... not. Death isn't. You take my meaning. Death is the ultimate negative. Not-being. You can't not-be on a boat.

ROS I've frequently not been on boats.

GUIL No, no, no—what you've been is not on boats.

ROS I wish I was dead. [*Considers the drop.*] I could jump over the side. That would put a spoke in their wheel.

GUIL Unless they're counting on it.

ROS I shall remain on board. That'll put a spoke in their wheel. [*The futility of it, fury.*] All right! We don't question, we don't doubt. We perform. But a line must be drawn somewhere, and I would like to put it on record that I have no confidence in England. Thank you. [*Thinks about this.*] And even if it's true, it'll just be another shambles.

GUIL I don't see why.

ROS [*furious*] He won't know what we're talking about.—What are we going to say?

GUIL We say—Your majesty, we have arrived!

ROS [*kingly*] And who are you?

GUIL We are Rosencrantz and Guildenstern.

ROS [*barks*] Never heard of you!

GUIL Well, we're nobody special—

ROS [*regal and nasty*] What's your game?

GUIL We've got our instructions—

ROS First I've heard of it—

GUIL [*angry*] Let me finish—[*Humble.*] We've come from Denmark.

ROS What do you want?

GUIL Nothing—we're delivering Hamlet—

ROS Who's he?

GUIL [*irritated*] You've heard of *him*—

ROS Oh, I've heard of him all right and I want nothing to do with it.

GUIL But—

ROS You march in here without so much as a by-your-leave and expect me to take in every lunatic you try to pass off with a lot of unsubstantiated—

GUIL We've got a letter—

[ROS *snatches it and tears it open.*]

ROS [*efficiently*] I see ... I see ... well, this seems to support your story such as it is—it is an exact command from the king of Denmark, for several different reasons, importing Denmark's health and England's too, that on the reading of this letter, without delay, I should have Hamlet's head cut off—!

[GUIL *snatches the letter.* ROS, *double-taking, snatches it back.* GUIL *snatches it half back. They read it together, and separate.*

Pause.

They are well downstage looking front.]

ROS   The sun's going down. It will be dark soon.

GUIL   Do you think so?

ROS   I was just making conversation. [*Pause.*] We're his *friends.*

GUIL   How do you know?

ROS   From our young days brought up with him.

GUIL   You've only got their word for it.

ROS   But that's what we depend on.

GUIL   Well, yes, and then again no. [*Airily.*] Let us keep things in proportion. Assume, if you like, that they're going to kill him. Well, he is a man, he is mortal, death comes to us all, etcetera, and consequently he would have died anyway, sooner or later. Or to look at it from the social point of view—he's just one man among many, the loss would be well within reason and convenience. And then again, what is so terrible about death? As Socrates so philosophically put it, since we don't know what death is, it is illogical to fear it. It might be . . . very nice. Certainly it is a release from the burden of life, and, for the godly, a haven and a reward. Or to look at it another way—we are little men, we don't know the ins and outs of the matter, there are wheels within wheels, etcetera—it would be presumptuous of us to interfere with the designs of fate or even of kings. All in all, I think we'd be well advised to leave well alone. Tie up the letter—there—neatly—like that.—They won't notice the broken seal, assuming you were in character.

ROS   But what's the point?

GUIL   Don't apply logic.

ROS   He's done nothing to us.

GUIL   Or justice.

ROS   It's awful.

GUIL   But it could have been worse. I was beginning to think it was. [*And his relief comes out in a laugh.*]

[*Behind them* HAMLET *appears from behind the umbrella. The light has been going. Slightly.* HAMLET *is going to the lantern.*]

ROS   The position as I see it, then. We. Rosencrantz and Guildenstern, from our young days brought up with him, awakened by a man standing on his saddle, are summoned, and arrive, and are instructed to glean what afflicts him and draw him on to pleasures, such as a play, which unfortunately, as it turns out, is abandoned in some confusion owing to certain nuances outside our appreciation—which, among other causes, results in, among other effects, a high, not to say, homicidal, excitement in Hamlet, whom we, in consequence, are escorting, for his own good, to England. Good. We're on top of it now.

[HAMLET *blows out the lantern. The stage goes pitch black. The black resolves itself to moonlight, by which* HAMLET *approaches the sleeping* ROS *and* GUIL. *He extracts the letter and takes it behind his umbrella; the light of his lantern shines through the fabric,* HAMLET *emerges again with a letter, and replaces it, and retires, blowing out his lantern.*

Morning comes.

ROS *watches it coming—from the auditorium. Behind him is a gay sight. Beneath the re-tilted umbrella, reclining in a deck-chair, wrapped in a rug, reading a book, possibly smoking, sits* HAMLET.

ROS *watches the morning come, and brighten to high noon.*]

ROS   I'm assuming nothing. [*He stands up.* GUIL *wakes.*] The position as I see it, then. That's west unless we're off course, in which case it's night; the King gave me the same as you, the King gave you the same as me: the King never gave me the letter, the King gave you the letter, we don't know what's in the letter; we take Hamlet to the English king, it depending on when we get there who he is, and we hand over the letter, which may or may not have something in it to keep us going, and if not, we are finished and at a loose end, if they have loose ends. We could have done worse. I don't think we missed any chances. . . . Not that we're getting much help. [*He sits down again. They lie down—prone.*] If we stopped breathing we'd vanish.

[*The muffled sound of a recorder. They sit up with disproportionate interest.*]

GUIL   Here we go.
ROS   Yes, but what?

[*They listen to the music.*]

GUIL [*excitedly*]   Out of the void, finally, a sound; while on a boat (admittedly) outside the action (admittedly) the perfect and absolute silence of the wet lazy slap of water against water and the rolling creak of timber—breaks; giving rise at once to the speculation or the assumption or the hope that something is about to happen; a pipe is heard. One of the sailors has pursed his lips against a woodwind, his fingers and thumb governing, shall we say, the ventages, whereupon, giving it breath, let us say, with his mouth, it, the pipe, discourses, as the saying goes, most eloquent music. A thing like that, it could change the course of events. [*Pause.*] Go and see what it is.

ROS   It's someone playing on a pipe.

GUIL   Go and find him.

ROS   And then what?

GUIL   I don't know—request a tune.

ROS   What for?

GUIL   Quick—before we lose our momentum.

ROS   Why!—something is happening. It had quite escaped my attention!

[*He listens: Makes a stab at an exit. Listens more carefully: Changes direction.*

GUIL *takes no notice.*

ROS *wanders about trying to decide where the music comes from. Finally he tracks it down—unwillingly —to the middle barrel. There is no getting away from it. He turns to* GUIL *who takes no notice.* ROS, *during this whole business, never quite breaks into articulate speech. His face and his hands indicate his incredulity. He stands gazing at the middle barrel. The pipe plays on within. He kicks the barrel. The pipe stops. He leaps back toward* GUIL. *The pipe starts up again. He approaches the barrel cautiously. He lifts the lid. The music is louder. He slams down the lid. The music is softer. He goes back towards* GUIL. *But a drum starts, muffled. He freezes. He turns. Considers the left-hand barrel. The drumming goes on within, in time to the flute: He walks back to* GUIL. *He opens his mouth to speak. Doesn't make it. A lute is heard. He spins round at the third barrel. More instruments join in. Until it is quite inescapable that inside the three barrels, distributed, playing together a familiar tune which has been heard three times before, are the* TRAGEDIANS.

They play on.

ROS *sits beside* GUIL. *They stare ahead.*

The tune comes to an end.

Pause.]

ROS   I thought I heard a band. [*In anguish.*] Plausibility is all I presume!

GUIL [*coda*]   Call us this day our daily tune. . . .

[*The lid of the middle barrel flies open and the* PLAYER's *head pops out.*]

PLAYER   Aha! All in the same boat, then! [*He climbs out. He goes round banging on the barrels.*]
Everybody out!

[*Impossibly, the* TRAGEDIANS *climb out of the barrels. With their instruments, but not their cart. A few bundles. Except* ALFRED. *The* PLAYER *is cheerful.*]

[*To* ROS] Where are we?

ROS   Travelling.

PLAYER   Of course, we haven't got there yet.

ROS   Are we all right for England?

PLAYER You look all right to me. I don't think they've very particular in England. Al-l-fred!

[ALFRED *emerges from the* PLAYER'*s barrel.*]

GUIL What are you doing here?

PLAYER Travelling. [*To* TRAGEDIANS.] Right—blend into the background!

[*The* TRAGEDIANS *are in costume (from the mime): A king with crown,* ALFRED *as Queen, Poisoner and the two cloaked figures.*

They blend.]

[*To* GUIL] Pleased to see us? [*Pause*] You've come out of it very well, so far.

GUIL And you?

PLAYER In disfavour. Our play offended the King.

GUIL Yes.

PLAYER Well, he's a second husband himself. Tactless, really.

ROS It was quite a good play nevertheless.

PLAYER We never really got going—it was getting quite interesting when they stopped it.

[*Looks up at* HAMLET]

That's the way to travel. . . .

GUIL What were you doing in there?

PLAYER Hiding. [*Indicating costumes.*] We had to run for it just as we were.

ROS Stowaways.

PLAYER Naturally—we didn't get paid, owing to circumstances ever so slightly beyond our control, and all the money we had we lost betting on certainties. Life is a gamble, at terrible odds—if it was a bet you wouldn't take it. Did you know that any number doubled is even?

ROS Is it?

PLAYER We learn something every day, to our cost. But we troupers just go on and on. Do you know what happens to old actors?

ROS What?

PLAYER Nothing. They're still acting. Surprised, then?

GUIL What?

PLAYER Surprised to see us?

GUIL I knew it wasn't the end.

PLAYER With practically everyone on his feet. What do you make of it, so far?

GUIL We haven't got much to go on.

PLAYER You speak to him?

ROS It's possible.

GUIL But it wouldn't make any difference.

ROS But it's possible.

GUIL Pointless.

ROS It's allowed.

GUIL Allowed, yes. We are not restricted. No boundaries have been defined, no inhibitions imposed. We have, for the while, secured, or blundered into, our release, for the while. Spontaneity and whim are the order of the day. Other wheels are turning but they are not our concern. We can breathe. We can relax. We can do what we like and say what we like to whomever we like, without restriction.

ROS Within limits, of course.

GUIL Certainly within limits.

[HAMLET *comes down to footlights and regards the audience. The others watch but don't speak.* HAMLET *clears his throat noisily and spits into the audience. A split second later he claps his hand to his eye and wipes himself. He goes back upstage.*]

ROS A compulsion towards philosophical introspection is his chief characteristic, if I may put it like that. It does not mean he is mad. It does not mean he isn't. Very often, it does not mean anything at all. Which may or may not be a kind of madness.

GUIL It really boils down to symptoms. Pregnant replies, mystic allusions, mistaken identities, arguing his father is his mother, that sort of thing; intimations of suicide, forgoing of exercise, loss of mirth, hints of claustrophobia not to say delusions of imprisonment, invocations of camels, chameleons, capons, whales, weasels, hawks, handsaws—riddles, quibbles and evasions; amnesia, paranoia, myopia; day-dreaming, hallucinations; stabbing his elders, abusing his parents, insulting his lover and appearing hatless in public—knock-kneed, droop-stockinged and sighing like a love-sick schoolboy, which at his age is coming on a bit strong.

ROS And talking to himself.

GUIL And talking to himself.

[ROS *and* GUIL *move apart together.*]

Well, where has that got us?

ROS He's the Player.

GUIL His play offended the King—

ROS —offended the King—

GUIL —who orders his arrest—

ROS —orders his arrest—

GUIL —so he escapes to England—

ROS   On the boat to which he meets—

GUIL   Guildenstern and Rosencrantz taking Hamlet—

ROS   —who also offended the King—

GUIL   —and killed Polonius—

ROS   —offended the King in a variety of ways—

GUIL   —to England. [*Pause.*] That seems to be it.

[ROS *jumps up.*]

ROS   Incidents! All we get is incidents! Dear God, is it too much to expect a little sustained action?!

[*And on the word, the* PIRATES *attack. That is to say: Noise and shouts and rushing about. "Pirates."*

Everyone visible goes frantic. HAMLET *draws his sword and rushes downstage.* GUIL, ROS *and* PLAYER *draw swords and rush upstage. Collision.* HAMLET *turns back up. They turn back down. Collision. By which time there is general panic right upstage. All four charge upstage with* ROS, GUIL *and* PLAYER *shouting:*]

At last!
To arms!
Pirates!
Up there!
Down there!
To my sword's length!
Action!

[*All four reach the top, see something they don't like, waver, run for their lives downstage:*

HAMLET, *in the lead, leaps into the left barrel.* PLAYER *leaps into the right barrel.* ROS *and* GUIL *leap into the middle barrel. All closing the lids after them.*

*The lights dim to nothing while the sound of fighting continues. The sound fades to nothing. The lights come up. The middle barrel (*ROS*'s and* GUIL*'s) is missing.*

The lid of the right-hand barrel is raised cautiously, the heads of ROS *and* GUIL *appear.*

*The lid of the other barrel (*HAMLET*'s) is raised. The head of the* PLAYER *appears.*

All catch sight of each other and slam down lids.

Pause.

Lids raised cautiously.]

ROS   [*relief*]   They've gone. [*He starts to climb out.*] That was close. I've never thought quicker.

1111

hey are all three out of barrels. GUIL *is wary and nervous.* ROS *is light-headed. The* PLAYER *is phlegmatic. They note the missing barrel.*]

[ROS *looks round.*]

ROS   Where's—?

[*The* PLAYER *takes off his hat in mourning.*]

PLAYER   Once more, alone—on our own resources.

GUIL [*worried*]   What do you mean? Where is he?

PLAYER   Gone.

GUIL   Gone where?

PLAYER   Yes, we were dead lucky there. If that's the word I'm after.

ROS [*not a pick up*]   Dead?

PLAYER   Lucky.

ROS [*he means*]   Is he dead?

PLAYER   Who knows?

GUIL [*rattled*]   He's not coming back?

PLAYER   Hardly.

ROS   He's dead then. He's dead as far as we're concerned.

PLAYER   Or we are as far as he is. [*He goes and sits on the floor to one side.*] Not too bad, is it?

GUIL [*rattled*]   But he can't—we're supposed to be—we've got a *letter*—we're going to England with a letter for the King—

PLAYER   Yes, that much seems certain. I congratulate you on the unambiguity of your situation.

GUIL   But you don't understand—it contains—we've had our instructions—the whole thing's pointless without him.

PLAYER   Pirates could happen to anyone. Just deliver the letter. They'll send ambassadors from England to explain. . . .

GUIL [*worked up*]   Can't you see—the pirates left us home and high—dry and home—drome—[*Furiously.*] The pirates left us high and dry!

PLAYER [*comforting*]   There . . .

GUIL [*near tears*]   Nothing will be resolved without him. . . .

PLAYER   There . . . !

GUIL   We need Hamlet for our release!

PLAYER   There!

GUIL   What are we supposed to do?

PLAYER   This.

[*He turns away, lies down if he likes.* ROS *and* GUIL *apart.*]

ROS   Saved again.

GUIL   Saved for what?

[ROS *sighs.*]

ROS   The sun's going down. [*Pause.*] It'll be night soon. [*Pause.*] If that's west. [*Pause.*] Unless we've—

GUIL [*shouts*]   Shut up! I'm sick of it! Do you think conversation is going to help us now?

ROS [*hurt, desperately ingratiating*]   I—I bet you all the money I've got the year of my birth doubled is an odd number.

GUIL [*moan*]   No-o.

ROS   *Your* birth!

[GUIL *smashes him down.*]

GUIL [*broken*]   We've travelled too far, and our momentum has taken over; we move idly towards eternity, without possibility of reprieve or hope of explanation.

ROS   Be happy—if you're not even *happy* what's so good about surviving? [*He picks himself up.*] We'll be all right. I suppose we just go on.

GUIL   Go where?

ROS   To England.

GUIL   England! *That's* a dead end. I never believed in it anyway.

ROS   All we've got to do is make our report and that'll be that. Surely.

GUIL   I don't *believe* it—a shore, a harbour, say—and we get off and we stop someone and say—Where's the King?—And he says, Oh, you follow that road there and take the first left and—[*Furiously.*] I don't believe any of it!

ROS   It doesn't sound very plausible.

GUIL   And even if we came face to face, what do we say?

ROS   We say—We've arrived!

GUIL [*kingly*]   And who are you?

ROS   We are Guildenstern and Rosencrantz.

GUIL   Which is which?

ROS   Well, I'm—You're—

GUIL   What's it all about?—

ROS   Well, we were bringing Hamlet—but then some pirates—

GUIL   I don't begin to understand. Who are all these people, what's it got to do with me? You turn up out of the blue with some cock and bull story—

ROS [*with letter*]   We have a letter—

1113

GUIL [*snatches it, opens it*]   A letter—yes—that's true. That's something . . . a letter
. . . [*Reads.*] "As England is Denmark's faithful tributary . . . as love between them
like the palm might flourish, etcetera . . . that on the knowing of this contents,
without delay of any kind, should those bearers, Rosencrantz and Guildenstern,
put to sudden death—"

[*He double-takes.* ROS *snatches the letter.* GUIL *snatches it back.* ROS *snatches it half back. They read it again and look up.*

The PLAYER *gets to his feet and walks over to his barrel and kicks it and shouts into it.*]

PLAYER   They've gone! It's all over!

[*One by one the* PLAYERS *emerge, impossibly, from the barrel, and form a casually menacing circle round* ROS *and* GUIL, *who are still appalled and mesmerised.*]

GUIL [*quietly*]   Where we went wrong was getting on a boat. We can move, of
course, change direction, rattle about, but our movement is contained within a
larger one that carries us along as inexorably as the wind and current. . . .

ROS   They had it in for us, didn't they? Right from the beginning. Who'd have
thought that we were so important?

GUIL   But why? Was it all for this? Who are we that so much should converge
on our little deaths? [*In anguish to the* PLAYER] Who are *we?*

PLAYER   You are Rosencrantz and Guildenstern. That's enough.

GUIL   No—it is not enough. To be told so little—to such an end—and still,
finally, to be denied an explanation—

PLAYER   In our experience, most things end in death.

GUIL [*fear, vengeance, scorn*]   Your experience!—*Actors!*

[*He snatches a dagger from the* PLAYER'*s belt and holds the point at the* PLAYER'*s throat: the* PLAYER *backs and* GUIL *advances, speaking more quietly.*]

I'm talking about death—and you've never experienced *that.* And you cannot *act*
it. You die a thousand casual deaths—with none of that intensity which squeezes
out life . . . and no blood runs cold anywhere. Because even as you die you know
that you will come back in a different hat. But no one gets up after *death*—there
is no applause—there is only silence and some second-hand clothes, and that's—
death—

[*And he pushes the blade in up to the hilt. The* PLAYER *stands with huge, terrible eyes, clutches at the wound as the blade withdraws: he makes small weeping sounds and falls to his knees, and then right down.*

While he is dying, GUIL, *nervous, high, almost hysterical, wheels on the* TRAGEDIANS—]

If we have a destiny, then so had he—and if this is ours, then that was his—and
if there are no explanations for us, then let there be none for him—

[*The* TRAGEDIANS *watch the* PLAYER *die: they watch with some interest. The* PLAYER *finally lies still. A short moment of silence. Then the* TRAGEDIANS *start to applaud with genuine admiration. The* PLAYER *stands up, brushing himself down.*]

PLAYER [*modestly*] Oh, come, come, gentlemen—no flattery—it was merely competent—

[*The* TRAGEDIANS *are still congratulating him. The* PLAYER *approaches* GUIL, *who stands rooted, holding the dagger.*]

PLAYER What did you think? [*Pause.*] You see, it is the kind they do believe in —it's what is expected.

[*He holds his hand out for the dagger.* GUIL *slowly puts the point of the dagger on to the* PLAYER's *hand, and pushes . . . the blade slides back into the handle. The* PLAYER *smiles, reclaims the dagger.*]

For a moment you thought I'd—cheated.

[ROS *relieves his own tension with loud nervy laughter.*]

ROS Oh, very good! Very good! Took me in completely—didn't he take you in completely—[*claps his hands.*] Encore! Encore!

PLAYER [*activated, arms spread, the professional*] Deaths for all ages and occasions! Deaths by suspension, convulsion, consumption, incision, execution, asphyxiation and malnutrition—! Climactic carnage, by poison and by steel—! Double deaths by duel!—! Show!—

[ALFRED, *still in his Queen's costume, dies by poison: the* PLAYER, *with rapier, kills the "*KING*" and duels with a fourth* TRAGEDIAN, *inflicting and receiving a wound. The two remaining* TRAGEDIANS, *the two "*SPIES*" dressed in the same coats as* ROS *and* GUIL, *are stabbed, as before. And the light is fading over the deaths which take place right upstage.*]

[*Dying amid the dying—tragically; romantically.*] So there's an end to that—it's commonplace: light goes with life, and in the winter of your years the dark comes early. . . .

GUIL [*tired, drained, but still an edge of impatience; over the mime*] No . . . no . . . not for *us,* not like that. Dying is not romantic, and death is not a game which will soon be over . . . Death is not anything . . . death is not . . . It's the absence of presence, nothing more . . . the endless time of never coming back . . . a gap you can't see, and when the wind blows through it, it makes no sound. . . .

[*The light has gone upstage. Only* GUIL *and* ROS *are visible as* ROS's *clapping falters to silence.*

Small pause.]

ROS That's it, then, is it?

1115

[*No answer. He looks out front.*]

The sun's going down. Or the earth's coming up, as the fashionable theory has it.

[*Small pause.*]

Not that it makes any difference.

[*Pause.*]

What was it all about? When did it begin?

[*Pause. No answer.*]

Couldn't we just stay put? I mean no one is going to come on and drag us off. . . . They'll just have to wait. We're still young . . . fit . . . we've got years. . . .

[*Pause. No answer.*]

[*A cry.*] We've done nothing wrong! We didn't harm anyone. Did we?
GUIL   I can't remember.

[ROS *pulls himself together.*]

ROS   All right, then. I don't care. I've had enough. To tell you the truth, I'm relieved.

[*And he disappears from view.* GUIL *does not notice.*]

GUIL   Our names shouted in a certain dawn . . . a message . . . a summons . . . There must have been a moment, at the beginning, where we could have said—no. But somehow we missed it. [*He looks round and sees he is alone.*] Rosen—?
Guil—?

[*He gathers himself.*]

Well, we'll know better next time. Now you see me, now you—[*and disappears*].

[*Immediately the whole stage is lit up, revealing, upstage, arranged in the approximate positions last held by the dead* TRAGEDIANS, *the tableau of court and corpses which is the last scene of* Hamlet.

That is: The KING, QUEEN, LAERTES *and* HAMLET *all dead.* HORATIO *holds* HAMLET, FORTINBRAS *is there.*

So are two AMBASSADORS *from England.*]

AMBASSADOR   The sight is dismal;
and our affairs from England come too late.

1116

The ears are senseless that should give us hearing
to tell him his commandment is fulfilled,
that Rosencrantz and Guildenstern are dead.
Where should we have our thanks?

HORATIO   Not from his mouth,
had it the ability of life to thank you:
He never gave commandment for their death.
But since, so jump upon this bloody question,
you from the Polack wars, and you from England,
are here arrived, give order that these bodies
high on a stage be placed to the view;
and let me speak to the yet unknowing world
how these things came about: so shall you hear
of carnal, bloody and unnatural acts,
of accidental judgments, casual slaughters,
of deaths put on by cunning and forced cause,
and, in this upshot, purposes mistook
fallen on the inventors' heads: all this can I
truly deliver.

[*But during the above speech, the play fades out, overtaken by dark and music.*]

DISCUSSION TOPICS

1. The possible meanings of the title of this play only gradually emerge. Nevertheless, it is good to ask immediately: Why does the title use the present tense *"are* dead"?

2. As with the title, the meanings of the coin-tossing game only gradually emerge. Having the same side of the coins come up heads ninety-two times is more than a good piece of stage action to grab the viewer's early attention. What hints of the play's themes does this early action provide? Why do the characters discuss probability? Logic? Why are syllogisms important?

3. What are the effects of preserving some of Shakespeare's lines?

4. What is the thematic significance of each of the following?

   a. The Player's comment that every exit might be looked on as "an entrance somewhere else."
   b. The Player's "death" when Guildenstern stabs him.
   c. The ship or boat imagery of the play.

5. Horatio's words close the play: "all this can I truly deliver." He seems quite sure that he has the facts. What facts are certain in the world of Stoppard's *Rosencrantz and Guildenstern?*

6. What evidence is there of personality disintegration within the play? (Perhaps it is equally valid to ask whether some of the characters had ever been inte-

grated in the first place.) Which characters seem most clearly to know who they are?

7. Discuss the Player's speech (to Guildenstern): "There's a design at work in all art—surely you know that? Events must play themselves out to aesthetic, moral, and logical conclusion."

8. How do you explain the fact that laughter and tears are never far apart in this play?

9. In what ways is the ship on which Rosencrantz and Guildenstern journey akin to "spaceship Earth"?

WRITING TOPIC

Shakespeare's *Hamlet* had a play within a play (other plays use the device also). This modern play takes *Hamlet* and adds, as it were, still another play, this one concerning two men who were nearly nonentities in Shakespeare's version. The result is that *Rosencrantz and Guildenstern Are Dead* is a quite different play. Show that this is so by analyzing what these two characters say about themselves.

Writing About Literature

Writing about literature is much like writing about any other subject. For most students this means it is a process that begins when they read a story, poem, or play and ends when they hand in the finished theme or essay. We have all known those exceptional people who seem to be able to go directly from the first step to the last with no apparent effort or even intermediate steps. Most of us, however, require time and careful planning to write successful papers. No two writers work in exactly the same way, and you must discover which method of composition is the most comfortable to you. But the following steps are fairly common and may provide you with a good plan for discovering your own technique.

1. *Read carefully.* If you are going to write a paper on a work of literature, you will want to know it very well. It is always a good idea to read the work at least twice and to mark your text by underlining or highlighting important words and details and by writing notes in the margins.

2. *Be sure you understand the writing assignment.* If you must discover your own topic or thesis, perhaps it would be best to begin by asking yourself the "twenty questions" in the checklist given in the Introduction. If there are problems you cannot solve or questions you cannot answer, these may be good starting places for further reading in the library and for your own written analysis.

3. *Commit your ideas to paper.* It is never too early to do so. One of the most important parts of any writing assignment is often revising and rewriting as you go along. You may begin with a thesis and outline, but do not be afraid to strike out in a new direction, to leave your mind open to new ideas and new discoveries.

4. *Organize your information.* After gathering together the information you want to use in your paper, you then arrange it into a well-organized essay with a clear subject or thesis and good supporting paragraphs that demonstrate or prove your point. The best short papers have only one main idea, so do not try to do too much in one paper. Leave out discussion of irrelevant details; make every word count. And avoid simply retelling the story or plot. A little summary may sometimes be helpful, but your thesis should aim at something more than a simple paraphrase.

5. *Write a clean, neat copy of your theme to hand in to your instructor.* This should give you one final opportunity to check your essay and make sure that it sounds finished and complete. It is a good idea to read the paper out loud and to imagine its effect on potential listeners or readers. Be certain that your readers can follow your arguments or demonstrations. Ask yourself whether you have provided enough information to be convincing and whether you have introduced your ideas effectively and persuasively.

Among the more common forms of writing about literature are *explications* and *analyses*. An *explication* (literally, an unfolding) is a line-by-line explanation of a work—in many cases a short poem. Although it may include a paraphrase, it is even more concerned with the ingredients of a closer reading and their combined achievement of some totality of meaning: definitions of words in context (since these often change radically over time); nuances of words (shades of meaning); connotations of words (what words suggest over and above what they literally mean); instances and functions of figurative language; images and patterns of imagery; rhyme; meter; and the relationship of all these things (and any other ingredients) to the theme of the work.

An *analysis* is a division of a piece of literature into parts and a discussion of those parts. Usually one part is examined in considerable detail. Such an analysis might take the form of a *character* study, which would describe not only physical appearances but also aspects of personality, motivations, and other psychological ideas. It would reveal whether a character is simple, complex, smug, tormented, frustrated, guilt-ridden, or ruthless. Analyses often focus on *plot;* that is, what actually happens in a work of literature. (How are the various actions of a work related to one another or to a central theme?) *Symbols* are frequently treated in analyses. (What do walls symbolize in "Bartleby the Scrivener," or a "khaki suit" in "Miniver Cheevy," or the road in "The Road Not Taken"?) Many poems, plays, and stories have clear connections with ancient *myth*. The "sacrificial" death of Hamlet to effect the "cleansing" of Denmark parallels the old Eastern myth of the "dying god-king," whose sacrificial death is necessary for the health and/or prosperity of the nation. A comparison of these connections sheds a special kind of light on the work under consideration, as would a discussion of the influence or effect of *setting* on a piece of literature. (What part does the Belgian Congo play in Joseph Conrad's *Heart of Darkness?* And since setting is not confined to *place* but also includes *time,* our discussion may seek to answer questions such as, how are Melville's "Bartleby the Scrivener," Owen's "Dulce Et Decorum Est," and Aristophanes's *Lysistrata* influenced by the period as well as the place in which they are set?)

Character, plot, symbols, myth, setting—all of these are clearly parts of the literary work; they are not the whole thing. But in writing about them, we can demonstrate how they fit in and to what extent the work is dependent on them. By looking at one of its parts in detail, we shall most likely better understand the work in its entirety.

Writing About Poetry

Let us see, though, what this definition and theory translate into in actual practice. Explication, that line-by-line scrutiny of every facet of a literary work, can probably be thought of as a necessary first step in any discussion of poetry. Some poems, of course, present virtually no serious problems for an explicator, yet the mere act of explicating may often "unfold" meanings hitherto missed or inadequately dealt with. Let us consider Richard Lovelace's "To Lucasta, on Going to the Wars":

Tell me not, sweet, I am unkind,
    That from the nunnery
Of thy chaste breast and quiet mind
    To war and arms I fly.

True, a new mistress now I chase,
    The first foe in the field;
And with a stronger faith embrace
    A sword, a horse, a shield.

Yet this inconstancy is such
    As thou too shalt adore;
I could not love thee, dear, so much
    Loved I not Honour more.

"To Lucasta, on Going to the Wars" is a Cavalier lyric with some of the qualities of the *dramatic monologue,* a speech by one person to another in a situation more or less dramatic (the second person does not speak in the poem). It is also written in three quatrains (or four-line stanzas), alternately iambic tetrameter and trimeter, rhyming *abab cdcd efef* (identical letters indicate similar sounds). A paraphrase would be as follows: A soldier, probably young, is taking leave of his beloved and going off to war. She has obviously been chiding him for leaving her, even accusing him of cruelty and possibly of infidelity. He denies guilt on both counts and justifies his action on the grounds that he could not love her as much as he does if he did not love one thing more—"Honour." Now let us look at an explication of the Lovelace poem:

"To Lucasta, on Going to the Wars": An Explication

"To Lucasta, on Going to the Wars" is set in an earlier day: Words such as "thy," "thou," and "thee" and such obsolete military hardware as "sword," "horse," and "shield" confirm this. The speaker is affectionate and tender, calling Lucasta "sweet" in the first stanza even as he defends himself against her charges. He is also eloquent and reasonable in seeming to admit that it does suggest a kind of insanity to leave the "nunnery" of her "chaste breast and quiet mind" and head for the chaos of armed combat. "Nunnery" is a particularly well chosen metaphor since it is the essence of feminine devotion to the teachings of the Prince of Peace. "Chaste" reiterates the idea of holiness and sexual purity. A "quiet mind" is precisely what the inhabitant of a nunnery would possess, a mind at peace with itself and others and decidedly not studying war. The young cavalier has thus paid his sweetheart high compliments on her purity, her pacific nature, and her religious devotion. The fact that Lucasta has upbraided him with "unkindness" rather than insanity implies that she is using an essentially feminine argument, perhaps even to the extent of tears and pouting—another indication that the poem depicts an earlier day: She is using the only argument available to her.

In the second stanza the soldier-lover elects a teasing tone and a humorous argument to oppose these feminine weapons, saying, ironically, that he is pursuing another love—the first enemy soldier he can catch sight of. He continues to banter Lucasta by saying that he means to "embrace" his horse, sword, and shield "with a stronger faith" (they will not be fickle and capricious like women; he will be able to rely on their trustworthiness). The last quatrain, containing the summation of his defense against these groundless charges, consists of two paradoxes. In the first, the speaker actually praises the "inconstancy" he has just confessed by saying that Lucasta herself will "adore" it when she understands what it is based on, another paradox: that his love for her is owing to the fact that he loves Honour more, Honour being a code comprehending such masculine virtues as nobility, integrity, physical courage, and loyalty to a cause such as King and country.

From this straightforward seventeenth-century espousal of traditional patriotism and male–female relationships, let us turn to a more difficult, modern antiwar poem, Randall Jarrell's "The Death of the Ball Turret Gunner":

> From my mother's sleep I fell into the State,
> And I hunched in its belly till my wet fur froze.
> Six miles from earth, loosed from its dream of life,
> I woke to black flak and the nightmare fighters.
> When I died they washed me out of the turret with a hose.

A number of characteristics make this poem more difficult than the earlier poem. One is that it relies less on logical, grammatical statement (however much embellished by figurative device) to achieve its meaning than on the juxtaposition of sharp images and their suggestive force in context. Another is that its allusions are more technical or private or obscure. A third is that its metaphors are more esoteric. This increased difficulty, however, is not so great that it prevents a paraphrase. The speaker is the disembodied spirit of a young World War II airman, a "ball turret gunner," killed in the war. He summarizes his brief life in five lines, climaxing and ending with his death from an enemy plane and antiaircraft fire and the ground crew's hosing the remains of his body out of the bomber. Randall Jarrell, the author, has appended the following gloss to the poem:

> A ball turret was a plexiglass sphere set into the belly of a B-17 or B-24, and inhabited by two .50 caliber machine-guns and one man, a short small man. When this gunner tracked with his machine-guns a fighter attacking his bomber from below, he revolved with the turret; hunched

upside down in his little sphere, he looked like the fetus in the womb. The fighters which attacked him were armed with cannon firing explosive shells. The hose was a steam hose.

Whereas an explication is a line-by-line examination of a literary text—customarily a short poem—an *analysis* is an examination of some particular part or aspect. You might be assigned a paper in which you are to discuss the function or the appropriateness of some figure of speech like personification or allusion in a given poem. Or you could be required to explain the structure of a sonnet, showing how it conforms to or departs from the criteria for the Shakespearean or Italian versions of that genre. The following is an analysis of one of the key images in Randall Jarrell's poem:

Analysis of the Birth Metaphor in "Death of the Ball Turret Gunner"

The first line of Jarrell's "Death of the Ball Turret Gunner" contains an arresting metaphor: "From my mother's sleep I fell into the State." It is apparently a birth metaphor, "sleep" referring to the twilight sleep produced by administering a painkiller and a sedative to a mother delivering a baby. The point here is that from the complete security of the womb, the future airman is transferred to another mother, the State —specifically its armed forces—which also provides a kind of security in its womb, the ball turret. The transfer from one womb to the other implies that the period of childhood and school is so brief that no real living can be done in such a span. In line 2, the young airman describes his new womb, the ball turret, and the frigid temperatures that freeze the fur lining of his flight suit. Line 3 begins the new birth and existence at altitudes suitable for a bomber, and the airman speaks of all that has gone before in his young life as a "dream," not as reality. Line 4 describes his delivery from the new womb, not by natural means assisted by medical science and its skilled practitioners, but by flak (an acronym for *Fl*iegera bwehr*k* anonen—German for "flyer defense cannons") and machine-gun bursts from fighter planes. It is in every sense a perverted birth, for it delivers the new creature not to life but to death. The last line provides the final tragic equation: a human being in war is on a par with debris: Fragments of Plexiglas, twisted metal and shrapnel combine with tissue, blood, and bone in a mess that a clean-up squad can remove, "sanitizing" as they go.

Just as the key figure of the poem is a birth metaphor, so the central image is a womb. The ball turret is shaped like a womb; the gunner hunches in that womb like a fetus. And in point of fact, though it does not appear in the poem, a ball turret gunner also had an "umbilical cord," a flexible tube that provided him with oxygen and served also as an intercom. It should be noticed that several words in the poem tend to "reduce" the gunner from his human status. The first is the verb "fell," which means "to become born" but is usually applied to lambs, not humans. (A similar usage would be the verb "drop," meaning "to give birth to" but used exclusively with animals.) Also one of the meanings of "belly" is "the undersurface of an animal's body"; and

1123

though it has also meant "womb," that is no longer the conventional term when referring to humans. It is natural then for the gunner's "wet fur" to suggest more a cub or whelp of some kind than a baby. The last line, equating the gunner's remains with debris, or afterbirth, completes this reductive theme.

Another common writing assignment in literature courses calls upon students to write papers of comparison and contrast. There are two different ways to accomplish such an assignment. One method is to compare and contrast the two works throughout your paper, mentioning different aspects such as the form, theme, or imagery of the two works in each paragraph of your paper. Another technique is to discuss the two works separately, first one and then the other. Sometimes it is more effective to combine these two methods. Let us consider the following example comparing and contrasting attitudes toward war in the poems by Lovelace and Jarrell.

"Death" and "Honour" in Two Poems About War

Richard Lovelace's "To Lucasta, on Going to the Wars" and Randall Jarrell's "The Death of the Ball Turret Gunner" present contrasting versions of a soldier's participation in warfare. On one level the poems record different moments in a soldier's life. The narrator of "To Lucasta" is saying farewell to his beloved before going off to war, while the narrator of "The Death of the Ball Turret Gunner" is describing his own death and its unceremonious aftermath. But even more important are the contrasting attitudes toward "death" and "Honour" in these two poems written 300 years apart.

The aristocratic young narrator of "To Lucasta" does not ignore the possibility of his own death. Even in the first stanza he acknowledges that he is flying from his mistress's embrace "to war and arms." And in the second stanza he mentions the "foe in the field" and "a sword, a horse, a shield." But the emphasis throughout is on a soldier's code of honor. In the final stanza the narrator excuses his "inconstancy" to his mistress by suggesting that she would not respect or "adore" him so much if he did not love "Honour more"—more even than he loves her, since he places that "Honour" above his love for this woman.

"To Lucasta" embodies a personal, aristocratic code of honor that places a soldier's duty to his country, or merely to the code itself, above his commitment to home and family, or at any rate to personal, sexual relationships. That code is entirely absent from the twentieth-century poem. The ball turret gunner appears to have been taken away from his home and his "mother" and deposited in an instrument of war, the "belly" of the bomber. There seems to be little personal choice in his participation, for he says in the poem's opening line "From my mother's sleep I fell into the State." "Six miles from earth," he awakens from his "dream of life" to the "nightmare" of war. And before he has a chance to come to terms with his participation in the war, he is being unceremoniously "washed . . . out of the turret with a hose."

"The Death of the Ball Turret Gunner" looks at war from a

different perspective from that of "To Lucasta." The seventeenth-century soldier embraces his personal code of honor and "flies" willingly to arms. But the ball turret gunner never appears to have made a conscious decision about his own personal involvement. He "fell into the State." He seems to have been the victim of circumstances outside his control. The "State" has decided his fate for him. And while he does not appear to question either the state's right to employ him in such a way or his own personal sense of duty, the poem raises questions in our minds about codes of honor such as that referred to in "To Lucasta." Where is the "Honour" in being washed out of the ball turret with a hose?

These two poems about war present contrasting attitudes toward a soldier's participation in warfare. "To Lucasta, on Going to the Wars" describes an aristocratic soldier who has made a personal commitment to his code of honor and the field of combat where he intends to win both glory and the admiration of his mistress. But the twentieth-century soldier in "The Death of the Ball Turret Gunner" seems to have been reduced to a pliant servant of the machines of warfare. There is no personal identity for the soldier, no personal commitment to a code of honor, and no chance for personal glory. At the poem's conclusion he has been reduced to human waste that must be washed out of the belly of the great war machine to make way for the next faceless soldier. Jarrell's poem records the reality of modern warfare and contrasts sharply with the attitude of Lovelace's celebration of "Honour."

Writing About Fiction

The structure of the short story may be said to consist of five basic elements; given in probable order of genesis, they are as follows:

1. *Theme:* the informing idea of the story—its "point," or, what Ray B. West, Jr., calls its "reducible meaning." We should recognize that no amount of translation into expository prose can take the place of the fictional experience itself, which is much like the poetic experience; nevertheless, we can infer some kind of paraphrasable meaning from this experience.
2. *Character:* the element that involves all the participants within the story, including animals and the narrator.
3. *Setting:* time as well as place.
4. *Plot:* the action of the story, psychological as well as physical; the plot may usually be charted in terms of rising action (enveloping action, exposition, complication, foreshadowing), climax, and falling action (denouement, resolution).
5. *Mood:* perhaps the most elusive element of the story; it is the emotional ambiance of the story, its atmosphere (e.g., irony, horror, melancholy, etc.); it is for the reader what tone is for the author.

In a well-written story these elements subtly enhance each other, coalescing to produce the essential conflict or tension that gives the work its impact.

The manner in which these structural elements are combined and articulated might be called *texture*. Texture here is meant to involve the author's distinctive style and technique, and it includes such devices as dialogue, imagery, symbolism, tone, and point of view. Imagery and symbolism function in fiction in much the same manner as in poetry.

Point of view needs a brief explanation. As mentioned earlier, every tale must have a teller: It must be narrated from someone's viewpoint. This "angle of narration," as point of view is sometimes called, may be third-person omniscient, third-person limited (sometimes referred to as the "central intelligence"), first-person, or stream-of-consciousness. This point of view is carefully chosen by the fictional craftsman to achieve a particular effect; moreover, the author may choose to vary the angle of narration for certain purposes within a particular story. One word of caution: The narrative point of view and the voice of the narrator should not be confused with the personal voice of the author. As in poetry, the narrator should be regarded as a mask or persona—even when the first-person "I" is used.

Generally speaking, *analysis* is more common than explication in writing about fiction since fiction tends to be the longer literary genre. The basic analytical principle, of course, remains the same: You are writing about some part of a short story or novel rather than explaining every line of it. And though poetry and fiction share many common topics, fiction treats them more elaborately, and the reader is enabled to trace development. To use an analogy with another art, fiction is painting on a broader canvas. For our illustrative analysis of a piece of fiction, let us look at William Carlos Williams's short story "The Use of Force." Although very brief, it is singularly rich in writing possibilities. One possibility has to do with the *theme* of the work, which the title of the following analysis indicates.

The Philosophical Theme of William Carlos Williams's "The Use of Force"

Everyone can agree that the use of force in illegal or immoral causes is wrong. By the same token, most people will agree that though it may be unpleasant or even have tragic consequences, the use of force in legal or moral causes is justified. "It is a social necessity." Williams's story easily illustrates this latter attitude. But who has the right to use force? Certainly a benevolent authority figure like the doctor. It never crosses the Olsons' minds to question this. They treat him with all deference. The mother apologizes for having him conduct the examination in the kitchen. The father, though holding the child in his lap, attempts to rise as the doctor enters. The doctor hears himself described as "nice," "kind," a man "who won't hurt you," though the parents are nervously resigned to the fact that he may have to hurt the child in order to treat her. Convinced of the doctor's goodness and authority, the parents in essence grant him *carte blanche* to examine the child's throat.

The doctor, on his part accepting the authority and responsibility that society invests him with, proceeds to fulfill the duties of his charge.

Since the child is willfully uncooperative, he drops his kindly pleading and warns that he will use force. He "orders" the father to put the child on his lap and hold her wrists. The child's screams of terror and pain cause the mother to weaken in her resolve. But the father obeys the doctor, who finally overpowers the child and effects the examination with a metal spoon. Because the doctor learns that the child has diphtheria, he can presumably treat her and save her life.

If this were all there was to the story, it would be simply another episode corroborating the apparently universal truth that in a benevolent, moral, socially humanitarian cause force is justified. But this is not all there is to the story. On the contrary, the story is both a psychological confession and an attempt to rationalize the sinister side of that confession. Human authority figures, like doctors, convinced of the righteousness of their ends and their motives, fall victim to some very common character flaws when they are not obeyed. There is a kind of pleasure or satisfaction that comes to them in bending someone to their own will, in forcing someone to obey for his or her own good.

When the Olson child does not tamely submit, she becomes a different being in the doctor's eyes: not a little girl, but a "brat" and a "savage" one at that. The encounter between doctor and patient ceases to be an examination: it becomes a "struggle," a "battle." At the same time that he confesses this belligerent dimension of the encounter, the doctor tries to explain it away by saying he "had to do it . . . had to have a throat culture for her own protection." In trying to force the wooden tongue depressor between the child's teeth, the doctor admits that he "had grown furious," that he "tried to hold [himself] down but . . . couldn't." The scientific detachment and the benevolent rationale of the ideal physician have given way to angry and brutal determination or stubbornness on the part of a passionately strong-willed human no longer in complete control of his feelings.

The doctor's description of his triumph by force reveals him to have been at the highest point of the struggle in a state not far removed from the hysteria of the child. The grim determination of the doctor's "We're going through with this" is followed quickly by "I too had got beyond reason. I could have torn the child apart in my own fury and enjoyed it. It was a pleasure to attack her. My face was burning with it." To be sure, the doctor never quite loses all control, and he continues his rationalization: He is "protecting" the child from her own "idiocy"; he is protecting others; it is a part of his sociomedical obligation. Still, he is himself aware of his "blind fury," his "adult shame, bred of a longing for muscular release."

The doctor has unaccountably chosen to chronicle these darker impulses, and his candor may help us and others in situations like his to examine carefully the reasons for using force in any given context. But we may safely conclude that the majority of the users of force infinitely less benevolent will not be so honest and will seek to rationalize even more convincingly their violent legal behavior. When Williams depicts how such license to employ force can affect the model of humane concern, the physician, we wonder what enormities it may produce in less altruistic hands.

Writing About Drama

Since drama, like fiction, is generally a more extended literary form than poetry, *analysis* rather than explication is the type of commentary more likely to be employed in discussing it. When you discuss drama as literature, however, rather than as theater, your topics and your approach will probably be similar to those of poetry and fiction. And, by and large, students in introduction to literature classes will be treating drama as literature. Let us look at an analysis that deals with a drama in this fashion.

In literary genres that have a strong narrative line, such as drama, the author customarily presents a "world," that is to say, a total context—an environment consisting of humans, objects, and attitudes. Eugene Ionesco's *The Gap* is a one-act play satirizing specifically the educational establishment—charlatans and corruption in universities and bureaucracies. But the larger implications of the play, like those of most plays, go far beyond the immediate limits of the world of the drama. They involve questions of values, of ethics, of human relationships, of moral obligations in a variety of areas. Ionesco uses a certain kind of "world" in which to make this statement. Let us look at an analysis of that "world" as a backdrop for the main satiric theme.

The World of The Gap

Eugene Ionesco's *The Gap* portrays the fall of a modern-day educational bureaucrat from the headship of his ministry or cabinet-level department (the setting seems to be France) to a thoroughly discredited phony who despite all sorts of honorary doctorates cannot pass a bachelor's degree examination that he has taken to eliminate a "gap" in his educational achievements. The play presents us with a symbolic microcosm of a world so shallow, corrupt, and absurd yet so recognizable that it is the perfect setting for the message the dramatist wishes to deliver.

The Gap is set in an "Establishment" world. The entire play takes place in the living room of a dwelling with "artistic pretensions": The Regency style of furniture testifies to the aspiring middle-class taste of the inhabitants, and the walls covered with diplomas of honorary degrees testify to their vulgar and tasteless boastfulness.

The characters of the drama have no names: They are simply called The Friend, The Academician, The Academician's Wife, and The Maid. Their clothes reinforce their facelessness and cipher-like anonymity. The Friend is dressed in the typical European civil servant's garb—hat, umbrella, stiff collar, black jacket and striped trousers, shiny black shoes—a uniform as prescribed and unalterable as a soldier's, the perfect attire for a bureaucratic lackey. He has brought to the Academician's residence the bad news of the Academician's failing his exam. The Wife has had to be roused from bed, so she is dressed in a robe. The Academician makes his entry fully dressed as a stereotypical military bureaucrat—chest covered with decorations, sword at his side.

The dialogue also reflects this absence of individuality. It is made up almost entirely of clichés; predictable, shallow, selfish responses; and contemptible psychological defenses. In response to The Wife's plea to be told the details of her husband's failure, The Friend answers, "I don't know what to say. . . . It's hard. I know . . . We had to expect it . . . be brave. That's life." The Wife upbraids her husband for being disgraced. He on his part doesn't manfully say, "I failed," but rather, "They failed me. The rats." His refusal to face hard reality is evidenced in his pathetic scurrying from one closed means of escape to another. He suggests that since the results of the exam were posted in the evening, perhaps the darkness prevented The Friend from seeing them accurately. The Friend's answer: "They had set up spotlights." When The Academician is told his low grade on the mathematics part of the exam, he offers the alibi that he had had no scientific training. For receiving the same mark in Latin and Greek, he excuses himself by saying that twentieth-century humanism is his forte.

The behavior of these human zeros helps to create the sleazy moral milieu of the "world" of *The Gap*. The long and successful record of The Academician was never attributable to true scholarly or administrative skills but to his ability to manipulate and survive at the last moment. He wonders why The Friend did not bribe someone to remove the grades from where they had been posted. He need not have wondered. The Friend had done that already—to no avail. The Academician decides to use his power as a commission chairman to rescind the new rules under which his examination was given only to be reminded by his wife that he had resigned the chairmanship before taking the examination. Rivaling The Academician's corruptness, The Friend enumerates dishonest ways in which The Academician might have passed the exam: using his high office to get the questions ahead of time, having a student take the exam for him, having his maid buy the questions on the black market. The complete ineptitude of The Academician is exemplified by his writing on the wrong question, writing on it badly, and, indeed, not writing much at all but merely scribbling. That a person of such dishonesty and poor scholastic abilities should head the education system of an entire country strains our credibility until we see The Academician's last ploy, his telephoning the President to ask him to intervene and declare the exam null and void. The President refuses to talk to him, saying that his "mummy won't let [him] make friends with boys at the bottom of the class."

We now sense that we are in a world where not just one segment is corrupt and shallow but where there is absurdity everywhere. Nothing has meaning. The Academician, a pompous, ignorant charlatan, is a three-time Nobel prize winner; he holds a university chair; he has lectured in the world's greatest universities; ten thousand theses have been written on his work; hundreds of critics have analyzed it; yet nothing makes sense; nothing seems right. Literature is filled with examples of grand hoaxes, perpetrated by brilliant and rascally con men. But a world presided over by imbeciles in politics and moral and intellectual morons in civil service and education is almost too painful to contemplate. That we can sympathize with the playwright's pessimism without succumbing to it may be owing to the satire's humor, biting though it is.

When Documentation Is Required

When writing about literature, you will often need to cite the work you are discussing so that your readers will know exactly to what passage you are referring and where it is located. You may also want to borrow ideas published in a book or article; you must acknowledge these for several reasons: for example, to give credit to their author and to indicate their source to readers who may wish to verify your citations or pursue the subject further. In addition, you are obligated to acknowledge your indebtedness whether you paraphrase the material or quote it *verbatim.* Your citations, which may be placed in parentheses in the body of the text, should include the name of the author, a short title, and page number(s). If any or all of these three items appear in the text, they should be omitted from the citation. Even the short title should be omitted if you cite only one work by that author since you will provide a full reference in the bibliography at the end of your paper.

Here are some examples to illustrate these forms of documentation.

> D. G. Gillham remarks that the "male 'worm' " and "female 'rose' " in Blake's "The Sick Rose" have " 'Freudian' significance" and "give rise in the speaker to the half-hidden feelings of indecency, guilt and fear so easily associated with sexual experience" (11).

Since the author's name is mentioned in the text, only the page number for the citation is given in the parenthetical reference. If you refer to more than one work by the same author, you must also include an abbreviated title (*Blake* 11) to distinguish among two or more works. References to journal articles are treated in the same way:

> Prospero's suite in "The Masque of the Red Death" has been described as "a metaphor of nature and mortality" (Vanderbilt 382). Walter Blair has pointed out the allegorical significance of the seven rooms that "connote the seven ages of man from the blue of the dawn of life to the black of its night" (239).

The author's name, Vanderbilt, is included in the first reference since no mention is made of him in the text.

At the end of your paper you should include a "bibliography of works cited" listed in alphabetical order by author. Here are examples of complete bibliographical entries for the book and articles previously mentioned:

Blair, Walter. "Poe's Conception of Incident and Tone in the Tale." *Modern Philology* 41 (1944): 228–240.

Gillham, D. G. *William Blake.* Cambridge: Cambridge University Press, 1973.

Vanderbilt, Kermit. "Art and Nature in 'The Masque of the Red Death.' " *Nineteenth-Century Fiction* 22 (1968): 379–389.

If your reference is to an article that appears in a collection of essays by various authors, you should follow the same procedure in your text. Your bibliography entry, however, would include the title of the collection and the name of its editor:

Leavis, Q. D. "Hawthorne as Poet." In *Hawthorne: A Collection of Critical Essays.* Ed. A. N. Kaul. Englewood Cliffs, N.J.: Prentice-Hall, 1966, 25–63.

When you quote from the story, poem, or play you are writing about, you should include references to the pages of the story (124), the lines of the poem (5–8), or the act, scene, and line numbers of the play (II.ii.45–51). Do not forget to include a reference in your bibliography:

Poe, Edgar Allan. "The Masque of the Red Death." In *LIT: Literature and Interpretive Techniques.* Ed. Wilfred L. Guerin et al. New York: Harper & Row Publishers, 1985, 16–20.

If you refer to or quote several works from the same collection, you may save time and space by including only the collection in your bibliography. But your parenthetical references in your text must guide your readers to the proper book. For example, if you refer both to "Araby" and "Indian Camp" from this anthology, you would include a parenthetical citation after the first reference or quotation from each work (reprinted in *LIT* 200, 239). Your bibliography should then include *LIT* but not the other authors and works.

LIT: Literature and Interpretive Techniques. Ed. Wilfred L. Guerin et al. Harper & Row Publishers, Inc., 1985.

GLOSSARY

This is not intended to be a complete glossary of literary terms. Such a list would be, rightfully, a book in itself, and adequate reference and source books of that sort are available. The terms given here do, however, appear in the present book—sometimes italicized to call attention to their being glossed here—and have special relevance for the types of literary interpretation that are discussed.

AESTHETICS.   The study of beauty (actually, a branch of philosophy). As the term is used in this book, it refers principally to the combination of feeling and thought stimulated by literary art. It does not concern what is merely "pretty" or picturesque, but what is effective. *See* ART and ARTIFACT.

ALLEGORY.   A narrative that has two meanings, one a literal or surface meaning (the story itself) and one a metaphorical meaning (the characters or actions or even the objects of which have a one-to-one equivalence with those of the literal narrative). Frequently the allegory has distinct moral, political, or philosophical implications embedded in its body of SYMBOLS. (Examples are John Bunyan's *Pilgrim's Progress* and the medieval play *Everyman.*)

ALLITERATION.   The repetition of initial sounds (e.g., "right as rain," "Kit-Cat Club," "the fickle finger of Fate").

ALLUSION.   Any reference, direct or indirect, to a person, place, event, or character in history, literature, mythology, or sacred books like the Koran and the Bible.

AMBIGUITY.   A vagueness, often intentional, that may enrich an author's MEANING by evoking any or all of a number of possibilities, which, when played off one against the other, heighten the dramatic or aesthetic effect. Sometimes, a deliberate ambiguity may be contained in puns or plays on words (e.g., "son" and "sun").

APOSTROPHE.   A figure of speech in which a person who is absent is directly addressed as if he were present (e.g., "Milton! thou shouldst be living at this hour"); also a form of personification in which a nonhuman or inanimate thing is directly addressed as if it were human or animate (e.g., "O Rose, thou art sick!").

ARCHETYPE.   An image, MOTIF, or thematic pattern that has recurred so regularly in history, literature, religion, or folkways as to have acquired transcendent symbolic force. According to Jungian psychology, archetypes or "primordial images" are MYTH-forming structural elements that are always present in the unconscious psyche; they are not inherited ideas but "belong to the realm of activities of the instincts and in that sense . . . represent inherited forms of psychic behaviour" (*Psyche and Symbol* [New York: Doubleday, 1958] xvi).

ART.   Generally, any concrete creation of the imagination that so blends FORM and content as to appeal to the emotions and the intellect of the perceiver in an aesthetically satisfying way.

1132

ARTIFACT (LITERARY). The literary work of ART itself: poem, drama, short story, novel; that is, a structure of words that is produced or created, just as a vase, a symphony, or a sculpture is produced.

ASSONANCE. Repetition of similar vowel sounds.

CATASTROPHE. The concluding action of a tragedy, wherein the principal character or characters meet death or other significant defeat. By extension the term may also designate an unhappy event in other forms of literature.

CATHARSIS. Aristotle's term for the purgation or purification of the emotions of pity and fear, a purgation that results from the viewing of a tragic drama. The term, itself a metaphor, has had varied interpretations. Perhaps the effect of tragedy would have been better described in terms of the beneficial stimulation of the viewer's total being —moral, emotional, and intellectual.

CENTRAL INTELLIGENCE. *See* POINT OF VIEW.

CLASSICISM. That aesthetic temper characterized by an emphasis on rational order, discipline, balance and symmetry, clarity and simplicity, and decorum. Generally, classicism is conservative, looking to the tradition transmitted from the past, especially from classical Greece and Rome, as a means of knowing man's limitations and the universality of human nature. Unlike ROMANTICISM, classicism downplays emotion, hyperindividualism, and subjectivism. *See also* REALISM.

COMEDY. Any literary work, but especially a play, that aims primarily to amuse and that ends happily. Note that the term is derived from the Greek *komoidos,* meaning a "singer in the [Dionysian] revels." *See* TRAGEDY.

CONNOTATION. An overtone of "evocative" meaning, the suggested or emotional meaning of a word as compared with its "dictionary" or "conceptual" meaning. For example, the connotative values of "home" may in some instances be more important than the denotative values. *See* DENOTATION.

CONSONANCE. Repetition of similar consonant sounds.

CONTEXT. The setting or frame of reference in which an event takes place, a speech is made, an idea is conceived, or a word is used.

DENOTATION. The literal ("conceptual" or "dictionary") meaning of a word, more objective than its connotation. *See* CONNOTATION.

DENOUEMENT. The conclusion of a plot, the unraveling of the mystery, the resolution of various strands of action in a DRAMA or a story. The denouement of a tragedy is often called the CATASTROPHE.

DIALECTIC. In formalistic criticism, a pattern of opposition between two attitudes, or character traits, or systems of ideas. Like PARADOX and TENSION, dialectic suggests a pull of opposed forces that, nevertheless, move toward synthesis or resolution. (In *Hamlet,* e.g., dialectic manifests itself on several levels, as in the disparity between appearance and reality, between things as they are and things as they should be, between the godlike in man and the complex of traits that Hamlet calls the "quintessence of dust.")

DRAMA. That genre of imaginative literature in which characters act out their roles, conventionally on a stage, although some dramas (called "closet dramas") are meant primarily to be read.

EXPLICATION *(explication de texte).* A line-by-line commentary and interpretation based on a close reading of a literary work.

FIGURATIVE LANGUAGE. A type of expression that achieves aesthetic effect by transcending or departing from the literal and conventional phrasing. *See,* for example, METAPHOR, HYPERBOLE, PARADOX, APOSTROPHE, and PERSONIFICATION.

FOIL. A character used to compare and contrast with another character, so that the more important character is better delineated. For example, Hamlet is better understood by our seeing him in relation to Horatio and Laertes. Customarily, the term is used for certain characters in drama, although it may be used in fiction as well. Thus, Tom Sawyer may be viewed as a "foil" for Huck Finn.

FORM. *See* ORGANIC FORM and FORMALISTIC; not to be confused with GENRE.

FORMALISTIC. A term used to describe that type of literary criticism having as its major concern the form of a work of art, ranging from its typography to the STRUCTURE its ideas build. The interplay of these variations of form results in a totality of effect that INFORMS or shapes inwardly the work and gives its parts a relevance to the whole and vice versa. (Related terms are *analytical, ontological,* and *New Critical.*)

FREUDIAN. *See* PSYCHOANALYSIS.

GENRE. A literary type: poetry, drama, fiction. To these basic ones may be added others like biography and the personal essay. Sometimes subdivisions of these basic types are also called genres, as with the novel and the short story as the main divisions of fiction, or tragedy and comedy in drama, or epic and lyric in poetry. A genre like ROMANCE may exist in both prose fiction and poetry.

GOTHIC. A term originally used to describe a particularly melodramatic and sensational kind of novel in the eighteenth century. Now used to refer to anything that is ghostly, eerie, mysterious, or horrifying (such as much of Poe's fiction and much of present-day fiction by Southern writers).

GUSTATORY IMAGERY. *See* IMAGERY.

HYPERBOLE. A type of figurative language characterized by exaggeration or overstatement for some special effect (e.g., John Donne's "Go and catch a falling star, / Get with child a mandrake root . . .").

IMAGERY. Any verbal appeal to any of the senses; a stimulation of the IMAGINATION through sense experience (note that "image" and "imagination" are cognates). *Visual* imagery, the type most familiar to readers at large, appeals to the sense of sight; thus any object that can be seen can be a visual image. Similarly, *aural* imagery is that which can be heard ("thunderous"). *Kinesthetic* imagery and *kinetic* imagery—perhaps more strange for the beginning student of literature, because the senses stimulated are not among the classical five—are closely related. We may make a distinction, however, if by "kinetic" we mean an appeal to a sense of motion and by "kinesthetic" we mean an appeal to a sense of muscular tensions and activity. Not only words, but prose and verse rhythms can create these effects (e.g., both kinetic and kinesthetic senses are stimulated in Browning's "I sprang to the saddle, and Joris, and he . . ."). Other types of imagery that may be perceived are *gustatory, tactile, olfactory,* and *thermal,* which make their appeals, respectively, to taste ("salty"), touch ("velvety smoothness"), smell ("stench"), and sensitivity to temperature ("scorch," "frigid"). Some of these tend to overlap, because what stimulates the taste often stimulates the sense of smell as well, and what can be heard can also suggest motion, and so on. In some writers (notably John Keats) the various sense experiences may be associated or mingled in such a way as to produce the effect of *synesthesia.*

IMAGINATION. That human mental faculty, distinguished from intellect, will, and memory, that, as Coleridge observed, shapes and fuses the perceptions brought to the mind; or, more generally, that level of the mind's activity at which things are created or conceived, or from which they begin to rise to consciousness in the mind of the writer, musician, painter, or thinker.

INFORM. To shape inwardly, to present the primary characteristic of an object or idea (not to be confused with the idea of simply presenting information). The term denotes an inner process that gives life to a particular entity. (E.g., when we say that Poe's single effect of "the redness and the horror of blood" informs "The Masque of the Red Death," we mean that this quality both pervades the story and gives it its essential MEANING.)

IRONY. A literary device, a manner of expression, a tone characterized by a duality wherein what is said or seen or otherwise perceived at one level is at another level either incongruous or misconstrued or diametrically opposed to what is expected. Note that there are several kinds of irony. *Socratic irony* is a dialectic technique using the pretense of ignorance to enable others to perceive their own logic and illogic (the word "irony" is derived from the Greek *eironeia,* meaning "dissembling, feigned ignorance"). *Verbal irony* means the opposite of what one says (e.g., Mark Anthony's famous oration following the death of Julius Caesar: "Brutus is an honorable man ..."). *Dramatic irony* is a device by which a reader or member of an audience is made aware of something the protagonist or characters do not know (e.g., the audience is aware, before the protagonist knows, that the murderer of Laius whom Oedipus is so intent upon discovering is Oedipus himself). This device is also called *tragic irony. Cosmic irony* (the *irony of fate*) is the manipulation of events by the gods or by destiny so that the protagonist is frustrated and mocked (e.g., the actual outcome of events is the opposite of that expected by the protagonist, as in *situational irony*). *Situational irony* (the *irony of events*) involves an unexpected turn of events, sometimes with cosmic overtones but often merely humorous or absurd.

JUNGIAN. *See* ARCHETYPE.

LYRIC. A major class of poetry, the subject matter of which is usually emotion, often subjectively perceived and presented, and the STYLE of which is highly charged with IMAGERY. Love and nature are two of the subjects with which lyric poets are frequently concerned.

MARXIST. *See* SOCIOLOGICAL.

MEANING. The content, the moral or intellectual or emotional signification, perhaps even the "message," of a given work, which is, however, integral to and inseparable from the work itself. Frequently the "meaning" of a work is stated by the critic in terms of the work's THEME.

MELODRAMA. A species of DRAMA that lays particular stress on emotion and pays little attention to the probability of action, accurate characterization, or genuine feeling. The typical "Western" story and the "mystery" tale offer familiar examples of melodrama. Now, more often than not, melodrama is a term of disparagement in literary criticism.

1135

METAPHOR. Broadly, FIGURATIVE LANGUAGE used to draw comparisons imaginatively, as opposed to literal STATEMENT. Specifically, a comparison of things essentially unlike, drawn without the use of words such as "like" and "as." (Metaphor occurs when one thing is directly called something else, as when Hamlet declares, "Denmark's a prison.")

METAPHYSICAL. In literary criticism and history, a type of poetry that flourished in the seventeenth century, the style of which has recurred since then, especially in the twentieth century. It is characterized by bizarre, grotesque, unconventional, even shocking figures of speech, and by wit and IRONY and a kind of detached intellectualism. (The term—actually borrowed from philosophy—received its classic literary definition in Samuel Johnson's *Life of Cowley.*)

METER. The pattern of stressed (accented) and unstressed (unaccented) syllables by means of which the rhythm of verse is conveyed (from the Greek *metron,* meaning "measure"). The basic unit of measurement within a line of verse is the foot; the standard feet in English verse are the *iambic* (an unstressed followed by a stressed syllable: *today*); *trochaic* (a stressed followed by an unstressed syllable: *colder*); *anapestic* (two unstressed syllables followed by a stressed syllable: *in the book*): *dactylic* (a stressed syllable followed by two unstressed syllables: *syllable*); and *spondaic* (two stressed syllables: *daybreak*). Lines of verse are designated by the number of feet within each line (one foot = *monometer,* two feet = *dimeter,* three feet = *trimeter,* four feet = *tetrameter,* five feet = *pentameter,* six feet = *hexameter,* seven feet = *heptameter*). Samuel Taylor Coleridge's "Lesson for a Boy" is often quoted as a device for helping students to identify the kinds of feet:

Trochee trips from long to short;
From long to long in solemn sort
Slow Spondee stalks, strong foot, yet ill able
Ever to come up with Dactyl trisyllable.
Iambics march from short to long;
With a leap and a bound the swift Anapests throng.

MOOD. The atmosphere or emotional effect generated by the words, images, situations in a literary work (the emotional ambiance of the work), for example, melancholy, joyous, tense, oppressive, and so on.

MOTIF. A THEME, an IMAGE, a type of action, or an ARCHETYPE that by its recurrent appearance traces itself through a work and heightens its aesthetic appeal. In literature, it may become a sign or index for the meaning or experience of a work.

MOTIVE. The reason for a character's action (i.e., his psychological motivation); the word is sometimes used also for what in this book is called MOTIF.

MYTH. In the traditional sense, an anonymous story reflecting primitive beliefs or explaining the mysteries of the natural universe. In more recent theory, myth is the symbolic projection of a people's collective values—a communal, almost instinctive, articulation of reality. Sometimes defined as the verbal aspect of ritual.

NEW CRITICISM. A critical position that emphasizes the literary ARTIFACT itself and tends to minimize matters such as the biographical and historical facts about an author and his work. It stresses close analysis of the literary work itself as an entity worthy of attention in its own right.

NOVEL. An extended, fictional, prose narrative that portrays characters in a PLOT. The novel may stress adventure for its own sake or character development or a partisan position on some issue or a blend of these and other emphases. The plot of the novel is more extended than that of the SHORT STORY, having usually many more episodes. In modern fiction it is possible to find novels that treat at length one or a few episodes in psychological depth and with a modified concept of time that plays down sequence and stresses relationship. Especially in our day, the distinction between a novel and a novella becomes difficult.

OBJECTIVE CORRELATIVE. A critical term made current by T. S. Eliot: external objects, situations, events that call forth a sensory experience and evoke a *"particular"* emotion.

OEDIPUS COMPLEX. A term used in Freudian psychology to denote the strong attachment, sometimes romantic, of a son to his mother. It may in some cases be sublimated and take conventionally acceptable channels; in others, it may give rise to feelings of jealousy of the father as a rival for the mother's love; in its extreme form it may result in incest. (The term derives from the classical MYTH of Oedipus, who unwittingly killed his father and married his mother.)

OMNISCIENT NARRATOR (OR AUTHOR). *See* POINT OF VIEW.

ONOMATOPOEIA. A figure of speech in which the sound echoes the meaning (e.g., "hiss," "tinkle," "crash").

ORGANIC FORM. The structural, necessary interrelationship of the parts of a literary work, which gives it, as it were, a life of its own that grows from within. The literary work becomes an organism.

PARADOX. A figure of speech containing a contradiction that is, nevertheless, somehow true. It is frequently used to express the complexities of life that do not easily lend themselves to simple statement. (Paradoxes abound, e.g., in the Scriptures: "For whosoever will save his life shall lose it: but whosoever will lose his life for my sake, the same shall save it.")

PERSONIFICATION. A figure of speech in which an inanimate object or an abstraction is treated as a living being or person, or in which a nonhuman being is treated as human.

PLOT. The action, that which happens—narratively speaking—in a literary work. Technically, it involves not only a sequence of episodes but their interaction and interrelation in a dynamic STRUCTURE.

POEM. A literary composition characterized by a high degree of verbal compression and FIGURATIVE LANGUAGE, in which pleasure, its primary end, is derived from an appreciation of the parts simultaneously with a perception of the whole. The poem should not be confused with mere verse; although, like verse, it may have a regular rhythm and rhyme, the poem achieves its identity through its heightened and compressed language rather than through mere jingle effects.

POINT OF VIEW. A device used in narration that indicates the position from which an action is observed and narrated. For example, a *first-person point of view* is that in which the narrator is a participant in the action; he may be a major character, perhaps even the central character; or he may be more of an observer, one who is on the fringes of the action. The OMNISCIENT NARRATOR is a kind of third-person narrator; he or she speaks with the authority of the creating author who knows all; he or she is not confined to what is seen or heard; he or she may even comment on or interpret action or character. Still another point of view, variously called *third-person limited* or *limited omniscient,* presents only that which can be seen or heard; it does not tell what the characters are thinking or feeling, although we may see the action more from the vantage point of one character (who may function as CENTRAL INTELLIGENCE) than another. The *scenic* or *dramatic point of view* resorts to dialogue even more than the others, resulting in the objective reporting of what is said. In all of these there is a possibility of overlap, and sometimes an author will shift from one to another within a story.

PROSODY. See METER.

PSYCHOANALYSIS. The diagnosis and treatment of mental disorder premised on the Freudian theory that such disorders are caused by repression of desires, desires that the afflicted person may have consciously rejected but that nevertheless persist strongly in his subconscious. A considerable body of modern criticism is based in large measure on the psychoanalytic theories of psychology pioneered by Sigmund Freud.

REALISM. A manner of presentation in literature that stresses an accurate, perhaps even factual, treatment of subject matter. The emphasis is on the rational and probable, as opposed, for example, to the romantic.

RHYTHM. The regular recurrence of stressed and unstressed syllables, and the approximately equal time intervals between those recurrences. *See* METER.

ROMANCE. A type of narrative fiction characterized by the fanciful, often idealistic, treatment of subject matter; love and adventure are often its principal themes. (The genre is an old one, including, e.g., prose and verse from the Middle Ages, such as the Arthurian stories, as well as later work such as Tennyson's *Idylls of the King.*) The romance may be contrasted with the NOVEL. (*See,* e.g., Nathaniel Hawthorne's Preface to *The House of the Seven Gables.*)

ROMANTICISM. The aesthetic temper or philosophy characterized by an emphasis on freedom from restraint; interest in the exotic, the far, the ideal, the past, the picturesque; subjectivism; and individualism. Often opposed to the tenets of CLASSICISM, Romanticism in the critical sense does not concern "romance" in courtship and sentimental love.

SCANSION. The process of identifying the meter of a verse by ascertaining the number and kind of poetic feet. *See* METER.

SENTIMENTALITY. An excess of sentiment or emotion beyond what the circumstances seem to call for; often a stereotyped response.

SETTING. A combination of locale; historical period, season, or hour; and spiritual, ethnic, and cultural background.

SHORT STORY. A short, fictional, prose narrative (which, according to Edgar Allan Poe, should work toward a single preconceived effect). As opposed to the tale, the short story in its most finished form fuses its few characters, its few episodes, and its details into a tightly knit STRUCTURE.

SIMILE. A figure of speech involving the comparison of two things essentially unlike by employing, usually, the words *like* or *as.*

SOCIOLOGICAL. A critical approach emphasizing the social, economic, or political context of a work of literature. For example, MARXIST critics would lay stress on the portrayal of class struggle. Not all sociological criticism, however, is Marxist. In fact, any critical approach emphasizing the interaction between social milieu and literary work may be labeled sociological.

SONNET. A fourteen-line LYRIC poem usually in iambic pentameter. The essential characteristic of most sonnets is the dynamic interrelationship of their parts: in the *Petrarchan* or *Italian* sonnet, the octave (the first eight lines) with the sestet (the last six); or in the *Shakespearean* or *English* sonnet, the three quatrains (four-line stanzas) with each other and the concluding couplet.

STANZA. A grouping of lines in poetry that results in formalized units held together by recurrent patterns of rhyme or sometimes only by thought or by the poet's decision to use units of a given number of lines. *See also* VERSE PARAGRAPH.

STATEMENT. In literary criticism, a first or surface level of communication; a paraphrase of the message or THEME or content of a literary work. The term is often opposed to "suggestion" or subsurface levels of MEANING and to the AESTHETIC quality of the art object.

STEREOTYPE. An oversimplified conception; something that duplicates something else without variation or individualizing characteristics. Contrast the stereotype, which is static and superficial, with the ARCHETYPE, which is dynamic and profound.

STRESS. In metrics, an accented beat in a verse line.

STRUCTURE. A formal pattern of words, images, actions, or ideas. *See* ORGANIC FORM, FORMALISTIC, INFORM, and TEXTURE. *See also* p. 1125.

STYLE. The particular way in which an author uses words; it is a manifestation not only of his or her vocabulary and rhetorical tendencies, but also of his or her personality. It might be influenced in given instances by POINT OF VIEW, SETTING, and other considerations that develop verisimilitude or other desired effects. In the hands of a skillful writer, style becomes an important key to MEANING (as in much of Hemingway's fiction).

SYMBOL. An image or object or action that is charged with meaning beyond its denotative value. Although the term presents difficulty and perhaps should be used with caution and for relatively concrete objects, it is not altogether inaccurate to speak of a character's being a symbol. In its most sophisticated forms, the symbol tends to become more and more indefinite in its meanings in contrast to the fixed meaning of ALLEGORY.

TENSION. Generally, a pull of opposing forces; in criticism, a quality of opposition that gives inner life to a poem or play or work of fiction by unifying its disparate elements. Thus we may point out the "tension" between THEME and FORM in a given work. *See* PARADOX, IRONY, and FORMALISTIC.

TEXTURE. The tone, connotations of individual words, or "felt life" of the literary work that combines with STRUCTURE to produce the total meaning of the work.

THEME. The underlying idea, relatively abstract, that is given concrete expression by the literary work.

TONE. A term used, sometimes broadly, to denote an attitude or feeling of the speaker or author as conveyed by the language in its artful arrangement (e.g., ironic, pensive, sly, acerbic, humorous). Tone describes the attitude of the narrator or *persona* of the work, whereas MOOD refers to the emotional impact felt by the reader of the work. Although often similar, these feelings are not necessarily the same.

TRAGEDY. A literary work (traditionally a drama) in which the protagonist is engaged in a morally significant struggle that ends in calamity or great disappointment. In his *Poetics* Aristotle defined Greek tragedy as "an artistic imitation of an action that is serious, complete in itself, and of adequate magnitude" involving a hero neither superlatively good nor wholly bad who, because of some human flaw such as pride *(hubris)*, was destined to be "brought low through some error of judgment or short-coming" *(hamartia)*. The proper tragedy, suggested Aristotle, would arouse emotions of pity and terror in the audience, leading to *catharsis* (a wholesome emotional purgation). Although later dramatists—particularly the modern playwrights—departed from many of the criteria set forth by Aristotle (concerning the unity of plot and action, e.g.), tragedy has continued to be viewed as a special genre informed by a serious mood and featuring a strong protagonist who challenges the gods or the forces of his environment with great courage and accepts his unfortunate fate with dignity.

VERSE PARAGRAPH. A grouping of lines in verse based primarily on thought content rather than on rhyme pattern. (*See* STANZA.) Conventionally, the verse paragraph is either indented or separated by some spacing device from preceding and following passages.

by George James Firmage. "r-p-o-p-h-e-s-s-a-g-r," from *No Thanks* by E. E. Cummings. Reprinted by permission of Liveright Publishing Corp. Copyright © 1935 by E. E. Cummings. Copyright © 1968 by Marion Morehouse Cummings. Copyright © 1973, 1978 by the Trustees for the E. E. Cummings Trust. Copyright © 1973, 1978 by George James Firmage.

Emily Dickinson: "After Great Pain, A Formal Feeling Comes," from *The Complete Poems of Emily Dickinson*," edited by Thomas H. Johnson. Copyright © 1929 by Martha Dickinson Bianchi; copyright © renewed 1957 by Mary L. Hampson. Reprinted by permission of Little, Brown and Company. "Success Is Counted Sweetest," "If I Shouldn't Be Alive," "I Taste a Liquor Never Brewed," "There's a Certain Slant of Light," "A Bird Came Down the Walk," "I Like to See It Lap the Miles," "Because I Could Not Stop for Death," "A Narrow Fellow in the Grass," "I Never Saw a Moor," "A Route of Evanescence," "Apparently with No Suprise." Reprinted by permission of the publishers and the Trustees of Amherst College from *The Complete Poems of Emily Dickinson*, edited by Thomas H. Johnson, Cambridge Mass.: The Belknap Press of Harvard University Press. Copyright © 1951, 1955, 1979, 1983 by the President and Fellows of Harvard College.

John Digby: "Shorter Biography of a Saint Circa 20th Century," from *The Structure of Bifocal Distance*, by John Digby. Copyright © John Digby 1974. Reprinted by permission of Anvil Press Poetry Ltd.

Isak Dinesen: "The Sailor-Boy's Tale," from *Winter's Tales*, by Isak Dinesen. Reprinted by permission of Random House, Inc., and The Rungstedlund Foundation of Denmark. Copyright © by Random House, Inc., 1942, and renewed in 1970 by The Rungstedlund Foundation.

Richard Eberhart: "The Groundhog" from *Collected Poems 1930–1976* by Richard Eberhart. Copyright © 1960, 1976 by Richard Eberhart. Reprinted by permission of Oxford University Press, Inc., and Chatto & Windus Ltd.

Lonne Elder III: *Ceremonies in Dark Old Men* by Lonne Elder III. Copyright © 1965, 1969 by Lonne Elder III. Reprinted by permission of Farrar, Straus & Giroux, Inc.

T. S. Eliot: "The Love Song of J. Alfred Prufrock" from *Collected Poems 1909–1962*, by T. S. Eliot, copyright © 1936, by Harcourt Brace Jovanovich, Inc., copyright © 1943, 1963, 1964, by T. S. Eliot; copyright by Esme Valerie Eliot. Reprinted by permission of Harcourt Brace Jovanovich, Inc., and Faber and Faber Ltd.

Harlan Ellison: "Shatterday" from *Shatterday*. Copyright © 1975 by Harlan Ellison. Reprinted by arrangement with, and with the permission of, the author and the author's agent, Richard Curtis Associates, Inc., New York. All rights reserved.

William Faulkner: "A Rose for Emily." Copyright © 1930 and renewed 1958 by William Faulkner. Reprinted from *Collected Stories of William Faulkner* by permission of Random House, Inc.

Carolyn Forché: "The Visitor," copyright © 1979 by Carolyn Forché and "The Colonel," copyright © 1980 by Carolyn Forché. Reprinted by permission of Harper & Row, Publishers, Inc.

Bruce Jay Friedman: "Black Angels." Reprinted by permission of the author and The Lantz Office.

Robert Frost: "Fire and Ice," "Stopping by Woods on a Snowy Evening," "Design," from *The Poetry of Robert Frost* edited by Edward Connery Lathem. Copyright © 1923, © 1969 by Holt, Rinehart and Winston. Copyright © 1936, 1951 by Robert Frost. Copyright © 1964 by Lesley Frost Ballantine. Reprinted by permission of Holt, Rinehart and Winston, Publishers. "The Road Not Taken," "Out, Out—," "Acquainted with the Night," from *The Poetry of Robert Frost* edited by Edward Connery Lathem. Copyright © 1916, 1928, © 1969 by Holt, Rinehart and Winston. Copyright © 1944, © 1956 by Robert Frost. Reprinted by permission of Holt, Rinehart and Winston, Publishers.

Gabriel García Márquez: "A Very Old Man with Enormous Wings" from *Leaf Storm and Other Stories* by Gabriel García Márquez. English translation copyright © 1972 by Gabriel García Márquez. Reprinted by permission of Harper & Row, Publishers, Inc.

Gary Gildner: "Sleepy Time Gal" was originally published in *The Georgia Review*, copyright © 1979 by the University of Georgia. Reprinted by permission of the author and *The Georgia Review*.

Allen Ginsberg: "A Supermarket in California." Copyright © 1956, 1959 by Allen Ginsberg. Reprinted by permission of City Lights Books.

Susan Glaspell: "Trifles," copyright © 1916 by Susan Glaspell. First published in *Plays*, Boston: Small, Maynard & Co., 1920.

ACKNOWLEDGMENTS

Louise Glück: "Gretel in Darkness," copyright © 1975 by Louise Gluck. From *The House on Marshland* published by The Ecco Press in 1975. Reprinted by permission.

Thom Gunn: "On the Move," from *Selected Poems 1950–1975* by Thom Gunn. Reprinted by permission of Farrar, Straus & Giroux, Inc. Copyright © 1958, 1979 by Thom Gunn. Reprinted from *The Sense of Movement* by Thom Gunn by permission of Faber and Faber Ltd.

Thomas Hardy: "Hap," "Drummer Hodge," "Neutral Tones," "The Man He Killed," "Convergence of the Twain," from *Complete Poems of Thomas Hardy,* edited by James Gibson, New York: Macmillan Publishing Company, 1978. Reprinted by permission.

Seamus Heaney: "Antaeus" and "Hercules and Antaeus" from *Poems 1965–1975* by Seamus Heaney. Copyright © 1975, 1980 by Seamus Heaney. Reprinted by permission of Farrar, Straus & Giroux, Inc., and reprinted from *North* by permission of Faber and Faber.

Ernest Hemingway: "Indian Camp" from *In Our Time.* Copyright © 1925, 1930 by Charles Scribner's Sons, copyright renewed 1953, 1958 by Ernest Hemingway. Reprinted with the permission of Charles Scribner's Sons.

Geoffrey Hill: "Lachrimae Coactae," "Lachrimae Amantis," from *Tenebrae* by Geoffrey Hill. Reprinted by permission of Andre Deutsch.

A. E. Housman: "Terence, this is stupid stuff," "When I Was One-and-Twenty," "To An Athlete Dying Young," "Is My Team Ploughing?" "With Rue My Heart Is Laden," from "A Shropshire Lad," Authorised Edition, from *The Collected Poems of A.E. Housman.* Copyright © 1939, 1940, © 1965 by Holt, Rinehart and Winston, copyright © 1967, 1968 by Robert E. Symons. Reprinted by permission of Holt, Rinehart and Winston, Publishers, and The Society of Authors as the literary representative of the Estate of A.E. Housman, and Jonathan Cape Ltd., publishers of A.E. Housman's *Collected Poems.*

Langston Hughes: "The Negro Speaks of Rivers." Copyright © 1926 by Alfred A. Knopf, Inc., and renewed 1954 by Langston Hughes. "Harlem" ("Dream Deferred"). Copyright © 1951 by Langston Hughes. Reprinted from *Selected Poems of Langston Hughes,* by permission of Alfred A. Knopf, Inc.

Ted Hughes: "A Dream of Horses," from *Lupercal* by Ted Hughes. Copyright © 1957 by Ted Hughes. Reprinted by permission of Faber & Faber, and Harper & Row Publishers, Inc.

Eugene Ionesco: "The Gap," translated by Rosette Lamont. Reprinted from *The Massachusetts Review.* Copyright © 1969 The Massachusetts Review, Inc.

Randall Jarrell: "The Death of the Ball Turret Gunner," "La Belle au Bois Dormant" from *The Complete Poems* by Randall Jarrell. Reprinted by permission of Farrar, Straus & Giroux, Inc.

Robinson Jeffers: "To the Stone-Cutters" Copyright © 1924 and renewed 1952 by Robinson Jeffers. Reprinted from *Selected Poetry of Robinson Jeffers,* by permission of Random House, Inc.

James Joyce: "Araby" from *Dubliners* by James Joyce. Originally published in 1916 by B.W. Huebsch. Definitive text copyright © 1967 by Estate of James Joyce. Reprinted by permission of Viking Penguin Inc.

Galway Kinnell: "The River That Is East" from *Flower Herding on Mount Monadnock* by Galway Kinnell. Copyright © 1964 by Galway Kinnell. Reprinted by permission of Houghton Mifflin Company.

Thomas Kinsella: "Girl on a Swing," "St. Paul's Rocks: 16 February 1832" from *POEMS, 1956–73* by Thomas Kinsella. Reprinted by permission of Wake Forest University Press.

Etheridge Knight: "Hard Rock Return to Prison from the Hospital for the Criminal Insane" from *Poems from Prison,* copyright © 1968 by Etheridge Knight. Reprinted by permission of Broadside Press.

Maxine Kumin: "How It Goes On" from *Our Ground Time Here Will Be Brief* by Maxine Kumin, copyright © 1967 by Maxine Kumin. Reprinted by permission of Viking Penguin Inc.

Donald D. Kummings: "The Contest Between Harmony and Invention." Reprinted from the *CEA Critic,* November, 1968, by permission of the author and the College English Association. Copyright © 1968 The College English Association, Inc.

Phillip Larkin: "Lines on a Young Lady's Photograph Album" reprinted from *The Less Deceived* by permission of The Marvell Press, England. "As Bad as a Mile" from *The Whitsun Weddings* by Phillip Larkin. "The Dancer" and "Love, We Must Part Now" from *The North Ship* by Phillip Larkin. Reprinted by permission of Faber and Faber, Ltd.

1142

D. H. Lawrence: "Snake," from *The Complete Poems* of *D. H. Lawrence.* Collected and edited by Vivian de Sola Pinto and F. Warren Roberts. Copyright © 1964, 1971 by Angelo Ravagli and C. M. Weekly, Executors of The Estate of Frieda Lawrence Ravagli. Reprinted by permission of Viking Penguin Inc.

Denise Levertov: "Sunday Afternoon" from *The Jacob's Ladder.* Copyright © 1961 by Denise Levertov Goodman. Reprinted by permission of New Directions Publishing Corporation.

Jack London: "The Red One" from *The Red One.* Permission granted to reprint by I. Milo Shepard, Trustee of The Trust of Irving Shepard.

Archibald MacLeish: "Ars Poetica," "End of the World" from *New and Collected Poems 1917–1976* by Archibald MacLeish. Copyright © 1976 by Archibald MacLeish. Reprinted by permission of Houghton Mifflin Company.

W. Somerset Maugham: "Appointment in Samarra" from *Sheppy* by W. Somerset Maugham. Copyright © 1933 by W. Somerset Maugham. Reprinted by permission of Doubleday & Co., Inc., and A. P. Watt Ltd. for the Estate of the late W. Somerset Maugham.

W. S. Merwin: "Proteus" from The Dancing Bears in *The First Four Books of Poems.* Copyright © 1975 W. S. Merwin. Reprinted with permission of Atheneum Publishers, Inc.

Arthur Miller: "Death of a Salesman" by Arthur Miller. Copyright © 1949 by Arthur Miller. Copyright renewed © 1977 by Arthur Miller. Reprinted by permission of Viking Penguin Inc.

Marianne Moore: "Poetry" by Marianne Moore. Copyright © 1935 by Marianne Moore, renewed 1963 by Marianne Moore and T. S. Eliot. Reprinted by permission of Macmillan Publishing Co., Inc.

Slavomir Mrozek: "Art" from *The Elephant,* translated by Konrad Syrop. Reprinted by permission of Grove Press, Inc. Copyright © 1963 by Grove Press, Inc., and 1985 by Grove Press, Inc.

Anais Nin: "Hejda" from *Under a Glass Bell* by Anais Nin. Copyright © 1948 by Anais Nin. Copyright renewed © 1976 by Anais Nin. All rights reserved. Reprinted by permission of the Author's Representative, Gunther Stuhlmann.

Joyce Carol Oates: "Stalking." Reprinted from *Marriages and Infidelities* by Joyce Carol Oates by permission of the publisher, Vanguard Press, Inc. Copyright © 1968, 1969, 1970, 1971, 1972 by Joyce Carol Oates.

Flannery O'Connor: "The Life You Save May Be Your Own." Copyright © 1953 by Flannery O'Connor, renewed 1981 by Mrs. Regina O'Connor. Reprinted from *A Good Man Is Hard to Find* by permission of Harcourt Brace Jovanovich, Inc.

Wilfred Owen: "Dulce et Decorum Est" from *The Collected Poems of Wilfred Owen.* Copyright © 1963 by Chatto & Windus, Ltd. Reprinted by permission of New Directions Publishing Corp.

Sylvia Plath: "Mirror," originally published in *The New Yorker,* "Daddy" from *The Collected Poems of Sylvia Plath,* edited by Ted Hughes. Copyright © 1963 by Ted Hughes. Reprinted by permission of Harper & Row, Publishers, Inc.

Katherine Anne Porter: "The Grave" from *The Leaning Tower,* copyright © 1944, 1972 by Katherine Anne Porter. Reprinted by permission of Harcourt Brace Jovanovich, Inc.

Ezra Pound: "In a Station of the Metro," "A Pact," "Alba," "Ancient Music" from PERSONAE, copyright © 1926 by Ezra Pound. Reprinted by permission of New Directions Publishing Corp.

John Crow Ransom: "Piazza Piece," copyright © 1927 by Alfred A. Knopf, Inc., and renewed 1955 by John Crowe Ransom. "Bells for John Whiteside's Daughter," copyright © 1924 by Alfred A. Knopf, Inc., and renewed 1952 by John Crowe Ransom. Reprinted from *Selected Poems,* 3rd edition, revised and enlarged, by John Crowe Ransom, by permission of Alfred A. Knopf, Inc.

Adrienne Rich: "Storm Warnings," "Mourning Picture," from *Poems, Selected and New, 1950–1974,* by Adrienne Rich, by permission of W. W. Norton & Company, Inc. Copyright © 1975, 1973, 1971, 1969, 1966 by W. W. Norton & Company, Inc. Copyright © 1967, 1963, 1962, 1961, 1960, 1959, 1958, 1957, 1956, 1955, 1954, 1953, 1952, 1951 by Adrienne Rich. "Paula Becker to Clara Westhoff" reprinted from *The Dream of a Common Language, Poems 1974–1977,* by Adrienne Rich, by permission of W. W. Norton & Company, Inc. Copyright © 1978 by W. W. Norton & Company, Inc.

ACKNOWLEDGMENTS

E. A. Robinson: "Mr. Flood's Party" from *Collected Poems* by Edwin Arlington Robinson. Copyright © 1921 by Edwin Arlington Robinson, renewed 1949 by Ruth Nivison. Reprinted by permission of Macmillan Publishing Co., Inc. "Miniver Cheevy," from *The Town Down the River,* copyright © 1910 Charles Scribner's Sons; copyright renewed 1938 Ruth Nivison. Reprinted by permission of Charles Scribner's Sons. "Richard Cory" from The Children of the Night. Copyright under the Berne Convention. Reprinted by permission of Charles Scribner's Sons.

Theodore Roethke: "My Papa's Waltz," copyright © 1942 by Hearst Magazines, Inc. from *The Collected Poems of Theodore Roethke.* Reprinted by permission of Doubleday & Company, Inc. "The Waking" copyright © 1953 by Theodore Roethke from the book *The Collected Poems of Theodore Roethke.* Reprinted by permission of Doubleday & Company, Inc.

Muriel Rukeyser: "Myth" from *The Collected Poems of Muriel Rukeyser* (1978). Copyright © 1973 by Muriel Rukeyser. Reprinted by permission of International Creative Management, Inc.

Anne Sexton: "Starry Night" from *All My Pretty Ones* by Anne Sexton. Copyright © 1962 by Anne Sexton. Reprinted by permission of Houghton Mifflin Company.

Charles Simic: "Forest" from *Dismantling the Silence* by Charles Simic. Copyright © 1971 by Charles Simic. Reprinted by permission of George Braziller, Inc.

Louis Simpson: "A Story about Chicken Soup," copyright © 1963 by Louis Simpson. Reprinted from *At the End of the Open Road* by permission of Wesleyan University Press. This poem first appeared in *The New Statesman.*

Isaac Bashevis Singer: "Getzel the Monkey" (tr. by Isaac Bashevis Singer and Ellen Kantarov) from *The Seance and Other Stories* by Isaac Bashevis Singer. Copyright © 1964, 1968 by Isaac Bashevis Singer. Reprinted by permission of Farrar, Straus & Giroux, Inc.

Stevie Smith: "Not Waving but Drowning" from *Selected Poems, Stevie Smith.* Copyright © 1964 by Stevie Smith. Reprinted by permission of New Directions Publishing Corporation and agents for the estate of Stevie Smith.

Sophocles: "Oedipus the King," edited and translated by Peter D. Arnott, from the Crofts Classics edition, *Sophocles: Oedipus the King* and *Antigone,* copyright © 1960. Reprinted by permission of Harland Davidson, Inc.

Gary Soto: "Graciela" from *The Tale of Sunlight* by Gary Soto. Copyright © 1978 by Gary Soto. Reprinted by permission of the University of Pittsburgh Press.

William Stafford: "A Sound from the Earth" from *Allegiances* by William Stafford. Copyright © 1967 by William Stafford. By permission of Harper & Row, Publishers, Inc.

John Steinbeck: "The Snake" from *The Long Valley* by John Steinbeck. Copyright © 1938 by John Steinbeck. Copyright renewed 1966 by John Steinbeck. Reprinted by permission of Viking Penguin Inc.

Wallace Stevens: "Sunday Morning," "Thirteen Ways of Looking at a Blackbird," "Anecdote of the Jar," "A High-Toned Old Christian Woman," "The Emperor of Ice-Cream" Copyright © 1923 and renewed 1951 by Wallace Stevens. Reprinted from *The Collected Poems of Wallace Stevens,* by permission of Alfred A. Knopf, Inc.

Tom Stoppard: "Rosencrantz and Guildenstern Are Dead," copyright © 1967 by Tom Stoppard. Reprinted by permission of Grove Press, Inc.

May Swenson: "Women" from *New and Selected Things Taking Place.* Copyright © 1968 by May Swenson. This poem originally appeared in *New American Review.*

Robert Swift: "Alter Egos," "Boxes and Cheese" by Robert Swift (unpublished). Printed by permission of the author.

John Millington Synge: "Riders to the Sea" from *The Complete Works of John M. Synge,* published by Random House, Inc.

Dylan Thomas: "A Refusal to Mourn the Death, by Fire, of a Child in London" and "Do Not Go Gentle into that Good Night" from *Poems of Dylan Thomas.* Copyright © 1945 by the Trustees of the Copyrights of Dylan Thomas. Reprinted by permission of New Directions Publishing Corporation and David Higham Associates, Ltd.

James Thurber: "The Secret Life of Walter Mitty." Copyright © 1942 by James Thurber. Copyright © 1970 Helen W. Thurber. From *My World and Welcome To It,* published by Harcourt Brace Jovanovich. Reprinted by permission of Mrs. James Thurber.

1144

Jean Toomer: "Reapers" and "November Cotton Flower" from *Cane* by Jean Toomer. Copyright ©
1923 by Boni & Liveright. Copyright renewed 1951 by Jean Toomer. Reprinted by permission of
Liveright Publishing Corp.

Richard Wilbur: "A Grasshopper," copyright © 1959 by Richard Wilbur. Reprinted from his volume
Advice to a Prophet and Other Poems. First published in *The New Yorker*. "Juggler," copyright © 1949,
1977 by Richard Wilbur. Reprinted from his volume *Ceremony and Other Poems*. First published in
The New Yorker. "Grace," from *The Beautiful Changes and Other Poems*, copyright © 1947, 1975
by Richard Wilbur. "Love Calls Us to the Things of this World" from *Things of This World*,
copyright © 1956 by Richard Wilbur. Reprinted by permission of Harcourt Brace Jovanovich, Inc.

William Carlos Williams: "The Use of Force" from *The Farmer's Daughters*. Copyright © 1938 by
William Carlos Williams. "The Dance" from *Collected Later Poems*. Copyright © 1944 by William
Carlos Williams. "The Red Wheelbarrow," "This Is Just to Say," and "Spring and All" from
Collected Earlier Poems, copyright © 1938 by New Directions Publishing Corp. Reprinted by
permission of New Directions Publishing Corporation.

Richard Wright: "The Man Who Was Almost A Man" from *Eight Men* by Richard Wright. (Thomas
Y. Crowell) Copyright © 1940, 1961 by Richard Wright. Reprinted by permission of Harper &
Row, Publishers, Inc.

William Butler Yeats: "The Lake Isle of Innisfree." "The Second Coming," copyright © 1924 by
Macmillan Publishing Company, Inc., renewed 1952 by Bertha Georgie Yeats. "No Second Troy,"
copyright © 1912 by Macmillan Publishing Company, renewed 1940 by Bertha Georgie Yeats.
"The Wild Swans at Coole," copyright © 1919 by Macmillan Publishing Company, renewed 1947
by Bertha Georgie Yeats. "Easter 1916," copyright © 1924 by Macmillan Publishing Company,
renewed 1952 by Bertha Georgie Yeats. "Sailing to Byzantium," "Leda and the Swan," copyright
© 1928 by Macmillan Publishing Company, renewed 1956 by Georgie Yeats. Reprinted with
permission of Macmillan Publishing Co., Inc., Michael B. Yeats and Macmillan London, Ltd. from
Collected Poems of William Butler Yeats.

Index